THUNDER AT PROKHOROVKA

A COMBAT HISTORY OF OPERATION CITADEL, KURSK, JULY 1943

David Schranck

Helion & Company

Helion & Company Limited
26 Willow Road
Solihull
West Midlands
B91 1UE
England
Tel. 0121 705 3393
Fax 0121 711 4075
Email: info@helion.co.uk
Website: www.helion.co.uk
Twitter: @helionbooks
Visit our blog http://blog.helion.co.uk/

Published by Helion & Company 2013

Designed and typeset by Farr out Publications, Wokingham, Berkshire
Cover designed by Paul Hewitt, Battlefield Design (www.battlefield-design.co.uk)
Printed by Gutenberg Press Limited, Tarxien, Malta

Text © David Schranck 2013
Maps © Helion & Company Limited 2013. Maps designed by Paul Hewitt, Battlefield Design (www.battlefield-design.co.uk)

ISBN 978 1 909384 54 5

British Library Cataloguing-in-Publication Data.
A catalogue record for this book is available from the British Library.

All rights reserved. No part of this publication may be reproduced, stored in a retrieval system, or transmitted, in any form, or by any means, electronic, mechanical, photocopying, recording or otherwise, without the express written consent of Helion & Company Limited.

For details of other military history titles published by Helion & Company Limited contact the above address, or visit our website: http://www.helion.co.uk.

We always welcome receiving book proposals from prospective authors.

Contents

List of maps		v
List of abbreviations		vii
Place name spellings		xi
Acknowledgements		13
Introduction		14
1	Prior to the start of Operation Citadel	17
2	July 4th on the Southern Salient	30
3	July 4th on the Northern Salient	40
4	July 5th on the Southern Salient	42
5	July 5th on the Northern Salient	82
6	July 6th on the Southern Salient	97
7	July 6th on the Northern Salient	128
8	July 7th on the Southern Salient	142
9	July 7th on the Northern Salient	165
10	July 8th on the Southern Salient	173
11	July 8th on the Northern Salient	203
12	July 9th on the Southern Salient	209
13	July 9th on the Northern Salient	237
14	July 10th on the Southern Salient	241
15	July 10th on the Northern Salient	268
16	July 11th on the Southern Salient	272
17	July 11th on the Northern Salient	309
18	July 12th on the Southern Salient	312
19	July 12th on the Northern Salient	373
20	July 13th on the Southern Salient	380
21	July 13th on the Northern Salient	398
22	July 14th on the Southern Salient	402
23	July 14th on the Northern Salient	415
24	July 15th on the Southern Salient	419
25	July 15th on the Northern Salient	428
26	July 16th-July 31st	431
27	August 1st-August 27th	454
28	Final Thoughts	464
Appendices		
I	German Order of Battle July 4th 1943	476
II	Soviet Order of Battle July 4th 1943	478
III	German Armored Strengths	483

IV	Soviet Armored Strengths	486
V	AFV Technical Data	488
VI	Ground forces strengths as of July 4th 1943	490
VII	Aviation Strengths	492
VIII	Casualties	493

Bibliography	495
Index	497

List of maps

Maps in colour section.

Map 1	Northern Salient, July 4th 1943 – midnight.	1
Map 2	Northern Salient, July 5th 1943 – midnight.	2
Map 3	Northern Salient, July 6th 1943 – midnight.	3
Map 4	Northern Salient, July 7th 1943 – midnight.	4
Map 5	Northern Salient, July 8th 1943 – midnight.	5
Map 6	Northern Salient, July 10th 1943 – midnight.	6
Map 7	Northern Salient, July 12th 1943 – midnight.	7
Map 8	Southern Salient, topographical.	8
Map 9	Southern Salient, July 5th 1943 – midnight.	10
Map 10	Southern Salient, July 6th 1943 – midnight.	12
Map 11	Southern Salient, July 7th 1943 – midnight. First major Soviet counter-attack.	14
Map 12	Southern Salient, July 8th 1943 – midnight. Second major Soviet counter-attack.	16
Map 13	Southern Salient, July 9th 1943 – midnight. 4th PzA resumes its attack.	18
Map 14	Southern Salient, July 10th 1943 – midnight.	20
Map 15	Southern Salient, July 11th 1943 – midnight.	22
Map 16	Southern Salient, July 12th 1943 – midnight.	24
Map 17	Southern Salient, July 13th 1943 – midnight.	26
Map 18	Southern Salient, Battle for Prokhorovka, July 11th 1943 – midnight. 2nd SS PzC's attempt to take Prokhorovka before 5th GTA fully arrived.	28
Map 19	Southern Salient, Battle for Prokhorovka, July 12th 1943 – midnight. The advance of 2nd SS PzC after Rotmistrov's assault failed to encircle the Germans.	29
Map 20	Southern Salient, Counter-attack of 1st TA, July 12th 1943 – midnight. The sector retreat of 48th PzC against 1st TA's counter-attack.	30
Map 21	Kempf's Offensive, July 12th 1943. 3rd PzC's advance.	31
Map 22	Orel Salient, July 11th 1943 – midnight. Deployments at the start of Operation Kutuzov.	32

Larger map sheets located inside rear cover of book.

Map 23	Southern Salient, large topographical.
Map 24	Southern Salient, Primary Axis, July 5th 1943. Opening day for 48th PzC and 2nd SS PzC.
Map 25	Southern Salient, July 8th 1943. Soviet armored counter-attack.
Map 26A	Southern Salient, July 9th 1943. 2nd SS PzC offensive.
Map 26B	Southern Salient, July 10th 1943. 2nd SS PzC offensive.
Map 26C	Southern Salient, July 11th 1943. 2nd SS PzC offensive.

Map 27   Southern Salient, July 12th 1943. Defense of Prokhorovka.
Map 28   Orel Salient, Operation Kutuzov, July 12th-August 16th 1943.
Map 29   Proposed alternate offensive, Southern Salient, July 12th 1943.

List of abbreviations

AAR	Anti-tank Artillery Regiment
AB	Artillery Brigade
AD	Assault Division
AGC	Army Group Centre
AGS	Army Group South
AR	Anti-tank Regiment
ATR	Anti-tank Regiment
CP	Command Post
DATR	Destroyer Anti-tank Regiment
DR	SS *Das Reich* Division
GA	Guards Army
GAD	Guards Airborne Division
GAR	Guards Airborne Regiment
GCC	Guards Cavalry Corps
GD	*Grossdeutschland* Division
GMRB	Guards Motorized Rifle Brigade
GMC	Guards Mechanized Corps
GR	Grenadier Regiment
GRC	Guards Rifle Corps
GRD	Guards Rifle Division
GRR	Guards Rifle Regiment
GTA	Guards Tank Army
GTB	Guards Tank Brigade
GTC	Guards Tank Corps
GTDR	Guards Tank Destroyer Regiment
GTR	Guards Tank Regiment
IC	Infantry or Army Corps
ID	Infantry Division
KSF	Komsomolets State Farm
LAH	SS *Leibstandarte Adolf Hitler* Division
MRB	Motorized Rifle Brigade
OP	Observation Post
OSF	Oktiabrski State Farm
PzC	Panzer Corps
PzD	Panzer Division
PzGD	Panzer Grenadier Division
PzGR	Panzer Grenadier Regiment
PzR	Panzer Regiment
RD	Rifle Division
RLR	Rocket Launcher Regiment
RR	Rifle Regiment

SD   Security Division
sPzAbt   Heavy Tank Detachment
sPzR   Heavy Tank Regiment
SSDR   SS *Das Reich* Division
SSTK   SS *Totenkopf* Division
StuGAbt   Assault Gun Detachment
StPzAbt   Assault Panzer Detachment
TA   Tank Army
TB   Tank Brigade
TC   Tank Corps
TDB   Tank Destroyer Brigade
TDR   Tank Destroyer Regiment
TK   SS *Totenkopf* Division
TR   Tank Regiment
VA   Air Army
VVS   Air Force (Soviet)

Code Source List
See bibliography for full details of each title.

Code	Author	Title
aaa		*Atlas of the Second World War (Collins)*
agk	Patrick Agte	*Michael Wittmann and the Waffen-SS Tiger Commanders of the Leibstandarte in WWII Volume 1*
asz	Albert Seaton	*The Russo-German War 1941-45*
awk	Alexander Werth	*Russia at War 1941-1945*
cbk	Christer Bergstrom	*Kursk: The Air Battle, July 1943*
cby	Chris Bellamy	*Absolute War: Soviet Russia in the Second World War*
cbz	Correlli Barnett	*Hitler's Generals*
dga	David M. Glantz	*After Stalingrad: The Red Army's Winter Offensive 1942-1943*
dgk	David M. Glantz & Jonathan House	*The Battle of Kursk*
dgn	David M. Glantz	*From the Don to the Dnepr: Soviet Offensive Operations, December 1942 – August 1943*
dgr	David M. Glantz	*The Battle for Kursk, 1943: The Soviet General Staff Study*
dlu	Didier Lodieu	*III. Pz.Korps at Kursk*
dpv	David Porter	*Fifth Guards Tank Army at Kursk 12 July, 1943*
eru	Erhard Raus & Steven H. Newton	*Panzer Operations: The Eastern Front Memoir of General Raus, 1941-1945*
evm	Erich von Manstein	*Lost Victories: The War Memoirs of Hitler's Most Brilliant General*
ezz	Earl Ziemke	*Stalingrad to Berlin : The German Defeat in the East*
fkk	Franz Kurowski	*Operation Zitadelle, July 1943*
fmz	F.W. von Mellenthin	*Panzer Battles: A Study of the Employment of Armor in the Second World War*

CODE SOURCE LIST

Code	Author	Title
fwl	Franz-Wilhelm Lochmann et al	The Combat History of German Tiger Tank Battalion 503 in World War II
fzk	Franz Kurowski	Panzer Aces
gjz	Geoffrey Jukes	Stalingrad to Kursk: Triumph of the Red Army
gmn	George M. Nipe Jr	Decision in the Ukraine: German Panzer Operations on the Eastern Front, Summer 1943
gnk	George M. Nipe Jr	Blood, Steel, and Myth: The II.SS-Panzer-Korps and the Road to Prochorowka
gnv	George M. Nipe Jr	Last Victory in Russia: The SS-Panzerkorps and Manstein's Kharkov Counteroffensive, February-March 1943
hjj	Hans-Joachim Jung	The History of Panzerregiment "Grossdeutschland"
hsz	Helmuth Spaeter	History of the Panzerkorps Grossdeutschland
hzs	Harold Shukman	Stalin's Generals
je	John Erickson	The Road to Berlin: Stalin's War with Germany Volume 2
jp	Janusz Piekalkiewicz	Operation Citadel: Kursk and Orel, the Greatest Tank Battle of the Second World War
kcz	Keith Cumins	Cataclysm: The War on the Eastern Front 1941-45
kfz	Franz Kurowski	Panzerkrieg: An Overview of German Armored Operations in World War 2
knz	Kamen Nevenkin	Fire Brigades: The Panzer Divisions 1943-1945
kuc	Karl Ullrich	Like a Cliff in the Ocean: A History of the 3rd SS-Panzer-Division Totenkopf
lck	Lloyd Clark	Kursk: The Greatest Battle
mck	Chris Mann	SS-Totenkopf: The History of the 'Death's Head' Division 1940-45
mhz	Mark Healy	Zitadelle: The German Offensive Against the Kursk Salient 4-17 July 1943
mjk	Michael Jones	Total War: From Stalingrad to Berlin
rb	Rupert Butler	Hitler's Death's Head Division
rck	Robin Cross	Citadel: The Battle of Kursk
rmk	Robert M. Citino	The Wehrmacht Retreats: Fighting a Lost War, 1943
sgf	Stephen G. Fritz	Ostkrieg: Hitler's War of Extermination in the East
snk	Steven H. Newton	Kursk: The German View
snz	Steven H. Newton	Hitler's Commander: Field Marshal Walther Model-Hitler's Favorite General
swm	Samuel W. Mitcham Jr	The Men of Barbarossa: Commanders of the German Invasion of Russia, 1941
vdp	David Porter	Das Reich Division at Kursk: 12 July 1943
vzz	Valeriy Zamulin	Demolishing the Myth: The Tank Battle at Prokhorovka, Kursk, July 1943: An Operational Narrative
wdk	Walter S. Dunn Jr	Kursk: Hitler's Gamble, 1943
wfz	Will Fey	Armor Battles of the Waffen-SS
wwf	Will Fowler	Kursk: The Vital 24 Hours

Code	Author	Title
zds	Dennis Showalter	*Hitler's Panzers*
zfk	Franz Kurowski	*Panzer Aces II*
zmb	Mark M. Boatner III	*The Biographical Dictionary of World War II*
zoc	Otto Carius	*Tigers in the Mud*
zom	Peter McCarthy & Mike Syron	*Panzerkrieg: The Rise and Fall of Hitler's Tank Divisions*
zow	Otto Weidinger	*Das Reich IV*
zra	Col Richard N. Armstrong	*Red Army Tank Commanders: The Armored Guards*
zrl	Rudolf Lehmann	*The Leibstandarte III*
zro	Richard Overy	*Russia's War: A History of the Soviet Effort: 1941-1945*
zsm	Samuel W. Mitcham Jr	*Panzer Legions: A Guide to the German Army Tank Divisions of World War II and Their Commanders*
ztc	Charles Trang	*Totenkopf*
zzk	Franz Kurowski	*Infantry Aces*
zzt	Thomas L. Jentz	*Panzertruppen 2: The Complete Guide to the Creation & Combat Employment of Germany's Tank Force 1943-1945*
zzy	John Pimlott	*The Atlas of World War II*
zzz	Simon Goodenough	*War Maps*

Place name spellings

Primary	Alternative
Alekseevka	Alexejewka
Berezovka	Beresowka
Berezov	Beresoff
Bolye Maiachki	Bol Majatschki
Butovo	Butowo
Bykovka	Bykowka
Cherkasskoe	Tscherkasskoje
Dubrova	Dubrowa
Gertsovka	Gerzowka
Grenoe	Gresnoje
Gremuchi	Gremutschy
Iakovlevo	Jakowlewo
Iasnaia Poliana	Jasnaja Poljana
Ivanovka	Iwanowka
Kalinovka	Kalinowka
Kartashevka	Kartaschewka
Kiselevo	Kisselewo
Kochetovka	Kotschetowka
Kozmo-Demianovka	Kisma Demanowka
Krasnyi Pochinok	Krassnyi Potschinok
Luchki North	Lutschki Nord
Luchki South	Lutschki Sud
Lukhanino	Luchanino
Malye Iablonovo	Mal Jablonowo
Malye Maiachki	Mal Majatschki
Mikhailovka	Michailowskoje
Nepkhaevo	Nepchajewo
Novenkoe	Nowenkoje
Ozerowski	Oserowskij
Petrovski	Petrowskij
Polezhaev	Poleshajew
Pushkarnoe	Puschkamoje
Rakovo	Rakowo
Rzhavets	Rshawez
Smorodino	Ssmorodino
Storozhevoe	Storoshewoje
Sukho Solotino	Ssuch Ssolotino
Syrtsev	Ssyrzew
Syrtsevo	Ssyrtsewo
Ternovka	Ternowka

Teterevino North	Teterewino Nord
Teterevino South	Teterewino Sud
Vasilevka	Wassiljewka
Verkhopenie	Werchopenje
Vesselyi	Wesselyi
Vinogradovka	Winogradowka
Visloe	Wissloje
Zavidovka	Savidovka
Zhimolostnoe	Shilomostnoje
Zhuravlinyi	Shurawlinyi

Acknowledgements

I would like to dedicate this book to my father and father-in-law who were both veterans and in their own way generated in me a deep interest and respect for the men and events of the Second World War.

I would also like to dedicate this book to my nephew Alex, who sadly left us much too soon. He will be in our hearts for always.

I would like to thank my friends Duncan and Paul, who provided sage advice and assistance when it was most needed. In addition, I would also like to thank my dear wife for her help, patience and understanding.

Introduction

This study, which focuses on the operational aspects of this important campaign and its far-reaching impact on the war, is trying to achieve two objectives. The first is to provide a comprehensive look at the battle events from within each corps sector driving down to divisional and wherever possible regimental level. With the action discussed chronologically from corps sector to corps sector, there are times when the discussion is hectic, multi-directional and sometimes a little perplexing. To assist the reader with this avalanche of information, a small amount of redundancy is introduced into the narrative to reduce the number of times the reader has to stop and go back to refresh his memory on a related thread of thought. For example on the boundary line between *LAH* and *SSDR* is a fortified hill protected with plenty of artillery that could strike both divisions. *LAH* fought and captured the hill in the morning. In late afternoon, which could be pages later in the book, *Das Reich* approached the nearby area that would have been under enemy artillery range prior to the *LAH* capture. As part of the discussion of *SSDR*'s activity in the area, a brief mention of *LAH* taking the hill earlier in the day and the impact it had on *SSDR* is also mentioned. There are also times during day-long engagements when different stages of the battle are mentioned, sometimes pages apart and a reminder is made of earlier events. There is also some overlap when different combatants review the same engagement from their perspective.

The battle zones for the northern and southern salient have different complexities and the story formats are laid out differently to respond to those complexities. In the north, where the engagements were fewer, more direct in nature and fought in a more confined area, the listings are separated only by day and time with no regard to corps sector. In the southern salient the battle zone was larger and the battle action was more plentiful, where actions in one corps sector would have greater impact on another corps sector. As such it is necessary to separate the battle action further to make the narrative easier to understand. So, in the south the battle action is divided by day and hour for each panzer corps sector. The coverage begins with the 2nd SS PzC followed by 48th PzC and it ends with the 3rd PzC. There is also coverage of the infantry corps on the extreme flanks which is included in the nearest panzer corps sector.

The narrative is driven by the German advance and as mentioned before is divided, at least in the southern salient, by the 3 primary panzer corps that participated in the assault. I believe viewing the overall campaign in the format chosen has certain advantages, providing a different perspective than strictly covering the battle sequence division by division or by sector by sector only. With the serious student studying this book along with the other key texts in the field, one can grasp some of the subtle nuances of the campaign that might have otherwise been overlooked. Choosing this format highlights the ordeals the corps commanders were facing on any given day. Knobelsdorff, Hausser and Kempf had different responsibilities and faced different problems and they, with their distinct experiences and resources, overcame the different terrain, weather and Soviet resistance in their own way. Soviet Generals Chistiakov, Katukov, Shumilov, Rotmistrov and Zhadov also receive a fair amount of attention but the most critical attention is given to Generals Hoth, Vatutin,

Rokossovsky and Model.

There is another complexity to consider. This campaign was dynamic, forever changing, attacks and counter-attacks occurring simultaneously within individual battles. During the day an objective achieved could be lost during the night with an enemy counter-attack. It happened many times that the Germans would have to recapture the same village or hill several times. The Soviets were tenacious about recapturing lost ground, attacking the flanks and getting behind the front line to wreak constant havoc on the Germans. By covering each of these episodes which could be pages apart may be a little confusing but it could not be helped if the story line was to be adhered to. If this complexity was not enough, the reader must also be aware of the blizzard of order changes Vatutin instituted from the very beginning of the campaign. To stay true to the chronology, these changes are also included in the narrative.

While the German side has the leading role, the Soviet side is far from neglected. I've tried to stay neutral, not favoring either side. The many counter-attacks ordered by Vatutin and Rokossovsky are given ample space.

The coverage is also extended beyond mid-July to almost the end of August and includes minor coverage of the events of Operation Kutuzov in the north and Operation Rumyantsev in the south. Regrettably it was not possible to give these operations as deep coverage as Operation Citadel. I just wanted to show that after Operation Citadel was cancelled, the Germans, in their weakened state, still had many problems to contend with.

The second objective is to create a handy reference guide for those readers who desire further study of this important, revealing campaign, enabling them to look-up key information on a select basis. To accomplish this goal an extensive index is provided and I've added a code or a series of codes to most paragraphs that will point the reader to other sources of related or supplemental material. In most cases this additional material is harmonious to this book but in a few cases the information is different. For example, one source quotes the number of panzers a certain division has or carries into a specific battle while another source quotes a higher number. Over the years the number of tanks available or destroyed has varied. I've chosen what I believe is the accurate number but the reader should be aware that other accounts exist. This annotation is an attempt to provide the reader with as wide a scope of information possible.

The code system is set up in the following manner. The prefix is three letters that designate the author and source. The accompanying number is the page number and where there is a "+" there are multiple pages to study. These references are not created equal. Some are in depth while others are fleeting. Some will be very helpful while others are less so – those marked with asterisks I found particularly useful. If the code ends with an "m" then it refers to a map that could be studied alongside the text. I've also supplied a series of maps and hopefully between my maps and the other provided map references, the reader's questions will be answered.

On my maps, the German front line represents the area where the Germans had reasonably firm control of the territory. In many situations a scouting party or small advanced combat group had gone beyond the represented line but did not control the countryside sufficiently for it to be considered German terrain. Conversely, within the recognized German territory there could be isolated pockets of resistance that could last for days after the front line moved north.

As described above this presentation revolves around the operational aspects of this critical campaign and while there are some anecdotal experiences included, it's not the primary theme of the book.

1

Prior to the start of Operation Citadel

March 1st
Zeitzler was thinking of ways to shorten the line and redeploy the troops more efficiently. The process was already underway when Kursk was discussed. Zeitzler knew Model would not have sufficient forces to reach Kursk so he decided to transfer forces from two outside areas to Kursk. The first source was at Demyansk. It was decided to finally evacuate the area with its nearly 100,000 men. Most of these men would head for Kursk. The other evacuation location was at the Rzhev salient. The evacuation of Demyansk began on February 7th and took ten days while elements of five Soviet armies tried to destroy the pocket. It was a brilliant maneuver. The Rzhev evacuation was called Operation Buffalo and it began on March 1st. This evacuation took 16 days and the line fell back as much as 90 miles in some places. Rzhev, Bely, Vyazma were left to the Soviets by no later than March 12th. Losing this salient reduced the German frontage by 230 miles and freed 21 divisions for duty elsewhere. swm126*. mhk46. asz354. asz357. zow130+.[1]

March 10th
Field Marshal von Manstein offered Hitler battle plans to attack and reduce the Kursk salient. When Hitler rejected his "backhand plan", the Field Marshal wanted the offensive operation to start in April. Hitler was having trouble with his allies; he needed an offensive that would regain the initiative, restore his image and ease the concerns for the Axis partners. Von Manstein's alternate plan to attack the salient looked like an offensive to achieve his political objectives. It was limited in scope compared to Operation Barbarossa but if it succeeded would destroy several Soviet armies, a lot of weaponry and shorten the front line. Between the loss at Stalingrad and North Africa, the Axis had lost 500,000 men, maybe more. Von Manstein, a veteran of WWI, quickly showed his ability as a talented strategist, one of the best in the *Wehrmacht* and rose in the ranks to Field Marshal and commander of an Army Group in relatively short order. The original plan was for 48th PzC to lead the assault toward Oboyan, which was the shortest route to Kursk. The 2nd SS PzC would strongly support the 48th PzC's right flank in its drive north. The 3rd PzC would parallel the SS Corps, providing flank protection. The 11th IC would protect the right flank and rear of 3rd PzC. It sounded like a good plan but when 3rd PzC could not keep up to the other corps, it damaged the integrity of the whole army and Hoth and von Manstein should have reacted but did not. lck176. awk679. zmb341+. ezz128+. zro198+. zro202. shn153. hsz106+. zrl202. zrl206+. asz353+. asz355m. asz358. zow131. dgk14.

March 18th
After recapturing Kharkov, the 2nd SS PzC supported by the *GD* moved toward Belgorod, capturing it after several days of heavy fighting. mhk48. dgn206+.

---

1   See page 15 for an explanation of these references, and pages viii-x for a key.

March 22nd
The British Ultra machine detected a communiqué containing details of Operation Citadel and it was immediately passed along to Stalin. lck182. shn155.

March 23rd
The Soviet Operation Star and von Manstein's counteroffensive that retakes Kharkov and Belgorod winds down. With the rainy season about to start both sides would be unable to move until mid-May or June and besides the fighting had been continuous for nine months and both sides were exhausted. Some German generals thought that it was the proper time and place to stay on the defensive, allowing the enemy to fight its way to attrition and a negotiated peace. These same generals also knew their dictator would never stay on the defensive, believing it was safer to attack and force the enemy on the defensive. This successful German counteroffensive formed the front line from which Operation Citadel started from. dgn209. hsz104+. zrl201. zow97.

April 6th
The 7th PzD was pulled from the front and sent to Barvenkovo, southwest of Izyum, for refit. Just like 6th PzD, the 7th PzD had a full complement of men but unlike 6th PzD's 6th PzR will be short a few panzers and other heavy equipment. While both of these divisions would start Operation Citadel with over 100 panzers, the 19th PzD would be down 30% from establishment. Hoth slowly began assembling his forces to the Kharkov area. knz214. fzk51. shn157.

April 8th
Marshals Zhukov and Vasilevsky submitted battle plans for the summer in the Kursk sector to Stalin. The plans not only included the defense of the Kursk salient but also the counter offensives called Operation Kutuzov and Operation Rumyantsev. The former operation would target AGC in the Orel sector while the later would target the southern half aimed at recapturing Belgorod and Kharkov.

Zhukov had been born into a poor family with no military heritage in 1896 in the small village of Strelkovka not far from Kaluga. He struggled desperately for an education and when WWI broke out he was called up for active duty. Over the years, he prospered in the service and would rise to be a Marshal and number two man, behind Stalin. He had major roles at Leningrad, Moscow, Stalingrad, and later Berlin, as well as helping form the battle plans for the defense of Kursk and the follow-up offensive. wwf30. hzs343+. zro198+.

April 12th
Stalin convened a war meeting in Moscow to determine what the summer offensive would be, to see if he could convince Zhukov and Vasilevsky to agree with his pre-emptive offensive. He was in favor of attacking the Germans first from the Kursk salient. Zhukov, Vasilevsky and *Stavka* wanted to stay on the defensive until the new German offensive petered out and then strike a weakened enemy as hard as possible. They favored the "backhand approach" that von Manstein promoted previously to Hitler. *Stavka* and Zhukov's presentation to Stalin was quite convincing and Stalin agreed with it.

I have often wondered how history would have played out if Stalin had attacked first. It's possible it would have benefited Germany more than actual events did if the Soviets, who had already started assembling men in the area, had launched in May or June when their logistics would not have been as complete as they had been in July or would not have had the benefit of the extensive defenses that were built. In the last three months before Operation Citadel was launched, 500,000 railway cars full of supplies and weapons were brought to the Kursk salient. German aerial recon detected many of these long trains heading from Moscow to the Kursk area. lck180. awk681. ezz128+. zro198+. shn155.

April 15th
From Munich, Hitler released Order # 6: Operation Citadel. Deployments and objectives were explained in much detail. The launch date for Citadel was set for May 3rd. Hitler told Knobelsdorff and von Mellenthin that 48th PzC would be the main spearhead to capture Oboyan and then Kursk. If the campaign was successful the front line would be dramatically redrawn; the line would run from east of Orel – Kursk-Maloarkhangelsk-Prokhorovka-Belgorod-Kharkov. The shorter line would free up divisions to be sent to Italy when the Allies struck. An officer at the meeting had the audacity to offer the idea that with the success of Operation Citadel, Stalin might be willing to sit down at the bargaining table. That idea was quickly quieted. Hitler and Zeitzler just wanted to destroy a few Soviet armies, straighten out the line and regain the initiative. The two biggest opponents to Operation Citadel were Generals Model and Guderian. Model wanted to rebuild his 9th Army before tackling such a large offensive and Guderian, the Inspector General of Armored Troops, did not want the offensive at all. He was instituting a program to revitalize the Panzer arm and needed more time to complete it. He knew if Operation Citadel went ahead, it would doom his program which he felt would be the only way of prolonging the war. Von Manstein also reminded his boss that Russia's tank production was about 1,500 tanks a month, so the longer the delay the more tanks would be faced in the salient. swm127. lck178. lck182. fmz212++. fmz216. vzz26. vzz33. ezz128+. kfz445+. zro198. pck89. zrl201. mhk50. asz354. dgk2.

Stalin already had a copy of the orders; it was obtained by the Lucy spy ring and delivered to Moscow. Using these plans, Zhukov devised a defense to neutralize the German offense. Zhukov had the time, about ten weeks, to supply the salient (about 500,000 freight cars worth) and to bring 20% of the Red Army to the area as well as 30% of the armor and 25% of the Red Air Force. He was determined to break the German spell of winning summer offensives. swm127. lck178. lck182. fmz217. mjk94. ezz133. shn153.

May 4th
During a conference in Munich between Hitler and his top officers, Col General Jodl once again asked Hitler to cancel the offensive. Jodl believed new forces would be needed in the Mediterranean and Balkans. Col General Guderian and Albert Speer also wanted to cancel Citadel. Guderian wanted the German Army to stay defensive for all of 1943 to allow a rebuilding of the entire Army. Model wanted to delay it further until more new panzers were available and his 9th Army could be rebuilt but Keitel, Kluge and Hitler wanted the offensive to launch sooner rather than later. Hitler was obsessed with the new panzers and was convinced that delaying the launch would be worthwhile to have more of these super weapons that "would easily penetrate the enemy's defenses". Even though Kluge was not a dedicated Nazi, he had a habit of following Hitler's lead. Kluge was born into an aristocratic Prussian family and it was unusual for Hitler to like and admire aristocrats, but

he apparently liked Kluge. Kluge was part of the invasion force of Poland as commander of 4th Army as he was in the invasion of France and Operation Barbarossa. Von Manstein had an aristocratic military background as well but understandably Hitler did not like him. swm130. cbz396+. mjk82. ezz129. fzk169. pck89+. mhk84. asz356+. dgk20. (May 4th)

By now the evacuation process of civilians in the Kursk salient was under way. 100,000 volunteers would remain to help build the defenses. lck207. shn155.

May 6th

The air war in the Kursk salient for the Soviets started in earnest for they expected Operation Citadel to begin within the week. For the next three days German airfields and important rail junctions were bombed. The Soviets claimed destroying 500 planes while losing 122 planes as well as destroying trains and disrupting German logistics. During this period the Soviet 2nd VA, 16th VA and 17th VA flew just shy of 10,000 sorties. nzk75. cbk12m. zro202.

May 7th

In retaliation for the recent air offensive in the Kursk salient by the Soviets, the *Luftwaffe* began an assault on three industrial complexes: the cities of Gorki, Saratov and Yaroslavl. An estimated 1,200 sorties were made and since this type of strategic bombing was unusual for the Germans, it came as a surprise to the Soviets and few planes were lost. Another 800 sorties were made at the rail junctions at Kostornoe, Kursk, Arkhangesk and Elets. The German escorts also claimed shooting down 163 Soviet fighters who tried to intercede at a cost of only seven planes. These attacks brought further escalation by the Red Air Force. nzk75. wwf48.

May 10th

The Panther production was experiencing problems and the panzer would not be ready in time, so Hitler had to postpone Citadel until June 12th. Albert Speer assured Hitler the production glitch was taken care of and that there would be 300 Panthers for the June 12th launch. Speer was too optimistic; by July 1st, only 12 Panthers were coming off the assembly line each week. There would be only 192 Panthers for Operation Citadel plus four recovery vehicles. By the end of 1943, Albert Speer had worked out the production problems and by the end of the war 6,000 Panthers had been built. Guderian knew of the problems associated with launching a panzer as complicated as the Panther and tried to convince Hitler to cancel Operation Citadel. Guderian also tried to have a MG mounted on the new Elefants but failed there as well. swm130. snk73. lck184. zpm184+. shn152+. vzz27. mhk135. zow131. dgk20.

In addition to the Panther, there were several other debuts for Operation Citadel. The "Elefant" tank destroyer was larger and heavier than the Panther, weighing in at 64 tons or more and sporting an 8.8cm 21 foot long gun. It had a thick hide (200mm in front) like the Tiger but its lack of machine gun made it vulnerable to infantry. Despite having two engines, it was slow, having a top speed of around 12 mph over ground. Another weakness with the Elefant was its tracks, which were not sturdy enough and were prone to mine damage. The three Elefant battalions would be deployed in the northern salient. The miniature tank like vehicle, named Goliath after its inventor, was used as a remote demolition tool. It ran on tracks like a panzer and was driven by two starter motors powered by batteries. It was five feet long, two foot high and almost three feet wide and most of them would carry a payload of 132 pounds of TNT. They would be used to clear a path in a minefield, clear barbwire entanglements, destroy MG nests and larger bunkers. wwf27. wwf19. lck189. pck40. asz364.

Going against Hitler's order not to build an extensive trench system in the Orel salient, Model began planning a trench system just like the one built at the Rzhev salient that successfully repulsed a massive Soviet offensive. Though Model had years of experience, he made his reputation by being a great defensive tactician and felt more at ease with that role. For the general to have to play offensive against an elaborate defense and a comparable commander like Lt General Konstantin Rokossovsky might have been asking too much. Though his strategy was different than Lt General Hermann Hoth, who released all his panzer divisions on the first day as compared to holding out four days before releasing all his reserve panzers, Model did use 300 panzers and assault guns the first day. snz257. mjk82.

Col General Heinz Guderian, still against Operation Citadel, went to see Adolf Hitler and once again tried to have the operation canceled. Hitler, though not confident to its success, refused the request. Hitler was also concerned about two other nearby areas which made the dictator more cautious and unwilling to take chances than usual. North of Orel and south of Kharkov were two areas in which the Soviets had concentrated large forces. Hitler could not afford to neglect these potential hotspots when dealing with Kursk. The refusal to release 24th PzC to von Manstein was a good example of his concern. Also intimidating the dictator was the fact that Axis forces were surrendering in Tunisia by the thousands and that it would be only a matter of days for the final capitulation and surrender. In all 130,000 Germans surrendered. The next day Hitler postponed Operation Citadel until July. fmz216+. ezz128+. dgk55. fkz169. kfz444++. zro202. zow134.

June 5th
General Jeschonnek of OKL reported to General Greim and Hitler that the *Luftwaffe* strength for Operation Citadel would be insufficient to guarantee control of the skies or to give adequate ground protection for all sectors all of the time. Hitler dismissed this information. Other generals tried to talk him out of this operation but he ignored all attempts. He had made up his mind on the offensive and nothing would change it. fzk169.

June 12th
Today was supposed to be the new start date for Operation Citadel but it was postponed again. Hitler set a new date; this time the start date would be between July 3rd and July 6th. The dictator wanted another 36 Panthers at the front. When FM von Manstein heard of another postponement, he strongly protested, claiming the Soviets had too much time to prepare and that no matter how many new panzers were available, the Soviet salient could not be taken. Even the OKW chimed in, which was unusual as Hitler deliberately kept them away from the business of the Eastern Front. Against Hitler's protests, the OKW also wanted to see the operation canceled. swm132. lck182+. lck212. ezz131. zro202. shn152+.

June 15th
During a meeting in Berlin, German intelligence briefed Hitler and his OKH staff on Soviet strength in the Kursk salient. The briefing was dismally inaccurate. For example, it was estimated that the Soviets had only 1,500 tanks instead of the approximately 5,000

tanks they actually had. They also anticipated Red forces in the sector to be about one million as opposed to the nearly two million actually present. (The above numbers include Steppe Front and other attachments to Voronezh Front.) lck211.

Hoth received aerial photos of the Kursk salient. It showed the 10th TC had arrived in the Oboyan region and other large columns moving west from Voronezh. Further concentrations of forces were seen at the Oskol River as well. The only conclusion Hoth could make was that the Soviets knew of Operation Citadel, and based on this knowledge, he adjusted his attack plan. Hoth liked the Oboyan route the best but did acknowledge some disadvantages to it. The terrain leading to the Psel River was rugged in spots; the river itself had swampy banks in many areas and there were only a few good crossing points. The ground to the north of the river was higher than the southern side, giving the Soviets a big advantage. As long as the 2nd SS Corps was south of the Teterevino-Gresnoe line, the Prokhorovka corridor was an ideal exit point for Soviet tanks to attack the 48th PzC's eastern flank as it tried to cross the Psel. He would need a formidable panzer force to stop the flank attack and that was why he chose the 2nd SS PzC for center duty. With the SS Corps heading to the northeast, it would be closer to 3rd PzC and the two corps could mutually assist each other in attacking Prokhorovka. The biggest change in the plan was after 48th PzC captured Cherkasskoe, the corps would also shift slightly to the northeast to parallel the SS in order to keep a unified front. The concept of a unified front was logical but in my opinion it was not executed very well. A true shift would mean to stay east of the troublesome Pena River valley and this clearly was not the case. In the Pena bend, the 3rd PzD and the 52nd IC got themselves into trouble and the *GD* division was called on to save them. This detour by *GD* killed their momentum to the Psel River and created a gap between the two panzer corps.

Once Prokhorovka and/or Oboyan were captured, Hoth had no formal plans to reach Kursk. The choices made would depend on circumstances. He thought the toughest part of the campaign would be fighting through the first defensive belts, the first 15 to 18 miles. Once past the Novenkoe-Teterevino North line the going should be easier. In theory it was practical but the 3rd PzC was too far behind the SS to gain much benefit from mutual support. The General was clearly wrong on this expectation though he was right to be concerned that 4th PzA did not have sufficient panzers or men to reach Kursk, especially after such a long delay. The receipt of 192 Panthers did provide some comfort; the machine had potential but was feared for its rumored shortcomings. snk72++. snk76. hjj112+. zrl202+.

After studying the aerial photos of every foot of the southern salient, Hoth and his staff worked out a carefully laid plan of coordinated fire between the artillery batteries of the different divisions. Air raids were also included in the plan. Hoth knew that carefully placed shelling and aerial bombing would be essential if victory was to be theirs. He had no false beliefs that this campaign would be easy. A rigid timetable for preparations before the launch was also followed. There was much to do before the attack and Hoth tried to be as efficient and organized as possible. The allotted batteries for the SS corps alone were over 24,000 shells and over 9,000 rockets for the first hour of the operation for 7/5, with explicit target instructions. Targets were chosen from aerial photos and information obtained from prisoner interrogations and Soviet deserters. fmz219. vzz32. zow135+.

Over the weeks the aerial photos kept arriving, showing how the Soviet defenses kept developing and greater force was building to the west of the attack zone (40th Army sector).

Von Manstein and Hoth considered moving the axis of attack further east which meant further south also to avoid the well organized defenses. They contemplated driving as far east as the Oskol River but then rejected the idea, staying with the original plan. This new plan would entail greater distances to travel and going deeper into enemy territory which meant greater risks of encirclement and destruction. After pleading his case to von Manstein, Hoth received *GD* and the new Panther Brigade for 48th PzC to aid in combating the expected resistance on the western flank of the original attack axis. Hoth anticipated that this extra armor would do well in capturing and holding Oboyan, creating a western bridgehead north of the Psel River which would allow the Panthers to strike eastward to assist the SS Corps when moving through the Prokhorovka corridor. Near the end of the month, Hoth sent new orders to his corps commanders that included the probable shift toward Prokhorovka. vzz32. zrl201+.

June 20th
Hitler set the new launch date of Operation Citadel to July 5th. At about this same time Marshal Zhukov, General Voronov, General Sokolovsky and Lt General M.M. Popov completed the final preparations for Operation Kutuzov. The generals had been planning this offensive since April. swm132. snk71. zrl209. dgk229+.

June 23rd
An officer from 2nd TC picked up a German deserter, Heinz Schroeter, who had a complete Order of Battle for both the Kursk and Orel salients. Though the Soviets already had knowledge of the campaign, this new confirmation was appreciated. zow132.

June 27th
Over the previous week, Soviet agents had been caught behind the line west of Belgorod, especially in the panzer bivouac trying to pick up intel. snk74.

June 29th
At night from the Kharkov-Akhtyrka area, the 4th PzA, 3rd PzC and *GD* began their journey northward to their final staging areas before Citadel began. The *GD* would settle near the Vorskla River northwest of Tomarovka. For *GD*, the recon photos showed their attack zone to be hilly, wooded terrain, cut by many streams and the lowlands extremely marshy; not exactly optimal panzer terrain. And north of this immediate ground was a long ridge that could not be seen past until captured. On the south side of the ridge it could be seen that the land was dotted with tank traps and heavily fortified bunkers. This ground had been reconnoitered up to this first ridge line and Hoth believed his forces could overcome any obstacles. There were two defensive trenches within the first defensive belt. One trench ran through Cherkasskoe and another to the north that ran through Dubrova. Hoernlein's *GD* would be the spearhead for the 48th PzC and would go straight for the high ground to observe for artillery. Its sector would be less than two miles wide. The 11th PzD would be on the right and 3rd PzD on the left. The 3rd PzD was assembling near Zybino. The rest of 48th PzC was stationed in the Bogodukhov-Akhtyrka area to the west of Kharkov. Taking a different route to avoid congestion it also started moving north. The front line was not the problem, it was the terrain near the Vorskla River and especially the Pena River where the terrain became really difficult. The area had received a lot of rain that summer and that

made those river valleys even worse. If these obstacles could be overcome then the Psel River to the north would have its own set of problems to be addressed. mhz192. fkk257+. kcz167. hsz108+. hsz112++. snk70. fmz218+ .zrl203+. zow135.

June 30th
The *GD* had been stationed near Moschchenoye, southwest of Tomarovka, and was now preparing to move to their jump-off points. hjj113+. hsz112.

While there had been a pause in the ground war the last three months due to the rainy season, plus the fact that both sides were preparing for Operation Citadel, the air war continued unabated. On the German side, the *Luftwaffe* made a determined effort to slow the building of defenses in the salient as well as the buildup of men, weapons and supplies that were being sent to Kursk sector. On the Soviet side, the Red Air Force was active in many sectors of the line, especially in the Kuban area where the 17th Army was wasting away and the *Luftwaffe* had to try to neutralize the threat. In the last three month period, the *Luftwaffe* reported losing 616 planes: 60% were bombers and the rest fighters. For Germany, this was a large loss; some of those lost pilots and planes were destined for Kursk and would be sorely missed during the campaign. nzk74. snk151++. mjk80.

It had been a productive month for Soviet partisans working behind the lines of AGC sector. In an attempt to slow the Germans from resupplying for Operation Citadel, they conducted over 800 attacks that destroyed nearly 300 locomotives, over 1200 railway cars and over 40 bridges. It actually made a major contribution to the cause for it slowed the German logistics, though General Model was still able to find ways to fill his bunkers. snk160.

July 1st
Stalin became the benefactor of an ever increasing flow of Lend Lease supplies. Four thousand tanks were delivered in 1942 as well as 120,000 trucks and jeeps and 2,400 planes. For all of 1942, 2.7 million tons of supplies and natural resources were delivered to Russia from the United States. In the last five months of 1943 another 158,500 vehicles would be received. During the first half of 1943, 1.5 million new soldiers were added to the roster and an even greater number of wounded returned to active duty. wdk32+. pck94.

By July 1st, the German Army had 243 active divisions and, despite initiating a vigorous draft program, on average each division was short 2,500 men. At Stalingrad, Hitler lost 19 divisions and the loss in North Africa earlier that year was not much better. The *Wehrmacht* would never recover from such losses. These losses were an epiphany of sorts for Hitler. He did try to boost his draft in and outside of Germany. German assembly lines now worked day and night; women now worked as well. Soviet volunteers were encouraged and armed to help fight partisan actions. Many non-Germans were now deployed around Germany, manning AA guns to assist in warding off Allied bombing.

It rained hard during predawn hours, making it more difficult for the trailing forces to reach their assembly area south of Tomarovka. wdk35++. zzk371. zow135.

Hitler invited his key commanders of Citadel to his Wolf's Lair for a final briefing and motivation session. He informed his generals that Operation Citadel would launch on July 5th. Some were pleased and some displeased. Luckily for all the generals their forces were well prepared and ready to go. The generals that were displeased were hoping Hitler would call off the operation. He also confided that aerial photos showed no new formations in the salient since mid June but there had been a redeployment of forces. The biggest change was an increase of men in the Pena River valley, especially northeast of Rakitnoye. Improvements in the defenses continued, which set most of the German generals with concern. Von Manstein had to postpone his trip to Bucharest Rumania to see General Antonescu to make this meeting. By the next day Stalin had been informed of the final date from the Soviet spy on Hitler's inner council. snk74+. pck20+. asz357. zow134+.

Hausser issued Order # 17 to Priess of *SSTK*. On the day of the launch the division, deployed to the immediate southeast of *Das Reich*, was to advance and capture Hill 216.5 while *Das Reich* was taking Berezov next door. Zhuravlinyi, north of Hill 216.5, would be the next objective. From there the division was to turn southeast and secure the Belgorod-Kursk Highway in the Shopino-Gonki-Erik sector. It was then to continue east and clear resistance between the key highway and the Lipovyi Donets River, extending its control to Smorodino. To assist the division against the many gun emplacements in the area, a Werfer battalion was attached to give *SSTK* more firepower. The *Luftwaffe* would fly in front of the advance, hitting the many guns and providing air cap against the Red Air Force. The attached Tigers would lead the ground assault. After regrouping it would attack Hill 227.4 and Hill 218. At the start of the campaign *SSTK* was only 65% of full strength. kuz192. vzz6m+. dgk95m. ztc268. zow135.

July 2nd
In mid afternoon, the *GD* division arrived at their pre Citadel assembly points northwest of Tomarovka. The HQ would be set up at Moshenoye, south of Tomarovka, while the division would wait in the woods to the west of the village. Attached to *GD* was 10th PzB which had approximately 192 new Panthers that were working when the train pulled into the nearby station. In total, *GD* had at least 350 and as many as 370 panzers on the eve of the launching of Operational Citadel. There are numerous sources that differ in numbers for the Panther brigade from 192 as the low figure and as many as 200 Panthers as the high figure. It seems that 192 Panthers were in working order and were able to start on 7/5. hsz112. hjj114. knz662+. pck27. zow136.

After the war conference with Hitler at Wolfsschanze, von Manstein flew to Bucharest and presented the Gold Crimea Shield to General Antonescu for his loyal support in the war. pck25. vzz88.

Vatutin and Khrushchev arrived at Katukov's HQ and informed the general that the German offensive would begin within the next three days. pck26+.

Saturday, July 3rd on the Southern Salient
The Kursk salient was located on an upland between the Oka and Don Rivers to the east and the Donets and Dnepr Rivers on the west. Also of vital importance would be the Psel River and the Pena River. Other rivers that fell within the battle zone were Lipovyi Donets, Koren, Razumnaia and Korocha which flowed southwards. Other rivers to contend with but to a lesser degree would be Desna, Svapa, Seim, Vorskla and Vorsokolets which flowed mostly south or to the southwest. The 48th PzC would have the toughest terrain to maneuver around, for the Vorskla, Pena as well as the Psel would have to be crossed. These rivers also had tributaries and marshy banks to fight as well. The 2nd SS PzC for the most part would advance between rivers, though *SSTK* would have to cross the Psel. The line the Soviets were holding in the salient was over 250 miles in length and at the

shoulders the distance was about 70 miles apart. The distance from the shoulder to the tip was almost 125 miles. The actual assault would fall within a 50 mile range of that 125 mile distance. Driving south from near Orel, AGC would fight its way to Kursk and meet up with AGS which was fighting its way north from Belgorod. Once linked, both army groups would begin to liquidate the several Soviet armies that would be trapped within the salient. dgk79*+. swm125. wdk112. lck176. hjj123m. zpm189. ztc268. zro198. hsz105+. vzz35.

To avoid the death and destruction of the linear trench warfare of WWI and to avoid the massive deaths of the current German blitzkrieg, the Soviets built defensive belts in the salient. These belts, which ran the entire German attack zone, usually consisted of three trench systems with each trench spread 100 to 400 yards apart. In this way infantry would be spread over greater distances, making artillery barrages by the enemy less effective. These belts also had the advantage that if the front trench was breached, the men could fall back to the next trench. The second and third trenches were constructed in such a way as to create kill zones if and when the first trench line was breached. There would be multiple layers of Pak fronts and dug-in tanks to stop the Tigers and Panthers breaking through. For example, in the south, 6th GA had four divisions in the first trench and three in the second. The 7th GA had three divisions in the first trench and two divisions in the second. In the southern salient, the second defensive belt was about five miles behind the first and the third defensive belt about ten to twelve miles behind the second. In the north, due to the different terrain features, the three defensive belts were closer together. These complex configurations were designed to mutually support strongpoints made up of infantry, armor and artillery. Oftentimes dug-in tanks were deployed to the flanks in order to strike the Tigers on their vulnerable side armor. Rokossovsky dug 3,000 miles of trenches while Vatutin had 2,500 miles of trenches. Strongpoints would usually be built every 500 to 800 yards that had the capacity to take down tanks as they approached. The heaviest defenses were built in front of 48th PzC and the 3rd PzC since these were the two best ways to reach Kursk. wdk104++. dgr34m. mjk80+. ezz133+. fzk170. vzz37+. asz360+. zow133+. dgk67.

The Soviets had all the advantages and it's a little surprising that 4th PzA did as well as it did. The Germans had a combined total of 900,000 men, as many as 2,700 panzers and assault guns, 10,000 guns and around 2,000 planes, half the number of field guns and many times less rocket launchers. The Soviets had 1.3 million men, approximately 3,300 tanks, 19,000 assorted guns, 2,600 assorted aircraft in the immediate area, more if needed, and 1,000 rocket launchers. Rokossovsky had the advantage over Vatutin in men and tanks. Central Front had 700,000 men and 1,800 tanks while Voronezh had 600,000 men and 1,500 tanks. If you include the numbers from Steppe Front then the numbers increase to 5,100 tanks, 31,400 guns and mortars, 3,500 aircraft and 1.9 million men. If you extend the range a little further when counting available planes then the Soviets had almost 6,000 planes. The Soviets also had the huge advantage of having months to prepare a sophisticated defense against the coming assault. The US, during 1943, supplied Russia with 35,000 radio stations, 380,000 field phones, and 956,000 miles of phone cable. The Red Army never had communications on this level before Kursk. In the first two years of the war, poor communications was one of the Red Army's major weaknesses and one reason for their poor results. The improvements in communications between the front line and HQs would have an incredible positive impact on how the Soviet forces responded to the German assault. wwf28+++. lck193+. swm131+*. lck185++. hjj112. mjk81. jp115. pck24+. rkz166*. sgf343. cbk12m. fzk170. kfz450. zpm191+. zro193+. zro201. vzz34. zow134.

The 5th GA was originally the 66th Army that fought bravely at the tractor factory in Stalingrad. Stalin awarded it with the new "Guards" designation for its valor. On 7/6/1943, the army was transferred from Konev to Vatutin. wwf92++. vzz54. asz360. (July 3rd)

The 5th GTA was created using the 3rd TC as its core. The 29th TC and 5th GMC were then added to it. In February of 1943 it received a full complement of tanks and became the 5th Guards Tank Army. In March it was assembled in the Ostrogozhsk area east of Prokhorovka as part of Konev's Steppe Front where it was reorganized, resupplied and trained. On 7/6/1943, the army was transferred from Konev to Vatutin. wwf92++. vzz54. (July 3rd)

The terrain features in the southern salient varied. In the 48th PzC sector there were the Pena and Vorskla rivers, which had difficult terrain as well as marshy basins that made tank movement difficult. In the center, the SS Corps had the best terrain and roads to travel, with roaming hills and few ravines to contend with. The *SSTK* would eventually encounter the Psel River, the crossing of which would be moderately difficult due to the above average rains. The location and contour of the river right next to the main corridor to Kursk favored the Soviet defenders. The *LAH* would have to cross the Solotinka, but that was a relatively small river. The 3rd PzC to the east had more favourable terrain than the 48th PzC but it did have to contend with a series of ravines and a number of rivers including the Donets, although there were clear access routes to reach the mighty river near Rzhavets. wwf97. gnk312m+. fmz219. hjj112. hsz112.

Stavka studied and analyzed German assaults and they were confident that Hoth would have his panzers lead the attack. To neutralize this threat it was decided to create Pak fronts. A Pak front was an assembly of at least ten guns, typically more, that were usually dug-in and waiting for a panzer formation to approach a key route. Tigers had greater firing distance on many of these guns and would have the advantage. That was why at least ten field guns would be deployed; the Tigers would hit some of these guns but the other guns would continue firing hoping to get lucky or perhaps hit an Mk that would be trailing the Tigers. Usually massive minefields and deep anti-tank ditches would be placed in front of the Pak fronts to slow the panzers even further. To make these Pak fronts even more formidable, a series of mutually positioned Pak fronts would be placed in order to overwhelm the German attackers. It was a clever concept and it was adeptly applied with excellent camouflage before the campaign was launched. This invention clearly made certain aspects of blitzkrieg less effective. It also made Mk IIIs and to some extent Mk IVs obsolete. The Germans found the best way to defeat Pak fronts were the careful modified use of *Panzerkeil* called *Panzerglocke*, or a special use of wedge formations with Tigers in the lead with coordinated use of air power. There would be a *Luftwaffe* observer with these Panzerglocke and when a Pak front was discovered a quick call would be made to the airfield for assistance. After the war even the Tiger crews hated the thought of going up against the large Pak fronts with either many guns or large guns. wwf77. wwf116. fmz230+.

Not counting assault guns, Hoth had over 1,200 assorted panzers that included, in round numbers, 100 Tigers, 200 Panthers, 500 Mk IVs, 400 IIIs and 50 Mk IIs. It was decided that the best way to penetrate the elaborate defenses would be to use a wedge formation with Tigers or Panthers in the lead and the lighter panzers trailing behind, providing flank screening. The 6th GA and 7th GA had 20 anti-tank guns per mile as well as 1,700 Voronezh Front tanks in the immediate area to stop the panzers. The *Luftwaffe* had 1,100 planes in the immediate sector to assist all ground forces. Extending the range a total of an estimated 1,830 planes that included bombers, fighters and reconnaissance aircraft were available to the Luftwaffe in the Kursk salient. These airfields ranged from Smolensk in the north to Kirovograd in the south. That 1850 figure was about 75% of *Luftwaffe's* resources on the Eastern Front. dgr239. gjz185. rkz166**. vzz29. wwf163m. snk73++. lck193. zpm191. asz358+.

In the last ten days, the number of daily missions flown by the *Luftwaffe* was between 100 to 150 sorties, down from a daily average of 400 sorties for the first three weeks of June. This was an attempt by OKH to hide the fact that the offensive was about to start. The Germans had 1,830 assorted aircraft spread out north and south of Kursk but most of the planes were stationed at the following fields: Bryansk, Smolensk, Orsha and Orel to the north and Belgorod, Kharkov, Stalino, Zaporozhe and Kirovograd in the south. This represented 75% of the air strength of the *Luftwaffe* on the Eastern Front. Nearly a combined total of 500 anti-aircraft guns and machine guns were also brought into the salient to protect their ground forces from Soviet planes. dgr238+.

The Soviet soldiers had been told the German offensive could start at any time and were now on high alert. All trenches were manned as well as the artillery. Reports were coming in from the Lucy spy ring in Berlin. pck28.

Hoth placed Ott's 52nd IC on his extreme western flank to protect the 48th PzC's western flank from attack in order to concentrate on their drive north. The 48th PzC had 535 panzers including 192 new Panthers from 10th PzB plus 66 assault guns. The 2nd SS PzC, to the east of 48th PzC, had a combined strength of 494 panzers including 42 Tigers and 104 assault guns. The far east flank protection was provided by Group Kempf, which had 344 panzers including 45 Tigers from the attached sPzAbt 503 and 25 assault guns. Overall von Manstein had 22 divisions which included six panzer and five PzGD and 1,514 panzers and assault guns. Hoth was already aware of the large tank concentration east of the Oskol River and was thinking of meeting them head on at Prokhorovka, 18 miles southeast of Oboyan, instead of having the Soviet tanks hit his flank as his corps headed up the Oboyan road. Some disagree with the claim that Hoth was fully aware of the size of the Soviet concentration to the east for if he had been aware he would have done things differently leading to the morning of July 12th. Hoth, who took over the 4th PzA in May 1942, had 223,900 men in 4th PzA and another 126,000 men in Kempf's Group. Hoth would be sacked by Hitler in November 1943 when Kiev fell quickly. dgk53**. pck52+. vzz28. vzz159. zsm259. zow132. zzt86+.

A statistic that is sometimes overlooked concerns medical care the soldiers received. Expecting large numbers of wounded, Vatutin and Rokossovsky had built or updated 450 hospitals or field stations. Their insight was warranted; all these facilities would be used. The Germans were not nearly as prepared. lck198.

As mentioned above, the 3rd PzC had 299 panzers: 6th PzD 106; 19th PzD 81; 7th PzD 112. sPzAbt 503 had 45 Tigers which were split into three companies and each panzer division of 3rd PzC received a Tiger company. There were also some StuGs. The grand total of fighting vehicles was 375. By 7/12 each of these units would be down to 50% or below in strength. It is estimated that these three divisions had less than 120 panzers along the Donets in the Ryndinka sector by 7/12. One reason for such a high loss of panzers was due to lack of infantry protection. Kempf started the campaign with only one infantry division, the 168th ID, for offensive purposes. A few days later the 198th ID arrived but was used mostly on the defense. When you combine a lack of air support, it quickly becomes clear that Kempf and Breith were working at a severe disadvantage and they had to start further south than the two other corps and cross the Donets as well. vzz411+. dgk287+. zzt92.

In the evening, Hoth received an aerial report that showed a concentration of 200 tanks south of the Psel River, straddling the Belgorod-Oboyan road. If Hoth had any doubts as to whether Vatutin could be surprised by the attack axis, they were gone now. Clearly Vatutin was expecting this main highway to be the main axis of attack for the Germans. zrl202.

Saturday, July 3rd on the Northern Salient
During the preceding month, Model had made sure his 9th Army was logistically prepared. The Army consisted of 335,000 men and for a campaign lasting ten days, large quantities of goods were assembled, including 5,320 tons of food, 12,300 tons of ammunition, 6,000 tons of fodder for his 50,000 horses and 11,200 cubic yards of fuel. wwf47. lck198.

Stavka was making last minutes changes to Operation Kutuzov. It had been planned and approved by *Stavka* in May. It was scheduled to launch no earlier than 7/12/1943. It was a counter offensive to encircle the 2nd PzA and 9th Army in the Orel salient. The Western Front would attack southward on the northern section while Central Front would attack northward on the southern arm of the salient. At the same time, the Bryansk Front would attack the eastern perimeter to keep all Germans busy. cbk83. dgk231m. snk433m++.

After receiving a few new replacements, the 9th PzD was short only 238 men and was considered at full strength. It also had 25 Mk IIIs, 34 Mk IVs as well as 275 armored vehicles and 46 guns. The panzers were made up of a mixture of short and long guns with 50mm and 75mm bores. The 9th PzD along with the 2nd PzD, 20th PzD and 6th ID made up the 47th PzC (Lemelsen) which was deployed in the center of the line and was tasked with breaking through the boundary line of the 13th and 70th Armies and reaching Olkhovatka and nearby Hill 274. The 6th ID and 20th PzD would launch the following day while 9th PzD and 2nd PzD would stay in reserve and wait for a penetration before attacking. That was the plan but when the penetration did not occur on the first day, Model would start his two panzer divisions earlier than scheduled to assist in the penetration. The corps was straddling the main road and railroad that led directly to Kursk. mkz116. wwf52. snk18. snk105+. lck116m.

Lt General Rokossovsky made a name for himself during the Battle of Smolensk in August 1941 when he commanded 16th Army and two years later he was commanding Central Front. It was not always good times for the General. In 1937, during the purges, Rokossovsky was imprisoned and tortured for three years. Being a son of a Polish father and Russian mother he also had to work to prove himself. By the end of the war, his star was almost as bright as Zhukov or Konev. lck192. zro200.

Just like Rokossovsky, General Konev made a name for himself during the Smolensk Campaign as leader of 19th Army and rose to become the Commander of Steppe Front in June 1943. Like Zhukov and Rokossovsky, Konev was smart and ruthless and would do most anything to defeat the *Wehrmacht*. Konev was also one of Stalin's few favorites. lck194. zro201.

2

July 4th on the Southern Salient

The Sunday morning was hot and muggy as the German soldiers moved to their launch points. Their morale was high and though they knew the campaign would be difficult, they were confident of reaching Kursk. fmz219.

In the south, Vatutin had two armies manning the front defensive belt: the 6th GA and 7th GA. Behind I. M. Chistiakov's 6th GA and Shumilov's 7th GA was 1st TA, 69th Army, 35th GRC, 2nd GTC and 5th GTC in second and third echelon. On the front line from west to east would be 71st GRD, 67th GRD, 52nd GRD and 375th RD closest to the Donets River. The 6th GA had almost 2,500 guns and mortars of varying sizes and 155 tanks and assault guns. The 6th GA also had the 96th TB with 61 tanks and the 230th TR with 39 tanks attached to it as well. Vatutin had another advantage over Hoth. Even though the Germans went through this area in 1941-42, Vatutin had lived much of his life in a village near Belgorod and knew the landscape better than the Germans; this would play an important role in the preparations. After the bitter fighting at Stalingrad, the 21st Army was renamed the 6th GA nzk34. wdk116+. lck193. asz361.

The starting line for the 48th PzC and 2nd PzC would be just north of the Borisovka-Tomarovka to just west of Belgorod. The 3rd PzC would start at Belgorod and along the Donets River to as far south as Maslovo Pristan and Ziborovka. The 6th PzD along with the 168th ID would be in the north at Belgorod. The 19th PzD would be to the immediate south followed by 7th PzD which was stationed in the Dorogobuzhino -Solomino sector. Further south, Corps Raus would cover the Toplinka-Ivanovka-Ziborovka sector. Toplinka, located on the western bank of the Donets River, was about midway between Solomino and Ivanovka.

To the east of 6th GA was 7th GA and it was commanded by M. S. Shumilov. His army was deployed on a 35 mile line that started to the east of the Donets River and swung south to the Neshegol River. Two divisions from 24th GRC and two divisions of the 25th GRC covered the front line. These divisions were the 36th GRD, 72nd GRD, 78th GRD and the 81st GRD. Another two divisions were in second echelon. The independent 213th RD was third echelon. Vatutin, expecting the Germans to use this sector as a main axis of advance, fortified Shumilov with many additional artillery batteries. In addition to the extra guns, Shumilov created huge minefields at the likely crossing points on the Donets. The army had over 1,600 guns of assorted sizes, mortars and rocket launchers. It also had almost 250 working tanks and assault guns. In addition to this hardware, three tank regiments were brought in to support the infantry. The 262nd TR supported the 81st GRD, the 73rd GRD had the 167th TR and the 148th TR was with the 15th GRD (24th GRC) which was in reserve the first days of the offensive but would be brought up several days later. nzk35+.

General Sepp Dieterich, the commander of *LAH*, released his command of *LAH* to activate the 1st PzC. In his place General Theodor Wisch would take command of the division. zow138.

Starting at the extreme left of the 48th PzC's attack zone, the first defensive belt for 6th

GA started just south of Dmitrievka-Korovino-Cherkasskoe-Trirechnoe across the Vorskla River-Berezov-Erik turning south until it reaches the Donets River. The 7th GA takes up the challenge from here and parallels the Donets River just east of the river. The second defensive belt beginning in the west follows the bend of the Pena River and then moved east to Lakhanino-Syrtsev-south of Pokrovka-Solonets-Nekhaevka- across the Lipovyi Donets River to Teterevino South. The biggest component of the third defensive belt was the Psell River. It then winds a little south and includes Hill 252.2, Komsomolets State Farm-Storozhevoe- across the Donets River- Rzhavets-Aleksandrovka-north of Kazache.

While 6th GA and 7th GA were on the front line, the 1st TA west of the Donets and 69th Army east of the Donets would be defending the second and third defensive belts. The 1st TA was run by M. E. Katukov, had 1,000 tanks and included 3rd MC, 6th TC and 31st TC and temporarily had 2nd GTC and 5th GTC. nzk36+.

From west to east, the German offensive would include the 332nd ID, 3rd PzD, *GD*, 11th PzD, 167th ID, *LAH*, *Das Reich* and *SSTK* closest to the western bank of the Donets River. Continuing the lineup on the eastern bank of the river would be 6th PzD, 168th ID, 19th PzD, 7th PzD, 106th ID and 320th ID. sPzAbt 503 had 45 Tigers and each company of the battalion was attached to each panzer division of 3rd PzC. nzk59.

Not only were the Germans at a great disadvantage with tanks but also with airplanes. Planes available within flying distance of Kursk were 1,830 for Germany and a massive 5,965 aircraft for the Soviets. Model would have 730 planes from Dessloch's *Luftflotte* 6 and Hoth would have 1,100 planes from Greim's *Luftflotte* 4 to support the ground campaign. The Soviets had a 3 to 1 advantage in tanks and a 4 to 1 advantage in planes. Before Operation Citadel started, Hitler ordered FM Richthofen and part of *Luftflotte* 4 to Italy as a defensive measure when the Allies attacked North Africa. lck190++. sgf343. cbk12m. zzk371. zow132+. The loss of these planes would be greatly missed for 3rd PzC would receive little air support during the campaign and is a major factor for their failure to keep up.

After being read the motivational letter from Hitler, a commando party led by Col Karck and accompanied by engineers with flamethrowers from *LAH* would launch its assault, after hours of preparation, at 2300 hrs. Its objective was to silently secure the OP on the hill west of Iakhontoff and to hold the outpost until relieved when the main attack began a few hours later. Without a moon the night was dark but the OP was secured. Once relieved the commando group was to be reinforced and would move along the nearby woods and capture Hill 228.6 while screening the right flank of *LAH* as it advanced. At the same time, the 315 GR of 167th ID also moved toward Streletskoe and secured the outpost in the village. After Iakhontoff was secured, early next morning the leading units were to fight their way to Iakovlevo. Hill 228.6 was important for it was to be the staging area for the Tigers to begin their assault. The Soviets wanted the hill also and countered with forces in the area but the attack was repulsed. zrl204+. zrl209. vzz6m. zow136+.

Preliminaries to the Kursk offensive started the same day, around 1500 hrs. The *Luftwaffe*, flying 800 planes, began bombing Soviet positions in and around the Kursk salient. Besides the air attack several advance teams were testing the Soviet line. The biggest incursion was in the south when Hoth's 4th PzA advanced on the 6th GA. A bad start when Hoth's Panthers did not show up due to the thick mud from the recent rains. Hermann Hoth, who was born in 1885 not far from Berlin, had been in command of the 4th PzA since June 1st, 1942, after Hoepner's dismissal. swm137. zmb240+. zzk371.

On Sunday morning at 1030 hrs, when Hoth's 4th PzA were moving into their starting positions, the Soviet 6th GA and to a lesser extent the 7th GA, delivered a crushing barrage that disoriented the Germans. The Germans regrouped and delivered an even heavier bombardment on Soviet positions in the afternoon. In the center of 48th PzC sector was the *GD* Division and it advanced toward the Syrtsev and Lukhanino area while the 3rd PzD and 11th PzD attacked on the left and right flanks. A few panzers moved forward during the shelling, trailing the infantry. bt81+*. hjj121m. wwf65.

At 1500 hrs, 75 bombers began the German offensive by striking the forward positions of the 52nd GRD and 67th GRD at Gertsovka eastward to Butovo. While the fighters circled overhead the Stukas dived and wailed as they were aiming at their targets. Soviet fighters sortied but they were stopped by German fighters and all bombers returned to base. Five squadrons dropped 2,500 bombs on an area two miles long and only 500 yards deep. German artillery began shelling Gertsovka, Butovo, Dragunskoe and Iakhontov which were defended by the 52nd GRD, 67th GRD and the 71st GRD. Under the screen of the shelling, panzers began to roll toward the first defense belt. The *SSTK* reached Butovo which was defended by 199th GRR of 67th GRD and fought their way into the village but were halted when some of their lead panzers were damaged. No matter how hard the *Luftwaffe* tried, Soviet shelling remained heavy, causing a lot of German casualties. The plan was to defeat the very front line positions with infantry and then have the panzers move up at night to lead the attack on the first main day of the assault, but a heavy rainstorm hit the area at night turning the already soft ground into muddy fields, delaying the panzers from reaching their start points. In certain sectors, the infantry would have to start without armor support next morning. fkk74+. pck30. hsz115. wwf44. fmz220. fmz221m+. gjz180+. fzk170. kfz450. pck50. zow139. dgk81.

After the bombings, preliminaries intensified with a massive shelling by the Germans and the Soviets quickly reciprocated. In the late afternoon, battalion-sized raiding parties went out to defending OPs and front line bunkers. At night German engineers crossed the front line deeper into no man's land to clear pathways through the minefields for the advance coming up in the morning. Often thousands of mines would be cleared each night. The Soviets had planted hundreds of thousands of mines and while the German engineers did their best to neutralize them, they missed many of them and the leading panzers, especially the new Panthers, paid for that shortcoming. Even if a panzer could be recovered from track damage or shell damage once stuck in a minefield, it would often take days to get the panzer back on the battlefield and while these panzers were in the repair shop, they would be greatly missed. lck233+. pck28.

With the Germans advancing in the afternoon and with the *Luftwaffe* flying larger missions than had yet occurred in the previous three weeks, Vatutin and *Stavka* believed the German assault would begin for real next morning. They would put into effect a plan that had been initiated two months earlier for a preemptive strike on German airfields at daybreak that would cripple German air support. dgr249. wwf163m.

The German aerial arsenal would include the FW 190, Hs 129, Ju 87, Bf 109G for ground attack while the He 111 and Ju 88 would be used for the more serious bombing runs. Some of the Hs 129s and Ju 87s were mounted with either a 30mm or 37mm cannon for hunting tanks. These cannon could penetrate the rear engine compartment, ruining the engine and usually engulfing the machine in a firestorm when the fuel lines and fuel tanks ruptured. The Soviets had for their lineup the La-5, Yak-1b, Yab-7b, Yak-9, P39, Pe-2 and the new favored Il-2 for ground attack. Most of the Il-2s at Kursk were the new model having a back seat for a rear gunner. The Soviet aircraft industry was more robust than the Germans' and the industrial scale of building planes dwarfed them.. These planes were a mixture of single engine and dual engine types and most were single seat with the exception of the Il-2m3 which had a second seat. nzk79+.

By dark the *LAH* had moved into their departure positions. The division had 11 working Tigers, 72 Mk IVs, 16 Mk IIIs and 31 assault guns. At 2300 hrs a commando team from 2nd PzGR launched its attack after several hours of preparation, taking out OPs in their sector that included Hill 228.6 and the hills west of Iakhontov, preparing the terrain for a quick departure for the panzers which would launch in a few hours. agk89. agk91m. agk94m. wwf59+.

At 2230 hrs, Soviet guns began shelling German positions along the front line on a prearranged schedule to disrupt the Germans' preparations. je98.

At 2300 hrs, a commando team from *Das Reich* left the line and, deliberately avoiding outposts, traveled to the edge of the fortifications surrounding Iakhontov. During the rest of darkness, engineers cleared mines in front of the town in preparation of the assault of this strongpoint next morning. Once the Germans were spotted, they had to clear mines under fire. German artillery was called up to answer the Soviet fire. By 0130 hrs on 7/5, Hill 228.6, a part of the Soviet strongpoint at Iakhontov, was captured by *LAH*. At 0245 hrs and not waiting for reinforcements the Bissinger Group of *Das Reich* captured Iakhontov. zow140.

The Red Air Force had a superiority of planes over the *Luftwaffe*. The 2nd VA had 881 aircraft, the 16th VA 1,052 and the 17th VA 735 planes. These three air armies had over 2,600 planes at their disposal. When you add in the 1st VA and 5th VA 2,800 planes the Soviets had access to nearly 6,000 planes if it was needed. On the German side only the 1st *Flieger* Division and the 8th *Flieger* Corps would participate in the campaign. The Soviets would have nearly a three to one advantage in numbers. One advantage the *Luftwaffe* had was experienced air crews and pilots. nzk76. kfz449.

Late at night a deluge of rain turned the soil into mud, hindering the movement of the German attack in the morning. bt82. gjz81. snk77.

In Berlin, Reinhard Gehlen of Fremde Heere Ost (German intelligence) reported to OKH that after looking at recon photos, there was no chance of victory at Kursk and that Operation Citadel should be canceled. The advice was ignored. Maj General von Mellenthin of 48th PzC had been thinking the same thing for weeks . He had seen the aerial photos of the salient and Kursk had been transformed into a fortress. Hitler was going to use a weapon of maneuverability as a battering ram and by mid June von Manstein, Guderian, von Mellenthin and a few others disagreed with their dictator. Hitler had made a mistake at Stalingrad and he was making the same mistake at Kursk. Friedrich von Mellenthin was born into a military family; his father had become a general, prompting his three sons to follow him into the officer corps. The Mellenthins were aristocrats living in Breslau; Friedrich was the youngest. wwf65+. fmz217. zmb355.

With Citadel starting the following day FM von Manstein and his staff moved from their headquarters at Zaporozhe by rail to near the front lines. The distance between Hoth and Model was 125 miles and von Manstein was still concerned the distance was too great. pck25. pck33.

Hoth started Operation Citadel with 1,269 working panzers: 102 Tigers, 192 Panthers,

563 Mk IVs, 416 Mk IIIs among other assorted panzers and assault guns. It's been claimed that the tank battles of Prokhorovka on 7/12 was the largest in history. It may have been the most important tank battle but by numbers alone, this was not true. In 1941, AGS fought a tank battle with Kirponos that had a combined number of 3,800 tanks. gjz185+*+*. fmz216.

Along the approximately 50 mile front of 6th GA and 69th Army, there were a limited number of routes the Germans could take to reach Oboyan or Prokhorovka. There were only four routes that had paved roads. Only half of this 45 or 50 mile front could be used by trucks and even fewer miles that the panzer could use. Going through Iakovlevo, which was a key road junction, gave the Germans the option of going either direction: toward Oboyan or Prokhorovka. Hoth chose the two key road networks as much as possible, avoiding whenever possible off road travel. They were the Belgorod-Prokhorovka Highway and the Belgorod-Oboyan Highway. The Soviets had the advantage of knowing the terrain and Vatutin had sufficient time to erect sturdy defenses along these axis routes. vzz89. dgk109. dgk114.

By the end of the day on the left flank of 6th GA, Vakhrameev's 23rd GRC was prepared to face the 2nd SS PzC when they attacked in the next day or two. It consisted of Nekrasov's 52nd GRD and Govorunenko's 375th RD. The 52nd GRD was defending one of the key paved roads leading north, the Tomarovka to Iakovkevo road to the Oboyan road. The line included Berezov and Gremuchi. The 375th RD defended the line: Petropavlovka to northwest of Chernaia Poliana. Further east, the 81st GRD of 7th GA and elements of the 92nd GRD were deployed along the Staryi Gorod- Blizhniaia Igumenka-Postnikov-Shliakhovo Station-Iar Orlov line. Russkikh's 94th GRD held the line from Iar Orlov along the Razumnaia River to Miasoedovo to the woods a mile east of Miasoedovo. vzz92. vzz247. dgr155m. dgr173m. dgr181m. dgr39m. pck59. vzz5m.

In addition to the Voronezh Front, Vatutin also had the resources of the 2nd Air Army and, if needed, access to the 17th VA of Southwestern Front. dgr238.

The large distance, about 12 miles, between the Soviet second defensive belt and the third defensive belt was due to the natural terrain features of the Psel River; its swampy river basin and its steep northern river bank. With the defenses behind the river it would make it harder for the Germans to cross against the swampy ground to the south and the high banks on the north side of the river. Each belt consisted of usually at least three trench lines as well as communication trenches that led to the rear. All the defense belts were built around terrain features that would give the Soviets a decided advantage; it would include a river line, a ridge line and a series of villages that could be fortified. Wherever possible, personnel trenches and anti-tank ditches, bunkers, MG nests with corresponding minefields and barb wire entanglements were placed in such a manner as to provide the greatest safety and results. The Soviets were masters at this and had several months to build these impressive defenses and yet the Germans would find a way to breach them. The real question would be how expensive would the Soviets make the task. vzz106. wwf31++. ezz133.

In the months before Operation Citadel launched the Soviets built three defensive belts between Belgorod and Prokhorovka and the Psel 'River. Each defensive belt would have as many as four trenches, usually two to three hundred yards apart. Rokossovsky also had three defensive belts positioned north of Olkhovatka. Between the two salients, there were almost 2,500 miles of trenches, both personnel and armor, along with 3,900 pill boxes, 9,300 artillery bunkers, 26,000, mortar positions and thousands of underground shelters.

There were 675,000 mines laid as well as miles of wire entanglements. Vatutin thought the main axis of attack would be between Shopino and Vorskla for the first defense line. The second defense line was between Luchki and Pokrovka. dgr277. dgr280m. swm132. nzk33. fzk170. ztc268.

Unlike Model, Hoth believed the application of localized concentration of armor would be what was needed to reach Kursk; the reason why he would launch with all his panzers at the beginning. The Soviets suspected that premise and placed as many armored units directly behind Chistiakov's 6th GA. Model would start his battle using mostly infantry to penetrate a gap in the line and then let his panzers drive through. Model also divided the Ferdinand Battalions among his panzer divisions. Keeping these heavy Battalions together would have provided a stronger punch through enemy lines. pck52+. pck33. swm137. fzk171.

In the Belgorod area, just north of the city, the Northern Donets River ran in a southwest to northeast direction and would play a major part in the Kursk battle.

From 3/28/43 thousands of Soviet engineers built nearly 2,000 miles of new roads to bring all the men, weapons, supplies and equipment to the battle front. In addition, new railroad track was laid to serve the new locomotives given to Russia through the Lend-Lease Program to help carry the men and supplies to the sector. dgr291.

The southern bend of the Pena River was 15 miles wide and presented a natural obstacle that the Soviets used to their advantage; a hardship to the Germans for the bend was practically the entire sector of the 48th PzC. At its southern point, it was 15 miles from Oboyan as the crow flies and another 35 miles to Kursk. The 90th GRD, 22nd TB, 27th ATR and the 3rd MC were dug in on the far side of the river. To make things harder for the Germans, there was a small marshy tributary with an impassable river-bed that flowed east through Lukhanino. gnk148. gnk162m.

The 2nd PzGR of *LAH* moved on Hill 228.6 northwest of Iakhontov to prepare the jump-off of the main force the next day. Unexpectedly the Soviets put up stiff resistance including hand-to-hand combat near the hill. The hill was the anchor of the 52nd GRD's sector which ran for only four miles to Hill 218.0. Defending a key highway to Oboyan as well as the important road junction of Iakovlevo, Vatutin knew the 52nd GRD's sector would be hot and deliberately gave the division a relatively narrow front to defend. By 0200 hrs Hill 228.6 had been captured and *LAH* was moving on the tank trench to the north as well as the village of Streleskoe. vzz92. wwf65. dgk109. dgk112. zrl209+

The 48th PzC of 4th PzA took the heights of Iakhontov-Streletskoe-Butovo-Gertsovka line northwest of Belgorod. From there the 52nd IC moved north following the panzers, pushing the Soviet 6th GA back. By midday, heavy rains and increased Soviet artillery had slowed the German advance. It would take 3rd PzD until nightfall to take Gertsovka and the surrounding high ground. It would be after 0200 hrs on 7/5 when the 3rd PzD and *GD* met, stabilizing the line. The bombardment was just an hour away to initiate Operation Citadel. pck28. pck32. dgr251.

German recon patrols had spotted weaknesses in the Soviet line in 48th PzC sector over the preceding couple of days. It was decided to start a limited assault a day early and head for Gertsovka, the rail line south of town and Hill 229.8, northeast of Gertsovka. As the lead German units launched, they noticed a quick stiffening of the line. The "easy" advance had cost 3rd PzD and *GD* more than what was expected. The 11th PzD made the best gains with the fewest casualties. Hoth decided that 4th PzA needed better artillery OPs before beginning the main attack the following day so he sent limited forces out to capture these key high ground targets. It had been argued by some in the *Wehrmacht* that 4th PzA did not have sufficient forces to reach Kursk. Hoth knew this and wanted to take advantage of every possibility and gaining these OPs would be a big plus. His artillery batteries would provide much better support from these key hills. The SS spearhead would start between Tomarovka and Belgorod. The 48th PzC would be west of Tomarovka driving north, straddling the Cherkasskoe-Butovo axis. In 48th PzC sector, the first important height to capture was at Zybino, southwest of Butovo where a heavy concentration of artillery was positioned. From on top of Zybino an observation post would be set up to assist in taking Gertsovka Station and Gertsovka to the immediate northeast. gnk65. snk19. snk75+. pck30+. dgk81.

Before reaching Butovo, a small creek with an impassable muddy bottom delayed both *GD* and 11th PzD from advancing. After getting a number of panzers stuck and barely able to pull them out, both divisions had to go around the creek which cost valuable time. After bypassing the creek, around 1500 hrs, while still raining *GD* launched again after withstanding a horrific aerial and ground bombardment and was able to quickly capture the hill west of Butovo which was defended by the 199th GRR. It was able to repulse Soviet counter-attacks, including attacks from the air. Soon afterwards the Germans placed their own OPs there. Even in this brief engagement, panzers were hitting mines and incurring track damage. The Panthers had not arrived yet but they would have their turn the following day. At the same time the high ground east of Butovo was captured by the men of 11th PzD. The *GD*, after Butovo was captured, did not stop their advance after dark but kept moving and during the pre-dawn hours of 7/5 captured the hills southeast of Gertsovka. (Gertsovka and Zavidovka would be attacked by 3rd PzD.) The day was successful for *GD* but it was also costly in men and panzers - taking Alekseevka and Lukhanino was expected to be fairly quick. Also at 1500 hrs other elements of the *GD* moved off for a preliminary attack against the Belgorod-Gotnya railroad and in the general direction of Gertsovka. The 3rd Panzer Battalion of *GD* was back at the starting line, waiting for its panzers to arrive at the railhead. The new 29 foot, 45 ton Panther, had a 75mm long barrel gun, armor up to 110mm and could travel as fast as 34 mph on a good surface but had not arrived yet either so the infantry had to rely on itself. pck31+. pck53+. fkk259+. dgr249. wwf65. snk77. gnk68m. fmz220. zpm184++. hsz114+.

A combat group from *GD* with elements of 3rd PzD guarding their western flank, advanced, heading north to secure the high ground west of Butovo before moving on the village. *GD* pushed the 67th GRD and 71st GRD (supported by the 27th TDB) deployed in front of Butovo back three miles toward Cherkasskoe, allowing *GD* to continue heading for the hill which they wanted to take first. With *GD* in control of the hill immediately to the west of Butovo and 11th PzD controlling the hill to the east, the village soon succumbed to German artillery. At 1645 hrs Butovo falls to the 11th PzD; the *GD* had already left the area heading north toward Cherkasskoe. Despite a Soviet counter-attack, by the end of the evening *GD* traveled three more miles and was subsequently fighting for Cherkasskoe. Trailing behind the panzer group the grenadiers of *Das Reich* captured the village of Berezov, about two miles north of the start point, driving elements of the 71st GRD back to Krasnyi Pochinok. wdk109. wdk118. dgr172m. hjj121m. pck31+. hsz114+. wwf44+. snk78. lck213.

The 3rd PzD's 394th PzGR and 332nd ID were not so productive for they ran into heavy shelling coming from Zybino hills. The divisions then had to endure attacks from the hills that lasted past dark.

The 11th PzD and the *GD* launched an attack against the strongpoints defended by elements of Nekrasov's 52nd GRD between Streletskoe and Berezov. An even larger battle took place near Gertsovka. At Gertsovka, the 213th RD put up fierce resistance, inflicting heavy casualties but by 2100 hrs the German attack had taken the town. The rest of 52nd GRD would be in front of *LAH*'s advance. Behind the 52nd GRD, Vatutin deployed 230th TR and 96th TB which together had 110 tanks. To the west of 230th TR was 245th TR which was facing *GD*. dgk81. gnk109.

The 52nd IC, to the west of 48th PzC, began its feint attack, hoping to draw forces away from 48th PzC but the attack failed, suffering heavy casualties. The 52nd IC was led by General Ott and consisted of the 57th ID, 167th ID, 255th ID and 332nd ID. snk70. snk77.

The 48th PzC also had additional panzers that were not counted for they were under long term repair and would not be ready for the campaign. *GD* had 51 panzers needing repairs and 11th PzD had 29 under repairs. wdk57+*. wdk112. snk73++.

It was not an auspicious beginning for the new Panther Brigade. Six of the new 45 ton panzers caught fire near Moschchenoye after leaving the rail station. gnk191. hsz113.

The 394th IR of the 3rd PzD was held up by defensive fire of the Soviet 71st GRD at Gertsovka Hills and did not reach their objective until dark. Gertsovka on the Belgorod-Gotnya railway line did fall later that night. dgk98. pck57. kfz451.

The 48th PzC consisted of 167th ID, 11th PzD, *GD* and 3rd PzD. A regiment of 167th ID would move with *LAH* and protect its flank. The 11th PzD would drive toward Butovo and then head for the eastern side of Cherkasskoe. The *GD* would drive straight toward the fortified town of Cherkasskoe while 3rd PzD, west of *GD*, would head for Gertsovka, Korovino and Krasnyi Pochinok. The overall main objective of the corps was to cross the Psel and drive on Oboyan, just 30 miles away. fkk247. gnk68m.

Before the campaign started, the 48th PzC had 61,700 men. This corps would include nearly 190 Panthers of 10th PzB attached to *GD* with the specific intention of defeating the 1st TA which was in the same sector. The 167th ID which was tasked with protecting the panzers' flank had 17,800 men. The 2nd SS PzC mustered 73,400 men. vzz91+*. dgk53+.

Hitler, against his generals' advice, had postponed the offensive for a month in order to have the latest batch of Tigers and Panthers in the battle, which subsequently gave the Soviets much more time to prepare. The Panthers were having mechanical troubles; the Germans had to replace axles on the trains as they drove east to Kursk.

The 1st TA consists of the 6th TC under Getman, 31st TC and 3rd MC which were deployed in the Belaia, Kurasovka and Bykonov region. The 5th GTC, a front reserve, was deployed to the rear in the Marino region. The total number of tanks was 930. The 1st TA was subordinated to 6th GA. While waiting for von Manstein to attack, the 3rd MC built a defense along the Studenok, Stalinskoe State Farm, Vladimirovka and Orlovka line while the 6th TC built a defense along the northern bank of the Psel River. 1st TA's combat zone included the boundary: the Oboyan, Ivnia and Trefilovka on the west and the Belgorod-Kursk railroad line on the east and the Psel River on the north. The coverage from east to west was 27 miles and the north south distance was 31 miles. dgr208++. dgr172m. dgr209m. kcz166+. dgk404.

A few Panthers died from mechanical failure before ever reaching their launch point.

46 Panthers died from mechanical troubles within the first two days of the battle but they were already in the repair shop and the mechanics were working as fast as possible to get them back on the battlefield. Though the front armor of a Panther was less than a Tiger, it still had an almost equal protection factor due to its angled plating. The 75mm L70 KwK 42 gun had high velocity that made it almost the equal of the Tiger's 88. The Panther, which was cheaper and quicker to build than a Tiger, once the bugs were worked out, would be an excellent tank but for this campaign it gave the *GD* division a lot of trouble. Vatutin had 105 KV-1s and a few SU-152s to combat the Tiger and Panthers. dgk18. snk73++. snk77. wdk53*. fkk258. zro193.

The offensive power of 48th PzC was *GD* division located in the center of 48th PzC. The new Panthers attached to this division were under the command of Major von Lauchert. On this morning these two battalions along with PzR 139 were joined to form PzB 10 (brigade). Decker was supposed to be the CO of the brigade but did not arrive until 7/11. Instead von Strachwitz commanded PzB 10. In addition to these Panthers, the division also had 15 Tigers and some 300 Mks that added to a total count of 535 panzers plus 66 assault guns. The 3rd PzD and 11th PzD were deployed on either side of *GD* and sported 90 panzers and 113 panzers respectively. The 11th PzD also had StuGAbt 911 attached and it had 31 machines. Von Knobelsdorff of 48th PzC had at his disposal over 700 assorted fighting vehicles. Hoth was so confident that he scheduled his forces to be at the Psel River, halfway to Kursk, by the end of day two; a passage of between 20 to 30 miles. According to the German timetable for Operation Citadel, the Soviets would have to be defeated in five days before additional reinforcements could arrive.

From my study of the campaign, it appears Hoth was too confident in defeating Vatutin and it made him a little too lax in choosing his attack route for 48th PzC as well as allowing the 2nd SS PzC to shift to the northeast toward Prokhorovka while maintaining the attack toward Oboyan. This shift in direction expanded the gap between the two corps, lengthened and thinned out the line. The general then compounded these errors by not closing ranks on the west flank when it was discovered Soviet resistance was stronger than anticipated. Abandoning either the Oboyan route or the Prokhorovka route seems logical. When you also consider the troubles of 3rd PzC and the difficulties of *Das Reich* and the fact that *SSTK* was stuck along the Donets for a couple of days, my choice would have been to abandon Oboyan and fully concentrate on the Prokhorovka corridor. wdk121. mhz201+. snk73. fmz218. hjj114. asz358.

By the end of the day, the recon forces of 48th PzC had pushed back the 6th GA having reached the line Gertsovka, Butovo, Hill 230.8 but the strongpoints at Dragunskoe and Iakhontov were still in Soviet hands. Artillery and men were moved up to secure these important OP areas. At dawn the next day, the 48th PzC resumed its attack on Dragunskoe, Iakhontov and nearby Zagotskot. dgr74. lck214. lck164m.

sPzAbt 503 arrived at their assembly area northeast of Belgorod, right next to the Donets River. It was soon discovered Kempf had decided to break up the battalion into companies, giving one company to each panzer divisions. The officers of sPzAbt 503 thought that was a mistake. They thought strength in numbers would be the best tactic; that the 45 Tigers working together driving down the main axis could plow through the enemy better and quicker than separate companies. Their pleas were ignored by Kempf. fwl110. fwl116.

The recapture of sections of the Donets as well as Belgorod during von Manstein's counter-attack in early 1943 allowed the Germans the chance to consider Operation Citadel. On April 1st, Kempf submitted a plan which would start within 30 days to retake the Kursk salient. The short delay would allow the AGC/AGS to regroup, be resupplied and wait out the rainy season. When repeated delays made it look like the offensive would begin in June or even July, Kempf turned sour on the offensive. erz210. fwl109.

At 2230 hrs, the Soviets delivered a series of disrupting barrages against 3rd PzC, east of Belgorod, especially on the only bridgehead on the eastern banks of the Donets at Mikhailovka. wdk121. dgk95m.

The 3rd PzC had the difficult responsibility of providing screen protection for the advancing 4th PzA while at the same time advancing along with the 4th PzA as it headed for the Psel River, Oboyan and Prokhorovka line. The responsibility was even more daunting when you consider the 3rd PzC had to start south of Belgorod as far south as the Nezhegol River and then head east as far as the Korocha River before heading north. On the extreme east flank was 11th IC or Corps Raus with his weakened 106th ID and 320th ID. Back in the first months of 1943, the 320th ID now commanded by Maj General Postel got caught behind the fast moving Soviet line and had to fight its way to the Kharkov line to escape destruction. In so doing, it lost most of its heavy guns, panzers and other supplies. It still had not fully recovered by July. To assist General Raus with overcoming these weaknesses, he received three flak regiments and five gun battalions. The three flak regiments totaled 72 88mm and nearly 900 smaller flak guns which would be used for not only aerial defense but also for ground support. erz199++. erz186m. hjj123m. hsz107+.

On the west bank of the Donets, Beaulieu's 168th ID made its final preparations for the following day's assault in support of 6th PzD. During the night of the 4th, Kempf's artillery expended most of it ammo in softening up the enemy. The Soviet 7th GA returned fire in the predrawn hours which delayed the 6th PzD, 7th PzD and 19th PzD crossing the Donets River next morning. The Tigers of the sPzAbt 503 which were to lead the other divisions also took casualties from the barrage. dlu10.

The 6th PzD entered this campaign with 16,200 men plus a few Soviet volunteers. It was commanded by Maj General Walther Hunersdorff who was a Knight's Cross recipient as of 12/22/1942. From recon photos it was known that his division had the toughest defensive barrier to crack in the Staryi Gorod sector. fkk277. fkk324m+. hjj112+.

The 19th PzD, which had fought two months earlier for the recapture of Kharkov and had been regrouping ever since, still was not up to full strength in either men or panzers. The CO was Lt General Schmidt, an experienced officer and recipient of the Knight's Cross with Oak Leaves. It would attack to the right of 6th PzD the next morning. The division would start the campaign with 70 panzers and 13,780 men. fkk286. vzz46. gnk86. dlu80. dlu115.

3

July 4th on the Northern Salient

See Map 1

In the north, Rokossovsky's Central Front had three armies protecting the front line. It included 70th on the western flank, 13th in the center and 48th on the eastern flank. All of 13th Army would see action and it would be fierce, while the two flanks would see fighting on part of their sectors. Pukhov's 13th had approximately 150,000 men defending a line nearly 20 miles wide by nearly the same distance in depth, along three defensive belts. From west to east the 8th RD, 148th RD, 81st RD and 15th RD would man the front trenches. In the second belt, the 74th RD, 307th RD and 6th GRD were deployed. The third belt would have five divisions: 2nd GRD, 3rd GRD, 4th GAD of 18th GRC and 70th GRD and 75th GRD of 17th GRC. In addition there would be either six tank regiments or brigades to support the infantry. As soon as the Germans showed their intended lines of attacks, Rokossovsky would redeploy these tanks to the appropriate locations. Behind the third belt would be many artillery batteries and additional reserves if needed. The 13th Army deployed over 3,000 guns of assorted sizes, rockets and mortars. It also had 200 operational tanks. Central Front had just over 1,100 tanks and then there was *Stavka* Reserve which meant more tanks. The largest unit would be 2nd TA which had two corps, the 3rd TC and 16th TC, and one brigade. Central Front also had the 9th TC and 19th GTC in reserve. The 2nd TA had 37,000 men and about 450 tanks. Rokossovsky also had 4th and 65th Armies in the sector. The 13th Army would be facing sPzAbt 505's 45 Tigers, which would lead the assaults for the Germans in a similar manner as the Elefants. The panzers that were following these giants would then exploit the gaps created. nzk32++. nzk85. dgk87m. lck192+. kfz449. zzt74+.

Rokossovsky set up his defensive belts in the following manner. The first belt from west to east consisted of Shepelevo-Izmanova-Verjh Tagino-Iasnaia Poliana-Ozerki-Maslovo-Krasnaia Slobodka. The second defensive belt was Malakhova Sloboda-Buzova-Probuzhdenie-Gnilets-Bobrik-Podolian-Butyrki-Aleksandrovka-Protasovo-Grinevka-Verkhne Gnilusha. Further south the third defensive belt started at Vetrenka- Berezovka-Krasavka-Samodurovka- Saburovka-Snovo-Ponyri-Maloarkhangelsk. There was one major difference between the defensive systems of the northern and southern salients; in the north, the defensive belts were closer together. For example, the key town of Olkhovatka, which sat behind the third defensive belt, was less than 15 miles from the front line. In the south, Prokhorovka was almost twice that distance from the front line. Another difference between the two salients was that even with a defense with less depth, Rokossovsky had built 500 more miles of trenches. (July 4th)

Model's 9th Army, a force of 335,000 men (including non combat and reserve), consisted of 21 German divisions broken down by 14 infantry, 6 panzer and one PzGD. The 9th Army also had 590 tanks, mostly Mk IIIs and Mk IVs, and 424 assault guns. It included the sPzAbt 505, sPzAbt 653, sPzAbt 654 (Ferdinands) and the 150mm self-propelled guns of StPzAbt 216. The 9th deployed its five corps in the following manner: 20th IC was on the western flank of the line while the 23rd IC was on the eastern flank. The three panzer corps from inner west to inner east were: 46th PzC, 47th PzC and 41st PzC. The 47th PzC was in the exact center of the line and had the primary responsibility of breaking through to Olkhovatka. Model also had a reserve force made up of the 4th PzD, 12th PzD and 10th PzGD which had a combine total of 184 panzers. They were deployed behind 47th PzC in second echelon. It has been argued that if the above mentioned heavy battalions had not been broken into the different divisions, these units would have been more effective as battering rams in breaking through the front lines. Capt Kageneck of the sPzAbt 503 in the south complained about same thing when his battalion was broken up between the 6th PzD, 7th PzD and 19th PzD.

In the Orel salient northeast of Model, the bulk of 2nd PzA was made up of the 55th IC, 53rd IC and the 35th IC. These three corps totaled 160,000 men in 14 divisions. It also had the 25th PzGD, the 5th PzD and 8th PzD in reserve plus two security divisions. To the west on the nose of the Kursk salient was Weiss's 2nd Army with 96,000 men and they were waiting to attack eastward once Hoth linked up with Model at Kursk.

General Model's rise in command was certainly dramatic. He started Barbarossa as CO of 3rd PzD then moved up to CO of 41st PzC and now two years later was the commanding officer of 9th Army, 2nd PzA and a favorite of Hitler. zpm189. dgk51++. lck116m. sgf343. fzk171+. kfz455. pck33. asz354. asz355m. zzt74+.

A German engineering team from 6th ID was clearing mines south of Tagino before the big assault that would begin just a few hours later, when a Soviet recon team apprehended one engineer and then interrogated the prisoner. Corporal Fermello told his captors all they needed to know. At 0110 hrs on 7/5, Rokossovsky opened his own barrage ahead of the Germans. pck33. dgk87m. lck116m. zro203. (July 4th)

The airmen of the 1st *Flieger* Division assembled in operation rooms at Bryansk and Orel airfields to learn their targets for the opening rounds. Most pilots thought it would be airfields but they were wrong. Maj General Deichmann would avoid the many air bases General Rudenko had set up in the Kursk area. The Soviet planes were spread out and the airfields were heavily defended. In May and June the *Luftwaffe* attempted to attack these fields suffering heavy losses and meager gains. Instead the pilots were directed to strike artillery batteries in the attack zones in the northern salient. The Division had 730 assorted aircraft but due to the shortage of fuel, missions were carefully scheduled whenever possible. In the south, the 8th Air Corps had just over 1,100 planes. Another important shortage the air groupings had was of AA guns, particularly the 88. For Model to defend his 9th Army against the expected heavy raid, quite a few 88s were pulled from nearby airfields and given to Model. This would reduce the air coverage at the airfields but at least 9th Army would have just over 100 precious 88s for their defense. cbk37. dgk54. cbk12m.

In addition to the Central Front, Rokossovsky also had the resources of the 16th Air Army. dgr238.

The German airfields in and around Orel had been established and improved since 1941 and included steel mesh on the runways. Some of the airfields west of Kharkov also had improvements. The fields were also protected with as many flak brigades that could be spared. cbk51. cbk12m. pck64.

4

July 5th on the Southern Salient

See Maps 9, 24

During the predawn hours, as many as 200,000 partisans launched their own attack, hitting convoys, rail lines, bridges and non-combat rear area soldiers. Railroad engineers and security divisions worked day and night to stop the attacks and repair the damage. The attacks were very successful and the supplies to the front fell dramatically. The timing of these attacks was another indication that the Soviets were well aware of the German plans. swm138. kcz169+.

The battle of Kursk formally began. After several delays, the German summer offensive was launched against the Soviet-held salient centered on Kursk. To the north of the salient, the German 9th Army (Model) attacks southward against the Soviet Central Front (Rokossovsky) on a front that would eventually expand to 25 miles. To the south, 4th PzA (Hoth) and Army Detachment Kempf strike northward against the Soviet Voronezh Front (Vatutin) on a nearly 40 mile front. The Soviet Steppe Front (Konev) was held in reserve. Zhukov and Vasilevsky were *Stavka* representatives for the battles in the north and south, respectively. The Germans hoped to eliminate the Kursk salient and with it a Soviet capability to launch an offensive in 1943. The Soviets had prepared extensive defenses and anticipated the German offensive. A disruptive bombardment was carried out shortly before the German forces were scheduled to begin attacking. When the offensive did get under way, progress was relatively slow and casualties were relatively high on both sides. After arriving at Kursk, Zhukov argued with Vatutin and Vasilevsky that the dug-in tanks should be unearthed and used in the offensive. The other two generals argued the defensive role was right for the moment. Stalin agreed with Vatutin. gjz184. hjj129. vzz26. vzz33. asz362+.

The German 9th Army attacked from south of Orel on the northern leg of the salient while the 4th PzA and Kempf Army attacked from Belgorod northward into the southern leg of the salient. Hoth and Kempf were using the traditional Blitzkreig with panzers in front contrary to Model's approach of leading with infantry. vzz26+.. dgk87m.

The first day saw penetrations of 11 miles on the southern salient and 6 miles on the northern salient. *Luftwaffe* estimated 432 Soviet planes were destroyed to the Germans' 26. A total of 1,450 German planes took part in the operation. Though the Red Air Force suffered greater casualties the above number for Soviet losses is high.

The German armies involved were Group Kempf, 4th PzA in the south and 9th Army and 2nd PzA in the north. There were 7 IDs, 11 PzDs and 3 assault brigades. In the south the main effort was led by 48th PzC and 2nd SS PzC with a total of 700 panzers. The Soviet 6th GA took the brunt of this force along the road to Oboyan. Despite the unfavorable weather, the *Luftwaffe* gave strong support throughout the campaign. The SS PzC was able to travel 11 miles, penetrating the 52nd RD line. Vatutin began sending reinforcements to plug the holes forming around Cherkasskoe and the Pena River. dgk94+.

At Kursk the Germans did gain ground but not enough to guarantee pocketing large numbers of POWs. There were six defense belts in the south and four in the north of the salient and von Manstein figured he had five days to secure them if victory was going to happen. They were already behind schedule. The plan called for gaining 18 miles a day. wdk124*.

During the day and night sPzAbt 505 destroyed 111 Soviet tanks while losing only three Tigers. By the end of the war, only 1,354 Tigers had been built. dgk18.

Even though Hitler thought this offensive would surprise the Soviets, the Soviets knew for months that the Kursk area would be the Germans spearhead and planned accordingly. The front line was 35 miles deep. By the end of the first day, Hitler and OKW knew the Soviets were expecting them. The field generals for months tried to tell Hitler this but he would not listen.

From interrogating a German soldier at 0110 hrs, Zhukov discovered the full invasion would begin at 0330 hrs. He immediately ordered all of his batteries to open fire on the German positions. 2,460 guns opened fire, causing heavy casualties on German assault positions. The Soviets claimed after the campaign the Germans had to delay the invasion for up to three hours to regroup but there was only a minor pause from their scheduled launch time. gjz180+.

Twelve miles east of Gertsovka at 0115 hrs, Hausser's 2nd SS PzC advanced under fierce fighting to capture forward positions at Iakhontov and on the southern slopes of the Erik River valley. The 2nd SS PzC received half of the 167th ID and the 48th PzC received the other half to help support the panzers. Hausser, a veteran of WWI, retired from service in 1932 but joined the SS when Hitler came to power in 1933. He is considered one of the best if not *the* best commanders of the Waffen SS. In 1941 while with *Das Reich* he lost an eye and wore a black eye patch. In 1944, he would be transferred to Normandy as CO of 7th Army. In August he was seriously wounded near Falaise and was replaced by Heinrich Eberbach. dgk84. snk75++. dgr280m.

Starting early, 2nd SS PzC launched from the line that included the Stepnoi, Sukhoi Verk and the nearby Hill 227.4 and Hill 218.0. The attack axis included Iakhontov, Hill 228.6 and Streletskoe but the main axis for *LAH* and *Das Reich* was straddling the Tomarovka-Bykovka road in order to reach their primary objective, the key junction at Iakovlevo The heaviest strike by *LAH* and *Das Reich* on the 52nd GRD was in a four mile section between Hill 228.6 and Hill 218.0. Just to the east of this sector was the important village of Iakhontov that the flank of *Das Reich* was heading for as well. Since the Soviets expected the Germans would travel down the paved road to Iakhontov, it was heavily covered with many anti-tank guns. The 52nd GRD was equipped with a special *flamethrower* battalion and had erected defenses on all sides of the village. Eventually, after a grisly fight by 1000 hrs the Soviets were forced from behind the anti-tank ditch south of Iakhontov and had to fall back to Hill 246.3. Engineers were brought up to clear minefields before more men or panzers could move in the direction of Iakovlevo. Heavy fighting would soon erupt for Hill 220.5 and Hill 217.1 near the farming village of Berezov which was also defended by 52nd GRD with 51st GRD in second echelon. gnk13. gnk56. vzz92++. vzz6m. vzz2m. cbk32. cbk12m. vzz39. zrk204+. zow135. zow139.

In order for *LAH* to reach Iakovlevo as quickly as possible, the *Luftwaffe* was tasked with clearing the resistance positioned in and around Berezov as well as both sides of nearby Hill 220.5 (1st PzGR). During this preemptive bombing and shortly after 0130 hrs the

2nd PzGR of *LAH* captured Hill 228.6 situated along the Tomarovka-Bykovka road. One hour later it took the high ground near Iakhontov. *Das Reich*, with 2nd PzGR of *LAH* on its left flank and heading for Kamennyi Log and Sadelnoe, took the village of Iakhontov at 0245 hrs but by 0510 hrs was still bogged down by tank ditches north of the village and counter-attacks by 52nd GRD which were trying to retake the town and hill. The attacks were repulsed. At the same time other elements of the 2nd PzGR were fighting their way into Streletskoe to the west of Iakhontov. Once the line Streleskoe-Iakhontov was achieved, the trailing units of *LAH* would advance. During this initial period, artillery batteries were nearly firing constantly on pre battle objectives or upon receiving new intel of troublesome Pak fronts or artillery concentrations, shifting to those new coordinates. Occasionally smoke screens would be ordered to help out a regiment in distress. agk93. gnk75. vzz92. vzz6m. vzz2m. zrl204+. zrl207. zow140.

At 0220 hrs in the Kursk salient on this Monday morning, the Soviets began shelling German positions to disrupt their assault preparations. Tanks remained silent to hide their positions. The 6th GA and 7th GA brought up 76mm guns to the first and second defense belts in the south to slow the expected panzer attacks. These guns were delivered by US trucks and caused the 167th ID some 600 casualties by the time the barrage stopped. The 167th ID had responsibility to guard the left flank of *LAH* as it traveled north along the east bank of the Vorskla River and had to fight hard to catch up with *LAH*. Further east, the 19th PzD defending the Mikhailovka bridgehead was also hit hard. In the north Model's front was especially hit hard, causing destruction in 90 batteries and 60 OPs. Also at this time, 180 German bombers attacked in front of the advancing 4th PzA. je98. dgk85+. rkz166. fkk75. agk87. agk91m.

At 0230 hrs, the 3rd PzR of *SSTK* captured Hill 218, southeast of Berezov, then repulsed several counter-attacks before moving on. By 1230 hrs, in fierce hand-to-hand combat, the grenadiers captured the nearby tank trench as well. kuz194. ztc268.

Before daybreak, German radar spotted approximately 400 planes heading toward Luftlotte 4 air bases. German fighters quickly scrambled to intercept the Soviet force. In the dogfight that pursued, many Soviet planes, about 120 in the north and as many as 432 in the south, were claimed to have been shot down. Even though aerial conflict on this day was one of the worst in the war on the Eastern Front, the totals that exclude this airfield disaster for the VVS were closer to 70 planes in the north and 150 planes in the south for the Red Air Force. The *Luftwaffe* lost just a fraction of these numbers, which gave them a temporary advantage in the air. The *Luftwaffe* claimed only 26 of their planes were downed. Many of the Soviet planes flew out of the Shumakovo airfield southeast of Kursk. Their main target was the Mikayanovka airfield, 34 miles southwest of Belgorod but Pomerki, Sololniki, Ostnova and Rogan were also targeted. Other airfields used by the Soviets were at Glinev, Novyi Oskol, Dubki and Pokrovskoye and some were as far as 60 miles east of Kursk. The Soviet mission failed primarily not by early radar notice alone but a combination of radar and the coincidental preparation of the German air crews for their own assault. With their planes all ready to fly, it took the German pilots only minutes to get into the air. Besides technique, Soviet radio equipment was inferior to the German equipment. dgk85. lck222+. cbk26*+. cbk34. cbk30. dgr249+. swm140. sgf344. wwf163m. cbk12m. pck63+.

In the predawn hours before Citadel began, the remainder of the 800 German airplanes of *Luftflotte* 4 were checked, fueled and loaded. These air fields were located at Barvenkovo,

Pomerki, Osnova, Rogan, Sokomki, Kramotorskaya and Mikayanovka. Just before 0300 hrs, these planes started to take off for their intended targets. mhz199+ mhz216. fkk51. fkk79. dgr249. cbk12m. hsz108.

After taking Hill 228.6 and repulsing a counter-attack around 0230 hrs, the Tigers of *LAH* along with the 2nd PzGR headed for Hill 220.5 near the Tomorovka-Bykovka road which was defended by the 151st GRR of 52nd GRD. At 0315 hrs, the eleven Tigers of Company 13 of *LAH* approached Hill 220.5. Hill 220.5 was heavily defended and would be much tougher to capture. In front of the hill was an anti-tank ditch that was heavily covered with mines and wire. Flamethrowers, anti-tank guns and dug-in assault guns were waiting for the Germans to attempt crossing the ditch. agk93+. agk94m. vzz92. zrl211.

Hausser's 2nd SS PzC launched its attack and met fierce resistance but still managed, with the help of the *Luftwaffe*, to advance 11 miles by dusk against 6th GA. The *SSTK* succeeded in attacking the 69th HQ at Iakhontovo, inflicting heavy casualties. Berezov, Gremuchi, Bykovo and Vosnesenskiall also fell to the Germans. The 6th GA was at a breaking point. By 1200 hrs all three divisions of 2nd SS PzC had penetrated the first defense belt. Katukov, Popiel and Chistiakov could not believe the speed of the penetration. The day's casualties would turn out to be the heaviest for 2nd SS PzC of the campaign. It proved to Hausser, who was observing much of the fighting that the initial shelling and bombing had little effect. It also told him that there would be no quick race to the Psel as Hoth expected. bt83. mhz210+. mhz216. vzz93. lck241.

When the Tigers and following infantry broke through the first line, Soviet anti-tank guns hiding in wait opened fired. The Soviet guns could not penetrate the Tigers so the big cats calmly stopped and started methodically picking off the Soviet guns. Tanks from the 230th TR moved up to challenge the Tigers. Wittmannn saw them first and immediately started moving toward the T34s. Other panzers moved toward the important hill and were stopped by a minefield and a tank ditch. While trying to free themselves, the Soviets shelled them heavily. It took the *LAH* until 1200 hrs to reach the top of Hill 217.1 and began securing the immediate area. Once the hill was secured other elements of the *LAH* moved up to the line. gnk66+. gnk74+. mjk88. vzz97+.

At 0315 hrs, *SSTK* artillery opened up and by 0400 hrs, at least 100 bombers and Stukas flew directly over the men in the trenches who were waiting for the word to go. When the bombers were done, the division jumped off with Tigers in the lead. As the men headed for and through the woods in front of Hill 216.5, many dogfights could be seen in the sky. Shortly after 0900 hrs, the regiment reached the approach to the hill. By noon the men had fought through the barbed wire and reached the first trench in front of the hill. Hand-to-hand combat erupted. Soviet artillery opened up when the assault guns were in range. The Tigers were safe against these small field guns but the assault guns were not so lucky and were taking casualties. During this engagement, the Tigers met up with the first SU-152. It was a hybrid T34 with a 15 cm howitzer built aboard. While the heavy guns were firing at each other, German engineers struggled to close down the trench in order for the panzers to make it across. Making things worse for the Germans, four Tigers found a minefield and lost tracks. The repair shop would have to make emergency repairs to get these machines moving again. The *SSTK* started the campaign with 115 assorted panzers and 39 assault guns that were in fighting condition. Excluding seven command panzers, 97 of those panzers were either Mk IIIs or Mk IVs. There were only eleven Tigers. gnk80+. kuz192+. ztc268.

Recon patrols from most German divisions moved out while still dark, infiltrated the very front trenches and eliminated a number of OP sights. The Soviets would be temporarily blind in a few sectors, giving the Germans a few minutes of advantage. wwf73.

Das Reich was unprepared for the launch. Many of their panzers had not arrived which meant Hausser would have to watch his grenadiers jump off without panzer support. Not a good start. Their artillery did begin on time. At 0330 hrs, it started firing on the low hills in front of Berezov which was defended by the 155th GRR and 156th GRR. At 0400 hrs, Stukas showed up to soften the front line as well. When the Soviets saw the Germans advance, a group of tanks went out to meet them with infantry on their decks. The Germans put up a wall of small-arms fire that targeted the mounted infantry. The fire was so bad that the Soviets had to jump from the tanks. After a vicious fight, *Das Reich* reached the first ditch in front of Berezov. Without panzers, *Deutschland* Regiment had to destroy one bunker at a time. It was slow going. Soviet artillery stationed at Zhuravlinyi Woods, north of Berezov, increased their mortar fire on the struggling Germans. With months to prepare, the Soviets were able to set up artillery positions that would cover their lines. The Germans were able to bring up their mortars to combat the Soviets but it still cost the Germans heavily. With their men stuck at the ditch, the big German guns shifted their aim from Berezov to Zhuralivni Woods where the biggest danger lurked. Without an OP, their aim was ineffective so Stukas were called in to quiet the Woods. gnk77+. vzz92. gnk69m. zow141.

At 0600 hrs, sappers led the advance of the 2nd SS PzC toward Berezov but *Das Reich*, traveling along the eastern bank of the Vorskla River, following the sappers were halted by heavy shelling from the west side of the river. Aerial bombing and additional shelling was requested. Their mission was to collapse the tank trench and clear the many mines in front of the town to allow the panzers quick passage. By 1000 hrs, the grenadiers of *Deutschland* penetrated the front line trench from the north of the 52nd GRD and were fighting hand-to-hand against the 151st GRR and 155th GRR. It was critical for the SS to gain control of the Tomarovka-Bykovka road and the Belgorod-Iakovlevo road in order to bypass much of terrible terrain along the Vorskla River that would greatly slow the advance and make the columns vulnerable to attack. By 1100 hrs *Eicke* Regiment of *SSTK* but temporarily attached to *Das Reich* entered the fight for Berezov by crossing the trench on the east side and fighting hand-to-hand with the defenders by 1230 hrs. The SS Corps also had the responsibility of screening 48th PzC's eastern flank. Part of that task was given to 167th ID. However Hoth placed *GD* with its 350 panzers directly in front of this terrible terrain and the first couple days fighting would have a disastrous effect on these panzers, causing the 48th PzC to fall behind the SS Corps. To make the situation worse for the attackers, some of the Soviet guns, like the 122mm, were using fragmentation bombs that would destroy all infantry or engineer in a 320 sq yard area. vzz89+. vzz94+. vzz221. vzz2m. gnk68m. gjz184. zow141.

Das Reich continued to fight for Berezov and eventually a hole erupted in the 52nd GRD's line and by 1400 hrs Berezov was being secured. The 156th GRR of 52nd GRD was hit the hardest and was forced to fall back to Hill 246.3. This was another example of a long and costly battle for a small strongpoint. This would be a pattern that would repeat itself over and over as the days went by. Leaving Berezov, a trailing battalion of the *Deutschland* Regiment headed for Hill 233.3, almost two miles north of the village to join the rest of the regiment that was locked in battle. As the lead Germans approached the

Hill, T34s came rolling down to meet their enemy. Though destroying a few of the leading tanks, the Germans had to halt their advance; Otto Weidinger was wounded and had to be carried to safety. He later recovered to lead his troops again. Panzers had still not arrived and infantry assault was in danger of being stopped. Other elements of *Das Reich* arrived and added their weight to the offensive. The German guns were now honing their aim on Hill 233.3 and Stukas would soon arrive to help out. At the foot of the hill, the Germans struck a minefield but by 1600 hrs they were on top of Hill 233.3 and mopping up the last resistance. Major Wisliceny of 3rd Battalion of *Deutschland* Regiment led the charge on the hill. He was awarded the Knight's Cross for his bravery and leadership that afternoon. Captain Schreiber and Master Sergeant Weber were also recipients of the Knight's Cross. *Das Reich* started the campaign with 98 assorted panzers including 12 Tigers, 18 captured T34s plus 43 assault guns. gnk78+. wwf149. gnk69m. hjj112. ztc268. vzz93. zow141+.

In the first hours of the campaign, the *Luftwaffe* struck the 52nd GRD extremely hard, inflicting many casualties. The 52nd GRD had the misfortune of being deployed in front of the route 2nd SS PzC was taking. The 67th GRD to the immediate west of 52nd GRD in the Olkhovka, Dmitrievka area and in front of 11th PzD and *GD* was also hit hard. The corps received high priority in aerial and artillery support. This extreme bombing also had disadvantages as well for there were so many shell holes that the new Panthers of the *GD* had trouble conquering the terrain. The *Luftwaffe* also had squadrons of fighters flying over Soviet rear areas trying to shoot down and prevent Soviet planes from entering the battle zone when they first started appearing in the skies after 0700 hrs. On the other hand, to the east when Kempf's forces attacked the 81st GRD at the Mikhailovka bridgehead not far from Belgorod, there was no *Luftwaffe* support. Without air support, the first couple days for Kempf were slow and tortuous. It is interesting to consider what 3rd PzC's advance would have been like if air support was provided. Would 6th PzD have been able to push 81st GRD back that first day with air support, instead of having to redeploy to the southeast the next day? The first day was a costly waste for 3rd PzC in general and 6th PzD in particular. Would the panzer divisions have been able to reach near Pravorot by 7/11 or 7/12 to assist *LAH* and *Das Reich* if the first two days had gone better for Kempf? cbk30+. dgk70m. dgr250.

On the east flank of 48th PzC was 2nd SS PzC. Hausser planned a narrow front from which his 400 fighting vehicles including 42 Tigers would smash through the Soviet lines on its way to Oboyan.

Elements of *LAH* launched shortly after first light and quickly ran into the Soviets' first defense belt that included tank and wire obstacles and a string of heavily armored bunkers. The lead panzers made little progress against this wall. So members of the 2nd PzGR, lead by Karck and using demolition charges, sneaked in and destroyed one bunker after another. The panzers rolled on. The 2nd SS PzC had an easier time than the 48th PzC for it received more support from the *Luftwaffe*. The Hs-129 twin engine heavily armored fighters with the 37mm cannon were in this sector. They were also using the new fragmentation SD-1 bombs that were simply horrific on infantry. The 151st GRR and 155th GRR were practically annihilated, leaving the Belgorod-Kursk highway open. pck60+. pck65++. lck232.

The 52nd GRD was deployed across the critical Tomarovka-Iakovlevo road on a line that included Trirechnoe-Gremuchi-Nepkhaevo-Berezov. The width of their sector was four miles. By 1000 hrs, the 2nd SS PzC broke through the first trench line. The 1008th

DATR, dug in on the second line at Hill 217.1, one mile northwest of Berezov, was waiting for the Germans to arrive. Vicious fighting between the Soviet artillery on the hill and the approaching panzers soon broke out. See Map 9. vzz92. vzz96. vzz2m. vzz3m. gnk66+.

North of Tomarovka in the 11th PzD sector where the 67th GRD was defending, several Fw 190s were shot down. In general on the first day of the offensive, the Soviet air response was slow and inconsistent but in this area the *Luftwaffe* was not heavily patrolling and the Soviet AF had better results. The German planes for the most part had control of the skies and lost many fewer planes than the Red Air Force this first day. Soviet fighter escorts would also fly at the same speed and altitude of the bombers and the German Bf 109s flying at a much greater speed and height had the advantage and destroyed more Soviet planes than they would lose today. Soviet observers were poorly trained and observation procedures and practices were delinquent and awkward, making for an extremely slow response. This failing was quickly recognized and was improved in the days ahead. On the other hand, German procedures were well formulated and followed well. When Soviet artillery threatened a German operation, the location was called in and the appropriate air response was made. This German routine worked well for the first days but as attrition wore down the *Luftwaffe*, their response was slowed and not as ubiquitous. cbk 29+. cbk31+.

The battle for Hill 220.5, the strongpoint of the Berezov sector, which was defended by the 151st GRR of 52nd GRD, started at 0315 hrs with a rocket barrage by the 55th Werfer Regiment. At 0405 hrs, the Stukas, while *LAH* continued to advance, came in to bomb the Hill as well. At 0430 the armored vehicles of *LAH* moved out while the shelling continued on the Butovo-Gertsovka line. Nearby, the fortified town of Berezov and its surrounding area was attacked again by *Das Reich*. The infantry of *LAH* moved on Hill 220.5 around 0700 hrs. It would take the Germans into the afternoon to take both of these objectives. Hill 220.5 straddled the Tomarovka-Bykovka road and was due west of Berezov by two miles. Hill 217.1, a mile north of Hill 220.5 also ran along the key Tomarovka-Berezov road and would also have to be taken before reaching Bykovka, further north. To the west next to the Vorskla River, the 2nd PzGR of *LAH* supported by the 315 GR of 167th ID was advancing against resistance at Sadelnoe and Kamenyi Log. The attack route for *LAH* was situated between the Vorskla River on the west flank and Berezov on the east. vzz92. gnk66. gnv75. agk90. vzz2m. gnk69m. zrl214.

At 0720, Vatutin ordered Kravchenko's 5th GTC to prepare to move forward. The CO was then ordered to move to and defend the Lunino, Teterevino, Petrovka line by next morning. With Gremuchi fallen, Burdeiny's 2nd GTC was ordered up to the line to fill the gap behind 5th GTC. They needed to be in place by 2400 hrs that night. Burdeiny had tentative orders to attack on the Teterevino, Bykovo, Rakovo axis if the Germans showed any weakness. vzz93. vzz105. dgk101.

During the day and especially during the morning hours, the Soviet AF concentrated their ground attacks in the Zybino, Moschchenoye, Tomarovka and Streletskoe areas in the west and in the Solomino, Bezliudovka areas east of the Donets against large panzer formations. dgr251.

At 0900 hrs, Il-2s attacked *Das Reich*. German Bf 109s greatly outnumbered the several groups of eight Soviet fighters and were able to shoot some down and chase the others away. cbk31.

The grenadiers attacking Berezov were taking heavy casualties and were making slow progress due to the hidden artillery in Zhuravlinyi woods which was directing accurate fire on *Das Reich* in front of Berezov and nearby *LAH*. The 55th Werfer and 1st Werfer Regiments turned their rocket launchers on the woods and started firing. The 55th Werfer Regiment was originally assigned to support 2nd PzGR of *LAH* and in particularly to screen the regiment from flank attacks emanating from the west bank of the Vorskla River. It was also positioned to support the assault on Bykovka, further north. Bykovka, situated near important roadways and the future site for *LAH*'s HQ, was also deemed to be a major aid station. A hospital had already been prepared in Tomarovka, west of Belgorod. The HQ for General Kruger of *Das Reich* was located at Redilovka but would relocate to just north of Kasazkaia after the operation launched. vzz93. dgk231m. snk433m++. dgk99. zrl208#. zow.134+. zow138.

At 0915 hrs, elements of *SSTK* approached Hill 216.5. In front of the hill was a trench and running behind the trench a series of bunkers the Germans had to take before reaching the top. With artillery firing ahead of the infantry, the Germans throwing grenades reached the trench. Without stopping, the trench was leaped and the men were heading for the bunkers. The defenders came out from behind their defenses to meet the attackers and a vicious hand-to-hand fight ensued. By 1600 hrs the *SSTK* had captured Hill 216.5 with the Soviet survivors falling back. Without waiting for the rest of *SSTK* to catch up, Haussler ordered his men to head for the Oboyan road. By late afternoon Haussler, his men and six Tigers reached Hill 225.9 which had a commanding view of the important road to Prokhorovka. A brief but costly battle with the 155th RR of 52nd GRD split the Soviet regiment from the rest of the division. This caused the regiment to fall back, leaving the division flank exposed and showing a gap with the 375th RD which was situated to the south. On the other side of 375th RD was 81st GRD of 7th GA which was currently fighting 6th PzD of 3rd PzC and was unable to lend a hand. The *Eicke* Regiment went on to capture nearby Erik, Gonki and Hill 198.3. gnk81+. zow145.

Lebedev's 96th TB was quickly ordered to Hill 225.9 when it was discovered *SSTK* was making good progress. The Soviets made it to the hill before the Germans could defeat 52nd GRD and though not well prepared, still put up stiff resistance. With night quickly approaching and without his full complement of panzers, Haussler chose to withdraw from the hill. He would attack it early next morning. This was a critical break for the Soviets. If it had been earlier in the day and with all of his panzers supporting, *SSTK* might have taken the hill and struck the 81st GRD in the rear at the same time 6th PzD had been attacking from the other direction. If 6th PzD had been able to break the 81st GRD line the first day, the 3rd PzC could have been a day ahead of schedule and potentially been able to link up with *Das Reich* by 7/12 for a coordinated attack toward Pravorot and Prokhorovka. Maybe? gnk83.

At 1435 hrs, *Eicke* Regiment of *SSTK* commanded by Knochlein attacked elements of the 52nd GRD defending the woods west of Hill 225.9. The assault was made difficult for the Soviets had dug a tank ditch in front of the forest as well as planting thousands of mines. German engineers were called up to clear the field; many pioneers lost their lives that afternoon to heavy small arms fire. Once past the minefield, the grenadiers were able to quickly overpower the defenders. The Germans could not finish clearing the woods before dark and stopped their advance in the woods. They would resume in the morning and hopefully reach Erik to the west by noon the following day. With less enemy fire, the engineers finally overcame the tank ditch and the panzers started rolling again, trying to catch up to the infantry. Once again the Soviet defenses, accurate artillery fire and an active air force had slowed the Germans' advance. *SSTK* flak guns downed many planes that day. *SSTK* had the lightest casualties of the SS Corps and still had 121 working panzers. gnk84.

The 1008th DATR and 538th TDR defending the road to Bykovka quickly destroyed six panzers, including three Tigers of *Das Reich* before being forced to retreat northward through town. Before the fighting was broken off, Kotenko claimed to have destroyed 33 panzers including 17 Tigers. Some of those destroyed by using Katyusha rockets pointed pointblank at the panzers. He lost 21 of his 24 tanks and 45 guns. The *LAH* joined in to help *Das Reich* subdue the Soviets which fell back to Hill 217.1. *LAH* then continued north hoping to cross the Vorskla and to try to breach the second defense belt near Iakovlevo. It failed its objective but would resume early next morning. dgk99+. rkz167. vzz95+.

The opening drive for the bulk of *LAH* was in the direction of Streletzkoye-Berezov which was defended by the 52nd GRD. Berezov, which was on the borderline between *LAH* and *Das Reich*, was captured by 1100 hrs. By this time the *Luftwaffe*, for the most part, had cleared or greatly reduced the skies of Soviet competition. cbk32. agk91m. lck164m. zow135.

To the northeast of Iakovlevo the terrain was open and flat up to the Komsomolets State Farm. With 2nd SS PzC fighting for Iakovlevo, just south of Pokrovka, Vatutin brought up the 31st TC to dig in and block the Germans' way. This area was part of the terrain between the second defense and third defense belt and there had been no trenches built in the area. The 1st TA was ordered to move up along a 19 mile sector between Melovoe and Iakovlevo and fortify the line. These redeployments of over 1,000 tanks were critical for this area was about to be attacked by two divisions of 48th PzC and one division of the SS which would have blown right past the original formations of 6th GA. See Map 9. vzz106+. lck241. vzz8m. lck164m.

In order for the panzers of *SSTK* to move past the swamp west of Erik, their engineers, taking point under fire from the Red Air Force and artillery coming from the Zhuravlinyi (Shurawlivny) Forest, were bridging the unsuitable terrain. gnk110. gnk69m. vzz3m.

The Pz Abt 2 attacked Nekhaevka, on the western bank of the Lipovyi Donets River and southwest of Teterevino, and the surrounding high ground, forcing the defenders to fall back. fkk134. vzz3m.

The 67th GRD, just to the west of 52nd GRD, was hard hit by the 48th PzC's 11PzD; Vatutin ordered the 6th TC and the 3rd MC up to the line to support the 67th GRD. Eventually the 67th would fall back to second echelon. kcz167. dgk95m.

Joachim Peiper and his fellow tankers that he was supporting contributed to the advance by breaking through the line east of Bykovka and opened the way to Iakovlovka and the future bridgehead across the Psel. fkk153. nzk85.

Hausser called in the *Luftwaffe* to hit the Zhuravlinyi woods in which Soviet artillery was hitting Berezov and Gremuchi hard. Hausser also called up the 55th Werfer Regiment which had been deployed with *LAH* and the 1st Werfer Regiment to shell the front trenches hard before the infantry stormed the line. Hausser also had the support of 400 planes from the 8th Air Corps. vzz93. vzz6m.

Once past the front line trenches, *Das Reich* captured Iakhontov by 1100 hrs and Berezov by 1330 hrs. Vzz92++. dgk99.

The 167th ID, deployed between *LAH* and 11th PzD, was tasked with giving *LAH*'s left flank protection but were locked in fierce combat just off *LAH*'s flank and could not move. The 167th ID had attached to it the 55th Werfer Regiment to give it greater punch. The infantry went after the towns of Sadelnye and Kamennyi which was defended by artillery of Kotenko's 1008th DATR that could hit *LAH* as it moved north toward Hill 220.5. Kotenko's regiment was one reason why Hill 220.5 was so difficult to capture. mhz216. gnk65.

At 1200 hrs, the *LAH* with the support of more than 30 panzers launched an attack along the road to Bykovka with lead elements reaching Hill 217.1, one mile northwest of Berezov. Half of the group split off and entered Berezov while a few panzers entered Gremuchi. Hill 217.1 was 500 yards northeast of Hill 220.5 and by 1400 hrs *Das Reich* had finished securing Berezov. At the same time *SSTK* was fighting for Gremuchi which had escalated from when the first panzers entered the village. The *SSTK* was trying to penetrate the line to reach the Belgorod-Kursk road by fighting through the woods south of Erik creek. At 1430 hrs, *Das Reich* moved out of Berezov for Zhuravlinyi and then Gremuchi. By 1600 hrs, *Das Reich* had cleared the Zhuravlinyi woods. vzz96+. gnk66. zow141.

A German recon force of over 2,000 men with support of 20 panzers from 11th PzD was advancing toward Butovo from the southeast. While the 11th PzD slowly pushed forward toward Butovo; their right flank, SS PzC, took the high ground near Iakhontov, forcing the elements of the 6th GA back from their outposts. At 1645 hrs, from this newly captured high ground, the 48th PzC and SS started shelling the depth of the first defensive belt. During the shelling the 48th PzC, supported by assault guns, rolled over Soviet defenses and reached Cherkasskoe southwest of Alekseevka by evening where a terrible battle erupted. Vatutin ordered Katukov to bring reserves up to the line that included Melovoe, Rakovo, Shepelevka from 6th TC while the 3rd MC was ordered up to the Alekseevka, Syrtsevo, Iakovlevo line and the 31st TC was supposed to move into the line that covered Studenok, Stalinskoe State Farm, Vladimirovka, Orlovka. In addition, the 2nd GTC were to move up to Sazhnoe, west of Krivtsevo, on the eastern bank of the Lipovyi Donets River and the 5th GTC were to move to the Teterevino South-Malinovka area. They would be in place by the following day. Around 300 sorties were flown on this afternoon to assist 48th PzC in their opening moves which was a big help considering most of the panzers had not arrived yet. An estimated 100 Soviet fighters were sent to stop the German formations but they were ineffective in stopping the attacks though ten German planes were shot down. Malinovka was a small village east of Teterevino South and west of Shakhovo. bt81+*. dgk81. hjj117m. dgr249. vzz105+. vzz5m+. vzz12m.

After capturing Berezov by 1300 hrs, the *Deutschland* Regiment moved north but not far from Bykovka engaged a group from 52nd GRD with a few American M3 tanks. After a while the Soviets were encircled and were putting up stiff resistance that was slowing *Das Reich* down. But they were running out of ammo and their survival would be lost unless help could arrive. Nekrasov planned a suicide tank attack as a diversion in order for his men to fall back to Bykovka. At 1400 hrs the tanks met four miles north of Berezov on Hill 233.3. A second group of tanks attacked *LAH* one mile south of Bykovka. Seven Soviet tanks were knocked out in the southern engagement but the 52nd GRD in the area continued to resist. At 1500 hrs, the *Luftwaffe* made another run on Hill 233.3, Hill 215.4, Bykovka, Kamennyi Log and Kozmo-Demianovka where the 52nd GRD HQ was located. Elements of two regiments of 52nd GRD that were encircled north of Berezov did not make Bykovka and were destroyed. By 1800 hrs, the garrison at Kozmo lost its communications with 6th GA HQ. vzz97++. gnk77+. gnk69m. vzz6m. zow141.

After the capture of Hill 233.3, both *LAH* and *Das Reich* were ordered to fight past dark and were informed their panzers were moving up. By 1800 hrs *Das Reich* following a ravine north of Berezov marched into a minefield. After extracting themselves the regiment had to back up and move through the Zhuravliny Woods to head toward Bykovka sector. zow142.

Following orders, the Thule Regiment of *SSTK* turned southeast after reaching the Gremuchi Valley around 1200 hrs heading for the Shopino area to secure the Belgorod-Kursk Highway as well as the nearby bridge over the Lipvoyi Donets. kuz194.

At 1220 hrs, a scouting party from *Der Führer* Regiment of *Das Reich* was headed toward Luchki South and by 1800 hrs was approaching its outskirts, having penetrated the gap in Chistiakov's 6th *GA*'s line. To the southeast, along with the *LAH*, a crossing was made but a bridgehead could not be established over the Lipovyi Donets River. During the crossing attempt IL-2 ground attack aircraft attacked the Germans. Eight planes were shot down. Lead elements of *Das Reich* were now almost 10 miles from their start line and not far behind *LAH*. Between *LAH* and *Das Reich*, the 52nd GRD had been hit hard and were falling back. fkk135. lck66m. pck66.

By 1200 hrs after nearly five hours of vicious fighting, Hill 220.5 fell to the Germans. The Tiger crews all mention when the battle was over that they had never experienced a wall of steel coming at them like that morning. It was an experience that would be carried throughout their entire lives. One of the Soviet units the *LAH* would be facing in this area was Dragunski's 1st MB which was supplied with the new panzer-killer, the 57mm gun. Flamethrowers and MG nests were positioned near minefields alongside wire entanglements to help stop infantry. There was also a tank ditch in front of the hill and as the German sappers cleared mines and took care of the ditch the panzers and infantry of *LAH* waited to pass took heavy fire, suffering heavy casualties. After Hill 220.5 fell to *LAH*, the 315 GR quickly moved up to the line and prepared to cross the Vorskla River and establish a bridgehead on the west side. While Hill 220.5 was being contested, other elements of 2nd PzGR advanced on nearby Hill 217.1, about half a mile northeast of Hill 220.5. After Hill 217.1, the grenadiers moved on toward Hill 215.4 situated a little over a mile south of Bykovka. agk87+. agk95+. agk94m. vzz92+. zrl214#.

After securing Hill 220.5, a part of the first defense belt and tearing a hole in the 52nd GRD line, the lead units of *LAH* with almost 100 panzers moved up the road toward Bykovka. Iakovlevo, a fortified village four miles further north of Bykovka and on the edge of the second defense belt would be next. It was expected of *LAH* to capture Iakovlevo from Maj General Tavartkiladze's 51st GRD before dark. The 51st GRD was deployed directly behind the 52nd GRD. Eventually the 230th TR which was harassing *LAH* northward gave up their attacks and moved northward toward the second defense belt to dig in. The German column just reached Iakovlevo at dusk and was immediately fired upon by the 28th ATB. With no artillery support and running low on ammo, the *LAH* decided to attack the village in the morning. The *LAH* had made the best progress of 4th PzA on this day by traveling eleven miles and reaching the outer edges of the second defense belt. gnk75+. dgk101.

Trailing its panzers, the 5th PzGR of *SSTK* crossed over the tank ditch southeast of Berezov at 1230 hrs, while the 6th PzGR cleared the woods southwest of Erik. The regiments of *SSTK* linked up and attacked and subsequently captured Hill 216.5 northeast of Berezov within the hour. The division then advanced and captured the villages of Kolchose Smelo and Kolchose Trudu situated near the Belgorod-Kursk highway by 1500 hrs. Eager to move on, a combat group from 6th PzGR split from the division and moved on the villages situated in the Hammer Woods after a brief shelling. Discovering a Soviet concentration in nearby Dragon Woods, the *Eicke* Group moved on it as well. During the last two hours, the *SSTK* Flak Abt shot down three planes using a combination of 37mm and 88mm guns. kuz194.

During the day, *SSTK* moved up to fill the critical east flank of 4th PzA; its main job to protect the 4th from being blindsided as it advanced northward. *SSTK*'s advance crashed into the dug-in positions of the 52nd GRD. By the end of the day, the Germans had eventually broken through and were continuing to advance but *SSTK* failed to reach the line held by the 375th RD. It did capture Iakhontovo by nightfall, forcing the 52nd GRD back. That was the CP for the Soviet 69th Army which evacuated very quickly. wwf77. lck241. dgk106m.

At 1240 hrs, Kraas's 2nd PzGR of *LAH*, with the support of 50 panzers, finally broke through the line that included Hill 217.1 and moved on toward Hill 215.4, a little more than a mile south of Bykovka. When the Germans were approaching Bykovka and Kosmo-Demianovka, the 51st GRD was ordered to move up to the line to support 52nd GRD. By mid afternoon and despite the 28th AAR and 1008th DATR moving up to help 52nd GRD defend the surrounding countryside, the town of Bykovka fell to *LAH* which by this time had seen both *LAH* grenadier regiments join forces. After taking Hill 215.4, *LAH* moved north but was met with horrendous fire, forcing the Germans to fall back to the reverse slope of Hill 215.4 to await reinforcements that were still coming up to the line from clearing Hill 220.5. fkk78+. wwf115. vzz6m. agk96. wwf112+.

Between the first and second defense belt, Michael Wittmann went to the aid of a fellow Tiger. By the end of the engagement Wittmann had destroyed eight T34s and seven anti-tank guns despite losing his mobility. Over the next eight days, Wittmann added another 20 tanks to his total. mhz215.

By 1400 hrs *Das Reich*, after getting off to a good start, was stopped by an extensive minefield which had to be cleared before moving on. A mile to the west *LAH* continued to advance and stormed the village of Bykovka. The rolling grasslands between the first defense belt and second defense belt were punctuated by copses which had been converted to Pak nests. The Tigers with their 88s took these in stride as they continue northward.

The 52nd GRD was still holding the line in the Pokrovka, Hill 254.2 area about six miles north of Bykovka but they would not be able to hold it for much longer against the constant pressure of *LAH* and *Das Reich*. dgk101+. vzz99. vzz2m. gnk113m.

In the afternoon, the *SSTK* was battling the 375th RD which was putting up stiff resistance. The *SSTK* had so far failed to cross the Lipovyi Donets and establish a bridgehead on the eastern banks and the odds that the river would be crossed today looked poor. vzz102. gnk82.

With the *LAH* splitting 52nd GRD in half, two regiments fell back along the western bank of the Vorskla River in the Voznesenski and Vorskla areas and the third regiment found solace along the Kamenski-Gonki line which was being defended by the still healthy 51st GRD. A small fraction made it north to Pokrovka and Bolshie Maiachki which was defended by the 49th TB and the 1st GTB. Once this action was discovered, Vatutin ordered the 51st GRD, which was deployed behind the second defense belt, to move up to the Solonets-Nekhaevka line to support the 52nd GRD. This quick response at Solonets, just a mile south of Iakovlevo, slowed the Germans from reaching Iakovlevo. There are many examples throughout the campaign where a small fortified village like Solonets delayed the German advance and collectively these delays tremendously helped Vatutin move reserves to these hot sectors. dgr75. gnk114. vzz6m+.

The 2nd SS PzGD, *Das Reich*, smashed through the defenses at Berezov and by nightfall its lead units had cut the key Oboyan-Belgorod road, cutting off the Soviet 155th GRR from its 52nd GRD. South of the *Das Reich*, the *SSTK* seized Gremuchi at 1430 hrs then wheeled to the right and drove the defending 155th GRR into the right flank of the 375th RD. The 155th fell back along the Belgorod-Oboyan road and with the help of 96th TB was finally able to hold the line and save the right flank of the 375th RD from being encircled. dgk100+. vzz105. zrl215.

In reaching the Oboyan-Belgorod road, the *LAH* had made a spectacular advance this first day and was now approaching the second defense belt but the Psel River was still at least 20 miles away. In so doing, it tore apart the 52nd GRD while destroying 15 tanks. The day's cost to *LAH* had been high: 97 dead, 522 wounded, 17 missing and about 30 panzers. The division would never make it past Prokhorovka if these losses continued. dgk100.

The *LAH* headed north, through the Soviets' second defense belt east of Iakovlevo, toward the Psel River to establish a bridgehead. The order to shift direction toward Prokhorovka had not been given so the divisional commanders were still planning on advancing toward Oboyan. Once past Iakovlevo the 1st PzR was ambushed near Hill 234.8 by the 28th Anti-tank Brigade. The Germans fell back to regroup and would resume their advance in the morning. The *SSTK* also made gains clearing the Zhuravlinyi woods. dgk100+. fkk133. zrl215.

East of the 52nd GRD sector, the 375th RD held a ten mile front leading southwest from Gremuchi and Berezov south to Belomestniai which was on the Belgorod-Kursk rail line. The 2nd SS PzC with its three panzer divisions and the 167th ID struck the 375th RD at Ternovka, quickly forcing the Soviets to fall back to the north to the west bank of the Lipovyi Donets River with the *SSTK* closely following. Not taking the time to destroy the 375th, the *LAH* continued north trying to maintain their schedule. By 1630 hrs, the *LAH*, fighting alongside 11th PzD, had advanced and was attacking Bykovka on the Vorskla River. The 51st GRD and the 230th TR were brought up to stop *LAH* but also failed. This town was six miles in from their start line. The other SS divisions had also reached the first defense belt. wdk119. dgk111. dgk222m. dlu63m. mhz207. agk91m.

LAH was driving up the road that ran through Bykovka flanked on the left by the 167th ID. *Das Reich* and *SSTK* were on the right, heading for the strongpoints of Berezov and Gremuchi. Hausser was losing Tigers to breakdowns as well from battle action and minefields. The *LAH* smashed through the 151st GRR's defenses and continued on toward Bykovka against stiff artillery fire which destroyed six panzers, including three Tigers. *Das Reich* continued toward Berezov. At 1630 hrs, the *LAH* received orders to head toward the Psel River but at 2000 hrs as it reached Hill 234.8 overlooking Iakovlevo it was hit by a severe artillery barrage that stopped its advance, forcing it to regroup for the night. The *LAH* had shattered Nekrasov's 52nd GRD in its advance but it lost 30 panzers doing it and this loss was already affecting the rate of the advance as well as the morale of its men. dgk99+. mhz207.

With the 52nd GRD in trouble between Berezov and Bykovka to the north, Kosachev's 28th Anti-tank Brigade was ordered from Pokrovka to Bykovka, six miles to the south. His arrival was too late for 1st PzGR of *LAH* had entered Bykovka and taken Hill 224.2, a little to the south, by 1630 hrs and many men of the 52nd GRD had been trapped and killed. Kosachev was delayed for he received his orders late plus he was attacked by *Luftwaffe* near the line Olkvatka-Hill 234.8 on the way to the encirclement. While 1st PzGR finished securing Bykovka, the 2nd PzR drove through on its way to Kozmo-Demianovka, less than a mile north of Bykovka and a mile east of Vorskla. With *Das Reich*, with the help of air support, keeping pace with *LAH*, its *Deutschland* Regiment captured Hill 233.3 at about the same time. The *LAH* grenadiers were then ordered to advance east of Iakovlevo toward the Psel River but the panzer regiment, being low on fuel, was ordered to stop early for the night and would resume next morning at first light. vzz99+. lck240. zrl214+. vzz6m.

By 1600 hrs, *Das Reich* overran the defenses on Hill 233.3, north of Berezov, and by 1630 *LAH*'s 2nd PzGR had entered Bykovka and was fighting street by street for its control. With Hill 233.3 in German hands the Bykovka area was untenable and by 1700 hrs the remains of 52nd GRD retreated to the Vorskla-Gonki area. By 1900 hrs, the SS troops captured the fortified Kozmo-Demianovka. Hausser ordered his divisions to continue through the night in order to either reach or secure a penetration of the second defense belt, have *LAH* link up with *Das Reich* in the Zhuravlinyi woods and disrupt the Soviets from organizing a stronger defense using the retreating soldiers. *LAH* reached the second defense belt at 1840 hrs and by 1900 hrs was heading for Iakovlevo. After taking Kozmo-Demianovka at 1900 hrs, *Das Reich* continued to fight after dark, trying to reach Hill 214.5 on the outer edge of the second defensive belt. When *LAH* stopped for the night it had reached Hill 234.8, just north of Kozmo-Demianovka. Elements of 167th ID to the west of *LAH* were heading to pass near Hill 254.4, west of Dubrova dgk100. vzz100+ gnk77+. gnk69m. ztc268.

By 1800 hrs, an element of the *LAH* approached the second defense belt and was fighting its way in. It was ordered to assist in capturing Hill 214.5 before pausing for the night. At this point the *LAH* had started fighting with Maj General Tavartkiladze's 51st GRD which was deployed behind the 52nd GRD near Hill 218.3, not far from Kozmo-Demianovka. The Germans continued to push the Soviets back and were able to capture the village of Vorskla, situated on the west bank of the river, before moving on the village of Solonets, a little further north on the west bank of the river and just south of Iakovlevo. The 96th TB moved up and attacked *LAH*, slowing it but not stopping it. The stragglers of the 52nd GRD, 151st GRR, 153rd GRR, which could not reach the second defense belt were crossing to the other side of the Vorskla River or in the other direction to 375th RD sector, but they would not find any safety there for the Germans were moving up there as well. The two regiments that reached the west banks dug in on a line that included Hill 233.6, Hill 238.4, and the ravine one mile west of Solonets. The 155th GRR, moving east, joined the 375th RD's 1243rd RR's defenses in the Nepkhaevo area. The two other SS divisions had not kept up and were along the line that included Zhuravlinyi woods but they would continue to drive past dark as well. vzz101+. agk95+. agk91m. vzz6m+. zrl215.

After capturing the four mile line between Hill 228.6 and Hill 218.0, the SS divisions quickly moved on. The *LAH* with the attached 315 GR of 167th ID protecting its left flank attacked the right flank of 52nd GRD while the *Das Reich* and *SSTK* struck the center and left flank of the 52nd GRD. With the full weight of the SS Corps on the 52nd GRD, the Soviets had to fall back but fighting the whole way. vzz92. dgk100. ztc268.

By late afternoon, *Das Reich*, inflicting heavy casualties on 52nd GRD, had penetrated the second defense belt at Iakhontovo but their speed had cost five Tigers, disabled to mines.

They would be recovered and repaired but these panzers would be missed in the meantime. With Tigers it would take at least two and sometimes three recovery trucks depending on terrain to bring it back to the repair shop. mhz216. nzk60.

By early evening Hausser's SS troops supported by the *Luftwaffe*, had split the 52nd GRD in half and penetrated almost 12 miles to the minefields and obstacles in front of the 6th GA's second defensive belt. Though the 52nd GRD had suffered heavy casualties, it doggedly resisted the panzers at this second line. Chistiakov ordered reinforcements to the line to arrive before morning. The 67th RD had to evacuate Cherkasskoe and fall back to Krasnyi Pochinok. Vatutin ordered a counter-attack for daybreak on the SS that was deployed a little south of the second defensive belt. Col Chernov's 90th GRD of 22nd GRC moved up to support the 52nd GRD from Aleksandrovka westward along the north bank of Pena River through Syrtsevo. The 51st GRD of the 23rd GRC held the line from Syrtsevo to Nepkhaevo on the Lipovyi Donets River with specific orders to block the Belgorod-Oboyan road, preventing the Germans from reaching Pokrovka. The 151st GRR and 153rd GRR were holding the ever extending western flank along the Vorskla River. A heavy rain began to fall during the night making travel difficult in the early morning. hjj121m. dgk222m. dlu63m. dgr209m. hsz120. lck240. vzz3m. dgk98. dgk101.

After pausing to regroup in the afternoon, Soviet planes at around 1800 hrs flew to the battle zone in an attempt to slow the SS advance. They were met by Bf 109s which had been flying cap over the ground forces pretty much for 15 hours. The Germans once again had their way with the Soviets, shooting down many more planes than they lost. Some of the German pilots had 8 to 10 victories while many had three, four or five victories. The favored technique was to come up from behind at a higher altitude and strike with MGs blasting. For the next hour wave after wave of new planes from both sides would escalate the air battle. It is estimated the kill ratio for that day was close to seven to one in the Germans' advantage. cbk32++.

By 1840 hrs, *LAH* had fought its way to within 500 yards of the second defensive belt between Iakovlevo and the Donets River on the east. Elements of 51st GRD along with 230th TR were moved to the penetration gap to close it but the attempt failed. The road congestion caused by the panzers moving up and trying to bypass other vehicles was bad and Hausser was forced to postpone the order for the panzers to move up until later in the evening. Luckily for the grenadiers of *Das Reich* little Soviet armor had been seen this day, but they were approaching the second defensive belt where General Vatutin had ordered several brigades from 1st TA to move up to and support the 52nd GRD and 51st GRD which were having trouble stopping 2nd SS PzC. wdk119. zow142.

After dark, when the battle died down for the day, there was still much to do. Damage to defenses had to be repaired, ammo had to be retrieved, machines had to be maintained and refueled, the wounded had to be taken care of and the dead had to be buried. Damaged phone lines had to be repaired alongside burying new mines and replacing destroyed wire entanglements. Planning for the following day's battle action also had to be worked out and the men had to be notified. If a unit was being redeployed they would have to travel to the new area. mjk87+.

While the *LAH* was struggling to get through the second defensive belt, the 315 GR of 167th ID on *LAH*'s flank attacked the 153rd GRR of 52nd GRD on the west bank of the Vorsklitsa River in the region of Streletskoe, Zadelnoe and Kamennyi Log in order to stop the shelling that was hitting *LAH*. The *LAH* was having trouble subduing several bunkers that resisted air attacks and shelling. Commandos came in using demo charges and flamethrowers to silence the defenders. The *LAH* was also battling the 51st GRD in the second defense belt in the Iakovlevo-Luchki South sector. At the same time, *SSTK* on 2nd SS PzC's right flank was still stuck against the 375th RD's defenses. This situation was made worse when 3rd PzC was struggling also and could not keep up with *SSTK*. vzz111. dgk100+. zow144.

Vatutin's forces were hit hard, suffering heavy casualties. His report to Stalin that night distorted reality, showing a more positive slant. He stated that 12,000 Germans were killed, 500 panzers destroyed and that the Germans were being pushed away from the Donets. gjz184.

After studying the day's results, Vatutin changed his deployment for the following day's battle. Tikhomitov's 93rd GRD was ordered to move to Prokhorovka by 0300 hrs and dig in behind Kositisyn's 183rd RD. The 92nd GRD and the 94th GRD were sent to bolster Shumilov's 7th GA facing 3rd PzC in the Korocha area. vzz108. hjj123m. dgk104.

By the end of the day Hoth, not counting those machines repairable, had lost 51 panzers totally destroyed, leaving 953 panzers and SPs still fighting. The penetration into the second defense belt occurred only in *LAH* sector; the forces on either side were behind exposing *LAH*'s flanks. This caused the division to divert forces to the flanks for protection and away from the front. Hoth's timetable was already behind schedule and at a cost far above expectation. His two flanks were falling dramatically behind, causing major tactical problems for the entire Army and yet he hesitated to make any major changes to rectify the situation and there were no reserves available to plug the gaps. Vatutin on the other hand had to release almost all of his reserves to the line by the start of the second day. 48th PzC and the Panther Brigade in particular were deployed in the wrong sector and the harsh results experienced by 48th PzC on this day should have been a wake up call, but it seems General Hoth slept through the alarm. mhz216. vzz111+.

At 2230 hrs Vatutin initiated a counter bombardment in 6th GA sector against the German guns that had been brought up to the new front and were now visible between Tomarovka and Belgorod.

By the end of the day, *Das Reich* had traveled almost five miles into the Soviet first defense belt but it was still another five miles from the second. The division still had to capture Hill 246.3 before reaching the second defense belt. Hopefully their late arriving panzers would catch up. Hausser for much of the day was not aware that many panzers still had not arrived and considered *Das Reich* poor showing compared with *LAH* due to the poor roads conditions and traffic control. Soviet artillery had proven accurate and their air force more active than expected and were also causing slowdowns. The SS Flak Abt 2 of *Das Reich* claim shooting down seven aircraft on this day. The *Deutschland* Regiment had taken point all day with *Der Führer* Regiment to the southeast in reserve. By next morning the *Der Führer* would be brought up to the line. Panzers were arriving late in 48th PzC sector as well. gnk80. pck53. zow143.

By the end of the day, the 2nd SS PzC had 334 working panzers and at least 44 assault guns. The 2nd SS PzC reported to Hoth destroying 7 tanks, 27 anti-tank guns, 300 anti-tank rifles and capturing 500 POWs. This booty was far below expectations. fkk133. vzz120*.

Fighting throughout the night and into the early morning hours of the 6th, *Das Reich* was being held up until infantry was able to catch up and protect the panzers. When it did arrive progress was made. *SSTK*, moving up the Belgorod-Oboyan road against the 375th RD made even less progress. The *LAH* was making the best progress but *Das Reich* was fighting throughout the night and by 0400 hrs on 7/6 was approaching the second defensive belt. wdk119.

Katukov's 3rd MC of 1st TA had battled with the leading SS Tigers the day before and suffered heavy casualties. Katukov knew his forces could not handle the panzer attacks at this stage and argued against a major counteroffensive that Vatutin wanted on 7/6. To complicate things, his 2nd GTC and 5th GTC were not in place or dug-in and would not be ready to attack for hours. Vatutin was not defensive in nature and his orders to attack this early in the campaign were a mistake; perhaps Katukov with the help of Stalin influenced his decision not to attack on a scale originally intended. vzz114+. cbk57. wwf82.

Stavka approved the transfer of Lt General Trofimenko's 27th Army from Steppe Front to Vatutin. It would take several days for the Army to get involved with the fighting in the Psel region. The 27th Army consisted of 71st GRD, 147th RD, 155th RD, 163rd RD, 166th RD, 241st RD and the 93rd TB among other attachments. kcz167. dgk324. lck263.

By the end of the day, elements of *LAH* approached Iakovlevo and had just begun fighting 51st GRD for the important junction. The terrain in front of 51st GRD was relatively flat, providing an easy access route to the north for German panzers, forcing Vatutin to give the 51st a narrow sector of about five miles to defend. The division had gone four miles further than 11th PzD and had its west flank exposed. The *Das Reich* on the east flank of *LAH* was two miles behind leaving the east flank of *LAH* exposed as well. *LAH* had to take assets meant for the front and redeploy them to cover their flanks until those other divisions caught up. The 167th ID was meant to cover the gap between 11th PzD and *LAH* but it was having trouble and was behind schedule. This would be a chronic condition that would plague the SS for the entire campaign. With 11th PzD already five miles behind *LAH* and 3rd PzC even further behind, the resistance on the flanks would bleed the SS dry. gnk111. vzz115. vzz119.

Late at night *Stavka*, en route via Vasilevsky, ordered the 2nd TC and 10th TC to move up to Prokhorovka. The 10th TC of 5th GA was sent to Iadova northeast of Prokhorovka and the 2nd TC from the Southwest Front was sent to Kamishevka on the Oskol River, east of Prokhorovka. Each of these tank corps was larger than a panzer division. The 5th GTA which was stationed over 200 miles away was ordered closer to Kursk and by the next evening was pulling into Staryl Oskol to the southeast of Kursk. The 2nd GTC at Korocha, 38 miles northeast of Belgorod, was ordered west to Prokhorovka to face *Das Reich* as well. It arrived at Gostishchevo the next morning to support the 375th RD against *SSTK*. The 5th GTC with 200 tanks arrived at Luchki South at midnight to support the 52nd GRD against *LAH*. That day another tank corps was sent to Prokorovski, 19 miles southeast of Oboyan. wdk127*. wdk132. fkk83. lck273. dgr82++. gnk245. kcz168. wwf121. dgr83m. hjj123m.

The 2nd VVS flew 1,322 sorties while 17th VVS few 569 sorties. The 1,891 total missions were all for the support of the 6th GA. wdk123.

Both von Manstein and Hoth were disappointed with the day's results. Their forces had made some gains but not enough or fast enough to encircle large groups of the enemy, like what was experienced in 1941. Hoth had scheduled the 4th PzA to have penetrated the second defensive belt on this day and only *LAH* had just reached the second belt, not gone through it. Especially troubling was the slow progress of *SSTK* west of the rivers and 3rd PzC on the east side of the rivers. Something had to be done but there were no reserves to send to the sector to speed the advance. Looking at the big picture von Manstein wanted Hoth and Model to meet at Kursk in four or five days but it would never happen if performance was not greatly improved. wdk124.

Throughout the day Hoth's radio operators listened to the air waves, listening for pleas of help from the front line Soviets, but there were not any such pleas which surprised the German general. It was an indication that the Soviet soldiers were expecting the assault and were prepared. pck57.

By midnight, with the help of the 315 GR of 167th ID, *LAH* forced a crossing over the Vorskla River in the sector Zadelnoe-Vorskla, an area of two miles deep which was originally defended by the 52nd GRD. After 17 hours of fighting the SS broke through the first defense belt in the area of the Belgorod-Kursk road and was now pounding on the second defense belt on a front four miles wide defended by Maj General Tavarikiladze's 51st GRD which moved up to the front and the remains of Maj General Nekrasov's 52nd GRD. Though lagging behind, the 167th ID played a key role today and throughout the campaign by closely supporting the panzer divisions. vzz102. wdk119. dgk111.

Kravchenko's 5th GTC assembled behind the 51st GRD on a seven mile front between Iakovlevo and the Lipovyi Donets River to the east. It was straddling two important roads: Butovo-Dubrovo road and the Belgorod-Kursk highway and these units would see fierce fighting over the next couple days. The 3rd MC moved to the second defensive belt, right behind 90th GRD. vzz107. dgk69.

The triangular shape of the Soviet salient encompassed Orel as the NE corner, Belgorod as the SE corner and Kursk as the Western corner. German strategy was to outflank the Eastern corners and encircle the Soviets. However the Soviets had planned carefully, were well dug in with multiple lines of defense and were determined to stop the assault, as the Germans were now finding out. In the case of Belgorod the defensive belts were 36 miles deep and included many tanks that were dug in. Even with all the preparations by the end of the day, the Germans made penetrations in the first defense belt. fmz225. zzz101m.

The *Luftwaffe* flew 1,958 sorties in the Kursk salient but it would drop to below 1,000 the next day. The Soviet AF was busy as well for they claimed destroying 100 German aircraft in the first two days. The Red Air Force was busy supporting the 6th GA. The 2nd Air Army flew 1,322 missions while the 17th VA flew 569 missions. The Red Air Force flew 1,274 sorties alone against 48th PzC. wdk123. rkz167. dgk104. dgr74.

In the south, the 8th Air Corps flew 2387 sorties. This number is higher than most other sources report. I think the difference considers the *Luftwaffe*'s defense of its own airfields outside the Kursk salient when the Soviets attempted a massive attack before dawn to destroy German air capacity. nzk77.

At Kursk, the *Luftwaffe* were using the 37mm cannon to stop T34s. The flying ace and the most decorated German officer of the war, Capt Rudel, stopped 519 tanks by war's end. On this day, Capt Rudel saw a company of Tigers (Kling, Wittmannn) being fired upon by a Pak front that was dug in and in front of Berezov. One of the Tigers had track damage and was immobile and vulnerable. Rudel and his fellow Stukas dived on the Soviet guns, destroying some of them while the Tigers advanced to better firing positions to finish off the rest. mhz215. lck273+. agk100. fzk306+. pck66.

By the end of the day, it was calculated that Model had lost 150 panzers though many would be repaired while Hoth lost 51 panzers. lck227.

By the end of the day, Hausser claimed his divisions shot down 17 Soviet planes by their flak guns. Many more were shot down from the air. wdk119.

During the night and into the predawn hours of 7/6, elements of 51st GRD deployed east of Iakovlevo moved south to Hill 243.2 to fortify an already strong position and to block *LAH* when it arrived the next morning. Hoth expected *LAH* to secure Iakovlevo today so it was imperative to capture it and the screening hill as early as possible the next day. agk99. gnk69m.

It was a tough day for the SS Corps; ground was gained but at a high cost. The *LAH* made the greatest gains and its lead units were north of Bykovka in the Olkhovka-Solonets area. Olkhovka sits on the banks of the Vorskla River and Solonets was about two miles northeast of Olkhovka. Leading the charge for *LAH*, Michael Wittmann destroyed eight tanks and nine guns today. He had to leave the fighting to go back and reload three times today. Each time 40 shells were stuffed into his Tiger and that did not include the reload of more shells, MG belts, fuel, oil and water at the end of the day before turning in. *LAH* suffered 97 dead, 522 wounded and 17 missing. *LAH* reported destroying 15 tanks, 3 planes and captured a disappointing 99 POWs. agk96. agk101. zrl215#..

At 0115 hrs, Hausser, the CO of 2nd SS PzC, sent out a recon force ahead of the main force in 6th GA's sector. By 0300 hrs, they had captured Iakhontov and moved onto the southern slopes of the Erik River Valley. The open fields in front of 2nd SS PzC were much more accommodating for the panzers than the terrain in 48th PzC sector and a principle reason for the SS's better progress. One has to speculate how the German advance would have played out if the Panther Brigade had been deployed with the SS or even with the 3rd PzC instead of a sector unsuited for armor. The engineers working throughout the previous night had better success in clearing mines, allowing the SS to move out quicker. A little later closer to daybreak, a violent thunder storm hit the 4th PzA's area, disrupting troop assembly. dgk84. mhz209+. dgr280m.

The 4th PzA recon force destroyed half of the outposts in front of 6th GA sector and forced the other outposts to be abandoned. Attack elements of the 167th ID, 11th PzD and *GD* reached their main objectives by 1800 hrs. However the 3rd PzD and the 332nd ID took heavy flanking fire from Zybino Heights and failed to take their objectives. They also had to defend against Soviet counters throughout most of the night. dgk84. snk75++. sgf346. nzk68+. dgr280m.

In the early hours of predawn *GD* sappers moved out into the open fields clearing paths through heavily encrusted minefields in order to speed up the panzers advance; a harrowing experience trying to defuse a mine in the dark while also trying to avoid the roaming bands of the enemy or a sniper. The engineers of the 48th PzC were in the fields as early as the SS engineers but due to the rugged terrain and rainy weather were less successful in finding and disarming mines; this failure would cause many panzers to be destroyed and troops to be killed or wounded. wwf66.

At 0245 hrs, the *Luftwaffe* carpet bombed an area two miles long near Butovo, an early objective for the 3rd PzR of 11th PzD and *GD* divisions. The air raid had the defenders in a confused state and the panzers made an easy penetration. By 0445 hrs, the Germans had control of the high ground and could see the Soviet defenses. Artillery would be quickly moved forward to take advantage of the better vision. West of Butovo near Gertsovka, Soviet resistance, 71st GRD, slowed the German advance and Zybino Heights, south of Korovino, was not captured until after dark. wwf71.

A small group of shock troops from 394th PzGR (3rd PzD) supported by 30 panzers from 6th PzR attacked the 71st GRD and elements of the 27th TDB at Korovino, the HQ for the 71st. The 67th GRD started to move up to the front line helping to slow the German advance. Elements of GD and 11th PzD shifted direction to help secure Cherkasskoe to the east of Korovino. While maneuvering for Cherkasskoe, GD drove into a minefield and damaged many panzers. The battle escalated further with the air force of both sides coming in to duel. An estimated 32 Red aircraft and 13 German aircraft were shot down. By 1300 hrs German panzers had reached a solid line between Geresovka-Cherkasskoe and by 1500 hrs had bypassed Cherkasskoe on both sides and were moving north with Tigers in the lead. By late nightfall the soldiers of GD following the panzers had the town but it had cost them dearly. The fight for Cherkasskoe was one of the toughest in the campaign and is just one of many examples why 48th PzC's attack route was too far west. fkk77+. fkk261+. nzk85. pck56. pck58+.

During the predawn hours, 14 engineers from GD cleared over 2,500 mines in front of the hills of Butovo without losing a person. It was also arranged that GD's artillery would provide a heavy rolling barrage to help clear the path for GD. Speed would be essential. fkk259. pck28. hsz113.

At 0400 hrs another wave of German bombers struck the front lines in the Korovino-Cherkasskoe area and the Streletskoe-Erik area. Hoth had begun his offensive with a two prong attack. The western prong would consist of the 332nd ID, 11th PzD and GD and attack the Novaia Gorianka-Butovo sector. The 3rd PzD would be in reserve. The eastern prong would consist of *LAH* and *SSTK*. The flank guard would be 167th ID and *Das Reich* for the most part would be in reserve. They would attack the Streletskoe-Erik sector. The repeated attacks in this area told Vatutin what axis the Germans would take and he made last minute changes to the deployments of the 52nd GRD, 67th GRD and 71st GRD defending these areas. Novaia Gorianka was situated on the southeast corner of Bubny. See Map 24. fkk76. lck232. vzz116. gnk111. gnk69m.

In front of the GD attack zone laid a deep ravine that ran from Gertsovka in the west all the way to the 11th PzD boundary line. It was sodden from recent heavy rains. In front of it lay a tank ditch and together these two obstacles would cost 3rd PzD and GD and its panzers many casualties on the opening day. The Soviets had placed many guns behind the ravine, waiting for the panzers to get stuck. The situation for the Germans would be made worse when the young panzer leaders rushed blindly into the trap, getting many panzers stuck in the deep mud. Decker's Panthers were not the cause of this panzer pileup for they had not arrived on the battlefield yet. It was Strachwitz in the lead at this time. The Panthers had been delayed the previous day by a blown bridge near Beresovyi. At midnight, leading into the fifth, the Panthers had just arrived at Moschchenoye, four miles south of the Beresovyi ravine and stayed until 0800 hrs on 7/5. They were still behind the lead units of the GD that were stuck in the mud and taking casualties. The GD had a narrow front that stretched from Gerzovka on the west to Butovo on the east. gnk92+. hsz119. hjj114. pck53+.

At 0400 hrs, the *Luftwaffe* bombed 6th GA sector, hitting the 67th GRD the hardest though the 71st GRD and 52nd GRD were also hit. Behind the 52nd GRD and 67th GRD was the 3rd MC with Krivoshein positioned in front of Iakovlevo. At 0500 hrs five battalions and 30 panzers struck the 71st GRD at Gertsovka. During the first hour of battle, the *Luftwaffe* flew 400 sorties in this area alone. Elements of the 332nd ID and 30 panzers struck west of Butovo gaining 2 miles against the 67th GRD and capturing the high ground west of Berezov and pushing the 71st GRD back north of Krasnyi Pochinok. A counter-attack was initiated on 332nd ID's west flank but it was repulsed. General Ott's 52nd IC made progress and would complete capturing Bubny, southwest of Gertsovka, early next morning. The 255th ID quickly moved up to the line to defend Bubny on its western flank. The Germans were trying to soften the line where 4th PzA would strike in a major way the next morning. Iakovlevo was12 miles northeast of Butovo, where the Germans were shelling ahead of their soon advancing panzers (3rd PzD). wdk117+. dgr172m. pck49. vzz116. dgr250. pck57.

At dawn, another wave of hundreds of bombers struck Soviet forces in the Syrtsevo, Gertsovka and Ternovka areas. A small corridor leading to Butovo and Dragunskoe was also hit. The Germans flew over 2,000 sorties on this day. For 15 hours the 52nd GRD was hit from the air for defending the planned attack route of the left flank of *LAH*. This heavy bombing was an important reason why some panzers made five miles. The Soviet fighters were slow to respond but by 0600 hrs, the Red Air Force began to take to the sky to deflect the Germans. They already had hundreds of planes flying against German airfields in a separate action. By the end of the day a combined total for both sides for both salients lost over 320 planes to heavy damage or complete destruction. A little further to the north and east in the *SSTK* sector, the *Luftwaffe* also attacked, but on a smaller scale, the line between the towns of Gremuchi and Gostishchevo which was defended by the 51st GRD. Dogfights erupted when Soviet fighters tried to intercept; the *Luftwaffe* lost several planes, more than the Soviets in this situation. This dogfight was so encouraging, Vatutin decided to initiate a bomb run into the rear of the German held territory around Tomarovka. dgr250+. cbk26+++. vzz2m+. cbk31. cbk41. vzz5m. cbk12m. asz362.

The 52nd IC's 255th ID was detached and sent to 48th PzC on the Vorsklitsa River and joined the 332nd ID in protecting the panzer's flank. The 48th PzC and the 2nd SS PzC jumped off at 0600 hrs after the planned two hour preparation. The *Luftwaffe* was a major help in subduing Soviet artillery. Maj General Fretter-Pico's 57th ID remained with 52nd IC in a defensive posture on the western flank. snk76+.

After an hour of preparation which included Nebelwerfer rockets, Hoth started his advance at daybreak with 48th PzC leading the way toward Zavidovka, Alekseevka and Lukhanino. Zavidovka, on the southern banks of the Pena, was reached first but 3rd PzD's initial attempt to take the village failed. Tigers would lead with IVs following in an expanding wedge helped take the town. Some of the divisional artillery had not arrived for 3rd PzD and *GD*, the corps lent them some of their guns. It was not a smooth beginning. Much of the corps artillery was supporting the 11th PzD and the 167th ID to the east of *GD*. Even before the German shelling started, Vatutin had started his own disruptive barrage, hoping to ruin communications and roads etc. The assault guns would follow. Some of these new guns were built without MGs so they were defenseless when enemy infantry attacked them. That night it rained hard. jp106. jp110. hjj121m. fkk80. gnk91. vzz2m. hsz121. dgk107.

At 0700 hrs a squadron of IL-2s came in low and attacked *GD* panzers which were stalled from thick mud and heavy fire. A little later a new wave of Il-2s came in low, targeting the 11th PzD and 167th ID. All three German divisions immediately called for air support. Messerschmidts were already responding to *GD*'s request and within minutes came flying in to intercept the Soviet fighters. Near Berezov a few Soviet bombers struck the *GD* HQ, killing three officers. cbk31+.

The 3rd PzD, with the 394th PzR in the lead, had to start without its artillery or panzers for the machines were being slowed by the muddy roads and had not arrived yet. Resuming their attack from the previous afternoon, the grenadiers launched at 0420 hrs toward Gertsovka. The 210th GRR of 71st GRD was defending the line between Gertsovka and Beresovyi. The German infantry made good early gains; the panzers started catching up to the men by 0600 hrs to give support in finishing the town off. By 0800 hrs the Germans had penetrated the Soviet defenses and were heading past the town. gnk97. gnk51.

At 0810, the 196th GRR countered at Cherkasskoe and started too regain ground. More panzers of the *GD* came up and with the support of the west flank of 11th PzD attacking east of Cherkasskoe, captured the town after a long difficult struggle that lasted all day. This town was three miles from the *GD* start line. In the sector east of 67th GRD, other units of *GD* hit the 52nd GRD in the center of their sector at Iakontov. The 11th PzD and 167th ID attacked the east flank of 52nd GRD at Berezov with over 100 panzers and air support. The 52nd GRD with support of the 1008th DATR and 538th TDR claim to have destroyed 18 panzers including ten Tigers but by 1600 hrs had to fall back four miles to Bykovka on the Vorskla River where it joined the 51st GRD. They held Bykovka overnight but had to continue to fall back next day. Korovino, Cherkasskoe, Zadelnoe and Gremuchi were the main spearhead sector for the 48th PzC. The *Luftwaffe* gave strong support to the advance. wdk118+. dgr74. dgr172m. pck56. zrl215. dgk69+.

Leaving Moscschenoye the 160 Panthers, of the nearly 190 that left Germany, reached the rail line south of Gertsovka by 0815 hrs but they still had to catch up to the infantry that had already launched. gnk93. hjj115.

At 0900 hrs, a third wave of IlL-2s came after *GD* forces, trying to liquidate the largest tank concentration that had been discovered. cbk31.

At 0900 hrs, the 11th PzD adjacent to *GD* reached Hill 237.7, west of Cherkasskoe then proceeded toward Hill 210.3, north of Cherkasskoe. In early afternoon a small squadron of T34s coming from Korovino attacked, slowing the advance. The T34s were liquidated by accurate shell fire and the advance continued. Nearby in the Gertsovka Valley, panzers of *GD* were stalled in a minefield and were taking heavy fire. The crews returned fire and desperately waited for sappers to come up and clear the mines. That morning the HQ was being overloaded by phone calls reporting mine damage or requesting help to clear mines. There were not enough sappers to handle the requests in a timely manner. At 1955 hrs, Cherkasskoe was reached and the escalating assault began with a pincer action. 11th PzD, using flamethrowers, speadheaded the assault and eventually entered the northern outskirts of town. A little later, members of the *GD* division neared the southwestern corner of town. To hold Cherkasskoe, Chistiakov moved two regiments of anti-tank guns toward the village next to the 67th GRD. When Tigers were brought up, the village fell and the Soviets had to fall back heading northeast for the relative safety of 90th GRD's line along the Pena River. wwf76. je100. dgk97. hsz115. hsz119. wwf74+.

In the 48th PzC sector, the *GD* division was assembling for its assault near Alekseevka when Soviet artillery opened up on them causing death and destruction. Not wanting to wait while under attack, the Panthers moved out and ran directly into a minefield in front of the Soviet first line of defense. The panzers stopped in the open field amid artillery and air patrols to allow the engineers to clear the mines. Some of the panzers were equipped with flamethrowers which helped suppress Soviet fire. lck233.

At 0900 hrs a direct hit on the *GD* HQ killed five officers. General Hoernlein was uninjured. hsz119.

After capturing Gertsovka, the lead units of 3rd PzD continued north and captured high ground south of Korovino during the night. Korovino was a fortified town that was the western anchor to the first defense belt, but it too fell that evening by the hard hitting 394th PzR of 3rd PzD. Knowing that the rest of the division was quickly moving up to Korovino, Col Pape of 394th PzR followed the retreating enemy and captured the village of Krasnyi Pochinok and reached the Pena River. To the left of 3rd PzD, the 255th ID and the Silesian 332nd ID continued to fight into the night in order to stay with the panzers and to screen their left flank. The Pena River marked part of the second defense belt and was about seven miles behind the first defense belt. Before reaching the Pena, the Vorskla and Vorsklitsa Rivers and accompanying swampland had to be negotiated. pck58+. vzz89++.

Westhoven's 3rd PzD on the left flank of *GD* was initially unable to break into Zavidovka, not far from Lukhanino, (protected by minefields and the 71nd GRD) despite repeated attacks. Eventually the village fell and once past Zavidovka, the 3rd PzD quickened its pace and quickly captured Krasnyi Pochinok. Lead elements of 3rd PzD, 40 panzers, attacked the only bridge over the Pena in the sector but were repulsed the first time by the 71st GRD. After bringing up more infantry, the second attempt penetrated the front line and the Germans were only 150 yards from the bridge when it was blown. The *Luftwaffe* had also raided the area. The bridge was damaged but it was fixed along with another bridge erected by next morning. A number of US M3 light tanks were destroyed in the engagement. The 332nd ID on 3rd PzD's left caught up to the panzers by nightfall. mhz210. fkk248. gnk148.

The 48th PzC had temporarily pocketed a large Soviet force southwest of Iakovlevo but without sufficient supporting infantry most of the Soviets escaped to head north. dgk99+. rkz167.

The 3rd PzD on the left and elements of *GD* continued to strike the boundary line between Col Baksov's 67th GRD and Col Sibakov's 71st GRD, trying to bypass two fortified strongpoints in their forward zone, the villages of Cherkasskoe and Korovino to the west. The Germans did succeed in creating a lodgment but then bogged down under increasing fire and huge minefields for the rest of the day. Only at midnight did the two main combat groups enter these two villages where house to house fighting was necessary to secure these villages. The 48th PzC which had only advanced about four or five miles, was still fighting its way through the first defense belt defended by General Ibiansky's 22nd GRC and was far behind the 2nd SS PzC. The German plan of using Tigers and Panthers as a spear was not working very well in this area due to the swampland and huge minefields that were covered by many anti-tank guns. It has been argued that Hoth's choice of concentrating all the Panthers in this small area was a mistake. So many panzers in such a small front gave the Soviet 2nd AF a real target of opportunity. It was discovered by the end of the first day that the Panther had a weak point that would cause the panzer to be set ablaze even with a superficial hit. Its fuel and oil lines were unprotected. Once this problem was alleviated, the Panther became safer but there were other issues that needed to be fixed as well. It was also quickly discovered that the Panther crews had not been trained properly and that would have to be rectified as well. vzz103+. wwf71. fmz228+. hjj112.

To reiterate, northwest of Belgorod at the boundary between the 22nd GRC and 23rd GRC, the 67th GRD the 52nd GRD of Chistiakov's 6th GA was defending against the

48th PzC and 2nd SS PzC. The 48th PzC's 550 panzers and assault guns struck the Soviet line with its 3rd PzD, *GD*, and 11th PzD. Defending the panzers were 332nd ID and 167th ID on the flanks. The *GD* attacked in a 2 mile front across the Berezov stream from Butovo to the fortified village of Cherkasskoe, the anchor point of the 67th GRD's defenses. The following Panthers ran into a minefield and were stopped. dgk94. dgk95m. wdk118.

Soviet planes had been hitting 48th PzC and especially *GD* hard around Berezov. Starting at 0730 hrs and for the next three hours, Soviet bombers and fighters would attack panzers and men. German pilots claimed shooting down 18 planes in this time period. The VVS claimed having 32 planes down in 48th PzC sector by 1200 hrs. To the right of 48th PzC, German planes struck the positions of the 52nd GRD which was blocking the main axis of *LAH*. During the day, the division suffered 2,400 casualties, many due to the air attacks. cbk32.

The leading elements of *LAH* moved on its objective, the village of Bykovka, situated along the Vorskla River. Afterwards the *LAH* approached Iakovlevo, also on the Vorskla River. The village was an important strongpoint in the second defense belt and was surrounded by mines which had to be cleared before moving on the village. Taking this village would provide flanking protection for the 48th PzC moving north. mhz215. mhz20m. gnk69m. lck164m.

To the west of *GD*, the 3rd PzD resumed its attack northward from Gertsovka toward Korovino.

The *GD* infantry, which would be supported by 350 panzers that had not shown yet, had to advance on their own determination. The lead panzer groups that had freed themselves from the mud were catching up. They advanced northward in a sector only two miles wide, between the Berezov stream and the dirt track of Butovo toward the fortified village of Cherkasskoe, the anchor point of the 67th GRD's defenses. The panzers, rushing to catch up to the infantry, ran into a minefield and waiting Soviet anti-tank guns. They got stuck and were being shelled heavily. While the engineers were clearing their back field in order for the panzers could fall back, the Soviets were firing. Germans used smoke to distract the enemy and artillery were called up to slow the Soviet attack. After two days of fighting, two thirds of *GD*'s panzers would be sidelined with battle damage, mechanical failure or were destroyed. This was a terrible debut for the Panther and it would not get much better for the Panther and *GD* that was depending so heavily on it throughout the campaign.

You have to wonder how *GD* would have performed if the panzers launched on time and avoided its careless movements and if the Panther had performed to its expectations. Perhaps 48th PzC could have crossed the Psel and driven on to Oboyan. If 48th PzC could have kept up with Hausser and supported the SS then the 2nd SS PzC might have taken Prokhorovka. dgk94. gnk92. dgr172m. gjz184. pck53.

Even after having to relaunch due to the mired Panthers, the *GD* and 11th PzD were fighting for the high ground that Gertsovka was located on. The Berezovyi stream, swollen from recent rains, and the soggy ground surrounding Gertsovka slowed the German attack. Many panzers got stuck and had to be pulled free by special recovery panzers and large halftracks. As the Germans gained ground on 6th GA, Chistiakov sent two anti-tank regiments to support the 67th GRD. With the help of flame throwing panzers, the 11th PzD still broke through the line east of the town. mhz205+. pck56.

The two pincers of *GD* launched from either side of the village of Butovo while Mickl's

11th PzD was on their right and 3rd PzD on the left. *GD* was heading for the fortified town of Cherkasskoe which was the Soviet lynchpin of the first defense belt and just three miles from the German start line. The defense belt was more of a belt than a line with a depth of a mile or more. Besides the massive minefield in front of Cherkasskoe, Lt General Chistiakov's elite 67th GRD was defending the town and sector. Even before reaching this point the Panthers started breaking down and between mechanical failure, the mines and swampland, 36 Panthers were lost before the fighting began. Most of these 36 damaged Panthers were recovered and eventually repaired. At 2,000 yards the Panthers opened fire and quickly destroyed a number of M3 Lees but before long the panzers were recalled to the start line where they shifted direction closer to 11th PzD and began again. mhz202++. mhz207. lck226. wwf71. wdk118+. pck55.

With the Panther Brigade late for the launch, the left flank of *GD* was stalled but the right flank was making progress. General Hoernlein transferred resources to the right flank to keep the momentum. The Fusilier Regiment shifted toward the northeast. pck55

At 1300 hrs, the 10th PzB of *GD* freed itself of marshy ground and minefields and attacked Cherkasskoe, slowly gaining control of the northwest corner of the town. At 1350 hrs, Soviet tankers driving east from Korovino toward Cherkasskoe to stop the invaders were they themselves attacked by the *GD*. Seven tanks were quickly disabled as a tank battle ensued. It would take until the next morning to capture Cherkasskoe and the surrounding area. This was an extremely costly battle for the Germans. Many officers and soldiers died as well as panzers being destroyed or damaged. Count Saurma of a Panther battalion died in this struggle, just one of the early victims of this campaign. The 11th PzD coming in from the east made a big contribution in taking Cherkasskoe. fkk263. pck54++. gnk68m. hsz112.

Furious fighting escalated near Cherkasskoe when the 11th PzD, on *GD*'s right attacked the artillery supporting the town that was emplaced on high ground east of town. With the artillery under attack, it lost its focus on protecting Cherkasskoe, making it easier to capture. The 11th PzD gained 5 miles today on its way to Oboyan. On *GD*'s left, 3rd PzD driving toward Korovino and the important high ground of Hill 220.5, south of Korovino made fewer gains. The 6th PzR drove on to Krasnyi Pochinok, the last major Soviet defensive position before the Pena River. During the night the 255th ID and 332nd ID joined the 3rd PzD for the next day's assault to resecure Hill 220.5. dgk98. hsz120. dgr74. wwf71. pck58.

In late afternoon elements of *GD* moved on Dubrova on the Lukhanino River, east of Lukhanino. Quickly breaking through the first trench line they were then stopped by a row of dug in T34s in the second trench. Infantry was called up and together cleared a path past the trenches and through Dubrova, allowing the Panthers to reach northeast of Hill 247.2 where they dug in for the night. The swampy terrain was now slowing the rest of *GD* as it approached Alekseevka and Lukhanino at night. The *GD* Panzer Regiment and attached Panther brigade had many new crew members, and though the battalion commanders, Decker and Lauchert, were experienced nobody had any experience in fighting with the Panther. Six Panthers were total losses within the first hour of battle due to engine failure which caused massive fires, killing most of the crews. See Map 23. dgk107. dgk154m. hjj114+. hjj121m. dgr209m. hsz122. gnk92+. wwf45.

The German engineers had been working fanatically constructing a bridge over Beresovyi ravine but by 1100 hrs only a dozen panzers had crossed. This meant that the attack on Cherkasskoe had been initiated by infantry without armor support. By 1600 hrs, 45 panzers had crossed the ravine and were heading north to join the action. The lead Panthers were still south of Hill 229.0 at 0945 hrs when Cherkasskoe was first attacked. The bottleneck at the ravine that included panzers and other vehicles was a golden opportunity for the Red Air Force which inflicted heavy casualties. Knobelsdorff considered changing the route into 11th PzD's territory but decided against it. gnk94+. wwf76.

In late morning, lead elements of *GD* were in bitter fighting with the 196th GRR at the cemetery just outside of Cherkasskoe. It was a stalemate until a few of Lauchert's Panthers arrived and, despite attacks from the air, gave the Germans the advantage, driving the defenders back into the northwest corner of town. The 611th ATR defending the sector with their 4.5 cm guns could not stop the new panzers and had to fall back. Once past the perimeter, the *GD* Grenadiers quickly moved through the northern part of town. After reaching the eastern edge of town, *GD* came under heavy fire from a nearby hill which was defended by the 245th TR and 1837th ATR. The 1837th had 8.5 cm guns which could penetrate the Panthers and they were forced to move back. While the fighting for Cherkasskoe continued, a small contingent of *GD* moved on to the northern suburb of Iarki. By dark the Germans were securing the area and would stop for the night in it. They were still fighting within the first defensive belt and at least three miles from the front edge of the second defense belt, and were therefore behind schedule and behind the SS Corps. It was an extremely expensive day for *GD* for the division lost 150 panzers. That total was made up of destroyed, damaged or simply stuck in the mud. The recovery teams would be able to put most of those panzers back on the battlefield but it would take time and in the meantime *GD* would be shorthanded. gnk95. gnk68m.

After an aerial bombardment the *GD* grenadiers, using flamethrowers and grenades, began clearing Berezov street by street. When the Germans entered the town Soviet mortar crews moved up and began shelling it.

By late morning, Vatutin ordered Katukov's 1st TA, the separate 2nd GTC commanded by Maj General Burdeiny near Gostishchevo and the 5th GTC under Maj General Kravchenko forward to support Chistiakov's 6th GA's second defensive belt which was already in trouble. The 6th TC of 1st TA, with 169 tanks, moved up along the Pena River behind the 90th GRD. The 3rd MC, equipped with 250 tanks would deploy eastward in positions extending from the Pena River valley to Syrtsevo, backing up 90th GRD's left flank. Kravchenko's 200-tank strong 5th GTC moved up behind the 51st GRD in the Iakovleo area. The 2nd TC with 200 tanks moved into the Gostishchevo area east of the Lipovyi Donets River, on the right flank of the advancing 2nd SS PzC. Chernienko's 31st TC with 196 tanks remained behind the 6th TC. The 2nd GTC using 60 tanks were to drive west and cut the Belgorod--Oboyan road and the Germans' supply line. All told, 1,000 tanks were moved up for the following day's fight against 4th PzA, to push it back and to restore the line. Vatutin would cancel the counter-attack and switch to a defensive posture when the Germans advanced too far to the north during the night for the Soviets tanks to assemble for their attack. Chistiakov would misuse these new forces and be severely reprimanded. dgk101+. gjz183. dgk222m. dlu63m. dgr209m. fkk248. vzz104++. vzz3m. vzz5m. zra58. pck75.

The 1st TA was to deploy along and east of Pena River in a defensive mode until the German advance petered out; then they could go on the offensive. During the night, the Germans were advancing too quickly for Vatutin to put his counter-attack measures in action and had to settle with the above defensive positions for now. The Germans had reached the Verkhopenie area and its important bridge across the Pena tonight, taking away Soviet assembly areas for their counterattack. General Vatutin was determined to launch a counter-attack but it would take until the 8th for it to materialize. The 48th PzC claimed 85 panzers were damaged or destroyed in today's heavy fighting. The corps had only 250 working panzers for resumption of the advance in the morning. dgk101+. hjj121m. dgr209m.

To the east of 90th GRD, the 51st GRD dug in along the high ground between Syrtsevo and Nepkhaevo on the Lipovyi Donets River, a tributary of the Northern Donets, with orders to block the Germans from reaching Pokrovka along the main Belgorod-Oboyan highway. Behind these two divisions, the 93rd GRD was deployed along the Pokrovka-Prokhorovka road. dgk101. dgk95m. hjj121m. dgk222m. dlu63m. dgr209m. lck247.

Elements of the *GD* were driving toward Hill 232.0 northeast of Cherkasskoe but were stopped before reaching it by Lt Col Okhrimenko's 20th GTB and the 6th GMRB. The hill was a strongpoint that covered Cherkasskoe, taking the hill first would make taking the town easier. hjj115. vzz121.

In the afternoon, the 151st RR and 155th RR of 52nd GRD near Sadelnoye, two miles southwest of Bykovka were encircled. At night the Soviets tried to escape suffering heavy casualties but some were successful. With the 52nd GRD falling back, the villages of Bykovka and Kosmo-Demyanovka fell to the Germans. With 52nd GRD falling back, the 375th RD with its now exposed flank had to fall back as well. The 51st GRD of 6th GA was called up to the new defense belt to slow the Germans. fkk79. vzz5m.

In late afternoon the 6th PzR raced forward at the junction of 71st GRD and 67th GRD and seized the village of Krasnyi Pochinok, three miles behind the front line. As the Germans were taking Krasnyi, the 71st fell back to the east and started building new defenses. To the east of 67th GRD, the 52nd GRD defending Iakontov were attacked by *GD* after a 30 minute barrage. The 11th PzD with its 100 panzers and 167th ID attacked the 52nd on its east flank at Berezov. Though losing some panzers, the 11th PzD was able to force the 52nd GRD back three miles to Bykovka on the Vorskla River. dgk97+. dgk95m. wdk119. dgr172m.

The last action of the day for 394th PzGR of 3rd PzD was driving due north about three miles from Gertsovka and storming Korovino which was defended by 210th GRR of 67th GRD by evening. Throughout the day the few tanks at Korovino would launch counter-attacks against the Germans that would eventually fizzle out when they proved ineffective. By 1430 hrs, the lead panzers reached the anti-tank ditch in front of Korovino. While the panzers were stalled at the ditch, several battalions were creeping their way through a ravine to the east of the village, hoping to surprise their flanking screen. It was an important town that anchored the west end of the first defense belt and the Germans felt it was important to control for flank protection. In the afternoon, the 6th PzR raced forward at the junction of the 71st GRD and 67th GRD and captured the village of Krasnyi Pochinok, three miles from the start line. This forced Sivakov to pull back his 71st GRD and to shift forces to plug the gap on his left flank. dgk98+*. dgk72. wwf76. pck57.

As ordered during the night, the 1st TA would move into the following positions: in the west they would occupy the Melovoe, Syrtsevo, Iakovlevo area just behind the 6th GA's forces. The 5th GTC were to move in along the Iakovlevo, Nekhaevka, Teterevino line and the 2nd GTC would head for the Rozhdestvenka to Druzhnyi area. With Korovino and Krasnyi Pochinok in German hands and the 3rd PzD reaching the Pena River, the security of the western flank was greatly secured. During the night, the 255th ID moved up to the line between 332nd ID and 3rd PzD to the north to strengthen it, but with the redeployments Vatutin had just initiated, the German advance would still be difficult. dgr78. dgr76m+. wwf82.

The village of Novaia Gorianka which was defended by the 210th GRR (71st GRD) put up stiff resistance, but was eventually overpowered by elements of *GD* and 3rd PzD and the village was captured before the Germans moved on to the fortified village of Dmitriievka in the Dragunskoe sector. fkk79. vzz115. gnk69m. dgk81. dgk98.

After dark as Cherkasskoe was falling to the Germans, the defenders of Dimitriievka were still holding on. It would take the Germans 17 hours before 67th GRD and 71st GRD crumbled to the German attack. With the Germans assaulting Dimitriievka and securing Cherkasskoe, they now had a gap in the first defense belt six miles wide by almost three miles deep. The fortified village Dragunskoe would be troublesome also. Hoth was hoping for more before the day ended; he expected the Panthers of *GD* to blow a hole in the Soviet defense that would allow them to reach the Psel River by the following day. He underestimated the defenses, the terrain and the men guarding them. This campaign would not be like Barbarossa. fkk78+. hsz119. gnk69m.

The defenders of Cherkasskoe had to fall back to the relative safety of the defensive position of Chernov's 90th GRD of 22nd GRC along the Pena River after *GD*, 11th PzD expelled them from town. The Pena was about six miles from the original Soviet front line. During the night, the 27th Anti-tank Brigade among other tank fragments, were brought up to help the faltering 67th GRD in stopping *GD*, 11th PzD and the nearby 3rd PzD from advancing. dgk98.

Providing additional details on Vatutin's redeployments for the next day: in the afternoon, Vatutin, the CO of Voronezh Front, ordered Katukov's 1st TA with its 31st TC, 3rd MC and 6th TC to move up to the second defense belt and to attack the 48th PzC which was traveling north on the Oboyan road. The 6TC moved behind the 90th GRD on the east, the 3rd MC behind the 67th GRD in the center and 31st TC was behind the 67th GRD and 52nd GRD on the west end as reserve. The 6th GA also received the 29th TDB, 1244th TDR, 869th TDR and the 309th RD from 40th Army. To support the 309th RD, the 59th TR, 60th TR, 203rd TR, 86th TB, the heavy 1461st SU Regiment, 12th TDR and the 1689th TDR. The 180th TB from Lt General Chibisov's 38th Army was brought up to Semenovka as another reserve unit for the west flank of 6th GA. The 161st RD was inserted into the west end of the line as well. The 6th TC consisted of 200th TB, 22nd TB, 112th TB and the 6th MRB.

It has been argued over the years that Vatutin had made several mistakes that allowed Hoth to gain as much ground as he did. One of those arguments concerns the placement of Lt General Moskalenko's 40th Army in the salient. The 40th Army was one of the strongest in the Voronezh Front; the Soviets knew where the attack zone would be so why was not 40th Army deployed in a blocking position? wdk126. dgr212. kcz167+. dgr76m. gjz182. dgk411+. vzz107.

With the heavy rains the leading elements of 48th PzC, traveling near the stream between Zavidovka and Syrtsev, were having trouble with the mud, the incoming shelling from 6th GA and the determination of the 27th TDB. Further south, after many hours of ferocious fighting, the forces of the 11th PzD and *GD* finally secured Cherkasskoe and would now have a chance to catch up with the rest of their divisions and fill in the gaps in the line. Its infantry and armor suffered crippling casualties in the minefields as well as from the shelling. Cherkasskoe was the boundary line between 67th GRD and 71st GRD. rc159. bt82. fkk76. gnk68m.

By 1930 hrs, the *LAH* had fought its way to within 500 yards of the southern edge of Iakovlevo. The village was a strongpoint on the second defense belt. It would have been nice to capture Iakovlevo that night and been able to advance from there in the morning, but it was decided it was too late and the attack would begin the following morning. By the end of the day, 48th PzC had also breached the outer defenses of the first Soviet defensive belt but it was slow going through it. Hoth and von Manstein agreed to change direction away from Oboyan toward Prokhorovka for it might be easier. Hoth also ordered *GD* and 11th PzD to quickly capture Olkhovka and Dubrova, catch up with *LAH* and link up with 167th ID to stabilize the line. Dubrova had been fortified and would not fall easily. wwf80. vzz115.

The trailing units of 11th PzD, *GD* and 3rd PzD were advancing on Cherkasskoe, attacking the right flank of Col Sibakov's 71st GRD and frontally on the 67th GRD when the 67th GRD shattered and started retreating. Outside of town, the two Soviet divisions regrouped and fortified the new defenses outside of town, blocking the Germans from leaving Cherkasskoe during the night. dgk97+.

After dark, Vatutin ordered Katukov's 1st TA to attack at dawn the following day but had to rescind the order when the Germans gained too much ground during the predawn hours, forcing the 1st TA to stay defensive. The 5th GTC in the area east of Luchki South and the 2nd GTC near Gostischtschevo along a six mile sector behind the Lipovyi Donets were given alert orders, but the coordinated attack was not realized either due to their untimely arrival at the launch point or poor preparation. It would be shown that Vatutin had a habit of rushing his counter-attacks before his brigades were ready and though these attacks slowed the German advance, the casualties were much higher than they needed to be. fkk81. vzz107. vzz114. gnk152. gjz183. kcz168. dgk106m. nzk85.

At night, with the battlefield situation changing, Vatutin altered his battle order for the next day by communicating 1st TA the following deployment: the 6th TC would move up to the second defense belt along the Melovoe, Rakovo and Shepelevka line before dawn the following day. The 3rd MC would deploy along the Alekseevka to Iakovlevo line and the 31st TC was to deploy along the Studenok, Stalinsk State Farm, Vladimirovka and Orlovka line for defensive purposes. These positions were achieved by early morning on 7/6. The 1st TA HQ was located at Zorinskie Dvory area. The 6th TC consisted of 200th TB, 22nd TB, 112th TB and the 6th MRB. The 31st TC comprised 237th TB, 242nd TB and 86th TB. The 3rd MC included 1st MB, 3rd MB, 10th TB, 1st GTB and 49th TB. The 5th GTC was to move to the Teterevino area while the 2nd GTC positioned themselves in the Gostishchevo area and prepared to launch an offensive toward Rakovo and Belgorod at dawn on 7/6. dgr211+. dgr209m. vzz3m. vzz5m.

At 2200 hrs, Vatutin transfered 160th TB, situated along the Oboyan road, to the control of 1st TA. The many reinforcements that were brought up to the front or were redeployed to another part of the front saved Vatutin when the Germans resumed their advance in the morning. dgr212.

Favoring offense, Vatutin gave secondary orders to 1st TA, 5th GTC and 2nd GTC in addition to their redeployment orders. Vatutin gave permission to these three units to attack the Germans if and when their advance stalled. The 1st TA was to drive toward

Tomarovka while 5th GTC drove toward Bykovka and 2nd GTC, which was deployed in the Gostishchevo area, would head for Gremuchi. Katukov of 1st TA tried to persuade Vatutin to delay the counter-attack order for it was clearly too early to attack; the 4th PzA was still too strong and would repulse the attack while inflicting heavy casualties. The order would be modified next morning. dgr78+. dgr76m+.

By the end of the day, Vatutin suspected the assault toward Korocha was a feint while the attack toward Oboyan was the main assault and moved his forces accordingly. Feeling more confident that the Oboyan road was the primary axis, at 1640 hrs Vatutin ordered the 6th TC and 3rd MC over to the Oboyan sector as part of the major redisposition of forces. To the southeast of there, closer to Belgorod, Vatutin brought up three divisions of 35th GRC to reinforce 7th GA, to cover the Korocha axis and eliminate the small German force that crossed the Donets River. Throughout the day along the whole salient 1,000 tanks and panzers were being brought into the action setting up, in days to come, the legendary tank battle. je100+. nzk85. hjj123m.

Decker accused Strachwitz of poor handling of his panzers which caused the traffic jamb plus the high casualties in the minefields. Strachwitz sent his panzers in too early before the infantry could clear a path through the mine-fields or before a gap was made in the line. This early friction created an atmosphere of distrust between the Panther brigade and Strachwitz. Strachwitz, though an experienced officer, did have a tendency to send his panzers into the fray too early and many of them received track and wheel damage as they ran into the minefields. Strachwitz was senior to Decker and had more experienced.. Strachwitz had received his Knight's Cross in August 1941, his Oak Leaves in November 1942 and his Swords in March 1943. Decker would be promoted to general in 1944 and command the 39th PzC but would never see the end of the war for he committed suicide in April 1945 when trapped in the Ruhr Pocket. With the high casualties of Panthers this first day and the next few days to come there was some basis for this condemnation of Col Strachwitz but the colonel did not change his tactics after losing so many in the early days of the campaign. In defense of the colonel, infantry and engineers were sparse at times and he probably had to use panzers as the breakthrough device. gnk96. hjj114. hjj131. zoc100. zsm69. zsm364.

Throughout the night and into the small hours of next morning, while *GD* was still securing the last resistance in and around Cherkasskoe, Hill 237.8 to the southeast of town was still firmly held by the Soviets and would have to be tackled in the morning. At night, Knobelsdorff decided 11th PzD should finish Cherkasskoe and Hill 237.8 so that *GD* could continue to move north. *GD* had such costly problems at the ravine and in front of Cherkasskoe due to the poor planning and preparations of General Hoernlein, who underestimated the Soviet defenses and the terrain, meaning that it would be fighting below par for the rest of the campaign.. While the fighting for Cherkasskoe raged throughout the night, the sappers were busy clearing mines for the trailing forces who would be heading for the front. After leaving Cherkasskoe, *GD* would head northeast toward Hill 237.8 and Dubrova. gnk96. hsz120+.

By the end of the day, the 48th PzC had penetrated the first defensive belt but had not gone far into it, reaching a line from Dragunskoe, Butovo to a point east of Cherkasskoe and then to a point southwest of Korovino. The 394th PzGR had just captured Korovino and were securing the village against possible counter-attacks during the night. The Soviet resistance was hard but the harsh terrain also was a problem. A claimed 40 of the 190

Panthers assigned to 48th PzC were out of action. The 3rd PzD and 52nd IC had trouble getting past Zybino. The 48th PzC received sporadically good air support but nothing matching 2nd SS PzC today. For the day the Germans captured few POWs and little material and it was believed the Soviets were no longer standing and fighting to the end but were falling back to the next defense belt. In fact the 71st GRD, which had defended near Cherkasskoe, had been pushed back and by the end of the day was defending the Bubny-Krasnyi Pochinok line. The 67th GRD had fallen back to the Krasnyi Pochinok-Trirechnoe line in the hope of stopping the Germans from expanding their western flank. The 52nd GRD, which was hit the hardest along the Kozmo-Demianovka axis, was split in two and had fallen back in disarray. Dragunskoe was two miles east of Kazatskoe and two miles north of Streletskoe. Trirechnoe was less than a mile south of Novo Cherkasskoe and six miles east and a little south of Krasnyi Pochinok. snk77+. wdk118+. vzz115. dgr172m. dgr75. wwf82. gnk68m. dgk95m. vzz2m.

By the end of the day the 48th PzC with the Panther Brigade attached, the strongest of the three panzer corps in 4th PzA, was scheduled to be approaching the Psel River, the third defensive belt but the divisions were still trying to penetrate and break through the second defense belt, some 12-15 miles further south. Even still the advance the Germans did make the first day caused Vatutin to call up almost all of his reserves including the 35th GRC to the front by the next day. When these forces arrived to the line, it still would not be enough and Vatutin would have to borrow from *Stavka* and other Fronts to meet the challenge. Hoth wanted the 48th PzC over the Psel and entering Oboyan by the second day at the latest. The plan was completely unreasonable. Hoth had made a major mistake in the route the 48th PzC would take; it slowed them down from the very start and the corps would never meet the schedule. It's possible the route planned was made because of the underestimation of the Red Army but that excuse holds no water for Hoth and von Manstein had photos of every foot of the salient and should have known better than to choose a route with such a poor terrain for panzers that also had extensive defenses with many strongpoints that would have to be captured. The 48th PzC had reached a line that just included Cherkasskoe. The line that Knobelsdorff reached was more than five miles behind Hausser. With the uneven advance of all three corps, flanks would be exposed and the front line would be longer than it had to be, thinning the forces of an army that started the campaign with dramatically insufficient forces. The performance of the Panther and 48th PzC would be one of the major setbacks for 4th PzA during the campaign. vzz109+.

By the end of the day, 2nd SS PzC had broken through 6th GA's defense and traveled nearly ten miles up the Vorskla River on its way to Oboyan. The southern German assault lost fewer panzers than the north, losing around 50 panzers which were unrecoverable. Even though 2nd SS PzC and 48th PzC both penetrated the first defensive belt they both fell short of their objectives and that worried von Manstein. The Germans were also questioning their practice of having Tigers and Panthers lead the charge. They were slow-moving targets that the Soviets had found a limited way to neutralize by the use of camouflaged Pak fronts. T34s, being much quicker and running in packs would out-maneuver the bigger tanks if not properly defended and disable them at their weak spots such as the tracks or engine compartment. Though Hoth intended all panzers to advance today, due to the late arrivals only about 800 eventually saw frontline action. Vatutin had more than that in 1st TA and access to another 1,000 in reserve. rc180+. dgk94. fkk79.

The Soviets quickly discovered their tanks were no match for the heavily armored

Tigers and rapidly used aircraft and big field guns to neutralize them. But the new German Panthers were having mechanical troubles with engines starting fires and having to be sidelined. It came at the worst possible time.

Throughout the predawn hours, German sappers of all panzer divisions searched for mines to clear in order to speed the way for the panzers at first light. Some of the mines were made of wood and the sappers had to use bayonets to find them. dlu25++.

At 0225 hrs, recon units and engineers of 3rd PzC crossed over the Donets south of Belgorod and ambushed the nearby railroad junction, but the gains had cost dearly in men for the defenders reacted quickly. rc177. shn157+.

In 7th GA sector, the 3rd PzC prepared to attack with almost 300 panzers that would spread out over a 35 mile front. It was originally tasked that once a secure bridgehead was established on the east side of the Donets, the panzers would drive to the northeast and capture Korocha on the eastern border of the intended axis. This objective would be changed to a less ambitious track once von Manstein saw the level of resistance his forces were up against. Von Manstein's changes were too slow, coming days later. hjj123m.

The 19th PzD was tasked with breaking through the first defense belt and heading for Uroshazah, near Kreida. The division had a bad start and did not fully achieve this modest objective. dlu25.

During the night, engineers completed a bridge at Pushkarnoye, which would allow the panzers of 19th PzD to cross the river once the grenadiers established a bridgehead across the Donets. Raus's 11th IC on the extreme eastern flank would cross over as well for their responsibility was to screen the panzers' right flank. wdk121+. hjj121m. fkk79. dgr155m. dgr173m. dgr39m. nzk85.

By 0225 hrs 3rd PzC and Group Raus had settled into their assault assembly areas along the Donets River from Belgorod to Maslova Pristani. It was still dark and the soldiers had to maintain silence. It gave a soldier time to think, think about his family and whether he'd ever see them again. He would wonder about his own mortality, whether that day would be the day that bullet caught up to him. Shortly afterwards, his introspection would be shattered as the 7th GA countered with artillery and air attacks.

The panzer divisions of 3rd PzC moved to the Donets at 0225 hrs, under support of artillery fire, in preparation for the crossing. The engineers and scouting parties were already across the river clearing mines and checking for the best routes to take. The plan was for 7th PzD to attack toward Solomino, the 19th PzD in the center of the front to attack south of Belgorod and the 168th ID on the left of Belgorod where a small bridgehead already existed would aim for Staryi Gorod. The 6th PzD with its heavy weapons supported the 168th ID and once the bridgehead was enlarged was supposed to drive toward St Gorodishche. The 7th PzD quickly crossed the river and established a bridgehead. The 19th PzD gained less ground and lost more panzers. The 168th ID did not gain ground and prevented the 6th PzD from advancing. The 2nd VA flew many sorties that day along the Donets, south of Belgorod, dramatically slowing the progress of the panzers of 3rd PzC. The *Luftwaffe* had little presence in the area, giving Soviet pilots no resistance at all. The 48th PzC and the 2nd SS PzC received all of their attention. The first day showed the *Luftwaffe* did not have enough aircraft to adequately cover all three corps and the situation only worsened as the campaign wore on. This was an extremely poor start for Kemp and his forces would not be able to catch up as the SS Corps battled its way toward Prokhorovka. By the end of the day, the gains were so small and the resistance so great that it could be seen that if that lack of progress continued, the whole campaign would be in jeopardy. Yet Hoth and von Manstein did nothing to improve the circumstances for 3rd PzC. shn157+. snk46. snk49. dgr198m. gnk86. dgr251. kcz167. erz201. dgk95m.

At Mikhailovka bridgehead, the heavy weapons of the 6th PzD would support the 168th ID and once the bridgehead was enlarged and the line penetrated the panzers were supposed to drive toward St Gorodishche and Staryi Gorod. The main force of 168th ID and 6th PzD were immediately stopped at breaking out by fierce resistance of the 81st GRD and supporting artillery but another smaller battle group of the 6th PzD took Chernaia Poliana, three miles northwest of Belgorod. Soviet reinforcements were brought up and the entire 168th ID / 6th PzD's advance was stopped. With no penetration, the 6th PzD had to cross on their own at a different location further south, following behind the 7th PzD which had made the biggest gains of the corps and ended the day near Krutoi Log. The 168th ID also shifted their direction a little toward the 19th PzD in order to avoid the impassable resistance of the 81st RD opposite Belgorod and to help support the 19th PzD. See Map 9. vzz5m. dgr76m. wdk22. fzk51. shn158. pck73. dgk136.

Group Raus began their assault south of 7th PzD with its line centered on Maslova Pristan. Shortly afterwards, the 7th GA countered with artillery and air attacks. The Germans crossed the Donets in eight places. The 6th PzD and 168th ID attacked toward Staryi Gorod, forcing the south flank of 81st GRD to retreat to the east but the rest of the 81st GRD remained firm and did not allow any gains to be made toward Staryi Gorod. Another battle group of the 6th PzD took Chernaia Poliana, three miles northwest of Belgorod. Reinforcements were brought up and 6th PzD's advance was stopped. The 19th PzD, attacking from their bridgehead at Mikhailovka southeast of Belgorod, made small gains on their bridgehead east of the river. During the night, engineers completed a bridge at Pushkarnoye which allowed the 19th PzD to bring their panzers to the line. Raus's 11th IC faced the 24th GRC as it advanced on the extreme eastern perimeter and would try to defend the panzers from attack from the east. wdk121+. hjj121m. fkk79. fkk324m. dgr155m. dgr173m. dgr39m. nzk85. vzz5m.

At 0225 hrs while the artillery preparation continued, the 7th PzD headed for the west bank of the Donets in the direction of Dorogobuzhino, seven miles southeast of Belgorod. After clearing a major traffic jam due to a minefield on the west bank of the Donets, the light panzers of 7th PzD crossed the Donets on a bridge northwest of Dorogobuzhino and marched on the village. Dorogobuzhino was quickly taken but the village of Razumnoe, a mile to the east, was prepared and would be more difficult to capture. In the first hour, when PzR Rothenburg was leading the advance, the 7th PzD destroyed 34 tanks. The engineers had to clear many mines before the troops could safely advance. They were working around the clock clearing the tens of thousands of mines that were planted over the previous few months. They also built another bridge over the Donets. The first attempt was destroyed from a rocket attack but the second attempt succeeded in large part to the grenadiers who were pushing back the enemy, enlarging the bridgehead and making it harder to reach the river by rocket. In one respect it was a bad day for 7th PzD for five of their key officers died in these early hour skirmishes as well as having some Tigers from sPzAbt 503 damaged by mines when they strayed from the cleared paths. fkk290. gnk88++. dgr155m. kfz451. zzt87+.

In the predawn hours, German engineers feverishly worked building a 24 ton bridge over the Donets, not far from Belgorod. At dawn it was 80% completed. The Soviet AF bombed it, putting the German advance in a state of confusion, especially Oppelin-Bronikowski's group of 6th PzD. The 19th PzD was already across when the bridge was destroyed but it did not go far without infantry against heavy resistance from 7th GA. Thirteen of the 14 Tigers of sPzAbt 503 attached to the 19th PzD were damaged; most by mines which were undetected by the engineers. Without the *Luftwaffe*'s support, the Red Air Force caused much damage to the Germans trying to cross the Donets. There was a heavy downpour in the early morning which also slowed the building of the bridges mhz217. gnk86. gnk88++. gjz182+.

At 0230 hrs while General Kempf was having a quiet moment near the river, Shumilov's 7th GA began a significant bombardment of 3rd PzC, especially at Mikhailovka where the Germans had their only bridgehead on the east side of the Donets. To the north at about the same time or a little earlier, Rokossovsky began his own disruptive barrage. mhz199+ mhz216. fkk51. fkk79. dgr249.

At 0330 hrs, after a 30 minute preparation, five divisions of Kempf's Group launched and eventually forced crossings at different points along the Northern Donets and from the German Mikhailovka bridgehead, which was situated across the river from Belgorod, southward to Maslova Pristan. Kempf's 168th ID was immediately stopped at breaking out of the bridgehead at Mikhailovka by the 81st GRD. The sites that were crossed were located at Pushkarnoe, Dalnie Peski, Dorogobuzhino, Solomino, Puliaevka, Maslova Pristan, Priiutovka and Bezliudovka. By 1300 hrs, screens were set up on the east banks of the Donets by the 6th PzGR and 7th PzGR and bridges were constructed at Maslova Pristan and Karnoukhovka to allow panzers and heavy equipment over the river. By the afternoon the Germans had consolidated their gains into a bridgehead seven miles wide and about two miles deep. By the end of the day, the 78th GRD was pushed back and was defending Hill 126.3 – Krutoi Log and the 72nd GRD and 213th RD the outskirts of Krutoi Log, Maslov Pristan and Priiutovka. Three of these sites were abandoned when the other crossings looked more promising. The 17th VA was called in to destroy the pontoon bridges across the Donets in order to isolate the 7th PzD that had made it across to allow 78th GRD to counter and destroy the remains. dgk103. dgr75. cbk33. erz203. dgr76m+.

In 19th PzD sector, the sappers had worked all the previous night to clear a path for the panzers. Early in the morning panzers of the 2nd Company of sPzAbt 503 began moving out but did not go far before three Tigers were damaged from mines that had been missed during the clearing. In all 13 Tigers were damaged but repairable to mine damage the first day. Two more were damaged by shellfire. The Tigers were being used as the spearhead because of their tough skin and long gun and they were in jeopardy to all the thousands of mines that had been planted. Four other panzers were lost to the 19th. Five Tigers were repaired by the end of next day but the other eight would take from two to four days to repair. Without these Tigers, the 19th PzD would not reach Hill 139.9 where the front observers were gauging the artillery distance. Without these Tigers, the 3rd PzC had little chance of reaching Prokhorovka on time. With the bridge just destroyed other panzers could not cross either and the infantry was left to fend for themselves and it was going badly. The division did not have any more 60 ton pontoons left either. dlu28+. gnk88++.

Elements of the 19th PzD, attacking from the southern border of the bridgehead at Mikhailovka southeast of Belgorod, made small gains on their bridgehead east of the river. The 19th PzD eventually penetrated the line near Razumnoe against Skvortsov's 78th GRD and the 81st GRD and approached the town by nightfall, losing many panzers in the process, most to mine damage. The 7th PzD escaped most of the shelling for the Soviets were targeting the 6th PzD and 19th PzD sectors where most of the bridge construction was taking place. See Map 9. fzk51. dlu40. shn158.

After crossing the Donets and penetrating the first defense belt, which was held by the 25th GRC's 81st GRD and supported by the 262nd TR, Kempf was to head northeast toward Kazache and then Korocha to block 7th GA from attacking 2nd SS PzC. gnk85. dgr155m. dgr77m. dgr87m. snk76. hjj123m.

Lt General Shumilov's 7th GA's 24th GRC and 25th GRC contained 76,000 men. It was also reinforced with the 27th GTB, 201st TB and a number of other tank regiments and mortar units. It also had 1,500 guns and a total of 245 tanks attached. The 3rd PzC had almost 300 panzers and additional 45 Tigers from sPzAbt 503. Instead of using sPzAbt 503 as a single massive battering ram, the battalion was broken up and split between the three panzer divisions. This has been heavily criticized throughout the years. gnk85.

Southeast of Belgorod on the east side of the Donets, the lead units of 7th PzD failed to take out Soviet OPs as they moved forward. This allowed the Soviets to have eyes on their shelling, making for lethal accuracy on the Germans crossing the river. gnk89.

While the Tigers attached to 7th PzD waited for the heavy bridge to be completed across the Donets, the grenadiers crossed over and headed for the rail line which was defended by Maj General Skvortsov's 78th GRD. The rail line and its protective embankment ran parallel to the river, about two miles east of it. By the afternoon, the infantry had torn a small gap in the line and proceeded to head inland. At this point Lt General Funck unleashed his panzers to expand the gap and extend the bridgehead. Their objective was now Razumnoe. Skvortsov of the 78th GRD ordered elements of the 81st GAB to plug the gap. gnk88+. dgr173m.

After being pushed out of Dorogobuzhino, the 78th GRD regrouped and initially stopped the Germans from advancing past the rail line running through Dorogobuzhino. The 73rd GRD joined in the defense but both divisions eventually failed to hold the village and were pushed back a mile to Razumnoe. After securing the village the 7th PzD resumed its march gaining another three miles and by nightfall reached a hill overlooking Krutoi Log. While the 81st GRD was deployed nearest the Donets, the 78th GRD was deployed to the southeast, closer to Krutog Log. The Germans were using their Tigers in the lead with the Mk IVs following. This formation lost the advantage of the long gun of the Tigers plus putting their highly prized panzer in more jeopardy. wwf82. dgk94. dgr39m. wdk122. dgr172m. dgr39m. gnk87+. dgr155m. wwf110.

In 7th PzD sector the lead Tigers of sPzAbt 503 expanded its bridgehead then traveled eight miles and was approaching Krutoi Log, situated on a plateau to the left of the panzer column. It was decided to attack in the morning and the 7th PzD camped for the night on the plateau. It had penetrated the first two defense belts. It was a relatively good day for the division, it had traveled about ten miles and casualties were low at 10 killed and 86 wounded but the other divisions of Group Kempf did not do very well and had incurred greater casualties. With their flanks exposed the 7th PzD was in a vulnerable position. dlu24. dlu63m.

From the Belgorod area, the 6th PzD under Hunersdorff and with 168th ID in the lead attack northwards toward Staryi Gorod. Elements reached Chernaia Poliana by nightfall but failed to reach their main objective of Gorod. Two important road junctions of Sabynino and Krivtsovo would be attacked before reaching Staryi Gorod. The 6th

PzD tried to reach Staryi Gorod but the minefields and heavy MG fire kept the Germans, including the Tigers, from entering the town. The 6th PzD had to withdraw to Chernaia Poliana. vzz179. gnk85+. vzz5m.

Once across the Donets River, the Kempf Group, led by 7th PzD, attacked the 7th GA and penetrated its line quickly in a few spots, drove on and reached the Koren River, establishing a bridgehead along with 19th PzD of seven miles wide and four miles deep. The gains were less than expected and 3rd PzC was still behind the 2nd SS PzC. It had cost Kempf several thousand casualties to establish this bridgehead. It turned out to be his costliest day of the campaign. The 7th GA had to fall back in this sector to its second line of defense to escape envelopment. dgk103+. dlu6m. gjz183. dgr78. dgk222m. dlu63m. gjz185.

Late in the day it was decided to move the 6th PzD southward during the night and cross the Donets in 7th PzD sector at dawn. Maj General Hunersdorff would then join the 7th PzD and together would exploit their strength against the river line defenses. The 7th PzD and 11th PzR of 6th PzD, with a total of around 200 panzers and assault guns, planned on attacking Soviet positions on the Razumnaia River line next morning. Meanwhile the nearby village of Krutoi Log, defended by 7th GA, repeatedly halted 7th PzD's attacks, these lasting late into the night. The 11th PzR was attached to 7th PzD with the specific task of taking Iastrebovo, two miles southeast of Blizhniaia Igumenka and leading the 7th PzD to Melikhovo, 25 miles northeast of Belgorod. The Belgorod-Melikhovo highway was critical for it would ease the advancement of the divisions to the front, speed up resupply and prevent 7th GA from using it.

Five miles south of Belgorod, there were still panzers of 7th PzD and the rest of 3rd PzC still waiting to cross the Donets on a new bridge that was being rebuilt, but the Tigers of sPzAbt 503 attempted to ford the river near the village of Solomino. When the leading #321 got stuck on the far side, the rest of the Tigers halted until a suitable bridge was available. When a 60 ton bridge was assembled, it was quickly destroyed by the Red Air Force. The bridge was repaired and the Tigers quickly crossed but soon ran into a bunker system that stopped their progress. Even with the very slow start with some of his forces still on the west side of the Donets, Kempf's Tigers had destroyed 30 T34s. wwf78++. mhz218. fkk278. dgr173m. kfz454. shn158+.

While the 6th PzGR and 7th PzGR of 7th PzD (Funck) had penetrated the front line of 7th GA and the 25th PzR was racing east to take the high ground west of Krutoi Log, Lt General Schmidt's 19th PzD, to the north in the wooded, swampy Pushkarnoye area near Milkailovka, was meeting stiff resistance. The infantry finally made progress in enlarging the bridgehead and the 71 panzers of the 27th PzR plus the attached Tigers of sPzAbt 503 launched from the 60 ton bridge that was just finished. Only a few panzers made it across before Soviet artillery and planes hit it. The Tigers had to wait to have the bridge repaired as the lighter bridge which the other panzers could cross would not hold up to the Tigers' weight. The light panzers were heading for Blizhniaia Igumenka which was captured by nightfall. snk49+. dlu24. dgk103. gnk89. erz203. dgr155m. wdk122. kfz451.

Having finally crossed the Donets, sPzAbt 503 was stopped at the Delnazhaya Igumenka bridge waiting for sappers to fortify it to handle the weight of the Tigers. The lighter tanks crossed over. While the Tigers were waiting for the bridge to be strengthened, the grenadiers crossed and established a bridgehead. After five hours, the Tigers crossed and headed for Razumnoe Station and then Dalnie Peski and the woods to the east. At Razumnoe, the Tigers were attacked by T34s. The first Soviet tanks were destroyed at

1,200 yards before they were within lethal firing range and the rest scattered. There were 45 Tigers in sPzAbt 503 and it would be broken up into thirds with one company going to each panzer division. Only the first 14 Tigers made it over the bridge before the Soviets shelled and destroyed the fortified bridge. The remainder of the Tigers had to wait again while the bridge was repaired. Most of the bridges in 3rd PzC sector had been damaged or destroyed at least once today, and with the Red AF in action, some had been hit several times, delaying the crossing dramatically. dlu10++. dlu28. dgr155m. dgr173m.

In front of the German bridgehead at Mikhailovka, the 15th GRD and 81st GRD of 25th GRC had created a huge minefield and erected formidable defenses. Add the heavy shelling in the predawn hours and 19th PzD and 168th ID paid a high price leaving the bridgehead and before reaching the Soviet line. At Mikhailovka and along the German line for 15 miles, the 72nd GRD and 36th GRD attacked, attempting to eradicate the bridgeheads that had just been developed. The bridgeheads at Besliyodovo and Priytovka were eliminated but the others withstood the attacks. German engineers were able to complete a bridge at Maslova by 1100 hrs and at Pristan by 1300 hrs. While the Mk IIIs and IVs rolled across the Donets, the Tigers had to wait until the heavier bridge was completed. The 262nd TR was attached to the 81st GRD to help equalize the balance against the panzers. The 73rd GRD and 213th RD were manning the second defense belt. fkk80. gnk85.

The initial charge across the Donets by 320th ID of 11th IC was successful but soon afterwards a group of 150 men were pocketed by a counter-attack by 7th GA. At Kempf's HQ, it was heard over the airwaves that the men were all executed after key interrogations. Those murders would set the bar for German reprisals for Soviet POWs. erz203. snk49.

By 1100 hrs, Kempf's 19th PzD, having deployed between the 6th PzD and 7th PzD, achieved a small penetration across the river opposite the Soviet fortified village of Razumnoe. Exploiting the opportunity, Lt General Schmidt's 73rd PzGR moved forward over a mile at the junction of the 78th GRD and 81st GRD. By nightfall the 19th PzD's 27th PzR joined the bridgehead on the Donet's east bank and completed routing the 228th GRR who fell back near Razumnoe. The 19th PzD was heading for Korocha but first it had to capture the heights overlooking Blizhniaia Igumenka. dgk103. dlu6m. dlu25*. dgr155m. dgr173m. dgr39m. dlu63m. hjj123m.

With the 3rd PzC making gains, even modest gains, Vatutin brought up the 213th RD and 27th GTB to protect the threatened Maslova Pristan area. Both formations attacked from the march. The Germans did succeed, encircling the defending 72nd GRD before reinforcements arrived and it took another 48 hours before the garrison was able to break out with the help of the reinforcements and head north. Vatutin thought that the only way Hoth could reach Kursk was with the linking of 3rd PzC with 2nd SS PzC and the subsequent destruction of 69th Army and he would do everything possible to prevent that from happening. The 69th Army started the campaign with nearly 61,000 men, 538 guns and 1,028 mortars. Why did Hoth not see this scenario? fkk80. vzz180.

South of 3rd PzC, Group Raus with the 106th ID and 320th ID made even less progress. The 106th ID did cross the river and reached the railway at Toblinka a few miles east of the river but their advance was stopped when attacked by the 72nd GRD and elements of the 213th RD. The 320th ID also crossed and reached the Belgorod to Maslova railroad line, a few miles south of Belgorod but the two German divisions had not mutually secured their flanks yet. wdk123.

The 7th PzD's 25th PzR crossed the Donets just west of Dorogobuzhino and as the infantry fought to secure the eastern side, the engineers built a light bridge to get the panzers and trucks across. The grenadiers made slow progress toward the village against the stiff resistance of the 78th GRD and 73rd GRD. Eventually both divisions had to pull back to Razumnoe allowing the 7th PzD to take over the village. wdk122. fzk170.

Vatutin gave Shumilov control of 69th Army's 111th RD and 270th RD which were in second echelon. Vatutin wanted Shumilov's 7th GA to attack in the morning to eliminate the bridgeheads that had been established that day. The two divisions would protect the line in case the Germans got past Shumilov's attack. vzz108*. dgr78.

Looking back over the day's action, the fighting around Belgorod was intense and losses were high on both sides. The panzers were halted not far from the key city. At night the 168th ID was ordered to advance with the 19th PzD against positions on the high ground northeast of Belgorod to penetrate the first defense belt. Comparing the results of 48th PzC and 2nd SS PzC, the 3rd PzC was clearly lagging for the other two corps broke through the first defense belt and or reached the second defense belt despite the rugged terrain.

The 35th GRC was ordered to send its 93rd RD forward to Prokhorovka for future deployment behind Kostitsyn's 183rd RD while Col Trunin's 92nd GRD and Russkikh's 94th GRD was sent to the Korodia area where it looked like the Germans were heading. The 7th GA under Shumilov was ordered to attack on two axes toward the Krutoi Log area where the 19th PzD and 7th PzD were making gains. This order to attack was rescinded as well in favor of a defensive posture that would wear down the attackers. fkk81. vzz107. vzz114. gnk152. gjz183. kcz168. dgk106m. nzk85.

During the night, 6th PzD moved southeastward away from the Lipovyi Donets River to follow 7th PzD over the bridges at Dorogobuzhino and Solomino. The maneuver weakened the vacated sector, allowing the Soviets to continue to apply harsh pressure on *SSTK* and 168th ID. The 6th PzD was originally tasked with taking Staryi Gorod and Chernaia Poliana but the resistance was too strong and the division decided it was better to find a different route. The 168th ID on the west bank of the Donets was guarding the 6th PzD's flank during the redeployment as well as shelling the Soviet positions on the east side. At the same time General Mattenklott's 42nd IC attacked across the Donets, south of the 320th, as a feint but it was unsuccessful. After dark Kempf and Breith conferred, trying to decide which line of attack 6th PzD should take after it crossed the Donets. Initially both generals thought the 6th PzD should pair up with one of the other panzer divisions to concentrate their strength but it was finally decided to have 19th PzD move more to the west and have 6th eventually move in between the other two divisions. wdk122++. dlu10. hjj121m. gnk141. dgk222m. dlu63m. fkk278. dgr155m. dgr173m. dgr39m. shn158+. snk47. vzz5m. fzk51.

During the night, Vatutin brought up the 111th RD and 270th RD of 69th Army to bolster the 7th GA's line at the second defense belt, east of the Koren River and to the rear of 24th GRC. He also sent the 93rd RD of 35th GRC to the Lipovyi Donets, west of Prokhorovka to prevent the 2nd SS PzC from linking up with Kempf. Kempf was at a disadvantage having to start his assault south of Belgorod and to have to cross the Donets from a standstill. In 3rd PzC sector, engineers had built two pontoon bridges across the Donets in this sector which allowed 100 panzers to cross before the Soviet AF destroyed the bridges. The bridges were finally completed and the rest of the 3rd PzC stuck on the west bank was able to cross over and race to catch up with their comrades. The disasters at the river in the morning were costly to Kempf, slowing his advance and he was never able to catch up. The Soviets played it well: extensive minefields, heavy artillery coverage and air support had a tremendous affect on 3rd PzC. dgk103+. dlu6m. gjz183. dgr78. dgk222m. dlu63m. gjz185.

By the end of the day 7th PzD's PzR 25 had traveled three miles and for the most part was still within the first defense belt. They were not close to reaching Korocha, their first day objective. gnk89. snk76. hjj123m.

The 106th ID of 11th IC made it across the Donets against heavy resistance, advanced slowly and by the end of the day reached the railway line at Toblinka, several miles east of the river when they were attacked by the 72nd GRD. The 320th ID, traveling south of 106th ID made it to the railway line after dark and then stopped for the night. wdk123.

Nearby Blizhniaia Igumenka by the end of the day, Funck's 7th PzD tentatively captured Krutoi Log. Krutoi Log was an important strongpoint on the second defense belt. Krieda, not far from Mikhailovka, had been destroyed when 7th PzD drove through it but resistance remained in the area. PzGR 74 also went through Krieda clearing residual resistance as it drove to the northeast. Between the accurate shelling and bombing, the 3rd PzC got off to a slow, costly start. The accompanying 11th IC lost heavily today, trying to protect 7th PzD's right flank. snk49+. dlu24. dgk103. gnk89. erz203.

Failing to reach its objective of Blizhniaia Igumenka against aerial attacks and stiff ground resistance by the end of the day, the 19th PzD suffered casualties of nearly 500, including 62 dead. dlu25.

By the end of the day, a bridgehead of seven miles wide and up to five miles deep (although averaging only two) was established but not all of his panzers or men had crossed over. Kempf's objective was Korocha but could only reach Koren. Knowing Korocha would be next, Vatutin brought up 35th RC to support the 7th GA for the next morning attack by the panzers. It was a costly, hectic day for 3rd PzC; Kempf's divisions were poorly deployed and 6th PzD had to catch up to bolster the front line and participate equally in the offense while guarding against the unexpected high resistance of frequent local counter-attacks.. rc177.

It was a bad day for 3rd PzC. Except for Dorogobuzhino, seven miles south of Belgorod, which was taken by 7th PzD, the Soviet first line of defense had not been penetrated very severely. The 19th PzD was close to breaking through southeast of Mikhailovka but 6th PzD and the infantry of 168th ID had been stopped by the 81st GRD and the 375th RD to the north. During the night, the 6th PzD was moved from close to the river eastward to follow behind the relatively successful 7th PzD, which was near Krutoi Log, but its advance was quickly brought to a stop by heavy artillery fire. Kempf was going to try to pocket the Soviets near Staryi Gorod by sending the panzers behind the Soviets instead of driving through them. The 3rd PzC had fallen behind which exposed the eastern flank of *SSTK*, forcing *SSTK* to concentrate on its flank instead of moving forward. The 167th ID was moving up to assist and then eventually replace *SSTK* on the flank but *SSTK* would still leave panzers behind to support the 167th ID. The 42nd IC, Kempf's infantry corps crossed the river but was immediately stopped by a minefield. This was a key development for Vatutin; with the stiff resistance of the 81st and 375th divisions, it forced *SSTK* to concentrate more on their flank than advancing to the north. It probably delayed *SSTK* two days to reach the Psel River which was a cruial development. wdk122. wdk130. dgr172m+.

hjj121m. fkk80. dgr155m. dgr39m. fkk320m. fkk324m. vzz5m.

By the end of the day, Gen Raus counted his casualties of 11th IC and it totaled 2,000 men. His corps, screening the 7th PzD from flank attacks, was heavily hit northwest of Shevekino which was a favorite jumping-off spot for the divisions of 7th GA to enter battle. General Raus was hoping his divisions would make it out of the first defensive belt by the following day where the resistance would lessen until he reached the second defensive belt. erz204.

It was only the first whole day of the campaign and yet General Vatutin was having to alter his battle plans and troop dispositions many times and would do so for every day of the campaign. It was a dizzying array of new orders and much credit must be given to the front line forces in keeping up with the changes. To proponents of the general, it could be said that they were watching a Grand Master move his pieces skillfully across the chessboard while detractors would say the general was out of his depth and was already floundering. The truth was probably somewhere in the middle.

5

July 5th on the Northern Salient

See Map 2

At 0110 hrs, Rokossovsky began a two-hour preparation along the entire line to disrupt the planned German assault. It also killed front line soldiers and cut communication lines. It was effective and the German launch got off to a slower start than expected but if Rokossovsky had started his barrage a little later, it would have been even more effective. This barrage was expected by Model for he learned through interrogations that Rokosovsky had learned of the invasion time and was trying to disrupt the start. wdk113. dgk87m. gjz179+. dgk92m. snz225+. zow140.

At 0230 hrs, the 13th Army began their own barrage that included almost 600 guns and lasted 30 minutes, in an attempt to cause havoc and confusion along the German line. dgr107. dgk87m. gjz179+. dgk92m.

The German initial objectives were Hill 253.5 at Butyrki heights, Hill 274 at Olkhovatka and Hill 272 at Teploe and the key panzer corps were specifically aligned to accomplish these objectives, once the infantry penetrated the front line. rc172. wf71. dgr198m. dgk87m. dgk92m.

At 0330 hrs over 200 planes, which included 60 escorts from Luftlotte 6, took off in three waves to attack Soviet positions at and near Maloarchangelsk, the largest city in the battle area. The first to attack were a formation of He 111s, then Ju 88s and finally Ju 87s. While in the air, Soviet fighters attacked the German formations but had little success against the escorts. At the same time, Model unleashed an 80 minute barrage against the same targets. These attacks hampered Soviet artillery preparation against Model's 9th Army opening assault on the city. There would be a constant rotation of planes attacking to slow the Soviet response. At 0530 hrs, the 9th Army moved out with 23rd IC on its east flank attacking the junction of 13th and 48th Armies making a small gap but at a heavy cost. Men and vehicles ran into thousands of mines that had been laid. In the north, the *Luftwaffe* flew 2,088 combat sorties to the Soviet nearly 1,200. Of those 1,200 sorties, 817 were fighters. An hour earlier some of these German planes had to scramble unexpectedly from their airfield when their radar picked up a large formation of Soviet fighters coming in to destroy them before the launch had even started. The pilots were ready for takeoff so their response was quick and they were able to defend themselves and the airfields. The Soviets were unsuccessful, losing many planes. The repeated bombing runs in the Maloarkhangelsk area tried to destroy the heavy defenses there and disrupt rail transport running through the city. The recently developed small caliber fragmentation bombs, the SD-1 and SD-2, were very accurate and many targets were destroyed during the first pass. snk163. dgk92m. rc170. je99. rkz167. lck222+. dgk87m. dgr250. cbk26++. gjz181. cbk55. nzk77. cbk12m. pck66.

The sPzAbt 656 was under the command of Major Steinwachs and was attached to 292nd ID. The sPzAbt 654 under Major Noak was attached to 78th AD. The sPzAbt 654 made a big difference in helping take Hill 239.8 the first day of battle. This Ferdinand regiment was credited with destroying over 500 tanks in the month of July. In addition to the 90 Ferdinands of sPzAbt 656, Model also had StPzAbt 216 under the command of Lt von Jungenfeldt. These StuGs would support and protect the Ferdinands. kfz460+.

While the German barrage was hitting the Soviet front line as well as the rear areas, German engineers were clearing pathways through the minefields. snz225+.

At 0430 hrs while Model initiated his own 80 minute preparation on just the Soviet front line, the 23rd IC launched a probing attack toward Maloarkhangelsk on the east end of the battle zone to hunt for weaknesses. The 13th Army continued to shell the Germans during the German barrage in an attempt to disrupt their imminent attack. It was partially successful. The 23rd IC then launched a feint attack to disrupt the Soviets while the rest of first echelon 9th Army made the real attack. The 23rd IC attacked the boundary between 13th and 48th Armies in the direction of Maloarkhangelsk which had an important road junction to all directions in the area. This area was defended by 8th RD and 148th RD of 15th RC. With the help of Stukas, the three divisions (78th AD, 216th ID, 36th ID) made a mile into the first defense sector but were then halted by a Soviet counter-attack. dgk86. dgk87m. nzk84. dgk92m. lck116m.

The current German artillery barrage that would last 80 minutes was directed to a depth of about two miles to the rear of the Soviet front line. It was an attempt to cut communications and to destroy entanglements, trenches and soldiers. During the shelling, about 100 German planes bombed the front to within a four mile distance. The 13th Army received the most of this abuse. Rokossovsky decided further shelling was needed and another barrage began at just past 0430 hrs, this time almost a thousand guns and mortars taking part. When Model launched his men, one spearhead attacked the 13th-70th Army boundary behind Krasnaia Slobodka and Izmailovo. A secondary demonstration occurred against General Romanenko's 48th Army in the Maloarkhangelsk-Panskaia sector which was defended by the 8th RD, 148th RD and 16th RD. In all the 48th Army had 84,000 men, nearly 1,500 guns and almost 200 tanks and assault guns. General Galinin's 70th Army had 96,000 men, almost 1,700 guns and 125 tanks. dgr107+. dgk59+. dgk87m. dgk92m. dgr108m.

At 0510 hrs the *Luftwaffe* launched another attack on positions held by the 13th Army along a 30 mile front between Trosna and Maloarkhangelsk, followed 20 minutes later by ten divisions. Unlike von Manstein and Hoth, Model was spearheading his attack with infantry followed by the panzers after a gap opened. The infantry was stopped and withdrew. An hour long bombardment ensued, then the infantry tried it again but with some Tigers this time. By 0930 hrs, Maj General Kessel's 20th PzD fought its way to Bobrik. Bobrik was defended by the 321st RR of 15th RD and when Bobrik fell, the 15th RD had to fall back in the sector. On its left was 6th ID which had crossed the Oka river to siege the village of Novi Chutor and to clear a path in the minefields for the panzers to pass. At this point, a few more panzers were brought up front to participate. Model was using this narrow front to plow men and tanks to overload the Soviet defense and he would continue to pour more resources to keep the Soviets busy. je99. dgr198m. fkk50. dgk87m. swm138. wwf48. dgk92m. lck116m. kfz454+. zsm155+.

After receiving a preemptive barrage by Rokossovky and a planned artillery and aerial barrage by 9th Army, the German main assault began at 0530 hrs against the 13th Army in the Maloarkhangelsk area. The lead corps were Lt General Friessner's 23rd IC and

Harpe's 41st PzC to the west. The 41st PzC had a narrow front; it was hoped that their concentration of forces would penetrate the front line quickly. The 78th AD of 41st PzC used many Goliaths to clear a path through the mine-fields to reduce the time to reach the front line. At 0630 hrs, Zorn's 46th PzC and Lemelsen's 47th PzC launched. The Soviets used massive shelling and air raids to slow the German advance. Initially, the Germans met little resistance from ground troops but when approaching the first trench a wall of small arms fire hit them hard. In front of the trenches the remote controlled Goliaths cleared paths through the minefields. wdk172. dgk86. dgk87m. swm136. dgk92m. kfz455.

On the eastern flank at 0530 hrs, the 292nd ID of 41st PzC and Maj General Hoffimeister's 383rd ID of 23rd IC attacked the 16th RD of 48th Army in the area north of Maloarckhangelsk. After a six hour battle, the Germans made little progress and gave up the attack. A regiment of the 383rd positioned at Panskaia on the north flank was counter-attacked by the 16th RD. The fighting was so fierce the regimental CO was killed. wdk174. dgk87m. dgk92m.

At 0530 hrs as the barrage was ending, Model left his HQ and headed for Lemelsen's 47th PzC's HQ. He wanted a personal update on how 20th PzD and 6th ID's assault began. The 292nd ID of 41st PzC launched with them and was screening their eastern flank. Their main objective was to reach Kashara by the end of the day. To give the 6th ID a little more muscle, a few Elefants (sPzAbt 656) led the advance. The main defender facing Grossmann's 6th ID was the 47th RR of Col Dzhandzhgava's 15th RD and Maj General Barinov's 81st RD. At the same time, the 18th GR had crossed the Oka River and captured Iasnaia Poliana. The 47th was putting up stiff resistance but were now slowly being pushed back. snz228. dgk92m. dgk88.

At daybreak around 0530 hrs the 6th ID, on the the right of 20th PzD, attacked along the valley of the Oka. The Tigers of sPzAbt 505 attached to the 6th ID destroyed a defensive screen of T34s before hitting the open flank of the 676th RR, and allowing the German infantry to advance behind it. Fighting much of the morning, the village of Novo Chutor was finally captured. By 1200 hrs, the Tigers had advanced and captured Butyrki, northeast of Bobrik, and were threatening to unhinge the 81st RD next door. The 81st RD (13th Army) was already being threatened by a frontal attack by the 292nd ID of Harpe's 41st PzC. sPzAbt 653, which had Ferdinands, was supporting the 292nd ID, had penetrated the line defended by 410th RR and were headed for Aleksandrovka. During this battle, Soviet sappers moved up and planted thousands of mines across the expected route of the Germans. Not expecting the mines, the Ferdinands and panzers drove right into the minefield, disabling many vehicles. The Germans' other axis of attack that morning was on the Panskaia-Maloarkhangelsk axis to the east which was also the boundary line between 13th Army and 48th Army. The 8th RD, 148th RD and 16th RD were hit the hardest but they were able to repulse the first attack. In the 16th RD (Latvian) sector, the Germans were able to penetrate the line and lunge a mile deep into the rear before the Soviets countered and pushed the Germans back. dgr110. pck42+. dgk87m. wwf48+. wwf50m. dgk92m. dgr199m. dgk88. lck116m. vzz12m.

At 0615 hrs, the panzers of von Kessel's 20th PzD drove into a massive minefield and were stuck there until the pioneers were able to clear the mines. The minefield was part of a massive tank trap. A Pak front was waiting for the trap to be sprung and started firing on the trapped panzers. It happened at a bad time for the 6th ID was beginning to get traction and was moving the Soviet line back. The 6th ID had also crossed the Oka River, advanced a mile and captured Novi Chutor. With the panzers stalled next to them, the 6th ID's momentum had soured. snz228+. kfz456.

At 0630 hrs after leaving Lemelsen, Model arrived at Harpe's 41st PzC HQ. The Army Commander was told the 508th GR of 292nd ID had gained some ground but was now stuck in a minefield, halting their advance. They were now taking heavy SA and mortar fire from Barinov's 81st RD (13th Army). Before Model arrived, Harpe had already ordered the 101th PzR of 18th PzD up to the line to help the drive reach the key objective of Ozerki. Lt General Josef Harpe was promoted to that position and became the CO of 41st PzC in 1942. He would rise to command the 9th Army and then the 4th PzA. snz229. zsm110. pck40.

About an hour after 23rd IC attacked toward Maloarkhangelsk, Lemelsen's 47th PzC and Harpe's 41st PzC with support from the air attacked the defenses of 29th RC's 15th RD (Dzhandzhgava) and Barinov's 81st RD northwest of Ponyri. The 120 panzers of 20th PzD breached the 15th RD's forward defenses by 0900 hrs. To the east, Friessner's 23rd IC was making a demonstration attack between the boundary line of 13th and 48th Armies in the direction of Maloarkhangelsk, an important traffic junction, but failed to make much progress. The 47th PzC, consisting of 2nd PzD, 9th PzD, 20th PzD and 6th ID, quickly made a shallow penetration between Podolian and Butyrki allowing the 20th PzD and 6th ID to head south toward Bobrik, Step and Saburovka on the Sevana. While the Ju 87s and He 111s hit ground targets, the Fw 190s effectively kept the Red Air Force out of the sector. Lt General Rudenko was hesitant in sending massive squadrons to counter the *Luftwaffe* and his air force paid the price. Realizing his mistake that night, he called for a stronger response the next morning. dgk86. snk105. lck249. lck252. dgk87m. dgr199m. cbk38+. dgk92m. lck116m.

At 0800 hrs and with 9th Army's expanding, gaining momentum, Pz Abt 21 launched from north of Lebedicha heading for Podolian by way of Tagino to join up with 20th PzD. Upon reaching Hill 218.2, the formation of assault guns were attacked from the air; stiff anti-aircraft fire downed several fighters and chased the rest away. Approaching Gnilets, a small band of Soviet tanks attacked the formation but were driven back. After dark the Abt 21 was fighting for control of Saborovka. The fighting went on way past dark and afterwards the supply trucks as well as the medics arrived to take back the wounded and to replenish fuel and ammo. Saborovka was about a mile south of Bobrik. zzt75+. dgk87m.

Between Bobrik and Gnilets, 20th PzD made initial gains by 0900 hrs. To extend these gains further reinforcements were brought up to add weight to the charge. The 47th RD was badly hit and was forced to withdraw. The 6th ID next to 20th PzD was helped by their success and also made gains, continuing to give cover to the panzers. The *Luftwaffe* also attacked both sides of Iasnaia Poliana. pc38+. dgr198m. dgk87m. dgr199m. dgk92m. lck116m. zzt75+.

On the left flank of 46th PzC, the men charging through the rye fields quickly discovered a minefield. It took them hours to clear a path for the men and panzers to get past no man's land. Tigers approached the edge of the rye field and fired shell after shell at the enemy line to give cover to the sappers clearing the mines. This delay affected the entire 46th PzC's momentum. pc36. dgk87m. dgk92m.

The 41st PzC struck the 81st RD hard and were unable to make initial gains, but eventually were able to push the Soviets back. The 70 ton Ferdinands were brought up to blast a path. These machines had no internal MG so the occupants would fire their MGs through the 88mm gun barrel for self-defense. In Berlin, Guderian had failed the Ferdinand road test but was overruled by Hitler who demanded these weapons be at Kursk. Guderian knew of the vulnerability of not having a MG so a make-shift sled was attached to the back of the Elefant (also called Ferdinand) with a tow chain and infantry would ride along and keep the enemy away from the vehicle. pc40+. dgk87m. wwf48.

After failing to penetrate the Maloarkhangelsk front line, the Germans pulled back at 0730 hrs and regrouped before attacking again. A new assault along the Soglasnyi-Arkhangelskoe-Iasnaia Poliana sector was launched that would eventually lead them to Olkhovatka. The very heaviest concentration was in the Verkhne Tagino-Arkhangelskoe area during this second assault. After a half hour of fighting, the leading German units reached the front line of the 81st RD and 15th RD and after a short time the Soviets slowly fell back. At the same time the *Luftwaffe* was pounding the line next door which was guarded by the 132nd RD and 280th RD of 70th Army. With 15th RD falling back, the right flank of 70th Army became exposed. The 712th RR of 132nd RD shifted direction east of Gnilets to face the gap. The 712th RR was not strong enough and they were pushed back into Gnilets but resistance stiffened and the Germans were not able to enter the town. The Germans expanded their attack area and hit the rest of 132nd RD and 280th RD as well and began to push them back. During this retreat in this sector, Soviet artillery poured down on the Germans, trying to slow their pursuit. The first axis of attack toward Maloarkhangelsk was still active but the advance was slowing down. By 1030 hrs, the divisions of 41st PzC had captured Nikolskaia 1, Ozerki and Iasnaia Poliana but the resistance of the 81st RD and 15th RD stiffened and the German advance was halted. Panzers were brought up and extended the gap before more reinforcements arrived. The panzers headed for Ponyri. Rokossovsky ordered the air force to attack the area of penetration to slow the Germans and by 1300 hrs reinforcements came into the area and stopped the attack. dgr110++. dgk87m. dgk92m. dgr199m.

At 0800 hrs, the 18th GR of 6th ID stormed the Church Woods, securing it then the Tigers of sPzAbt 505 drove past the infantry toward Podolian and the hills to the south and southeast with the 6th ID following. Before going very far, the Tigers were attacked by T34s that were hidden in nearby cornfields. Soviet infantry was also hidden in those fields and the 6th ID had to go in and clear it and at great cost in life and time. The Tigers had made an important breakthrough and if the 2nd PzD or 9th PzD had been activated and trailing close behind the Tigers, a critical follow-through could have been made. As it was those two panzer divisions did not arrive until next morning and it was too late as Rokossovsky had plugged the gap. The left flank of 6th ID was struggling and falling behind but it did manage to reach Hill 245 and Heart Woods. However, with the line on its left at Ozerki even further behind, it put extra pressure on the 6th ID. fkk52. lck251. fkk102m. dgk87m. dgr199m. dgk92m. lck116m. kfz456+.

The 292nd ID of 41st PzC with support of six Ferdinands moved up to Aleksandrovka, three miles deep into enemy territory and half way to Ponyri. pc41. dgk222m. dlu63m. dgr111. lck116m. dgk87m. dgr199m. dgk92m. dgr199m.

At 0830 hrs, Rokossovsky, continuing his redeployments, ordered the 74th RD up close to the front line at Protasovo, just west of Maloarkhangelsk, to protect the town's west flank. dgr111. dgr108m. dgk87m. dgk92m. dgr199m.

While 46th PzC and 47th PzC were making their coordinating attacks, the 23rd IC under Friessner and consisting of the 78th AD, 216th ID and 383rd ID, continued their attack toward the heavily fortified strongpoint of Maloarkhangelsk. Plenty of engineers were with the assault to help with the minefields. The 23rd IC was to join up with 41st PzC east of Ponyri. The 20th IC under Roman, consisting of the 45th ID, 72nd ID, 137th ID and 251st ID, stayed behind the front line to protect against the Soviets getting behind and rolling up the front forces, primarily the 46th PzC. snk106. dgk87m. dgr199m. nzk84. dgk92m. lck116m. zzk372.

On the west flank, the 258th ID, 31st ID, and 7th ID of 46th PzC attacked the 280th RD and 132nd RD of 70th Army at 0930 hrs in the Tureika area. The 7th ID soon occupied Tureika, driving the 175th RD back about 2.5 miles. In the west, the 258th ID took Obydenki Ismailovo, a mile from its start line but was halted by the 280th RD as the Soviets shifted forces to the southwest to meet the threat. At 0900 hrs, Lt General Hossbach's 31st ID took the high ground north of Gnilets, southeast of Tureika, driving the 132nd RD south about four miles. Another important duty for 46th PzC was to protect the right flank of 47th PzC which had the main responsibility of breaking through and driving to Kursk. The general plan of attack for 46th PzC was on the axis: Smitrovsk-Orlovski-Chern Creek-Tysnokoye-Fatezh. The 20th IC on 46th PzC's right flank would drive down the Svapa Creek line. wdk172+. fkk55. fkk102m. dgk87m. snk18. snk106. dgk92m. pck39m.

It was a little after 0900 hrs when Maj General von Kessel's 20th PzD was approaching Bobrik. The commander ordered his artillery be redirected toward Bobrik to soften the village. pck38. pck39m.

At 0930 hrs, after four hours of fierce fighting, the Germans penetrated the Soviet line in two places: Arkhangelskoe and Verkhne Tagino sectors. That morning, Rokossovsky ordered the 2nd TA to move up to the center of the line to plug these gaps. By noon the tankers were on the road and moving toward their new positions, reaching them after dark. Besides plugging the gap, the 2nd TA along with the 16th TC and 11th GTB was tasked with destroying any panzers that were now south of that line and heading for Kashara-Olkhovatka. The 19th TC was subordinated back to 2nd TA and was also moving up to join 2nd TA, arriving at around 1900 hrs. The 16th TC would attack next morning toward Step and Butyriki from the Ponyri II, Kutyriki area. Maj General Sinenko's 3rd TC would attack from the Poselka-Gorodishche line along with Lt General Bondarev's 17th GRC. The 17th GRC was in second echelon and it would take them time to reach their launch point. They would be delayed longer than expected for the *Luftwaffe* had discovered their long convoy in the rear areas and were hitting it as hard as possible to prevent it from reaching the front. The 19th TC would attack toward Saburovka and Podolian but it was late starting as it ran into a minefield that had to be cleared. The 17th GRC consisted of 6th GRD, 70th GRD and 75th GRD. dgr201++. cbk42. nzk87. dgk92m. dgk91.

At 0930 hrs the 15th RD, being pressured by both 47th PzC and 41st PzC in defending the three villages of Iasnaia Poliana, Ozerki and Nikolskaia (not far from Arkhangelskoe) and not having any air support, was forced to fall back about a mile to save itself. Concerned for the quick breakthrough, Rokossovsky ordered a massive aerial counter-attack. At 1000 hrs an air battle took place over Ponyri. The Germans still had the advantage but by noon the Soviets were bringing more planes into the sector and doing a better job in defending themselves and the ground assets. The Germans would still have the advantage by the end of the day but at least the Soviets were realizing the magnitude of the *Luftwaffe* response and trying to meet it. cbk39. dgk87m. dgk92m.

Along a six mile front in the vicinity of Vekh Tagino and running to the Orel-Kursk railway, the 20th PzD began to make progress toward their important objectives of Teploe and Olkhovatka. Model decided to use this as the main axis and directed the 6th ID, 86th ID and 292nd ID to capture those towns which were defended by 15th RD of 13th Army. Lt General Grossmann called sPzAbt 505 to come up to the line to help the infantry reach Teploe. mhz226. dgr198m. fkk102m. zzz101m. dgk87m. dgk92m. lck116m.

East of the 81st RD sector, along the rail line leading to Ponyri, the 86th ID of 41st PzC with support from Maj General Schlieben's 18th PzD and a few Elefants advanced southward toward the town. The 29th RC and the 129th TB stopped the German advance in front of the town four times but the fifth time, the Germans broke through. The 148th RD, deployed northwest of Maloarkhangelsk had to pull back when the 81st RD and the 29th RC fell back to help defend each other's flanks to avoid any flank exposure. The break in the line was near Tosna, northwest of Maloarchangelsk. When Rokossovsky heard of the breakthrough, he sent 350 planes to stop the Germans as well as ordering up several tank brigades from reserve to the area. dgk89. dgk87m. dgr199m. wwf50. dgk92m. dgr111. dgk92m. lck116m. pck41+.

The 23rd IC with Lt General Traut's 78th AD and Maj General Schack's 216th ID supported by Major Karl Noak's sPzAbt 654 (Elefant Battalion) attacked the east flank of the 13th Army defended by the 8th RD and 148th RD. Major Noak was a respected commander and a recipient of the Knight's Cross with Oak Leaves. Assisted by good air support, the 78th AD pierced the first defense belt, advancing six miles to the road from Protasovo to Maloarkhangelsk and continued south of the road, driving the 148th RD back. The 216th ID, despite receiving heavy artillery and mortar fire, advanced due east to Ielisaveto, over six miles from their start line, driving back the 8th RD. The area between Trosna and Protasovo on the Maloarkhangelsk road between the spearheads of the 78th AD and 216th ID was still held by the Soviets. This separation of German divisions could prove deadly if they're not careful. At night, a tank-supported counter-attack in the Trosna area surprised the Germans. Trosna, northwest of Maloarkhangelsk, was north of the main axis of 23rd IC's attack, so the attack hit the vulnerable left flank. Model would spend the next couple days taking Trosna and eliminating the flank threat. wdk174. wdk177+. dgk87m. dgk92m. dgr110. dgr108m. dgr199m. lck116m. zzk372+. pck42.

In the 23rd IC sector, the Ferdinands of sPzAbt 654 would draw near the front line but stop outside the minefield and start firing on the front line. While this firing was taking place, many Goliaths were brought up to clear paths in the minefield to allow the Elefants and infantry move on the line. These "mini remote control tanks" did not always work but when they did, the results were usually impressive. It was important for 23rd IC to capture Maloarkhangelsk by the following day to help screen the Soviet reserves that were already moving forward from reaching and impeding 47th PzC's assault. zzk372+. pck43.

By 1030 hrs, the good beginning was already slowing down along the entire line of the 47th PzC and 41st PzC sectors. In 6th ID sector, the 332nd RR had moved up to the line and countered the Germans, completely stopping their advance. While still at Harpe's HQ, Model called up fire control and redirected the entire battery group of 23rd IC to support the 47th PzC. Model would redirect fire to other sectors throughout the campaign. For now, the 47th PzC had the priority over 23rd IC so despite the hardship placed on 23rd ID, the redirection took place without a moment's hesitation by Model. He also called additional engineers to free up the stuck panzers and men from the minefields. snz229+.

From information gained through prisoner interrogations, Model learned that his initial barrage inflicted heavy casualties on 15th RD and 81st RD. To exploit this weakness Model ordered additional shelling on this line before sending in the 6th ID along with some Tigers. The Tigers were to cross the shallow Oka River and head for Podolian and Butyrki and into the exposed flank of 676th RR. After crossing the Oka but before reaching Iasnaya Poliana the Tigers were ambushed by a large number of T34s in a desperate attempt to destroy them. For the next three hours the two sides fought bitterly but the Tigers, though outnumbered, were getting the upper hand. When the 6th ID arrived the Germans forced their way through the line and then stormed the village of Butyrki shortly after noon. The 15th RD had to evacuate along with the T34s but 42 T34s were destroyed in the fighting. Mk IIIs and Mk IVs followed in the wake of the Tigers and were able to capture the village of Podolian. mhz227. fkk52+. fkk102m. dgk87m. dgr199m. dgk92m. lck116m. zro203.

With the flanking exposure of the 132nd RD on 70th Army's eastern flank, the Germans concentrated the *Luftwaffe* and artillery of the 46th PzC on this area to make a breakthrough. The infantry of the 46th PzC attacked but were met by stiff small arm fire and a deadly minefield, suffering heavy casualties and were forced to fall back. As the battle raged on the ground, a huge air battle took place near Maloarkhanglsk that included German bombers and their escorts and the Soviet fighters. The German escorts won the battle forcing the Soviets from the area after shooting down 100 Red planes. The 46th PzC badly needed this air support and while it did receive some, greater support in the west could have added the extra boost needed to break through. Just like in the south, the *Luftwaffe* did not have sufficient assets in the sector to cover the entire line. dgk90. dgk87m. dgk92m.

On Model's left flank, 23rd IC under Friessner also made modest gains. Using Ferdinands and Goliaths, a two-foot high remote controlled vehicle carrying over 100 pounds of explosives, a path through the minefield was cleared, allowing the spearhead, the 78th AD, to advance. They advanced through heavy fire to the road junction leading to Maloarkhangelsk. Also alongside the Goliaths were the B-IVs which were more useful. These were larger versions that could carry 1,000 pounds of explosives and could clear a larger path of minefield or destroy a larger bunker. Outside of Maloarckhangelsk 8 larger B-IVs cleared the 400 yards on mines to the city limits. pck42. dgk87m. dgk92m.

Despite the lethal support of the Elefants, the 78th AD and 216th ID faced heavy resistance from behind well-constructed defenses, supported by massive artillery deployed to the rear. The assault grenadiers reached their secondary objective of Hill 249.7 but failed to capture their main objective of Hill 255.6. This hill made an excellent OP, allowing for views for miles in any direction. Model wanted that hill and his orders were to take it next morning. The flank attacks coming from Trosna persisted throughout the day and the commander wanted that cleared up as well. zzk372+.

The Ferdinand anti-tank guns escorted the Tigers to protect them but without Infantry to protect the Ferdinands, Soviet infantry were destroying both weapons with satchel charges. In addition to the Ferdinand, Model also had 45 Hornets carrying 88mm assault guns. These Hornets were used by the Pz Abt 655. In the south, Kempf was given the Pz Abt 560 which also sported 45 Hornets. This machine did a splendid job at Kursk and received little attention for its efforts. wdk87+. pck36.

By 1100 hrs, the Germans had penetrated the line and were now approaching Podolian. The 15th RD was taking heavy casualties and was in trouble. On the 15th's right flank the

132nd RD lent them the 712th RR to help protect east of Gnilets. The 712th RR soon found itself in trouble and had to retreat inside Podolian where they were able to repulse the German attack. By this time the other two regiments of 132nd RD were in trouble and were backing up into the other side of Gnilets. Nearby the 280th RD was being pushed back as well. The *Luftwaffe* had switched sectors from 13th Army to 70th Army and their assistance had made a big difference in the gains now being made. By the afternoon, the 81st RD and 15th RD were now forming defenses along the Semenovka-Shirokoe-Boloto-Saburovka line while the 132nd RD and 280th RD were forming up along the southern outskirts of Bobrik, Gnilets, Probuzhdenie, and Izmailovo. The 74th RD had moved up and plug the gap between the boundary between 148th RD and 81st RD. dgr111+. dgk87m. dgr199m. dgk92m. dgr199m.

In 47th PzC sector, the Tigers of sPzAbt 505 were brought in to attack Iasnaia Poliana, just south of Tula, after the air strike and quickly penetrated the Soviet line defended by 15th RD. pc39. dgk87m. dgk92m.

Tigers of sPzAbt 505, supporting the 6th ID, had crossed the Oka River attacking the open flank of 676th RR of 15th RD at dawn. The infantry was following. After capturing Novo Chutor the division headed for Butyrki but the 6th ID had to shift its left flank toward the rear to protect itself from an attack coming from Ozerki forest. Despite this counter the infantry, 6th ID, was able to capture Iasnaia Poliana and reached Hoopoe woods. This Soviet attack was a delaying attempt to allow Soviet reserves to come up and block the panzers and Elefants from reaching Butyrki. Model still held back the 2nd PzD, 4th PzD, 9th PzD and 18th PzD and without their support the German advance started slowing down as the Soviet reserves reached the front. Elefants were new mobile assault guns with thick hides but had no self-defense, which greatly reduced their usefulness; with the withholding of four experienced panzer divisions, the combination was already causing the German advance to start slowing down. At Aleksandrovka, many Elefants were damaged by Soviet infantry. bt82. dgk222m. dlu63m. fkk51+. dgk88. dgk87m. dgk92m. lck116m. kfz456+. pck39.

At noon two additional panzer divisions, the 2nd PzD and 9th PzD, were called up and later that afternoon struck the west flank of the 15th RD, driving the Soviets further south. The east flank of the 15th RD in the Maloarkhangelsk area was hit by another 60 panzers, supported by the 292nd ID of 41st PzC. The 292nd ID had penetrated the first defense belt, reaching Ozerki, about three miles from their start line. Now with the help of the panzers, one regiment of 292nd ID continued on and by 2200 hrs traveled another three miles reaching Butyrki, which had been taken by the Tigers earlier. The line in this 15th RD sector was being threatened but Model did not respond quickly enough with his panzer divisions and Rokossovsky brought up reserves first and plugged the forming gap. To the west, Lt General Weidling's 86th ID encountered minefields and heavy shelling from the 5th Artillery Division that stopped their advance. By the end of the day, the 86th ID had reached Otschki on the road to Maloarkhangelsk, six miles from their start line but the whole division was now stalled. The 41st PzC on this first day penetrated the first defensive belt but were only halfway to the second line that included the important town of Ponyri. wdk173. dgk87m. dgr199m. snk19. pck39. lck116m.

After repeated assaults, the 15th RD and 81st RD of 13th Army's eastern flank continued to give ground; 15 Tigers were at the Oka River firing as they moved along with the lighter Mk IVs to break through the Soviet line of infantry. By noon Rokossovsky could tell the main assault was changing from the Ponyri axis to further west at Olkhovatka, though the Ponyri axis remained important. He moved up 2nd TA and 17th GRC into position to counter the Germans' main assault area at Olkhovatka and the weaker Ponyri axis as well. Model was now attacking along a 25 mile front against Rokossovsky's Central Front. As part of 2nd TA, 19th TC and 9th TC were brought up to the line as well. Three hundred planes were currently supporting the German attack though Model would have liked twice that number. The German front in the north would be about 31 miles wide by the end of the campaign. If the opportunity arose the following day, Rokossovsky had given permission to 2nd TA and 17th GRC to attack in the area between Olkhovatka and Ponyri II. The 19th TC would attack Saburovka and Podolian only. Later in the day, Rokossovsky changed his assault to limit only part of 2nd TA to go on the offensive. The 3rd TC, deployed along the Polsela Goriannova-Gorodishche line, would stay defensive. je100. gjz181. fkk102m. dgr107. dgr112+*. dgk87m. dgr199m. kcz167. dgk92m. dgr199m. dgk88. pck39.

To the east of 47th IC, the 6th ID supported by sPzAbt 505 under the command of Major Sauvant smashed through a defensive screen of T34s and penetrated 15th RD's right flank held by 676th RR. By noon, the Germans captured the villages of Butyrki and Aleksandrovka and threatened the neighboring 81st RD with encirclement on its left flank. On the 81st RD's right flank northwest of Ponyri, the 41st PzC with support of Elefants was decimating that line as well. The *Luftwaffe* was also supporting the 47th PzC in its advance. The Germans were using B-IVs to clear minefields. These were remote control vehicles that usually carried 500 pound bombs or sometimes 1,000 pound bombs and would drop them and move on before the device was detonated. A series of detonations would clear a lane for panzers and infantry to pass fairly quickly. dgk89. snk107. lck251++ lck255. dgk87m. dgr199m. dgk92m. lck116m. kfz457.

The 15th RD and 81st RD were being pushed back at the Semenovka-Shirokoe-Boloto-Saburovka line but then joined forces with 132nd RD and 280th RD who were at Bobrik and Gnilets and together stopped the German attack. The 74th RD moved up to Protasovo to help close the gap between the 148th RD and 81st RD. These six Soviet divisions had been pushed back but were now stiffening their resolve and were slowing the German advance. dgr112. dgr103m. dgr199m.

Near Bobrik the 20th PzD, with the help of engineers clearing mines, pushed forward making penetrations into Rokossovsky's 17th GRC near Olkhovatka. Rokossovsky had placed his main force near Ponyri but the Germans swerved direction, heading toward Olkhovatka. The Soviet 16th TC and 19th TC had to quickly redeploy to meet the new threat. Other redeployments in the north involved moving more of the 17th GRC and 18th GRC eastward near Maloarkangelsk where the 23rd IC was making slow progress. Only later in the day when 41st PzC also engaged Ponyri did the Germans make progress; Rokossovsky had to contend with that as well. rc164. dgr198m. fkk102m. dgk87m. dgr199m. dgk92m.

The 46th PzC under Zorn launched a supporting attack to the right of the main struggle led by 47th PzC along the Smitrovsk-Fatezh line. The 7th ID and 31st ID slowly advanced toward Gnilets against 132nd RD but failed to reach it today. Elements of both divisions after running into a clover field found it was littered with mines. Clearing the mines took time and destroyed the momentum the Germans had. The main objective for the corps was reaching the Svapa Creek line. Once the attack had made some gains the 12th

PzD would come up between the two corps to help secure the Svapa Creek area near Fatezh. The corps also had the 102nd ID and 258th ID. At the same time, the 41st PzC under Harpe and consisting of the 18th PzD, 86th ID, 292nd ID would advance along both sides of the Orel-Kursk highway. The Svapa generally ran east-west just north of Samodurovka. dgk89. snk106. fkk104m. zzz101m. dgk87m. dgr199m. dgk92m. lck116m. pck36.

At 1400 hrs, Model escorted by Zorn of 46th PzC moved up to the line to see how 7th ID and 31st ID on the west flank of 20th PzD were doing. The 46th PzC not only had the responsibility of keeping up with 47th PzC's advance to the south, it also always had to block 70th Army from attacking the flank of 47th PzC. Model left shortly after giving Zorn a little pep talk. His next stop would be the HQ of Friessner's 23rd IC on the far eastern flank. Arriving, Model quickly learned the 78th AD and 216th ID divisions had also stalled against stiff resistance. snz230.

The 86th ID and 292nd ID along with the 45 Ferdinands of sPzAbt 654 breached the minefields of the first defense belt and together were able to make some progress southwards. Venturing too far from the infantry, some of the Ferdinands were destroyed by Molotov cocktails and demolition charges. The Soviet infantry would hide in their trenches until the Ferdinands had passed and then would attack them from the rear where they were most vulnerable. These panzers would often use their valuable 88 shells to shoot down roaming teams of these human tank killers. Inside the tank to save their shells, they would use their MGs shooting out the barrel to stop the attackers. mhz227+. dgk87m. wdk85. dgk92m. lck116m.

When the drive on Maloarchangelsk slowed, Model sent sPzAbt 653 with its 45 Ferdinands to the 78th AD in the hopes that a gap could open up. Even with the extra fire power the 18th GRC's three divisions held the line against the German onslaught. The Germans were able to capture some of the fortified villages in front of the critical city. The Ferdinands left the village of Glasunovka but were slowed dramatically by the many minefields that led to Hill 257 which was the Soviet lynchpin of the first defense belt. Rokossovsky had predicted the two important axes of attack for the Germans would be through Olkhorvatka and Ponyri and built his defenses accordingly. To combat these elaborate defenses, the 78th AD using a dozen Sd Kfz 301 remote control explosive carriers tried to clear a path for the Ferdinands to make it to the top of Hill 257. By the end of the day only 12 of those 45 leading Ferdinands were still fighting. mhz221+. dgk87m. dgr199m. wdk85. dgk92m.

Where the remote control explosive carriers were clearing a path for the Ferdinands, one of them was hit by a shell and exploded causing a chain reaction, destroying two other carriers and a StuG III as well. mhz225. dgk87m. dgk92m.

At 1630 hrs Model arrived back to see Harpe to find out if the extra panzers of 101st PzR (18th PzD) were making a difference in reaching Ozerki. The 508th GR started moving again but still would not reach Ozerki by nightfall. Before Model left, Harpe suggested that the 51st PzGR and 101st PzGR of 18th PzD should be brought up during the night and be ready at first light to help the 6th ID and 292nd ID. The 18th PzD had very few transport trucks left and the infantry attached to the division really were not mobile and would be better suited to support other infantry. Model knew already that extra support would be needed in this sector if the second defensive belt were to be penetrated, but he held off giving Harpe a decision until later that night. snz230.

By late afternoon, the German 86th ID had reached the outskirts of Ponyri. The 86th was then joined by the 216th ID and 78th ADs and launched an attack against the heavily defended road leading to Maloarkhangelsk from Ponyri. The Germans made initial gains but the Soviet 129th TB was brought up and stopped the attack. By the end of day, 47th PzC and 41st PzC had penetrated 4 – 6 miles into the Soviet defensive belt but at great cost. The 292nd ID captured Ozerki and 86th ID, both from 41st PzC, captured Ochki. dgk87m. dgr199m. nzk84. dgk92m. lck116m.

Probably the largest dogfight in the northern salient occurred in the early evening. After an hour of fierce fighting to repulse German attacks, a reported 42 Soviet planes were shot down while only a couple German escorts were destroyed. cbk40. dgk92m.

By late in the afternoon, Model still had the bulk of five panzer divisions waiting to enter the battlefield. It was a decision that would be contested. mhz229. dgk87m. dgk92m.

At 1700 hrs, Model arrived at 47th PzC's HQ to adjust Lemelsen's attack orders for the following day. Model could see the resistance was greater than expected and he would have to accelerate the plan. He told Lemelsen the entire 9th PzD and 2nd PzD would enter battle in the morning. snz231.

While attached to Grossmann's 6th ID, sPzAbt 505 captured the town of Butyrki late in the day and was threatening to unhinge the left flank of the 81st RD of 13th Army which was already under pressure from the 292nd ID of the 41st PzC. The Tigers and Elefants drove through the 81st RD reaching Aleksandrovka. During the battle, Soviet sappers planted more mines with great success, putting 100 vehicles out of action. wwf50. dgk87m. dgk92m. lck116m.

In the 47th PzC sector, the 20th PzD and 6th ID attacked with strong panzer support that included Tigers and air support. The Germans quickly penetrated the first defense belt and by noon was fighting for the second defense belt. By 1900 hrs, the 132nd RD and 280th RD were defending the second defense belt southwest of Bobrik, seven miles south of the German start line. One German regiment reached Saburovka, eight miles south of the start line. By 2000 hrs the Soviet rifle divisions were supported by the 167th GLAR and 206th GLAR from the 1st GAD. The 70th Army also released several tank regiments to the area. wdk173. dgr198m. dgk87m. dgr199m. dgk92m. lck116m.

After being on the road all day, Model arrived at his own HQ at 1900 hrs to discuss with Elverfeldt, his Chief of Staff, plans for the following day. Model actually had more confidence in Harpe than Lemelsen but the master plan had the 47th PzC, the strongest in 9th Army, with primary responsibility of reaching Olkhovatka. Walter Model decided to redirect all *Luftwaffe* support destined for 41st PzC to 47th PzC for the next day. A breakthrough had to happen soon and this was the best way to achieve it. Model never told FM Gunther Kluge of AGC of the many changes he instituted for the following day so it was not surprising Kluge called up later that night complaining that he learned about the changes from a corps commander. Model had been discouraged about the chances for a victory at Kursk after the several postponements, but he was still determined to reach Kursk. Only the 6th ID and the 292nd ID had made it through the first defensive belt and were fighting toward the second belt by the end of the day but at last he realized it would take more than his infantry to reach Olkhovatka. It could also be seen by the end of the first day that 9th Army did not have enough troops or artillery to defeat the Soviet defenses. Late in the day Model did introduce segments of the 20th PzD and the 101st PzR of 18th PzD along with sPzAbt 656 among several other Gun Battalions that contributed to the approximately 500 panzers and assault guns that had been released onto the battlefield, although only about 300 panzers opened the assault. It could be argued that without better air support to speed the advance, putting any more panzers into the attack would have caused even greater traffic jams, presenting the Soviet AF with easy targets. However with judicious planning and allocation of armor and anti-aircraft batteries that heightened risk should have been reduced to the arriving armor. It is also argued that keeping the Tiger and Elefant battalions together instead of splitting them among the divisions might have provided a more concentrated attack along the three main axes of Maloarkhangelisk, Ponyri and Olkhovatka and thus have delivered better results. snz231++.

By the end of the day, many field officers believed Model was mistaken to use just the 20th PzD, sPzAbt 505 and the Elefants for the initial attack. Kessel's 20th PzD, fighting through minefields, barbwire and trenches had made about four or five miles but the advance was narrow and not very convincing. The front was not heavily defended at first but by the start of the second day, Rokossovsky had reinforced it. If the Germans had made it pass the first line on a wider front, it was believed Olkhovatka sector could have been captured resulting in a better chance to reach Kursk. fkk52. fkk102m. dgk87m. dgk92m.

It was almost dark in the second defense zone near Podsoborovka, when the 27th GTR counter-attacked but did not get anywhere. While the 27th GTR paused to refit before attacking, Model had sent panzers to the area in preparation for their next assault. The 27th GTR was overwhelmed. wdk173. fkk102m. dgk87m. dgk92m. dgk120.

The 17th GRC was delayed moving up to the line for the offensive planned for next morning when the *Luftwaffe* struck several times at the moving formation. It was in position in the Ponyri II, Kutyrki area and the Snovo, Samodurovka area by 2030 hrs despite the attacks. dgr113. dgk87m. dgr108m. dgr199m. dgk92m.

At the end of the day Rokossovsky knew his forces had suffered heavy casualties. After dark he traveled along the line giving praise and encouragement to his men. At the same time the corps commanders of 9th Army were staying up late, studying maps and end of day reports, trying to figure out a way to speed their advance. Model, knowing Rokossaovsky's abilities, planned his assault in a cautious manner, not wanting to risk all his panzers until his infantry had created a gap. By the end of the day, the German corps commanders were questioning that logic, believing brute force was the way to go and General Model was beginning to change his mind as well. Model called Lemelsen and told him to bring up the complete 2nd PzD, 9th PzD and 18th PzD and insert them in the Butyrki-Bobrik sector where the Soviets showed the greatest weakness. Rokossovsky had built an amazing defensive system that included trenches, minefields, bunkers, MG nests and wire entanglements and even with these three panzer divisions, it would still be a difficult task to reach Kursk. mjk85. pck43+.

By the end of the day, 41st PzC with the aid of the *Luftwaffe* had reached the northern outskirts of Ponyri. Aerial reconnaissance also discovered major formations of armor moving up from Livny area to Maloarkhangelsk, Ponyri and Olkhovatka. The 120 panzers of 20th PzD of 47th PzC breached the front line of 29th RC by 0900, pushing the Soviets back and then capturing the village of Bobrik. It was stopped shortly afterwards, after arriving at the trench line of 17th GRC's 6th GRD which was in second echelon and supporting 29th RC. The sky was black and vision was poor from the many bombs, shells and mines that were exploding on both sides of the line. pc41++. dgk86**+. dgr198m. fkk102m. dgk87m. dgr199m. dgk92m.

In the north Model's 9th Army advanced six miles on an almost 25 mile front. Starting west of Maloarchangelsk in 23rd IC sector, the infantry breached the Soviet's first line of defense against the 15th GRD and 81st RD. A few other divisions to the west had reached and were fighting for penetration of the second defense but during the afternoon and throughout the night Soviet reserves were moving up to bolster this line and stall the attack. See Map 1. gjz181. dgk92m.

On the extreme left flank of the sector, Lt General Hocker's 258th ID and Lt General Rappard's 7th ID of General Zorn's 46th PzC advanced toward the Kursk-Orel highway, their first objective, but were stopped after nearly two days of trying by the 280th RD. The 7th ID on its flank also met stiff resistance and was stopped. In front of this advance, 9th Army artillery pounded the 13th and 70th Armies and yet the Soviets held the line. Model regrouped his infantry and sent the 20th PzD to attack on a narrower front against the 13th Army's 15th RD which finally had to fall back to the ridge line west of Ponyri. With the 15th RD falling back, the right flank of 70th Army became exposed. The main thrust would now be on the Teploe-Olkhovatka axis. The 23rd IC was still tasked with taking Maloarchangelsk but without a panzer division for support, it would be impossible. bt82. dgk89. mhz220+. dgr198m. fkk102m. zzz101m. dgk87m. lck116m. dgk92m.

Rokossovsky had spent a lot of time on this day planning a counter-attack for next morning to push the Germans out of the penetration zone. This counter-attack was premature and disrupted their defenses more than helped. The Front commander correctly deduced that the attack on his eastern flank was secondary and the attack in the Ponyri-Olkhovatka area was the primary action and took the proper counter measures. Ponyri was 30 miles northeast of Kursk while Olkhovatka was about 25 miles north of Kursk. dgk91. dgr112+. dgr108m. dgk87m. dgk92m. dgr199m. mjk84+.

In the evening, Rokossovsky sent the 3rd TC of 2nd TA to defend the Polsela Goriannova-Gorodishche line. Next morning from the Ponyri II area, it was to attack along with the 16th TC, the 11th TB in cooperation with 17th GRC in the direction of Step and Butryki, in order to plug the breach on the left flank of 13th Army. Once those two villages were captured, this formation would join the 19th TC and attack westward toward Saburovka and Podolian. In addition to the upcoming attack, the 148th RD, 74th RD and 81st RD were brought back to the line with the rest of 13th Army. Rokossovsky was making sure that his line was strong in case the offensive failed. The 19th TC would take so much time to prepare for the attack that it would be late to launch next morning and, without consulting, Rokossovsky abandoned the attack. Step was east of Bobrik and south of Butyrki. See Map 2. dgr113+. dgk116m. dgk87m. dgr199m. dgk92m.

Luftflotte 6 would fly 2,088 sorties today in support of 9th Army's assault. Unlike Hoth, Model planned on using the bulk of his panzers on 7/6 after his infantry made gaps in the line and he was counting on the *Luftwaffe* for another full day of coverage when more of his panzers were deployed. The sPzAbt 505 and Elefant battalions were also on the line. The Soviet 16th AF started out slow but by the afternoon it competed with the *Luftwaffe* almost on an even basis. Tomorrow would be no different. mhz220. dgk87m. dgk92m.

By the end of the day the 23rd IC, though it advanced about five miles into the east flank between the 13th and 48th Armies, failed to roll up the sector. Model wanted to take this sector for the Kursk railroad ran through it and also to disable this flank and prevent it from attacking 47th PzC on its flank when it drove south through Olkhovatka or Ponyri. The theory was logical but Model, just like Hoth in the south, did not have enough men to accomplish both objectives. dgr112. dgr108m. dgr198m. dgk87m.

By the end of the day, Model's forces had broken into the first defensive belt at the junction between 70th and 13th Armies, creating a lodgment nine miles wide and five miles deep, just west of Ponyri. Model had lost many panzers, some say 200 which seems high, but many of them were retrieved at night and repaired. The 46th PzC, 47th PzC and 41st PzC all contributed to the count. During the night Rokossovsky sent reinforcements to the line in the Olkhovatka-Ponyri area where it was obvious Model was using as his main spearhead sector and by next morning resistance had increased. This is where Model went wrong. His first day's assault force was inadequate and it could not break through which gave Rokossovsky time to reinforce the line over night. By next morning the line in the Ponyri-Olkhovatka sector was stronger than it was on the first day. dgk91. snk107. dgr113. dgk87m. dgr199m. dgk92m.

The 47th PzC made five miles the first day but its flanks were being attacked and it was being seriously threatened. The 23rd IC on the 47th's east flank was fighting reserves coming up as well as 350 planes attacking the advance. dgk87m. dgk92m.

The 9th Army gained about six miles that day. It would turn out that it was the best daily gain in the operation for Model and half of the total ground gained. One has to wonder what kind of progress 9th Army could have made that day if more of the panzer divisions led the charge. Personally, my hunch is that it would have made a big difference in reaching and controlling the Olkhovatka heights but the Soviets had too many reserves and would have been able to stop the Germans from reaching Kursk regardless. If the Soviets had had to retake Olkhovatka it would have been horrifically expensive and probably would have impacted their planned counter offensive on the 12th. Model allowed Rokossovsky time to bring up heavy reinforcements during the night to degrade the momentum Model was trying to generate. wdk174. dgk87m. dgk92m.

By the end of the day, Model had one of the worst days of his career. His men and panzers were ravaged, with approximately 7,200 casualties and 60 panzers either destroyed or so severely damaged it would take a long time to repair them. Another 100 panzers were lightly damaged and would be quickly back in the field. One reason for such high panzer damage can be attributed to the new Soviet PTAB bomb. The PTAB was sort of a high velocity cluster bomb that could cover a 3,000 square yard area with one bomb load from an IL-2. It is unimaginable what these cluster bombs could do to the infantry. Model could thank the 1st *Flieger* Division for much of 9th Army's gains. The divison flew almost 2,100 sorties that included nearly 650 from Stukas, 600 from bombers, 520 from fighters and the remainder by mostly recon and transport planes. The Red Air Force flew just over 800 sorties. The 7,200 casualty figure represented 20% of the combat strength of 9th Army. cbk40+. nzk77. dgk92m. snz242+. hsz106.

By the end of the day, the 47th PzC and 41st PzC, positioned in the middle of the line advanced between four to six miles but were still fighting within the first defensive belt. wwf51. dgk92m.

6

July 6th on the Southern Salient

See Map 10

During the predawn hours the 2nd VA bombed the German ammo depot at Tomarovka as well as reserves stationed there. Other targets included Borisovka and Pushkarnogo. At dawn another squadron bombed the *SSTK* positions northwest of Belgorod. Without the presence of German planes, the Soviets had an easy time with the mission. After a horrendous day the day before and with the new day starting out cloudy, Major General Seidemann allowed his pilots an extra hour of rest. At 0900 hrs when most of 4th PzA launched for the day, the *Luftwaffe* was ready to support. About 200 sorties targeted the 52nd GRD and 67th GRD again. The Soviet divisions suffered heavy casualties the previous day but were still giving *LAH* and 11th PzD a tough time. Just west of 67th GRD, the 6th TC was getting hit hard from a second wave of German planes. For the day the *Luftwaffe* flew 1686 sorties. cbk56.

As part of Vatutin's deployment adjustments, the 35th GRC at 0300 hrs started moving its 93rd GRD forward from behind Prokhorovka to the Petrovka-Oktiabrski-Pravorot line behind 69th Army's 183rd RD. They were in place before the end of the day. The other two divisions of the 35th GRC, the 92nd GRD and 94th GRD were sent to 7th GA in the Korocha region to stop 3rd PzC. dgr78. hjj123m. dlu44+.

At 0300 hrs in the Iakovlevo area the Soviet 1st TA's 3rd MC and 5th GTC as well as the 51st GRD were locked in battle with the *LAH*. The Germans launched repeated attacks against the Soviets with more than a 100 panzers when the 31st TC with 160 tanks under artillery fire came up to support. In spite of the reinforcements, by 1100 hrs the Germans had fought their way past, trying to cross the small Pena River. At which point additional tanks and additional artillery joined the battle. By 1500 hrs the Soviets had to withdraw to their second defense belt, allowing the *LAH* fighting along the Cherkasskoe-Pokrovka axis to capture the Alekseevka and Lukhanino areas in which the second defense belt was situated. Even though it was afternoon, so much smoke, fire and dirt was in the air it looked like dusk. Later that afternoon, the 1st GTB of 3rd MC moved up and engaged the *LAH*, slowing its advance. A battalion from the 49th TB, which was currently in reserve, was also brought up to help. The 31st TC consisted of 237th TB, 242nd TB and 86th TB. jp149. dgr212+. dgr209m. lck265. vzz114.

German panzers of the 2nd SS PzC attacked the right flank of Voronezh Front's 2nd GTC west of the Lipovy Donets slowly forcing them back during an all day battle. Throughout the day Soviet fighters would fly in to disrupt the panzers but the *Luftwaffe* was quick to respond, bringing in their own fighters and the Soviet aerial assault was muted each time. The biggest aerial battle over the 2nd GTC occurred toward dusk. Bf-109s shot down many IL-2s but an accurate count is not forthcoming from the German side. Soviet records show 59 planes were shot down in the sector that day. At 2300 hrs, the 5th GTC was brought up to assist the 2nd GTC from falling back any further. While the extra tanks slowed the Germans, it did not stop their advance. cbk57.

In 4th PzA sector the recently arrived forces of the 6th GA include 51st GRD, 89th GRD and 90th GRD were moved up closer to the front line. The 89th GRD would be deployed behind 90th GRD. vzz108. dgk108.

The 6th PzGR of *SSTK* launched near daybreak, around 0400 hrs, toward Hill 225.9 which overlooked the Belgorod, Iakovlevo, Oboyan highway. The Germans intended to take the hill and then cut off the escape route going east from Erik. Launching from the hill, *SSTK* was also planning to attack 375th RD which was guarding the Lipovyi Donets passage to 3rd PzC. The hill and the important road were heavily defended from the woods nearby in the direction of Gonki which was attacked at the same time by 5th PzGR. To make things worse for the Germans, the *Luftwaffe* was not available to lend a hand until later. It would not be an easy engagement. Hill 225.9, nearby Hill 198.3, the woods, Gonki and Erik all fell that afternoon which limited access to the river for the Soviets who were pulling back. At this same time, General Hausser ordered Priess to send a recon group north toward Luchki South to link up with *Das Reich* which was currently engaged with 2nd TC which had crossed the Lipovyi to join battle. gnk130. kuz194. ztc269.

As dawn broke in *LAH* sector, the 1st PzGR was fighting for control of the hills south of Iakovlevo. The 2nd PzGR was defending against a counter-attack for control of Olkhovka, west of Kozmo-Demianovka, and the 315 GR of 167th ID, which was still attached to *LAH*, was fighting in the ravine south of Bykovka. In the afternoon the 315 GR would return to the 167th ID. The Soviets were trying to reclaim ground lost the previous day. zrl216.

The Tigers attached to *SSTK* led the charge for Hill 225.9. The panzers ran over wire entanglements as they were shooting at MG nests and larger bunkers in front of the hill. Other panzers and then grenadiers were following. Eventually the Stukas showed and bombed the top of the hill, causing much destruction to the defenses and the dug-in tanks. By 0630 hrs the hill was in German hands. After taking the hill the Tigers moved south in the direction of Shopino and Ternovka which were the primary sites where the Soviets were crossing the Lipovyi Donets. The 96th TB and the 496th AR were protecting the crossings and started firing on the Tigers with their Paks when the tanks were in range. By 1700 hrs after a hard struggle, the *SSTK* was fighting on the edge of Shopino limits. Soviets in the sector came to help the Shopino garrison but the German artillery was too strong and their attempts failed. Additional tanks were coming across the river and the *SSTK* was being threatened near Smorodino until the German artillery was redirected, stopping the Soviet advance. gnk130. gnk140+. gnk69m. ztc269.

On the southern flank of *SSTK*, the *Eicke* Regiment was advancing toward Erik which was southwest of Hill 225.9. Knowing that *SSTK* was closing in on the sector, the garrison at Erik evacuated southeast toward Shopino. Erik was captured fairly quickly despite the intervention of elements of 2nd GTC which were arriving in sector and *Eicke* Regiment started to secure the surrounding area. gnk140.

The *SSTK* resumed its advance against 375th RD which was defending Visloe, Shopino and Erik which were on the west bank of the Lipovyi Donets. The Germans were trying to squeeze the 375th RD between the 2nd SS PzC and the 3rd PzC. The 275th RD's left flank had to fall back a little before it shattered. vzz115+. dgr80+. dgr155m. dgr173m. dgr280m.

Other elements of *SSTK* pushed Govorunrnko's 375th RD back as it headed east toward Shopino, Ternovka and the Lipovyi River to link up with Kempf. The 375th RD, along with Maj General Lebedev's 96th TB, was able to repulse the attack. This defeat on the perimeter of the battlefield would weigh heavily against the Germans in the days to come; without linking up, it would slow Kempf's progress as well. dgk111. wdk129. dgk222m. dlu63m. dgr155m. dgr173m.

By 0400 hrs, the 2nd SS PzC marched due north against the 6th GA's 52nd GRD with 250 panzers and assault guns, while elements of the *LAH's* left flank advanced up the main road toward Bykovka. The 167th ID's 315 GR was on its left flank and *Das Reich* on the right headed for Berezov and Gremuchi. The *LAH* smashed through the line of the 151st GRR and headed for Bykovka. The *LAH* fought its way into the town but lost 33 panzers, including some Tigers, doing so. The Germans lost so many panzers because the 5th Guards Mortar Regiment had depressed their rockets all the way to fire on the incoming panzers but the panzers had destroyed 21 of the 24 launchers and half of the regiment. At 1610 hours Bykovka fell to the 2nd SS PzGR which then sent a recon patrol to cross the Psel River by nightfall. By 1800 hrs the 2nd SS PzGR captured Kozma-Demitankovka and was within striking distance of the key objective Pokrovka. dgk99+. dgk109*. dgk106m.

The 2nd SS PzC began shifting its axis from Oboyan toward Prokhorovka leaving its intended route from Iakovlevo to Syrtsevo the responsibility of the 48th PzC and to the capture of Oboyan all on its own. The 2nd SS PzC had already engaged the 51st GRD just south of Iakovlevo, quickly forcing it to fall back suffering heavy casualties. Meanwhile, the 11th PzD and *GD* were straddling the Butovo-Iakovlevo road in the region of Olkhovka and Dubrova in order to link up with the 167th ID's 315 GR that was guarding 2nd SS PzC's left flank. If this move could be accomplished quickly, there was a good chance of encircling the 67th GRD and 52nd GRD's 153rd RR in the Novo Cherkasskoe-Trirechnoe-Dragunskoe-Veselyi region. The 2nd SS PzC would be keeping the 51st GRD too busy to come to the aid of these divisions while the *SSTK*, trying to force Col Govorunenko's 375th RD across the Lipovyi Donets in the region of Visloe, Shopino and Erik, would be blocking their way from helping the encircled. Dubrova was east of Lukhanino on the southern banks of the Lukhanino River. vzz115. vzz118. vzz2m. dgk101+. dgr155m. dgr173m. dgr280m. nzk87.

By early morning the 5th GTC had arrived in its assigned area: Teterevino, Ozerovski, two miles northeast of Luchki South, to support the 6th GMRB against the advancing SS divisions. The 21st GTB and the 48th TR also deployed in the Ozerovski area to the left of the east flank of 3rd MC. The 2nd GTC was on the other side closest to the Lipovyi Donets River. vzz125. vzz121+. dgk109.

Kravchenko's 5th GTC, which just moved up, counter-attacked the advancing *Das Reich* in support of 51st GRD south of Iakovlevo but were forced to withdraw with heavy losses. The 51st GRD also withdrew with the tanks. Next to the 51st, the 3rd MC's 1st GTB clung to the fortified towns of Pokrovka and Bolshie Maiachki against the SS PzC's left flank. dgk109.

Krivoshein's 3rd MC was defending the critical Butovo-Dubrova road, the Belgorod-Kursk road and the fortified villages in the Lukhanino, Dubrova and Iakovlevo area, as well as indirectly defending Syrtsevo as the Germans would be coming that way. German troops of the 2nd SS PzC that were moving up would pass through the Iakovlevo sector also, so the 3rd MC had large responsibilities. vzz117+. dgr212. lck265.

At daybreak elements of the *SSTK* launched an attack toward the villages of Nepkhaevo and Sashenkovo, trying once again to force a crossing of the Lipovyi Donets and to screen the rest of 2nd SS PzC's east side. At 0900 hrs after a bitter fight, the *SSTK* captured the two villages from the 155th GRR of 52nd GRD. Burdeiny's 2nd GTC was moving into the area and would try to take the villages back. vzz127. dgk100+. dgk111.

The Soviet line had decidedly stiffened from the redeployment of Katukov's 1st TA during the pre dawn hours to forward positions along the line running from the villages of Melovoe, eastward through Syrtrsevo and on to Iakovlevo. This line was already defended by the 6th GA but Vatutin wanted it stronger to stop the Germans here at the second defense belt. Vatutin had even sent Kravchenko's 190 tanks of 5th GTC to this line to be added with Katukov's 525 T34s and 109 T70s. Burdeiny's 2nd GTC was sent forward to occupy positions near Gostishchevo to the east of the Lipovyi Donets River. The right flank of 2nd SS PzC would be heading in this direction and Burdeiny just beat them to this area only by hours. This was an extremely lucky turn for the Soviets because the chances of *SSTK* crossing the river without the blocking presence of 2nd GTC was high and if the *SSTK* crossed the river, it would have had major impact on the defenses of 69th Army and a corresponding beneficial effect on 3rd PzC. Vatutin had originally planned a counter-attack for today but the German drive the previous day was so strong he rescinded the attack for these defensive actions. Vatutin, though wanting a major counter offensive, approved these local attacks in order to slow the German advance and allow his forces to prepare better defenses. mhz230. vzz3m. cbk56. vzz5m.

Hoth had begun his assault with Tigers and/or Panthers in the lead and with the IIIs and IVs in the rear and he would continue this practice throughout the campaign. This maneuver nullified the advantage of the Tiger's longer range gun and put these valuable weapons at the mercy of the strong anti-tank defenses of the Soviets. The 48th PzC and 2nd SS PzC were moving along converging roads through Pokrovka and leading to Oboyan. Chistiakov's 6th GA would take the brunt of these two corps. The panzers were to cross the Psel and establish a bridgehead by the end of the day but grossly failed to achieve this objective. dgk94*. dgk106m.

Although losing some 15 panzers the previous day, the 2nd SS PzC was fielding a greater number of panzers on the battlefield on this day due to the repair shops returning panzers to the field. Advancing along a narrow frontage of six miles that lay between the rivers Vorskla and the Lipovyi Donets, the *LAH* and *Das Reich* bit hard into the Soviet defenses. The key objectives for the day were to secure a number of key heights. *LAH* assaulted Hill 243.2 held by 1st GTB and 51st GRD to the east of Iakovlevo, a key road junction, in a bid to outflank the heavily fortified village. With the support of artillery, the *LAH* advanced toward the hill in four columns marching across the Chapaev-Shepelovka area where Katukov's artillery began shelling them. Even against the heavy shelling, 1st PzGR of *LAH* captured Hill 243.2 by 1130 hrs. The 2nd PzGR was then called up to assemble on nearby Hill 232.0 before moving out. The *Der Führer* Regiment had the lead to take this hill but got hit by heavy shelling which slowed their advance making it impossible for the regiment to reach the hill. They were redirected toward Luchki South. This hill and Hill 246.3 were surrounded by open ground and were an ideal attack route for the panzers. To the west and east of this area you had the swamps of the Vorskla or Lipovyi Donets Rivers. At this point it is estimated that the 2nd SS PzC, with the attached Tigers, had 334 panzers and 44 assault guns. Of these, the *LAH* had 99 and *Das Reich* had 121 while *SSTK* had just over 100 panzers. Shepelovka was located on the eastern bank of the Pena River about midway between Zavidovka and Lukhanino and was a mile north of the twin villages of Krasnoe and Alekseevka. mhz232. dgr209m. vzz120+. zrl216. zow143.

Maj General Tavartkiladze's 51st GRD was defending the sector that included

Solonets, Iakovlevo, Luchki South, Teterevino South, Malinovka as well as Hill 229.4, Hill 226.0, Hill 243.2, Hill 246.3 and Nekhaevka. The sector had a front of ten miles, longer than normal, but it did have the 52nd GRD supporting it and right behind these two divisions were a number of tank brigades that had moved up to the second defensive belt during the predawn hours. Within this ten mile range there were only a number of areas that could support panzer travel and Tavarkliadze, gambling, deployed most of his troops in these likely spots. The 51st GRD started the campaign with nearly 11,000 but it had quickly fallen to under 9,000 men. As expected, *LAH* and *Das Reich* were assembling over 100 panzers for the assault on the 51st GRD on a four mile front where the terrain was relatively flat. That optimal sector that would take the SS through Iakovlevo and Solonets was defended by Lt Col Sushkov's 154th GRR and when the Germans plowed through this sector, the 154th GRR would suffer heavy casualties.The Werfer Regiment, using their rocket launchers, hit Hill 243.2 and Hill 246.3 before *LAH* launched their attack. *Das Reich* was late arriving and could only launch a small portion of the division against the right flank of Hill 246.3. *Das Reich* was really needed for this difficult operation and, with the bulk of the attack falling on *LAH*, it cost them heavily. The Germans made three unsuccessful attacks before pulling back and letting their artillery soften up the Soviet line. Then 150 Stukas came in and dropped their loads on the position. Around noon the 2nd SS PzC launched another attack from Kozmo-Demianovka toward the hills which failed also. An hour later the Germans shifted direction a little and attacked Luchki South. By 1500 hrs, Luchki South and Nekhaevka were in German hands. The 51st GRD had to withdraw to the northwest. Hill 210.7, closer to Teterevino, was still defended by the 158th GRR. vzz118+. vzz6m+.

The previous day, the 51st GRD had moved south from the second defense belt in order to slow the 2nd SS PzC after penetrating the first line. Early on this day, while still preparing defenses, the *LAH* and *Das Reich* resumed its attack through the second defensive belt. wdk129.

On the east bank of the Lipovyi Donets, the west tributary of the Donets, the 155th RR of 52nd GRD and elements of the 2nd GTC were holding a defensive position against *Das Reich* and *SSTK*. To the south along the (Novi) Lipovyi Donets, the 375th RD, 496th TDR and the 96th TB were defending Shopino and Ternovka against the south flank of the *SSTK*, straddling the Belgorod-Kursk road. After dark, the Soviets countered with infantry riding on T34s but the attack failed and the Soviets suffered heavy damage. wdk129+. dgk222m. dlu63m. fkk135.

At 0730 hrs the 1st PzGR of *LAH*, supported by the 55th Werfer Regiment, attacked toward Hill 243.2 (west of Hill 246.3 and Luchki South but east of Iaklovlevo) but were repulsed by heavy artillery fire. Heavy German artillery countered the Soviets and by nightfall *Das Reich* moved up to assist in capturing Hill 243.2 and clearing the road to Luchki South. Panzers moved through and started driving toward Prokhorovka. From Pokrovka to Bolshie Maiachki, the 3rd MC with support from the 51st GRD countered, trying to block the Germans. To slow the Germans, Soviet aircraft and artillery fired on the German column to give time for the 6th GA and 69th Army to reach Prokhorovka. The Soviet attempts slowed but did not stop the German advance. rkz167. dgr209m. vzz2m. vzz3m. lck266. gnk114. gnk112m+. zrl216.

Though busy in the western sector, Siedemann diverted part of the 8th *Flieger* Corps of *Luftflotte* 4 to the east when Kempf signaled a desperate request for air support. With not enough planes or fuel, the *Luftwaffe* could not handle the needs of all the ground forces at the same time. When the planes went east, the support in the west declined, especially in 48th PzC sector, allowing Soviet fighters to temporarily take control of the skies in the west and knocking down ten aircraft in a short period of time. cbk56.

After an artillery preparation, the *LAH* attacked and quickly tore a two mile gap in the line in the 51st GRD sector that would eventually lead toward Prokhorovka. By 0945 hrs, *LAH* was ordered to Hill 243.2 to assist *Das Reich* which was having trouble in reaching it from the east. Nearby, the 2nd GTC sent a tank company to the line Hill 243.2 – Hill 246.3 to try to plug the gap and another tank company to the line Petrovski-Nekhaevka. With the threat of the 2nd GTC moving in from the river, *Das Reich* left Hill 243.2 to *LAH*, moved east and focused on Hill 246.3, Luchki South and the 6th GMRB of 5th GTC and the supporting 2nd GTC defending the area. The defenders put up stiff resistance but were overwhelmed and had to scatter. *Das Reich* did not stop to clear the village and moved on toward Kalinin where Kravchenko's 5th GTC's HQ was located. The staff had to quickly retreat to Iasnaia Poliana when German panzers were seen suddenly approaching the town. The German pressure was too much and the garrison soon followed. When Vatutin heard of this breakthrough, he ordered the 1st TA, 2nd GTC and 5th GTC to counter-attack immediately but events did not turn out the way Vatutin planned, for the Germans were moving too quick and the Soviets had to stay defensive. Hill 243.2 was east of Iakovlevo while Hill 246.3 was just southeast of the fortified town of Luchki South. See Map 23. vzz121*+. vzz125. vzz7m. gnk114+. agk99+. kcz168. dgk106m. dgr209m.

The leading combat group of *LAH* resumed its advance northward from Teterevino South and by 0900 hrs had reached the anti-tank ditches in front of Hill 258.2 and along the road to Prokhorovka, southwest of the Komsomolets State Farm, when they were ambushed by many T34s of 5th GTC. *Das Reich*, to the right of *LAH* and little behind it, was also later attacked by 2nd GTC. The attacks were repulsed and by 1000 hrs, *LAH* had captured Luchki North and on its western flank was now approaching the village of Pokrovka while *Das Reich* continued to try to liquidate a number of tanks from 5th GTC that were pocketed. Despite both divisions advancing they were constantly defending their flanks which did slow them down. By the end of the day, *LAH* reported to Hausser that 75 tanks were destroyed and 123 POWs captured. *LAH* also reported 84 dead, 384 wounded and 19 missing. The 285th RR of 183rd RD was defending Hill 258.2. See Map 10. fkk136. vzz3m. vzz8m. vzz130. nzk87. zrl217.

The 2nd PzGR of *LAH* was ordered to march to Luchki North and secure it. The regiment would then screen the rest of the division as it moved further north as well. wwf85.

With all the recent rains, the roads were still very bad and *Das Reich* was behind schedule in starting its attack at the scheduled 0730 hrs. At 0930 hrs *Das Reich* resumed its attack on Hill 246.3 which was situated on the outer edge of the second defense belt. The assault of the hill would be led by Schulze's *Der Führer* Regiment. As *Der Führer* was advancing toward the hill, artillery pounded the ground to the north of it, softening the resistance. Once a penetration was made, additional forces would come in to add support. The first attack was repulsed but after Stukas bombed the front line, a second attack was successful. At this point Kruger ordered Reitzenstein's panzers to move out and exploit the gap at Hill 246.3. Once over the hill, the panzers shifted direction and headed for Luchki South. By 1400 hrs, the lead panzers had reached Hill 232.0 and were less than a mile from their objective. While the panzers were traveling the long way around the town, the

Grenadiers took the direct route. Despite being attacked at Hill 232.0, they both attacked the town on time and by 1500 hrs, Luchki South was in German hands. There is some confusion about the Hill designation. One source calls it 232.0 and another source calls it 232.6. gnk124. vzz3m.

As the *LAH* was advancing northward, Tigers from 13th Company were approaching Luchki South when they were fired on by a battery of 15cm guns. Taking evasive measures, Wittmann and his four fellow Tigers moved in on the big guns and were able to silence them without losing a man. Once past the destroyed guns, the Tigers entered Luchki and were ambushed by waiting tanks. Kleber's lead Tiger was hit and could not move; Wittmann and Warmbrunn moved up to protect Kleber while he repaired his track, and to fire on the enemy tanks. Four assault guns were destroyed. Without pausing, the five Tigers moved on toward Luchki North, a couple miles away. This time the company was not so lucky. Approaching Luchki North, the Tigers were ambushed by hidden KV1s. The lead Tiger was hit hard, erupting into flames. The crew jumped out and were running for cover but were killed by machine gun fire. The remaining four Tigers were able to move in and take out the two heavy tanks. fzk307+.

It had rained during the night and by sunrise the roads were still muddy but by 1030 hrs, the Soviets were moving. Supported by 30 tanks, they attacked *LAH* near Nasiana Poliana but were repulsed. *LAH* was also attacked northwest of Teterevino. *Das Reich* sent a battalion of panzers up to assist *LAH* in repulsing the attack. fkk134.

Vatutin had already formulated German intentions. The Oboyan route would be primary and it would be attacked in a two pincer formation using 48th PzC taking the western route and the 2nd SS PzC taking the eastern route. The Germans, on their way to Oboyan, would try to encircle as much of 1st TA and 6th GA and destroy. In order to prevent this from happening, Vatutin brought up tank reserves. The 1st TA would now defend the Melovoe-Syrtsevo-Iakovlevo sector while the 5th GTC would have the Iakovlevo-Nekhaevka-Teterevino area. The 2nd GTC would have the Rozhdestvenka-Druzhnyi line. Rifle divisions from 6th GA and 69th Army were also being moved up. Druzhnyi, on the eastern bank of the Lipovyi Donets River, was south of Rozhdestvenka, not far from Gostishchevo. dgr78+. dgr76m+.

After taking Hill 243.2, the 2nd PzGR of *LAH* moved along the east bank of the Vorskla River trying to recon the area. The 1st PzGR spotted the Soviets falling back toward the Olkhovka-Dragunskoe area as they headed north. The next few miles the Germans would move quickly against light resistance. Panzers, which included a few Tigers in the lead and motorized infantry, were immediately ordered to fill the vacuum of the retreating Soviets. Before long the German convoy saw tanks, about 40, from Major General Kravchenko's 5th GTC moving toward them. Tigers opened up and destroyed the leading tanks but they still kept coming, all the while Soviet guns kept firing on the panzers from a nearby hill. The Tigers kept firing and the T34s had to reverse course and head east or northeast to avoid being destroyed. The range advantage of the Tigers was hard to overcome. gnk115+. gnk112m+. vzz6m.

On the way to Luchki, Wittmann and his fellow Tigers were accidently strafed by the *Luftwaffe*. Wittmann, thinking fast, opened his hatch and brought out his Nazi flag, placing it on top of the engine compartment to stop any further collateral damage. agk102.

At 1130 hrs, the *LAH* and *Das Reich* resumed their attack along the Iakovlevo line and found little resistance in 51st GRD which was already falling back into Dubrova, a key part of the second defense belt. The gap that was created between 51st GRD and 52nd GRD was quickly filled in by elements of 31st TC and the 1st TB of the 3rd MC, north of Iakovlevo. *Das Reich* was also attacked by the 230th TR east of Iaklovlevo but both attacks were uncoordinated and were repulsed. The Soviets attempted a counter but it was repulsed. The 100th TB of 31st TC moved up to Bolshie Maiachki behind the 52nd GRD. By 1400 hrs, *Das Reich* was still stalled at Luchki South by 5th GTC using Churchill tanks. *Das Reich* fell back, regrouped and attacked again in late afternoon. At the same time the 2nd GTC, supported by the 48th GTR east of Luchki, also attacked *Das Reich*'s southern flank and the north flank of *SSTK*, and together the Soviets stopped *Das Reich*'s advance on the west bank of Lipovyi Donets River. After dark *Das Reich*'s left flank was able to move another mile north of Iakovlevo against 5th GTC. At midnight *Das Reich* stopped for the day and went defensive. Later that day, north of Iakovlevo, *Das Reich* eventually met up with the 122nd GAR of 5th GTC. A battle ensued but Kruger did not want to fight so late and had his forces move back for the night. The enemy would still be there in the morning and his men would be more rested for the fight. He would also have time to move artillery up closer to the line to assist when the battle was renewed. wdk129. dgr212. dgk222m. dlu63m.

After failing in taking Iakovlevo, *LAH* regrouped and after a 90 minute barrage launched another attack by 1130 hrs on the village. Repeated attempts failed but by next morning *LAH* finally forced the defenders out of town. Iakovlevo was the boundary line between 3rd MC and 5th GTC. The 1st GTB of 3rd MC was hit the hardest but still held the line while other elements fell back, allowing the town to be entered. The 49th TB would be sent after dark to bolster the line with 1st GTB. At 1430 hrs the Germans advancing along the Cherkasskoe-Pokrovka axis succeeded in capturing Alekseevka and Lukhanino which were also defended by the 3rd MC. The 10th MB had put up fierce resistance and the Germans had to call in the *Luftwaffe* for assistance before the Soviets started pulling back. From the Olkhovka area, the Germans repeatedly attacked the 1st MB but failed each time. Olkhovka was southwest of Iakovlevo and northwest of Vorskla situated on the east bank of a tributary of the Vorskla River. dgr80. dgr212+. vzz2m. dgk108.

The only force of Vatutin's that was able to attack as originally planned was Burdeiny's 2nd GTC. The 2nd GTC's 200 tanks moved into the Gostishchevo area, east of the Lipovyi River and prepared to attack 2nd SS PzC when it arrived. The other units who were to attack found themselves in defensive roles. dgk102+. vzz3m. vzz5m.

Das Reich was not only busy attacking northward; its eastern flank was struggling to hold its line against repeated attacks from the 155th GRR of 52nd GRD and elements of 2nd GTC along the Lipovyi Donets River. South of 52nd GRD, the 375th RD, 496th TDR and the 96th TB were trying to block *SSTK* from entering Shopino and Ternovka, a little further south. wdk130. dgr76m. dgr86m. dgr93m.

The *LAH* then attacked 10th MB of 3rd MC but the tankers absorbed four attacks from many panzers as well as air attacks. At the same time the 1st MB held back eight attacks from the Germans advancing toward Olkhovka. The Germans, having lost many panzers, eventually pulled back to regroup. Leaving a small screen there, the *LAH* shifted direction and attacked 5th GTC on its flank and by 1800 hrs captured Luchki South, driving the tankers back to the north and northeast. Before stopping for the night, the *LAH* also captured Kalinin and Ozerovski and was threatening to split the boundary line between 1st TA and 5th GTC. After hearing Luchki had fallen, Vatutin ordered at 2050 hrs the 31st TC to deploy into the Krasnaia Poliana area. To strengthen the 31st TC, the

29th Anti-tank Brigade was attached. dgr213 dgr209m. vzz116. dgk108.

The 2nd SS PzC was ordered to complete capturing the second defense belt. As the *LAH* headed north it was slowed by intense fire near Iakovlevo on the Oboyan highway by the 3rd MC of 1st TA. After ten hours of fighting without taking the village, elements of the *LAH* and *GD* on either side of the village went around and headed in the direction of Luchki South and Teterevino So. A little later Iakovlevo also fell. Katukov quickly responded by sending Col Morgunov's 200th TB of 6th TC, 29th Anti-tank Brigade and part of 31st TC to block the Germans northeast of Iakovlevo, while all of 5th GTC prepared to attack at Teterevino. Before the 5th GTC could attack, *LAH* was able to push the 200th TB and 31st TC back to the north of the town in some of the worst trench warfare of the campaign, finally securing Teterevino by nightfall, around 1700 hrs. The infantry of the 183rd RD were defending the line between Teterevino and Iasnaia Poliana before being evacuated from their trenches. It had been raining and the trenches had deep water in them. Nearby, the *Das Reich* was assaulting the railroad embankment at Belenikhino. Despite suffering heavy casualties, Commander Kruger captured the railroad section. fkk82+. fkk133. lck274. wwf85. gnk113m. dgk129.

By 1200 hrs, Vatutin sent orders to 1st TA and 6th GA to attack next morning. The Germans advanced too far in the afternoon and Vatutin had to cancel the offensive with orders to stay defensive. By the end of the day, all reserves of Voronezh Front had been committed to the second defense belt. dgr82.

On two hills near Iakovlevo, about 1,100 yards apart, 1st TA and *LAH* were firing at each other. After an hour of shelling, twelve T34s were in flames; they could not compete with the thick skins and long guns of the Tigers. With a crisis building the 5th GTC was moved from the northeast into an area just east of the Donets River in the Prokhorovka area. wwf83++.

While *LAH* and *Das Reich* were driving north, a large contingency of *SSTK* were fighting off repeated attacks on the flanks by 2nd GTC and 96th TB. Leading elements of *SSTK* initiated a small break in the Soviet line and penetrated to Iakhontovo. The German engineers, while under fire, were busy clearing mines for the Tigers to proceed. By nightfall the *SSTK* had crossed the important Kursk-Belgorod rail line. The *SSTK* was now only twelve miles from the southern bend of the Psel River but it was concerning Hausser that so many forces of the *SSTK* were being used on the flanks and not for the drive north. By the end of the day, the 167th ID was still tied down helping 11th PzD from its predicament and unable to take over flank protection as it was originally tasked. mhz233. cbk57. gnk113m.

The *LAH* and *Das Reich* were gaining ground in the middle of their sector. By 1200 hrs, the *Der Führer* Regiment of *Das Reich* had captured Luchki South, driving the 6th GA back. The *LAH* was even further north than *Das Reich* and had traveled 20 miles since the previous day, but now these divisions were engaging with tanks of the 1st TA and their advance would slow. *LAH*'s first encounter with 1st TA was near Iakovlevo between two hilltops. wwf83.

The *Das Reich* of 2nd SS PzC had entered the village of Luchki South by 1200 hrs, 12 miles in from their first defense belt in the 6th GA sector. The 5th GTC made several counter-attacks but were repulsed each time. Other deployments were being made as well. The 49th TB was moving to Pokrovka while 31st TC was on its way to Bolshie Maiachki. The 2nd GTC and the 96th TB were moving along the Lipovyi Donets continuing to attack 2nd SS PzC's east flank in order to dilute its northward lunge. Next door in *LAH* sector, the Pz commander, Michael Wittmann, in his Tiger knocked out 8 tanks and 7 anti-tank guns this day alone against the 6th TC. Teterevino, southwest of Prokhorovka, was entered and in the process of being secured as darkness fell. At the end of the day, Vatutin ordered 6th TC back to form a new defense line south of Oboyan. rc176. dgk94. dgk109. dgr209m. lck267.

The 2nd SS PzC's *LAH* punctured the second defensive belt of 6th GA and were heading northeast toward Teterevino North but, with infantry trailing, the panzers were poorly protected. Aerial reconnaissance spotted two enemy columns moving toward this sector. The first column was heading south toward Teterevino North and the other column had crossed the Lipovyi Donets River near Nepkhaevo and was heading west. This second column if not stopped could maneuver behind *LAH* and between the two forces trap and destroy the German force. Hausser ordered a reinforced battalion that was currently at Luchki South to immediately head north and slow if not stop the second enemy column. The panzers near Teterevino North would have to handle the first column on their own. Before reaching the town the panzers hit a minefield, knocking out four panzers and a blocking defense that was too strong to take. It was just about dark so the Germans pulled back and set up a defense for the night; the 1st PzR would try again in the morning when more of the division arrived. Even with little progress, the 2nd PzC claimed to have destroyed 173 tanks and captured 1609 POWs on this day. dgk109+. dgk124m. zrl217.

At 1300 hrs after driving the Soviets out of Luchki South, *Das Reich* was closely following the retreating 51st GRD and 5th GTC. Breaking into two combat groups, the first group headed for Ozerovski and the second group in the direction of Sobachevski and Kalinin. With *LAH* and *Das Reich* in the area, it was clear Hausser was trying to encircle the 5th GTC. The isolated attack by 22nd TB from the Kozinka woods in the direction of Hill 232.0 and from Luchki South failed. Kravchenko sent the 21st TB and the 48th GTR to help the 22nd TB but without artillery support even working together could not stop the 2nd SS PzC. The Germans crushed the 22nd TB near the villages of Ozerovski and Kalinin while the other two units had been encircled near the Kozinka woods. Afterwards, the 2nd SS PzC attacked toward Belenikhino Station and Storozhevoe. The 5th GTC lost 110 tanks in engagements that afternoon. The *Luftwaffe* was busy here and across the entire line, having flown about 1500 sorties. vzz123+. vzz7m.

The 2nd PzGR of *LAH* were struggling to move north. Soviet tanks from the 49th TB coming from Pokrovka continued to harass the infantry at every turn. Nearby the 315 GR of 167th ID was still mired in fighting to clear the Vorskla River bank in the Streletskoe area. Resistance was finally lessening as the Soviet defenders started to fall back toward Pokrovka. In the afternoon with the *LAH* making progress, Katukov ordered Chernienko's three tank brigades of 31st TC to attack the lead units of *LAH*. By late afternoon five tank brigades (100th TB, 49th TB, 1st GTB, 242nd TB and 237th TB) were attacking *LAH*'s west flank. Wisch had no reserves to send Lt Frey and ordered him to take care of the situation on his own. Frey stopped his advance and went defensive. The fighting continued into the night but the Soviets were not unable to roll the flank up. One Tiger was destroyed by a direct hit from a KV1 at 600 yards; the whole crew was killed. The other Tigers continued to fire at the flashes; Wittmann fired at the tank that killed his comrades and destroyed it. The Tigers destroyed all the dug-in tanks and many of the mobiles before the rest bugged out. The flak guns that were part of the convoy continued to fire at Soviet fighters while the tank battle ensued. Toward evening, Chistiakov pulled his men along the

Vorskla River from all towns south of Pokrovka, enabling the 315 GR to move up. gnk118+. zrl216.

After taking Hill 243.2, a combat group from *LAH* shifted to the northwest and headed for Hill 230.5, north of Iakovlevo. *Das Reich* was still tied down on the right side of Hill 243.2 near Luchki South under terrific fire by 52nd GRD and 67th GRD. Stalling in this sector delayed the whole division. The Germans brought up additional artillery and assault guns and with the help of the *Luftwaffe* pounded the Soviet positions for 90 minutes before trying another attack. When the attack began the Soviets could not hold and started to fall back to positions currently held by 1st TA. By midday, Luchki South (*DR*) and Iakovlevo (*LAH*) had been taken. Initially the 51st GRD was able to stop *LAH* several times but eventually the 51st GRD fell back to just south of Sukho Solotino and Malye Maiachki. Hill 230.5 to the north of Iakovlevo still had to be taken before *LAH* could move further north. A garrison from *LAH* remained at Iakovlevo to keep it from falling back into enemy hands, for there were still raiding parties in the area looking for easy prey. mhz232+. dgr209m. vzz120+. vzz7m. zow144.

Four Tigers attached to *LAH* that were approaching Luchki North landed in a minefield. Wittmann in the lead Tiger was struck by a mine which caused track damage to his right side and loss of mobility. Waiting T34s started firing on the damaged Tiger. There was no damage to the panzer but the men could not evacuate it to fix the track due to the heavy fire. A second Tiger moved up behind Wittmannn and its men jumped out while still under fire and hooked chains between the two Tigers. With Wittmannn being pulled, the two Tigers started moving back to a place of safety. The three working Tigers resumed their advance toward Luchki North while Wittmann's crew repaired the track. A small defensive battery position in front of Luchki North started firing on the Tigers. The Tigers started to return fire and by 1400 hrs had destroyed the Soviet battery and forced its men back into town. The Tigers entered the town and a new line of tanks, including KV1s from Kravencho's 203rd TR, started firing on them. The Tigers systematically destroyed every Soviet tank before moving north of town. While this action was occurring, Soviet fighters were attacking German fighters who were trying to soften the defenses that the ground forces were heading for. gnk117+. agk100.

The left flank of 6th GA (51st GRD, 52nd GRD and 67th GRD) had suffered heavy casualties and was in disarray. When Katukov was ordered to counter-attack toward Iakovlevo, Luchki South and Teterevino to stop *LAH* and *Das Reich*, which had penetrated the line, it was not an easy task. The 2nd SS PzC was heading for Gresnoe, Bolshie Maiachki and Kochetovka where Katukov was stationed. Katukov still had to defend his other sectors but he did the best he could. By 1330 hrs, Krivoshein's 3rd MC was ordered to race the 49th TB to the aid of 1st GTB (Col Gorelov) in the area north of Iakovlevo to plug the gap. The 31st TC was ordered to send its 100th TB to the north of Iakovlevo at the collective farm at Mikhailovka where it was to attack 1st PzGR. *LAH* was moving too fast; they were already at Luchki North and the 100th TB had to intercept the Germans in the area of Ulianov, Bolshie Maiachki and Iablochki. The 1st PzGR of *LAH* had not done quite as well but it did capture the difficult Hill 230.5, 2.5 miles northeast of Iakovlevo where other elements of *LAH* were still clearing the last of the resistance in house to house fighting. The 1st PzR of *LAH* had reached the Luchki South-Teterevino South line by 1300 hrs and were advancing for Teterevino North. Teterevino North, a short distance south of KSF, was 11 miles north of Teterevino South. At this moment, *Das Reich* was in the Luchki South sector approaching Teterevino South while *LAH* was fighting toward Teterevino North. vzz123. vzz127+. lck269. zrl216. zow144.

At 1315 hrs, elements of the 51st GRD and supported by 38 tanks, driving southeast from Iakovlevo, counter-attacked the 1st PzGR of *LAH* near Hill 243.2. The Germans were able to repulse the attack while destroying eight tanks. agk100. vzz2m.

LAH was ordered to move to Luchki North to give support to *Das Reich*, which had just taken the town but was still meeting stiff resistance. The Germans had opened a gap in the 6th GA line and were well on their way to gaining ten miles today. bt84. dgr209m.

Vatutin had to bring up most of his reserves to plug the gap south of Oboyan as well as shift the 38th Army to 40th Army sector where they were needed. Tomorrow, Vatutin would have to tap the reserves of those two armies as well. Later that night, Stalin agreed to release the 5th GTA to Vatutin but it would take days to arrive. With reinforcements arriving to the front, Vatutin ordered the 52nd GRD to the rear. Katukov of 1st TA ordered the 31st TC to seal off 2nd SS PzC's advance from the west. To help with this assignment, Col N.M. Ivanov's 100th TB was brought up to the line at Bolshie Maiachki. Once the 100th was deployed, the battered 52nd GRD would fall back to regroup. dgk113. dgk111. dgr209m. vzz159. gjz183+. cbk56+. zro206+.

After taking Luchki South and the surrounding area, elements of *Das Reich* (2nd SS PzC) advanced on Belenikhino Station, where the makeshift tiny garrison put up stiff resistance, repulsing the larger attacker which fell back to Kalinin to regroup. Tanks from Lt Col Okhrimenko's 20th GTB and the remains of Col Occharenko's 21st GTB of 5th GTC started arriving around 2000 hrs, turning the station into a strongpoint. vzz126. vzz7m.

The *LAH* and *Das Reich* were making decent gains that day and by 1400 hrs had both reached the Prokhorovka road axis, at great cost to the Soviets. Lead elements of *Das Reich* with the support of *LAH* had captured Hill 230.5, nearly three miles northeast of Iakovlevo which was still being secured by the bulk of *LAH*. Several Soviet divisions were hit hard; for example the 51st GRD lost 2000 men and 5th GTC lost many tanks. Chistiakov was severely reprimanded for his deploying his tank brigades piecemeal and losing so many tanks. *Das Reich* had pushed the 51st GRD out of Luchki South and were currently pursuing the rearguard, as the bulk of the 51st GRD was heading for Ozerovski and Kalinin to the northeast. The 22nd TB was ordered to attack toward Hill 232.0 to slow *Das Reich* in chasing the 51st GRD but the assault was quickly repulsed. Vatutin also ordered Burdeiny's 2nd GTC which had recently arrived in sector to cross the Lipovyi Donets River and get behind the SS and cut the Belgorod-Prokhorovka road. vzz127+. zrl216.

The 1st PzR had to slow its advance due to running low on ammunition, but at 1430 hrs the supply trucks arrived and the panzers were refueled and reloaded. The panzers were to link up with 1st PzGR and together would head north. zrl216.

The 2nd GTC launched another counter across the Lipovyi Donets River against the 2nd SS PzC's right flank in the Rozhdestvenka-Kriukovo-Novye Lozy area. A reserve battalion was called up to deploy at Luchki near the Lipovyi Donets, to help cover the panzers' flank, when it was discovered additional Soviet tanks (5th GTC) were coming up to the line from the west on Vatutin's orders. Even more tanks from the 31st TC were brought up to cover the line at Bolshie Maiachki. dgk110+. dgk222m. dlu63m. dgr209m. dgr80.

It was after 1530 hrs when the Soviets, probably the isolated companies of 52nd GRD, attacked the garrison that was left at Kozmo-Demianovka but the assault was repulsed with heavy losses to the Soviets. zrl216.

At 1630 hrs, the right flank of 1st PzR was north of Luchki and heading toward Teterevino North. Before reaching Teterevino, the panzers hit a minefield that was covered by artillery and dug-in tanks hidden behind a tank ditch. The air support officer riding with the panzer column called for air support to cover the panzers as they tried to back out of the minefield. The panzers were able to fall back with the aid from the air, and after dark the Soviet tanks attacked but were beaten back. The 1st PzR was lucky that afternoon, escaping with only minor losses. zrl217.

At 0600 hrs, with the original defenders falling back to Iasnaia Poliana after losing Kalinin, elements of the 5th GTC were ordered to Kalinin to defend the area. Having arrived in the Kalinin area by 1700, they were attacked by the *Luftwaffe*. Though receiving heavy casualties, five German planes were shot down. At 1800 hrs panzers attacked; the Soviet AA guns were then used to stop the panzers. At 2000 hrs, Soviet defenders were still trapped but continued to fight until dark when they made a break. The ones that escaped headed north. vzz125+. dgk134+.

At 1700 hrs Kravchenko (5th GTC) ordered Okhrimenko's 20th GTB, which was stationed near Teterevino, to the encirclement near Hill 246.3 and Hill 243.2 (northeast of Iakovlevo) and the woods to the northeast, in the hopes of freeing the encircled 21st GTB, 22nd GTB (5th GTC) and 48th GTR and stopping 2nd SS PzC from getting any closer to Belenikhino Station or Prokhorovka. Attacking from the woods north of Sobachevski, the 20th GTB struck the grenadiers within sight of the station. At 2300 hrs the few remaining tanks in the pocket launched an attack to breakout of their trap, which succeeded by next morning, and drove east of Belenikhino Station, stopping in the woods on the way to regroup. During the breakout only a dozen tanks survived; most of the light T70s were destroyed. vzz124++.

At 1700 hrs, aerial reconnaissance discovered a column of 30 tanks crossing the Donets near Soshenkov. The 3rd PzR of *SSTK* was ordered to intercept and destroy. The 3rd PzR attacked the column of British Churchill tanks and quickly destroyed 15. At 1900 hrs, the Soviet survivors turned and headed for the river. It was learned from prisoner interrogations that the column was from the 48th GTR. The 3rd PzR would meet the 48th GTR next morning when they tried to attack the panzers again. kuz194. vzz7m. zow145.

German planes coming back from recon patrol reported seeing a Soviet convoy of over 150 vehicles approaching the east bank of the Donets River. It turned out the convoy was the 26th GTB of 2nd GTC. The rest of the convoy was not far behind. By next morning Vatutin would have another 200 tanks and 50 more guns to stop the Germans. This was alarming news for *Das Reich*. It was thought that the Soviets would try to encircle *LAH* by going through *Das Reich*. Hausser decided to keep *Das Reich* panzers near the Luchki South-Kalinin-Ozerovski area instead of moving further east until the Soviet intentions were known. gnk125.

In general Hoth's 4th PzA made three penetrations into the Soviet line today, gaining about seven miles. Hausser made more progress but then the Soviets stiffened their defense and stopped Hoth's overall advance. 1st TA with its original 640 tanks was dug-in behind 6th GA which the Germans were passing by, but the 1st TA was determined to repel all attacks. wwf82. dgk94. dgr39m. dgk106m.

With 6th GA in trouble, the responsibility of stopping 2nd SS PzC fell on Katukov and his 1st TA. He planned to crush 2nd SS PzC by attacking from the west and pushing them against the defenses along the Lipovyi Donets. The 3rd MC, 31st TC and the 237th TB would drive from the north and northeast. The 1st GTB, the 49th TB, the 100th TB and the 242nd TB would drive east from west of Pokrovka against the narrow salient the SS had formed. At the same time, elements of the 2nd GTC, 5th GTC, 375th RD, 89th GRD and 93rd GRD would stay in place along the Lipovyi River to make sure the Germans would be trapped. The front line defenses were able to keep the bulk of *LAH*'s infantry south of the Belgorod-Oboyan road for the rest of the day and night. This armor attack would begin in the morning. The attacking units had a combined strength of 383 tanks and that did not include the tanks waiting in the east. The *LAH* would also move forces up to the line during the night and it was a good thing they did; they would be needed to withstand the coming assault. vzz133+. dgr80. dgk106m.

SSTK slowly advanced up the Belgorod-Kursk road on this day, capturing Erik and the adjacent Hill 198.3. Resistance increased as night fell; the panzer regiment stopped at the bridge site west of Shopino to defend it while the grenadiers were bedding down a mile northeast near Ternovka. Shopino was east of Iakhontov, not far from the west bank of the Lipovyi Donets River. After a brief rest, a recon patrol which included panzers were to move out toward Luchki to check out the enemy and to see if *Das Reich* could be found. fkk135. dgk106m. dgk222m. kuz194.

Despite being all alone in the front and being pressured by the heavy resistance, Hausser pushed the *LAH* toward Teterevino North which was almost eight miles from Prokhorovka. gnk119+. gnk113m. dgk106m.

At 1830 hrs Vatutin, talking to Stalin, delivered a sitrep and then asked for more armor, infantry and air support. Vasilevsky seconded the request. It was quickly agreed he would get it. Stalin, against Konev's protests, released Rotmistrov's 5th GTA and 5th GA from Steppe Front reserve to Vatutin's Voronezh Front. It was currently deployed in the dense forest around Ostrogozhsk and the adjacent Kuzmenkov and Kamenka sectors. It had orders to be on the road by daylight of the 7th and to arrive in the Prokhorovka sector as quick as possible. The 5th GTA consisted of the 29th TC, the 5th GMC and the newly attached 18th TC. The only possible reserve Hoth might have, the 24th PzC, was not even in sector. The 23rd PzD and 17th PzD were a part of 1st PzA and preparing for a battle to capture Lischansk in the south. The 5th SS PzD, Viking, was in reserve and not prepared to fight. It was a discouraging thought to General Hoth that he had no realistic reserves left and that he would have to complete the campaign with his existing exhausted forces. gnk151. mhz239. lck272. dgr220. vzz268++. pck74. vzz161.

Once past Teterevino North, *LAH* was approaching Hill 258.2 when the 183rd GRD, which was defending it, opened fire on the leading panzers and the transport vehicles carrying infantry. The panzers continued to advance and ran into another minefield. The Germans had already lost many panzers to mines and yet they continued to be reckless about approaching defenses. Hill 258.2 was situated on the outer limits of the Soviet third defense belt. gnk119. vzz129. gnk113m.

Besides talking to Stalin, Vatutin also wired *Stavka* with a situation report and asked for additional tanks and planes, despite his glowing report of destroying many panzers and stopping the German advance. Vasilevsky recommended the request. By 1900 hrs the next day, Burkov's 10th TC with 165 tanks plus assault guns (Steppe Front), Maj General

Popov's 2nd TC with 168 tanks (Southwestern Front) and the 17th VA were arriving in sector. Both tank corps had been reinforced with anti-tank guns with 85mm barrels and two motorized rifle regiments. Stalin also ordered Konev to release 5th GTA to Vatutin as well. The 5th GA was also being sent with the 33rd RC leading the convoy. With the 5th GTC and 2nd GTC already in sector and fighting along the Donets Rivers, *Das Reich* and *SSTK* were being forced to spend much of their resources fighting flank battles and not fighting to the north to support the *LAH*. In the first two days the Germans had lost many panzers; the 48th PzC was already falling behind and not supporting *LAH* as ordered and besides, the Germans just did not have enough men or panzers to reach Kursk and it was already showing. The additional Soviet tank corps would not be fully assembled in sector for 24 hours but when ready for battle would present a noticeable increase in resistance and greater threat to the German advance. vzz159. gnk152+. gnk245. gjz184+. nzk88. wwf91. wdk132+.

Around 1900 hrs, the *SSTK* was fighting along the Belgorod-Kursk road when the Soviets counterattacked. The Germans were able to repulse the surprise attack, destroying 15 tanks in the process; 12 tanks were American made lightweights. wdk130.

At night the SS, probably *Das Reich*, headed for the Kilovy Donets. Elements of the 2nd GTC crossed the river in order to stop the enemy from reaching the Lipovyi Donets River in the Luchki South area. At 2000 hrs a battle erupted that forced the *SSTK* to halt their offensive and send panzers northward to assist *Das Reich*. Eventually the Germans gained the advantage and the 2nd GTC had to retreat back across the river.

Kempf's responsibility was to protect Hoth's right flank on his northerly advance but since Kempf was way behind, the *SSTK* had to act as flank guard against 2nd GTC and 5th GTC. This caused the SS, and especially Kempf, to fall behind schedule. The *Luftwaffe* was practically absent east of the Donets on the previous day, allowing the Soviets to control the skies. The Soviet planes frequently attacked the German bridgeheads and the forces that had made it across the river. Without consistent air support the 3rd PzC would continue to fall behind against these aerial attacks as well as against artillery strikes. Kempf's frequent requests for air support finally paid off as the *Luftwaffe* arrived and the ground forces made better progress. By the end of the day, 3rd PzC's lead forces were now eight miles from Belgorod at Miasoedovo and the rear units were able to cross the river. Even with the *Luftwaffe* support the Soviet defenses in this area were going to be tough to break. Kempf would need even greater air support if he was to catch up - but he would not get it. The lion's share of air support would go to the SS Corps with the remainder going to 48th PzC. The *Luftwaffe* did not have sufficient resources to maintain adequate cover to all the panzer corps and this would be a contributing factor for not reaching Kursk. It cannot be overstated how much this failure of Kempf to keep up with the SS impacted the overall campaign in the south and how it highlights the flawed strategic plan by von Manstein and the execution of that plan by Hoth. dgk113. cbk57.

During the day the Soviet AF began sending larger numbers of escorts along with their bombers to give greater protection. It helped but it was decided to send even larger numbers of escorts to give greater protection for the rest of the campaign. Hoth and his corps commanders were already aware that they lacked sufficient men and panzers to defeat the Soviet defenses and were already using the *Luftwaffe* as fire brigades. cbk58+.

SSTK, on 2nd SS PzC's right flank, broke through Soviet defenses and gained 12 miles to the north. By dusk, *SSTK* had crossed and cut the Belgorod-Oboyan highway, stopping for the night astride the Belgorod-Kursk railway. Their objective had been to cross the Psel River with at least a battalion and establish a bridgehead on the north bank by the end of the night, but they failed to do it. dgk94.

With the *LAH* getting too far ahead of either flank and with the increased Soviet resistance at Hill 258.2, Hausser officially ordered *LAH* to fall back to Luchki North for the night to avoid becoming isolated. Kravchenko's 5th GTC was on the northeast corner of *LAH* while the 31st TC was on the northwest corner and the 1st GTB and 49th TB was in the middle. It was a wise decision by Hausser to pull back his premier division. To make it more difficult for the Germans, the 2nd GTC had been ordered to the Psel sector and would arrive next morning. gnk121.

German pilots, flying the new Hs 129Fs, were now using the new 1000 AB Bombs. These bombs contained hundreds of bomblets that could destroy many soldiers when detonated. The area covered could be as large as 30 yards by 60 yards. cbk57.

At 2300 hrs, General Rotmistrov received written orders to move out as soon as possible, assemble at the Oskol River and await further orders that would include fighting at Prokhorovka. That was a distance of at least 150 miles from their original assembly area. Parts of the 5th GTA were on the road by 0130 hrs on 7/7 while others would be a half day behind. Originally the 5th GTA consisted of the 29th TC and the 5th GMC, but with this new deployment order the 18th TC was attached to Rotmistrov. The 5th GTA started arriving at the river on the morning of 7/8 after traveling 125 miles in 24 hours. At 0100 hrs on 7/9, Rotmistrov was ordered to reach the Bobryshevo, Bolahaia Psinka, Prelestnoe, Aleksandrovski and Bolshie Seti region, north of Prokhorovka, and be prepared to repel attackers. This new deployment was another 60 miles away. The 5th GTA had under its command approximately 800 tanks: 501 T34s, 261 T70s and 31 Churchills plus assault guns. dgr220++. fkk167. cbk77. bt84. kcz170. wwf121. vzz162++. vzz166+. vzz180. dgr86m.

At night, *Das Reich* attacked the rail embankment at Belenikhino but the first attempt failed. Regrouping, the second attempt was able to scatter the defenders. fkk134.

After receiving a recon report that a column of tanks were crossing the Donets at Soshenkov, *SSTK* moved forces toward the village to intercept the Soviet tanks. *SSTK* found and engaged the Soviets and was able to knock out 15 tanks before the remainder crossed back to the east bank of the river. It was discovered from POW interrogations that it was again the 48th GTR and most of its tanks were Churchill tanks. By the end of the day the *SSTK* reached the Shopino-west of Ternovka-southeast of Smorodino line. That was a common practice for the Soviets – assemble east of the Lipovyi River then cross just before launch time. fkk135. dgk106m. vzz7m.

By the end of the day, the 2nd SS PzC had broken through the second defense belt between Luchki North and Iakovlevo. *LAH* had noticed earlier in the day the first tank reserves showing up in sector between Iakovlevo-Teterevino North; the 5th GTC. This news disturbed Hoth for he was hoping reserves would not arrive for several more days. It was also noticed in the 48th PzC sector that Katukov's 1st TA had brought tank reserves south as well. The 31st TC, northwest of *LAH*, was preparing defenses and, along with the 3rd MC, prepared for a fight at Pokrovka. The 2nd GTC on the west bank of the Donets was now fully engaged with *Das Reich* and *SSTK*. The 90th GRD and 67th GRD, with support of the 3rd MC, had done a good job of slowing the 48th PzC's advance. gnk151.

By the end of the day, the 2nd *SS* PzC had gained on average five miles and more in some places as well as penetrated further into the second defensive belt at Iakovlevo and Luchki So but the 4th PzA was falling further behind schedule. wdk130.

During the night, Kling's Tigers were called to duty. It had been recently discovered that a column of enemy tanks were moving south toward Teterevino. Hs 129s with their 30mm cannon and the Tigers were to stop the advancing enemy. The strafing damaged or destroyed a number of tanks from 5th GTC and before the Tigers arrived, a squadron of Fw 190s flew in and supported the first squad of aircraft. The fragmentation bombs that were dropped scattered the closing infantry. The four Tigers finally joined the battle, firing on the hidden tanks that the aircraft had missed. After two hours of fierce battle, the tanks were destroyed and the riflemen pulled back to the north. All four Tigers had been disabled and would need to be towed back for repairs. The recovery teams prepared the Tigers for recovery while under fire from Soviet snipers still in the area. These tanks were believed to be part of the column heading for Teterevino North earlier in the day that 1st PzR had fallen back on when stopped at the fortified tank ditch. fzk309+. zrl217.

By the end f the day *LAH* had only four working Tigers and *Das Reich* had ten. gnk152.

At the end of the day, the three divisions of the SS collectively reported to Hausser of destroying 173 tanks and capturing 1,600 POWs. The capture of tens of thousands of POWs, as in 1941, was not being repeated. The Soviets finally got wise to their mistake of standing and fighting to the death and besides, the defensive fortifications that had been built allowed the infantry to fall back to the next trench very easily. wdk130.

In the south, the *Luftwaffe* flew only 899 sorties down from almost 2,000 missions the previous day. The reported sorties the Soviet AF flew are uncertain. One source claims 1,958 sorties, while another claims 1,278. wdk130. dgr81.

By the end of the day, the Germans had gained only from six to nine miles which was half or a little more of what was planned. Hoth was still 67 miles from Kursk. Soviet reinforcements were already moving to the third line and in some cases the second line. It was a bad sign that this early in the operation the Germans were already behind schedule and would be facing an increasing number of reinforcements. wdk132.

The first two days of fighting had been costly; Hoth estimated that hundreds of panzers had been destroyed, damaged or were malfunctioning. The *GD* had been hit the hardest with 270 panzers of its original 350 being removed from the battle field due mostly to mechanical troubles or mine damage. The 2nd SS PzC had 110 panzers down and 48th PzC lost 134 panzers in this day's fighting alone. A large number of these casualties would be repaired but while so many panzers were in the repair shop, the German advance would clearly suffer. lck272. cbk57.

After fighting all day the 375th RD had to fall back but was still on the western banks of the Lipovyi River defending between Visloe and Shopino. dgr80.

While the 3rd PzC was slowly pushing 7th GA back, the *LAH*, *Das Reich* and *SSTK* divisions had penetrated 20 miles, and crossed the Belgorod-Oboyan highway. It halted that night astride the Belgorod-Kursk railway to reqroup, but before dawn (7th) they would be on the move. While still dark, the nearly 400 panzers attacked the 1st TA. The Soviets were overwhelmed but the air force was called in. Despite the air raid that destroyed some of the panzers, the Germans broke through the center of the line shattering the 51st GRD and a number of tanks. The 1st TA's tanks withdrew and came around and attacked the flank of the panzer formation in the Syrtsevo-Iakovlevo sector. wwf85. je104. hjj121m. dgr209m.

In the south the *Luftwaffe* reported having eleven planes damaged but repairable and another eleven completely destroyed. The 2nd VA reported 45 destroyed aircraft and 17th VA lost another 37 planes. On average German pilots had far more experience than their Soviet counterparts and in most instances of the air war it showed in the early days of the campaign but by August many Soviet pilots would be the equal of his enemy. cbk58.

By the end of the day the second defensive belt had been penetrated in the SS sector but with the reinforcements that Vatutin brought up on this and the previous day, the German advance would be more difficult from this point. The mini-salient that *LAH* started the day before grew even larger , exposing more of their flanks and forcing Maj General Wisch to invest even more of his forces on the flanks and away from the spearhead. The northern front of the salient had just reached the Prokhorovka road, north of Luchki and Bolshie Maiachki, and on the verge of capturing Malye Maiachki, Teterevino and Isania Poliana. The salient that *LAH* and *Das Reich* were carving out extended from the Vorskla River in the west to almost the Lipovyi River in the east. The towns captured on the northern perimeter included Petrovski, Pokrovka, Kalinin, Teterevino South and Luchki North. I wonder what progress could have been made the first days if *Das Reich* had been fighting on the northern front instead of protecting *LAH*'s eastern flank. Now that Vatutin had brought up many reserves and would call up even more the following day from other armies, the German pace was about to dramatically slow. General Hoth understood the impact the Soviet positions deployed along the Donets Rivers were having in breaking up the solidarity of the eastern flank and yet he did little to overcome it. He was obsessed with making sure the 48th PzC would fulfill their mission to reach Oboyan.The 48th got off to a relatively bad start and never came close to fulfilling its responsibilities. Instead of scaling back the sector and modifying the battle plan, the general threw more resources on a losing sector. The 48th PzC was the most powerful corps in 4th PzA but the 2nd SS PzC outperformed it. zrl217.

Vatutin reported to Stalin that an estimated 332 panzers and 80 planes had been destroyed that day, and over 100 planes in the previous two days. These estimates were high.

There was enough light during the night for the *Luftwaffe* to send out bombers to soften up the expected route *LAH* would take in the morning. The primary targets of the Ju-87s and Ju-88s were the 51st GRD and 52nd GRD between Teterevino and Prokhorovka. Other key targets were Belenikhino, Iasnaia Poliana, Ivanovski Vyselok and Stalinskoe State Farm. wwf85. vzz3m.

In the early days of the campaign the famous German Stukas did much of the work. The first two days of aerial fighting saw 1,864 sorties from Ju-87 Stukas dive bombers. On this day alone 1,023 sorties were flown in the north, while in the south 1,686 sorties were flown against Soviet positions. cbk59. The Soviet Air Force reported 1,632 sorties. nzk77. wwf85. vzz3m.

The 4th PzA, over the last two days had gained from six to as many as twenty miles (but the average was about half that amount) but still had not attained freedom of movement or a secure rear area. The question was whether the situation would get better or worse as the salient they were building grew deeper. Time would tell. dgr81+.

After securing Teterevino, a group of ten panzers from *LAH* drove north to recon what was ahead for next morning. After breaking through the quickly prepared defenses of the 285th RR of 183rd RD, the panzers headed for Komsomolets. wwf85.

In an attempt to catch up to 2nd SS PzC the 48th PzC, which was still struggling to get past the first defense belt along the Korovino-Cherkasskoe-Hill 246.0 line which was defended by the 67th GRD and 71st GRD, launched at 0300 hrs against Chistiakov's divisions (6th GA). It had rained all night and the ground was muddy as the *GD* and 11th PzD drove north along the Butovo-Iakovlevo road in the Olkhovka-Dubrova sector, in order to meet up with 167th ID which was guarding 2nd SS PzC's left flank. The Germans could not afford to have any exposure in their line that the Soviets could exploit. vzz115. dgk84. snk75. hsz120.

In 1st TA sector (right behind 6th GA), Vatutin ordered a counter-attack to slow 48th PzC. He had ordered many reinforcements into the area; many had arrived during the night and more would be arriving later today. The 2nd GTC and 5th GTC would lead the assault but the assault would be uncoordinated and would garner poor results. wdk128++. dgr212. cbk57.

Knobelsdorff wanted an early start for his corps in order to reach the main Oboyan road which would lead north for the Psel River. There was a smaller yet important road that left Cherkasskoe, skirted the Pena River and went through Lukhanino and Syrtsevo before intersecting the Oboyan road. The 48th PzC had to take the several strongpoints along this route that day to reach their primary objective and at the same time keep the Soviets from crossing the Pena and attacking the 48th's flank. *GD* and 11th PzD would have the northern front while 3rd PzD and 52nd IC maintained the western flank. There was a delay for the bulk of the 48th PzC to advance beyond Lukhanino. The 11th PzD was still mopping up resistance at Cherkasskoe. Also, a little ways north of town, the fortified Hill 246.0 was blocking the route north and 11th PzD was tasked to take it as well. In the fight for Syrtsevo, Hoth lost one of his key regiment commanders, Heinz Klostermeyer. He was with the Grenadier Regiment of *GD* and would be missed by all his men. gnk150. wwf43+.

While securing Cherkasskoe, the rest of 48th PzC would prepare to move toward Zavidovka and Alekseevka as well as Olkhovka, Dmitrievka and Syrtsevo to the northeast. After two hours of bitter fighting with almost 300 panzers, the 71st GRD had to evacuate Krasnyi Pochinok, falling back to a new line. The 3rd PzD, moving north was able to capture Rakovo and Zavidovka, which straddled the Pena River, but were not able to go further. The Germans tried from Chapaev to Shepelevka to the north to establish a bridgehead on the western banks of the Pena but failed against the stiff resistance of the 6th TC and 90th GRD. It was in the Pena area that the Soviets used suicide dogs to destroy panzers. In the 169th GRR of 67th GRD area not far from Berezov, 16 dogs were able to stop 12 panzers. vzz116+. vzz2m. dgr213.

The 11th PzD and *GD* had the lead in penetrating the second defense belt in the western sector. During the night of 7/5, the divisions were still finishing the securing of the Cherkasskoe area and the bulk of these forces could not move north until the strongpoint was fully secured. Near daybreak, with the help of flame throwing panzers, the forces finally did leave the town and headed northeast along the eastern edge of the Pena River. *GD*'s objective was eventually Dubrova, but first Lukhanino on the outer edge of the second defense belt had to be captured. It was defended by the 67th GRD. The 3rd PzD was to clear resistance from the Pena River and it would have the support of the 52nd IC to protect its flank. After leaving Cherkasskoe, it was nearly noon when *GD* began its advance toward Lukhanino by attacking Hill 210.7. gnk146. gnk112m. hsz120.

At first light the engineers of 11th PzD had started clearing mines on the Cherkasskoe to Butovo road; it would be heavily used and the Germans could not afford the time or vehicles in finding the mines the hard way. gnk146.

Following a rain-soaked night, elements of *GD* began to clear the area southwest of Cherkasskoe. While this clearing took place, Soviet artillery shelled the Cherkasskoe area being held by the Germans. At the same time, other members of *GD* headed toward Dubrova which also contained heavy Soviet resistance. Before reaching Dubrova, *GD* had to clear Hill 237.7 and then Hill 241.1. Another group of *GD* headed through the river valley west of Yarkity for the villages of Kalashnoye and Lukhanino which lay northeast of their line of departure. During the night, the boundary with the 11th PzD which was attacking on the right had been established on the new line: Butovo village-Dubrova road. The 3rd PzD, which was a little behind *GD* on its left flank, was attacking the village of Zavidovka which was important for it had a standing bridge over the Pena tributary which the 48th PzC needed. hsz120+. gnk312m.

Two battalions of the 11th PzD left Cherkasskoe before daybreak and attacked Hill 246.0 by 0330 hrs. By 0630 the Germans were on top of the hill and the defenders were falling back. With the Soviet artillery on the hill quieted, Knobelsdorff sent additional forces of the 11th PzD toward Lukhanino. A mile north of Hill 246.0 an additional Soviet battery fired on the recon forces moving north. After a brief skirmish, the Germans continued north. By 0830 hrs the bulk of the 11th PzD was on the move and heading for Syrtsevo. gnk150.

The trailing units of 11th PzD of 48th PzC pushed northward along the Butovo-Cherkasskoe road, east of Butovo, against stiff resistance reaching the outskirts of Cherkasskoe. Despite the fact that the Germans were finishing securing Cherkasskoe, the countryside was still teeming with the enemy and the marching grenadiers still had to be on high alert. Their main objective was the heights at Zybino. With the 3rd PzD attacking 71st GRD from its flank and 11th PzD attacking frontally both the 71st GRD and the 67th GRD, the Soviets had to start falling back into the 52nd GRD's rear. Nearby, the 196th GRR supported by the 611th Anti-tank Regiment were defending near the ruined village of Cherkasskoe but had to fall back to the northwest after dark to the safety of the 90th GRD defending the Pena River. By night, the 3rd PzD reached the Pena River at Rakovo. The swampy land prevented the panzers from crossing until next morning. Zybino was due south of Novaia Gorianka and due west of Loknia. dgk97+. dgk105. snk75+. dgr172m. hjj121m.

With the fusiliers of *GD* capturing Lukhanino, Knobelsdorff ordered 3rd PzD north to occupy the town, capture nearby Zavidovka and then establish a new bridgehead across the tributary of the Pena River. He then got the temporary assistance of the *Deutschland* Regiment to head northwest to capture Syrtsevo on the east side of the Pena. At the same time, elements of 11th PzD continued to shrink the pocket around Dubrova. Lukhanino straddled a tributary of the Pena River and was not far (east) from Zavidovka, which had a standing bridge over the Pena the 48th PzC could use. Directly across Zavidovka on the Pena's north shore was Rakovo. gnk147+. gnk162m. vzz2m. nzk88.

The *GD* resumed its attack toward Hill 241.1, southwest of Dubrova, but before reaching this objective had to overcome an anti-tank trench and a minefield. By 1400 hrs, Hill 241.1 was captured. Between this hill and Hill 247.2, northwest of Dubrova, the *GD* met up against about 90 tanks, half of them dug-in. During the engagement in a friendly fire incident a Panther was hit, killing its entire crew. By the end of the day, *GD* had lost 37 Panthers to battle action and mechanical failure. During the day's advance, *GD* became separated from 11th PzD but roaming patrols from both divisions linked up. The distance between the two divisions was not great but it gave the Soviets a chance to exploit the gap if it was discovered. hjj116. hjj117m. mhz235. hsz122. gnk312m.

At 0830 hrs, Westhoven's 3rd PzD assaulted Zavidovka on the southern bank of the Pena. As the panzers neared the village Soviet artillery opened fire. With the 3rd PzD taking ground, there was a chance the only bridge over the Pena in the sector could fall in German hands; Soviet engineers blew the bridge. Zavidovka and the other villages along the Pena had been fortified and would be costly to capture. The 52nd IC's 332nd ID was moving up to take 3rd PzD's previous position and the rear units of 3rd PzD were now moving up to the Lakhanino area. Originally Lt General Westhoven had the responsibility of crossing the Pena River in this sector but with such stiff resistance, Knobelsdorff decided to shift 3rd PzD eastward and head for Lakhanino. gnk148+. gnk162m.

On the west side, 52nd IC's 255th ID and 57th ID started the day attacking northward west of Bubny to protect 48th PzC's western flank while it was on the march. At 0830 hrs the 48th PzC resumed its assault and pushed back the 71st GRD, 67th RD and 52nd GRD to the second defense belt inflicting heavy losses on the Soviets. At 1400 hrs the 332nd ID on the west flank of 48th PzC attacked the 71st GRD at Krasnyi Pochinok, which was five miles from the German start line. Following the 71st GRD, the 332nd ID pushed them out of Korovino and back to the Pena River near Rakovo which was part of the second defense belt. The 90th GRD moved up and filled the gap between the 71st GRD and 67th RD while next door the 6th TC and 3rd MC were slowing the advance of *GD* at and to the east of Lukhanino, as the *GD* was moving northeast toward Dubrova; both sides suffered heavy casualties. While some of the German planes that were originally meant to support 48th PzC were sent to help Kempf, a large portion of the remaining aircraft was sent in to attack 6th TC. Despite having several raids on the tankers, the German planes were unable to cause heavy damage and the 6th TC held their ground. Fewer German planes striking Soviet artillery in the 48th PzC sector allowed the Soviet artillery to take a more active part against the German ground forces. Also, the Soviet tankers were helped by repeated waves of fighters interfering with the German sorties. wdk128. cbk56+. dgr172m.

With the 332nd ID and 225th ID moving up to the Krasnyi Pochinok-Cherkasskoe area, the *GD*, 11th PzD and 3rd PzD drove north attempting to clear resistance west of the Vorskla River. At the same time the *LAH* and *Das Reich* pushed forward along the Belgorod-Kursk rail line while *SSTK* provided flank protection in the east. The 167th ID provided flank protection for *SSTK*. These two pincers, one on each side of the Vorskla River, succeeded in encircling and destroying some Soviet forces but not to the degree that was expected. Von Manstein expected his two main corps to break into the second defense belt along the Luchki South-Iakovlevo-Dubrova-Lukhanino line at such a pace that many Soviet defenders would be encircled and destroyed. While the 2nd SS was advancing fast enough, the lagging 48th PzC prevented any such encirclement. fkk81+. gnk111. gnk112m+.

After a 90 minute barrage, elements of *GD* supported by some panzers as well as air support head toward Pokrovka, but bumped into the 71st GRD near Krasnyi Pochinok at 1130 hrs. After a bitter fight the village and the nearby villages of Novo-Ivanovka and Mikhailovka fell to the Germans. With the Germans gaining this line, the 40th Army sent the 309th RD's 294th RR to the Kobylevka-Razdol line. They arrived late at night to help block the 52nd IC from expanding to the west or northwest. dgr79. dgr39m. wwf44.

A disruptive barrage caused parts of the 4th PzA to get a late start but by 1000 hrs the entire army was on the move. Charging from Cherkasskoe, the 48th PzC in general would head for Pokrovka while the 2nd SS PzC and 167th ID would leave from the Kozmo-Demianovka area and head for Bykovka with the aim of surrounding the 67th GRD and 52nd GRD. Some of the panzers of 48th did split off to head northwest toward Krasnyi Pochinok which was defended by the 71st GRD. Not only did Krasnyi Pochinok fall but also Novo-Ivanovka and Mikhailovka soon thereafter. With these villages falling, 40th Army sent 309th RD's 294th RR to the Kobylevka-Razdol line to block the Germans. dgr79. dgk106m. dgr76m+.

Attacking from near Cherkasskoe, the 48th PzC would take Alekseevka, Lukhanino, Podimovka and Zavidovka by mid afternoon. The 11th PzD assisted *GD* in taking Zavidovka located on the southern bank of the Pena. Podimovka was south of the Pena River bend, just northwest of Zavidovka. The 3rd PzD reached Rakovo. dgr213 dgr209m. vzz116. dgk106m.

The initial attack from the Krasnyi Pochinok-Cherkasskoe area was repulsed by the 71st GRD, the 67th GRD and the 27th TDB. The Germans pulled back and tried again at 1300 hrs. This time the assault penetrated the line in the Setnoye-Sartytoie-Zavidovka area. Just as the Germans were approaching the Rakovo area, the 6th TC of 1st TA arrived and stopped their advance by knocking out several Tigers and Panthers. Undeterred, the Germans shifted direction and headed east for Olkhovka and reached the Vorskla River north of Kosmo-Demianovka where they were threatening to encircle the front line units that were trying to regroup. fkk82.

In the late morning, the 1st PzGR advanced north toward Dubrova on the Lukhanino River but was unable to initially reach the village because of the many tank ditches and the Soviet armor that was brought up to protect them. Despite the fierce fighting, by nightfall the Germans were able to advance past Dubrova and arrived at Hill 247.2 where they dug in for the night. This German penetration was not widespread and with this small salient, the 1st PzGR of *LAH* was in a precarious position. dgk107. dgk106m.

By 1100 hrs after clearing Cherkasskoe, the bulk of *GD* moved towards Hill 237.7 and Hill 241.1. These hills were also hard to capture but finally were taken before moving on Hill 247.2 due east of Dubrova. This hill would be necessary if the fortified town of Dubrova was going to be taken. Assaulting Hill 247.2 would be difficult; the task of taking it would be given to Maj Remer of Group Remer but the hill had to be taken before moving on Dubrova. With Soviet guns on Hill 247.2, Dubrova would be difficult and costly to capture but with Germans on that hill, their artillery could target Soviet defenses inside Dubrova. The taking of the hill plus moving guns on that hill was expected to take hours. The attack on Dubrova was therefore scheduled to start next morning, which would allow a lengthy preparation on the town before the attack was launched. The guns would continue to fire on the town while the attack progressed. At the same time, the 11th PzD was attacking Hill 237.8 east of Cherkasskoe. After taking it, the division moved a little north and attacked Hill 246.0 which was due east of Cherkasskoe. fkk264. gnk96. gnk68m. gnk312m. hsz121+.

At 1130 hrs as most of the 11th PzD was advancing from Cherkasskoe sector toward Lukhanino, Dubrova and Olkhovka, a combat group soon split off from this group and headed south for Trirechnoe. dgr80. dgr76m.

By midday, the 29th Anti-tank Brigade, being transferred from 40th Army, deployed between 1st TA and 5th GTC. dgr84.

Knobelsdorff's 48th PzC shifted direction for better tank terrain between Alekseevka,

Lukhanino and Syrtsevo along the Tomarovka-Oboyan road. In late afternoon the 11th PzD and 3rd PzD, trying to split the Soviet forces that were blocking the way to Oboyan, engaged Chernov's 90th GRD and Krivoshein's 3rd MC along the Lukhanino River. The Germans were unsuccessful. At night, Vatutin brought up the 35th MC to help 90th in stopping the German advance. dgk105. hjj121m. dgr209m.

West of *GD*, the 3rd PzD's 394th PzGR attacked due north from Gertsovka toward Korovino, striking Col Sibakov's 71st GRD's 210th GRR which was defending this sector and 67th GRD's left flank. Breaking through the right flank of 67th GRD by afternoon, the 394th PzGR had captured the high ground overlooking Korovino and by evening had expelled the 210th GRR from the town and the immediate area. The 70 panzers of 6th PzR of 3rd PzD raced past the boundary of 71st GRD and 67th GRD and resecured the village of Krasnyi Pochinok, three miles to the rear of the original Soviet front line. To prevent encirclement, the 71st GRD had to fall back. The attack was successful and the 3rd PzD, *GD* and 11th PzD breached the line and entered the gap heading northeast toward the Pena River and the 2nd defense belt. The 48th PzC under Knobelsdorff had torn a big hole in the line and the Soviets were unable to close it. dgk98+. dgr172m. dgk106m. gnk112m.

With the trouble the 48th PzC was having with navigating the Pena River Valley, Knobelsdorff ordered this corps to the east of Alekseevka through Lukhanino and Syrtsevo. The corps was slowed again as it approached Lukhanino with its huge minefield to the south of town. lck270+.

Schimmelmann's panzer group of 11th PzD was heading for Syrtsevo but by 1230 hrs as they approached Hill 241.1 the panzers were stopped by a tank ditch and firing from the hill. Under the cover of smoke, the panzers backed off and called for engineers to take care of the ditch. Not wanting to wait for the panzers, two battalions bypassed the hill despite several ambushes and by 1800 hrs were on their way north again. By this time the ditch had been filled in and the panzers were fighting for the hill. Other engineers were busy clearing mines on the road to Dubrova. gnk150.

While the *GD* and 11th PzD continued their northbound route to Oboyan, the 3rd PzD screened *GD*'s left flank while the 332nd ID continued to screen 48th PzC's far left flank south of the Pena River. Soon, all panzer divisions would meet up with 10th TC that were spread out across their path. By this point both 11th PzD and *GD* were overextended and exposed and needed time to regroup, but the orders were to continue. The 11th PzD near Dubrova attacked the 67th GRD and 1st MB / 3rd MC, with 70 or more panzers and by nighttime had pushed the Soviets from the front line into Dubrova which was on the road to Oboyan. This caused Hoth to order the 3rd PzD even closer to *GD* in the Syrtsevo area. In addition to the 3rd MC defending Syrtsevo, there was the infantry of the 67th GRD and 90th GRD to deal with. snk79. wdk129. hjj121m. mhz235. dgr209m.

The 11th PzD and *GD* met fierce resistance from Col Baksov's 67th GRD and Col Nekrasov's 52nd GRD as they fought their way northward. By 1700 hrs, these two German divisions captured the fortified villages of Novo-Cherkasskoe, Alekseevka, Tiriechnoe, Dmitrievka and Olkhovka. With the Germans gaining control of these villages, the two Soviet divisions fell back, fighting a rear guard action back to the Syrtsevo-Dubrovka line at the rear of the second defense belt. The 11th PzD, *GD* and *LAH* were quick enough to catch and destroy many of these soldiers in the Vorskla and Vorsklitsa River valleys while the survivors were able to slip past the German line during nighttime hours. Moving forward, the 48th PzC headed for the fortified villages of Zavidovka, Syrtsevo and Lukhanino further east but still within the Pena River basin. These villages were defended by the 90th GRD, 6th TC and 3rd MC which put up stiff resistance. The 3rd PzD was slowed by fighting in the Podimovka-Alekseevka area and had further trouble when attacking Zavidovka. Initially the resistance was too much and the 3rd PzD pulled back to regroup. The 67th GRD was situated in the middle between 52nd GRD on their eastern flank and the 71st GRD on the western flank and defended a nine mile line crossing the Vorskolets River Valley to the western bank of the Vorskla River. The 52nd GRD was on the eastern side of the river and handled a four mile stretch while the 71st GRD defended an equal amount to the west. vzz117. dgr80. dgk72+. dgk106m. dgr76m.

The leading edge of 48th PzC moved north into the second defensive belt that contained many dug-in T34s and artillery. The 10th PzB had many Panther failures today caused mostly by the rough terrain and the muddy ground that slowed *GD*'s advance. The 11th PzD captured several villages and reached the Pena River line north of Cherkasskoe. By the end of the day, the 48th PzC had penetrated through the first defensive belt, advancing along the general line to the southern banks of the Pena River eastward to Lakhanino. Knobelsdorff regrouped the corps during the night, with the exception of elements of the *GD* and 11th PzD, which were sent northward along both sides of the road to Oboyan. The 167th ID was the only unit in the sector that made any progress today without suffering heavy casualties. It secured Dmitrievka by afternoon where it was attached to 2nd SS PzC. snk77. snk79. dgr172m. dgk124m. gnk112m.

By 1500 hrs, when the issue of who controlled Hill 247.2 was settled, the right-hand regiment of *GD* was approaching Dubrova when they came upon a strongpoint in front of town among the cornfields and rolling hills. It was part of the outer edges of Vatutin's second defensive belt and contained a maze of trenches, bunkers, MG nests and buried Pak guns. German artillery was directed on the site, a shock group with flamethrowers was brought up and each bunker, trench and fox hole had to be vanquished one at a time. It was a costly ordeal but it was accomplished. hsz121.

In the Lukhanino-Syrtsevo-Hill 247.2 sector, the Germans repeatedly tried, with the help of up to 200 panzers, to break through the defenses of the 90th GRD, 1st TA's 6th TC and 3rd MC but failed. This was part of the second defensive belt; the defenses were well prepared and Vatutin was bringing up 1st TA to support the 6th GA. 48th PzC was beginning to shift northeastwardly, putting greater pressure on 3rd MC and less on 6th TC. The 3rd PzD reached the fortified village of Lukhanino despite heavy resistance from 6th TC. It was decided after seeing aerial photos of Lukhanino that it would be better to shell it first before attacking. Once the attack began, it would be necessary to clear one fortified house at Olkhovkatime until all the units made it to the stream, north of the village. The Soviets began shelling Lukhanino while friendlies were still fighting. The shelling plus the discovery of a new minefield caused Lt General Westhoven to order his forces in the town to pull back until the shelling stopped. Traveling along the Lukhanino stream, the 3rd PzD was able to reach the east bank of the Pena River by evening. In the same sector the 1st MB successfully defended Olkhovka against many attacks by *GD* that lasted all day. See Map 23. dgk108. dgr209m. fkk248. vzz7m. gnk442.

In late afternoon, the *GD* pivoted east between Lukhanino and Alekseevka before shifting toward the river and after a brief but fierce fight created a small bridgehead across the Pena River. Further west, the 3rd PzD was taking heavy fire and had to pull back to Cherkasskoe which secured the left flank of *GD* between Cherkasskoe and Iaoki. Later and still against heavy resistance, the 3rd PzD also crossed the Pena River. To the right of *GD*, the 11th PzD struck the 67th GRD at 1130 hrs and by 1500 hrs had pushed the Soviets back through Trirechnoe and Dmitrievka to Oikova, over six miles from the start line but at least a mile from the second line. The 11th PzD also pushed the 52nd GRD back to the second defense belt at Dubrova. American built M3 tanks were being used by the Soviets; six were destroyed in this engagement. The panzers of *GD* were being hampered by excessive muddy fields and only some of them took part in the assault on the fortified villages of Lukhanino and Kalesnoie. *GD* had just captured Hill 237.0 and had gone on to attack the more important Hill 241.1 which overlooked Dubrova. The defenders were determined to keep the hill and it was taking more from the grenadiers to reach the top. As more of the division reached the sector, it was sent in to assist. This sector was part of the second defensive belt and as such there were many strongpoints the 48th PzC had to clear before moving on. While the main roads and strongpoints were cleared, the surrounding areas were still infested with the enemy. The Germans would never have a moment's rest from partisan attacks in the rear areas. Lying south of Dubrova and to the north of Cherkasskoe, these hills lay directly along the line of advance to the key village of Syrtsevo which was defended by the 250 tanks of Krivoshein's 3rd MC. wdk128+. dgr172m. hjj115. hjj121m. mhz234. dgr209m. gnk312m. dgk106m. dgk95m.

The 48th PzC moved north toward the Psel River bend which was an important objective for the day. The 11th PzD was advancing well and its commander, Mickl, thought his recon patrol might reach the river by tonight or most likely the next day. Nearby, *LAH* and *Das Reich* moved on to Gresnoe. Northeast of Cherkasskoe after fighting fiercely all day, 11th PzD was able to reach and capture the village of Olkhovka with the support of the 167th ID. By the end of the day on the west side of *GD*, the 3rd PzD had reached the Pena River but had failed to cross it in any significant way. mhz236. dgk94. dgk106m.

During the predawn hours, Vatutin released the 72 gun 27th ATB and other units to move into 67th GRD and 90th GRD sectors along the Pena River to bolster the line against the 48th PzC. dgk98.

Strachwitz's panzer group was only three miles north of Cherkasskoe when it was attacked by tanks of the 245th TR. The Panther Brigade which was to stay in communication with Strachwitz, who was nowhere to be found. Decker was still angry with Strachwitz for his blunder at the ravine the previous day and did not want his machines to fall under a commander that had different views of fighting a battle. Strachwitz had been slowed down in front of a tank ditch located in front of Hill 241.1, west of Dubrova. Knobelsdorff was getting angry with the slow progress and was trying to motivate his officers. He also had to contend with the increasing friction caused by the arguing Strachwitz and Decker. Decker had made some accurate accusations that Knobelsdorff should have acted on but did not and it caused the loss of many Panthers over the next week.

By 2100 hrs, the Grenadiers of *GD* reached the edge of Dubrova and were fighting to enter the town. At the same time the Fusiliers of *GD* captured Hill 210.7 north of Cherkasskoe and by 2100 hrs had captured Lukhanino and created a small, tenuous bridgehead on the other side of the Pena River. gnk146+. (July 6)

At night, FM von Manstein ordered the 2nd SS PzC to gain 12 miles the next day and reach the third defense belt which stretched from just south of Oboyan to Prokhorovka. The panzer corps would have to drive to the northeast, cross the Psel River as well as continue on the road that led to Prokhorovka. The Psel River ran about 25 miles southeast from

Oboyan before turning to the northeast, passing three miles northwest of Prokhorovka. The river provided an excellent natural defense for the Soviets. The 48th PzC on the west flank was also ordered to reach the Psel River between Schipy and Olkhovski then cross the river and head for Oboyan. wdk133.

The 3rd PzD, 11th PzD and the *GD* divisions moved north and, with the help of the *Luftwaffe*, pushed the 67th GRD back into the 52nd GRD's defense belt which was fighting the SS panzers to the east of 48th PzC's sector. By evening both the 67th and the 52nd RDs had to fall back to beyond the second defense belt leaving just the 90th GRD and 3rd MC defending the sector. Reaching the second belt the 48th PzC made repeated attempts throughout the night, gaining some ground but failing to break all the way through. dgk105.

It was only at Lukhanino by the end of the day that *GD* was able to penetrate the second defense belt. The 3rd PzD was still at the Pena River and the 11th PzD was west of Bykovka. mhz236. lck271.

As it started to get dark, Group Remer of *GD* bypassed the heavily fortified Dubrova and captured Hill 247.2 where they dug in for the night. They would attack Dubrova in the morning. hsz121.

The 11th PzD along with elements of 167th ID stopped for the night just west of Bykovka. lck271.

By the end of the day, the 48th PzC had linked up with 2nd SS PzC near Iakovlevo. This German salient was tentatively heading straight for Oboyan. The 48th PzC had reached a line that touched the Pena River and reached Syrtsev in the east. Syrtsev was due west of Solonets which the *LAH* had reached the previous night. In other words, the 48th PzC was a full day behind the SS. Solonets was just one mile south of Iakovlevo. In the preceeding two days, the 48th PzC claimed to have lost 300 AFVs. Though many of these vehicles would be repaired, the time off the battlefield would be considerable and would have a definite impact on the German advance. The *Luftwaffe* had lost 100 planes in the previous two days. dgk111+. dgr172m.

In the 48th PzC sector, the Soviets were now striking the flanks as well. Vatutin wanted a major counter-attack and Katukov, which had moved his 1st TA up to the second defensive belt during the predawn hours, tried to persuade his commander to delay the attack as the Germans were still too strong. Vatutin would not change his mind, so Katukov talked to Stalin. Stalin then ordered Vatutin to delay the attack for at least another day. Vatutin, though downsizing the attack, still ordered a few local attacks to launch next morning. The 1st TA had been assembled in reserve, north of the Psel River not far from Oboyan. It was a 20 mile trip that Katukov's hundreds of tanks made in a half of a day. The 6th TC and 3d MC led the trip with the newly formed 31st TC following. The 112th TB of 6th TC brought up the rear and was considered the reserve. Katukov sent a speedy recon patrol ahead to reconnoiter the second line and report back to him; he did not want any surprises when his army arrived. It was not long after 6th TC and 3rd MC arrived at the line that the Germans arrived and attacked, quickly penetrating both corps, especially the 3rd MC sector. Katukov has been criticized for having 3rd MC in first echelon instead of 31st TC. zra59+. zow145.

The 4th PzA had reported a net loss of 263 panzers to AGS for the first two days of the campaign. The figure had been higher but the repair shops were working around the clock to repair and get the panzers back to the battlefield. mhz238.

With Knobelsdorff aware of the bickering between Strachwitz and Decker, the corps commander took steps to rectify the issue by removing Decker from command of his brigade and giving the entire Panther brigade to Colonel Strachwitz. The resolution was controversial for the first two days; *GD* lost two-thirds of their 300 panzers. gnk148.

By the end of the second day, *Das Reich* had traveled 13 miles, penetrated two defense belts and was heading toward the third. *LAH*'s move was comparable, maybe a little better. The advance was good but it was only on a ten mile front which meant it was fragile. Hoth had called Knobelsdorff with explicit orders to make sure 11th PzD's right flank caught up and linked with the left flank of *LAH*. On the Soviet side, the 6th GA's defenses had been penetrated in several places, had heavy losses of men and its HQ had lost control of its divisions. vzz131. vzz133. dgk100++. dgk109+.

Vatutin, in order to safeguard the western approaches to Oboyan, ordered 40th Army to move its forces along the Proletarski-Vengerovka line to block any possible expansion on the Korovino-Rakitnoe axis. dgr78. dgr76m+.

By the end of the day, the three divisions of 48th PzC had failed to reach their objective of the Psel River. The repeated attacks by the Soviets on Knobelsdorff's flank caused more resources to be diverted from the front to the side. As the ground battle heated up, the demands on the *Luftwaffe* increased and it was becoming increasingly difficult to get air support in a timely manner. The mobile flank formations were also being used for ground attack where a huge amount of ammo was being expended. Despite the increasing resistance, Hoth's 4th PzA was able to gain six miles in many places. dgk108. mhz233+. dgr214.

At 0300 hrs, the panzers of 3rd PzC resumed moving to the northeast from Belgorod area toward Korocha, their primary objective. hjj123m.

During the predawn hours, the 6th PzD crossed the Razumnaia River at Miasoedovo, 11 miles east of Belgorod, and redeployed behind the 7th PzD before shifting direction toward Melikhovo to fill the gap between 19th PzD and 7th PzD. While the 19th PzD and 7th PzD had crossed the Donets in strength early that morning, it would not be 6th PzD's turn until midday. The line followed the Belgorod-Korocha road 13 miles northeast of Belgorod. The three panzer divisions then attacked and, despite having 300 panzers, progress was slow against heavy artillery. South of 7th PzD, Group Raus and the 42nd IC broke into the Soviet first defense belt despite stiff resistance, especially from the 78th RD, between the Donets and Koren Rivers. A little later in the day the 106th ID was attached to 7th PzD at Krutori Log, 10 miles southeast of Belgorod and advanced due east driving back the 73rd GRD to the second defensive belt that ran north-south about 11 miles east of the Donets. By noon the 106th reached the second line at Poliana, five miles southwest of Krutoi Log. The 106th ID and the 320th ID next door could not advance any further that day against 24th GRC. wdk131+. dgr172m. mhz240. dgr155m. dgr173m. erz204. hjj123m.

In 7th GA sector, further reinforcements were brought up. Col Trunin's 92nd GRD, Maj General Tikhomirov's 93rd GRD and Col Russkikh's 94th GRD of Maj General Goriachev's 35th GRC moved up and were in place by 0300 hrs on 7/6. The 111th RD, 183rd RD and 270th RD of 69th Army moved into the Prokhorovka area, north of town. Other tank brigades moved closer as well stopping in the Batratskaia Dacha area, 10 miles east of the Donets River to block the path of 19th PzD. Other units stopped at Gremuchi and the Poliana State Farm near Krutoi Log to block 7th PzD. Elements of Maj General Vasilev's 24th GRC (213th RD and the 27th TB) stopped at Maslova Pristani to block 320th ID and another group, while the 15th GRD and 111th RD moved into Nekliudovo-

Churaevo area on the eastern side of the Koren River. On the southeastern flank against 11th IC and 7th PzD, Vatutin sent the 25th GRC supported by 31st TDB, the 167th TR and the 1438th SU Regiment to the Batratskaia Dacha sector, right behind the second defensive belt. A second reinforcement group was sent to block 19th PzD, further northeast of the first group. It included the 1529th SU Regiment, the 1669th TDR and this formation would assemble near Gremiachi to block 19th PzD. Gremiachi is roughly eight miles south of Batratskaia Dacha. dgr77m wdk130+. vzz108. lck247.

Following orders before daybreak Shumilov, using his 7th GA's second echelon forces, attacked the new bridgehead that Kempf established the previous day near Belgorod on the east banks of the Donets. Advancing from near Gremuchi and the Poliana State Farm the Soviets drove toward Krutoi Log where the 7th PzD bivouac for the night. vzz108. gnk141.

The 6th PzD, following orders, reached the Razumnaia River at Solomino aiming to attack Generalovka before moving on to reach within a mile south of the strongpoint village of Iastrebovo, which was defended by elements of the 92nd GRD and 94th GRD. The division made relatively good time and was able to cross the Solomino bridge by 1430 hrs. Generalovka was a village on the southern bank of the Razumnaia River, due south of the larger town of Blizhhaia Igumenka. Iastrebovo was a little east for those two sites and vertically in the middle of the two. dlu34. dgr155m. dgr173m. dgr39m. dlu30. dgk136. nzk88. zzt88+.

During the predawn hours, the 7th PzD was frequently attacked by Soviet fighters which slowed the German preparations but caused little death. At 0615 the division launched with the support of the Tigers of sPzAbt 503. After a brief but fierce battle, the 7th PzD broke through the front line and headed for Krutoi Log along a narrow axis, clearing any resistance left over from yesterday. gnk141.

Advancing along the Razumnaia, a large slow moving river, the lead elements of the 7th PzD climbed the ridge and attacked and captured Krutoi Log to the southwest. The advance was resumed along the river. At Batratskaia Dacha, the division was stopped by strong artillery. The subsequent counter-attack along the wood line south of the village was repulsed. The lead elements of 7th PzD would have to wait until the next day when more of the division arrived before pushing on toward the fortified village of Miasoedovo. fkk293+. dgr39m. dgr155m.

After the capture of Krutoi Log, the 7th PzD tried advancing northward, to clear the area around Hill 216.1 to the west of Batratskaia Dacha Kolkhoz. The advance was stopped by heavy shelling from in front of the hill. The *Luftwaffe* was called in to assist. The advance was able to continue after the Stukas had been called in. This area was wooded and the Soviets had set up numerous ambushes which slowed the advance though the lead units of the division still made it six miles north of the captured town of Krutoi Log by late afternoon. dlu35+. dgr39m.

During the night and predawn hours, the 6th PzD moved to its new launch point further south of Belgorod. They did not get permission to start until later in the morning but by 1200 hrs the bulk of the division was on the east side of the Donets and heading through the corridor that 7th PzD had cleared for Krutoi Log. Within minutes of the crossing, the 6th PzD was attacked from the air as well as shelled. By 1800 hrs, the 6th PzD joined 7th PzD and together attacked Hill 216.1. Elements of the infantry moved out and headed for Hill 207.9, a mile north of Batratskaia Dacha but it would take until midnight to secure the two hills and the village. The two divisions stopped their advance for the night and would resume at daybreak. gnk143. snk20. dlu30. dlu31m. zzt88.

The German attack east of Belgorod, especially around the enemy stronghold of Kreida, was very difficult and made no progress. The Soviets countered through the woods west of Koren with several RDs and a tank brigade driving to the Shevekino-Belgorod road against the 106th ID but were stopped with the help of 11th IC's assault guns which inflicted heavy losses. The main Soviet attack was between Poliana and Shcholokovo and while determined, it was uncoordinated. During the battle the 198th ID was brought up to help and in the days to come played a pivotal role in defending 3rd PzC's flank. Raus's 11th IC was making the smallest gains. The failure of 3rd PzC to quickly capture the Kreida-Staryi Gorod stronghold would have immense negative impact for the German campaign in the days to come. wwf83. snk51*+. nzk88.

Trailing elements of the 7th PzD also advanced leaving the 106th ID and 320th ID of 11th IC to guard its flank. Heavy fighting erupted as the Soviet Volchansk Group attacked 11th IC. The Bezlydovka bridgehead along the Donets was abandoned in order to narrow the front and concentrate the forces of 11th IC. bt84. erz204.

Still on the west bank of the Donets, the 106th ID remained on the defensive. The 6th PzD had redeployed from Staryi Gorod to the southeast behind the 7th PzD, which was the only unit making progress in 3rd PzC sector. The panzer divisions were able to finally break through the Soviet line to gain the high ground at Miasoedovo and then toward Melikhovo. Coordinating its attack with 7th PzD, 11th IC captured the high ground between Koren and the Donets before turning northeast, waiting for the expected counter-attack. snk50. dgr172m. dgr155m. dgr39m. vzz5m. dlu37+.

The 6th PzD, after being redeployed behind 7th PzD, shifted direction a little and headed for Melikhovo by way of Iastrebovo. shn159. dgr155m. dgr155m. dgr173m. zzt88+.

Advancing between Razumnoe, which had been captured in costly fighting by 19th PzD and Krutoi Log, the 7th PzD pushed aside the 233rd RR of 78th GRD, trapping forces north of Krutoi Log before being ambushed by the 73rd GRD. During this day and the following day, the 7th PzD repeatedly attacked the defenses of Col Kozak's 73rd GRD but were repulsed each time until the 6th PzD arrived to the line between 7th and 19th PzDs and rolled up the right flank of the Soviets, forcing the 73rd GRD back to the low ridge running from Gremuchi through Batratskaia. Though the 74th PzGR was making some progress, the 442nd PzGR of 168th ID was assigned to 19th PzD to speed its advance through this difficult section. dgk111+. dgr172m. dgr39m. dlu43+.

The Kempf Group, with 7th PzD and 19th PzD leading the way, crossed the Northern Donets the previous day and attacked 7th GA. The 6th PzD joined the column this early afternoon after redeploying. The 19th PzD wheeled northwestward against the left flank and rear of the 81st GRD. Despite heavy resistance by the 81st GRD and supporting tanks, the Germans succeeded in seizing Kreida Station and to the north of Generalovka the key town of Belovskoe. Afterwards a splinter group broke away from 19th PzD and headed for Belovskaia and the nearby State Farm. While this group advanced on the Farm, Soviet aircraft made repeated attacks on the column. The Germans continued to advance but hit a minefield that quickly damaged 14 panzers. While the Germans were trying to escape this trap, Soviet artillery from the 114th Guards Artillery Regiment damaged another four panzers. By 1500 hrs, the panzers and men of 73rd PzGR that could free themselves shifted direction to bypass this strongpoint. The 74th PzGR moved up to continue the fight for the State Farm, for the Germans could not allow the Soviets to stay behind. While the fighting continued, German engineers cleared pathways through the minefield. Seeing the 19th PzD making progress, Vatutin shifted the 78th GRD and Col Kozak's 73rd GRD to block the panzers' path. dgk111+. gnk142.

East of the Donets where dense forest lay, the 7th PzD, 19th PzD and then the 6th PzD were being bombarded by either artillery hiding in the trees or by minefields. It was relatively slow going for the Germans. In one example of the day, the lead Tigers of the sPzAbt 503 were caught in a minefield but the Mk IIIs and Mk IVs to the flanks had missed the minefield and attacked to reduce the shelling on the Tigers. As it turned out both the Tigers and the Mks were heavily shelled. mhz240.

Elements of the 198th ID were deployed on the western flank of 3rd PzC near the Donets River. For the previous two days and for the next few days to come, while fierce fighting was occurring in this section, additional units of 198th ID would be arriving from Chuguyev. The additional troops helped but the front line still could not be significantly penetrated against fierce resistance. erz206. dgr97.

sPzAbt 503 attached to 6th PzD destroyed 21 various tanks and several guns today. By late afternoon after fighting all day, the 6th PzD was able to turn the left flank of 73rd GRD, forcing it to pull back from the ridge north of Germuchi to the fortified village of Batratskaia Dacha. At this point the 6th PzD could go no further. The 11th PzR of 6th PzD bedded down for the night near Hill 209.9 and was ambushed twice but was able to repulse both attacks. Next morning the 6th PzD was heading for Generalovka to support the 19th PzD in its attack of Blizhniaia Igumenka. The 6th's recon team was already at Kolonozh-Dubovzh. dlu34. dgr155m. dgr173m. dgr39m. lck269.

Working not far from 7th PzD's influence, the 11th IC's 106th ID with some difficulty captured the high ground west of Korek. The whole sector centering on Kreida was a Soviet stronghold and difficult to clear. Even when a section was cleared, the Soviets would fanatically try to take it back. Nothing was going easy for 106th ID or the 11th IC. Raus had taught his infantry a technique to separate the Soviet tanks from the protection of its infantry and it seemed to be working quite well on the Soviet counterattacks. The German infantry would allow the Soviet tanks to penetrate the front line without resistance and then once past would mow down the Soviet infantry following in its wake. The 88 batteries in second echelon would destroy the T34s as they neared. Many tanks were destroyed in this manner. erz204+.

The 168th ID, now under Hunersdorff, caught up with the 6th PzD and were taking some of the pressure off the panzers. The 6th PzD was trying to cross the Razumnaia River at Solomino before the Soviets destroyed the bridge. Once across, the panzers headed for Generalovka with the ultimate goal of reaching Iastrebovo by night. With ten Tigers in the lead, Generalovka was eventually attacked. The Soviets responded with heavy artillery and fighters coming in to support. Neither action stopped the Tigers and after a while, the panzers were overrunning the Soviet position. 17 Soviet tanks and many guns were destroyed in the engagement. Some panzers broke off and drove to nearby Solovzhev Kolkhoz to secure that as well. They hit another minefield on the way and needed help from the sappers to clear the field. Some sappers were killed in the process, for the minefield was being covered by artillery. dlu30+. dgr39m.

During the predawn hours, Vatutin brought up Kozak's 73rd GRD plus attachments to the Batratskaia Dacha sector, which included two important hills, to block the path of 7th PzD. The hills were Hill 216.1 and Hill 207.9 and were defended by the 31st Anti-tank

Battalion. During the day and into the early evening, the 7th PzD fought for this sector but failed each time. Eventually Hill 207.9 fell, soon followed by the other hill, and then by 2200 hrs the village fell. gnk142. dgr77m. dlu33.

After dark, 7th PzD reached Iastrebovo. With 7th PzD in the lead and the 6th PzD trailing, they were being hit the hardest on their flanks from Soviet ambush. The area was wooded, encouraging Soviet ambush and hindering the panzers' speed. The panzer divisions were hit by the new assault guns that sported a 122mm gun, the SU-122. It made quite an impression on the German tankers. shn159. dgr155m.

At night, the newly arrived 111th RD replaced 15th GRD on the front line between Shebekino and Volchansk in order for the 15th GRD to deploy between Nekliudovo and Churaevo along the eastern bank of the Koren River. The 270th RD which moved up with the 111th RD the previous night was sent to defend the Shebekino area tonight. dgr78++. dgr100m.

The 3rd PzC fought its way slowly northeast of Belgorod. Its 6th PzD and 168th ID were embroiled in bitter fighting along both banks of the Donets River, a battle that raged for the next three days. The 168th ID finally broke through the first defense belt southeast of Mikhailovka, Belgorod and was able to head toward Staryi Gorod three miles northeast of Belgorod. The right flank of 168th, following behind 19th PzD and clearing the residual, was making better progress. The two divisions were trying to expand the Milhailovka bridgehead but were having little success. The 6th PzD moved to Dorogobuzhhino and launched an attack to the northeast. The 19th PzD, deployed between the 168th ID and 6th PzD to the east, was able to push the 78th GRD back to Blizhniaia Igumenka, over six miles northeast of Belgorod. bt84. dgr81. dgr39m. dgr77m. vzz5m. dlu44.

The 3rd PzC's main assault, the 7th PzD with the 6th PzD close by, advanced from Nizhni Olshanets toward Krutoi Log. By the end of the day, it had captured and secured the Krutoi Log area and also Razumnoe, Generalovka and Belinska. The day's fighting for 3rd PzC would be one of the hardest days of the campaign, for each of these villages had been turned into a strongpoint with plenty of supporting artillery. The 81st GRD had fallen back to the Den Urozhai Collective Farm; the 78th GRD and the 73rd GRD fell back to the line: Belovskaia, Batratskaia Dacha State Farm and the Korenskaia Dacha. The 213th RD and 72nd GRD occupied the line from Gremuchi to Priutovka. wdk131. hjj121m. dgr155m. dgr173m. dgr39m. wwf89. bt84. dgr81. dlu33.

The Kempf Group, despite lack of air support, was able to slowly advance to the high ground between the Donets and Koren Rivers but the 3rd PzC was unable to secure the east bank of Korocha River and while leaving resistance on their flank had to strike north to secure the east flank of Hoth's 4th PzA. Kempf was falling too far behind the 2nd SS PzC by extending its east flank so von Manstein changed the attack boundaries to avoid going too far east. Even at this early stage, it could be seen the east flank would have its troubles and not contribute to the degree that it had to for the campaign to be a success. FM von Manstein should have been more proactive in adjusting the battle plan and in supervising General Hoth. hjj123m.

More Soviet planes flew in the Kursk battlefield on this day, having a greater affect on the attacking Germans. The Red Air Force claimed they downed 100 planes while reporting 1,632 sorties flown in the south. dgk93. rkz167.

7

July 6th on the Northern Salient

See Map 3

The 4th PzD was called up from reserves ahead of schedule and would travel from Tagino to Novotroitzki to the Oka River arriving at their assembly point by 0100 hrs on 7/7 to await further orders. fkk56. dgk87m. dgk92m. lck116m.

On the previous day, Model released only one full panzer division (plus assault guns and other attachments), the 20th PzD, which gave Rokossovsky time to determine more fully which axes of attack to defend against. During the predawn hours many reinforcements were brought up to the line, making Model's job so much harder. Model should have attacked harder in a concentrated effort along his primary axis to reach Olkhovatka by the end of the first day. lck256. dgk87m. dgk92m.

At 0200 hrs, Grigoryev's 16th TC began an assault on 20th PzD and the accompanying Pz Abt 21 at their bridgehead at Saburovka. At 0350 hrs, the infantry of 17th GRC joined the attack as did the planes of Rudenko's 16th AF. By 0600 hrs a fully fledged battle was occurring between Saburovka in the east and Samodorovka in the west with the Germans losing ground, but by 0900 hrs the Germans had stopped the attack and stabilized the line. Panzer companies were sent out in an independent action to scout out weaknesses in the Soviet line near Hill 230.4 which was near the southern edge of Saburovka. The company of assault guns came upon the battle that 20th PzD was in and without orders joined the melee with its three StuG IIIs. Model saw a chance to reach Olkhovatka and sent the two panzer divisions still in reserve, the 2nd PzD and 9th PzD, to exploit this weakness. The skies were clear and the temperature was in the high 80s by afternoon and the air forces of both sides were out looking for targets of opportunity. The 16th TC brought up reserves and exerted greater pressure on the men of the 20th PzD. So much pressure that once the Germans reached the key road south of Hill 230.4 they halted and started digging in. The battle raged for hours and some of the panzers had to go back to Saborovka to be resupplied. The 2nd PzD deployed almost 100 panzers and, with sPzAbt 505's 24 Tigers, were added to the mix for a total of 300 panzers now fighting in an area of seven miles wide and two deep that had expanded between Saburovka and Ponyri. Tanks from both sides, but more Soviet, were littering the countryside by now but by 1800 hrs a new wave of 50 T34s came racing onto the battlefield. This was the early hot spot of the campaign and General Rokossovsky was trying to blunt the attack before it got out of hand. The new tanks were attacking the western flank, trying to turn the line, and eventually the flank was threatened. General Model sent reserves to Bobrik to block the attack. mhz242. fkk55. fkk102m. lck290. wwf51+. dgk87m. dgr199m. dgk92m. lck116m. kfz457. dgk93. zzt75+.

At 0230 hrs on that rainy Tuesday morning, the *Luftwaffe* attacked Soviet positions in front of the advancing panzers. Their targets were tank columns coming up to the front line. These same planes made raids the previous night on the same positions. At that time the Germans had to fight off many Soviet fighters. The Germans claim knocking down 162

Soviet planes while losing only seven. fkk54. dgk87m. dgk92m.

After Rokossovsky brought up reinforcements during the predawn hours to bolster the second defense belt, the Germans had a much harder time. The 16th TC went to Olkhovatka to face 47th PzC, the 19th TC to Molotyschi against 20th PzD, the 17th GRC to Kashara north of Olkhovatka against 6th ID, the 18th GRC to Maloarkhangelsk against 78th AD and the 9th TC to advance into the Central Front reserve. The 60th and 65th Armies on the west face of the Kursk bulge sent the 11th GTB to the 2nd TA and two other regiments. The 48th Army sent the 2nd AB to the 13th Army. The attempted counteroffensive by 2nd TA and the western elements of the 13th Army was premature, uncoordinated and was repulsed with the help of the infusion of the 2nd PzD and 9th PzD during the predawn hours into the line west of Ponyri. After the 2nd TA launched, the 104th TB and 164th TB moved closer to the line. If they were needed, it would take them only minutes to react. The two brigades did enter battle but were quickly shattered and had to pull back. See Map 3. wdk174. kcz168. dgr198m. dgk87m. wwf51+. dgk92m. lck116m. kfz458.

During the predawn hours, Rokossovsky ordered Rodin's 2nd TA to deploy to just north of the Teploe-Olkhovatka-Ponyri line. It was the second defense belt. The army with its attachments had nearly 600 tanks and 50,000 men. The 17th GRC was sent to the Ponyri sector and 18th GRC was sent to the Maloarkhangelsk sector. The 19th TC was moved closer to Olkhovatka sector. lck227. dgk87m. dgr199m. wwf51. dgk92m.

In the 47th PzC's sector, the Soviets had brought reinforcements up to the line to plug the gap as well as 200 tanks. A major tank battle ensued that lasted for days. The Germans inflicted heavy casualties and pushed the Soviets back to the Nikolskoe-Olkhovatka-Ponyri line where another series of strongpoints had been built. snk107. fkk102m. dgk87m. dgr199m. dgk92m.

Model penetrated the first defensive belt the previous day with his infantry. On this day the second defensive belt that included Ponyri, Olkhovatka and Samodurovka would be his next objective and he would use his panzers to exploit that gap near Gnilets. During the predawn hours, Rokossovsky reinforced this line and it would be twice as hard to crack than the previous day. The 2nd TA and 16th TC were deployed between Ponyri and Olkhovatka while the 17th GRC dug in between Saburovka and Samodurovka. Other units were also brought up. The Soviet AF received additional planes and it would not be long before the *Luftwaffe* would lose control of the skies in the northern salient. Gnilets was west of Ponyri and north of Teploe/Samodurovka. It was also on the boundary line between 41 PzC and 47th PzC. By the end of the day Model had suffered 25,000 casualties and 200 panzers were either damaged or destroyed. It was a large price to pay for such small returns. lck289+. dgk87m. swm138. lck116m. dgk92m. zro204.

Working throughout the predawn hours Lt General Rodin's 2nd TA completed its redeployment to the Teploe and Olkhovatka area. His 19th TC, recently attached and commanded by Maj General Vasilev, was on the west while Maj General Sinenko's 3rd TC was on the east, closer to Ponyri. Between these two corps was Maj General Grigoyev's 16th TC which was finishing up refueling and preparing for the expected battle at daybreak. One distinctive feature of Rokossovsky's defense at his three critical points of Olkhovatka, Ponyri and Maloarchangelsk was that with each passing day, shelling increased against each German assault on the villages of the second defense belt. Rokossovsky spent almost twice as many shells as Vatutin. Survivors of the Ponyri battles would liken it to a small scale Stalingrad. mhz242+. mhz246. mhz19m. dgr198m. fkk102m. dgk87m. dgr199m. wwf51.

dgk91. dgk92m.

Rokossosky began his opening barrage before his counter-attack was launched. Model during the night had assembled the 2nd PzD and 9th PzD along with sPzAbt 505 into new positions for his planned attack in the center of the line but were struck hard by the Soviet barrage. With both sides reinforcing their line, the upcoming escalated tank battle would last for four days along the empty ridges west of Ponyri Station and would be the second largest tank battle of the campaign. Between Ponyri and Saburovka, over a thousand tanks of both sides, accompanied by infantry and artillery firing over open sights, determinedly fought for possession of the key villages of Olkhovatka, Samodurovka and nearby Hill 274. dgk91+. dgr198m. fkk102m. dgk87m. dgr199m. mkz118. dgk92m. lck116m.

At 0330 hrs, the 47th PzC resumed its attack, striving for a decent penetration of the Soviet line. On the left flank, Grossmann's 6th ID along with the grenadiers of the 18th PzD and the panzers of 9th PzD attempted to bypass the fortified village of Saburovka and head for Hill 274 and Olkhovatka. At this point, Model was confident that the villages of Ponyri, Olkhovatka, Kashara and Teploe would be captured that day with the increased presence of the two panzer divisions. On 47th PzC's left flank, the 292nd ID and 86th ID continued to drive toward Ponyri. Lt General Luebbe's 2nd PzD with its 140 panzers plus assault guns would secure Gnilets and Bobrik on their way to Hill 272 and Teploe. Von Kessel's 20th PzD and 31st ID of 46th PzC would advance southwards along 2nd PzD's west flank. It turned out that 20th PzD reached Gnilets first and by 0830 hrs was fighting inside the village. By 0900 hrs, Gnilets was under German control. The secondary attacks by 46th PzD in the west and 23rd IC in the east were scaled back in order to use their artillery in the center. mkz117. dgk92m. lck116m. snz233++. snz239.

At 0350 hrs, Rokossovsky began a heavy preparation along much of the attack line to soften up the Germans before his land assault began. At 0400 hrs, Soviet fighters passed over 17th GRC and 16th TC sector looking for opportunities when the *Luftwaffe* showed. A major dogfight ensued but despite casualties on both sides neither side gained the advantage. At 0500 hrs, the 17th GRC finally started to get an advantage over the enemy, forcing them to fall back. The Soviets were able to reach the Druzhovetski-Step-Saburovka line (northeast of Samodurovka). On the right of 17th GRC, the 148th RD and 74th RD was fighting, making modest progress toward Trosna and Semenovka. Once past Druzhovetski, Lt Col Teliakov's 107th TB of 16th TC headed for Butyrki but before reaching the village it was ambushed by panzers which were able to destroy 46 tanks before the 164th TB could come up to support. They also incurred heavy casualties and together the two Soviet brigades of 16th TC pulled back between Olkhovatka and Ponyri. With 16th TC severely damaged, 13th Army sent up other mobile forces to strengthen the line. After repulsing the tanks, the Germans advanced toward Olkhovatka against 17th GRC. By 1300 hrs, the 17th GRC and the remaining supporting tanks made a fighting withdrawal back to the second defense belt near Olkhovatka where they were able to stop the German advance. dgr114. dgr108m. lck116m. dgk87m. dgr199m. cbk42. nzk87. nzk86m. dgk92m. dgk93.

At 0350 hrs Rokossovsky launched his counterattack which was supported by fighters. The Soviet forces pushed out of the Olkhovatka area to the north and with the 19th TC from Samodurovka to the northwest. This action was meant to restore the left wing of 13th Army and the right flank of 70th Army. After the Soviet counter was halted, the 9th PzD and 2nd PzD, with the support of sPzAbt 505, resumed their advance between Ponyri

Station and Saburovka for their main target of Olkhovatka but were stopped once again. During the night, Rokossovsky interpreted German actions and redeployed his forces. The 18th RD was sent to Maloarkhangelsk and the 3rd TC was sent to Ponyri but was released to battle in increments. The 17th GRC reinforced the 13th Army and the 19th TC was positioned west of 16th TC to cover any thrusts toward Olkhovatka, though the 19th TC had not completed its redeployment. wwf51. dgk91++. dgr198m. fkk102m. dgk87m. dgr199m. dgk92m. lck116m. pck45.

East of Olkhovatka, the Soviet 148th RD, 81st RD and 74th RD attacked the 292nd ID and 86th ID at Ponyri at 0350 hrs after an artillery preparation. A fierce battle developed around the largest of the three Ponyri villages as both sides added reinforcements, including 9th Army's reserves: the 12th PzD and 10th PzGD. The 307th RD was attacked by elements of the 292nd ID, 86th ID and 78th AD supported by 170 panzers. sPzAbt 656 with Ferdinands supported the 86th SD east of Ponyri. Nearby the 107th TB fought a hard battle with a Tiger battalion; 203rd RR of 70th GRD stopped a Tiger with anti-tank grenades. The 205th RR of 70th GRD was attacked by 60 panzers and destroyed three Mk IVs with anti-tank grenades at close range. The 84th GTDB of 75th GRD was attacked by panzers, including Tigers, and managed to destroy five Mk IVs with 45mm anti-tank guns. A battery of the 729th TDB claimed five panzers at Ponyri. The German 41st IC claimed 28 tanks, most of them T34s. wdk175. dgk87m. dgr199m. dgk92m. lck116m.

The 13th Army and the 2nd TA launched a massive counterattack along the entire front of 13th Army. The Soviets had a 2 to 1 superiority in men and brought over 750 tanks to the assault. wdk174. dgk87m. dgk92m.

The tank battle escalated in the 20th PzD's sector between Saburovka and Samodorovka. Lt General Rodin threw in elements of 3rd TC to support 16th TC that had started the fight. The battle raged into the next day and when it was over the enlarged German counterattack had been stopped and 18 of the 24 Tigers had been stopped as well. The Germans had failed to reach Kashara which was part of the second defense belt. A big factor in stopping the Germans was 19th TC's attack into the flank of 20th PzD near Bobrik. Without the use of the 27th Army which was sent south to Vatutin, Rokossovsky pulled divisions from Lt General Cherniakhovsky's 60th Army and Lt General Batov's 65th Armies which were deployed in quiet sections.The piecemeal fashion that Model sent his panzer divisions into battle was probably the biggest reason why 9th Army gained so little ground compared to 4th PzA in the south. mhz242++. dgr198m. fkk102m. lck290. dgk87m. gjz185. kcz167. dgk92m. lck116m. lck263. dgk59.

At dawn, the Soviets expanded the counter-attack against the advancing German line, spearheaded by 2nd PzD and 9th PzD, near Olkhovatka. The 3rd TC, 16th TC, 19th TC advanced toward the Germans and ran into a minefield the Germans laid the previous night, stopping the advance and forcing them to go defensive. Tigers of sPzAbt 505 came at them, aiming for Hill 274 but they reached only Saburovka by nightfall. Model thought if he could take Hill 274 then he could reach Kursk. Rokossovsky ordered the rest of 2nd TA to move up and dig in and wait for the next assault. He also brought infantry and supplies from 60th and 65th Army sector, from the quiet sector on the front of the salient, to help out. It was a tough day for the 2nd PzD, 9th PzD and sPzAbt 505 which led the assault against the stiff Soviet resistance which inflicted heavy casualties on the Germans. je101+. fkk102m. dgk87m. wwf53. dgk92m. lck116m.

In furthering developments in the center of the front, elements of the 17th GRC's 70th

GRD, 75th GRD, supported by the 16th TC and 9th TC, attacked the 2nd PzD of 47th PzC between Bobrik and Saburovka, six miles from their start line. In short order, elements of the 17th GRC pushed 2nd PzD back to the Druzhovestsky-Step-Saburovka line but were then stopped by a counterattack now being supported by a squadron of Fw 190s that pushed them back to their start line. The 17th GRC entered the battle between Teploe and Olkhovatka, attacking the 47th PzC. The 1st GAD provided strong artillery support to the 17th GRC. All of the 17th GRC had not reached the front line so the units that did reach it had to set off by themselves. Before the ground forces launched, the Red Air Force initiated a heavy bombing run. This scale of aerial attack was unusual for the Soviets which alerted the *Luftwaffe* a major attack was imminent. The *Luftwaffe* at the Orel-West scrambled in the hopes of catching Soviet bombers in the air and helping their own ground forces against the attack. The Soviet AF got lucky on one of their raids, timing it perfectly. The *Luftwaffe* that had been there, left the area to refuel and reload before a new wave of planes arrived; the Soviet planes being unmolested attacked the 47th PzC with deadly affect, inflicting heavy casualties. A little later the roles were reversed and the 17th GRC got hit hard. Both sides continued to escalate throughout the morning, bringing more planes into the area until there was a massive air war taking place over the massive ground war. For one raid, the 15th VA sent planes from airfields east of Orel to assist the 16th VA. Both sides had heavy casualties though the Germans still had the advantage. The Soviets had control of skies in this area early morning but by late afternoon, the Germans had recovered and were at least on par with the Soviets. wdk175. dgr198m. dgk87m. cbk43++. nzk87. dgk92m. lck116m. cbk12m.

Not liking the failed attempt to control the skies plus having Stalin criticize him during the previous night's report, Rokossovsky ordered a much heavier presence of the 16th VA. Rokossovsky had planned a nearly front-wide counteroffensive for today and ordered Rudenko to heavily bomb the German positions ahead of the launch, especially in the center, north of Ponyri. Sergei Rudenko, a Ukrainian, escaped Stalin's purges of the late 30s and was one of the leading architects of revitalizing the Soviet Air Force after horrendous losses during the first weeks of the war. He would retire a Marshal of Aviation. cbk42+. dgk92m. hzs199++.

At 0500 hrs, General Harpe called Model asking for more armor to support 20th PzD which suffered heavy casualties the previous day. Model sent two companies of sPzAbt 505 from 23rd IC sector to the 41st PzC. snz236.

At daybreak, the assault force of the 292nd ID and 86th ID and then later 18th PzD resumed its fight for Ponyri. It had entered Ponyri Station the previous night but was stopped today by the 29th RC without making any appreciable gains. Later at night another attempt was made but the combined efforts of 292nd ID, 86th ID and 18th PzD ground to a halt again due to the stiff resistance of the 29th RC's 307th RD commanded by Maj General Enshin which was dug in around Ponyri Station. The three German divisions were trying to split the boundary line between the 13th and 48th Armies, but without proper air support were not making much progress. At the same time just to the east of Ponyri, the 86th ID ad 78th AD advanced toward Hill 253.5 and the village of Prilepy which was southeast of Ponyri. The 4th PzD was the last panzer reserve Model had and he would be forced to bring that up as well. dgk93. lck293. lck116m. dgk87m. dgk115. dgr199m. cbk47. kcz168. dgk92m.

At daybreak, the 78th AD resumed its attack toward Hill 255.6, having to clear trench by trench, dugout by dugout, foxhole by foxhole but by 1100 hrs, the 14th AR of 78th AD was on top of that hill. Model now had eyes on this hill and could see south and east as to the approach by the enemy. The Soviets would attack this hill repeatedly for days to get it back. With the capture of this hill, the Trosna valley became untenable and the defenders would have to fall back to the east to avoid encirclement. Some 1,300 POWs were captured in the Trosna area on this day. The 23rd IC had penetrated the first line but the second defensive line would be even harder. zzk273+.

Harpe's OPs discovered a large concentration of enemy soldiers of 13th Army assembling for an attack. Model was called and asked for artillery assistance. If this shock group got past 292nd ID, it could easily attack the flank and rear of 47th PzC. Model immediately turned more guns on the coordinates; having 47th PzC attacked from the rear was the worst possible scenario imaginable and had to be prevented. snz237.

At 0540 hrs, General Kluge called Model for an update. General Model predicted the high ground around Teploe, Kashara, Olkhovatka and Ponyri would be captured. If these key objectives could be taken that day then reaching Kursk would be easy. These were ambitious goals and I wonder if Model actually felt that confident of his predictions. He did not like sending the two panzer divisions of 2nd PzD and 9th PzD up to the line to create the gap for he knew casualties would be high and was concerned the remaining panzer divisions would not be enough to exploit the gap and reach Kursk. The 4th PzD, 12th PzD and 10th PzGD were still in reserve behind 47th PzC. As early as this day, Model considered forming a shock group from all three divisions under the control of General Esebeck. Kluge was not in favor of this shock group. He wanted a panzer division to remain in reserve in case 2nd PzA needed help. The 2nd PzA consisted of mostly infantry divisions; the 5th PzD which was in reserve was the only division with panzers – 93 panzers that 2nd PzA had. The 8th PzD had already been ordered up to the salient but would not arrive until 7/12. Model was aware of the risks of using the reserve divisions on 7/7 but that would be the only possible way of capturing those key heights. FM Kluge informed Model that he was arriving at the Front that morning for an appraisal of the battlefield before giving his consent to use all three reserve divisions. snz237+.

At first light, artillery and Stukas bombed the Ponyri villages and the railroad station before the 292nd ID and 78th AD began their assault. The fighting was extremely vicious. A balka and a stream ran through the villages and were a terrain feature the Germans had to overcome. From the north, behind the infantry, the panzers of 9th PzD drove toward the railroad station. There were 60 Mk IIIs and Mk IVs, all with the long barrel 75mm guns. The remaining Ferdinands of sPzAbt 654 were there also. To the east of Ponyri the towns of Goreloie and Prilepy, located on high ground, were also heavily fortified and would also be a tough target for sPzAbt 653. Before taking these villages, the Germans had to capture Hill 253.5 to their north. By the end of the day Hill 253.5 was captured but the Germans could go no further against increasing Soviet resistance. Even with the help of nearby 86th ID, little progress was being made in this sector. mhz246. zzz101m. dgk87m. dgr199m. dgk92m. lck116m. kfz459.

Rokossovsky enhanced his attack plan of the previous night. Elements of 13th Army would hold its defenses near Maloarckhangelsk; the rest of the army along with 48th and 70th Armies and the recently arrived 2nd TA would attack. The 13th Army would attack westward toward Ponyri and Saburovka while the 17th GRC and the 16th GRC with support of the 2nd TA would attack from Orlinka, Prilepy, Bitiug and Kashara eastward toward Ponyri, Ladyrevo and Koshelevo in an attempt to encircle and destroy the Germans attacking southward toward Ponyri. At the same time the 48th Army was advancing toward Panskaia, Shamshin and Zmievka. The 70th Army's left flank advanced toward Kromy through Probuzhdenie and Gorchakovo. The 19th TC and 9th TC, a part of 2nd TA, were moving into the Arsenevski, Trubitsyn and Sergeevskoe area and would move toward Verkhne Smorodnoe, Ponyri II, Stanovoe and Samodurovka upon orders. The 19th TC was running behind schedule and could not begin when the 17th GRC attacked, which greatly diluted the effectiveness of 17th GRC. Only elements of 19th TC launched about noon, while the rest of corps had to support the 70th GRD and 75th GRD. dgr112+. dgr108m. lck116m. dgk87m. dgr199m. dgk92m. dgr199m.

Unlike Hoth, Model was sending his panzer divisions into battle in a piecemeal fashion. The 2nd PzD, 9th PzD, 20th PzD and 18 PzD had been brought into battle little by little over the previous two days. This left the 4th PzD, 12th PzD and 10th PzGD in reserve, though they had been moved closer to the line. The 4th PzD would be called up and enter battle the following day in the Samodurovka area. dgk87m. dgk92m. lck116m.

The 9th PzD, 18th PzD, 86th ID and 292nd ID continued to push south towards Ponyri. So far Model's units had advanced no more than six miles but suffered over 10,000 casualties. bt84. dgk87m. dgr199m. dgk92m. lck116m.

On the right of 6th ID after an hour of fighting, the 112th PzGR of 20th PzD penetrated the woods north of Podolian, allowing the panzers to reach the southern edge of Krasniye Ugolok by 0830 hrs. At the same time, after the mines were cleared, the Tigers of sPzAbt 505 were rolling through the hills southeast of Podolian with elements of the 20th PzD following. fkk53. fkk102m. dgk87m. dgr199m. dgk92m. lck116m.

The 41st PzC reached the outskirts of Ponyri with the help of Elefants. Fierce man to man combat ensued. The 2nd PzD, 9th PzD, 18th PzD were being deployed between Saburovka and Ponyri to support the advance and help take Ponyri. The high ground of Ponyri was the objective; taking it would give the Germans an edge. Hill 272, southwest of Teploe, Hill 274 northeast of Olkhovatka and Hill 253.5 east of Ponyri were the key targets. The battle for the heights would last four days and be fierce. rc184. dgr198m. fkk102m. dgk87m. dgr199m. dgk92m. lck116m.

Shortly after 0900 hrs, 46th PzC discovered that 16th TC and 19th TC had moved up to the line and it was assumed would be attacking shortly. Model was not notified of this development for he was on the road visiting his corps commanders. By 1000 hrs, Model reached Luebbe's 2nd PzD's HQ. Still not knowing that 2nd TA had moved up to the line, Model considered Luebbe's plans for the day excessively cautious but did not comment on it at the time. At 1030 hrs, Model reached Grossmann's HQ (6th ID) to attend a meeting with FM Kluge and General Lemelsen. This was where he discovered 2nd TA was on the line. This development forced Model, with Kluge's approval, to release 10th PzGD and 12th PzD from reserve. Three miles away at von Kessel's HQ (20th PzD), Model was informed that Bobrik, not far from Gnilets, was about to be captured. Gnilets had to be captured quickly because 150 Soviet tanks were moving into sector. Maj General von Kessel was promised Ferdinands from sPzAbt 505 but they were very late in arriving. After learning that many of 2nd TA's tanks were in the western quadrant facing 20th PzD, Model believed there would not be tank reserves moving against 2nd PzD, giving it a chance to break through. Heading toward Lt General Luebbe, Model intended to give the commander some moral backing. He stayed there until 1900 hrs when he returned to his HQ. The 2nd PzD was ordered to take Olkhovatka that day but failed. It gained only a mile and captured Snovo against stiff resistance but could not go any further. The 47th PzC had a dismal day as 9th PzD, 20th PzD and 6th ID also had only modest gains. Model had been criticized for being out of touch with his HQ staff for six hours, claiming the needs of 9th Army was more important than only Lt General Luebbe's 2nd PzD. For example, after Maj General von Kessel's 20th PzD captured Gnilets, the division moved on and captured Bobrik at 1530 hrs before heading toward Podolian. It has been suggested that if Model was at HQ at 1530 hrs, he could have ordered the 2nd PzD and 9th PzD to shift their axis to the southwest to parallel 20th PzD instead of advancing due south, providing all divisions greater gains than actually were achieved that afternoon. When Model found out about 20th PzD at 1630 hrs, he realized it was too late to shift 2nd PzD and 9th PzD, so he tried the "next best thing" by shifting the artillery of 9th PzD to the southwest to support 20th Army. In the time that that artillery was shifted away from 9th PzD, they suffered heavy casualties. This scenario was a good example of the fog of war; taking one direction could lead to totally unexpected consequences. snz239++. snz244.

The Germans made initial progress against Maloarkhangelsk on the first day but Soviet counter-attacks had pushed the Germans back which caused a split between forces at Maloarkhangelsk and Ponyri. This split could give the Soviets an opportunity to drive a wedge between the two groups. Model knew from aerial recon that the Soviets were moving massive reserves into the area. Even this early into the campaign Model's forces were spread out and disorganized. Model called in the *Luftwaffe* to help even the score. dgk87m. dgr199m. dgk92m.

Soviet reinforcements brought up during the predawn hours were able to stop the 23rd IC of 9th Army at Maloarchanglek. The 23rd IC made such a poor showing, Rokossovsky, emboldened, transferred forces from in front of 23rd ID to the Ponyri sector. The 47th PzC was able to reach Teploe-Olkhovatka area before being stopped. The 41st PzC joined up and together were able to move forward again. aaa125m. dgr198m. fkk102m. lck256. dgk87m. dgr199m. dgk92m.

On the right side of 20th PzD, the 31st ID was falling farther behind due to stiff resistance and was still north of Krasnaia Saria which was their first major objective. Finally by 0930 hrs the village was taken. At about the same time, the 112th PzGR of 20th PzD captured the village of Podolian before moving on to the hills south of the village. During this whole time the Red Air Force launched many sorties against the attackers. At 1830 hrs, the 31st ID was able to push through Gnilets, which was a sector objective of the day. At 1905 hrs, the 20th PzD was able to penetrate as far as Saburovka where another five T34s were destroyed and developed a bridgehead over the Svapa. About 18 T34s were destoyed in the engagement. fkk53++. fkk102m. fkk102m. dgk87m. dgr199m. dgk92m.

The 20th PzD battled its way through the 70th Army line and reached Gnilets, the boundary between 15th RD and 132nd RD, and established a gap in the Soviet defense. Once Model learned of the gap, he ordered the three panzer divisions in the area to exploit it. The 2nd PzD and 20th PzD would be in the immediate attack zone while the 9th would be on their eastern flank. Rokossovsky anticipated Model's tactics and had ordered the 2nd TA to come up to the line during the predawn hours. The tanks were waiting for the Germans when they launched at daybreak. dgk87m. dgr199m. swm138. dgk92m. lck116m.

As part of a coordinated effort to reach the critical heights surrounding Hill 274, the 2nd PzD launched an attack on this morning from Nizhnee Tagino to the south towards the Olkhovatka area. For the next seven days, it along with the other panzer division involved made limited gains and on 7/12, the assault was stopped. knz98. dgk87m. dgk92m. lck116m.

After heavy fighting, the 23rd IC was held up before reaching Maloarchangelsk by 13th Army. Rokossovsky had brought up new artillery batteries in this area during the predawn hours and this new strength was having a detrimental affect on the Germans. Many new mines were also laid during the night. These actions plus the stiff resistance of the 294th RD and 254th RD prevented the 23rd IC from going beyond Protasovo. With the ever increasing demands placed on the *Luftwaffe* for support in the Ponyri-Olkhovatka axis meant 23rd IC to the east were not receiving much help from the air. The 23rd was even having trouble protecting the boundary line on its west shared by 41st PzC. The number of German sorties flown for both salient boundaries dropped from 4,298 the previous day to 2,100 on this day. Not having sufficient planes, the *Luftwaffe* was limited to tactical situations of the highest priority. Strategic bombings of rail and road leading to the battlefield were not possible any longer. bt83. mhz248. fkk102m. dgk87m. dgr199m. swm138. dgk92m.

The 9th Army north of Olkhovatka, regrouped and advanced again toward the city but General Rokossovsky brought up the 65th Army to fill in the gap between 13th and 17th Army in the attempt to stop the German advance. He now had 3,000 guns, 5,000 MGs and over 1,000 tanks defending this line. The odds would be slim for a major German breakthrough. Rokossovsky fired more than twice as many shells at the enemy as did Vatutin and Rokossovsky always claimed that was Vatutin's error in execution and why Hoth gained more than twice as much territory as Model. fkk102m. dgk87m. dgk92m. zro206.

As the Germans were approaching Olkhovatka, Rokossovsky ordered the 16th TC and the newly arrived 19th TC of Rodin's 2nd TA to the area to support the 70th GRD and 75th GRD. If Model controlled the high ground it would be a disaster for Rokossovsky. The Soviet general would do anything to prevent that from happening. At 1730 hrs the 19th TC entered battle by attacking west of Olkhovatka but it had the misfortune of attacking at the exact time a large squadron of German planes flew over and attacked. The tankers were hit hard and had to immediately fall back to the Teploe, Knasavka line. The 75th GRD was a tough division having as its core veterans of Stalingrad. dgk117. fkk102m. dgk87m. cbk48. wwf51. dgk92m. mjk85.

Next to 16th TC, the 19th TC would also attack the 47th PzC when they started to make some progress in the morning. The two tank corps had 150 tanks between them and their weight slowed the German advance and inflicted heavy casualties. In the early evening and with the help of sPzAbt 505, Lubbe's 2nd PzD captured additional ground which included Hill 230.0. The 2nd PzD put all its effort into taking Kashara, due north of Olkhovatka and a part of the second defense belt, but was unable to take the fortified town by itself. Vollrath Lubbe had been promoted to Major General in October 1942. He had been with panzers for years but in 1944 he was transferred to infantry, which he considered a demotion. fkk55. fkk102m. lck292. dgk87m. kcz168. dgk116m. dgk117+. lck116m. zsm49.

As the fighting developed the 2nd PzD repelled a fierce counterattack by 6th TC. A massive artillery duel also erupted between 13th Army and Model's 9th Army in the same sector. bt83. dgk92m. lck116m.

On the right of the advancing 17th GRC, the 18th GRC supported by the 3rd TC attacked 9th PzD and 6th ID. The fighting was difficult but the 9th PzD was able to drive back the 81st RD to Berezov Log along the rail line to Ponyri. The 2nd PzD and 9th PzD supported by infantry and artillery penetrated the line and took high ground on both sides of Olkhovatka against the 17th GRC. wdk175. dgr198m. dgk87m. cbk43. mkz119. nzk87. nzk86m. dgk92m. lck116m.

On the far eastern flank the Germans assaulted the boundary line between 48th Army and 13th Army which was defended by the 81st RD. The Germans started to gain some ground but elements of the 307th RD shifted direction and the 103rd TB of 3rd TC was brought up and were able to plug the forming gap. To the west on the boundary line between 13th Army and 70th Army, the Germans were able to penetrate the second defense belt, striving to reach the heights of Olkhovatka. Though Model did gain a little in the center, the 2nd TA and 17th GRC did a good job of preventing a rout. The tenacious fighting by both sides is difficult to imagine but it was horrible. dgr115. dgr108m. dgk87m. dgk92m.

In the afternoon, a reserve unit of 9th PzD was brought on line to attack Ponyri, which was defended by Jenshin's 307th RD, and later joined by other elements of Lt General Pukhov's 13th Army to stop the advance. Reserve Soviet tanks of 3rd TA continued moving to the front line to battle the panzers. jp151. bt83. dgk87m. dgr199m. mkz118. dgk92m. lck116m.

At 1500 hrs, the 112th PzGR (20th PzD) finally captured Bobrik before moving into the Gnilets, Podolian area. By 1630 hrs, Model concentrated his artillery in the 47th PzC sector for the expanded assault there. He still wanted the main penetration to be with the 47th PzC. fkk53. fkk102m. fkk102m. dgk87m. dgr199m. dgk92m.

Though taking Gnilets, west of Podolian, the 31st ID was now stuck in front of Hill 236.7 and Hill 234.1. The 12th GR and 17th GR were able to take the hills west of Krassny and Saria. At 1500 hrs it asked for help. After taking Bobrik at 1530 hrs, the 20th PzD attacked from near Bobrik toward Hill 231.7 (in the direction of Gnilets and Podolian) in the attempt to help the stalled 31st ID. Twenty T34s came over Hill 231.7 and countered the 20th PzD and the Germans failed to take the hill. If the 2nd PzD and 9th PzD had been ordered to change their direction from south to west, there would have been a real opportunity of encircling 16th TC but 47th PzC was not aware and a golden opportunity was lost. Model became aware of the situation around 1700 hrs and it was too late to shift his divisions but he ordered his artillery to shift and fire in front of von Kessel's combat group to attempt to speed his advance. With the shift in artillery, the 6th ID and 9th PzD lost their support and were then at the mercy of the attacking Soviets. They suffered heavy casualties. fkk55. fkk104m. dgk87m. dgr199m. mkz118. dgk92m. lck116m.

Attacking toward Butyrki at the deepest German penetration of the day, Lt Col Teliakov's 107th TB of the 16th TC fell into an ambush by Tigers of sPzAbt 505, losing 46 of their 50 tanks within minutes. The 164th TB, pulling up on the 16th TC's left to assist, was also mauled, losing 23 tanks. As the Soviet tanks retreated, the panzers of 47th PzC followed and reached the Soviet second defensive belt, defended by the 13th Army. The panzers were stopped at this point by 17th GRC's 70th GRD and 75th GRD guarding their well prepared defenses. At 1800 hrs the 150 tanks of the 19th TC moved passed the 2nd defense belt and entered the fray with the panzers of the 2nd PzD and 20th PzD in the Bobrik-Samodurovka sector, just north of Teploe. By night the 2nd TA which started the campaign with 465 tanks was now in a shambles and the remnants had to fall back. Sinenko's 3rd TC was brought up to the line to replace 2nd TA but it was also brought up in piecemeal fashion and was not as effective as it could have been and suffered heavy casualties. Teploe was west and a little north of Olkhovatka. Butyrki was west of Ponyri. (sPzAbt 505 and StuGAbt 909 were part of the 21st PzB). dgk93. mhz19m. dgr198m. fkk53. fkk102m. dgk87m. cbk43. dgk92m. lck116m.

At 1630 hrs Model made a decision that would have dreadful effects on Lt General Scheller's 9th PzD. He ordered 9th PzD's artillery to shift their fire from covering their division over to von Kessel's 20th PzD which was deployed further west in the Bobrik-Pololian area. While the 9th's artillery battalions were supporting 20th PzD, 9th PzD who were attacking toward Ponyri, was severely damaged by a mauling from 307th RD's artillery and supporting tanks. The 9th PzD started the campaign with a full complement of panzers but over the proceeding few days would lose all but a handful of them. mkz118+. dgk92m. lck116m.

At 1700 hrs, Model ordered Lemelsen's 47th PzC to redirect the 2nd PzD,which originally had 140 panzers and 50 SPGs, and 9th PzD, to assist 20th PzD, which had been fighting since the first day to exploit the boundary line it had just discovered to be poorly defended. In the primary attack zone, the 20th PzD was on the right flank, 6th ID and 2nd PzD in the center and 9th PzD on the left near Ponyri. The 31st ID was on the far right with orders to take the high ground south of Gnilets and to push forward to the Nikolskoe-Samodurovka line. On the left of this main spearhead was sPzAbt 505 which was now moving into the eastern part of Saburovka but also had to stop for the rest of the line to catch up. The 47th PzC claimed destroying 157 tanks on this day. fkk54+. fkk102m. pck45. dgk87m. dgr199m. dgk92m. lck116m.

The Germans were bringing up the last of the reserves to feed the line for the following day's assault. It included 4th PzD, 12th PzD, 10th MD and 36th MD. je102. dgk87m. dgk92m. lck116m.

To the northwest of Maloarckhangelsk, the 15th RC, with tank support, attacked the 216th ID from the area around Trosna. Just north of the 216th ID, the 383rd ID defended against repeated counter-attacks from 48th Army. The German 20th IC on the west flank had a quiet day. wdk176. dgk87m. dgk92m. lck116m.

At 1830 hrs General Model, in an OP near the front, studied the 9th PzD's progress and decided that 4th PzD would not advance the following day behind the 9th PzD as originally planned, but would attack to the west of it and 2nd PzD. At 2130 hrs, the army general returned to his HQ where his staff tried to persuade him that the 4th PzD should move behind 9th PzD because of the many casualties of 9th PzD, but Model refused to change his mind. Instead Model combined the 18th PzD with the 9th PzD to help the 9th PzD get past Ponyri by attacking Snovo, which was defended by 16th TC. After taking Snovo the 9th PzD and 18th PzD would stop its advance and go defensive while the 4th PzD and 2nd PzD attacked Teploe, west and a little north of Olkhovatka. The 86th ID and 296th ID would then attack Ponyri. mkz119. dgk92m. lck116m.

At 1830 hrs on the west end of the front, 19th TC attacked through the 132nd RD and 175th RD toward Podolian hitting the 46th PzC's 7th ID and 31st ID the hardest. The Germans were able to repulse the attack and counter-attacked, reaching a line less than a mile south of Gnilets and almost five miles from their start line. Heavy artillery and air attacks cost the Germans dearly for their progress. After regrouping the Germans launched another attack at 1900 hrs and were able to create a bridgehead across the Svapa River, seven miles from their start line. The Svapa ran east-west, north of Samodurovka. The 19th TC was to attack again in the morning with the other forces but was delayed mostly through ineptness which did not please the Front commander. dgr114+. dgk87m. dgr199m. dgk92m. wdk175. fkk102m. dgk87m.

Model left 2nd PzD at 1900 hrs and instead of going straight to his HQ and without informing his Chief of Staff, stopped off to see Lt General Buffa of 12th Flak Division to discuss providing greater protection to 47th PzC. Model finally showed up at his HQ at 2130 hrs. It has also been said that Model needed to delegate more. His staff tried again to convince him to place 4th PzD in the Ponyri sector as was originally planned but he continued to consider the issue. He wanted the division in the Olkhovatka sector and would not budge from that decision. The 2nd PzD, 18th PzD and 9th PzD could have used 4th PzD in the Ponyri-Ponyri II sector and with the support of 4th PzD probably could have broken through, but Model considered Olkhovatka to be the prime sector and 4th PzD would stay close to 20th PzD in that quest. With 4th PzD relatively fresh, Model believed Olkhovatka would be theirs by the end of the day. Even though Olkhovatka was the primary target, Ponyri and the important nearby Hill 253.5 and Hill 239.8 could not be left behind and therefore the attack in the Ponyri sector was also necessary. He spent far too much time away from his HQ receiving valuable information too late to respond to it. With the heavy fighting in the first quarter of the year, 4th PzD was down 2,500 men. The division was also low on transport trucks so AGC gave it 2,500 horses to assist carrying their supplies. By mid March it also had only 36 panzers working, though at the start of Operation Citadel that number had risen to about 100 panzers. Lt General von Saucken also had 13,166 men on the roster. snz245. snz248+.

At night in the Saburovka area, elements of the 46th PzC, supported by Tigers, stormed the city on the northern defense belt. More and more Soviet tanks were brought up until 1,000 tanks were involved as the Germans tried to move on the crucial hills of Olkhovatka with Hill 274 its central point. For the Germans to take Kursk they had to control this high country and the Soviets knew it as well. That is why so many tanks and anti-tank guns were involved. The *Luftwaffe* was called in but due to fuel shortages their raids were not expansive or effective. The Soviet infantry was using their anti-tank rifle to deadly success. fkk102m. dgk87m. dgk92m.

At the end of the day, Model's forces would find themselves just beginning to encounter Rokossovsky's strongest forces defending between Saburovka and the Olkhovatka heights. Rokossovsky originally believed the axis toward Ponyri would be the main attack zone while Olkhovatka would be secondary. While these two axes were most important for Model, it was Olkhovatka that was the primary. Rokossovsky had both axes defended sufficiently and when panzers did not attack in earnest until 7/6, the Soviets had time to mobilize their forces. If Model had used all his panzers the first day while Rokossovsky kept his massive reserves to the rear, Model would have had a better chance of taking Ponyri and Olkhovatka. The slow piecemeal introduction of his panzers gave the Front Commander time to move his reserves to key axes of attack, sealing Model's fate. mhz229. fkk102m. dgk87m. dgr199m. dgk92m.

The combined efforts of 292nd ID, 86th ID and 18th PzD (41st PzC) failed to capture Ponyri after an all day fight. The village was being defended by the tenacious 307th RD. dgk93. dgk92m. lck116m.

The divisions of 47th PzC made no penetrations and barely budged the Soviet line. Over the following couple of days, the 2nd PzD and 9th PzD suffered heavy casualties and would not be able to contribute much for the rest of the campaign. Model did have the 4th PzD, 10th PzGD and the 12th PzD still in reserve but he would call them up much sooner than expected. mkz117. dgk92m. lck116m. snz235+.

By the end of the day in the 41st PzC's sector, despite heavy fighting in the Ponyri area, the Germans were unable to break through the second defense belt. On the east flank, the 78th AD of 23rd IC fought hard to secure Protasovo on the road to Maloarkhangelsk six miles from their start line. In the evening, the 78th AD repulsed a strong counter-attack at Protasovo. Fighting for much of the night the Germans, after fighting house to house, cleared the town then marched another three miles toward Maloarckhangelsk. wdk176. dgk87m. dgr199m. cbk53. dgk92m.

That morning Model had been confident that a breakthrough would occur but when it did not, he became concerned. After dark, General Model called FM Kluge of AGC to request the 4th PzD be released for duty. Kluge was hesitant for he wanted to save 4th PzD for when the Orel Salient came under attack. After a lengthy argument the 4th PzD was released to Model's command. fzk172. kfz457.

Model ordered 9th PzD and 18th PzD to assemble in the Snovo area to block 19th TC which was heading in that direction. With these two divisions at Snovo with a defensive posture, it left only 2nd PzD and 4th PzD to attack toward Teploe while the 292nd ID and 86th ID attacked toward Ponyri. This was potentially a risky maneuver. If either or both sides gained ground while 9th PzD and 18th PzD stayed stationary, then flanks could be exposed. Model came up with an unusual modified attack plan that included the *Luftwaffe* as an important ingredient. The *Luftwaffe* would attack in the 20th PzD/4th PzD sector for two hours then shift to the east to support the 292nd ID and 86th ID then rotate back to the west. In the afternoon, air support would be given to 23rd ID in their attempt to take Maloarkhangelsk. The 9th Army just did not have the force to push the enemy back or the planes to support all the sectors at one time. Rokossovsky had always prided himself that he outmaneuvered Model but the true fact of the matter was that less than 70,000 combat troops to go up against Central Front was just not adequate. snz245+.

The heavy air battles in the northern salient were causing the *Luftwaffe* to use its precious fuel too quickly. It could not keep up the pace. One important air raid that the *Luftwaffe* performed after dark was a raid of 35 bombers on the rail junction at Yelets, northeast of Kursk. All through the night and into the predawn hours of 7/7 the Red Air Force, not having fuel problems, flew missions. Over the last two days General Rudenko was desperately working on communications and procedures for OPs reporting vital information that the Red Air Force needed on a timely basis. Also of concern to General Rudenko was improving escort protection of his bombers. cbk49. aaa63m. aaa106m. dgk92m.

In the north, the Red Air Force flew 779 fighter sorties down from 817 the previous day. cbk55. dgk92m.

Included in the Soviet air arsenal was a squadron of Douglas DB7 Bostons that were part of the American Lend-Lease program. The Boston was a two engine attack bomber that performed well for the Soviets. During the morning attack on 2nd PzD, it inflicted heavy casualties but a couple of them were shot down. Overall the Soviet AF did well that morning against the *Luftwaffe*, while the 17th GRC attacked the 47th PzC in the center of the line. cbk43. dgk92m. lck116m.

By the end of the day, Model's forces made further modest gains in the center of the line and had penetrated the second defensive belt. The 78th AD on the right flank of 23rd IC captured Protasovo. Model was still frustrated because his 9th Army was still behind schedule; he'd hope to have been in Olkhovatka by the end of today. 9th Army had casualties of 3,000 men, half of the previous day but still fairly high when you consider the few gains made. The 292nd ID and 86th ID in 41st PzC sector made the best gains on this day, despite that these divisions had little armor support. The CO of 292nd ID suggested the rugged terrain and the extensive defenses worked against the armor while infantry, having greater flexibility, could maneuver in ways the panzers could not. The 20th PzD war diary for this day complained of not having sufficient infantry to protect its panzers. Even though Model wanted to conserve his armor for the big breakthrough, he knew 9th Army did not have sufficient infantry to easily defeat Central Front. Even though 9th Army had a ration strength of over 200,000, combat strength was only 69,000. That was the biggest reason Model tried to talk Hitler in delaying this offensive, in order to build up and train replacements.

Model's staff estimated that during the first two days of fighting, Rokossovsky lost four tanks to every panzer that was destroyed or severely damaged. Red armor was able to slow or stop the German advance but had been unable so far to push the Germans back. snz242+.

The German 9th Army had advanced about 6 miles into the first Soviet defensive belt, pushing back the 2nd RD, 67th RD and 71st GRD, but the panzers were approaching Soviet tank ambush sites where many Pak guns and tanks were dug-in. In the south, the forces of AGS had penetrated at least ten miles into the Soviet defenses. There was heavy rainfall on the southern battlefield. dgk87m. dgk92m.

During the night additional reinforcements were brought up to the line in the Ponyri sector. The 11th Mortar Brigade, 46th Artillery Brigade, 2nd Anti-tank Brigade's 12th Artillery Regiment are examples. The 43rd TR and 58th TR were moved to the Maloarkhangelsk area. This Kursk defensive gives some indication on how far the Red Army had improved their armor and heavy divisions over the past year. The wealth of artillery and mortar units in both the southern and northern salients had a profound impact in stopping the Germans. The prepared defenses were excellent and for the most part, infantry was trained and prepared to take on this German juggernaut. dgr115. dgr108m. dgr119.

8

July 7th on the Southern Salient

See Map 11

After three days of fighting in the Kursk salient, it was calculated by Soviet estimates that German losses were 1,500 panzers and 600 planes. 20,000 Germans were killed. These figures were overstated. You will find that statistics coming from the Soviet government, especially during and right after the war, were overstated when referring to German casualties and understated when referring to Soviet casualties. OKH estimated that 460 Soviet tanks had been destroyed by the end of this day.

Top *Luftwaffe* ace, Lt Hartmann, shot down seven Soviet fighters over Kursk salient. It brought his kill total to 352 planes.

The Red Air Force slowly began to gain equality in the air, increasing *Luftwaffe* casualties. dgk118.

It was past midnight leading into 7/7 and elements of the *LAH* were still in combat near the hamlet of Teterevino. The several Tigers that arrived quickly destroyed three T34s and chased the remaining tanks away. For the next two hours, the *LAH* met up with harassing fire but when it started raining, making it difficult to identify friend from foe, the action died down. The heaviest fighting of the day (7/6) occurred when it was light and *LAH* launched an attack from the Pokrovka area toward Bolshie Maiachki, Malye Maiachki and Gresnoe in the attempt to reach their objective of the bend in the Psel River at Krasnyi Oktiabr. As part of 1st TA's major counter-offensive to isolate the SS, the 31st TC driving south crashed into *LAH*. For five hours a bitter battle raged with the largest engagement occurring at Bolshie Maiachki. By evening the 100th TB of 31st TC had to fall back from the village. The *LAH* entered the village but was unable to advance further from the still heavy resistance in the area. While this fighting was occurring, other elements of *LAH* captured Gresnoe. The 2nd SS PzC also advanced toward Krasnyi Oktiabr, south of the Psel River, but failed to reach it. Vatutin expected this major armor attack would push *LAH* and *Das Reich* into the Lipvoyi River but instead the SS divisions were still able to repulse the attacks and gain ground at the same time. mhz251. vzz134+. zrl217.

During the predawn hours the Soviets made repeated attacks on the small garrison left by *Der Führer* on the small town of Petrovski. The pressure became so great that the Germans had to fall back to the south to avoid destruction. zow145.

Joachim Peiper spent all of the previous afternoon and evening moving his panzers and trucks toward Teterevino North after advancing through the village of Luchki North. At 0130 hrs on 7/7, Peiper and his battalion were in a hedgehog defense for the night when 16 tanks attacked. As the battle raged and more T34s arrived, Peiper reacted quickly, got his panzers started, engaging the T34s and destroying five tanks, but he was eventually surrounded and needed help. fkk153. gnk163m. zrl217.

At 0130 hrs, Rotmistrov's 5th GTA was driving west but was still 150 miles away from Prokhorovka. The 18th TC and 29th TC were driving down parallel roads in the lead while 5th GMC was trailing in second echelon. Each convoy was 15 miles long. In Moscow, *Stavka* gave the green light to General Rodion Malinovsky and General Tolbukhin, the commanders of Southwestern Front and Southern Front, to make final preparations for their offensive south of Belgorod to pin down German divisions and prevent redeployment to the Kursk area. This would be part of Operation Rumyantsev. For this operation, the Soviets would have 71 rifle divisions or 1.2 million men and 2,800 tanks. mhz260. dgr82+. dgr83m. zra346.

Before dawn, 163 Soviet heavy bombers attacked German rear areas northwest of Belgorod for the second straight night. A little later another 269 sorties of light bombers attacked the same area. The Germans were also active during the night, sending out 50 planes in two groups looking for targets of opportunity. cbk58.

Hoth ordered Hausser to press his attack toward Prokhorovka and take control of the heights along the Prokhorovka-Kartashevka road to the northwest of the rail junction. Knobelsdorff was ordered to stay east of the Pena River and close up on *LAH*. The Germans must maintain a unified line if they were to have any chance of defeating Vatutin. To free up *SSTK* from flank duty, Hausser ordered Lt General Trierenberg's 167th ID to break its current engagement and take over *SSTK*'s position along the Lipovyi Donets. Once accomplished, *SSTK* would redeploy to the west of *LAH* and have the responsibility of crossing the Psel and establishing a bridgehead north of the river. The *SSTK* had to reach the Prokhorovka-Kartashevka road and also to protect *LAH*'s flank as it made a run for Prokhorovka. Hausser reminded his division commanders that frontal attacks should be avoided and to use encircling tactics only. The German generals knew of their panzer weakness and tried to conserve where possible. The relief of *SSTK* from the Lipovyi Donets line would take two days. In the meantime, *SSTK* would continue to clear the ground to the north, along with *Das Reich*. This shift toward Prokhorovka was not a surprise for Hausser. Hoth informed him of that possibility on 5/31. gnk159. agk102. wdk137. vzz30+.

The lead panzers of *LAH* reached Teterevino North for the night where defense procedures were initiated. They were well ahead of the division and were leery about ambushes. A panzer on sentry duty discovered three enemy tanks driving into town and was able to destroy each of them. At daybreak when those three tanks did not return, 30 tanks attacked the town. By then a battalion of 2nd PzGR arrived and with the help of the panzers were able to repulse the attack. With the capture of Teterevino North, *LAH* had traveled about 18 miles from its start point. agk101. nzk90. gnk163m. zrl217+.

By 0400 hrs, General Kruger completed the relocation of his HQ to the woods just south of Hill 246.3. Hill 246.3 was north of Iakhontov. zow145.

At 0400 hrs, the 10th TC left its reserve area in the Staryi Oskol region, east of Prokhorovka, and by 1900 hrs had reached the Prokhorovka area. dgr84. dgr83m. nzk90.

During late night a column of Soviet tanks had crossed the Lipovyi Donets River at Rozhdestvenka and had infiltrated the Nekhaevka-Smorodino area. At 0430 hrs, after discovering the incursion, Maj General Priess sent the 3rd PzR to the area to secure it. zow146.

The leading elements of 2nd PzGR of *LAH* moved north past Luchki South to intercept the roving tank column as ordered the previous night. At 0500 hrs, they engaged the Soviet tanks and for the whole day had to defend themselves against repeated attacks. Without supporting armor, five Soviet tanks were destroyed and their path had been blocked from wrecking havoc further west but the battalion size German force suffered heavy casualties in the blocking maneuver. zrl218.

Just before daybreak, the 52nd GRD and as much of the 23rd GRC that could manage were to redeploy along the line Kliuchi-Hill 226.6-Polezhaev (north of the Psel River) and prevent Hoth from securing a bridgehead north of the Psel River. wwf85+. vzz1m.

The day before, the *LAH* had reached the Luchki North-Teterevino North line but stopped for the evening as the surrounding countryside had not been cleared. During the very early hours of the 7th, Soviet ambush teams went looking for easy prey behind the German line. They were lucky in some instances but unlucky at other times when they went up against superior numbers. After daybreak, the 3rd MC, 1st GTB and 31st TC continued to hit *LAH* along this front sector. During the predawn hours, Pak guns were brought up to the line to support *LAH* against attacks and to give support when the advance got started. Frey's 1st PzGR was able to push the 1st GTB out of Pokrovka last night. Katukov ordered the 49th TB with support from the 100th TB to advance and retake the town. The Soviet tanks were approaching the battle zone when a squad of roaming German planes looking for targets of opportunity saw the tanks and immediately dived for them. The Germans at Pokrovka had no panzer support for it was at Teterevino fighting off an attack there, but the unexpected planes causing confusion and destruction among the Soviet tanks had no doubt reduced the casualties among the waiting infantry. The tanks got within MG42 range and many of the Soviet soldiers riding on the tanks were killed. With the *LAH* north of Teterevino North, German artillery was being moved to Teterevino North to provide cover for the advance on the Psel River and Prokhorovka. gnk159. gnk164. gnk163m. pck67. pck67m. zrl217.

While the *LAH* fought to secure the Pokrovka-Teterevino North line and the 48th PzC advanced along the shallow Lukhanino River between Alekseevka and Pokrovka (exclusive), the 167th ID tried hard to repair the gap between the two corps. Lt General Trierenberg knew of the division redeployment and wanted the front line to be stable before he left for the river. To help 3rd MC, the 40th Army released the 309th RD to Katukov's 1st TA. They would arrive next morning. Krivoshein's 49th TB was moving up to the river to support the defenses in front of Pokrovka. The 1st GTB was already in mortal combat with 2nd SS PzC at Pokrovka. To the west of the village, elements of 2nd SS PzC was still clearing the area since 0600 hrs while 6th TC was defending the Pena River and the road leading to Oboyan. The 86th TB was sent to 1st TA and the 9th Anti-aircraft Division to 6th GA to help defend the Pena River valley. The 48th PzC resumed its advance on the east side of the Pena River and along this road and struck the 6th TC. dgk126++. dgr85. dgr209m. dgr176m. nzk90. wdk135.

While the 49th TB attacked Pokrovka, the 1st GTB defended Pogorelovka and Mikhailovka, south of Pokrovka but 100 German planes arrived and started to attack the villages but failed to push the Soviets from their defenses. Pogorelovka was just northeast of Iakovlevo. gnk165. vzz7m. dgr111.

LAH panzers repulsed repeated attacks from 5th GTC along the line that included Teterevino North. While the Soviets attacked, *LAH* was unable to resume their advance toward Prokhorovka. *Das Reich* also was busy fighting off attacks from 2nd GTC and did not gain any ground during the attacks. gnk165.

Elements of *Der Führer* had entered Iasnaia Poliana, not far from Luchki North or the Prokhorovka railroad to the east the previous night. By 0540 hrs the Soviets had organized a counter-attack to retake the town. Several armored trains rolled up and started firing their guns while a small contingent of men and tanks attacked the town under the cover of fire. A small hunting party of Stukas flew by attacking the trains, destroying one of them. zow145.

At 0545 hrs, the *LAH* and lead elements of *SSTK*, moving from north of Luchki North, headed across fields of hay toward the village of Gresnoe, south of the Psel Bend. To the east, *Das Reich* headed east from Luchki South toward Teterevino South, the last significant fortified settlement in the second defensive belt in this sector. Teterevino, roughly eight miles southwest of Prokhorovka, was the gateway on the land bridge between the Rivers Psel and the Donets to reach Prokhorovka from the south. The 1st TA repeatedly attacked *LAH* soon after leaving Luchki North and its fellow *LAH* column around Teterevino and Bolshie Maiachki. *SSTK* was also involved in these battles and between the SS divisions claimed many tanks destroyed. Stukas were called in and claimed a number of tanks also. Red planes finally showed up and attacked the panzers moving on Teterevino. By the end of the day, Hoth claimed only three Tigers had been destroyed among others being damaged but repairable. Hoth was surprised by the increased presence of armor reserves attacking his 4th PzA. He expected it would take Vatutin a few more days to bring his reserves to sector, giving him more time to reach the Psel, which was taking much too long to reach. The *LAH* claimed destroying 75 tanks, 12 planes and 23 guns that day as well as capturing 244 POWs. *SSTK* claimed destroying 50 tanks of 2nd GTC. A number of working T34s were also captured. mhz257+. dgr209m. gnk163m. zrl220. zow147.

Hoth concentrated hundreds of panzers along the northern front in order to reach and then penetrate the third defense belt. At 0600 hrs, the trailing elements of *LAH* on the left and *Das Reich* on the right moved out from the second defense belt at Iakovlevo and Pokrovka, east of the Oboyan road, with strong support from the Luftwaffe's 8th *Flieger* Corps. The two divisions, driving in open country, were pushing the weary 51st GRD to the north. Nearing noon, elements of 5th GTC, with less than 60 tanks, from northwest of Iakovlevo struck *LAH*. At Mikailovka north of Iakovlevo on the Oboyan road, the 1st GTB was attacked by 100 German planes then 30 panzers and a battalion of infantry. A few miles north of Mikhailovka at Pokrovka, the 49th TB delayed the *LAH* but the *LAH* did push on and captured Pokrovka. As part of Vatutin's armor counter-attack, other tank brigades also tried to stop the *LAH* at Ulianov just east of Pokrovka but were driven north over six miles to Gresnoe. Ulianov has been called Ulianovka by some. wdk133+. hjj121m.

The two western panzer corps incurred greater losses the day before when the *Luftwaffe* diverted planes to 3rd PzC. On this day, the 48th PzC and 2nd SS PzC would receive highest priority. In the early morning the *Luftwaffe* attacked the Dubrova, Lukhanino and Gremuchi areas where the ground forces were trying to completely break through the second defensive belt. Of special interest to the pilots were dug-in tanks and artillery. cbk59. pck69.

At the start of the day, *Das Reich* was positioned from Ozerovski in the north to Teterevino South in the south. The panzers of *Das Reich* were to drive north, secure Teterevino North and then continue to drive further north in order to screen *LAH*'s east flank while it drove on Prokhorovka. The panzers moved out at 0600 hrs and initially met little resistance but it was discovered that a large group of tanks from 5th GTC was assembling near Iasnaia Poliana, southeast of Teterevino North. At 1030 hrs, 40 tanks from Col Zhilin's 22nd GTB attacked Reitzenstein's panzers. After two hours of fighting and suffering heavy casualties, the Soviet tanks fell back to Iasnaia Poliana. The *Luftwaffe* swept in and destroyed more tanks; the remaining tanks escaped further north allowing

Das Reich to reach Teterevino North. In two days of fighting, the 5th GTC had lost almost half of its 200 tanks. While the panzers were busy to the north, the *Der Führer* and *Deutschland* Regiments were fighting a mostly defensive battle all day and did not gain much. *Der Führer* did capture Kalinin and then extended their gains a mile further east to the Belgorod-Prokhorovka rail line but the gains were much less than expected of the division. At the end of the day, *Das Reich* panzers numbered 88 and were deployed near Teterevino North. gnk166++. gnk163m. zow145.

The panzers of *SSTK* were stationed near Gonki, north of Belgorod. The division was supposed to hand over this sector to 167th ID the next morning. Throughout the predawn hours the 26th, GTB harassed the division. Soviet resistance along the river was strong and the infantry moving in would have their hands full. To make it as easy as possible on the 167th ID, Priess ordered a preemptive attack on the Soviet tanks to cull their numbers. The Germans launched but Soviet artillery and planes slowed the German advance. At the same time German artillery fired on Shopino and Nepkhaevo in preparation of an infantry attack on those two villages. *SSTK* did reach Shopino, setting up defenses, but soon Soviet artillery started hitting the village. At 2200 hrs, a series of small recon raids were made in the Gonki area; the Soviets were looking for weakness. gnk171. gnk175.

It was 0700 hrs on the Teterevino-Prokhorovka road and Peiper had been in battle for five hours trying to break out from being surrounded. He had radioed for relief but before it arrived two Tigers came to relieve the trapped men. When Ribbentrop's panzers arrived he engaged the superior force and destroyed six more tanks. Peiper had minor wounds and was taken to an aid station before going back to his outfit which was already on the road. fkk153. zrl219+.

The two previous days the weather had been hot and clear but later that day the temperature had cooled dramatically with a heavy overcast. For the next week the temperature would remain cool and there would be intermittent downpours. mhz251.

The 3rd PzR of *SSTK* moved out from their nightly defense quarters near Shopino and ran into the 48th GTR. After a five hour battle, the remains of 48th GTR once again retreated to the east bank of the Lipovyi Donets. During the day, Maj General Priess moved his HQ to Zhuravlinyi, north of Gonki and not far from the line. kuz194. vzz6m. zow147.

To the right of *LAH*, *Das Reich* reached Kalinin from South Luchki by 0730 hrs and had now covered five miles from its morning start point. At 0920 hrs the Soviet infantry, supported by 35 T34s, attacked *Das Reich* from the northwest but were repulsed by 1030 hrs as were the other tank battles initiated by 2nd TC between Kalinin (*DR*) and Teterevino (*LAH*) throughout the morning. The *Das Reich* advanced over six miles that day and reached Teterevino on the Prokhorovka road but it was still six miles short of the third defense belt. While *Das Reich*'s panzers attacked northward, the *Der Führer* Regiment had to set up defensive positions east of the panzers to protect them from flank attacks. The *Luftwaffe* helped *Das Reich* near Iasnaia Poliana northeast of Teterevino. The 2nd SS PzC by the end of the day were at least six miles ahead of either flank. wdk134. dgk124m. dgr221m.

With having stopped the *LAH* during the night and having taken heavy casualties, the 5th GTC allowed reserves to pass through and then fell back behind the Pokrovka-Teterevino North line. dgr80.

At 0815 hrs, a small German force from *LAH* was holding Luchki North, three miles northeast of Pokrovka. The first Soviet assault failed but the second attempt with 30 tanks succeeded in breaking the line and reaching Luchki North. Additional *LAH* troops, coming from near Iakovlevo, drove through Pokrovka and then recaptured Luchki North. With the slow progress Model was making and the difficulties he was having in the north, Hoth, who was already concerned with his advance, began to have doubts about the success of this operation. The Soviet resistance and depth of defense was far greater than expected. dgk125. dgk124m. dgk95m. snk81. dgr209m. gnk163m. zrl218.

Heading for nearby Pokrovka from Makhailovka, a combat group from *LAH*'s 1st PzGR was attacked by the 49th TB but by 1000 hrs, the 49th TB had to break off the attack and flee to the north. It was a busy morning for *LAH* for it had just repulsed an earlier attack against 1st GTB, north of Iakovlevo as it was heading for Mikhailovka. After defeating the 49th TB and capturing Pokrovka, *LAH* continued its trek toward Luchki North to resecure it before moving toward the third defensive belt as ordered. Just minutes past Pokrovka as it headed for nearby Ulianov, elements of 31st TC, supported by the 29th TDB and 1244th TDR, attacked with 80 tanks and assault guns to prevent the Germans from driving through Ulianov. The attack failed and the 31st TC had to fall back past Gresnoe to the north side of the Belgorod-Oboyan road. By 1500 hrs, *LAH* was able to reach Luchki North, three miles east of Ulianov. The *LAH* had been spread out today and would be for the next several days. Their line covered from Iakovlevo in the southwest to Pokrovka-Bolshie-Maiachki (1st PzGR) to Luchki North to Teterevino North (1st PzR and 2nd PzGR) and just west of Ivanovski Vyselok and Iasnaia Poliana (1st PzR) in the northeast. wdk134. zrl218+.

By 1000 hrs the 1st PzGR had occupied the important Iakovlevo and a little later the village of Pokrovka to the northwest. agk101. gnk163m. gnk69m.

With the advances of the previous two days, the *LAH* and *Das Reich* created a nine mile gap between the two divisions. *Das Reich* was moving east toward the Lipovyi Donets before moving north while *LAH* was moving more north on an axis that included Iakovlevo, Malye Maiachki and Gresnoe. Hausser ordered the two divisions to stabilize the line and close the gap before resuming their advances. This was another example of 4th PzA not having sufficient forces to follow the plan of moving toward Oboyan and Prokhorovka and considering the troubles of 3rd PzC falling even further behind and creating an even greater gap with 4th PzA, it was time for General Hoth to reconsider his alternatives and make some important changes but he did not. Hoth further errored by ordering the 48th PzC, which was already miles behind the SS, to expand his sector to the west of Berezovka, which thinned General Knobeldorff's forces and slowed his northern advance even more. vzz132+.

Starting at 1030 hrs and lasting most of the day, the 2nd PzR (*DR*) defending the Iasnaia Poliana-Teterevino North sector was repeatedly attacked by multiple groups of 30 tanks but while the regiment took casualties, it did repulse each attack. At the same time to the northwest of Teterevino North, elements of 1st PzR (*LAH*) with the support of the *Luftwaffe* was repulsing similar attacks. The oppressive heat of the day plus the fumes made fighting inside those tanks a real torture. zow147.

While *LAH* was fighting a losing battle to take Krasnyi Oktiabr near the Psel River, *Das Reich* was also failing to reach Belenikhino Station and the Komsomolets State Farm which was being defended by the 20th TB and the 6th GMRB of 5th GTC. When the 2nd SS PzC could not take their objectives against the major offensive that Vatutin instituted, they halted their attempts in the afternoon after gaining some of their objectives, and respectively pulled back to Kalinin and Ozerovski, going defensive in order to regroup and hopefully let the Soviet tankers exhaust themselves. If the 2nd SS PzC had achieved a breakthrough at a key site like Gresnoe or Iablochki just north of Bolshie Maiachki, their offensive would have probably continued throughout the day and evening. Despite holding the Germans back, Vatutin wanted to fortify the line further. Getting the 29th DAB and 309th RD from 38th and 40th Armies, they were in their new defensive positions shortly after dark, supporting 5th GTC. Vatutin was also receiving Maj General Popov's 2nd TC from Southwestern Front and it would be at Pokrovka by the afternoon of 7/8. German aerial recon patrols spotted Popov's tanks and trucks traveling north during the predawn hours of the 8th but the column was never attacked by the *Luftwaffe*. vzz136+. dgk109.

On the east flank of *SSTK*, aerial reconnaissance discovered two new tank corps moving to support the existing 2nd GTC on their western flank that stretched to the Oboyan road. The Soviet Air Force was increasing their assaults as well. Now that 4th PzA was past the second defense belt and moving toward the third line, Vatutin was increasing the pressure by bringing in more reinforcements. The 2nd SS PzC claimed to have destroyed 121 tanks and captured 499 POWs that day. wdk136+.

The lead units of *LAH* crossed the Luchki North-Teterevino road and headed for Gresnoe, southwest of Prokhorovka and the gateway to the land bridge between the Psel and Donets Rivers. pck67+.

Elements of the *LAH* and *Das Reich* further south, driving up the road toward Prokhorovka, push Kravchenko's 5th GTC through and past Teterevino North. The advance was halted when the Soviet tank brigades attacked the flanks and the Germans had to shift forces from the front to the sides. To make contact with the 48th PzC, the attack zone was narrowed once reaching the Novoselovka-Luchki-Bolshie Maiachki area. In the Pogorelovka and Mikhailovka region, the Germans, supported by 100 panzers, resumed their attack on the 1st GTB but the line held. The advance of the 2nd SS PzC was slowing down due to the increasing resistance of the 31st TC and other brigades along their growing flanks, which meant forces from the front line had to shift toward the side. Though Teterevino North and Gresnoe were captured on this day, parts of the 2nd SS PzC were still fighting within the second defense belt. dgk124m. dgk125*+. lck275. zzz101m. vzz7m.

The 31st TC had just disengaged as ordered and were moving east to their new positions but were stopped at 1400 hrs when the tanks were ambushed by both *SSTK* and *LAH*, west of Krasnaia Poliana. After a brief battle, the 31st TC had to fall back to the Malye Maiachki line. By the end of the day, 4th PzA gained about three miles. The 5th GTC and 2nd GTC continued to resist 48th PzC's attempt to reach Oboyan but the 3rd MC had suffered greatly and had little strength left. The 6th TC, despite its many battles, was still strong; its 180th TB had just moved out of reserve and into the Urochishche Stanovoe area, closer to the front. Reserves from 40th Army were beginning to arrive on the western flank, making Hoth's job even harder by having to devote more resources to the flank. dgr215.

With the breakthrough of the 51st GRD's line and the subsequent 5th GTC's partial encirclement near Kalinin, the right flank of 2nd GTC was exposed so Vatutin ordered Burdeiny to the eastern side of the Lipovyi Donets. Before retreating, the 2nd GTC with 165 tanks attacked *Das Reich* in an attempt to relieve 5th GTC but was unsuccessful in pushing the Germans back. However 5th GTC, fighting throughout the night, was able to escape though it suffered heavy casualties in the process. This action also meant the second defense belt had been completely breached and the 2nd SS PzC was approaching the third defense belt in the sector. This included the Komsomolets State Farm and Teterevino North, which were defended by the 285th RR of 183rd RD. *Das Reich* had managed to reach the Teterevino North to Ivanovski Vyselok road. It had also sent 10 panzers to the woods south of the State Farm to check conditions. At this point these panzers were within range of Soviet guns. Several panzers were hit and the remainder fell back to Hill 258.2 which was just captured. The Germans were now only six miles from Prokhorovka but now were up against the third defensive belt which would be a tough nut to crack. To the northwest, *LAH*'s right flank was also attacked in this engagement. Other elements of *LAH* deployed near Luchki North were attacked by tanks of 31st TC coming from the northwest which caused heavy casualties but the attacks, with the help of the *Luftwaffe*, were eventually repulsed. Other grenadiers from *LAH*, deployed further west, captured Pokrovka by mid morning. After the battle for the village, tanks from 31st TC driving south attacked the village trying to retake it but failed. Pokrovka was five miles west of Luchki South and about 15 miles southwest of Prokhorovka Station. vzz129. vzz8m. gnk119. gnk113m. zow147.

Some of the riflemen manning the front line would report back to their commanders of the craziest circumstances they ever witnessed. They would see Tigers deliberately drive into anti-tank ditches and, attacking the far wall at an angle, would claw their way using their weight and wide tracks to grind up the far wall, eventually climbing up and out of the ditch. mjk87.

After forcing the 48th GTR to cross to the east side of the Donets the previous day, *SSTK* shifted to the west and fought its way to the Iasnaia Poliana line where the 168th ID was stationed. By the end of the day, *SSTK* had knocked out another 41 tanks and SPGs. fkk136.

The 29th Anti-tank Brigade heavily engaged the 2nd SS PzC but, despite the determined effort, by late afternoon the panzers had taken Teterevino North and the Soviet brigade was virtually wiped out. bt85.

The *Luftwaffe* made repeated runs in the *LAH* sector that day as the SS division drove toward Prokhorovka. The *LAH* admitted that without air support no gains would have been made. cbk61.

By the afternoon, leading elements of the *LAH* had reached Teterevino North while *Das Reich* on its right had reached a position between Petrovski in the south and Kalinin in the north. The *SSTK* and 168th ID were still providing security on the east flank along the Lipovyi Donets. Kalinin was almost due north of Teterevino South on the west side of the Lipovyi Donets River. It was also just west of the Belgorod-Prokhorovka railroad. wdk138*+. dgr209m. hjj121m. dgk222m. dlu63m. dgr221m. vzz7m.

Even now, so soon into the campaign, it was going as General Hoth had envisioned, at least in regard to the advance of 2nd SS PzC in the direction of Prokhorovka. Originally the Oboyan route was primary but the general thought the Prokhorovka corridor route though longer to Kursk could turn out to be advantageous. On the road from Pokrovka, southwest of Luchki North, to Prokhorovka, Hausser's 2nd SS PzC were making modest gains against the second defense belt held by Chistiakov's 6th GA and Katukov's 1st TA, which were strongly entrenched along the Pena and Lukhanino Rivers and in front of Prokhorovka. This move by 2nd SS PzC was moving away from the main objective of Oboyan. The 48th PzC continued to move toward Oboyan while trying to protect 2nd SS PzC's left flank. *SSTK*, on 2nd SS PzC's right flank, was pushing Soviet forces back toward the Lipovyi Donets River and still had not been able to contribute to the northern attack. As the corps neared the Psel line, the 168th ID would be forced to defend the flank on its own to allow *SSTK* to move up alongside *LAH* for the final push across the Psel. By nightfall the Soviet 49th TB of 3rd MC and 100th TB of 31st TC slowly gave ground around the key Pokrovka and Bolshie Maiachki sites, withdrawing toward the Psel River. This situation was brought about by the failure of 3rd PzC to clear the Donets Rivers in the first few days, allowing elements of 69th Army and certain tank corps to continue to harass 2nd SS Corps. dgk123+. dgk95m. dgk222m. dlu63m. dgr80.

The *SSTK* and 168th ID were guarding the east flank in the Shopino area on the Lipovyi Donets River. Defending the west bank of the river was 375th RD and 2nd GTC. At 1900 hrs, the *SSTK* reached the highway west of Shopino and drove the Soviets across the river. The Soviets countered around 2300 hrs with air attacks and heavy artillery, stopping *SSTK* on the high ridge one mile west of the river where they ended their day of advancement. Before retiring for the night, the division spent couple hours building a defense against possible ambushes. wdk134. dgk222m. dlu63m.

In addition to the other reinforcements brought up to the second defense belt, the 242nd TB and 237th TB of 31st TC were brought forward to defend the Ozerovski area. dgr80.

At night, Priess of *SSTK* reported to Hausser that his division had destroyed only 41 tanks and assault guns and captured only a few POWs, weapons and supplies. It was a meager return. Most of those tanks were from the 48th GTR. kuz194.

By the end of the day, *LAH* had reach Luchki North about three miles northeast of Ulianov. The 31st TC retreated north on the Oboyan road with 3rd MC. The 52nd GRD had also retreated eight miles to the north bank of the Psel River at Polezhaev. General Vatutin was alarmed by the 2nd SS PzC's advance and was trying to break their momentum. wdk134. dgk124m. dgr221m.

In the southern salient, the 8th *Flieger* Corps reported downing 96 planes, 1 train, 44 tanks, 20 guns and 50 vehicles. These claims, especially the destroyed planes, were high. According to Rudenko, the Soviets lost only 63 planes. cbk61+.

It was only the third day into the operation and Hausser's 2nd SS PzC's right flank was exposed due to Kempf's inability to keep up with the advance on the east side of the Donets. The 2nd SS PzC made little gains for it was busy defending both flanks. By the end of the day Hausser had secured a line from Teterevino to a point northeast of Rozhdesdevskoye. The 48th PzC, after breaking through the initial defense zones, also transferred the rest of 167th ID to 2nd SS PzC. Rozhdesdevskoye was just west of the Donets River. snk77+. dgk124m. vzz497.

Wittmann and his SS Panzers had destroyed many T34s on their way to Teterevino. A motorcycle company accompanying the panzers captured a Soviet brigade HQ before entering Psyolknee where the Soviets counter-attacked but were repulsed. The SS divisions were making progress on a narrow front but their flanks could not keep up which gave the Soviets the opportunity to attack the SS panzers from the sides as well as the front. Vatutin was sending up reserves to stem the gains of the panzers. Stalin made it clear that the Germans could not make it to Oboyan. rc197.

By the end of the day, more of Vatutin's reinforcements had arrived in sector, slowing the German advance, and more reinforcements would be arriving over the next few days. Vatutin was planning on using these reinforcements for another major assault in the morning but some of these forces arrived late and the major assault turned piecemeal and confused. Hoth wanted to be at Oboyan by now but was not close to that objective and the general did not make any dramatic changes to his deployments to achieve this. Hoth had always claimed the 2nd SS PzC was scheduled to move toward Prokhorovka but with the scale of resistance the Soviets were exerting against all three corps, those pre-campaign plans should have been reconsidered. The troubles that 3rd PzC was having on the eastern flank just made things worse and the terrain that 48th PzC had to traverse as well, as the pressure the Soviets were exerting on its western flank, was slowing it down. To make the situation even worse, Model's 9th Army was doing poorly and reserves meant for Rokossovsky were now heading for Vatutin – 27th Army. vzz138. dgk123+.

German intelligence sent a report to von Manstein that estimated 500 Soviet tanks had been destroyed since the start of the campaign but that Vatutin had another 1,500 remaining.

The Soviet 5th GTA under Rotmistrov was ordered to continue their march to Prokhorovka but also had auxiliary orders to head for the Protochino area if Prokhorovka fell before they arrived. This was the expected route the panzers would take to reach Kursk and Rotmistrov was ordered to stop them, no matter the cost. His leading tanks would cross the Oskol River to the west side by the next morning. The 5th GTA was still a day, probably two days out from its assigned area. Stalin also provided a large air cap to prevent the *Luftwaffe* from getting near and identifying the size of the columns or to harass the tankers. dgk121+. jp156. zra346+.

By midnight east of the Donets, Kempf Group was making little progress, alarming 4th PzA. It allowed Vatutin to redirect his 2nd TC westward to attack 2nd SS PzC on its east flank near Gostishchevo. Gostishchevo, situated on the important Belgorod-Prokhorovka rail line, was midway between the Lipovyi Donets and the Northern Donets Rivers. vzz3m. vzz5m.

Kruger's *Das Reich* had to expand its front to accommodate *SSTK*, shifting forces further east to handle the increase resistance on the east flank along the Lipovyi Donets River. dgk125. dgk222m. dlu63m.

At night Vatutin ordered Lt General Chistiakov's 6th GA in the west and Lt General Kriuchenkin's 69th Army in the east to prepare during the predawn hours to counterattack toward the Iasnaia Poliana, Pokrovka and Iakovlevo region next morning. Vatutin became concern for Kriuchenkin who appeared to be losing control of the situation and his army, but allowed him to command this attack. The assembly included the 2nd TC, 2nd GTC, 5th GTC,10th TC, 6th TC, 31st TC, 3rd MC and the 89th GRD and 375th RD with the objective of driving a wedge between the SS divisions and encircling as many forces as possible to destroy. The 2nd GTC along with 89th GRD crossing the Lipvoyi Donets would attack toward Luchki South from the east, cutting off the Germans north of that village from those that were south of it. While the other units would attack toward Vasilevka, Komsomolets State Farm and Belenikhino in order to drive a wedge between *LAH* and *Das Reich*. The 5th GTC was in a terrible condition, having lost half of their tanks the day before, but had about 100 tanks still working. Deployed just north of 2nd GTC, the 5th GTC would head almost due west toward Luchki North. The 2nd TC which hasn't arrived in sector yet would attack just north of 5th GTC. The 10th TC which was currently arriving would attack along the Prokhorovka road toward Teterevino North. The 6th GA, 3rd MC and 31st TC defending the Psel bend would drive south toward the Gresnoe, Malye Maiachki and Bolshie Maiachki area forming the northern boundary of the intended encirclement of the 2nd SS PzC. On the west flank, the 6th TC would attack 48th PzC in order to prevent that corps from sending units to assist 2nd SS PzC. Just like the offensive launched on this day, the planned offensive for tomorrow would fail to reach its objectives and for the same reasons: the new brigades coming into the sector did not have sufficient time to prepare or to study the intended battlefield and therefore could not fine tune their attack on the enemy. Most importantly the attacks were uncoordinated with several brigades arriving and beginning their attacks many hours too late. One of General Vatutin's faults was his impatience. He frequently forced an offensive before the participants were ready and the big offensive scheduled for tomorrow is a prime example. Half of the tank brigades were not even at their launch points or resupplied for the attack. Needless to say the attack the next day would not go as it was intended. The offensive should have been postponed a few hours to allow for better coordination and preparation. vzz139+. vzz143+. vzz8m.

The *Luftwaffe* had sporadically supported the 3rd PzC for these first three days. Sometimes the support would be strong and helpful and at other times non existent, but due to attrition and the needs of 48th PzC and 2nd SS PzC, air support would diminish dramatically on the eastern flank after today. If the *Luftwaffe* could have supported the 3rd PzC properly, there would have been a good chance that Kempf could have linked up with *Das Reich* by 7/12 and entrapped large numbers of 69th Army. I' have wondered how the campaign would have evolved if 48th PzC and the SS Corps had stayed defensive once the Hill 260.8-Hill 241.6-Komsomolets State Farm line was reached in order to regroup and temporarily devote more air and panzer resources to 3rd PzC for Kempf to catch up. Vatutin would have had to devote additional resources against Kempf, relieving a little pressure off the other two corps when their advance resumed. The greatest air activity for both sides occurred in the Malye Maiachki, Verkhopenie, Iakovlevo, Teterevino, Novoe Oskochnoe, Verkhni Olshanets, Melikhovo and Kazache areas. dgr254++.

By the end of the day, the *LAH* continued to extend its salient northward. The grenadiers had reached the important town of Gresnoe, captured Teterevino and Iasnaia Poliana and were within sight of the important Komsomolets State Farm that was situated along the road to Prokhorovka. The west side of the salient had narrowed from the previous day as the *LAH* concentrated on moving toward the important rail junction to the northeast.

Hoth was extremely disappointed with the day's progress. He thought the Soviet defense was about to collapse and expected his coordinated attack would finally shatter the line. All three corps made little progress and continued to fall behind Hoth's estimated schedule. *GD* had broken through the second defense belt, reaching the Belgorod-Oboyan road and had the appearance of finally taking off but all of a sudden, the 6th TC appeared and halted *GD*'s advance. Hoth was especially disappointed with the high failure rate of the Panther. There were so many Panthers still on the battlefield that the recovery teams were not able to bring them back in a timely fashion to be repaired. *GD* had a net loss of 220 panzers including the Panthers in the four days of fighting. To help *GD* get back on course, Hoth ordered the SS panzers to disengage during the night and assemble north of Teterevino North and be prepared to attack to the northwest toward the Solotinka River into the flank of 1st TA that was blocking *GD*. This action would also assist in protecting *LAH*'s west flank. With the benefit of hindsight, this move by Hoth to send *LAH*'s panzers over the next two days to the Solotinka region was to be a poor decision and is a perfect example of the fog of war. This will be discussed further with the coverage of 7/9. See Map

11. gnk186+.

By the end of the day, *LAH* had only 41 assorted panzers working. They started the campaign with 92 panzers. Quite a few of the 51 downed panzers were repairable and would see further action in the days to come. In fact by the 12th, *LAH* would have half again as many panzers on the field. The *LAH* had gained some ground and was now five miles ahead of 48th PzC which meant *LAH*'s west flank was exposed. The mini-salient that *LAH* was carving out was growing, exposing more of its flanks to the enemy. The division was spending more of its resources to protect their flanks. This was an issue that is repeatedly mentioned in this book. Hoth had to have seen this salient from the first day. He clearly knew the problems associated with a salient. He could see 48th PzC and especially 11th PzD could not keep up with 2nd SS PzC and yet he did not do enough to correct it. His solution was to send the panzer regiments of *LAH* and *Das Reich* to the northwest the next morning to clear the resistance on the boundary between 11th PzD and *LAH*. While there were some beneficial results of this action, it clearly was not sufficient. The patient was given a band-aid when he needed an operation. The tank recovery and repair teams for both sides performed super human feats to have as many tanks on the battlefield as possible. gnk166. gnk117.

There was a downside to sending SS panzers to the northwest the next day to help 11th PzD. By trying to help 11th PzD, the momentum of both *LAH* and *Das Reich* was hampered and any benefit that accrued to the operation was temporary. The exact same thing happened to *GD* when it had to turn west to help 3rd PzD. With the three Fronts that Stalin sent to the Kursk salient there probably was not any way the Germans could have won but if I was von Manstein, a constriction of the flanks would have been tried by 7/7 and in fact with the dismal start the 3rd PzC had on 7/5, the constriction would have started on 7/6 by moving Kempf back to the west side of the Donets. This would have freed *SSTK* to head north several days sooner which would have helped both 11th PzD and *LAH*. The 167th ID could have been redeployed as well – either with the *SSTK* or to the west to support the 3rd PzD. Admittedly, making such a redeployment during battle would not be easy but it could be done and with beneficial results. It would not have been any worse than the redeployments that were being planned for Operation Roland. Better yet than constricting 3rd PzC would be to constrict 48th PzC sector. The three armored divisions of the 48th were not strong enough to advance on such a wide front and still handle flank duties at the same time. A withdrawal was in order.

By the end of the third full day of fighting, Hoth had suffered 10,000 casualties. The *Luftwaffe* had still retained control of the skies but just barely. The Soviet pilots were tenacious and would not give up. The 8th *Flieger* Corps flew 1,829 sorties while the VVS flew 1,536 sorties. cbk61. nzk77.

During the night after receiving Vatutin's new attack orders for the next morning, his corps commanders prepared their forces. Maj General Burkov's 10th TC with nearly 200 tanks moved south on the Prokhorovka-Teterevino North highway and directly attacked *LAH*. Burdeiny's 2nd GTC, using 140 tanks, moved to the river to attack *Das Reich* south of Teterevino North while Popov's 2nd TC with 168 tanks was to give support to Burkov as soon as it arrived in sector later in the morning of the 8th. Kravchenko's 5th GTC with only 100 tanks also moved to the river near Belenikhino. Almost 600 tanks would be attacking *LAH* and *Das Reich*'s east flank next morning. There were 400 more tanks attacking from the north and west and at the very least Vatutin wanted to isolate the SS divisions from their supply lines but was really hoping for nothing less than the complete destruction of the SS Corps. gnk187.

At 0300 hrs after hours of shelling and air raids, the *GD* along with the 3rd PzD and 11th PzD on each side resumed its attack up the Oboyan road. At the same time, *Das Reich* and *LAH* began their advance from west of Belenikhino toward the northwest. At 0400 hrs, these two groups engaged 1st TA. Katukov asked for air support and the aircraft attacked the Germans in the Olkhovka-Iakovlevo-Kozmo-Demianovka area. A second wave of Luffwaffe showed up and ignited a dogfight which saw many planes fall from the sky, many of them Soviet. fkk83+. vzz115+.

The 11th PzD on the right flank of 48th PzC launched at 0300 hrs and took the high ground a mile east of Dubrova, driving back the 67th GRD. The *GD* in the center broke through the defenses and finished securing Dubrova and its immediate countryside before moving north on the Oboyan road and at 1430 hrs after repulsing an armor ambush crossed the Pena River. A little later the 11th PzD and the *GD* met up with 3rd MC and the 31st TC of 1st TA on the Oboyan road. It is claimed that T34s knocked out five Tigers at close range in this engagement. Nearby, not far from Syrtsevo, the 112th TB of 6th TC blocked *GD* north of Syrtsevo claiming to have knocked out 15 panzers which included six Tigers. These claims of destroying so many Tigers seem high. The 48th PzC had orders to penetrate through the second defense belt by the end of the day but it did not seem possible. Verkhopenie, west of the Oboyan road, was six miles away, Pokrovka on the east side of the road was nine miles away and the 48th PzC was falling behind the 2nd SS PzC with every hour. The 48th PzC had greater resistance to overcome and it was getting worse with all the reinforcements Vatutin was bringing to the line. The 86th TB with 60 tanks had joined 1st TA. These attacks by 1st TA were in support of 6th GA which was falling back in this important sector. The 112th TB was Katukov's last reserve; any further help would have to come from Vatutin or *Stavka*. wdk135*. hjj121m. dgr209m. zra61. pck69. hsz122.

Though *GD* and 11th PzD started early, by 0400 hrs, the entire 500 plus panzer force of 4th PzA resumed its attack against Chistiakov's 6th GA, between Syrtsevo and Luchki South. A rolling artillery barrage fell in front of the panzers to clear the way as they moved north. Stukas were flying above looking for target opportunities: tank columns, manned trenches or artillery. The boundary line between 1st TA and 5th GTC was between the villages of Luchki South and Gresnoe and would be a prime target. This coordinated attack was immediately reported to Vatutin, His main concern was for his forces (1st TA) in front of 48th PzC and he quickly reacted by sending all available reserves up to bolster the line as well as redeploying troops from "quiet" sectors to combat *GD* division and 11th PzD. mhz251+. mhz260. dgr209m.

Unlike the first night, the previous night and predawn hours saw *GD* stop their advance and throw up a defensive posture. They were in the middle of the second defense belt and they were surrounded. Tanks of Krivoshein's 3rd MC were redeploying on the west bank of the Pena River and could easily be heard. The 3rd MC consisted of the 1st TB, 3rd TB and the 10th MRB located here and the 49th TB which was to the east fighting *LAH* along with 1st GTB. Katukov's brigades had suffered heavy casualties and requested from Vatutin additional reserves. Vatutin ordered anti-tank units from the 38th and 40th Armies which were situated further west of the Pena River. Katukov's last mobile reserve, the 6th TC was moved eastward to block *GD*'s northward march. The 112th TB was in the lead as the 6th TC and already engaged *GD* and part of 11th PzD. gnk182.

JULY 7TH ON THE SOUTHERN SALIENT   155

At dawn the 48th PzC launched an attack northward, with Tigers in the lead and with air support, from the Dmitrievka and Olkhovka area against the 1st TB and 3rd MB of 3rd MC and 31st TC. Eventually the Germans broke into the 1st TB line, forcing the Soviets to fall back to Syrtsevo. The *Luftwaffe* was called in and made several critical runs that inflicted heavy casualties on the Soviets. Before long the 3rd MB had to fall back as well. The retreat of both brigades was covered by the 49th TB but without assistance they fell back as well. To assist 3rd MB at Syrtsevo, Vatutin redeployed 112th TB of 6th TC to Syrtsevo while 200th TB was sent to Verkhopenie, north of the current line in case Syrtsevo fell. The 180th TB which had just arrived at Oboyan was sent to Stanovoe Woods. The 67th GRD was still retreating but would make a stand between Syrtsevo and Verkhopenie. Other artillery formations were brought up to Verkhopenie as well. dgr214+. cbk59. cbk61. dgk404.

At dawn, the 3rd PzD began marching toward Lakhanino as ordered, arriving there by 0600 hrs. On the way to the town, the 3rd PzD could hear Stukas hitting the surrounding area. The 3rd PzD was still having trouble with getting their big guns up to the line and the air support was critically necessary. By 1430 hrs, the 394th PzGR of 3rd PzD was crossing the small tributary of the Pena River, northwest of the Lakhanino area. At the same time, the 3rd PzGR assaulted Lakhanino to clear the last resistance from the town. Engineers were brought up with flamethrowers and satchel charges to go house to house. After clearing the town, the engineers built a bridge over the stream to allow the remaining panzers to cross while still dark. gnk184. cbk61.

Mickl's 11th PzD, to the right of *GD*, launched at dawn. They were ordered to penetrate through the second defense belt and reach the Oboyan road. Two fortified hills, Hill 229,4 and Hill 245.2 were key strongpoints in this sector that Mickl would have to take. The attack started at 0330 hrs and by 0730 hrs Hill 229.4 on their right flank was captured. Taking this hill weakened the line and before long the Germans were making good gains. The lead panzers found another minefield that slowed their advance but with the help of engineers they cleared a path through and Hill 245.2 was next to fall. The battle for Hill 245.2, on the boundary line with *GD*, initially gave the Germans a lot of trouble but it eventually fell. *Luftwaffe* aerial recon tried to hurry Mickl's advance as the planes spotted 50 tanks leaving Pokrovka heading his way and if the hill was not secured before the Soviets arrived, the division would be in a critical position. Additional bombers were brought in from other sectors to help soften the hill. With the extra help of the *Luftwaffe* the hill was taken and the lead panzers went ahead, reaching the important Belgorod-Oboyan road then traveling another mile to reach the Hill 251.2, northwest of Pokrovka, by late afternoon. gnk185+. gnk163m.

At 0500 hrs, Katukov's 1st TA with 100 tanks launched an attack on *GD*, 11th PzD and *LAH* as they were pushing north from around the Iakovlevo area in 6th GA sector. This battle raged for hours with the T34s being the victims of the longer shooting guns of the panzers. Before the battle was over the air forces of both sides were brought in, causing further casualties. The *LAH* claimed destroying 20 tanks. Krivoshein's 3rd MC was hit hard as was 6th TC, both falling back toward Syrtsevo and Gremuchi. Soviet artillery covered the retreat well, slowing the Germans from following. With 48th PzC approaching Syrtsevo, Katukov brought up the 67th GRD to help defend the critical strongpoint. With the heavy fighting of the last days plus the minefields and mechanical failures, *GD* had only 40 of the original 192 Panthers still working. Most of the 148 Panthers would be recovered and repaired to fight again. Besides the mechanical problems, it was quickly discovered the Panthers had poor radio comms. mhz253+. dgr209m.

Strachwitz started the day with only 73 working panzers, half of them were from Col Lauchert's Panther Brigade. Seventy-six Panthers were out of action due to mechanical troubles; most of the others had wheel and track damage due to mines. There were only a few Panthers destroyed from tank battles. Just before daylight the Grenadiers and engineers of *GD* penetrated the tank ditch and encircled the village of Dubrova. The panzers moved closer to support but the Soviet defenses were still too strong; Strachwitz requested air support. At 0800 hrs after an hour of aerial bombing, the panzers launched toward Dubrova. Finding some weakness on the eastern perimeter, the Germans shifted their attack. Hill 254.5, not far from the road to Dubrova started firing on the German attack. A few panzers moved toward the hill but were repulsed. The Panthers ran into a minefield and were damaged by mines; unable to move, the Soviet guns on the hill started pounding the panzers on their thin side armor. All the panzers, around five or six, were destroyed. gnk182. dgk127. dgk409. pck69.

Once *GD* made it past the tank ditch, the advance toward Hill 254.5 was still tortuous for the heavy fire continued. The remaining two Tigers hit mines as soon as they passed the ditch and were out of action. It was now up to the Panthers to reach the top of the hill. While the hill was being fought over, Strachwitz's other panzers made it past Dubrova and headed north. Just before noon and a few miles north of Dubrova and east of Syrtsevo, Shrachwitz's panzers approached and secured Hill 230.1. Without much trouble the panzers rolled through, past Syrtsevo, and were nearing Hill 218.5 when they were ambushed by 112th TB of Maj General Getman's 6th TC. Thirty tanks from the north and 20 tanks from the south were trying to encircle and destroy the lead panzer group. Strachwitz was able to fall back and regroup without losing too many panzers. While this was going on, the Fusiliers of *GD* to the southeast were fighting for the town of Syrtsev, just northwest of Dubrova. The Red Air Force was called in but had little success for the Fusiliers penetrated the front line and was fighting within the town by nightfall. From within the center of the town, the Soviet garrison, with support of their new 12.2 cm assault gun, staged a counter-attack which failed. Soviet artillery and aerial bombing continued; it was decided to pull back from town and try again in the morning. Hill 230.1 was also four miles south of Verkhopenie. gnk183+. gnk214. vzz2m. wwf45. dgk127+.

Shortly after capturing Dubrova Group Strachwitz's Panthers drove into a minefield where many panzers were damaged. As the Germans were trying to extract themselves from the field, Soviet artillery and tanks were firing on them. Most of them that were recovered could be repaired but it would take time and slow their advance. After Dubrova, *GD* moved north to Syrtsev and Point 1.2 north of Syrtsev. Point 1.2 was taken only after fierce hand-to-hand combat. Both objectives were costly, especially after two waves of IL-2 aircraft came in low, battering man and panzer. After securing the village on 7/8, it was discovered the Soviets had built underground bunkers three stories high. The Soviet garrison at Syrtsev fell back to either Gremuchi or Syrtsevo to the west. hsz122. fkk265. pck69. dgk127. wwf45. wwf86.

Moving north with *GD*, the 11th PzD was north of Dubrova and now twelve miles from Oboyan. Reaching this far meant the panzers had breached the Soviet second defense belt, dividing a wedge between 1st TA and 5th GTC. *GD* broke through on both sides of Syrtsev, pushing its defenders back into Syrtsevo and Gremuchi. With the Soviets concentrated in a small area, the German artillery found them easy prey. In the afternoon, the panzers were moving on Syrtsevo but hit a minefield and had to stop when Soviet artillery fired on them. bt85.

On the west flank, the 48th PzC was still struggling to penetrate through the second defense belt. The 3rd PzD provided security for the western boundary in the morning as the rest of 48th PzC drove toward Oboyan. In the afternoon the 332nd ID relieved the 3rd PzD in order for the panzers to help with the spearhead. Once on the front line, the 3rd PzD attacked the 90th GRD north of Lukhanino on the Pena River. To the east, the 3rd PzD attacked the Soviet position a mile northeast of Iakovlevo, pushing the 52nd GRD northward. This was another example that showed the Germans were constantly under attack in one way or another. Capturing strongpoints was not a guarantee that the area behind the moving front line was secure. The Germans were constantly having to clear areas multiple times. wdk135.

In an attempt to curb the progress that *GD* and 3rd PzD were beginning to make, the Red Air Force sent a large squadron of assorted planes to attack, including 82 IL-2s and 122 fighters. This large attack force overwhelmed the few German planes in the sector and inflicted heavy casualties on the ground forces. This group by the end of the day, making repeated attacks, dropped 10,000 PTAB bombs on the enemy. cbk60.

Vatutin ordered the 309th RD, 9th AD and 86th TB to be transferred to the control of 1st TA and be deployed in the Ivnia and Zorinskie Dvory area. This line was north of the German front and was intended to be a blocking force. dgr215+.

The 2nd SS PzC and the 48th PzC attacked the 6th GA and the 1st TA with almost 500 panzers defending along the Pena and Lukhanino Rivers and as far as southeast of Pokrovka. Expecting trouble, Vatutin brought all the reserves within reach during the night. For the following two days, bitter fighting would rage as 2nd SS PzC found a weak spot along the highway leading northwest from Pokrovka to Prokhorovka. This shift away from Oboyan was said to be unscheduled by the Soviets. The 48th PzC to the west of 2nd SS PzC was still heading for Oboyan but also had to expand its front in order to protect the SS's left flank as it shifted to the east. Priess's *SSTK* continued to push the 49th TB and 100th TB eastward as it advanced into the Lipovyi Donets Valley. The *LAH*, with air support, attacked again the defenses around the Pokrovka and Bolshie Maiachki areas, forcing the 49th TB and 100th TB back. dgk123. dgk222m. dlu63m. dgk95m.

The *GD* occupied the important Hill 230.5 against strong resistance. The Hill would be a good jumping off point to attack Syrtsevo. Other elements of *GD* reached Verkhopenie further north, forcing the 3rd MC back. At midnight the 112th TB reached the river near Syrtsevo and attacked *GD* while 200th TB moved along the bank opposite Verkhopenie. dgk128. hjj121m. dgk222m. dgr209m. dgk95m.

On this sunny day, *GD* continued its attack on the heavily fortified Syrtsevo. A Soviet counter with the newly arrived elements of the 67th GRD and 60 tanks from 6th TC attempted to push back the Germans in front of Syrtsevo and Group Strachwitz which was on nearby Hill 230.5, but it was unsuccessful. Outmaneuvering the Soviets during a severe rocket barrage, *GD* entered Syrtsevo by 1400 hrs and started clearing the village which would be secured next morning. The 6th PzR of 3rd PzD joined in to clear the village. The defenders fought to the death instead of surrendering. hsz123. hsz117m.

In late morning the 48th PzC briefly paused to reqroup, allowing the 200th TB and 112th TB of 6th TC and 3rd MC to be taken off the line to rest. The 6th MRB and 22nd

TB remained on the front line. dgr214+.

The 48th PzC launched an attack from the Syrtsevo- Iakovlevo area toward Krasnaia Dubrova. At the same time a smaller group attacked toward Bolshie Maiachki. Yet another group, probably *LAH*, attacked from the Teterevino State Farm and Ozerovski area against Gresnoe. The objective of these attacks was to penetrate the line and encircle a large portion of the 1st TA and 6th GA. By the end of the day, the 1st TA still held most of the second defense belt that included Lukhanino-Krasnaia, Dubrova and Bolshie Maiachki, just outside of Malenkie Maiachki and Gresnoe. A small German wedge had reached the back of the second defense belt at Bogoroditskoe and Ivanovski Vyselki. dgr84. nzk90.

Getting a late start, the Fusilier Regiment of *GD* launched an attack from Lakhanino to the northeast toward the heavily defended Olkhovaya Gorge and the hills west of Syrtsev. Accompanying Panthers drove into another minefield and were stuck there until engineers could clear a path. The *Luftwaffe* came in first to soften the Soviet positions but not much later Red planes arrived and a deadly dogfight ensued. As the Fusiliers moved up, very tortuous hand-to-hand fighting occurred and the advance was very slow but eventually Syrtsev was entered, forcing the Soviet defenders to retreat toward Syrtsevo. By evening, several battalions of *GD* succeeded in occupying Hill 230.5 against strong armor forces. Hill 230.5 was a great observation point and a good jumping off point to attack Syrtsevo from the east. At 1350 hrs these elements of *GD* and the 6th PzR of 3rd PzD captured Syrtsev. hsz122+. dgr209m.

In addition to expanding 48th PzC's sector to the west, Hoth also ordered the 11th PzD, which was heading northwest for Oboyan, to expand its sector to close the gap with 2nd SS PzC which was now heading to the northeast. The 3rd PzD and *GD* were to clear all Soviet resistance within the Pena River Valley to beyond Berezovka. With these orders, the Germans did not gain much ground. The thinning of the line by expanding the sector for 48th PzC only guaranteed its failure to reach Oboyan. Once again the Germans did not have the resources to defeat the Soviets in this salient. Hoth should have realized that and contracted the battle zone not expanded it. The 52nd IC under the command of Maj General Fretter-Pico and 3rd PzD under Lt General Westhoven drove west of the Pena River where the resistance was too strong and *GD* had to come to their rescue which slowed their momentum to the north. This reversal of sorts should have been a signal to General Hoth to be cautious on his western flank where the resistance was greater than expected, but he ignored the evidence and continued to probe westward, weakening his northern advance. vzz132+.

General Vatutin was once again moving his forces. To bolster the line in front of Prokhorovka, the 183rd RD of 69th Army was moved to the south of town. To the west the 161st RD was quickly moved into the area to help the 71st GRD stop the 255th ID and 3rd PzD. At the same time, Mainstein was moving his forces as well. The 3rd PzD on the western boundary was moved as close to the Pena River and at Krasnyi Pochinok, north of Korovino, to allow the panzers to fight northward. The 52nd IC was ordered to move up as close to 3rd PzD in order to relieve some pressure off the 255th ID. Elements of 167th ID was moved east to relieve *SSTK* near Shopino so *SSTK* could redeploy toward the Psel River. Later that evening, von Manstein emphasized to Hoth and Kempf of the urgency to quicken the pace but with 9th Army in the north doing badly, Hitler diverted three air groups, roughly half of the 8th Flieger Corps, from the south to the northern sector, jeopardizing von Manstein's forces even further. wdk136.

The 48th PzC, predominately the *GD*, gained five miles on this day, culminating in taking Dubrova and advancing toward Verkhopenie by bypassing Syrtsev on both sides. The garrison at Syrtsevo, without putting up much resistance, retreated to the north toward Gremuchi or Syrtsevo on the Pena River. The corps' next objective was Hill 260.8, south of Novoselovka. It would be crested by Group Schimmelmann of 11th PzD on 7/9 and secured during the night, forcing the 3rd MC to fall back. Just north of Hill 260.8 but south of Novoselovka, the 309th RD which had just dug in was able to stop the lead combat group of 11th PzD from reaching Novoselovka. Other elements of *GD* would then join up with 11th PzD to take on Syrtsevo which was the last fortified position in the second defense belt before reaching Oboyan. After taking the towns the 40th Army counter-attacked the 3rd PzD of the 48th PzC, halting its progress. The first few days of fighting, the 48th PzC had to struggle against tough and sodden terrain but on this day they found open ground more suited for panzers. Heavy shelling of these panzers in the open caused frequent delays and casualties. Though securing Verkhopenie and with 3rd PzD lagging behind, *GD* was still under fire from Soviet guns from the west bank of the Pena River. Add stiff resistance from the 10th TC and 6th TC and it is understandable that *GD*'s advance to the Psel was slowing down. Much of 3rd PzD was still in the Lukhanino area which was only six miles from their start point. dgk142. dgk222m. mhz252. mhz272. dgr209m. vzz157. gnk312m. cbk61. fmz221. vzz2m. pck72.

The 48th PzC's *GD* and 11th PzD, attacking along both sides of the Oboyan road, ruptured the 1st TA's defenses as well as the flank of 31st TC to the east. Right from the beginning the Soviets attacked 48th PzC's flanks, preventing the corps to attack with full strength to the north. A Soviet counter-attack on 48th PzC's weakened left flank at Krasnopolye especially slowed their progress. The *GD* and 11th PzD, with the support of nearly 200 panzers and air support, had previously pushed the 1st MB and 3rd MB back off Hill 254.2 and to the outskirts of Syrtsevo and Gremiuchi, a distance of 3 miles. Northeast of Syrtsevo on Hill 230.5, the 112th TB was able to repulse a panzer attack. The Soviets lost 15 tanks in the engagement. Both sides had heavy casualties. The Germans were unable to take Syrtsevo this day. Hill 254.2 and Pokrovka were about six miles north of Bykovka. dgk126+. dgk131. snk80. hjj121m. dgr209m. vzz99. vzz2m.

To reiterate, *GD* succeeded in reaching the crucial Hill 230.5 on both sides of Syrtsevo, inflicting heavy losses on the 6th TC as it retreats northward past Gremuchi. By nightfall *GD* reached Verkhopenie. The Germans were initially stopped at Hill 230.5 due to heavy mining and anti-tank artillery. Once past Hill 230.5, the 11 PzD wheeled northwest toward Syrtsevo, the last major Soviet defense before Oboyan. North of Gremuchi, Hill 230.5 was finally taken at 1330 hrs. On its left flank, 3rd PzD closed on Berezovka. It was a good day for the Germans, who were making modest gains in all areas and it appeared a major breakthrough was close. The Soviets were moving up reserves and by the next day or two they would have the upper hand. *GD* fighting near Syrtsevo was attacked by more dug-in tanks. While the tanks fought, the German infantry continued north. One Tiger was taken out by a mine. Once Syrtsevo was secured, *GD* paused to form a combat group to lead the way to Hill 260.8, south of Novoselovka. To the right, the 11th PzD was able to stay with *GD* but on the left side the 3rd PzD was falling behind, potentially exposing *GD*'s flank. *GD* would have to stop its advance and help the 3rd PzD to catch up. This happened during the whole campaign. The assault on the flanks was so fierce, it prevented the lead units from concentrating entirely on the attack to the north. The 4th PzA just did not have enough men to defeat its enemy and the mechanical troubles of the Panther exacerbated the situation. The odds of *GD* reaching Oboyan were becoming slim. wwf86+. rkz168. hjj116. hjj121m. mhz255. dgr209m. vzz128.

As night fell, the 11th PzD forced Soviet tanks off a hill north of Gremuchi as well as Hill 230.5, east of Syrtsevo. The panzers had moved forward to secure the right flank of *GD* and to provide a stronger defense against a night attack. The 3rd PzD was behind the others and *GD*'s left flank was exposed because of 3rd PzD's slow progress. mhz255. dgr209m.

The forces of Hoth's 4th PzA nearly broke through Voronezh Front defenses around Syrtsevo but Soviet 31st TC counter-attacked, slowing the German advance and preventing the 48th PzC from fully exploiting the weakness in the Syrtsevo-Hill 230.5–Gremuchi line. lck283.

The inexperience of the new Panther crews was showing and causing more to be destroyed or damaged than usual; one ploy of the Soviet gunners was to attack from the side where the armor was only 40mm. The Panther crews would often angle their gun at a target without considering pointing the front armor which was the thickest at the enemy. It was decided after the battle to have Mks ride farther to the sides and more to the front to protect this weakness. rkz167. mhz255.

Later that night after regrouping, Col Leonov's 112th TB came up and again attacked the 48th PzC near Syrtsevo. Syrtsevo was still held by Soviets but it was surrounded by the enemy. At the same time, the 200th TB occupied positions farther north along the Pena River's west bank opposite Verkhopenie. As the Germans advanced the Soviets were able to take most of their field guns with them. The recently arrived 112th TB had been active all day, making repeated attacks against *GD* and 11th PzD. dgk129. snk80. hjj121m. dgk222m. dgr209m.

Vatutin, throughout the day, was trying to scrape together every possible man to block the expected route of 48th PzC's advance. Attacking along both sides of the Oboyan road, *GD* and 11th PzD penetrated through 1st TA's defenses while turning the flank of 31st TC, which was also battling 2nd SS PzC's left flank. As many as 300 panzers, including 40 Panthers and supported by Stukas, attacked the Soviets, pushing them back 3 miles to Syrtsevo and Gremuchi. Hill 230.5 and Hill 254.2 east of Syrtsevo were attacked as well. The Germans suffered greatly for their advance but did capture Hill 230.5. By night the Soviets prepared to evacuate Syrtsevo for Gremuchi or along the bank of the Pena River, south of Verkhopene. The lead units of *GD* were following close behind, heading for Novoselovka. dgk126+. dgk129. hjj121m. dgk222m. dgr209m. vzz2m. fmz223.

On this day, Hoth's 4th PzA was tasked in capturing the high ground near the road Prokhorovka-Oboyan. Hoth unleashed hundreds of panzers against 1st TA. The panzers were surrounding the Soviets. The infantry of 48th PzC in particular was needed to complete the circle but their slow advance allowed many Soviet tanks to escape. rkz167.

At 1700 hrs, the 17th VA launched an attack toward the important airfield at Rogan. Pilot error missed Rogan and the group attacked Vararovka by mistake. The surprise attack only destroyed one Fw 190 while the Soviets lost five planes. cbk61.

Late at night, with the big offensive planned for next morning, Lt General Katukov traveled to all his brigade commanders checking their readiness and providing motivation. zra61.

Germans had overrun Dubrova earlier on this day but lost many panzers doing so. By the end of the day, the 48th PzC had penetrated the 2nd defense belt in several places, which could have been a good omen, but it was not for it cost them too many panzers and men. The defenders of Dubrova, the remains of Krivoshein's 6th GA and 6th TC, started to fall back to Syrtsevo on the Pena but were hit hard by German artillery causing even greater casualties. dgk127+. pck69.

By the end of the day, the 90th GRD supported by the 3rd MC, 6th TC and 31st TC occupied the front line from just north of Lukhanino-Krasnaia Dubrova-Malenkie Maiachki-Gresnoe. The 52nd GRD had fallen back to the northern bank of the Psel in the Kliuchi-Polezhaev sector. To look at it from the German view, the 3rd PzD and 332nd ID made no appreciable gains and were still hampered by the Pena River defense. The *GD*-11th PzD combo had gained a little, moving from the Lukhanino-Syrtsev line up to Syrtsevo. The 167th ID that was sent up to the line to plug the gap between 11th PzD and *LAH* made no significant ground. dgr85. dgr86m.

By the end of the day, only 40 Panthers out of 192 were still operating. Seventy-six were in the repair shop due to mechanical breakdowns or mine damage. I wonder what the 10th Brigade's performance would have been like if the Panther had been a perfected tank that had been reliable and/or been placed in a sector more appropriate for its armor. Having nearly 200 mechanically reliable medium weight tanks with a superior gun and better communications, with crews experienced, commanders who actually worked together, and deployed on advantageous terrain, it's quite possible the 48th PzC could have beaten the SS across the Psel River or at the very least made it to the river. gnk191.

The natural barrier of the Psel River and its marsh land caused Vatutin to place the third defensive belt an unusually long distance of 18 miles behind the second defense belt. There was no alternative as the space between the second and third defensive belts was flat, open ground and difficult to defend. gjz185.

With the Soviets counter-attacking in force today, especially in 2nd SS PzC sector, the Germans made only modest gains and could only stabilize the line after taking several key sites. The first few days, before Vatutin's reinforcements arrived, saw better gains for the Germans. Hausser had been hoping for a breakthrough in the Iablochki area or east of Gresnoe where the 237th TB was defending and if it had occurred, he would have had his divisions fight throughout the night to exploit the success. Before the campaign started both Hausser and Hoth were confident that the Germans had enough armor to defeat the Soviets, but doubts had since been growing that they underestimated the strength of the Soviet army. Besides the stiff resistance the Soviets had been able to generate, German aerial recon reported seeing hundreds of tanks along the SS front. It was true that the 48th PzC and the SS Corps drove deep salients in their respective zones but the salients were narrow and the Soviets had enough strength to still control the overall battlefield situation. vzz137+. dgk109+.

After hard fighting against the 19th PzD the previous day and being threatened with encirclement, the garrison at Kreida evacuated in the predawn hours. Soviet resistance in the area was still strong and the commanders of 19th PzD and 6th PzD agreed to work together to penetrate the Soviet defenses that were giving all three panzer divisions trouble. The 19th PzD would drive north along the western bank of the Razumnaia River and the 6th PzD would be on the east side. Each division would use the other for flank protection as well as the river. They both launched at daybreak, around 0400 hrs. By 0500 hrs, the Germans were attacking Kreida and the surrounding area after the 81st GRD moved in. gnk178.

Leaving the Batratskaia Dacha area while still dark and heading east, Group Schulz of 7th PzD, supported by a number of Wespe guns and panzers, traveled unmolested through the woods west of town. Leaving the woods they approached Hill 216.1 then started shifting to the north to drive toward Sheino. Soviet artillery began pounding the German column. It was decided that the panzers would engage while the infantry tried to bypass this strongpoint. Sheino was seven miles north of Batratskaia Dacha and only two miles south of their main objective, the village of Masikino. The Soviet resistance was too strong, forcing the panzers to pull back into the woods. The Soviet defenders were a recent attachment to 7th GA – 167th TR and 262nd TR. gnk175. gnk178. kfz451.

In the 3rd PzC sector, the main spearhead was driving in the direction of Iastrebovo and Sevriukovo. Fighting the whole day along the Razumnaia River, the 3rd PzC had captured Belovskaia, Iastrebovo and Sevriukovo areas but Melikhovo to the north remained in Soviet hands despite repeated attacks. Vatutin ordered the 111th RD and 270th RD into blocking positions north of Sevriukovo dgr85. dgr155m. dgr173m. dgr39m. nzk90.

During the predawn hours, 6th PzD assembled in the area near Generalovka, still behind the 7th PzD. At daybreak the division moved out and by 1130 hrs had captured the fortified towns of Iastrebovo and Sevriukovo. The captures were difficult and included house to house fighting. Both sides suffered heavy casualties. By late afternoon the 6th PzD was crossing the Razumnaia River to the east bank on a repaired bridge at Iastrebovo when they were ambushed. The attack was repulsed and the division was able to complete its crossing. Once again Soviet resistance slowed the German progress; the Germans were still behind schedule. At this point the 19th PzD and 6th PzD linked up and wisely continued north together along the Razumnaia River. The divisions were using the river and each other as flank protection. gnk178. dlu31. dlu51. dgk136.

Lead elements of the 19th PzD, the 73rd PzGR, were advancing toward Blizhniaia Igumenka. To reach the village, the Germans had to pass through a small wooded area. These woods were the beginning of the second defense belt in the sector and it was heavily defended. As the Germans entered the woods, the Soviets put up a wall of fire that drove them back. The Pz Abt 19 and 27th PzR swung around and attacked the village from the east while the 74th PzGR moved north about a click from Blizhniaia Igumenka and attacked Hill 215.5. Once the woods were penetrated, the village and hill were taken quickly. Without pause, the 74th PzGR headed for Hill 212.1 which was not reached until after dark. The hill was taken but throughout the night, Soviet artillery shelled the hilltop. gnk179. gnk182. dlu48+. dlu66. dlu68m.

On the east flank Kempf shifted his assault to the north which exposed his eastern flank. The 168th ID was brought to the line to guard the flank, replacing 19th PzD which would lead the charge to the north, closest to the river. The front line was now at Mikhailovka, a heavily fortified sector held by the 81st GRD. Its 235th GRR took the brunt of 19th PzD assault but that afternoon it destroyed five panzers and had to fall back three miles to the east. Other elements of the 19th PzD struck the 92nd GRD and 94th GRD of 35th RC around Blizhniaia Igumenka, six miles northeast of Mikhailovka. The 6th PzD, three miles east of 19th PzD drove north reaching a position a mile north of Serukovo. The 7th PzD, protecting part of the east front along with the 106th ID, suffered heavy losses against the 25th GRC's constant pressure and the attacks by the 17th VA. In these engagements, Group Oppeln-Bronikovski lost eight panzers. The 429th GR of 168th ID, now attached to 19th PzD, shifted direction to clear Kreida of resistance before moving back with the panzers. At the same time, the 73rd PzGR of 19th PzD headed for Kolch but was ambushed in the woods south of its objective and suffered heavy casualties, forcing Kohler to turn his men back. wdk133. dgr155m. dgr173m. dlu35. dlu46+. dgk136.

In the Kursk salient, the weather was warm and sunny and the roads were drying and in good condition. In the south on the east flank, Group Raus using his 88 batteries, were trying to repulse a counter-attack led by tanks. The main assault struck the 320th ID which was defending the important bridgehead at Bezliudovka. It repulsed numerous attacks with the help of corps artillery deployed near the Donets. The two divisions of 11th IC, the 320th ID and 106th ID, were trying to stay in contact with each other for mutual protection against the murderous fire from 24th GRC. These two divisions were being overwhelmed and could barely make any headway today. The 7th GA, which was defending against Kempf, had the 35th GRC, the 92nd GRD and the 31st TB transferred to it but it would take up to a day to have them in position. wdk132.

The 7th PzD captured Miasoedovo despite heavy resistance and many Soviet tanks. The bulk of 6th PzD was still held up in Iastrebovo. The 168th ID and 19th PzD were still cornered not far from Belgorod. The two divisions wheeled northwestward against the flank of 81st GRD. It was decided to shift 7th PzD to the west to attack Soviet positions from the rear to relieve the 168th ID's flank. To do this the Melikhovo-Dal Igumnovo area had to be secured first. Contacting 11th IC to the west was also necessary. The area that von Manstein wanted taken on this eastern flank was too ambitious, too unrealistic. Kempf did not have the resources necessary to achieve AGS's objectives and it showed from the very first day, but von Manstein was slow to respond to this reality. shn159. dgk136.

After a hard fight, Raus's 11th IC of the Kempf Group reached the high ground four miles east of the Belgorod-Volchansk railroad line. In the woods on the west bank of the Korenye brook, 11th IC finally was forced to go on the defensive. Dug-in T34s, anti-tank guns, flamethrowers and artillery were too much resistance to continue the advance. snk20.

After a Stuka raid, Group Oppeln-Bronikovski of 6th PzD advanced from Hill 207-Belinska area toward Sevriukovo-Iastrebovo, after crossing the Razumnaia. The Germans pushed the defenders out of town and captured the high ground west of Sevriukovo. The Soviet counter-attacks were repulsed while German engineers repaired the damaged bridges leading out of town. wwf88. dgr155m. vzz154.

On this Wednesday, the 3rd PzC driving northward was trying to get behind 81st GRD and destroy it before crossing the Donets and catching up to Hausser's 2nd SS PzC. It was tough going for 3rd PzC against well prepared defenses and reinforcements that were coming up to the line. The 213th RD and 72nd GRD were also counter-attacking the 106th ID and 320th ID defending the right flank near Maslova Pristan, preventing the Germans to break away and head north to support LT General Funck's 7th PzD. The 7th PzD was stuck at Batratskaia Dacha and unable to move to support 6th PzD's assault toward the northern region. The 7th PzD after a brief pause during darkness, resumed its attempt at clearing the area before following 6th PzD. After securing Batratskaia, the 7th PzD drove north, following the east bank of the Razumnaia River. Their next objective before shutting down for the night was the village of Masikino. dgk135+. gnk175.

While fighting off repeated attacks to the north and northeast in the direction of Melikhovo, the 106th ID drove Soviet troops into the 7th PzD to the west and together pocketed elements of several divisions. While the remainder of these divisions were able to escape, much equipment and heavy weapons were left behind. erz206.

The 6th PzD under Hunersdorff drove into Miasoedovo, pushing the Soviets back. sPzAbt 503, leading other elements of 6th PzD, secured Iastrebovo. Both the 6th and 503rd moved up against the 92nd GRD and 94th GRD of 35th GRC which had moved up to support the sagging 25th GRC under Maj General Safiullin. Lt General Schmidt's 19th PzD on the 3rd PzC's left flank reached and secured Blizhniaia Igumenka by 1600 hrs in the 81st GRD's rear. The Germans took no mercy on the defenders as they started to fall back, deliberately running over the soldiers with their panzers. The 168th ID was still stuck south of Staryi Gorod, east of the Donets River, was unable to remove the defenders. Panzers of the 19th PzD did arrive and Staryi Gorod finally fell by 1800 hrs. by the joint efforts of the 168th in the west and the panzers moving in from the east. dgk136. dgr95. hjj121m. vzz108. dgr155m. dgr39m. vzz5m. dlu48. shn159.

Off and on all day there were dogfights in 3rd PzC sector. In the late afternoon a group of IL-2s returned to the area after reloading to find the *Luftwaffe* was gone, leaving the skies to the Soviets. The planes strafed the front line of the 320th ID in front of the 7th GA which was launching an attack in the Melekhov-Chiornaya Poliana area. The aerial attack inflicted heavy casualties and confusion on the infantry at an ideal time. The air attack also interfered with the 106th ID from relieving 7th PzD at its current position in order for it to move north and assist 6th PzD when it attacked the Rzhavets area. cbk60+.

While the 168th ID with the help of 19th PzD tried to outflank elements of the 81st GRD defending the river bank, the eastern elements of 3rd PzC after crossing the Koren River, also started receiving increased Soviet resistance to the south by counter-attacking the 106th and 320th ID near Maslova Pristan. These attacks by the 213th RD and the 72nd GRD with support of heavy artillery caused heavy casualties on the Germans. At the same time elements of the 7th PzD and the 6th PzD, in the center of the line, had launched from Batratskaia Dacha toward Miasoedovo. The 117 panzers including 45 Tigers of the sPzAbt 503, after escaping a minefield, drove the Soviets northward from Iastrebovo. The 35th GRC was quickly sent to stop the advance and its lead units started shelling the German engineers trying to build a bridge over the Razumniaia River. The 7th PzD made the best gains on this day and were further north than the other two panzer divisions, but that situation would probably change the next morning as the bulk of the 94th GRD had just arrived in sector. dgk135+. dgr155m. dgr173m. dgr39m. dlu51+. shn159. shn156m.

The 3rd PzC made slow but disturbing progress against the flank of 7th GA, undermining the Soviet positions. Alarmed, Vatutin brought up the artillery from 38th and 40th Armies to cover the the flanks of 6th GA and 7th GA sectors, in an effort to halt the German attack. General Shumilov was ordered to attack on the flanks as much as possible. dlu57.

At 1430 hrs, the 111th RD was ordered to move north and occupy the line between Churaevo to Shebekino to Volchansk. The 270th RD was to defend the line between Nekliudovo and Churaevo, replacing the 15th GRD. The 15th GRD would defend the Novo Troevka, Nekliudovo line. dgr85. dgr100m.

9

July 7th on the Northern Salient

See Map 4

For the first two days, Model's 9th Army forces made only a small advance in the Central Front defenses. Not satisfied with the gains near Ponyri, Model ordered his troops to resume their advance toward Maloarchangelsk. He was hoping this feint would take some of the pressure off Ponyri. Rokossovsky continued to redeploy his forces to meet the changing battlefield. Elements of the 60th and 65th Armies were moved to support 13th Army in this area. dgk87m. dgr199m. dgk116m.

At dawn, Model's 9th Army renewed its attack in the middle of Central Front's sector, attempting to penetrate its second defense belt around the town of Ponyri and north of Olkhovatka, six miles to the west. Ponyri was an important railroad junction leading to Kursk. The 18th and 9th PzDs and 86th ID were in the lead. Ponyri would see some of the fiercest fighting of the campaign at the station and the nearby Hill 253.5. The 18th PzD and 292nd ID attacked the town 5 times and were repulsed each time by the 307th RD of 13th Army, with the support of tanks and artillery. At 1000 hours, the Germans, with 50 panzers, entered the northwest corner of the town but were then thrown back. On the east side of town, the Germans captured the May 1st State Farm. dgk115. fkk102m. dgk87m. dgr199m. nzk88+. nzk89m. dgk116m. lck116m. zro204.

During the predawn hours 18th PzD assembled next to 9th PzD in front of Ponyri II. The two battered divisions with the support of elements of 6th ID would head for ground between Ponyri II and Olkhovatka beginning around 1100 hrs. The 2nd PzD and 20th PzD from west of Snovo would also advance toward Ponyri II against 17th GRC which was holding the second defense belt in this sector. This sector was being defended by the 6th GRD. A small *Luftwaffe* squadron provided protection from above. Rudenko sent a large group of fighters to attack the concentration of panzers. The Soviets did inflict casualties on the panzers but even with the German planes outnumbered, they were able to knock some of those Soviet planes from the sky. Most of the 70 panzers of 18th PzD, which were now deployed on the right flank of 41st PzC, were the long barreled Mk IVs. A few Mk IIIs had the short barrel 50mm or 75mm. At the same time and farther to the west, the 2nd PzD and 20th PzD would attack southward between Samodurovka and Kashara. mhz260+. mhz19m. dgr198m. fkk102m. dgk87m. dgr199m. cbk50. mkz119. nzk88. nzk89m. dgk116m. lck116m.

West of Ponyri the 9th PzD pushed the 6th GRD back to occupy the woods. Despite this advantage, the Germans were only able to wrestle part of Ponyri from the Soviets. Further to the west of town, the 47th PzC, with support from 6th ID drove southward toward Olkhovatka and the ridge, which was a key objective of Model's. Rokossovsky wanted to keep this high ground and had prepared a strong defense with the 70th RD and 75th RD to keep it. dgk115+*. fkk102m. dgk87m. dgr199m. dgk116m. lck116m.

The 2nd PzD shifted direction, heading for the ground between Samodurovka and

Olkhovatka. Along with 20th PzD, both of Lemelsen's 47th PzC's divisions attacked but despite the shift the Germans were hard hit from the determined 13th Army. The Germans were going for the important high ground, Hill 274. From this hill, you could see all the way to Kursk and it was the best observation point in the sector. Whoever controlled this high ground would also control the land between the Oka and Seim Rivers and put its enemy at a disadvantage. To the right of 2nd PzD, 46th PzC failed to break through 70th Army's line after repeated attacks. dgk117+. dgr198m. fkk53. fkk102m. dgk87m. dgr199m. cbk54. dgk116m. lck116m.

Not wanting to be late for the party as they were the previous day, the planes of the 1st *Flieger* Division were raiding Soviet positions along the front as well as flying recon patrols at first light. Fw 190s were looking for easy targets. Yesterday, Model's 47th PzC suffered casualties because Soviet planes arrived at the front first. A little later Soviet bombers, heavily escorted, started hitting the German lines. Wave after wave would hit the line. Of course this Soviet increase caused an escalation of the *Luftwaffe* to protect its ground forces. cbk49+. dgk116m.

Ninety panzers of 4th PzD along with Tigers and Ferdinands were poised south of Podsoborovka waiting for orders to attack. The Stukas opened the attack and at 0505 hrs, the panzers moved out. Despite being under heavy shelling and an exposed left flank, the 4th PzD captured the eastern portion of Samodurovka, just south of the Svapa River as well as attacking Hill 238. fkk58. fkk104m. dgk87m. dgr199m. dgk116m. lck116m.

At dawn, the Germans attacked toward the important town of Ponyri while to the west the assault on Olkhovatka continued. The Soviet 307th RD backed by tanks repulsed all attacks on Ponyri. At 1000 hrs, the Germans did reach the railroad embankment on the edge of town but were forced back. At 1100 hrs after regrouping, the Germans attacked again and in hand-to-hand combat advanced and captured the village of May First before moving on and entering the northern outskirts of Ponyri. Calling for help from all units near Ponyri, the 307th RD countered and once again pushed the Germans out of Ponyri. The Germans shifted direction, bypassing Ponyri and attacked the 17th GRC's right flank, 6th GRD, between Ponyri and Olkhovatka and by 1200 hrs had penetrated the line. By 1230 hrs, the Germans captured the woods west of Berezovyi Log. By 1930 hrs, the Germans were approaching Ponyri II and nearby Hill 257.0, threatening to penetrate the flank of 75th GRD which was positioned west of Snovo. The 75th GRD shifted and then counter-attacked, stopping the German advance and forcing the Germans to retreat. fkk102m. dgr116+. dgk118+. dgk87m. dgr199m. dgk116m.

At 0530 hrs, the 20th PzD resumed its attempt to enlarge their Svapa bridgehead. Slowly they fought their way to the east-west road one mile south of Saburovka but had to stop there for its right flank was too far behind to protect the panzers' own flank. fkk54. fkk102m. fkk104m. dgk87m. dgk116m.

In the early morning, the Soviets began a counter-attack but the Germans were able to repulse it and inch its way toward Teploe-Plkhovatka-Ponyri, about six miles to the south. The attack was nearing its critical stage; Model brought up the 12th PzD and 36th ID to break through the last major defensive belt and gain the important high ground. The 46th PzC heading southwest was in the lead. snk107+. dgr198m. dgk87m. dgr199m. dgk116m. lck116m.

In the 46th PzC sector on the west flank, elements of the 31st ID and 7th ID fought for high ground west of Gnilets in the Soloschonki area against the 280th RD of 70th Army.

The 31st ID took the hill but lost it to a counter-attack that was supported by tanks. Both sides sent reinforcements. The 12th PzD, moving out of reserve, was ordered to the area. The 70th Army sent the 175th RD up as well, moving into the Fatezh road area and then into the line between the 280th RD and the 132nd RD. With the help of the 175th RD the Soviets were able to hold the hill west of Gnilets. wdk177. fkk102m. dgk87m. nzk87. dgk116m.

The Soviets counter-attacked and made progress toward Bolkhov, pushing the Germans back three miles on a narrow front. The retreat went all the way back to Podolian; it was a devastating setback. Elements of all the other panzer divisions had to send panzers there to stop the Soviet advance. fkk61. dgk87m. dgr199m. dgk116m.

Heavy fighting the previous two days forced Rokossovsky to take units from 65th and 60th Armies to reinforce the hard pressed 13th Army in the Ponyri-Olkhovatka area. At Olkhovatka 300 panzers from the 2nd PzD, 4th PzD, 20th PzD, 18th PzD and 9th PzD crashed into 16th TC and 19th TC. The 292nd ID and 86th ID were in support as well as the entire *Luftflotte* 4. At Ponyri, the Germans advanced into the village becoming embroiled in bitter hand-to-hand fighting in the school House, Tractor Depot, railway station and water tower. The bitter fighting lasted all day with both sides making attacks and counter-attacks. Model had to call up more ammo for his forces. Model was convinced that the only way to defeat Rokossovsky was through the heights of Olkhovatka and the plains south of the village where the panzers would have an advantage over the Soviet tanks. bt84. je102. fkk102m. lck296. dgk87m. dgr199m. dgk116m. lck116m.

The 4th PzD was brought from reserve the previous night and attacked toward Teploe in the morning but could not go very far due to the heavy resistance of the dug-in T34s. The tanks forced Kahler's 33rd PzR back from Teploe. In the open fields the panzers, including the Tigers, were easy targets to Soviet artillery; to make it harder for the Soviets, the panzers rode at max speed. The nearly 100 panzers the 4th PzD had were mostly 75mm long gunned Mk IVs. The day's assault would see five panzer divisions advance within a ten mile front, running from Molotychi-Samodurovka eastward through Ponyri. The 20th PzD, 4th PzD, 2nd PzD, 9th PzD and 18th PzD would attack with 300 panzers of the Mk III, MK IV variety. sPzAbt 505 with its Tigers would lead the attack. The 21st PzB would be attached to 4th PzD. During the night Rokossovsky brought up two RDs, three armor brigades and placed them between Teploe and Olkhovatka where much of the German forces would attack. Once again Rokossovsky correctly anticipated Model's intentions. mhz281. dgr198m. fkk60+. fkk102m. lck302. dgk87m. dgr199m. dgk116m. lck116m. fzk172.

The 20th IC on the west flank of 9th Army's attack zone had the primary duty of preventing any breakthrough from the west that would endanger 46th PzC. Today it was also given other responsibilities. General Roman was to create three combat groups and achieve a number of objectives. The first group would launch from Sevsk and advance toward the Dmitryev-Lgovsky line. The second group would launch from Kamarichi and advance to Deryugino. The last group would start at Dmitrovsk-Orlovski area and head for Mikailovka and gain control of the Svapa Creek area from the northwest. snk107. vzz4m. dgk116m.

At 0830 hrs on this already hot day, the 4th PzD and the rest of 47th PzC resumed its march on the high ground south of Samodurovka-Kashara-Bitiug line on both sides of Olkhovatka. Elements of 4th PzD and 20th PzD were sent to support the 6th ID in their advance. The bulk of 20th PzD resumed its attack on Hill 231 and eventually captured it. The hill was a good observation point looking south. The 21st PzR of 20th PzD continued to support 31st ID in attacking Hill 234 as the remainder of 20th PzD maneuvered around Hill 234, heading to capture the area along the Svapa River. The Svapa Valley one mile west of Saburovka was reached and after a brief fight pushed the Soviets out of the area. The bulk of 4th PzD was being deployed between 20th PzD and 2nd PzD. Model had made the decision that Olkhovatka was the key objective and placed 4th PzD directly north of the village at the expense of 9th PzD and 18th PzD which needed help near Ponyri. fkk56. dgk87m. dgr199m. dgk116m. lck116m.

The 20th PzD of 47th PzC and 4th PzD made repeated attacks toward Samodurovka, seeking to penetrate the ridge line of defenses at the junction between 70th and 13th Armies, with 17th GRC taking the brunt of the attack. The 81st RD was mauled badly the previous day and Rokossovsky put them in reserve directly behind 17th GRC. With cloudy skies, the *Luftwaffe* made few runs. The ridge line was anchored by Hill 257, north of Olkhovatka. It was also necessary for Rokossovsky to bring up Maj General Kiselev's 140th RD to assist Lt General Galanin's 70th Army's right flank from repeated attacks. dgk118. dgr198m. fkk102m. dgr115++. dgk87m. dgr199m. nzk88. nzk89m. dgk116m. lck116m.

Model's 9th PzD and 18th PzD attacked on a narrow sector west of the Ponyri railway line towards the high ground east of Olkhovarka. The 2nd PzD, with its fewer than 100 panzers, and 20th PzD attacked further west in the direction of Samodurovka. The sPzAbt 505 joined this assault as well. Repeated German attempts failed to break through this second defense belt held by 13th Army's 132nd RD and 140th RD but eventually the Germans were able to push the defenders back. Another panzer assault force was heading for Ponyri. Model was developing his plan to take the high ground of Olkhovarka which would give him the advantage over the Soviets, while driving south of the town. His observations and artillery support would have the advantage. The thousands of mines the Soviets planted and buried tanks were effective, destroying many panzers and men alike. Taking this area would not be easy. Model did not have many routes his forces could take to reach Kursk and Rokossovsky still had forces to block the Germans' path. je102. dgk117. dgr198m. fkk102m. dgk87m. dgr199m. dgk116m. lck116m.

The 132nd RD was deployed west of Gnilets facing 31st ID. Next to the 31st ID on its eastern flank was 20th PzD. The 31st ID was trailing the panzers which were already south of Bobrik and approaching Krasavka. To keep the line secure, the panzers of the 21st PzR had to keep some forces behind to stay in contact with the 31st. Next to the 132nd RD was the 775th RD and 70th RD. When a penetration occurred in the 132nd RD sector, these two divisions shifted some forces north of Teploe, enabling them to close the gap and inflict heavy casualties on the leading Germans of 20th PzD who were trapped at Teploe and could not make it back to their comrades in Samodurovka. Samodurovka was midway between Teploe and Krasavka. dgr117. dgr199m. dgk116m.

At 1000 hrs on the 41st PzC front, the Soviets finally lost some ground at one of the Ponyri villages. Elements of the 10th PzGD pushed back 4th GPD a short distance at Polevaia. On the east flank of 41st PzC, the 86th ID supported with panzers attacked 307th RD. Backed by artillery support and the 13th TDB, the 307th RD counter-attacked, claiming to have destroyed ten Tigers and twelve Mk IVs while pushing the Germans off the high ground. In the afternoon, the 86th ID attacked again and recaptured the hill.

On the western flank, the Pz Abt 21 had just endured an air raid that had caused too much damage but it was now 1000 hrs and the formation was late for its advance. The assault guns were south of Saborovka and were now heading for Hill 234.1 and Hill 228.9, respectively south and southwest of Gnilets. As the group was approaching the woods southwest of Gnilets, 30 T34s came racing out and ambushed the assault guns. Reaction time was slow but the Germans recovered and engaged; before long the Soviet tankers disengaged and went back into the woods, allowing the Germans to continue for their hills. The Germans had discovered minefields were everywhere and many panzers would be disabled with track damage. Sometimes the crew could make repairs in the field but most times the panzers would have to be towed back to the shop for repairs. These repairs could take several days and the division would have to make do without for that period. At times there were many panzers waiting for repairs and the division would be at an extreme disadvantage for the duration. zzt84.

As the day progressed, while the 47th PzC were fighting inside Bitiug, other elements drove toward the high ground south of Bitiug and Kashara, five miles southeast of Bobrik. Once secured, it was to drive another three miles south and capture high ground on either side of Olkhovatka. With the 9th PzD and 6th ID in the lead, the 47th PzC attacked the 17th GRC. At noon, two regiments of 6th ID supported by 50 panzers of 9th PzD struck 6th GRD at Bitiug. Nearby, 30 panzers of 9th PzD made some gains against 75th GRD and 3rd TDB at Ponyri, two miles south of Bitiug, as well as capturing Berezovyi Log. The Soviets countered, trying to retake lost ground, and a ferocious battle ensued where both sides suffered heavy casualties. The 18th PzD also advanced on a section of Ponyri but the 307th RD, situated on the Orel-Kursk rail line, was able to repulse that attack as well. With 17th GRC being pushed back, the 43rd TR and 58th TR were ordered to the area to stop the 47th PzC. While Model's assault on the first day was less than maximum, his attack had geared up and with this day's efforts he was putting everything he could in attacking the central sector between Ponyri and Olkhovatka. Bitiug was south of Snovo and west of Ponyri. wdk177. dgr198m. lck300. dgr115. dgr108m. dgk87m. dgr199m. nzk90. nzk89m. dgk116m. lck116m.

The 3rd TC attacked toward the concentration of Germans at Ponyri and just east of it while the 18th GRC, further east, attempted to push back the 78th AD that was marching southeast toward Maloarckhangelsk. The 16th TC, 19th TC and the 17th GRC was assigned to 2nd TA and ordered to attack 47th PzC. Model ordered all five corps of 9th Army to resume their attack; the 78th AD of 23rd IC struck the 74th RD toward Luninka, three miles southwest of Maloarchangelsk and then formed a defensive position. The 18th PzD of 41st PzC was heading for the Snovo River, west of Ponyri. Once there they would cross the river and establish a bridgehead. The 2nd PzD of 47th PzC was heading for Fatezh west of Olkhovatka. The 4th PzD, coming out of reserve, would assist 47th PzC in its drive south of the Svapa River. The 46th PzC was to head for the new bridgehead over the Svapa River and for the high ground west of Bobrik. Model already knew that surrounding the northern defenses were too optimistic and changed to more modest objectives. wdk176. dgr198m. dgk87m. dgr199m. dgk116m. lck116m.

To the left of 20th PzD, the 2nd PzD took Kashara, northeast of Olkhovatka. Samodurovka, to the west was also an objective and currently being shelled. This appeared to Model as a penetration of the Soviet third defense belt. At the same time the 6th ID stormed the hills to the east of town. The fighting had been very hard these first three days. Model estimated casualties of 10,000 men which were not easily replaced. Ammo shells for the panzers were almost all gone; Model urgently requested more from Berlin. The newly arrived 4th PzD was following behind 20th PzD with orders to take the chain of hills from Hill 253.5 to Hill 279. To the left of 4th PzD, the 2nd PzD with the support of sPzAbt 505, after taking Kashara, was to storm Hill 234.1, Hill 274, Hill 258. With the current progress Von Saucken, the CO of 4th PzD, moved his HQ to the woods north of Podolian. At the same time a little to the east, the 9th PzD and 18th PzD were fighting toward Olkhovatka but were making little progress. fkk56. dgk87m. dgr199m. kcz168. dgk116m. lck116m. asz364.

At 1200 hrs, the 6th ID, supported by nearly 50 panzers (47th PzC), attacked toward Bitiug which was defended by 6th GRD. After a fierce fight the 6th ID fought its way into the northern section of the village. mkz119. dgk116m. lck116m.

By midday, the 4th PzD were able to make a gap in the Soviet line about two miles long between the villages of Samodurovka and Kashara, both north of Olkhovatka. The fighting was hard and several officers were killed. Von Saucken was injured. The 2nd PzD and 20th PzD began to drive through and headed for the area around the key village of Teploe, 2.5 miles to the southwest. The hilltop town of Olkhovatka was just three miles further south. Rokossovsky asked for air support to help plug this critical gap. At the same time three miles to the east at Ponyri, the 9th PzD and 18th PzD were being repulsed. Rokossovsky continued to send artillery to the area. Maj General Enshin's 307th RD continued to put up stiff resistance against the two panzer divisions. Every night the Soviets would continue to lay mines in front of their positions so the Germans would have clear old territory everyday. mhz264+. dgr198m. fkk59+. fkk102m. dgk87m. dgr199m. dgk116m. lck116m.

The 20th PzD resumed its advance southward, aiming to capture Samodurovka. By noon the 2nd PzD and 20th PzD had ripped a two mile hole in the Soviet line between Kashara and Samodurovka. Tigers poured through first then the other panzers of the two divisions, forcing the 6th GRD back. From here, Model would try to take Olkhovatka. The 17th GRC were preparing to meet the Germans when they reached the slopes near Olkhovatka. Like the Germans, the Soviets were now using 30mm MGs on their planes and they were eating up the Mk IIIs and Mk IVs. Samodurovka was west of Kashara and north of Teploe lck298+. dgk87m. dgr199m. dgk116m. lck116m.

At 1430 hrs, the 12th AD delivered a heavy barrage on the 78th AD at Protasovo. The 78th AD was supported by a dozen Ferdinands and the new 150mm Sturmpanzers and was able to repulse the subsequent attacks by 74th RD. The 78th AD was also fighting to the north near Trosna against the 2nd GPD and were able to take a hill southeast of town. To the north of Trosna, the 383rd ID was defending against a heavy attack supported by tanks, repulsing the attack. wdk180. dgk87m. dgk116m.

Fighting in the Berezovyi Log area, the Germans with the help of air support, were able to push the 6th GRD back and by 1530 hrs was attacking Hill 257.0 and the Kashara sector. Afterwards the Germans, after receiving reinforcements, shifted back to Ponyri and attacked 17th GRC again and by 1900 hrs finally started pushing 307th RD back. The 307th RD reformed their line between Bazhenova and south of Ponyri and additional reserves were brought up. In the Kashara sector, the 4th PzD, 2nd PzD and to a smaller extent the 20th PzD lead the charge. In the Ponyri sector it was 18th PzD and to a lesser extent 9th PzD in the lead followed by several divisions of infantry. dgr116+. dgr108m. dgk87m. dgr199m. dgk116m. lck116m.

The 18th PzD, 86th ID and 292nd ID launched a coordinated attack on both sides of Ponyri. The defending 159th GAR claimed to have destroyed two Tigers and five other panzers. At 1900 hrs, after a pause to regroup, the Germans attacked again, with support of 60 panzers, against the stubborn defenses of 307th RD. The fighting around Ponyri PC surged back and forth. To the left of 86th ID, the 36th ID reinforced with Ferdinands suffered heavily from the fire of 12th AD and the counter-attack of 148th RD. wdk178. dgk87m. dgr199m. dgk116m. lck116m.

At 1700 hrs, the 18th PzD and 9th PzD with its remaining 30 panzers attacked toward Ponyri II and began pushing the 75th GRD and elements of the 3rd TDB back when a group of IL-2s showed up and attacked the panzers with their newly equipped 37mm cannon. The Soviet planes attacked the rear of the panzers where the armor was the thinnest and were able to stop many of the panzers which stopped the panzer attack. mkz119. dgk116m. lck116m.

The men of 41st PzC made limited gains taking much of Ponyri and the surrounding countryside but no further south while the panzers further west advanced and captured Teploe, northwest of Olkhovaka. cbk53. dgk116m.

On the east flank, the 78th AD of 23rd IC repelled eleven attacks from the 74th RD. The Soviets with the support of the 12th AD were trying to retake Protasovo on the Maloarkhangelsk road. The 41st IC sent a company of Ferdinands to assist. Despite hard fighting by the Germans today along the whole front, they were unable to penetrate through the second defense belt. Soviet artillery and well position anti-tank guns were a major cause to the little progress made by the Germans. The Germans would not gain much beyond this point. After three days of fighting the Germans were almost out of panzer shells and requested 100,000 more. With 500 panzers remaining, that was 200 shells per panzer. wdk178. lck311. dgk87m. dgk116m.

While the Germans made very little progress in the center today, it did push back the 17th GRC a little, capturing Teploe. The 70th GRD and 75th GRD did regroup and with the help of 140th RD in late afternoon attacked from Samodurovka, hitting the flank of 4th PzD and slowing the advance near Teploe and Kashara. dgr117. dgk87m. lck116m.

The fighting in the north cost 9th Army another 2,800 casualties, bringing the three-day total to 13,080. After the war, it was estimated that Central Front had over 30,000 casualties, lost more than 150 tanks and 185 assorted aircraft in the first three days of fighting. During the campaign, German intelligence estimated the casualties at twice those figures, leading Model to believe that 9th Army had a chance to reach Kursk. snz247+.

The Red Air Force continued to bomb after dark targets of opportunities. When the movements of 4th PzD were discovered they attacked the formation. Over 500 sorties were made at night and into the predawn hours of 7/8. It was not a pleasant night for the men of the 4th PzD. The men were soaked and exhausted, being shelled and fired on from the ground and from the air. On the west side of 47th PzC front, the 4th PzD had been inserted into the line near Teploe and, with the support of 2nd PzD, attacked late at night. Heavy rain fell, slowing the Germans' advance. The Soviets counter-attacked with the 43rd TR, 58th TR and elements of the 2nd TA.

In the northern salient by the end of the day, the 1st *Flieger* Division had flown 1,687 sorties against 16th VA's 1,185 and 15th VA's 185 sorties. Of the Soviet total, 731 sorties were fighters. The Germans still had the edge in the sky but the gap was quickly shrinking. In fact, the Soviets had more fighter sorties than the Germans on this day in the north. In the north, the Germans still had a victory ratio of five to one. By the end of the day 1st

Flieger Division estimated destroying 43 planes, 14, tanks, 60 other vehicles, 20 guns and a number of ammo sites. cbk50. cbk55. nzk77. dgk116m.

10

July 8th on the Southern Salient

See Maps 12, 25

The German advance in the north was less than one mile on this day. To the south the German commanders remained hopeful of a breakthrough, but the rate of attrition remained high. Soviet strongpoints proved difficult to overcome. Meanwhile, Red Army counter-attacks, with armor, prevented substantial gains. The enemy tanks started shooting at about a mile or less. The T34s did well against IIIs and IVs, but the Tigers were immune to most strikes from a T34. The Soviet anti-tanks with larger guns had better kill ratios but there were not many deployed. The Soviets were sporting a few American made Shermans and British Churchills that were given on lend-lease. The Germans also found as they expanded their control of the battle zone, bunkers filled with American canned food and supplies. jp127. hjj122. kuz194. zow176.

In Berlin, the OKH decided to continue the assault at Kursk. It was clearly not going as well as planned but the Germans still had hope for improvement.

In Berlin, a German intelligence report was given to Hitler that despite the increase in German campaigns on partisans in May and June, their destruction on critical communication lines had actually increased three fold in some sectors.

In the Kursk area, *Luftwaffe* had made 4,000 sorties in support of the troops. That day, a claim of 193 Soviet planes were shot down while losing eight planes. Ground forces were also hit hard from the air. Casualties estimated vary widely depending on which side they're from but OKH claimed the *Luftwaffe* had shot down 700 planes in the previous four days. 700 tanks had been claimed as well.

During the predawn hours and with the rains having stopped, the roads were drying out as the 40th Army was marching closer to the battle sector to support the flagging 6th GA and 1st TA. bt85

Now that 4th PzA was nearing the critical Psel River-Prokhorovka line, Hoth spent most of his time strengthening the front line and reaching the point of departure to cross the river and capture the rail town, in order to gain access to the all important corridor that leads to Kursk. Hoth felt 48th PzC needed help to move beyond the Psel River so he ordered Hausser's SS to pause their attack toward Prokhorovka and shift direction to the northwest, cross the Solotinka River and get behind 1st TA and 6th GA to squeeze the Soviets against 48th PzC, south of the Psel River. At the very least they should strengthen the boundary between 11th PzD and *LAH* which was the Solotinka River. The Solotinka River was a tributary of the Psel running south about ten miles and was three miles east of the Oboyan road. When Vatutin saw the SS panzers heading west past the Solotinka River, he assumed the SS was fortifying 48th PzC's attempt to reach Oboyan. While sending a number of reserves to reinforce 1st TA, Vatutin thought this redirection favorable to his upcoming armor attack, which would be primarily but not exclusively directed east of the river against *LAH* and *Das Reich*. The panzers had assembled away from the front line during the night and Vatutin believed the grenadiers on the line were vulnerable. What the general did not realize was that many German guns had been brought up and were now supporting the men. gnk191. gnk193m. gnk196. gnk230. gnk227m.

The *LAH* had an arduous schedule that would see the three regiments going in different directions. The 1st PzGR would head north toward Gresnoe while the the 2nd PzGR would head to the northeast in the direction of Prokhorovka while the 1st PzR along with *Das Reich's* 2nd PzR advanced to the northwest.

On the southern bank of the Psel River at the villages of Vasilevka and Andreevka, the 99th TB of 2nd TC were waiting for *SSTK* to reach the river. The best tank ground on the north side of the river could be reached from between these two villages. To the east the other sector favoring tanks was east of Storozhevoe woods. The 285th RR of 183rd RD and the 169th TB of 2nd TC defended the village of Storozhevoe to the railroad line. All the brigades of 2nd TC were also ordered to be prepared to attack toward Gresnoe or toward Hill 255.9 upon order, but that would be difficult since some of the tanks were dug in. vzz183+.

At 0500 hrs the 167th ID was moving to the line to relieve *SSTK* from the Lipovyi Donets sector. The *SSTK* started making preparations to leave to the northwest toward the Psel River sector where they now had the responsibility of crossing the river and establishing a bridgehead. The 2nd GTC attacked late morning and a large part of the *SSTK* had to stay to support the 167th ID in defending the line from Nepkhaevo in the south to Teterevino in the north. Hausser had received early aerial reports of tanks approaching but, not knowing the full details of strength, he still ordered his divisions to begin redeploying to fulfill Hoth's orders to assist 48th PzC. The battle for *SSTK* lasted throughout the night and *SSTK* did not begin to move out in earnest until next morning. lck282. gnk191+. gnk193m. gnk196. gnk227m. ztc269. pck77. zow153.

The preparations for the major counter-attack by 10th TC, 5th GTC, 2nd GTC and 6th TC along the 4th PzA's front, and especially on the Prokhorovka-Teterevino road axis, was going poorly and the situation only got worse when those preparations were preempted and the three divisions of the 2nd SS PzC attacked first. The 183rd RD, the remains of 52nd GRD and the 11th MRB had moved up to the line to support the tank brigades in their planned offensive and were hit hard as well. First to initiate their counter-attack, the 10th TC with nearly 200 tanks began launching an attack on 2nd SS PzC along the road from Prokhorovka to Teterevino. Kravchenko's 5th GTC with 100 tanks later joined the engagement from the east, crossing the Lipovyi Donets and advancing past Belenikhino, aiming for Kalinin. The tank corps initially made modest gains but were repulsed by Duetschland Regiment in front of Kalinin. Still later, Burdeiny's 2nd GTC with 140 tanks deployed south of the 5th GTC, joined in attacking from Nepkhaevo but quickly lost 50 tanks in a devastating attack by the *Luftwaffe* and retreated. The tankers were protected on the right flank by the 11th MRB and the 52nd GRD as they attacked along the banks of the Psel River southward from Krasnyi Oktiabr. The 10th TC was surprised by an even stronger attack by *SSTK* and *Das Reich* that disrupted the Soviet attack, and inflicted heavy casualties. dgk134. dgk124m. dgk222m. dlu63m. zow151++.

The Soviets tried to regroup the best they could while under the German assault and counter-attacked but the situation was chaotic, losing momentum, and they failed to regain their composure. While many of the brigades attacked the SS, the 6th TC attacked *GD* near Iasnaia Poliana but had little success against the *Luftwaffe's* supported counter-attacks. *LAH* was also on the offensive early and reported destroying 82 tanks. All of 2nd SS PzC claimed destroying 121 tanks. General Theodor Wisch also reported 66 dead and 178 wounded. On the Soviet side, close to 200 Soviet tanks were claimed lost in these engagements by the end of the day. The objective Hausser was trying to achieve included a 2nd SS PzC link up to 48th PzC at Sukho-Solotino in order to strengthen the line and assist in clearing the southern banks of the Psel and then to establish a bridgehead on the other side. dgk134+. dgk124m. dgr89. zrl222.

At 0500 hrs, one combat group of the *LAH* resumed its attack to the northeast from Pokrovka, southeast of Verkhopenie, aiming for the junction of the Oboyan and Prokhorovka roads. The rest of the division would head either north or northwest as ordered. *LAH* quickly met up with nine tanks and destroyed one before chasing the rest away. By 0800 hrs, the combat group passed through Malye Maiachki, nearly ten miles north of the second defense belt and continued to drive toward Gresnoe. Southwest of Veselyi, the *LAH* was attacked by the 31st TC, 192nd TB, 29th TDB and elements of the 51st GRD. The battle lasted all day and ranged in the Luchki, Pokrovka and Bolshie Maiachki area. The *LAH* destroyed eight tanks in the first two hours and captured Malye Maiachki around 1430 hrs. At 1500 hrs Gresnoe fell and the 31st TC fell back to Kochetovka. The *LAH* captured Veselyi by 1700 hrs but then withdrew to the southwest to Luchki North for the evening. Before reaching Luchki North they were ambushed. Two Tigers were hit by anti-tank fire but were not severely damaged and the column continued to Luchki. Elements of the 167th ID and 11th PzD that were nearby were shifted to help *LAH* for the day. *LAH* reported destroying 19 tanks and 5 planes. wdk139. hjj121m. fkk86. dgr209m. vzz7m. dgk130m. gnk193m. gnk227m. zrl221.

During the predawn hours, the panzer group of *LAH* assembled in the Teterevino North area and at 0800 hrs, after learning Malye Maiachki had been captured by grenadiers, launched an attack toward the Solotinka River which ran north to south from the Psel River and past Malye Maiachki and Gresnoe. This small river was part of the boundary line between the 11th PzD and the SS Corps. The *LAH* was supposed to join up with 48th PzC east of Novoselovka which was located on the Oboyan road. Panzers of *Das Reich* were to launch at the same time and protect *LAH*'s right flank. Hoth also provided additional air support to 48th PzC. This maneuver was intended to encircle and destroy 3rd MC and 6th TC; pushing them back was not enough for they would regroup and attack at the river. *SSTK* was also being redeployed to the Psel River sector that day and would add its weight to the offense later in the day or next morning. Much of Hoth's plan dissolved when Vatutin's tank corps attacked *LAH* and *Das Reich* that morning. The Germans had to quickly turn defensive for their own survival. The launching of this attack by the SS Corps took them out of defensive mode and helped the Soviets when they attacked. If the Soviets had been prepared and coordinated as Vatutin had wished, the Soviets could have inflicted heavy casualties on the SS. gnk191+. gnk193m. vzz3m. gnk227m. zrl221.

Flying ten yards above the ground and using their new 30mm cannon, the *Luftwaffe* inflicted heavy casualties, about 50 tanks, on the 2nd GTC. This was a record number of tanks destroyed in a single mission by the Lufftwaffe and the only time German air power was able to stop an armor advance. Once the Soviet resistance died down, Hausser continued his advance toward Oboyan. *Das Reich* panzers stayed with *LAH* to protect its right flank as it headed for the Solotinka area. The *SSTK* that had redeployed to the northwest were trying to inch their way to the bend of the Psel River. Hausser was scheduled to meet up with 48th PzC further north at Sukho-Solotino to join forces and cross Psel River to attack Oboyan together. Popov's 2nd TC and Burdeiny's 2nd GTC were busy in their own sectors and could not assist 10th TC which was having the hardest time. The *Luftwaffe* were flying out of the Mikonaiovka air field near Kharkov when they spotted the moving column and attacked. dgk135. dgk130m. dgr221m. fkk145.

The day began warm, humid and partly cloudy as the panzers of the *LAH* prepared for their trek west to assist 48th PzC. The panzers did not leave on time due to the Soviet attack but once it was rebuffed, the *SS* panzers moved out to their individual objectives. The grenadiers had also been delayed but had resumed their missions ahead of the armor. Each regiment of *LAH* was going to advance in separate directions. The grenadiers were moving north and northeast while the panzers were heading to the northwest. The grenadiers were to capture Malye Maiachki, west of Teterevino North and located near the Solotinka River, before the panzers actually launched. Other Grenadiers moved southwest on a line from Teterevino North to Luchki North to protect the flank from roaming bands of marauders. The sector at this point was far from being secure. The Grenadiers met resistance immediately after leaving Teterevino North and did not get to Malye Maiachki until 0730 hrs where they proceeded to launch an attack from the march. By 0800 hrs the town, which had been abandoned, was in German hands. Katukov had ordered his 31st TC which was defending the area to move north along the Oboyan road where the 242nd TB (31st TC) was already stationed. When Wisch learned the Soviets had pulled back in the area, he immediately ordered his panzers to advance and fill the void before Soviet reinforcements could be called in. When the panzers of *LAH* approached Malye Maiachki, the tankers of 242nd TB attacked. A small panzer group from *Das Reich* was paralleling *LAH* a mile to the north and when the Soviets attacked both German groups responded. The moving battle was confined to the Bolshie Maiachki-Veselyi area. While the bulk of the 242nd TB fought the panzers, a small group splintered off and attack Luchki North. Wisch finally realized that the scope of the Soviet attacks may have been larger than thought and ordered his remaining panzers south to Luchki North, a key jumping off site to the north, where the defenses were better. After two hours of making no gains, the Soviet tanks pulled back beyond Veselyi. The *LAH* panzers quickly occupied Veselyi and nearby Hill 239.6 with the support of *Der Führer* which happened to be in the area. A new column of Soviet tanks charged from the northeast to engage the trailing 2nd PzR. The Sturm Abt 2 was in the area and quickly moved to the battle to support the panzers in repulsing the attack. After the attack, the assault guns split off from 2nd PzR and drove north toward the Psel River. Surprising the enemy, this assault group captured Krasnyi Oktiabr and the nearby hamlet of Prokhorovka next door. gnk194++. gnk193m. vzz3m. agk102. agk105. gnk227m. zrl221. zow148.

At 0500 hrs, a second coombat group of the *LAH* resumed its drive north from Pokrovka heading for Bolshie Maiachki which was captured two hours later by 1st PzR after a fierce tank battle. The panzers had moved on and the grenadiers were now moving in to secure the area. The bulk of the *LAH* and *Das Reich* panzers moved out from near Teterevino North to the northwest, heading for the village of Kochetovka on the Solotinka River. *LAH* had the lead and *Das Reich* was following on a parallel course to screen their flank. A formation of 40 Soviet tanks from 10th TC, which had just been transferred from 5th GA to Vatutin, drove down the Teterevino-Prokhorovka road to intercept them. After nearly a three-hour battle and losing a number of tanks, the 10th TC moved off looking for easier prey. They found the 2nd PzGR east of Pokrovka while the panzers continued to advance toward the Solotinka River. This early advance by the Germans disrupted a planned counter-offensive by Vatutin. The fresh 10th TC which was to spearhead the attack was used to try to blunt the Germans' advance, but the early advance by the Germans forced the Soviets to attack before they were fully prepared. The 2nd TC would attack the flank hours after the engagement started with 10th TC. mhz267. fkk137. fkk319m. lck282. agk102. gnk203+. vzz121++. wwf91. vzz7m+. dgk130m. gnk193m. gnk227m. zrl221. ##

After the 242nd TB pulled back from the engagement with *LAH* and elements of *Das Reich* to the fortified hills just east of Veselyi, the Germans did not immediately follow; they needed time to regroup. Veselyi, Hill 227.4 and Hill 239.6 were being manned by the remains of the 3rd MC and Chernienko's 31st TC. Hoth had made it a point to attack the boundary line between 3rd MC and 31st TC and the plan was successful. gnk196. kcz168. kcz17m.

Shortly after daybreak, elements of Burkov's 10th TC left Prokhorovka for Teterevino North for a frontal attack on *LAH*. With *LAH*'s panzers already on the road to the west, there were only two crippled Tigers which could barely move due to track damage plus a small garrison to defend the town. A column of Soviet tanks penetrated the German line, held only by grenadiers, north of town and was headed for town. Seeing the damaged Tigers, the Soviets headed for their prey. The Tigers opened up first and the battle was joined. When it was over the two Tigers had destroyed 17 T34s. Stunned by the loss, the 10th TC moved to the northeast to regroup. By the afternoon, the Soviet tank attacks in the *LAH* sector had stopped but air recon had still spotted large numbers of tanks north of the Psel bend which was probably the tardy 2nd TC late for the launch. After this day's battles, *LAH* had only 40 working panzers. Wisch ordered all of them to pull back behind the Teterevino North-Luchki North line to regroup. Frey and his panzers were ordered west again the next morning to gain control of the Solotinka River area. After dark Frey moved his panzers into a deep ravine where he would launch his attack in the morning. *Das Reich* panzers would also take part in the attack. Both divisions were to cross the river and meet up at Kochetovka. The Soviet tanks continued to attack *Das Reich* early in the morning from Teterevino North to Gostishchevo and Kruger was forced to keep some of his panzers on the front line. gnk199++. vzz3m. vzz5m.

Priess was preparing his *SSTK* to move out for the Psel River sector. He still had 99 working panzers that included 35 Mk IVs, 52 Mk IIIs and seven Tigers. The division was currently holding a 13 mile sector from Petrovka to Shopino in the south. A few of the panzers were regrouping several miles behind the line at Gonki on the road that would take them north through Iakovlevo. The 167th ID was slow in moving in to replace *SSTK* and that was making Priess even later than scheduled. While preparing to leave, Burdeiny's 2nd GTC with 40 tanks attacked *SSTK* in the Visloe-Ternovka area. German artillery stationed south of Visloe started shelling 2nd GTC's rear area to prevent reinforcements from coming up to the line. Bochmann was ordered to take his panzers up to the line and block the attack. This was another example of the Soviets having perfect timing of attacking the Germans when they were least prepared. Just past Hill 209.5 the panzers ambushed the advancing T34s. A small group of tanks got past Bochmann but were stopped by guns located on the hill. The *Luftwaffe* came back and helped *SSTK* with the enemy tanks. The fighting continued late into the night and yet *SSTK* would still make it to the Psel River by the following day. At the same time to the north, the 5th GTC was launching an attack against *Das Reich*. Vatutin, using several additional corps was trying to separate, isolate and destroy the three divisions of the SS Corps but with the support of the *SSTK* panzers and the heavy support of artillery for *Das Reich*, the two German divisions managed to repulse much of the attack without their lines disintegrating. gnk207++. gnk193m. vzz3m. gnk227m. kuz195. zow151.

The small contingent of *Das Reich* tanks was heading west toward Gresnoe, less than three miles south of Veselyi, to join up with *LAH* west of the Solotinka River. At first there was little resistance but when the Germans approached Gresnoe, they heard the sounds of guns firing on *LAH* as that division was preparing to attack the Soviet position. Hill 239.6 and Hill 227.4 were nearby and were also objectives. *Das Reich* neared the arena and the 31st TC started firing on them as well. With their batteries set up and firing, the *Das Reich* advanced toward Veselyi and Hill 239.6, west of Vesselyi. By noon Hill 239.6 was captured and *Das Reich* was moving toward the Solotinka River and then Kochetovka. *LAH* was taking care of Hill 227.4, south of Veselyi, during this battle. Before reaching Kochetovka, *Das Reich* saw nearly 200 tanks of the 10th TC crossing the Psel River and heading for Teterevino North. After reporting the Soviet column, the panzers continued west and within an hour reached Krasnyi Oktiabr where the lead panzers could see 11th PzD attacking Kochetovka. When the panzers became visible, additional tanks came out to meet them and a small but vicious battle ensued. The supporting Grenadiers were just crossing the Solotinka River, still trying to catch up to the panzers. gnk201. gnk193m.

By 0800 hrs the lead tanks of 2nd TC began reaching the Kamyshevka-Pravorot area and began the assembling and preparations to attack *Das Reich*. The eventual attack did not begin for 2nd TC until 1600 hrs; it was too late to be of much help to 10th TC. Vatutin's plan for the concerted tank offensive was flawed for it did not allow its participants enough time to reach their launch points. to stock up provisions or to study the battlefield. Vatutin had done this several times throughout the campaign and his tank brigades paid dearly for their premature attacks. The lead elements of 5th GTA started arriving in their designated areas north of Prokhorovka. Hoth estimated that his forces destroyed 212 tanks that day. Around 500 Soviet tanks had been destroyed in the preceeding four days. dgr83+. gnk203+.

At 0900 hrs, 40 T34s resumed their attack on the *LAH* which was advancing on Veselyi, a small strongpoint located midway between Sukho-Solotino and Gresnoe that was heavily defended. At just past noon, the *LAH* had advanced and was now attacking into the town, but during the previous hour the Germans were stalled against heavy fire. What broke the issue was the maneuvering of the Tigers to the Soviet flank, destroying the line of dug-in assault guns. At 1000 hrs, another 40 T34s attacked the eastern flank of *Das Reich* which was marching on a line between Teterevino and Kalinin. Both Soviet attacks failed to stop the German advance. With Tigers also leading the way and with Stukas supporting, the *LAH* later attacked Hill 237.6 near Veselyi and Rylski. By the end of the day, the *LAH* had driven a wedge between 31st TC and 3rd MC that penetrated almost to the village of Solotino. Also by the end of the day the fighting had been so fierce along the SS front, Hausser reported having 40 panzers damaged while destroying a total of 121 tanks. In this sector alone 45 tanks were destroyed. mhz267++. dgr221m. dgr209m. fkk137. fkk319m. agk102. nzk91. gnk199+. gnk193m. zrl221.

In the southern salient, the biggest air battle of the day took place over the sector where 2nd GTC attacked the SS. While German fighters were keeping the Red AF busy, Stukas and Hs 129s, with their 37mm cannon, attacked the tanks of 2nd GTC which were advancing from the safety of the nearby woods near Gostishchevo, surprising the grenadiers. Fw 190s dropping the new bomblets that each could cover an acre of ground were mowing down the supporting infantry. In addition to the losses in the air, an estimated 50 tanks of 2nd GTC were severely damaged or destroyed. The 2nd GTC pulled back to the woods spoiling Vatutin's big counter-attack. cbk66+. fzk173. pck68+. pck76. zow150+.

The 48th PzC ended their advance at Pokrovski, three miles west of Malye Maiachki. This left a gap on their right flank as the *LAH* made greater gains today and were north of Luchki North. A shock group of *Das Reich* left Teterevino and attacked 5th GTC and after a stiff battle continued on, shifting direction to the northwest away from Prokhorovka to cut behind the Soviet defenders in order to reach a hill east of Veselyi by 1100 hrs. It was a march of six miles. After securing the hill, the panzers of *Das Reich* moved on for another two miles and fought another hard battle east of Kochetovka. The third defense belt was now just a few miles north of Kochetovka. wdk139.

As part of the major tank offensive on the flank of 2nd SS PzC, Kravchenko's 5th GTC began its attack toward Kalinin and then Belenikhino at 1100 hrs after an hour preparation. Under a rolling barrage, the first wave of thirty T34s attacked with masses of infantry following behind. The *Deutschland* Regiment waited until the tanks were only 500 yards away before firing. Seven Soviet tanks went up in a fireball but the attack continued. A small group of T34s managed to penetrate the line, drive through the town and head for Luchki North and the vital road that fed the front line. Next door to *Deutschland*, *Der Führer* Regiment was also being attacked. Many of the Soviet tanks that made it to the rear in both sectors were destroyed by German artillery that had to lower their barrels to point blank range. 1100 hrs was late but not as late as Popov who would not launch his first wave until 1350 hrs. Despite air support, the first wave failed. After regrouping, a second wave was again launched at Teterevino South which was also defended by *Das Reich*. A few tanks made it into town but were hunted down by elite teams and destroyed by either satchel charges or magnetic mines. Further south at Nepkhaevo, Burdeiny's 2nd GTC attacked but was met with the *Luftwaffe*'s new 3.7 cm guns flown on Henschel's 129s. The planes inflicted heavy casualties on the first wave of tanks. When the planes left, the tanks regrouped and attacked toward Hill 209.5. gnk204++. gnk193m. nzk91. zrl221. zow149.

Around midday, a coordinated assault was made by the panzers of *LAH* and *Das Reich* against Hill 227.4 and Hill 239.6, which lay east and southeast of Veselyi. While the panzers of *LAH* fought the thirty T34s that came around Hill 227.4, Peiper and his mechanized force was ordered to take the village of Rylski which was providing flanking support. *Das Reich* had similar problems when the 237th TB rolled down Hill 239.6. Rylski fell fairly quickly though resistance remained around it but Veselyi, further north, was more difficult. Kling and his four Tigers had to outflank the front defenses and attack the town from the east. The Soviets did not have anything that could stop a Tiger and all the dug-in tanks were systematically destroyed by the Tigers. Rylski was a small village near the east bank of the Solotinka River, southwest of Veselyi. gnk196+. gnk200. gnk193m.

After taking Hill 239.6 in late morning, Reitzenstein's Panzer Group headed for the Solotinka River. By 1300 hrs, the panzer column was approaching the river and the 11th PzD contingent was waiting for them on the western bank. Within sight of the small river, a Soviet tank force rushed out from hiding and attacked Reitzenstein. Fighting for positional advantage, the small engagement turned fierce but after an hour the Germans were able to outflank and then repulse the enemy who retreated north along the Solotinka for the safety of the Psel River defenses. gnk202. gnk193m.

At 1350 hrs exploratory units of the 2nd TC repeatedly attacked Kalinin but were repulsed each time by the *Deutschland* Regiment of *Das Reich*. With the panzers moving ahead, *Das Reich* infantry fell behind, unable to support the panzers or be supported by them, and the *Luftwaffe* could not take up the slack. For the entire afternoon, *Das Reich* was repeatedly attacked by 2nd TC. Two pincers with 40 tanks each attacked German positions at Teterevino North and Luchki North. With the help of a nearby *SSTK* battalion, the attack at Luchki North was repulsed but the situation at Teterevino was more serious and once again the *Luftwaffe* was called in to help. Even though the Germans gained ground that day, the Soviets began increasing their counter-attacks with the increased reinforcements that had arrived that day and the night before. Along the long ridge stretching from east of Teterevino North, the third battalion of *Deutschland* Regiment was defending against these attacks. *Das Reich* also stopped another attack, this time infantry, that was heading toward Veselyi and by 1100 hrs had taken the high ground to the east. In the early afternoon a small tank group from 2nd TC made it past Kalinin and were heading toward Luchki North with the objective of cutting off the critical supply route that fed the front sectors of both *LAH* and *Das Reich*. As the six Soviet tanks were approaching Ozerovski, German artillery batteries were able to destroy all six tanks, squelching the potential threat of isolation. fkk138+. wdk140. dgr221m. fkk319m. vzz139++. fkk138. vzz3m. vzz7m. gnk193m. gnk205. zrl221. zow149.

A small combat group from *SSTK* was advancing through the Petrovski-Sabachevski area when they were ambushed. They made a fighting withdrawal against the larger force without suffering too many casualties. kuz195.

It was noon and it had not rained that day. The hot sun was beginning to dry the ground and the panzers and trucks were beginning to move a little easier. wwf89.

A strong counter-attack in the Hill 258.2-Komsomolets State Farm area, where almost 150 tanks from 2nd TC attacked the *LAH* and *Das Reich*, startled Hausser with the scale of the attack in combination with the ongoing actions. He ordered the lead units of *LAH* and *Das Reich* that had gotten ahead of everybody else (near Kochetovka, Gresnoe and Malye Maiachki) to pull back to the line (losing a two mile area) to avoid having those forces split apart and encircled. The 2nd SS PzC was now packed into a tight corridor in the Iakovlevo-Luchki North-Ozerovski-Teterevino area. The modest success of the Soviet attack can be attributed to hard fighting of Maj General Chernienko's 31st TC near Gresnoe, along with 2nd TC and 5th GTC to the east of Hill 258.2 but all three corps suffered heavy casualties. They failed to force Hoth to shift forces from 48th PzC over to Hausser but it made Hoth more conservative with his orders for the next morning. Ozerovski was just west of Kalinin. vzz150++. vzz3m. zrl221.

Vatutin, suspecting a shift toward the important Prokhorovka, started deploying some of his reinforcements that were arriving in sector there; his tankers would try to clear the territory held by *LAH* down to the Teterevino-Kalinin-Nekhaevka line. The other tank corps also headed for *Das Reich* between the hills northeast of Luchki South and Teterevino. fkk141. vzz153.

At noon south of Luchki South, one regiment of the *SSTK* with 30 panzers was attacked by elements of the 2nd GTC. By 1245 hrs, 40 tanks supported by infantry attacked Visloe and Ternovka, not far from Shopino, on the Lipovyi Donets River. By 1445 hrs another 25 Soviet tanks arrived and the battle continued. Additional help from two regiments of the

167th ID arrived in the afternoon to help the German cause. With the new forces, *SSTK* was able to repulse the attacks and, moving throughout the night, reached their assigned launch point west of *LAH* for the next morning attack. By now all 2nd SS PzC's reserves had been called up; there would be little chance for additional help. The division destroyed a number of T34s in the engagement and forced the Soviets to cross over to the east side of the Donets. The *SSTK* started the operation with 164 panzers and assault guns but by the end of the day had only 112 panzers and assault guns and some of these were in the repair shop. Only five of the original eleven Tigers were working; a couple had been destroyed and the rest were in the repair shop. wdk140+. dgk222m. dlu63m. fkk139. fkk144. fkk322m+.

Vatutin counter-attacked the German formations nearing the Psel River. One pincer launched from the northwest near Tomarovka while the second pincer would strike from Shopino (southeast) along the Kursk-Belgorod highway. Vatutin was hoping the two formations would meet in the middle and isolate the German front line. Hoth already had his forces on the move when the Soviets struck. With new Tigers in the lead, the Germans blasted through the Soviet line of 3rd MB and 31st TC allowing 100 panzers to head for Sukho-Solotino. The 10th TC and other units were called up from an endless reservoir of reserves to block the Germans from reaching Oboyan. je104+. dgr155m. dgr173m. dgk130m.

Along the long ridge stretching from east of Teterevino, the third battalion of *Deutschland* Regiment was defending against repeated attacks from Soviet tankers. Some of the tanks broke through the German positions and it was necessary to call for help. Thirty minutes later the *Luftwaffe* flew by and helped stop the attack. fkk138.

At 1345 hrs, Hoth assigned the following day's tasks to the 2nd SS PzC. The task was clearing both sides of the Gresnoe and the Solotinka sector. The 48th PzC was to advance northwest of the Solotinka sector to cross the Psel River in the Ilinski-Shipy sector. It was also to protect the west flank of 2nd SS PzC. A minute later, Hausser called back to Hoth to inform him that *Das Reich* was in fierce battle in the Kochetovka Hills and that Recon forces were in possession of the hills at Krasnyi Oktiabr, while other patrols were approaching the suburbs of Prokhorovka. fkk140. fkk323m. dgk130m. vzz1m.

Between the main forces of 2nd SS PzC and 3rd PzC, the *LAH* wiped out a pocketed Soviet force that included tanks near Prokovski which was located just southwest of Teterevino South and the Prokhorovka rail line. The *LAH* moved on along the railroad line toward Prokhorovka but was stopped before reaching Bogorodits. snk81. dgr76m. gnk163m.

As part of the major offensive, the 2nd GTC launched hours late from Petrovski, Kriukovo and Chursino and drove toward Luchki. In conjunction with the assault of 2nd GTC, Col Seriugin's 89th GRD would attack also on a line that would include the capture of Visloe, Shopino and Erik. Another combat group consisting of elements of the 26th GTB, 4th GMRB and 89th GRD would attack toward Hill 209.5 and the nearby State Farm. While these battles were raging, the 48th PzC to the west, were modestly gaining ground against 1st TA in the Gremuchi-Verkhopenie area. vzz143+. vzz147+. vzz8m. vzz330+. vzz7m. dgk135.

GD reported to Knobelsdorff but the report that was sent up the line stated they had arrived at Verkhopenie. This was an error for they had arrived at Gremuchi, three miles south of their real objective. Hoth thought *GD* was further north and in line with 11th PzD and *LAH*, which were at the Solotinka River, so the *GD* division was ordered east to join up with 11th PzD and elements of *LAH*; together they would force the Psel River, destroying the remnants of the 31st TC. With the misguided intel that *GD* was further ahead than they really were, Hoth later that night decided to send *LAH* panzers back from the Solotinka area east the next morning to resume their attack toward Prokhorovka. With the heavy tank attacks against *Das Reich* to the east, *Das Reich* panzers that deployed alongside *LAH* heading for the Solotinka River had already been ordered back to the Teterevino North sector for defensive purposes against the four tank corps that were attacking along their entire sector. *Das Reich* was frequently attacked on their way back east but was able to repulse each attack. By this time the 2nd TC under Popov had not completely arrived with its 168 tanks but was being deployed to the left of Burkov's 10th TC piecemeal. The 10th TC (200 tanks) driving south on the Prokhorovka road therefore had poor eastern flank support. Kravchenko's 5th GTC's 100 tanks were next, driving toward Belenikhino and Iasnaia Poliana. Burdeiny's 2nd GTC's 140 tanks were deployed further south in the Nepkhaevo area. If this Soviet attack had been better prepared and coordinated and ready to launch at daybreak it would have caught the defenses of *LAH* and *Das Reich* less prepared while their armor was heading for the Solotinka. The piecemeal launch of the Soviet offensive negated much of the potential. gnk193m. vzz2m+. gnk227m. gnk203+*.

It is estimated that Popov's 2nd TC did not arrive in sector until 1350 hrs. It cannot be overstated that if Popov's forces had been in place by 0900 hrs to assist 10th TC on its drive on Teterevino North that it was almost certain the Soviets would have penetrated the *LAH* / *Das Reich* line and caused massive trouble for 4th PzA. gnk204. gnk193m. gnk227m.

As part of the planned major offensive, 2nd TC also launched late at 1600 hrs against the 2nd SS PzC with its 169th TB and 26th TB in the lead and with 99th TB following. They were unprepared and driving blind toward Hill 258.2-Teterevino North-Luchki North. When the 169th TB reached the Komsomolets State Farm, the hiding Germans ambushed them with dug-in panzers and mortars, inflicting heavy casualties. At the same time, the *Luftwaffe* was flying by and attacked the tanks on open ground. Some of the planes were the Ju-87G, carrying the new 37mm cannons that could destroy T34s by hitting the engine compartment and igniting the fuel. Without Soviet fighters, the Germans had free access to the tanks. The remnants of 169th TB which made it to Hill 258.2, as well as the rest of 2nd TC, fell back to Iar Zaslonnyi or Stalinskoe State Farm when the advance stalled in large measure to the effective air attacks. The strength of this day's attack, especially after the large losses suffered yesterday, startled Hausser. He immediately recalled the combat groups of both *LAH* and *Das Reich*, fighting on their western flank against 31st TC, back to their original positions to the east. vzz145++. pck68+.

The 169th TB of 2nd TC attacked south of the Komsomolets State Farm near Hill 258.2 where Tigers in the lead saw them attacking and started firing before the T34s could shoot back. Stukas were in the area and flew in attacking the tanks as well, having no Soviet fighters to contend with. German artillery on nearby Hill 224.5 as well as Hill 258.2 also contributed. At 1800 hrs the air attack escalated with even more Ju 88s and Ju 87s attacking, forcing the tankers to fall back. With fighting that had firing from all directions, chaos reigned until after dark. When some of the Soviet tankers fell back to the woods near the State Farm others were able, with the help of the infantry, to establish a small position on the southeastern corner of Hill 258.2. The SS expecting another attack during the night started erecting greater defenses on the hill. vzz143+. vzz147+. vzz153. vzz8m. vzz330+. vzz7m. dgk135.

Having just lost Teterevino South, *Das Reich* regrouped and proceeded to advance toward the village. Forty T34s rolled out of the village on a frontal attack. Quick recovery by artillery and anti-tank guns along with aircraft helped the panzers destroy 11 tanks and repulse the attack. Four other Stukas were sent out on a second wave to the north of Teterevino to attack Soviets that were assembling. The *Luftwaffe* did lose three planes in both engagements. While *Das Reich* was defending itself from this attack, three battalions supported by twelve T34s were attacking toward nearby Luchki from Sabachevski. Hausser sent a battalion and a few panzers from *SSTK* to Luchki to support the local garrison. During these engagements, German artillery was brought closer to the line and started shelling Vyselyi and Ternovka, near the Lipovyi Donets River, where the Soviets were assembling. fkk141+. fkk322m+. gnk205. gnk193m.

The *SSTK* was less than a mile east of Hill 209.5 and one mile southwest of Visloe and was engaged with Soviet tanks of 26th GTB over control of the hill. The German pressure was too great when the 3rd PzR showed up to support the grenadiers and the T34s began falling back to east of Ternovka, not far from the Lipovyi Donets River. The 4th GMB which were supporting the tanks fell back also. Other elements of the StuGs crested Hill 209.5 to the west and headed north while enemy tanks were firing on them from northwest of Gonki. Hill 209.5 was not far from Visloe which is a mile north of Ternovka. By 1430 hrs, *LAH* had cleared north of Bolshie Maiachki and Hill 252.5, 2.5 miles north of Iablochki but south of Vasilevka. Two small hills, Hill 220.4 and Hill 251.2, not far from Hill 252.5 were key targets as well. A little later, elements of *SSTK* counter-attacked a Soviet group of tanks southwest of Visloe and destroyed most of the 25 attackers. The many local armor attacks throughout the day were not overtly successful but they did slow the 2nd SS PzC's advance. fkk140+. fkk319m. vzz283. vzz143. kuz195. ztc269.

The 31st TC reinforced with the 192nd TB fought all day with the *SSTK* and *LAH*. By 1500 hrs, the Germans had pushed the 237th TB of 31st TC back to Kochetovka. Elements of the 86th TB, 59th TR (a part of 1st TA) were in the area and deployed next to 31st TC. Renewed resistance by the Soviets prevented *SSTK* from establishing a bridgehead on the northern banks of the Psel when the forward units of 10th TC arrived. The 10th TC was transferred from Steppe Front. The panzers of *Das Reich* along with elements of *Der Führer* had made it most of the way to Kochetovka when the 31st TC retreated to the north. By the end of the day, the Germans had advanced about five miles. This rate of advance was far behind Hoth's estimate of reaching Oboyan by the 7th at the latest. Vatutin estimated the Germans lost 129 panzers on this day. dgr216. zow149.

Up till now the primary axis of attack for 4th PzA had been toward Oboyan but there was a possibility that the main axis could shift east toward the corridor next to Prokhorovka. Marshal Vasilevsky discussed with General Vatutin about redeploying some of his forces to block such a possibility. wwf90.

The Pz Abt 2, on the northern flank of the advance of 2nd SS PzC, reached the southern bend of the Psel River. The battalion of Tigers stormed the village of Prokhorovka and then forced its way into Krasnyi Oktiabr on the southern banks of the Psel. During the brief struggle, some of the Soviet tanks had gotten past the Tiger screen, heading south and reaching the village of Iablochki to harass the garrison there. The *LAH* and flanking *Das Reich* columns of panzers advancing south of the Pz Abt 2 toward Kochetovka were attacked by the Red AF, slowing their pace as they had to defend themselves again. The Soviets also lost numerous T34s today going up against the Tigers. At 1230 hrs, the *Das*

Reich discovered another large concentration of tanks in the woods east of Iasnaia Poliana which slowed *SSDR*'s advance. Another formation of Soviet tanks from 5th GTC attacked and penetrated the thin German positions in Kalinin and made it to the Ozerovski area. German artillery stopped their advance and forced them back to their starting point. They lost seven T34s in the engagement. The reinforcements Vatutin ordered to the line were now being felt by the Germans and their advance was clearly slowing down. The major offensive Vatutin had intended did not materialize but the Soviet tankers still succeeded in several local penetrations. Even when the coordinated armored offensive was considered over, the Soviet corps along the Lipovyi continued to launch local attacks. fkk137. gnk193m dgk130m. vzz3m. zow148.

Elements of the *LAH* cleared resistance from Bolshie Maiachki and nearby villages which were defended by the 31st TC during the day. Later in the day but before dark, *LAH* near Teterevino attempting to regroup after a tough day was attacked probably by elements of 5th GTC and infantry support of the 183rd RD. Panzers were quickly dispatched as well as an air raid by the *Luftwaffe*. The battle was joined for most of the night; the new panzers and air attacks destroyed a number of Soviet tanks but the Soviets were still able to penetrate the German defenses and rout *LAH*'s supply depot in the rear. The Soviets were eventually pushed back. During the afternoon the *SSTK* pushed 31st TC's flank back past Gresnoe and pushed on toward the Psel River. *Das Reich* had to cover the right flank of *LAH* near Teterevino. dgk134. dgk124m. wdk140. gnk193m. gnk227m. zrl221.

The principle objective Hausser was trying to achieve included a 2nd SS PzC link up with 48th PzC at Sukho-Solotino in order to assist in clearing the southern banks of the Psel and then to establish a bridgehead on the other side. The Soviet counter offensive prevented that objective from being fully realized as well as threatening to breach the Teterevino North-Iasnaia Poliana sector that was being defended by the infantry of *LAH* and *Das Reich*. This lack of success occurred even with heavy support of the Red Air Force. Kravchenko's 5th GTC and Burdeiny's 2nd GTC suffered heavy casualties for their effort. The 4th PzA reported destroying 212 tanks today. dgk134+. dgk124m. dgr89.

After the unsuccessful struggle for Gresnoe and nearby Veselyi which lasted past dark, the *LAH* fell back to near Luchki North, about three miles south to reduce the exposure to its flanks. Learning that this village was not taken, Hoth ordered the 2nd SS PzC to go defensive for the next morning to regroup. The 2nd SS PzC was supposed to fight its way to the south bank of Psel by the end of the day but while a recon battalion made the objective, the rest of the division was still at least six miles from the river. The *LAH* was also to reestablish a link with 11th PzD at Kochetovka, west of Kozlovka on the Solotinka River, and *SSTK* was to clear all Soviets south of the Psel from Kozlovka, just west of Vasilevka. The 167th ID was tasked to close the gap between 48th PzC and the 2nd SS PzC. The panzers from the *SSTK* were to be pulled back and maintained for the upcoming battle for Prokhorovoka, while its infantry were to cross the Psel and establish a bridgehead on the northern bank. The infantry moved into attack positions during the night and at first light would force the river. wdk145+. hjj121m. dgr209m. fkk137. vzz187++. vzz8m. gnk227m.

At 1800 hrs, the infantry of *Das Reich* reached Iasnaia-Poliana, about ten miles southwest of Prokhorovka, but ran into strong resistance at the railroad east of town. By 2000 hrs the situation stabilized near the town but *Das Reich* had to send an assault gun battalion to reinforce the right flank which was still having trouble. wdk140.

Hausser and his panzers of 2nd SS PzC would be delayed in meeting up with 48th PzC near the Solotinka River because Kempf Group, fighting east of the Northern Donets River, was being weighed down by fierce resistance by 7th GA and 69th Army and 3rd PzC could not protect Hausser's right flank. Hausser had to invest too many of his forces on the flanks which weakened his forward movement. Kempf was trying to get around the stubborn 81st GRD and ambush it from the rear but that was not going well either. dgk135+.

At dusk, a small group of T34s broke away from the main battle and headed for Visloe, which *SSTK* panzers were holding. The two sides started firing on each other when a squadron of German attack planes came in and strafed the T34s. Several of the tanks were destroyed and the remainder immediately pulled back. After dark Soviet planes came over Visloe and, using the burning buildings as beacons, zeroed in on German positions, inflicting some damage on the enemy. Hausser received orders to have *SSTK* on the road by first light and to reassemble at Luchki South. gnk210. gnk193m. vzz3m. gnk227m.

With most of the panzers of *LAH* and *Das Reich* moving toward the Solotinka River, the remaining Tigers and assault guns stayed in the Teterevino North area where Soviet resistance the last two days had increased. At 1800 hrs southwest of Hill 252.2 two Tigers were ambushed by a group of assault guns and though a few of the T34s were destroyed, both Tigers received track damage and were unable to move. A recovery caravan was quickly dispatched during the ensuing battle to bring them back; the remaining panzers and assault guns in the area pulled back and went defensive after disengaging from the Soviet tanks. zrl222.

With the 2nd SS PzC trying to thrust forward over the Psel into the rear sectors of 1st TA, Vatutin, recognizing the danger sent the 2nd GTC from the woods near Gostishchevo to repeat the counter-attack on the flank and rear of 2nd SS PzC. Vatutin was not only trying to reduce the pressure on 1st TA but also cut off the Germans' supply line. The SS PzC was surprised and unprepared for the ambush and would have been in deep trouble but the *Luftwaffe* came in and caused much damage to the Soviet tanks before they could reach the outnumbered panzers. The 31st TC's line had been penetrated and its forces were falling back without permission. When Khrushchev, the political officer of 1st TA, heard this he went to Katukov with an order that all forces would stand and die if needed or they would be shot. If the Germans got behind 1st TA then it could destroy it and Oboyan and maybe even reach Kursk. Khrushchev then went to Vatutin to have reinforcements sent.

Khrushchev was a miner before the revolution but converted quickly being in favor of the ideology of Communism. He was born in Kalinvoka in 1894 which was located in the Kursk salient so he was another local boy fighting for his home and country. He was a political commissar from 1941 to 1944 and was not afraid to push Vatutin when it was called for. After the war he remained actively in politics and in 1955 after Stalin died took over the reins of the country and lead it for nearly a decade during the Cold War years. Shortly after the Cuban Missile Crisis he was ousted from power in 1964 by Brezhnev who took over. He died relatively poor on Sept 11, 1971 just outside of Moscow. fkk145+. pck68. pck75+. rc198. lck284. wwf90. vzz3m. vzz5m. zmb274. zow150.

Earlier in the day, Burdeiny's 2nd GTC was deployed near Gostishchevo to block Kempf's forces from meeting up with 2nd SS PzC, but Vatutin ordered the tankers to shift 90 degrees and attack the right flank of 2nd SS PzC and the 167th ID. For days the 167th ID would be hit hard to reduce their support to 2nd PzC moving forward. As the 2nd GTC cleared the woods and came out into the open still a few miles from engaging the Germans, the *Luftwaffe* flying by and looking for opportunities dived onto the tanks and inflicted heavy casualties, destroying 50 tanks and causing Burdeiny to cancel the operation. These Soviet tanks had been undiscovered by the ground forces and if they had been able to attack would have caused heavy casualties on the Germans. The 2nd SS PzC reported with the help of the *Luftwaffe*, destroying 212 tanks that day. That brought the total to 502 since the start. mhz276++. bt86. wwf90. fkk140. vzz5m. pck76+. zow150++.

The 10th TC and the 3rd MD continued to attack *SSTK* after dark. Since 7/5, the 2nd SS PzC had losses of 202 panzers leaving 249 capable of fighting the next morning. But with repaired panzers that were brought back for the next day the number jumped to 272 panzers. mhz294.

At 2030 hrs Hausser ordered the 2nd PzGR, the bulk of which was deployed near Luchki South, to immediately move north to the Teterevino North area to safeguard the new line from roaming bands of shock troops looking for a weakness in the line. *Das Reich* was having trouble and General Hausser was forced to expand *LAH*'s sector to just south of Teterevino North. On the other *LAH* flank, the 1st PzGR was ordered to move further west and cover Sukhno Solotino. At night Maj General Wisch moved his HQ north to within three miles south of Iakovlevo. zrl222+.

Late at night, *Stavka* attaches Rotmistrov's 5th GTA to Vatutin's Voronezh Front while the 5th GTA was moving into assembly areas near Staryi Oskol for the trip west during the early morning of 7/9. They would then move on Prokhorovka with their 630 tanks. Bakharov's 18th TC was also attached to 5th GTA. These tanks would deploy east of Oboyan to the northeast of Prokhorovka as soon as possible. In less than three days the army covered 150 miles. Zhadov's 5th GA became under control of Voronezh Front and would move in to protect the Psel River in front of 5th GTA. To prevent the *Luftwaffe* from destroying the tank column, Stalin sent air cover the whole way to Prokhorovka from the Oskol River area. It would take 5th GA until 7/10 to deploy in front of Prokhorovka; the 5th GTA would be a little later. The 5th GTA would assemble in the Priznachnoe region, six miles east of Prokhorovka. The Soviet third line of defense ran just in front of the town to and along the Psel River. To soften up the 4th PzA, the Soviet AF flew many missions. Also the rest of 2nd TC was called up to the same location. *Stavka* hoped these reinforcements would prevent the Germans from reaching Oboyan and ruining their third defensive belt, which was holding up with only several penetrations. In the north, it was decided by *Stavka* that Rokossovsky did not need any further help in stopping Model's 9th Army. dgk138+. wdk139 vzz160++. vzz166+. vzz182. gnk220. gnk227m. cbk67. zro206+.

At night Vatutin, realizing that the Germans were heading for Prokhorovka, began sending forces to the sector. The 10th TC under Burkov was sent to the left flank of 1st TA nearest Prokhorovka. The 5th GTC was ordered to redeploy from their Teterevino-Komsomolets line and head northwest to defend the corridor west of Prokhorovka. To strengthen the river sector further, Vatutin ordered the 5th GMC to defensive positions in the Psel-Zapselets River sector on the right flank of where the 18th TC would assemble. The 18th TC deployed along the northern bank of the Psel from Veselyi-Polezhaev-Prelestnoe to the southern edge of Aleksandrovski. This could have been an error on Vatutin's part to move these three corps in this manner, weakening the defenses directly south of Prokhorovka in favor of the line further west. Other redeployments occurred as well near the Donets River area. Vatutin figured his current forces could and would hold back 4th PzA for a couple more days until 5th GA and 5th GTA fully arrived to destroy his enemy. The *LAH* and *Das Reich* had to be slowed and prevented from capturing the important rail station until reinforcements arrived, but were these deployments the correct response? vzz177*. vzz8m. vzz1m. gnk193m. gnk227m.

To strengthen the 7th GA sector, Vatutin ordered the 49th RC of 69th Army to 7th GA. At 2200 hrs, Vatutin ordered the 183rd RD (69th Army) to redeploy from the Vinogradovka-Novoselovka (east)-Shipy line to the Prokorovka rail line running in the Komsomolets-Iasnaia Poliana-Teterevino line. wwf92.

After dark Stalin called Vatutin with orders to stop 4th PzA's advance now, for the major counter offensive to capture Orel was dependent on both 9th Army and 4th PzA being exhausted and incapable of any further advance. The consequences of failing to stop 4th PzA was well understood by Vatutin. wdk146.

To sum up the day's results of the Soviet armor offensive: At 1000 hrs, the major Soviet counteroffensive officially began with the objective of splitting up and encircling the 2nd SS PzC but the fighting actually began earlier when these tank corps had to defend themselves from the German preemptive attack. This Soviet offensive was quickly planned, poorly reconnoitred and poorly coordinated. The unit commanders had little time to prepare or to regroup from the losses of the previous two days and the two new corps had to go into battle from the march with no preparation at all. Besides, the attack was premature for the Germans were still too strong and too well entrenched to be defeated and the situation for the Soviets became further confused when the SS preempted their attack. By 1500 hrs the 5th GTC had recaptured Kalinin and reached the Ozerovski-Scbachevski line and a hill south of Sobachevski. The 2nd TC to the right of 5th GTC and the 2nd GTC on the left were unprepared and delayed their attack, failing to exploit the success of 5th GTC, and made no gains. The 10th TC had inflicted pain and casualties but failed its objectives as well. The success that occurred would be the result of the determination of the combat troops that were supporting the tanks and the tankers that started on time. vzz140++. vzz7m. zow149.

By the end of the day, the 2nd SS PzC had reached the following line: *LAH* reached the Kochetovka-Teterevino North road and was well on its way in securing the ground between the two important villages. It also covered the ground from Teterevino North south to Ozerovski. *Das Reich* had formed a line from Ozerovski southward to a little ways south of Teterevino South. The *SSTK* took over from here to Ternovka just west of the Lipovyi Donets River. The SS had been moving to the northeast following the Belgorod-Prokhorovka highway but Hoth, despite the increasing resistance in front of *LAH*, would order most of the panzers of *LAH* and even order *Das Reich* to resume its northwest trek the following day and secure all the ground to the Solotinka River in order to reduce the pressure on 11th PzD's exposed right flank. This shift to the west has been criticized for it slowed the momentum of the *LAH* toward Prokhorovka for basically two days. There were alternative choices but Hoth was apparently blind to them. With the 4th PzA so far behind schedule and the Soviet defense so much tougher to crack than expected, it was wrong of Hoth to continue his diverging attack toward both Oboyan to the west and Prokhorovoka to the east. When you add the extreme trouble 3rd PzC was having to the equation, it made sense to contract the battle zone not expand it. In my opinion it is viable that 48th PzC and 52nd IC should have contracted their attack zone, shifting eastward to strengthen thier defenses and to assist the SS anyway it could instead of independently moving along the Oboyan road. Or instead of contracting the western flank, Hoth could have contracted 3rd PzC sector closer to the Donets Rivers, although it was getting late in the campaign for that measure. Contracting and not expanding 48th PzC sector would have been easier and safer to accomplish and would have made unnecessary this impromptu trek to the Solotinka by the SS armor. The two days the SS armor spent in the Solotinka area could have been better spent in forcing the Psel and entering the Prokhorovka corridor ahead of the 5th GTA's arrival. This action by Hoth would seem to signify that he was unaware of the 5th GTA's movement toward Prokhorovka. If Hoth had known, it would have been more logical to establish a bridgehead north of the Psel-OSF-Prokhorovka line, allowing his 2nd SS Corps to defend itself and making it as difficult as possible for the Soviet reinforcements to assault them. This side excursion is another indication that 4th PzA's front was too wide. wdk138+. gnk193m. vzz8m.

At night, Lt General Trierenberg's 167th ID moved up the Belgorod-Kursk rail line to the right of 2nd SS PzC, under the protection of heavy artillery fire from the 238th Artillery Regiment situated on high ground near Luchki South. With the Germans holding this sector, it enabled Hausser to push his battalions northwards toward the Psel River. rc201. dgk94. dgr209m. pck77.

Hausser reported to Hoth that his corps had 121 panzers that were either destroyed or damaged to the point they had to be pulled from the field for long term repair. He also reported that his corps did not have compensating gains today for those casualties though there were a few important ones. General Hausser had been 2nd SS PzC's first commander when it was formed in July 1942. The division was original deployed in France but transferred to the Eastern Front in early 1943 where it participated in the battle for Kharkov. vzz155. zsm261.

The 80,000 men of 5th GA under Zhadov started arriving at the Psel River from a forced march of 70 miles to take part in the Prokhorovka battle. It would take until the following night before the bulk of the two corps were in place. They would defend a 20 mile sector between Oboyan and Prokhorovka. Other armies were being repositioned between Oboyan and Kursk in case of a breakthrough. je106. dgk139. vzz167.

The *SSTK* spent much of the day trying to redeploy from the Lipovyi Donets area to the left flank of *LAH* in order to force a crossing of the Psel and screen *LAH*'s left flank when it made a run on Prokhorovka. The preparations to move northwest were going very slowly due to heavy attacks that were aimed at *SSTK*. When *SSTK* did leave the next day, the partial 167th ID found it difficult to maintain the line and *Das Reich* was forced to assist. The transfer was meant for this day but with the repeated attacks the changeover was not possible. By the end of the day on 7/9 when *LAH* and *Das Reich* were north and northeast of Belenikhino Station, the lead units of *SSTK* would almost have caught up to the left flank of *LAH*. lck282. kcz169. snk20.

By the end of the day, the Soviets had mobilized many of their reserves but operable front line tanks were down dramatically until 5th GTA arrived. They were weakening and yet the front line would not retreat, knowing more reserves were coming. Despite the modest results of his armor attack on this day, Vatutin still wanted to increased the number of counter-attacks to weaken the enemy further. The narrow salient Hoth was excavating captivated Vatutin; he was sure that eventually it would crumble, especially when 5th GA and 5th GTA arrived. That day's attacks which included seven Soviet tank corps were nearly on the scale and voracity of the coming tank battle of 7/12 but since it did not produce the results of the other attack, it's not nearly as well remembered. It did however exhaust the Soviet tank corps, allowing the 4th PzA to gain key ground in the next several days when they resumed their attack in the morning. fkk84. vzz155.

German intelligence discovered a series of large columns of tanks and trucks moving west toward Prokhorovka. Other tank concentrations were already assembling at Kochetovka, Gresnoe and Solotinka. Knowing this, Hausser pulled back *LAH* from the northern salient it had carved out until *SSTK* and *Das Reich* caught up. The 4th PzA made fewer gains that day; the impact of those Soviet reinforcements was beginning to be felt. The Soviet counters were strengthening and the Germans were being forced to either make a tactical retreat or go defensive. The 1st TA was becoming more aggressive, with 3rd MC and 6th TC launching larger and more frequent attacks. The 5th GTC and 2nd GTC had been attacking also, with less success but still at great cost. fkk143+.

Hoth reported another 125 panzers had been destroyed or severely damaged today, bringing the total to just over 400. It was also reported that another 300 Soviet tanks had been destroyed or captured. The 2nd SS PzC claimed to have destroyed 183 of those tanks, bringing its four-day total to 401. The Germans gained very little ground today but still levied a heavy price on the Soviets. mhz267. lck311. wdk141.

With the determined efforts of the counter-attack from elements of the 2nd TC, 2nd GTC and 5th GTC, it had prevented 2nd SS PzC from gaining much ground or achieving many of its objectives. The following day, when these tankers stayed on the defensive, the 2nd SS PzC would gain from three to eight miles. vzz259.

Von Manstein, through recon photos, became aware of the large numbers of tanks that were moving south toward the Psel River. For example Rotmistrov's 5th GTA arrived at their assembly area near Stary Oskol early that morning and would be still heading west for another day. Zhadov's 5th GA was being redeployed to support the 5th GTA when it was ready to attack near Prokhorovka. It is not clear if this sighting was 5th GTA moving to Prokhorovka or one of the corps which was already in sector but being redeployed. The 5th GTA was still east of Stary Oskol when the sighting was made so unless the aerial recon patrol was considerably farther east than usual then it was probably a corps redeploying to the west of Prokhorovka. The fact that the *Luftwaffe* knew of this concentration of tanks, whether 5th GTA or some other corps, and did not interdict it proves how shorthanded the *Luftwaffe* really was. mhz279. aaa124m.

In the last three days of fighting, 4th PzA and Group Kempf had fought their way through the first and second defense belts and were in the six to eighteen mile zone between the second and third defense belt. Progress on this day was better than in the previous days for Kempf but they had traveled only 13 or 14 miles from their start line and still had over 60 miles to reach Kursk. In the first four days, the Soviets had brought up many reinforcements and had seven tank corps and even more brigades. They had lost 500 tanks but still had 1500 more tanks to prevent von Manstein from reaching Kursk with even more forces coming. Vatutin still had more than Hoth and Hoth had lost some Tigers which degraded his spearhead attacks. Von Manstein was unaware of these forces and believed he still had a chance to reach Kursk. It just would not happen. wdk143+*.

At Teterevino, a German crew, picking up their repaired Tiger, was just in time to defend the village against an attack of 40 T34s. This one Tiger destroyed 22 T34s between several attacks before the Soviets fell back. When the AP rounds were expended, Staudegger started using HE. There was a waiting list of 100 more panzers in this sector that were being repaired as fast possible, but in many cases the crews had to wait for days to get their machines back. Though the Germans were fortunate to have recovered all those panzers, it was still a hardship fighting a campaign, awaiting the use of those 100 panzers. mhz268. agk103+. sgf346.

It is estimated that in the last two days the *Luftwaffe* flew 1481 sorties while the Soviet AF flew 2,600. According to Niklas Zetterling in *Kursk 1943*, these sortie numbers are low and that the German number was about the same as the Soviet number. lck315+.

By the end of the day, *LAH* had only 57 working panzers, most of them were Mk IVs. The Tiger battalion attached to *LAH* commanded by Kling was down to its last working Tiger. Wittmann was in charge of it. Ten were in the repair shop. gnk228.

In the southern salient, the 8th *Flieger* Corps reported destroying 43 planes, 84 tanks, 5 guns, 2 rocket launchers and 40 vehicles. Another 21 tanks were damaged but recoverable. cbk67.

The VVS reported flying 1,185 sorties in the southern salient. This was a drop of 350 sorties from the day before. The *Luftwaffe* reported flying 1,686 sorties, a drop of only 143. cbk64. nzk77.

By the end of the day and after five days of heavy fighting, the lead units of 48th PzC and 2nd SS PzC had each carved out a salient into the Soviet line about 18 miles wide and 12 miles deep. It covered from the salient 48th PzC had made at Verkhopenie in the west to *LAH*'s that had almost reached the Komsomolets State Farm and included Gresnoe and Malye Maiachki. With the panzer raid that saw *LAH* and *Das Reich*'s panzers move to the northwest toward the Solotinka River, *LAH*'s salient on the west expanded. Hoth had scheduled in his plans to be even further along than this at the end of the first or perhaps second day as a worst case scenario. Hoth and von Manstein were really worried at this point that the campaign would fail. wwf90.

During the predawn hours, the VVS flew 275 sorties in the southern salient. The attacks, which included biplanes, attacked along the Donets and Pena Rivers. At the Pena, the pontoon bridge erected by 3rd PzD engineers was destroyed which dramatically slowed that division's clearing of the resistance in the bend. cbk62.

Verkhopenie was a long slender village that ran along the eastern bank of the Pena River. Since it also had a heavy bridge across the river, both sides wanted to control the village. The Soviets had turned the sleepy little village into a strongpoint that clearly would not be easy to take. There was an extensive trench system in front of it and a Pak front defending it, as well as many tanks from 1st TA dug-in on the western bank of the river to stop the Germans. The 3rd PzD and elements of *GD* brought up their own artillery, Panthers and other panzers to take Verkhopenie away from the defenders. The Germans would eventually wrestle the village away but in the process of fighting the bridge would be damaged and the engineers of 39th Engineer Battalion would have to work throughout the night to have the bridge ready for panzers and trucks to cross in the morning. wwf89. pck71.

Early in the morning, General Hoth's 4th PzA resumed its advance along the main road toward Oboyan to reach the Syrtsevo-Gresnoe area before Vatutin could bring up additional reserves. The *GD* advanced northward along the eastern bank of the Pena River while 3rd PzD followed on *GD*'s immediate left flank. The 3rd MC attacked *GD* with forty T34s in the lead but the attack was repulsed, destroying ten tanks before they were in firing range. Later, 6th TC's 112th TB arrived and attacked the German position but failed to dislodge them as well. The 200th TB of 6th TC was stationed two miles to the northeast at Krasnaia Poliania, one mile northeast of the Oboyan road, waiting for orders but was not brought in for this engagement. That night Soviet reserves would be brought up to Oboyan. je103. hjj121m. lck284. dgr209m. gnk214. gnk227m. pck70.

While the main force of *GD* headed directly toward Syrtsevo, Hausherr's company of tanks screened their flank. Not realizing it, these four panzers drove into a trap set up by Soviet tanks hiding from plain view. Within minutes all four panzers were destroyed and Lt Hausherr was killed. A little later, the Remer Group broke away from the rest of *GD* and headed north, aiming to reach the Oboyan road. Though attacked from the air, the little ground resistance north of Syrtsevo, afforded a quick advance until they were within sight of the highway and approaching Hill 241.1, two miles east of Verkhopenie. This area was defended by the 192nd TB and 200th TB and upon sighting, the panzers attacked the enemy head on. gnk214+. gnk193m.

Syrtsevo, on the east bank of the Pena and defended by 6th TC and 90th GRD, was attacked by *GD* again but the line initially held. Another attack was launched from the south and east that broke into the village around noon with the help of 6th PzR of 3rd PzD. By 1330 hrs, the village was cleared. At the same time another group of the *GD* division advanced toward Verkhopenie by way of Gremuchi. Once north of Gremuchi, the *GD* was ambushed by 50 Soviet tanks. As the battle raged, additional panzers were ordered to the area to give urgent support. The panzers made it to Hill 230.5, east of Syrtsevo, but were struck again by a new group of Soviet tanks. With the help of the *Luftwaffe*, this German column made it into Verkhopenie but it lost panzers from Soviet fire of the 200th TB from the west bank of the Pena and fell back. Being in the open, the returning *Luftwaffe* planes destroyed many of these Soviet tanks. dgk131+. dgk95m. hjj121m. dgk222m. dgr209m. fkk267+. dgr217. gnk193m. gnk227m.

At 0530 hrs, *GD* and 3rd PzD were driving north toward the fortified village of Syrtsevo. Two panzer formations were heading north: the first group was heading straight for Syrtsevo and the other group for Hill 230.5, just to the east of the village. Defending the area that both panzer formations would meet up against were the 3rd MC (1st MB, 3rd MB), 6th TC (112th TB, 200th TB) and 90th GRD who were putting up fierce resistance. To help the attack, the *Luftwaffe* was giving close support. Waves of 50 planes each were coming in every 30 minutes attacking the many dug-in tanks, MG nests and bunkers that were deployed to the east and west of the Pena River to defend Verkhopenie and Syrtsevo. Even with the air support the *GD* division was taking terrible casualties while gaining ground slowly. All morning the fighting continued and it was nearing noon when *GD* entered the village and another 90 minutes of street fighting to clear the village.

The air war over the fortified village of Syrtsevo heated up when a Red fighter group came flying in, looking for a way to stop the massive losses the German planes were causing. German escorts saw the Soviet planes and vectored to intercept. Soviet fighters, although outnumbered, shot down five Stukas and one Bf 109 while losing even greater numbers before they had to evacuate the area, leaving the skies to the Germans. With improved Soviet planes and better pilots, the Ju-87 was showing its age and would be used less in the future on the Eastern Front. When Vatutin realized Syrtsevo would probably fall, he ordered elements of the 38th and 40th Armies under Moskalenko to move east and attack 48th PzC's western flank in order to reduce pressure on Syrtsevo. The remainder of the two armies would move northeast of Syrtsevo to in front of the Psel River along with the fading 6th GA to stop the frontal attack by 48th PzC. They would not be in place until the next morning. mhz267++. dgr221m. dgr209m. fkk137. fkk319m. gnk214. cbk62.

The 48th PzC was finally able to link up with *LAH* at Iakovlevo while the 3rd PzC was still miles behind, causing an exposed right flank for the 2nd SS PzC which the Soviets were exploiting. lck282.

Mickl's 11th PzD resumed its advance later than usual that morning. It had stopped after dark, building a defense for the night between Pokrovka to the Oboyan road, east of Syrtsevo. *GD* was on its left and *LAH* was on its right. The panzers had been at Hill 251.2, east of the highway, for the night. The two panzer regiments, 110 and 111, straddled the highway as the division moved north around 1000 hrs. The 31st TC had moved back to the other side of the Oboyan road and Mickl wanted to fill the void. Gresnoe was their next objective which would help support *SSTK*'s left flank as they were moving into the Psel River area. The lead units of 11th PzD reached Bolshie Maiachki, joining up with elements of *LAH*. As the bulk of the division was approaching Krasnyi Poliana, 40 T34s from the 192nd TB appeared to block their path. Air recon also discovered that additional tanks, probably the 112th TB, were heading for Syrtsevo. The 167th ID caught up to the 11th PzD and together they advanced northward, past Pokrovka and by 1300 hrs had reached Hill 249.3. Not stopping, the 11th PzD continued to advance, trying to reach the area east of Verkhopenie. On the east flank while the rest of the division was engaged, Pz Abt 11 headed for Krasnyi Poliana which was defended by the 192nd TB. Also in the area was the 49th TB and remnants of 3rd MC that the 11th PzD had to be also concerned about. gnk217+. gnk219. nzk91.

As 11th PzD neared Verkhopenie, traveling on the Oboyan road, Soviet resistance dramatically increased. The 192nd TB, 49th TB and the 3rd MC had dug in and were waiting for the German approach. Vatutin wanted to stop the Germans south of the Psel and Verkhopenie was the first of four major strongpoints that would try to stop the Germans south of the river. The panzers and half tracks of the leading group of the 11th PzD reached Hill 242.1, southeast of Verkhopenie when Soviet artillery opened up on the column. Bigger Soviet guns started firing as far away as Ilinski, a mile northeast of Verkhopenie. Minutes later, 40 T34s came down the hill to attack the panzers at point blank range. While this engagement was going strong, the rest of 11th PzD tried to come up to the line to straddle the road to help out. When it was getting dark, General Mickl decided to withdraw his troops for the night and try again in the morning. In the last three days of fighting the 11th PzD had lost 35 panzers and were now working with only 37 left. gnk219. gnk227m.

The lead units of *GD* were ordered to Verkhopenie to appraise the situation but because Syrtsevo was still unsecured, the Germans had to go through Gremuchi to the east. At Gremuchi a battalion was left to protect the bridge before moving on. Shortly afterwards a Soviet column attacked from the northeast but was repulsed, suffering heavy casualties. Meanwhile Strachwitz with his few remaining Panthers advanced past Hill 230.5 to the north. By evening *GD* was approaching Verkhopenie and in battle with the defenders south of the village. With Strachwitz having trouble, a battalion of *GD* that was left at Syrtsevo was ordered north to Verkhopenie to assist. By late night with the help of the *Luftwaffe*, Strachwitz had taken Verkhnopenie. The village, which ran in a north-south direction along the banks of the Pena River, was difficult to capture and a big part of that success went to the Flak Battalion of *GD* that destroyed a number of T34s and Soviet aircraft as well. hsz124. hsz117m. gnk193m. gnk113m. gnk227m. pck70+.

In an attempt to stop *GD*, the 200th TB attacked, but after an all day fight had to fall back to behind the Pena River where it started to dig in its tanks. With this pullback it looked like the 48th PzC was about to break through to drive on Oboyan. Along with the 200th TB, the 3rd MB and 49th MB of 3rd MC continued to grind away at *GD*. The 31st TC was also being pushed back by the 2nd SS PzC and was trying to build a defense north of Verkhopene across the Oboyan road and along the Solotinka River, forward of Sukho-Solotino and Kochetovka to the Psel River. The 2nd TC, 10th TC and 5th GTC were still attacking the 2nd SS PzC which would give enough time for 31st TC to finish this new defense line. Besides sending some of its forces to the west to help 3rd PzD and 52nd IC, *GD* was also ordered to advance three miles and capture Hill 260.8 which would make an excellent observation point overlooking the Oboyan road. Clearly *GD* was asked to do too much and sent in too many directions to accomplish too many objectives. It is another indication that 4th PzA did not have sufficient forces to get the job done. With additional troops of the 48th PzC and 52nd IC approaching the Pena River along the Oboyan road, Vatutin ordered the 200th TB of 6th TC and the remains of 3rd MC and Chernienko's 31st TC to fall back north of the Pena River and along the Solotinka River to the Psel River. To keep pressure on Hausser, the 31st TC then attacked southeast from Malye Maiachki against the flank of 2nd SS PzC. The newly arrived 10th TC was ordered to continue its attack in the afternoon along the Prokhorovka road toward Teterevino to help neutralize *LAH*'s attack. dgk133. lck283. vzz139++. dgk141m. dgk222m. fkk84+. dgr209m. gnk312m. gnk193m. kcz168. gnk227m.

In the morning, the *GD* division approached Hill 260.8 then wheeled west to cover the panzers of the 3rd PzD of the 48th PzC coming up after bypassing Verkhopenie. When the panzers were set to attack the nearby Hill 243.0, the infantry of *GD* group attacked Verkhopenie with its bridge across the Pena. The panzers were repulsed on the Hill while the infantry made only modest inroads to the town of Verkhopenie. When the Soviets counter-attacked from Hill 243.0, they were repulsed. Assault guns were brought up to aid *GD* and after a vicious three-hour battle the town was entered. 35 Soviet tanks were destroyed in this latest engagement. Some US supplied M3 tanks were destroyed. While *GD* was fighting for Verkhopenie, major elements of 3rd PzD were moving northward clearing the ground from Lukhanino to Verkhopenie to prevent Soviet forces from exploiting the gaps in the line and getting behind *GD*. The 3rd PzD was not moving fast enough and elements of *GD* would be tasked to stop their advance and turn south to help 3rd PzD. rc199. wwf89++. bt85. dgk222m. dgr209m. pck72. gnk219. gnk193m. gnk312m. gnk227m. fmz223. fmz222m.

In addition to the 2nd GTC, 5th GTC, 2nd TC, 10th TC and 31st TC, a number of other formations were also preparing for the coordinated armor offensive that would start at 1030 hrs after a 30 minute preparation. The 6th TC would launch from west of the Pena River toward Iakovlevo. To the north of the 6th TC, the 31st TC and 3rd MC moved into the Hill 260.8 area, just south of Novoselovka, to prepare for the assault. To the south of 6th TC, the 161st RD and 71st GRD, now attached to 40th Army, would attack to the east toward Gertsovka. The Germans surprised many of these formations by striking first and the coordinated attacked never took place, though individually some did advance while the others had to stay defensive. With the different axes of attack, Vatutin was hoping to split up 4th PzA into pieces before destroying it but results, due to lack of preparation and poor timing, were clearly disappointing for Vatutin. It was mostly Vatutin's fault for the poor results. He rushed his forces, not giving them time to prepare or reach launch point on time or communicate with the other corps. A few regiments from 38th Army were also transferred to north of the Psel River in the Semenovka to Goianino area as reserve. Though these Soviet assaults ultimately failed their primary objectives, it did have an important secondary benefit. While the Germans were desperately trying to break out of the second defensive belt to reach the Psel, these numerous counter-attacks the previous two days had caused the Germans to scale back their attacks to defend themselves against the Soviets. This fanatical action would be seen numerous times throughout the campaign; the Soviets, regardless of the costs, would counter-attack on the flanks that caused the Germans to transfer forces from the northern front to the sides to save themselves. The Germans just did not have sufficient forces on hand in either salient to defeat the large pool of Soviet reinforcements defending a well developed defense and the many counter-attacks. dgr88. dgr86m. vzz151. gnk193m. dgr127.

In addition to the massive attacks by the different tank corps, the 309th RD of 40th Army launched an attack eastward to cut off the 48th PzC marching north on the Oboyan road. The 309th was supported by the 86th TB and the 36th GMR was to march east and capture the Hill 251.4, Hill 240.4 and Hill 207.8. The attack was not successful and the 309th RD and the others had to pull back by evening and defend the Verkhoenie-Hill 261.0-Sukho Solotino line while the 31st TC held the line east of Sukho Solotino, Kochetovka and the left bank of the Solotinka River. dgr88. dgr86m. dgk412.

In front of the 3rd PzD, the 3rd MC had regrouped and were now in the following deployment from left to right: the 67th GRD, the 201st TB, 22nd TB, 112th TB, the 6th MRB and the 90th GRD. These forces were deployed within the Pena River bend and attempted to block 3rd PzD from advancing north to link up with *GD*. fkk251.

The 3rd PzD advanced in the Pena bend, turned to the southwest and breached the sector from the rear in the vicinity of Berezovka, forcing the Soviets back toward Rakovo. Taking advantage of this success, the 332nd ID crossed the Pena River and captured the area to the southern edge of Melovoe. The 332nd ID was not strong enough to encircle the garrison and the Soviets escaped northward. During this fighting to clear the Pena bend, both divisions which were flanking both sides of *GD* fell behind while *GD* continued forward, exposing their flanks. A 60 ton bridge was constructed across the Pena at Rakovo which was completed on the morning of 7/11. For the next two days the 48th PzC moved in and cleared the woods north of the Pena River in the Rakovo-Melovoe area. The Soviets counter-attacked at dark but were repulsed. snk81+. dgr172m. dgk222m. mhz290.

About three miles north of Syrtsevo and not far from Verkhopenie, the Germans were beginning to break through the line to reach the eastern outskirts of the village. It was defended by the 3rd MB, 200th TB and the late arriving 180th TB, 49th TB plus elements of the 51st GRD and 67th GRD. These uncoordinated forces attacked the 3rd PzD that were there plus the *GD* that were just arriving. It is claimed the Soviets engaged 100 panzers including 28 Tigers and inflicted heavy casualties. The 48th PzC claimed destroying 95 tanks in the engagement. On the extreme west edge of the salient, the 52nd IC was moving up as well and were at Alekseevka when they were attacked by elements of 40th Army. The 332nd ID destroyed three tanks near Korovino that belonged to the 71st GRD. The 255th ID at Bubny were also attacked by the 161st RD. Verkhopenie, north of Syrtsevo but south of Novoselovka, was on the Pena River and because of its bridge was heavily fortified and the German advance was clearly slowing because of the increased resistance. The above numbers for panzer engaged, especially the Tigers seem high and are suspect. wdk138.

hjj121m. mhz20m. fkk86. dgr209m. pck70+. nzk91. gnk193m. gnk227m.

The 48th PzC resumed its advance northward along the east bank of the Pena River and straight up the Oboyan road, pushing the remnants of the 3rd MC out of the way until approaching Ilinski, when Soviet anti-tank fire stopped the advance. Despite the heavy shelling, the 3rd PzD came alongside the Soviets and outflanked them, causing 3rd MC to fall back from the river. dk131.

The *GD* front advanced along the Oboyan highway from Syrtsevo to Krasnaia Poliana sector. Elements of the 3rd PzD and 11th PzD took part in the attacks also. *LAH* attacked to the west while *Das Reich* attacked more to the north from the Malyie Maiachki-Gresnoe sector. Two small assaults were launched into the Gresnoe-Vasilievka-Syrtsevo-Berezovka areas in order to protect the flanks of the main group. Every available panzer was in this operation and the count was about 400. The Germans were stopped just north of Syrtsevo by the 112th TB, the 10th MB and 1st MB. The 90th GRD were quickly dispatched to the area as a backup. fkk85. dgr209m.

For the battle of Syrtsevo, 40 tanks attacked *GD* as the formation approached the town. After quickly destroying ten tanks, the remaining T34s withdrew. By midday, Syrtsevo had fallen to the combine efforts of 3rd PzD and *GD*. After passing through Syrtsevo and while heading for Verkhopenie, more dug-in tanks fired on the formation. After regrouping and with the aid of 40th Army, the Soviets countered, trying to retake Syrtsevo but the attempt failed. When its infantry arrived at 1500 hrs and with the help of the arriving 6th PzR of 3rd PzD as well as the *Luftwaffe*, *GD* was able to fight its way into Verkhopenie but at a cost of losing two Mk IVs and severely damaging another. Once there, Group Strachwitz of *GD*, with only nine panzers left, paused to regroup before attempting to travel the last seven miles to the village of Oboyan. At the same time the 3rd PzD was still trying to clear the west bank of the Pena River but was having a hard time by itself. Other combat groups of *GD* quickly moved ahead from Verkhopenie: one group was trying to capture Hill 240.8 while the other was sent toward the village of Novoselovka and nearby Hill 260.8, but both groups were being blocked by heavy artillery. East of Hill 260.8, 11th PzD was preparing to advance due north attempting to help reduce resistance for the other two combat groups in their charge northward. With Syrtsevo fallen and *GD* continuing to move north, the Soviet defenders were forced to head west across the Pena River. With the Soviet counter-attack at Syrtsevo, parts of *GD* which were scheduled to advance toward Verkhopenie had to stay behind and defend Syrtsevo, again slowing the German advance northward. hjj118. mhz289. dgr209m. pck71. vzz427. gnk312m. gnk214+. wwf89+. gnk193m. gnk227m.

By midday on this Thursday after six hours of fighting, Syrtsevo, not far from where the Strachwitz Group was fighting, had fallen to *GD* and 3rd PzD, which had moved up to assist. However, a counter-attack by the 40th Army forced the 48th PzC to send more panzers to the village. *GD* lost four panzers plus others were damaged in this latest battle. After a while forty T34s engaged the Tigers of 3rd PzD and quickly ten T34s were destroyed near Hill 230.5 before the rest could leave the field, withdrawing to the other side of the Pena River. Verkhopenie, to the north and a little west, was *GD*'s next target. With the help of the *Luftwaffe*, which inflicted heavy casualties on 200th TB, the lead elements of *GD* arrived in the vicinity of Verkhopenie that night. Other elements of *GD* along with elements of 3rd PzD had headed east toward Syrtsevo. Beyond Syrtsevo was open ground that led to the third defense belt. It is estimated that *GD* started the day with only forty working Panthers but with the heavy fighting throughout the day, a few more were down. For the afternoon, *GD* was spread out from between Gremuchi to just south of Verkhopenie with the Soviets attacking this entire flank. It made it extremely difficult to defend themselves against the many ambushes the Soviets were good at. The gap between *GD* and 11th PzD had not been closed and the Soviets were taking advantage of that also. It is estimated the Strachwitz group destroyed 50 Soviet tanks that afternoon. By the end of the day Verkhopenie was still held by the Soviets. wwf89. dgk131+. dgk130m. hjj118. hjj121m mhz271+. dgr209m. fkk266. pck70. lck275. lck285. hsz122+. gnk214+.

In the afternoon, while the battle for Syrtsevo was raging, other elements of *GD* had moved north and attack Verkhopenie, three miles northwest of Gremuchi. After the village was taken, Soviet tanks made repeated attempts to get it back but failed. Just north of Gremuchi, Group Franz had pocketed a portion of the attackers. When the pocket was cleared, Major Franz claimed destroying 53 tanks and assault guns. dgk132. hjj121m. dgk222m. dgr209m. gnk193m. gnk227m.

Elements of 3rd PzD, with the help of a *GD* Regiment, finally took Syrtsevo, forcing the garrison to fall back across the river. The smoke from burning tanks, grass fires and shelling reduced visibility to virtually zero. Meanwhile other elements of *GD* were storming hills further north and were now only six miles from Oboyan. Soviet reinforcements were arriving and their resistance was slowing the German advance. The 3rd PzD were also pushing the enemy back west and north between Verkhopenie and Berezovka. This area would see plenty of hard fighting in the days to come. hjj121m. dgr209m. fkk250+. nzk91. gnk193m. gnk227m.

The 48th PzC had advanced three miles on the Oboyan road on this day but failed to reach its objectives of securing Schipy and crossing the Psel River. It had taken the high ground between Novoselovka on the west and Kochetovka on the east while forcing the 3rd MC and 31st TC to retreat northward. wdk147+. hjj121m. gnk191. gnk193m. gnk227m.

The 2nd TC, 10th TC and 5th GTC were attacking the 2nd SS PzC which would give their comrades enough time to finish a new defense line that included north of Verkhopenie across the Oboyan road and along the Solotinka River forward of Sukho-Solotino and Kochetovka to the Psel River. dgk133. dgk141m. dgk222m. fkk84+. dgr209m. gnk312m. gnk193m. kcz168. gnk227m. vzz139+. dgk412.

Up until around 1300 hrs, the 1st MB of 3rd MC and 112th TB of 6th TC were able to hold the superior German force of Strachwitz's panzers and infantry but then had to fall back across to the west side of the Pena River. The 200th TB of 6th TC at Krasnyi Poliana would also fall back after numerous air attacks and were digging in when a new squad of Stukas flew by and attacked, causing further damage to the corps. The 3rd MC, also blocking the Oboyan road, had to fall back three miles to the north but by the end of the day was still able to hold on to Hill 260.8. With 10th TC arriving in sector that morning, Vatutin sent elements of the 10th TC to the troubled sector of 3rd MC to help close the gap. dgr216. gnk214+*. gnk312m. cbk64. zra62.

Still advancing north toward Oboyan, the 48th PzC was striving to reach the Psel River but was coming under attack on its left flank from 6th TC. With *GD* and 11th PzD in the lead, they advanced on Hill 260.8 to gain the advantage of height. 3rd PzD was to shift to the west and attack the enemy west of Verkhopenie. *GD* was then to attack Hill 243 which overlooked the flank of the Soviet defenses at the Pena River, taking it away from 6th TC. Nearby Hill 247.2 would be the next objective. These engagements were made to eliminate the threat to the left flank of 48th PzC as it moved north toward Oboyan. The moves were timed to coincide with 2nd SS PzC consolidating their advance onto the Prokhorovka axis. dgk133+. dgk222m. dgr209m. gnk193m. gnk312m. gnk227m. fmz221m.

Westhoven's 3rd PzD was still having trouble advancing against stiff resistance. Trailing elements of the division were still in Lukhanino removing the last remnants of resistance, while the rest of the division was a little further north fighting to secure Syrtsevo and safeguarding *GD*'s left flank. The Soviets had strong defensive positions on the west side of the Pena, including many dug-in tanks, that were clearly having a slowing influence on Hoth's left flank. gnk216. gnk242+. nzk91. gnk193m. gnk227m.

With additional troops of the 48th PzC and 52nd IC approaching the Pena River along the Oboyan road, Vatutin ordered the 200th TB of 6th TC and the remains of 3rd MC and Chernienko's 31st TC to fall back north of the Pena and along the Solotinka River to the Psel. To keep pressure on Hausser, the 31st TC, after regrouping, then made a local attack southeast from Malye Maiachki against the flank of 2nd SS PzC. At the same time, the newly arrived 10th TC was sent south along the Prokhorovka road toward Teterevino to slow *LAH*'s advance. dgk133. lck283. vzz139++.

The 4th PzA would make relatively good gains against new reinforcements, reaching the third defense belt, but the advance would get even harder as 4th PzA penetrated into the third defensive belt, crossing the Psel River and capturing Hill 226.6, Hill 241.6 and Hill 252.2 against the soon arriving 5th GA and 5th GTA. On the 48th PzC front, most of the Soviets were west or north of Syrtsevo on the Pena River three miles north of Lukhanino. The 1st TA was still tenaciously blocking their path to Oboyan. With the help of the *Luftwaffe*, the 3rd PzD crossed the Pena River after breaking through the second defense belt north of Lukhanino. At 1800 hrs, they ran into a battle at Syrtsevo with the 90th GRD and 100 tanks from elements of the 112th TB of 6th TC and the 1st and 10th MB of 3rd MC. The 3rd PzD did cross the Pena River in limited numbers; the left flank of 3rd PzD finished securing Berezovka about three miles to the north of the bend while driving back the 6th TC. wdk137. hjj121m. dgr209m. vzz2m.

Burkkov's 10th TC and Popov's 2nd TC arrived in the Psel River area from the Staryi Oskol area to prepare for an attack on 2nd SS PzC in the Prokhorovka area. Together they brought 358 tanks. The 35th GRC was also brought up to bolster 7th GA's line. On the west side, three additional TBs were brought up and positioned between 1st TA and 5th GTC. These units were going to be ordered by Vatutin to stop the SS PzC by attacking their flanks. The 6th TC and 3rd MC would be tasked to lead Vatutin's forces against 48th PzC. The 10th TC was part of the 5th GA and Zhadov protested vigorously against *Stavka*'s decision to give the corps over to Katukov's 1st TA. This was the second major counter-offensive in two days that had as its major objective to isolate and then destroy the 2nd SS PzC. Both offensives were poorly planned and executed and much of the blame should and would fall on General Vatutin. Though the attacks did slow the Germans, it cost the Soviet tankers more than it should have and failed to return the expected results. dgk114+. mhz239. vzz139+.

Fighting all day with 48th PzC to prevent the Germans from reaching the Psel, the 6th TC and 3rd MC were able to stop the Germans, despite the air support, from reaching Verkhopenie and Hill 260.8. Hill 242.1 along the Oboyan road was also held. Once again Soviet artillery would prove too much to penetrate. dgr88+. dgr86m. gnk193m.

Lt General Franz Westhoven of 3rd PzD moved his HQ to Sirtsev, a village southeast of Syrtsevo and only a mile northwest of the former Soviet strongpoint of Dubrova. He ordered the Pz Abt 3 to the Verkhopenie area to protect the division's right flank. Westhoven had been promoted to Lt General in April 1943. fkk251. vzz2m. zsm57.

The *GD* had reached the outskirts of Verkhopenie where it was attacked by 3rd MC. On the right flank of 48th PzC, the 11th PzD was attacked by 50 tanks from the 5th GTC coming from Pokrovka. By the end of the day, the 48th PzC had gained six miles but that was half of what was needed. The 1st TA and the 6th GA with the help of recent reinforcements were still putting up strong resistance despite the high attrition. wdk138. hjj121m. dgr209m.

By the end of the day, Knobelsdorff reported to Hoth and later relayed to OKH, that there were only forty working Panthers. In four days of fighting, nearly 75% of the Panthers were either destroyed or incapacitated. Many of these panzers were repairable and would be fighting again in a few days. wwf92.

Looking back at the day, the 48th PzC was attacked by the 6th TC, 31st TC and 3rd MC. Knobelsdorff barely held his position against these fierce attacks. The 3rd PzD did cross the creek near Valdimirovka to move toward Kruglik but it became apparent that the Soviet tank strength was formidable and growing by the day in the Pena bend and that a coordinated attack by *GD*, 3rd PzD and 52nd IC would be necessary to vanquish it. The hold of Kruglik, if taken the following day, would be precarious at best unless greater resources came into the area. With the new Soviet reinforcements coming in from the west and north, the road to Oboyan was firmly closed. The Germans had no chance to reach the town and some of the German officers were already aware of it. Through prisoner interrogation, radio intercepts and his own recon reports, Hoth knew his forces were facing the 2nd GTC, 3rd MC, 5th GTC, 10th TC and 6th TC but he was still under the false belief that Oboyan could still be reached. snk81. wdk138.

Though the plan for SS panzers to head west and help 48th PzC trap the Soviets west of the Solotinka River failed, the 48th PzC did make modest gains when the panzers of *LAH* and *Das Reich* pushed the 31st TC to beyond the Psel River. Hoth decided to return the panzers of *LAH* and *Das Reich* to their sectors in order to refit and to help defend against the resumption of tank attacks on the SS's eastern flank that started that day. With the 167th ID now in defensive positions along the east flank, *SSTK* would be moving toward the Psel River at first light. gnk225. gnk227m.

Knobelsdorff sent orders to his divisions for the following day. The 11th PzD was to drive north and capture Ilinski, a mile northeast of Verkhopenie. *GD* was to capture Verkhopenie and secure the area while the 3rd PzD was to complete taking Lukhanino. After taking Verkhopenie, *GD* was to shift to the west and link up with 332nd ID and together they would advance five miles and attack Dolgi. The 11th PzD, after taking Ilinski, would stop their advance, go defensive and prepare for the inevitable counter-attack. After capturing Lukhanino and with *GD* heading west, the 3rd PzD was also tasked with clearing resistance between Lukhanino and Verkhopenie. Also all 4th PzA artillery was moved up to Syrtsevo area and the *Luftwaffe* was put on high alert to help with the assaults. gnk219.

Looking back at the day, the 3rd PzD continued to have trouble advancing against stiff Soviet resistance. By the end of the day, the division had not crossed the Pena River in any meaningful way. Knobelsdorff was planning to have *GD* stop their northern assault and turn west and help 3rd PzD cross the river and catch up. gnk242+. gnk193m. gnk227m.

The 111th Guards Artillery Regiment, 66th RLR and the 12th TDR from 40th Army moved south to reinforce the 6th GA. The 1st TA received 180th TB, 222nd TDR and the

38th RLR from 38th Army; the 59th TR, 60th TR and 4th AR from 40th Army while the 438th TDR and 38th RLR came from the Steppe Front. The 5th GTA was moving and would be in place in several days waiting for further orders when it assembled six miles north of Prokhorovka after a 220 mile trip. The 5th GTC had already arrived, seeing action, and 10th TC with its 200 tanks would be there soon. Later that night the 5th GA, which was also transferred from Steppe Front to the Vatutin's Voronezh Front, was making a night march and would soon be in second echelon between Prokhorovka and Oboyan. The 47th Army was ordered to move from near Rossoch, 60 miles east to the Korocha area, about 35 miles northeast of Belgorod, to reinforce the third defense belt behind 7th GA. wdk143*. bt85. hjj123m.

By *Stavka's* order in the predawn hours, 47th Army of Steppe Front, moving closer to Prokhorovka, traveled from the Olkhovatka, Krivonosovka, Kamenka region to the Khmelevoe, Korocha, Bulanovka region. dgr87+. dgr83m. hjj123m.

The 6th PzD's 11th PzR and sPzAbt 503 launched at 0645 hrs and made good early progress until reaching the tank ditch and mines in front of the fortified town of Kalinina, due south of Melikhovo. Between Kalinina and Melikhovo another tank ditch and defense line had been erected. Maj General Hunersdorff sent his two panzer groups around these obstacles and attacked Melikhovo from the east and west. Artillery was also brought up and while the Soviets were under heavy shellfire, the engineers came up, neutralized the ditch and cleared a path through the minefields. By the end of the day, Melikhovo was captured and the Soviets in the area had to fall back to regroup. Thirty assorted tanks were captured. The shelling from both sides was so heavy, the Grenadiers called Melikhovo "Little Stalingrad". After the fall of Melikhovo, Group Oppeln-Bronikovski moved north and blocked the Belgorod-Korocha road to prevent resupply. The 7th PzD was still forced to devote many assets in protecting the east flank of the corps from repeated attacks and were not making much progress to the north. gnk212. nzk91. dgr89. hjj123m. dlu59+.

The reduced northerly progress for 7th PzD was due to the repeated attacks of 94th GRD along the Miasoedovo, Hill 206.9, Batratskaia Dacha line. At 1000 hrs, elements of the 96th TB arrived and added their weight to the attack. Next door, the 92nd GRD also attacked the flank of 7th PzD. At the same time, a panzer group from 19th PzD split off from the main force and drove toward Dalniaia Igumenka which was strongly protected by a major tank ditch and minefields. Becker, though wounded, was able to take the village after a fierce struggle. Still another combat group was formed from the 19th PzD which drove toward the fortified forest south of Blizhniaia Igumenka. The Soviets were able to repulse the attack, retaining Blizhniaia Igumenka and then generated their own attack that pushed the Germans back. Keeping the forest and the village gave the Soviets a good jumping off area to thrust against the German western flank in the morning. The Soviet AF increased their sorties to 1,500 a day which slowed the German advance. The Red Air Force was beginning to take control of the skies. The area between Blizhinaia Igumenka to the west and Miasoiedovo in the east, which the Germans controlled, was just three to five miles in breadth which gave the Soviets a chance to cut off the salient and destroy the two panzer divisions; not very secure to say the least. Regardless of the threat, Kempf had orders to extend the salient and reach the Sabynino-Verkhni Olshanets area as soon as possible. Von Manstein also gave Kempf higher pirority of *Luftwaffe* assets to help expand their ground, especially along the Donets. dgk136+. dgr155m. dgr173m. gnk211+. dgk222m. dlu63m. dgk95m. vzz3m. dgr89. dgr87m.

The 3rd PzC driving north was able to penetrate Soviet defenses between Razumnaia and the Severny Donets Rivers, up to the Belgorod-Korocha road but were stopped there when Soviet reserves were brought up. bt86. dgr39m.

Vatutin was trying to funnel the 3rd PzC into a corridor from which his 7th GA and 69th Armies could encircle the panzer divisions. Along with the 92nd GRD and 94th GRD, Vatutin also had deployed three other divisions (213th RD, 270th RD and 15th GRD) along the eastern bank of the Koren River in order to confine the Germans' march to the northeast. Kempf ordered the 198th ID to come alongside the 7th PzD to provide flank protection in the Miasoedovo-Batratskaia Dacha area if and when those Soviet divisions countered. The Soviets were attacking the German flanks in all three sectors which caused the Germans to use panzers as flank protection. With the panzers on the flanks, they were not helping on the drive north.To further combat this increased resistance, artillery from 11th IC was sent north as well. gnk211. dlu81.

Kempf sent a combat group led by Colonel Oppeln-Bronikowski that included 100 panzers toward Blizhniaia Igumenka and Sevriukovo with the ultimate goal of capturing Melikhovo, ten miles northeast of Belgorod. The sector was defended by the 92nd GRD and 94th GRD. The 6th PzD advanced northward and after fighting a 150 minute battle with Soviet reserves, took Melikhovo from the south after neutralizing an attack of thirty T34s advancing from the town. Major Bake's Panzer Battalion led the charge against those thirty tanks and was able to stop the attack. The 19th PzD, with support of the 168th ID and advancing in parallel with the 6th PzD, also gained ground, both divisions being between the Northern Donets and the Razumnaia Rivers. This German force was squeezed for the most part into a tiny three mile front in order to enter these villages but the surrounding countryside was still in Soviet hands. One of the biggest reasons for the advances was due to Hoth concentrating his armored forces into a powerful spearhead. The Germans may have destroyed 26 tanks in advancing to Melikhovo by 1600 hrs but the Soviets were forming new defenses just to the north with 35th GRC as the main defender and were determined to stop the Germans. The town and the surrounding area would not be secured until next morning. The 6th PzD suffered 100 dead in the day's fighting. fkk279. dgk95m. vzz154+. vzz247. dgr155m. dgr173m. dgr39m. gnk211. fzk52. dlu59++. dlu65+.

On the east side of the Donets, the 168th ID had made little progress and was still only two miles from Belgorod as it resumed its attack against 81st GRD defending Staryi Gorod. To its right, the 19th PzD and 6th PzD launched an assault against the 35th GRC, which included the 92nd GRD and 94th GRD. By noon the 6th PzD gained some ground but the 19th PzD was initially held up by heavy artillery. By 1300 hrs the 19th PzD was east of Blizhniaia Igumenka, three miles northeast of Staryi Gorod, and by 1600 hrs struck the 81st GRD at Staryi Gorod with 100 panzers and air attacks. After a vicious fight that required using flamethrowers, incendiary grenades and redirecting artillery, the 19th PzD finally pushed the 81st GRD out of Blizhniaia Igumenka. Nearby the 168th ID was finally making good progress and with help of 19th PzD captured Staryi Gorod.. dgk136. hjj121m. wdk142. dgr95. dgr155m. dgr173m. dgr39m. vzz5m.

By noon after briefly regrouping and having more of the trailing forces of the divisions reach the front, the 6th PzD and 19th PzD, with 200 panzers and assault guns, resumed its attack on the second defense belt in front of Kalinina and Melikhovo, eventually driving the 35th GRC northward. They were now 12 miles from their start line of 7/5. Elements of 19th PzD eventually turned west and cleared Soviet troops from their defensive positions around Dalniaia Igumenka. By 1900 hrs the Germans were in complete control of the Melikhovo area. Raus's corps of 198th ID and 106th ID on the extreme east flank could not keep up and 7th PzD had to hold back forces to assist the infantry which slowed their progress. Even still by the end of the day a gap opened between 7th PzD and 198th ID. The 94th GRD with tanks supporting attacked the 7th PzD north of Melikhovo while 92nd GRD attacked 6th PzD when the 305th RD came up to support the line between the two divisions. wdk142. dgk95m. dgr155m. dgk130m. dlu63+.

East of the Donets, elements of 6th PzD and sPzAbt 503 drove five miles and captured the key road junction of Melikhovo after a three hour battle against the 92nd GRD, 95th GRD, and the 96th TB. The 2.5 mile wide salient that was being created was potentially dangerous for the Germans. Vatutin was well aware that if Kempf was able to join up with Hausser for his attack on Prokhorovka, it would place his forces, especially his 48th GRC, at a grave disadvantage and made the destruction of this salient the highest priority. The 19th PzD, on 6th PzD's left, was slowed by the fight at Blizhniaia Ignumenka and was falling behind the 6th PzD. The 7th PzD was stopped between Miasoedovo and Batratskaia Dacha against the 94th GRD. The 7th PzD also attacked Soviet positions between Koronio and Miasoedovo. The 3rd PzC had to cross the Lipovyi Donets if it was to be able to attack the Soviet position near Belgorod that was still thwarting the 168th ID. dgk136+. dgk222m. dlu63m. vzz153. lck282. dgr155m. dgr173m. dgr39m. shn159. dlu63m.

Southeast of the heavy battle that included the fighting of 2nd GTC and *LAH*, a smaller but still vicious dogfight was occurring at Shakhovo. Shortly after 1300 hrs the two sides broke off the engagement and pulled back, each side losing planes. cbk67.

East of the Donets, the Germans who were advancing along a narrow 2.5 mile front against the 92nd GRD and 95th GRD, captured the village of Melikhovo after dark. The 96th TB was originally stationed there and between the three units kept the Germans at bay for three hours before being forced to fall back. The Germans tried advancing toward the villages of Blizhniaia Igumenka and Dalnaia Igumenka but were prevented by the renewed resistance of the 92nd GRD and 96th TB. The 94th GRD and 31st TDB prevented the Germans from diverting to the east. Vatutin sent the 305th RD to bolster the line in the 96th GRD sector in case the Germans advanced that way. Even though the 3rd PzC and especially Corps Raus were making little progress, it did force the Soviets to devote large resources in this area and away from the areas west of the Donets. The 198th ID, which was a reserve unit for 1st PzA, was being held near Belgorod and could be used better elsewhere so von Manstein released it to Kempf earlier in the day. fkk87. fkk255. dgr155m. dgr173m. zzt88+.

Late at night von Manstein, knowing that 3rd PzC could not catch up to 2nd SS PzC by way of Korocha, ordered Kempf to turn 6th PzD and 19th PzD west to encircle and destroy the thin salient of Soviets along the Donets that were between the two corps. Also, not having sufficient reserves he canceled the objective of taking Korocha to the east and gave Kempf orders to catch up with 2nd SS PzC to the west by hugging the sector closer to the river. This should have been part of the original battle plan as long as Group Kemp was basically by itself. It could be argued Kempf spun his wheels for three days needlessly trying to drive too far east. During the evening the 2nd TC had been withdrawn from the salient and moved north to put pressure on *Das Reich* south of Prokhorovka. wdk142+. aaa124m++. zzz101m. snk424m++. dgr94+. hjj123m.

At 2200 hrs, elements of the 69th Army were redeployed to the Sovkhoz railroad line from the Vinogradovka area in anticipation of a German assault the next day. wwf92.

On the extreme east flank, Kempf's 3rd PzC was still trying to close the gap with *SSTK* and surround the Soviets defending the Donets River sector but was having trouble moving against stiff resistance. wdk141.

By the end of the day after an especially bitter fight around the Melikhovo area, the 7th GA was deployed on the following lines: The 81st GRD continued to hold Staryi Gorod and Blizhniaia Igumenka, not far from Belgorod. The 92nd GRD along with the 96th TB was deployed along the Andreevski-Shliakhovo line while the 94th GRD with 31st Anti-tank Brigade held the Ushakovo-Miasoedovo line. The 305th RD defended the Sabynino-Ushakovo line. During the predawn hours of the 9th, the 107th RD was moved up to protect the Verkhni Olshanets-Gremuchi-Ploskoe line. The 3rd PzC had created a narrow salient by capturing Melikhovo but the Soviets still had confined Kempf quite convincingly and the two strongpoints of Blizhniaia Igumenka and Miasoedovo while being threatened were still held by the Soviets and a continued threat to the German rear areas. Kempf would devote many resources on 7/9 in capturing Khokhlovo and Staryi Gorod areas adjacent to the Donets River. Kempf also had to be especially concerned about a Soviet counter-attack that would cut off this narrow salient and isolate much of his forces. With that regard Kempf paused his northward march and turned west toward the Donets to widen his salient and destroy the Soviets at Staryi Gorod to free up the 168th ID. dgr94. dgr155m. dgr173m. dgr39m. vzz5m. dgk163.

The 45 Tigers of sPzAbt 503 had been split up evenly between the three panzer divisions of 3rd PzC. Capt Kragenak calculated that by the end of this day 34 Tigers had been disabled: 7 were hit by shellfire, 16 disabled by mines and 9 had mechanical troubles. Two more were complete write-offs. Most of the 32 tanks would be fixed within eight days but a couple of them had to be sent back to Germany for repairs. zzt93.

In the evening, Kempf ordered Hunersdorff to send part of his division westward next morning and eliminate the stronghold of Dalniaia Igumenka that 198th ID could not tackle on its own. The 198th ID would then continue north along the river, clearing resistance. gnk212.

During the last two days, Shumilov's 7th GA had repeatedly attacked the 3rd PzC's right flank. In second echelon, Shumilov still had the 15th GRD, 270th RD and 111th RD waiting. He also shifted the 92nd GRD and 94th GRD of 35th GRC to attack the Germans advancing on the Lipovyi Donets River. Lately, the Soviet AF had been averaging 1,200 sorties a day but the Germans the previous two days had averaged only 725 sorties. The Germans still barely controlled the skies but that would change on 7/11. dgk137. dgk222m. dlu63m.

11

July 8th on the Northern Salient

See Map 5

East of Ponyri, the Germans continued to try to take Hill 253.5 but were not having much success. In the village, vicious fighting continued at the water tower, railway station, school and tractor factory. The 292nd ID suffered heavy casualties in the house to house, hand-to-hand combat that saw waves of attacks and counter-attacks. Nearby to the west, the 9th PzD was being hit hard by repeated runs from the Red Air Force. The Soviet air force was starting to use large bore cannons, 37mm, to attack panzers from the rear to destroy them. mhz285. dgk87m. dgr199m. nzk91. dgk116m. lck116m.

The initiative would move to the Soviets on this day. Reserves were brought up to the Ponyri area to stop the 41st PzC. The 70th Army sent the 140th RD and 162nd RD to Teploe while it moved the 181st RD closer to the front. It also sent orders to 229th TR and 259th TR to prepare to move up to reinforce 13th Army. It was obvious to the Germans the Soviets were planning a major offensive that day and tried to prepare for it. Artillery shells were brought up and the front line went defensive. wdk179. dgk87m. dgr199m. dgk116m.

The battle for Ponyri Station continued. At 0600 hrs, the 307th RD with support from a few tanks counter-attacked, trying to regain the station; both sides stubbornly bringing reinforcements up to battle. By the end of the day, the Germans controlled most of the town. During the evening, Model recalled and regrouped his forces near Olkhovatka to prepare for a major effort to take the important town. The fresh 10th PzGD was brought up during the night to add its weight to the battle. Rokossovsky brought up the 3rd GAD, 4th GAD and 51st TB of 3rd TC and the heavy 27th GTR to stop the expected assault the next morning. dgk120+. dgr118. fkk102m. dgk87m. dgr199m. nzk91. dgk116m. lck116m.

On a partly cloudy hot day, the 20th PzD fought a furious battle near the village of Samodurovka, suffering huge casualties. At the same time, panzers of von Saucken's 4th PzD, heavily supported from the air, drove between 2nd PzD and 20th PzD, smashing through the Soviet defenses at the junction of the 175th GRD and 70th GRD, and seized the small village of Teploe, west of Hill 274. For the following three days a fierce battle would be fought for this village and the surrounding high ground. Rokossosky brought up reserves such as the 3rd Anti-tank Brigade under Rukosuyev and the Germans were unable to take the nearby ridge for any length of time. The 33rd PzGR of 4th PzD reached the top of the ridge but was then pushed off by a Soviet counter-attack. Nearby, the 6th ID reached the foot of Hill 274, just north of Olkhovatka, but could go no further. The narrow avenue of approach to the hill and Olkhovatka was an extreme disadvantage to the Germans. Between the well-built defenses and the aerial attacks, many Germans and panzers were lost. The weather in the south of the salient was also clear and warm, the roads had dried from the last rains and the panzers were moving better. dgk118+. wdk137. fkk63+. dgr198m. fkk102m. lck302. dgk87m. dgr199m. swm139. nzk90. dgk116m. kfz459. lck116m. zro204. pck46+.

After an initial barrage at 0800 hrs, the 9th PzD, 18th PzD, 2nd PzD, 20th PzD and 4th PzD with 6th ID renewed their attack along the sector running from Ponyri, Kashara, Kutyrka, Pogorelovtsy to Samodurovka towards Olkhovatka and Hill 274, which was defended primarily by the 17th GRC. The Soviets opened up with a huge artillery barrage that caused heavy casualties on the attackers. The supporting *Luftwaffe* flew in ahead of the panzers to soften the line. By midday, despite the minefields and heavy artillery, the Germans broke through the front line and the remaining 200 panzers flooded south toward Teploe and Olkhovatka. The fighting would rage in this area for the next two days. Model was determined to take the high ground. On the other hand, Rokossovsky understood the advantage he had and would fight to keep it. All four of the above divisions of 47th PzC, along with 18th PzD of 41st PzC plus the 4th PzD that was attached to 47th PzC, resumed their attack. The German force was tasked with advancing five miles to reach a line between Ossinovi to the south and Leninski village east of the Snovo River. Despite pushing back the 6th GRD a little, the 47th PzC never reached their objective but reached only a small section of the Olkhovatka-Ponyri road, about a mile from their start point that morning. The 16th TC and 19th TC came up to support 17th GRC, stopping the Germans. mkz120. dgk120. dgk116m. je102+. mhz281+. dgr198m. fkk102m. dgk87m. dgr199m. swm139. lck116m.

The 7th ID and 31st ID of 46th PzC deployed to protect the western flank of 47th PzC by attacking in a southwest direction toward the Svapa River, north of Samodurovka. In this sector, elements of the 175th RD and 132nd RD supported by tanks launched early in the morning to counter the German advance. The Germans destroyed two KV1s and two T34s in the engagement. wdk179. dgk87m. dgr199m. dgk116m.

During the predawn hours, the Germans had assembled six divisions in front of the Soviet 13th Army sector, with the heaviest concentration from Snovo to Podsoborovka to Saburovka where the 47th PzC was deployed. At 0800 hrs moving from this position the Germans advanced against fierce resistance toward the sector from Samodurovka to Ponyri II. The repeated attacks, centered on Hill 257.0, were repulsed by 17th GRC, inflicting heavy casualties on the attackers but by 1700 hrs the Germans were able to capture Hill 257.0. It was too late in the day for the Germans to advance further and they were prevented from reaching Olkhovatka and its surrounding high ground for another day. dgk120. dgr198m. fkk102m. dgk87m. dgr118. dgr108m. dgr199m. dgk116m.

Just before dawn German radio interceptors picked up an order for a large attack on 41st PzC near Ponyri. The 1st *Flieger* Division was going to be scrambled from bases near Orel to meet the new threat. The Soviet air attack was in coordination with a counter-attack led by 307th RD, the 51st TB and 103rd TB. The ground attack began on time but the planes on both sides were held up when heavy rains hit. The planes did not take off for three hours. In those three hours the 307th RD retook the village of Maya in bitter fighting. cbk54. dgk116m.

Lt General Esebeck took charge of a newly formed combat group made from the 31st ID and 20th PzD, with the express orders of taking the hills around Olkhovatka. This group was on the right flank of 47th PzC. Knowing the importance of keeping these hills, Rokossovsky brought up the 9th TC during the afternoon to stop the German advance. nzk90+. dgk116m.

The 3rd TDB, working in the 17th GRC's sector, counter-attacked the German formation of several hundred panzers at 0830 hrs, destroying one Tiger and three other panzers. With the support of the *Luftwaffe*, the Germans continued to attack, inflicting further losses on the Soviet brigade before moving on. East of Ponyri, the Soviets with air support and 50 tanks, attacked the 292nd ID. The shattered division held its line until it was relieved by the 10th PzGD and was sent to the rear. Also east of Ponyri, the 307th RD, 129th TB, 51st TB and the 27th GTR attacked the 86th ID but were repulsed. The Germans claimed destroying 50 tanks in this area. Further east in the 23rd IC sector, the 74th RD began a series of attacks. wdk179+. dgk87m. dgr199m. dgk116m. lck116m.

Pz Abt 21 got a late start on this morning, preparing for the coordinated attack on the Krassavka-Samodurovka line. The Soviets pre-empted the attack with one of their own. Pz Abt 21 had to halt their advance and defend themselves at Hill 225.4. The other divisions in the attack resumed their advance. By late afternoon the Pz Abt 21 was fighting on the approaches to both Krassavka and nearby Teploe zzt84. dgk116m.

The 200 panzers from assorted units of 47th PzC reached Kashara and Samodurovka as they aimed for Olkhovatka. Ten miles to the east, the fighting at Ponyri continued with both sides losing heavily. In the late morning and early afternoon the rains slowed, the 1st *Flieger* Division was able to blanket this area with 650 sorties. Another 523 sorties were made to the rest of the line. The 20th PzD's 112th PzGR, like the other divisions of the 47th PzC, suffered heavy casualties. Some of the veterans claimed the fighting on this day was as bad as it was in front of Stalingrad. Without the full support of the *Luftwaffe*, the German ground forces were hit hard by artillery when it was unmolested by aerial attacks. A few flights also covered the 41st PzC to the east. During this early morning rainy period the Soviets did fly a few bombing missions at select targets but a mere fraction of what was scheduled to fly. je102. dgr198m. fkk102m. dgk87m. cbk54. nzk77. dgk116m.

North of Olkhovatka many of the 200 panzers of the day's assault were supported by artillery and *Luftwaffe* attacked the boundary between the 13th and 70th Armies, trying to build a larger wedge between them but failed. Ferocious fighting developed around the Teploe area as 4th PzD tried to take the village. North of Teploe lay Hill 238. As 4th PzD's panzers crested this hill, they were slammed by waiting T34s and a battery of anti-tank guns which inflicted heavy casualties. Fighting raged for two plus days as the Germans struggled against the minefields and heavy shelling. bt85. mhz281+. dgr198m. fkk102m. dgk87m. dgk116m. lck116m.

In another example of poor communications because of his excessive travels, Model was not aware of the way Lemelsen planned on using 4th PzD that day on the battlefield. Model had intended 4th PzD to remain together and to advance next to 20th PzD in the Teploe-Olkhovatka area. Lemelsen detached the 35th PzR from the division and attached those panzers to the shock group formed from Luebbe's 2nd PzD and Burmeister's sPzAbt 503. With the three panzer units working together they had 200 panzers. The grenadiers of the division would then be inserted in the line next to 20th PzD without any internal armor support. Lubbe did give StuGAbt 904 to von Saucken. Though Lemelsen had made an enemy of Model on this day, he was still a recipient of the Knight's Cross with Oak Leaves. In late 1943, General Lemelsen was transferred to Italy. snz249+. zsm69.

The 47th PzC sent in the 4th PzD to relieve the 20th PzD which was placed temporarily in reserve at Bobrik. The 2nd PzD, 4th PzD and 9th PzD with most of the available air support continued to attack the 17th GRC with the objective of reaching a line about five miles south from Ossinovi to Leninski, west of the Snovo River. The Germans made some gains against the 6th GRD west of Ponyri II but failed overall to achieve their objective of crossing the road from Ponyri II to Olkhovatka only a mile from their morning start line. The 16th TC and 19th TC counter-attacked, stopping the German advance. Although this section was already well defended, the 11th TB of 2nd TA and 4th GPD as well as the 129th TB from the Maloarkhangelsk area were sent to this area for added security. wdk179. dgr198m. dgk87m. dgr199m. dgk116m. lck116m.

Rokossovsky brought up his last reserve Tank Corps, the 9th TC, to defend Hill 253.5 to the east of Ponyri and the village of Ponyri from the south. Meanwhile the 9th PzD and 18th PzD attacked the two objectives but were repulsed. The heavy rains this day made it impossible for the panzers and Model ordered them to halt their advance. At the same time, the 20th PzD captured Samodurovka on its way to help 4th PzD take Hill 272. The panzers were helped by Stukas dropping 550 pound bombs on Soviet positions. dgr198m. fkk102m. dgk87m. dgr199m. dgk116m. lck116m.

The 3rd company of 14 Tigers of sPzAbt 505 arrived and were put directly into the field near Teploe to assist in taking the critical Hill 274. By the end of the day, three of the Tigers were destroyed while only three were still fighting; the rest needed repairs. A couple miles to the east, vicious fighting continued around Hill 274, the lynchpin of the western sector that if it could be taken would give the Germans a better chance to take Olkhovatka just south of it. But as hard as the Germans tried, the repeated attacks continued to fail. Before the day ended, sPzAbt 505 was pulled from the line to rest and to repair their Tigers. They would be forced to attack the following day but at least they would have 29 working Tigers, more than what they had on this day. mhz285. lck305. dgr198m. fkk102m. dgk87m. dgk116m. kfz458.

In the north during a conference with Model, Kluge made some disposition changes and ordered the 8th PzD from Velize to the Orel sector. The 12th PzD was also attached to 47th PzC. General Model knew 9th Army had lost its chance for victory; it was now fighting for survival. wdk180. zzz101m. dgk87m. dgk116m.

At 1230 hrs Model arrived at 4th PzD's HQ where he learned the 35th PzR had been detached and that General von Saucken and several other officers had been wounded while up at the Front during an air raid. Model exploded when he heard the news, convinced that Lemelsen had acted incorrectly. He immediately called his corps commanders with explicit instructions that divisions were not to be split apart without his permission. The 35th PzR would be coming back to 4th PzD. Model was at 4th PzD for four hours to oversee operations. The division did capture Teploe but not the important hills surrounding the village. The division had suffered horrendous casualties and without any apparent chance of capturing those hills for it was later learned Rokossovsky had brought up additional artillery batteries to the sector. At this time Model decided to pause the assault the following day in order for his battered divisions to regroup. He was sure that he would never see Kursk; he was also sure that Hitler would reject his request to halt the campaign. General von Saucken was a competent officer and would eventually command the 39th PzC in July 1944. snz250+. zsm264.

At Ponyri II during battle, the 10th PzGD moved up to the line to support the exhausted 292nd ID against a renewed attack. As soon as it was possible, the 292nd ID was ordered back to second echelon for rest. wdk180. dgk116m. lck116m.

In the afternoon, elements of the 9th PzD and 18th PzD fought their way into Ponyri. The worst fighting occurred at the train station, tractor building, schoolhouse and water tower where the defenders were able to stop the German advance. The grenadiers were also able to capture some of the hills around Ponyri except the most important one, Hill 253.5 which was heavily defended by artillery and the 1032nd RR. mkz120. dgk116m. dgr108m. lck116m.

While Pz Abt 49 of 4th PzD was defending Hill 234.0 from a Soviet tank attack, the rest of 4th PzD resumed its attack to regain lost ground and to capture East Teploe and the nearby Hill 272.9. The division had the help of sPzAbt 505 and the *Luftwaffe*. To prevent flanking fire against the 4th PzD, sPzAbt 505 would take Hill 274.5 next door. The 33rd PzR of 4th PzD would drive east from Teploe against 253 while the Burmeister Group attacked farther to the left Hill 272.9 and Hill 274.5. First Battalion of 35th PzR would join the battle as well. The 20th PzD was committed to the right where it covered 47th PzC's flank and was to advance against Samodurovka West at 1515 hrs. This was a coordinated effort to capture several strongpoint villages and the surrounding hills northeast and northwest of Olkhovatka. If successful, Olkhovatka and its high ground would be next. The Soviet resistance was so fierce that the German offensive was stopped about 100 yards north of Teploe. The Germans were able to repulse a counter-attack but forward movement was impossible and the panzers fell back a ways. fkk62+. dgk87m. dgr199m. dgk116m. lck116m.

At Hill 257.0, the 17th GRC defended against repeated attacks from German panzers numbering upwards of 100 units The attacks were initially repulsed but slowly the determined Germans by 1700 hrs gained the top ground but were unable to go any farther, failing to take Olkhovatka. dgk120. fkk102m. dgk87m. dgk116m.

East of Ponyri elements of the 307th RD, 129th TB, 51st TB and the the 27th GTR attacked the 86th ID. During the all afternoon battle the Germans claimed destroying or capturing 50 tanks. wdk180. dgk116m. lck116m.

The 78th AD was advancing slowly against 2nd GAD defending in front of Trosna, northwest of Maloarkhangelsk. The Germans were able to capture a hill southwest of Trosna. At 1800 hrs to the northeast of 78th AD, the 383rd ID was stalled by heavy artillery from the 48th Army. wdk180. dgk116m. lck116m.

In the north at night, 20th PzD captured Samodurovka, northwest of Olkhovatka where panzer formations gained some ground but still could not reach the key city. Despite the fact that the bulk of the 9th Army was deployed in the central sector of the front, it could not gain more than 3 miles in four days. dgr198m. fkk102m. dgk87m. dgr199m. dgk116m.

In the north the 1st *Flieger* Divison flew 1,173 daylight sorties while the 16th VA and 15th VA flew a combined 1070 sorties. The Soviets flew 613 fighter sorties as part of the total. With the daily attrition, the Soviets were dropping their fighter sorties with each passing day. Losses for the day are difficult to estimate due to exaggeration but it appears the Red Air Force lost about 50 planes and the Germans lost about a dozen. Though losing a lot of planes, the Soviet AF was playing a vital role in stopping Model from reaching Kursk. cbk55. nzk77. dgk116m.

General Rokossovsky noted that the Germans were making better progress in Vatutin's sector than his sector. He placed the blame on Vatutin's mismanagement and not on the ability of the Germans. He was quite vocal on the subject. Stalin and Zhukov were also concerned. jp156. dgk87m. dgk116m.

By the end of the day, 9th Army suffered another 3,200 casualties and not one division gained a mile. Making the situation worse was that the vehicles were in great need of maintenance and all the men were exhausted but man and machine would be forced to continue fighting. The 2nd PzD, 4th PzD and 9th PzD had suffered the worst with all three divisions below 50% strength. snz251.

12

July 9th on the Southern Salient

See Maps 13, 26A

Stavka was convinced that to have a successful counter-offensive, the Germans must be stopped before reaching Kursk from either direction and the salient must be kept in place. To this end, Vatutin brought up his last reserves to block the advance. He also ordered his forces to step up attacks on the German flanks for this slowed the advance. The Germans never had a chance to succeed because of the heavy flanking action. The 600 tanks and the many guns of the 5th GTA were being brought up to the front to deploy behind the Psel and block the passage past Oboyan or Prokhorovka. The Germans had already decided to shift directions from Oboyan toward Prokhorovka. The action on this day would be the death knell of the German army. *Stavka* still had two armies in reserve if they were needed that were intended for the counter-offensive. dgk138. dgk147.

Despite its modest setback the day before, Hoth ordered the 2nd SS PzC to resume its attack in the Gresnoe-Solotinka area before heading for Prokhorovka as he decided to do before the campaign started. The 48th PzC was to continue its drive north of Solotinka to the Psel River in the Ilinski-Shipy sector. After reviewing the results of the Hill 258.2 combat, Hoth changed his orders for 2nd SS PzC and 48th PzC. The 2nd SS PzC were to attack Soviet positions northeast of Beregovoe and seize the eastern bank of the Solotinka on both sides of Kochetovka. The 48th was to attack along the Iakovlevo-Oboyan road with the intent of capturing the series of hills between Kochetovka and just south of Novoselovka. Afterwards the corps would turn and rout the Soviet positions on the west bank of the Pena. The new plans, especially concerning Hill 260.8 and Hill 240.4, were less ambitious showing the waning confidence in Hoth as Soviet reserves continued to appear and as his casualty list increased. vzz152+. gnk193m. gnk227m. dgk143.

At 0100 hrs, the 5th GTA was ordered to move to the Bobryshevo-Bolshaia-Psinka-Prelestnoe-Aleksandrovski-Bolshie Seti area. The 5th GTA had traveled 60 miles in less than 23 hours. dgr222. wwf92. dgk411. dgk415. dgr86m.

By daybreak, the 2nd PzGR had redeployed to their new sector, just north of *Das Reich*, as ordered. zrl223.

Hoth was still trying to strengthen the boundary between his corps but with 2nd SS PzC heading toward Prokhorovka that task was becoming harder, not easier. Additionally, in the previous two days Hoth saw a resurgence of armored attacks from reserves that dramatically slowed 4th PzA's advance and he had to rekindle his forces' forward momentum if they were to penetrate the third defensive line and advance past Prokhorovka and Oboyan. At 0200 hrs the *LAH* linked with *Das Reich* between Teterevino South and Luchki South and in that respect fortified the eastern portion of the line a little. In the morning the 2nd SS PzC was allowed to regroup while the commander completed his battle plans. Hausser reduced the number of attack points to simplify operations and ordered the 167th ID, which still had the support of a few assault guns from *SSTK*, to expand their sector to Luchki South and relieve *Das Reich* of part of their sector. The 167th ID now had to defend the line that *SSTK* had covered, as well as a small part of the line that *Das Reich* was defending. *Das Reich* could now concentrate on the Teterevino-Kalinin-Iasnaia Poliana area. After moving from the east flank of the corps to Luchki North sector, *SSTK* created two combat groups. One headed in the direction of Malye Maiachki, Veselyi and Kochetovka with the intention of pushing the 31st TC to the west, away from the intended crossing point of the Psel. The second group headed for Krasnyi Oktiabr, Ilinski, Kozlovka and Vasilevka in order to force the Soviets out of those villages and their defenses on the south side of the river. Hausser ordered Kruger of *SSDR* to concentrate on moving northeast toward Pravorot in order to screen *LAH* as the assault on Prokhorovka and the main corridor continued. During the previous day's fighting, Hausser practically had each regiment of his divisions attacking on its own axis; *LAH* had been abused the worst. Though on the western flank, the 52nd IC was ordered to stay defensive along the Pena River bend in order for 48th PzC to stabilize the northern line and link up with the SS. vzz155+. gnk210. gnk227m. wwf96. dgr95.

The night before, the Soviets were repulsed from Visloe but they had not given up on the area. It seemed like a good spot for penetration of the remaining *SSTK* and to close off the Belgorod-Oboyan road and so they would try again. At 0230 hrs from east of Hill 209.5, Soviet forces that included tanks from the 2nd GTC launched another assault toward Visloe. The surprise attack gained ground and succeeded in reaching Hill 225.9, just east of the important roadway. The *Eicke* Regiment along with a battery of guns were at nearby Gonki. They rushed the couple miles to the west to Visloe and confronted the attackers, enabling them to stop the attack and push them back. Priess had orders to redeploy his *SSTK* to the west of *LAH* but the transfer was going slowly due to repeated attacks by 2nd GTC. gnk210. gnk193m. vzz3m. gnk227m.

At 0300 hrs, four German weather planes sortied to get the latest intel on the weather. All four planes never came home. They were the victims of roaming Soviet fighters looking for targets of opportunity. This was a bad start for the *Luftwaffe*. cbk67.

It was discovered the previous day during the heavy fighting that there was a gap at the boundary between *LAH* and *Das Reich*, not far from Teterevino North. During the predawn hours elements of *Deutschland* moved north to strengthen the boundary. zow154.

In the very early hours while it was raining, *SSTK* was relieved of their current deployment by 167th ID and sent to the west of the Teterevino North-Luchki North area to attack alongside *LAH*. *LAH* headed for Sukho Solotino to link up with 11th PzD while *SSTK* advanced toward Kochetovka. The 167th ID moved along the Lipovyi Donets as far north as Smogodino with *Das Reich* guarding the line north of that village. Around noon *LAH*'s 1st PzGR captured Rylski on its way to its main objective and, along with leading elements of *SSTK*, captured Veselyi. Following Veselyi, the *SSTK* cleared the east bank of the Solotinka River as well as the village of the same name. After leaving Rylski the 1st PzGR headed in the direction of Solotino, clearing the ground as it went. At 1300 hrs, the 3rd PzR was attacked by about 50 tanks from the 24th GTB west of Gresnoe, but the attack was repulsed with 14 T34s smoldering on the battlefield. Nearby the Sturm Abt 3 was fighting with 40 tanks for control of Hill 224.5. The battle cost the Soviets 14 more tanks. Rylski was a small village west of Malye Maiachki and Teterevino North and south of Veseyli and Sukho Solotino which straddles the Solotinka River, not far from Kochetovka. fkk146+. fkk319m. lck317. agk121. agk121m. wwf96. vzz5m. gnk193m. gnk227m. ztc269. zrl223. zow154.

At the start of the day, Hausser estimated having 202 panzers damaged or destroyed which left 249 still working. Some of those 202 damaged panzers would be fixed and deployed onto the battlefield. lck318. vzz177.

In the *Das Reich* sector it was foggy in the early morning and visibility was poor but their listening outposts could clearly hear Soviet tanks moving. In the predawn hours, the 10th TC and 5th GTC had redeployed and the 2nd TC and 2nd GTC had moved in to replace them. At first light, German planes were up to search for the tanks and found them assembling in the woods east of Kalinin and Iasnaia Poliana. An attack would soon follow. The panzer battalion of *Das Reich* had been moved off the front line and was at Ozerovski to regroup. Ozerovski also housed the panzer repair station for the SS. German intelligence also discovered Soviet concentrations in front of 167th ID which was deployed south of *Das Reich* near Petrovski. The Soviets started shelling *Das Reich* and 167th ID. *Das Reich* started shelling the Soviets to disrupt their preparations and to slow their progress in building a bridge over the Donets. While the panzers were at Ozerovski, *Deutschland* was defending Teterevino North and *Der Führer* was at Kalinin, south of Ozerovski. gnk230+. gnk193m. gnk227m.

Shortly after daybreak, Soviet tanks moved through the village of Ivanovski Vyselok after leaving the woods near Storozhevoe, heading straight for the *Deutschland* Regiment. A few minutes later a group of 25 Soviet fighter bombers flew over the front line aiming for the HQ area of *Das Reich*, just south of Kalinin. A few minutes later a second squadron of Soviet planes attacked the panzers near Ozerovski. For the rest of the morning, the Red Air Force bombed this sector repeatedly, causing death and confusion, and did not receive any resistance from the *Luftwaffe*. While the aerial bombing continued, Soviet tanks and men maneuvered through a ravine toward Kalinin, getting closer to the *Der Führer* Regiment. The T34s left the ravine heading straight for the Germans. The German Pak 40s were ready and destroyed a number of tanks in the first minutes of the engagement. The remainder of the T34s reversed course and headed back into the ravine. The 7.5 cm Pak 40 gun using high velocity AP rounds could penetrate the T34 front armor. At the same time that Kalinin was under fire *Deutschland*, defending Teterevino North, was also under attack. The German counter fire was so hot the infantry riding on the Soviet tanks had to jump off. Mortar and artillery fire found the distance and added to the resistance on the Soviet force which forced the Soviets to fall back into the woods. *Das Reich* had more Pak guns (5.0cm and 7.5cm) than *SSTK* and *LAH* combined and it was these guns that prevented a penetration of the front line today as well as the previous day. At 1130 hrs a third smaller attack ensued further south near Nepkhaevo against *Der Führer* but that was repulsed also. The sector was quiet for the rest of the day. gnk231+.

The 1st PzGR of *LAH* and the only working Tiger launched its attack toward the Solotinka River to help slow down the Soviet flank attacks on 11th PzD and *GD*. Much of the *Luftwaffe* was redirected to assist the 48th PzC but a few planes remained with the SS and they would fly cover for the ground assault. By 0830 hrs the regiment had reached the approaches to Rylski and nearby Sukho Solotino on the banks of the Solotinka River which was their primary objective. Malye Maiachki, a little further off was also important. Using the cover of a ravine the men got as close to their targets as possible; about a half mile. At 1000 hrs, artillery began and the men launched in three different groups. The first two objectives, still burning from earlier shelling, had been abandoned. The Soviets blew the bridge before leaving Sukho Solotino. The panzer group advancing on Malye Maiachki was led into a trap. A Pak line had been set up in the woods next to the village. When the panzers neared the woods, the Soviet guns opened up. Two panzers were destroyed in the first volley. The rest of the panzers regrouped and started firing at the Soviet guns. The grenadiers moved on the woods and after a while the Soviet guns were silenced. gnk228+. nzk92. gnk193m. gnk253m. gnk227m. dgr91. dgr86m.

The 52nd GRD was now north of the Psel River and was defending from the hill north of Kliuchi to Hill 226.6 and to Polezhaev. The 285th RR of the 183rd RD along with the 11th MRB of 10th TC were defending in front of Vasilevka, Molozhavaia gully (north of the KSF), Komsomolets State Farm, Ivanovski Vyselok and Storozhevoe. Malov's 99th TB of 2nd TC was defending from Vasilevka to Andreevka. vzz182+. vzz187. gnk312m. nzk92.

Pz Abt 3, attached to *SSTK*, left their old position which was being taken over by 167th ID along the Donets River and headed for Gresnoe. With the heavy rain and Soviet shelling, the ride took three hours to arrive. To the west and north of Gresnoe, the ground was dry and the column continued on toward Kochetovka but was stopped before reaching the Solotinka River by heavy ground fire. Additional battalions were beginning to approach the Gresnoe area around this time, about 0830 hrs. Air support was called in to slow the shelling and take control of the skies. *SSTK* had to make it across the river in force without suffering heavy casualties. Hoth knew this and was quick to send the *Luftwaffe*. However Group Baum taking a separate route, reached Vesselyi, east of the Solotinka River by 1130 hrs without incurring many casualties. A detachment was sent west of the river to find the 11th PzD to see how big a gap in the line would expose each division's flanks. As the recon team, supported by a company of panzers, approached Hill 224.5, east of Kochetovka, a small group of Soviet tanks ambushed them. After disabling three Soviet tanks, the 237th TB retreated. A second, larger attack occurred later that surprised the Germans from a different direction. They fell back to near Hill 224.5 to regroup after losing several panzers and then reengaged after calling for artillery support. After several hours of fighting, 14 T34s were billowing smoke and fire while several more panzers were destroyed. When the Soviets pulled back, Biermeier's battalion resumed its march toward Kochetovka. At the same time the trailing Baum Group was entering Luchki North. When leaving the ravine as the panzer column neared Kochetovka, it could be seen that the town was busy with tanks and vehicles and men redeploying, preparing for a fight. The Germans saw their chance to exploit the Soviets who were not ready to respond and started firing into the town. gnk233++. zow154.

After repulsing the many tank attacks and destroying so many tanks in the first days of the campaign, Hoth believed this day would be easier and that his SS Corps would finally take Prokhorovka as well as establish a bridgehead on the north bank of the Psel River. It was not meant to be as the Soviets, despite heavy casualties the previous day planned on keeping up the heavy resistance on the ground and in the air today. The Germans did make gains in all sectors in the south but at a high cost. The Soviet AF was almost at parity with the *Luftwaffe* and would try again to gain control of the skies. cbk67.

From 0700 hrs, repeated sorties of IL-2s were accidentally made against the 183rd RD within the area that included Vasilevka and Hill 241.6. Casualties were never made public but the Soviet defenses were said to be hit hard. vzz288+. vzz1m. gnk193m. gnk227m.

SSTK had orders to cross the Psel River on this day near Krasnyi Oktiabr and establish a bridgehead on the northern banks. The key objective one mile north of the river was Hill 226.6. The hill was an excellent OP and it was strongly defended. From on top of the hill, artillery would have an easy time shelling *LAH* as it headed for Prokhorovka, just seven miles away. *SSTK* had to take the hill for their own needs as well, for while the hill was in Soviet hands, they could also shell the new bridgehead. While *SSTK* fought to establish the bridgehead as well as clearing the southern bank of the river, the panzers of *LAH* continued their advance along the Solotinka River area. It was a difficult proposition for *SSTK* for their division was spread out over miles with much of the division still south of the river. In addition, some of the assault guns stayed with the 167th ID to help defend Hill 209.5 against repeated Soviet attacks. Priess moved his HQ to the woods just south of Luchki North which was still within range of the Soviet guns. gnk232. gnk227m. snk78. dgr95.

The weather was cloudy but warm and dry shortly after daybreak. There would be heavy local thunderstorms later in the morning and the roads slowed but stayed passable. The *LAH* resumed its advance to the northwest and moved through Ryliski to just south of Sukho-Solotino on the Oboyan road. A small *LAH* group moved directly north and by evening reached the Psel River, a mile east of Kochetovka, after driving back the 31st TC. Despite strong defenses, the *SSTK* cleared the 51st GRD and 52nd GRD from the area northwest of Gresnoe by 1000 hrs. Grenadiers in half tracks drove west and crossed a branch of the Psel at Veselyi and another group reached high ground a mile east of Kochetovka where it encountered Soviet tanks. A third group drove north six miles to reach its objective, Kozlovka, on the southern bank of the Psel River and began building a bridge as ordered. *SSTK* had orders to cross the Psel today and establish a bridgehead so the panzers could cross the next day. Though artillery was brought up close to the river, it would still be a difficult assignment to accomplish for just the infantry as Vatutin had assembled a heavy concentration of guns in the area. Nevertheless, it appeared, based on early results, that it could be achieved. gnk236+. gnk227m. ztc269. zow154. wdk146+. fkk319m.

LAH resumed its forward march but was constantly being attacked by 2nd TC and 5th GTC along the road to Prokhorovka. *Das Reich*, with a regiment of the 167th ID, held its ground on the east flank of the corps against repeated attacks from the north and east by 5th GMC and elements of 2nd GTC. The rest of 2nd GTC attacked the remaining two regiments of 167th ID but the terrain in the sector was harsh and not suitable for tanks and 2nd GTC failed to penetrate the line. Despite reinforcements during the day, the Soviets failed to push *Das Reich* back. The 5th GTC was ordered to travel at night to the west and deploy near the Orlovka area, three miles south of the Psel. Vatutin was making sure that 48th PzC would never reach Oboyan. dgk142. snk81. wdk147. dgk222m. dgr209m. gnk312m. nzk92. gnk193m. gnk227m.

The *LAH* and *SSTK*, attacking at the same time, smashed through the shattered 3rd MC and drove Chernienko's 31st TC back to Kochetovka. The *LAH* crossed the Solotinka River and seized Sukho-Solotino, linking up with 11th PzD, forcing the Soviet tankers beyond Kochetovka. By day's end, after being relieved by 167th ID on the east flank, *SSTK* reached the Psel River and after a sharp fight captured the village of Krasnyi Oktiabr from the 52nd GRD and the 11th MRB of 10th TC. A little further north and to the east *Das Reich* was still being repeatedly attacked by 5th GTC and 2nd TC and could not devote total resources to the frontal attack either. By the end of the day, the 192nd TB was still holding Hill 251.2 and Beregovoi. *Das Reich* and 167th ID tried to protect the eastern flank along the Lipovyi Donets River for most of the day and were able to prevent 5th GTC from capturing Kalinin and 2nd GTC from reaching Nekhaevka. All available *Luftwaffe* planes supported the advance. The Red AF was busy also, flying over 1,000 sorties in 4th

PzA sector alone. dgk140+. dgk141m. snk81. dgk222m. mhz288. vzz185. dgr89. dgr86m. dlu63m. wwf96. vzz280. zra62. zow154+.

Hoth's panzers were making small gains toward Oboyan but at great cost of men and panzers against 1st TA's determined armor. It has been suggested by some that he diverted his main axis toward Prokhorovka in an attempt at finding easier prey; Oboyan was to be bypassed. His dwindling panzers and assault guns were to attack from the west and south toward the Prokhorovka corridor. This steerage change could also aid his right flank in protecting itself against a flank attack from the east. His goal was also to envelop, with the support of the 3rd PzC, the Soviets between the Donets and Lipovy Donets Rivers and then capture Prokhorovka before major reinforcements arrived. The 69th Army under Lt General Kriuchenkin was repositioned in the Prokhorovka-Donets area to prevent the above from happening while 5th GA and 5th GTA was in transit. dgk139. rkz168.

All the Tigers of *LAH* were in the shop near Teterevino North being either maintained or repaired. agk120.

The *SSTK* and *LAH* continued to advance against 3rd MC, southeast of Oboyan; the 31st TC had to withdraw behind the Solotinka River near Kochetovka as well. At the same time, the 2nd TC continued its attacks against German troops along the approaches to Prokhorovka. *Das Reich* and 167th ID were inching ahead against the 2nd TC and 5th GTC for most of the day when the 5th GTC disengaged and started moving west as per Vatutin's orders. The 3rd PzC to the east was still way behind schedule and no help to Hausser. The 204th RD under Col Baidak of 38th Army was called up to help block the way to Oboyan behind the shattered 3rd MC. Vatutin also attached units from 38th Army to Katukov's 1st TA. dgk142. dgk139+. nzk92. dgk130m. gnk193m. gnk227m. rc201. dgk222m. dlu63m.

In the afternoon, Burkov's 10th TC began withdrawing from its position north of the Prokhorovka road and began its march westward to join Katukov's 1st TA which was blocking the Oboyan road. It left its 11th MRB in place, to defend along the Psel River from Krasnyi Oktiabr to Mikhailovka, with the 52nd GRD and its 178th TB, which defended on Popov's 2nd TC's flank north of the Prokhorovka road. It was the 11th MRB's fierce resistance that slowed *SSTK*'s and *LAH*'s crossing of the Psel River as well as reaching Hill 241.6. Heavy thunderstorms also slowed the German advance giving a little more time to improve defenses. Popov had deployed his force astride the road, forward of Komsomolets State Farm and the rail line running south past Iasnaia Poliana. With the 5th GTC also moving west, the only other tank corps facing *Das Reich* was 2nd GTC which was deployed south of 2nd TC. To help fortify this section of the line, Vatutin moved the 93rd GRD and 89th GRD closer to the Lipovyi Donets River. In addition to these two divisions, the 51st GRD was deployed west of Krasnyi Oktiabr and the 52nd GRD was deployed east of Kransyi Oktiabr to Polezhaev while the 183rd RD defended the corridor just east of the Psel River and the 11th MRB protected the area that included Komsomolets State Farm and Storozhevoe. When the 9th GAD arrived it would further bolster this sector. dgk166+. dgk222m. vzz185+. vzz8m. wwf109+.

Attacking after being redeployed, elements of the *SSTK* headed north and quickly captured Veselyi, north of Malye Maiachki, before advancing toward Hill 224.5 one mile south of Kochetovka where the fighting intensified. At 1300 hrs, Group Becker of *SSTK* struck out from west of Ozerovski toward Krasnyi Oktiabr with the intent of capturing the village on the southern bank of the Psel west of Kozlovka and Vasilevka before establishing a bridgehead on the north bank of the Psel. Late in the day, the 10th TC had to evacuate Krasnyi Oktiabr for Kozlovka because of this advancement. The Germans left the village heading for the river but were halted one mile from Ilinski. Shifting their direction the group captured Kozlovka at 1845 hrs but were stopped again before reaching Vasilevka. By the end of the day, the *SSTK* controlled almost a four mile stretch of the southern bank of the Psel River but failed to establish a bridgehead on the northern bank and there was still active resistance on the southern bank. The German engineers brought up the bridging equipment to Luchki North for when the bridgehead was established against the 52nd GRD. To help with the task, Hausser found a battalion of rocket launchers and artillery to bolster the *SSTK*. At the same time, the 48th PzC continued to hit against the 1st TA along and north of the Pena River in order to protect 2nd SS PzC's left flank. vzz156+. vzz7m. vzz9m. gnk237. gnk227m. zow154+.

Around midday, Hausser's 2nd PzR of *SSTK* arrived at Gresnoe on its way to the Psel River. The artillery batteries stopped just north of Gresnoe and started setting up their guns. Soon afterwards, Karl Ullrich's 3rd PzR reached Gresnoe on their way to Krasny Oktiabr. gnk235+. gnk253m.

In the afternoon, von Manstein's forces advanced toward Oboyan in the west and Korocha to the east. The Germans had a 20 mile breach in the line in the Oboyan area and a six mile breach near Korocha; von Manstein was sending his forces through those gaps as quickly as possible. Once again Rokossovsky thought Vatutin was in error. He had spread his 6th GA forces too thin against a too long of a defense belt instead of choosing key strongpoints and protecting those points more fully. The Germans had made gains of 20 miles or more in this sector. With the decision to have 2nd SS PzC shift direction toward Prokhorovka, it was critical that Hausser capture the rail town before 5th GTA arrived. Von Manstein canceled the drive to Korocha and turned Kempf north to help cover the SS's flank. mhz297. dgr98. dgr93m. hjj123m. pck67m. vzz261.

A controversy had sprung up since the battle concerning the motives for shifting the main axis of attack from Oboyan to Prokhorovka. Vatutin's and the Soviet position has always been that the shift was due to stiff resistance of 6th GA and 1st TA, causing an unacceptable slowing of the advance of 48th PzC; it forced Hoth to his secondary axis, toward Prokhorovka. Hoth on the other hand stated that he had planned on shifting to the Prokhorovka axis since before the campaign. I personally believe there is some truth to both sides. Hoth considered the Oboyan route the primary and considered the possibility of using Prokhorovka only if the main axis was failing and thats exactly what happened. I find it hard to believe Hoth's intentions were to automatically change axes without ample reasons to do so and that conviction was helped along by the success the *LAH* was having. His actions concerning the 48th PzC's attack toward Oboyan stayed steadfast after 7/8 though he was forced on the defensive by the repeated attacks from the west. He still pushed the 48th to the northwest while *LAH* and *SSTK* launched their offensives to the northeast. If the Prokhorovka axis was truly the primary axis, the handling of 48th PzC should have been different. If this theory has some truth to it then one can argue Hoth's handling and deployment of 48th PzC, especially the Panther Brigade, from the beginning was faulty. The *GD* and the 11th PzD were the two driving forces of the corps while the 52nd IC and to some extent the 3rd PzD were basically on flank protection. With 48th PzC heading northwest toward Oboyan and the SS Corps heading northeast to Prokhorovka, the German line was actually expanding, making it much more difficult to advance and protect themselves from counter-attacks at the same time. This goes against one of the key axioms of attack; a concentration of strength. dgk146.

The Thule regiment of *SSTK* attacked and captured Vasilevka and Kozlovka by late afternoon from the 52nd GRD, but was halted there by the increased Soviet resistance of the arriving 11th MRB and had to defend itself throughout the night at these villages. Some of the men of the *Eicke* Regiment made it to the northern bank of the Psel in the predawn hours of 7/10 but when it was shown the division was not ready to support them, they were recalled to the southern bank. While the men were crossing the river, a friendly fire incident happened. One of the German rockets fell short and landed among the men but fortunately for them there were no fatalities. From Gresnoe to Kochetovka, the *SSTK* lost 18 panzers including three Tigers and had casualties of 88 men including 19 dead. By the end of the day, *SSTK* still had 81 working paners and most of the 18 damaged panzers could be repaired. fkk147. gnk236+. gnk193m. gnk253m. gnk227m.

The Soviet 5th GTA among other tank units were still working their defenses in the Prokhorovka area. They had 800 tanks there. je105. gjz185. fzk54.

After fighting for hours, the *SSTK* and *LAH* drove the 31st TC to the north bank of the Solotinka River and the 6th PzR of *SSTK* had seized more of the southern bank of the Psel near the villages of Krasnyi Oktiabr and Vasilevka. Pushing the enemy back in this sector also helped relieve some of the pressure off 11th PzD which also had a good day. By the end of the day the corps had passed through the second defensive belt and was knocking on the door to the third defensive belt; the Psel River. The gains that day were seven miles in some places, outpacing yesterday's gain that had actually lost ground in some places. However Vatutin, with two reserve armies approaching, was still confident that his forces could contain the Germans as it was costing the Germans far too much for the small gains they were making the last three days. The previous two day's armor assaults had been successful in stopping the German advance and with the 5th GA and 5th GTA quickly approaching, Vatutin began planning a new armor assault that would finish off the 2nd SS PzC. As the 4th PzA advanced northward and the salient grew longer, the German flanks extended, and that meant more resources would be allocated to flank protection. The advance was clearly slowing down and with no further reserves, there was little chance of reaching, let alone defending, Kursk when the forces got there. It seemed illogical to continue the campaign.

Unlike at Stalingrad, where Marshal Zhukov had planned months in advance to draw the Germans into the vortex that was Stalingrad in order to encircle and destroy the enemy, neither General Vatutin nor the *Stavka* appear to have had the foresight this time. It seems to me that the third defensive belt would have been the ideal location and timing to spring another Operation Uranus on the Germans. Hoth had carved out a deep enough salient and had suffered enough casualties to make his remaining forces vulnerable to a massive flank attack from east and west that would be the equal of the original Operation Uranus. Using the five armies (5th GA, 5th GTA, 27th, 47th and 53rd) of Steppe Front along with 7th GA, 6th GA, 1st TA, 69th Army and 40th Army that were already deployed should have been enough to encircle the entire front line of 4th PzA after penetrating the flanks. vzz157+. vzz258+. gnk193m. gnk227m. dsk111.

Near Teterevino North, elements of *LAH* panzers headed by Rudolf von Ribbentrop, the son of the Foreign Minister, were moving north when 40 T34s attacked. Ribbentrop's Mk IVs attacked, quickly destroying six tanks and causing the rest to retreat. Moving on, the elements of *LAH* and elements of 11th PzD joined forces south of the village of Solotino by midday and attacked the village, pushing the defenders to the north. More and more *SSTK* troops were moving west from the east flank duty, relieving some of the frontage from *LAH*. Their task was to clear resistance from south of the Psel in order to make the crossing as easy as possible. Their first focus was the fortified village of Kochetovka which was defended by the 6th GA where the fighting was terrible. Kochetovka, the HQ location of 6th GA, was captured that afternoon, forcing Chistiakov to move his HQ to the north with 1st TA. The Soviets would regroup and always counter-attack every gain the Germans made, making this battle another war of attrition. mhz294+. swm141.

The 2nd GTC continued its attack on 2nd SS PzC's right flank (*Das Reich*) along the Lipovyi Donets, south of Teterevino North. Though persistent, Burdeiny did not have much success and ordered his tanks back to their start positions. dgk167. dgk130m. dgk124m. dgk222m. dlu63m.

To be closer to his division, Maj General Wisch moved his HQ to the woods south of Luchki North, arriving there by 1600 hrs. zrl223.

The Soviets began seeing the Germans change their tactical behavior that evening along the entire line. The Germans were becoming more defensive in thought (digging in and building wire obstacles) as if they were running out of steam and needed a fallback position in case their attack fizzled. It also seemed the protection of the flanks had higher priority. This action was noticeable on Hill 258.2 and at Nekhaevka and Luchki South. vzz153. vzz185. vzz3m.

At night von Manstein ordered *LAH* panzers to continue their trek to the northwest toward the Solotinka River to relieve the pressure off 11th PzD's east flank. The *LAH* grenadiers on their east flank were ordered to continue their drive toward Vinogradovka, a little over four miles south of Prokhorovka. The grenadiers inflicted heavy casualties on the 2nd TC and 183rd RD who were blocking their way. *Das Reich* would continue its drive to the east against 2nd GTC, 375th RD and 81st GRD. The *SSTK* had even more demanding objectives. It was to cross the Psel River, establish a bridgehead on the north side and build a bridge across to allow the panzers over as well. wdk150.

Fighting all day, while lead units of *SSTK* crossed the Psel and established a small bridgehead on the north bank, the bulk of the division tried to follow but was stopped at Hill 241.6 which was defended by the 11th MRB. The 2nd TC moved into a defensive position along the Prokhorovka road near Iasnaia Poliana after their attack failed. To make matters worse, Bolshie Maiachki was taken from the 242nd TB of 31st TC early in the morning. The 237th TB of 31st TC had to fall back behind Gresnoe to the Psel River, all the while protecting its flank at Teterevino which was being attacked by *Das Reich*. dgk166. dgk134. dgk211m. nzk92. dgk130m.

At 2030 hrs, General Hoth radioed his corps commanders that a large armor column was seen heading west from Stary Oskol and that it was more important than ever to take Prokhorovka and cross the Psel the next day. He then transmitted formal orders for the following day. *LAH* was to drive on Prokhorovka while *SSTK* crossed the river and drove on Hill 226.6, and if possible reached the Kartashevka road. *Das Reich* was to stay defensive while protecting the right flank of *LAH*. The 48th PzC was to continue clearing resistance from the Pena Bend. Hoth had anticipated that reinforcements would drive to Prokhorovka from the east since before the campaign started and he expected Kempf to intercept, providing a screen for the SS driving north, but Kempf had made little progress and was too far behind to help the 2nd SS PzC and yet Hoth did little to resolve the issue. zow155.

Late at night the *LAH* redeployed and was in a better position to begin their assault toward Prokhorovka with *Das Reich* in the morning. To the left of *LAH*, *SSTK* was still tasked to clear the southern banks of the Psel River area in the morning despite not having the entire division on the front line. Hoth had called General Priess during the night to reinforce the need to establish a secure bridgehead over the Psel and be prepared to support *LAH* in its drive on Prokhorovka. The Germans had to be in control of the corridor before the 5th GTA arrived. *Das Reich*'s first objective after securing Teterevino was to travel the Teterevino-Prokhorovka road which paralleled the railway for nine miles and capture Hill 252.4, located a mile and half to the northwest of Prokhorovka. This plan was never launched or realized. wwf92. dgk222m. mhz305. vzz1m. vzz11m. nzk92.

At 2215 hrs Maj General Wisch ordered that once 2nd PzGR had penetrated the line of the Komsomolets State Farm next morning the Recon Battalion of *LAH* was to move forward and, avoiding as much fighting as possible, sneak past KSF, Hill 241.6 and Oktiabrski State Farm and then attack and capture Hill 252.4, northwest of Prokhorovka, directly situated in the center of the corridor to Kursk. The order was over ambitious and illogical and it never succeeded. vzz177. vzz9m.

Late at night, the lead units of 5th GTA moved to the Bobryshevo area north of Prokhorovka to wait for the German force that had just captured Kochetovka and was inching toward the corridor to Kursk. The 5th GA also moved up. Vatutin committed 1st TA but was worried his tank forces would not hold up. With the modest gains made in the area the last few days, Hoth also redeployed their forces for the coming major assault. Hoth started the day with 599 panzers but they were down to 501 working panzers by the end of the day and any major assault would be difficult with the 5th GA and 5th GTA now close to Prokhorovka. He also estimated that at least 500 Red tanks had been completely destroyed in his sector. Hoth was still confident that his forces were still strong enough to reach Kursk, still 50 miles from his current front line. Hoth and von Manstein underestimated Soviet reserves and in reality did not have much of a chance of reaching Kursk at their present rate, especially with Kempf lagging behind and with *SSTK l*eaving the Lipovyi region for the Psel sector. wwf92. bt86. mhk288. nzk92. gnk193m. gnk227m. dgr86m.

The German offensive was short on panzers and infantry. While they were using the panzers on the front attack, artillery was being used as a substitute for lack of panzers on the sides. From near Hill 219.8, where several German soldiers were captured, it was also learned from prisoner interrogations from that rear area that non-combat personnel were being brought up to the line; a clear indication that 4th PzA was running out of combat troops. It was a fact that made Vatutin, after reading a report of the interrogations, smile for the first time today. vzz260.

Shortly before midnight Hoth, after receiving the latest air reconnaissance report, called Hausser to inform him that a large group of Soviet tanks (5th GTA) were spotted near the Oskol River heading west and reminded him that it was critical to take Prokhorovka and Hill 252.4 before the tanks arrived in sector. The next day Hoth received additional evidence from recon patrols that new reinforcements (5th GA) were moving into the bend of the Psel River. Hausser, relaying the news, then emphasized the importance of taking control of the Psel River and Prokhorovka before these new forces became operational to his division commanders. vzz296+. pck53. vzz181.

By the end of the day the German advance was bogging down. The active Soviet defenses were wearing down the attacking German forces.

At 2300 hrs, Rotmistrov ordered the 18th TC to deploy north of the Psel River along the villages of Veselyi, Polezhaev, Prelestnoe and Aleksandrovski. In addition, the 5th GMC was sent to the Zapselets River area, near Veseyli, to guard 18th TC's western flank where *SSTK* was making progress. Much of the 5th GTA had arrived or would arrive within the next twelve hours. The 5th GA had arrived in the Prokhorovka area today as well. The 32nd GRC and 33rd GRC of 5th GA had deployed since 0430 hrs that morning and were currently building a defense. The 5th GTA would deploy for the most part behind these corps. While the 5th GA was unprepared for battle, the 52nd GRD, 11th MRB as well as the 26th TB and 99th TB of 2nd TC would defend the front line near the Psel River for the next 24 hours. The 169th TB to the east was currently in the Storozhevoe area. Between Storozhevoe and along the Psel River, the 5th GMC and 18th TC were the primary mobile units defending. The 5th GTC, which was in terrible condition by this time, was pulled off the line and sent to Krasnoe. The 10th TC defending the Prokhorovka axis had been ordered west to the Psel but was unable to quickly disengage, disrupting Vatutin's timetable. The 32nd GRC consisted of 13th RD, 66th GRD and 6th GAD under the command of Maj General Rodimtsev who played such an important part in keeping 6th Army away from the Volga long enough for Marshal Zhukov to launch Operation Uranus. The 33rd GRC consisted of the 95th GRD, 97th GRD and 9th GAD under the command of Maj General Popov. vzz180++. wwf94.

At night Hoth revised orders for 2nd SS PzC. *LAH* in its drive for Prokhorovka was to narrow its attack axis and concentrate its strength at the tip of the spear while *Das Reich* was to put pressure on their eastern flank to relieve pressure off of 3rd PzC in order for Kempf to advance more quickly. Hoth did not like the terrain south of Oboyan which gave the Soviets an undue height advantage plus the Psel River was also another obstacle that he did not favor. He would have to advance north of the Teterevino-Novenkoye line, 16 miles south of Oboyan, to gain a suitable battle ground. Also the Soviets were building a concentration of tanks at Prokhorovka, about 30 miles northeast of Belgorod. If Hoth continued toward Oboyan these tanks could attack Hoth's right flank putting him in severe trouble without the aid of Kempf. Also by moving toward Prokhorovka, the 2nd SS PzC and 3rd PzC would remain closer and be able to help defend each other. Making Oboyan such a high priority for 48th PzC was a mistake, considering the many strongpoints and terrible terrain it had to traverse. It has been suggested that if 48th PzC had taken the eastern flank instead of 3rd PzC that 48th PzC could have made greater progress than 3rd PzC, linking with *Das Reich* before 7/12 and together could have supported *LAH* in taking Prokhorovka on that pivotal day. If in this new scenario 3rd PzC had stayed east of the Vorskla River line, they could have avoided the hazardous terrain of Pena River valley where so many strongpoints had been built, giving them a better chance to defend the west flank along with 52nd IC. dgk146. snk67. snk72+. dgk124m. lck320+. kcz168+.

The 52nd GRD was once again deployed along a critical sector. The 151st GRR of 52nd GRD was holding the line from north of Kliuchi to Hill 226.6. The 155th GRR held the line from southeast of Kliuchi to Hill 226.6. The 153rd GRR deployed from Hill 226.6 to Polezhaev. The 52nd GRD displayed courage and fortitude throughout the campaign and deserving of Vatutin's gratitude. vzz182. gnk312m.

By the end of the day, the 1st TA and 6th GA and supporting reserves, for the most part, had so far contained the German advance in front of the third defensive belt. It is also true that 3rd PzC had failed to penetrate the line and engaged the rear of 7th GA and 69th Army along the Donets Rivers in any meaningful way. dgr95. dgr92m.

The 8th *Flieger* Corps flew 1,621 sorties and claimed losing eleven aircraft. nzk77.

SSTK forces broke into the third defensive belt and were planning by next day to cross the Psel River, the last major natural barrier to Kursk. A small bridgehead was quickly established on the north bank by Ullrich's grenadiers by taking Vasilevka, Kozlovka and then Krasny Oktiabr before the Soviets could counter-attack. Priess was first to report to Hausser the condition of his panzer regiment. There were 114 working panzers and assault guns which included 32 assault guns. rc201. wwf95. vzz1m. gnk193m. gnk227m. ztc269.

The lead units of 5th GTA started arriving in the Bolshie Seti-Pristennoe-Glafirovka area, about 15 miles north of Prokhorovka. Of the 721 tanks and SPGs that started the trek 227 tanks broke down and needed repairs. By 1700 hrs on 7/11, 101 tanks were repaired and on their way to Prokhorovka. The 18th TC was then ordered to deploy behind the infantry in front of Prokhorovka. vzz167. ick319.

By the end of the day, *LAH*, now with the help of *SSTK*, had widened its salient to include Sukho-Solotino in the west and captured Krasnyi Oktiabr in the north which was near the southern banks of the Psel. *LAH* did not gain a lot of new ground but spent much of the day on defense, reducing resistance in the area they already had. *LAH* counted its casualties since the start of the campaign: 283 dead, 1,282 wounded and 30 missing. With the advances made by 48th PzC and the 2nd SS PzC today the Germans controlled the area between the Pena River in the west and the Lipovyi River to the east and to the north; the Psel was so tantalizingly close. lck318.

LAH claimed the destruction of 17 tanks while the other two SS divisions claimed another 38 tanks and assault guns. This clearly showed the corps was trying to stabilize its position before advancing further. wdk149.

The forward units of the 5th GTA began arriving behind the Psel River-Prokhorovka line after dark. Trailing units were still in the Bobryshevo-Marino area, up to 50 miles behind. It would take the next 24 hours for 5th GTA to complete their trek. dgr90. dgr86m.

Hoth let his 4th PzA rest and regroup for the morning and ordered their advance in late afternoon toward Prokhorovka, but could make only marginal progress in the Verkhopenie-Sukho Solotino-Kochetovka sector. The 4th PzA had elements of 5 panzer divisions along with 4 IDs protecting their flanks and it was making it difficult to drive along the Oboyan and Prokhorovka roads with such a large force devoted to the flanks and not the main axis. je104. dgk222m. dgr209m.

SSTK, after taking Kochetovka (HQ of 6th GA), moved east to assist *LAH* by attacking the fortified ridge, Hill 241.6, that had a commanding view of the Psel River area to the north as well as the corridor to Kursk. The Germans pounded the ridge before attacking and were able to push the Soviets off it. The 24th GTB regrouped, launching a counter-attack that lasted past dark, but eventually *SSTK* prevailed and the Soviets tankers had to fall back. The tanks of 5th GTA were desperately needed but most were still 60 miles away. Zhadov's 5th GA with its 80,000 men were coming to help defend the Psel River. By the end of the day, with the reinforcements coming, the Germans diverted their forces toward Prokhorovka and with 48th PzC focused more on their flank than front, Vatutin was becoming confident that the worst was over and that his forces were in control.

It has been argued that Hoth faulted in sending panzer regiments from *LAH* and *Das*

Reich toward the west that day. By the end of the day, the SS's successful defense of its eastern flank against the major tank offensive gave it a real opportunity to capture Prokhorovka the next day when the Soviet tank corps were in disarray, if the full panzer regiments were not near Solotinka. The panzers of both divisions were too far west to advance early the next morning to take Prokhorovka. The heavy rains during the night and into the morning of the 10th only made logistics worse. gnk251++. gnk193m. gnk227m.

In general the 4th PzA's line had fully penetrated the second defense belt and extended the front line that included from west to east: Novoselovka, Kochetovka, Verkhopenie, Berezovka, Iakovlevo and Teterevino North. The quest to this point for the Germans was tortuous and costly and their momentum was slowing. It is estimated that 4th PzA had only 500 working panzers plus some in the repair shop. wwf96. gnk193m. gnk227m.

At 0035 hrs, General Burkov's 10th TC was relieved of its defenses between Vasilevka and Komsomolets State Farm in order to concentrate its forces to the west in the Vladimirovka area, a few miles south of Oboyan, to strengthen the defenses blocking the Oboyan road. The 2nd TC took over their original position. Col Baidak's 204th RD of 38th Army was also transferred to 1st TA into this area for further strengthening. Other formations were also brought up to this area. Col Dremin's 309th RD was moved to the line that included from Oboyan road east to Peresyp located on the Psel River, a few miles west of Veselyi. General Vatutin was putting too much faith in 5th GA, and especially 5th GTA, in defeating the SS and was sending too many forces from the corridor over to in front of Oboyan. He had already sufficient forces in the west to handle the 48th PzC and some of the units moved from the eastern corridor would have been better utilized where they were against the SS. dgr90. gnk245. dgk139.

At 0400 hrs, elements of *GD* resumed their march toward Verkhopenie. By 0700 hrs, they slowly fought their way into the fortified village having to fight a house to house battle to clear it. The eastern half was secured by 0830 hrs but the western side was harder and took longer. When the east side was secured, elements of *GD* were released to head north toward Novoselovka and Hill 260.8. Colonel Strachwitz did not get far when a column of T34s coming from Hill 240.4, just west and a little south of Novoselovka, attacked. Strachwitz was able to push the Soviets back to the village but the prepared defenses at the village were able to stop the German advance. Strachwitz pulled back and waited for reinforcements. mhz289. dgr209m. lck314. gnk239. gnk193m. gnk312m. gnk227m. pck71. dgk143.

General Mickl's 11th PzD launched at 0400 hrs; the 111th PzGR on the right and the 110th PzGR in the center as they traveled north along the Oboyan road. The Schimmelmann panzer group was on the left. The division discovered a minefield south of Ilinski which was quickly cleared. The column then crested a hill just past the village and the remains of the 3rd MC defending Hill 260.8 opened fire on the Germans. The barrage was so intense that the panzers had to back up behind the hill they had just climbed to save themselves. *GD* had been ordered to take the hill that day but failed to do so. Knobelsdorff brought corps artillery to bear on the hill and ordered the *Luftwaffe* which had hit the hill earlier to hit it again. Once the barrage had ended, the two German units assaulted the hill. Attacking this hill was the first time the Germans saw the devastating power of a SU122 assault gun. Two direct hits on panzers utterly destroyed them. While the panzers were waiting for the shelling and aerial bombing to end, the 110th PzGR attacked the 51st GRD at Pokrovski, northeast of Verkhopenie, forcing the Soviets to fall back to the north. To the east of Verkhopenie, the 339th PzGR captured Krasnyi Poliana before moving on and occupying the nearby village of Beregovoe, just to the north. At the same time that Pokrovski was captured by the 110th PzGR, the 111th PzGR was driving toward the village of Sukho Solotino, due north of Krasnyi Poliana. gnk244+. gnk193m. vzz2m. gnk227m. dgr91.

After dawn under a cloudy sky, the Fusilier Regiment of *GD* resumed its advance from Verkhopenie to the northeast toward Novoselovka and Hill 240.4, north of Novoselovka . Before arriving at its objective, the regiment was attacked and halted. Other elements of *GD* were on the road as well and were heading for Hill 260.8, south and a little east of Novoselovka which stretched along the road to Oboyan. The 11th PzD on the east of the road was preparing to launch an attack northward as well. Another battalion of *GD* stayed at Verkhopenie to clear the last resistance from the town and the west bank of the Pena River. By 0900 hrs, the fortress town of Verkhopenie was secured. As the Fusiliers approached Hill 240.4, Soviet tanks came over the rise and attacked but were repulsed. *GD* continued past Hill 240.4 and was approaching Hill 243.0 when they were attacked again. After a brief battle, *GD* captured Hill 243.0 but stopped on the hill to regroup. They lost three panzers in the engagement. hsz125+. fkk269. gnk193m. gnk312m. gnk227m. dgk143+.

During the predawn hours, 3rd PzD's engineers completed a bridge over the tributary of the Pena River, just west of Lukhanino. The division was planning to move north to help support *GD* but the Red Air Force flew over just before dawn, destroying the bridge. Westhoven, frustrated by the slow progress, changed his attack plan on taking Lukhanino. He ordered his panzers to move from the south of town to the east which meant the panzers had to drive through Dubrova before turning toward the east side of Lukhanino. The 394th PzGR remained in the south to continue to keep the southern defenses occupied. By 1400 hrs, Westhoven's panzers had fought their way to Hill 218.5 east of Syrtsevo. At the same time on the west flank, Pz Abt 3 failed to take Alekseevka against strong resistance. By the end of the day and despite modest gains made by 394th PzGR and the panzer group, Lukhanino was still in Soviet hands. The 3rd PzD started this campaign with less than 100 panzers and just did not have the strength to hold their own against such strong resistance. gnk216. gnk193m. gnk227m.

At 0600 hrs, a squadron of German planes bombed the Verkhopenie-Novoselovka area in front of the advancing *GD* division. At the end of the day, Knobelsdorff signaled Major General Seidemann of the excellent coverage the *Luftwaffe* provided for the 48th PzC. *LAH* also received quality air support as it shifted its advance to the northeast toward Prokhorovka. Vatutin must have brought up additional flak guns, as the *Luftwaffe* pilots bitterly complained of increased resistance. By the end of the day, the 8th *Flieger* Corps reported downing 38 Soviet aircraft but also losing 28 planes. The VVS reported losing 32 planes. By providing better escort protection, the Soviets were able to reduce the number of planes being lost. They also had improved their recon reporting and the VVS was now responding to sectors who needed air support quicker. cbk68+.

At 0700 hrs, Soviet bombers and fighters made repeated strikes against German concentrations at Verkhopenie, Krasnaia Poliana, Sukho, Sukho-Solotino and Kochetovka. At 0800 hrs, Soviet infantry drove toward German positions along this line. At 0830 hrs, the *Luftwaffe* arrived and escalated the battle. By 1130 hrs, 60 panzers had penetrated the line and reached the southeast outskirts of Verkhopenie and a little later a second pincer attacked the southern border. The 3rd MC and the 67th RD defending the town fought back and repaired the gaps in the lines but eventually to the west of Verkhopenie, the 67th RD was forced to fall back to Kalinovka by *GD*. The panzers were able to fight through Verkhopenie which was defended by 1st TB, 49th TB, 180th TB and the 203rd TR and head for Novoselovka. Other elements of *GD* followed 67th RD but were unable to break into Kalinovka. Before reaching the town, the 86th TB and 67th RD moved up and stopped the German advance. Just outside the town, 31st TC denied any passage that got by the 86th TB. At 1500 hrs, 60 Stukas and fighters flew in and attacked the 3rd MC and 31st TC that were defending the Oboyan Highway. fkk88. fkk323m. dgr209m. gnk193m. gnk227m. dgr91. dgr86m.

At the same time that Soviet planes made bombing runs along Verkhopenie, the leading elements of *GD* resumed their attack on the town after having pulled back to regroup for the night. These battalions were hoping the rest of the division would show up but when they did not, they had to advance without them. Fortunately, soon after moving forward, Group Strachwitz arrived with their 39 panzers and started firing on the northern half of the town from the southern edge of town. The town was being defended by elements of the 200th TB. The *Luftwaffe* also appeared and started bombing the shrinking pocket. Strachwitz had ten Tigers and ten Panthers remaining. As more of the division arrived, they were directed past the town toward Hill 260.8. gnk240+. cbk64..

The 48th PzC ordered the *GD* and 11th PzD, with support of the *Luftwaffe*, to advance on and capture Hill 260.8 which was defended by 6th TC. The 3rd PzD and 332nd ID would join in and attack Soviet defenses west of Verkhopenie. Then *GD* would move on Hill 243.2 (northwest of Verkhopenie) which overlooked the Pena River and Hill 247.2 which overlooked the withdrawal routes along the Berezovka-Ivnia-Kruglik road. The 48th PzC would then move on Oboyan at the same time 2nd SS PzC moved on Prokhorovka. *Das Reich* was currently advancing along the Lipovyi Donets River, trying to reach Pavorot. From there it would drive north to protect *LAH*'s east flank when attacking Prokhorovka but even with giving up front to the 167th ID, *SSDR* was still having trouble advancing against such stiff resistance and would not be there to help their comrades. dgk133+. dgr172m. dgk222m. dlu63m. fkk269. dgr209m. gnk312m. snk78. fmz221m.

The 48th PzC was tasked with continuing its drive north along the Oboyan road, pushing the enemy back to the Psel River and capturing the ridge between Kochetovka and north of Novoselovka. The corps was also responsible for encircling and destroying the 6th TC while it was on the west side of Pena River. The 52nd IC was to engage the enemy at and south of Berezovka and at the same time assist 48th PzC in the destruction of 6th TC on the banks of the Pena. The 2nd SS PzC was to continue its drive in the Pokrovka-Beregovoe-Sukho Solotino sector. *Das Reich* was to hold the Luchki-Teterevino line against all attacks. With more infantry and armor crossing to the southern banks of the Psel, 2nd SS PzC would find their assignments hard to accomplish. The *Luftwaffe* was active on this day, flying an estimated 1,500 sorties in support of this major drive by 48th PzC. fkk143+. fkk323m. dgr91. gnk227m.

By 1000 hrs, the 309th RD, originally of 40th Army, had reached its new defensive position on the west flank from Malinovoe woods through Melovoe woods to just outside of Olkhovka. dgr90. gnk245.

Von Manstein moved the panzers of 3rd PzD along a six mile front toward Berezovka. The 3rd PzD made progress on the left flank west of Rakovo-Kruglik road and thus gained a better position for an enveloping attack from the left against Berezovka. Fighting all day and into the night, it took 3rd PzD about 15 hours to take the fortified town. The *GD* in the center of 48th PzC sector made less progress than expected against increased resistance. dgk222m. dgk130m. gnk193m. wwf92. gnk227m.

The 10th TC attacked along the Hill 258.2-Berezovka front which was defended by 3rd PzD. Pz Abt 3 launched several flanking counter-attacks, destroying several T34s and driving the Soviets back near Hill 258.2. The 10th TC eventually fell back from their attack to regroup before trying a second time to dislodge the 3rd PzD from this important area. When they failed again, the 10th TC would be back the next morning to try again. fkk254+. fkk323m. gnk193m. gnk227m.

In the morning, *GD* and 11th PzD of Knobelsdorff''s 48th PzC advanced on a broad front from Krasnaia Dubrova toward Novoselovka but by the day's end did not capture the town due to the stiff resistance of the 309th RD, 86th TB and the many tank ditches that were dug in front of the town. The 11th PzD had advanced on the road to Oboyan, penetrated the 3rd MC and captured Hill 260.8, south of Novoselovka and linked up with *LAH*, north of Sukho-Solotino. This was an important linkage because the 6th GA had been attacking this exposed flank the last two days. The boundary between the two German divisions still was not strong but at least it was an improvement. The *GD* on 11th's left also advanced past Verkhopenie to the northeast toward Novoselovka and Hill 240.4 to the west of town. At Hill 240.4, a vicious tank battle ensued with the 86th TB. Stukas were called in to assist. The 3rd PzD had been stopped in front of Hill 244.8 and could not assist. dgk142+. dgk222m. dgr209m. gnk312m.

On this Friday morning, the *GD*, next to the 3rd PzD, was now situated northwest, northeast and west of Novoselovka but south of Hill 244.8 which also lay alongside the Oboyan road. Major elements of *GD* deployed north of Verkhopenie were about to assault Novoselovka when they received new orders. While the part of *GD* that was farthest north would screen for Soviet reinforcements moving south, the rest of *GD* would veer 90 degrees to the west and head for Hill 251 and Hill 247.2, northwest of Verkhopenie to help 3rd PzD against the constant attacks from 6th TC and 90th GRD. After helping 3rd PzD, the *GD* moved north of Verkhopenie again and by 2200 hrs had reached Point 1.3 where they were attacked. Instead of engaging, *GD* fell back a little and waited for morning. *GD* had a relatively good day that day, helping itself in its northerly trek while helping 3rd PzD, but the division still had not secured Hill 240.4, west of Novoselovka, which was an objective for the day. With *GD* moving west to help 3rd PzD, it had put greater strain on 11th PzD to hold the northern line. With the blockage of the Oboyan road fairly secured, Vatutin was moving reinforcements to the far west to attack the flanks of *GD*, 3rd PzD, 255th ID and 332nd ID of 52nd IC in order to keep them from helping the northern advance. dgk144+. dgk222m. fkk87. dgr209m. dgr155m. dgr173m. hsz126.

On the extreme western flank, the Soviets had ceased their attacks on 52nd IC which allowed the Germans to recapture Voskhod, southwest of Korovino. It was then learned that Soviet reserves were being brought up and this quiet time meant the Soviets were preparing for a larger attack. vzz170.

By 1030 hrs and after fighting since the day before, 3rd PzD had captured half of Syrtsevo. While the infantry fought for the rest of the village, German engineers were already building a bridge over the Pena tributary that would allow Schmidt-Ott's 56 panzers to cross the river and head north. When the bridge was finished the panzer regiment crossed and headed slowly due to the muddy roads toward Verkhopenie. On the way to their objective two small hills were taken. By the time the panzers reached Verkhopenie, much of the fighting was over and *GD* was finishing the securing of the town. By the end of the day, the 3rd PzD was still fighting to secure both Syrtsevo and Lukhanino. With the delay of 3rd PzD in taking these villages, they were unable to drive north of the Pena River to support *GD* from flank attacks, which in turn slowed *GD*'s northern advance. gnk243. gnk193m. nzk92. gnk227m.

GD and 11th PzD had a coordinated attack in the Verkhopenie sector. Both divisions were to launch at the same time and later in the morning link up to begin phase two of their operation. Panzers attached to *GD* attacked from near Hill 242.1, west of the Oboyan road and three miles south of Hill 260.8 but were immediately stopped by heavy shelling from the hill. It took *GD* 90 minutes to get past the hill and start their drive in securing Verkhopenie and the immediate surrounding area on the east side of the river. Soviet artillery was still in the northern part of town and causing much havoc with 11th PzD to the east. Not knowing *GD* had been delayed, 11th PzD proceeded to attack and capture Ilinski but once there started receiving heavy shelling from Soviet artillery from Hill 260.8, nearly three miles north of Verkhopenie. The hill had complete dominance over the flat land to its immediate south and the Soviet artillery forced the 11th PzD to fall back until help arrived. This lack of communication by *GD* was inexcusable. They did not even report their delay with Corps HQ. When Knobelsdorff heard of 11th PzD's problem, he switched air support from *GD* to the 11th PzD. Elements of *GD* advanced past Verkhopenie and started marching toward Hill 260.8. By this time most of the *Luftwaffe* supporting this sector was directed toward this hill. gnk240+.

While *GD* fought for control of the Verkhopenie sector, 11th PzD was advancing on its west flank in order to join up with elements of *GD*. Together, after Verkhopenie was secured, they were to drive north and capture the fortified village of Dolgi on the west side of the Berezovka-Kruglik road, just south of the Tolstoe Woods. While *GD* and 11th PzD advanced on Dolgi, the 3rd PzD resumed its attack on the Pena River line. The 332nd ID was also advancing toward Dolgi. Knobelsdorff was planning on squeezing the Soviet forces deployed within the Pena River bend between these four divisions. The Germans could not allow Soviet forces to remain in this sector if they had any chance of reaching Oboyan. The flaw in the plan was thinking the 332nd ID without any armor support could travel the five miles to Dolgi through Soviet held territory. When the 332nd ID launched, it soon bogged down; Hoth found *Luftwaffe* support to get the division started again. The 332nd ID never made it to Dolgi. The Germans did pocket some Soviet forces but fell far short of the intended objective. gnk239+. gnk193m. gnk227m.

The 1st TA and 6th GA facing 48th PzC made only minor attacks and in some cases fell back. The 3rd MC was still holding the line on the Pena River from Krasnaia Dubrova in the south to Novoselovka on the north, with the 67th GRD opposing the west flank of the 48th PzC. Some of the pressure on the west flank was relieved when the 3rd PzD, using all its panzers, fewer than 100 panzers, forced the 6th TC across the Pena River, west of Krasnaia Dubrova, after repeated attacks. From north of Krasnaia Dubrova up to Novoselovka, the western line was still being defended by 200th TB of 6th TC and 67th GRD. The 3rd PzD followed, crossing the river north of Alekseevka while continuing its attack in the Syrzevo area on the east bank of the river. wdk148. hjj121m. hjj117m.

On the road to Oboyan, six German divisions including three panzers made an all out attempt to breach the third Soviet defense belt before Oboyan. Two columns, one with

200 panzers and the other with 60, tried to batter their way through T34s, infantry and obstacles, and with the Soviet air force trying to stop them. The Germans penetrated the line and reached Kochetovka, the HQ of Chistiakov who fell back with his 6th GA. Chief of staff, Penkovsky, stayed with the troops while Chistiakov set up his new HQ further to the rear. The Germans were now within 12 miles of Oboyan but the last few days had been costly in men and panzers and their momentum was quickly slowing. The German axis was shifting from Oboyan to the northeast to the high ground at Prokhorovka. There, the Germans could bypass Oboyan. je104+. kcz168+.

Knobelsdorff sent much of his 48th PzC to capture Novoselovka but after fighting all day the village remained in Soviet hands. The 11th PzD under Michl drove up the Oboyan road, broke through 3rd MC and seized Hill 260.8, south of Novoselovka and linked up with *LAH* north of Sukho-Solotino. They were stopped by the 309th RD and heavy artillery fire south of Novoselovka. Novoselovka was northeast of Verkhopenie. The 48th PzC and 2nd SS PzC were being slowly separated as the 2nd SS was heading toward Prokhorovka. dgk142. snk81. wdk147. dgk222m. dgr209m. gnk312m.

East of the Oboyan road, a combat group from 11th PzD under General Balck and with the support of panzers from *GD* in the area, took Hill 260.8 which was the area's highest elevation and an important stepping stone to advancing on Novoselovka. Group Strachwitz of *GD* resumed his drive northward in the direction of Hill 240.4. West and north of Verkhopenie, *GD* was slowed by heavy flanking fire on Hill 243.0, delaying its arrival at Hill 260.8 to help secure it and the surrounding area with 11th PzD. The Hill was difficult to take due to the many dug-in tanks waiting there. With the help of the *Luftwaffe* and the rocket regiment, the Soviets were forced off the hill. Three panzers were lost in the capture. After the hill, *GD* moved on toward the fortified village of Novoselovka. The nearby Hill HF was captured in the process of assaulting Novoselovka. Other elements of *GD* moved off toward Hill 258.2, three miles west of Verkhopenie to secure it, which would help 3rd PzD catch up. At 1900 hrs *GD* resumed its advance north of Verkhopenie but was quickly blocked by 30 tanks. Instead of tackling the tanks, Strachwitz pulled back for the night, deciding to do battle in the morning when his men were rested. Only 25 tanks were destroyed by *GD* that day. hjj119. dgk142+. dgr209m. fkk269. gnk193m. gnk312m. dgk141m. gnk227m.

As the 48th PzC inched northward, its 3rd PzD and the 332nd ID attempted to protect the west flank. Lately the fiercest fighting was on its western flank not its northern front. *GD* linked up with 11th PzD and moved toward Kochetovka but they were stopped by the reinforced 10th TC. dgk140+. dgk141m. dgk222m. dlu63m.

GD had veered west as ordered to close up and protect the flank of 3rd PzD while it secured Verkhopenie, capturing it after a hard fight. The hill at Verkhopenie, Hill 258.2, was also captured as was Hill 244.5 on the road to Oboyan. This would be the deepest penetration 3rd PzD had of the campaign. During the night German engineers reinforced the original bridge over the Pena and built a new 16 ton bridge as well. Also in sector, the 3rd PzD, north of Verkhopenie, regrouped during the night and was prepared to advance at first light. While pausing at Verkhopenie, the Germans discovered near the Kubaossvski ravine, northwest of Berezovka, a concentration of tanks and by next morning that concentration grew to include the hills north of that defile. Pz Abt 3, located on the ridge west of Verkhopenie, discovered the tankers as well. The Soviet tanks grew at an alarming rate; elements of 3rd PzD were ordered back to Hill 258.2, west of Verkhopenie, to defend it and prevent an ambush into the rear areas of all the divisions of 48th PzC. fkk251++. gnk216. gnk227m.

At 1130 hrs, elements of *GD* and 3rd PzD escalated their attack on Verkhopenie sector from the west between Krasnaia Dubrova and Novoselovka, with 100 panzers and close air support, against the 67th GRD and 200th TB of 6th TC which were heavily bombed but still put up stiff resistance. Despite destroying five panzers and damaging two Tigers, the Soviets had to fall back five miles to the north. The 309th RD of 40th Army was moving up to assist the 67th GRD in slowing the German advance but had not arrived in any real strength yet. However, by the end of the day the whole division would be assembling behind 67th GRD. Nearing dusk, the division saw action when the 67th GRD was forced to fall back into the line with 309th RD. wdk148. gnk216. hjj121m. hjj117m. dgr209m. dgr217. gnk227m. dgk409+. pck70.

At 1130 hrs after fighting for almost a day, the 200th TB of 6th TC started slowly to evacuate Verkhopenie and the surrounding countryside toward the west. With Verkhopenie falling into German hands, a gap opened on the east side of the Pena River that Hoth, not responding quickly enough, was not going to exploit. After the recent heavy fighting, Katukov ordered the 31st TC to fall back to the northern side of the Oboyan road. Any unit to the south of the road was being threatened with encirclement. Vatutin also ordered the 309th RD and 29th ATB, plus other attachments from 40th Army, to move east and bolster the Oboyan road defenses against *GD* and 11th PzD. gnk215+. gnk193m. gnk227m.

As the 48th PzC (11th PzD) moved north between Verkhopenie and Solotino, 16 miles from Oboyan and west of Prokhorovka, Soviet reserves were moving to the line, slowing the German advance. The *GD* and elements of 11th PzD attacked again from the Krasnaia Dubrova area toward Novoselovka against the 3rd MC and the 67th GRD. By noon the presure became too great and the Soviets began to pull back. This retreat forced the nearby 31st TC to fall back as well to avoid being ambushed on their flank. The 3rd PzD, attacking in the Pena bend, advanced up the Rakovo-Kruglik road past Berezovka, but trying to move north after taking the village failed because the Soviets were heavily dug-in in the area woods. The 52nd IC had been unable to cross the Pena River and Hoth was hoping *GD*, by moving to the west, could force the Soviets to fall back to avoid encirclement. Vatutin's response to this ploy was to send reinforcements from 40th Army. 11th PzD was completely halted. In the woods between Malinovoe and Melovoe, the newly arrived 309th RD and the 51st GRD were also able to stop the German advance to the northeast. East of the Donets, the advance of 3rd PzC had lengthened its flank and Kempf had to commit greater forces to protect it which slowed his northward march. General Hoth could clearly see the impact the lengthening salient was having on his flanks and his corps' inability to maintain the northward advance while guarding against the hordes of Soviets trying to cut off the salient and isolate his army. Apart from asking his superior for reinforcements which he knew were not available, and except for a few minor actions to safeguard the SS from the ravages of 5th GTA that was now nearing the battlefield, Hoth did not institute any major changes to his strategy. dgr91. rc 202. bt86. dgr209m. gnk216. fmz223+.

The 10th TC was arriving in position south of Oboyan and preparing to block 48th PzC from reaching the important town. The 204th RD and 184th RD were also arriving in sector as well as numerous other tank units. The Soviet AF was also giving the sector top priority. On the east flank, Vatutin moved the 69th Army alongside 7th GA between the two branches of the Donets River. To the east the 69th Army, consisting in the main of 81st GRD, 89th GRD, 92nd GRD, 93rd GRD, 94th GRD, 107th GRD, 183rd GRD, 305th GRD, 375th GRD, 2nd GTC, 148th TR, 96th TB, 30th TDB and 27th Anti-tank Brigade was moving closer to the line. Regardless of the area some units would deploy or redeploy in forward positions but most would be behind the third defensive belt at this stage of the campaign. wdk149+. nzk92.

At 1200 hrs in Verkhopenie, the 200th TB began to quicken its evacuation, heading north. Other Soviets deployed in the area moved west and crossed the Pena River. At this time, Group Strachwitz left the mopping up of Verkhopenie to the grenadiers and started heading for Hill 260.8 on the east side of the Oboyan road and the retreating Soviet tankers. On the way to the hill, more T34s appeared and attacked Strachwitz from the flank. Without calling for air support, Stukas flew by attacking the Soviet tanks. A dozen tanks were destroyed and with the threat of more panzers arriving, the rest of the T34s pulled back to Hill 260.8. At the same time, the lead units of *GD* who had been marching north approached Novoselovka and Hill 240.4, east of the fortified town. Soviet artillery on Hill 260.8 started shelling the German column, stopping it in its tracks. T34s then attacked but Stukas came in to repulse the attack. The small panzer group continued and by the end of the day was two miles north of Novoselovka. It had been a difficult but modestly successful day for *GD*. The division had been given several assignments that broke the division into several combat groups, spreading them out and breaking up their already deteriorating cohesion and overall attack strength. Verkhopenie had been a difficult objective and there had been several Soviet tank groups roaming the area looking for easy prey to contend with as well. The *Luftwaffe* played an important part in *GD*'s advance that day, destroying many tanks. gnk241+. gnk193m. gnk227m.

At noon, von Manstein ordered 1st PzA to send the 24th PzC, which included the 23rd PzD and Viking, up to Kharkov. The 24th PzC arrived the next day with less than 150 panzers but since the 48th PzC had only 132 working panzers, it would be a doubling of strength. Von Manstein knew it would be difficult to get Hitler's release of the 24th PzC but it was the only way the 4th PzA would reach Kursk. wdk150. vzz158. gnk157. gnk220.

From north of the Petrovka area, leading elements of the 5th GTC attacked *LAH* but were repulsed each time. North of Berezovka, the 332nd ID was attacked while other attacks at Dmitrievka against 255th ID were being made. The 332nd ID was eventually able to push back the 90th GRD westward beyond Zavidovka and trailing elements of the 3rd PzD reached Rakovo on the west bank of the Pena by noon. These divisions were trying to repair the line that the Soviets had ravaged from earlier attacks. Another section of the line for 332nd ID however was pushed back. The 52nd IC, fighting on the west flank, was ordered to send men to the east flank. The Soviets were giving so much trouble to 52nd IC's flank that Hoth requested the 2nd Army to the west initiate an attack on 38th Army, and 40th Army to reduce the pressure on Hoth's west flank. Von Manstein refused the request. The 2nd Army had been hit hard in the early months of 1943, against the Soviet winter offensive that pushed them back from the Don River, and still had not recovered. Von Manstein felt the two rifle divisions and one tank brigade facing 2nd Army was too much to handle. Hitler refused to counter von Manstein's order as well. wdk147. hjj117m.

The 3rd PzD, using only Mks, was really struggling to push back Soviet resistance at Berezovka near the Pena River. Hoth had to stop *GD*'s northward advance altogether and shift a large part of the division to the west again in the same day to assist 3rd PzD in stopping the ever-growing resistance on the western flank. The rest of the division would stay in place and block any attempts by the Soviets to penetrate the line. This sideways fighting would last a week which meant that the whole *GD* division would never move forward in the campaign. With Hill 243.0 and Hill 247.2 being used to such an advantage by the Soviets, it was decided *GD* would capture those hills while trying to assist 3rd PzD. With elements of *GD* helping 3rd PzD at Berezovka, the village fell but as soon as the panzers returned to *GD* in the north, the 3rd PzD was halted again. It was not strong enough to go it alone. The 332nd ID had similar troubles at Berezovka, Alekseevka and Mikhailovka. Hoth continued to be uninspired in thinking of a new strategy for the 48th PzC; arguably this lack of insight for 48th PzC would play a major role in 4th PzA's undoing. mhz290. lck314. vzz2m. gnk193m. gnk227m. fmz221m.

Bitter fighting raged between Verkhopenie and Solotino as 4th PzA continued to strike the 1st TA and 6th GA, trying to find weakness as well as to stablize their line. While much of *GD* fought for the town, 11th PzD continued north to meet with *LAH* at Sukho-Solotino. During the battle for Verkhopenie, a tank battle raged nearby on Hill 243.0. Group Wietersheim took the hill and then moved north, heading for Hill 240.4 and Novoselovka. This was part of a major offensive von Manstein initiated to put pressure on the two armies. Von Manstein thought the Soviets were about to break and wanted to exploit their weakness. The 48th PzC and 2nd SS PzC advanced along a ten mile front with hundreds of panzers leading the way. dgr209m. lck312++. lck318. gnk312m. dgk144.

The 11th PzD was the only panzer division of 48th PzC that was concentrating its full effort in moving north to clear the southern Psel River area. Vatutin was preparing to send 1st TA and 6th GA south to split the 48th PzC in half. mhz295+. dgk211m. vzz261++. dgk130m. gnk193m. gnk227m.

Group Strachwitz of *GD* moved out from south of Verkhopenie to the northeast toward Novoselovka. It passed Hill 260.8 aiming for Hill 240.4, just west of Novoselovka. At the same time, the 11th PzD on the east side of the Oboyan road also headed for Hill 240.4 but both divisions ran into Soviet armor before reaching that important hill. The tank battle escalated quickly with the long firing guns of the Tigers getting in the first kills, but the T34s were moving quickly, trying to get in close to outmaneuver the bigger panzers. The Germans broke through the Soviet screen and were able to reach Novoselovka and Hill HF despite additional attacks. The lead column was able to reach Hill 244.8 on the road to Oboyan. fkk270. gnk312m. dgk143.

After leaving Verkhopenie but before reaching the northern Novoselovka sector, Col Strachwitz received new orders. As soon as possible, he was suppose to turn west again and assist 3rd PzD. As part of its trek westward to assist 3rd PzD, Group Strachwitz of *GD* advanced toward Hill 251.4 and Hill 247.0 before moving on and attacking 6th TC which was blocking 3rd PzD's advance. Strachwitz had 39 assorted panzers which included ten Tigers and ten Panthers. Both *GD* and 3rd PzD asked for air support but with a lack of planes, only *GD* received it. Elements of *GD* were heading north toward Novoselovka and the resistance was tough. By the end of the day, Novoselovka fell to the Germans, forcing the 3rd MC to pull back behind the 309th RD. By the afternoon, the 3rd MC and 31st TC were in a confused state and it was a golden opportunity for *GD* to break through to reach Oboyan. However the 10th TC began arriving in sector and slowed the Germans down until more of the corps could arrive. lck314+. dgr217.

The 11th PzD pushed forward into the Kochetovka area and westward along the road to Oboyan. Part of the 48th PzC was defending the Pena River line and Vatutin moved the 10th TC into position to attack the 48th PzC if necessary. A heavy rain started which would slow the tanks down. rc201. dgk139+. dgk222m. dlu63m.

In mid afternoon, the *GD*, *LAH* and 11th PzD continued the attempt to penetrate the line south of Novoselovka, finally overrunning a stubborn 86th TB which caused the 31st TC to quickly fall back to the line defended by 309th RD to prevent encirclement. The line was from Novenkoe to Kalinovka and included Hill 251.4, Hill 240.0, Hill 235.9 and Hill 207.8. This deployment would strengthen the defense across the road to Oboyan. fkk89. dgk410.

After 3rd PzD drove the 6th TC across the Pena River, the *GD* and 11th PzD followed with the intention of finishing off the tank corps near the Oboyan road at Novoselovka, 12 to 15 miles away from Oboyan. Elements of the 3rd PzD stayed at the Pena River and began clearing the swampland of the many Soviets still hiding there. The lead units of *GD*, heading for Novoselovka, were already northeast of Verkhopenie and were approaching Hill 240.0 when they were shelled and had to stop to wait for artillery and reinforcements. While fighting with the 6th TC, the *GD* cleared the area east of Verkhopenie, and a mile or two north of Syrtsev. The 48th PzC gained some ground on this morning against the 3rd MC, the 31st TC and 6th TC. The Germans claimed destroying 101 tanks along the Oboyan road. The Soviets claimed to have destroyed a total of 295 panzers but these numbers seem high. wdk148. hjj121m. hjj117m. mhz289. dgr209m. fkk251.

After receiving orders the day before, the 5th GA started deploying along the north bank of the Psel River between the Oboyan road and Prokhorovka and were ready for the coming fight by dark. The 5th GTC, which had been defending the Belenikhino-Teterevino sector, was ordered to the west along the Oboyan road near Orlovka. They arrived on site at 0100 hrs on 7/10. The 40th Army's 219th RD was ordered to move north from Rakitnoe area to Kruglik area. The 204th RD, 10th TC and 67th GRD were ordered to occupy the Kruglik-Malinovoe line by next morning. These actions were taken due to the Germans reaching the Gresnoe, Ozerovski and Iasnaia Poliana line by the previous night. wdk150. dgr97. dgr93m.

Elements of *GD* were trying to clear the last of the resistance from the fortified town of Verkhopenie and Hill 260.8. At the same time, the 11th PzD to the east of the village were heading north, while the *Luftwaffe* was bombing the west side of the Pena in order to soften up the area. Leaving Verkhopenie, the *GD* recon group moved out but quickly bumped into the 86th TB. A battle ensued and with the help of the passing *Luftwaffe*, the 86th TB fell back and the *GD* was able to reach Hill 243.0, one mile west of Verkhopenie. When 3rd PzD was stuck west of Verkhopenie, elements of *GD* had to be diverted to help 3rd PzD get free. They were needed further north. Together they broke out and were able to head north. Both German corps made disappointing progress in places that day and it looked like *GD* would be needed on the flanks and that would greatly be felt by the front line divisions. Verkhopenie was eventually cleared. dgk143+. dgk222m. dgr209m. fkk269. gnk193m. gnk312m. vzz439. gnk227m.

In the afternoon, Lt General Knobelsdorff started receiving recon reports of two major Soviet tank concentrations in the Verkhopenie-Novoselovka area. The first tank grouping was three miles west of Verkhopenie, while the larger tank group was heading south near Vladimirovka but still north of Novoselovka. This last group was Burkov's 10th TC. With the 3rd PzD spread thin along the Pena River, the first sighting caused Knobelsdorff to order the 3rd PzD to go defensive until greater clarity was resolved. In the northern case, *GD* was ordered to postpone their current mission, assemble as much as possible and be prepared to defend against a major attack. A little later an order from Hoth reached Knobelsdorff that canceled all offensives for *GD* until the tactical conditions improved. They would never improve and that day's advance was basically their last to the north. Next morning, more of *GD* would veer to the west to assist 3rd PzD in repulsing the frequent Soviet attacks on their flanks. By expanding their battle zone further west over the last couple of days, Hoth had enlarged the line and weakened his defenses and yet he made no real attempt to correct the over indulgence when it was proven that 3rd PzD needed the frequent help of *GD* to curb the Soviet incursions. gnk242. gnk193m. dgr172m. gnk227m. dgk412.

On its left flank, the 3rd PzD was being harassed so much that it could not contribute to the advance northward. The lead units of the division did manage to reach Hill 244.8 on the road to Oboyan but it was at a heavy cost. To the east of 48th PzC, the 2nd SS PzC was meeting heavy resistance as well from the 10th TC (before leaving the area) and 31st TC along its entire line. In support of the ground advance, the *Luftwaffe* carried out 1,500 sorties. dgk144+.

From north of the Novoselovka area, while fighting the 309th RD and the 3rd TC, *GD* turned west, staying north of Verkhopenie, toward Hill 232.8 to assist 3rd PzD against the 6th TC. The 10th TC with elements of 67th GRD deployed along the line Kruglik, Kalinovka and Malinovoe were ordered to prepare for battle and attack *GD*'s flank as they traveled west. At the same time, Soviet positions near Lakhanino and Shepelovka were being aggressively attacked as well. Hoth was convinced flank resistance had to be reduced before crossing the Psel. Lt General Hoernlein was ordered to turn west then south and, with the support of 3rd PzD driving north, to encircle and destroy 6th TC, which had been causing much trouble on 48th PzC's west flank. vzz261. dgr91. dgr217.

The 11th PzD attacked the 31st TC and the 51st GRD defending Orlovka, located eight miles southwest of Oboyan. The total count for German panzers in the south at this stage was fewer than 500 operable but there was a backlog of damaged panzers that would be repaired. The 11th PzD would travel over five miles on this day, moving toward Pokrovski on the east side of the Oboyan road. In the evening *GD*, now driving in a northwest direction to the Pena River, reached Novoselovka after advancing six miles. wdk148+. hjj121m.

At 2200 hrs Hoth signed Order No. 5, describing the objectives for the following day. The 48th PzC would continue along the Oboyan road while *LAH* made a direct run from the Teterevino area on Prokhorovka and the high ground to the west. *SSTK* was supposed to establish a bridgehead across the Psel while *Das Reich* remained defensive. The 3rd PzC which was concentrated in the Melikhovo sector was to drive toward and cross the Donets River. The 52nd IC was supposed to cross the Pena River and clear the west bank of resistance. At this point the 4th PzA had fewer than 500 panzers and assault guns, with 2nd SS PzC having 294 of them. The opening stage would start tomorrow. Crossing the Psel River was the first obstacle and with the recent heavy rains the river was swollen, making it harder to forge and to erect a bridge over it. All the work done on this day was in preparation for the final lunge across the Psel and the capture of Prokhorovka and the southern corridor to Kursk. wwf97. vzz170++*. lck321.

Hoth visited Knobelsdorff in the field and reprimanded him for the slow progress of the 48th PzC and especially 3rd PzD. Hoth then visited Westhoven to motivate him as well. Hoth wanted the 3rd PzD to cross the Pena *en masse* the following day and no excuses would be tolerated. gnk244.

It had been a pretty good day for the Germans, at least on some of their axes of attack. The 48th PzC had captured Verkhopenie, Sukho-Solotino and Gresnoe which were located on the swampy river basins of the second defense belt that had slowed the panzers down. The two previous days with the heavy reinforcements, the 1st TA and 6th GA had slowed the Germans' advance but with the heavy casualties of those armies, the 48th PzC had gained seven miles that day and was breaking out of this second defensive belt into the open. However, it had cost the 48th so much in men and panzers to get to this point that they might not have enough left to penetrate the third defense belt. The arrival of the fresh 10th TC enabled the Soviets to halt the 48th's advance. The 48th had less than 140 working panzers but if von Manstein could get Hitler's approval to use 24th PzC, another nearly 150 panzers could be deployed. With the gains that day, the 48th PzC was almost abreast of the 2nd SS PzC which had been miles ahead. vzz157+. vzz258+.

With it getting dark, a splinter group of *GD*, still south of Novoselovka, stopped for the night. A patrol was formed to head west during the night to recon the Kruglik area. Stukas had been periodically bombing Hill 260.8 for most of the day but *GD* failed to take it. Later in the afternoon, the panzer regiment of 11th PzD arrived and after continued shelling and aerial bombing, the Soviets were forced off the hill. The Germans then drove several more miles north of the hill before stopping just south of Hill 244.8. Mickl reported to Knobelsdorff that he had 57 assorted panzers still working including the obsolete Mk II, Hummels and flame-throwing panzers. gnk241. gnk244+. gnk301.

Late at night, 3rd PzD cleared Berezovka by way of the Rakovo-Kruglik road of enemy troops from the west. The Soviets stopped the 48th PzC after leaving Berezovka for Kruglik at the southern edge of a little woods north of Berezovka. wwf92. dgk222m. mhz305.

Late at night, Soviet infiltrators from the west bank of the Pena slipped back into Verkhopenie to cause havoc. fkk269.

At night, Vatutin redeployed his forces to meet new expected threats in the morning against the shifting *GD*, 3rd PzD, 255th ID and 332nd ID. Going against Zhukov, the 1st TA dug in their anti-tank guns and went defensive. Vatutin, after receiving reinforcements and making these recent redeployments, felt confident the Germans would be defeated. He was relying on 69th Army, which had recently been moved up into the Donets' triangle, to stop 3rd PzC. Von Manstein knew a tank column (5th GTA) was moving west to engage and he ordered Kempf to speed his advance and intercept Rotmistrov to prevent him from attacking 2nd SS PzC in front of Prokhorovka. The 2nd SS PzC received their orders late at night to advance on Prokhorovka and to establish a bridgehead over the Psel River in the morning. Though the Germans were aware of tanks moving into sector, they were not sure how many tanks were coming. dgk145+. nzk92.

The last three days the 38th Army and 40th Army had transferred to Vatutin the following: two rifle divisions, one AA division, three tank brigades, four tank regiments, three AA brigades, eight anti-tank artillery regiments and one gun artillery regiment. It's no wonder the Germans were slowing down. dgr90.

By the end of the day, *GD* was approaching Novoselovka and in fact had captured some ground to the north of the town, while to the east of the Oboyan road, the 11th PzD had reached north of Pokrovski, which meant north of Verkhopenie. Both German divisions had gained about six miles. It was a good day for 48th PzC for it had pretty much caught up with the SS, though the boundary between 11th PzD and *LAH* was still in jeopardy. The 3rd PzD did gain some ground along the Pena River. wdk149. nzk92.

There are a number of alternative strategies that would have worked better. One such alternative would have been to narrow the attack axis for 48th PzC so that *GD*, switching places with 11th PzD and being on the direct flank of the SS, would have attacked to the north while the other divisions of 48th PzC could have provided flank protection. The strength of *GD* alongside *LAH* in the early days and then next to *SSTK* in the later stage would have been extremely compelling. With part of 11th PzD safeguarding *GD*'s right flank and the rest of the division assisting 3rd PzD, the western flank would have fared better as long as it did not stray too far west beyond the Pena River, especially when you consider Vatutin would have had to devote more assets to the northern line and fewer on the western line. With a small attack zone, these divisions would have had many fewer strongpoints to capture. In my estimation, if 48th PzC had stayed east of the Vorskla River line, avoiding the Pena River valley, they could have avoided frontal attacks on the tough strongpoints of Cherkasskoe, Syrtsevo, Lukhanino, Dubrova, the Pena River crossings, Berezovka, Tolstoe Woods, Verknopenie, Novoselovka and a number of strongly held hills. Despite the heavy casualties in men and panzers in the early days, Hoth still ploughed on with his original axis of attack. Even after taking these strongpoints, while his strength dramatically fell, the Soviet resistance remained strong due to the ready reserves of 38th and 40th Armies situated to the west coming into sector. The previous night and again the following morning, Hoth received intel that additional infantry and tanks were coming to the salient. A major counter-offensive was coming and all Hoth did was to push Knobelsdorff to do more of the same before the Soviet attack was launched. Perhaps it was too late by the 9th or 10th to make major changes in 48th's deployment but Hoth's obsession in attacking along the Berezovka-Kruglik road over the coming several days seemed not the best strategy if Prokhorovka was now the primary axis.

Kriuchenkin's 69th Army moved up to defend the Prokhorovka-Lipovyi Donets River sector between 6th GA and 7th GA. At the same time other Soviet units were stopping 3rd PzC east of the Northern Donets. dgk139. dgk222m. dlu63m.

With the 3rd PzC turning north and west, Vatutin, over this and the following day, transfered many divisions of 7th GA to the control of the commander of 69th Army where they would try to block the apparent new path of the Germans and prevent the 3rd PzC from joining up with *Das Reich*. With 6th GA weakening, 69th Army received greater responsibility in covering a larger sector that now extended as far west as Vasilevka and as far south and east as Belnikhovo, Shopino, Kiselevo, Shliakhovo and Miasoedovo. One of the first changes 69th Army made was to move 2nd TC and 93rd GRD from the Rozhdestvenka area further north to the Leski-Shakhovo-Dalni Dolzhik areas. These redeployments would be completed by next morning. The 7th GA continued to be active in attacking the flanks of 7th PzD and 11th IC in the far east. dgr97. dgr93m. dgr155m. dgr173m.

After leaving Melikhovo for Khokhlovo, the 6th PzD was quickly stopped by stiff resistance from Lebedev's 96th TB in the grove near Hill 217.4. By 1800 hrs, after a four-hour fight and running out of ammo, the remaining few T34s fell back to Kiselevo leaving the grove of trees on that hill to the Germans. Despite the modest gains, neither the 6th PzD nor the nearby 19th PzD could' break through to the Donets and were still trying to penetrate through the second defensive belts. vzz248. vzz3m. dgr155m. dgr173m. dgk162+.

zzt90.

In 3rd PzC sector, the 6th PzD led the advance with its nearly 100 panzers and assault guns against 92nd GRD, taking the high ground north of Melikhovo, 12 miles northeast of Belgorod and crossed the Belgorod-Korocha road. The nearby villages of Cholchlovka and Schischino were also eventually captured but at a high cost. The 19th PzD and 7th PzD advanced on either side of 6th PzD, providing flank protection. Later in the day north of Melikhovo, the Soviets counter-attacked, forcing part of 6th PzD to go defensive while the rest of the trailing 6th PzD crossed the Razumnaia River east of Olkhovatka. To the south and only a few miles from Belgorod, the 168th ID was still trying to overcome the strong defensive positions around Staryi Gorod. Raus was still providing protection on the extreme east flank against strong resistance and was not making much progress either. The 7th PzD along with Lt General Forst's 106th ID also attacked toward Kasikino. fkk89. dgr155m. dgr173m. vzz5m. wdk149. hjj121m. dgr39m. wwf96. vzz5m. hjj123m. dlu80.

On the east side of the Donets north of Melikhovo, the 6th PzD finally seized the heights south of Shliakhovo. Then the 6th PzD and 19th PzD linked and finally captured the village of Kelekovo which led to the destruction of two Soviet RDs and the fall of Belgorod Heights, which subsequently allowed Kempf's force a little more maneuverability in moving north. The difficulties Kempf's forces met with was shown by Group Westphalian's 6th PzD's losses. The division started the campaign with 117 panzers but by the end of the day, there were only 35 panzers still fighting. This day was the worst day of the campaign, losing 48 panzers. Many of these losses were due to mine damage but most of these machines were recovered and repaired. sPzAbt 503 had 34 of its 44 Tigers damaged or destroyed; 16 of them by mines. Twenty-two Tigers would be repaired and on the field later that day. Eight other Tigers would be repaired within eight more days and a few more would have to be sent back to Berlin for repair. The supply road Belgorod-Korocha also fell into German hands. shn160. lck327 mhz307. hjj123m.

The rest of 69th Army moved up to the line between the two Donets Rivers. The army included 81st GRD, 89th GRD, 92nd GRD, 93rd GRD, 94th GRD, 107th RD, 183rd RD, 305th RD, 375th RD, 2nd GTC, 148th TR, 96th TB, 30th TDB and 27th Anti-tank Brigade. wdk150.

The heaviest fighting of the day east of the Donets occurred in the sector defended by 81st GRD and 92nd GRD. After multiple attempts to penetrate the line, the Germans outflanked the 282nd GRR, broke through the line and reached Hill 185.7 on the road running from Staryi Gorod to Dalniaia Igumenka. The village of Postnikov was also captured but Shishinl and the high ground east of the village stayed temporarily in Soviet hands. It was discovered that the 81st GRD, 92nd GRD and 375th RD by 2200 hrs began pulling back to the Kiselevo-Hill 211.5-Shliakhovo-Sabynino line. The 81st GRD was eventually redeployed with the 48th GRC along the Donets River on the Hill 147.0-Hill 213.4-Novo Oskochnoe-Shcholokovo line. Vatutin also sent reinforcements to defend Kiselevo-Hill 211.5–Olshanets. The 73rd GRD, 375th RD, 89th GRD, 107th RD, 305th RD and 92nd GRD with support of the 4th MRB of 2nd GTC would sacrifice everything to stop the 19th PzD from getting through to the Donets and linking up with *Das Reich*. The 69th Army had few tanks and most of the burden to stop the panzers lay on infantry but so far they had prevented the Germans from penetrating the second defense belt. Novo Oskochnoe was due west of Kazache and northeast of Krivtsevo. vzz248++. vzz3m. dgr155m. dgr173m. dgr39m. nzk92. vzz5m.

The 6th PzD regrouped at Melikhovo before it moved north with the 19th PzD in the direction of Postnikov, while 7th PzD struggled to defend its line east of the Northern Donets River against increasing Soviet hostilities. Kempf still struggled, far behind his schedule, being little help to 2nd SS PzC. By the end of the day, the 6th PzD had only 40 panzers and four captured T34s working. sPzAbt 503 which was working with 6th PzD had 15 working Tigers. It was at this point that Hoth changed his battle plan to alter the axis from Oboyan to Prokhorovka. One advantage this direction shift would have was that the SS divisions would drive closer to the 3rd PzC which would help take some of the pressure off 3rd PzC. dgk145+. fkk280. vzz247. lck327. dgr155m. dgr173m.

At 2200 hrs, after losing Blizhniaia Igumenka, Postnikov, Dalniaia Igumenka and Shishino the 81st GRD, 92nd GRD and 375th RD were officially ordered to fall back to avoid being encircled by the 6th PzD and 19th PzD. They were to reform to the northwest nearer to the Donets River along the Kiselevo, Hill 211.5, Shliakhovo and Sabynino line. These divisions would have to hurry because the lead units of the 6th PzD and 19th PzD were moving quickly through the gaps toward this line. Shortly after noon, the 19th PzD captured Hill 211.5. At the same time, the 442nd GR, defending Blizhniaia Igumenka was being heavily attacked and was in danger of losing the village and opening a gap in the rear of 19th PzD. Schmidt immediately recalled several battalions from the 168th ID to return to the village to assist the 442nd GR. The village held with the extra support. At Andreevski, Group Bieberstein (Major) was up against a stiff defense but was slowly getting the upper hand. After losing these key sites, Maj General Goriachev's forces had to fall back and set up new defenses along the line from west to east: Sabynino, Shliakhovo,Sheino and Ushakovo. Units involved with this new line included the 305th RD, 375th RD, 92nd GRD, 96th TB and 107th RD and were deployed in two echelons. The second line included Novo Oskochnoe, Verkhni Olshanets, Komintern, Shukhtsovo and Hill 221.0. Vatutin reminded Goriachev that it was critical to delay Kempf as much as possible and that the 3rd PzC must not link up with *Das Reich* before Rotmistrov launched his attack. vzz249+. vzz10m. vzz1m. nzk92. dgr155m. dlu80. dlu88+.

In the 3rd PzC sector, 6th PzD, 7th PzD and 19th PzD made minimal gains. Schmidt of 19th PzD at the end of the day decided it would be prudent to move back to Blizhniaia Igumenka for the night. Kempf's main objective was to capture the road junction at Korocha and to divert 69th Army away from the Donets and the SS, but he was not close to doing it. This slow progress also meant Kempf would not intercept and stop 5th GTA from reaching Prokhorovka. dgk145+. dgk222m. fkk87. dgr209m. dgr155m. dgr173m. hjj123m.

At night General Breith established Group North, which was comprised of most of 6th PzD and elements of 19th PzD. Two battalions of artillery were also attached. It would be commanded by Hunersdorff. His orders were to penetrate the Soviet line north of Melikhovo and then to drive on Dalniaia Igumenka and destroy the tank concentration deployed near there. Once achieved, Hunersdorff would drive to the Donets River near Shcholokovo and into the rear of 81st GRD, which was blocking 168th ID's advance, and between the two German forces destroy the 81st GRD and as much of the nearby 375th RD as possible. The remainder of 19th PzD also shifted west to join up with 168th ID to form Group South, under the command of Schmidt, and between the two combat groups crushed the 81st GRD. Schmidt's first objective was to capture Blizhniaia Igumenka and the surrounding area and then to destroy the Soviet infantry deployed in the woods a mile south of the village. At the same time, the 198th ID was ordered to move up and replace the

7th PzD in protecting the eastern flank. The 7th PzD was badly needed in 3rd PzC's drive north to link up with 2nd SS PzC which was by now just south of Prokhorovka. See Map 13. gnk237. vzz12m. nzk92. dgr155m. dlu74+.

13

July 9th on the Northern Salient

With only a few local offensives, Model had some of his forces rest and regroup for the renewed fighting that would start the following day, but he could not allow the Soviets a complete day of rest. The local attacks on key targets were launched mostly in preparation of gaining better launching positions for the following day's big offensive. Rokossovsky used the slow day to prepare for the major offensive that would start in three days time in the Orel salient. By the end of the day, the line was pretty much where it started; the Soviet line, from east to west, ran along the Trosna, Protasovo, Bazhenova, Ponyri, Hill 257.0, Samodurovka, Hill 250 and Buzova line. dgr118. dgr108m. dgr199m. nzk91+.

At dawn, around 0500 hrs, General Rudenko sent a squadron of over 170 planes to attack 47th PzC's rear areas near Saburovka while the Germans were preparing to attack. The low front that blew in the day before was still hanging over the salient. The sky was still overcast and more rain was expected a little later. Many of these pilots were from 15th VA and were green rookies. The attack was confused and disoriented and little damage was inflicted on the 47th PzC, but it did cause enough of a confusion to cause a delay in their limited attack. When the air attack began, German fighters scrambled but by the time they arrived it was too late as the Soviets had already left. While eight Soviets who had strayed from the formation had been downed, a golden opportunity for experienced German pilots to attack rookies had been lost. Due to weather conditions, sorties for both sides were down. The 1st *Flieger* Division flew 877 sorties while 16th VA had 327 bomber missions along with 448 fighter sorties. cbk70. nzk77.

After a predawn barrage that struck the defenses at Olkhovatka, the 47th PzC attacked. At first light nearly 200 panzers of 2nd PzD, 4th PzD and 20th PzD, 9th PzD plus the men of the 6th ID charged the ridge north of town from their assembly point in the Teploe-Kashara area. The ridge was defended by the fresh forces of the 162nd RD of 70th Army. This ridge was part of the second defensive belt and had been extensively built up; it would be extremely hard to take. The corps fought all day but made no progress against heavy artillery. On the Olkhovatka-Ponyri road to the east of the ridge, the 2nd PzD, 9th PzD and 6th ID were engaged in heavy fighting. Shelling came from between Ossinovyi and Leninski further south. wdk181. dgk121.dgk138.dgk147. fkk102m. dgk87m. dgr199m. lck116m.

Just east of Teploe on the left flank of 4th PzD, the 70th GRD counter-attacked with support of tanks from 237th TR but the attack was repulsed. Next to the 4th PzD, the Pz Abt 21 deployed northeast of Samodurovka also received the attention of the 237th TR but it was able to repulse the attack as well. The Pz Abt launched their own attack toward Hill 274.5, southeast of Teploe which was initially defended by a line of dug-in T34s. The small arms fire was so fierce that German infantry could only advance sheltered behind their panzers. Casualties were horrendous. As was the Soviet SOP; they would engage and tie up the attacking force with these dug-in tanks and when the time was right a mobile force of tanks would attack from behind the hill as was done here. fkk65. dgk87m. lck116m. dgk116m. zzt84+. (July 9th)

GnMaj Deichmann was appraising the performance of his Fw 190 pilots over the past four days in regards to their ability in penetrating escort cover to reach and destroy Soviet bombers. His pilots for the most part had not been as successful as expected. The Soviet pilots had stepped up their performance. cbk70.

The 2nd PzD and 9th PzD once again tried to breach the Olkhovatka-Ponyri road but after fighting all day failed again. At 2200 hrs, the 6th GRD launched a counter-attack along the road just east of Olkhovatka, gaining an upper hand. This would be the deepest the 9th PzD would advance; the days to follow would see the division being pushed back. mkz120+. dgk116m. dgr108m. lck116m.

In the 46th PzC sector, the 31st ID and 20th PzD working together launched an attack across a ten mile front that saw a small penetration of the line between Gnilets and Bobrik and in front of Samodurovka. The Soviets quickly closed the gap at a hill south of town. The rest of 46th PzC remained on the defensive. On the 41st PzC front, the 18th PzD and 292nd ID launched an attack at 0630 hrs and after overcoming stout resistance the Germans, with the help of Ferdinands, breached the defensive belt on a 500 yd front at Ponyri PC. The Soviets counter-attacked in the afternoon but were unable to push the Germans back. The *Luftwaffe* was brought in to help shut down the Soviet counter. wdk181. dgr198m. fkk102m. dgk87m. dgr199m. wwf48. lck116m.

At the meeting with Kluge, Lemelson, Harpe and others, Model informed of the latest offensive that would start next morning. The 47th PzC would capture the hills near Olkhovatka by going through Teploe and Molytyschi, due south of Teploe and due west of Olkhovatka. The attack would involve the 2nd PzD, 4th PzD and 20th PzD and they were moving into attack positions as the meeting was proceeding. If the breakthrough did not materialize, the 10th PzGD, 12th PzD and 36th ID would be released from reserve to join the battle. Rokossovsky knew this axis of attack was critical for the Germans and would bring new reserves each night. Tha German attack began after a preperation and included the front between Teploe and Samodurovka. That evening, OKH released the 12th PzD and 36th ID to Model and a new plan was created. This latest planned attack never launched for the Soviets countered on 7/11. fkk336+. lck305. dgk87m. dgr199m. lck116m. snz252.

The 6th ID, supported by assault guns, assaulted Hill 253.5 near Ponyri. Hill 274 further west was also attacked but both attacks were repulsed. The heavy fighting at Olkhovatka and Teploe continued with the Germans making minor gains. Much of the German fighting that day was defensive or tactical as Model called for a day to regroup before resuming the offensive on 7/10. During the predawn hours, 4th PzD was ordered to defend the Samodurovka-Teploe-Hill 240-Hill 234 line. In the past two days of fighting the 35th PzR of 4th PzD had lost 50 of its 90 panzers and desperately needed this day off to make some repairs. They had also used 94 tons of ammo and that needed replenishing because 4th PzD along with 2nd PzD would lead the assault the following day. Some of the front recon units near Samodurovka and Hill 238 had lost comms with HQ and that had to be corrected as well. dgr198m. fkk65. fkk101m+. dgk87m. dgr118. dgr199m. lck116m. bt86. (July 9th)

The 508th GR captured Hill 239.8, east of Ponyri. It was one of a few minor successes the Germans had all day and it gave them hope that Ponyri could be taken and kept. Before

Ponyri and Olkhovatka could be taken the fortified hill, Hill 253.5 north of Prilepy, had to be taken first. Hill 253.5 was east of Ponyri but it could not be left in Soviet control if a successful march south of Ponyri was to be accomplished. The regiment with the help of Ferdinands captured the important Hill 253.5 later in the day. Once south of this hill, the Soviets launched an attack that stopped 508th GR's advance. They fell back to Hill 253.5. With the capture of these two hills, Model anticipated his forces would soon take Ponyri and the surrounding countryside. mhz286. fkk102m. dgk87m. dgr199m. wwf54. dgk115. pck47+.

At Ponyri, the railway embankment was captured by 292nd ID then the division waited for the 18th PzD and 9th PzD to struggle with the rest of the village. The panzers did eventually take Hill 253.5 east of the village but failed to take the remaining ridge which was defended by the 1032nd RR. The Germans were in Ponyri but it was not secured. wwf54. dgk87m. dgr199m. lck116m.

Soviets were finally driven from Teploe but at great cost to the Germans. Hill 272 was still held by 3rd Antitank Brigade with dug-in T34s. Within 48 hrs, 3rd PzR and 35th PzR had captured the hill but the Soviets would not give up the hill and counter-attacked. The Germans would take the hill twice before finally losing it to the Soviets. 6th ID fought its way to the bottom of Hill 274 but could go no further. dgr198m. dgk87m. lck116m.

At Kursk, Zhukov spoke with Stalin and both agreed the German offensive was near its end and that it was time for their long-awaited offensive to start. Operation Kutuzov, the attack toward Orel, would begin on 7/11 or 7/12 at the latest. At the same time, a meeting with Model, Kluge, Harpe and Lemelsen concluded the northern attack had failed but the offensive must continue in the Olkhovatka sector to prevent Rokossovsky from sending forces south to help Vatutin. The 47th PzC would attack the high ground southwest of Olkhovatka while the other panzer divisions would attack the high ground in the Molytychi to Teploe area. mhz286. mhz19m. dgr198m. fkk336. lck306. fkk102m. zzz101m. mkz121. kfz459.

At 1830 hrs, 90 He 111s struck the Soviet lines in the center of the line that was facing 47th PzC. Results were mixed. This air attack was in preparation for the big offensive planned for next morning. cbk71. (July 9th)

The 41st PzC, while struggling with the enemy, was trying to protect the east flank of 47th PzC and remain contact with 23rd IC on its eastern flank. Rokossovsky would not allow the Germans a moment of rest; if his forces were not attacking the Germans, his artillery would shell them. The Soviets attacked the 41st PzC along the railroad east of Ponyri II. In the 23rd IC sector, the Soviets sent small raiding parties against the 78th AD and 216th ID that went into the night. In the center, the 47th PzC was defending its small gain while the 46th PzC was still in defensive mode. Model ordered a pause in the afternoon to rest and maintain the panzers for another attempt at breaking the line next morning. wdk180+. dgk87m. dgr199m. lck116m.

The 9th Army gained a couple of miles and penetrated the Soviet third defensive belt but the advance was stopped before reaching the important Olkhovatka. The 9th Army had only gained eleven miles since it started the campaign. The Tiger Battalion, sPzAbt 505, was expected to clear the way but it had failed against the horrendous shell fire of thousands of Rokossovsky's guns. sPzAbt 505 was sent into reserve for the night and the 46th PzC took its place in the line. fkk102m. dgk87m.

General Model knew by the end of the day his offensive had failed and he also anticipated an attack against 2nd PzA northeast of Orel any day. He was receiving aerial reports of the Soviets massing for an attack. He just did not have the air assets to attack the concentrations. To keep up appearances and to keep Rokossovsky from sending troops to Vatutin, the assault would continue for two more days. Rejecting Hitler's orders, Model started quietly moving forces to Orel. mkz121. lck116m.

14

July 10th on the Southern Salient

See Maps 14, 26B

The Allies landed on Sicily on this day. Hitler felt threatened and decided to cancel Operation Citadel in order to send forces to Italy. The Allies landed 160,000 men and 600 tanks on the island. Some historians say that using the Allied invasion was a way for Hitler to save face and to close down Citadel before a conclusive or disastrous result. While this was a secondary issue, Hitler sent more forces to the south and north of Kursk to help stop Soviet offensives than he sent to Italy; Orel and Mius River areas being the two most important. dgk151. lck338. lck376. gjz188. cbk74. sgf350. fmz229. zro210. asz365. zow130.

Since most of the men on the assembly lines had now been drafted, Hitler ordered that foreigners in occupied territories be sent to Germany to work in the factories.

During the predawn hours, greater numbers of tanks from 5th GTA began arriving north of Prokhorovka. Also arriving south of Oboyan was 38th Army's 204th RD. Vatutin was making it impossible to reach the town for the Germans. dgr94. dgr92m. zro207.

Von Manstein ordered Hoth before dawn to move a panzer division from 4th PzA to 3rd PzC to quicken its pace of advance. Hoth, not wanting to comply with his order, talked his way out of it as it would interfere with Panzer Order No. 5 that had already been circulated to the corps commanders. That was the order that commanded Hausser to shift the SS to the northeast toward Prokhorovka. Hoth had intended to shift directions before the campaign started and as he had always asserted it was not the result of stiff resistance in front Oboyan or the deployment of 5th GTA to the Prokhorovka sector that was his primary reason for the shift. gnk252. snk83.

Das Reich would play a mostly defensive part in the day's action as well as protecting *LAH*'s east flank. The *Deutschland* Regiment was closest to *LAH* while *Der Führer* was further south. The 167th ID was further south of *Das Reich* but would be expanding their sector so *Der Führer* could move further north. The 167th ID would complete their expansion by late afternoon. From south to north would be 331st GR and 315th GR, and 339th GR would be on the north end. The shift in 167th ID to the north was completed by the end of the day. *Der Führer* then started to move to their new sector during the predawn hours of 7/11. The redeployment for *Der Führer* was made most difficult by the constant pressure of small Soviet attacks. The panzers were in reserve not far from Ozerovski which was a mile behind the front line. On July 8th, *Das Reich* had 94 panzers but it would start the day's fight with only 56 panzers, which included only one Tiger and seven confiscated T34s. Fighting in the Solotinka area the previous day had been costly. The Soviets had the 10th TC and 5th GTC in the area and to the south the 2nd TC. The 5th GTC would be redeployed to the west along the Oboyan road that day to block the 48th PzC. The 93rd GRD also moved into the line in order for 2nd GTC to move further north. Vatutin continued to move his forces like chessmen closing in on the endgame. gnk260+. zow157.

As a tactical concern, the width of the Psel River at the bend was about 30 yards but the swampy ground on the southern banks of the river was up to 200 yards wide, making the crossing difficult while under fire. The engineers of *SSTK* would have a difficult time building bridges while under fire from ground and air forces. vzz187+.

The panzers of *Das Reich* and *LAH* had returned to the Teterevino North area after their advance to the Solotina River. That day, *LAH* would be responsible for straddling the Prokhorovka road and capturing the important rail junction. *Das Reich* would attack to the east and northeast to help relieve some of the pressure off *LAH*. At the same time *SSTK* would advance on Kochetovka and, if possible, cross the Psel River and establish a bridgehead on the northern banks. The 11th PzD on *SSTK*'s left flank would also advance, attempting to solidify the boundary between the two divisions. zrl224.

The 6th GA and 69th Army were preparing for the major assault of 2nd SS PzC. The morale of these two armies after fighting five vicious days was still good as the soldiers knew major reinforcements were about to arrive. Their boundary line was the Psel River. On the west side of the river, the 51st GRD of 6th GA was defending Hill 211.9 and Hill 207.8 while 52nd GRD was holding Hill 226.6-Polezhaev sector. The 183rd RD and the 11th MRB of 10th TC lay in front of *LAH* and *Das Reich* on the Vasilevka, Komsomolets State Farm, Ivanovski Vyselok and Storozhevoe sector. The 2nd GTC and the 6th GMRB of 5th GTC were defending the line northwest of Belenikhino to Teterevino to Zhimolostnoe. The 2nd GTC at that point had 141 working tanks. The 2nd TC had 116 working tanks which including 43 T70s and a few Churchills. vzz187. vzz8m. vzz1m. gnk253m. gnk312m. wwf110.

At 0500 hrs, the 93rd GRD started moving up to the line to face the SS Corps between Vasilevka in the west to Belenikhino in the southeast replacing 2nd GTC so that the tankers could move further south and east and have coverage of Belenikhino, Leski, Shakhovo and Dalni Dolzhik. The 89th GRD was moved to the line that included Kalinin east to the Lipovyi Donets and Hill 187.7. The 6th GA would remain stationary. The 51st GRD would defend Hill 211.9, Hill 207.8 and Ilinski. The 52nd GRD would be deployed between Hill 226.6 and Polezhaev on the northern banks of the Psel. The 285th RR of 183rd RD and the 11th MRB of 10th TC would confront *LAH* and *Das Reich* on the line: Vasilevka-Molozhavaia gully-Komsomolets State Farm-Ivanovski Vyselok-Storozhevoe. The 2nd GTC and 6th GMRB of 5th GTC held the line northwest of Belenikhino to Teterevino South to Zhimolostnoe. The 285th RR of 183rd RD would be right behind the 2nd GTC. Vatutin was well on his way to having his forces deployed for the major offensive slated for the early morning on 7/12. vzz186+. gnk312m. wwf110. zow157.

Around 0500 hrs, a small contingent of *SSTK* moved to the river to reconnoiter the northern shore and try to force the river and establish a bridgehead. The small combat group launched a probing attack at dawn that initially failed to cross the Psel. After several hours of persistent fighting, the now battalion-sized force still could not cross the Psel River. Stopping the attempt to secure a lodgment, the small combat group pulled back and waited for the rest of the grenadiers to arrive before trying to secure the northern banks. dgk164. vzz187+.

The *SSTK* was behind schedule clearing the southern banks of the Psel with the muddy conditions and the stiff resistance of the 11th MRB and 33rd RC. Eventually the leading Tigers cleared the way to the river on 7/9 and the *SSTK* formation prepared to cross and tentatively capture the village of Kliucki on the northern bank of the Psel, southeast of

Veselyi in the predawn hours. From Kliuchi the formation would then head further north on a line that included Veselyi, Hill 226.6 and Beregovoe to give further screening for *LAH* as it made its final run on Prokhorovka. The *Luftwaffe*, sparingly at first but expanding their missions as the skies cleared, preceded *SSTK*, bombing Hill 226.6 and the extended ground northwest of the bend in the Psel River. The initial attack failed due to heavy shelling coming from the hill and the grenadiers had to fall back. Priess was organizing a larger force for the second attempt at 1000 hrs in the morning. The attack force would consist of a pincer action and included Group Becker and Group Baum who would attack along the Kozlovka-Krasnyi Oktiabr sector. While the attack launched, every gun from *SSTK* and some from *LAH* would try to shut down the batteries on top of Hill 226.6. The *Luftwaffe* would support the attack. Stukas would attack the hill while ground attack aircraft would assault the defenses along the northern bank of the river. Low cloud cover and a flash thunderstorm finished the *Luftwaffe*'s participation almost from the very start. In the afternoon the cloud cover improved and Stukas were out, bombing Hill 226.6. By the end of the day a bridgehead had been established, Kliuchi had been captured and Hill 226.6 tenuously captured as well. mhz305. fkk148. fkk319m. vzz1m. gnk312m. wwf109. zrl224+. zow156+.

In an attempt to stop *SSTK* from crossing the Psel and *LAH* from reaching Prokhorovka, reserve elements of the 183rd RD supported by tanks and artillery, were brought up to defend the line: Vasilevka-Komsomolets State Farm-Ivanovski Vyselok. The 1st PzGR of *LAH*, which had been driving toward the Psel to link up with *SSTK* and solidify the front line before moving on Prokhorovka, had stopped and were regrouping before advancing. vzz189+. vzz8m. dgk167. zrl224.

A little northwest of Ivanovski Vyselok, the 183rd RD of 48th RC was defending the trench in front of Komsomolets State Farm. They were waiting for the advancing 2nd PzGR and hoping their guns would whittle the enemy down before it reached the front trenches. *Das Reich* was fighting to penetrate the Soviet positions along the Storozhevoe forest and break through to Iamki as well as protecting *LAH*'s eastern flank. Elements of Popov's 26th TB, deployed at Oktiabrski State Farm about a mile away to the north, had orders to strike toward Hill 241.6 and Hill 258.2 to the south of Komsomolets, to relieve the pressure on the 183rd RD when the Germans were encountered. This tank force, plus forces already in the area coming together, plus artillery on the Psel banks would be able to slow but not stop *LAH* from driving through the farm. The 2nd PzR of *LAH* with air support was having better luck against the Churchills and their 57mm guns than the T34s which were more prominent. The 15th GHTR moved up at 1330 hrs and momentarily slowed the Tigers further in front of Hill 241.6 but lost 11 of their 12 tanks to the Tigers and the *Luftwaffe* above. vzz192+. vzz3m. gnk253m. zow157.

At 0530 hrs, the Thule regiment of *SSTK* resumed its advance from Vasilevka and Kozlovka to the Psel River to contribute with the rest of division in crossing the important barrier. Air recon showed the Soviets were quickly erecting new defenses north of the Psel, after an earlier probing attack crossed the river but failed to establish a bridgehead. While *SSTK* was crossing the river and advancing toward Beregovoe, *LAH* would drive for the high ridge three miles east of Kartaschevka and along the line with Prokhorovka before descending on the rail town. A small combat group of *LAH* supported by a few tanks and rocket launchers had assembled in the Molozhavaia gully to the north of Komsomolets State Farm and was preparing to make another run toward Prokhorovka. Popov of 2nd TC discovered the Germans and was preparing to repulse the attack. Even with the help of the *Luftwaffe* the attack was repulsed by the artillery of 285th RR and *LAH* had to fall back to their starting point. While the defense of this section was occurring, Vatutin had initiated his own offensive to disrupt *Das Reich* from maintaining *LAH*'s eastern screen The 2nd TC was called on to make this strike. fkk147+. vzz188+. vzz8m. fkk323m. gnk253m. dgr99. zrl224.

During the predawn hours, Lt Colonel Akopov's 245th TR was attached to 52nd GRD and by 0600 hrs, was occupying the line on the northern slopes of Hill 226.6. The regiment had eight light US tanks. vzz195. gnk253m. gnk312m.

At 0600 hrs and for the next three hours, German planes, flying below the clouds, strafed the 285th RR on the northern bank to soften the Soviet defense while *SSTK* brought up more men and weapons to the river. This German deployment was slowed by muddy conditions and against heavy resistance of the 52nd GRD and artillery coming in from near Vasilevka and Andreevka. The Germans chose the location of the crossing correctly, for the bend in the river reduced the amount of flank fire but it was still difficult. As a result of prisoner interrogations, plus spotting vehicle traffic in the area the night before, reinforcements were being sent to the Psel River near Vasilevka and Andreevka. Elements of the 99th TB were sent also along with the infantry.

After repulsing the small attack of *LAH*'s shortly after daybreak, Popov's 2nd TC along with the 183rd RD charged down the Prokhorovka road into the defenses of *LAH* and *Das Reich*. The battle was fierce and the Soviets had to fall back, suffering heavy casualties. Popov would regroup and try again. Not far away to the southeast, the 2nd GTC under Burdeiny was also pulled from the line and sent to Maloe Iablonovo to regroup after suffering heavy casualties as well. The 93rd GRD took its place. When the 10th TC was ordered west to block the way of the 48th PzC to Oboyan, the 2nd TC was ordered to block the road to Prokhorovka. dgk167. wwf110. vzz188+.

Hausser ordered his 2nd SS PzC to penetrate the third defensive belt and reach the Prokhorovka Station-Hill 252.4-Beregovoe- Hill 243.5- Kartashevka- Hill 236.7 line. At this stage of attrition and with the length of the flanks that had to be defended, that task would seem nearly impossible, as during the last few days the SS had failed to accomplish the task. To meet these objectives and do it before the armored column arrived, each division would have to advance between five to eight miles that day through the third defensive belt. If these objectives could be accomplished, it would allow the 2nd SS PzC to then turn south and destroy 69th Army's 48th RC along with the help of 3rd PzC. Then the two German corps could turn north again and head for Kursk. Hill 252.4 less than two miles northeast of Prokhorovka and Hill 243.5, one mile northwest of Korytnoe, would be key objectives. *LAH* would advance toward Prokhorovka-Hill 252.4 while *Das Reich* headed for the high ground one mile southeast of Ivanovski Vyselok before turning north toward Iamki-Pravorot then Prokhorovka. The *SSTK* was to extend their bridgehead to the northeast along the Psel River. Later in the day, *Deutschland* Regiment did capture Ivanovski Vyselok after a hard fight but the assignments for *SSTK* and *LAH* were too ambitious at this stage in the campaign. *Der Führer* Regiment, south of *Deutschland*, had a longer sector to protect from Iasnaia Poliana to Nekhaevka and was unable to gain much ground. *SSTK* would follow the west bank of the Psel northward to guard *LAH*'s left flank. If possible, Schipy to the west and only six miles from Oboyan would also be captured, though neither *SSTK* nor 11th PzD ever got close to accomplishing this objective. The 48th RC under Maj General

Rogozny consisted of 183rd RD, 93rd RD and 89th RD, among other attachments that would be blocking the way. Kartashevka was two miles north of Veselyi and three miles north of Krasnyi Oktiabr. Korytnoe, which was another key objective, was about two miles north of the Kartashevka-Prokhorovka road. vzz175++*. vzz185. vzz1m. vzz130+. vzz3m. vzz11m. wwf101. dgk184m. wdk154. zrl224. dgk146.

South of Prokhorovka, heavy rains in the predawn hours prevented the attack force of *LAH* (including panzers which were having troubles in the mud) in reaching their designated launch area near Teterevino North, by 0600 hrs as planned. Wisch, the CO of *LAH*, wanted to wait for rest of his division to assemble before attacking toward Prokhorovka but was ordered by Hausser to attack as soon as the artillery preparation was over, piecemeal if he had to. Their objectives would be to clear the ground west of the railroad, Ivanovski Vyselok, the Komsomolets State Farm and Hill 241.6 located along the road to Prokhorovka, which all had to be taken to have a chance of taking Prokhorovka. While *LAH* traveled north along the railroad track toward KSF, *Deutschland* Regiment was to attack to the east toward Ivanovka and Vinogradovka. If these objectives could be taken that day and if *Das Reich* could make comparable gains, then both divisions could assault Prokhorovka together the next day. *Deutschland* gained about a mile that day but failed to reach either town. *Der Führer* also attacked but made it only to the railroad opposite Belenikhino. zow157.

Kraas's 2nd SS PzGR moved into position between Teterevino North and Ivanovski Vyselok and waited for the signal to begin its march toward Ivanovski Vyselok before moving toward the rail line, KSF, Hill 241.6 and if possible Prokhorovka. During this time, Frey's 1st PzGR was withdrawing from the Solotinka River area back to Teterevino North. When the entire coordinated 2nd SS PzC's offensive resumed later that morning, the boundary line between *LAH* and *Das Reich* included Teterevino North, the forest east of Ivanovski Vyselok, Storozhevoe and Iamki. The boundary line between *LAH* and *SSTK* included north of Teterevino, Vasilevka and the other villages running along the Psel River. The sectors were triangular with Teterevino North being a common point. zrl224.

In the early morning hours, a small Soviet squadron attacked the airfield at Vararovka, not far from Belgorod. Approaching the airfield a thunderstorm arose, making visibility difficult but the mission continued. The ambush was a complete surprise and the Germans were not prepared. The bombers and fighters destroyed a number of Junkers, including several that were trying to scramble. Though most of the Soviet planes received flak damage none were shot down. cbk74.

The defense of Ivanovski Vyselok and the Komsomolets State Farm, as well as Vasilevka and Kozlovka to the west, was critical for the Soviets as the Germans would be passing through this corridor to reach the Psel River's northern region and Kursk. Vatutin would load this sector with every gun, mortar and tank he could find to stop Hoth at this third defensive belt. The State Farm was two miles southeast of Kozlovka which was a mile south of the river and had the relative flat terrain needed by the panzers. vzz189. vzz7m.

LAH's attack toward the Prokhorovka rail embankment started late; it was 1030 hrs. *LAH* was going to reach the rail line then follow it to Prokhorovka. The 2nd PzGR was in the lead and would have to secure Ivanovkski Vyselok first. On approaching the village, two Soviet tanks rushed out from the nearby woods and tried to ambush the column. The Soviets did destroy several trucks but grenadiers, using shaped charges, destroyed both tanks. The grenadiers had at this time no panzer support. After an hour march the regiment reached the rail line then shifted to the northeast toward Prokhorovka. Within minutes the regiment, now supported by a platoon of assault guns, saw the big Komsomolets State Farm ahead. Just north of the farm was Hill 241.6 which was next to the railroad and defended by the 11th MRB. The rail embankment was as high as 30 feet above the ground in places and the Soviets exploited that height factor to the maximum. The grenadiers and guns moved onto the farm and discovered a minefield in front of it. Soviet artillery immediately started firing from Hill 241.6. The Germans were in the open and helpless but then four Tigers appeared, heading directly toward the hill. The Soviet shelling moved from the grenadiers to the Tigers, giving the soldiers time to regroup and move ahead. The engineers continued to clear the mines. Kling's Tigers were taking many hits to their front armor; it was having no effect but as the Tigers came within range of the entrenched T34s they started aiming for the thinner side skin of the panzers. The Tigers stopped and systematically destroyed each tank before moving on. gnk255+. vzz3m. vzz9m.

The southern attack by 4th PzA and Army Detachment Kempf had sufficiently reduced the forces of Vatutin's Voronezh Front to justify the release of the Soviet 5th GTA from the Steppe Front. If Vatutin had waited another day before asking for 5th GTA or if General Rotmistrov had taken longer to arrive at Prokhorovka, the chances that the combined efforts of the 2nd SS would have taken Prokhorovka by 7/12 were much improved and would have placed tremendous pressure on 69th Army, which was trying to hold back 3rd PzC driving north.

The 5th GTA started arriving in the Prokhorovka area in greater numbers that day; Rotmistrov, before his entire army had arrived, dispatched available tanks along the Psel River and positions west of Prokhorovka. He also redeployed his 40,000 men along the Psel from Oboyan to Prokhorovka. This process would take two days to complete. The 3rd PzC continued to slowly advance northward. After the earlier attack on *LAH* at the KSF, Popov's 2nd TC moved west to defend Kochetovka against the SS. While the SS was being attacked, the 1st TA disposed along the Oboyan road was preparing to move against the 48th PzC along the Pena River if the opportunity arose. dgk138+. dgk168.

Traveling at night, the 24th PzC, arrived at Belgorod from the Donbas to participate in the coming attack on Prokhorovka if so ordered. je105*.

As two of the divisions of 2nd SS PzC were heading for Prokhorovka along both banks of the Psel River, it was down to less than 300 panzers while 3rd PzC to the southeast was down to less than 200. Rotmistrov's 5th GTA which was moving toward this area would have 830-850 tanks, including its new attachments. To the west, the 48th PzC and 1st TA collectively had another 700. In the next few days, as many as 1,250 tanks would fight along the eastern flank of the Kursk salient and about 570 on the field immediately west and south of Prokhorovka, mostly between the Psel and Lipovyi Donets Rivers. These tank numbers do not include the hundreds battling against each other in 48th PzC sector. dgk151+. dgk222m. dlu63m. zpm195.

Lt Col Malov's 99th TB and Col Borodkin's 11th MRB counter-attacked *SSTK* and by 1100 hrs had pushed the Germans back from Prokhorovka, Kozlovka and parts of Vasilevka, foiling *SSTK*'s attempt to expand their bridgehead and link up with *LAH*. The Prokhorovka mentioned above was between Krasnyi Oktiabr and Kozlovka and was a different village six miles west of THE legendary Prokhorovka (Station). vzz189. vzz5m. dgk164. dgk165m.

At 1030 hrs, the *LAH* launched their main attack toward Prokhorovka. Group Becker headed straight for the southwestern corner of Komsomolets State Farm while Group Sandig headed east toward the rail line before turning north. At the same time, *SSTK* launched another more aggressive attack toward Kozlovka and Vasilevka in order to keep the Soviets from concentrating their artillery on *LAH* and hopefully to keep Vatutin from sending reinforcements there as well. *SSTK* was met by a Soviet counter-attack by the 99th TB and the 11th MRB which drove the Germans back from Kozlovka. vzz189. zrl227.

The start time was delayed by four hours due to the heavy rains that slowed both grenadier regiments of *LAH* in reaching their individual start points. After refueling, the 1st PzGR began its drive toward Prokhorovka from near Sukhno Solotino at 1045 hrs. Hausser deliberately gave the regiment a late start because of the heavy fighting it had been in the previous day. By 1300 hrs and having been constantly attacked by Popov's 2nd TC, the *LAH* regiment finally reached and stormed the Komsomolets State Farm from the southwest. The left flank of 2nd PzGR had already engaged the defenders from the south and east and together both regiments were finally pushing the defenders off the Farm. Immediately afterward the division attacked the fortified Hill 241.6 with its many dug-in tanks. There was no time for rest; the grenadiers had to silence those guns that were causing so much damage. The Tigers in the division had already begun to attack the hill in order to reduce the shelling of the grenadiers at the farm. Being greatly outnumbered, the remaining four Tigers took on a host of T34s in front of the hill. Vatutin had anticipated the attack toward Prokhorovka and during the night deployed every gun that could be rounded up to prevent the Germans from reaching Prokhorovka. In spite of Vatutin's efforts, by 1630 hrs the hill was in German hands. They counted 53 tanks and 23 Pak guns destroyed on the hill, in addition to 197 POWs captured. Before the hill could be manned and defenses improved, sappers cleared mines from the approaches. A total of 367 mines encased in wood were cleared. *LAH* lost 26 killed, 168 wounded and 3 missing in today's fighting. mhz306. mhz314. fkk87. dgk166. vzz8m. gnk253m. gnk312m. zrl224. zrl230. dgk165m. zow156.

The infantry of *LAH* made little progress in advancing toward Prokhorovka as Soviet artillery on the Psel River and to the east at Vinogradovka were deadly accurate. The 2nd PzGR made it to the railroad northeast of Teterevino North and drove another mile toward Prokhorovka. Despite being attacked by the recently arrived 183rd RD, 10th TC and the 93rd GRD, this regiment was able to join up with *SSTK* by nightfall. The panzer regiment of *LAH* was fighting to the east in the Malye Maiachki and Gresnoe area where they pushed back the Soviet defenders another three miles. wdk151.

At the Komsomolets State Farm, Kling's Tigers (one had turret damage and was only partially functioning) crossed over the tank ditch the engineers had filled in and were initially aiming their anger at the bunkers in front of the State Farm. The grenadiers and assault guns shifted direction, cutting across the farm and advanced on Hill 241.6 which seemed the more dangerous of the two positions and by 1430 hrs Hill 241.6 was in German control and being fortified against counter-attacks. Some of the Soviet defenders surrendered while others were able to escape. gnk257. gnk260. zrl227.

By mid morning, *Das Reich* resumed its difficult advance to the northeast from east of Teterevino North, trying to cross the Prokhovrovka rail line to reach Storozhevoe. After a hard day's fight, it failed to reach its objective but managed to reach and secure Ivanoski Vyselok, a small village lodged in a long ravine south of Prokhorovka road and just southwest of Storozhevoe. To facilitate the coming tank battle, the last regiment of 167th ID moved from Pokrovka, west of Luchki, to the Lipovyi Donets to relieve *Der Führer* of *Das Reich* protecting the southern flank of the Lipovyl Donets line, in order that the full division could participate in the battle for Prokhorovka. dgk166. dgk184m. dgk95m. dgk222m. dlu63m. dgr209m. vzz3m. gnk253m.

Das Reich had troubles also. Its drive toward the village of Storozhevoe was slow with the heavy resistance of 2nd TC, fighting them every inch of the way. *Das Reich* was ordered toward Storozhevoe to relieve pressure off *LAH* at Komsomolets and to assist *LAH* in the final run for Prokhorovka. mhz306. mhz314. fkk87. vzz8m. gnk253m. gnk312m.

Throughout the morning, the *LAH* made repeated attempts to take Komsomolets State Farm, just northwest of Ivanovski Vyselok, but were repulsed by fierce shelling from the 99th TB, 11th MRB and the 1502nd DAR, located on the left bank of the Psel River. The 26th TB also supported from near Hill 241.6 which was a mile south of Andreevka on the southern banks of the Psel River. Eventually *LAH* broke through the line near Hill 258.2, defended by 285th RR, and headed for Ivanovski Vyselok. The 26th TB deployed just north of the KSF and Hill 258.2 sent tanks, which included Churchills, to block the SS from reaching their objective but the tanks could not stop the Tigers leading the assault and eventually the two hills and state farm were captured. vzz192+. vzz8m. dgk167.

West of the corridor several hours after the recon force tried to breach the river, the two infantry regiments of *SSTK* attacked across the Psel to secure a tentative hold on the bridgehead before seizing Hill 226.6, the key high ground just east of the small fortified village of Kliuchi. The advance was slow against the 52nd GRD and 11th MRB. This failure of a quick expansion of the bridgehead north of the Psel made it difficult for *LAH* to drive northeast, forcing Hausser to delay the larger attack planned that included *LAH*'s drive on Prokhorovka. By noon, *SSTK* was free and had secured a foothold on the river's northern bank east of Kliuchi and the rest of the corps resumed its attack. Hausser rushed *LAH* in attacking toward Prokhorovka when the division was not properly prepared and they paid for that impatience. Having waited another four hours would have given the General better results. The Soviets paid a high price for their assault the previous day and were not prepared for another attack if the division had attacked as one. dgk164. dgk124m. dgk222m. lck326. gnk312m. wwf99 ztc269. dgk165m.

When *SSTK* failed to take Hill 226.6 during the previous night, the *LAH* combat group had to wait to see if it was captured during daylight. That morning *LAH* was concerned that if it launched from Hill 241.6 (not yet captured) toward Prokhorovka, the Soviet artillery on Hill 226.6 would find them. Despite the concerns, *LAH* could not wait any longer and at approximately 1100 hrs began their advance anyway. By 1300 hrs, the 2nd PzGR reached and was fighting for Hill 241.6 and the woods next door to the east. In front of the hill a long line of dug-in tanks were waiting for the coming attack. Tigers were in the lead and started firing AP shells against the tanks and HE rounds against the MG bunkers. The fighting was fierce but with the help of the Tigers, the 2nd PzGR captured the hill by 1630 hrs. Hill 241.6 was about a mile due south of Andreevka which was on the southern bank of the Psel River. This hill was critical for the Germans for it was a great OP and an equally good launching point to attack Hill 252.2 and Prokhorovka. The 1st PzGR had a hard day the previous day, in gaining control of Sukho Solotino so Hausser gave them the morning to regroup. agk122+. vzz1m. wwf100. zrl227.

Since the day before, *Das Reich* had been struggling to capture Kalinin, east of the Lipovyi Donets River and not far from Ozerovski. A regiment from 167th ID moved into positions in the Kalinin area to relieve *Das Reich* so it could shift direction to the northeast in order to concentrate its power toward Storozhevoe and Iamki. It would also take some of the pressure off *LAH* as the 10th MC and 5th GMC were attacking them along the Prokhorovka road. Other elements of 167th ID were fighting in the Shopino area, about six miles north of Belgorod, against the 81st GRD and 375th RD, in order to relieve some of the pressure off 3rd PzC. A small group from *Das Reich*'s right flank had actually made it across the Lipovyi Donets near Petrovski and were fighting against the same two Soviet divisions. The German pressure in this area, along with the recent success of 6th PzD and 19th PzD along the Donets, was an important contributing factor causing the 69th Army to begin their retreat to the north. The *SSTK*, fighting for control of both southern and northern banks of the Psel, were meeting up with the 5th GA which was beginning to enter the sector. wdk152. vzz3m. dgr86m. dgr93m. vzz7m.

While in the field in the late morning, Staudegger, the hero at Teterevino North two days earlier, received his Knight's Cross. He was then flown to Prussia to see Hitler before going on leave. agk123.

At about the same time, the 2nd PzGR was fighting its way toward Hill 241.6. The remainder of the two grenadier regiments of *SSTK* were working their way across the Psel River to bolster the forces already over there. Once across the river and after securing the bridgehead, Hill 226.6 and Kliuchi would be targeted. German intelligence had identified seven batteries of assorted guns on and behind that hill that could reach both *SSTK* and *LAH*. Slowing the redeployment even further were the heavy rains that turned dirt roads and the countryside to deep mud. Not only the panzers but the artillery batteries would be late arriving at their jump points. Priess of *SSTK* calculated that it would be 1000 hrs before the remainder of his regiments would move across the river, that was hours later than both Hoth and Hausser expected. The village of Kliuchi, southwest of the hill and Hill 226.6 itself were also prime targets for the *Luftwaffe* when cloud cover lifted. Besides the heavy rains during the predawn hours, the skies were so overcast in the early morning that the *Luftwaffe* could not fly. Even with the repair crews working throughout the night, *LAH* had only 45 assorted panzers operational for the day's attack. Forcing the river, securing a bridgehead and capturing Hill 226.6 in quick succession was a necessity if *SSTK* was going to provide flank protection to *LAH*, but they got a late start and would run further behind schedule as the day wore on. Though capturing their targets, the division was running hours behind schedule and it threw off the entire SS's timetable as the *SSTK* were supposed to drive north in parallel with *LAH* to protect their flank. vzz176.+ gnk254+. gnk253m. vzz1m. zrl227.

At 1200 hrs *SSTK* launched a larger attack to force the Psel but failed the first attempt due to heavy shelling and small arms fire. With the support of the mortar teams to suppress SA fire from the north bank, and using rubber rafts, the shock troops succeeded in crossing the river north of Kozlovka by 1700 hrs and within an hour had secured the first trench line of the village of Kliuchi. *SSTK* made modest gains that day as Vatutin made it difficult to cross the Psel and had blocked the German advance from reaching Kartashevka, which would be *SSTK*'s anchor point before turning east to help *LAH* with Prokhorovka. Once Kartashevka was secured, the *SSTK* had planned on crossing the Psel to the east side at Petrovka which was only three miles northwest of Prokhorovka. Once on the east side *SSTK* could screen *LAH*'s west flank. vzz196. gnk263. vzz11m. fxk311. vzz244.

Since 0600 hrs, *LAH* was taking heavy shelling from the west bank of the Psel River and from the southeast area of Vinogradovka. Despite this shelling a combat group of 2nd

PzGR made it to the railroad line due west of Belenikhino. Reaching this point spurred greater Soviet tank assaults from the direction of Storozhevoe. The *LAH* was still able to reach Hill 241.6 against the fierce resistance of 285th RR (183rd RD) by 1400 hrs, capturing it later that afternoon and by dusk they had reached the woods directly north of Storozhevoe. The 169th TB was also pressured and fell back from Ivanovski Vyselok but the *LAH* was stopped by the tanks defending the route north of Stalinskoe State Farm. *LAH* also expanded its left flank in order to make contact with *SSTK* for the night when 1st PzGR resumed its advance in the afternoon. The Stalinskoe State Farm was southeast of Hill 252.2 and on the fringe of the northeast corner of Storozhevoe Forest. fkk149. vzz1m. vzz8m. vzz176. vzz191. gnk326. gnk253m. gnk323m.

The Pz Abt 3 of *SSTK*, fighting its way into Kochetovka, joined forces with 11th PzD at the church near the center of the town as ordered. zow157.

As ordered, the *LAH* panzers resumed their attack northward while the grenadiers of *Das Reich* attacked east toward Vinogradovka, about four miles southwest of Prokhorovka. *Das Reich* and two regiments of 167th ID would maintain pressure on the Lipovyi Donets to pin down the 2nd GTC, the 375th GRD and 81st GRD while 3rd PzC moved north. *SSTK* would continue for the high ground on both sides of the Psel northwest of Prokhorovka. After completing the heavy bridge on the 11th (1420 hrs) it would then move toward Petrovka along the corridor's edge, also northwest of Prokhorovka. The 48th PzC continued to battle 6th TC in its attempt to reach Oboyan. wdk150. dgk222m. dlu63m. lck328. kuz195.

Hill 226.6 was the important high ground east of the village of Kliuchi which was also defended by the 52nd GRD and the 11th MRB. The first attack on the hill failed but by early afternoon and despite the muddy conditions from the predawn rain, *SSTK* secured a small lodgment at its base. It was a precarious position and the division had to crest the top if it did not want to be destroyed. Meanwhile the garrison at Kliuchi was preventing *SSTK* from advancing northward along the western edge of the sector. While Kliuchi was in enemy hands, *SSTK* would have to worry about flank attacks and though the critical timetable was already behind schedule, the time would have to be invested in taking the strongpoint on the western edge of the line if Soviet flank attacks were to be prevented. More of the *SSTK* division finally was crossing the Psel and expanding the small bridgehead on the north side toward Kliuchi. Still more of the division would have to cross before expanding the bridgehead to beyond Hill 226.6. The *LAH* had to postpone their launch until almost noon, to make sure *SSTK* would make it across the river and keep the Soviets busy so they would not attack *LAH*'s left flank when it made its final run on Prokhorovka. wwf100. dgk222m. lck325. gnk253m. gnk312m. nzk94. vzz1m. vzz8m. vzz244.

It was not until nearly 1400 hrs that *Deutschland (Das Reich)* was able to launch their attack to the northeast. They were to move north and screen *LAH*'s east flank as it drove past Hill 241.6 which had just fallen. *LAH* had to attack with an exposed east flank; the Soviets took full advantage of this and it cost *LAH* greatly. *Das Reich* did not go far before the Soviets, hiding in the Storozhevoe woods, ambushed them and slowed their advance further. This lack of coordinated effort by these two divisions is another example of the Germans costing themselves assets that they could not afford to lose. gnk263. gnk253m. vzz10m.

In the afternoon the skies cleared and the *Luftwaffe* was able to support *SSTK* in forming a bridgehead on the north side of the Psel and advance a modest way. The bridgehead centered on the light bridge erected by engineers and extended a half mile directly northwest of Mikhailovka to Hill 226.6, northeast of Bogoroditskoe, and Kliuchi. Kliuchi was a half mile east of Krasnyi Oktiabr. fkk149. vzz1m. vzz176. vzz191. gnk312m.

By 1200 hrs, the *LAH* advance that had started near the Teterevino North area to the northeast had cleared the bend in the rail line leading to Prokhorovka, and by 1400 hrs, from the railroad embankment, the 2nd PzGR of *LAH* had been able to penetrate the first trench in front of Komsomolets State Farm against the 169th TB of 2nd TC, although it was then held up. After fighting for three more hours, KSF and Hill 241.6, just north of the Farm and sitting beside the rail line, was captured despite fierce shelling by the Soviets from several hilltops and repeated tank attacks originating from the Stalinskoe State Farm. The Soviet line from Ivanovski Vyselok to Storozhevoe was still being held by 1400 hrs but *Das Reich* continued to increase the pressure and Ivanovski Vyselok was teetering. vzz189+. vzz8m. dgk167. vzz196. zrl227.

By 1500 hrs, the 2nd PzR of *LAH* drove the 285th RR from the west front trenches of Komsomolets State Farm, clearing the farm as it headed north. At the same time, the lead Tigers of *LAH* approached Hill 241.6 to the immediate northeast of KSF while the 2nd PzGR continued to attacked the rear of 285th RR and 169th TB, which had redeployed in the woods north of the Farm. Soviet tanks coming from Stalinsk to the north rushed to support the 169th TB but after four hours of hard fighting were unable to reach the crest of Hill 241.6 and the remainder of 285th RR had to fall back to the 99th TB's position at Vasilevka. The *LAH* was also able to force the tankers to abandon Ivanovski Vyselok and head for Storozhevoe. Losing Komsomolets and Ivanovski Vyselok was a serious threat for the Soviet defenses in front of Prokhorovka, less than six miles away, but Storozhevoe was still holding even though *Das Reich* continued to fight for it until midnight, as did *SSTK*, for greater control of the bridgehead. The Germans moved quickly onto the ground just evacuated by moving along the railroad embankment, using its 20-foot height for cover. vzz191+. vzz196*. vzz8m. dgk171.

While the two grenadier regiments of *SSTK* were securing a bridgehead on the northern shore of the Psel River, the panzer regiment had rolled in to Krasnyi Poliana from Gresnoe. Without a bridge to cross the Psel, the panzers were isolated. The Pioneer Regiment 680 after pausing at Gresnoe earlier in the day had been shelled shortly after leaving Gresnoe for the river. They had to wait the shelling out in a ravine and were late in arriving at the river to assist with bridge building duties. gnk268. gnk253m. fzk311.

The bulk of *SSTK* had moved to the corps' left flank and had crossed the Psel north of Kozlovka, resuming its attack at 1600 hrs under air support and light rain against Group Pantiukhov's 52nd GRD in the bend of the river. The first penetration of the trenches of 155th GRR occurred a mile southeast of Kliuchi. The Soviet regiment could not withstand the pressure of the larger force and had to fall back toward the woods northeast of Oktiabrski State Farm. A half hour later at 1800 hrs, lead elements of *SSTK* advanced toward Kliuchi which was defended by the 151st GRR. A brief but vicious battle erupted but the 151st GRR also had to fall back. Once Kliuchi fell, the *SSTK* headed for Veselyi. From Kliuchi, Group Baum attacked the nearby woods. Group Becker headed for Hill 226.6. Hill 226.6, northeast of Kliuchi, was reached by midnight. Though 52nd GRD was pushed back from its front trenches it, along with the attached 245th TR, gave up ground grudgingly and did stop *SSTK* from taking Hill 226.6. At 2030 hrs, Hausser was informed that *SSTK* established a bridgehead at Krasbyi Oktiabr and had linked up with 11th PzD at

Kochetovka. Hausser ordered the panzers and heavy equipment to cross the river that night so that the division could attack early next morning. There was still a strong contingent in the Kliuchi area and after regrouping the Soviets would counter-attack the village later that day. Kliuchi was located on the northern banks of the Psel River across from Krasnyi Oktiabr. vzz193+. vzz195+. vzz1m. vzz8m. gnk312m.

Under an umbrella of heavy artillery and air support, the *SSTK* had forced a crossing of the Psel River and then created a small bridgehead on the north side at the same time as other members of *SSTK* captured the villages on the southern banks of Vasilevka, Kozlovka and Krasnyi Oktabyr, all within six hours. While fighting on the north side of the river the artillery and the rest of *SSTK*, despite the pouring rain, came across as well. The *Eicke* regiment engaged the critical Hill 226.6 and eventually secured part of the hill by evening. Stukas continued to fly missions as late as possible to soften up the remainder of the hill. *SSTK* suffered 430 casualties that day, the highest total for any day in the campaign. mhz306.

Late in the afternoon the rain stopped in the Prokhovoka sector and the skies improved to partly cloudy. Stukas took to the air but by this time, the day's heavy fighting was history. The *LAH* suffered heavy casualties on this day, having 197 either killed or wounded, and gained less than two miles in most places. gnk257. gnk260.

In the *Das Reich* sector, east of *LAH*, the division continued to repulse repeated attacks in the Belenikhino and Kalinin areas. An attack by *Deutschland* Regiment was able to reach the bend in the railroad line near Ivanovski Vyselok. At night and in preparation of aiding *LAH* in the morning, the right flank of *Das Reich* was relieved by the 331st IR of 167th ID. In addition, the rear area of *Das Reich* had made contact with 11th PzD earlier in the day and now occupied the line Hill 227.0-Hill 235.9-Hill 248.3 and the road fork on Hill 232.8 at Kochetovka. The entire 167th ID was ordered to move up closer to the right flank of *Das Reich* to safeguard its flank when it attacked in the morning. fkk149+. lck327. fkk323m.

Trierenberg's 167th ID moved into defensive positions along the railway line, just north of Luchki South. With the help of the *Luftwaffe* the division was able to hold off repeated attacks by Soviet tanks. The division had no panzer support and had to rely on its artillery to stop the tank attacks. pck77.

After attacking Kliuchi, the *SSTK* Recon Battalion heads for Veselyi, which was about a mile to the north, to inspect the battlefield but were stopped before reaching it. vzz194. vzz1m.

With the Germans threatening Prokhorovka, the 24th Army and 4th TC moved to Kursk to stop the advancement if the Germans made it pass Prokhorovka.

At 1930 hrs Regiment CO, Becker, radios Priess (*SSTK*) informing him that the bridgehead was established and that the lead units were at the foot of Hill 226.6 and would continue to fight for the hill during the night. Just before dark, the *Luftwaffe* finally showed to help the grenadiers with Hill 226.6. Panzers were still on the southern bank of this shallow river, waiting for the bridges to be completed. Without the panzers and with cloudy skies to prevent heavy use of air support, the infantry had to rely on mortar and artillery fire for support. Though the *Luftwaffe* was hesitant to fly, the Red Air Force flew many missions against *SSTK* that day. Later in the evening, Soviet defenders began to back away from the river, allowing the Germans to modestly enlarge the bridgehead and begin sending more forces across the river. *SSTK* still had 78 panzers working plus a few assault guns. gnk267. gnk253m. vzz1m. vzz8m.

By 2100 hrs while *SSTK* was securing Kliuchi and a recon team was advancing on Veselyi, the rest of the division was establishing a small bridgehead at Krasnyi Oktiabr on the north side of the Psel. Other members of *SSTK* made contact with 11th PzD. It had been a hard day for *SSTK*; it lost 430 men. It was the worst single loss of the campaign for the division. The day was cloudy and rainy but the roads remained usable (barely) in this area which allowed *SSTK* to stay active. After dark, the Soviets made repeated attacks on the fledgling bridgehead and for a while it looked like *SSTK* would be pushed into the river but it held on to a small piece of turf. That night the light panzers, trucks and guns were sent across the river; Priess wanted his division to get an early start in the morning in expanding the bridgehead. vzz194. nzk94. ztc269. zrl227. dgk164+.

Additional reserve units were coming up to the line. Vatutin sensed a climax was coming and he brought up as many resources as he had along the line between Oboyan and Prokhorovka. In this small area, he had 850 tanks and would try to encircle and destroy his enemy. je106. rkz168.

During the night, the 7th GAAR of Col Sazonov's 9th GAD, which was located at Staryi Oskol, was ordered to the Prokhorovka area to the left of the rail line by 0400 hrs next morning. It was a 75 mile trip but the regiment made it thanks to the Studebaker trucks they were driving. They had to erect defenses and communications from scratch but they were ready by 0700 hrs on 7/11. The rest of the division would be dug-in in front of Prokhorovka by the next night. vzz239+. vzz9m. wwf110.

In the SS sector by the end of the day, the Soviets controlled the area east and southeast of Teterevino North, the area just outside of Leski and Belenikhino, the area just outside of Vinogradovka and the area south and north of the railroad west of Storozhevoe and east of Hill 241.6. The Soviets were hugging the German line, not giving anything away for free. fkk150. fkk320m. fkk232m. vzz8m.

Determined to take Prokhorovka, Hausser, late at night, renewed his orders for both the 1st PzGR and 2nd PzGR of *LAH* to attack toward the important rail station in the morning. The Germans had to gain control of the rail line and the corridor leading to Kursk and Prokhorovka had to be theirs if it were to fall. For *Das Reich* to support *LAH* better, the 167th ID was ordered again to increase their sector to the north so that *Das Reich* could reduce their sector and concentrate more force in the Storozhevoe area. *SSTK*, which was currently in the Gresnoe area, was ordered to clear the villages along the southern bank of the Psel River and prepare to secure the bridgehead on the north side. wwf101+. vzz8m.

By the end of the day, von Manstein summarized his Army's results. The first two days of battle saw penetration of the first two defense belts. On the third day, 48th PzC broke into open territory about six miles from Oboyan and headed for the third defense belt. Soviet reinforcements started arriving to the line in greater numbers on this third day. On 7/11, the 2nd SS PzC was north of the Psel River and making a final drive on Prokhorovka. fkk151.

The Soviet counter-attacks in the areas where the Germans had made inroads in the south were increasing and the German advance was petering out. The Soviets took back Novyi Oskol in the south, among several other important villages along the Psel River. Even without the influence of 5th GA and 5th GTA, Soviet resistance had dramatically slowed the Germans along practically the entire battle sector. Nothing had been easy that day and it would get a lot harder once the two Soviet armies deployed.

The Germans made few gains on this day while Soviet reserves continued to build up. Von Manstein still saw Oboyan as the primary initial objective, while the 2nd SS PzC would be tasked with destroying the newly arrived 69th Army. He also had to have Kempf and Raus catch up if they were to be successful. With this in mind, von Manstein had canceled the advance on Korocha to the east and directed Kempf more to the west to assist 2nd SS PzC. Von Manstein also wanted the 24th PzC to join the fighting by 7/17 on the east flank of 4th PzA. He was also trying to get the 8th PzD and 12th PzD into the sector as well as infantry from 2nd Army which was to the west. It would be a difficult job to persuade Hitler to release any of these units. The original plan to reach Korocha was a mistake strategically and waiting this long to change the plan was also a mistake. After the first few days of experiencing heavy resistance from 7th GA, von Manstein should have made changes. wdk154. aaa124m+. snk424m+++. dgk113. dgk146. hjj123m.

Along the Prokhorovka road after briefly regrouping, the 2nd TC counter-attacked again and became enmeshed in a running battle with *LAH* and *Das Reich*. By the end of the day, the Soviet defenders were pushed back from Hill 241.6 and the nearby Komsomolets State Farm. During the night, the bulk of 5th GA arrived to support Popov. Sazonov's 9th GAD, which would play an important role over the next few days, started arriving that night and began digging defenses in front of Prokhorovka. The 33rd GRC of 5th GA was brought up to block the path of 2nd SS PzC. Its 95th GRD and 97th GRD dug in directly behind the shattered 51st GRD and 52nd GRD to the west of 9th GAD. Maj General Bobrov's 42nd GRD, which was held in reserve, prepared to assist either of these divisions or the nearby 9th GAD. Vatutin also ordered greater air support in order to prevent any expansion of the northern bridgehead. With the Soviets concentrating on 2nd SS PzC a slight relief was given to 48th PzC. After dark, the 183rd RD shifted position to relieve the 5th GTA in order that it could move over to bolster 1st TA. dgk167*. dgk130m. snk82. gnk260. vzz322. gnk284. gnk293. gnk193m. wwf110. gnk227m.

LAH, advancing between the Prokhorovka road and the railroad, made good progress until reaching the first trench in front of the Komsomolets State Farm but eventually captured KSF by 1500 hrs. It was a major win for *LAH* for it set up the division to move on Hill 241.6 and then Hill 252.2. After KSF they shifted a little east and assaulted Hill 241.6 and initially were stopped by tanks that were dug-in, but by nightfall with the help of Tigers the Hill fell to the Germans. The *LAH* had destroyed 53 tanks, 23 guns and captured a few prisoners. The Komsomolets State Farm was two miles south of Kozlovka and the village was one mile south of the bend of the Psel where *SSTK* was planning on crossing in force. Hill 241.6 was a little northeast of Komsomolets State Farm and defended by 11th MRB which was also being attacked by the 2nd PzGR. After both KSF and Hill 241.6 were captured, the entire 2nd PzGR moved up to the line between the hill and the rail line and began building new defenses against the counter-attacks that would be coming. The line west of Hill 241.6 all the way to the *SSTK* boundary was more thinly defended but was more stable after the successes of 1st PzGR made the day before. Though both *LAH* and *SSTK* made few gains today, they were critical ones that would help the divisions assault in the morning. It would be another tough day driving deeper into the third defense belt. dgk166+. snk81. wwf100+. vzz187++. vzz8m. lck327.

By the end of the day, Soviet forces exhausted as ever, knew the Germans could not win. In the north since the start of the campaign, the Germans gained only twelve miles on a ten mile front while in the south, the Germans gained 30 miles on a 30 mile front. The two

German fronts were still over 50 miles from each other. jp169.

By the end of the day, 4th PzA had gained up to 30 miles since the start of the campaign and had crossed the Psel, establishing a small bridgehead before moving toward Oboyan but certain generals knew the assault was nearly over and their objectives would never be met. wwf90.

The 2nd SS PzC gained only two or three miles on this day but it had several successes. It captured the Komsomolets State Farm, captured Hill 241.6 and it established a small bridgehead on the northern banks of the Psel. Lt General Kriuchenkin of 69th Army had no further reserves so during the night he had to redeploy active forces from other areas to these two key hot spots. He sent Morozov's 81st GRD to help 48th RC along the line: Hill 147.0-Volobuevka-Sazhnoe-Krivtsevo-Shcholokovo. He was in second echelon and was ordered to prepare to counter, along with 2nd GTC, in the direction Belenikhovo and Malye Maiachki into the left flank of *Das Reich* when the order was given. Volobuevka was near the eastern bank of the Lipovyi Donets River, north of Rozhdestvenka.

The 81st GRD only had 3500 men so it was reinforced with the 227th RR of 183rd RD by moving 18 miles into a flanking position on the line at Storozhevoe-Vinogradovka-Zhimolostroe to protect Prokhorovka Station and in preparation for if a counter-attack was ordered. This attack would hit the flank of the *LAH* driving through their main axis of Komsomolets State Farm-Hill 241.6-Oktiabrski State Farm. The *LAH* suffered casualties of almost 200 soldiers but it destroyed a claimed 76 tanks and assault guns as well as capturing a few POWs. Shchlolkovo straddled the Donets River about three miles south of Ryndinka. dgr102. dgk165m. gnk253m. vzz196++. wwf101. vzz12m.

The previous day had been pretty good for 4th PzA and the salient had grown to 25 miles long, but it was running out of fuel and ammunition and its men were exhausted. Though important objectives had been captured, the progress on this day was minimal and Maj General von Mellenthin wrote in his journal: "It could no longer be doubted that the back of the German attack had been broken and its momentum gone." wwf90.

By the end of the day, the German salient that Hoth was excavating had not grown much. The 48th PzC had reached just south of Kruglik, Kalinovka and Kochetovka while *SSTK* had secured more of the southern bank of the Psel. *LAH* was now at Komsomolets State Farm and just west of the Storozhevoe. *Das Reich* was just outside Belenikhino.

Vatutin ordered his forces to prepare for a major counter-attack on either 7/11 or 7/12 at the latest. The 6th TC, 10th TC, 31st TC, 3rd MC, 5th GTC, 204th RD and 309th RD would attack south toward the Kruglik-Olkhovatka line and once reaching Novenkoe, shift direction and head for Iakovlevo-Pokrovka area to meet up with 6th GA and 5th GTA in order to encircle a large portion of 4th PzA. dgr219.

While the *LAH* moved towards Prokhorovka, trying to capture the important rail junction before 5th GTA could intervene, the *SSTK* moved into the Corps' left flank, crossed the Psel River and by dusk had taken Krasnyi Oktiabr and set up a small bridgehead. After dark, while the divisions were making preparations and General Hausser completed last minute details for the attack on Prokhorovka the next morning, General von Manstein tried to commit 24th PzC from reserves to assist in taking Prokhorovka but Hitler refused. rkz168. pck77. pck83.

In the south, the 8th *Flieger* Corps flew only 682 sorties. nzk77.

During the predawn hours, Maj General Getman's 6th TC along with the weakened 90th GRD, the 3rd MC's 1st TB and 10th TB regrouped along the Psel River and southward along the Pena River. Vatutin knew the 48th PzC was exhausted and was planning on exploiting it. These Soviet forces were nearly prepared when *GD*'s panzers showed up. The 10th TC moved a little south and deployed along the Kruglik-Kalinovka line and across the Oboyan road in support of the remnants of the 3rd MC (1st GTB, 49th TB, 3rd MB). The 5th GTC was also attached to the 1st TA and deployed in the Zorinskie Dvory and Orlovka areas. Vatutin released the 204th RD from reserve and sent it over to the 1st TA to block 48th PzC from reaching Kruglik. dgr217. wwf103.

Burkov's 10th TC was also brought up to reinforce the shattered 1st TA north of Novoselovka. During the previous day's battle, Knobelsdorff of 48th PzC noticed the weakness between 6th TC and 3rd MC near the road to Oboyan and moved forces during the night to the area. The 6th TC had no more than 100 tanks left but during the night 10th TC would move in behind and add another 120 tanks to the coming battle. The 48th PzC and its attached 10th PzB was down to below 200 running panzers. During the predawn hours, the 5th GTC also arrived to block 48th PzC's advance on the Oboyan road. Vatutin was making sure that Knobelsdorff would never make it to Oboyan. gnk242. wwf111. dgk152+. dgk222m. dgr209m. wwf103.

During the predawn hours, additional reinforcements arrived from outside the sector to bolster 6th TC. The 60th TR from 38th Army and 66th GMR plus others from 40th Army arrived to solidify the line north of Verkhopenie. At thismoment, Verkhopenie and Kalinovka were unoccupied.

With the support of the *Luftwaffe*, the panzer grenadiers of 48th PzC launched an attack against the high ground south of Kruglik and against the road leading north through Kruglik. Both were being defended by 6th TC. While the rest of 4th PzA, under Hoth, attacked in the direction of the Psel River and Prokhorovka, elements of *GD* broke through to the north on the road to Oboyan, inflicting heavy casualties. lck322. hsz128.

The *GD*, though exhausted, had continued to swing to the southwest to defend from the ever increasing threat on its flank, as the 3rd PzD was not up to the task. This slowed its northward progress. Their new objectives were Hill 243.0, northwest of Verkhopenie, and further west Hill 247.0, south of Kruglik. After taking the high ground, *GD* moved to the forests north of Berezovka to help the 3rd PzD at Hill 251.5 and Hill 247.0 who were stymied by stiff resistance. It smashed into the blocking Soviet force and together the *GD* panzers and 3rd PzD broke through the Soviet line. The Soviet tankers defending those hills fell back to those same woods near Berezovka. The *Luftwaffe* came in to support. The rest of *GD* was ordered to standby on Hill 260.8 along the Oboyan road and 3rd PzD took over the lead flanking position. This was stretching 3rd PzD's capacities as Tolstoe woods was a Soviet strongpoint where many attacks against the 3rd PzD were initiated from. The 52nd IC was then to move up as well. dgk157. fkk270+. fkk321m. gnk253m. nzk94. wwf103. fmz225+. fmz221m. fmz224m. hsz127.

During this cloudy and rainy day, Col Dremin's fresh 309th RD moved up to support the shattered 3rd MC and the recently arrived 5th GTC, along the Oboyan road. Knobelsdorff of 48th PzC detected the weak junction between 6th TC and 3rd MC and throughout the night shifted forces of *GD* and 3rd PzD to attack it at daybreak. The remaining 11th PzD would have responsibility in advancing on the Oboyan road to protect *GD*'s western and southern movements. The 11th PzD's 110th PzGR had deployed on Hill 232.8 and stayed in contact with *GD*, stationed just outside of Kalinovka. The 111th PzGR was defending east of Hill 244.8 to the Melovoe Woods. Mickl's panzer group was

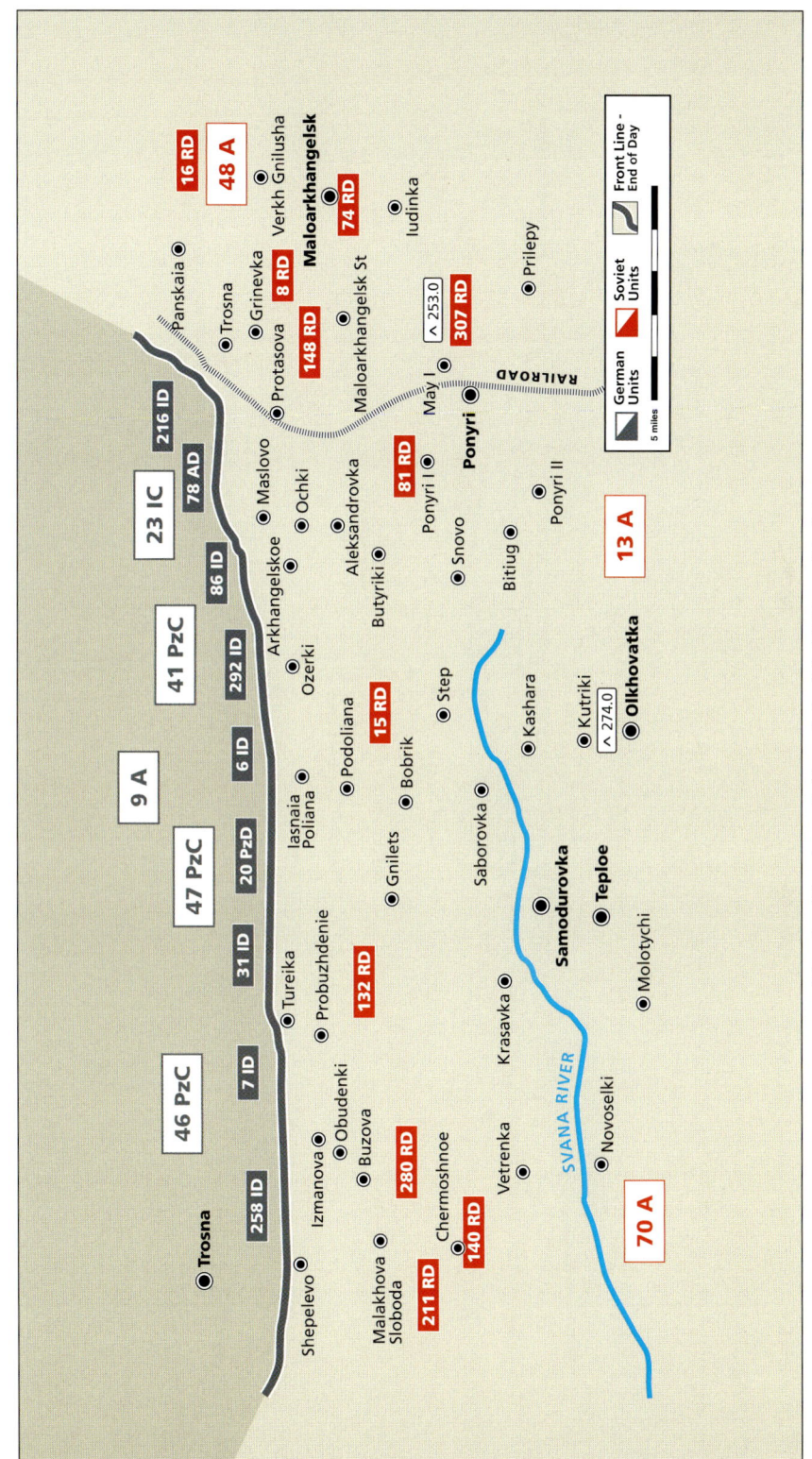

Map 1   Northern Salient, July 4th 1943 – midnight.

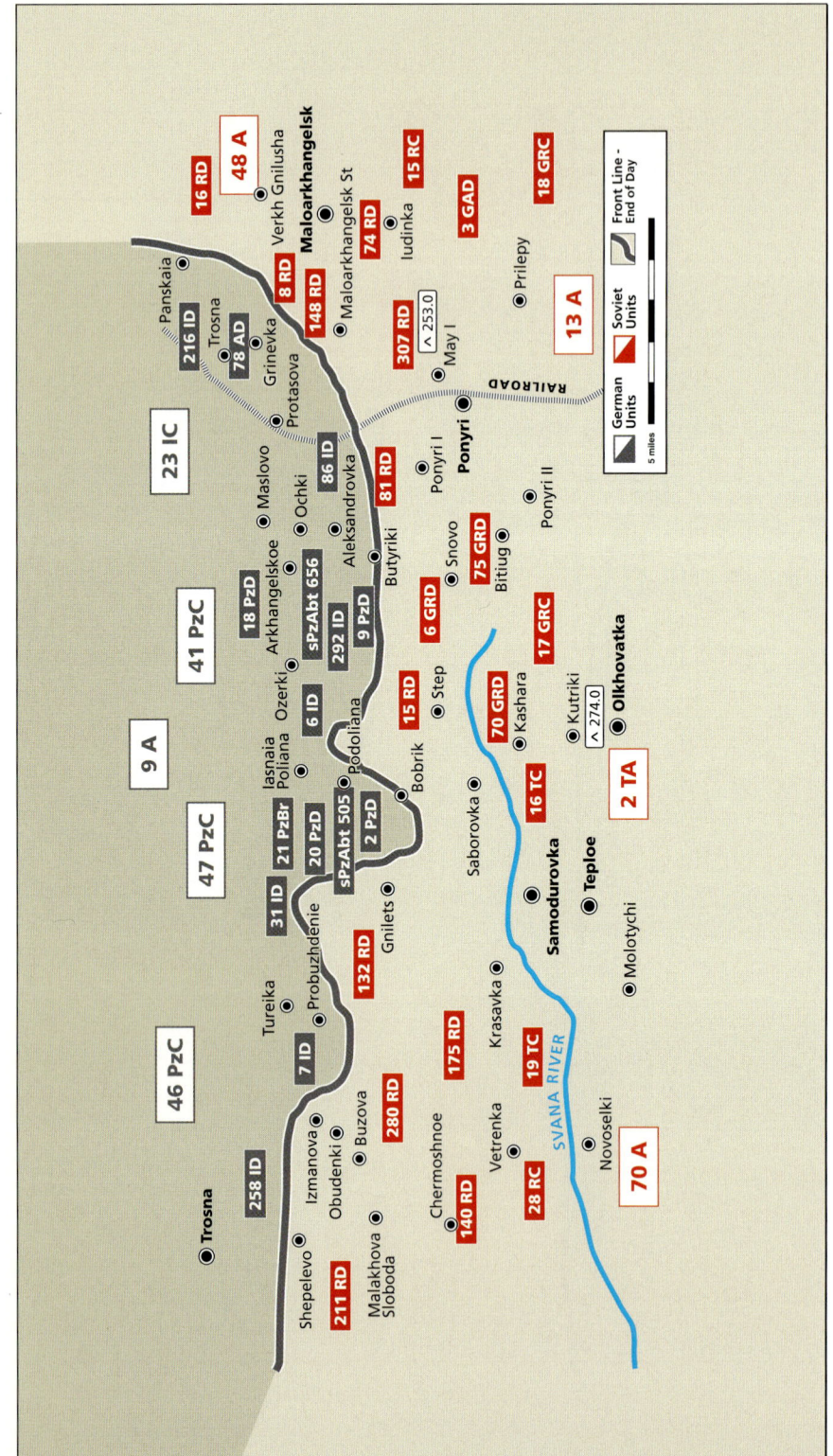

Map 2   Northern Salient, July 5th 1943 – midnight.

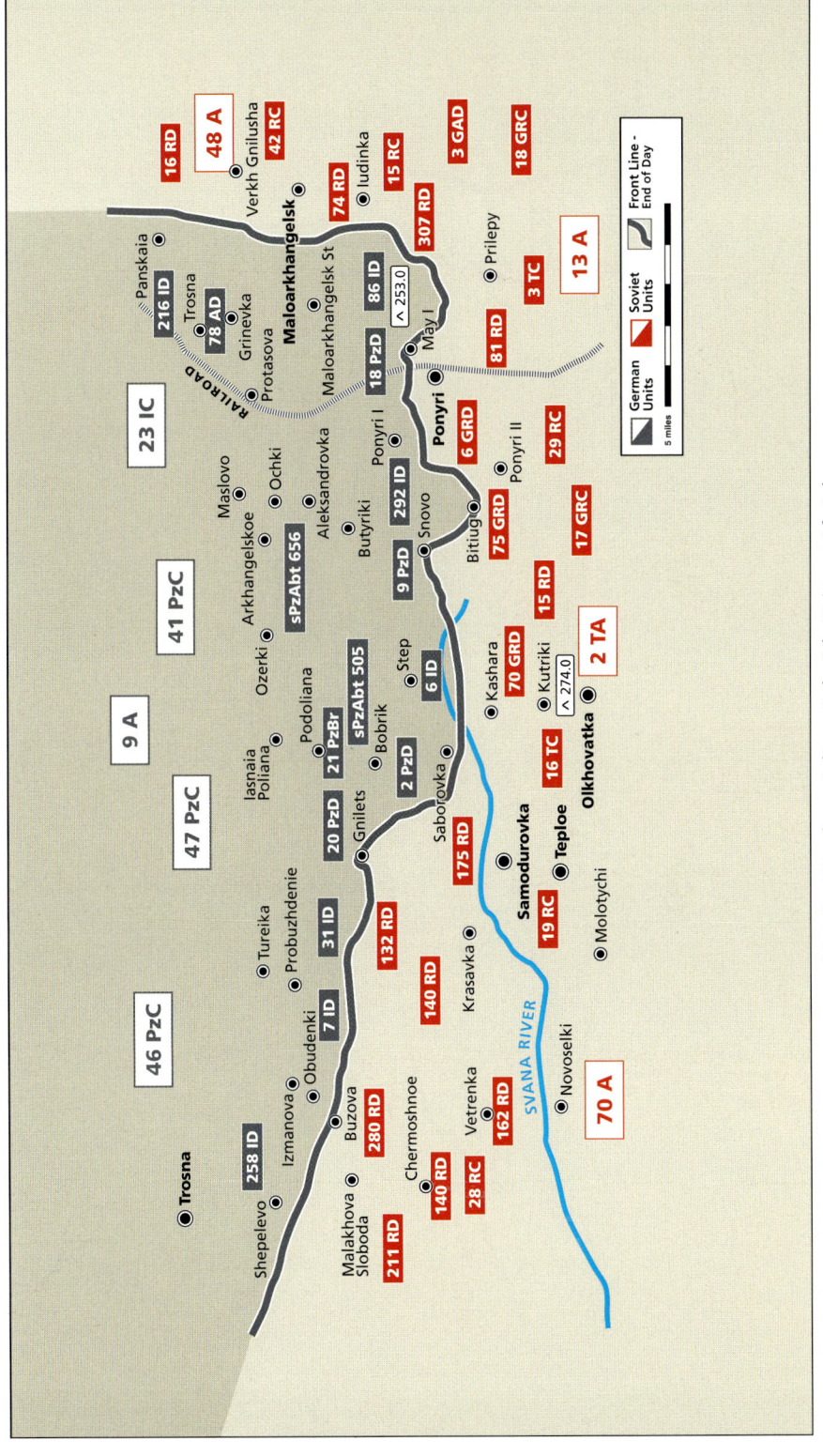

Map 3   Northern Salient, July 6th 1943 – midnight.

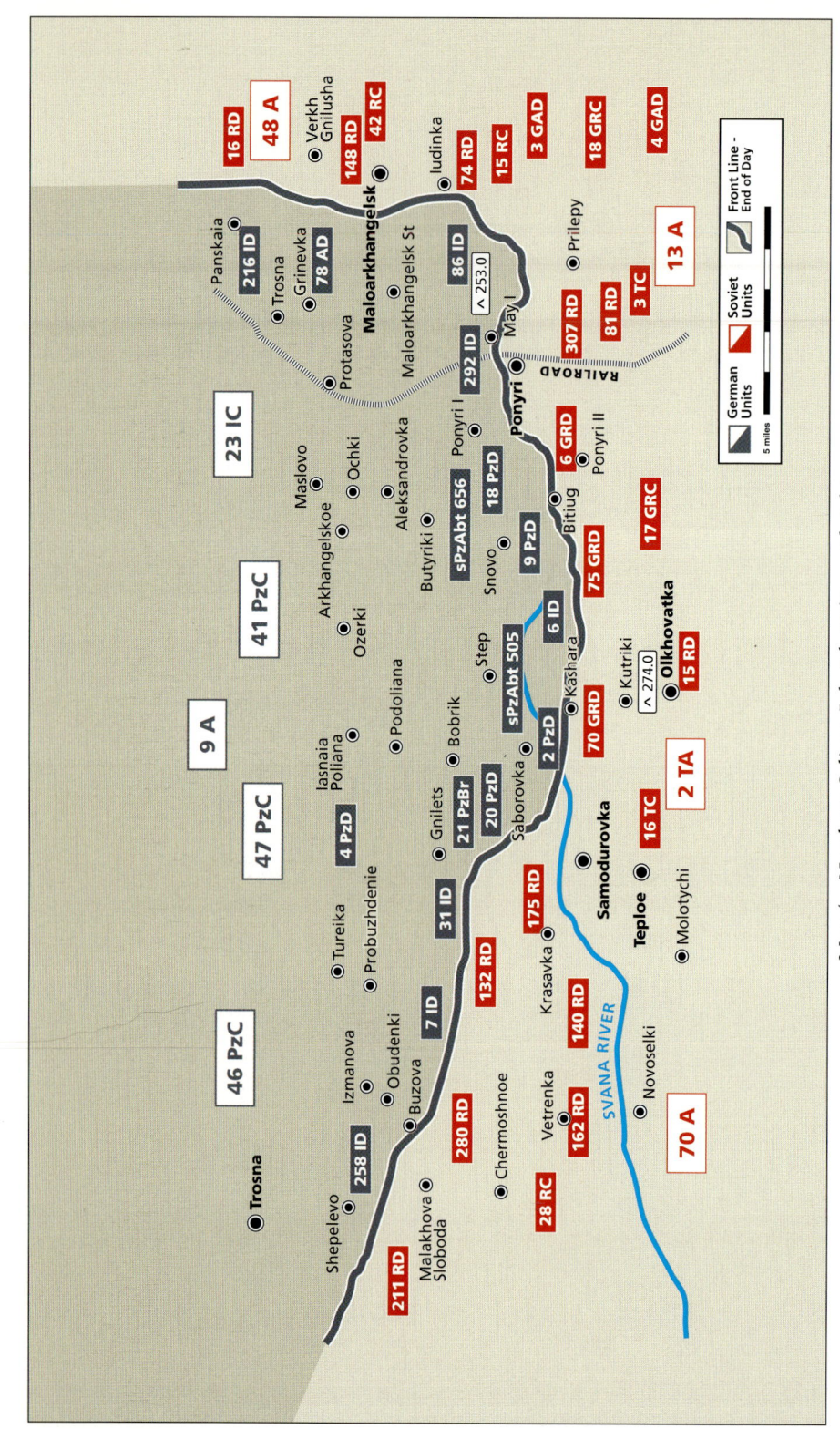

Map 4 Northern Salient, July 7th 1943 – midnight.

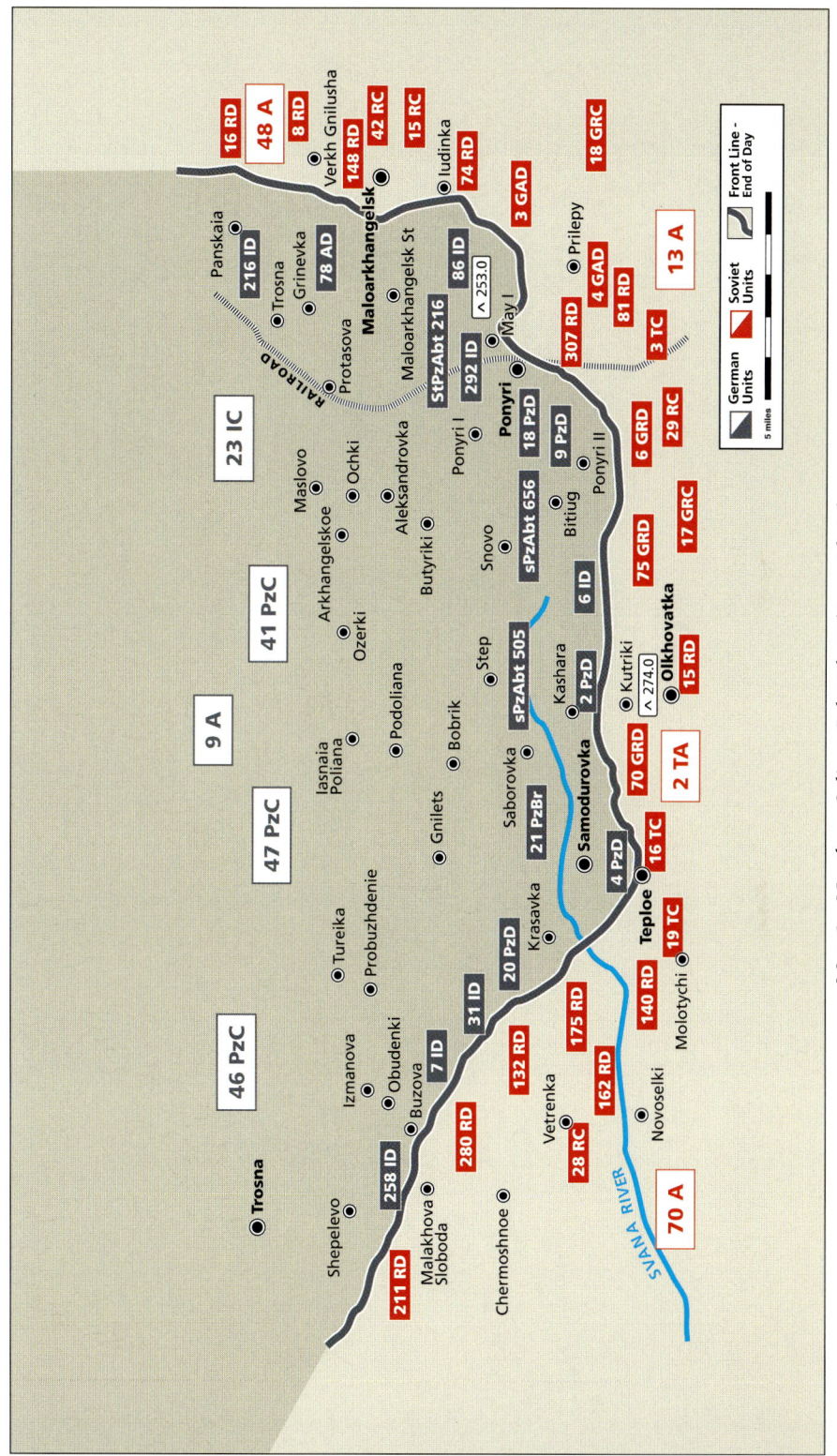

Map 5   Northern Salient, July 8th 1943 – midnight.

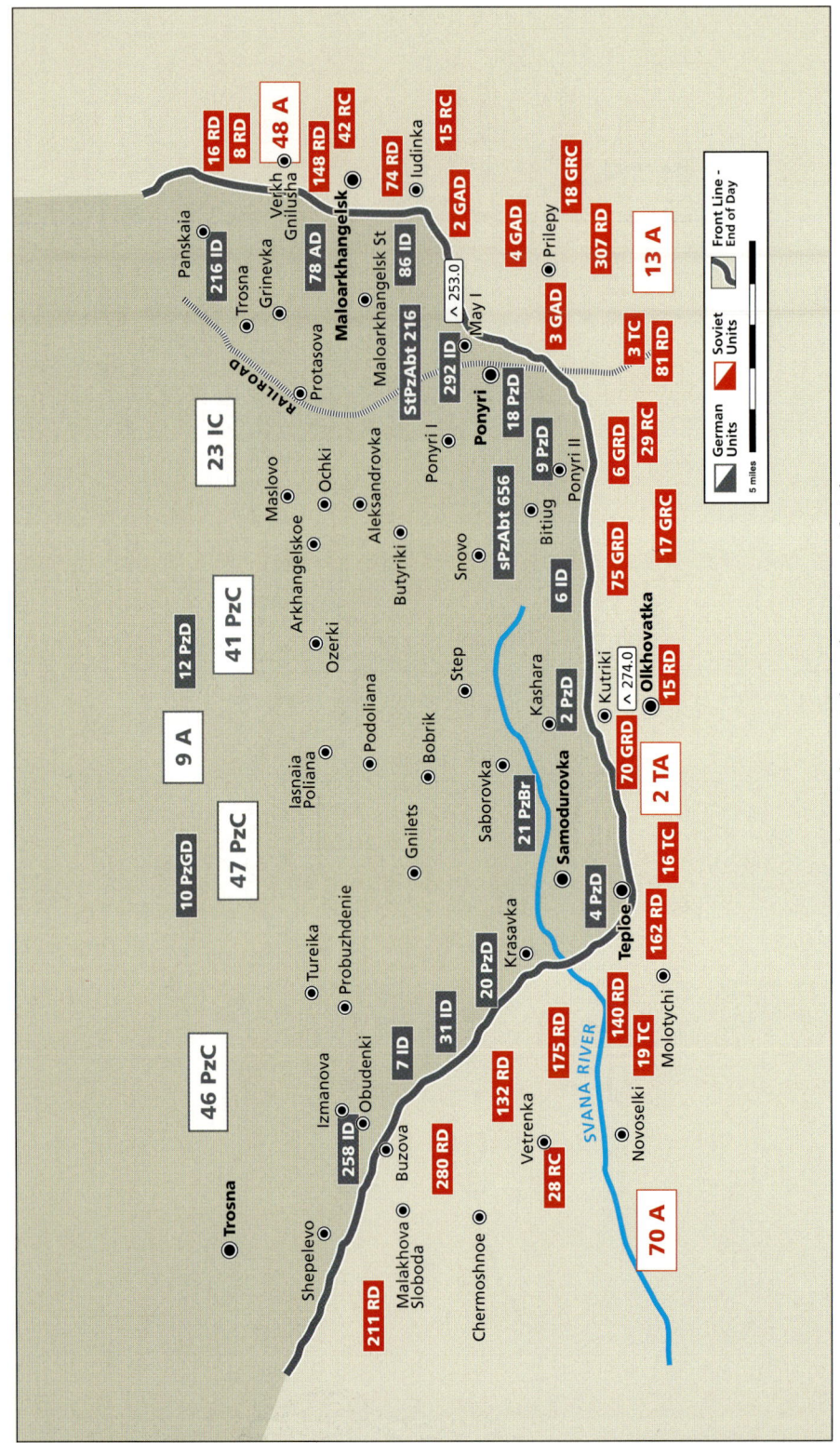

Map 6 Northern Salient, July 10th 1943 – midnight.

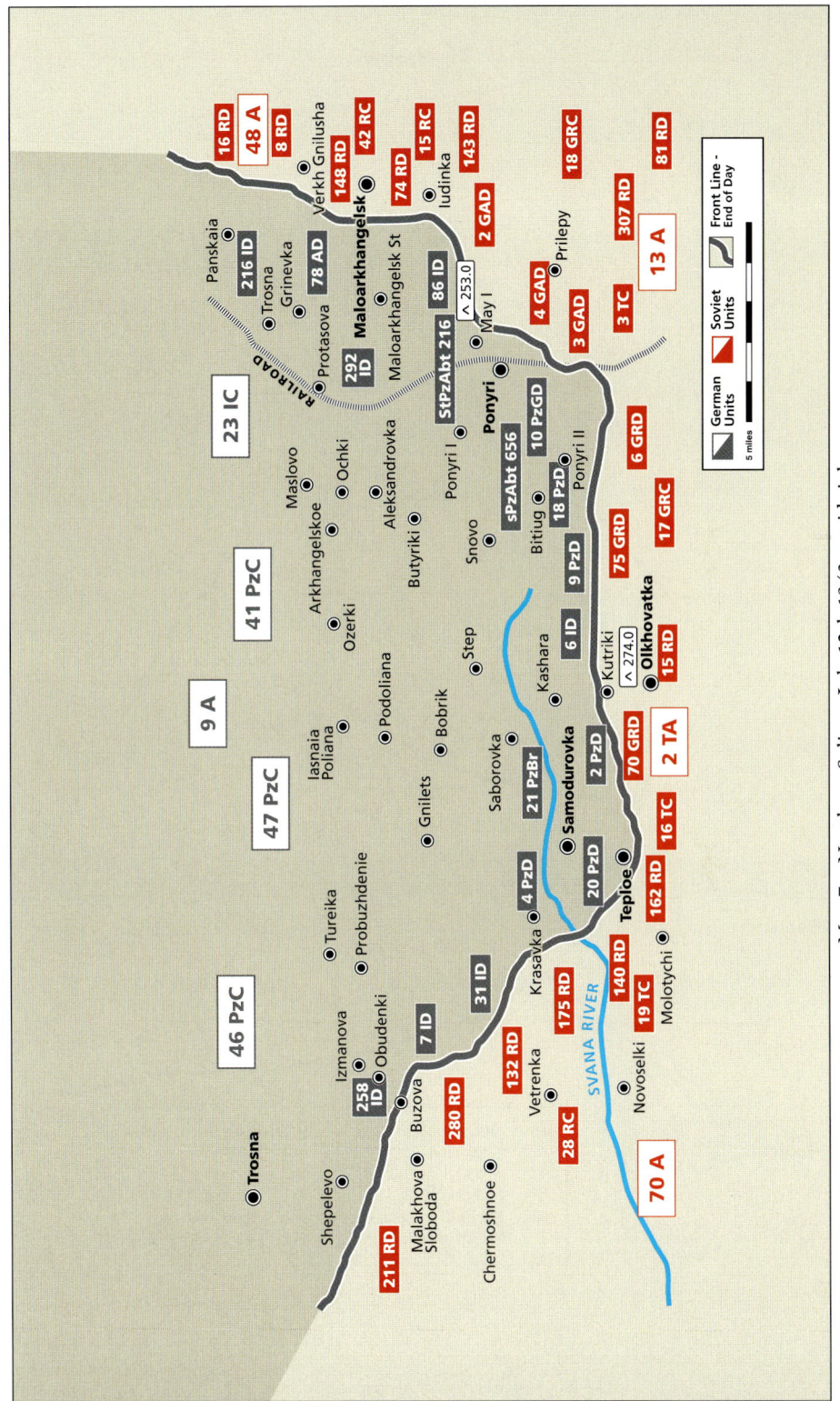

Map 7   Northern Salient, July 12th 1943 – midnight.

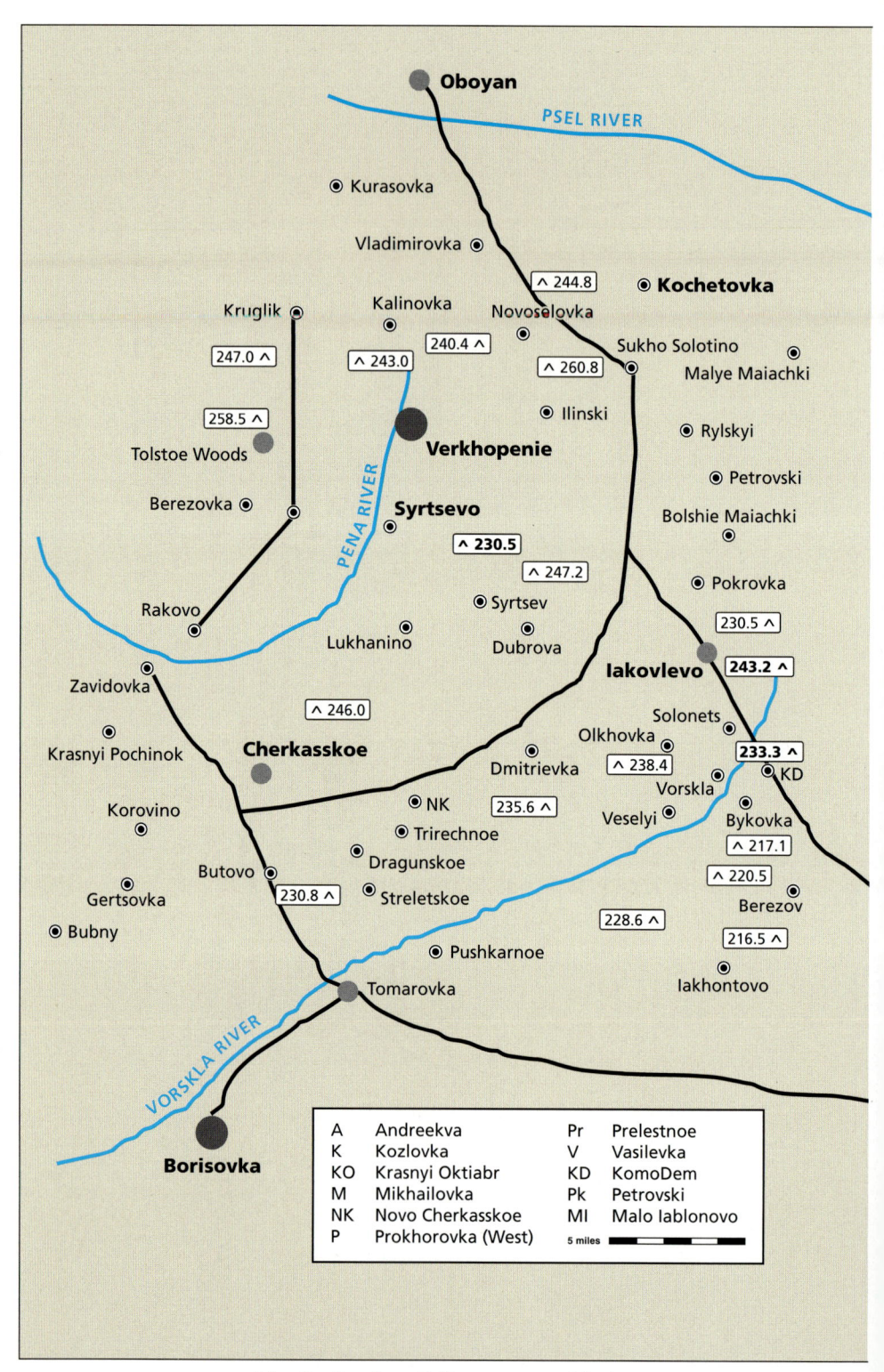

Map 8   Southern Salient, topographical.

Kartashevka
Korytnoe
236.7
Beregovoe
Polezhaev
Petrovka
Veselyi
252.4
N
226.6
Prokhorovka
Kliuchi
Pr
OSF
252.2
230.5
KO
M
KSF
P
K
V
A
Iamki
Storozhevoe
241.6
Ivanovka Vyselok
Pravorot
Gresnoe
234.9
Vinogradovka
258.2
Belenikhino
Novoselovka
Teterevino No
Iasnaia Poliana
Avdeevka
232.6
Ozerovski
Kalinin
Luchki No
210.7
Ivanovka
MI
Plota
DONETS RIVER
Teterevino So
Leski
Luchki So
Pk
Shipy
Vypolzovka
246.3
Shakhovo
Ryndinka
Rzhavets
241.5
Nechaevka
Rozhdestvenka
Aleksandrovka
Smorodino
LIPOVYI DONETS
Alekseevski
Gostishchevo
Nepkhaevo
Krivtsovo
Kazache
Zhuravlinyi
230.3
Verkh Olshanets
Sabynino
Visloe
Gonki
Lomovo
211.5
Ternovka
Kiselevo
Shliakhovo
Gremiache
218.0
217.4
RAILROAD
Shopino
Melikhovo
Erik
Khokhlovo
Sheino
Dalniaia Igumenka
Ushakovo
Miasoedovo
Blizhniaia Igumenka
Staryi Gorod
Belgorod
Iastrebovo
Makhailovka
Kreida
Generalovka
Dorogobuzhino
Krutoi Log
DONETS RIVER
Razumnoe
Solomino
Maslova Pristan

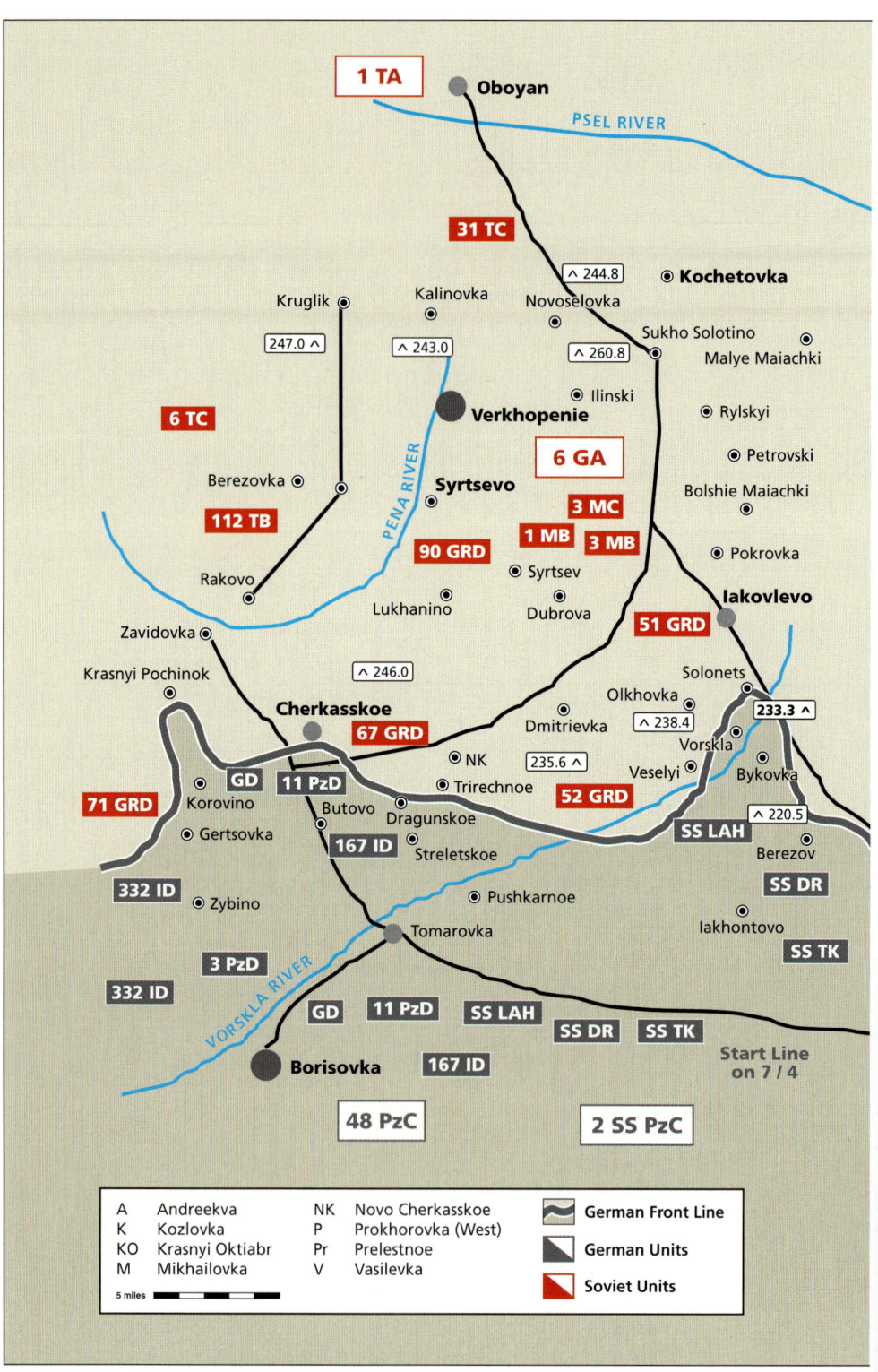

Map 9   Southern Salient, July 5th 1943 – midnight.

Kartashevka
Korytnoe
Beregovoe
236.7
N
Polezhaev
Petrovka
Veselyi
252.4
226.6
Prokhorovka
Kliuchi
Pr
OSF
252.2
230.5
KO
M
P
K
V
A
KSF
Storozhevoe
Iamki
69 A
183 RD
241.6
Ivanovka Vyselok
Pravorot
Gresnoe
234.9
Vinogradovka
258.2
Belenikhino
Teterevino No
Iasnaia Poliana
232.6
Ozerovski
Kalinin
Ivanovka
Luchki No
210.7
DONETS RIVER
Plota
5 GTC
Teterevino So
Leski
Luchki So
Shipy
Vypolzovka
246.3
Shakhovo
Ryndinka
Rzhavets
241.5
Nechaevka
Rozhdestvenka
Aleksandrovka
Smorodino
LIPOVYI DONETS
Gostishchevo
Alekseevski
Nepkhaevo
Krivtsovo
Kazache
89 GRD
2 GTC
230.3
Verkh Olshanets
Sabynino
Gonki
Visloe
211.5
Lomovo
Ternovka
Shliakhovo
Kiselevo
96 TB
RAILROAD
217.4
Gremiache
Erik
Shopino
Melikhovo
Khokhlovo
375 RD
Sheino
Dalniaia Igumenka
Ushakovo
Miasoedovo
168 ID
Staryi Gorod
Blizhniaia Igumenka
81 GRD
Iastrebovo
Belgorod
Makhailovka
73 GRD
7 GA
6 PzD
Kreida
Generalovka
78 GRD
Krutoi Log
Dorogobuzhino
Razumnoe
DONETS RIVER
Solomino
213 RD
19 PzD
7 PzD
Maslova Pristan
3 PzC
106 ID
72 GRD
320 ID

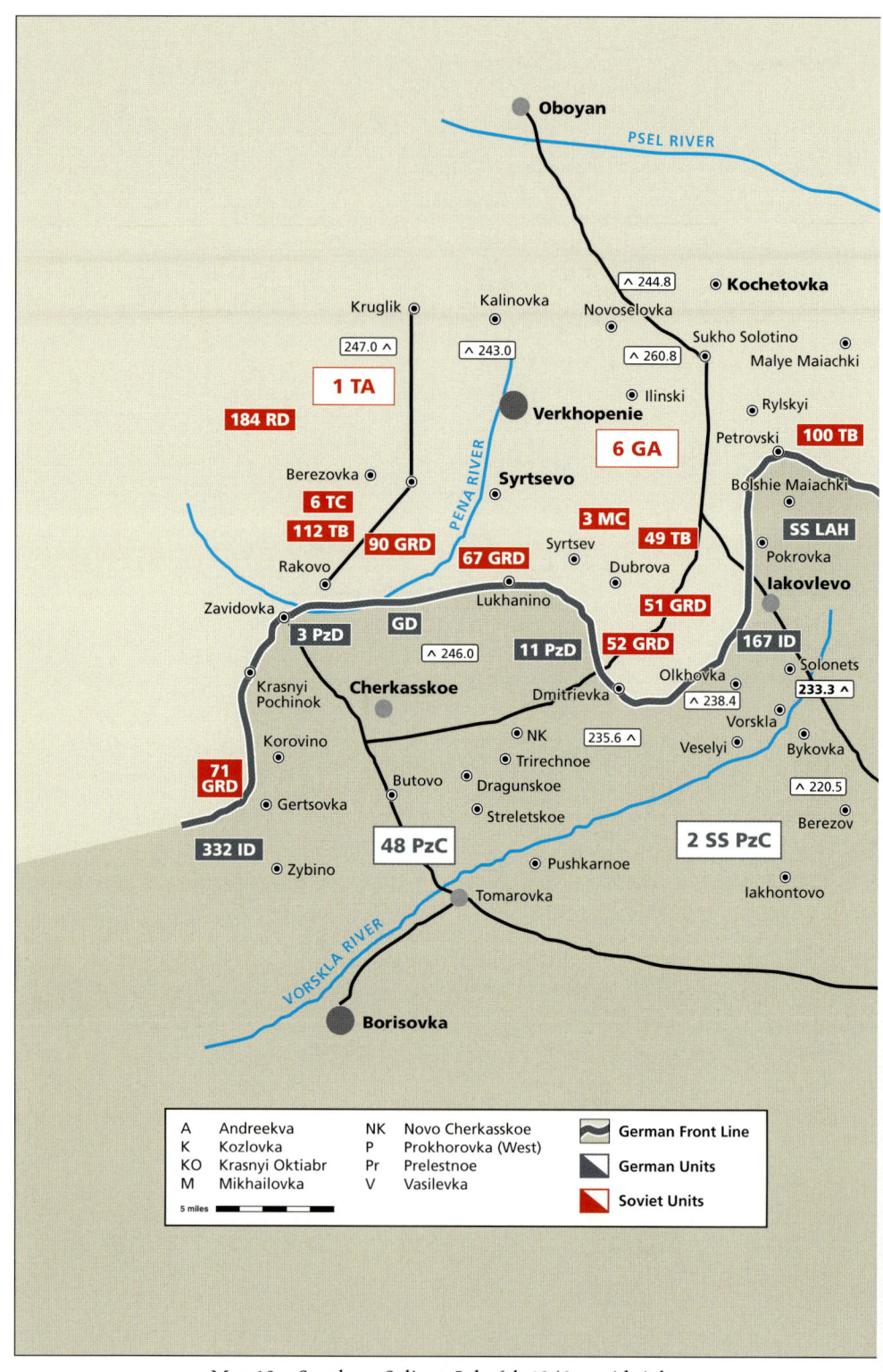

Map 10   Southern Salient, July 6th 1943 – midnight.

Kartashevka
236.7
Korytnoe
Beregovoe
Polezhaev
Petrovka
Veselyi
252.4
226.6
Kliuchi
Pr
OSF
Prokhorovka
M
252.2
230.5
KO
P
K
V
A
KSF
Storozhevoe
Iamki
241.6
Ivanovka Vyselok
Pravorot
69 A
Gresnoe
234.9
Vinogradovka
258.2
183 RD
93 GRD
Belenikhino
Teterevino No
20 GTB
Iasnaia Poliana
232.6
Ozerovski
5 GTC
Kalinin
Ivanovka
Luchki No
210.7
21 GTB
Teterevino So
Plota
Leski
DONETS RIVER
RAILROAD
305 RD
22 GTB
Shipy
Luchki So
Vypolzovka
246.3
Shakhovo
Ryndinka
Rzhavets
241.5
Nechaevka
Rozhdestvenka
Aleksandrovka
Smorodino
LIPOVYI DONETS
Gostishchevo
Alekseevski
Nepkhaevo
SS DR
Krivtsovo
Kazache
2 GTC
230.3
89 GRD
Verkh Olshanets
94 GRD
Sabynino
Gonki
Visloe
211.5
92 GRD
Lomovo
Ternovka
Shliakhovo
Kiselevo
375 RD
SS TK
217.4
Gremiache
Erik
Melikhovo
Khokhlovo
Shopino
15 GRD
Sheino
Dalniaia Igumenka
Ushakovo
81 GRD
Miasoedovo
168 ID
Staryi Gorod
Blizhniaia Igumenka
73 GRD
Iastrebovo
7 GA
Belgorod
19 PzD
78 GRD
Makhailovka
Kreida
Generalovka
6 PzD
Krutoi Log
Dorogobuzhino
Razumnoe
DONETS RIVER
Solomino
7 PzD
213 RD
106 ID
3 PzC
Maslova Pristan
72 GRD
320 ID
N

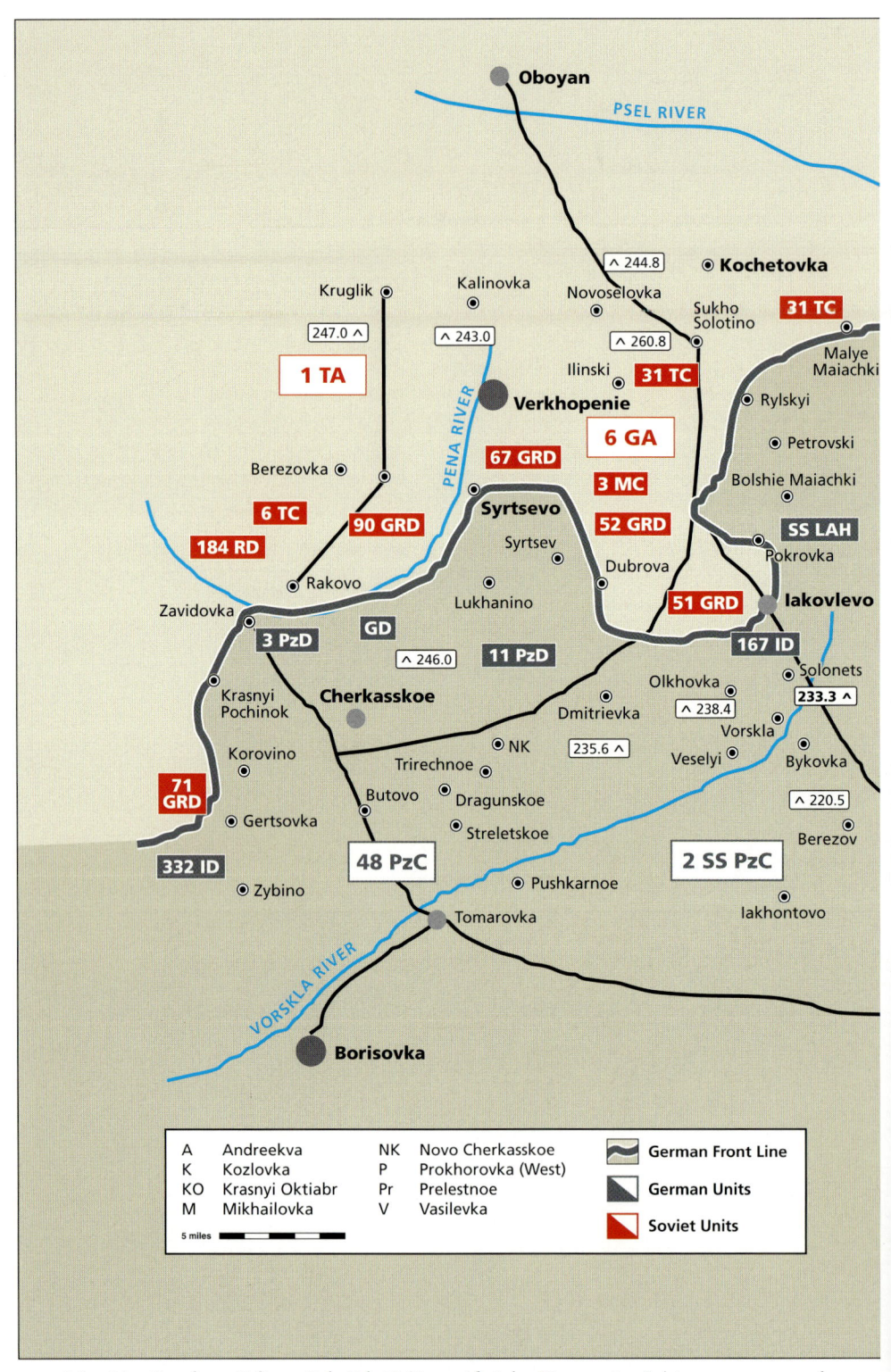

Map 11   Southern Salient, July 7th 1943 – midnight. First major Soviet counter-attack.

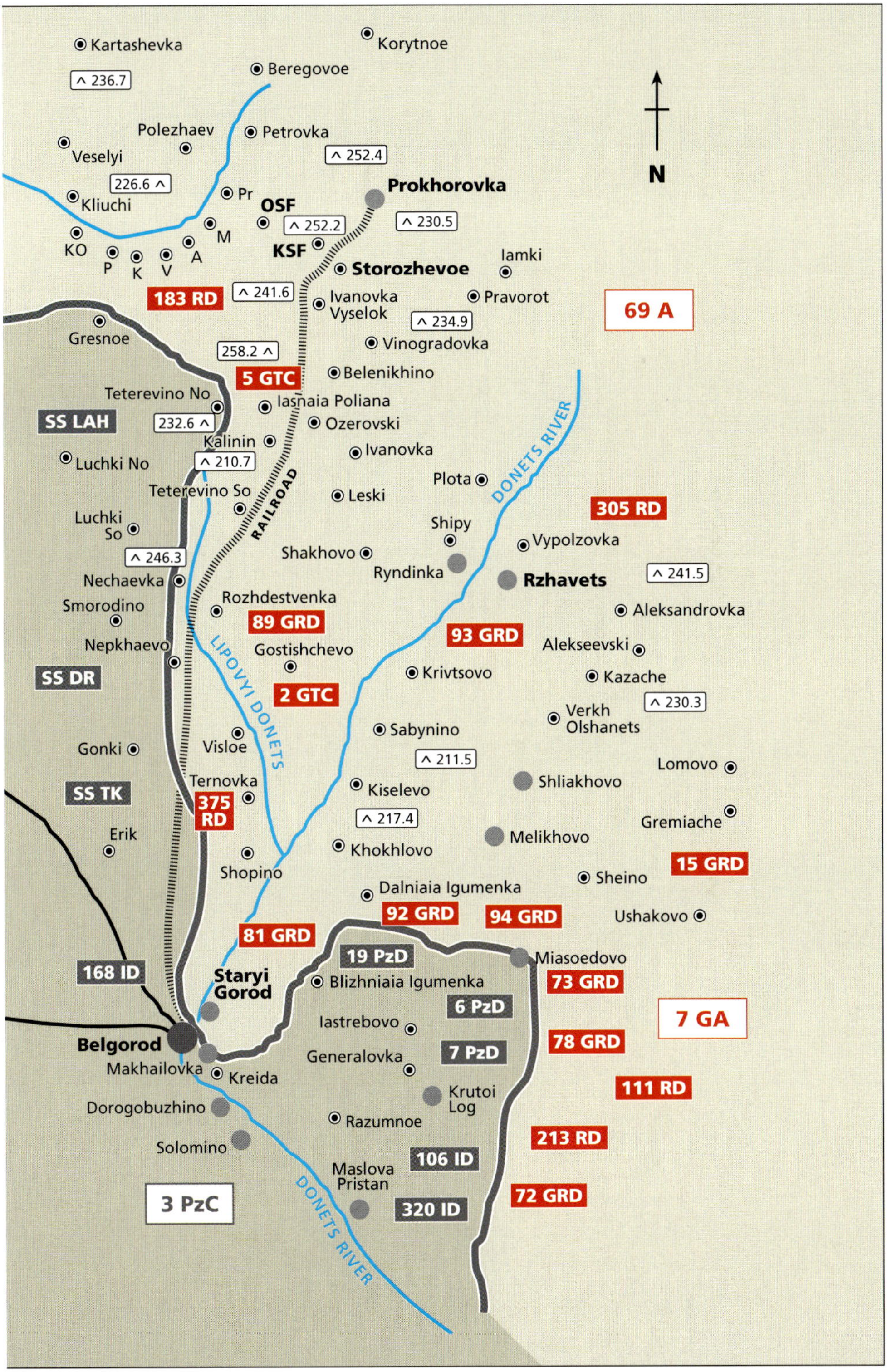
Kartashevka
Korytnoe
Beregovoe
236.7
Polezhaev
Petrovka
Veselyi
252.4
226.6
Kliuchi
Pr
OSF
Prokhorovka
252.2
230.5
KO
M
P
K
V
A
KSF
Storozhevoe
Iamki
183 RD
241.6
Ivanovka Vyselok
Pravorot
69 A
234.9
Gresnoe
258.2
Vinogradovka
5 GTC
Belenikhino
Teterevino No
Iasnaia Poliana
SS LAH
232.6
Ozerovski
Kalinin
Ivanovka
Luchki No
210.7
Plota
DONETS RIVER
Teterevino So
Leski
RAILROAD
305 RD
Luchki So
Shipy
Vypolzovka
246.3
Shakhovo
Ryndinka
Rzhavets
241.5
Nechaevka
Smorodino
Rozhdestvenka
89 GRD
Aleksandrovka
93 GRD
Alekseevski
Nepkhaevo
Gostishchevo
LIPOVYI DONETS
SS DR
Krivtsovo
Kazache
2 GTC
230.3
Verkh Olshanets
Sabynino
Gonki
Visloe
211.5
Lomovo
Ternovka
SS TK
375 RD
Kiselevo
Shliakhovo
217.4
Gremiache
Erik
Khokhlovo
Melikhovo
15 GRD
Shopino
Sheino
Dalniaia Igumenka
92 GRD
94 GRD
Ushakovo
81 GRD
19 PzD
Miasoedovo
168 ID
Staryi Gorod
Blizhniaia Igumenka
73 GRD
6 PzD
7 GA
Iastrebovo
Belgorod
78 GRD
Generalovka
7 PzD
Makhailovka
Kreida
111 RD
Krutoi Log
Dorogobuzhino
Razumnoe
213 RD
Solomino
106 ID
Maslova Pristan
3 PzC
320 ID
72 GRD
DONETS RIVER
N

Map 12   Southern Salient, July 8th 1943 – midnight. Second major Soviet counter-attack.

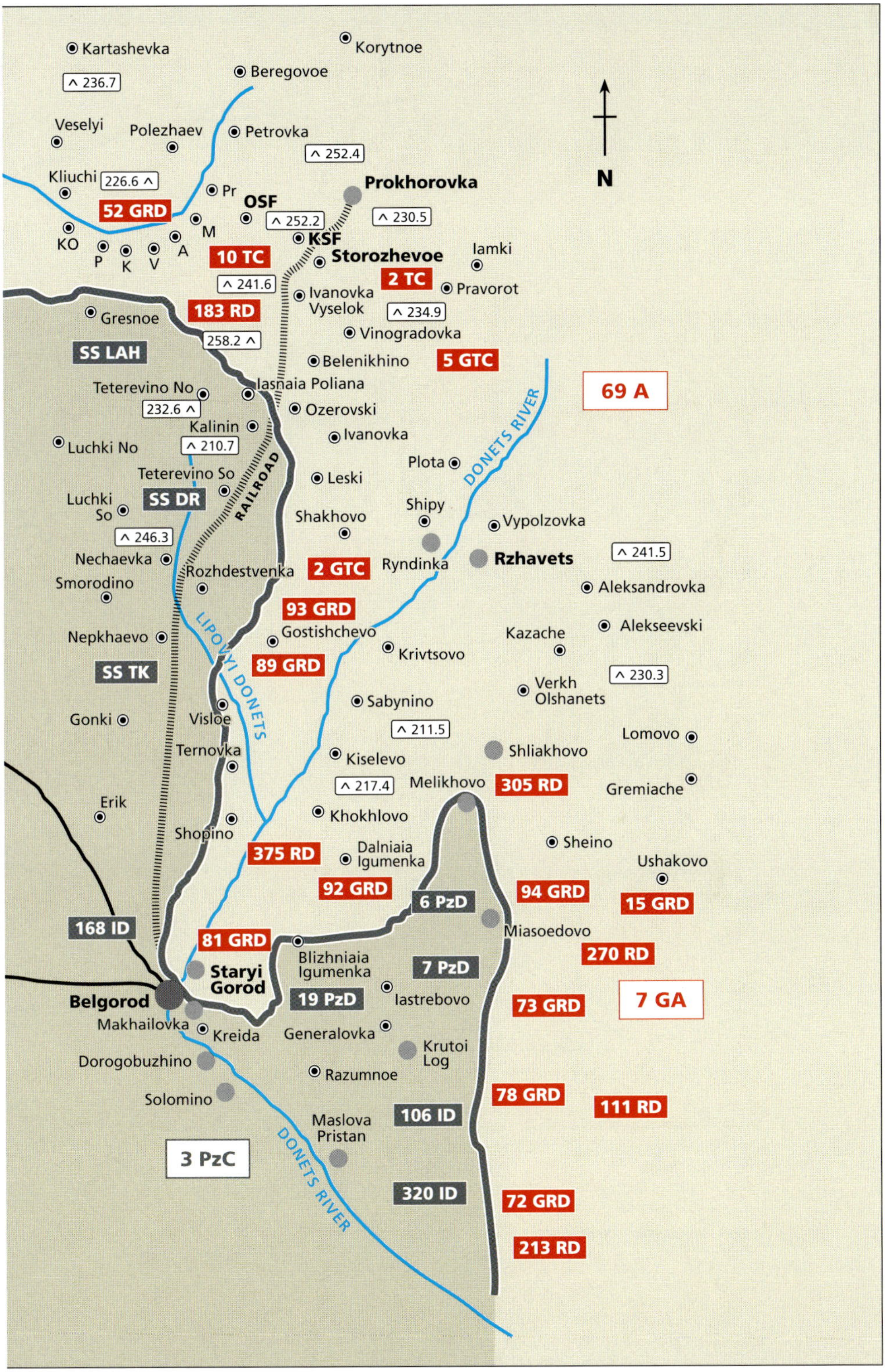
Kartashevka
Korytnoe
236.7
Beregovoe
Veselyi
Polezhaev
Petrovka
252.4
Kliuchi
226.6
Prokhorovka
N
Pr
OSF
52 GRD
252.2
230.5
M
KSF
KO
A
10 TC
Storozhevoe
Iamki
P
K
V
241.6
2 TC
Pravorot
Ivanovka Vyselok
183 RD
234.9
Gresnoe
Vinogradovka
258.2
SS LAH
Belenikhino
5 GTC
Teterevino No
Iasnaia Poliana
69 A
232.6
Ozerovski
Kalinin
Luchki No
210.7
Ivanovka
Teterevino So
Plota
DONETS RIVER
RAILROAD
Leski
Luchki So
SS DR
Shipy
Shakhovo
Vypolzovka
246.3
Nechaevka
Ryndinka
Rzhavets
241.5
Smorodino
Rozhdestvenka
2 GTC
Aleksandrovka
93 GRD
Alekseevski
Nepkhaevo
Gostishchevo
Kazache
Krivtsovo
89 GRD
SS TK
230.3
Verkh Olshanets
LIPOVYI DONETS
Sabynino
Gonki
Visloe
211.5
Lomovo
Ternovka
Shliakhovo
Kiselevo
Melikhovo
305 RD
217.4
Gremiache
Erik
Khokhlovo
Shopino
Sheino
375 RD
Dalniaia Igumenka
Ushakovo
92 GRD
94 GRD
6 PzD
15 GRD
168 ID
Miasoedovo
81 GRD
270 RD
Blizhniaia Igumenka
Staryi Gorod
7 PzD
Belgorod
7 GA
19 PzD
Iastrebovo
73 GRD
Makhailovka
Kreida
Generalovka
Krutoi Log
Dorogobuzhino
Razumnoe
78 GRD
Solomino
111 RD
106 ID
Maslova Pristan
3 PzC
DONETS RIVER
320 ID
72 GRD
213 RD

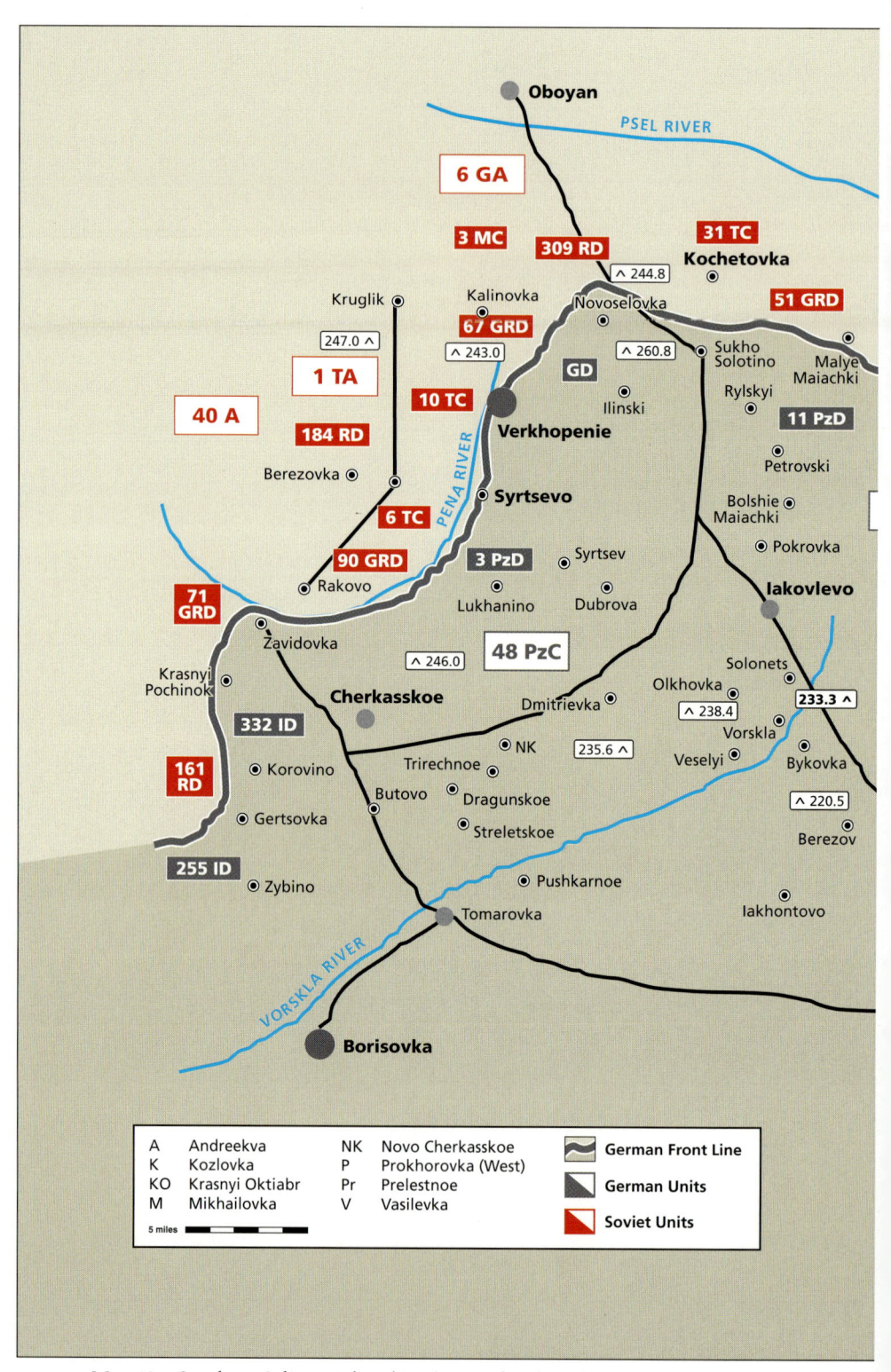

Map 13   Southern Salient, July 9th 1943 – midnight. 4th PzA resumes its attack.

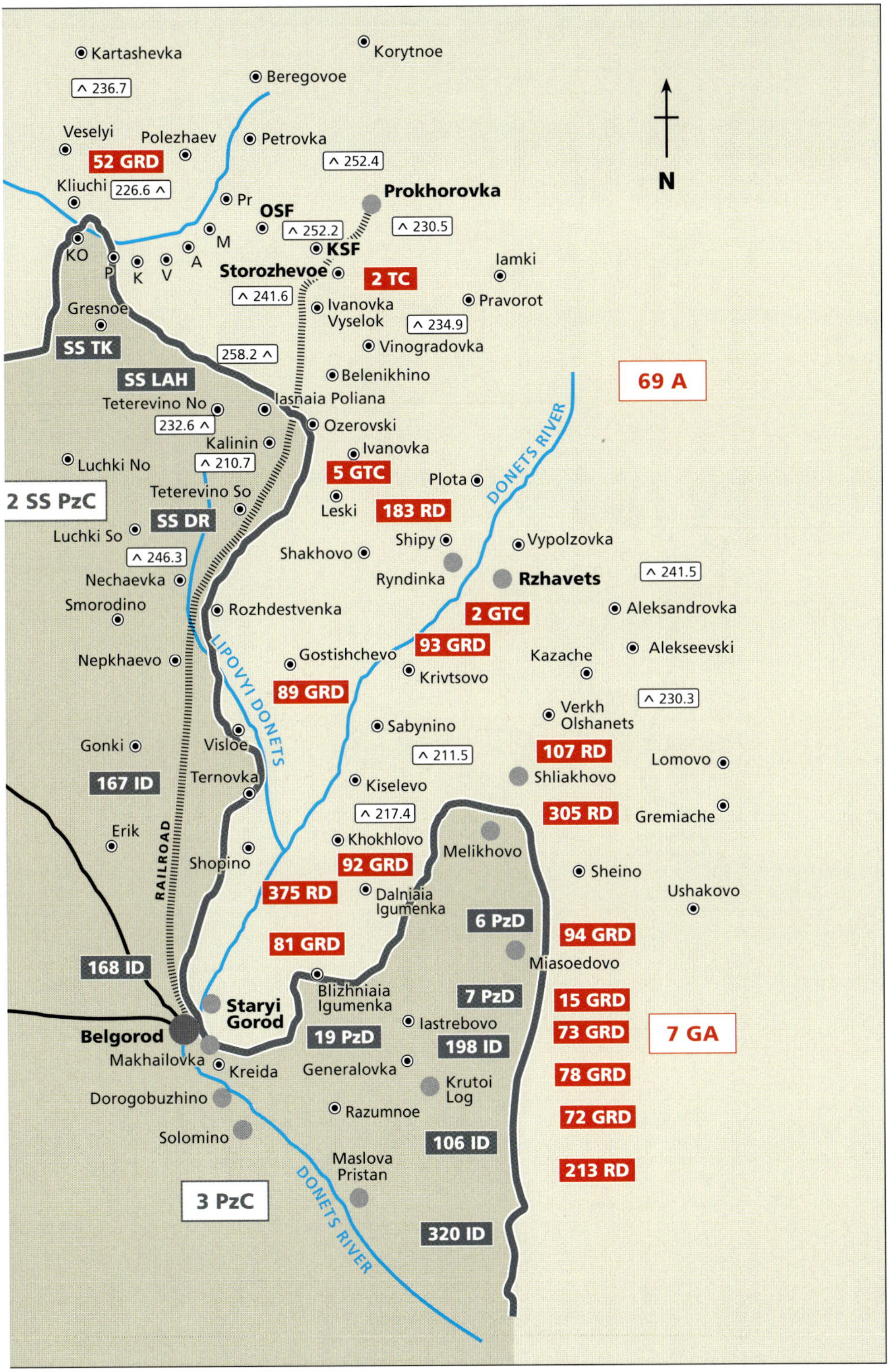
Kartashevka
Korytnoe
Beregovoe
236.7
N
Veselyi
Polezhaev
Petrovka
52 GRD
252.4
Kliuchi
226.6
Pr
Prokhorovka
OSF
252.2
230.5
M
KSF
KO
P
K
V
A
Storozhevoe
2 TC
Iamki
241.6
Ivanovka
Vyselok
Pravorot
Gresnoe
234.9
SS TK
Vinogradovka
258.2
69 A
SS LAH
Belenikhino
Iasnaia Poliana
Teterevino No
232.6
Ozerovski
Kalinin
Ivanovka
Luchki No
210.7
DONETS RIVER
5 GTC
Plota
2 SS PzC
Teterevino So
Leski
183 RD
SS DR
Luchki So
Shipy
Vypolzovka
246.3
Shakhovo
Rzhavets
241.5
Nechaevka
Ryndinka
Smorodino
Rozhdestvenka
2 GTC
Aleksandrovka
93 GRD
Alekseevski
Nepkhaevo
Gostishchevo
Kazache
LIPOVYI DONETS
Krivtsovo
89 GRD
230.3
Verkh
Olshanets
Sabynino
Gonki
Visloe
211.5
107 RD
Lomovo
167 ID
Ternovka
Kiselevo
Shliakhovo
217.4
305 RD
Gremiache
Erik
Khokhlovo
Melikhovo
RAILROAD
Shopino
92 GRD
Sheino
375 RD
Dalniaia
Igumenka
Ushakovo
6 PzD
94 GRD
81 GRD
Miasoedovo
168 ID
Blizhniaia
Igumenka
7 PzD
15 GRD
Staryi
Gorod
Iastrebovo
73 GRD
7 GA
Belgorod
19 PzD
198 ID
Makhailovka
Kreida
Generalovka
Krutoi
Log
78 GRD
Dorogobuzhino
Razumnoe
72 GRD
Solomino
106 ID
Maslova
Pristan
213 RD
3 PzC
DONETS RIVER
320 ID

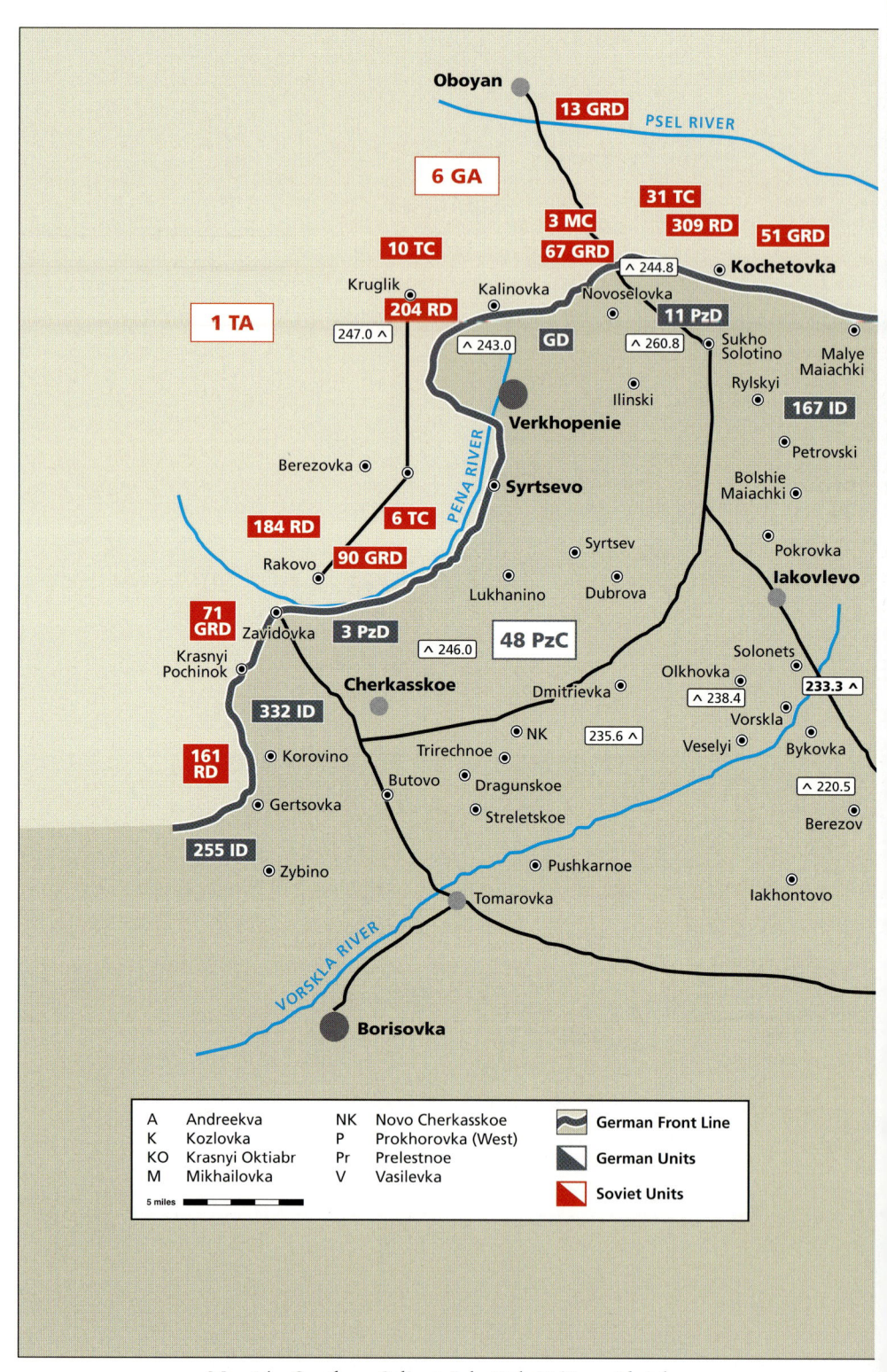

Map 14   Southern Salient, July 10th 1943 – midnight.

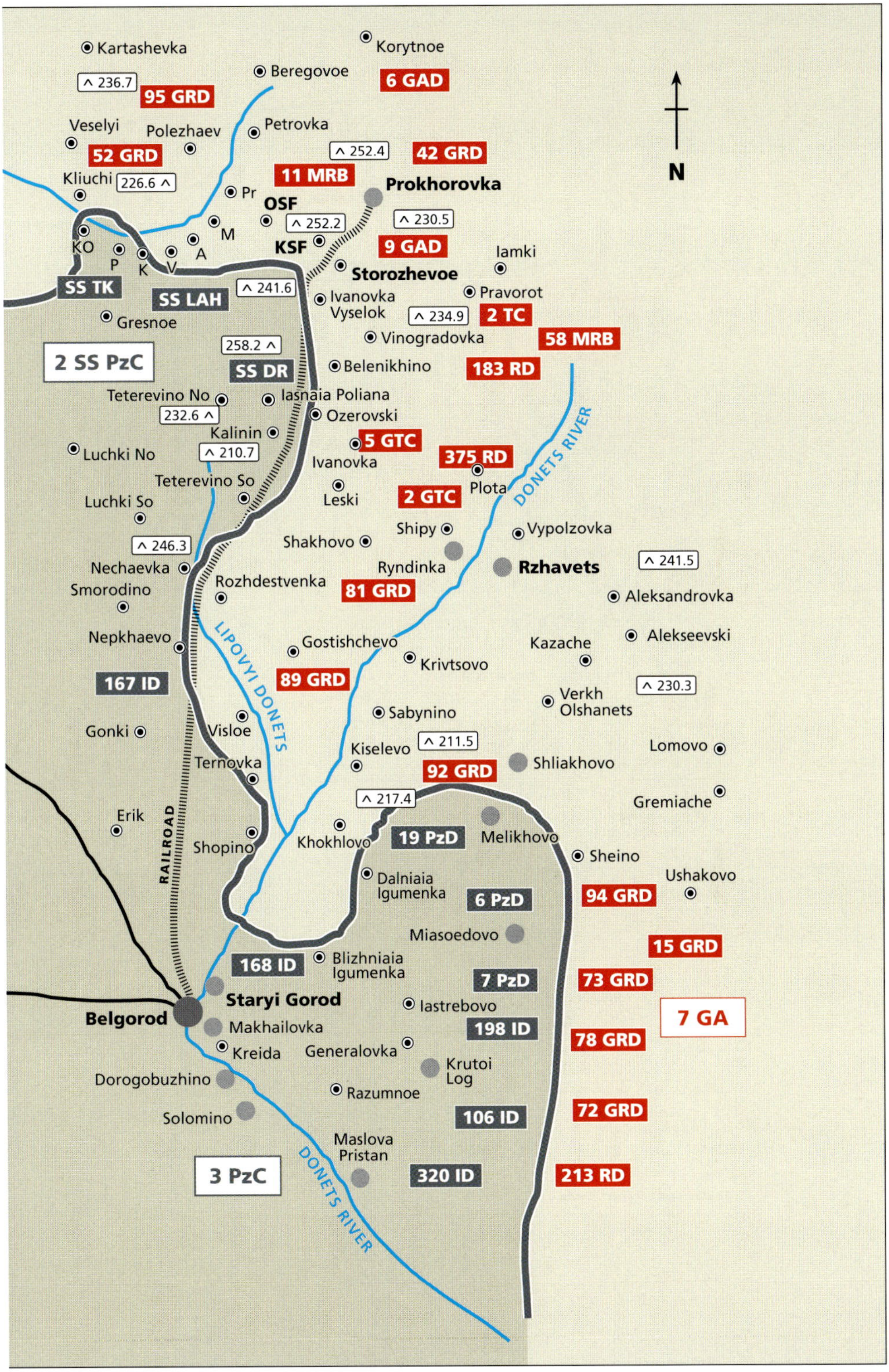
Kartashevka
Korytnoe
236.7
95 GRD
Beregovoe
6 GAD
Veselyi
Polezhaev
Petrovka
52 GRD
252.4
42 GRD
Kliuchi
226.6
11 MRB
Prokhorovka
N
Pr
OSF
KO
P
K
V
A
M
252.2
230.5
KSF
9 GAD
Iamki
Storozhevoe
SS TK
SS LAH
241.6
Ivanovka Vyselok
Pravorot
Gresnoe
234.9
2 TC
Vinogradovka
58 MRB
2 SS PzC
258.2
SS DR
Belenikhino
183 RD
Teterevino No
Iasnaia Poliana
232.6
Ozerovski
Kalinin
5 GTC
Luchki No
210.7
375 RD
Ivanovka
Teterevino So
Plota
Luchki So
Leski
2 GTC
DONETS RIVER
Shipy
Vypolzovka
246.3
Shakhovo
Nechaevka
Ryndinka
Rzhavets
241.5
Smorodino
Rozhdestvenka
81 GRD
Aleksandrovka
Nepkhaevo
Gostishchevo
Kazache
Alekseevski
LIPOVYI DONETS
Krivtsovo
167 ID
89 GRD
Verkh Olshanets
230.3
Sabynino
Gonki
Visloe
Kiselevo
211.5
Lomovo
Ternovka
92 GRD
Shliakhovo
Gremiache
Erik
217.4
RAILROAD
Khokhlovo
19 PzD
Melikhovo
Shopino
Sheino
Dalniaia Igumenka
Ushakovo
6 PzD
94 GRD
Miasoedovo
15 GRD
168 ID
Blizhniaia Igumenka
7 PzD
73 GRD
Staryi Gorod
Iastrebovo
7 GA
Belgorod
Makhailovka
198 ID
78 GRD
Kreida
Generalovka
Krutoi Log
Dorogobuzhino
Razumnoe
Solomino
106 ID
72 GRD
Maslova Pristan
3 PzC
320 ID
213 RD
DONETS RIVER

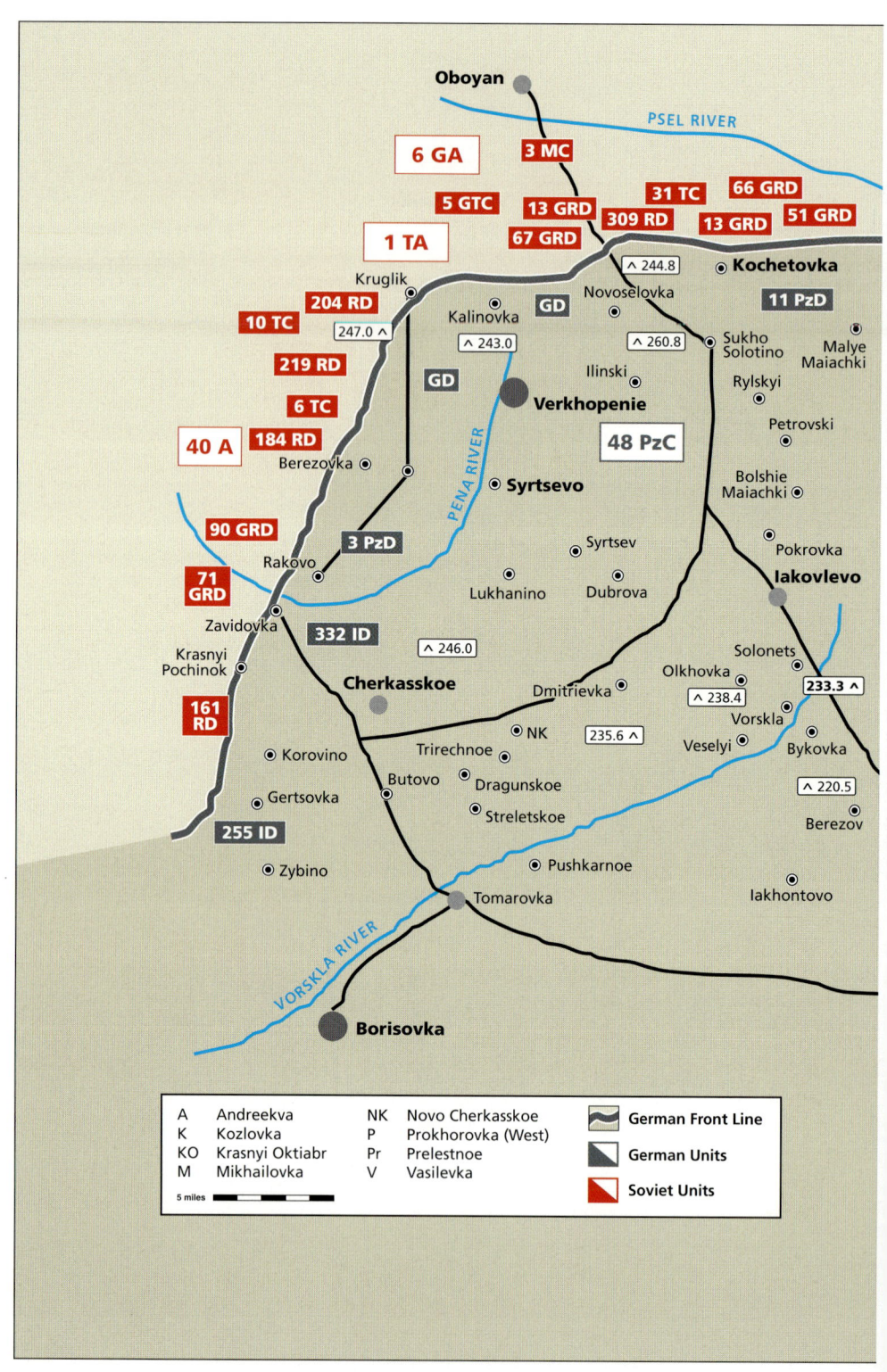

Map 15   Southern Salient, July 11th 1943 – midnight.

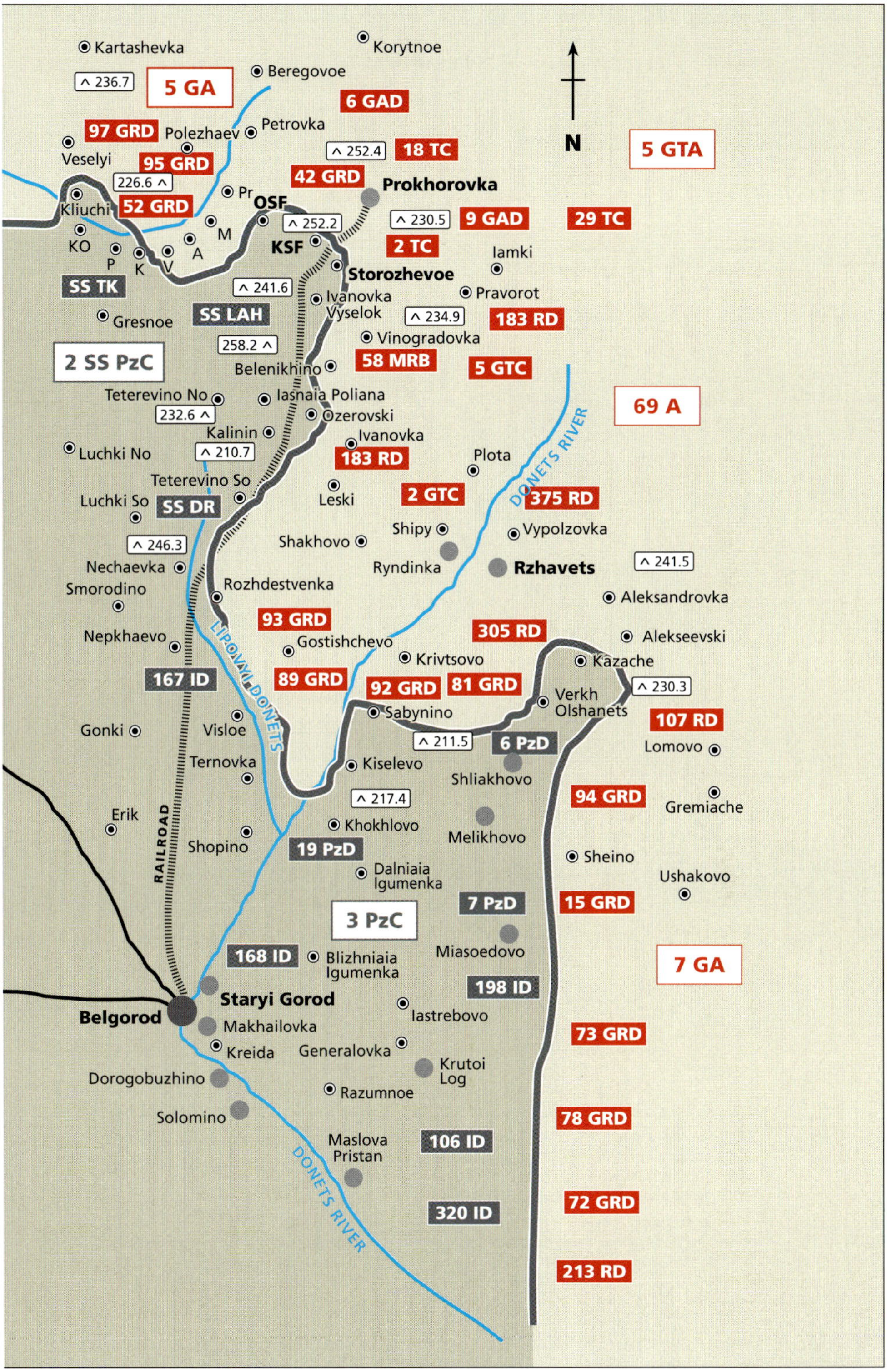
Kartashevka
Korytnoe
Beregovoe
236.7
5 GA
6 GAD
97 GRD
Polezhaev
Petrovka
Veselyi
95 GRD
252.4
18 TC
N
5 GTA
226.6
42 GRD
Prokhorovka
Kliuchi
52 GRD
Pr
OSF
252.2
230.5
9 GAD
29 TC
KO
P
K
V
A
M
KSF
2 TC
Iamki
SS TK
241.6
Storozhevoe
Ivanovka
Vyselok
Pravorot
Gresnoe
SS LAH
234.9
183 RD
258.2
Vinogradovka
2 SS PzC
Belenikhino
58 MRB
5 GTC
Teterevino No
Iasnaia Poliana
69 A
232.6
Ozerovski
Kalinin
Ivanovka
Luchki No
210.7
183 RD
Plota
Teterevino So
Leski
2 GTC
DONETS RIVER
375 RD
Luchki So
SS DR
Shipy
Vypolzovka
246.3
Shakhovo
Nechaevka
Ryndinka
Rzhavets
241.5
Smorodino
Rozhdestvenka
Aleksandrovka
93 GRD
305 RD
Nepkhaevo
Gostishchevo
Alekseevski
LIPOVYI DONETS
Krivtsovo
Kazache
167 ID
89 GRD
92 GRD
81 GRD
230.3
Verkh Olshanets
Sabynino
107 RD
Gonki
Visloe
211.5
6 PzD
Lomovo
Ternovka
Kiselevo
Shliakhovo
217.4
94 GRD
Gremiache
Erik
Khokhlovo
RAILROAD
Shopino
Melikhovo
19 PzD
Sheino
Dalniaia Igumenka
Ushakovo
7 PzD
15 GRD
3 PzC
Miasoedovo
7 GA
168 ID
Blizhniaia Igumenka
198 ID
Staryi Gorod
Belgorod
Iastrebovo
Makhailovka
73 GRD
Kreida
Generalovka
Krutoi Log
Dorogobuzhino
Razumnoe
Solomino
78 GRD
Maslova Pristan
106 ID
DONETS RIVER
320 ID
72 GRD
213 RD

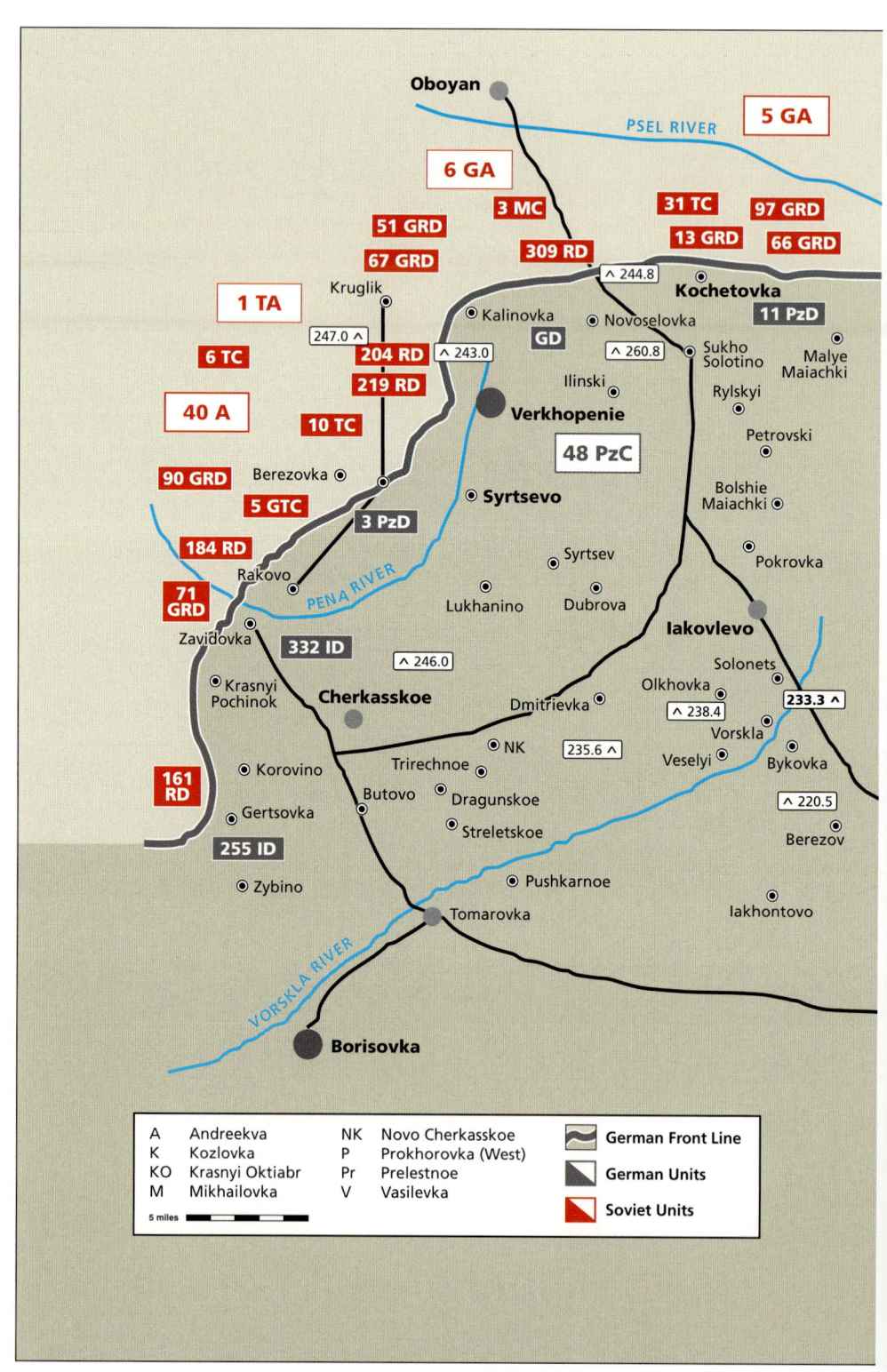

Map 16   Southern Salient, July 12th 1943 – midnight.

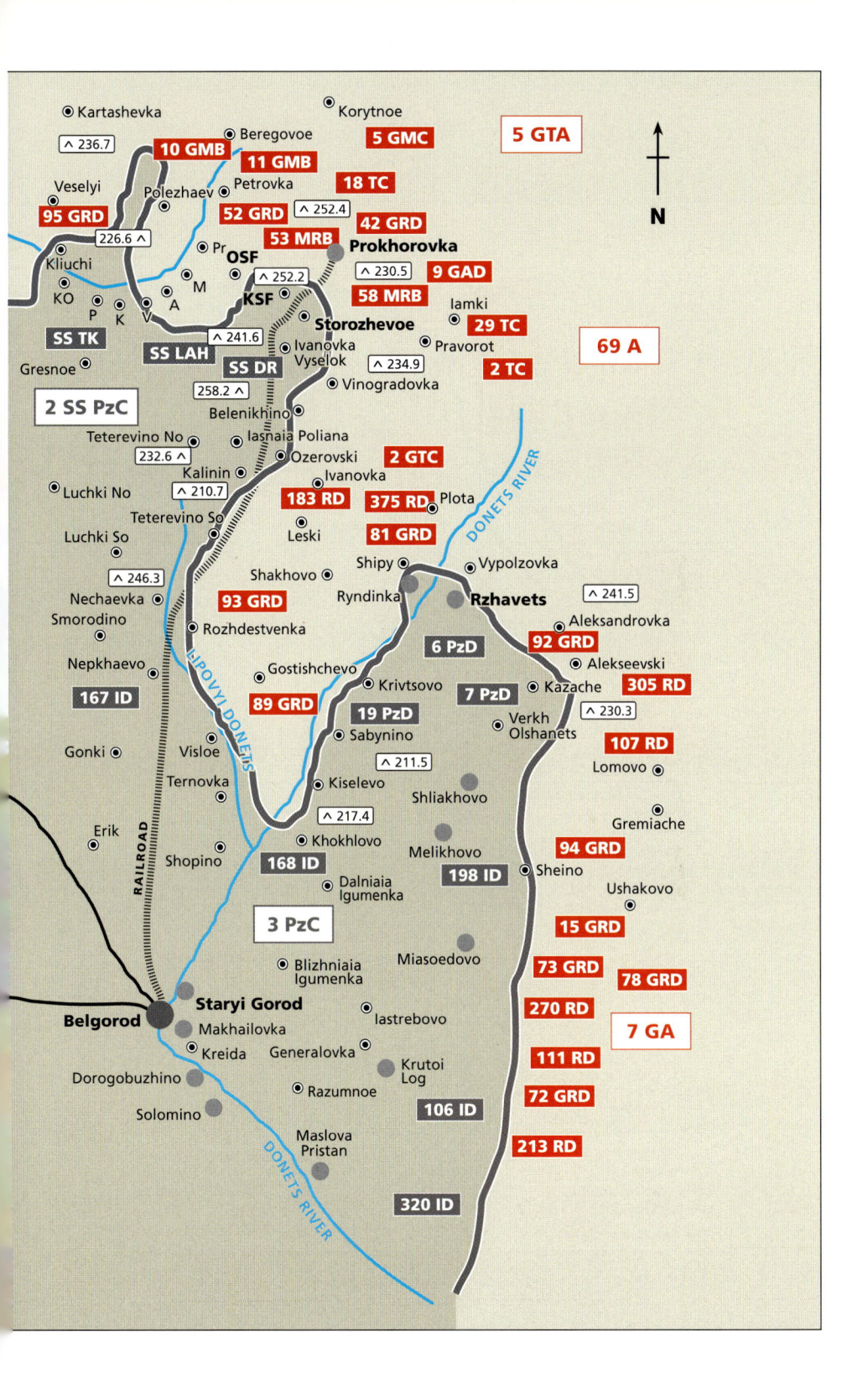

Map of the Prokhorovka/Belgorod area showing military unit positions.

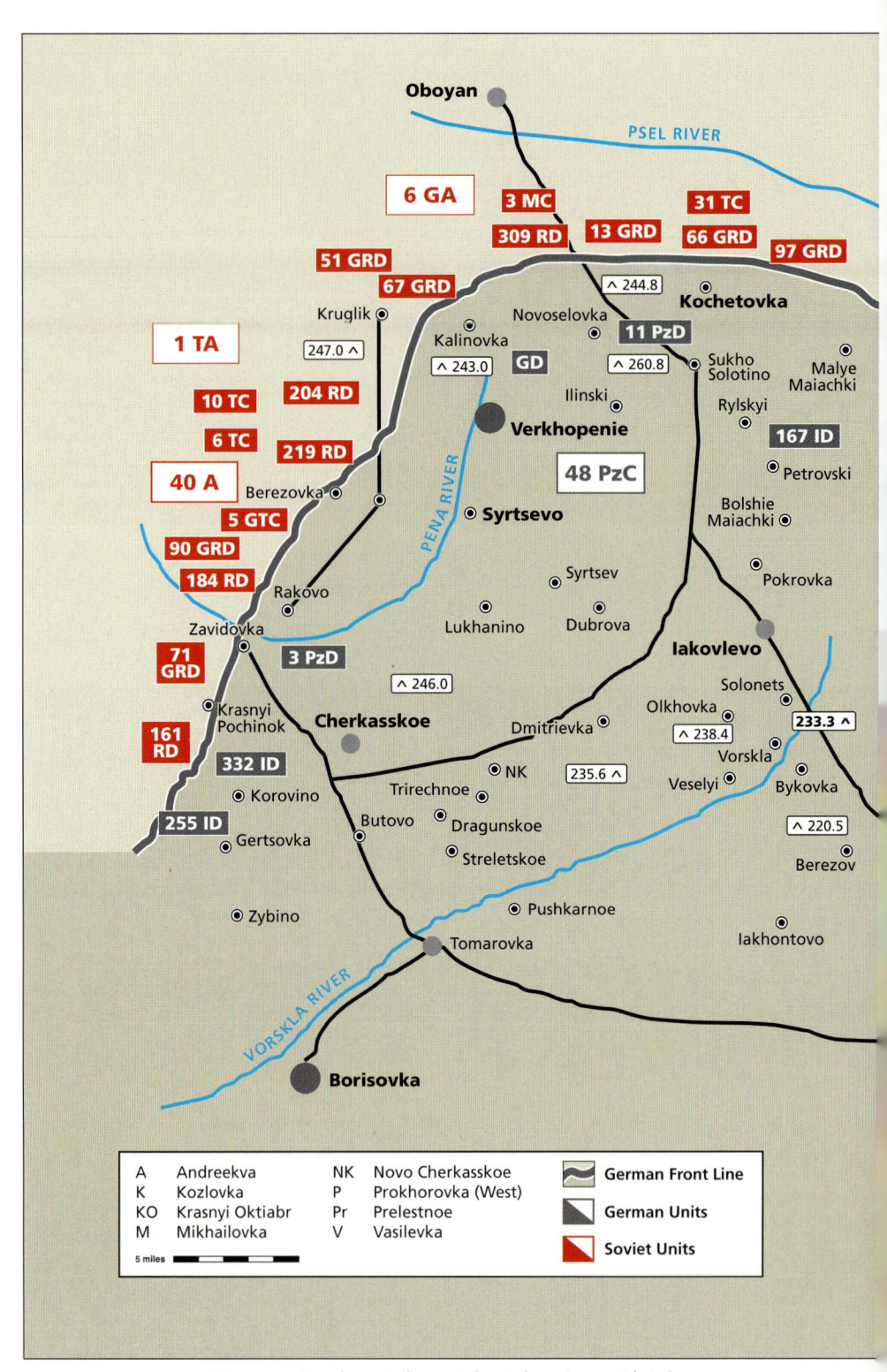

Map 17   Southern Salient, July 13th 1943 – midnight.

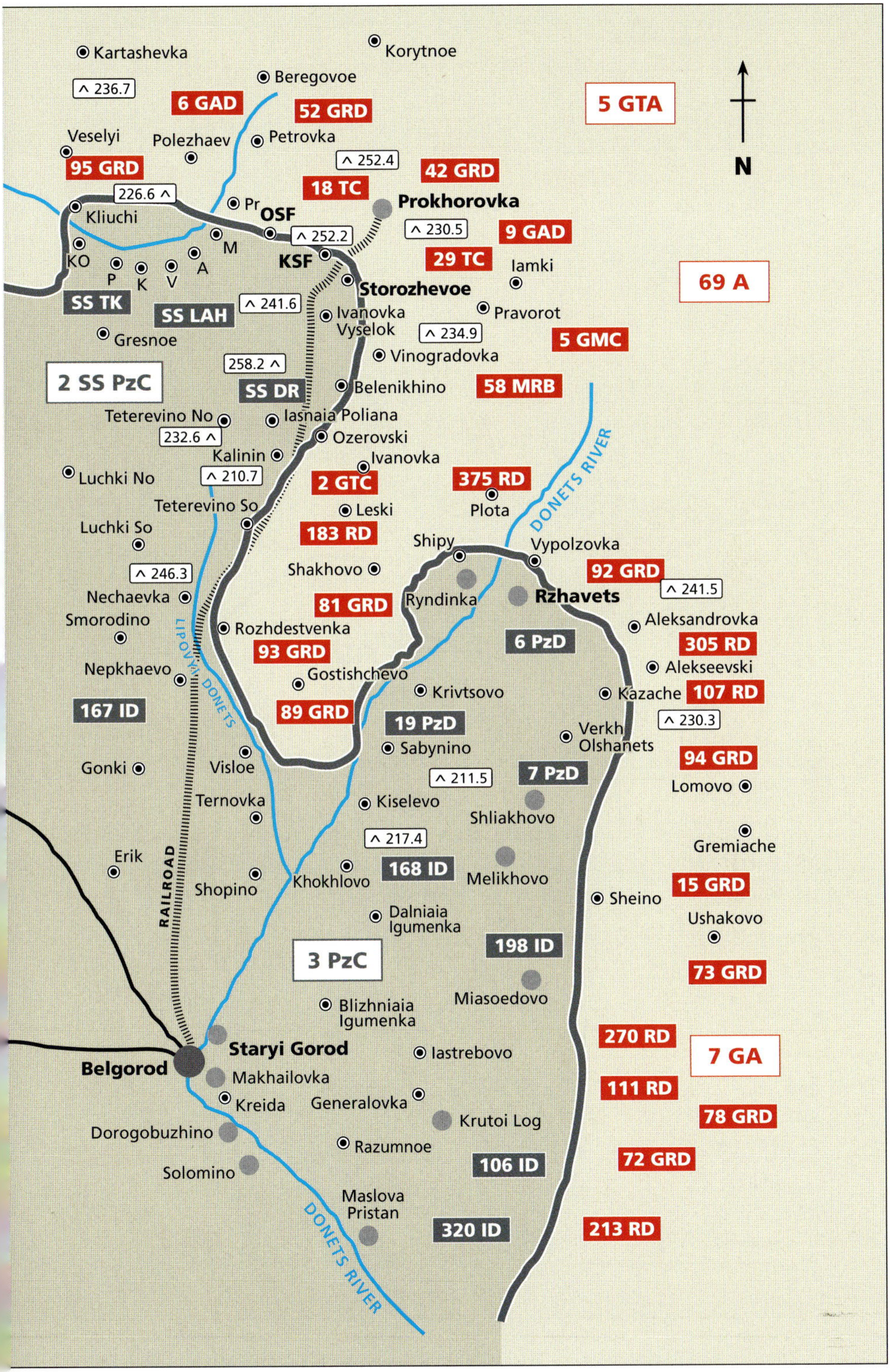
Kartashevka
Korytnoe
Beregovoe
^ 236.7
6 GAD
52 GRD
5 GTA
N
Veselyi
Polezhaev
Petrovka
95 GRD
^ 252.4
42 GRD
226.6 ^
18 TC
Prokhorovka
Kliuchi
Pr
OSF
^ 230.5
9 GAD
M
^ 252.2
KO
P
K
V
A
KSF
29 TC
Iamki
69 A
Storozhevoe
SS TK
SS LAH
^ 241.6
Ivanovka Vyselok
Pravorot
^ 234.9
5 GMC
Gresnoe
Vinogradovka
258.2 ^
2 SS PzC
SS DR
Belenikhino
58 MRB
Teterevino No
Iasnaia Poliana
232.6 ^
Ozerovski
Kalinin
Ivanovka
Luchki No
^ 210.7
2 GTC
375 RD
DONETS RIVER
Teterevino So
Leski
Plota
Luchki So
183 RD
Shipy
Vypolzovka
^ 246.3
Shakhovo
92 GRD
^ 241.5
Nechaevka
Ryndinka
Rzhavets
Smorodino
81 GRD
Aleksandrovka
Rozhdestvenka
6 PzD
305 RD
LIPOVYI DONETS
93 GRD
Alekseevski
Nepkhaevo
Gostishchevo
Kazache
107 RD
Krivtsovo
167 ID
89 GRD
^ 230.3
19 PzD
Verkh Olshanets
Sabynino
94 GRD
Gonki
Visloe
^ 211.5
7 PzD
Lomovo
Ternovka
Kiselevo
Shliakhovo
Gremiache
^ 217.4
Erik
168 ID
Melikhovo
15 GRD
RAILROAD
Shopino
Khokhlovo
Sheino
Ushakovo
Dalniaia Igumenka
198 ID
3 PzC
73 GRD
Miasoedovo
Blizhniaia Igumenka
270 RD
Staryi Gorod
7 GA
Iastrebovo
Belgorod
111 RD
Makhailovka
Kreida
Generalovka
78 GRD
Krutoi Log
Dorogobuzhino
Razumnoe
72 GRD
106 ID
Solomino
Maslova Pristan
320 ID
213 RD
DONETS RIVER

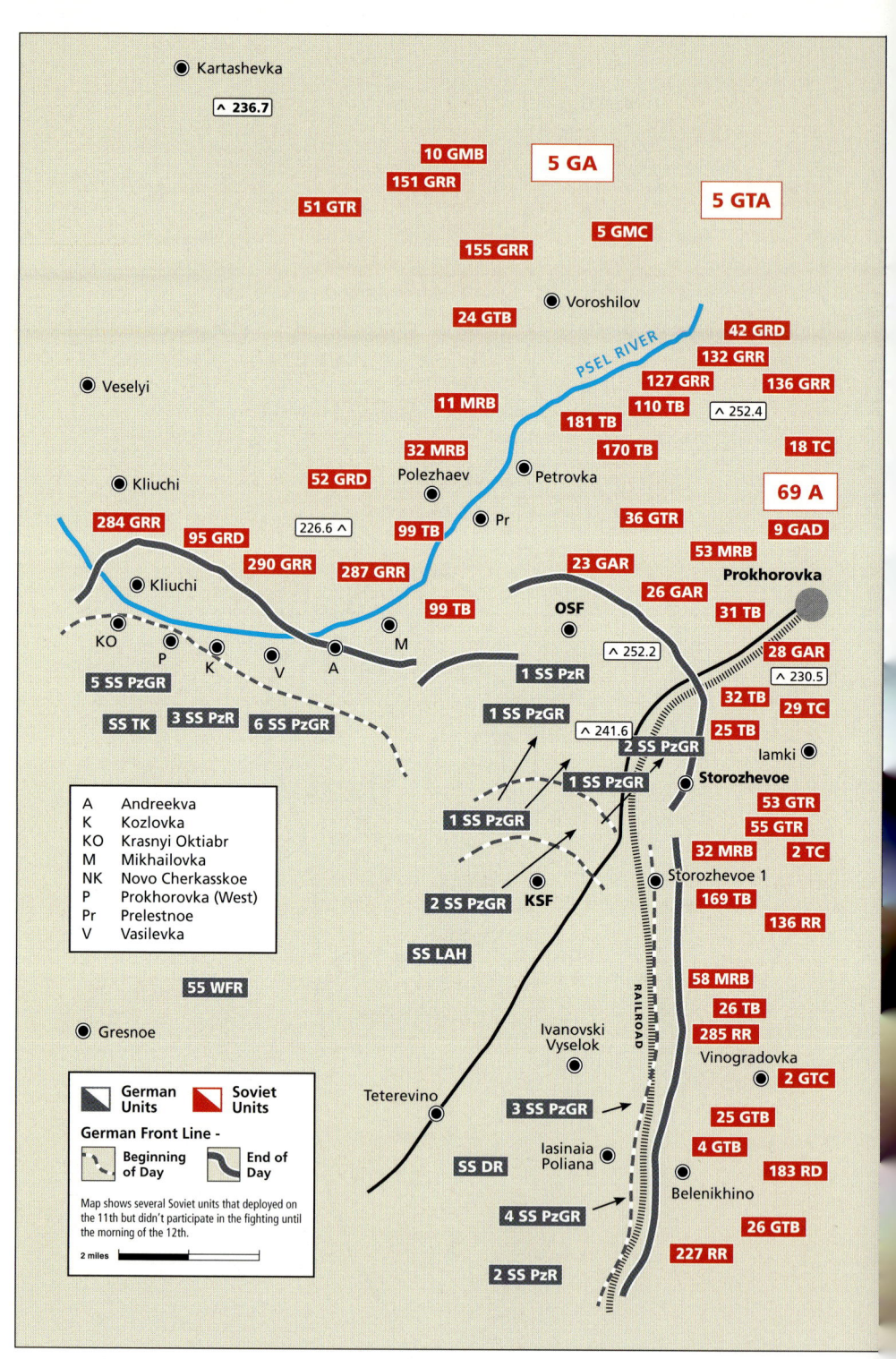

Map 18 Southern Salient, Battle for Prokhorovka, July 11th 1943 – midnight.
2nd SS PzC's attempt to take Prokhorovka before 5th GTA fully arrived.

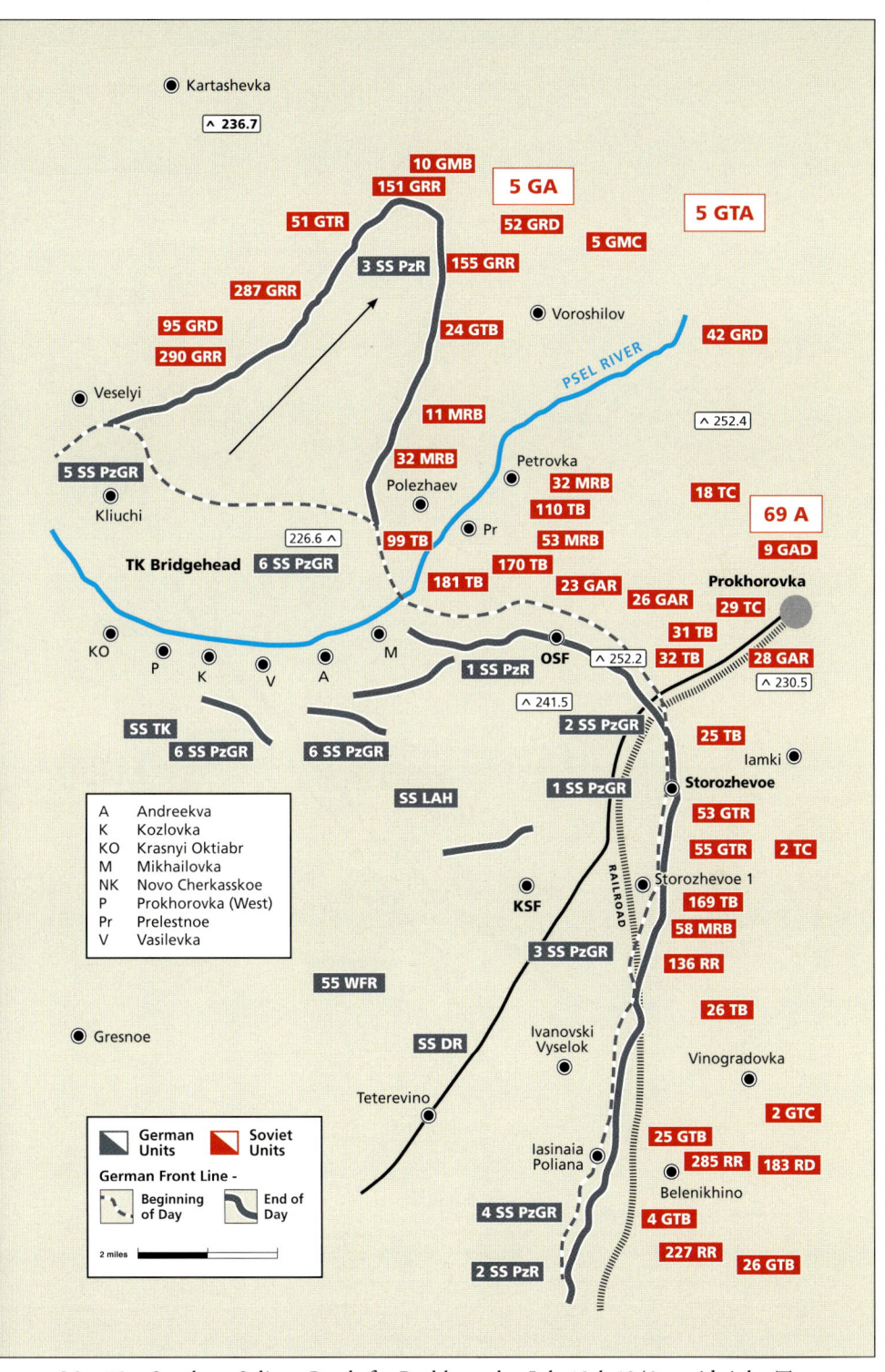

Map 19 Southern Salient, Battle for Prokhorovka, July 12th 1943 – midnight. The advance of 2nd SS PzC after Rotmistrov's assault failed to encircle the Germans.

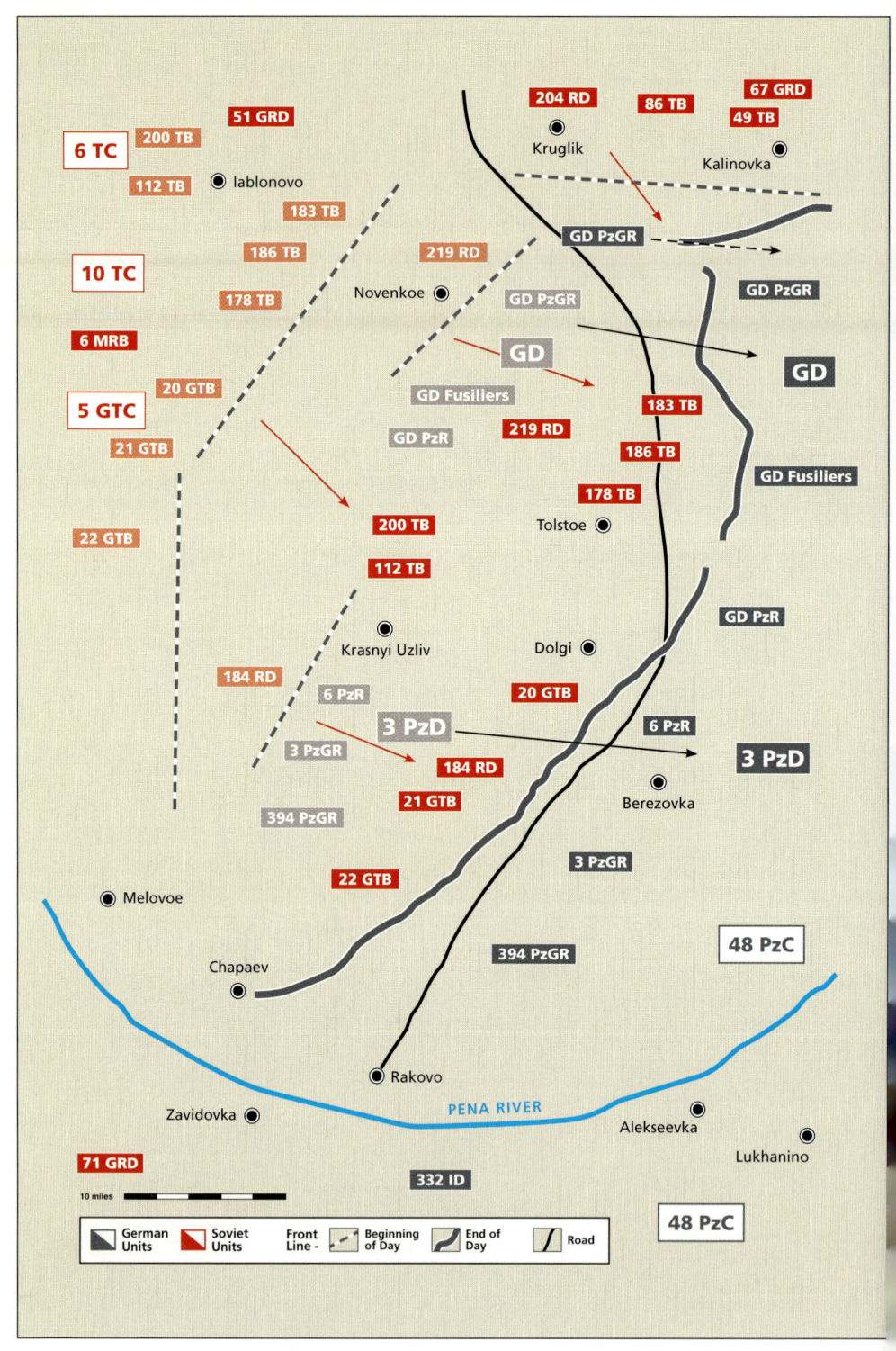

Map 20 Southern Salient, Counter-attack of 1st TA, July 12th 1943 – midnight.
The sector retreat of 48th PzC against 1st TA's counter-attack.

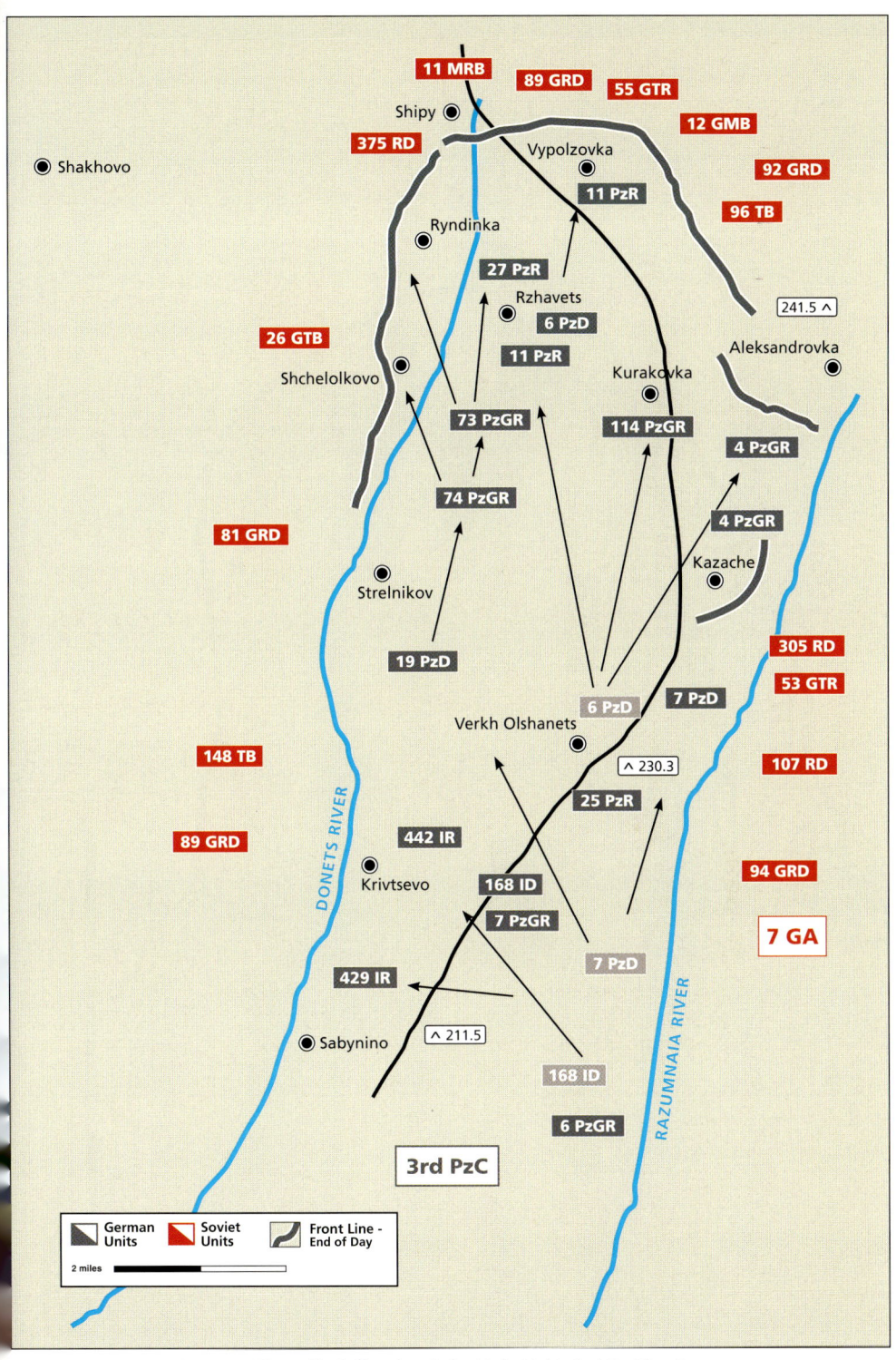

Map 21   Kempf's Offensive, July 12th 1943. 3rd PzC's advance.

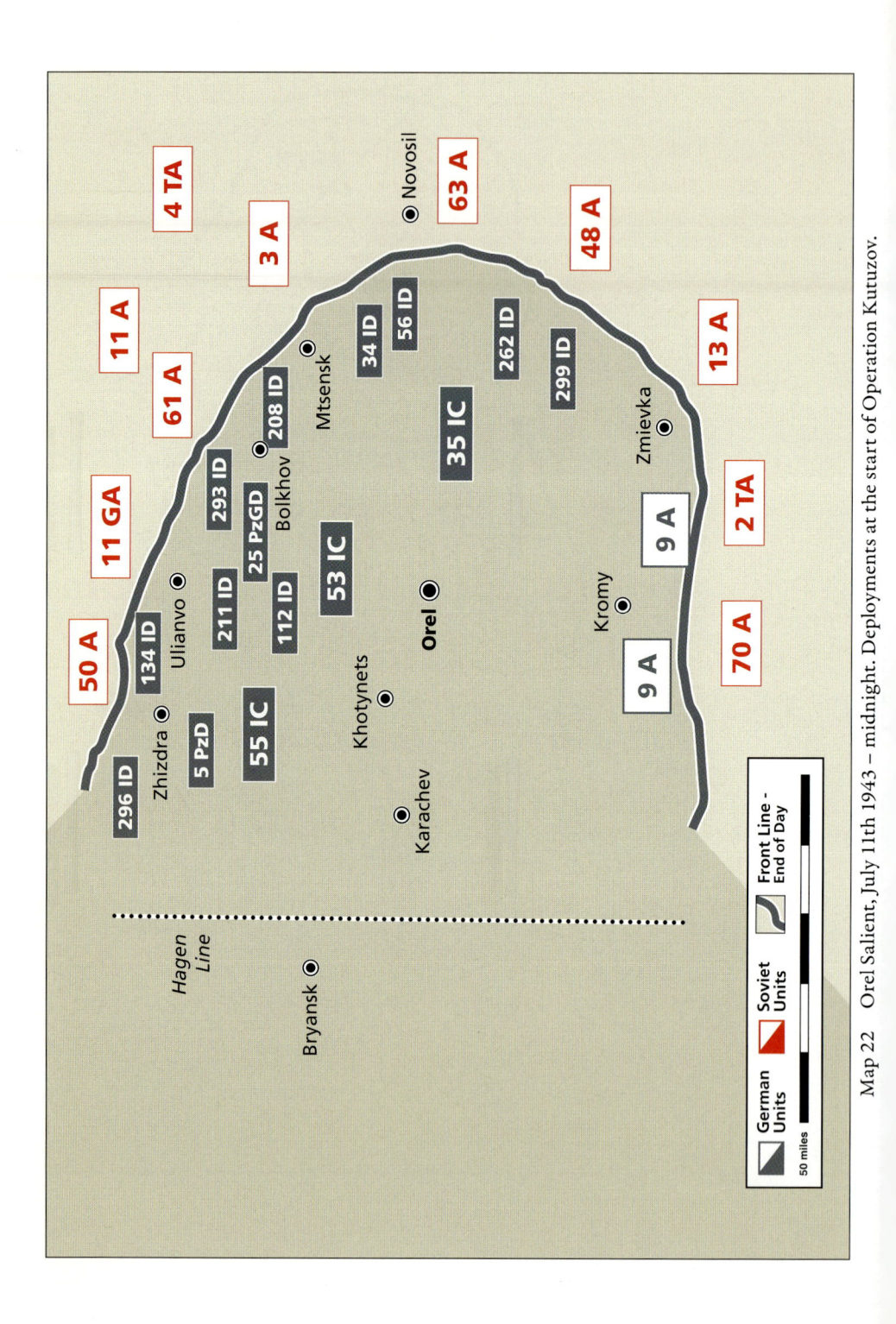

Map 22 Orel Salient, July 11th 1943 – midnight. Deployments at the start of Operation Kutuzov.

approaching Hill 244.8 to join up with Strachwitz's group when Soviet tanks and infantry crested the hill and attacked. By the end of the day, 48th PzC was now down to an arguable 173 running panzers. This number included 30 Panthers, some of which were in the repair shop. dgk153. dgr218. gnk245. gnk274. wwf104. dgr99.

The bulk of *GD* assembled during the predawn hours near Hill 244.8 to regroup. The hill was about six miles southwest of the bend in the Psel River but the division would never go beyond the hill. At daybreak, Knobelsdorff ordered the *GD* to head south on the west side of Verkhopenie near Hill 258.5 and the Tolstoe woods (referred to sometimes as Tolstoe Woods) to crush the Soviet defenders in the Pena bend. The defenders consisted of 3rd MC, 6th TC and the remnants of 67th GRD and 90th GRD. If this could be accomplished then 48th PzC would have a good chance to reach Oboyan against lighter resistance on its west flank. Hoth knew the operation was running out of time but felt this delaying operation was necessary for the overall success of Operation Citadel. Von Manstein and Hoth at this point felt the Germans had a chance of reaching Kursk, not realizing that 5th GTA and 5th GA were nearing the sector. gnk270. gnk253m.

At 0330 hrs *GD*, attacking the boundary line between 6th TC and 3rd MC, fought a hard battle with 200th TB of 6th TC southwest of Novoselovka, in rugged terrain that limited armor movement. Early in the fight, the 16th VA sent a squadron to slow the Germans down. The planes did cause the 48th PzC to halt temporarily and to pull back but, after the *Luftwaffe* intervened forcing the Soviet planes to leave the sector, the Germans resumed their advance. During the battle that *GD* was winning, Vatutin brought up reinforcements; the 112th TB, 6th MRB and the 60th TR, but still could not stop *GD*. *GD* continued to advance and took Hill 247.0 south of Kruglik along the Kruglik-Berezovka road after daybreak, severing Getman's 6th TC's communications with HQ and 10th TC and threatening the viability of his entire force. *GD* moved on and after the three-hour fight with 10th TC, captured Hill 243.0 northeast of Verkhopenie but suffered heavy casualties doing it. Colonel Graf Strachwitz was injured and handed command over to Captain von Wietersheim. Getman's 6th TC was shattered, having only 35 tanks left in the exchange, and had to fall back. Leading elements of *GD* approached the village of Kruglik but were then fired on by Soviet rockets, halting the advance and forcing the panzers to fall back. During the night, Vatutin sent up the remnants of four tank regiments to support 6th TC. dgk153++. vzz594. dgk154m. dgr172m. dgk222m. fkk84. dgr209m. cbk74. wwf105++ jp168. wwf105+. gnk253m. zra62. fmz221m. hsz128.

While elements of *GD* attacked toward Hill 243.0, other elements of the division launched from near Novoselovka heading for Kalinovka and Vladimirovka, which were defended by the 10th TC. The 10th TC attacked the Germans, inflicting heavy casualties and forcing the *GD* to fall back to regroup. Kalinovka was west of Novoselovka while Vladimirovka was a few miles north of Novoselovka along the road to Oboyan. dgr218. dgr172m.

Leading elements of *GD* were pushing ahead toward Kruglik which, if captured, would cut off the Soviet'Russians' supply route to the south. South of Kalinovka and east of the Berezovka-Kruglik road, Group Strachwitz carried out its assigned task of screening the right flank of the main thrust driving on Hill 247.0, south of Kruglik, by attacking Hill 243.0. Kruglik and Kalinovka were important fortified strongpoints in the west and when they were approached by recon forces of *GD* after Hill 243.0 was captured, T34s came out of their hiding places and attacked after an ambush by rocket fire failed to stop the Germans. The *GD* could not move further so they dug in east of Kalinovka and south of Kruglik to regroup and to block the path if Soviet reinforcements left Kruglik. Before Group Strachwitz attacked Hill 243.0 at 0500 hrs, it had to defend itself against an ambush southwest of Novoselovka at Point 1.8. hjj120. mhz292. hsz127+. fkk271+. gnk270. gnk275. wwf103++. fmz221m.

By 0700 hrs, Shractwitz had captured Hill 243.0 but its advance had been stopped when the 112th TB and 200th TB counter-attacked. With the help of the rocket regiment the Soviets were repelled. While on the hill, the Germans regrouped and then resumed their advance after 1300 hrs. By the end of the day, 48th PzC had reached Novenkoe, creating a salient in the positions of 6th TC and 184th RD and threatening to roll the Soviets up. dgr218.

The 3rd PzD joined *GD* as darkness fell at Verkhopenie but the 3rd PzD had to split its 70 panzer group into two to defend against two threats. While being ordered to join up with *GD* to defend Verkhopenie, the 3rd PzD sent some panzers and men south to Berezovka, where the left flank of 6th TC renewed its attack. When the 3rd PzD's panzers approached the northern edge of Berezovka they surprised the battered 6th TC, encircling a number of tanks and destroying them. It was a bad day for 6th TC, who by the end of the day had only 35 tanks and assault guns still running and only half of them were T34s. The tank corps had started the day with 100 tanks and the campaign with 200 tanks. During the day other Soviet tankers joined the fray.

Southeast of Kalinovka around 1000 hrs, elements of *GD* were attacked when trying to make contact with 11th PzD and were forced to go into a hedgehog defense. Shifting direction to elude the heavy fire, the *GD* Group moved on the intersection near Hill 258.5 but found heavy fire there also. The 3rd PzD to the southwest, and trying to advance, was also struck by heavy fire and could not provide assistance. In early afternoon the 2nd APC Squadron and a assault gun battalion passed through the Kubaossovski Valley, the road to Kruglik to Hill 258.5, about 1,000 yards southeast of Hill 247.0 to assist. The Soviet supply road to this wooded area at Hill 258.5 was finally severed, allowing *GD* to capture the hill. Hill 247.0, Hill 243.0 and Hill 258.5 were captured on this day but these important victories were tempered by the huge cost. The woods to the west of Hill 258.5 and Kruglik would be the next important objectives but both were heavily defended and would not be easy to take either. More of the Fusiliers were arriving to the area and that would help. The Strachwitz Group had captured Hill 243.0 but was now meeting heavy fire on its west flank. The rest of the day was used to bring more troops up and to stabilize the line. By the end of the day, *GD* Division was spent, making any further meaningful gains in the future suspect. See Map 23. rc203. dgk222m. hsz127+. fkk271+. fkk323m. dgk154++. fmz221m.

During the predawn hours, Katukov's 1st TA reorganized itself along the Psel River to the Oboyan road and southward along the Pena River. Getman's 6th TC, 90th GRD and 3rd MC defended along the Pena River on the 1st TA's right flank. The tank battle between the reinforced 1st TA and 48th PzC's left flank intensified and would continue for the next four days, preventing the 48th PzC from advancing or helping 2nd SS PzC. dgk152.

At 0400 hrs, while Strachwitz and his panzers were waiting for 11th PzD to show near Hill 244.8 to be relieved, the Soviets launched an ambush from behind the hill. It was during this engagement that Strachwitz had his arm crushed and was forced to hand over his command to Wietersheim. Several other panzers were hit as well but the Soviet attack was repulsed. When the 11th PzD did arrive, *GD* broke up into two groups: the panzers headed toward Kruglik while the grenadiers headed for Kalinovka, due east of Kruglik, to set up new defenses. Kalinovka lay in the middle of a valley that terminated to the south near Hill 258.5. Unknown to *GD*, Getman's 6th TC was defending that valley. To the north of Kalinovka, the 10th TC, with 100 tanks, had just moved there and was awaiting orders to attack. Between the two Soviet corps, the *GD* grenadiers were greatly outmatched. It was raining during the German match and it did slow them down. The panzers had driven past Kalinovka on their way to Hill 258.5, located west of Verkhopenie near Tolstoe Woods, when they were ambushed near Hill 232.8. The attack was repulsed and the Soviet tanks of the 200th TB of 6th TC headed back in the direction of Kalinovka. The panzer group continued on in the rain but it was attacked again by another Soviet force just north of Hill 258.5. After several hours of fierce fighting, the panzers started pushing the Soviets back though the battle was still engaged. gnk270+. gnk283m. dgk155+. wwf103. vzz594. hsz129+.

Elements of the Fusilier Regiment of *GD* and the 11th PzD were driving toward the Psel River when they were ambushed by the 10th TC and elements of the 31st TC coming in at both flanks. The Germans, though outnumbered, were able to repulse the attacks and move forward to capture Hill 244.8 which lay astride the road to Oboyan north of Novoselovka, just 13 miles from Oboyan. The Germans dug in on top of the hill and repulsed the counters that came. When more of *GD* arrived next day, they would attempt to cross the Psel. At the same time other elements of *GD* a little to the west of the important road were hit hard by a rocket attack that came from just south of Kruglik. They were currently fighting with 6th TC when the rockets started falling. mhz293. lck324. gnk301. pck72.

Fighting for Syrtsevo continued throughout the predawn hours but by dawn the Soviets fought a grudging withdrawal to the northwest. It was discovered that day from an interrogation of a captured general that the Soviets knew all about Operation Citadel and had prepared for it. gnk273. gnk253m.

Vatutin sent his 22nd GRC into the western flank of 48th PzC in order to prevent it from entering the heated battle west of Prokhorovka. rkz168.

The 11th PzD, from northeast of Verkhopenie and southeast of Novoselovka, had been fighting all day along the road to Oboyan and by evening had gained three miles, reaching Kochetovka to meet up with *SSTK*. The left flank of 11th PzD had gained only one mile to Kalinovka where it tied in with *GD*. *GD* was on the west side of the Oboyan road and advanced three miles to reach Kalinovka, about three miles north of Verkhopenie. To the left of *GD* from 0800 hrs, the 3rd PzD had to defend itself all day from Soviet counters but by the end of the day had advanced to a point over a mile northwest of Berezovka, south of the *GD* position. wdk152+. hjj121m. dgr209m. gnk253m.

In the 52nd IC sector, the 332nd ID eliminated most of the 6th TC and had driven the newly arrived 184th RD out of Alekseevka on the Pena River. The south side of the river was now clear of Soviets. Further south of Alekseevka, other elements of the 332nd ID were defending themselves against repeated attacks northwest of Korovino by the 71st GRD, while the 255th ID defended against two attacks southwest of Bubny by the 100th RD of 40th Army. With the bad weather, air raids by both sides were reduced and the roads were deteriorating, making travel difficult. It was another difficult day for 3rd PzD; it fought all day and could only reach two miles north of Berezovka near Dogi and Tolstoe Woods. It continued to be unable to stay with *GD*, which forced *GD* to stop its advance, turn back and support 3rd PzD. wdk153. gnk253m dgr98. dgr93m.

The 255th ID, 332nd ID would continue to provide flank protection. To the west of *GD*, 3rd PzD, which started the campaign with 70 Mk IIIs and IVs, was now down to 23 working panzers and was struggling to defend itself let alone advance. mhz306. mhz314. fkk87. vzz8m. gnk253m. gnk312m.

A shock group from *GD* and a few assault guns advanced through the Kubaossovski Valley and finally reached the road to Kruglik from Hill 258.5 by dark. The group was now 1,000 yards south of Hill 247.0 and had effectively blocked the supply route from Kruglik to Tolstoe and Berezovka. This shock group would also stop any reinforcements coming from the north to assist the defenders of Tolstoe Woods when the 3rd PzD and elements of *GD* attacked it. hsz128.

The weather turned against the Germans; it was cloudy with thunderstorms, making the roads almost impossible for trucks. The *Luftwaffe* was also restricted. By 1600 hrs, elements of *SSTK* had penetrated the line at Kozlovka and at Kochetovka, enabling them to join up with 11th PzD. A second light bridge across the Psel was completed at Krasnyi Oktiabr after 6th PzGR captured the town. wdk151. gnk253m. pck77+.

Northwest of Berezovka, the 3rd PzD broke through the Soviet line holding the Rakovo-Kruglik road and succeeded in outflanking the Soviet forces, which included the 112th TB (6th TC), forcing them to fall back into the nearby woods. With *GD* nearby, the two divisions were able to encircle the small Soviet force. The *Luftwaffe* flew in to help clear the pocket. It is estimated that 48th PzC was down to 219 panzers and assault guns when the day started. Another 46 panzers were lost that day, leaving 173 panzers working. In the last week of fighting the 48th PzC had lost 263 panzers. Only 25 of the nearly 200 Panthers that *GD* received were total write-offs; the rest needed repairs from mechanical failure or battle damage. 20 Panthers were ready to go back into the field by next day, raising the count of working Panthers to 38. *GD* had only 87 panzers including the 38 Panthers still running. In a few days' time, when Citadel was canceled, there would be 44 operable Panthers. Of the remaining 120 Panthers that were recovered, 80 were in the repair shop due to mechanical failures and the rest had battle damage. mhz291+. hsz130. nzk177+. hjj120.

Vatutin, realizing his front line in the west was shattered, brought up reinforcements the night before and continued to do so in the morning. Besides the 10th TC, 184th GRD and 204th GRD, the 309th RD, the weakened 67th GRD and the 5th GTC were brought up to block the way to Oboyan. A little to the east, Chernienko's 31st TC was also brought up to cover the banks of the Psel River where the 51st GRD and elements of the 309th RD were dug-in. Most of these units would now be under 1st TA leadership. wff103+.

The threat to 48th PzC's western flank was becoming so severe that most of *GD* had to assist the 3rd PzD in safeguarding the flank, leaving the 11th PzD the sole responsibility of pushing across the Psel to reach Oboyan. It was a task that one weakened division would be unable to accomplish. wwf104.

The 48th PzC resumed its attack northward, taking the village of Pokrovski then moving on to the hill five miles to the north and capturing it. The northern combat group of *GD*, after clearing resistance east of Verkhopenie, turned southwest to destroy the Soviets that were withdrawing west of the Pena. At the same time, the 3rd PzD retook Syrzevo and the high ground to the south. fkk255. fkk323m.

At 1130 hrs General Guderian arrived at Knobelsdorff's HQ to receive a personal sitrep and to discuss the new Panther. Guderian agreed with the field commander that the crews of the new Panthers were poorly trained and that the machine went into battle before all the bugs were worked out. It was also pointed out that the side armor was too thin but the new gun was very potent. The fuel lines were also in need of extra protection to reduce the chance for fires. When General Guderian returned to Berlin, he completed a critical report summarizing the good and bad points of the Panther. Speers used this report to make improvements in the machine. gnk275. zzt98+.

After a brief but bitter battle, the 332nd ID captured Vosschod and then had to defend it from a Soviet counter-attack. The Soviets were also unsuccessful in blowing the bridge at Zavidovka. On the right flank of the 52nd IC, the 255th ID were being pushed out of their defenses in the woods southwest of Bubny where it was lost in hard hand-to-hand combat. The outposts in the village of Trefilovka were pulled out as well. fkk255.

The 48th PzC struck the 6th GA and 1st TA as it tried to push closer to Oboyan. *GD* wheeled south and cleared Soviet forces on the left flank of the corps. *Luftwaffe* assisted with raids. bt87.

The 52nd IC moved north, crossed the Pena and joined with 3rd PzD against the Soviet 40th Army.

While the *GD* panzer group was fighting off the 6th TC north of Hill 258.5, it was discovered that another Soviet column of 40 tanks was heading south from Kalinovka. Not capable of handling both Soviet forces, Wietersheim requested 3rd PzD dispatch a panzer group from Verkhopenie to intercept the large force. Knobelsdorff agreed and sent the order. Despite a heavy air cap of Soviet planes in the sector, 3rd PzD sent a panzer column west to intercept. Driving into another thunderstorm, the ground turned to mud and slowed their progress but at least the Soviet planes had to move off. When Schmidt-Ott's panzers (3rd PzD) reached *GD*, just north of Hill 258.5, the battle was still raging. By 1900 hrs, the two German forces had forced the 6th TC to evacuate the hill and were securing the top for any last resistance. The 6th TC lost 65 of its 100 tanks and the survivors of the 200th TB and 112th TB hid until dark before heading south for the Berezovka area where the 184th RD was stationed. gnk271+. pck72. hsz130.

After helping the Strachwitz group capture Hill 258.5, the Schmidt-Ott group of 3rd PzD moved further south and renewed its attack on Soviet positions on Hill 243.0. The *Luftwaffe*, which had been absent all morning, finally showed up and struck the guns on top of the hill. By 1800 hrs it was estimated another 50 tanks were destroyed between the panzers and the Stukas. Almost 100 tanks were destroyed between the fighting for Hill 258.5-Hill 243.0 area. With the heavy losses, the Soviets fell back to the north, while the panzers of the 3rd PzD continued south toward Berezovka to join elements of *GD* clear that sector. Schmidt-Ott's panzers were traveling south opposite the Tolstoe woods along the Kruglik-Berezovka road, south of Hill 258.5, when a battery of Soviet guns opened fire on the column. The panzers had to immediately leave the road and head cross country to the east to avoid the barrage. Schmidt-Ott stopped for the night off the road and would resume his march to Berezovka in the morning. No further action occurred that night for the tired panzer group. See Map 23. gnk273. pck72.

When it was discovered that the Soviets had abandoned the area immediately west of Solotinka, Mickl ordered his panzer group to secure Hill 232.8 and then move east toward the boundary with 2nd SS PzC, which was advancing to secure the northern side of the Psel River. Pz Abt 11, attached to 11th PzD, attacked Hill 232.8 and after a three-hour battle drove the defenders off. As this battle was raging, the Germans could see Soviet tanks and infantry heading for nearby Hill 244.8. It appeared the Soviets had not given up on that hill. When Hill 232.8 was captured, the Germans considered attacking toward Hill 244.8 to intercept but quickly rejected that thought when it was determined that nearly 50 Soviet tanks had assembled there. gnk275.

While part of *GD* had moved south to Hill 258.5, the remainder of the division, along with elements of 11th PzD, stayed in the Kruglik-Kalinovka area. The Germans were split between these villages, trying to block the Soviets from sending reserves and supplies further south. The original plan was to have *GD* approach Kruglik and bring artillery to bear on any convoy that left the town but when Major Frantz saw the extreme activity within the town, he decided to attack and capture the town if possible, or destroy as much as possible and fall back if the Soviet response was too strong. Just before dusk, he launched and got within 300 yards of the village before the Soviet guns and rockets started firing. The town could not be captured for lack of infantry and the assault guns pulled back to the south and established a blocking position. It had been a hard day for *GD*. They avoided a potential catastrophe at Hill 258.5 but they gained little ground and could not capture Kruglik or Kalinovka, though they maintained blocking positions to the south. After starting the campaign with 300 assorted panzers, *GD* was now down to 20. gnk272.

Two Soviet shock groups were being prepared for a massive counter-attack. The first group was being assembled in the Novye Lozy-Belenikhino-Prokhorovka-Polezhaev-Veselyi-Kochetovka area and included the 5th GTA, a rifle corps of 69th Army and two rifle corps of 5th GA. The second, smaller group which consisted of the 6th GA and 3rd MC of 1st TA, was assembling in the Melovoe, Novenkoe, Kruglik Kalinovka and Hill 244.8 areas. To the east, the 49th RC of 7th GA was preparing an attack along the line Hill 209-Gremuchi-Hill 202.8. vzz261++. vzz268. vzz428.

The 48th PzC was now no more than twelve miles from Oboyan, the lynchpin of the Soviet defenses on the southern salient. It began massing its panzers along a five mile front west of Prokhorovka. Hoth intended the SS to join up with the Kempf Army to the east and capture Prokhorovka while the 48th PzC took Oboyan. Kempf's advance was meeting stiff resistance from many Soviet units. The 24th PzC was just released from reserves and was now traveling north from the Donbas to clear resistance north of Belgorod and would then move on to assist at Prokhorovka. That was with Hitler's permission. With the extreme resistance the Soviets had generated and with the state of exhaustion and attrition his forces were experiencing, I argue that both Oboyan and Prokhorovka were not attainable and that Hoth should have changed his plans to one or the other, preferably Prokhorovka. Von Manstein did not have the resources for both objectives as well as trying to encircle the 48th RC with the help of 3rd PzC in the Donets River sector. rc204.

By the end of the day, Hoth had become slightly more confident that after *GD* had taken two important hills and blocked Kruglik and Kalinovka, that 4th PzA had a chance of reaching Kursk. This attitude of Hoth alone clearly shows he did not understand the scale of reinforcements that would soon be arriving. *GD* was now approaching Kruglik and there had been little resistance; the Germans started to believe the Soviets had evacuated when all of a sudden, hundreds of rockets poured from the village against the panzers. The first attack failed against such resistance and *GD* had to fall back. Also, in the 3rd PzC sector it looked like the Soviet salient along the Donets River was finally beginning to recede. Even at this late date, Hoth was not aware a tank force the size of 5th GTA and an army the size of 5th GA were now preparing a major counter-attack. Hoth had wasted too much time fighting in the Pena River area instead of redesigning his attack plan while he had adequate forces to reach Prokhorovka and beyond. Now it was too late. gnk281. wwf103.

Friction was building between von Manstein and Hoth. Von Manstein wanted Hoth to give more attention and assets to 3rd PzC while Hoth seemed obsessed in clearing the Pena River region. Hoth suggested to von Manstein that 24th PzC be deployed east of the Donets in order for 3rd PzC to catch up. Looking back it can clearly be seen that von Manstein was right and Hoth was wrong about concentrating so much effort in the Pena River area. The Pena River region was a black hole that ate up the 48th PzC and contributed to the corps stalling its advance due to high casualties in men and panzers. It also prevented the 48th PzC from crossing the Psel River and supporting *SSTK* which badly needed that support. When 24th PzC was still held back, Hoth continued to neglect Kempf and concentrate on the Pena River area. Hoth seemed to forget his timetable and the possibility that Vatutin had more reserves that could be brought up, and von Manstein had confronted Hoth for the last three days about the east flank and allowed Hoth to neglect it. gnk275.

At 0600 hrs as part of Group South the 19th PzD, minus its panzers which were with Group North, moved out and attacked Blizhniaia Igumenka from the southwest. The Red Air Force flew low over the village and strafed the German infantry that were now just entering the village and fighting house to house. Schmidt, seeing the Soviet planes and knowing his men were in trouble, sent the waiting Pz Abt 19 in to support the attack. After defeating the remaining bunkers that ringed the village, the panzers entered the town and together wih the infantry were able to push the Soviets out. This is just one of many examples that show the 3rd PzC received little air support. With greater air support, Kempf might have been able to reach Prokhorovka by the 12th. gnk239.

After the bitter fighting the previous day, Kempf paused most of his forces on this morning to regroup and to bring his artillery closer to the new line. The 3rd PzC could not pause too long for it had to catch up to 2nd SS PzC in order to divert enemy strength away from Prokhorovka. vzz251.

During the predawn hours, Vatutin had to recall the 92nd GRD back up to the line next to the 305th RD; it had been sent to the rear for rest the previous day but a gap formed between Kiselevo, Hill 122.5, Shliakhovo and Hill 224.4 and they had to plug it. These preparations were needed as the 3rd PzC, with 19th PzD in the lead, would attack in the morning between the Donets and Razumnaia Rivers. The 168th ID would be on the left next to the Donets and heading for Khokhlovo and Kiselevo. The 6th PzD to the right of 19th PzD would launch from the Melikhovo area toward Kazache and eventually Rzhavets. Next to the 6th PzD on the right flank was 7th PzD and protecting 7th PzD's flank was 198th ID. To reduce the flank frontage of 7th PzD, the 326th GR of 198th ID had to increase its frontage. The increased frontage proved too much and Maj General von Horn had to send other elements of the 198th ID northward to help the 326th before it shattered against the constant pressure. The 7th PzD was at Miasoedovo and it had to break through the 94th GRD's defenses along the heights north of town if it was to catch up and then protect the 6th PzD's flank. It spent the entire day trying to break loose but it failed and stayed in the Miasoedovo sector. Kempf wanted the 7th PzD to be more involved with the drive north instead of using most of its resources in defending the eastern flank. He ordered the 198th ID to expand its sector to take over more of the east line for 7th PzD. Additional corps artillery was moved up to assist 7th PzD in its move north. Kiselevo was two miles north of Khokhlovo. vzz251+. vzz3m. dgr155m. dgr173m. dgr39m. vzz3m. dgk170m. gnk268+. dlu83. dlu87. shn160.

At 1200 hrs from just north of Melikhovo, Hunersdorff launched his Group North toward Hill 230.3. Within an hour the hill was his and he was driving west toward Sabynino, southwest of Hill 230.3. All the while, the 168th ID launched into the western edge of the Soviet salient along the Donets River. Other elements of the combat group tore through the Soviet line near Dalnaia Igumenka and, driving southwest, reached the State Farm where a group of T34s were stationed to keep the corridor open to allow the assorted Soviet forces to escape the pocket that Breith tried to form. Most of the Soviets had gone north, evading the closing noose. The Germans had been too slow in closing the pocket but at least the Soviet stronghold along the river had been broken. The 168th ID could now move north with the panzers and by the afternoon had reached Blizhniaia Igumenka. Von Manstein wanted the *Luftwaffe* to go after the fleeing Soviets but all of the *Luftwaffe* was busy in the other two corps' sectors and could not assist. It had taken 3rd PzC four days to clear an area that was scheduled to be taken in the first day of operations. Kempf would never catch up and it would be a critical failing as *Das Reich* would be forced to protect its flank and was never much help with *LAH* in taking Prokhorovka. The situation could have been different if Kempf had been able to keep up with the advance of the SS and protect their flank. Though risky, the two divisions of 24th PzC that were in the area should have been deployed by 7/6 or 7/7 to help clear this Soviet salient near the river for it was causing an impossible condition for the SS moving north. It has also been argued that Kempf should have received some of the new Panthers in helping to screen the far eastern flank or perhaps had greater priority with *Luftwaffe* support. These and many other indicators show the Germans just did not have enough panzers, planes and men to succeed in this operation. gnk237+. gnk253m. vzz3m.

At 0700 hrs, the 375th RD counter-attacked the 168th ID. Maj General von Hutner was preparing to attack when the assault came. Instead of going defensive, he ordered his 168th ID to attack. It had been discovered that the Soviets were crossing the Donets, heading for the Shopino area and building new defenses. Kempf wanted this escape route blocked in order to trap as many of the enemy as possible on the east side. The Soviet counter had been repulsed and the 168th had gained ground, capturing hundreds of POWs and destroying many tanks. It was finally looking like 3rd PzC would catch up to *Das Reich* and stabilize the line. dlu90+.

Kempf's 3rd PzC was still struggling with 7th GA. Its failure to stay up with 2nd SS PzC was putting a drag on the SS's advance. While 48th PzC had to contend with just the left flank attacks, the 3rd PzC had both east and west flank attacks. The 19th PzD and the 168th ID had to defend against the enemy along the Northern Donets and Lipovyi Donets Rivers as they advanced northwards. Kempf also had to defend his long right flank southward to Maslovo Pristan, which had just been captured, against even stronger resistance. This struggle forced the 2nd SS PzC to use its 167th ID and *Das Reich* to protect its unguarded right flank along the Lipovyi Donets River. dgk161. dgk222m. dlu63m. lck246. dlu90.

The 6th PzD, which started this campaign with 105 working panzers with a few more in the repair shop, entered a minefield and lost several more panzers. By the end of the day, there were less than 40 panzers left in the division including several Mk IIIs with either

37mm or 50mm guns. A couple of converted T34s were part of the arsenal as well. rkz168. lck327. gnk269. gnk253m. fzk52.

It was another frustrating day for Kempf and Breith for their 7th PzD and 19th PzD were still tied down defending themselves against repeated flank attacks. The trailing units of 6th PzD, which were deployed to the right of 19th PzD, were able to drive northward a little as they headed for Melikhovo; 19th PzD along with the 168th ID were trying to clear the eastern bank of the Donets and protect 6th PzD's flank at the same time. On the other side of 6th PzD, 7th PzD was tied down assisting Corps Raus in guarding the far eastern flank. Shumilov gave orders to 81st RD and 375th RD to start pulling back to avoid being encircled and to help block the Germans in front of Prokhorovka. When the 6th PzD launched from Melikhovo, it was attacked near Hill 230.3 by Soviet tanks and infantry which it repulsed. A second group attacked near Shliakhovo, south of Hill 230.3, penetrating 6th PzD and threatening to encircle part of the division further south. The trapped panzers fought their way out and caught up to the bulk of the division but it was a costly affair. Earlier, with the help of engineers, 6th PzD was able to cross the tank ditch two miles from Melikhovo. mhz308. lck328. dgr155m. dgr173m. gnk269. vzz3m. vzz10m.

The 7th PzD remained east of Razumnoe to protect the rest of 3rd PzC's right flank as it drove northwards. The division was finally relieved by 198th ID when it moved up into the line. The 6th PzD and 19th PzD would stop for the night to regroup near Melikhovo. The two panzer divisions fought all day but could not advance much against stiff resistance. They were to attack Shliakhovo, two miles to the north, early next morning but would get a late start due to the critical need to regroup. The 168th ID was finally able to move quickly on the west flank of 3rd PzC along the east bank of the Donets River, arriving at Khokhlovo while its recon team reached Kiselevo. This lack of overall progress clearly shows 3rd PzC needed greater support yet Hoth, despite von Manstein's urgings, continued to ignore 3rd PzC's plight. shn160. dgr155m. dgr173m. dgr39m. vzz248. vzz3m. dlu83.

The 7th PzD covered Kempf's long eastern flank to Miasoedovo and lent support to Corps Raus which was under constant pressure. Additional pressure in the Rzhavets region was provided by the 72nd GRD and the 213th RD. Nearby, Shumilov's 15th GRD was moving toward Batratskaia Dacha which was defended by the 320th ID and 106th ID, which had already lost 40% of its strength. While helping the infantry the 7th PzD was unable to assist 6th PzD which was also having trouble. The pressure was to lessen a little when the 375th GRD and 81st RD was moved to north of Melikhovo, where 6th PzD was struggling to break through. The 89th GRD remained in the area to harass Raus. It was Vatutin's plan for 15th GRD to penetrate the line near Batratskaia Dacha as the 3rd PzC continued to advance northward past Melikhovo area. dgk162+. dlu63m. dgr155m. dgr173m. dlu87.

At 1400 hrs after clearing corridors through the minefields, the 19th PzD attacked toward Kiselevo from Khokhlovo and Hill 217.4 against the stiff defense of the 4th MRB and the 92nd GRD. Along this line 100 tanks were dug in, slowing the German pace noticeably. The flanking Hill 211.5 had Soviet artillery and they were firing on the German advance as well. Several Churchills tired to outmaneuver the panzers but the lead Tiger stopped two tanks in their tracks, forcing the remainder to retreat. After several costly attempts, the 19th PzD captured Kiselevo by 1600 hrs. The capture of this important strongpoint brought the 3rd PzC one step closer to reaching the Donets. See Map 23. vzz253. vzz3m. gnk253m.

On the east side of the Donets, Group Kempf went defensive against the counters of 25th GRC and the 35th GRC, which allowed the trapped contingent in the sliver of a salient next to the Donets to head north, allowing Kempf to make some progress in this area. The 17th VA made repeated bombing runs against the Germans to help the 25th GRC and the stragglers who were heading north. The 7th PzD was still holding a defensive front between Melikhovo and Miasoedovo, 13 miles northeast of Belgorod on the Razumnaia River, facing the 94th GRD. North of Melekovo, the 6th PzD repulsed a Soviet counter that was supported by 50 tanks. The 19th PzD was attacked at Dalnaia Igumenka by 92nd GRD while the 168th ID drove back an attack by the 81st GRD at Staryi Gorod. Unbelievably, the 168th ID was still only a few miles from Belgorod. The Germans were able to pick up much needed supplies in the field that were left when the Soviets quickly evacuated this strongpoint. wdk153. hjj121m. dgr155m. dgr173m. dgr39m. cbk69. vzz5m.

The 19th PzD had seen such heavy fighting in the opening days of the campaign that its two grenadier regiments only had a total of 400 combat soldiers each. Kempf again asked von Manstein for the 24th PzC as a replacement but the request was denied. It was not von Manstein's fault; Hitler would not allow the release. gnk269.

While the two other panzer divisions of 3rd PzC had been busy clearing the salient near the Donets, the 7th PzD had a relatively easy morning. The Soviets had not attacked while the 198th ID moved in to replace the 7th PzD. This was the first chance the panzers had to receive some maintenance. The division was now down to 50 panzers, including three Tigers. gnk239.

At 1700 hrs, Morozov's 81st GRD, now a part of General Rogozny's 48th RC, was ordered to the line: Hill 147.0-Volobuevka-Novoselovka (east)-Krivtsovo-Shcholokovo and instructed to be prepared to attack along with the 2nd GTC toward Belenikhino and Malye Maiachki on orders. After fighting for four days at Staryi Gorod to block the passage of 168th ID and 19th PzD, the 81st GRD had lost much of its heavy equipment and many men. The survivors were exhausted but were still determined to stop the Germans. The 227th RR of 183rd RD was sent further north to Storozhevoe, Vinogradovka and Zhimolostinoe line in order to keep *Das Reich* or 3rd PzC from passing. Knowing the SS would resume their attack northward the next morning Vatutin also tried to reinforce the line from the Psel River to Prokhorovka. vzz198. vzz5m.

At night, the Soviets made repeated armored assaults with mounted infantry in the Petrovski-Sbatshevski area (northeast of Belgorod) but were repulsed each time, at great expense. fkk151. vzz7m.

The Kempf Group pushed northwards as the enemy continued to attack their east flank. The corps stopped along the Belovskaia line for the night. The 4th PzA gained as much as six miles on this day on certain axes and once again the Kempf Group could not catch up.

According to Hoth's original plan, the 3rd PzC should have reached Prokhorovka, setting up a defense against further reserves coming into the sector from the east to protect the 2nd SS PzC as it drove through the corridor. General Breith was still 20 miles south of this area with dim prospects of reaching Prokhorovka and yet Hoth did little to assist his eastern flank. pck72+.

Kempf, knowing he was behind schedule, still allowed his divisions to regroup for much of the day. Trailing forces and artillery were brought up closer to the line and panzers received a quick maintenance check. He did send out recon forces to reconnoiter but not much beyond that. This pause allowed the Red Army to make changes in their deployment.

The 92nd GRD brought up its 280th GRR (Lt Col Novikov) alongside the 276th GRR (Maj Simonov) along the Kiselevo-Hill 211.5 sector. The Germans were heading straight for this sector to gain control of more of the Donets River as they drove north. Hill 211.5 was northeast of Kiselevo. vzz251. vzz10m.

The 198th ID, a part of Corps Raus, continued to hold back the many attacks launched by 7th GA but with the accumulated attrition, it was becoming harder and harder to do so against an enemy that seemed to have a bottomless well of reinforcements. lck327.

Kempf claimed to have destroyed 170 tanks and battering several tank regiments and four rifle divisions since the start of the campaign. The Soviets were still bringing up replacements and it was only a matter of time until this new pressure would implode 3rd PzC. The 111th GRD, 78th GRD, 270th RD and 15th GRD were all positioned east of the Koren River ready to deploy against Corps Raus and 7th PzD. wdk153+.

15

July 10th on the Northern Salient

See Map 6

The Germans were stopped far short of cutting the Orel-Kursk railroad line but Model did not have reserves to make another attempt at the important rail line. zzz101m. dgk87m. dgk122m.

In the predawn hours, the 15th VA attacked airfields near Orel but were unsuccessful and lost a few planes in the process. Destroying German planes on the ground would not only help Rokossovsky defeat 9th Army, it would also make it easier to defeat 2nd PzA when Operation Kutuzov began. cbk71. dgk122m. cbk12m.

In the 4th PzD sector near Teploe where the Germans were being pushed back, Kahler's 33rd PzR regrouped and resumed its attack, reaching Hill 260. In tough hand-to-hand combat, the 33rd PzR was able to crest the hill but under heavy shelling the Soviets immediately counter-attacked. In this engagement alone the regiment had over 100 casualties. For the day the entire division suffered 500 casualties while it expended 200 tons of ammo. The costs of reopening the gap toward Olkhovatka were high and the return was miminal. fkk68. dgk87m. dgk122m. lck116m.

While the 47th PzC made no gains, the 46th PzC with the 258th ID, 7th ID and 31st ID in the lead, attacked the east flank of 70th Army. The 258th ID attacked the 280th RD but were repulsed and then were counter-attacked. The 7th ID made a little progress but then the 175th RD counter-attacked and the Germans had to retreat. Both divisions failed in their objective of reaching the Kursk-Orel highway. Six T34s were reported lost. In the early hours on the east flank, the 74th RD and 148th RD, with support from tanks and planes, attacked the 78th AD of 23rd IC at Protasovo. The Soviets lost 12 tanks but did gain some ground. Throughout the whole day, the 78th AD and 216th ID received heavy shelling from the 12th AD. Despite this, elements of the 78th AD with the help of Ferdinands took a hill near Trosna and another group took the town by 1300 hrs, capturing 824 POWs. wdk182. dgk87m. dgk122m. lck116m.

The 41st PzC's 86th ID and 10th PzGD suffered heavy shelling from the 5th Artillery Division and the Soviet AF before being attacked by the 307th RD at Ponyri PC. At 1800 hrs, a small raiding squad of eight T34s took a hill near Ponyri PC but were then hit by Stukas and driven off. According to Soviet POWs, they had suffered heavy casualties during this operation. wdk182. dgk87m. dgr199m. dgk122m. lck116m.

After a brief pause, the 47th PzC which had the most panzers, resumed its attack with the objective of traveling through Teploe and traveling three miles to gain control of the high ground near Molotyschi. The Burmeister Brigade which included 2nd PzD, 4th PzD and 20th PzD, after initiating the attack, were to remain behind at Samodurovka north of Teploe in reserve until needed. The terrain north of Teploe was difficult and the 47th PzC had a tough time in advancing through it against heavy artillery shelling. By noon the assault was canceled and the 47th PzC moved back to its start line. The Soviets followed the retreat with elements of the 2nd TA, 19th TC, 40th GRD, 70th GRD, 75th GRD and the 1st GAD. wdk182. dgr198m. fkk102m. dgk87m. dgr199m. dgk122m. lck116m.

Von Saucken's 4th PzD with the support of sPzAbt 505 resumed its advance to capture Teploe. Afterwards, other panzer units would drive through the gap and head for Olkhovatka. The 33rd PzR of 4th ID finally took the town after hard house to house fighting where the CO was almost killed by snipers. Nearby at Hill 235, Stukas bombed it before an assault force with Tigers leading the way moved in. Twenty-two T34s were destroyed when Soviet hunter/killer teams moved in on the Tigers which were not yet defended by other panzers or infantry, but the German assault failed anyway. Because of some confusion in 4th PzD's command, the infantry was brought in too late and a good chance to penetrate the line was missed. The Red Army responded quicker and by 1700 hrs, had brought up more tanks and men and countered driving 12th PzR back east of Teploe. Pz Abt 49 was nearby and helped slow the Soviets, giving 12th PzR time to dig in and the line to stabilize a little. Pz Abt 49 arrived at 1900 hrs to assist and was able to establish contact for HQ with these forces. fkk65+. dgk87m. dgk122m. lck116m.

Stavka ordered Operation Kutuzov to begin in two days' time but with one major change in the plans. With Central Front suffering so many casualties it would delay its attack for several days in order to regroup. The Western Front and Bryansk Front would begin on 7/12, though probing attacks started a day earlier. The objective of the offensive was to attack the flanks of 53rd IC and drive inward, surrounding it and the 35th IC in the center of the line. With Central Front starting late, it gave Model a few days to transfer forces from quiet sectors to the hot sectors which greatly helped the shattered 2nd PzA, at least for a few days. When Central Front joined the offensive, the Germans would be forced to eventually pull back to save itself. cbk83. mkz121. dgk231m. snk433m++.

The 9th PzD took Snovo, Bityug and Berezovyi Log then crossed the Snovo and reached the northern part of Ponyri II. North of Olkhovatka, they broke through both defense belts and yet in the previous four days, the Germans had gained only seven miles. fkk102m. dgk87m. dgr199m. dgk122m. lck116m.

Model relieved Col General Rudolf Schmidt of 2nd PzA for his criticism of Model's running of Citadel. The Gestapo arrested and escorted the General back to Berlin. This would prove a horrendous mistake, for two days later the Soviet offensive began. General Clossner of 53rd IC was in the position to replace Schmidt but Model did not think Clossner was qualified so Model took over while 2nd PzA was stationed near Orel. No replacement was immediately named as the unit was expected to go to Serbia but by 8/15 when the 2nd PzA was still fighting near Orel, General Lothar Rendulic became CO of 2nd PzA. The 5th PzD was Model's only panzer reserve to back up 2nd PzA for the Orel salient. The OKH also had the 8th PzD and 2 IDs deployed to the rear in reserve as well. dgk232. dgk87m. dgk122m. lck116m. snz238. zsm259. swm139+.

A small group of German fighters, looking for easy prey, attacked a squadron of 30 bombers near Fatezh. Five Soviet planes were shot down. It is theorized that this Soviet group was heading for the nearby German airfield and the German ambush saved the airfield from attack. cbk71. dgk122m.

While 2nd PzD and 4th PzD were assembling, German artillery opened fire on the high ground at Olkhovatka. *Luftwaffe* attacked battery positions as well. Regardless of the heavy rain, the panzers advanced against heavy fire. Despite the fire power of 200 panzers, the Soviets held their positions near Ponyri though the grenadiers of 4th PzD did capture

Teploe after hours of house to house fighting. bt86. dgr198m. fkk102m. dgk87m. dgr199m. nzk94. dgk122m. lck116m.

Rudenko wanted to stop the German advance before reaching Olkhovatka which was defended by the shattered remains of 2nd TA. His recon patrol discovered a panzer assembly area near Kashara. Before noon the general sent 208 planes to destroy the panzers. Despite a heavy flak defense, the Soviet planes swooped down and destroyed a number of panzers, vehicles and an ammo dump. The German assault was delayed by the attack. cbk71. dgk122m.

The 12th PzD and the 36th MD was moved up closer to the line, soon to be inserted into the fighting. The 5th PzD and 8th PzD were moved to the Trosna-Fatezh road and were preparing to drive south along it. nzk94. dgk122m. lck116m.

After losing their tenuous hold on the hill, the Germans tried once again to take the heavily fortified Hill 253.5, northeast of Ponyri. This time the Ferdinands of sPzAbt 654 led the charge but again the attack failed. The wall of steel coming down that hill was too much, even for Elefants. mhz286. dgk87m. dgr199m. dgk122m.

Fearing that the Soviets would move any day against the Orel salient, Kluge sent the 8th PzD to Orel to bolster the 200,000-man 2nd PzA, while the 9th Army still had almost 300,000 men. The 2nd PzA had no panzers left and only a few assault guns. cbk83. dgk231m. snk433m++.

The right flank of 9th PzD reached the base of the ridge at Olkhovatka but could not go any further. If you study the engagements in capturing hills between the northern sector and southern sector, you have to ask why was Hoth so much more successful than Model? Hoth had tough hills in front of him like Hills 230, 241, 252, 260 and 244, just to name a few, but these were conquered while Hills 274, 253 and a few others in the north were never securely captured. Did Hoth's forces have more determination or were they more cunning in the attack? It is possible but doubtful. Did Hoth have a better attack plan than Model? The answer to this question would be yes, but was it the only factor to consider? Were there extenuating terrain or defense features that made a difference? It's possible in some cases but definitely not all cases. Central Front had an advantage in men and weaponry over Voronezh Front but was it the main reason for Model's hard-fought but in the end dismal performance? Arguably this leads me to consider that Rokossovsky's command decisions had a clear impact among the other considerations just mentioned and the reason why 9th Army gained less than half the distance that 4th PzA did and why 9th Army had greater casualties as well. fkk102m. dgk87m. dgk122m. lck116m.

On the eastern front of the Orel salient, it was discovered that the Soviets had deployed 200 batteries in front of the 262nd ID sector (35th IC). The 432nd GR, which had to defend a six mile front, would be the hardest hit. To assist the 262nd ID, Rendulic redeployed corps artillery to the sector and moved a few battalions from other sectors there to help out. This added strength would save thousands of soldiers and slow the Soviet 'Russians' assault when preliminaries began the next day. fkk340. dgk231m. snk433m++.

The OKH allowed the 9th Army a morning of rest to regroup and the last of Model's reserves, the 10th PzGD, was ordered up to the front to assist the 292nd ID in the Ponyri-Prilepy line to make one final attempt of breaking through. Even though the divisions were less than 20 miles from the front, it took two days to reach the launch areas. Bodenhausen's 12th PzD and Golnick's 36th ID arrived a day earlier. Even with the help of the *Luftwaffe*, which had been reinforced from airfields further north, these two divisions could not penetrate the minefields and bunkers that were strewn along this line. The day was windy and rainy, making it harder on the panzers and planes to navigate. This new PzGD had seven artillery battalions, and a Nebelwerfer Regiment which was desperately needed but the attack still failed. During this movement, a Soviet tank brigade attacked the Germans in Ponyri but was repelled, never getting close to the village. The Germans had Ponyri but were now facing the last and the heaviest defended line yet. What was to come would be worse than what had already been experienced. Stalin believed that if the Germans captured Kursk, Hitler would then drive toward Moscow. This perception was crucial in why the Central Front was fortified to a greater extent than Voronezh Front. dgk87m. dgr199m. gjz191. mhz287. cbk71. nzk94. dgk122m. lck116m. snz253. cbk12m. kfz459. pck48.

The German 9th Army gained only a mile today. Model decided to go from offensive to defensive expecting a Soviet counter-attack. Still hopeful, Model was already planning the next offensive after the Soviet counter-attack. The *Luftwaffe* claimed another 126 Soviet planes shot down. dgk87m. gjz191. dgk122m.

The 1st *Flieger* Division reported losing only seven aircraft on this day on flying 1136 sorties. During the day and despite the bad weather, the Luffwaffe's 1st *Flieger* Division flew 661 sorties just in the Teploe area. Any visible artillery battery or tank concentration was attacked. The *Luftwaffe* did lose one of its best aces: Major Resch with 94 victories was shot down and killed on this day. The 16th VA flew only 301 missions. cbk71++. nzk77. dgk122m.

The Soviet pilots had flown nearly around the clock since the start and were now exhausted and tired of battle. Some of the pilots when flying their patrols would avoid the battle zone and just skirt it to avoid a fight. When Rudenko found out about the practice he informed his pilots that anybody caught in such a cowardly act would be either transferred or arrested. There was so little contact between the two sides in the north that day that 1st *Flieger* Division reported losing only seven planes. cbk73. dgk122m.

16

July 11th on the Southern Salient

See Maps 15, 18, 26C

German intelligence estimated 1,227 Soviet tanks had been destroyed thus far in Operation Citadel, raising Hoth's confidence about tomorrow's attack. fkk151.

Anticipating a major battle in the next day or two, Vatutin lined up every artillery piece he could find from the bend of the Psel, from Prelestnoe to Oktiabrski State Farm, along the railroad to Lutovo. He concentrated a hundred guns and almost 200 mortars along this section. vzz205+.

North of the Psel River throughout the previous night and the predawn hours, the *SSTK* were defending their precarious hold on their bridgehead against constant attacks by the 31st TC and elements of the 33rd GRC of 5th GA, which were still arriving in sector. With little heavy equipment in the bridgehead, the attacking T34s had to be destroyed by demolition teams. The engineers desperately worked throughout the night and early hours against heavy rains and heavy artillery in building a light bridge to accommodate the trucks and light panzers. It was completed at daybreak. The engineers then started working on a heavy bridge to get the Tigers over. Once the whole division was across, their main objective would be Hill 226.6 and then Hill 252.4 in order to give *LAH* flank protection when they moved on Prokhorovka. Hausser wanted these objectives captured that day but the Soviets were not cooperating. While the bridgehead was being defended, the *Eicke* Regiment continued to clear the southern bank of the river of Soviet resistance. There was a large concentration of Soviet artillery on Hill 252.4 that was stopping *LAH*'s advance. Hausser made the hill a priority for *SSTK* to take. Hoth was asking too much of *SSTK* and in fact of 2nd SS PzC. The *SSTK* never got close to Hill 252.4 and the Soviet artillery on that hill played havoc with the SS for the rest of the campaign. Hill 252.4 was northeast of Hill 226.6 and almost due north of Hill 252.2. See Map 23. mhz319. mhz343. vzz218+. lck334. vzz226. gnk312m. agk124. vzz202. vzz1m.

Maj General Popov's 33rd GRC of Zhadov's 5th GA had been ordered to the line to defend Prokhorovka and the corridor to the west of it. Traveling all night, the lead units of the 33rd reached their destination at daybreak and began digging in. Liakhov's 95th GRD and 97th GRD deployed along the north bank of the Psel River on the line Veselyi-Polezhaev to support the depleted 51st GRD and 52nd GRD. The 9th GAD was also brought up to defend Vasilevka, Prelestnoe and Iamki. The 9th GAD had nearly 9,000 men, the highest count of the seven divisions in 5th GA but it had the least number of anti-tank guns at about 75. To bolster the division's artillery weakness, Popov attached the 301st Destroyer Anti-tank Regiment to it. The 9th GAD consisted of three regiments: 23rd GAR, 26th GAR and 28th GAR. dgk167**. vzz200+. vzz204. gnk260. vzz214.

At 0330 hrs, elements of the 97th GRD, which had just arrived in sector, attacked the extreme western end of the *SSTK* bridgehead, not far from Kliuchi. It was a probing attack to search for weak spots in the line. The *SSTK* had preceded this attack with one of their own and without stopping took on this second group of Soviets. At the same time on the southern banks of the river, the *Eicke* Regiment was defending itself and the rear area of *SSTK* near the village of Vasilevka against a surprised counter-attack. At about 1300 hrs, German artillery started shelling the village before *Eicke* advanced. Surprisingly, the 99th TB with its T34s and KV1s attacked first after the German shelling stopped. Krivoshlein ordered their own shelling to continue with the Soviet tanks barreling down at the village. The new German rocket barrage turned the tanks, which headed back to the northeast as well as stopping the garrison inside the village from supporting the once advancing tanks. There was still a gap between *SSTK* and *LAH* on its right and Maj General Priess was concerned that the Soviets would try to exploit that gap again as the 99th TB just did. The heavy bridge over the Psel had still not been completed and the panzers were waiting impatiently to cross the river and head for Hill 226.6. gnk293++. gnk283m. zrl233.

Even with the continued barrage, Priess did not believe Knochlein's battalion of T34s could take Vasilevka on its own. A battalion of panzers that had recently arrived at the river and was waiting for the bridge to be completed was sent to do battle with the T34s that were in the area. Meierdress's panzers arrived shortly after 1400 hrs and Knochlein would give additional support to his battalion in fighting the panzers and by 1500 hrs had entered the western edge of the village. gnk296+. gnk283m.

After dark and into the predawn hours of 7/11, the 58th MRB after traveling over 100 miles were arriving in sector. It was the only reserve left of 2nd TC and it was brought up to the line: Mikhailovka, Andreevka, the woods northwest of Storozhevoe, Hill 245.8 south and west of Prokhorovka. Their arrival was timely for it helped repulse a panzer attack by *LAH* just hours later. The 99th TB, 26th TB and 169th TB then moved up to this line and fortified it. The 33rd GRC of 5th GA were deploying behind this line in second echelon. vzz200++. vzz222. vzz9m.

A combat group from *SSTK* launched at 0415 hrs with the intention of closing the gap west of Prokhorovka and linking up with *LAH* after capturing Andreevka and Mikhailovka. At the same time *SSTK* was attempting to secure and expand a bridgehead over the Psel. All of the previous night and early on this morning, the remains of 10th TC that were still in the area had attacked the *SSTK*'s bridgehead over the Psel River but without success. Further slowing up *SSTK* was an attack on its left flank between Kochetovka and Kozlovka by 31st TC at the same time as the Germans were beginning their advance against the 51st GRD and 52nd GRD. At 0830 hrs, another tank attack hit the bridgehead and with the roads being bad, the *SSTK* ran out of artillery shells before more could arrive. At 1420 hrs, another new bridge across the Psel River between Bogorodizkoye and Veselyi was opened. The new bridge could handle Tigers but the roads were so bad from the rain that expansion of the bridgehead was slow and difficult. *LAH* was driving toward Kozlovka and Vasilevka with tentative plans to reach as far west as Kochetovka. Hausser had wanted to concentrate *LAH*'s strength for the run on Prokhorovka but could not due to the gap between *SSTK* and *LAH*. It had to be closed first. Planes were restricted due to the cloud cover. wdk155. pck78. vzz188+. vzz8m. gnk283m.

By 2100 hrs of the previous night the 151st GRR of 52nd GRD and the 245th TR countered at the second trench line and forced *SSTK* back to the first line at Kliuchi but were stopped there momentarily. The *SSTK* still had the bridgehead that inclued Krasnyi Oktiabr, just outside of Kliuchi and the southern slopes of Hill 226.6, northeast of Bogoroditskoe. By the end of the day, SS 5thPzGR and 6th PzGR had captured Kliuchi and were in partial possession of Hill 226.6 to the east of the village and north of the Psel River. The fighting continued and by 0400 hrs of 7/11 the Germans were pushed out of the first trench line of Kliuchi with the help of the first tanks of 5th GTA's 18th TC. However, they failed to push the Germans from the bend in the river. The ground to the immediate north of the hill was still in Soviet hands. Kliuchi was a half mile east of Krasnyi Oktiabr. wwf100. dgk169. dgk184m. dgk222m. vzz1m. vzz195. vzz8m. gnk253m. gnk312m. zow159.

The 2nd SS PzC and especially the *LAH*, had gained more ground the day before than Rotmistrov anticipated with regards to his launch point and was now occupying the ground that 5th GTA was originally going to assemble and launch their attack from. At 0415 hrs on 7/11 Vasilevsky arrived at the 2nd TC observation post to study the landscape to see if changes should be made to Rotmistrov's original offensive plans. Rotmistrov had arrived to Prokhorovka before his tanks to make plans, though the lead tanks were now arriving during the predawn hours. Within 24 hrs his whole army would be in sector. Quite an accomplishment for such a large army to travel so far in just a couple of days. vzz208. wwf111+. dgk179. vzz245.

In the Prokhorovka area before dawn on this Sunday, the 3rd PzC made its big push north for Prokhorovka using 6 divisions. They had to catch up with *Das Reich* to form a stable line. Several hours later at 0900 hrs, the *LAH*, *Das Reich* and *SSTK* launched as well. At the same time, the 48th PzC was attacking toward Oboyan in order to keep the Soviets from sending reinforcements to Prokhorovka. During the entire battle in the Hill 252.2 area, heavy rains and strong winds buffered the field. Shortly after noon, up to100 panzers were straddling the road to Prokhorovka; later still more panzers arrived between Prokhorovka and Storozhevoe. These towns were not only in jeopardy from the rising numbers of panzers but also the rear of 5th GTA was at risk as it was assembling in the area for the following day's offensive. je106+. dgk184m. gnk283m. vzz9m.

Before dawn, the 6th PzGR of *SSTK* passed through the murderous fire of Soviet artillery commanding the heights on the north side of the Psel. The Germans proceeded to storm the village of Krasnyi Oktiabr, establishing the beginning of their expanded bridgehead over the river. They held the village from repeated counter-attacks and then began to expand it. The rest of the division waited, especially the heavy armor, until the bridge was completed. fkk152. fkk320m.

A violent thunderstorm hit the Teterevino North sector before dawn where the *LAH* were preparing to advance toward Prokhorovka. The heavy rains slowed the preparations, turning the roads to mud and making cross country travel almost impossible. Three miles to the northwest was the Psel River and to the northeast Prokhorovka was about the same distance. Along the banks of the Psel was a series of fortified villages that housed Soviet artillery that could reach *SSTK* or *LAH*. Those villages included Kozlovka, Vasilevka, Mikhailovka, Prelestnoe, Petrovka and Polezhaev. These strongpoints would be attacked on this day and be involved in heavy fighting with the SS as they were strategically situated. These villages lined the western side of the corridor to Kursk, while Prokhorovka was the anchor to the eastern entrance to the corridor. Located in the center of this corridor, but closer to Mikhailovka, was the giant Obtiabrski State Farm. The farm had many cinder block buildings and the Soviets had turned it into a fortress that would be difficult to take. Just to the east of this farm was Hill 252.2 which was also heavily defended by the 52nd GRD and 183rd RD who could also fire on the attackers of the farm. Both sides had many casualties fighting for Hill 252.2. Hill 245.8 on the eastern side of the tracks, north of the Storozhevoe woods and next to the Stalinskoe State Farm, was also another key height that was well defended by the 58th MRB and supporting tanks and artillery. Each of these strongpoints also had minefields and anti-tank ditches to protect it. Teterevino North was just two miles west of the railroad embankment while another key village, Ivanovski Vyeselok, was just on the other side of the embankment with a road that led directly to Prokhorovka. See Map 23. gnk281+. gnk283m. vzz1m. vzz8m. mjk89. zow157.

In the early plans of the defense of the southern salient, Hill 252.2 was recognized as an important part in the third defense belt. It was the guardian to the entrance of the land corridor to Kursk by way of Prokhorovka. Trenches were built in front of it, to the sides and on it to protect the artillery that was planned to be emplaced there. During the predawn hours, the 9th GAD arrived at the hill and immediately began expanding the trench system and adding their own artillery. When the Germans overran this hill, they would take advantage of these defenses. Hills 241.6, 242,5 and 231.3 would also be fortified in time to stop 5th GTA on 7/12. vzz320+.

As soon as the German artillery laid down a covering barrage, Kraas' men moved into the open field in front of Hill 252.2. The Soviet small arms response was absolutely murderous; then the artillery had its turn. The guns on Hill 252.4 to the north started firing and a few minutes later the guns from the Storozhevoe woods began to fire. The entire Soviet defense had been built on mutually protecting strongpoints. When one was attacked, another one and usually multiple other sites would fire on the attackers. The Germans were marching into a kill zone and at a time when their panzers were in short supply. The fire was so bad the grenadiers had to stop and dive for cover; a shell hole, depression or the occasional ravine would do. There was a lucky break for *LAH* attackers as the skies started to clear. The Stukas were up in the air and prepared to pound the heavily bunkered Hill 252.2 and the surrounding countryside. By 0830 hrs the grenadiers had reached the foot of the hill where it was discovered another minefield had been placed. While it was raining bombs from all directions, the engineers moved up and started clearing the mines. Once past the mines, the pioneers found a tank ditch that had to be taken care of. The few Tigers under Kling's command moved up and past the ditch, blasting the many bunkers linking the top of the hill, ignoring the many hits from the small Pak guns. Riding in a V formation, the assault guns screened the Tiger's flanks. Stukas were called in again and without air support Hill 252.2 would have probably stayed with the Soviets. Despite having a *Luftwaffe* liaison officer, a friendly fire incident happened that killed a number of grenadiers. gnk285. gnk288. gnk283m. vzz9m. cbk75.

At first light in the Prokhorovka area, Soviet airplanes dropped 200 tons of bombs to halt the Germans from reaching the village. On the German side, Hoth ordered the *Luftwaffe* to spend all their resources supporting the 2nd SS PzC. This made it especially difficult on 48th PzC. The *LAH* and *Das Reich* were currently only 4.5 miles from Prokhorovka and only one mile from Iamki. Hoth wanted to take the town before the additional reserves could block the advance. At 0500 hrs in rainy weather, the *LAH*'s 2nd PzGR resumed its attack along the road to Prokhorovka with its remaining four Tigers in the lead. Two miles ahead, its first objective was the heavily fortified Hill 252.2. As they approached the hill, Soviet artillery from near the villages of Petrovka and Prelestnoe to the north opened fire on the German column. As the Germans got closer to the hill, T34s coming from Andreevka and Iamki attacked the flanks of *LAH*. rc222. mhz315. vzz1m.

agk123. zrl231.

As the battle for Hill 252.2 heated up and the German Tigers were ascending the hill while the assault guns were still at the base, the tanks from 169th TB advanced from a nearby copse of trees to attack the assault guns from the east. The T34s were redlining and the mounted infantry could barely stay on the tanks. The German assault guns, which were not immune to the T34 shell, kept their composure and turned to face the charging enemy. During the engagement, Commander Kling was wounded and had to be evacuated. His second, Schultz, took command. Schultze was then wounded and Wittmann was in charge of the Tigers. Engineers with shaped charges were taking on the Soviet tanks as well. The tank attack petered out and the surviving T34s fell back to the woods while the Tigers crested the hill, grenadiers following. Both sides suffered heavy casualties. By 1430 hrs Hill 252.2 was in German control and the last resistance silenced. Leery of a counter-attack after dark, the grenadiers decided to defend the top of the hill and resume their advance in the morning. Later that night, orders came down instructing the 2nd PzGR to stay on Hill 252.2 and enhance its defenses. This hill would be used as a anchor to launch from when driving north through the corridor. The recently promoted Lt Col Frey's 1st PzGR would resume clearing the Storozhevoe woods which was turning out to be extremely difficult. gnk288++. zzk320.

Under a cloudy sky and a rolling fog, a combat group from Lt Col Kraas' 2nd PzGR of *LAH* along with Tigers and assault guns attacked from west of the rail embankment, moving over muddy ground, heading straight for Hill 252.2 and the Oktiabrski State Farm, which were defended by the 26th GAR of the 9th GAD. If possible, the rest of regiment would not linger at the hill but head toward Prokhorovka. Once the hill was taken the rest of the panzers of 1st PzR would move up and attack the OSF along with the others. Farther out from the hill, mines were sporadically placed; a soldier never knowing when his next step would be his last. The pioneers were in the lead, doing the best they could to find and clear the mines. The last four Tigers of the division followed behind the engineers. The combat group would attack the northwest corner of the hill. The other 52 panzers of the division were back at Teterevino North waiting for Hill 252.2 to be secured before moving out to run the gap and head for Prokhorovka. At the same time, Frey's 1st PzGR headed east, closer to the rail line, toward Storozhevoe Woods to clear the resistance that was constantly harassing the east flank of *LAH* and *Das Reich*. The woods which were defended by the 169th TB of 2nd TC and supporting infantry were located northeast of Ivanovski Vyselok. If they could be cleared then Hill 245.8 would be the last natural obstacle between *LAH* and Prokhorovka. Hausser wanted these two regiments to capture their initial objectives then both move on Prokhorovka together from two directions: south and southwest. Stukas had been ready to strike the hill before the assault force reached it, if the skies had permitted. The 55th Werfer Regiment began shelling the villages of Prelestnoe and Petrovka which had artillery that could reach in front of Hill 252.2. gnk284. wwf112+. zrl232.

By 0600 hrs, the 18th TC, which still had eight US M3 light tanks, was deploying on the northern slopes of Hill 226.6 and trying to keep 6th SS PzGR from securing the hill. vzz195. vzz8m.

At daybreak, the 11th MRB, with support from elements of the 99th TB and the 1502nd DAR of 2nd TC, were attacked along the southeastern outskirts of Andreevka-Mikhailovka and the small hill one mile southwest of the Oktiabrski State Farm by heavy tank and artillery fire from the left flank of *LAH*. The defenses included a minefield and an antitank ditch in front of Hill 252.2 which was heavily covered by the 9th GAD. When the ditch was reached at 0625 hrs, the Germans increased the covering fire to keep the defenders busy while they prepared a way across it. Failing to cross the ditch, 2nd PzGR of *LAH* was forced to pull back against the withering fire. At the same time 1st PzGR moved to Luchki North and was about to attack toward Storozhevoe including the positions held by 227th RR. Wisch, the CO of *LAH*, fearing a counter-attack against his 2nd PzR during their withdrawal, ordered the 1st PzR to stop its attack and defend the flank of 2nd PzGR while it moved back. The 55th Werfer Regiment was called up and started shelling the artillery positions along the river to assist the fall back. vzz212+. vzz218. vzz9m. gnk283m. zrl231.

After a few minutes to regroup, the 2nd PzGR attacked again toward the hill and 1st PzGR resumed its advance to the east. The battle for Hill 252.2 intensified as *LAH* had just overcome the tank trench in front of the hill, allowing trailing battalions to move up. As German planes struck and artillery narrowed in on their targets, more Soviet tanks came pouring in from Andreevka and Mikhailovka to counter the German pressure. At the same time, about 0630 hrs, elements of the *LAH* were fighting to clear the woods north of the village of Storozhevoe II. The Germans could not leave enemy troops hidden in these woods behind as they moved toward Prokhorovka. By the end of the day the woods had been cleared but the Germans were slowed before reaching the village of Storozhevoe. Fighting throughout the night, the Germans penetrated into the village, fighting house to house. The state farm at Storozhevoe I would not be reached today either. *Das Reich*, which was to work with *LAH* in taking the hill, was stuck south of the village of Vinogradlovka against a determined enemy, the 26th TB of Popov's 2nd TC. mhz317. vzz218+. lck333++.

At 0630 hrs, elements of 1st PzGR joined the attack with 2nd PzGR, and with the support of a company of Tigers, attacked Soviet positions at Storozhevoe. At the same time, Soviets, using a two pincer action, attacked eastward from Andreevka the original *LAH* group defending its western flank. The *LAH* penetrated the 183rd RD and 169th TB's line, forcing it back toward Prokhorovka and the 52nd GRD's defenses. The *Luftwaffe* was called in to help the western flank by attacking the Soviet assault force plus their batteries, placed in villages along the Psel. The 28th GAR moved into position south of Prokhorovka to block the 2nd SS PzC. The *LAH* followed with the support of the *Luftwaffe*, finally capturing Hill 252.2 after a bloody fight that lasted hours. From the Hill, the panzers drove toward Oktiabrski State Farm, reaching it by 1530 hrs but were stopped by massive artillery fire and the newly dug-in 9th GAD placed practically along the entire *LAH* sector. All the while that *LAH* was defending itself, corps batteries were shelling OSF, Hill 252.2 and Lutovo with the anticipation that *LAH* would repulse the attack and then move on the above objectives. The skies were already beginning to clear and it would be a hot and muggy day. dgk171+. dgk184m. dgr222. gnk284. wff112++. zrl232.

At 0630 hrs, the 1st PzR of *LAH* was preparing to advance from the Bolshie Maiachki area toward Luchki North. The 55th Werfer Regiment would fire on the banks of the Psel in order to reduce Soviet shelling during the operation. At 0730 hrs an additional preparation started on the right side of the line in this sector. At 0900 hrs, the Group Krass of 2nd PzGR launched their attack with Tigers in the lead on the right side. By 1000 hrs, the Germans had pushed the 227th RR of 183rd RD back north of the railroad embankment and into the defensive belt of the 26th GAR of 9th GAD in front of Hill 252.2 and the Oktiabrski State Farm. Elements of *LAH* were now about two miles from the outskirts of Prokhorovka but Hill 252.2 had to be captured first before the railroad junction was attacked. vzz214. vzz217+. gnk284 zow158.

With the support of 50 Ju-87s hitting the hill, the *LAH* eventually secured Hill 252.2 and the subsequent success in keeping it against the counter-attacks of 29th TC. The Oktiabrski State Farm was their next objective. During this battle a squadron of He 111s attacked Soviet positions north of Prokhorovka, losing two planes to heavy flak. The 8th *Flieger* Corps lost 16 planes while shooting down 23 planes. However, the *Luftwaffe* was more successful against ground forces, allowing the 2nd SS PzC to make modest but important gains. mhz319. vzz218. lck332++. cbk76.

At 0650 hrs, the 2nd PzGR of *LAH* which had paused to allow a group of panzers and assault guns to arrive, launched again slowly along the woods one mile southwest of Iamki toward Prokhorovka, against the 227th RR and 287th RR (183rd RD), elements of the 58th MRB and tanks from 169th TB. The attack was repulsed by heavy artillery fire from just beyond Hill 252.4, Prelestnoe and Petrovka. Soviet tanks countered from the woods, six miles southwest of Prokhorovka, after a few of the panzers were struck and burning from the shelling. At 0900 hrs, 80 planes attacked the Soviet artillery positions near the woods but there were so many guns in the area that it did not slow the shelling much when some of the guns were destroyed. The Germans pulled back but tried six more times to break through along both sides of the railroad but failed until the Peiper Group was able to get across the line at the boundary between the two regiments and then headed for Hill 252.2 and the Oktiabrski State Farm to the northwest of the hill. When Group Becker reached the tank ditch in front of Hill 252.2, the shelling was so severe that Becker had to back away and asked for air and artillery support. The *Luftwaffe*, over the next couple of hours, made repeated attacks on the Soviet positions. For the previous few days when the 2nd SS PzC reached the Prokhorovka axis, Vatutin had set up a kill zone leading to Prokhorovka. Heavy artillery concentrations had been established on both sides of this corridor of death the previous night and the fire was worse than it had been. On the west side near Vasilevka, Andreevka and other villages close to the river and on the east side along a line that includes Storozhevoe also received extra guns. vzz210++. vzz226+. vzz1m. cbk75. wwf112. zrl231.

Supported by only a few assault guns, elements of the *LAH*, traveling south and east of the Psel River came under heavy artillery fire when assaulting Hill 241.6, south of Vasilevka and Andreevka. The Soviets had dug in many tanks on the hill and it was a formidable defense. *SSTK* forces near Mikhailovka remained in contact with the *LAH* but could not provide much assistance. Though it cost *LAH* severely, 76 Soviet tanks were claimed destroyed during the assault for the hill. At the same time Col Lipichev's 53rd MRB attacked the *LAH* recon forces south of Oktiabrski State Farm and north of Komsomolets State Farm. The rest of *LAH* with a company of Tigers in the lead marched along the Prokhorovka rail line past Hill 252.2 heading to the northeast. dgk164+. vzz207. vzz8m. dgk165m. dgk189+.

At 0700 hrs the clouds started to dissipate and the sun would begin to dry the land as a new wave of 25 German bombers, flying with escorts, bombed the Soviet line from Storozhevoe to Oktiabrski State Farm in preparation for the continuing assault by 2nd SS PzC. Nine more waves came in until 1300 hrs. Facing east along the Kalinin-Petrovski line and heading for Prokhorovka, elements of *LAH* and *Das Reich*, with support of almost 100 panzers in the Teterevino North-Ivanovski Vyselok-Komsomolets area, launched their combined attack. The Germans drove directly toward the 227th AR and the 285th RR who had just moved into the Vinogradovka area. Ivanovski Vyselok was just south of the Komsomolet State Farm and Vinogradovka was a little south of Ivanovski Vyselok. The Red Air Force was busy also; bombing the lead units of *LAH* in the same general area. The grenadiers could not wait for the skies to clear and launched before any air support was provided but were still appreciative when their bombers showed up. vzz209+. vzz234. vzz3m. vzz215. vzz7m.

At 0700 hrs Priess radioed General Hausser requesting an emergency shipment of artillery shells; the division did not have enough to last the day. The warehouse at Tomarovka, west of Belgorod, sent 1,000 10.5 cm shells to Gresnoe but the shipment did not arrive until late the next day. Without the ammo, the northern bridgehead was seriously threatened by the depleted but aggressive Soviet force that was made up of the 51st GRD, 52nd GRD and the 11th MRB. German intelligence also discovered additional reinforcements were moving south into blocking positions: 33rd GRC of 5th GA. General Hausser was also told that the bridge over the Psel River would not be completed until late morning which delayed the panzers from crossing and put added strain on the Grenadiers. gnk293. gnk283m.

At 0830 hrs *LAH* approached Hill 252.2, not quite two miles southwest of Prokhorovka, *LAH* penetrated the Soviet first line of defense then shifted direction to the northwest for less than a mile to capture the heavily fortified Oktabriski State Farm, before moving back to the road and Hill 252.2 from the north. The 9th GAD had moved into position south of the town the previous night and was waiting to stop the Germans when they arrived. These airborne troops were the vanguard of Zhadov's 5th GA. Just behind Zhadov was Rotmistrov's 5th GTA, arriving and preparing to add their weight to the coming offensive. As the *LAH* began assaulting Hill 252.2, the Soviet response in artillery was so intense that *LAH* immediately called for assistance. Despite low clouds and recent rain, the *Luftwaffe* quickly arrived and started pounding the hill. At 0900 hrs, additional German artillery moved into range and started shelling the hill. General Hoth knew this hill had to be taken and quickly and all available resources were being used. At 1330 hrs, the Soviets counter-attacked Peiper's battalion on the south slope of Hill 252.2 along with Kling's four Tigers. The fighting was fierce but Kling and Peiper and his men were able to repulse the tankers with the help of planes that were circling overhead. mhz316. fkk152. vzz1m. agk123+. wwf116.

Rotmistrov and his staff arrived early in the morning to the Prokhorovka area ahead of his forces but as the day progressed, units of the 5th GTA and 5th GA would be arriving. The 42nd GRD plus tank and artillery units arrived in the Oktiabrski area. His general plan was to drive in a southwest direction from Prokhorovka toward the Komsomolets State Farm Pokrovka area and, with the help of 1st TA and 5th GA, would encircle the 2nd SS PzC and destroy it. At this point General Rotmistrov thought the 2nd SS PzC was being held and that he would have time to complete the fine details of his counter-offensive plans. Later when Rotmistrov was discussing his plans with Valsilevsky, the Germans broke through the line not far from Belenikhino and the woods next to Storozhevoe which were defended by 169th TB and the 285th RR of 183rd RD. The 5th GTA's 18th TC and 29th TC had to throw those plans away and charge in a chaotic fashion to stop the *LAH*, *SSDR* and *SSTK* divisions. To make conditions worse for Rotmistrov, Kempf was finally moving and was now only 12 miles from Prokhorovka and could potentially attack 5th GTA's flank later the following day. It turned out Kempf was close enough to Prokhorovka as

Rotmistrov did change his plans. He had to send tanks and artillery toward 3rd PzC which diluted his main attack against 2nd SS PzC. wdk155. mhz322. mhz329. vzz368+. vzz8m. wwf118+.

Vatutin was making last minute changes to his plans for the major offensive which was scheduled to begin the next day. Most of the 80,000-man 5th GA was expected to arrive late that night or early the following morning. The 5th GTA had already begun to arrive and were preparing for the assault as well. He wanted his current forces to hold the line in order to give 5th GTA a good launch point but the SS foiled Vatutin's plans by reaching Hill 252.2-OSF area. lck320. lck164m. lck260m. lck308m. vzz9m. gnk283m.

The Germans believed the Soviets were out of reserves and believed their progress would improve starting that day. However the *SSTK* had trouble in crossing the Psel River due to the fact that the 5th GA was just arriving in sector and were already helping the shattered 51st GRD and 52nd GRD defend the line. wdk158.

Before Vatutin could commence his counteroffensive near Prokhorovka, 2nd SS PzC launched its attack with the support of *Luftwaffe*. From Hill 241.6, *LAH* starting at dawn, struggled forward along the Prokhorovka road with *Das Reich* protecting its right flank against the 2nd TC fire. *LAH* had initial success but was then stopped at Hill 252.2, just southeast of Oktiabrski State Farm. During this struggle, the 99th TB harassed the Germans near Andreevka. Tigers were called up to support 1st SS PzGR and with their help they were able to force the 2nd TC to retreat up the road. Vatutin gave 2nd TC and 2nd GTC to Rotmistrov to bolster his 500 plus tanks when he attacked 2nd SS PzC in the morning. The two tank corps were to attack in the Vinogradovka and Belenikhino areas. dgk169+. dgk184m. dgk222m. vzz218+. vzz1m. wwf111+. gnk283m.

During the predawn hours on the east flank of 2nd SS PzC, the 167th ID relieved *Das Reich* from flank duty south of Kalinin. The 167th ID took over a section of the line from *Das Reich* so that the SS could concentrate their strength and penetrate the stubborn resistance to the northeast. Soviet artillery hidden in the woods would also fire on the *LAH* assault on the Stalinoe State Farm and Hill 252.2 and the artillery had to be silenced as well. *Das Reich*'s panzers had returned from the Solotinka River assault and were resting at Ozerovski and would be a contributing factor to the advance as well. This would be the first major attempt to clear the Storozhevoe Woods and the Germans were expecting a vicious fight. *Das Reich* still experienced hard fighting against 2nd TC at Ivanovka, north of Kalinin but southwest of Prokhorovka. The 167th ID, in their new position, was being attacked by the 81st GRD and 375th RD and had to start withdrawing to the south of Shopino. wdk156. dgr209m. hjj121m. dgr221m+. gnk284. gnk283m. vzz9m.

On this Sunday morning, FM Vasilevsky and Lt General S.P. Ivanov arrived at Vatutin's HQ at Oboyan to supervise the next day's action. Vasilevsky would stay close to 5th GTA while Ivanov would move further east to Korocha to watch over 7th GA. dgk175. mhz322++. mhz329. hjj123m.

The 2nd PzGR on the east flank and inching its way northward, was attacked by tanks coming from Iamki. The engagement occurred near the anti-tank ditch south of Oktiabrski. The *Luftwaffe* entered the battle by attacking the artillery on top of Hill 252.2. The 2nd PzGR was able to advance past the several trenches to reach the foot of the hill. The panzers were firing from a distance as the pioneers cleared lanes through the minefields for the panzers to advance. As the lanes were cleared, Peiper's half tracks rolled forward, attacking the southern slope. Between the panzers, motorized infantry and infantry, not to mention the aerial and artillery support, the defense on Hill 252.2 was finally weakening with its defenders beginning to fall back to the OSF, though it would take several more hours before it was secured. It was one of the bloodiest engagements of the campaign but the grenadiers could not rest because the Oktiabrski State Farm next door had to be captured and the fighting there would be the equal of the hill. agl123. vzz9m. gnk283m.

At 0905 hrs after a heavy artillery barrage plus air strike, *LAH*'s 2nd PzGR resumed its drive toward Prokhorovka. With the help of a few Tigers the *LAH* regiment reached the base of Hill 252.2 and the village of Lutovo, not far from the Oktiabrski State Farm and southwest of Prokhorovka by 1000 hrs, but was stopped by stiff resistance of the 26th GAR defending the hill. dgk172. dgk184m. vzz218. vzz205. zrl232.

At 1115, 40 tanks driving from Iamki and 40 tanks from Petrovka attacked *LAH* positions at Stalinskoe State Farm near Hill 252.2. After two hours, the attack was repulsed and the Soviets lost 40 tanks. Afterwards the remainder of the tanks plus elements of 31st TB of 29th TC and 170th TB of 18th TC attacked the Oktiabrski State Farm which had just been infiltrated. vzz321.

At 0930 hrs, two regiments of *Das Reich*, supported by nearly 100 panzers and assault guns, attacked the 2nd TC and elements of the 69th Army defending the flank of Komsomolets State Farm, southeast of the railroad about three miles southwest of Prokhorovka. Other elements of the 2nd TC attacked the south flank of *LAH* in the Vinogradovka area about six miles southwest of Prokhorovka but it was repulsed by the *Deutschland* Regiment. wdk155+.

The *SSTK* was still clearing the southern bank of the Psel River. By midmorning the grenadiers had captured the village of Vasilevka which had been defended by the 99th TB. The 99th TB retreated to the southeast and ran into an *LAH* Pz Abt. The ensuing battle lasted into the night. The *SSTK* made little gains on this day; its only success was the taking of Vasilevka but Vatutin was already planning to take it back. The villages to the north of Vasilevka, Prelestnoe, Mikhailovka and Petrovka were all in Soviet hands and their artillery would go after both *SSTK* and *LAH* in the morning. The big guns were still safely secured on Hill 252.4. The Soviets were making good use of thousands of anti-tank guns in this sector, the corridor that the Germans had to pass through; there were more guns per mile here than anywhere in the salient. For the rest of the day, the SS was defending itself against constant counter-attacks. This was not a good sign for the Germans. gnk290+. gnk283m.

By 1030 hrs after regrouping, the 2nd PzGR of *LAH* attacked up Hill 252.2 again. This time with the help of sappers, the panzers made it across the antitank ditch and started climbing the slopes while German artillery bombed the crest and reverse slopes as well as the Oktiabrski State Farm where a large concentration of Soviet artillery was deployed. The *Luftwaffe* returned and hit the hill and state farm as well. In the afternoon, the German assault led by the panzers of Peiper's Group finally gained traction and were able to move almost a mile northward to the crest of the hill. vzz217+. zrl232.

In the morning, *Das Reich*, with support of artillery, launched an attack from Teterevino on the axis Ivanovski Vyselok-Storozhevoe. After a bitter fight a few panzers and infantry fought their way into the outskirts of Storozhevoe but were stopped after fighting for hours at the edge of the village. vzz243. vzz3m. vzz9m.

Peiper's battalion launched a drive from the southern portion of Hill 252.2 toward the OSF and as the formation was moving up the hill, the *Luftwaffe* flew by and accidently bombed the formation, damaging couple panzers including the one that Peiper was in.

Without a pause for the incident, Peiper charged the hill with MG42s blasting and crested the hill at 1300 hrs against the 287th GRR. Eventually, after repeated attacks and with the assistance of the rest of *LAH*, he entered the Oktiabrski State Farm next door by 1400 hrs. The fighting continued for a while but it was finally "secured" and was where he stayed for the night after repulsing a strong counter-attack and preparing for the big tank battle expected the following morning. *LAH* Grenadiers arrived and took control of the state farm, clearing resistance in the immediate area. All the while the *Luftwaffe*, in small waves of 15 to 20 planes every 20 minutes, bombed the sector: Hill 252.2, Hill 252.4 a little further north, Barchevka and the Oktiabrski State Farm which was defended by the 26th GAR. The 26th GAR was running out of ammo and had to resort to picking up ammo from the fallen. After dark, the artillery of the 9th GAD arrived in sector. The 23rd GAR, also of 9th GAD, was deployed behind the 26th GAR in Prokhorovka as reserve. Even though the Germans had control of the farm, the Soviets had not fallen back very far and were expecting to take back the farm in the morning when the massive counter-attack began. fkk154+. vzz214. vzz218++. vzz229. vzz8m. gnk284. gnk283m.

By early afternoon and while Peiper's panzers and motorized infantry were attacking Oktiabrski State Farm from the west and south, the 2nd PzR of *LAH*, led by a few Tigers, was attacking the farm from the north and east, shattering the left flank of 287th RR and forcing it to retreat toward Prelestnoe. After overcoming two trenches, the Tigers continued forward past the farm and entered Petrovka, which was also defended by elements of 287th RR. The Soviets had lost many tanks on this day defending Hill 252.2 and the nearby OSF which worried Vatutin; the loss meant their offensive the following day would have less punch. vzz224++*. vzz1m. vzz9m. gnk283m. dgk177+. See Maps 18 and 23.

Due to the famous Kursk Magnetic Anomaly, a group of Yak-9s got lost and five of the planes had to make emergency landings when they ran out of gas. Members of the 31st TB of the 29th TC (5th GTA) complained that they received no air support before 1300 hrs. cbk81.

Lead elements of the *LAH* advanced on the Oktiabrski State Farm (not far from Hill 252.2) but had to retreat back to Hill 215.4 from heavy artillery fire on their first attempt. In front of the farm a tank trench was built preventing passage. Sappers were called up and after a short while of using explosives to fill in the trench, *LAH* continued toward the farm. They would wait until more of the division arrived before trying to take it. dgk174.

The *SSTK* expanded their bridgehead on the northern bank of the Psel and reached Hill 226.6. The division also cleared Soviet resistance on the south bank that was attacking the left flank of *LAH*. The village of Kliuchi was taken but when reinforcements from 95th GRD, supported by Ivanov's 100th TB (31st TC) came up, the drive of the *SSTK* was stopped and the Germans had to fight to keep Kliuchi. While the *SSTK* had captured part of Hill 226.6, the 290th GRR thwarted all attempts to complete the capture of the hill. *SSTK* captured Vasilevka on the south bank of the Psel, forcing the 99th TB back, but it was unable to drive further when elements of 95th GRD came up to support the 99th TB. To the right of *LAH*, *Das Reich* cleared Ivanovskii Vyselok but could not reach Vinogradovka in the valley beyond. dgk176+. dgr172m. dgk222m. vzz227+. vzz9m. gnk283m. gnk312m.

As the *LAH* of 2nd SS PzC advanced up the Prokhorovka road, it bumped into the new defensive position of the 9th GAD near Oktiabrski State Farm, a short way west of Prokhorovka. Since late the previous night, the 9th GAD had hastily moved into defenses at the farm that had been started by 183rd RD along the line south of Prokhorovka, but had not completed its disposition when the *LAH* attacked next morning. Still, the artillery fire was so fierce in this sector from all the guns that were deployed across the corridor that *LAH* had to fall back to the reverse slopes of Hill 215.4 to regroup. The defenses on Hill 252.2 and the village of Lutovo, also south of Prokhorovka, were being shelled as the panzers approached. Elements of the 95th GRD defending Hill 252.2 had to fall back as *LAH*'s 60 panzers crested the Hill. Hill 252.2 was less than a mile southwest of Prokhorovka. The Germans were advancing on such a narrow front and were creating a mini-salient which the enemy might try to cut. Lutovo was midway between Hill 252.2 and Prokhorovka. dgk171++. dgk184m. snk81. vzz218+. vzz320. lck336. nzk95. wwf115. wdk155.

The 2nd SS PzC would record destroying 125 Soviet tanks that day, in their desperate struggle to capture Prokhorovka. It was being supported by the *Luftwaffe* as it made its way north toward Prokhorovka. The *SSTK* struggled to expand its bridgehead which was anchored on Hill 226.6 near the northern bank of the Psel River, while the *LAH* drove forward from Hill 241.6 along both sides of Prokhorovka road which was defended by the 2nd TC's 169th TB. *Das Reich* was still protecting *LAH*'s right flank. Two hour's later, the *LAH* had traveled two miles against stiff artillery fire before being stopped in front of Hill 252.2, just southeast of Oktiabrski State Farm and north of Iamki. *LAH* was down to 90 AFVs. The Soviets also had a good tank recovery system and some of the tanks that could be reached on the battlefield were recovered and repaired or salvaged. dgk178. dgk169+. dgk184m. vzz1m. gnk312m.

Reacting to the latest battle action, Hausser submitted new orders to his commanders. Priess's *SSTK* had to expand its bridgehead north of the Psel, complete clearing Hill 226.6 and protect *LAH*'s flank as it moved on Prokhorovka. Kruger's *Das Reich*, advancing on *LAH*'s right, would have to clear Storozhevoe and capture Vinogradovka before moving on to help *LAH* take Prokhorovka. The *LAH* would move past Storozhevoe, capture Iamki before moving on Prokhorovka. The key to the success of the plan was *SSTK* quickly capturing Hill 252.4, which had a large concentration of artillery, and the subsequent protection of *LAH*'s left flank. Without this, there was little chance for success. Hausser brought up every gun he could to cover *SSTK*'s advance. Hill 252.2 was southwest of Prokhorovka and west of Iamki while nearby Hill 252.4 was further north and near Beregovoe II. See Map 18. mhz320+. vzz218. vzz1m. vzz9m. gnk283m. gnk312m.

While fighting in the northwest corner of the Storozhevoe woods, a small contingent of Soviets were able to manuever behind *LAH*'s 1st PzGR and were threatening to do much damage. A couple of the assault guns supporting the grenadiers acted quickly, cutting back and engaging the enemy, forcing them to fall back while grenadiers were brought up to cover their flank better. By 1700 hrs much of the large woods were in German hands. The grenadiers then moved toward the town of Storozhevoe but the shelling coming from nearby Leski, Vinogradovka and Pravorot quickly stopped the advance and the 1st PzGR had to fall back to the safety of the woods. A little further south, *Das Reich* reached the railroad, capturing the woods, ravine and hill southeast of Ivanovski Vyselok. zrl232+. zow158.

At 1330 hrs, the 26th GAR and the 169th TB counter-attacked toward Hill 252.2 and the village of Lutovo, southwest of Prokhorovka, against 2nd PzGR of *LAH*. The 99th TB, having been forced out of Vasilevka by *SSTK*, joined the attack on Hill 252.2. While still engaged that night, Col Liakhov's 95th GRD shifted forces and joined the battle. Additional panzers and planes were called up and overpowered the Soviet forces between the boundary of the 95th GRD and 9th GAD, making them fall back to the west. The Germans were now only a mile from Prokhorovka. By the end of the day, the *LAH* had smashed the 2nd TC and isolated 99th TB in the Psel valley after driving it out of the village of Vasilevka. The 29th TC and 18th TC were setting up defenses along the forest border near Storozhevoe for the expected advance the following day by the 2nd SS PzC. The smoke and sounds of battle at the Komsomolets State Farm just two miles to the right were present. Even before the fighting died down for the night, the Germans were bringing guns and rocket launchers closer to the line; they were determined to take their objectives the next day and they might have if 5th GA and especially 5th GTA had not arrived in sector and begun settling into defensive positions. Vatutin was feeling the pressure that the Germans were exerting and felt compelled to have his two new armies attack in the morning. It is possible, even probable, that better results could have resulted if the two new armies had stayed defensive behind this third defense belt and worn down the enemy. With many fewer Tigers and panzers in general and fewer shock troops, the German assault force, while still effective, did not have the punch that it had had the first few days, which meant the two new armies had a real chance of stopping the SS without a suicidal attack. The SS objectives for the next day included Prokhorovka, Hill 252.4, Hill 236.7 and all the ground up to the Karashevka-Prokhorovka road. See Map 8. dgk173++. dgk184m. vzz218+. cbk75. vzz202. wwf118. zrl233. dgk179.

At 1300 hrs, the Soviets launched a small attack from east of Teterevino North, skirting *Das Reich* and heading northwest toward 1st PzGR of *LAH*, which was deployed from between an area north of Storozhevoe and Hill 252.2. Discovering the Soviet assault force, elements of *Deutschland* Regiment of *Das Reich* attacked the Soviet flank. After an initial German surge, the Soviets regrouped and then repulsed the attack and by dark the *Deutschland* was falling back. By the end of the day *Das Reich* had 88 working panzers and 58 Pak Guns. *LAH* reported having 60 panzers and 30 assault guns. The 2nd PzGR of *LAH* also reported destroying 21 tanks and 45 guns plus capturing 320 POWs. The regiment also reported 21 killed and 203 wounded. gnk292. gnk283m. zrl233+. gnk292. gnk283m.

After five hours of fighting, additional panzers arrived at Hill 252.2 and by 1330 hrs, Lt Col Kashpersky's 26th GAR was being forced off the hill and was retreating to the north to the OSF. To stop this retreat, Vatutin sent some of the tanks from 18th TC to strike the right flank of the German assault and to block the panzers from reaching the Oktiabrski State Farm. The *LAH* quickly consolidated their gains and prepared to move off the hill and head for the Oktiabrski State Farm to the northwest, which was also heavily defended by artillery. When it was first thought the hill would be captured, artillery was immediately sent toward the hill. Counter-attacks were expected and Hausser did not want to lose the hill and fight again to regain it. The thought of such an event sickened him. The counter-attacks lasted into the evening. dgk172. dgk184m. vzz218. vzz205. zrl233.

At 1410 hrs, the *LAH* was finally overpowering the defenders of Hill 252.2 but since *SSTK* and *Das Reich* were lagging behind, the *LAH* would soon have to stop their advance into the corridor for fear of isolation. However, with the momentum of *LAH*, OSF would be attacked that day regardless of the consequences. With so much Soviet artillery on Hill 252.4, taking Prokhorovka would be difficult; clearing the hill first was necessary but Hausser, seeing the modest advance of *SSTK* and *Das Reich*, did not want *LAH* extending itself to Hill 252.4 and getting cut off. The attack on Hill 252.4 would have to be for the following day after *SSTK* made further gains, but Vatutin would have other ideas and the 5th GTA would attack in the morning. While the bulk of *LAH* were fighting in the Hill 252.2-Hill 245.8 area, the 1st PzGR of *LAH* traveled through the woods north of Storozhevoe on a more direct route to Prokhorovka. vzz226. vzz1m. vzz9m.

On the Psel River, it was a frustrating day for *SSTK*. Only part of the division was on the north side and the remainder of the division was on the south side waiting for the bridge to be completed. It was ready at 1420 hrs but by then it was raining hard and the ground was muddy. The division had to be satisfied by just crossing the river and preparing the bridgehead for the panzers and artillery that would be coming over early next morning to participate with the rest of the division in expanding the bridgehead. fkk155. fkk320m.

While the *LAH* was slowly advancing from Hill 241.6 toward Hill 252.2 and the OSF, the *SSTK* was expanding its bridgehead on the northern bank of the Psel. *SSTK* crossed a Psel tributary, gained a foothold on Hill 226.6 and advanced toward the villages of Kliuchi and Veselyi to the west of Hill 226.6 but were stopped at Kliuchi when the 284th GRR of 95th GRD, supported by the 100th TB moved up to engage. The 290th GRR were being pushed off the hill but with new reserves were trying to retake it. The Luftwaffe made it a priority to support the 2nd SS PzC on this day, especially the *SSTK*. In order for the *LAH* to take Prokhorovka, the *SSTK* had to advance northward to gain control of Hill 252.4 and the Psel River in the area of the hill. Hoth and Hausser were giving the division as much help as they could to accomplish this key job. The 55th Werfer Regiment was also moved up to KSF to support the assault of OSF. See Map 18.

At 1450 hrs, Hausser informed Hoth that the heavy bridges over the Psel were completed but the panzers and heavy equipment of *SSTK* would not be crossing until next morning. It was too late in the day to begin operations and it was not smart to send panzers across to a bridgehead that was not fully secure. Priess was also low on fuel and to begin a difficult assault with the chance of running out of fuel was suicidal. The fuel would arrive in the morning. The southern banks of the Psel for as much as 500 yards were normally soft but the recent heavy rain caused the ground to be extremely muddy, making it difficult for panzer, truck and man to negotiate. It was not a good day for *SSTK* because of the delay of the engineers, arriving so late to complete the bridges. It also gave the 5th GA and 5th GTA time to prepare for their major offensive. It may have been a wasted day for *SSTK* but it was costly, the division experienced 75 dead and 375 wounded. By the end of the day, *SSTK* had 94 working panzers, including ten Tigers. It also had 21 assault guns. gnk296+.

Maj General Wisch of *LAH* moved his HQ again; this time it was within the town limits of Luchki North. Hausser called Wisch at his new HQ and persuaded him to point all his artillery on Hill 226.6 next morning to assist *SSTK* in securing the hill and the surrounding area. zrl233. dgk177.

Von Manstein ordered the 2nd SS PzC to continue toward Prokhorovka but to shift off the main road in order to avoid the heavy defenses blocking them. *LAH* would travel through the Komsomolets State Farm and along the railroad line to reach Prokhorovka. Once the hill was secured, *SSTK* would attempt traveling along both banks of the Psel River to reach their objectives of Shipy and Kartashevka and Hill 252.4. The third regiment of the 167th ID was still advancing to Luchki to free up elements of *Das Reich*, in order for the grenadiers to take part in the drive north on the east side. While the main action was near Prokhorovka Hoth was trying to stablize his west flank for tomorrow's offensive as well. On the extreme western boundary, the 52nd IC was attempting to clear the 90th

GRD from the Rakovo area, just north of the Pena River to relieve the pressure off 3rd PzD and *GD* so they could focus on driving north. The weather had cleared from the previous night and conditions were improving for the German assault. The *Luftwaffe* was expected to assist but shortly after daybreak heavy rains came, turning the roads to mud and making it difficult to fly. Toward the afternoon the weather did improve, still partly cloudy with strong winds but the planes started flying to support the ground forces.

In addition to the fighting at the Oktiabrski State Farm the *LAH* advanced along a two mile front between nearby Iamki State Farm and Andreevka with the support of assault guns and planes, trying to drive a wedge between the 95th GRD and the 9th GAD near Prelestnoe and the southern edge of Petrovka to clear the entrance to the corridor. With the State Farm falling around 1700 hrs, the Soviets pulled back to the southwestern slopes of Hill 252.4, less than two miles northwest of Prokhorovka. The advance that day of *LAH* that smashed the defenses of 2nd TC and isolated its 99th TB in the Psel valley also drove a wedge between 95th GRD and 9th GAD. This created a salient toward Prokhorovka that was not duplicated by *Das Reich*, *SSTK* or 48th PzC which meant *LAH*'s flanks were exposed. When the *LAH* captured the OSF, it quickly enhanced its already good defenses, including laying mines and bringing up more artillery to assist in the following day's attempt to take Prokhorovka. Hill 241.6, Hill 242.5 and Hill 231.3 were also fortified. The *SSTK* was late in crossing the Psel River at Petrovka and advancing on Hill 252.4 to silence the guns there that would give *LAH* a chance to take Prokhorovka. *Das Reich*, on the other side of *LAH* was also having trouble in providing protection. dgk174+. dgk184m. vzz320+. vzz325. vzz9m. lck336. gnk283m. gnk292.

After a fierce fight, 2nd PzGR of *LAH* captured Hill 252.2 on the western side of the Prokhorovka corridor. With Prokhorovka only a mile to the east, Hill 252.2 was an excellent OP, being able to look into the village. Peiper's battalion was then ordered to defend the hill against counter-attacks throughout the night while the rest of the division moved back because of its exposed flanks. Lt Col Peiper was isolated after *LAH* retreated for the night. Lt Ribbentrop's panzers had backed off south of the hill. The closest friendly was *SSTK* at Vasilevka, about three miles to the southwest. To the southeast, *Das Reich* was two miles away, deployed north of the Storozhevoe woods but completely tied down to its sector and unable to assist *SSTK* if the need arose. So the Germans did not have a strong presence at the entrance of the corridor to start the next morning. Though there were no counter-attacks, Peiper could hear Soviet tanks moving closer throughout the night within the three mile corridor from the Psel River in the west to Prokhorovka to the east. He knew an attack was coming in the morning and tried to prepare his men but they could never be prepared for the Soviet tidal wave that would be unleashed shortly after daybreak. The corridor was fairly flat fertile ground that saw many wheat and sunflower fields growing. It was through this corridor that hundreds of Rotmistrov's tanks would advance the next morning. gnk315+. cbk76. sgf347. cbk12m. zrl232.

Even though two light bridges had been completed across the Psel River near Bogoroditskoe, travel across them became impossible. It had rained so much in the last few days that the road leading up to the bridge was so deep in mud that not even panzers could navigate it. Priess informed Hausser of the road conditions at 1420 hrs. With the rain and cloud cover, air support was also canceled. Both generals agreed that the major assault north of the river would be on 7/12. Priess agreed with Hausser's analysis that the following day would be the last day for *SSTK* to expand the bridgehead and move the division over.

JULY 11TH ON THE SOUTHERN SALIENT   287

After 7/12 the Soviet reinforcements would make crossing the river impossible. zow158+.

By 1700 hrs, the line held by the *LAH* ran from Storozhevoe to the nearby forest (1st PzGR) to northwest of Hill 252.2 (2nd PzGR) to the hill west of Oktiabrski State Farm (1st PzR) and it would not change much by the end of the day. dgk177. dgk184m. zow158.

At 1700 hrs, while the main force of *SSTK* was driving toward Petrovka, a small combat group with a dozen panzers was forcing the Psel further west and trying to capture Krasnyi Oktiabr which was defended by 290th GRD. The diversion failed and the 290th GRD pushed the *SSTK* south of the river. At the same time south of the river, with *SSTK* attacking from its right flank and *LAH* from its left flank, the *SSTK* penetrated the line defended by Lt Col Malov's 99th TB and was able to fight its way into Vasilevka. The 99th TB regrouped and then countered and was able to push *SSTK* out of Vasilevka. During this engagement the 99th TB's CO, Lt Col Malov, was killed in action. After regrouping themselves, the Germans launched another attack and were able to penetrate the left side of the line, hitting the 287th GRR hard and causing them to fall back. With the 287th GRR of 95th GRD falling back, it exposed the flank of 99th TB and allowed *SSTK* to encircle elements of the 99th and to reach Petrovka. The 99th TB fought throughout the entire night to save itself. To the east, the *LAH* fell back also but after regrouping was able to finally take Oktiabrski State Farm by the evening. vzz235. vzz231. vzz1m. vzz8m+. dgk174.

At 1700 hrs, the 2nd TC and 2nd GTC came under the control of 5th GTA. With over 200 tanks that these two corps had, Rotmistrov now had a gross total of 931 tanks: 581 T34s, 314 T70s and a few SUs. There would be 707 tanks ready to launch in the morning. 558 tanks would be in first echelon, spread along a narrow five mile front, while the remainder would be in reserve. There were also a little over 100 tanks that broke down in transit that would be made available in the next two weeks. The 18th TC would drive between the Psel River to the east of Prelestnoe and Hill 241.6 while the 29th TC would launch between Hill 241.6 to Storozhevoe. The 5th GTR would be in reserve. When the Germans gained ground the previous day, the Soviet tank corps had to start a little further back but still in this general area. The plan would be for the Soviets' pincers to meet in the Luchki North and Iakovlevo area. Vatutin was placing extreme pressure on Rotmistrov's assault in the morning to stop the German assault then to split and encircle a large portion of 4th PzA. When the Germans reached Hill 241.6 that day, the plan had to change; the boundary line became the Oktiabrski State Farm and because of the terrain, the 18th TC's front narrowed to less than two miles. The plan and the hope was too ambitious and had little chance of complete success. vzz277++.

With Burdeiny's 2nd GTC now under the operational control of 5th GTA, Rotmistrov gave Burdeiny his orders for the major offensive in the morning. The 4th GTB was currently engaged north of Belenikhino and the 25th GTB was fighting near Storozhevoe. Both units started to disengaged and move back to prepare. The 26th GTB was in reserve at Shakhovo but moved out after dark and would be ready to attack east of Vinogradovka by morning. Nearby, additional artillery was moved to Hill 252.4 to support the 95th GRD's 287th GRR in the Petrovka area in the morning. The 26th GTB would have its orders changed and would not participate in the attack against *Das Reich*. Rotmistrov would send it south toward the Donets in the Ryndinka sector to block 3rd PzC from linking up with *Das Reich*. vzz235. vzz10m. vzz3m. dgk193.

At 1900 hours, Rotmistrov finished his revised attack plans for the 5th GTA and the 5th GA for the following day. With the Germans approaching Prokhorovka, the Soviet assault would be led by the 29th TC and 18th TC in the Prokhorovka-Belenikhino area and would travel alongside the forest adjacent to Storozhevoe. Further west the 18th TC would parallel the Psel River. The lead units of *LAH* beat Rotmistrov to his launch areas that day and would have to start further north, placing his tanks at a great disadvantage. The whole Soviet attack plan had to be revised. dgk175+. dgk168+. dgk184m. dgk222m. vzz11m.

Even after *LAH* had taken the Oktiabrski State Farm, the resistance remained fierce as the 29th TC had been deployed just to the north of the farm for its assault in the morning. The Germans could go no further and went defensive. lck335. vzz9m.

General Kruger of *Das Reich* completed moving his HQ to the woods east of Luchki North by 1745 hrs. Soon after arriving, he received the daily action report from his staff. The report showed the division had 69 working panzers and 27 assault guns available for the start of the big offensive in the morning. zow160+.

The *LAH* had made some difficult progress that day by taking Hill 252.2 and the nearby OSF but by 1900 hrs, the day's fighting had expired. The primary effort by *LAH* had been centered on the farm but the flanking areas were still in Soviet hands. If *LAH* was not careful or prepared, this salient could disappear in a flash as well as a large part of the division. In other words, *LAH* had carved out a mini-salient with its sides exposed, so Hausser ordered *LAH* not to attempt any further advancement and instead ordered the division to go defensive and to protect itself from counter-attacks during the night and early next morning. Trenches were dug and artillery brought up. This salient split the 95th GRD and 9th GAD's defense line in two and isolated the 99th TB of 2nd TC with its other brigades to the east; this was a huge advantage to the Germans if the salient could be held. Kashpers's 26th GAR of 9th GAD had been split as well and now most of the regiment was on the east side of OSF running east to Iamki south of Prokhorovka. The 28th GAR and the 23rd GAR were deplored behind 26th GAR in the second and third trenches respectively. Behind the regiments was the 57th GTR with its 21 KV1s and anti-tank guns. wwf116+.

By resuming its attack along the road to Prokhorovka by 0500 hrs, the *LAH* had made some progress today but since *SSTK* and *Das Reich* were struggling, it found its flanks, in addition to the mini-salient in the center, exposed. Consequently, Maj General Wisch decided to halt the advance and go defensive until the other divisions caught up. mhz319. vzz218. lck332++. cbk76. zrl233.

In the early evening, around 1900 hrs, Marshal Vasilevsky visited General Rotmistrov to receive a situation report and found that the Germans were further along than expected, spoiling the original attack plan. Vasilevsky called Stalin with the bad news and the dictator became concerned and angry. Vasilevsky ordered Rotmistrov to run another recon before assembling his troops to the start point. While the first revision of 18th TC's attack plan of assaulting next to the Psel River remained the same, due to the smaller assembly area the attack axis for the 29th TC was expanded to include not only driving down the Prokhorovka road toward Teterevino North, retaking OSF and Hill 252.2 but also to advance north of the Storozhevoe woods toward the Komsomolets State Farm. Potentially this was a better plan, which would give the 29th greater freedom of movement as well as putting pressure on several key points. This change to the north in the launch point would have a devastating effect on the following day's offensive for 5th GTA. Vatutin was pressing Rotmistrov to attack before 3rd PzC could link up with *Das Reich*. He did consider two other alternative plans for Rotmistrov's offensive but rejected them in favor of the "corridor" route. The first alternative considered attacking *SSTK* near Hill 226.6, pushing them back to the southern banks and then driving on Iakovlevo. It was rejected because of the difficulties associated with crossing the river and its bordering swampland. The other attack route was in 69th Army sector on the Shakhovo-Iakovlevo axis. Without giving much of an explanation Vatutin rejected this route also. I seriously wonder what would have happened if both 5th GA and 5th GTA had stayed defensive on that fateful 7/12 instead of attacking from a compromised position. The farther north the 4th PzA drove, the thinner their flank defenses became and the longer Soviet resistance wore down the German army within the third defensive belt, the more productive the Soviet counter-attack should have been when it occurred. vzz228. wwf118+. zro208. pck79+. dgk175+. vzz241. dgk179. vzz271.

Marshal Vasilevsky, after studying the situation report, ordered Rotmistrov to send the 18th TC to Petrovka to assist the 9th GAD. The Germans had already stopped their advance for the night in this sector and would not resume it until near daybreak. However, when Vasilevsky was inspecting the defenses with Rotmistrov in another area, they ran into panzers that were charging ahead which shocked both officers. Rotmistrov had to redeploy his tanks further north as a launch point for the morning offensive. Maj General I.I. Popov of 33rd GRC ordered the 9th GAD and the 95th GRD not to wait for dawn and to attack the German salient during predawn hours. The attack was launched in the direction of the Oktiabrski State Farm but it failed against the strong defenses the Germans had erected. Under this noise of this battle, Rotmistrov moved his tanks to their new start positions. vzz241+. lck337+.

At 1920 hrs, and despite heavy rains and muddy terrain, an armored combat group attacked along the southern banks of the Psel, drove through Mikhailovka and attacked Hill 252.2 . It was a last minute attempt to weaken the Soviet line within the corridor before the big offensive began in the morning. During this advance the Germans met with the greatest resistance from the 233rd AR south of Petrovka. Though taking casualties, the Germans pushed the artillery regiment north of Petrovka. The 48th RC under Rogozny, 2nd TC and 2nd GTC prepared to counter-attack and retake the hill. Additional artillery was moved to the top of Hill 252.4. Other redeployments were taking place as well, as part of major offensive that would start in the morning. The 4th GTB was moved along the rail line north of Belenikhino while the 25th GTB was attacking toward Storozhevoe and the Stalinskoei State Farm. The 26th GTB was moving from Shakhovo to the woods east of Vinogradovka. Elements of the 95th GRD were sent to the area north of Oktiabrski State Farm to bolster the 287 GRR. The discovery by the 2nd PzGR of *LAH* of the buildup north of Oktiabrski State Farm caused the Germans to abandon Petrovka. With the reinforcements north of Oktiabrski State Farm, the *LAH* stayed at the farm, developing defenses and disrupting the attack plans of 5th GTA for the morning. vzz234. vzz9m.

In addtion to the orders given to 5th GTA and 9th GAD to attack the northeast quadrant of 4th PzA tomorrow at 0830 hrs, Vatutin also ordered the following - the 52rd MRB and elements of the 9th GAD would support Shumilov's 7th GA's 49th RC (73rd GRD, 270th RD and 111th RD) in an attack to stop Kempf's forces east of Razumnoe in the morning and to prevent Kempf from joining up with 2nd SS PzC. Neither commander wanted a frontal attack but the 2nd SS PzC were getting too close to the Psel and Prokhorovka to do anything else. Other elements of Zhadov's 5th GA were to attack 48th PzC and prevent them from crossing the Psel River or sending troops to help the SS.

dgk179+*. dgk184m. vzz200. vzz8m. dgr39m.

At night, Hausser ordered the Hill 226.6 area and all along the SS line to be fully secured by morning and that extra sentries were to be posted during the night to prevent surprises. *Das Reich* received special a incentive to attack early, to completely seize Storozhevoe and Vinogradovka and strike Belenikhino while protecting *LAH*'s left flank. *Das Reich's Deutschland* Regiment was able to capture Ivanovski Vyselok but failed to reach Vinogradovka. The 2nd SS PzC recorded 125 Soviet tanks destroyed today. The Germans had inflicted heavy casualties on the Soviets - the smashing of 2nd TC, which was to play an important part in Rotmistrov's assault next morning, was especially destructive. See Map 18. dgk177+. dgk184m. dgr172m. dgk222m. mhz317++. vzz227.

By nightfall, lead elements of *LAH* entered the village of Storozhevoe but had to spend the rest of the night clearing Soviet resistance street by street as well as the nearby woods. The *Das Reich* was unable to keep up with *LAH*'s advance, thus exposing *LAH*'s right flank to attack. *LAH*'s advance had inflicted heavy losses on 2nd TC as well as isolating 99th TB in the Psel valley and threatening the separation of 9th GAD. The losses to 2nd TC on this day would have an effect on the big tank engagement of the next few days. dgk174+. dgk184m. mhz317+. wwf116.

The tank battle near Prokhorovka would see 294 panzers from 2nd SS PzC including 26 captured T34s plus Kempf's 135 panzers, if they could get there in time. The 5th GTA deployed 642 tanks and 30 SP guns for a numerical advantage of 3 to 2, though less than 500 tanks would be in first echelon. The ratio would be 2 to 1 if Kempf did not arrive on time. This did not include tanks that were not targeted for this campaign. The 5th GTA also had 40,000 men to add to the offensive. The *LAH*, which was to take the brunt of 5th GTA's assault, had only 70 working panzers and was the weakest of the three SS divisions. Between the 1st TA and 5th GTA, they would have 1,000 tanks going up against the entire 2nd SS PzC and 48th PzC from between Kruglik to the bend of the Psel River to Prokhorovka to Belenikhino, south of Prokhorovka. It was a distance of about ten miles and much of it was rolling hills. The largest of the tank battles would be between *LAH* and 18th TC and 29th TC, and would be held between the bend of the Psel River and the Prokhorovka rail line. Vatutin added the 2nd TC and 2nd GTC, plus other units, to 5th GTA for the big assault next morning. Zhadov's 5th GA was also to cross the Psel River and drive the Germans back. dgk160**+. dgk169. dgk184m. gjz186. mhz330. fkk155. vzz9m. vzz11m. dgk287. rc205. vzz264.

At night, the 1694th Anti-aircraft Artillery Regiment was redeployed to the eastern bank of the Psel River near Vyshniaia Olshanka, northeast of Hill 226.6 to help defend against the *SSTK* crossing the river and joining up with *LAH*. vzz274. vzz9m. dgk213m.

At 2215 hrs, Zhadov brought up his 6th GAD to the Sredniaia Olshanka-Hill 243.5-Ostrenki line. Vatutin needed heavy reserves as his first echelon was greatly weakened and near collapse. The 52nd GRD had only 3,300 men and the 10th TC's 11th MRB had only 1,400 men. The healthiest division in the sector was 95th GRD which had 8,700 men and was in second echelon between Veselyi and Kluichi. vzz383*. vzz9m.

At night, elements of the *LAH* infiltrated the woods just northeast of Storozhevoe and brought up anti-tank guns, setting an ambush for the next day. Col Volodin's 25th TB and Capt Lunev's 1446th AR had assembled in Iamki and their route of attack for the next morning would take them into this trap. The infantry of the 25th MRB would follow behind the tanks but they were expected to fall behind and unable to protect the tanks.

vzz332+. vzz9m. dgk191.

At 2000 hrs a small contingent of *LAH* and a few supporting panzers broke through the line at OSK and headed for Prokhorovka. By 2200 hrs, this force broke through the outer defenses of the village held by 183rd RD and headed for the inner ring. They were stopped by the 23rd GAR and the 28th GAR just 500 yards from the outskirts of Prokhorovka and a mile from the brick factory located inside the village, but the incursion was pushed back by a desperate counter-attack near Hill 252.2. The *LAH* had originally launched that day from Hill 252.2 and had made some important gains but it was decided by 2400 hrs that their position was too exposed and subsequently some units fell back to the trenches on either side of Hill 252.2, negating most of the gains made. Working through much of the night, the Germans enhanced the trench system near the hill as well as near the villages of Prelestnoe, Mikhailovka and Andreevka (*SSTK*). These defensive actions would turn out to be wise, for it was in these areas where the 18th TC and 29th TC would attack in the morning. At the same time, the far western flank of the SS also slowed its advance and settled down in the Krasnyi Oktiabr-Kozlovka area to prepare for the final push to take Prokhorovka the next morning. dgr222. dgr93m. vzz236+. vzz238++. vzz9m.

After learning the 2nd SS PzC had captured Komsomolets State Farm and Ivanovski Vyselok, Burdeiny ordered the 755th DAB, with the new 85mm AA guns, to support the line on the nearby high ground to keep Vinogradovka and Storozhevoe from falling. vzz243. vzz9m. vzz3m.

During the day, fierce fighting occurred east of the Storozhevoe woods, near and on the approaches to the Stalinskoe Branch of the Oktiabrski State Farm which straddled the rail line and was defended by the 227th RR of 183rd RD. With the help of the 169th TB and the 58th MRB, the 183rd RD was able to keep the Germans from gaining much ground, though the Stalinskoe State Farm was captured by *LAH* and the 169th TB was nearly encircled near Storozhevoe by *Das Reich*. At 2030 hrs, Burdeiny ordered the 25th GTB to deploy near Storozhevoe to protect the 169th TB and to prevent any further penetration by the Germans. When the Komsomolets State Farm fell, Burdeiny also sent the 755th DAB from Shakhovo to the hill one mile east of Vinogradovka, to contain any further breakout. Shortly after arriving in sector, the Germans attacked toward Vinogradovka but after a brief, ugly fight had to pull back. By the end of the day, 1st PzGR was knocking on the edge of Storozhevoe its woods and the Prokhorovka road, while 2nd PzGR held from the road to just northwest of Hill 252.2 and 1st PzR held Oktiabrski State Farm. vzz242+. vzz9m. dgk177.

In addition to Rotmistrov's multiple prong counterstrike against the 2nd SS PzC, the tanks of 1st TA were to attack the bounday line between *GD* and the 11th PzD in the Kalinovka sector, the area around the Kubaossovski gorge up to Hill 258.5 area and then drive into the interior and join up with 5th GTA along the Krasnaia Poliana- Iakovlevo line. The 5th GMC, stationed at Priznachnoe east of Prokhorovka, was in reserve and would be used to exploit the first penetration and then head in the direction of Luchki and Pogorelovka. The primary tank corps would occupied jump-off points along the Prelestnoe, Storozhevoe and Maloe Iablonovo line by midnight leading into 7/12. With the fighting easing on this day, positions did not move much after dark. dgr223+. dgr209m. fkk273. zzz101m.

After dark, the 9th GAD launched a counter-attack from Petrovka toward the Oktiabrski State Farm at the same time as the 95th GRD droves south to eliminate the

SSTK bridgehead north of the Psel River. Both divisions failed and had to fall back to their start positions by daybreak of 7/12. Vatutin was trying to move the line to improve the launch point for 5th GTA in the morning. vzz323. vzz467. vzz9m. vzz11m.

At 2250 hrs, Hausser transmitted revised orders containing minor changes to reflect the latest battlefield conditions to his divisions: The *SSTK* would move from its bridgehead and capture the hills to the northeast, travel along the Psel River and, while protecting *LAH*'s left flank, reach the Prokhorovka-Kartashevka road. *LAH* on *SSTK*'s right flank would finish capturing Storozhevoe and the woods to the north of it, then move on Stalinskoe State Farm, Iamki and the ridge one mile to the east. *Das Reich* would capture Vinogradovka and Ivanovka then move and capture the hills southwest of Pravorot and the hill one mile east of Storozhevoe. It is significant that only *SSTK* was to initially launch with its full division against a sector while the other two divisions were to launch with only a regiment or two, leaving the rest to stay on the defensive. This seems to signify Hausser's awareness that the Soviets were going to launch an offensive. The small bridgehead that *SSTK* held north of the Psel was shelled for most of the night and into the early hours of 7/12. vzz297. vzz9m. ztc269.

Both von Manstein and Hoth believed Vatutin had used most of his reserves and that the Germans did not have to worry about major reinforcements coming into sector. This assumption resulted in Hoth's deliberate attention in spending the previous several days clearing up flank resistance at the expense of not gaining any appreciable ground toward the Psel. Von Manstein's desire to pocket and destroy 69th Army between the two Donets Rivers consumed his attention. It can be argued that both decisions were their achilles heel but some will say that it was an absolute necessity to relieve this pressure before moving on. By the following day and certainly before the end of the month both officers would see their choices were not possible. Again this severe resistance on the western flank and along the rivers to the east showed that von Manstein did not have enough forces to defeat Vatutin. In addition to 5th GA and 5th GTA redeploying to Prokhorovka, the remainder of Konev's Steppe Front was beginning to move toward Prokhorovka, which would be part of the major counter offensive that would start in a few days. wdk158. dlu92+.

Most of the day for *Das Reich* was one of defense and redeployment. The division was preparing for a major assault on the following day. The sector south of Kalinin that was held by *Der Führer* was now being taken over by the 339th GR of 167th ID. Pz Abt 238 would support the infantry. The 315th GR took over the Petrovski sector and the 331st GR was on their right flank. *Der Führer* would move north and take over part of sector currently held by *Deutschland*, south of Storozhevoe. This would free *Deutschland* for the assault on Storozhevoe and the woods to the north. The 167th ID would then advance eastward toward the Donets River in an attempt to link up with 168th ID and pocket Soviet forces that had been giving 3rd PzC trouble. gnk292. gnk283m. vzz7m. dlu90.

While waiting for 5th GTA to arrive at Prokhorovka, Vatutin had several days to study the best route for Rotmistrov to take on his offensive. With *LAH* driving up the Prokhorovka road and with *SSTK* being redeployed to the Psel River, it seemed obvious to the Soviet commander that General Hoth had decided on the Prokhorovka corridor to reach Kursk. Never one to avoid a confrontation, Vatutin, thinking he had the advantage in numbers, believed the best way to handle the greatest threat, SS Corps, was with a head-on frontal offensive; strength against strength. For Vatutin, this was a change in thinking, for up until that moment his strategy had been flank attacks with the objective of getting behind the front line, isolating and then destroying the corps. To rush nearly 400 tanks down a narrow corridor into a well-prepared defense of the strongest corps of 4th PzA, bristling with many guns and Tigers, seems like a bad decision. A continued flank attack would have been more sensible. With a severe penetration by 5th GTA on either flank (48th PzC by way of the extreme western and northwestern sector or 3rd PzC by way of passing through 69th Army sector) would have caused Hoth to stop his northern advance and try to repair the damaged line before the situation became desperate and irrevocable. While the Germans were in a temporary state of confusion and redeployment, Vatutin could have escalated the offensive with his five other armies. There was just no way General Hoth could ignore the potential destruction of either corps. vzz262+. vzz267++. dsk111.

This campaign would be another example in a growing list where the Germans were "a day late and a dollar short". Moscow and Stalingrad are two easy examples where it is shown that the German Army just did not have the resources to put the Soviets away, but there are more. The SS were attacking a critical area on this day that was being heavily reinforced by the arrival of 5th GA and 5th GTA. If the 4th PzA had been a little stronger, deployed differently and had greater air support then it's a reasonable theory that the SS could have been fighting for the third defensive belt two days earlier, before the reinforcements arrived. Hoth lost some air support when a squadron of planes were sent north to help Model. If 24th PzC had been involved in the fighting from the beginning. If the Panther had proven more reliable. If Hoth had deployed 48th PzC and 3rd PzC differently. If Knobelsdorff had not run out of artillery shells. If it had not rained so much. If Hitler had not delayed the offensive so much. All these "ifs" would play against 4th PzA, allowing the 5th GTA on scene in time to block Hausser's path to Prokhorovka.

In order to protect the newly arrived 5th GA and the 5th GTA from air attack, Vatutin brought up the 29th and 6th Anti-Air Artillery Divisions to cover the respective armies. These divisions were broken up by regiments and spread across the sectors from Iamki in the east to the Psel River valley in the west. The 5th GA had already been deployed for a day and had already taken advantage of this air cover. vzz289+. vzz9m.

In preparation for the major offensive the following day, the VVS grounded all bombers for the day, allowing just the fighters to make raids. The bombers were being maintained and repaired and their pilots given a few hours' rest. The Soviet fighters flew many sorties on this day and the skies over the southern salient saw many dogfights. The largest air battle occurred in 3rd PzC sector where Kempf was beginning to make gains. Vatutin wanted to stop the advance; he could not allow the 2nd and 3rd corps to join. When the Soviet fighters started attacking the panzers, Kempf called for air support and to his surprise received it. In the north the *Luftwaffe* flew 933 sorties while the Red Air Force flew 595. cbk76. nzk77.

In the fierce fighting for Oktiabrski State Farm, a few panzers and supporting infantry of *LAH* broke through the line of the 26th GAR and headed east for Prokhorovka but were slowed by the second trench defended by the 23rd GAR. The critical arrival of the Red AF stopped the advance, forcing the Germans to fall back. The heaviest fighting of the day ocurred in this small area between Oktiabrski State Farm and Storozhevoe, involving *LAH* and *Das Reich* against various Soviet units. The *LAH* attacked the axis that included the state farm while *Das Reich*, beginning from Teterevino, attacked along the axis Ivanovski Vyselok-Storozhevoe. The recent arrival of the 755th DAB to this area slowed the Germans' advance. vzz228. vzz242+. vzz9m.

By the end of the day, 2nd PzC had seen a full day of heavy fighting and showed few gains for their effort, but they were important gains. Overall the 2nd SS PzC had gained three miles the previous two days; *LAH* had captured the Komsomolets State Farm, Oktiabrski State Farm and Hill 252.2. *Das Reich* was finally making progress in the direction of Storozhevoe while *SSTK* crossed the Psel and were moving toward Hill 226.6. A part of the 2nd TC had been encircled on the southern banks of the Psel in the Mikhailovka area, suffering heavy casualties. Heavy rains that day made it impossible for *SSTK* to launch its major offensive from its small bridgehead on time and it was a hardship on the other two divisions in trying to maneuver. While the Germans had made several penetrations of the first row of northern defenses, the second line was still strong. General Vatutin had become concerned about the German progress the past two days but he was wagering everything on General Rotmistrov's offensive beginning the next morning to destroy the enemy. On the other side, the key successes his army gained in the preceding days gave encouragement to General Hoth. He now believed Prokhorovka and other key objectives would be taken the following day. On the Prokhorovka line, two German columns were nearing Prokhorovka, one from the west and the other from the south. On the western flank, the 48th PzC had not gained a lot of territory lately but was able to repulse most of the many counter-attacks that were launched between Berezovka and Kruglik, assaults aimed at separating and then destroying them the next day. Hoth believed his western panzer corps would continue to hold off the enemy while the 48th made several key offensives tomorrow. vzz244. vzz9m. gn312m. zow158. Je107++.

By the end of the day, the German line in SS sector consisted of Kochetovka, Krasnyi Oktiabr, Vasilevka, the northern slopes of Hill 252.2, Oktiabrski State Farm, Komsomolets State Farm, the western edge of Storozhevoe, Ivanovski Vyselok, Iasnaia Poliana, Belenikhino and all the way south to Gostishchevo II. Hoth was putting pressure on Hausser to have *SSTK* catch up to *LAH* in order to screen *LAH*'s left flank during the final run for Prokhorovka. *SSTK* had to secure the Hill 226.6 area and capture 252.4 in order to achieve his orders. Hausser was sending every available gun to *SSTK* to help support Priess's advance. Though a lot of ground was not captured today, key objectives were and the SS were favourably deployed to move on Prokhorovka in the morning. The 48th PzC did not gain much either for it spent much of its efforts on the western flank protecting its gains of the last two days. The 11th PzD gained a little north of Kochetovka today. The 3rd PzD was making gains west of the Pena River. The salient of 48th PzC and 2nd SS PzC was now 20 miles across. vzz227. gnk312m. vzz272. vzz3m. vzz5m.

Near midnight, Vasilevsky returned to Rotmistrov's HQ and ordered the 5th GTA to be prepared to attack as early as 0300 hrs the next morning. While many of the tanks of the 5th GTA had arrived, it would be 0130 hrs of the 12th when the final tanks arrived. There would not be much time to maintain the tanks and prepare for the assault. vzz245. vzz442. vzz9m. dgk179+.

The heavy fighting of the past week brought the count of planes working for 2nd VA down to 472 aircraft: 266 fighters, 140 bombers and the remainder were fighter bombers. The 17th VA had just over 300 assorted aircraft. For the big offensive the next day, the 2nd VA would attack 4th PzA and 17th VA would attack 3rd PzC. Going up against 17th VA would be 8th *Flieger* Corps which was tasked with helping Kempf reach *Das Reich* in order to have a coordinated attack toward Pravorot and the Prockhorovka. cbk78.

After investigating the terrain of the intended assault, the Soviet reconnaissance team recommended to Rotmistrov attacking along the Shakhovo-Iakovlevo axis which was defended by the 167th ID. This route was rejected because of terrain difficulties for the tanks. It was decided the main attack would be carried out between the Psel River and Storozhevoe on a front that would be less than five miles wide. vzz271. gnk283m.

The three regiments of 9th GAD, which would play an important role in the following day's fighting were deployed: Kashpersky's 26th GAR was dug in between Oktiabrski State Farm to Hill 252.2 to Lutovo. The 23rd GAR was deployed between Kartashevka and the Prokhorovka Station in second echelon while the 28th GAR was dug in to the southwest of the station in first echelon. The 9th GAD's artillery for the most part was deployed along the railroad. The 287th GRR defended from Prelestnoe to Oktiabrski State Farm and between the four regiments, a line four miles long was covered. vzz205*+. vzz11m. lck333.

Vatutin's plan for the assault in the morning against the two western German corps involved Katukov's 1st TA, Chistiakov's 6th GA, Rotmistrov's 5th GTA and Zhadov's 5th GA. Shumilov's 7th GA with its 49th RC would attack Group Kempf to prevent Kempf from linking up with *Das Reich*. Vatutin repositioned his 10th TC in order to attack 3rd PzD with its 23 working panzers in the morning. dgk197. dgk183m. lck332.

By the end of the day, The 4th PzA completed its second phase of operation by nightfall, which was highlighted by the successful defense of the expected Soviet counter-attack around the Pena River valley area. This flank had to be stable before next morning when the big offensive launched. The 48th PzC claimed 7,000 POWs, 1,300 enemies killed and 900 destroyed or captured tanks since the start of the campaign. It was estimated that von Manstein's forces in the south, since the start of Citadel, had fatally lost 116 panzers. The remainder of the damaged panzers were repairable and would fight another day, but not necessarily in this campaign. The 4th PzA destroyed 1,000 planes and collected other booty from the bunkers and villages that were captured as well. snk83. sgf347. gnk309. gnk283m.

The beginning of the third defensive belt was just south of Prokhorovka westward along the Psel River. The fourth defensive belt was 13 miles north of this line on the Seim River. Vatutin was determined to stop the Germans at the third defensive belt. If the Germans penetrated the third belt, Vatutin would lose many men fighting a rear guard action back to the Seim River. Besides, he figured Stalin would sack him if he could not stop the Germans at Prokhorovka. vzz233+.

With the orders Hoth issued for the next day, it seems apparent that he and von Manstein were aware of a counter-attack but unaware of the size of the reinforcements that had arrived in sector in the last 24 hours. Had he been aware, his primary attention would have shifted from the 48th PzC to the SS and the attacks for 48th PzC in the Pena River bend would have been postponed until clarification of the battlefield was determined. It would have been prudent for the SS to have gone completely on the defensive instead of receiving new local attack orders. This was clearly an intelligence failure on the part of the Germans; Hoth was beginning to feel confident that his 4th PzA could reach Kursk but that attitude would change within 24 hours. gnk304. gnk309. gnk283m.

Hoth had given Hausser general orders to take Prokhorovka, leaving the corps commander to plan the details of the attack. Hausser wanted *LAH* to take the rail town from the north and south with the help of *SSTK*. His plan was too optimistic as *SSTK* was obligated to secure Hill 226.6, defend the line to Veselyi and take Hill 252.4, Polezhaev, Petrovka and the Kartashevka road before attacking Prokhorovka from the northwest. Once *SSTK* started crossing the Psel then *LAH* and *Das Reich* would begin their advance.

The *LAH* would advance straight up the Prokhorovka road and capture Storozhevoe Forest and the Stalinskoe State Farm while *Das Reich* would advance eastward between Vinogradovka and Ivanovka and capture the high ground just east of those villages, before shifting toward Pravorot and screening *LAH*'s east flank. Considering the stiff resistance the Soviets had put up the last few days and the modest gains the SS had made, these plans seem far too optimistic. gnk310. vzz1m. vzz11m. gnk283m. wdk154.

With elements of the 11th PzD approaching Hill 244.8, a small Soviet tank group ambushed the lead vehicles but after three Soviet tanks were destroyed, the rest of the tanks fell back to the hill. A little later, a larger Soviet tank force supported by infantry launched again and this time broke into the defenses of the 11th PzD; hand-to-hand combat ensued with the grenadiers protecting the mortar crews. The 11th PzD had planned on attacking the hill right after sunrise but with the muddy roads much of the division was stretched out for miles behind and had to wait until 1100 hrs when it was better prepared. Mickl was to split his forces and attack from the south and north. The southern group would attack first but it would be a feint; the northern group would be the main assault force. The skies were mostly cloudy and the Lutfwaffe was not much help with the assault; the 11th PzD was hit hard by the large concentration of guns on the hill and it was forced to retreat, suffering heavy casualties. The low lying fog also prevented accurate shelling by the Germans as well. General Mickl did not want to attack the hill under these conditions, and especially without air support, but Knobelsdorff overruled. Von Mellenthin, Hoth's Chief of Staff, claimed the attack failed due to poor planning and poor execution, especially artillery support. Mickl wanted to tackle Hill 239.6 to the east and next to the Dist Melovoe before attacking Hill 244.8. General Mickl was offered greater artillery support to take Hill 244.8. Instead of attacking the hill, Mickl 's panzer group moved toward the low lying hills southwest of Orlovka, just three miles from the Psel River. The 111th PzGR moved out and headed for the Solotinka area and Kochetovka. At Kochetovka the Germans could see about 50 tanks of the 5th GTC redeploying on the north side of the river. Hoth also ordered 52nd IC to finish capturing Rakovo on the north bank of the Pena River before closing up on 3rd PzD. gnk301. cbk75.

During the predawn hours, German artillery was moved up to cover the Berezovka-Tolstoe areas to help screen the big attack on Berezovka scheduled for first light. The Stukas would be part of the assault as well. gnk273. gnk283m.

The *GD* of 48th PzC, after fighting all day, pushed the remains of 6th TC and 90th GRD out of Kalinovka, where they stopped for the day and prepared for the assault the next day on the Psel River with 3rd PzD and 11th PzD. The two Soviet formations fell back to the west of Chapaev-Novenkoe-Kruglik line which was being defended by the 184th RD. The 11th PzD, on *GD*'s right, secured Hill 260.8 which ran alongside the Oboyan road, not far from Novoselovka. While regrouping behind the defense belt held by 184th RD, the 204th RD was able to fend off the German attack near Kalinovka and Kruglik. Hoth would ask Knodelsdorff to succeed in crossing the Psel River the following day; it was a task he was unable to do that day and the Soviets would be even stronger in the morning. It was not an enviable assignment. dgk158+. dgr99+. gnk312m.

On the morning of the 11th, the 48th PzC launched a coordinated three-pronged attack to finally destroy the 6th TC, which had caused so much trouble the last few days. The first prong left Zavidovka and attacked Col Elin's 6th MRB while the second prong struck from Syrtsevo toward Berezovka. The third prong launched from Tolstoe Woods area toward

Krasnyi Uzliv and Chapaev. This concentric attack had as its sole aim the encirclement and destruction of 6th TC. By noon, the first prong heading for Zavidovka reached and captured Rakovo. The second prong was nearing Berezovka and the third group did capture Krasnyi Uzliv. The 6th TC found itself partially encircled with shell fire coming down on it from three sides and was taking heavy casualties. They tried to disengage but the Germans would not let go, however after dark the remains of 6th TC was able to break loose and head west for Novenkoe. dgr218. dgk170m. dgk184m.

Hoth was convinced that the Pena River bend had to be cleared before moving north to Oboyan but the 3rd PzD and 52nd IC had failed to budge the Soviet defenses. At 0600 hrs, the *Luftwaffe* struck targets south of Hill 258.5 to soften up the defenses for the upcoming attack. While the planes were bombing the different sites, the lead units of *GD* and its pioneers were approaching the hill to clear it of mines. Hill 258.5 was due west of Verkhopenie and just due east of the Tolstoe Woods. The main battle group was approaching Hill 237.6, south of Hill 258.5 and one mile north of Berezovka. Hearing the air attacks on the hill, this battle group speeded up its march and joined the overall attack without further preparation. Before reaching Hill 237.6, panzers, upwards of 60 Mk IIIs and Panthers attacked the Soviet defenses on Hill 243.8, four miles south of Hill 258.5 and one mile west of Lukhanino where for the last three days, the 3rd PzD had been desperately trying to clear the town and the surrounding territory. Hearing the Germans nearing Berezovka, the Soviets in the area began evacuating to the west but waited too long and were shelled as they escaped, trying to reach the Tolstoe woods where a heavy concentration of tanks and infantry deployed. The heavy thunderstorms of the predawn hours and into the first hours of the day made moving difficult and slow which once again was a disadvantage to the Germans. gnk298+. gnk312m.

After capturing Hill 237.6 and Hill 243.8 and approaching Berezovka, Knobelsdorff ordered 3rd PzD to join *GD* in attacking Berezovka. gnk299.

After helping 3rd PzD the previous day, major elements of *GD* resumed their advance toward Oboyan while an armored combat group stayed behind to support 3rd PzD west of the Pena River. The 3rd PzD and elements of the 332nd ID cleared Soviet resistance from the Berezovka area and forced the 71st GRD westward from Rakovo and Chapaev along the Pena River and closed up to the 184th RD's defenses extending southward from Novenkoe to Melovoe on the Pena. Katukov sent the remains of 10th TC to Novenkoe to bolster the right flank of 1st TA. The 219th RD also arrived from reserve. dgk157+. dgr172m. dgr92m. dgk222m.

The 11th PzD took a hill two miles north of Kochetovka. The Soviets countered, trying to retake the hill but failed. The *GD* was clearing up resistance along the Pena between Berezovka and Verkhopenie. The 1st TA and 6th GA remained defensive, content just to keep the Germans from advancing. On the 52nd IC front in predawn action, the 332nd ID defended itself against a counter-attack against 90th GRD and 184th RD at Zavidovka. The 332nd ID was still able to cross the Pena at Alekseevka in the morning and was at Rakovo by noon. The 255th ID defending near Bubny repulsed battalion-size attacks from the 161st RD. wdk157+. hjj121m. gnk193m. dgr209m. gnk227m.

In the morning, the 5th GA's 32nd GRC began moving into defensive positions on the north bank of the Psel river in the Oboyan-Olkhovatka sector. In front of them were 1st TA's 31st TC and 10th TC with elements of 6th GA's 51st GRD which were already in battle with the enemy. The 33rd GRC were being deployed along the Semenovka-Veselyi line behind the 52nd GRD. vzz168. dgr96. dgk170m. dgk184m.

At 1000 hrs on this Sunday morning, *GD* was able to finally capture Hill 243.0. Soviet POWs stated the Psel was being fortified and that Vatutin would try to stop the advance at the river. The 3rd PzD moved up to support *GD*. It was a fairly quiet day in 48th PzC sector. No major offensives were planned, only small skirmishes to improve the current line: the crossroads south of Hill 248 to Hill 233.8 by 11th PzD and the boundary of *GD* to the hills east of Kalinovka to Kubaossovski Gorge to Hill 247.0 (south of Kruglik) to Hill 258.5 by 3rd PzD. On the other side of this line elements of 69th Army and 1st TA were waiting to stop them. hjj120. hsz129+. fmz221m.

At 1200 hrs, the panzers of *GD* arrived at Berezovka to help the 3rd PzD with the Soviet garrison. The panzers broke up with half attacking from the west. The Panthers went to the south of town and attacked. The 394th PzGR and 3rd PzGR crossed the Pena at Syrtsevo and followed. The 3rd PzD had already entered the town on the east side. Sensing weakness in the northeast quadrant, 6th PzR shifted to that axis. While the battle for Berezovka was raging and the pioneers were clearing the last of the minefields on Hill 243.8, guns could be heard at nearby Rakovo, on the banks of the Pena River, at its most southern point. The 332nd ID was now attacking it but the initial assault had been repulsed. An element of 332nd ID swung around to the north of the town and linked up with panzers from *GD* near Hill 243.8 at around 1500 hrs. Hill 243.8 was four miles west of Lukhanino and four miles south of Hill 258.5. gnk299. gnk283m.

The 10th TC and the remains of the 5th GTC, with a combined total of 200 tanks, would launch their offensive into the western flank of 48th PzC the following morning. Instead of hitting the *GD* division as planned, it would strike the lead units of 3rd PzD which was currently moving up to cover *GD*'s flank at Kalinovka. Part of the 3rd PzD, the 394th PzGR, was still in the Berezovka sector trying to clear the last resistance that lingered. By late morning the resistance had been reduced and the bulk of the division would head north. The 332nd ID was already moving up to defend the sector from Soviet attacks coming from west of the Pena River. gnk301.

The 3rd PzD and the 332nd ID cleared Soviet resistance from the Berezovka region, forcing the 71st GRD westward from Rakovo and Chapaev along the Pena River to close up with the 184th RD at Novemkoe-Melovoe on the Pena. Elements of the 10th TC were redirected to support the 1st TA around the Novenkoe area. At the same time, *GD* attacked the Kalinovka-Kruglik line at Kalinovka in its pursuit to head north. Meanwhile, the 204th RD fended off the German probes. While the 2nd SS PzC headed toward the northeast, the 48th PzC continued its slow advance toward Oboyan. See Map 23. dgk158. snk81+. dgr172m. dgk222m. nzk95.

Chistiakov's 6th GA, strengthened with the 10th TC and 5th GTC, as well as 1st TA's 3rd MC, prepared for the major offensive starting the next day that would encircle the 48th PzC. The 22nd GRC of 6th GA would lead the advance and consisted of the 90th GRD, 184th RD and 219th RD. Starting from the Kruglik-Chapaev-Novenkoe line, it would drive south then east along the Syrtsevo-Iakovlevo axis and meet up with 5th GTA, encircling the bulk of the 48th PzC and 2nd SS PzC. The 184th RD and 219th RD of 40th Army were to deploy behind 10th TC and clear resistance after the tankers drove through but Lt General Moskalenko resisted giving his divisions up and they were late arriving for the start. This delay was most helpful to 48th PzC. Next to the 22nd GRC, the 23rd GTC (204th GRD, 309th GRD and 67th GRD) would also start near Kruglik and drive past

Verkhopenie toward Pokrovka. The 71st GRD would guard the corps right flank and 51st GRD would be reserve. vzz427+. kcz168. dgk106m. dgr99. dgr93m.

The Soviets would always counter-attack after losing a strongpoint in the attempt to recapture. The Germans were well aware of this practice and part of the German tactical MO would be to quickly set up defenses in order to repulse these attacks. This was a part of phase two of an operation. It became second nature for the Germans to go defensive, especially in the later days of the campaign.

As part of 6th GA, the 5th GTC's 21st GTB and 22nd GTB would attack from the Novoselovka and Kuznetsovo forest area in the direction of Hill 208.0, Sukhodol forest, Shepelevka, Lukhanino and Iakovlevo. Iakovlevo was the center of the German attack zone. Handing over its defense belt to 204th RD, the 10th TC would advance from Novenkoe, Tolstoe woods, Verkhopenie and Hill 251.4 and capture Krasnaia Dubrova, Pokrovka and Ulianov, Hill 237.6 and Hill 254.5. The 183rd TB would launch from near Novenkoe and head for Verkhopenie and Hill 251.4. The 186th TB in second echelon would head for Pokrovka and Ulianov. The 178th TB would attack along the axis: Novenkoe, Hill 237.6 and Hill 254.5. All this action was in an attempt to get behind and isolate the German front line (48th PzC). The basis for these different axes of attack was to carve up the German territory in order to destroy 4th PzA more easily but after days of heavy fighting, all of these tank brigades were greatly weakened and their orders were too ambitious. Those two Soviet tank brigades suffered heavy loses on 7/6, north of Iakovlevo. vzz428+.

To get a head start, 6th GA and 1st TA launched their offensive today, the 3rd MC's 31st TC, 204th RD and 309th RD would hold the current line in case the Germans counter-attacked and penetrated the first line. The 3rd MC could only go on the offensive if 48th PzC was retreating. By next morning this order would change and the 3rd MC along with the 204th RD and 309th RD would launch with the rest from the line: Kalinovka-Malinovoe-Hill 211.9. The combat group would attack *GD* and 11th PzD. vzz429.

Vatutin formed a plan for 1st TA to counter-attack that would start out by attacking the left flank of 48th PzC and then destroy 4th PzA by meeting up with 29th TC and encircling much of the 4th PzA. Knobelsdorff realized the Soviets were preparing a major counter and tried to prepare his forces for it. The 255th ID moved up to the southern bank of the Pena to screen the left flank of the 48th PzC. Near the Pena River, the 3rd PzD engaged Soviet tanks in a fierce but short battle that allowed the Germans to capture 100 tanks. This insight of moving the 255th ID further north to tighten the line by Knobelsdorff would be helpful in the 48th PzC's attempt in repulsing the coming major offensive. In the morning, the 7th GA and 69th Army would drive west and south against Kempf with the objective of having the two pincers meet and encircle 3rd PzC. dgk159++. snk82.

At night, the 11th PzD and *GD* advanced on Hill 260.8 and Hill 244.8 along the Oboyan road. This was the important high ground leading to Oboyan that would give 48th PzC a great observation post and artillery position. Only the Psel River was the last natural barrier before the town. A far worse barrier would be the counter-attack toward Gresnoe, Iakovlevo and Bykovka that Vatutin was preparing, which would start the next morning with the objective to stop the advance before the Kruglik-Olkhovatka line and at the same time have the 6th GA counter-attack toward Iakovlevo and Pokrovka. This attack would impede the *GD* from helping 11th PzD and 3rd PzD with the assault on Oboyan and that failure would restrict 48th PzC from getting involved in the big tank battle planned for the next day near Prokhorovka. dgk159+. fkk102m. gnk312m.

In the 48th PzC sector, both 11th PzD and *GD*, moving in tandem, advanced northward along the Oboyan road. The 11th PzD captured Hill 260.8 while *GD*, with the help of 11th PzD, captured Hill 244.8. The hill was an important OP and both sides wanted it. After losing some ground, the Soviets regrouped and were able to stop the Germans from any further progress. The progress made by the 11th PzD allowed them to shrink the gap with *LAH* to their right, which eased the pressure on both divisions by a little bit. dgk159. lck331. gnk312m. vzz428.

In the Prokhorovka sector, the attack of the 2nd SS PzC gained only a little net ground, yet the *SSTK* was able to seize and stabilize a bridgehead over the Psel, moving northward. Nearby, the 48th PzC captured 100 working Soviet tanks abandoned with empty fuel tanks. Though there were exceptions, General Hoth considered some of today's gains important ones, but with the 9th Army to the north at a standstill, the benefits of Hoth's successes were questionable. snk83.

Late at night and into the early hours of 7/12, the 3rd PzD, 332nd ID and 255th ID relieved *GD* in the west so it could prepare for the big assault planned for the morning. All three divisions were weak and exhausted and would be unable to fully stop Vatutin's counter-attacks which began that same day. During this redeployment, the 3rd PzD replaced the *GD* on the southern slopes of Hill 260.8, east and southeast of Kalinovka. The Soviets quickly counter-attacked and drove the 3rd PzD off the Hill. *GD* was going to lead the attack across the Psel River next morning and was moving to its jump-off point. The 2nd SS PzC had already crossed the river and Hoth was placing a lot of pressure on the 48th PzC to catch up and straighten out the line. Kalinovka was due west of Novoselovka but due east of Kruglik. rc210. hsz129. fkk271. dgr209m. gnk312m. mhz314. fmz226. fmz227m.

Besides relieving *GD* near Hill 260.8, the 3rd PzD also had responsibility for defending the Berezovka-Verkhopenie area and the 332nd ID filled in 3rd PzD's former lines north of the Pena River forward of Rakovo. The 255th ID stretched its lines northward to Mikhailovka. These redeployments were meant to strengthen the front lines in the hot areas but it also weakened the flanks which Vatutin would take advantage of. The *GD* was concentrated west of the Oboyan road, working the flanks and not the northern front. The dilemma of 48th PzC being stretched too far, clearly shows that 48th PzC like the 4th PzA, and like 6th Army at Stalingrad, just did not have enough panzers and especially men to defeat the Soviets. dgk204+. dgk211m. dgr172m. dgk222m. dgr209m. gnk312m.

It had been a mildly successful day for *GD*, 3rd PzD and 332nd ID for they had taken several key hills, and then cleared Rakovo and Berezovka. In addition, a number of counter-attacks were repulsed. The Soviets were still strong in the area for they had been reinforced by elements of 40th and 38th Armies to the northwest. They were especially strong at Tolstoe Woods woods which ran along the Berezovka-Kruglik road, where they would harass Germans as they passed by. At Kalinovka, to the north, *GD* had just been able to enter the town but was unable to defeat the local garrison and was forced to pull back. The 3rd PzD was ordered to Kalinovka to free *GD* elements there in order to resume its advance. It was estimated that 6th TC, which had been battling 48th PzC for days, was now down to 35 working tanks. The accompanying 3rd MC was in worse condition. *GD* was now ordered to reassemble north of Novoselovka by next morning, to attack and push the recently arrived 10th TC north of the Psel River. gnk300. wwf121. gnk283m.

Vatutin was already redeploying his forces for the following day's big offensive. He moved the 10th TC and the 5th GTC from in front of *GD* over to the west and was planning on attacking *GD*'s west flank and slicing through it in order to reach the Iakovlevo-Pokrovka area where it was planned to join up with the 29th TC, coming from the east to surround a major portion of 4th PzA. The plan was audacious and unrealistic but that was a trademark of Vatutin, Zhukov and the Soviet generals. gnk300. gnk283m.

For the previous two days, Hoth's main focus had been on 48th PzC in order for them to catch up and align themselves with the SS Corps. The front line had to be solid with no gaps if they were to reach Kursk. Hoth continued to be slow and deliberate, neglecting the timetable that was so important at the beginning of the campaign. It seems the general was over confident after inflicting heavy casualties on 1st TA, 3rd MC and 6th TC and apparently was unaware of the size of the reinforcements that had just begun to arrive: 5th GTA and 5th GA. The Germans could not afford to thoroughly recon the sector to get a more definitive picture of what was facing them and it made Hoth make poor choices. While the *LAH* and *SSTK* were attacking in the north, part of 48th PzC would still be clearing the Pena bend which would take another few days. With the extremely muddy terrain, Hoth understood why 48th PzC, trying to cross the Psel, made only modest gains against increasing resistance but what made him think that without any additional support for the 48th PzC the next day that the situation would improve? It was critical for the 48th to cross the Psel and join the 2nd SS PzC in expanding the bridgehead and forming a unified front north of the river. gnk303. gnk283m.

Other elements of Konev's Steppe Front were ordered to deploy north of Psel River line to block any further incursions toward Oboyan and to prepare themselves for the major counter-offensive that would soon be coming. It would take couple days for the reinforcements to arrive in sector. wwf91.

Late at night and into the very early hours of 7/11, a combat group from the 7th PzD was moving west to the south of 6th PzD, which was currently deployed around Melikhovo, and in concert with 19th PzD at daybreak drove along the Donets toward Khokhlovo, Kiselevo and Sabynino trying to overpower the stubborn Soviet line. shn160. dgk162.

At 0200 hrs from northwest of Hill 217.4, in the Dalniaia Igumenka sector, a massive preparation began that lasted three hours. Then the *Luftwaffe* came in low and strafed the Soviet lines before Kempf launched his forces. It was a two-prong attack with the objective of taking Kiselevo, Khokhlovo and Sabynino, situated along the Donets River. At 0930 hrs, the 19th PzD along with 168th ID drove along the Donets while the 7th PzD, further east, was driving from the northern outskirts of Miasoedovo to the northwest toward the same villages. Their axis of attack was defended by the 94th GRD. The resistance from Kiselevo with its surrounding minefields and the adjacent Hill 211.5 with its maze of trenches was horrendous. By 1400 hrs, the 19th PzD had made three attacks against the 92nd GRD but failed each time. After moving artillery on Hill 217.4 and gathering 50 panzers, another attack was made and by 1525 hrs, the panzers were able to break through and enter Kiselevo where they fought hard to secure it. Khokhlovo fell soon afterwards. With the fall of these two villages, the 19th PzD had reached the Donets and were now facing the 375th RD, which had just received orders to fall back. The 74th PzGR, after dark, tried to take the maze of trenches nearby but failed. Kempf was under orders to catch up to *Das Reich* and contribute to the capture of Prokhorovka but the 69th Army and 7th GA were putting up unbelievable resistance. The 3rd PzC, though making good progress that day, did not move fast enough to encircle any large concentrations of the enemy. The 92nd GRD along with the 96th TB fell back to the Vypolzovka-Alekseevski Vyselok line. See Map 23. vzz252++.

vzz3m. dgr102+. dgr155m. dgr173m. dgr93m. dlu100.

While the 73rd PzGR fought for Kiselovo, the 429th GR attacked the 89th GRD. The regiment penetrated the line and advanced on the village of Petropavlovka which was quickly captured, though the 73rd PzGR had to defend the village against a counter-attack. It then moved on nearby Belomestnazha, Hill 190.5 and Hill 211.6, capturing those as well. The regiment then tried to secure the woods to the north of the hills but got bogged down in heavy fighting and could not make any further progress that day. dlu100+. dgk163.

With the success 19th PzD, 168th ID and 7th PzD was having in clearing the eastern bank of the northern Donets River, the 375th RD and 81st GRD on the western side were ordered to pull back to the north side of the Lipovyi Donets and defend the Kiselevo to Krivtsovo line. It was felt that if this raid along the Donets was successful it would help the 6th PzD break loose as they headed north from Melikhovo toward Kazache. dgr103. fzk52. dlu96+ shn160..

With the combat group heading toward Sheino, the rest of Lt General von Funck's 7th PzD moved northward toward Melikhovo, trying to screen 6th PzD's right flank while 6th PzD prepared for its assault northward from Melikhovo. The 6th PzD was delaying their attack to see if enemy forces were leaving their sector for the river to help stop 19th PzD. The 429th GR of 168th ID was still attached to 19th PzD due to its weakened condition. dlu96.

At dawn, the 6th PzD with support from the sPzAbt 503, which had just had its three companies reunited, launched their attack northward from Melikhovo toward Shilakhovo and was able to penetrate the line of 305th RD and the 107th RD deployed directly behind it. The 6th PzD was then able to drive eight miles northward through the line and seize Olkhovatka, Olshanaia, Oskochnoe and Kazache. A wedge was also cut into the prepared defenses of 107th RD and the entire division had to fall back. This sudden move north also made 89th GRD's position untenable just south of Gostishchevo and it had to fall back as well. To allow this retreat, Kriuchenkin ordered the shattered 81st GRD rear guard duty for the general exodus of the area. The 81st fell back to the Krivtsovo-Ryndinka line. Even with this successful advance, Kempf was still 15 to 20 miles from Prokhorovka. Kriuchenkin shifted his exhausted 375th RD to block this new gap at the line: Shakhovo, Zhilmestne and Novoselovka (east). The 375th RD would bolster the line that 2nd TC had generally reached yesterday. The 305th RD and 107th RD fell back to the Balka Razumnaia-Gremiache line. The 94th GRD fell back behind the Koren River in the Sheino-Ushakovo area, just north of the 15th GRD. dgk162+. dlu63m. vzz251++. vzz3m. gnk298. nzk95. vzz5m. vzz12m. dgr93m. dgr155m. dgr173m. dgr99. dgr103+. fzk52. dlu82. shn160. zzt90.

With the securing of Miasoedovo, the 7th PzD's front covered from Miasoedovo in the north down to Raus's sector. The 11th IC was having trouble in the Rzhavets (southern)-Batratskaia Dacha area with 72nd GRD and 213rd RD. The 15th GRD had just arrived and was adding their weight to the battle. The 198th ID was brought up to help 320th ID and 106th ID hold the line. The 326th GR, positioned at Batratskaia Dacha, was particularly under a lot of pressure. At 1700 hrs after a pause to regroup, the 15th GRD attacked Batratskaia again with tanks in the lead, followed by infantry. During the pause, German sappers laid new mines in front of their position which disabled a number of tanks during their charge. The Soviets, with fanatical spirit, were able to advance to the town limits where, with bayonets fixed, fought man to man to destroy the enemy. At dusk, failing to penetrate the line, they started to fall back. The 198th ID lost over 100 men that day.

dgk162+. dlu63m. dgr103. dgr155m. dlu87+. dlu97+.

In the morning, von Manstein visited Kempf at his HQ at Dolbino to give him a pep talk and to explain how important it was for 3rd PzC to catch up with *Das Reich*. Kempf argued that he needed 24th PzC but Hitler would not release it. lck329.

By the end of the day, the Kempf Group had set up defensive positions for the night and when the Soviet 5th GTA's massive offensive launched in his sector the next morning, Kempf was able to repulse it. In one sector, General Kempf was then able to penetrate the boundary between 107th RD and 305th RD, northeast of Belgorod, that allowed a few panzers to race north along the Donets. jp174. lck330.

To recap, the morning started east of the Donets with Kempf jumping off with 6th PzD, 7th PzD and 19th PzD, supported by elements of three infantry divisions, paralleling the river. To the northwest, 48th PzC renewed its drive on Oboyan. The 2nd SS PzC began to fight its way towards Prokhorovka. Heavy rains during the night made it slow going for the panzers and infantry alike. Before long, the Germans were penetrating the defenses of the 5th GTC in front of Storozhevoe, southwest of Prokhorovka. rc206. dgk184m.

With Rzhavets and Ryndinka being threatened by the advance of 6th PzD, a battalion of the 375th RD was sent to Shakhovo to block 6th PzD from reaching Prokhorovka from that axis. To stop the Germans from expanding their bridgehead, the 92nd GRD was ordered to cross and defend the west bank of the Donets between Shcholokovo to Vypolzovka (near Ryndinka) while the 305th RD was to cross the Donets between Kolomytsevo and Novo Slobodka. By midnight, the German line was generally Kiselevo-Khokhlovo,-Verhne Olshanets but they had salients that went further north. Vatutin had wanted to transfer several antitank units from this sector to 5th GTA but with this breakthrough had to leave these forces near the Donets. Shcholokovo is on the west bank of the Donets about three miles south of Ryndinka. vzz408++. dgr221m.

At the same time as the 19th PzD was driving north along the Donets, the 6th PzD headed east to the Razumnaia River before shifting north to follow along the river. It was important for the 6th PzD to capture the bridge over the river at Komintern to prevent the Soviets from resupplying their forces west of the river. This bridge was almost ten miles from the bridge at Rzhavets. To secure the 6th PzD's left flank, the 19th PzD supported by the 168th ID would attempt to capture the bridge over the Donets at Sabynino. gnk269+. gnk283m. vzz10m. vzz3m.

The 2nd SS PzC just barely broke through the third defense belt near Prokhorovka but the 5th GTA was coming up to push the Germans back. The 42nd GRD had already arrived and several tank brigades would arrive by early evening. Vatutin expected the 5th GTA, when all units arrived, to lead the major assault to push back the SS Corps the next day. To the east, Vatutin ordered his armies to stand and fight to the last man. It was critical to prevent 3rd PzC from joining up with *Das Reich*. To make this happen, the 89th GRD of 69th Army was sent in to stop the 168th ID advancing north along the railroad east of the Lipovyi Donets River. Advancing north of the river the 168th ID would be able to attack the flank and rear of the forces struggling with *Das Reich*. It could be catastrophic for the Soviets if the 168th could reach the 167th ID and *SSDR*. The 107th RD was sent to Kazache to hold back the north flank of the 7th PzD. wdk158. dgk222m. dlu63m.

Group Horst of 19th PzD began its drive north, paralleling 6th PzD which was further east. After penetrating the Soviet line, Horst advanced over three miles and from a fighting march, attacked Kiselevo. He and Group Schmidt attacked from the south and east. By

1900 hrs the town fell. Horst resumed his advance toward Sabynino, just east of the Donets and next to the fortified Hill 211.5 which it would reach the following day. The village was a strongpoint, as was the hill, and they were close enough to each other to give mutual support. The 19th PzD would have its hands full with this engagement. gnk298. vzz3m. vzz10m.

In the afternoon, a meeting was held between von Manstein, Hoth, Kempf and Breith at the Dubino HQ. The discussion was about what to do with the flagging 3rd PzC. Von Manstein suggested that the entire corps redeploy to the west of the Donets and go completely defensive. This would allow *Das Reich* to concentrate entirely on a northward advance, fighting side by side with *LAH* toward Prokhorovka. Kempf, who had had a negative outlook on the role of 3rd PzC since the beginning after the long delays, wholeheartedly endorsed the proposal. Lt General Hermann Breith being more optimistic favored staying the course; von Manstein, liking what he heard, agreed. In the next eight days, Kempf would repeatedly try to have his corps stay defensive and each time it would be rejected. Hitler was disappointed with Kempf's attitude and it's not surprising that Kempf would lose his command in the near future. Prior to Kempf becoming CO in November 1942, Breith was CO of 3rd PzD. erz208. snk22. zsm57.

This decision to stay the course for 3rd PzC was tough to make. There was some logic in going defensive on the west side of the Donets but it was too late in the campaign to redeploy, with the major offensive to take Prokhorovka scheduled the next day. I would have been in favor of deploying 3rd PzC west of the river from the start of the campaign and it would still have made sense up to the end of 7/6 when little progress was made and it was obvious the resistance would be costly to overcome without adequate resources.

Attacking to the north from Dalniaia Igumenks and Melikhovo areas the 6th PzD, heading for Shliakhovo, a key anchor near the rear of the second defensive belt, was trying to split the boundary between 276th GRR and the 1004th RR. After capturing Shliakhovo, the panzers cleared Hill 230.3 and Olkhovatka. The hill was difficult for it had a number of batteries stationed there, but sPzAbt 503 and the Bake Group quickly captured it. After capturing Shliakhovo and Olkhovatka, the 6th PzD would ultimately head for Kazache, hopefully capturing the important town before quitting for the day. Before capturing the main objective of the day, the 6th PzD had to capture Hill 233.3 and the village of Snamenka which turned out to be difficult. It had been raining that morning and the panzers were hampered by the muddy ground. Olkhovatka was a tiny village due north of Skliakhovo and west of Komintern. vzz254+. vzz10m. dgr155m. dgr173m. dgr93m. dlu95+.

At 1300 hrs, 3rd PzC artillery began to shell Shliakhovo; toward the end of the hour, the *Luftwaffe* dropped their deadly cargo. At about 1415 hrs, the ground attack on Shliakhovo began with the attacking forces driving along both sides of Razumnoe River with the main effort toward Shliakhovo. The 6th PzD, west of Razumnoe River, attacked to the north and seized Shliakhovo and later Olshanaya, Oskochnoye and finally Kazache. At the same time driving to the east of 6th PzD, the 7th PzD attacked toward Shieno. The 3rd PzC had now penetrated the Soviet second defense belt and was in a position to operate in open terrain. At 1530 hrs, the 282nd GRR launched a counter in the direction of Sabynino and Kiselevo but it was stopped, with GRR suffering heavy losses when the *Luftwaffe* flew in low strafing the advance. The left flank of 276th GRD had to fall back to behind Hill 230.3 but were pushed aside when the 6th PzD came through. At 2300 hrs, the 35th GRC ordered its troops back to the line from Vypolzovka to Aleksandrovka. The

19th PzD protected 6th PzD's flank during the attack and was also able to reach Soyshno and then Saverskoye. The 3rd PzC was then ordered to cross the Donets and support the SS Corps in its envelopment of the 69th Army. shn160. dlu63m. dgr39m. vzz5m. shn160. dlu63m. dgr39m. vzz5m.

Along with the success of the two other panzer divisions and after a hard fight by 6th PzD to capture Shliakhovo, the 6th PzD without pause advanced on Verkhne Olkhanets. With this pressure, Soviet defenses collapsed along the Sheino-Shliakhovo-Kiselevo line allowing the 3rd PzC to move further along the Razumnaia and Donets Rivers. This retreat was critical as the 69th Army was getting squeezed and Vatutin scoured the area for reserves to bring up to save his men and stop the advance from reaching Prokhorovka. With this advancement, FM von Manstein moved his reserves (24th PzC: 17th PzD, 23rd PzD and Viking) closer to the front, closer to Belgorod. Generally speaking, the 3rd PzC, on a line, moved from Melikhovo area to Verkhni Olshanets area; it was a good day for 3rd PzC. jp170. jp172. mhz309. dgr209m. dgr102. dgr155m. dgr173m. vzz3m. vzz5m.

With the Germans approaching Oboyan, Prokhorovka and Rzhavets, the Soviet 5th GTA, its attachments and reserves, including the 2nd TC and 2nd GTC, moved to their assembly areas for the counter-attack in the Belenikhino and Prokhorovka area. Also included in the 850 tank total was the 5th GMC's 212 tanks, which would be in reserve. Besides the reserve Vatutuin had to send an armor group south to ward off the 3rd PzC, leaving his main attack group down to 500 tanks. The 3rd PzC, now gaining momentum, was south of them, waiting for the 4th PzA to attack the Soviet tanks from the front so they would have a good chance to encircle them from the rear. As the 4th PzA neared them, the Soviets realized their dangerous position and retreated from the envelopment, giving the Germans an easier advance to Prokhorovka. The Soviets regrouped to add reinforcements and attacked the Germans, who were trying to complete the takeover of Prokhorovka. With more of the arriving 6th PzD and 19th PzD in the sector, the Germans drove the Soviet tanks back. The two divisions pursued the Soviets creating a bridgehead over the Donets after taking Rzhavets. Using two captured T34s as lead tanks, the Germans passed through Soviet lines and were able to reach and capture Rzhavets without much of a fight. Eventually the Soviets discovered the truth and attacked the German column inside the city district but it was too late and the German combat group took control of the city. It was a major coup for the audious Germans. jp176+. dlu63m. dgk222m. mhz328*. je106. rkz168. pck80. gnk309. fzk172?. zow160.

A few hours later after capturing Kazache, into the predawn hours of 7/12, a special combat group of 6th PzD captured Rzhavets, surprising the garrison. The 6th PzD had broken through the second defensive belt. With today's progress, the 19th PzD moving toward Sabynino and 6th PzD scattered between Kazache and Rzhavets had created a larger pocket by pressing the 81st GRD in the Rzhavets, Strelnikov, Krivtsovo, Sabynino sector against the banks of the Donets. The lead units of 6th PzD were now less than 11 miles from Prokhorovka and becoming a real threat to 5th GTA's flank. vzz255. vzz10m. dgk106m. vzz3m. dgr155m. dgr173m. gnk283m. dgr99.

The 7th PzD launched at 1000 hrs against the 15th GRD and 94th GRD of 35th GRC along the line from west of Miasoedovo eastward to Sheino. The Soviet infantry, with support of artillery, were able to repulse the first few attacks. By 1500 hrs the boundary line between the two Soviet divisions was detected between Miasoedovo and Sheino and exploiting this weakness, the 7th PzD with the support of up to 50 panzers, attacked again. By 1700 hrs, the Germans had reached the rear area of 283rd GRR and 288th GRR and were threatening encirclement. Fighting through darkness and with the help of an ambush attack from Maj Chuev's 286th GRR, the other two regiments were able to escape the closing pocket but had suffered heavy casualties in the process. At the same time as the division attacked Miasoedovo, a small combat group rode up the road to Sheino and another group launched an attack into the woods between Kalinin and Miasoedovo. The success the three panzer divisions had on this day was encouraging and Kempf believed that a link-up with *Das Reich* was now possible and with that link-up the 48th RC of 69th Army could begin to feel the German pincers slowly closing around them. vzz255. vzz10m. dgk106m. vzz3m. dgr155m. dgr173m. gnk283m. dgr99. fzk171.

Colonel Russkikh's 94th GRD, supported by tanks, counter-attacked the southern flank of 7th PzD at Sheino. The Soviet resistance was less that day but the rearguard of 69th Army was only three miles to the north preparing and waiting for the Germans to arrive. To the extreme east, the 15th GRD arrived in front of the 106th ID. The 270th RD moved in behind them and the 111th RD was behind the 213th RD. wdk157. vzz3m. vzz5m. vzz10m.

In the north, Model's 9th Army had been stopped. In the south, the Soviets were fighting bitterly and 2nd SS PzC's advance was slowing down. The attrition and exhaustion was clearly having an effect. The SS claimed 94 tanks destroyed, mostly by 2nd TC at Komsomolets. Only 309 Soviet POWs were captured and only five Soviet airplanes shot down due to the bad weather. In the 3rd PzC sector, the Soviets were withdrawing, giving Kempf an easier time in advancing north. While the 6th PzD and 7th PzD were still strong, the 19th PzD had sustained heavy losses. Von Manstein discussed with Hoth that with Model's failure, a rethinking of their plans and objectives would be necessary. Von Manstein again told Kempf how important it was for 3rd PzC to reach Prokhorovka in order to help 2nd SS PzC defeat 5th GTA. snk84. wdk156. mhz287. mhz309.

As part of the coordinated attack on the line that included Kiselevo and Shliakhovo by 19th PzD and 6th PzD, by 1600 hrs Shliakhovo was being cleared and elements of 6th PzD had broken through the line west of Shliakhovo and headed past Verkhni Olshanets and Hill 230.3, in order to reach Kazache for the night. Rzhavets was their main objective, which the lead units would reach in the early hours of the next morning. vzz402. dgr155m. dgr173m. vzz254+. vzz3m. dgr103.

Group Schmidt of 19th PzD with the support of the *Luftwaffe*, broke through the line held by 280th GRR of 92nd GRD and by 1600 hrs captured Kiselevo. Horst and Schmidt were attacking the town from different angles and Schmidt on the eastern axis was luckier than Horst to enter the town first. From near Kurakovka northwest of Kazache, the 89th GRD moved up to Kiselevo and counter-attacked 19th PzD. The 92nd GRD stationed at Sabynino was also ordered south to Kiselevo. The 96th TB at the original line regrouped and was heading for Kiselevo as well. The combined Soviet strength stopped Schmidt and were trying to encircle him. Kempf, realizing the importance of 19th PzD's mission, at 1900 hrs sent the *Luftwaffe* in to support. After the air raid, Schmidt attacked. The 89th GRD started to fall back but ran into the lead units of 6th PzD which were also heading for the river. With the 48th RC in disorder, the 168th ID on the left flank of 19th PzD was able to cross the Donets and head toward Gostishchevo which was captured from 89th GRD later that night. Kempf was now across the Donets in two places, though not secured, and raising havoc with 48th RC. With the day's progress, the 19th PzD and 6th PzD had created a larger pocket by pressing the 81st GRD in the Rzhavets-Strelnikov-Krivtsovo-

Sabynino sector against the banks of the Donets. vzz255. vzz10m. dgk106m. dgr155m. dgr173m. gnk283m. dgr99. vzz403++. vzz3m. vzz5m. vzz406. vzz5m.

Toward dusk the 3rd PzC moved into position from the south to make a run on Prokhorovka in the morning as well. During the night, elements of the 5th GTA arrived in the area to take part in the engagement next morning. The SS PzC was not aware of the scale of 5th GTA and 5th GA that had already arrived and were threatening the SS. Though the presence of 3rd PzC deployed near Ryndinka did have a modest impact on Vatutin, if Kempf could have been just five miles closer it would have had a much greater effect on the dispositions of 5th GTA for tomorrow's offensive. bt88.

After dark, Hunersdorff's 6th PzD supported by Capt Kageneck's sPzAbt 503, captured Kazache, 8 miles from the Donets River. They then moved toward Aleksandrovka, with the main objective of capturing Rzhavets 12 miles away and the other key crossing site over the Donets next morning. By 1900 hrs, the 6th PzD making the biggest gains, broke through the 92nd GRD line, scattering its forces and by dark had reached and captured Kazache at the rear of the second defensive belt. A few hours later, into the predawn hours of 7/12 the 6th PzD captured Rzhavets and broke through the second defense belt. The lead units of 6th PzD were now less than 11 miles from Prokhorovka and becoming a real threat to 5th GTA's flank. At the same time next morning, Schmidt's 19th PzD would ford the Donets, drive on Krivtsevo and join 6th PzD at Rzhavet by night time. Facing both panzer divisions would be the 81st GRD, 89th RD, 92nd GRD, 93rd GRD and the 305th RD which were supported by tanks. dgk198. dgk222m. dlu63m. gnk298+. vzz3m. dgr103. fzk52.

At 2000 hrs, with the *Luftwaffe* flying cover, the Germans advanced from Shliakhovo toward Lomovo against elements of the 35th RC. German bombers were hitting Kazache, Verkhnil Olshanets and Novo-Oskochnoe much of the day. By 2200 hrs the Germans broke into Verkhnil Olshanets, east of the Donets and near Hill 230.3. vzz236. vzz3m.

At sundown the 3rd PzC pushed forward into the area north of Sheino. German intelligence informed FM von Manstein that Soviet reserves that were assembled east of Kharkov were now moving north.

In order for the Kempf Group to continue to screen 2nd PzC's east flank, it had to advance northward between Ushakovo and Sobyshno which was strongly held. They were having trouble keeping up but did break through the defenses near Aleksandrovka, just south of Hill 241.5. After breaking through Razumnoe and the Donets at Rzhavets, the drive on Skordnoye would require all of 3rd PzC if it were to fall. Once captured, it could then help 4th PzA in clearing out the Donets triangle. The 4th PzA was being frontally attacked to the point where it could not clear the triangle by itself. Von Manstein considered ending 3rd PzC's attack and redeploying it west of the Donets River to be linked with 2nd SS PzC but decided against the move. snk52+. vzz417. dgr39m. erz208. vzz12m.

On the eastern flank the 19th PzD supported by 168th ID on its left begun to saturate the Khokhlovo-Kiselevo sector, about 12 miles northeast of Belgorod on the Lipovyi Donets River. Unable to withstand the pressure and fearing the 167th ID would cross the river to encircle, the 375th RD began withdrawing northward about ten miles, allowing the 168th ID to advance. The 19th PzD continued north on the east side of the Donets, passing through Khokhlovo in the morning then Kiselevo by midday, ending the day with its lead combat group over 19 miles northeast of Belgorod and a gain of 8 miles for the day and showing the Soviets were finally giving ground. To the east of 19th PzD, the 6th

PzD leading the charge also had a good day, penetrating the Soviet line at Shliakhovo and driving the 305th RD and the 92nd GRD back ten miles to in front of Rzhavets where a new line was forming. See Map 15. wdk156. dgk222m. dlu63m. vzz10m. vzz3m.

With the penetration of Kazache, the 6th PzD was now eight miles southeast of the northern reaches of the Donets. If the Soviet 69th Army's front continued to give way, Kempf, as the plan was developed, could cross the river barrier to take what would be 5th GTA in the left flank and rear and roll up the entire left flank of Voronezh Front. Blocking Kempf's advance was the fortified town of Rzhavets with its bridge over the river, but he had plans for taking the city as well. aaa125m. dlu63m. pck83. gnk298. cbk76. vzz3m. fzk52+.

By the end of the day, the three panzer divisions of 3rd PzC penetrated the defenses of 96th GRD and 305th RD, both of 35th GRC among others, in the sector that included Shishino, Khokhlovo, Kiselevo, Sheino, Miasoedovo and Kazache. This advance was now deep into the second defense belt. Next door, the 92nd GRD and 96th TB held the line despite heavy losses. The 3rd PzC, since the start of the operation, had advanced between the Donets River in the west, past the Razummaia River and half way to the Koren River in the east. In the north face of the salient, the 3rd PzC started the day along the line south of Khokhlovo-Dalniaia Igumenka to the Razummaia River. With this day's gains, the 19th PzD advanced along the Donets as far north as Sabynino. The 7th PzD had secured Melnikhovo and moved up to Shliakhovo. The 6th PzD, in the center of the line made it past Melnikhovo and Shliakhovo all the way north to Kazache, carving out a mini-salient of only a few miles wide that sat on top of the larger salient that 3rd PzC was building. In the lead for the 6th PzD were the remaining 19 Tigers of sPzAbt 503. These Tigers, plus the 6th PzD's 11th PzR's 40 panzers, made an effective battering ram. The 7th PzD had about the same number of working panzers while 19th PzD had about 25. vzz402. dgr155m. dgr173m. dlu93.

The 3rd PzC continued its advance and was able to reach the last Soviet defensive belt. It wass estimated that in the previous week, the corps captured 24,000 POWs, destroyed or damaged 1,800 tanks, 1,080 assault guns and 267 guns. FM von Manstein still held the reliable but weakened 24th PzC in reserve but was considering using them to back up the 3rd PzC if he could get Hitler's permission. fzk316. kfz452.

Later that day, it was decided that Rotmistrov would release the battalion of KV1s from 5th GTA in order to move south and attack the Tigers of sPzAbt 503 that Breith had leading his forces toward Prokhorovka.

With the Germans now in the Aleksandrovka area, Kempf was now pushing his commanders harder than ever to join up with *Das Reich*. The 11th IC had to stop the expected attack that would be coming to break through its lines and attack the panzers from the rear, and so prepared itself for it. The 6th PzD would be used as the eastern screen while the rest of 3rd PzC moved northward. As the 7th PzD and 19th PzD attacked toward Shakhovo, the 2nd GTC counter-attacked but with the aid of the 167th ID on the west side was able to repulse the Soviet attack. The panzer group did cross the Donets, establishing two small bridgeheads. The attack on village of Shakhovo would begin the following day, after taking the wooded area south of Gostishchevo. 1,000 POWs and large amounts of weapons and ammo were captured at Gostishchevo. Gostishchevo was ten miles north of Belgorod. See Maps 15, 23. snk53+. lck283. vzz3m. erz208. vzz5m. vzz12m.

17

July 11th on the Northern Salient

A major Soviet counter-attack got under way. The 41st PzC at Ponyri PC received the heaviest attacks but the 46th PzC and 47th PzC were also hit hard. The Soviets were targeting the panzer corps for destruction. Elements of the 23rd IC defending Trosna fought hard but were driven back. In the evening, Kluge released the 12th PzD and 36th ID to the 46th PzC in the hope of a breakthrough of the second defense belt the next morning. At night, a German attack on Olkhovatka failed and the attackers retreated to their start line. The entire 9th Army was now defensive. sPzAbt 653 and sPzAbt 654 stopped all offensive action and went defensive. wdk183. fkk336. dgk87m. dgr199m. lck116m.

Though the gains from the previous day were small, the Germans were still hopeful that Olkhovatka, just a few miles to the south of the present line, could be captured. But this success depended on regaining the flanking Hill 253.5 which was lost the day before. With all the Soviet guns emplaced on this hill, the Soviets could tear to shreds any advance on Olkhovatka the Germans would make and Rokossovsky was bringing more guns to the front by the hour. Between Olkhovatka and Ponyri an impenetrable wall of guns had been erected over the last couple days and 9th Army just did not have the resources to overwhelm it. By the end of the day 33rd PzR of 4th PzD would have just 347 men still fighting but thanks to the repair shops, the panzer count of 35th PzR was now up to 60; sPzAbt 505 now had 11 Tigers ready for combat. fkk69. dgk87m.

FM Kluge finally released 12th PzD and 36th ID to Model. Model immmediately ordered both divisions to travel through the night and assemble next to 4th PzD north of Olkhovatka in order to participate in the renewed attempt to take the critical town and the surrounding countryside which was planned to get underway shortly after daybreak. Model hesitated and inserted just a regiment of 12th PzD into the day's fighting. He expected trouble at Orel and was preparing to send forces to the salient. nzk95.

As fighting at Ponyri-Olkhovatka died down, the Soviets began probing attacks in preparation for Operation Kutuzov, the planned destruction of the German forces in the Orel salient. Units of the Western Front and Bryansk Front attacked the 55th IC, 35th IC and 53rd IC of 2nd PzA. Once the penetration occurred, the 3rd TA would punch through and roll into the German rear, threatening the positions of 9th Army on the southern face of the Orel salient. For the offensive the Soviets had accumulated over a million troops from three fronts. The smallest army was 50th Army of Western Front, which had only 54,000 men. bt87+**. zzz101m. dgk87m. dgr199m. lck116m.

East of Orel while the probing attacks were underway, the Soviets opened a surprise bombardment on 2nd PzA (formerly under Schmidt but now under Model) that would precede a counter-attack beginning next morning, more massive than any previous attack in the area. The attack by 11th GA was launched from Sukhinichi in the north. It was the ideal choice to attack. The 2nd PzA was extremely weak there and just to the north of the German line a huge woods allowed the Soviets to assemble their forces without being observed. FM Kluge initially dismissed the attack as unimportant but by the end of the day, when the attack continued, he changed his mind and called up what few reserves were left to the area. Meanwhile further south, the Soviets had planned for several reserve units to join the front lines on another counter-attack and expected them to be in place by the start of the attack but they were delayed, weakening the assault. The Germans, with the full support of the *Luftflotte* 6 repelled the Soviets, forcing them back but the woods were effective in concealing the Soviets and the German planes did little damage to their original launch area. Next day, the assault only increased around the salient. In this northern sector, the Soviets appeared to be aiming for Khotynets in order to cut the critical Bryansk-Orel highway/railroad. For days the *Luftwaffe* kept the Soviets at bay until artillery and AGC reserves could be brought up. The German planes did make strikes against the rail towns of nearby Kozelsk and Kaluga to the north, in the hopes of interrupting the Soviet logistics. The *Luftwaffe* were now using armor-piercing shells that could penetrate Soviet tank's' rear plating, either knocking out the engine or hitting the fuel tank. See Map 22. jp172. je108. snk168 zzz101m. aaa125m. aaa106m. dgk231m. snk433m.

In the afternoon in the 2nd PzA area, the Bryansk and Western Fronts started increasing pressure on the German line north and east of Orel. Some Soviet reserves were still being held back with potential to increase the pressure on the Germans. The Soviets still outnumbered the Germans by over 2 to 1 in most categories. AGC ordered the 9th Army to the south to halt its advance, go defensive and be ready to shift troops to help the 2nd PzA. jp173. zzz101m. dgk231m. snk433m.

Probing attacks by Bryansk and Western Fronts in the Orel salient had begun. The reconnaissance troops were looking for points of weakness from which to attack in force the next day, when the offensive would begin for real. Model immediately understood the meaning of these attacks and that night started sending forces from 9th Army north to the Orel salient. kcz169. dgk231m. snk433m.

The 47th PzC was worn out and battle weary; any further attacking by the corps was impossible. Kluge assigned the 12th PzD to help bolster the sector from the expected counter-attacks. The 5th PzD and 8th PzD would also be coming over to the sector. wdk183. dgk87m. dgk231m.

In the late afternoon on the northern flank of the Orel salient, the 11th GA was gaining ground toward Khotynets. A flak battalion was sent from nearby Karachev as a stopgap measure to prevent the enemy from cutting their supply line. Using their 88s and their 20mm guns, the battalion was able to hold off the attack until the *Luftwaffe* came back and more artillery could be brought up to plug the hole. When the Soviets were approaching Khotynets, Model shifted the entire air support from 9th Army to protect this sector. Without air support, the 9th Army would have to go defensive. It was critical to hold this rail line, not only for supplies and troops coming into the salient but the railroad would be needed when evacuation orders were given. There was a huge supply depot at Orel and Model wanted to take as many supplies as possible with him, not leaving anything for the Soviets. See Map 22. snk169. dgk231m. snk433m.

Rendulic's 35th IC of 2nd PzA was deployed along the line about 30 miles east of Orel. Much of the line was deployed behind a narrow but deep river that was impossible for tanks to navigate without a bridge. But once past this obstacle the terrain was mostly flat and ideal for tanks. His corps was down to less than 40,000 men, 200 guns and no panzers. His area of responsibility was 80 miles long and was divided between the 34th ID, 56th

ID, 262nd ID and the 299th ID. The Soviets had been concentrating forces in the Novosil area and by 7/11 had 16 RDs and 300 tanks plus another 1,100 tanks along the line in the general area. snk218+. zzz101m. dgk231m. snz259+. snk433m.

On the eve of the full start of Operation Kutuzov, the Soviet 2nd VVS made massive bombing runs across the line from its Bryansk Front, hitting German batteries and panzer concentrations. The operation's objective was to drive into the rear of the 9th Army by going through 2nd PzA defenses in the Orel salient. This counter-offensive had been planned for months thanks to the Lucy Spy ring that informed the Soviets of the German offensive that would start by 7/6. The Soviets waited until 9th Army was exhausted then launched a limited attack on a ten mile front, hoping to surprise the Germans while their concentration was on Kursk. Model had to use reserves intended for the salient on this assault. rc221. dgk230. zzz101m. dgk231m. snk433m. mkz121. lck116m.

Late at night, Model ordered his last reserves of the 9th Army, the 10th PzGD under Schmidt and the 31st ID, to attack in the central part of the line near Ponyri. They repelled a strong Soviet counter-attack at the rail station at Ponyri but were unable to hold hold the town. By this point, even the Germans knew Kursk could not be won but Model would not give up. With the probing attacks by the Soviets to the north and east of Orel beginning, these would be the last resources sent to the Kursk salient. je108*. mhz287. zzz101m. dgk87m. dgr199m. swm139. lck116m.

By the end of the day, total casualties for 9th Army since the start of Operation Citadel were estimated to be 22,273. It was also estimated that the five panzer divisions of 41st PzC and 47th PzC had suffered over 6,500 casualties which gives an indication how bad the infantry divisions were hit. The figures for unrecoverable panzers were modest and planes of *Luftflotte* 6 were extremely light at only 94 planes for having flown over 10,000 missions. snz254.

18

July 12th on the Southern Salient

See Maps 16, 19, 20, 27

The first objective of the day for 1st PzGR and 1st PzR was to move out at dawn and capture the Stalinskoe State Farm near Hill 252.2 and then to move east and capture Iamki, south of Prokhorovka. The 2nd PzGR was to wait until *SSTK* had advanced past Hill 226.6 and was attacking toward Hill 252.4, before moving north from Hill 252.2. The 2nd PzGR was to help squeeze and destroy the Soviet defenders between itself and *SSTK* before shifting east and attacking Prokhorovka from the north, while 1st PzGR was attacking from the south. zrl233.

In the predawn hours, elements of the 95th GRD and 9th GAD launched an attack on *LAH* in order to push them back to give 5th GTA a little more room to maneuver in the morning attack, but the attempt was repulsed. Under the noise produced by this assault, the tanks of 5th GTA moved up to their ultimate starting areas. vzz241.

This was a big day in the campaign as both sides expected to deliver the victorious assault, the knock-out punch that would doom the other side and allow themselves to complete their intermediate objectives. Von Manstein expected his forces to capture Prokhorovka and secure the important corridor leading to Kursk, secure and enlarge their bridgehead over the Psel River and be ready to launch an attack on Oboyan in the next day or two. He also expected 3rd PzC to catch up to *Das Reich* and close the pocket around elements of 69th Army and consolidate the line. Vatutin on the other hand, expected with the massive armor of 5th GTA to break the back of the 2nd SS PzC and begin pushing back the 4th PzA. While there was intense fighting on this day, by the end of the day both Generals were disappointed, with neither side achieving their objectives. While it cost Vatutin much more in men and tanks and did not break the back of the SS, he was able to halt the German offensive and would eventually, over the next two weeks, push the 4th PzA back to their starting point. dsk111.

At midnight and into the predawn hours, the tank corps of 5th GTA begin moving into their launch positions for next morning's grand offensive. The area where nearly 400 tanks were being positioned was about seven miles in length by two miles wide and many of them only one to two miles from the German line. The German sentries all along the line could hear the commotion of so many tanks and dreaded the coming of the morning. HQ was quickly informed of the tanks and reinforcements were sent to the key sectors and in place by daybreak. After the Soviet tanks were in place, the men of the 9th GAD facing *LAH* and 95th GRD facing *SSTK* moved into position. vzz295. vzz341. wwf123.

Priess was ordered to secure Hill 226.6 at dawn before moving on to other objectives, so while the Soviets were busy deploying, the men and panzers of *SSTK* were also getting into position. The role for *SSTK* became critical. It was imperative for the division to expand its bridgehead, secure Veselyi, Hill 226.6 and Hill 236.7 (1.5 miles north of Veselyi) before reaching the Prokhorovka-Kartashevka road. It was then to advance and preferably capture

Hill 252.4 before *LAH* reached Prokhorovka. In this way the division could protect *LAH*'s left flank as it made a run for Prokhorovka. These three hills would make great OPs for either side but were now defended by 51st GRD and 52nd GRD with 95th GRD in second echelon. North of Hill 226.6, the 95th GRD also covered Hill 243.5, east of the Voroshilov State Farm. As of the night before, Vasilevka on the southern bank of the Psel was in the control of the 99th TB and that would have to be taken by *SSTK* also. The village could be used as a launch point of advance by the Soviets to retake the river crossing and then *SSTK* would be in big trouble on the north side of the river. Priess was also aware of the tank situation on the other side of the river and was concerned for the coming morning. vzz341. vzz382+. vzz442. vzz1m. gnk343++. gnk313m.

Also important for the east flank of 2nd SS PzC, *Das Reich* had to secure Storozhevoe, its woods and Pravorot to the east in order to secure *LAH*'s right flank. All three divisions had to be in line if they were to secure Prokhorovka. vzz341. vzz382+. vzz442. vzz1m. gnk312m.

Elements of *SSTK* also deployed at Vasilevka and along part of the Psel River bank. There was an extensive assault plan for the SS that day and it depended on *SSTK* enlarging the bridgehead as far north as the Kartashevka road, before turning east to protect *LAH*'s western flank when it attacked Prokhorovka, but Priess also had to defend the southern bank of the river. Hearing extensive tank noise during the predawn hours did not make Priess over confident about his upcoming offensive but the panzers launched pretty close to plan and the grenadiers would have to rely on the *Luftwaffe* and their artillery to stop any attack. By 0900 hrs, the 3rd PzR was crossing the Psel to bolster its comrades and to initiate the attack when ordered. Priess also did not know Maj General Popov's 95th GRD and 97th GRD of 33rd GRC of 5th GA had moved in and bolstered the shattered 52nd GRD on the front line. Behind the 33rd GTC was 42nd GRD and the 11th MRB defending the Kartashevka road. It would be a very difficult day for the *SSTK*. gnk343++. gnk313m. vzz341. vzz1m. ztc270.

At 0030 hrs *LAH* conducted a recon in force that included men and a few panzers, starting from the woods northwest of Storozhevoe and attacking north toward Lutovo. The garrison at Lutovo, made up of the 25th TB of 29th TC and its 25th MRB, were prepared and counter-attacked quickly, repulsing the Germans who fell back to Storozhevoe within the hour. The previous day there were no tanks at Lutovo; this told Hausser that new tanks had been brought to the line and would soon attack. Lutovo was situated so that a tank offensive would run past Stalinskoe State Farm, Komsomolet State Farm and Storozhevoe. Hausser immediately ordered a platoon of assault guns to set up an ambush on this expected axis. Hoth, also suspecting a major counter-attack, ordered an unusual number of recons during the predawn hours. By daybreak Hoth would have a good understanding that an attack was coming and would postponed his advance until the Soviet offensive was beaten back. Lutovo was northeast of Hill 252.2, about halfway between the hill and Prokhorovka. vzz295+. vzz444+. dgk184m.

The day began with the Germans deployed along the following line: The 167th was half mile southwest of Gostishchevo to Soshenkov. *Das Reich* was from northeast corner of Kalinin to southeast corner of Iasnaia Poliana to Storozhevoe. *LAH* deployed from Storozhevoe, Oktiabrski State Farm and Hill 252.2 to just east of the villages on the southern bank of the Psel River where *SSTK* took over along the Psel River. The *GD* was half mile southwest of Hill 243.0 to a mile west of Verkhopenie. The 11th PzD was between

SSTK and *GD*. The 332nd ID was from Hill 237.6 to Berezovka to north of the woods east of Chapaev to Chapaev, and the 3rd PzD deployed north of 332nd ID to the boundary line with *GD*. vzz438*+*. vzz3m. vzz5m. vzz7m.

Rotmistrov's attack plan for the day was ambitious but straight forward; it contained three main axes of attack. His tank corps, with the infantry of 5th GA following, would attack along the seven mile front held by 2nd SS PzC but the main thrust of his tanks would be on three axes from three directions that would meet in the general area bordered by the Gresnoe, Komsomolets State Farm, Teterevino North triangle to dissect and then destroy the SS. The first axis would involve 18th TC (181st TB, 170th TB) driving southwest along the Psel River clearing the villages on the southern bank as far as Vasilevka before turning to the southeast and heading for Pokrovka, Gresnoe and Komsomolets. By taking the villages, it would isolate the *SSTK* bridgehead north of the river, which would be vulnerable to the 5th GA driving south. wwf133+. kuz95.

When the offensive began, the second axis, that of the 29th TC (25th TB, 31st TB 32nd TB) to the east of 18th TC, would straddle the Prokhorovka road, past Iamki to Komsomolets State Farm. Penetrating *LAH*'s eastern flank and upon reaching the farm would isolate *LAH* from *Das Reich*. The third axis was 2nd GTC and the corps had deployed to the southeast in the Zhimolostnoe-Invanovka area and would drive west and a little north to the Teterevino-Komsomolets area to get behind *Das Reich*. With the support of 29th TC to the north and 2nd TC on the eastern perimeter, the three corps would destroy *Das Reich*. The infantry following the tankers would squeeze and eliminate the last of the resistance. Vatutin was even more ambitious, wanting to take a bigger chunk of the 4th PzA by having his forces meet in the Iakovlevo area after the 2nd SS PzC was destroyed. Skvortsov's 5th GMC (10th GMB,11th GMB,12th GMB) was originally held in reserve but that would change when Rzhavets fell. There were additional tank brigades involved in this offensive and those will be discussed as the offensive evolves.

The plan for 29th TC, which had its greatest concentration of tanks near the brick factory just outside of Prokhorovka, was to drive south along the road/railway to the east of 18th TC and attack between the Oktiabrski State Farm and Iamki. The 33rd GRC of 5th GA and 32nd MRB and 53rd MRB of 5th GTA would follow the tanks to secure the area. Between the two main pincers of the 18th TC and 29th TC, along a front of almost four miles, a total of 234 tanks were in first echelon, hundreds more would be second echelon and more in reserve. The 29th TC with its 170 tanks, consisting of 32nd TB, 25th TB and 31st TB, would have the tough responsibility of taking the well-fortified OSF and then the KSF. The 18th TC with its 140 tanks in first echelon consisted of 181st TB, 170th TB and the 32nd MRB and would have to neutralize Hill 252.2 as well as capturing the key villages on the southern bank of the Psel. Both brigades would have the support of the 127th GRR of 42nd GRD. The 32nd MRB and 53rd MRB, as well as several mortar regiments, would be in second echelon. Khliupin's 110th TB and the 36th GTR of 18th TC, with a combined total of around 100 tanks, were in corps reserve. The 5th GMC with 228 tanks would be in 5th GTA reserve. After sending some of his tanks to block Kempf, Rotmistrov still had as many as 600 tanks (not all in first echelon) to contend with the 294 panzers and assault guns of 2nd PzC. For that day's assault the 5th GTA with its recent attachments had 501 T34s, 261 T70s and 31 Churchill tanks as well as a few assault guns; that would tip the scales at just over 800 vehicles, poised near Prokhorovka preparing for the coming tank battle. wwf94. dgr222+. vzz309. vzz441+. gnk309+*+. gnk313m. gnk320. vzz318. vzz341.

wwf121. sgf348. wwf133++. wwf140.

If Hoth and Hausser had not expected a counter-attack and gone on the defensive, not bringing artillery closer to the line during the night, Rotmistrov's plan might have been more successful but the fact is that every available gun was brought up to the line and contributed greatly to the German defense during the Soviet assault.

By the end of 1942, Great Britain had stopped sending the heavy Churchill tank to Stalin, who thought little of it and did not want any more of them. The tank had a 12 cylinder gas 350 horsepower engine and a top speed of 16 mph. The ones at Kursk were among the last of the 301 tanks that were sent to Russia. wwf95.

According to Rotmistrov's plan, 18th TC on the west side of Oktiabrski State Farm was heading southwest along the the Psel River to strike *SSTK*'s position straddling the river and to separate *SSTK* from *LAH*. The 29th TC's 25th TB would break through Oktiabrski State Farm and Komsomolets State Farm and head for Luchki North and Iakovlevo, in order to isolate *LAH* from *Das Reich*. Part of 29th TC, mostly the 25th TB, along with 2nd GTC to the southeast would then drive behind *Das Reich* while 2nd TC would attack the division from the front. Rotmistrov would discover by the end of the day that preparations had been poor and that cooperation and coordination between the different tank corps, and between tank corps and infantry, was terrible and would produce miserable results. vzz298. dgk180. fkk327.

Even with the Germans advancing faster than expected the night before, Rotmistrov had been able to change his plans and communicate those changes to his corps commanders concerning the attack, especially the launch position against SS 2nd PzC later that morning. In the original plan, the OSF was still in Soviet hands and the attack was to begin along that line, but with the farm in German hands, Rotmistrov had to start further back in the corridor and then attack two strongpoints like Hill 252.2 and the OSK. This aspect change was one of the major reasons for such a costly assault. The 18th TC and 29th TC with under 300 tanks in first echelon would take the lead position against *LAH* and *SSTK*. The 25th TB of 29th TC would attack in the Storozhevoe sector and Burdeiny's 2nd GTC would attack further south against *Das Reich*, while Popov's 2nd TC remained on the defensive to screen against *Das Reich*'s advance toward Iamki from south of Storozhevoe. These last two emancipated corps still had 187 tanks. Along with the secondary brigades, Rotmistrov's 5th GTA would have just over 800 tanks at his disposal, though only 600 tanks participated in the day's offensive. Now the primary front would be diluted by sending the 26th GTB and others to Trufanov in order to face both the 2nd SS PzC and 3rd PzC. In the Prokhorovka area, at most 1,100, probably fewer tanks fought. This was not the largest tank battle recorded. During the first month of the war in the Brody-Dubno sector, a tank battle between Southwest Front and 1st PzG involved about 3,800 tanks, maybe more. gjz186+. wwf94. dgr222+. mhz327. pck80+. lck344. sgf348. wwf111+. zra348+. zow160. vzz554.

In the predawn hours, 2nd GTC regrouped its remaining 97 tanks in an area east of Belenikhino. These tanks would attack *Das Reich* defending positions from west of Vinogradovka along the rail line to Belenikhino later that morning. While the 18th TC and 29th TC had the primary position and responsibility, the role for 2nd GTC was also important, for it was to assist the 25th TB further north to isolate and destroy *Das Reich* on the eastern flank of the 2nd SS PzC sector. The 29th TC was the center of 5th GTA's front and it would for the most part attack down the Prokhorovka road. The weakened 2nd TC, positioned between 29th TC to the north and 2nd GTC to the the south, would try to join the line by protecting the flanks between Storozhevoe and Ivanovski Vyselok. The 21 KV tanks of the 53rd GTR which were originally ordered to protect Burdeiny's flank between Storozhevoe and Ivanovski Vyselok were redirected southward to support the thinning ranks of Popov's brigades. These KV1s would however deploy against Kempf if the 6th PzD and 19th PzD broke through the front line blocking the 3rd PzC from reaching Prokhorovka. Elements of Skvortsov's 5th GMC with a total of 228 tanks would be in reserve.

The 3rd PzC was desperately needed to support *Das Reich* in reaching Prokhorovka but Kempf was at Rzhavets, 12 miles away, with his forces just crossing the Donets. From Rzhavets, a scouting party left after dark heading east toward Kurakovka and Alexsandrovka. Before reaching Alexsandrovka, the Germans discovered a large armor formation assembling outside of town; it had to quickly reverse course and head back to Rzhavets to report its findings. After the report was given, the 11th PzR of 6th PzD was rounded up and sent to Kurakovka after dark to prepare an attack on this Soviet armor group. General Hunersdorff could not afford to have a strong armor group to his rear while advancing over the Donets toward Prokhorovka. Eliminating this threat to the 6th PzD's rear was essential but it diluted and delayed 3rd PzC's advance toward Prokhorovka, reducing the pressure off 69th Army for a few hours. dgk180+. dgk184m. dgr172m. dgk222m. pck82+. vzz366+. lck365. zzt90.

By morning, the bulk of Zhadov's 5th GA had fully arrived in the Prokhorovka sector but with Zhadov in second echelon his forces would have to enter the battle with virtually no tank support. The 10th TC had been part of the 5th GA but on 7/9 it was attached to 1st TA. The 11th MRB of 10th TC was still however defending near the key Hill 226.6. Zhadov's left flank, consisting of the Col Sazonov's 9th GAD and Maj General Bobrov's 42nd GRD would attack between the Psel River and Storozhevoe behind the tanks of 5th GTA. The right flank, consisting of 52nd GRD, 95th GRD (33rd GRC) and 97th GRD would attack *SSTK* in the bend of the river to eliminate the bridgehead currently centered on Kliuchi, southwest of Hill 226.6. It would also attack 11th PzD in the Kochetovka area. When 33rd GRC broke into Kochetovka, it temporarily severed the link between 11th PzD with *SSTK*. The 33rd GRC was to keep *SSTK* north of the river busy while 18th TC swept behind the Germans south of the river and encircled them. The left flank would then head for Gresnoe, Malye Maiachki and Iakovlevo. Following behind the 33rd GRC would be 32nd GRD's 13th GRD and 66th GRD alongside 33rd GRC's 97th GRD. These plans did not materialize as Priess's *SSTK* attacked first, after putting down a small probing attack. *SSTK* had to gain ground quickly in order to catch up and screen *LAH*'s advance. vzz322+. vzz380+*. vzz1m. gnk312m. nzk96. kuz193. zrl234. zow161.

In addition to the ambitious attack plans for 5th GTA and 5th GA, Vatutin also had important attack plans for 1st TA and 6th GA. The 5th GTC and 19th TC, on separate axes, would drive through the western front of 48th PzC, dividing the German corps into thirds, against which 6th GA would follow up and finish crushing the 48th PzC. The two tank corps would link up at Iakovlevo along with the corps of 5th GTA after their separation of the 2nd SS PzC into thirds. Together all these tank corps would form a impenetrable wall that would roll up the Germans as they tried to avoid destruction from the infantry heading south. As customary with *Stavka* planning, their plan was too ambitious and lacked coordination and sufficient preparation. wwf132+.

The fall of Rzhavets and the crossing of the Donets by the Germans were threats that could not be ignored and Vatutin and Rotmistrov had to act without delay by transferring forces to the river. Since there were not sufficient mobile reserves in the sector, front line brigades would be pulled from the main attack force. This weakening of Rotmistrov's forces by over 100 tanks and several Pak batteries would sorely be felt. Rotmistrov's reserve now consisted of 10th GTB and the 24th GTB which only had a total of 96 tanks. By 0515 hrs, the 5th GTA was at its modified start line Prelestnoe-Storozhevoe-Maloe Iablonovo and waiting for the launch signal. The attack was originally scheduled for 1000 hrs but Valsilevsky wanted to control the battlefield and beat the German panzers to the field, so the attack was moved to 0830 hrs after a 30-minute preparation. The barrage came from near the Oktiabrski State Farm, Komsomolets State Farm, Storozhevoe and Stalinskoe State Farm. So much was happening to the 5th GTA in the early hours that it was chaotic and this was compounded by new COs working together for the first time and lacking the initiative to think beyond the orders when it was necessary. At the end of the day, many Soviet officers would complain that the preparation was poorly focused and not aggressive enough. The same would be said for the VVS, which was delinquent for such a major offensive. vzz300+. vzz306++. wwf136.

During the predawn hours, the *Luftwaffe* sent 61 planes out on special missions to help ease the advance of the ground forces shortly after daybreak. Seven bombers bombed the railway station at Staryi Oskol, east of Prokhorovka, in the hopes of slowing reinforcements and supplies reaching the battle zone. The raid was successful and large explosions could be seen erupting. The remainder of the German planes attacked Soviet positions behind the front line on the routes that the 2nd SS PzC would take in the morning. The importance of these missions was telling, for the skies were heavily overcast. cbk76+. cbk78.

In preparation for their offensive, the 2nd VA and 17th VA flew 240 bombers against German positions along the line Malye Maiachki, Bolshie Maiachki, Pokrovka and Gremuchi. This was the general area where 29th TC, 18th TC and 2nd GTC were to meet in a encirclement attack. Additional planes from 17th VA attacked 4th PzA's supply routes southwest of Belgorod. cbk77.

During the predawn hours, thunder, lightning and heavy rains hit the *Das Reich* sector, causing delays. After *LAH* finished capturing the area north of Storozhevoe, *Das Reich*'s *Deutschland* Regiment was to conduct an advance eastward in the direction of Iamki. For that matter, the entire *Das Reich* division along its whole sector from Storozhevoe to Teterevino South was to attack but the muddy conditions slowed their pace. The panzer regiment in the center of the sector would head for Vinogradovka and Ivanovka. The attack by 2nd GTC and to a lesser extent 2nd TC, was an important part of the main offensive by 5th GTA that pre-empted the Germans, forcing them to go defensive. Hausser had warned his divisions of a pending attack, instructed them to stabilize their lines ahead of time and, with only a few exceptions, had gone defensive. gnk340. gnk313m. wwf123.

At 0300 hrs, elements of the 29th TC along with the attached 10th TB launched a probing attack to the right of Hill 252.4 in the direction of the woods north of Komsomolets State Farm to the northern outskirts of Bolshie Maiachki to Hill 251.2, in preparation to the main attack which would start at 0830 hrs. Their objective was to reach Grushki-Storozhevoe-Hill 223.4-Pogorelovka and destroy the German positions on Hill 255.9 northeast of Teterevino and then Hill 258.9. Behind the 29th TC, the 53rd MRB would follow, advancing toward Hill 258.8 and nearby Storozhevoe. The important Hill 252.4 which bristled with Soviet artillery, was one and a half miles northwest of Prokhorovka and would support the attack. A number of other smaller attacks between the Psel River and just south of Storozhevoe were initiated to prepare for the major attack as well. vzz272+*. dgk174. dgr224. vzz8m. zrl234.

At 0315 hrs on this Monday morning, the *SSTK* drove, in pouring rains with the ground quickly turning to mud, into the city limits of Vasilevka, engaging in house to house combat. Soviet tanks coming from Petrovka entered Vasilevka from the east.

Tigers had a longer range of fire than the Soviet tanks, so the Soviets rushed in and fought the Germans up close, trying to equalize. In one example, a Soviet commander died after being hit twice by a Tiger but the driver was still alive. With the T34 burning and belching smoke, the driver accelerated to full speed and rammed the evading Tiger. The crash of a 100 tons shook the ground. jp184.

The *LAH* started the day with only four operational Tigers under the current command of Michael Wittmann. Rotmistrov believed the Germans had up to 100 Tigers and he schooled his drivers to race in and shoot at point blank range in order to neutralize the Tiger's thick hide and powerful gun. Rotmistrov was lucky that there were only a handful of Tigers available, otherwise it is hard to imagine how few tanks would have survived the day. gnk310.

During the very early hours, the engineers of the 51st Motorized Sapper Battalion cleared pathways through the extensive minefields across the Prokhorovka rail line to speed the attack by 2nd GTC. vzz362+.

At first light, Soviet bombers and fighters bombed and strafed German positions in the attack zones of the coming offensive. After the air strikes, Soviet guns opened up to further soften the German line. Of special interest to the Soviets were *SSTK*'s bridgehead north of the Psel and *LAH*'s position on Hill 252.2 which was only a mile west from the edge of Prokhorovka. Any Germans near the rail line were also hit. gnk315+.

At 0450 hrs moving out from near Hill 241.6, a group of the 1st PzR of *LAH* launched toward Stalinsk, capturing it. With the help of *Das Reich*, Storozhevoe and Iamki would be next. The combat group then moved to defend the Prokhorovka road until reinforcements came. *Das Reich* was in the process of clearing and strengthening the area between Storozhevoe and Vinogradovka before launching their main attack eastward. These villages were part of the southern approach to Prokhorovka and were important to control. The 3rd PzC was too far south to give any direct assistance to the operation but von Manstein was hoping that the 3rd PzC was close enough that it might be able to divert Soviet armor away from Prokhorovka. The 26th GTB of 2nd GTC was diverted from the Storozhevoe area to stop Kempf from enlarging his new bridgehead near Ryndinka. dgk178+. dgk184m. dgr172m. vzz362++. dgr221m. gnk365m.

Just before daybreak, the east flank of *LAH* was preparing to launch their attack northeastward with the objective of taking Storozhevoe, the woods north of it, Stalinskoe State Farm and Iamki and then advance on the hill one mile east of Storozhevoe-Iamki. With the aid of *SSTK* after clearing the Psel River, both divisions would move on Hill 252.4 and Prokhorovka. *Das Reich*, screening *LAH*, was to march forward and make contact with *LAH* at Storozhevoe, clearing the hills northeast of town while the rest of *Das Reich* also moved on Vinogradovka-Ivanovka. They were then to hold the line: Ivanovka-the ridge southwest of Pravorot- hill one mile east of Storozhevoe. If *LAH* and *SSDR* succeeded in their plans and 3rd PzC could continue advancing, the tank corps attached to 5th GTA and the infantry of 69th Army would be in real danger of being pocketed. fkk157+. gnk313m.

Dawn broke on this Monday and it was heavily overcast throughout the southern sector with heavy local showers, making it difficult for both sides to maneuver. zow161.

At 0500 hrs, the *LAH* joined up with *SSTK* in the attempt to strengthen the boundary line but with daybreak the Soviet air fleet bombed both groups, slowing their progress. At 0600 hrs north of Hill 226.6 the SS repulsed a Soviet regiment at the Prokhorovka-Petrovka line with the help of strong artillery support.

Nearing daybreak along the seven mile front from west of Hill 226.6 to Hill 252.2 to Vinogradovka, the 2nd SS PzC were completing preparations for their major assault and were moving into the front line positions. Hoth suspected the Soviets would launch an offensive this morning so the previous night he had ordered his corps commanders to fortify defenses and only launch after the Soviet attack had been repulsed. In addition, all available artillery and ammunition was made ready. Gresnoe and Hill 241.6 were especially well prepared and fortified. Hoth may have expected an assault, but not nearly to the scale that occurred. Sunrise was 0502 hrs. lck343. vzz309. gnk312m.

During predawn hours, Soviet recon forces reported their findings to HQ. The Germans showed heightened activities at Komsomolets State Farm, Storozhevoe, Oktiabrski State Farm, Hill 241.6, Vinogradovka, Ivanovski Vyselok and Teterevino. Storozhevoe appeared to have fallen and the Germans were heading further east toward Zhimolostnoe. vzz443.

At 0525 hrs, the *SSTK* launched their attack from Kliuchi northward in a two-pincer formation. The left group headed for Veselyi and Hill 236.7 which was defended by the 151st GRR of 52nd GRD, while the right group headed northeast for Hill 226.6, Hill 235.3 and then Polezhaev. Between these two points, two well-placed trench lines were built which would not be easy to defeat. This area was defended by 155th GRR. The western group was able to break through the line and was heading for Veselyi but heavy artillery stopped the Germans and forced them to fall back. This German attack was searching for weakness and when it did not find any in the west, retreated and then the division concentrated its efforts on Hill 226.6 to the east. The *SSTK* and *LAH* regained comms with each other and when the 5th GTA attacked they both went defensive. At around 1100 hrs, the bulk of the Soviet offensive had dissipated and *LAH* resumed its advance. When Priess discovered *LAH* was on the march, he resumed his offensive toward Hill 226.6/Polezhaev. He had been ordered to reach the Kartashevka road today but it did not look promising. Though Rotmistrov failed to destroy the SS, he was able to stop the German advance for most of the morning plus inflicted heavy casualties on the enemy. Hausser's forces had lost all real momentum and would be unable to accomplish all of the their objectives. vzz385++. vzz383. vzz11m. gnk312m. kuz193+.

The 95th GRD was called up to the front line in the bend of the river. The 151st GRR and the 155th GRR stayed on the north side to stop *SSTK* from expanding their bridgehead while the 153rd GRR was crossing the river and attacking the villages of the southern bank to push *SSTK* out. Mikhailovka would be first. The 126th GRR of 42nd GRD would join the battle for Mikhailovka. vzz384+.

At 0530 hrs, a large squadron of German bombers flew over the Soviet front looking for targets of opportunity in preparation for the coming assault by *LAH*. Spotting tanks, probably 29th TC, the pilots dived against heavy flak toward the visible tanks. vzz298.

By daybreak, the 5th GA had fully assembled in the bend of the Psel River. It consisted of seven divisions, almost 63,000 men ready for battle and 1,800 field guns and mortars of varying sizes, but almost no tanks. With much of the *SSTK* north of the Psel with its panzers, the 5th GA would be at a disadvantage. It was critical for *SSTK* to be successful today if Hoth were to have any chance of reaching Kursk. The *SSTK* had to secure Hill 226.6 and reach the Prokhorovka-Kartashevka road without suffering heavy casualties and be prepared to take Hill 252.4 to protect *LAH*'s flank. vzz380. gnk312m.

At 0600 hrs Burdeiny of 2nd GTC, situated east of Ivanovka, instructed his crews to prepare for battle. They would try to penetrate past the Komsomolets State Farm and head for the Pokrovka-Iakovlevo area where it was discovered by air recon a concentration of panzers were stationed. German bombers and fighters flew by and attacked, slowing their preparations. lck343+. gnk313m.

Despite shelling, air raids, rain and mud, the engineers of *SSTK* finished the repairs on the 60 ton bridge over the Psel River by dawn. The few remaining Tigers were now able to cross over and join the division for their march toward Hill 226.6 which was defended by the depleted 52nd GRD of 6th GA, 31st TC of 1st TA and the recently arrived 95th GRD of 5th GA. Additional units of Zhadov's 5th GA would be arriving in the area that day as well. Priess's *SSTK* had only its men and 121 panzers to take that hill, expand their bridgehead which, currently measured 2.5 miles wide and 1.5 miles deep, as well as protect the left flank of *LAH* as it drove to Prokhorovka. It was a daunting task and Hausser knew it, pouring as many assets into the sector as could be found. With the support of artillery and the *Luftwaffe*, *SSTK* pushed the defenders in front of the hill and finally attacked it by midday. Despite fanatical resistance by the Soviets, the hill was in German hands by 1330 hrs. After regrouping, Priess continued his march to the northeast and despite heavy rains, the *Luftwaffe* continued to fly sorties as late as it could. mhz343. clk359+. gnk312m. wwf124.

At 0600 hrs, Rotmistrov's 18th TC and 29th TC were just starting their engines, preparing to beat the Germans to the punch in their assault southward away from Prokhorovka. However while Rotmistrov was standing at his observation post on Hill 230 just southwest of Prokhorovka, he saw German tank activity. His pre-emptive strike appeared lost and his men would have to fight without the advantage of surprise. The panzers had an umbrella of artillery preceding their advance but they would soon move into observed range of the Soviet guns and the response would be expectedly heavy. The Soviet Air Force was alerted as well but were slow to respond and would miss the opening. A German recon plane spotted the Soviet tanks of 18th TC getting ready to move out and dropped a purple smoke shell to warn the oncoming *LAH* tanks. Within minutes the panzers saw hundreds of tanks coming at them. Rotmistrov had reached his observation post in an orchard at daybreak and was watching all the action. He had sent his key staff officers to the brigade HQs to oversee their actions. mhz231+. lck343. lck346. dgk187. vzz298+. mhz335. zrl234+.

Shortly after daybreak, while Rotmistrov was preparing his attack, Soviet artillery opened up along the line with 2nd SS PzC, in the hopes of disrupting German assault preparations and communications. vzz298.

At 0600, the *Das Reich* were waiting in the woods south of Prokhorovka to advance and at 0630 hrs Stukas bombed Soviet positions across from *Das Reich*. Before long, Soviet fighters came in and drove the bombers away which initiated a bombardment of German positions. When the bombardment finished, tanks from 29th TC moved out to confront the grenadiers and the few panzers supporting them. The T34s would try to close in on the panzers and especially the Tigers where the panzers lost their some of key advantages.

Rotmistrov was under the impression that his forces would face 100 Tigers but in reality there were only a handful left.

Priess, the CO of *SSTK*, though needing every panzer north of the Psel decided to keep a company of panzers south of the river to protect his bridges at Bogoroditskoe and to prevent a Soviet assault south of the river from isolating the forces north of the river. vzz341. vzz348.

Though the lead units of *SSTK* had crossed the river and were advancing before daylight, it was not until 0900 hrs or a little later that *SSTK*'s 3rd PzR had crossed the Psel and started attacking northward against the 151st GRR of 52nd GRD. The 95th GRD in second echelon was beginning to move up to bolster and then replace 52nd GRD, but the *SSTK* attacked too soon while there was confusion in the ranks. It penetrated the line northeast of Kliuchi and began spreading out heading for Hill 226.6 and the secondary objectives of Polezhaev and Veselyi. Fierce fighting erupted between Hill 226.6 and Veselyi. After regrouping the 52nd GRD countered toward Kliuchi, Kozlovka, Bogoroditskoe and Vasilevka but were stopped. vzz384+. vzz442. gnk312m. dgk184m. vzz348.

Even before *SSTK* could advance from its bridgehead, the Soviets launched a small probing force from Vesselyi. The ambush was small but effective and Priess had to act quickly to plug the gap before it grew too large. Meierdress's battalion of panzers was sent and was able to plug the gap by 0730 hrs. Soviet planes showed up and started pounding the German defenses around Vasilevka. When Meierdress returned, he was then ordered to be part of the assault across the Psel. By 0900 hrs, the whole panzer regiment of *SSTK* had crossed the river heading north and within the hour a small contingent had slipped past Hill 226.6 and was heading for the Kartashevka road. gnk344.

Just after daybreak, Peiper on Hill 252.2 and elsewhere along the line could hear many Soviet tanks being started. Peiper knew it would not be long before he saw them moving toward the hill and ordered his men to prepare for the assault. They would be facing the 32nd TB of 29th TC and the outer edges of 170th TB of 18th TC. gnk317.

At 0600 hrs a Soviet recon probe was launched against *LAH* to check the strength of its defenses. The attack was quickly broken off and the men fell back. At 0630 hrs, *SSTK* near Vasilevka saw large assembly of men and tanks growing one mile east of Petrovka. At 0830 hrs *SSTK* saw 40 tanks and less than a division of men gathering east of Vasilevka. By 0900 hrs *LAH* positions saw 200 tanks or more in groups of 30 to 50 moving out of the corridor straight at them and along the line from Vasilevka to Storozhevoe. The 29th TC was spreading out to cover ground between Hill 252.2, the nearby state farms and the Storozhevoe Woods to the east, while the 18th TC covered the western side of the corridor as far as Vasilevka. Before long even more tanks were attacking the flanks of SS Corps. gnk317. zrl234.

At 0600 hrs, Burdeiny of 2nd GTC received a message from Rotmistrov stating 6th PzD had crossed the Donets at Ryndinka. Burdeiny immediately pulled the 26th GTB which was facing west and preparing to attack with the 25th GTB against *Das Reich*, and redeployed the brigade southeastward near Plota to prevent 6th PzD from expanding their bridgehead. With 26th GTB's 44 tanks heading for Plota this meant 2nd GTC had only 97 tanks left to strike *Das Reich*. The 11th MRB and 12th MRB were also sent to stop 3rd PzC. vzz363. dlu102.

By 0630, air traffic control reported to General Hausser that 150 enemy sorties had already been counted in the *SSTK/LAH* sector. This was more than usual for this time of day and it was an indication that the Soviets were up to something. zow164.

The 1st PzGR of *LAH* launched at 0650 hrs advancing eastward south of the rail line, clearing Soviet resistance from the Storozhevoe area. Their ultimate objective was the capture of Iamki, less than two miles southwest of Prokhorovka. dgk182. dgk183m.

At 0710 hrs, the Soviet bombers reached their target area which centered around Luchki North. The German fighters tried to intercept the bombers but the Soviet escorts kept them at bay. cbk78.

At 0730 hrs, the 2nd PzGR on the left flank of *LAH* moved out with the intention of reaching Hill 252.2 and Oktiabrski State Farm to secure the front line before advancing deeper into the corridor. They arrived at the farm at 0815 hrs and after a small pause continued their trek northward but at 0830 hrs, the 18th TC and 29th TC charged their position with infantry following behind. A huge battle erupted between the few panzers that were already on the line and the 1st PzR that was still coming up to the line as well as the 2nd PzGR that had just arrived. dgk182. dgk183m.

In the early morning under cloud cover and recent heavy downpours that turned the roads to mud, the Soviets shelled *SSTK* as it advanced to the northeast on the northwest bank of the Psel River. Using hit and run techniques, T34s would ambush the German column, hitting quick and hard and then running off. The division tightened its formation and kept on going and by evening would reach the hill directly west of Polezhaev, not far from the Psel River. At the hill, the Soviets attacked again. The attack was repulsed with 14 T34s being destroyed. On the right flank of the 2nd SS PzC, *Das Reich* was advancing from near Storozhevoe, also defending itself from frequent tank attacks. Despite losing many tanks, this frequent attacking by the Soviets seemed to be working as the German advance on the flanks was definitely slowing. This went on all day. The three divisions reported to Hausser at the end of the day that 244 Soviet tanks had been destroyed. fkk158+. zow162.

Rotmistrov's 18th TC, in a narrow attack zone east of Petrovka in the Psel valley, faced *LAH* and the right flank of *SSTK*. The 29th TC would begin their attack between the Oktiabrski State Farm and Storozhevoe. Further Soviet guns were brought up during the night to support the attack next morning. Vatutin's master plan was to have his eastern and western pincers drive south and meet in the Iakovlevo-Bykovka area to encircle 4th PzA. The 5th GTA would drive through Petrovka, Brochorovka and Belenikhino toward Potrovka, Iakovlevo and Bykovka. The 1st TA and 6th GA would advance to Bolshie Maiachki and Iakovlevo. The 7th GA would conduct a secondary attack southeast of Belgorod toward the west. The plan was highly over-optimistic and had little chance of success. dgk180*. fkk327.

By 0800 hrs, after warming their engines and reloading the ammo racks, the remaining 1st PzR of *LAH* with its 67 panzers began moving north toward Hill 252.2 and the Oktiabrski State Farm, to secure the front line with 2nd PzGR before moving further north. One of the objectives for the day was to capture Hill 252.4 and neutralize the guns there that would be used to cut down the grenadiers advancing on Prokhorovka. Before reaching beyond Hill 252.2, the 18th TC and 29th TC appeared. The Germans discovered Soviet tanks had massed on the ridge between themselves and the Prokhorovka-Petrovka line. The lead German units fired purple warning shells to alert other units of the impending danger. The sun had been up only two hours and the day was already warm, humid and overcast. Though early rains had made the ground difficult, a new storm expected this afternoon would not impede the major tank battles occurring that morning in the *LAH* sector, but would influence those a little to the east in *Das Reich* sector where the ground was softer, the rain would impede the tanks of both sides for the tank battles continued into late afternoon and early evening. dgk163+. dgk182+. dgk189. dgk184m.

At 0800 hrs, a column of 30 T34s was heading for the forest near Storozhevoe. The 1st PzGR of *LAH*, heading for Storozhevoe, spotted the column. German artillery opened fire on the column destroying several tanks but the column made it to the forest. Soon a purple smoke canister fell from a recon plane showing the Germans another Soviet column moving toward them. This column had 45 tanks. All of a sudden these different tank groups launched with support from artillery making things difficult for *LAH*. Another group of tanks from the 53rd GTR showed up and all together over 100 Soviet tanks were swarming toward the German positions. German artillery saved the day, destroying many tanks. The lead tanks were from the 25th TB of 29th TC; the trailing tanks were from the 2nd TC's 169th TB. The 169th had been ordered to stay back and provide additional fire power to the attack. Soon the air force of both sides were having their own duel in the sky. Before long, 400 tanks from 5th GTA were in the fight all along the 2nd SS PzC sector. dgk186++. dgk184m.

The *LAH* had most of its panzers to the south of Hill 252.2, with only a few on the front line when the Soviets attacked. Ribbentrop's company of only seven panzers which were deployed near Hill 252.2 were awakened by the noise of tanks and quickly prepared for battle. Minutes later, purple smoke was seen in the sky, a signal that enemy tanks were coming and minutes after that Tarasov's 170th TB, about 60 tanks, were heading straight for Ribbentrop. Tarasov's 170th TB was east of the 181st TB and would cover the ground as far east as Hill 252.2. In minutes the hill would be hit by the 170th TB on the west and 29th TC's 32nd TB on the east. Tarasov leading his brigade would not survive the day. dgk185. gnk317+. agk124+. vzz311. wwf126+. fzk174++. zrl234.

Shortly after 0800 hrs, when the leading tanks of 5h GTA attacked, the barrage that had started earlier and included the dreaded Katyusha rockets escalated to a thunderous din that shook the ground and quickly left a lingering cloud of smoke hovering above the ground. dgk187+. gnk326+.

At 0830 hrs when the 76th GMR fired its last rocket down the road from Prokhorovka, the 18th TC and 29th TC began their main assault with a regiment of the 42nd GRD mounted on their tanks. The 32nd MRB of 18th TC and the 53rd MRB of 29th TC in their transports were following closely behind but the walking infantry could not keep up. By 1000 hrs the infantry fought their way to the outskirts of the Oktiabrski State Farm but they was running out of ammo and the rest of the 42nd GRD was elsewhere preparing their own attack. Things became confused. The assault on the farm and toward Hill 252.2 (defended by the 2nd PzR of *LAH* and Peiper's battalion) slowed, but a little to the east the 32nd TB (Col Linev) of 29th TC had reached the Komsomolets State Farm. Once hearing of this penetration, Rotmistrov ordered elements of the 5th GMC, in reserve, to join the battle and exploit the first break of the day. It was around 1400 hrs when Col Mikhailov's 10th GMB of 5th GMC was called out of reserve to deploy in the Ostrenki area to strengthen the line, while at the same time Col Ovcharenko's 21st GTB was sent to the Voroshilov State Farm, to the northwest of Prokhorovka, to prevent the *SSTK* from linking up with *LAH* or attacking the rear areas of 5th GTA. vzz322++. lck343+. dgr226. vzz307. dgk188+.

At 0830 hrs, elements of Burdeiny's 2nd GTC made probing attacks with part of its approximately 100 tanks allocated to this sector. It was casually supported by the 183rd

RD and together they moved out to attack the southeastern flank of 2nd SS PzC with the objective of eventually attacking with the support of the 29th TC to encircle *Das Reich*, with at most its 95 panzers and assault guns, along with the eastern flank of *LAH*. The *Deutschland* Regiment of *Das Reich* had left Ivanovski Vyselok and was heading toward Storozhevoe to assist *LAH* in its eastward advance, as well as strengthen the line there in case an offensive began that day. It did not travel far before being ambushed by 25th GTB. While *Deutschland* was busy with the 25th GTB, the 4th GTB rushed past the engagement and struck the flank of *Der Führer* Regiment, which was defending the Belenikhino area. *Das Reich* was using T34s confiscated from Kharkov earlier that year to help repulse the Soviet assaults. In one instance, a column of German-held T34s moved toward T34s preparing to attack *Das Reich* and when they were close enough, started shelling the startled victims of 2nd GTC. The fighting intensified on *Das Reich*'s right flank as the 2nd GTC expanded the assault, driving a larger wedge between *Das Reich* and 3rd PzC to the south. With the armor of 3rd PzC so far behind *Das Reich*, *Das Reich*'s southern flank was somewhat exposed and needed the 167th ID to protect it. dgk192. dgk184m. wwf137+. zow162+.

The initial success of the 32nd TB of 29th TC in bypassing the Oktiabrski State Farm and breaking into the Komsomolets State Farm was short lived, even with elements of 29th TC's 53rd MRB giving ground support. The Germans counter-attacked from the OSF to the north and surrounded many of the troops of the 53rd MRB at KSF. Though the Soviets suffered heavy casualties in this moving pocket, the free remnants of 53rd MRB moved back into the now vacant trenches on the OSF, which the Germans had initially abandoned, and could not be expelled. The soldiers on the east side of the farm that were not encircled but could not get back to their lines fell back toward Iamki. Nearly 400 soldiers died and another 700 were injured from the 53rd MRB in the fighting at or near the Komsomolets State Farm on this day. A few T34s were rounded up for a counter-attack to relieve the pocket but on their way along the railroad were ambushed by German assault guns and all the tanks were destroyed. The 32nd TB, one of the units that defended Tula in 1941, carried only T34s. vzz326+. vzz442. vzz61.

By 0830 hrs, the primary corps of 5th GTA, having formed two pincers, launched their assault that intended to penetrate the German line, head to the rear areas and then encircle *LAH* and *SSTK*, and perhaps more of the SS. The western pincer would be Maj General Bakharov's 18th TC and the eastern spearhead would be led by Kirichenko's 29th TC. The 18th TC's 181st TB and 170th TB would be responsible for the lead in the area between the Psel River and Hill 252.2 inclusive. The 29th TC would have the land east of Hill 252.2 and the village of Iamki to the east. The 32nd TB would lead the assault and to the east, the 25th TB would head for the Storozhevoe sector. In second echelon, the 9th GAD, 42nd GRD and 31st TB would follow the lead tanks and clear the remaining resistance. With the German artillery primed and waiting for the offensive to begin, these lead brigades suffered heavy casualties in the first minutes. vzz309+.

The 181st TB, commanded by Lt Col Puzyrev who was closest to the southern bank of the Psel River, was tasked to eliminate *SSTK* from the villages on the southern banks. Afterwards they were to shift directions, and with any support from the 170th TB, head for Gresnoe and Malye Maiachki and then join up with the 29th TC and 2nd GTC to encircle the SS Corps including the heavily defended Hill 241.6. The observers on Hill 241.6 were looking out at the fairly flat landscape to the north. On their left was the Psel River's big bend that eventually headed to northeast. Directly in front looking up the corridor, the roaming hills could be seen and on the right the Storozhevoe woods blocked part of the view of the 30-foot high railway embankment that led to Prokhorovka. Further south of the Storozhevoe woods, an observer would be able see the low roaming hills turn into a landscape of rugged gullies and ravines around the Belenikhino area. The villages along the Psel river, west of OSF included Prelestnoe, Andreevka, Mikhailovka and Vasilevka. wwf123.

The terrain in the corridor favored tanks closest to the Oktiabrski State Farm and the bulk of the tanks of 170th TB were concentrated in this area. The Germans took advantage of this concentration with their artillery and before the 170th TB reached the Oktiabrski State Farm, many of the tanks were hit. The *Luftwaffe* also flew many sorties despite partially cloudy skies. The Me 110s and Stukas were a deadly combination. Air support and a strong artillery presence were two major reasons for 5th GTA's heavy casualties during the day. The 127th GRR of 42nd GRD was following the tanks and suffered from the air strikes as well. The 36th GTR was to follow as well but when its commander, Lt Mitroshenko, was seriously wounded from the air strike, the 36th GTR paused to recover and have Maj Plissov take the lead. Other reasons for the poor results included poor intelligence that missed the newly built fortified defenses on the morning of 7/12 and poor coordination of infantry and armor as well as the lack of effective support from artillery and air with the armor. vzz319+. vzz323. vzz340++. gnk347+.

It was expected that the 32nd TB would have fought its way past Oktiabrski State Farm and would be fighting for Komsomolets State Farm by 1000 hrs. The 2nd GTC was ordered to launch a full scale attack at 1000 hrs against *Das Reich* along the Iasnaia Poliana-Kalinin-Ozerovski-Sobachevski line to support the 32nd TB. With these two pincers, Rotmistrov wanted to encircle the *LAH/SSDR* forces in the Storozhevoe-Iamki area. This would be the start of the separation of *LAH* and *SSDR*. The left flank of 2nd GTC was to break through and make its way to Iakovlevo to block any Germans from retreating. This was an over-optimistic plan that had little chance for complete success. Hausser was quick to respond to penetrations with reinforcements and artillery coverage, which prevented deep penetrations. The *Luftwaffe* was also quick to vector planes where they would do the most good. The 25th GTB, which would be the lead tankers for this attack, were stationed near Vinogradovka. Several mortar and artillery regiments would stay there to support the tankers attack. vzz361+.

To the left of 25th GTB was its sister brigade, the 4th GTB under Col Brazhnikov. The 4th GTB would attack at the same time toward Kalinin, due south of Iasnaia Poliana and southwest of Vinogradovka. To add punch to the attack, Maj Zotov's 1500th DAR and Maj Sereda's 1695th AAR were brought up to contribute the fire power of their guns. Col Savchenko's 4th GMRB would attack toward Sobachevski and Luchki. Both brigades would be supported by the 273rd Mortar Regiment and the 755th Destroyer Anti-tank Artillery Battalion. The Red Air Force would also attack German concentrations in the Ivanovka and Vinogradovka areas. The 26th GTB was originally planned to assemble behind Lt Col Bulygin's 25th GTB for the attack but with the crossing of the Donets by 6th PzD at Rzhavets, the 26th GTB was held back in case it was needed to block the advancing 3rd PzC. The 16th Guards Mortar Regiment was attached to the 2nd GTC to assist in clearing a path for the tankers with its rockets. In addition, the 32nd TB and 53rd MRB were preparing defenses at the Komsomolets State Farm. General Vatutin was bringing up to the front every gun he could find to prevent any breakthrough during Rotmistrov's offensive. vzz362. vzz3m.

When the 18th TC and 29th TC launched that morning, they had to travel at least a mile on open ground before engaging the panzers. The 8th *Flieger* Corps was already in the air and was planning on raiding Soviet positions in preparation for 2nd SS PzC's attack. When the squadron of Hs 129s, Ju 87s and Fw 190s spotted the row of tanks on the ridge, they immediately dived on the vulnerable tanks. The Soviet flak guns in the sector opened on the planes. An estimated 248 sorties were flown by the Germans for the benefit of the 2nd SS PzC that morning. The Hs 129s and the Stukas with the 37mm cannon were especially deadly to the Soviet tanks. The 32nd TB, and to a lesser extent the 31st TB of 29th TC which was further north, was especially hit hard. Capt Rudel was credited with 12 tanks that day using his single cannon. It was a favorite practice by German pilots to attack the external fuel tanks on the tanks, which was usually good enough to light the whole vehicle ablaze. At that moment, the Red AF was absent but Soviet artillery tried to take up the slack and slow the German panzers which were now in sight. cbk79. zow148.

At 0835 hrs, the 170th TB advanced across the small valley southeast of Petrovka, smashing into the advanced positions of *LAH*. The engagement, just north of Oktiabrski State Farm, quickly became chaotic with neither side making any appreciable gains until the 1000th AAR came up to support the 170th TB. Together they forced the *LAH* to slowly fall back to Oktiabrski. Despite losing 30 of its 60 tanks mostly from the few panzers that were up front and artillery that had been brought up to the line during the night and aerial attack, the 170th TB still followed the *LAH* and engaged again. vzz341.

The 170th TB drove closer to Hill 252.2 than 181st TB with the intentions of heading toward the gap between *SSTK* and *LAH*. Ribbentrop's seven panzers saw the Soviets coming and began to scale the hill to gain any advantage on the larger force. As the panzers were moving up Hill 252.2 they saw another group of Soviet tanks about a kilometre away to the northeast of Oktiabrski State Farm, heading south; they were part of 29th TC. Ribbentrop stopped his company and started firing on the Soviets. His panzers were Mk IVs with the high velocity gun and even at that range could stop a T70 or even a T34 with a side hit, but within minutes more tanks from the 170th TB were heading directly toward Ribbentrop. This was his main concern and he had to breakaway from the first group to the right and concentrate on the new threat. The T34s were instructed to rush in and attack the panzers at close range to nullify their longer range advantage, but the Soviet tankers would find the Germans were also good at arms-length fighting and would destroy many of the T34s. vzz311. zrl235+.

Before reaching the Oktiabrski State Farm, the panzers of 1st PzR (*LAH*) were moving toward the front line in the vicinity of Hill 252.2 when they were attacked by Soviet tanks racing toward them from positions on the last defensive ridge on the Prokhorovka-Petrovka line. The T34s using their speed tried to outflank and out-maneuver the panzers. The Germans stopped where they were and starting firing at the T34s, about 800 yards away, quickly knocking out several tanks. North of Oktiabrski along the Prokhorovka-Petrovka line, the lead panzers of 1st SS PzR who had arrived and 2nd PzGR were attacked by another 60 tanks from about 1,000 yards away. During the three-hour battle the 1st SS PzR inflicted heavy casualties on the Soviets as their tanks tried to close the gap and fight at point blank range. Eventually the Soviets did succeed in getting close, inflicting casualties on the Germans. Similar small tank attacks were launched along the entire line of 2nd SS

PzC. dgk185.

At 0830 hrs, the 5th GA attacked southward heading toward its eventual objective of Gresnoe while other elements of the 32nd GRC and 33rd GRC with 40 tanks headed for Kochetovka, west of Gresnoe and a important strongpoint on the boundary between *SSTK* and 11th PzD. Some penetration of *SSTK/LAH* line allowed the Soviets to attack artillery positions of the *LAH* to the rear. The *SSTK*, while inflicting heavy losses on the Soviets, eventually did advance to the northeast along the Psel to within six miles of Prokhorovka, with the capture of Polezhaev which was defended by elements of 95th GRD. At 2000 hrs, the 67th GRD moved up to break the stalemate, which forced the 2nd SS PzC to stop its advance and go defensive. Also at this time, the 11th PzD and *SSTK* attacked the 52nd GRD, defending alongside 5th GA with 100 panzers and motorized infantry plus air support. A couple hours after daylight the *SSTK* finally had its Tigers across the Psel, struggling to catch up with the other panzers in order to extend their bridgehead northward. wdk160. dgr221m. dgr225. gnk313m..

Michael Wittmann, working with *LAH*, and his company of Tigers were south of the Oktiabrski State Farm when he saw many tanks from the 18th TC moving southwest past Ribbentrop's position heading for Andreevka. In the open field, Wittmann, Kling and their fellow Tigers opened up at 1,800 yards, knowing the Soviets would not shoot until they reached 500 yards or closer. The Mk IVs, idling behind the Tigers, would have to wait until the tanks got within 800 yards for a lethal shot. The T34s maneuvered to get in close using their speed and agility but with the few Mk IVs screening the Tigers, the Soviet attempt against the Tigers was suicidal. Before long, four of the Mks were hit from a distance of less then 225 yards. Though many Soviet tanks were down, some Soviets broke through this German screen and headed west where they met up with shellfire from German artillery at Gresnoe. mhz333++. fzk173+. fzk311++. zrl235+. zow164+?.

As the Soviet offensive gained traction, the 18th TC's 181st TB, traveling southwest along the Psel River's southern bank, headed for Andreevka and Vasilevka when the *Luftwaffe* showed up looking for targets of opportunity. They dived on the tanks through cloudy skies, inflicting casualties but the tankers continued on without hesitation. Near their launch point, the 18th TC had to contend with a number of ravines that ran west and east. Because of this, the 181st TB moved further east closer to 170th TB but after passing those ravines, the 181st TB was able to move closer to the river as ordered. gnk344+. gnk313m. vzz342. mjk92.

To the left of 18th TC was Maj General Kirichenko's 29th TC. It was comprised of Lt Col Linev's 31st TB, Col Moiseev's 32nd TB and Volodin's 25th TB and launched at the same time. The 32nd TB, leading 31st TB, drove between Hill 252.2, the Prokhorovka rail line and Iamki while the 25th TB attacked from east of Iamki toward Storozhevoe and its woods in support with 169th TB of 2nd TC. Each of these brigades of the 29th TC had approximately 60 tanks. All would be used in the attack, with none left in reserve. The 31st TB and 32nd TB had the misfortune of attacking *LAH* at its strongest point, the Oktiabrski State Farm, and would pay the price for that bad luck. The 53rd MRB under Lipichev would be in second echelon. dgk189. vzz342+. wwf125. zrl234.

Das Reich was heading for Iamki when 40 tanks came rushing in with their guns blazing. *Das Reich* was southeast of Stalinskoe State Farm and was trying to secure the right side of the woods and along the railroad line leading to Prokhorovka. Then a second wave of tanks were spotted; this time with enough lead time the German artillery started shelling before the tanks were in their own firing range. At the end of this second wave, Soviet artillery which must have just been moved up, started firing on the German forces. The attacks had escalated quickly. fkk161+.

Once past Ribbentrop, elements of the 170th TB, driving more to the east of 181st TB and closer to Hill 252.2 and Oktiabrski State Farm, aimed for the territory on the western end of *SSTK*'s sector and attacked Kron's Pz Abt 3 as it approached Kochetovka. Additional Soviet riflemen were moving up and the fighting became fierce. Kochetovka was on the west flank of *SSTK*, west of Vasilevka on the Solotinka River. The Solotinka River was a tributary of the Psel River. Kron's battalion was also screening the eastern flank of 48th PzC's 11th PzD and was quite isolated. If not careful, his group could be encircled and destroyed. gnk344+. gnk313m.

Within minutes of the opening engagement near Oktiabrski, and with more tanks arriving from both sides every minute, the open field was ablaze with burning tanks and moving tanks maneuvering and firing as quickly they could. Some of the Soviet tanks were behind anti-tank defenses, firing at easy targets as additional waves of Soviet tanks, 30 to 40 strong, arrived as the battle developed; fewer panzers were coming up. This tank battle of maneuverability lasted over three hours and by dark 192 T34s and T70s were left behind with their hulls spurting flame and smoke. Among the dead tanks lay hundreds of dead soldiers and on the perimeter of this tank field lay many impromptu foxholes in which some of the living wondered if the battle was really over. It was truly an eerie sight. The tank recovery teams were already on their way to salvage as many panzers as possible as the *LAH* retained control of the field. fkk163++.

Despite the fierce tank battle west and south of Prokhorovka, the 73rd PzGR captured the nearby town of Sabyno at 0900 hrs. jp195.

In the morning, the *LAH* was driving north along the Petrovka-Prokhorovka road when 50 tanks attacked, hitting directly on Peiper's battalion of panzers, igniting a fierce battle. By 0900 hrs, Peiper had stabilized the German position and counted 15 burning Soviet hulks in front of him. fkk159.

Kurt Sametreiter and his Tiger crew (of *LAH*) deployed west of Iamki, knocked out 24 tanks of the 29th TC on this day and was awarded the Knight's Cross. agk124.

In the afternoon the situation was becoming untenable. The 5th GTA was forced to discontinue its attack and go on the defensive. The 2nd SS PzD lost momentum but the motorized infantry in the Prokhorovka sector was able to repulse the Soviet attacks and then counter-attack to the north at the Psel bridgehead.

North of the Psel River, *SSTK* had now assembled its nearly full complement of 121 panzers and assault guns of the 3rd SS PzR and was driving northward from Hill 226.6 in order to break through the newly erected defenses held by 6th GA's 52nd GRD and by 1st TA which held positions further west. By 1300 hrs the Hill 226.6 sector had been cleared and the bulk of the panzers were trying to catch up with the leading Tigers that had already taken off for the Kartashevka Road. Before reaching the Tigers, the Mark IVs were attacked by the 95th GRD who were heading for the hill to retake it. With the help of a second *Luftwaffe* attack, *SSTK* pushed the 95th GRD back to Polezhaev. The Soviet resistance regrouped and stiffened and the Germans were halted at Polezhaev. The 95th GRD was now shattered and Rotmistrov sent the 42nd GRD to bolster it. Nearby, the 24th GTB of 5th GMC was sent to nearby Voroshilov State Farm to stiffen the line with 18th TC and 5th GA against the Tiger formation that was roaming the area. dgk193+. vzz1m.

gnk312m+. kuz195.

The series of tank battles evolving from the Soviets' three main axes of attack would encompass an arc about 12 miles long that started south of Prokhorovka near the villages of Ivanovka and Leski on the southeast corner to the south bank of the Psel River in the northwest corner. The weather was cloudy and, with recent heavy rains, made the dirt roads difficult in spots for wheeled vehicles which impacted the Germans worst. With the *SSTK* on the northwest and *LAH* and *Das Reich* to the east and southeast, the 2nd SS PzC drove to control both sides of the road to Prokhorovka as well as expand their bridgehead north of the Psel. The Soviets estimated that the SS Corps had 500 panzers including 100 Tigers and Ferdinands but this number was too optimistic. The number was closer to 300 panzers, assault guns and a handful of Tigers and all the Ferdinands were in the north with Model. wdk158+. hjj121m.

Since daybreak and before the main Soviet offensive began and again after the initial Soviet armor attack, a detachment from *Deutschland* Regiment of *Das Reich* (left flank) had tried to secure Storozhevoe and its surrounding lands from the west in order to stabilize their line, but failed each time. It was defended mostly by the 169th TB of the 2nd TC. *Das Reich* had captured the southwest corner of the woods, west of the village but it needed reinforcements if greater progress was to be made. A few more members of *Deutschland* arrived and together along with artillery support entered the village and were fighting street by street for control of the village. The remainder of *Deutschland* Regiment was in the process of leaving Ivanovski Vyselok and heading toward southern Storozhevoe to support *LAH* and the rest of its regiment but did not travel far before being ambushed by tanks of the 25th TB (29th TC), with soldiers of the 9th GAD riding on its decks and the 55th GTR. The panzer regiment was further south near Belenikhino and unable to help but the regimental artillery was able to target the oncoming tanks and started firing. Several waves of 30 tanks each attacked their positions and the Germans were greatly outnumbered and fighting for survival, being pushed back to the village of Vinogradovka where the Germans had erected a speedy defense. *Das Reich* had captured 26 new T34s in March when recapturing Kharkov and were now using those machines against the Soviets. mhz341. vzz3m. gnk325++. zow162.

The 2nd SS PzC was now fighting along its entire sector. While *SSTK* was being attacked in the Vasilevka/Andreevka area and *LAH* attacked near Hill 252.2 and the Oktiabrski State Farm, *Das Reich* and the right flank of *LAH* were being attacked by Volodin's 25th TB of 29th TC, the 169th TB of 2nd TC, 55th GTR and the men of the 28th GRR along the Storozhevoe sector, including the nearby forest that *Das Reich* was finally penetrating. With tanks in the lead, the T34s would fire on the move to prevent the more accurate panzers from hitting them and would therefore often miss their target. With the commander of the tank the gunner as well, his vision was limited and he could not see the targets or the threats as well as the German tank commanders could. gnk326+. vzz321. vzz1m. kuz193.

As part of Vatutin's plan of attacking 2nd SS PzC on its flanks, Rotmistrov's tanks attacked *LAH* and *Das Reich* from the Prokhorovka railway embankment south to Storozhevoe and Belenikhino. South of Prokhorovka east of the rail line, the 29th TC's 25th TB with the support of the 9th GAD attacked and inflicted heavy casualties on *Das Reich*'s left flank, while it was already in battle with the 2nd TC and 2nd GTC, which were attacking its central and southern flank. The 25th TB had made a brief penetration near the Komsomolets State Farm but it was quickly closed. Near Storozhevoe, the 136th GRR (42nd GRD) and 26th TB counter-attacked, trying to push back the SS, but the Germans were able to hold the line with the help of the *Luftwaffe* which inflicted heavy casualties on the 136th GRR. A little south of 25th TB and the 2nd TC, the 2nd GTC repeatedly attacked *Das Reich* for most of the day. The fighting the last two days may have been a tactical success for the Germans, for they punished the Soviets but it was a strategic success for the Soviets who were able to hold the advance and recover from their heavy casualties while the Germans could not. fkk329. lck361+. vzz339.

The first to break through the German screen at Oktiabrski State Farm and Hill 252.2 was a group of 15 T34s from 32nd TB. Once past the line, the Soviet tankers continued past the woods, Hill 242.5 and Hill 241.6 and broke into the outskirts of Komsomolets State Farm from the south. It was a distance of three miles into the German rear area. Elements from the 53rd MRB tried to follow but were attacked from the air and lost touch with the tankers. Despite allowing some of the tanks of the 32nd TB to pass the farm and Hill 252.2, after an hour of fierce fighting, the Oktiabrski State Farm was still controlled by *LAH*'s 2nd PzGR (Krass). Each SS division had experienced a minor penetration of their line but this was the worst. It was not critical yet but Hausser had to close the gap before Soviet reinforcements could arrive in strength. vzz314. vzz319. vzz441. dgk189++.

At 0920 hrs, after stabilizing the line after the first wave of Soviet attacks, the *LAH* began their drive up the Prokhorovka road, when a wave of tanks with mounted infantry came barreling down the road and attacked. It was the remains of 32nd TB of 29th TC with 35 tanks in the formation as well as the 31st TB. agk124+.

At 0920 hrs, the 32nd TB attacked along the Prokhorovka road against the road junction southwest of Swch. Quickly six panzers from *LAH* were put out of commission at 220 yards but the remaining panzers and artillery knocked out 19 tanks. While this battle was raging, a small tank squad with infantry riding on top ambushed the supporting battery on Hill 241.6. The gunners had to depress their guns and fire point-blank range at the oncoming tanks. The attack was repulsed. dgk179+.

As the tank battle escalated, the tanks became so close to each other that shells sometimes penetrated both the side armor as well as frontal armor. In some cases, the shell inventory of the victim tank would blow as well, blowing off the turret which would land many yards away. It does not bare thinking about what happens to those inside. As the commanders of both sides realized the scope of the tank battle, they each called in air support. In the air, the many dogfights became almost as impressive as the land battle, where nearly 1,100 tanks were battling in a small area south and southwest of Prokhorovka. While the Germans were advancing slowly against the Soviet front, Soviet tanks attacked on the sector running from Petrovka to the station at Belenikhino, southwest of Prokhorovka, and along the line of the Psel. Once again as per Rotmistrov's orders, the T34s rushed inside the Tiger's lethal range and fought the heavier panzers at point blank range; it was a long shot with poor possibilities for success. jp183. je109*. dgk222m. mhz328+.

The initial *LAH*/29th TC tank engagement escalated when a second group of Soviet tanks appeared. The Soviets, moving south from Prokhorovka with 35 tanks from 32nd TB, hit first and a short time later a second formation of 40 tanks from 31st TB clashed into *LAH*. The left German pincer meant to screen the right pincer as it headed for Prokhorovka from near Oktiabrski. The two enemies met north and northeast of Hill 241.6. The Germans started firing at 800 yards but the Soviets, using T34s and T70s, were able to get in close, about 500 yards, and destroy a number of the panzers. This was the second time that morning that *LAH* was attacked by 29th TC. The 32nd TB had fallen back and regrouped before attempting this second attack. The Germans claimed destroying 62 Soviet tanks in this series of engagements along this critical roadway. See Map 27. dgk190.

Many of the Soviet tankers did not stay to fight it out with Ribbentrop or the arriving panzers of 1st PzR; they would fire on the panzers as they drove by for they had a timetable to keep, but they were slowed once they arrived at the first tank ditch, south of Hill 252.2. The trench was originally dug by the Soviets but it was enlarged the previous day after it was captured to form a tank ditch to trap and destroy the Soviet tanks when they were forced to stop. By the end of the day, Ribbentrop lost five panzers: two were repairable, plus his own, but two were completely destroyed along with their crews. Ribbentrop drove back to behind his lines, picked up a repaired panzer and returned to the battle. It is estimated that 100 Soviet tanks were either destroyed or were confiscated at the ditch when the crews abandoned them. It is claimed by some of the German survivors that some of the T34s going at full speed that fell on top of tanks that had already fallen into the ditch were able to back out undamaged. This feat was especially impressive to the German soldiers firing at them. This enlarged tank trap was dug out of the conviction that the Soviets were planning a major offensive that day. By this time a new wave of Soviet planes flew in to drop their deadly cargo as the German flak guns opened up on them. gnk319++. gnk320. gnk328. sgf349. vzz295+. vzz327.

At 1000 hrs from southwest of Hill 252.2, 20 panzers exited a ravine and headed straight for the newly erected 9th GAD position. At 800 yards the Soviet guns opened up with the panzers (no Tigers) returning fire. The panzers created a small gap in the line and elements of the 28th GAR fell back toward Prokhorovka. vzz239+. vzz11m. mjk92.

Popov's 2nd TC, having already lost more than half its tanks since the start of the campaign, was the weakest corps in 5th GTA. Even with their mechanics working throughout the night, the corps had only 52 working tanks to start the day. Even worse, its brigades had been deployed thinly between Storozhevoe, Pravorot and Iamki. Its assignment for the day was to hold the line between 2nd GTC on its left and 29th TC on its right. The 2nd TC was only allowed to attack if its two neighbors made major penetrations. The bulk of 58th MRB, which had received tanks from 2nd TC, was defending Iamki and Storozhevoe. Even though the 2nd TC did not go on the offensive until later in the morning it still had a difficult day; it defended in the Storozhevoe, Ivanovka, Belenikhino Station and Teterevino areas against the advances of *Das Reich* and 167th ID. The 2nd TC consisted of the 58th MRB, 26th TB and the 99th TB. vzz368*++.

The 2nd GTC, with elements of the 183rd RD of 69th Army securing their right flank, launched from the Vinogradovka-Belenikhino area, attacking toward Kalinin. On its southern flank, it hit the southern boundary between *Das Reich* and the 167th ID, though *SSDR* was hit harder. The Soviet tanks came in waves but eventually more than 50 tanks made the assault. The battle lasted all day, though the 2nd GTC was able to approach Kalinin by 1430 hrs but was unable to capture it and had to eventually fall back. wdk160. dgr221m. dgr225. vzz11m. gnk313m.

Around 1000 hrs and heading south, the 31st TB of 29th TC after being released from reserve entered battle, heading past Hill 252.2 from east of the Oktiabrski State Farm. The German artillery using 105mm and 155mm guns from Hill 252.2 and Hill 241.6 opened fire on the tankers. Shortly afterwards the *Luftwaffe* came in, adding their weight to the battle. The 31st TB drove into a wall of steel and suffered heavy casualties. The 25th TB on 31st TB's eastern flank also suffered heavy casualties from intense shelling from Hill 241.6. Already bloodied in battle, the 32nd TB, after briefly regrouping, moved southwest along the rail line, meeting stiff resistance as the Soviet tanks, paralleling the 31st TB, tried to maneuver close to the panzers. Their advance quickly stopped but they did not fall back. Digging in they returned fire but soon lost 40 tanks and 350 men with their exposed location. After a three-hour battle, 62 Soviet tanks were smoldering on the immediate battlefield. lck357. vzz316++. dgk191. gnk313.

By 1030 hrs, elements of four tank brigades and their supporting infantry were still stuck at the Hill 252.2-Oktiabrski State Farm barrier. Rotmistrov had to capture the hill and farm if he was going to move forward in any major way; he could not bypass it and leave such strongpoints in his rear area. A small group of tanks from the 32nd TB of 29th TC did slip by the farm and was now fighting its way into the Komsomolets State Farm. The intelligence arms of each side let the military down. The Germans expected a counteroffensive and built defenses to stop it but Hoth had no idea how large the attack would be. On the Soviet side, Vatutin and Rotmistrov had no idea how well the Germans had built their defenses. This, coupled with the short planning and preparation period, would clearly show poor results by the end of the day. vzz325. vzz342+.

The 181st TB was approaching Vasilevka on the southern bank of the Psel River by 1000 hrs when German 88s, panzers, mortars and rockets opened fire. By 1100 hrs the tank brigade, despite the heavy resistance, had determinedly fought its way to the town limits. In order to prevent the town from falling as well as having their communications severed, Tigers from Hill 226.6 were called back and together with the *SSTK* were able to push the 181st TB out of Vasilevka and back to Andreevka by early afternoon. After clearing the river villages, the 181st TB was supposed to turn south and clear Gresnoe and Malye Maiachki where German artillery was emplaced before turning north again to isolate the *SSTK*'s northern bridgehead and block the retreat path of the SS along with the 29th TC, when they had succeeded in their penetration attempts. However, at this point it was looking doubtful that either would happen. It was a costly day for *SSTK* as it suffered over 300 casualties including 69 dead and 20 armored vehicles lost, but their assault reached the heights north of Polezhaev and inflicted heavy casualties on 31st TC. vzz340++. gnk347. ztc270. pck81+.

The 2nd SS PzR, stationed near Ozerovski, launched eastward toward Vinogradovka. Once captured it was to turn south toward Ivanovka. gnk340. Vzz3m.

The 25th TB with the support of the 25th MRB and 169th TB launched their attack from Iamki but soon found itself in a tank trap that *LAH* had created the previous night. The Germans had antitank guns waiting and when the 25th TB passed by, the Germans attacked the column. Of the 32 T34s in the column, 26 were destroyed. The survivors made it to the southeast of Storozhevoe, which was still in Soviet hands, to regroup. The 25th TB was now the size of a battalion with mostly T70s. At 1200 hrs, the remaining elements of 25th TB attacked toward Ivanovski Vyselok and while the *LAH* had encircled and were reducing elements of the 32nd TB plus the 53rd MRB at Komsomolets State Farm, *Das Reich* had a protective screen that stopped the 25th MRB from freeing the encircled Soviets. By the end of the day the 25th TB had lost 50 of their 69 tanks and were positioned defensively southeast of Storozhevoe. vzz332++. gnk323.

Following the left flank of 168th ID, the 167th ID crossed the Lipovyi Donets River heading north. From west of Teterevino South and from Nepkhaevo, the Soviets countered the 167th ID on its left flank but were repulsed. A little further north in the fiercest fighting for *LAH*, they were able so far to plug the penetrations at the Oktiabrski State Farm and regained lost ground, but it did not gain any new ground. Elements of *SSTK* that were guarding the Psel bridgehead at Bogoroditskoe, just west of Vasilevka, repulsed all attacks by 18th TC. vzz438+. dgk184m.

By 1100 hrs, elements of the 25th GTB of 2nd GTC under Burdeiny (supposedly supported by the 183rd RD that had launched from the Vinogradovka area along the Iasnaia Poliana-Kalinin-Ozerovski-Sobachevski axis) with the help of 29th TC to its north, was supposed to split the 2nd SS PzC. To ensure success with the operation, the 273rd Mortar Regiment was positioned at Ivanovka to lend a hand. The 183rd RD did not launch until the afternoon and it was not much help to the 25th GTB. One wonders how the Soviet attack would have gone if the 183rd had launched on time and with determination. The 26th GTB had unexpectedly been dispatched to stop Kempf from enlarging his bridgehead on the Donets near Ryndinka. Its right flank was originally supposed to secure the Storozhevoe area and its left flank was to penetrate to Iakovlevo by 1700 hrs. During the predawn hours, Soviet engineers had cleared paths in the minefield near the Prokhorovka tracks, which speeded the assault for 25th GTB and its infantry in this attack. vzz362++. lck369. dgr221m. dgk184m.

The battle with *Der Führer* Regiment of *Das Reich* and 25th GTB began with a wave of 30 tanks driving from the direction of Belenikhino, but 25th GTB was unable to initially break through the German defenses to reach its target, Iasnaia Poliana. However, it did reach and secure the woods near Iasnaia Poliana by 1300 hrs and the small village of Ozerovski after that. The small Soviet force set up defenses in the village and were determined to hold the village until reinforcements arrived, but the Germans counter-attacked and wiped out the defenders. Diverting some of their tanks, the Soviets drove through the nearby woods and attacked the German artillery batteries, destroying them, but were unable to travel much further after hitting a line of dug-in anti-tank guns. At 1130 hrs, other elements of the 25th GTB attacked *Das Reich* first from the Komsomolets State Farm-Ivanovski Vyselok area with 20 tanks but were the victims of a heavy rocket attack that inflicted heavy casualties. Soon afterwards the *Luftwaffe* flew in and strafed the Soviet formations, forcing the Soviets back. Shortly afterwards when little progress had been made, Burdeiny ordered his 25th GTB back to the woods southeast of Vinogradovka to regroup. The Germans had this area under shellfire and the 25th GTB had to maneuver toward the woods east of Ivanovka. The 4th GTB and 4th GMRB, to the south of 25th GTB, angled its attack toward Luchki in an attempt to help encircle a large part of 2nd SS PzC, with the help of the other brigades. The *Luftwaffe* showing up when it did was propitious, for if the 25th GTB was not forced back and was able to continue the fight for KSF along with the penetrations by the 18th TC from the west and 29th TC from the northeast, the farm might have fallen and put a dangerous hole in the *LAH/Das Reich* line. vzz363+. vzz441*. dgk184m. lck363+. dgr104. dgr221m. gnk313m. vzz11m. zow162.

At 1100 hrs on the left flank of *LAH* where few panzers were supporting the attack, the 18th TC broke through, allowing some tankers from the 110th TB to drive south before the gap was plugged. At 1130 hrs a small penetration occurred near Hill 252.2 by the 32nd TB but that gap was also filled. After regrouping and adding the strength of the 9th GAD, the Soviets made another attempt for the hill and the adjacent Oktiabrski State Farm and at

1300 hrs pushed the Germans back. By morning, the Germans had withstood Rotmistrov's gigantic attack but by this time in the campaign were unable to exploit it for further gains. The Soviets maintained their defensive resistance. lck357+. vzz327.

Das Reich's *Deutschland* Regiment had advanced from Ivanovski Vyselok hours before, when it was struck by lead units of Bulygin's 25th GTB. It was now 1100 hrs and both sides had continued to bring reinforcements to the area and the skirmish had turned into a vicious battle. The 25th had heavy artillery support that hit the Germans hard. While the *Deutschland* Regiment was defending itself, Brazhnkiov's 4th GTB had swept pass the front line, crossed the rail line north of Belenikhino and into the eastern outskirts of the village of Iasnaia Poliana, attacking the northern flank of *Der Führer* Regiment. The regiment was now being attacked by elements of several tank brigades and it had little armor to support it. It did have strong artillery support from near KSF, which saved it from destruction, but the Soviets did force the regiment to fall back into Iasnaia Poliana in an orderly retreat. At the same time, the 25th GTB driving from Vinogradovka made it south of Belenikhino but was counter-attacked and had to fall back to the east of Iasnaia Poliana and Kalinin. By 1430 hrs, *Das Reich* sent reinforcements to support its threatened right flank; the Soviets disengaged and fell back for the night. It started raining hard and the dirt roads were turning to mud, discouraging both sides from traveling in the dark. The 26th GTB under Col Nesterov (2nd GTC) had been redeployed toward Plota-Ryndinka to help stop the 6th PzD and 19th PzD from expanding their new bridgehead on the west side of the Donets. *Das Reich* was lucky for the 26th GTB was sent south toward Plota; if it was not for the transfer, the 26th GTB would have exploited that gap between German divisions. 25th TB was part of 29th TC while 25th GTB was part of 2nd GTC. dgk192+. dgr221m. vzz362+. vzz364+. dgr39m. wwf137.

In and around the village of Vasilevka, *SSTK* artillery was winning the battle against the 18th TC's 181st TB and it had to fall back to Andreevka, where the brigade joined up with elements of the 170th TB. Together they moved east, having the 23rd GAR riding on their decks, back to attack and get behind *LAH* in the corridor. This time the Soviets would be facing Wittmann's company of four Tigers. Wittmann saw the tanks racing toward him from over a mile away and, despite being greatly outnumbered, moved to intercept. Wittmann started firing when the tanks were a mile out, long before the Soviets could fire. When the Soviets were just 1,000 yards away, almost every Tiger round hit their target and the Soviets had to get closer still before having a chance to destroy a Tiger. In this exchange, a damaged T34 had gotten close to a Tiger and was going for a suicide run to destroy it. It did ram the front of the Tiger but before the ammunition in the Soviet tank detonated, the Tiger was backing up and when the T34 exploded, the Tiger was only five yards away but survived the experience. gnk329++. vzz11m. vzz323. wwf123+. fzk311. fzk314.

Moiseev's 31st TB, despite suffering heavy casualties in its opening engagement, struck Hill 252.2 and for several hours tried to push the Germans off. Linev's 32nd TB, after pausing to regroup, moved up to support the 31st TB. Even the 9th GAD had to launch an attack that reached the foot of the reverse slope of Hill 252.2. The 9th GAD tried to give cover to the tank crews trying to escape the tank trap. In front of the trap and after fighting for hours against superior numbers, Ribbentrop was still alive and fighting on top of the hill, destroying T34s at 30 yards, as quick as the loader could work. In the desperate struggle to keep the hill and the eventual withdrawal Peiper lost 20 of his half-tracks and trucks. Ribbentrop claimed the reason for the Soviets' poor kill ratio was the fact the commander of the tank was also the gunner and does not have the time or visibility to match the German proficiency. gnk322. zrl235+.

Resuming his advance at 1100 hrs after realizing the worst of the Soviet tank counteroffensive was over, Priess's *SSTK* with a group of up to 60 panzers had fought its way to the base of Hill 226.6 by 1200 hrs as well as to the outskirts of Krasnyi Oktiabr, which was defended by 11th MRB. By 1215 hrs, 40 panzers and 200 motorcyclists made it to Hill 226.6 and then crested the hill, driving elements of the 52nd GRD back in disarray toward Olshanka as well as losing its comms with 5th GA. By 1300 hrs, Hill 226.6 was loosely secured along with the first line of trenches north of Kliuchi. Not staying long on Hill 226.6 except for a security detachment, *SSTK* started moving toward Hill 236.7 which had a commanding view toward the north and east. Hill 236.7 was due north of Hill 226.6 with its crest just south of the important Prokhorovka-Kartashevka road. The hill would be tough to take because some of 95th GRD's artillery was placed there. Zhadov's HQ was there as well. With Hill 226.6 in German hands, Col Karpov's 24th GTB of 5th GMC was called up to the Voroshilov State Farm to block the advancing panzers from reaching the critical Kartashevka-Prokhorovka road. Where was the *Luftwaffe*? They had been absent in this sector all day. The *Luftwaffe* did support *SSTK* a little but not as much as the two other SS divisions, especially *LAH*. vzz387++. vzz400+. dgk194. vzz1m. gnk312m.

The 25th TB and 28th GAR attacked German positions south of the rail line to Storozhevoe, where they penetrated the German line and drove to the Prokhorovka road. They were met by waiting panzers who drove them back into Storozhevoe and along the southern slopes of Hill 252.2 to the fields just outside of Iamki. While the Soviets did not gain ground in this sector on this day, they certainly halted the German advance on Prokhorovka. At a cost of 53 killed and 321 wounded, *LAH* claimed to have destroyed 192 tanks and 19 anti-tank guns while losing half of their panzers. *LAH* also claimed capturing 250 POWs. The 18th TC was hard hit but not as hard as the 29th TC. Both corps were in a precarious position as 2nd TC on 29th TC's left flank was unable to move due to *SSDR*'s advance eastward. It was typical of Soviet tank crews to stay with their tank when immobilized and fire off the remainder of the shells before evacuating. A stationary tank was easy prey for panzers, with their superior optics and guns; many tanks were destroyed in this fashion. dgk191+. dgk184m. vzz333*. zro209.

The 2nd SS PzC continued its advance toward Prokhorovka but its line was becoming disorganized due to the many Soviet attacks from all directions. The *LAH* had been hit hard in theTeterevino-OSF-Hill 252.2 area today while at the same time *SSTK* had forced the Psel River and struggled with clearing Hill 226.6 and beyond. It was the important high ground needed to attack the fortified village of Kliuchi. The initial attack failed and the 52nd GRD retained the ground. This failure also strained the German line as the main assault of *LAH* was trying to advance on the road to Prokhorovka. The *SSTK* had to take Hill 226.6 and several other hills to the north to reduce the shell fire on *LAH* as it drove on Prokhorovka. dgk164. dgk124m. dgk222m. gnk312m.

The *LAH*, driving up the road to Prokhorovka, broke into the village but was quickly counter-attacked by the newly arrived 29th TC, which was being pressured by both *LAH* and *SSDR* south and west of the railroad. The 25th TB and then the 18th TC joined the fight, which escalated into a pitch battle. The 18th TC with T34 tanks in the 181st TB and 170th TB, penetrated to Oktiabrski by 1430 hrs and was greeted by a few Tigers, which inflicted heavy casualties on the two TBs as they were pushed back into Prokhorovka. By the evening the *LAH* had been pushed out of the rail junction. wdk160. vzz332+.

With the 18th TC and 29th TC fighting hard in the Prokhorovka, Vasilevka and Kalinin areas, Vatutin brought elements of the 10th TC closer to the front in case it was needed by the other two tank corps. The 18th TC also brought up the 110th TB, which was waiting in reserve, to protect its right flank against the possibility of *SSTK* in the northern reaches of their bridgehead turning south to attack 181st TC in the rear or flank, while it attempted another attack in the Vasilevka area. At 1300 hrs, the 110th TB moved up next to the 32nd MRB east of Prelestnoe and was waiting for the order to attack toward Valsilevka, Gresnoe and Mikhailovka. At the same time, the 170th TB and 181st TB were ordered to resume attacking toward Andreevka. The 110th TB, along with the 36th GTR, had not gone far in moving to their designated positions when cruising *Luftwaffe* spotted them and attacked. By late afternoon it is estimated the 18th TC and 29th TC, after falling back, had a combined total of roughly 200 tanks. Most of them were concentrated near Petrovka, northwest of the Oktiabrski State Farm. They would try to block *SSTK*'s panzers from crossing the Psel River and supporting *LAH* near Prokhorovka. The 9th GAD and 42nd GRD would be in support in this Petrovka sector. fkk169. vzz347. vzz1m.

By 1100 hrs, elements of the 25th GTB (2nd GTC) were falling back toward an area southeast of Storozhevoe to regroup. The 29th TC and its attachments, along with the 136th GRR of 42nd GRD which was following, had also stalled a half mile east of the Oktiabrski State Farm and were fighting a static defense. In less than three hours of fighting the 29th TC had lost 60% of its tanks. The 32nd TB had lost 40 tanks, 25th GTB lost 48 tanks and the 31st TB lost 30 tanks. They suffered casualties of nearly 2,000 men as well. vzz334+. vzz11m. dgk192.

Elements of the 18th TC attempting a second run and driving from the Andreevka area, ambushed the defenders on the critical Hill 241.6. Reacting quickly, the *LAH* sent reinforcements to the hill but the Soviet tanks inflicted heavy casualties on the artillery batteries before being repulsed. Tankers from the 170th TB and the 181st TB had split off and were attacking toward Ivanovski Vyselok and had almost reached *Das Reich*, south of the Komsomolets State Farm. At the same time at the Komsomolets State Farm, elements of the 29th TC and 32nd MRB were trapped and fighting for survival. The two Soviet forces could not link up and were fighting separately. With the situation stabilizing for *LAH* in their center, Hausser motivated their right flank at the Komsomolets State Farm to greater heights. Within the hour, the *LAH* was able to retake lost ground and re-established control of the Komsomolets State Farm. vzz351. zrl236+.

Just before noon after regrouping, the 26th TB (2nd TC) attacked *Deutschland* Regiment near Storozhevoe before it could mount a counter-attack. After repulsing two Soviet attacks, *Deutschland* was able to initiate their own assault toward Storozhevoe in the early afternoon. By 1400 hrs, Major Blissinger's battalion reached the southern edge of the town and began to fight its way in. After an hour of fighting in the town, the Germans controlled the majority and were now clearing the last resistance in the town. *Das Reich* and *LAH* were now linked together more securely. gnk340.

At around midday, at the railroad line east of Iasiana Poliana, *Das Reich* repulsed an attack with Soviet infantry while its left flank resumed its attack on Storozhevoe against strong resistance. Elements of the *LAH*, stationed at KSF two miles southwest of Prokhorovka, held against repeated tank attacks. At the same time to the west, *SSTK* elements repulsed repeated attacks aimed at destroying their bridgehead over the Psel at

Bogorodiskoye. The bulk of *SSTK* was still fighting to secure and enlarge their bridgehead north of the Psel and for control of the hill to the north of Hill 226.6, just west of Polezhaev. fkk169. dgk184m. gnk313m.

By 1200 hrs, the German command knew their assault on Prokhorovka would fail and decided to support the main assault force driving toward Oboyan. A shock group from *SSTK* with almost 70 panzers was dispatched along the northern bank of the Psel River in the Krasnyi Oktiabr-Kozlovka region; their task to envelop the flanks of 6th GA and 1st TA and then to reach the region north of Prokhorovka in the rear of 5th GTA. With the help of air support, this German assault group had penetrated the line defended by the weakened 52nd GRD. By 1300 hrs they had crested Hill 226.6 and the line to the west of the hill but just to the north, the 95th GRD was waiting and attacked the moment German panzers crested the hill. At 1800 hrs, when the Germans could not break through, 95th GRD stopped its assault and pulled back to regroup. At 2000 hrs after an air raid, the Germans attacked the 95th GRD again and this time succeeded in pushing them back and capturing Polezhaev, but were unable to advance further along this axis because the remains of 18th TC had been ordered to stop the Germans at the river. After losing the hill, the 52nd GRD countered to try to recapture but fell back when it could not wrestle the hill from the Germans. The 52nd GRD was able to halt *SSTK* from advancing past the hill to the west. dgk194. dgk222m. dgr225. vzz1m. gnk312m.

In the area north of Kochetovka and Krasnyi Oktiabr, west and southwest of Prokhorovka, the 32nd GRC of 5th GA pushed the Germans back, reaching the high ground between Kochetovka and Krasnyi Oktiabr. The Soviet advance was brought to a stop with a German counter-attack. The 294th GRD reached the outskirts of Kochetovka and tried to enter the village, fighting hand-to-hand but another German counter-attack pushed the 294th out. The 95th GRD and 52nd GRD, with the attached 181st TB and 170th TB, had to shift direction to assist the 294th GRD in stopping the German counter-attack and preventing encirclement of some of their troops. fkk329. gnk193m. gnk227m.

Von Manstein ordered the *LAH* and *SSTK* to clear the Petrovka area. *SSTK* was to then move from Beregovoe to Kartschevka and force a crossing of the Psel River, advancing into the prime corridor next to the Petrovka area where *LAH* was stationed. This was the preliminary part of a master plan to encircle and destroy the Soviet forces between 2nd SS PzC and 3rd PzC to the east. *LAH* was down to 50 panzers while *Das Reich*, after repairing some, had 83 panzers and *SSTK* had 54. Assault guns were 20, 24 and 20 respectively. Hausser estimated his corps lost between 60 and 70 panzers that day, but some would be recovered and repaired. See Map 16. dgk209. dgk212. dgk213m. vzz11m

While *Deutschland* was fighting for control of Storozhevoe, *Der Führer* Regiment was defending the line between Iasnaia Poliana to Kalinin against a mostly tank and infantry attack by 2nd GTC. Around noon the 4th GTB, with at least 50 tanks, found the boundary between *Deutschland* and *Der Führer* and attacked, trying to exploit the weak sector. It quickly penetrated the line and drove toward Iasnaia Poliana. As the tanks approached the village, German MGs opened on the Soviet infantry riding on the the tanks, killing many. The tanks kept coming. gnk340. gnk313m.

By early afternoon and without much pause to regroup, the *SSTK* had launched from Hill 226.6 with the rest of its panzers toward Hill 236.7. This hill was an excellent observation site and both sides wanted it. A fierce battle ensued as the panzers drove toward the crest. The Germans were repulsed, with 16 panzers burning along with motorcycles and infantry laying on the battleground. *SSTK* had to fall back. While this hill was being contested, the 11th MRB had regrouped and was attacking Hill 226.6, trying to regain control of it. vzz388+. gnk312m.

At noon, elements of *LAH* infiltrated the woods north of the village and captured Stalinskoe State Farm, while other elements of *Das Reich* driving from Ivanovski Vyselok tried to complete the circle from the south and southeast of Storozhevoe. With *LAH* successful in repulsing the attacks at the Oktiabrski State Farm and the *SSTK* finally gaining traction and pushing the Soviets back in the bend of the river, Hausser, trying to achieve the initiative, launched attacks against the flanks of 18th TC, while at the same time motivating *Das Reich* to complete taking Storozhevoe and reach Pravorot further east. Shortly after 1200 hrs, the 29th TC's 25th TB passed through the line and attacked *Das Reich* but failed and had to fall back. The 169th TB, 58th MRB and the 55th GTR fought alongside the 25th TB. Quickly following, *Das Reich* entered the western outskirts of the village of Storozhevoe by 1400 hrs and had secured it by dark. By gaining control of Storozhevoe, *Das Reich* had closed the gap between itself and *LAH*. Storozhevoe was south of Hill 252.2 and the Oktiabrski State Farm. vzz372++. gnk366. dgk191. dgk184m. vzz349. zow163+.

With Model having trouble to the north, including the new Soviet offensive in the Orel sector, von Manstein visited Hoth to get a first hand account of the situation in the south. He wanted to see if Hoth could continue the offensive, keeping Vatutin busy in order to prevent forces from moving north against Model, as well as to destroy the Soviet divisions of 69th Army fighting between the Donets Rivers. vzz440.

At 1300 hrs, more than three hours after 2nd GTC had launched, the 183rd RD of 48th RC launched its attack toward the Kalinin-Ozerovski-Hill 232.0 line which was defended by *Das Reich*. If the 183rd had launched with the tankers, results may have been dramatically different. As the 183rd RD approached the line in front of Kalinin, the Germans fired a rocket barrage that inflicted heavy casualties. After a brief fight, the 183rd RD fell back. At the same time Tikhomirov's 93rd GRD attacked the 167th ID's line between Teterevino South and Soshenkov. The battle extended into the night and the 93rd GRD had broken through the line northeast of Smorodino but had to fall back after it ran low of ammo. At Soshenkov elements of the 93rd GRD crossed the Donets and established a small bridgehead on the east side. The 627th Pioneer Battalion was called up and were able to block the Soviets from heading west toward Petrovka. Soshenkov was south of Rozhdestvenka. vzz367+. vzz574. vzz7m.

By 1300 hrs the 95th GRD and 42nd GRD in the Krasnyi Oktiabr-Kozlovka area, southwest of Hill 226.2, had fought all morning and then did their best to disengage and withdraw. The *SSTK* continued in a northeasterly direction toward the Veselyi-Polezhaev line to destroy the elements of Zhadov's 5th GA that were regrouping. In response to this break in the line, Zhadov ordered the 24th GTB of the 5th GMC to the Voroshilov State Farm where it would cooperate with the 18th TC and the infantry of 5th GA to stop the enemy arriving at Polezhaev. The *SSTK* had not only repulsed the attacks by 5th GA and the tank corps of 5th GTA, it had gained some ground and was within shelling distance of the important Kartashevka-Prokhorovka road. With these gains that threatened the penetration of the third defense belt, Zhadov and Rotmistrov cobbled together forces along this road where they finally stopped *SSTK*. dgk194. vzz460. dgk222m. vzz1m. wdk160. gnk313m.

In the early afternoon, 2nd GTC and 2nd TC had broken into the woods west of Belenikhino and the farms east of the village of Kalinin near the Lipovyi Donets, taking the railway embankment from the Germans in fierce combat. Later in the afternoon, *LAH* and *Das Reich* launched a counter-attack in the Kalinin-Belenikhino-Storozhovoe area that lasted far into the night. dg134. je110. dgk222m. dlu63m. dgr221m.

The 167th ID had been busy that day defending itself and the southern flank of *Der Führer* against repeated attacks. Near Smorodino a Soviet attack penetrated the line but the gap was closed with a German counter that inflicted heavy casualties. German artillery made the difference that day and was a prime factor for the Germans holding their lines. vzz368. vzz7m.

At the same time that Hill 236.7 was being attacked by *SSTK*, another combat group of *SSTK* was fighting for Hill 235.5 to the southeast, not far from the Voroshilov State Farm. This hill was also defended by the 95th GRD and artillery. Keeping both these hills just south of the Prokhorovka-Kartashevka road was critical for the Soviets if they were to keep *SSTK* from joining up with *LAH*. The *SSTK* made its deepest penetration toward the important road at 1730 hrs and from that point on was fighting a static battle as the Soviets brought up more artillery, which finally stopped the Germans. The 95th GRD suffered heavy casualties as well as the artillery personnel in stopping the Germans. The 24th GTB of 5th GMC was ordered to the Voroshilov State Farm arriving at 2030 hrs, while the 10th GMB was sent to the Ostrenki area in case *SSTK* resumed its advance. The 51st GTR was sent to Malaia Psinka at 2310 hrs to block *SSTK* from advancing but by then the *SSTK* had stopped for the night. The *SSTK* lost 46 tanks that day including ten Tigers. Many of these panzer losses were caused by artillery and rockets that had been brought up on the day and were firing from across the Psel River. All Tigers were recovered and were repaired and returned to the field starting 7/14. In the 5th GA sector, Zhadov kept his forces on alert all night in case of a night attack. Hill 236.7 straddled the important Kartashevka-Prokhorovka road that stayed in Soviet hands. vzz391++. vzz396++. vzz401. vzz1m.

At 1300 hrs, when the two leading tank corps of the 5th GTA were beginning to make inroads into the Oktiabrski State Farm, a friendly fire incident happened that set the Soviets gravely back. A small group from the 2nd VA, looking for targets to hit, mistakenly believed they were striking German troops defending the farm but in reality it was Soviet troops who had fought their way into the farm. The planes, using their 30mm MGs and the PTAB bombs, wreaked havoc and destruction on their tanks and men. vzz329.

At 1300 hrs after fighting for hours, two brigades of 29th TC along with 28th GAR captured Hill 252.2, pushing the German panzers back 2 miles and capturing Sovkhoz Okatybrski as well. However, at the same time the German forces penetrated 33rd GRC in the Krasniy Oktiabr-Ochetovka area, forcing the two Soviet divisions north of the Veselyi-Polezhaev line. Once there the Germans threatened the right flank of the 5th TR but the 24th GTB was called up to strengthen the right flank. As part of the coordinated attack by 5th GTA, the 29th TC attacked again with its right flank along the railroad toward Komsomolets State Farm. Though capturing Hill 252.2, the 32nd TB and 31st TB could not drive further due to increased resistance from dug-in panzers and assistance from the *Luftwaffe*. Before the hill was recaptured, the 1st Battalion of 32nd TB was encircled and destroyed south of Hill 252.2. dgr224+. dgk191. vzz8m. jp198. vzz1m.

With the likelihood of Prokhorovka not falling today, General Hausser was ordered to form an armored combat group from *SSTK's* 3rd PzR and with the support of the *Luftwaffe* shift direction to the west and attack the flanks of 6th GA and 1st TA in an attempt to take pressure off the 48th PzC's bid to cross the Psel. This left the Tigers, a few Mark IVs and most of the grenadiers of the division to tackle the defenses north of Hill 226.6 along the Veselyi-Polezhaev line to themselves. This is the general area where the 200 tanks of 18th TC and 29th TC would fall back to when their overall offensive was canceled but local attacks would continue past dark. *SSTK* would not advance beyond this point. dgk193++. dgk222m. vzz1m. gnk312m. dgk231m. snk433m.

Lipichev's 53rd MRB, in second echelon, came up to support 31st TB when it stalled in front of KSF and together they penetrated *LAH*'s line southwest of Oktiabrski and into the Komsomolets State Farm. Exploiting this success, the remains of 31st TB and the 53rd MRB advanced and by 1730 hrs had entered into the Komsomolets State Farm. After the center of the farm, Soviet forces pulled back from its salient to Hill 252.2 to stabilize the line next to 25th TB and to avoid encirclement during the night. The Soviets had penetrated the *LAH* artillery line on Hill 241.6 and had not known it, but with a little further advance they could have encircled *LAH*'s HQ which was also stationed on Hill 241.6; a golden opportunity lost due to the fog of war. dgk190+. vzz8m. vzz333*. gnk332.

At 1300 hrs with all the fierce fighting happening at Oktiabrski State Farm and Hill 252.2, the 170th TB plus the infantry of the 9th GAD and 42nd GRD finally infiltrated the front line at the farm, forcing 1st PzGR of *LAH* to fall back about a half mile to the south from the Oktiabrski State Farm. With the heavy artillery support from Hill 241.6, the Soviets still had a hard time in taking the rest of the farm but with the Germans losing some ground, it made it easier for the 181st TB to move southwest along the river toward the villages that they were supposed to clear. By this time the lead units of the 181st TB had captured Mikhailovka and these reinforcements along with the 36th GTR would support the second attack on Andreevka and Valsievka. At 1400 hrs, with his brigade stalled in front of Andreevka, Bakharov called the 32nd MRB to the line to help break the stubborn defense. dgk191. vzz347+.

By 1300 hrs the first of the 150 tanks of 5th GTA that broke down on the way to the battle zone arrived at Prokhorovka. It would take a week for all of them to arrive. Without these additions, the 18th TC, 29th TC and 2nd GTC in first echelon, Rotmistrov had about 450 tanks attacking that morning. With 5th GMC and 2nd TC in second echelon or reserve, another 300 tanks would be at Rotmistrov's disposal. wdk159.

After being pushed out of Storozhevoe by 1400 hrs, the Soviet remnants of the 25th GTB, the 285th RR of 183rd RD and a battalion of 58th MRB continued to defend a line east and southeast of Storozhevoe. At 1505 hrs, two battalions and a dozen panzers from *Das Reich* (*Deutschland*) split off and headed from the woods north of Ivanovski Vyselok toward the northeast. At the same time, after stabilizing KSF, two battalions and 14 panzers of *LAH* attacked the 285th RR and quickly forced them to fall back toward Pravorot. With these two successful actions, Storozhevoe was just about encircled. Vatutin was also worried that if Storozhevoe and Pravorot fell then *Das Reich* could turn south and link up with Kempf, encircling 48th RC of 69th Army. To prevent that from happening, Rotmistrov ordered the remains of 5th GTA to resume the attack regardless of the condition of the individual corps. The 169th TB would act as a screen while the 26th TB and the 58th MRB would attack from Ivanovka along the rail line toward Hill 234.9 (east of Belenikhino), Belenikhino and Teterevino. The advance failed but it did slow the Germans' advance. vzz375++. vzz574. vzz365. vzz369.

Elements of Maj General Tikhomirov's 93rd GRD created a bridgehead on the east bank of the Donets, heading for Petrovka, but the 627th Pioneer Battalion of 167th ID blocked their way and inflicted heavy casualties on the 93rd GRD. vzz368.

At 1400 hrs Savchenko's 4th GMRB, driving west next to 4th GTB, reached the Sobachevski-Ozerovski line but was immediately halted by heavy artillery fire. vzz363.

Around 1330 hrs after leaving Hill 226.6, elements of the *SSTK* made it to the western bank of the Psel north of Polezhaev and tried to force a crossing into the rear of the assembling 18th TC. After an hour of bitter fighting, the 18th TC repulsed *SSTK* from forming a bridgehead on the eastern bank. At 1530 hrs, 30 additional panzers left Hill 226.6 and advanced in the direction of Polezhaev but were repulsed by the 153rd GRR and artillery. Moving away into the ravine west of the village, the German column resumed moving north toward Hill 236.7. The hill, defended by elements of the 95th GRD, was attacked but again the Germans were repulsed and had to fall back by way of the ravine. This was a critical tactical victory for the 95th GRD; the hill was a valuable OP in the Soviet third defensive belt and if it had been lost, it would have been a major coup for the Germans. After regrouping, the *SSTK* tried to capture Polezhaev again and by 2000 hrs had captured the town. Despite the hour, the troops dug in to defend against possible ambushes during the night. The next day the 95th GRD was withdrawn from the line to regroup and the 31st TB and 32nd TB would be reinforced with the 53rd MRB and elements of 9th GAD. vzz390. gnk312m. dgk194+.

After taking Hill 226.6 just north of the Psel River from 155th GRR and 11th MRB, *SSTK* continued to drive in a northeasterly direction and by dusk, the division, with the help of air support, had been able to capture Polezhaev while the Tigers had moved on to try to secure the Beregovoe-Kartaschevka road by dusk. This success against 5th GA alarmed Rotmistrov and since his only armor remaining was in reserve, he called on Karpov's 24th GTB of 5th GMC to move to the vicinity of the Voroshilov State Farm and nearby Hill 228.3 to support the 5th GA and block *SSTK*'s advance by attacking the German northern flank. In addition, the 10th GMB was deployed just north of the Kartashevka road to either defend the road or to assist 24th GTB in attacking *SSTK*'s panzers. Rotmistrov also sent the 6th GAD to assist 24th GTB. When the rest of the division was unable to join the Tigers at the critical road, the Tigers were called back. vzz383. mhz343+. fkk169. lck369. gnk372. gnk312m. gnk365m. vzz11m. kuz195.

At 1400 hrs, the 5th GTA finally pushed the *SSTK* westward enabling the Soviets to liberate Vasilevka after a fierce battle that saw the Germans suffer heavy casualties. jp199.

Despite the cloud cover, the Soviet AF made 893 sorties compared to the *Luftwaffe*'s 654. The *Luftwaffe*, despite the lower count, still dominated the air in the south. lck356.

From southeast of Kalinin, Soviet tanks, believed to be 2nd GTC, broke through the line and headed for Luchki but were stopped by heavy tank fire from *Das Reich*. Eight Soviet tanks were destroyed. Until 1500 hrs, 2nd GTC tried to reach Luchki when the Germans countered, stopping the advance. The Germans then tried to penetrate to the rear and roll up the tank corps' right flank. At 2000 hrs, Burdeiny ordered a stop to the offensive and to go defensive. Hausser had received reports earlier in the day that a tank concentration was forming to their east and he ordered *Das Reich* to stop its advance and go defensive. This order probably saved many Germans while inflicting heavy casualties on Burdeiny. The 2nd GTC lost 54 of its 94 tanks. One reason for Burdeiny's failure against *Das Reich* was due to the lack of coordination with 183rd RD and 6th GMRB. vzz365++.

While *LAH* was overcoming the offensive by the 18th TC and 29th TC, *Das Reich* had pushed aside the right flank of the 2nd GTC as well as elements of 25th TB and had managed to fight its way to Storozhevoe, where it was currently fighting street by street to expel the 169th TB and elements of the 58th MRB from the village. By the afternoon, the only area of concern for Hausser was the repeated attacks by 18th TC on *SSTK* at the boundary line with *LAH*. By 1430 hrs, *SSTK* was fighting on the outskirts of Andreevka against the 36th GTR which was supplied with Churchill tanks. The division would enter the village within the hour and start securing it street by street. At the same time, the village of Vasilevka was being secured and defended against a counter-attack by elements of 18th TC. Elements of the 18th TC had diverted from Andreevka along the nearby ravine and was currently fighting for the important Hill 241.6 with its central location. Elements of *SSTK* tried to follow but were stopped by heavy artillery fire. There was give and take for most of the day. One side would make some gains in one sector but give it back when the other side regrouped or received reinforcements. This exchange of ground was often repeated; the villages south of the Psel, the OSF, KSF and Storozhevoe were prime examples of this savage back and forth. vzz349++.

Elements of the 28th GAR of 9th GAD of 33rd GRC was following behind 29th TC. While the tankers were stalled in combat, the infantry continued to move and by 1400 hrs had passed the southwest edge of the Stalinskoe State Farm and had reached the northeast edge of the woods to the west of Storozhevoe. By 1700 hrs, the regiment had reached the southern edge of the woods and was heading for Ivanovski Vyselok when it was attacked. After a brief skirmish, the 28th GAR had to fall back into the woods. Also included in 33rd GRC was the 52nd GRD and the 95th GRD. These two divisions, along with the 11th MRB of 10th TC, were defending the belt north of the Psel River that included Hill 226.6 against the advance of *SSTK*. After crossing the river, *SSTK* after realizing that the Soviets were striving to reach Gresnoe, Malye Maiachki, Teterevino North and the Komsomolets State Farm, increased their artillery barrage, putting up a wall of steel against the penetrators. If successful then Pogorelovka and Iakovlevo would be next, but those objectives would never materialize for 5th GTA that day. vzz335++. vzz380+. vzz1m. gnk312m. vzz8m+.

After losing Oktiabrski State Farm and with Komsomolets State Farm being infiltrated, Hausser called up for air support. At around 1300 hrs, small groups of planes totaling 150 fighters/bombers, Me 110s and Ju 87s, showed up and for the next hour attacked Soviet formations, especially the 31st TB. Hill 254.5 on the northwest edge of the farm was of special interest to the pilots. Both Soviet infantry and tanks were pinned down and unable to advance. When the planes left, the Soviets pulled back. With the bulk of 18th TC and 29th TC squeezed into the area between the Psel River to the west and the Storozhevoe woods to the east, the *Luftwaffe* had plenty of targets to hit. vzz328++. vzz283.

Small groups of Soviet aircraft had made repeated attacks along the Prokhovoka road as well as the small airfield at Luchki North. Each time there was little German interference with the attacks. The Soviets dropped their loads and returned home to reload, but with the next run their luck ran out for the *Luftwaffe* were waiting for them. Within minutes, a half dozen planes were down and the remainder of the Soviet planes bugged out. It was a relatively strange day for the air war in the southern salient. The VVS had most of their assets on the two flanks which controlled the skies, while in 2nd PzC sector the *Luftwaffe* had control. This air support for the SS divisions was a major reason for their repulsing so many enemy tanks. The *Luftwaffe* reported losing 19 planes while downing 16 enemy planes. cbk81.

By 1400 hrs after fierce fighting, the 170th TB of 18th TC along with troops of 5th GA had nearly recaptured the Oktiabrski State Farm while the 181st TB of 18th TC was fighting in the Vasilevka-Andreevka area with its right flank, where it encountered strong resistance from *SSTK*. It was able to push back *SSTK* to Kozlovka and briefly recapture Vasilevka by 1800 hrs. The 18th TC tried to move further south but was stopped by heavy shelling coming from Gresnoe. By late in the day and to avoid being pocketed, the 18th TC had fallen back and was defending the Petrovka, Prelestnoe and Andreevka line. This would be one of the major tank battles of the day that would contribute to the legend, but it was not as large as the battle in the Hill 252.2 sector. dgk182+. dgk189. dgk184m. dgr224. gnk312m. gnk347. dgr222. dgr224. vzz1m. lck346. kuz195.

After realizing that the Soviet plan to entrap *SSTK* on the north side of the Psel had failed and that the Soviet attack was losing steam, Hausser ordered an attack to keep the Soviets on the defensive. Besides, Hausser had many objectives to accomplish on this day and he could not wait any longer to achieve them. At 1430 hrs, shelling increased and the 2nd SS PzC began their counter-attacks. The *SSTK* broke through the 52nd GRD, overran the 95th GRD's 284th GRR and emerged on the riverbank near Polezhaev. In the process *SSTK* encircled the 11th MRB, plus the leading Tigers were able to shell the column of 110th TB that was on the other side of the river and heading for Mikhailovka, destroying several tanks. The Germans resumed their attack toward Andreevka and Mikhailovka while another battalion headed for Vasilevka from Kozlovka. By 1400 hrs, *LAH* had also repulsed the 29th TC's attack on Hill 252.2 and elements of the 32nd TB, 53rd MRB at the Oktiabrski State Farm had been pocketed and were being reduced. The Soviets had not given up on the hill or the farm and it was not guaranteed the Germans would still hold them by the end of the day. The remnants of the 25th TB had been thrown back to their start positions. It was recognized by both sides that the 29th TC's advance had failed its main objective of getting behind the SS and pocketing it. vzz348+. vzz11m. ztc270.

At 1430 hrs, the 2nd GTC with 25 tanks and with the support of the 456th MRB, broke through the German defensive belt and reached the outskirts of Kalinin where it engaged the *Das Reich* garrison. The Germans countered and with the Soviets disorganized had to fall back. Von Manstein was quoted as saying this was the moment of climax where he would win or lose. He still had the 24th PzC and the 17th PzD in reserve and thought that he could still win in the south. jp199. hjj121m. vzz367. vzz441. dgr221m.

Das Reich was up against repeated attacks from all flanks; Kruger called for air support. Ju 88s and Ju 87s were vectored in against 2nd GTC's 4th GTB and 4th GMRB, which were closing in on Kalinin. After the air raid, the Soviets pulled back to regroup but resumed the attack on a smaller front. vzz331.

By 1500 hrs, a small group of tanks from the 4th GTB, advancing from Vinogradovka, reached the outskirts of Kalinin but were quickly destroyed by a superior force from *Der Führer* waiting for their arrival. Additional tanks from the 4th GTB arrived too late to save the lead units, but were then attacked by a passing squadron of planes, forcing the Soviet tanks back to the southeast of the village. At the same time that the attack on Kalinin was repulsed, *Deutschland* Regiment launched an attack on Storozhevoe and the nearby woods to finish the job that *LAH* and they had started this morning in clearing the important village. The village was secured by 1600 hrs. vzz364.

During a slow moment when the Soviet tanks had pulled back to regroup, *Das Reich* resumed its advance and was approaching Vinogradovka when 40 German planes struck the 4th GTB defending the village as well as the 4th GMRB, which was defending near Kalinin. All the while other elements of *Deutschland* of *Das Reich* continued to clear the ground around Storozhevoe. As the battle was moving toward Kalinin and with the help of 4th GMRB, the 4th GTB was able to repulse the initial attack on its flank. By 1800 hrs, with the support of 339th IR of 167th ID, the 2nd PzR of *Das Reich* attacked the exposed flank of 4th GMRB while the 4th GTB was falling back toward Belenikhino. The 4th GMRB stayed to screen the retreat and had to endure a panzer attack as well as a *Luftwaffe* strafing. To make the situation worse, the Red Air Force came by and accidently bombed the 4th GMRB as well. The brigade suffered almost 300 casualties before it could disengage and fall back. Just like *LAH*, *Das Reich* for the most part had started the day in a defensive position, but once the line was stabilized by early afternoon, it went on the attack in earnest. Though attacking throughout its entire sector, *Das Reich* concentrated its primary efforts at Storozhevoe and in the Vinogradovka sector. Without the aid of air support that day, *Das Reich* would have suffered much greater losses and would have fallen back in an attempt to close the several brief gaps that had appeared that would have been exploited by the Soviet tankers. vzz365+. zow163.

By the afternoon with the high casualties of the armored offensive, Rotmistrov's right flank was under severe pressure. The 18th TC was on the verge of collapse near Petrovka; Rotmistrov brought up 10th GMB of 5th GMC to the Ostrenki region and the 24th GTB was moved to Voroshilov State Farm area to ward off a German attempt to penetrate into the 5th GTA rear area, west of Prokhorovka. These Soviet reinforcements caused Hausser to go on the defensive. Voroshilov was an important road junction a little ways northwest of Prokhorovka. Ostrenki was four miles due north of Petrovka. Konytnoe was three miles due north of Petrovka. rc215. aaa125m. dgk184m. dgr226. vzz398. vzz11m.

By mid afternoon, another severe thunderstorm hit the *Das Reich* sector making movement over ground difficult. The 2nd TC and 2nd GTC, who had been battling with *Das Reich* since early morning, decided to fall back to the east of the railroad embankment. Late in the day after all the losses, Burdeiny who was disgusted that he lost 26th GTB when it was sent to Ryndinka to stop 6th PzD from joining up with *Das Reich*, pondered what the results would have been with this extra brigade against *Das Reich*. Burdeiny lost 44 tanks of the 26th GTB which he intended to use to open a gap between *Das Reich* and 167th ID and get behind *Das Reich* to destroy it along with his other brigades. However, by now he was no longer able to go on the offensive due to the losses and immediately set about preparing new defenses for the coming counter-attack of *Das Reich*. Soviet tanks, which had extra fuel tanks on the side, were often targeted by German gunners and planes. Soviet brigades lost many tanks on this day when these external fuel tanks were targeted and the fiery fuel mixture enveloped the engine compartment. gnk341+.

At 1600 hrs, another small group of panzers, around 20, left Hill 226.6 heading north for Hill 236.7, which was still defended by the 95th GRD. Soon after leaving the hill, the panzers entered a deep ravine in order to avoid contact with the 11th MRB or 52nd GRD which was in front of the hill. Reaching Hill 236.7, the panzers exited the ravine and started firing on the hill. vzz390. gnk312m. vzz1m.

Malov's 99th TB of 2nd TC, which had only 19 tanks left, was fighting for its survival after being encircled in the Vasilevka-Andreevka area. The 99th TB would wait for nightfall before trying to breakout to the east. The remaining 26th TB was regrouping at Grushki while the repair crews worked on their tanks. The 99th TB's HQ was at Krasnoe, east of Storozhevoe, and communications were not always in tact. vzz369.

In 25th TB and 2nd TC sector, *Das Reich* finally captured Storozhevoe by 1600 hrs, expelling the last resistance that had doggedly fought on for the last two days. At 1930 hrs Rotmistrov ordered Popov's 2nd TC to attack from Belenikhino toward Ivanovski Velselok and Komsomolets State Farm, into the right flank of *Das Reich*. Rotmistrov also ordered Bakharov's 18th TC to attack from the west and link up with Popov near KSF. The order at this late stage in the day was desperate considering the circumstances. The 18th TC tried to break out of Vasilevka but was unable and the attempted encirclement of *LAH* failed almost from the very beginning. At about this same time, the 1st PzGR was attacked from the east side by the infantry of 9th GAD and the support of the 25th TB. The tanks did not lead the charge but stayed behind and continuously fired along with artillery while the infantry advanced. The assault was repulsed. By the end of the day, the 18th TC lost 56% of its tanks and had only 65 machines still working. Post battle evaluations of Bakharov, the commander of 18th TC, were negative. It is claimed he had been slow to respond to battlefield conditions and made several errors in judgement; he would lose his command shortly, but would prove his ability and eventually would command the 9th TC later in the year. It has been suggested that if the Red AF had a more prominent role on this day, the number of tanks lost would' have been smaller. Another condition that had a negative influence of 5th GTA's attack was its starting position, which had been too far north where ravines played havoc with the tanks. Bakharov also believed his corps did not receive enough artillery support and that this was the real cause for his corps' casualties. vzz355. vzz358*+. gnk366. zrl237.

In the afternoon, the 36th GTR and the 1000th AAR was ordered up to the line to support the 170th TB, who were now fighting *SSTK*'s right flank and threatening to rupture their line and sever the boundary between *LAH* and *SSTK*. In addition to sending a Tiger company from near Hill 226.6 to assist, German batteries at Gresnoe shifted their shelling to this hot spot. This artillery battery stationed at Gresnoe hit the Soviet forces hard, forcing them back as well. During this engagement, Michael Wittmann and his Tiger company stood fast against many T34s roaring down on them. dgk188+. snk84. lck349. gnk312m. fzk311+.

While the *SSTK* grenadiers were fighting to keep Vasilevka, a panzer group had left Hill 226.6, traveling northeast, and was fighting with 95th GRD for control of Polezhaev, near the west bank of the Psel River. Just before midnight the Tigers reached the Kartashevka-Prokhorovka road and were now only three miles northwest of Prokhorovka. After dark the tanks disengaged from west of Vasilevka, and Bakharov began regrouping the 18th TC, making preparations to counter-attack along the southern bank of the river in the morning. Bakharov's 32nd MRB on the northern bank of the Psel River was still struggling with elements of the *SSTK*. The panzers were also short on fuel and ammo which forced the Germans to be cautious. During the hard fighting that day, *SSTK* lost the use of 45 panzers, including all ten Tigers. Many of these could be repaired if retrieval was possible. With this loss, *SSTK* had 56 working panzers. There were also 316 casualties including 69 dead. gnk348++. vzz1m.

Exploiting the brief, modest success of 18th TC when earlier a few of its tanks fought their way to the edge of KSF,, the 53rd MRB, an attachment to 5th GTA, advanced quickly and by 1730 hrs had entered the Komsomolets State Farm. A German counter proved too strong and the 53rd MRB had to fall back to Hill 252.2, which had been recently recaptured and was now defended by the 25th TB. As part of this coordinated offensive, the 2nd GTC was attacking from Vinogradovka and Belenikhino region in the direction of Kalinin by 1430 hrs, but before reaching its objective, was attacked by a tank column of *Das Reich* moving north, which would prevent the 2nd GTC from reaching Kalinin. With the 29th TC falling behind, exposing 2nd GTC's right flank, the corps commander decided it would be wise to fall back until the new line stabilized. The 2nd GTC had lost half its strength since the start of the campaign and was down to 100 tanks by the end of the day. dgr225. vzz8m. vzz333*. gnk313m.

Late in the afternoon, when the 53rd MRB lost its tank support and failed to take Hill 241.6, which was heavily defended by artillery with guns up to 155mm, it fell back north of Hill 252.2. Bakharov then ordered his 18th TC reserve, the 110th TB and 36th GTR to form a new line south of the 53rd MRB, 181st TB and 170th TB, allowing them to regroup. The new deployment for 110th TB was north of Vasilevka, where Vatutin expected the Germans to launch a renewed attack northward. The Germans did not wait until the following day, but launched late that afternoon. The *SSTK*, north of the Psel, attacked Bakharov's 32nd MRB, which was able to slow *SSTK*. While this new engagement was evolving, the 31st TB of 29th TC struck *LAH* between Oktiabrski State Farm and Storozhevoe for one more time, but it struck the *LAH*'s strongest sector and did not make any gains. The 170th TB joined in and attacked the *LAH* on its left flank. After regrouping, the 32nd TB later joined in and together the three brigades were able to push the *LAH* back in the Oktiabrski area, but at a terrific cost. It had been an extremely long day for the men of both sides and yet the fighting continued in certain key sectors. In the other sectors, the men were eating, cleaning their weapons and getting resupplied. dgk189+*+. dgk184m. vzz8m. gnk333++. gnk313m. vzz348. vzz1m.

At night, north of the Psel, Rotmistrov's forces attacked *SSTK*, but the attack was uncoordinated and failed. His tanks had to withdraw. *SSTK* had broken off battle with 24th GTB in late afternoon and had dug in for the night when they were attacked again. The 18th TC and 29th TC had also broken away early in order to regroup its 200 tanks in preparation for resuming the attack in the morning. Bakharov's 170th TB, 181st TB and 110th TB was ordered to attack Vasilevka in the morning. The 6th GAD was ordered out of reserve to join the attack in the morning. dgk212. dgk195+.

On the left flank of 167th ID, nearest to *Das Reich*, many penetrations were occurring, but every time a counter-attack closed the gap. The 167th ID, under Trierenberg, and *Das Reich* were the northern prong while 3rd PzC was the southern prong that were trying to encircle 69th Army's 48th RC. The *Das Reich* was trying to drive east from Storozhevoe toward Pravorot before heading south to capture Vinogradovka and Leski. The 167th ID, which was already south of *Das Reich*, was supposed to reach Leski and protect *Das Reich*'s flank and rear. The Soviets had attacked *Das Reich* since early morning and had prevented the Germans from reaching Pravorot but they had failed to destroy, or even push back, the enemy as ordered. Though the Soviets were being pushed back slowly, *Das Reich* would try again for Pravorot in the morning. vzz365. vzz474. dgk183m.

By 1700 hrs, Bulygin knew his 25th GTB's attack on *Das Reich* had failed and his scouts had informed him that German reinforcements were on the way. He ordered his tanks to disengage and fall back to the east. The German artillery followed the retreat and the 25th GTB had to fall back farther than it wanted to avoid the shelling. vzz365.

It was late afternoon just south of the Oktiabrski State Farm and the death and destruction of the largest tank battle of the campaign was basically over and the combatants had fallen back to lick their wounds. A lonely soldier was sitting in a shell hole, trying to reclaim his wits and stop shaking. It was still daytime but it was hard to tell from where he was sitting. Within his view he could see at least 50 maybe 60 spires of smoke and flames bellowing from destroyed tanks, darkening the sky above the field. Add the thousand or more explosions and the dirt thrown up into the air and you have shades of armageddon around you. The day had been hot and muggy and the pollution hung just a short ways off the ground. The soldier was giving thanks for still being alive but could not understand his luck; so many of his comrades had died that day. If he made it through the war, it would be an experience he would never forget no matter how long he lived. dsk111.

By 1800 hrs, the 18th TC had captured Vasilevka and reached Kozlovka but between Hill 217.9 and Hill 214.6, a distance of two miles, the Germans had dug in and were able to stop them. German artillery from Gresnoe was adding its support in stopping the tankers. The 18th TC along with the 36th GHTR and 32nd MRB set up defenses along the line Vasilevka-Mikhailovka-Prelestnoe to just outside of Petrovka. The 18th TC had been able to penetrate three miles behind the German line; it was the best performance of the day for 5th GTA. While the 5th GTA had made some early gains across the line the Germans figured out the Soviet intent and countered with heavy aerial and ground artillery which was able to push the Soviets back, except for this progress of the 18th TC. Elements of the 5th GMC was still available but Rotmistrov chose not to use them to support the 18th TC. After reaching Kozlovka, the 18th TC and 36th GTR fell back and stabilized the line closer to Vasilevka. vzz354+. vzz343.

In the late afternoon, the 169th TB with the other remains of the 2nd TC launched an attack from Ivanovka to the northwest toward Teterevino. The Soviet force was unable to reach Teterevino and had to stop and go defensive, despite destroying several panzers. vzz378. dgk213m.

The 24th GTB of 5th GMC, the 18th TC and the 5th GA attacked German defenses at Polezhaev while Mikhailov's 10th MB moved to Ostrenkov, six miles north of Prokhorovka, to block the German advance. The 6th GA next to 5th GA was to wait until the Germans were exhausted then counter-attack east of the Oboyan road, eastward to the Psel River. In the meantime, the *SSTK* dug in to its advanced positions and forced the 18th TC to divert part of its force to the Psel River's northern bank to assist the 11th MRB. For the day 5th GTA while diverting the German advance had not stopped it. Popov's 2nd TC and Burdeiny's 2nd GTC were now ineffective as a fighting unit, leaving the shaken 18th TC and 29th TC with a total of 200 tanks to resume the fight. The 18th TC had to contend with three deep ravines running through their sector, making their job of planning and executing that much tougher. dgk195. dgk205+. dgk212. vzz342. vzz1m.

After dark, recovery teams of both sides commenced bringing damaged tanks from the field to be repaired as quickly as possible. Other teams were out bringing in the wounded, the dead or looking for prisoners to interrogate. Later still, sapper teams went out in front of their line and planted additional mines for the next day's battle. vzz445++.

Much was expected from 2nd GTC, despite losing 26th GTB to Trufanov; it was the left pincer in the attack to isolate *Das Reich*, but not only did it fail that task, it was pushed back two miles from its starting position. It also lost 54 of its nearly 100 tanks that took part in the operation. Though having good artillery support, the corps had poor cooperation with the infantry of the 48th RC's 183rd RD and the 6th GMRB which was defending the sector and this was one of the reasons for the poor performance. vzz367.

At night, Hausser sent his division commanders orders for the next day. *Das Reich* was to go defensive and improve their line and be prepared to help 167th ID if the Soviets attacked them. *LAH* was ordered to stay in place and try to improve their boundary with *SSTK*, but to be prepared to assist *SSTK* if needed when they launched their attack to the east. *SSTK*, with the only offensive in the works, were to cross the Psel and squeeze the Soviets between themselves and *LAH*. The *Eicke* Regiment was to resume its advance along the southern bank of the Psel, clearing resistance while *SSTK*'s panzer group headed for Prokhorovka along the Kartashevka road. This was highly optimistic as the remnants of 5th GTA, around 200 tanks, were being concentrated around Petrovka, just south of the key road and near the Psel River. gnk364. gnk365m.

Late at night on the Prokhorovka battlefield, the noise, except for pouring rain, finally ceased. Counting the burning carcases one could see hundreds of tanks, field guns and trucks lying wrecked on the steppe; more than half of 5th GTA lay broken in the same fields but it could at least say it had halted the Germans. At Oboyan the Germans were stopped as well. For the next three days, the Germans made feeble attempts at Prokhorovka, but they all failed. On the northern boundary, Rokossovsky had also stopped the Germans and did so without using a lot of his reserves. je110+.

At night, von Manstein visited Hoth's HQ but the general was with Hausser at the time. Von Manstein ordered von Mellenthin to send the 167th ID across the Donets to help the 168th ID and 3rd PzC quicken their pace. Von Manstein wanted Hoth to do this days earlier but Hoth found ways to avoid doing it. Von Manstein also wanted *LAH* to stay in place until *SSTK* had crossed the Psel River at Petrovka and then together they would attack toward Prokhorovka. Petrovka, just on the outside western edge of the corridor, was four miles west of Prokhorovka. Much of the remains of 5th GTA's tanks were blocking the way of both German divisions and it would not be an easy advance since the Germans would be outmatched again. gnk364. gnk365m. kuz195.

Sch.G1 of 8th *Flieger* Division reported losing eleven aircraft caused by heavy flak while fighting over Prokhorovka. Six of those planes that were totaled were Hs 129s. In other sectors, the Germans reported knocking down 12 planes in dogfights. cbk81.

After dark it started raining, turning everything to mud and putting the finishing touches to von Manstein's hopes of encircling the 48th GRC between the rivers. lck370.

The heaviest tank battles of the day occurred in and around the Oktiabrski State Farm/Hill 252.2 area, the Valsilevka sector and the Storozhevoe/Vinogradovka sector and included the 300 panzers of 2nd SS PzC and collectively over 650 tanks of 18th TC, 29th TC and 2nd GTC, plus their attachments during the repeated waves of attacks. The claims of up to 2,000 tanks engaged at a single battlefield are exaggerations. At most, there were 1,100 tanks spread out on three separate fields within a six mile radius. The Germans, while having fewer panzers, did have one advantage; all panzers had radios while on the Soviet side only the COs had radios. The German crews knew only Soviet command tanks had radios, so they would search for antennas and target the tank for destruction. vzz319+.

After dark, Hoth ordered *SSTK* to continue its expansion of the Psel valley with the subsequent objective to assist *LAH* in taking Prokhorovka and Hill 252.4. By the end of the day, around 2230 hrs, *SSTK* artillery was firing on the important Prokhorovka-

Kartashchevka road but this lead force was nearly isolated and in real danger of being encircled if the defenders decided to attack. When *SSTK* approached this road, it represented the farthest point north 4th PzA achieved. Almost as soon as the lead panzers reached the key road Priess ordered them back to the bridgehead to avoid being isolated by the growing number of reinforcements coming into the sector. Priess was listening to the Soviet communications, hearing the orders to have new units move to the Polezhaev sector. vzz455. vzz460. kuz193. ztc270. ztc270m+. zow166.

By the end of the day *Das Reich*, having been on the defensive most of the day, had not made any impressive gains and did not come close in capturing Pravorot but they did inflict heavy casualties on the the Soviet tank brigades. General Kruger was encouraged that the following day would be better, especially if it was dry. gnk342.

It had been a costly day for both sides but especially for Rotmistrov, who estimated having 400 tanks destroyed or badly damaged. He still had the 24th GTB with about 100 tanks and the 10th GMB of 5th GMC to use in the morning. Vatutin also moved the 6th GAD of 5th GA up to the Kartashevka road to stop *SSTK* in the morning when they resumed their advance. German air reconnaissance noted the fresh reserves and informed Priess who dreaded the coming battle for his exhausted men. gnk350. gnk313m. rc215. bt89. gjz186. dgr222*. zec270. ztc270m.

Ribbentrop's company of tanks was a disruptive influence on the Soviet tankers near Hill 252.2 and gave the other panzers of *LAH* time to move up and confront the larger force on a more equal term. Between the fierce fighting for Hill 252.2 and the kill zone that was set up at the tank ditch near the hill, Rotmistrov's attack lost much of its momentum. By the end of the day, Hill 252.2 was still German. Ribbentrop destroyed 21 tanks and for this feat he was awarded the Knight's Cross on July 15th. gnk329. gnk333. fzk174++. fzk184. zrl235+.

By the end of the day, the 181st TB suffered heavy casualties from the pounding it received from the *SSTK* artillery in the early morning plus the damage caused by *LAH* Tigers, other panzers and tank destroyer teams for the rest of the day. Its brother, the 170th TB was only a little better. Late in the afternoon, the 170th TB was ordered to pull back from Hill 252.2, redeploy to the west with the 99th TB and resume the attack on Vasilevka. Most of the *SSTK* artillery had been stationed at Gresnoe all day and stopped this new attack as well. The Soviet tanks pulled back to Andreevka to avoid the barrage. When the Soviets pulled back *LAH* did not pursue and stayed behind their defenses to regroup. Gresnoe was southwest of Vasilevka by four miles. Lt Col Kazakov became the CO of 170th TB after Lt Col Tarasov died when his tank was destroyed by a shaped charge. gnk332. gnk335. gnk313m. pck81+. dgk188+.

The tank battle of Prokhorovka, the so-called largest tank battle in human history and a major part of the Battle of Kursk, was the pivotal battle in the southern salient. On the north bank of Psel, on Hausser's left flank, *SSTK* fought a series of savage close quarter tank and infantry engagements with the 31st TC and 33rd RC. In the center, the 18th TC and 29th TC attacked mostly *LAH* but also the *SSTK* force guarding the southern bank of the Psel. On 2nd SS PzC's right flank, the Soviet 2nd GTC slammed into *Das Reich* across the gap which Citadel's timetable had required to be closed by Kempf Corps, still some 12 miles from Prokhorovka, stalled by the forces which General Rotmistrov had sent south on Vatutin's orders. By dusk, the 2nd SS had to withdraw, incurring heavy losses. rc214+. bt89*.

When the scope of the Soviet counter-attack is considered and the meager results made compared to the expectations, credit must be given to Hausser and Hoth for their insight of the coming attack and the subsequent preparations made to cope with it. Recon reports from the *Luftwaffe*, spotting the many reinforcements coming from the east and north, helped in their evaluations. On the other hand, Vatutin claimed that even if his offensive did not achieve the planned goals, it did stopped the Germans' advance and at a cost that would prevent them from reaching Kursk. vzz440. vzz444+. vzz452+.

The 27th and 53rd Armies of Konev's Steppe Front along with the 4th GTC, which had 400 tanks, were redeployed to the Oboyan-Kursk area and would take part in the counter-offensive. The 27th Army, which was stationed at Elets, was originally ordered to Rokossovsky but Zhukov, who was now at Kursk, decided Vatutin needed it more and redirected Lt General Trofimenko's 27th to the southern salient, closer to Prokhorovka. Lt General Managarov's 53rd Army, which had been deployed defensively along the Kshen River, was sent to the Bunino-Nekhaevo sector along the Seim River north of Prokhorovka. vzz168. dgr96. dgr242m. dgk221. dgk241. gjz181. kcz167. nzk92. dgk79. dgk424.

During the night and into the next morning, SS troops continued to hammer at the Soviet infantry between Veselyi and Polezhaev, but at 1000 hrs on the 13th, the 5th GTA counter-attacked, stopping the Germans from moving past those villages. je112. vzz1m.

Stalin was not satisfied that the SS had been stopped today, and was livid with Vatutin and Rotmistrov for losing so many tanks and shattering the once mighty 5th GTA. The generals were lucky to keep their jobs, thanks in part to the intervention of Vasilevsky and Zhukov.

It is estimated that up to 400 tanks of 5th GTA were either damaged or destroyed over the next couple days. Late at night after hearing of the tremendous losses Rotmistrov's 5th GTA suffered today, Stalin ordered Zhukov to Kursk to oversee the regrouping of their forces and to make sure the German offensive was really finished. In his usual manner, Stalin bypassed Vatutin and talked directly to Rotmistrov and Vasilevsky before calling Zhukov. Rotmistrov was supposed to have encircled 2nd SS PzC that day and eliminated it, but that clearly did not happen. If Rotmistrov had really been as successful as Soviet doctrine claimed, there would have been no need to get Zhukov up in the middle of the night to run to Kursk. He arrived at Kursk the next afternoon. Vasilevsky, before heading south to a less critical sector, stuck up for Rotmistrov which probably saved him from execution for this debacle. Khrushchev was in trouble as well. mhz347+. vzz457. gjz188. kcz169. wwf140+.

By the end of the day, the SS Corps made some small but important gains after 5th GTA's offensive exhausted itself. Moving from Hill 226.6 north of the Psel, the *SSTK* advanced past Polezhaev to just south of the Kartashevka-Prokhorovka road where it was halted by reserves moving into the area and heavy artillery. The *LAH* advanced to the east and northeast along the road to Prokhorovka and though it got close to the village, it was prevented from entering the village by some fanatic resistance by the local garrison. The *Das Reich* made it past Storozhevoe but was stopped soon afterwards as well as being halted along the route south to Vinogradovka and Zhlomostnoe. A little further south, Belenikhino was threatened but never captured. By nightfall, the German salient had increased in two small areas. The first was a sliver that grew from *SSTK*'s bridgehead north and the second was on the northeastern flank carved out by *LAH* and *Das Reich*. The Germans had done well that day to keep from imploding from the massive counter-offensive and still make gains, but the fact is that the German forces had suffered relatively large losses, had not captured much of the enemy and its forces were totally exhausted. While the Soviet forces were also exhausted, they had more men and tanks and would be able to hold the Germans basically along the lines of that night until Steppe Front moved in and their major counter-offensive started. zow166.

Maj General Wisch of *LAH* reported his losses for the day to Corps HQ. Men killed amounted to 48 with five missing, while wounded were 321 in number. Hausser was also informed that 192 tanks, 3 planes and 19 guns were destroyed. General Hausser visited Wisch on the battlefield and verified the number of destroyed tanks. zrl238.

The less than stellar results of the Soviet counter-offensive can be attributed to the lack of planning and coordination of the 5th GTA and 5th GA. The 42nd GRD and 9th GAD provided poor support to the tanks. It is estimated that 5th GTA had casualties of over 5,500 men including 1,500 killed. The 29th TC suffered the worst tank destruction of all the corps, losing 103 tanks while the 18th TC lost 84 tanks. The 5th GMC lost almost half of its 207 tanks. The 2nd GTC lost 54 tanks and the 2nd TC lost 22 tanks. In all, the 5th GTA lost about 400 tanks that day and more than half of them were irrecoverable. The above corps still had 366 working tanks including those that broke down on the road to Prokhorovka and had been repaired but had not arrived on site. The losses the 5th GTA suffered that day were greater than the 1st TA and 6th GA lost in the first week of fighting but to be fair to Rotmistrov he had no time to prepare or plan the offensive or the authority to rebuke Vatutin's desperate plan. The 2nd SS PzC lost about 850 men and 70 panzers at best, but some of those panzers could be recovered. Casualties estimates run as high as 163 panzers by other sources. cbk81. vzz344. vzz440+. gnk363.

West of the Donets, the Germans gained little and while Kempf gained some ground, the gains were meaningless with Prokhorovka still in Soviet hands. The Soviets launched their counter-offensive north of Orel that day which added a whole new dimension to the Germans' problems. wdk163. vzz438. wwf142++. zzz101m.

With the great losses in tanks and men suffered that day, both sides during the nighttime hours tried to regroup their men and recover as many tanks off the battlefield as possible. Many tanks were recovered in the Andreevka, Hill 241.6, Oktiabrski State Farm and Stalinskoe State Farm areas. It was a busy night after a horrendous day of fighting. vzz445+.

The 4th PzA had been able to break into the first defensive belt on the first full day of the assault, but it took three days to break through the second defensive belt to reach the third defensive. In the coming days, the 2nd SS PzC would break into the third defensive belt but would be unable to break through it and head for the Seim River, halfway to Kursk. Even if the 2nd SS PzC had been able to capture Prokhorovka that day and had begun traveling north along the corridor to Kursk, it would have had to take on several rested armies as well as two other tank corps that were only days away if they were needed. wdk170+.

The Soviets were quick to point out that even if Prokhorovka fell, there were still numerous strongpoints leading to Kursk, with the Seim River fortifications the most heavily defended to clear before reaching Kursk. It's a feat that could not be accomplished by the Germans after losing so many panzers and men. dgr223.

With the Soviets beginning their major counter-offensive toward Orel that day, it was critical for the Germans to take Prokhorovka and race toward Kursk, which would force Rokossovsky to redeploy and potentially ease the pressure off Model. pck83. zzz101m.

The Soviets prepared for their major counter-offensive toward Belgorod and Kharkov. Konev's Steppe Front began to deploy. The 47th Army, the 3rd GMC and 1st MC began to move out for the Novyi Oskol-Velikomikhailovka area. vzz502.

After the tank battle for Prokhorovka was finished, the Germans counted over 400 destroyed or damaged tanks on the battle field. The tanks that could be immediately recovered by the enemy were quickly destroyed so that Vatutin's recovery teams could not repair them. The legend that claims *LAH* lost hundreds of tanks that day is patently false. The next morning, *LAH* and *Das Reich* reported to Hausser that their combined total of working panzers had actually increased from the day before and were now up to 190 panzers, thanks to the repair crews working throughout the night. Hoth was skeptical of the numbers of claimed destroyed tanks so he visited the battlefield near Prokhorovka. In an area of only 500 yards by 1,000 yards but when the general counted 90 smoldering enemy tanks, he became a believer. He then traveled south to the front lines in front of *Der Führer* sector. Looking east toward Belenikhino and using a scope he witnessed the same destruction but on a smaller scale and congratulated Lt Col Stadler for a job well done. The job of stopping a superior tank force with practically no panzers impressed FM von Manstein and over the next few days he awarded 250 Iron Crosses to the division. To the south of *Der Führer*, the 2nd PzR also performed well against 2nd GTC while assisting 167th ID in stopping the attacking tankers. One of those Iron Crosses went to Capt Mennel who had, in just three days, 24 victories in the Teterevino, Luchki, Kalinin and Iasnaia Poliana area. sgf350. kuz193. fzk173. fzk313+. pck82. zow163. zow167. zow170.

For such an important day on the ground, it was relatively quiet in the air regarding dogfights. The 2nd VA and 17th VA ran 893 sorties against the 8th *Flieger* Corps' 654. This was the first time the Soviets flew more sorties than the Germans in the south. With the attrition of the past week, the *Luftwaffe* spent most of its assets in 2nd SS PzC sector. The other two corps received only occasional support. cbk78+. nzk77.

Soviet offensive further south of Kharkov, near Taganrog and Stalino seriously threatened the German line so Hitler refused to release 24th PzC to von Manstein.

After dark east of Kalinin, *Das Reich* was rebuilding their defenses against a renewed tank attack that was expected by next morning. zow164.

By the end of the day, Vatutin believed the Germans had been broken, though fighting would continue. Soviet forces had stopped the German advance, claiming to have captured 70,000 men and destroying 2,952 tanks and 5,000 trucks in the Battle of Kursk. The Soviets claimed losing 2,800 tanks and 24,000 POWs just on the southern salient. The figures quoted by the Soviets are high for the German side but were presented for the purposes of Soviet propaganda. FM Kluge signaled the OKH that 9th Army was exhausted, had suffered 30,000 casualties and could not fight anymore. It was estimated that Col General Hoth had casualties of 29,000. After the campaign, Col General Kirovsheev estimated the three fronts that were directly involved with the defensive phase of Operation Citadel suffered casualties of nearly 178,000 men. The Voronezh Front had the most casualties, followed by Steppe Front which nearly had as many casualties. The Central Front had less than half as many casualties as either of the other two fronts. je112. fzk316. dgk274+.

By the end of the day, the *LAH* held the following line: Starting at the southeast quadrant it shared defending Storozhevoe then, moving north and west, the line ran through the Storozhevoe woods (1st PzGR), Hill 252.2, the edge of Oktiabrski State Farm westward to Andreevka (2nd PzGR and 1st PzR) zrl238.

The fighting within the confines of Operation Citadel would continue for a few more days but the line at the end of the day would not change much during that period. The fighting for the next few days would be anticlimactic. After studying Operation Citadel closely, it can be argued that General Guderian was correct, that Citadel never should have launched. Even after draining the rest of entire Eastern Front to a minimum, von Manstein and Kluge still did not have enough men or panzers to get the job done. With the extreme resistance Hoth (and Model) met the first few days, it should have been realized Operation Citadel was a mistake, for even if Oboyan or Prokhorovka and Olkhovatka to the north were captured, the continued resistance on the extended flanks would have spelled 4th PzA's and 9th Army's doom in the long run. That flank protection could never be maintained and 2nd Army on the "nose" of the salient was not strong enough to influence the outcome. They could have launched Citadel in early May as von Manstein, Kempf and others wanted to prevent the Soviets having time to fortify the salient as they did, but an early start would have presented problems for the Germans as well.

Though the 5th GTA and 5th GA received most of the attention in this day's literature, the fact is that the 1st TA and 6th GA fighting the 48th PzC deserved recognition for their contribution in the repeated attacks and their resilience in stopping the 48th PzC from advancing past the Psel River. dsk111. wwf108.

During the predawn hours, the 5th GTC moved into launch position along the Novoselovka-Kuznetsova Woods line and would attack eastward along the Shepelevka-Lukhanino axis. At the same time the 10th TC was moving along the Novenkoe area and preparing to attack toward the Berezovka-Syrtsevo line. The 204th RD moved up into 10th TC's old position alongside 309th RD, 3rd MC and 31st TC to prevent a German breakthrough in case the offensive failed. dgr219+.

General Knobelsdorff was preparing his corps for the attack when the Soviets preempted him. *GD*, six miles south of Vosnessenovka on the far left flank, was to drive north to the village, pushing the Soviets back as they advanced and then shift to the northeast in order to concentrate the Soviet forces and encircle them with the help of 11th PzD. While *GD* was marching north and before engaging the enemy, the artillery of the 5th GTC started shelling the German column. After a while, the 10th TC drove from hiding places and attacked. gnk351.

At 0620 hrs from west of the line Kruglik-Hill 254.5-Hill 247.0, Soviet tankers attacked the side of the *GD* column which was heading north from Hill 247.0. The Germans were overwhelmed and had to retreat southward. At the same time, other elements of *GD*, which were heading for Kalinovka, were attacked from the front. They quickly found themselves in trouble, in fierce hand-to-hand combat that inflicted heavy casualties on both sides and forced the Germans to withdraw, but eventually they turned the situation and regained lost ground. The deepest penetration was by the 183rd TB of 10th TC, which got close enough to Verkhopenie to feel the shelling that the German garrison was firing. With the many attacks on *GD* that day, their offensive plans were canceled and the division began to regroup and prepare to resume the attack next morning. The 3rd PzD had a tough day as well, for the Soviets countered and retook the villages of Gertsovka and Berezovka. If the Soviets could penetrate the 3rd PzD's line, they could race to the east and encircle the 3rd PzD and perhaps even *GD* and the 11th PzD. The 3rd PzD regrouped and would launch an attack the next day through Kubaossovski Gorge toward Hill 243.0 and help defend and mitigate the threat from the concentration of Soviet forces at Kalinovka. hsz129. fkk271++. vzz431+. vzz176. gnk163m. gnk312m. fmz221m.

In the early morning, the 10th TC, now temporarily commanded by Maj General

Alekseev until Burkov's wounds healed, with 100 tanks and supported by the 219th RD, launched an attack from west of Novenkoe toward Berezovka and Syrtsevo. Before reaching Berezovka, the 10th TC engaged elements of *GD* and 3rd PzD at Tolstoe woods. The Soviet tankers were able to push the Germans aside, forcing them to fall back to the east to the Pena River. To the south of 10th TC, the 5th GTC supported by the 184th RD launched an attack from near Melovoe toward Shepelovka and Lukhanino. Lukhanino was in the general area where Vatutin wanted his forces to converge after penetrating the front line and separating the German divisions. On the east of the Oboyan road, the 6th GA's 23rd RC, 3rd MC and 31st TC were ordered to defend the road on the first German assault but then counter-attack after the German advance sputtered out. dgk205. vzz431. dgk211m. dgr172m. hjj121m. dgk222m. dgr209m.

Along with the panzer group of *GD* moving north along the Berezovka-Kruglik road, the Fusiler Regiment of *GD* was also moving north, leaving behind the Pz Abt 3 to defend its old position. The Soviet tanks waited long enough for the Fusiliers to travel north away from sight and sound and then attacked the panzer battalion. It quickly penetrated the line and forced Pz Abt 3 back toward Kalinovka. gnk351. gnk312m.

After the 332nd ID moved up to 3rd PzD's old position, the 394th PzGR of 3rd PzD started advancing northward along the Berezovka-Kruglik road, when they were hit by a vicious barrage that included rockets. Without waiting for the shelling to stop, Soviet tanks from the 5th GTC attacked the defensive positions of 332nd ID. The men of the 332nd started to panic and began to fall back. Seeing what was happening, Schaefer put up a line of blockers to stop the retreat before it turned into a rout. Knobelsdorff ordered elements of the panzer regiment of *GD* deployed at Berezovka to head toward the 332nd ID and stem the Soviet attack. The panzers arrived and restored order, helping the infantry restore the line that stretched from Tolstoe Woods to the Pena River. A rout was avoided but it was not an auspicious beginning. At the same time next door, the Pz Abt 3, which had also just moved up into the old *GD* positions, was attacked by the 204th RD and the 86th TB and were forced back in the direction of Kalinovka, which was being held by *GD* Grenadiers. Penetrating the gap that had developed with the retreating Pz Abt 3, the Soviet tanks drove toward and attacked Kalinovka. The Germans on the west side of town were forced back from their front trenches. Major Bethke, leading the counter-attack, forced the Soviets back and reoccupied their outer defenses. gnk351.

Vatutin wanted to crush the 48th PzC for once and for all. He already had his current deployments attack 332nd ID, Pz Abt 3 of 3rd PzD and the Fusiliers of *GD* along the Berezovka-Kruglik road, but now he also brought the 10th TC into the sector as well. The 183rd TB reached Tolstoe Woods while the 186th TB drove past the Tolstoe woods and attacked Hill 258.5. The two brigades had immediate success and were threatening to cut 48th PzC's supply lines. Hastily, the 394th PzGR of 3rd PzD and the Pz Abt 327 were redeployed west of Verkhopenie to block the Soviet progress. The Soviet tankers were moving fast, not having any resistance in front of them, and soon reached and attacked the 394th PzGR. The Germans surprised the tankers by launching their own attack which successfully halted the Soviet attack and forced the T34s backwards. A disaster had been averted but the 3rd PzD had been too weak to stand on its own since the start of the campaign and the division was getting weaker by the day. Knowing the Soviets had brought in reinforcements to the Tolstoe Woods area, Knobelsdorff ordered Lt General Hoernlein's *GD* to redeploy the panzer group to the Tolstoe woods-Hill 258.5 area to help

Westhoven's 3rd PzD clear the area. The *GD* would not advance any further north than that day's positions. gnk352.

At dawn in the 11th PzD sector, the Soviets attacked the division's right flank. It was a diversionary attack that was hoped would pull more German troops from the main attack sector, the center of the 11th PzD's line. At a little past 0800 hrs, the main attack was launched on both sides of the Oboyan road. There was no artillery preparation. During the predawn hours, a Soviet ambush squad had infiltrated the German lines and hid in a nearby woods. When the main attack was launched, this small commando team attacked the grenadiers from behind and started a panic. The Germans quickly pulled back, leaving a gap in the front line. Mickl sent a group of panzers to the gap to close it and to stabilize the situation. The counter-attack was successful and the line was stabilized, but the 11th PzD had lost contact with *SSTK* at Kochetovka to the northeast. gnk353.

At 0800 hrs after an artillery preparation, Katukov's 1st TA along with other attachments attacked the 332nd ID defending near Chapaev; fighting lasted for most of the day when Kravchenko's tanks reached Rakovo but could not force the 332nd back over the Pena River. Novenkoe, west of Verkhopene, was first cleared and then the assault force of Col Andrushchenko's 183rd TB moved on to Verkhopene. Afterwards they severed the Berezovka-Kruglik road. At the same time the 178th TB and 186th TB was pushing the 3rd PzD back into Berezovka, despite fierce counter-attacks. By the end of the day, 3rd PzD had only 40 working panzers and were no longer much help to the troubled *GD*. dgk206. dgr172m. dgk222m. dgr209m. vzz2m. gnk312m.

The 48th PzC was beginning its attack across the Psel River when 22nd GRC supported by elements of the 10th TC attacked. Knobelsdorff immediately had to halt his advance on the river to defend himself against the ambush. The 48th PzC eventually repulsed the attack but by then it was too late to cross the river as Operation Citadel was being canceled. The lead units of *GD* were east and southeast of Kalinovka and were waiting for 3rd PzD to relieve them in order to move to Hill 260.8 for the intended attack shortly after daybreak. The first units of 3rd PzD arrived at Hill 247.0, south of Kruglik but would not relieve *GD* along the Oboyan road starting with the Berezovka-Verkhopenie sector until next morning. That night a sudden barrage killed Lt Bremer of *GD* before his scheduled relief. The 332nd ID took over 3rd PzD's former position north of the Pena River, forward of Rakovo. In turn, the 255th ID moved into the Mikhailovka area. A PzR was dug in at Kalinovka and was waiting for 3rd PzD to come to clear the potential threat of being pocketed that was facing them. On the way, the lead elements of 3rd PzD were struck at Hill 247.0, south of Kruglik, but by morning were able to free the trapped PzR. The newly-arrived 9th RD and 13th GRD also participated in the attack west of Prokhorovka against the right flank of 11th PzD. Near Krasnopolye, the 219th RD tried to push back the west flank of 48th PzC. Both of these attacks failed, causing many casualties for the attackers. dgk204+. dgk222m. dgr209m. fkk273. gnk312m. dgk159. cbk79.

It had been a difficult day for 48th PzC; the Soviets launched many attacks along their entire line, penetrating it in numerous places and forcing the Germans back to save themselves. If General Hoth had any aspiraions to reach Oboyan, those dreams were now shattered. It was time to retrench and go on the defensive.

Vatutin continued to put pressure on the enemy by sending reserves to the front. While the 18th TC and 29th TC struck at 2nd SS PzC southwest of Prokhorovka, and the newly arrived 5th GMC began a counter-attack against the new bridgehead near Ryndinka, the newly arrived 219th RD (40th Army) attacked the 48th PzC on its western flank near Krasnopolye. snk84. wdk120. zzz101m. vzz11m.

At 0900 hrs, the 5th GTC with elements of the 184th RD launched a counter offensive that smashed through German lines and approached Chapaev near the southern bend of the Pena River by 1300 hrs. Elements of the 332nd ID fought hard but had to fall back from a superior force. By 1700 hrs, Soviet tankers reached the northern outskirts of Rakovo on the northern bank of the Pena but were halted by fierce rocket fire coming from the town. At the same time further north, the 10th TC which had 120 tanks drove into *GD*, pushing it back and occupying Tolstoe Woods. The Germans regrouped and were able to stop the 10th TC in the woods. The 3rd MC, 31st TC and 309th RD of 40th Army also launched an offensive but failed to gain any ground, being stopped by heavy artillery fire. By the end of the day, the 5th GTC would have only 14 working tanks. The *GD* driving west of Verkhopenie were ambushed and fought off the 3rd MC and 67th GRD. In the afternoon, the 6th GA continued to attack west of the bulge with the 204th RD and 309th RD. By evening the panzer divisions of the 48th PzC were on the defensive from the combined attacks of the 6th GA and 1st TA on both sides of the Oboyan road. However, the left flank of 309th RD was counter-attacked by the 11th PzD, stopping their advance. West of *GD*, the 3rd PzD holding the west flank of 48th PzC, was hit by the uncoordinated efforts of elements of 10th TC, the 204th RD and 309th RD of the 23rd GRC southwest of Kalinovka. Just west of the Oboyan road and north of Verkhopenie, the 3rd MC and the 31st TC launched an attack on the 3rd PzD at 0830 hrs in the direction of Novoselovka. The 3rd PzD was halted but it did well not to lose ground against this double attack. For the next two days the 1st TA continued its offensive but did not gain any ground. On 7/15, the 1st TA went defensive and handed its sector over to 5th GA and 6th GA. On 7/16 1st TA went into second echelon. wdk160+. hjj121m. vzz434. dgr209m. gnk313m. dgr220. dgr92m. vzz430*. vzz2m. dgk424.

As part of the major offensive that Vatutin instituted, the 71st GRD, on the west flank south of the 5th GTC and 10th TC, launched an attack in the Korovino-Krasnyi Pochinock area. Afterwards all three units would drive on Rakovo, Berezovka before ending up at Iakovlevo. Just as with 5th GTA, the 1st TA/6th GA were to strike on multiple axes and meet in the Iakovlevo area. Elements of 23rd GRC, the 3rd MC and the 31st TC rolled along the road toward the south from the Kalinovka area. The 255th ID, 332nd ID, the 3RD PzD, 11th PzD, and *GD* offered stubborn resistance. The Soviets made over a mile's advance before the Germans regrouped and were able to halt them along the line by nightfall. fkk328+.

On the far western flank, the 52nd IC was defending its full 12 mile front against repeated attacks. Lt General Schaefer's 332nd ID at Chapaev was being pushed back, but the attacks against Zavidovka and the woods west of Korovino were being repulsed. At Mikhailovka and Krasnyi Pochinok, the Soviets had entered the villages but were thrown out with German counters. Lt General Poppe's 255th ID, defending southwest of Bubny, repulsed all attacks. The 57th ID was quiet all day. The cloudy sky and frequent rain storms reduced air activity for both sides. fkk170.

At 1000 hrs, a squadron of IL-2s attacked German artillery positions in the Sukho-Soloino-Pokrovka-Ozerovski area, which was as much as ten miles behind the front line. German fighters attacked but the Soviet escorts did a good job of keeping the bombers safe. By this point, with the attrition the Soviet fighters experienced there were just enough fighters to be used as escorts. There were no longer Soviet fighters flying independently, looking for targets of opportunity. cbk81.

At 1000 hrs, additional elements of the 5th GTC launched their attack on Chapaev. They had only one regiment from the 184th RD to support them. The 22nd GTB was on the right while the 21st GTB was on the left. The advance went slowly as the *Luftwaffe* made many attacks, plus the ground was littered with mines and the Soviet sappers had to clear a corridor. By 1400 hrs the 21st GTB slowed near Chapaev but the 184th RD was catching up to the tanks. With the help of the infantry, Chapaev fell, inflicting heavy losses on the battalion of 332nd ID defending the town. A small contingent of 184th RD stayed at Chapaev while the rest moved toward Rakovo. After three hours of hard fighting the Soviets got to within a mile of Rakovo but were halted by a fierce artillery barrage. Rakovo was on the north bank of the Pena River. vzz430. gnk312m. vzz2m.

While the *GD* slowly advanced along the west side of the Oboyan road, 3rd PzD continued defending the Berezovka-Verkhopene sector. The 332nd ID moved in to the vacated area that was filled by 3rd PzD, along the north side of the Pena River north of Rakovo. The 255th ID was stretching its lines northward to Mikhailovka. While this arrangement strengthened 48th PzC's northern side, its southern side when facing westward was as weak as ever. The 10th TC, with 100 tanks remaining and supported by Kotelnikov's 219th RD, had regrouped during the night and advanced that morning on the outskirts of Novenkoe and then to Berezovka and Syrtsevo. At the same time to the south, the 5th GTC with 70 tanks and 184th RD advanced toward Shepelovka and Lukhanimo. The shattered 6th TC with 50 tanks was following the infantry. Vatutin's new offensive in the west was now in full swing. dgk205. dgr172m. hjj121m. dgk222m. dgr209m.

Southwest of the Psel River, the 97th GRD of 33rd GRC of 5th GA, repulsed an attack by 11th PzD and then launched its own attack at the boundary line between the 11th PzD and *SSTK*. Without tank support, the 97th GRD was stopped after making modest gains. The *SSTK*, seeing there were no tanks in the Soviet attack, continued to attack northward against the adjacent 95th GRD. The 31st TC with its 70 tanks, was available but was never called up to assist the 97th GRD or the 95th GRD. Though it was a small measure of risk to send the 31st TC forward, it was a mistake not to allow the 31st TC to also attack the boundary line, for it was very weak and vulnerable. vzz435.

Smaller Soviet attacks on German positions at Zavidovka on the southern banks of the Pena and in the woods west of Korovino were repulsed, but the attack on elements of the 332nd ID near Chapaev caused heavy casualties and the garrison had to pull back. It tried to regroup and requested reinforcements to retake the lost ground. Other elements of 332nd ID were able to hold Hill 237.6 and Berezovka. The villages of Mikhailovka and Krasnyi Pochinok were recaptured when the Germans counter-attacked. The 255th ID defending Bubny successfully repulsed several attacks. The 57th ID saw no fighting along their front. *GD* maintained a hold of Hill 243.0 not far from Verkhopenie. The weather was cloudy with scattered rains but the roads remained manageable. See Map 23. vzz439.

On 5th GA's right flank, the 32nd GRC's 13th GRD and 66th GRD was able to keep 11th PzD of 48th PzC gains to a mile in the Kochetovka-Hill 174.0-Hill 227.6-Bobryshevo area. Nearby, the 97th GRD of 33rd GRC was able to limit the infantry to two miles, stopping them along the Malaia Psinka-Hill 246.4 line. vzz399+. nzk96.

About midday, the 3rd PzD, trying to advance along the Oboyan road, was attacked and its line penetrated. The panzers, which had come off the line and fallen back to resupply, had to make an emergency run back to Hill 258.5 near Tolstoe to prevent 3rd PzD's left flank from being rolled up. Hill 258.5 was retaken but the panzers waited there for the infantry to arrive before moving on to the woods near Tolstoe. In this engagement a number of US tanks were destroyed as well large caches of US rations captured. hjj122. hjj123m.

On the high ground 2.5 miles west of Verkhopenie, the 11th PzD held off repeated attacks while 3rd PzD was trying to plug the gap that the Soviets had opened west of Verkhopenie. Elements of *GD* were trying to clear the woods west of Verkhopenie. fkk169.

By late morning on the western flank of 48th PzC, the coordinated attack by the 5th GTC and 10th TC against the 332nd ID and the 3rd PzD were making gains and disrupting the Germans, especially the 3rd PzD. The panzer's front line in the Verkhopenie-Berezovka area was being perforated and eventually its left flank shattered. The Soviets were able to reach *GD* and 11th PzD as well. Some units started falling back, trucks heading south on the Oboyan-Belgorod road creating a road jam, giving the Soviet Air Force easy targets to destroy. It was clear the offensive in 48th PzC sector was at an end. This is another example of a German flank not keeping up against too much resistance and supporting the SS. It is also another example of the German Army not having sufficient forces. lck366++.

The 1st Storm Aviation Division was brought up and attacked German lines at Verkh Olshanets, Shliakhovo and Melikhovo, while the 291st Storm Aviation Division attacked toward Verkhopenie, Syrtsevo, Dmitrievka, Novo-Cherkasskoe, Dubrova, Iakovlevo and Petrovka. Much of the Soviet air support was away from the immediate Prokhorovka axis. There were friendly fire incidents on both sides but more so on the Soviet side. With the air forces of both sides active that day, many tanks were destroyed or damaged from air attacks. vzz329+*. dgr155m. dgr155m. dgr173m.

On the left flank of 5th GTC, the 10th TC, which started with 100 tanks, also found the going slow. Even with the support of the 219th RD, the formation was halted at the Tolstoe woods by heavy artillery fire from 3rd PzD and *GD*. vzz430+.

After the bitter fighting the day before, in which 48th PzC inflicted heavy losses on 6th TC, 3rd MC and 90th GRD, Knobelsdorff ordered his corps to regroup that morning and prepare to resume the attack in the afternoon. *GD* was to assemble on the Oboyan road by 1500 hrs to resume its attack northward. The 11th PzD already assembled to the east of the road would join in the attack to cross the Psel River. The 3rd PzD was moving to fill the vacancy of *GD* south of Kruglik near Hill 247.0 while 52nd IC's 332nd ID and 255th ID was also being redeployed closer to 3rd PzD. So when the 6th GA and 1st TA launched their offensive, the 48th PzC was in the process of regrouping and ill-prepared to defend against a major attack. The Germans reacted quickly but still suffered heavy casualties. vzz429.

Over the last couple of nights, Vatutin had ordered mortar crews up to the line to participate in today's offensive. From Korovino in the south to Vasilevka in the north these mortar crews using the larger M20 rockets caused much death and destruction during this assault. The foot soldiers of the 332nd ID and the panzer crews of the SS were the recipients of this destruction, and dreaded the weapon. vzz396+. gnk312m.

The 48th PzC fought hard against stiff attacks, but had not lost much ground by the end of the day. Near Novenkoye, 10th TC made some gains but the 48th PzC countered and recaptured lost ground. snk84.

At 1600 hrs after spending nearly seven hours with Hausser, von Manstein arrived at Knobelsdorff's HQ. After learning the SS had gone defensive that morning, the field marshall found out his 48th PzC lost some ground and was forced on the defensive as well. While his boss was present, Knobelsdorff issued orders for the next day. No major offensives were listed; instead the corps would clean up the line and improve their defenses. It was important that 11th PzD link up with *SSTK* and have a continuous line. *GD* and the 3rd PzD would try to clear resistance from between the Kalinovka and Hill 258.5 areas. Once achieved, the combined combat group would fight its way south to the Pena River, cutting off the supply lines of the 5th GTC. With 5th GTC's lines of communication cut and with 332nd ID, 3rd PzD and the *GD* group closing, it was hoped the 5th GTC would be pocketed and destroyed. Hausser gave similar orders of cleaning up the line for the SS as well. These defensive measures were a clear indication of Hoth's surprise and concern over the day's developments. He had planned on taking Prokhorovka that day as well as expanding the Psel bridgehead, with the 48th PzC following in just a few days but instead the 4th PzA was stopped that day, suffering heavy casualties. *GD* ended the day with only 47 working panzers while 11th PzD had 34 panzers and 3rd PzD had 23 panzers. At this stage, the thought of continuing northward was impossible. It would take everything the 48th PzC had to survive further attacks. gnk353+ gnk363+. gnk365m. zow162.

South of the Pena River at Rakovo, the 52nd IC was attacked again by the 22nd GRC, supported by tanks. The 184th RD and 219th RD of 40th Army also joined the battle. At 1100 hrs, the 71st GRD resumed its attack at Korovino and Krasnyi Pochinok and drove into the south flank of 332nd ID. At 1700 hrs, the 219th RD and the 5th GTC drove into the north flank of 332nd ID, while the 90th GRD hit the center of 332nd ID at Rakovo. With four divisions attacking at once, the 332nd ID was having a hard time keeping its integrity. wdk161. gnk312m.

Late that afternoon, Maj General Mickl got permission to have his 11th PzD move back to a better defendable position and to shorten the line. The division was just beginning to move back when it was attacked on its right flank as the Soviet tanks and infantry were aiming to reach Hill 235.9, not far from Kochetovka. gnk353. vzz460.

In the early evening, the 3rd PzD moved up to forward positions to relieve *GD*, which would move to Hill 260.8 to launch toward the Psel River. To the right of *GD*, the 11th PzD were to try and clean and stabilize the line near Kochetovka. Later that night after *GD* pulled out, the Soviets attacked 3rd PzD, forcing them to fall back. The 48th PzC was in dire straights by this time and there was little chance for further advancement. wwf132. wwf135m.

Maj General von Mellenthin, the Chief of Staff for 48th PzC, wrote in his diary: "The situation on the left flank had deteriorated to such a degree that an attack northwards was no longer possible." cbk81. fmz226.

Von Manstein, not wanting to give up on reaching Kursk, ordered the 24th PzC, with almost 150 panzers, to move from Kharkov to Belgorod over night. With so many Soviet reserves, the addition of an under strength corps would have made little difference. The Germans had thinned out the entire line before Citadel started, so von Manstein could not ask the other army groups for assistance. The 2nd Army for example was holding a sector 37 miles wide while 4th PzA with twice as many men covered a similar distance. wdk163+. mhz297. vzz453. vzz455. aaa124m+.

Von Manstein had planned to deploy 24th PzC (Viking, 23rd PzD and 17th PzD) to Prokhorovka but when the Soviets launched a major offensive south of Kharkov across the Mius River and toward Izyum, those units had to be deployed there instead. The 48th PzC on the western flank was also stopped by now. Hoth wanted to stop 2nd SS PzC's advance, shift units and break through in the west. Kempf also lost the 7th PzD, which brought him to a stop as well. The offensive was just about finished. snk54. dgk423+.

By the end of the day, the 48th PzC lost ground on its western flank from the Chapaev-Rakovo area in the south to the Novenkoe-Kruglik area in the north.Looking back on the day, all the offensive plans Knobelsdorff had ordered for his corps were all pre-empted by Soviet attacks. The 48th PzC spent the whole day on the defensive. gnk353.

For a German victory at Prokhorovka to mean anything, the 48th PzC had to secure the road to Oboyan. That was the German plan; to attack Kursk from the axis of Oboyan and Prokhorovka. Vatutin would do everything possible to prevent that. Late in the afternoon and into the night, elements of 5th GTA and Popov's 2nd TC and others were repositioned to block the 48th PzC from expanding their bridgehead on the Psel River. dgk179*+.

In the predawn hours, instead of a direct daylight attack on Rzhavets, the 11th PzR of 6th PzD with a captured T34 in the lead of the column, drove into Rzhavets, capturing the important city after a sharp but brief fight with very little loss and capturing the critical bridge across the Donets. The 92nd GRD and 96th TB of 69th Army were guarding the town as well as the town of Aleksandrovka, six miles to the east which was also attacked. At daylight, not knowing the town had been captured, the *Luftwaffe* attacked Rzhavets, inflicting injuries on Hunersdorff and his staff. The 6th PzD, attacking toward Aleksandrovka, was being repulsed at every attempt to take the town. 19th PzD would be called in to help. Sending 19th PzD to assist 6th PzD slowed their forward progress to cross the Donets. The 114th PzGR was sent to the bridge to secure it. dgk198+++. dgk202. dgk222m. dlu63m. gnk383. nzk96. wwf152+. dlu102+.

Before dawn, elements of 6th PzD under Major Bake's command took the important town of Rzhavets, with its bridge over the Donets, by stealth. While Rzhavets was being captured, the bulk of 6th PzD was six miles further east attempting to take Aleksandrovka against elements of the 96th TB to remove resistance on their flank when Rzhavets was secured. The 6th PzD also captured Vypolzovka and the Ryndinka bridgehead by the 114th PzGR, but the hold was tenuous. The Soviets at Aleksandrovka pinned the 6th PzD, precluding a quick crossing of the Donets and joining up with *Das Reich* to take Prokhorovka. At the same time, the 19th PzD was trying to cross the Donets at Shcholokovo against Maj General Morozov's 81st GRD (7th GA). A number of brigades from 5th GMC and 2nd GTC were transferred from 5th GTA toward the Donets to curb these crossings. Artillery and 161 tanks were taken away from 5th GTA for their offensive with this action. The 89th GRD at Kurakovka were losing traction and being pushed back. rc207. dgk183m. pck83++. fkk281++. vzz236. vzz300*. vzz402++. vzz407+. vzz419+. lck363+. dgk201. dgk221+. dlu63m. fzk53+.

In the predawn hours, Vatutin and Rotmistrov learned the 6th PzD had taken the bridge at Rzhavets and the 19th PzD had also crossed the Donets River at Shcholokovo, south of Rzhavets, where the 81st RD was trying to stop the German advance. Rotmistrov would have to send part of his reserve, the 5th GMC, and the 53rd GTR to the river to help Trufanov stop the new threat. Vatutin, around 0500 hrs, also ordered a brigade from 2nd GTC to the Hill 243.8–Hill 242.7 sector, west of Podolkhi, to block the Germans' path on the west side of the Donets. This dilution to his main attack in the corridor against the SS was unnerving, for Rotmistrov knew he would need every asset possible to defeat the Germans. With these and other dilutions, the general kept the 10th GMB with its 51st

GTR and the 24th GTB as reserve. Already in the southeast sector was the 92nd GRD and the 96th TB, which would link up with the new reserves and join the battle. In addition to these ground forces, Vatutin increased his air strikes near the river. Vatutin, seeing how close Kempf was to Prokhorovka, also sent 200 Pak guns to 69th Army to slow 3rd PzC further. A battalion of 24 KV1s were the main power of the 53rd GTR and were also sent to face the Tigers of sPzAbt 503. gnk311. gnk314*+. gnk313m. vzz300. nzk96.

In the early hours of the morning after Bake captured Rzhavets, General Hunersdorff and some of his officers were standing just outside of 11th PzR's HQ when a He 111, mistakenly thinking the CP was Soviet, bombed it. Fifteen died and 49 were wounded. Hunersdorff was slightly wounded but stayed with his command. Colonel Oppeln-Bronikowski was more seriously wounded and had to give up his command to Major Bake, who also suffered minor wounds. Major von Bieberstein and 14 junior officers died. This friendly fire incident was a disaster to the division, but to make matters worse, two days later the General would be hit by a sniper and succumb to his wounds. These two events crippled the command structure of the 6th PzD, from which it never fully recovered. fzk55. dgk201. zzt91.

With the Germans near Rzhavets and with Gostishchevo in German hands, the Soviet defenders (48th RC), during the predawn hours, started falling back from the line between Sabynino and Shliakovo to avoid encirclement. At the same time, elements of the 375th RD in reserve were sent from the Zhimolostnoe sector to the Ryndinka area to block the 6th PzD or 19th PzD from reaching *Das Reich*. With 6th PzD taking Rzhavets before dawn and the 27th PzR of 19th PzD advancing along the Donets River toward Ryndinka, the 89th GRD and the leading elements of 375th RD were falling back to escape encirclement. When *Stavka* heard of the unauthorized retreat, they immediately stopped it as a counter-attack was planned after daybreak and this disorderly retreat was counter-productive. The 7th PzD was ordered to the Kazache area to support 6th PzD. vzz408+. erz209. vzz5m. dlu101+. dlu103m.

During predawn hours, 69th Army regrouped after its retreat to escape encirclement. The 93rd GRD held the Rozhdestvenka-Druzhnyi line and the 81st RD held the Northern Donets line from Krivtsevo to Ryndinka. The 89th GRD held the southern sector of the Donets from Kiselevo to Krivtsevo. The 92nd GRD with the 96th TB occupied a prepared defense belt along the front Vypolzovka-Novo-Alekseevskii Vyselok. The 107th RD and 305th RD held the line that included Razumnoe and Gremiache while the 94th GRD defended the Shliakhovtsevo-Sheino-Ushakovo line. dgk163. dgk405. dgr209m. vzz3m.

Before daybreak, Soviet recon forces east of the Donets reported their findings to HQ. In 69th Army sector, the Germans showed heightened activities at Rzhavets where they' were crossing the Donets and heading for Shipy and Shakhovo. Kazache had fallen and the surrounding area was currently being cleared. This information was then relayed to Rotmistrov and Vatutin. vzz443. pck83.

At 0500 hrs, after learning the startling coup de main at Rzhavets, Vatutin ordered Rotmistrov to send additional armor to the Ryndinka-Avdeevka-Bolshie Podiarugi area to block Kempf from reaching Prokhorovka. Col Grishchenko's 11th GMB and Col Borisenko's 12th GMB of 5th GMC and the 26th GTB of 2nd GTC was sent to bolster Trufanov's forces. These reinforcements would be under the command of General Trufanov. The 92nd GRD and one regiment of 375th RD was also sent to support the armor. They were in position by early afternoon. The 3rd PzC finally started making headway after five days of crawling its way toward Prokhorovka, but this new Soviet force sent early that morning would slow Kempf at the river. dgr104. dgr93m. vzz413+. cbk81.

At dawn, 6th PzD struck with the support of a few Tigers from the sPzAbt 503, in a coordinated effort with 19th PzD, along the eastern banks of the Northern Donets driving through Khokhlovo, Kiselevo and Sabynino. A rearguard at Sabynino was making it difficult for 19th PzD to capture it. Moving on after Sabynino, the lead elements of 19th PzD met up with 6th PzD south of Rzhavets around 1630 hrs. They were then ordered to Ryndinka. The advance had penetrated the line of 305th RD and bumped into the 107th RD, six miles to the rear. The 89th GRD also had to fall back to the south of Gostischchevo. The battered 81st RD tried to protect 89th's retreat by stopping the German advance at the Donets from Krivtsevo to Ryndinka. Other tank brigades moved up along the eastern bank of the Koren River to put additional pressure on the panzers. Trailing elements of Kempf Group were still 15 miles from Prokhorovka and the Raus Corps was unable to provide adequate screening. The pressure was getting worse with more reserves moving up. The rest of 69th Army fell back and regrouped after dark. Sabynino was on the east bank of the Donets, south of Krivtsovo. dgk163. vzz252+. vzz12m. vzz3m. erz209. dlu108.

After taking Rzhavets and the bridge across the Donets, Hunersdorff, the CO of 6th PzD, quickly sent the 114th PzGR across the river to Ryndinka to protect their northern flank and secure the bridge from sabotage. gnk315. fzk53+. dlu102+. pck86.

In an attempt to plug the gap made by Kempf's three panzer divisions, Kriuchenkin's 69th Army during predawn hours made the following deployments. The 89th GRD occupied positions between Kiselevo and Krivtsevo. The 81st GRD defended the western bank of the Donets from Krivtsevo to Ryndinka while the 92nd GRD with the 96th TB occupied the line between Vypolzovka and Novo Alekseevski Vyselok. The 107th RD and 305th RD occupied defenses along the line Razumnoe ravine-Gremuchi. The 94th GRD with the 31st AB defended the line Ploskoe-Novoselovka (east) and along the eastern bank of the Koren River. To the left, 7th GA's 15th GRD continued to defend along the line Sheino-Solovev State Farm. The 93rd GRD remained on the line between Rozhdestvenka-Druzhnyi. dgk163. dgr209m. vzz3m. dgr39m.

Shortly after 0500 hrs Maj General Burdeiny ordered Col Nesterov to redirect his 26th GTB southward toward the Avdeevka-Plota area to stop the 3rd PzC from crossing the Donets and reaching Prokhorovka. (The brigade would be sent further south once its in sector.) This greatly weakened the attack planned on *Das Reich's* southern flank near Belenikhino-Leski area. Burdeiny now had less than 100 operable tanks to begin his original planned assault. Plota was three miles northwest of Ryndinka. vzz362+. gnk354.

At dawn, the bridgehead at Rzhavets on the southern bank of the Donets was reinforced by a Panzer Grenadier Regiment. Preparations were being made to break out of that bridgehead and to bring the rest of the division across the river. Just as the German column was moving on the bridge, the Soviets blew the bridge. The Soviets also counter-attacked in a delaying action and the 6th PzD had to postpone their crossing until the attack was put down. The lead units of 6th PzD found a crossing six miles from Rzhavets; advancing units made the crossing but were struck by friendly fire from *Luftwaffe* aircraft. Rzhavets was 11 miles south of Prokhorovka. At dawn Rzhavets was still not completely secured, so 6th PzD had to take time to secure it before breaking out. At 1115 hrs, near Rzhavets, Vypolzovka was captured, pushing the Soviet defenders toward Avdeevka. This new bridgehead west of the Donets worried Vatutin. He had to divert a part of Rotmistrov's forces to the sector and away from the main assault. rc209. dlu63m. vzz412. dgr221m. fzk53+. pck86.

At daybreak, the 69th Army was still fine-tuning their positions and was now holding the line where the German spearhead was making the most progress. The 305th RD and 96th TB was holding the line: Vypolzovka, Aleksandrovka, Alekseevka and Ploski. The 92nd GRD was falling back during the night to this line and would support the 305th RD during the daylight hours. The 81st GRD was holding the line to the southwest between Ryndinka, Shcholokovo and Strelnikov. Even with all of the new deployments of the last few hours, Vatutin was still worried about a breakthrough. vzz410+.

During the previous day, 6th PzD captured Kazache, eight miles south of the Donets, and early this morning, with the support of Tigers from the sPzAbt 503, started moving toward Aleksandrovka to clear the division's rear while Bake moved on Rzhavets. The key crossing sites over the Northern Donets would be for the following day. At the same time, the 19th PzD advanced along the southern banks of the Donets heading toward Krivtsevo. They would link up with 6th PzD after dark at Rzhavets, south of the Donets. At Rzhavets, the tank battle near Prokhorovka could be heard. With German controlled T34s, the first defense belt of Rzhavets was penetrated. Soon the Soviets discovered their error and started shooting. By 0500 hrs, Vatutin had ordered elements of 5th GTA detached from the main attack to head south to block the northern and western perimeter of Rzhavets. Aleksandrovka was located on important high ground six miles east of Rzhavets. Major Bake led the stealth thrust of the 11th PzR into Rzhavets and took the credit for keeping his men cool when the lead tank stalled in front of the Soviet garrison guarding the road. The 6th PzD would have extreme trouble clearing Aleksandrovka and that difficulty was a clear signal of 3rd PzC's deteriorating condition, and the impact that would have on the rest of the campaign. dgk198++. dgk202*. dgk222m. dlu63m.

Elements of 6th PzD (3rd PzC) launched early this morning from the Kazache area toward Novo-Alekseevski Vyselo, capturing it later in the afternoon. Another attempt to take Aleksandrovka failed when 96th TB counter-attacked. dgr104. dgr93m.

The 26th GTB of 2nd GTC was traveling toward Plota as ordered when Trufanov, the area commander, called the brigade with a possible change of orders. If needed, the 26th GTB would head further south for Shakhovo to provide further fire power in case 81st GRD, defending nearby Shcholokovo, needed help. It turned out 81st GRD needed help and the 26th GTB was sent south to assist. Both areas were being attacked by 19th PzD. Once in the area, a defense was quickly built on Hill 228.4 that overlooked the important Shakhovo-Ryndinka road. At 0955 hrs, the 11th GMB arrived from Krasnoe in the Rzhavets, Vypolozovka, Shipy area. Within this area, Hill 135.0 was captured by the Germans and a battery of rocket launchers deployed there. The 11th GMB was ordered to recapture the hill. The 12th GMB along with the 92nd GRD were tasked to retake Kransnoe Znamia and Vypolzovka. At the same time, the 53rd GTR was to attack Hill 241.5, north of Aleksandrovka, before moving on to Aleksandrovka. A little later, the 3rd MB of 5th GMC arrived on the Shipy-Ryndinka road, where both the 19th PzD and *Das Reich* were heading toward. Trufanov now had 157 tanks in his make shift combat group. Kransnoe Znamia was east of the Donets, a mile north of Vypolzovka. See Map 21. vzz414+. vzz423. dgr104. dgr221m.

6th PzD was attempting to enlarge their bridgehead in the Ryndinka sector, while to the south the 19th PD was attempting to force the Donets near Shcholokovo. This penetration in this sector took on urgent proportions for 2nd GTC; Burdeiny sent his deputy commander, Col Poloskov, to 26th GTB which had moved into this area to fortify the line. Upon surveying the area, Poloskov ordered 26th GTB to set up defenses on Hill 228.4, situated along the important Shakhovo-Ryndinka road. vzz414.

General Kempf ordered Maj General von Horn of 198th ID to immediately relieve 7th PzD, the bulk of which was deployed in the Razumnoe valley. Lt General von Funck was ordered to drive most of his 7th PzD westward and link up with *Das Reich* to stabilize the line and clear any lingering resistance in the pocket that would be formed. General von Funck had been commander of 7th PzD since 1941 but, despite being a competent panzer commander, would be transferred to the 23rd IC later that year. In September 1944, Hitler would fire him; the reason was thought to be because of his aristocratic background. dlu104. zsm84+..

Southeast of Prokhorovka, elements of the 6th PzD and 7th PzD were still advancing northwards toward Ryndinka and Rzhavets, while the lead units were now only seven miles from the SS PzC attacking Prokhorovka. Rotmistrov ordered reserves down to block these trailing divisions from reaching the Plota line. Part of 7th PzD had to stay behind to support 11th IC being attacked and was faltering. je109. dlu63m. nzk96. dgr221m.

At 0745 hrs, Battle Group Horst attacked Sabynino in order to break through the last flank position of the Soviet defensive belt.In the Pena salient area, Soviet formations penetrated German lines forcing the 48th PzC to go on the defensive.

At 0900 hrs, the 49th RC of 7th GA (73rd GRD, 270th RD, 111th RD) attacked Kempf's right flank, elements of 7th PzD, east of Razumnoe at the Solovev State Farm and the Poliana State Farm. This was an attempt to slow down 3rd PzC from helping guard 2nd SS PzC's right flank. The Soviets only achieved partial success by reaching Hill 207.9 and Hill 191.2, less than a two mile gain. But it was good enough to disrupt Kempf from linking up with Hausser's 2nd SS PzC. By the end of the day Kempf was still nine miles from Prokhorovka. After losing Rzhavets this morning, the Soviets quickly rallied and were able to prevent 3rd PzC from gaining much ground today. dgk197. dgr104. dgr39m. dgr93m.

The 7th PzD had to provide security for the east flank of 3rd PzC because of lack of infantry for flank guards. On Kempf's southeast boundary, Corps Raus held a 13 mile front, holding back an increasing number of divisions assigned to the 49th RC of 7th GA, including four fresh divisions that arrived the previous day. The 73rd GRD, 270th RD and 111th RD of 49th RC with support of the 27th GTB attacked Corps Raus at 0900 hrs. Just like in 4th PzA's sector, there was not enough infantry to protect the flanks and drive forward. wdk162+.

In the 3rd PzC's sector, the 17th VA flew 134 sorties to help the 69th Army repulse an attack by the panzers. The low cloud cover restricted German bombers from taking to the air in the way they should have. cbk79.

Elements of the 19th PzD were sent to reinforce the bridgehead on the Donets at Rzhavets-Ryndinka, about twelve miles from Prokhorovka. The rest of 19th PzD was trying to cross the Donets near Shcholokovo with the intent of capturing the village. The 69th Army had just received the 35th GRC, which filled the gap between Prokhorovka and Rzhavets. As the day progressed east of the Donets, the 92nd GRD, 94th GRD and 305th GRD were able to contain trailing elements of 6th PzD from reaching Kazache. The 6th PzD, which had been badly mauled, needed help to break out but the 19th PzD and 7th PzD had been unable to give assistance until later. The 19th PzD, along with the 168th

ID, did make progress clearing the area along the Donets in the Khokhlovo, Kiselevo and Sabynino areas, but 7th PzD, further east, made few gains. The distance between Belgorod and Prokhorovka was about 30 miles. dgk162+. dgk165m. dlu63m. vzz413+. dgr155m. dgr173m. vzz12m.

Traveling from Krasnoe, the 11th GMB reached the Rzhavets, Vypolzovka, Shipy line by 1000 hrs and started preparations to attack 6th PzD at Ryndinka. Elements of the 375th RD would support the tankers in pushing the 6th PzD to the east bank of the Donets. Maj General Trufanov, who was in charge of forces in the Donets area, was at a big disadvantage as he was commanding a hodge-podge of units without the aid of a HQ staff and the situation was chaotic. It would be even more difficult to take Ryndinka, for the Germans had artillery on nearby Hill 135.0. The attackers concurrently attacked the hill along with the town. In mid afternoon, a large formation of *Luftwaffe* came swooping in and caused much havoc on the Soviets. At the same time the 92nd GRD and the 12th GMB would attack toward Vypolzovka, Avdeevka and the 53rd GTR would advance along the Hill 241.5-Aleksandrovka axis. The 12th GMB arrived in the Avdeevka area at daybreak on 7/12 and were then ambushed. While part of the 12th GMB engaged the ambush, the rest of the brigade attacked toward Avdeevka. Both sides suffered heavy casualties. vzz415++. vzz478.

In 7th GA sector and jumping off from Hill 202.9, Hill 209.6 and Gremiache, Maj General Terentev's 49th RC's 111th RD and 270th RD with the support of the 201st GTB, 27th GTB and the 73rd GRD, launched an attack in the direction of Krutoi Log, Razumnoe and Dalnie Peski. During the assembly before the attack, the Germans launched their own rocket attack that caused confusion and delayed the Soviet attack. The assault was disorganized and went off in piecemeal fashion. The Soviets gained a mile or two in places before heavy German artillery fire was able to halt their advance. Not wanting to give up these meager gains, the Soviets dug in and waited out the shelling. vzz437. dgr39m.

With the 6th PzD at Rzhavets and the bridge that crossed the Donets River, Kriuchenkin of 69th Army regrouped his forces for the expected battle at daybreak of the 13th. The new line would include 93rd GRD on the Rozhdestvenka-Druzhnyi line, southwest of Gostishchevo. The 89th GRD occupied the new line between Kiselevo and Krivtsevo while the 81st GRD defended the western bank of the Donets from Krivtsevo and Ryndinka. The 92nd GRD and 96th TB defended the line from Vypolzovka, north of Rzhavets, to Novo Alekseevski. The 107th RD and 305th RD occupied the line between Razumnoe to Gremiache. The 94th GRD and the 31st Anti-tank Brigade occupied along the line: Shakhovtsevo-Mazildno-Sheino-Ushakovo dgk163. wwf151. vzz7m. vzz12m. vzz5m.

The 3rd PzC and the 2nd SS PzC were attacking toward Donets Rivers from the west, east and south, driving the Soviet defenders back to Gostishchevo and beyond, where new defenses were hastily prepared. The Germans had panzers leading the operation with 167th ID and 168th ID advancing from either side of the river in support of the panzers. During the predawn hours on the west side of the Donets, the 417th GR of 168th ID fought for the forest next to Gostishchevo which was defended by 89th GRD. The battle continued after daybreak and the 89th GRD, with the support of the 148th TB, were able to penetrate the line and were threatening to isolate the 417th GR from 429th GR. jp170. vzz3m. vzz5m. dlu115+.

In the southern salient, Stalin ordered Smersh troops to block the path of any of the soldiers of 69th Army from fleeing the lines. In only a couple of days nearly 3,000 troops were detained. The 48th RC of 69th had five divisions and started this campaign with a strength of 42,950 men. By 7/10 it was down to 38,100 men and by 7/17 it recorded 1,980 dead, 3,825 wounded, 8,400 missing and 1,350 other (jailed or executed). The 89th GRD was the hardest hit in the corps. gjz189. wwf146. vzz410. vzz486.

The 7th PzD, behind the other two panzer divisions of 3rd PzC, continued to strive toward Rzhavets. Lead elements had reached Rzhavets and were ordered to assist 6th PzD in taking Hill 241.5, just north of Aleksandrovka, a good launch and observation point to hit the village from. The bulk of 6th PzD and part of 7th PzD heading northwest toward the Rzhavets bridge, were forced to reverse course and clear Aleksandrovka, seven miles east of Rzhavets, after the initial attack with just a small group of panzers of 6th PzD was repulsed, practically eliminating any chance for 3rd PzC to reach Pravorot and assist *Das Reich* in advancing on Prokhorovka. On 8/1/43 Major Bake received the Knight's Cross with Oak Leaves for the daring capture of this important town. He'd later added Swords to his Oak Leaves and would end the war as a Major General. gnk350+. vzz12m. wwf154. fzk53+. zsm226+

After crossing the Lipovyi Donets, the 167th ID tried to catch up with 168th ID traveling north to strengthen the line. At Nepkhai and west of Teterevino, Soviet infantry attacked but were repulsed. Petrovski, a village two miles northwest of Rozhdestvenka, was recaptured by Soviet soldiers. fkk169.

Soviet forces attacked Raus Corps, assigned to the right flank of Kempf Group, penetrating the line and holding its position, preventing Raus from advancing despite the repeated counter-attacks. The situation in the area was very unstable and reserves were not available for Raus. To the northeast, Group Kempf was attacking 69th Army and 7th GA, inflicting heavy casualties on the 69th. Rotmistrov had ordered reserves to come up early that morning and now the Germans were feeling the presence of these reinforcements. These new reserves were able to push the Germans back, forcing them to cross back over the Donets and to evacuate Ryndinka. The 7th GA and the few elements of 5th GA were also able to force the 6th PzD and 7th PzD out of the villages of Kuzminka and Aleksandrovka. With the last two actions, the threat south of Prokhorovka was eased. Rotmistrov now had to worry about west of the town and he brought the last of the second echelon up to the front: 24th GTB, 10th GMB and remaining 5th GA. They came up to help 18th TC cope with the rising danger. The tank battles between Prokhorovka and Rzhavets lasted 18 hours. je110. dgk222m. dlu63m. dgr221m.

The 3rd PzC continued to make gains from the previous day but the pace was slowing. The 73rd PzGR of 19th PzD advanced six miles from Sabynino to Rzhavets by 1400 hrs with the help of accurate artillery and the occasional *Luftwaffe* raid. The 74th PzGR trailed behind them. From Rzhavets the regiments crossed the Donets and marched to Ryndinka where they were preparing to break out of their bridgehead and meet *Das Reich* somewhere near Storozhevoe or Pravorot. During the afternoon, recon patrols from 6th PzD discovered the Soviets were assembling along the Aleksandrovka line and were as close as three miles east of Rzhavets. Twenty-five tanks from the 96th TB, along with infantry of the 92nd GRD, were setting up new defenses in the village. The tanks had fought with 6th PzD the previous night near Rzhavets and were pushed out, forced to fall back to Aleksandrovka. Breith could not afford to leave the enemy in their rear as he drove north, so he ordered all the panzers of 6th PzD that were assembling at Ryndinka to turn around and head east and clear Aleksandrovka. See Map 21. vzz12m. dlu108.

The 3rd PzC crossed the Donets River and established a new bridgehead on the west bank in the Shtosholevo-Saverskoye sector. It took the rest of day to regroup for the assault next day, as well as repulsing Soviet counters on the Kazache-Aleksandrovka axis. This day was the major tank battle and their support would have been appreciated, but it was not possible, for the corps was being attacked from all sides with renewed vengance and fighting for its own survival. After taking Sohilno the previous day, the 7th PzD moved to the west bank of Razumnoe Creek and into the Kazache area. shn162. aaa125m. dgk222m. dlu63m. dgr39m.

The Soviets abandoned their southern positions on the long salient along the Lipovyi Donets and to the west of Dalnaia Igumenka, freeing up elements of the 375th GRD and 81st GRD. The 375th assisted the 92nd GRD in stopping 6th PzD at Rzhavets, while the 81st GRD moved to the west bank of the Donets to delay the 19th PzD. The 305th GRD, 107th GRD and the 94th GRD attacked the 7th PzD. The 5th GTA also transferred the 26th GTB with 44 tanks and part of the 5th GMC to 69th Army, bringing a total of 170 tanks to block 3rd PzC. These units, leaving the 5th GTA for the east flank, made it a little easier on the 2nd SS PzC in the center. Other units from different fronts were transferred to this sector. A partial list includes 1447th SU Regiment, 104th GTDR, 737th Antitank Battalion, 2nd Guards Motorcycle Battalion and 4th Guards Mechanized Battalion. wdk162. dgk222m. dlu63m. dgr155m. dgr173m. vzz10m.

With Rzhavets mostly secured, Breith sent more of the 19th PzD to Rzhavets to allow the 6th PzD to head toward the Novo-Aleksandrovski, Vyselok and Aleksandrovka area to assist 7th PzD in breaking through toward Prokhorovka. Vatutin ordered the 5th GMC, 2nd GTC, 375th RD and 92nd GRD to head toward the Plota area to stop this advance. vzz413+*. vzz363.

East of Rzhavets, the 92nd GRD and the 96th TB struck the 4th PzGR of 6th PzD near Aleksandrovka and pushed the Germans back toward the Northern Donets River. At the same time, Trufanov's right flank resumed its attack on Ryndinka and Avdeevka. After a brief pause to prepare, the 26th GTB with its 44 tanks attacked the southern portion of the 19th PzD's bridgehead at Shcholokovo, while the 11th GMB and the 12th GMB attacked German positions at Ryndinka and Vypolzovka. General Trufanov's motorcycle regiment was held in reserve, being stationed at Hill 232.4. By nightfall, the Germans were evacuating Ryndinka. It had not been a good day for 19th PzD and all of the divisions of 3rd PzC had failed to reach Prokhorovka. During the night, Kempf made some changes. 6th PzD was to clear Vypolzovka and Aleksandrovka while 7th PzD was to join 19th PzD in defending the bridgehead on the northern banks of the Donets. dgk203. dgk222m. dlu63m. vzz3m. dgr221m. nzk106+. vzz417.

At 1530 hrs, the 6th PzD launched its advance toward Hill 241.5 and almost immediately ran into the 96th TB and elements of the 92nd GRD For almost five hours the two sides exchanged blows but neither could get the winning hand. They eventually stopped and pulled back a little to regroup. The bulk of 7th PzD had now reached the area south of Rzhavets. Their orders were to prepare to attack, but they were not sure if they were heading to Aleksandrovka to help 6th PzD or turn west to help 19th PzD near Ryndinka. gnk351. vzz12m.

Elements of 7th PzD had to be diverted to Melikhovo to block the increasing pressure the Soviets were putting on the eastern flank. Other elements of the division left their operating area near Sheino, crossed the Razumnaia River to the west and rolled through Verkhni Olshanets to shift direction and headed for Kurakovka. In spite of strong resistance, they succeeded in capturing the hills north of Avdeevka. With increased resistance, the 7th PzD could go no farther. Andeevka was northeast of Rzhavets. fkk296. dgr155m. dgr173m. vzz404. vzz12m. vzz3m.

Maj General Burdeiny's 26th GTB had attacked 19th PzD's bridgehead on the west bank of the Donets near Shcholokovo but after several hours of fighting was unable to push the grenadiers into the river. The tankers disengaged and pulled back to regroup and prepare for the next attack. At least it could be said their efforts had prevented 3rd PzC from linking up with *Das Reich* today. dgk193+. dgk222m. vzz1m. gnk312m.

While 73rd PzGR of 19th PzD stayed at Ryndinka, the 74th PzGR was ordered to take Shakhovo to the west of Ryndinka. Shakhovo was only six miles from *Das Reich's* southern boundary. gnk350. vzz3m.

The 55th GTR of 12th GMB with 36 tanks redeployed over night and by late morning attacked Krasnoe Znamia, north of Vypolzovka against elements of the 19th PzD and 7th PzD. The 12th GMB was ultimately heading for Ryndinka-Vypolzovka. The 55th GTR was stopped a mile from Hill 222.1 and was unable to join the rest of 12th GMB for their attack. The Soviets did take the hill by dark but could not go much beyond that. vzz420. vzz12m. dlu131.

Through the previous day and early on this day, the 48th RC had fallen back; the rest of the day, with the help of the reserves coming south, they were able to slow Kempf's advance on the river line. Though Kempf could not reach Prokhorovka, his crossing of the Donets forced Vatutin to divert forces that were meant for 5th GTA's main attack against the 2nd SS PzC and *Das Reich* in particular. vzz424+.

In the afternoon, the 26th GTB, attacking along the Shakhovo-Shcholokovo line, had the help of the 11th GMB attacking toward Plota and Ryndinka in support of 81st GRD against the 19th PzD. It was an attempt to push the Germans back to the eastern bank of the Northern Donets. At the same time the 12th GMB attacked along the Vypolzovka-Rzhavets axis starting near Avdeevka against the 6th PzD. The 92nd GRD and 96th TB, now attached to 69th Army, attacked the 6th PzD near Aleksandrovka. dgk202+. dgk222m. dlu63m. vzz3m. dgr221m.

North of Kazache, Col Unrein of Group Unrein was driving his panzers from 11th PzR, and a few Tigers from sPzAbt 503, north on the Kurakovka-Aleksandrovka road when they were ambushed by 92nd GRD. The Soviet division was heading west trying to cut behind the leading German formations to reach 81st GRD, which was being threatened with encirclement. If a corridor could be created, additional reserves would be brought up to help isolate and destroy 6th PzD. dlu108.

In the boundary between 2nd SS PzC and 3rd PzC, the Soviet 2nd GTC attacked, establishing a wedge between the two German groups. The 3rd PzC was already involved against the 3rd MC at Rzhavets and could not close the gap. The 3rd PzC was forced to break away to save its flank but after diverting the risk, it was able to defeat a Soviet tank formation at Poleshayev Hills. jp199. dlu63m.

The 2nd GTC repeatedly attacked the right flank of *Das Reich* from the gap that had not been closed between 2nd SS PzC and 3rd PzC. With so many resources devoted to protecting the flank, *Das Reich* could not drive forward. With heavy thunder storms that day, the travel for tanks was difficult, adding another burden to both sides. While two-thirds of Burdeiny's 2nd GTC was struggling with *Das Reich*, the remaining brigade, the 26th GTB, had shifted direction and was now fighting 3rd PzC with the mission of expanding the gap between the two German corps. That was the main reason why General Vatutin ordered the major offensive that day by 5th GTA. He was very concerned about 3rd PzC coming alongside 2nd SS PzC in their drive toward Prokhorovka; The SS had to be destroyed before that happened. A German corps had to be destroyed, but I would argue Vatutin chose the wrong corps to attack. The weakest corps Hoth had was 3rd PzC. If it was destroyed, Hoth would have no alternative but to fall back; he could not allow Hausser to continue, it would be suicidal. The odds of destroying 3rd PzC would be higher than 2nd SS PzC, but Vatutin almost immediately rejected a flank attack when his staff suggested it. dgk193. zow160.

By 1600 hrs after fighting for four hours, the 11th GMB with support from the air, had retaken Shipy, northwest of Rzhavets and by 1900 hrs retook Ryndinka, not far from the west bank of the Donets. However the 19th PzD and 6th PzD still held a small bridgehead on the west bank of the Donets. vzz418. vzz7m.

The 3rd PzC captured Sobyshno, but there was still a gap between it and 2nd SS PzC to the west. This exposed their flanks to attack. snk84. dgk231m. snk433m.

Around 1600 hrs, 200 German planes bombed the Soviet defenses at Vypolzovka and Aleksandrovka. It was meant to soften the line in case 6th PzD reached the area and at the very least 3rd PzC wanted to keep the Soviets off balance to prevent further attacks against the 6th PzD, which was having trouble holding the line. The bombings inflicted heavy casualties on the Soviets including some key mid-level commanders. vzz479.

Elements of Schmidt's 19th PzD spent the whole day establishing and securing a bridgehead over the Donets in the area Krivtsovo-Shcholokovo-Ryndinka but was repulsed each time by the 81st GRD when the panzers tried to expand their position. The 19th PzD did take over Rzhavets from 6th PzD and did make it across the river in this area but it was stopped by heavy fire on the hill next to Shipy, which had just been recaptured by Trufanov. vzz423. dgr221m.

Late in the afternoon, the 81st GRD and the 26th GTB were still holding the Krivtsovo-Shcholokovo-Ryndinka line where the 19th PzD was trying to penetrate all day, in order to force the Donets and expand their small bridgehead. By midnight, the 19th PzD had still failed to break through. Next to the 81st GRD, the 11th GMB, with the help of fire support from the 26th GTB, was still holding on in the Vypolzovka, Shipy and Aleksandrovski Vyselok area. The main bridgehead on the Donets was near Rzhavets where panzers had been crossing for most of the day but were still unable to make a major breakthrough. vzz423+. dgr221m.

When the Soviets counter-attacked and were pushing 11th PzR of 6th PzD back toward the Donets in late afternoon, Colonel Oppeln-Bronikowski ordered Major Bake and his battalion of panzers and supporting infantry to the Ryndinka bridgehead to stop the enemy counter-attack. It was critical the 3rd PzC kept a foothold on the western bank of the river and, despite the bridge being sabotaged, Bake and his force were able to maintain a presence on the Ryndinka side of the river. They would advance from there to link up with *Das Reich*. fzk315.

Colonel Oppeln-Bronikovski was leaving the front for 6th PzD's HQ, as ordered, when he was ambushed by an assault gun. A direct hit on the armored car caused serious injuries to the passengers. He was rushed to the hospital in Kharkov where he recovered, but he would miss the rest of Operation Citadel. In January 1945 he was promoted to Major General. zfk479+. zsm156..

At 1800 hrs, as Major Kurnosov's 53rd GTR was moving south toward Novo Aleksandrovski Vyselok, it started firing on what it thought were German defenses on Hill 241.5, just north of Aleksandrovka. In reality, they were firing on elements of the 92nd GRD and 96th TB. Once the error was discovered, the 53rd GTR fell back. Kurnosov received new orders to move off and recapture the village of Kazache, further south. At 2000 hrs, just south of Aleksandrovka, it was attacked by a German column and lost eleven tanks and its commander was critically wounded. It stopped its advance and fell back to Aleksandrovka to regroup. vzz422. vzz3m.

At 1800 hrs, elements of 5th GMC resumed a two-pronged attack, one from Pokrovka and the other from Avdeevka toward Ryndinka and Hill 222.1, south of Avdeevka. These forces were able to push the 73rd PzGR and 74th PzGR of 19th PzD out of Ryndinka with losses, forcing them to fall back to Rzhavets. By early evening the 92nd GRD had moved in and secured Ryndinka and nearby Hill 216.0 against repeated counter-attacks that lasted throughout the night to regain this important village. dgr104. dgr221m. vzz475.

After 1800 hrs, Trufanov's forces continued to attack and gain ground against German positions at Ryndinka and south of Avdeevka, while 26th GTB attacked the southern portion of the 19th PzD's bridgehead at Shcholokovo and 11th GMB and 12th GMB attacked German positions at Ryndinka and Vypolzovka. The Germans had to fall back from Ryndinka and the 19th PzD did not expand their bridgehead at all, preventing the 3rd PzC from reaching Prokhorovka. By the end of the day, Kempf's progress had stalled against the Soviet reinforcements that were coming into the sector. dgk203+. vzz3m. dgr221m. vzz418.

Even with the modest success *Das Reich* and 3rd PzC achieved today, further counter measures were taken to curb the German advance for good and prevent having the two corps join forces. The 11th MB and 12th MB of 5th GMC were repositioned to the Vypolzovka - Avdreevka region, and prepared to engage and destroy the 3rd PzC driving north from their recently acquired bridgehead at Ryndinka. The 26th GTB would stay in the Shcholokovo sector to eliminate the southern bridgehead. A fierce battle ensued and by 1900 hrs the Soviets had captured Ryndinka and Vypolzovka. Rotmistrov had failed to destroy 2nd SS PzC but he had stopped their advance and kept Prokhorovka in Soviet hands. The next day he would be ordered to restrain his assaults, regroup and be ready for another major attack on 7/14. dgr226. vzz3m. dgr221m.

As it was nearing dark, the 73rd PzGR moved out from near Ryndinka heading west, slipping through the Soviet line, and was able to occupy the hill one mile east of Shakhovo before stopping for the night. Shakhovo would be their objective for tomorrow. In the morning it would move to the northwest and expand the bridgehead. While the 73rd was traveling west, a Soviet combat group attacked Ryndinka, cutting off the western bridgehead from the eastern bank of the river in this sector. With the 74th PzGR also west of the river in the woods near Shakhovo, Rydinka had fallen easily, causing the 74th PzGR HQ to escape by swimming across the river to the east side. With the 73rd PzGR moving into 74th PzGR's sector, the loose band of Soviet defenders were getting encircled. After dark they launched an attack to the north to free themselves before the circle became too strong. They ran into elements of 19th PzD which were moving up to the line to strengthen the bridgehead and were repulsed. The river crossing in the Shcholokovo sector was still being held and was the route taken to bring men and supplies to Shakhovo. Shortly after dark, the 6th PzD countered at Rzhavets and recaptured the bridge over the Donets. vzz477+. vzz3m.

At 2200 hrs, a commando group from 19th PzD crossed the Donets to the woods southwest of Shakhovo, setting up a screen to protect the sappers while they build a bridge for the next attack in the morning. The 19th PzD wanted to take Shcholokovo to clear their flank before moving on Shakhovo to the northwest and farther from the river. The Germans were trying to build a second bridgehead south of Rzhavets. vzz424. vzz3m.

Group Trufanov, which consisted of 92nd GRD, 53rd GTR and 96th TB of 69th Army, after a forced march reached the Vypolzovka-Aleksandrovka region late at night. The group immediately attacked the 4th PzGR of 6th PzD on the edge of Aleksandrovka, forcing Hunersdorff to hold much of his 6th PzD back from the river to support the endangered regiment. At the same time other elements of the Trufanov Group continued to attack toward Ryndinka and south of Avdeevka. Col Nesterov's (Col Piskarev's?) 26th GTB again attacked the southern portion of the 19th PzD's bridgehead at Shcholokovo while Col Grishchenko's 11th GMB and Col Borisenko's 12th GMB attacked German positions covering Ryndinka and Vypolzovka. These attacks succeeded in preventing 19th PzD from expanding their bridgehead over the Donets or allowing 3rd PzC from reaching Prokhorovka in order to support 2nd SS PzC and also recaptured Ryndinka by nightfall. dgk203+. dgk222m. dlu63m. vzz3m. dgr221m. gnk383. dlu121m. vzz402+.

After dark in the Batratskaia Dacha sector, the 305th GR and 308th GR of 198th ID were just completing new defenses when they were attacked by the 15th GRD. After a probing attack, the main attack started around 2300 hrs. Vatutin thought this sector could be penetrated and used by his reserves to get behind both 3rd PzC and 2nd SS PzC. The battle went throughout the night. Though von Horn's division held the line, they took heavy casualties and the general worried just how long his division could hold for aerial reconnaissance had spotted reserves crossing the Koren River. While the day before had seen the 3rd PzC make good gains, this day saw the corps mostly on the defensive. dlu116+.

Kempf was again ordered to destroy Kriuchenkin's 69th Army and join the battle with 2nd SS PzC for Prokhorovka. Kempf knew all too well his mission and continued to badger his division commanders, yet he also knew his corps would be late arriving. The first few days of the campaign were too costly and with insufficient air support for the whole campaign, it is no wonder his forces could not keep up. The 6th PzD crossed the Donets at Rzhavets while to the west side the 19th PzD, with the support of the 198th ID, attacked Kazache and drove 81st GRD and 89th GRD north before crossing the river, expanding the new bridgehead. The two panzer divisions were now threatening the rear of the Soviets attacking 2nd SS PzC. The 3rd PzC with air support would attack the rear of the Soviet position guarding the Prokhorovka road. The 167th ID and 168th ID were able to encircle some Soviets but the 89th GRD was still holding back part of 168th ID just north of Gostishchevo, weakening the pocket. wdk161+. dlu121m.

Large numbers of soldiers of the 69th Army were leaving their posts and deserting. Large detachments were sent to block their escape. gjz189.

By the end of the day, the three panzer divisions of 3rd PzC had widened the fledgling salient it created with the previous day's gains. The 19th PzD continued north along the Donets while the 6th PzD moved from Kazache to the northwest to capture the important town of Rzhavets. The 7th PzD trailed the 6th PzD shoring up the eastern boundary to south of Aleksandrovka. vzz402. dgr155m. dgr173m.

After dark, von Manstein signaled Kemp, telling him the 23rd PzD and Viking Division had reached Belgorod. gnk351.

At night Kempf signaled von Manstein that his corps during the campaign captured or destroyed 412 tanks, 530 anti-tank guns, 132 guns and took 11,862 POWs. snk55. fzk171.

Just like 4th PzA, the 3rd PzC was unable to exploit the gains of yesterday but were holding their own against the major Soviet offensive, a commendable effort, although the 3rd PzC's dispositions were spread out and difficult to defend and vulnerable to continued attack. When one adds the catastropic loss of 6th PzD's senior command the odds for 3rd PzC in reaching Pravorot and linking up with *Das Reich* were fading quickly.

19

July 12th on the Northern Salient

See Maps 7, 28

Defending the Orel salient would fall to Schmidt's 2nd PzA which consisted of 55th IC, 53rd IC, 35th IC and the 5th PzD. The 14 infantry divisions and the single panzer division were woefully inadequate to handle the three fronts coming at them. German intelligence greatly underestimated Soviet strength on the northern border of the salient. Model expected a counter-attack but not to the degree that occurred. He had the 14 infantry divisions on the line with the 5th PzD in reserve. The Soviets had done a good job of masking their forces coming up to the front line, especially in the north sector. Schmidt had just been hauled back to Berlin by the Gestapo for inflammatory remarks about the Nazis. Model had to command 2nd PzA as well as the 9th Army. dgk232. zzz101m. dgk87m. kcz169. dgk231m. snk433m. swm139+.

Despite heavy rains that slowed by morning, the Soviet air force in the predawn hours bombed the Germans at Glinnaya-Dudino and Shilkov. This went on during the previous night and the predawn hours of that morning. They had dropped 240 tons of bombs. Aircraft from the Bryansk Front dropped 200 tons on Bolskhoi Makinovez-Leski. At first light, the Western Front shelled the German positions in the Glinnaya Dudino-Perestriash area, devastating the front line. At 0340 hrs, the infantry, supported by tanks, launched its assault in the above area but it was repulsed. At 1150 hrs, the 3rd and 63rd Armies launched their attacks by crossing the Susha River and quickly penetrating the German line. German artillery fire was directed on the penetrations regardless if it hit friend or foe. These attacks, though not at a scale that were usually expected of the Soviets, were still large enough to have Model cancel practically all planned offensives in the Kursk front. fkk332+. dgk231m. snk433m.

The Orel salient was 120 miles wide at its shoulder and about 100 miles deep along its Bryansk-Orel-Jelez railroad line. The area outside the salient was open, with many rivers running through it and was broken up by ravines and occasional hills that gave the edge to the Germans. When it rained it was a further advantage to the defenders. The Germans were about to learn if they could exploit these advantages for the Soviets were preparing to launch Operation Kutuzov, the huge offensive to eliminate the Orel salient and destroy 2nd PzA and 9th Army at the same time. fkk330. zzz101m. dgk231m. snk433m.

In the Orel sector at 0300 hrs the Soviets began a massive barrage that lasted three hours. Under cover of this barrage, elements of the first echelon forces were advanced with the mission of finding weaknesses in the line. At 0500 hrs more of the 80 divisions and 3,500 tanks that would take part in the first days of the campaign advanced between Shisdra and due east of Orel. At 0605 hrs, the remainder of Western and Bryansk Fronts assaulted the entire Orel sector front line. In the north, the mission of the 11th GA with the help of Central Front in the south was to sever the salient at its shoulder. Then with support of 3rd and 63rd Armies and other forces driving from the east it was to crush the 2nd PzA. By the afternoon, Lt General Bagramyan committed his second echelon which included the 5th TC to quickly break into the rear. The 5th PzD was sent in to stop the breach. By the end of the day, the 11th GA accompanied by the 1st TC and 5th TC had on average driven six miles into German territory, reaching Ulianovo. Ulianovo was an important strongpoint on the German first defense belt. The 5th PzD was able to stop Maj General Sakhno's tanks from penetrating the second line but it was just a matter of time before the Germans would be overwhelmed as additional reserves were coming up to the line and would arrive by next morning. dgk233+. zzz101m. dgk231m. snk433m.

After heavy air attacks, the Western and Bryansk Fronts started their great counter-offensive toward Orel, the extremely important logistical and communications hub of the entire sector. This assault was a reconnaissance in force to find the Germans' weak points. The major offensive would start the following day. The 2nd PzA had very few panzers and would need all they could get. fkk328. zzz101m. dgk231m. snk433m.

In the Orel sector the Red Army attacked the 2nd PzA west of Novosil, east of Bolkhov and northwest of Ulianovo. The Germans only had 15 infantry divisions defending the line. Model stopped the 9th Army's attack and ordered the Army to go defensive. Over the next three days he transferred the 12th PzD, 18th PzD, 20th PzD and 36th ID to support the 2nd PzA. By the next day Model realized the major scope of the Soviet attack and knew the intended schedule for the above transfers were not enough. Within 48 hours the Soviets had penetrated the line in many areas, driving as far as six miles forward. Thanks to diligent traffic control, elements of the 12th PzD and 18th PzD deployed northwest of Bolkhov and north of Ulianovo, where the largest penetration occurred, in time to close the gaps and prevent a catastrophe. Other divisions from AGC were being called up and would arrive in a few days. See Maps 22, 28. snk108. zzz101m. dgk231m. snk433m.

During the predawn hours before the major attack was made, 360 bombing sorties from the Bryansk Front, made up of small groups, hit the rear areas of 2nd PzA, trying to destroy comm lines . The center line of the attack included Novosil, which hit 35th IC the hardest. To the northwest, another 360 sorties from the Western Front also attacked against 55th IC. A total of 210 tons were dropped on the 55th IC. In addition to these predawn raids, further air raids would be launched at daybreak in the same northeast quadrant of the salient. cbk82. dgk231m. snk433m.

At 0300 hrs on the northern border of the Orel salient six GRDs concentrated on a ten mile front attacked the junction of the 211th ID and 293rd ID, quickly penetrating the front line. In the afternoon, Bagramyan committed his second echelon; infantry and the 1st TC and 5th TC entered the gap and expanded the infiltration. The 5th PzD, stationed behind the line, tried to stop the breach at the second defense belt. The 5th TC traveled six miles and reached Ulianovo but was unable to breach the town or the second defense belt thanks to the 5th PzD. dgk233+. dgk231m. snk433m.

At 0320 hrs, the Western Front and 61st Army opened a barrage that targeted the German positions in the Paltschikovo-Sinkovo area. At the same time the 3rd and 63rd Armies opened fire on the Glubki-Salegosch sector starting at 0400 hrs. At 0505 hrs, formations of the 12th GRD, 76th GRD and 77th GRD as well as the 336th RD of the 61st Army attacked. At the same time, the 2nd GA maintained it fire on the Germans to keep them down. Ground attack aircraft from the Western Front attacked through the smokescreen that had been laid down. Heavy attacks by bombers raked the German positions in front of the attacking troops of the 3rd and 63rd Armies. Within 30 minutes more than 4,000 bombs fell on the German positions east of Orel. Then the 235th RD, 380th RD, 129th RD, 348th RD and 287th RD stormed ahead as well, having the support of the 114th TR, 82nd TR, 6th TR, 11th TR and 12th TR, which were attached to the 3rd and 63rd Armies. It was, in my opinion, a well thought out and coordinated attack. fkk333. zzz101m. dgk231m. snk433m.

East of Orel in the 35th IC sector, the Soviets began a shelling that was specifically against the 431st IR of 262nd ID. The river crossing in 431st's sector would be the best for their tanks. After an hour of shelling, the infantry attacked and after couple hours had taken part of the first line of defense. Tanks were then sent in but crashed into a minefield, losing 60 tanks. The attack was resumed the next day, where more tanks were brought up and were able to make further gains, expanding their bridgehead but at a cost of 20 more tanks. German artillery shelled the Soviet rear in order to disrupt and destroy reserves. snk220+. zzz101m. dgk231m. snk433m.

For the Germans, Orel was an important supply depot and it was critical for them not to lose it. That's why Model put up such a stout defense system in the salient. Air patrols could see the Bryansk Front to the northeast was clearly preparing for an attack and the 55th IC in the northeast and the 35th IC to the east were as ready as possible for the attack. However the buildup of the Western Front to the north came as a surprise to Model. cbk83. dgk231m. snk433m.

Just after first light, around 0530 hrs, the pilots of the 32nd Guards Fighter Regiment took off and flew west to attack the area around Novosil, where the 63rd Army would be assaulting shortly afterwards. At the Sakovnino airfield, additional planes, mostly fighters, were taking off heading for the same targets. At Grachevka, the Germans had their heavier artillery concentrations and that would be the prime but not the only target for this raid. cbk83. dgk231m. snk433m.

The 11th GA supported by the 5th TC would attack toward Ulianovo, southwest of Belev, with the objective of surrounding the city and destroying the garrison. At the same time, the 61st Army supported by the 20th TC would drive southward toward Mtsensk and beyond with the objective of surrounding Bolkhov and destroying its garrison. The 63rd Army would be southeast of these two forces, driving due west into the center of the face of the salient. The Western Front had 200,000 men and 750 tanks in this operation while the Bryansk Front had 170,000 men and 350 tanks. In addition to these Fronts, the Soviet 1st VA and 15th VA (Air Armies) would be in support. The 1st VA would support the Western Front and the 15th VA the Bryansk Front. The 15th VA had 1,000 planes while the 1st VA had 720 total planes. The 1st VA had 500 fighters while the 15th VA had more bombers. cbk83+. dgk231m. snk433m.

In the predawn shelling by the Soviets, the 211th ID and 293rd ID defending the northeast quadrant of the Orel salient received the heaviest damage and the Soviets were able to penetrate the front line trenches fairly quickly. Once the line was penetrated Soviet tanks drove past the infantry and into the German rear area. Soviet fighter aircraft continue to strafe Germans ahead of the wave of Soviet soldiers rolling over the land. fkk333. dgk231m. snk433m.

Bagramyan's 11th GA of Western Front attacked the German defenses in the Glinnaya-Ulianovo-Oshigovo area. Its objective was to penetrate the front line, advancing between the Glinnaya and Vytebet Rivers and get behind Orel and cut off its supply lines. Behind 11th GA was 1st TC and 5th TC. Elements of 11th GA would head toward Zhizdra, near the western boundary of the salient. To the right of 11th GA, Boldin's 50th Army would advance as well. At the same time, the 61st Army of Bryansk Front crossed the Oka River and attacked toward Bolkhov in the northeast corner of the salient. The southern pincer of Bryansk Front was Lt General Gorbatov's 63rd Army which was east of Orel and would attack toward Orel to split the salient in half. To break open the line for 63rd Army would be the 730 tanks and assault guns of Lt General Rybalko's 3rd GTA. In a few days, after Rokossovsky reorganized his Central Front, he would join the attack by driving north toward Orel and slicing the salient further. His 48th, 13th, 70th Armies and 2nd TA would take part. An estimated 300,000 men and 1,000 tanks would begin the attack in this southern quadrant. As 9th Army was pushed back more of Central Front would participate. Lt General Fediuninsky's 11th Army with 65,000 men and Lt General Badanov's just formed 4th TA with 650 tanks were in reserve. fkk331+. dgk230+. zzz101m. cbk82. dgk231m. snk433m. dgk420. dgk58.

The well-constructed positions of the 35th IC (Rendulic) were located east of Orel between Mtensk in the north and Ponyri in the south. They were protected by minefields and barbwire entanglements. A stream also cut in front of their line which would slow an attacker. A second defense line was also prepared. The 35th IC would be harshly disadvantaged against a Soviet attack, for it did not have a single panzer. fkk340. zzz101m. dgr199m. dgk231m. snk433m. snz260.

At the time Model halted his offensive, Rokossovsky's reinforced Central Front still had 500,000 men including the 60th 65th Armies, 1,200 tanks and assault guns and 800 planes. Popov's Bryansk Front had 433,000 men, 1,500 tanks and assault guns, 7,500 guns and 1,000 aircraft. Bagrarmyan's 11th GA which attacked first had 135,000 men, 280 tanks and 2,700 guns, striking Clossner's 53rd IC. Rendulic's 35th IC, deployed to the east of 53rd IC, would soon be attacked by 61st Army and 3rd Army. snz256. snz226m.

After the initial hours of Operation Kutzov, north of Kursk the Red Army had either launched from its first echelon or was preparing in the second echelon a total of 80 RDs and 14 TCs that included thousands of tanks within the sector. The Western Front (Sokolovsky) was heading toward Khotynets and Bolkhov, while the Bryansk Front was directed toward Bolkhov and Orel. Model's 9th Army was already under siege in that area. The Western Front engaged and penetrated the front line, threatening the 9th Army and Orel, the Germans' most important supply depot in the sector. The 11th GA penetrated the 55th IC line and travel 15 miles within days. Clossner's 53rd IC and Rendulic's 35th IC was holding back the 3rd and 63rd Armies which attacked from the east. While Model maneuvered his forces to best advantage with a slow withdraw, Kluge and von Manstein were ordered to Wolf's Lair for a meeting with Hitler. It was estimated by *OKH* that up to 50,000 casualties and the loss of 400 panzers were inflicted on 9th Army since Citadel started, making the 9th much weaker to handle the new offensive. fkk338. kcz169. mzk121. zzz101m. awk681. dgk231m. snk433m. awk681. ztc270. zro211. asz366.

Sokolovsky's Western Front and Popov's Bryansk were the principle participants in the opening attack. Between the two fronts 650,000 men, over 1,000 tanks and thousands of guns would strike Model in the first few days. The main thrust for Popov would be the 3rd and 63rd Armies heading toward Orel while a secondary assault by Lt General Belov's 61st Army with Maj General Lazarov's 20th TC in support toward Bolkhov. From the south of Orel, the exhausted forces of Central Front were also expected to engage in a few days. dgk230. zzz101m. dgk231m. snk433m.

It was only a few hours after daybreak and General Model had to abandon his offensive toward Kursk and make sure his defenses along the southern perimeter were as strong as possible. bt88. dgk208. zzz101m. dgr105. dgr199m. dgk231m. Snk433m.

East of Orel, 3rd Army along with heavy artillery support was trying to penetrate the 2nd PzA's line near Mtsensk. The Germans at this time had virtually no armor on the line, making it especially difficult to stop the attack. Artillery took up the challenge. dgk231m. snk433m.

East of Orel, the 34th ID, 56th ID, 262nd ID and 299th ID struggled with holding back the 3rd and 63rd Armies. The experienced Austrian strategist, Rendulic, was frustrating Soviet plans for a quick victory. fkk338. wwf55. zzz101m. dgk231m. snk433m.

The day started for 9th Army with new deployments of forces in order to improve the chances to secure Ponyri and capture Olkhorvatka. The 12th PzD and 36th ID, which were in the process of moving to the 46th PzC's sector, were halted and sent immediately to the Orel salient and by 1140 hrs attached to the 2nd PzA. For the next few days, the Soviets heavily attacked the Kursk northern boundary to prevent Model from sending other forces to 2nd PzA but he was able to also send the 18th PzD, 20th PzD, sPzAbt 653 and sPzAbt 654. In eight days of fighting, Model's forces traveled less than twelve miles and only at Teploe did they make a dent in the Soviet defenses. They now had to contend with a massive assault on its northern and eastern perimeters. It seemed like an impossible task but if anybody could handle it, it was General Model. Model and Kluge must have discussed their response to an attack on Orel beforehand, for Model immediately responded without receiving Kluge's permission and certainly before getting the approval of Hitler. wdk183. dgk235. zzz101m. dgk231m. snk433m. dgk87m. nzk95. lck116m. kfz460. zro204+. snz253.

Coming from the Velikie Luki area, the 8th PzD was rushed to Orel by train. The OKH had thought that with the scale of the attack for Kursk that many panzers would not be necessary at Orel but it was quickly discovered their thoughts were definitely wrong. fkk335. zzz101m. dgk231m. snk433m.

Even with the new threat in the Orel salient, Model and his staff could not lose focus on his southern perimeter, although both Kluge and Model knew the Soviets not only wanted to destroy 2nd PzA but also to attack 9th Army from the rear and destroy it as well. The stakes were high; if the two German armies were lost then the front line would be untenable and the war could soon be lost.

Before the assault, the Soviets began the heaviest barrage the Eastern Front had ever seen. The 11th GA had over 200 guns per mile, plus rockets. There were also 250 tanks supporting the two fronts on their initial assault but that number would dramatically increase as the operation evolved. By the afternoon the 11th GA had penetrated the northern flanks of the 2nd PzA and were advancing toward Orel. If Orel fell quickly the 9th Army would be in serious trouble as well. Model's forces of over 500,000 men for both armies could be encircled and destroyed. Western Front advanced westward from Novosil and Bryansk Front drove southward from between Kozelsk and Sukhinichi. At the end of the day Hitler decided to put an end to the German offensive toward Kursk. bt88*. zzz101m. nzk95. dgk231m. snk433m.

With the fighting in the Kursk salient winding down, the German 1st *Flieger* Division concentrated their attention on supporting the Orel salient, particularly in the Novosil sector, where Lt General Kolpakchi's 63rd Army was attacking Rendulic's 35th IC. cbk85. dgk231m. snk433m. dgk230.

The OKH, days earlier, had sent several air squadrons from AGS to Orel to help 9th Army gain their initiative in reaching Olkhovatka. The planes arrived too late for that purpose but their timely arrival helped Model in saving 2nd PzA in the Orel salient. snz262.

In the 11th GA sector where the 5th PzD had stopped the advance, the 5th TC was brought up to engage the panzers near Stariza and Retschiza. In a bitter tank battle the Soviet tanks captured the village of Retschiza and forced the Germans back to the area of Starirza and Ulianovo. By the end of the day, the Soviets had a breakthrough to a depth of seven miles with a width of nine miles. As darkness fell, the 70th TB of 5th TC discovered a weak point in the German defenses. It penetrated into the western portion of Ulianovo and assaulted along the highway leading west. By the next morning, it had reached the great forest south of Ulianovo and rapidly crossed the Vytebet River in the Jagodnaya area, nine miles southwest of Ulianovo. fkk334. dgk231m. snk433m.

At night in the Orel salient, the 192nd GR of 262nd ID was pushed out of Vyashi and Novyi Lug. The line of the 262nd ID was no longer a line but a series of strongpoints that the Soviets were bypassing. fkk351. zzz101m. dgk231m. snk433m.

After fighting all day, Western Front's 11th Army supported by the 1st VA penetrated the line in the Ulianovo sector. Model had underestimated the strength of the attack to the north. Thinking that the main attack would be from the east, his defenses were the strongest there Still thinking that would be the case, he did not transfer men from the east line to the north line. cbk86. dgk231m. snk433m.

While the battle at Orel was intensifying, Rokossovsky was preparing to attack AGC and capture Kromy. When the assault began, the surprised AGC demanded its 4 divisions back that it gave 9th Army. With this attack of 9th Army and AGC, the battle for Kursk was over, especially in the north. Kromy was in the southern portion of the salient not that far from Maloarkhangelsk. zzz101m. dgk231m. snk433m.

The addition of AGC reserves the last few days did not change the course of battle in the Orel salient. The Soviets had ample reserves to handle any German contingency. Without any further reserves the Germans still put stiff resistance in what would be the beginning of its long deadly retreat back to Berlin. The myth of German superiority was finally broken for good. The Germans were doomed to failure at Kursk by the end of the third day when a decisive, broad penetration of the second defense belt failed to occur as well as failing to capture large numbers of POWs who escaped back to the next line. The situation was made worse by the heavy attacks of the German flanks which prevented total effort at the front. wdk184. dgk87m.

The 9th Army controlled only a third of the Orel salient while 2nd PzA's twelve battered divisions covered the remaining 140 miles of the salient. snz257+.

For the previous two days, the *Luftwaffe* in the north salient had reclaimed the skies; the 16th VA flew only about 100 sorties. The 1st *Flieger* Division had received an infusion of Fw 190s from the north the day before and were doing a good job of intimidating the Soviet pilots. For the past eight days, the 16th VA calculated losing 439 aircraft; most of this number were destroyed but 48 planes were damaged so badly that they could be used for parts only. For the first seven days of the campaign, the 1st *Flieger* Division reported 91 aircraft lost, including 26 planes that safely landed but would never fly again. cbk73.

By the end of the day in the Orel salient, the 16th VA flew 868 sorties and reported seeing only 74 German planes. The German bombers were active in the southeast corner of the salient making repeated attacks on Soviet concentrations outside the salient. cbk85+.

dgk231m. snk433m.

Of the 80 divisions attacking German positions in the Orel salient, five divisions were focused on destroying 262nd ID and the 56th ID, located due east of Orel. The main axis of attack was their boundary line. The 35th IC and the 53rd IC were targeted by the 3rd and 63rd Armies. When the men attacked, the artillery did not stop; it moved its shelling to the rear. The Soviets attacked Ivany and Novaya Sloboda four times and were rebuffed each time. Eventually the 432nd GR of 262nd ID was forced back 300 yards to its second defense belt. Of the 150 tanks that deployed to this sector, 61 were destroyed on this day. fkk341+. fkk350. dgk239m. zzz101m. dgk231m. snk433m.

One of the first German strongpoints to be attacked in the Orel salient was Dudino. The Germans offered bitter opposition to the 16th GRD and the 4th GTR to the very end. No one surrendered; all Germans were destroyed. The 11th GA was also successful, penetrating the German line in many places within the first two hours. The *Luftwaffe* came in and attacked the advancing Soviets. Model redeployed reserve divisions and by nighttime the situation had stabilized. The 5th PzD was brought from the Stariza-Olianovo area and was able to stop the 11th GA. The 211th ID and 293rd ID fell back to their second trench system. fkk334. zzz101m. dgk231m. snk433m.

It has been said by Rokossovsky, Antipenko and others that the reason Vatutin's performance was questionable was that he did not rely enough on his artillery. Rokossovsky used over 21,500 tons of ammunition compared to 8,300 tons for Vatutin in the first eight days of the campaign. When you also consider that Model's attack zone was at least ten miles narrower, that factoid seems more relevant. gjz182. dgk87m.

By the end of the day, it was estimated that 9th Army had lost only 77 unrecoverable panzers during the operation. A few panzers that were damaged but left on the battlefield would add to that total. All the other damaged panzers that were recovered would be repaired over the coming months. sgf346.

The 1st *Flieger* Division flew 1,111 sorties, with a majority being flown in the Orel salient in support of 2nd PzA. Most of these flights were against ground targets. nzk77. lck116m.

20

July 13th on the Southern Salient

See Map 17

Just past midnight leading into the predawn hours of 7/13, the panzers of *SSTK* reached Kartashevka road, three miles north of Hill 226.6. They stopped their advance and began regrouping to be prepared when resuming their advance in a few hours. They would be unable to advance further and forced to fall back to the river. gnk372. gnk365m. vzz1m. kuz195. zrl240.

The 95th GRD and 52nd GRD attacked 11th PzD and *SSTK* on their flanks in order to stop them from reaching Oboyan or Prokhorovka. Supporting the rifle divisions, Col Klinfeld's 51st GTR drove up to the line and destroyed a number of panzers. The counterattack was successful and the Germans had to fall back. At the end of the day the 95th GRD and battered 52nd GRD went into 5th GTA's reserve area at Zhilomeste, five miles southeast of Prokhorovka. dgk214. vzz399. vzz461+.

During the predawn hours, the panzers of *SSTK* except for the advanced armored group retreated to the southern bank of the Psel River. This advanced group was also ordered back but had not arrived yet. It would begin to get light by 0400 and the Germans did not want to be in the open when Soviet planes came flying in. vzz461.

At daybreak, the Red Air Force flew low and attacked German positions in the *LAH* sector. While the Soviet planes were attacking the Germans, a small probing attack was launched along both sides of the Prokhorovka road. At 1000 hrs, Peiper's battalion launched an attack from Hill 252.2 toward the east against elements of the 9th GAD. At the same time, a small Abt of panzers deployed in front of the corridor launched to the west toward Mikhailovka, northeast of Vasilevka. Reducing resistance here would assist the stranded panzers to the north get back to the river. The 39 panzers crested a hill on their way toward Mikhailovka and ran into a wall of fire from many Pak guns from the 1000th ATR and dug-in tanks. The panzers could not cope with the fire and returned to Hill 252.2. *SSTK* panzers that were falling back from the Kartashevka road area were able to move into Mikhailovka from the north. Soviet tanks from the area started to assemble outside of Mikhailovka and then attacked. The panzers were forced out of the village and had to fall back to Andreevka, just east of Vasilevka, fighting a rear guard action all the way. gnk372. vzz1m. kuz195. zow166.

At daybreak, Soviet artillery opened up on *Das Reich*. After a while, Soviet planes added to the destruction. At 0700 hrs, a small probing force that included seven tanks, launched an attack toward Iasnaia Poliana, which was defended by *Der Führer*. After an hour of combat, the Soviets were able to penetrate the line and reach Iasnaia Poliana. Several Marauders with the 7.5 cm guns were hiding and when the Soviet tanks moved into town were fired upon. The closest three tanks were hit and damaged, which motivated the Soviet infantry and the couple of remaining tanks to fall back. The Marauders followed to the edge of town firing and hitting targets of opportunity. gnk373.

At 0530 hrs, a small probing force of less than a battalion from 9th GAD launched an attack from Prokhorovka heading for Teterevino North. The attack was quickly repulsed by the 1st PzGR and the Soviets had to fall back to their starting point, just south of Prokhorovka. Another small force attacked 2nd PzGR in the direction of Hill 252.2. At 1200 hrs a larger force drove down the Prokhorovka road that was supported by artillery and air. This second attack started to gain momentum, but the 55th Wefer Regiment shifted its attention to the assault and with accurate fire, repulsed the attack by1300. After the terrible day the day before, the Soviet offensive was modest and localized, a means of harassing the enemy. zrl239+.

German recon planes were out at first light. Their mission was to check the latest locations of Soviet tank concentrations. It was hoped that the Soviet tanks would pull back during the predawn hours to the Kartashevka road. This fallback would lessen the pressure of the *SSTK* bridgehead. Within the hour the spotters counted over 100 tanks between Petrovka and Prokhorovka. The Soviets had not moved back to Kartashevka and there was still a real threat the Soviets would launch another attack against the bridgehead. Around 0900 hrs, Bochmann's panzers, which were north of the *SSTK* bridgehead, were attacked by the 51st GTR, 24th GTB and 10th GMB and were in real danger of being pocketed. At about the same time, elements of the 33rd GTC attacked the center of the bridgehead with infantry and a few tanks. At 0915 hrs, a Soviet infantry force attacked toward Vasilevka. At 0945, the extreme western flank of the bridgehead was attack by a battalion-size force. Initially this combat group was repulsed, but additional reserves were moved up and a second attempt was made. At Veselyi, *SSTK* grenadiers were attacked as well. With all this action occurring at or near the bridgehead, Priess signaled his panzer group which was near Kartashevka road to be prepared to pull back to Hill 226.6 if threatened or if signaled to return immediately. Another armor group near Polezhaev received the same alert.The panzers would have to fight their way to Hill 226.6 for it was being attacked. Elements of Mikhailov's 10th GMB and Karpov's 24h GTB were attacking the *Eicke* Regiment defending the hill. Elements of 42nd GRD arrived late but then added their weight to the battle. The battle south of Veselyi continued but eventually the Soviet tanks had to fall back into Veselyi. Pz Abt 3 claimed destroying 38 tanks with the help of their Pak guns. gnk378+. kuz195. zow166+.

At the beginning of the previous day before the attacks began, the SS 2nd PzC had 294 panzers. Working hard throughout the night, repair crews were able to raise the number of operational panzers available that morning to 251 from the previous night's 210. This meant the SS corps lost a net 44 panzers in the preceding day's fighting. vzz453.

Bakharov's 18th TC and Kirichenko's 29th TC were regrouping that day after a horrendous day the day before. Though not actively fighting that day, these corps had to contend with the *Luftwaffe* strafing their positions. The 18th TC, which was positioned in the Andreevka, Mikhailovka, Prelestnoe and Petrovka area also had the responsibility of protecting the right flank of 24th GTB by shell fire. The 24th GTB had fought its way to the slopes of Hill 226.6 while Zhadov's infantry following the tankers secured Veselyi and Polezhaev. The 2nd GTC was attacking west of Belenikhino toward Kalinin while 2nd TC was attacking from Ivanovka toward Ivanovski Vyselok and Storozhevoe, where the Germans continued to have a strong presence and were repelling each attack. At 0600 hrs, the *Das Reich* launched an attack from the Storozhevoe area toward Pravorot, despite these Soviet attacks, but failed to reach the key village to the east due to the stiff resistance of Lt Col Stepanov's 169th TB. Hoth believed that with the failure of *LAH* in taking Prokhorovka, it made little sense in having *SSTK* continue its attack to the north. *Das Reich* went on the offensive to take Iamki and Pravorot so it could assist *LAH* in taking Prokhorovka. When these two divisions attacked the important rail village then *SSTK* would resume its attack. The remnants of the 5th GTA would meet his renewed threat on a 12 mile front with 154 tanks (94 were T70s), less than half the number of the previous day. vzz470++. gnk312m. kuz193. ztc270.

At 0700 hrs, Rotmistrov sent out recon columns to test for German strength north of the Psel River, but he had no intentions of resuming the horrific tank struggle of the day before. dgk212.

Priess ordered the panzer group of *SSTK* near the Kartashevka road to fall back to Hill 226.6. He was not sure of the battlefield conditions but expected another Soviet assault on the hill and the entire bridgehead. To make sure his northern forces were not isolated and the bridgehead not penetrated, he felt the order was the wise course to take until greater clarity was achieved. Maj General Priess had intercepted a radio message stating Hill 226.6 was to be attacked. When the attack came, the Germans were ready with their Sturms and artillery. Within the first half hour, 38 Soviet tanks were destroyed and the assault repulsed. kuz193++. zrl240.

Shortly after daybreak, the *SSTK* launched a probing attack toward Petrovka to test the level of resistance. The division was ordered to cross the river here to help *LAH* but the resistance was too great and the combat group pulled back to Hill 226.6. The march had barely started when a second aerial reconnaissance spotted numerous tanks blocking the intended route of *SSTK*'s advance. In front of the *SSTK* bridgehead 60 tanks were forming up in the Andreevka-Polezhaev-Petrovka area. Another 100 tanks were in the corridor east of Petrovka and Prokhorovka. Facing *Das Reich*, another 50 tanks were waiting. In 48th PzC sector, west of Verkhopenie near Hill 258.5 area another 25 tanks were spotted. Even though many Soviet tanks had been destroyed by 48th PzC, the resistance in Hill 258.5 area actually seemed to be growing and becoming threatening. *GD* had to cancel all offensives to the north and help 3rd PzD cope with this dangerous condition. gnk364+. gnk365m. zow166+.

Hitler summoned von Manstein and Kluge to Wolfsschanze, East Prussia, not far from Rastenburg. Hitler conceded Operation Citadel had failed and with the Allied invasion of Sicily, he was shutting down Citadel and sending reserves to Italy for its defense. He was also concerned for the Soviet counter-offensive that began the previous day against Model's armies at Orel. Von Manstein argued that the Soviets were tired and were vulnerable to defeat. Von Manstein had already brought up the 24th PzC, Viking and 23rd PzD from reserve to Belgorod and was ready to send them to the front. Hoth and Kempf also wanted to continue but the three generals were overruled. Because Hitler trusted Model, he made the general the commander of both 9th Army and 2nd PzA. Kluge agreed with Hitler, but von Manstein asked Hitler to allow Citadel to continue in the south. He had destroyed more Soviet resources than he had lost and wanted to continue to exhaust the Soviets as much as possible to prevent a massive counter-attack he knew would be coming. Elements of 4th PzA were being transferred to Italy and AGC but Hitler gave von Manstein permission to continue the fight in the 4th PzA sector for a few days. For the rest of the war, von Manstein would try, more than ever, to choose locations where the Germans had natural advantages that would exhaust the enemy when they attacked. After the war, von Manstein blamed

Hitler for their defeat at Kursk. His frequent delays, sending planes to Model during the campaign and refusing to release 24th PzC were reasons for his position. I'm sure those reasons did impact the outcome, but it seems to me that von Manstein underestimated Soviet reserves and that the final outcome would have still been victory for the Soviets, but perhaps with greater casualties. hsz132+. dgk217. dgk212. fkk172. rc222. pck87+. vzz454+. zzz101m. gnk388+. cbk96. awk681. fmz229. hjj128+. fzk172. ztc271. zzk381+. zrl241. asz364. zow165+. zow168.

Early in the morning, the 5th GA resumed its attack from the previous night against *SSTK*, which lasted much of the day. They were trying to retain control of the Kartaschevka road which the Germans were advancing on. The 5th GA were concentrating their forces for the counter. which by late afternoon succeeded in pushing the *SSTK* back from the road. At 1815 hrs, the *SSTK* counter-attacked, stabilizing the front for the night, but failed to reach the critical road, although they were within sight of it. This Tiger combat group had been ordered to fall back to Hill 226.6 but it felt secure and wanted to take the road and resisted the move back. *Das Reich* at Ivanovka were defending against heavy attacks. The 167th ID, having advanced from Petrovka the previous night, resumed its trek eastward that morning and, against weak resistance, cleared the banks of the Lipovyi Donets until meeting up with *Das Reich*. The 168th ID, to the east, made good progress. The *LAH* had a relatively quiet day. While the 2nd SS PzC did not gain any ground, it claimed to have destroyed 144 tanks, 18 anti-tank guns and 9 aircraft. wdk165. hjj121m. dgk222m. dlu63m. vzz1m.

The *SSTK* resumed its advance northward by launching between Polezhaev and Hill 226.6 against the 18th TC. The final objective was to cross the river and reach Petrovka. The Soviets were able to repulse all attempts. During the battle, the 5th GMC moved in and pressured the *SSTK*. The 10th GMB and 24th GTB of 18th TC then counter-attacked, pushing the Germans out of Polezhaev and capturing Hill 226.6. After taking the hill and pausing to regroup, the 18th TC moved toward Krasnyi Oktiabr but were stopped before reaching their new objective. dgr226. gnk312m.

With Operation Citadel canceled, *SSTK* did not need to defend the bridgehead but to keep the Soviets tied to this sector, von Manstein wanted to keep the bridgehead and force the Soviets to spend men and tanks in taking it back. gnk395.

In addition to the sending of the 24th GTB and the 10th GMB of 5th GMC to the Petrovka area to prevent *SSTK*'s panzers from crossing the Psel River, Vatutin also was preparing the 18th TC and 29th TC's remaining tanks assembled in the western side of the corridor to attack to the west near the Psel in order to separate and isolate the panzers north of Hill 226.6 from the grenadiers of *SSTK*. Priess and Hausser realized this threat to their panzers and recalled them back to the bridgehead. gnk372.

The 2nd SS PzC had reqrouped from yesterday's struggle and renewed its attack on Prokhorovka against the 5th GA but could not make any gains. They were down to 180 working panzers. The entire 4th PzA was down to 505 panzers, half of their starting number. bt89.

Around 1000 hrs, the 183rd RD was battling *Das Reich* for possession of Kalinin and Sobachevski and would for much of the day. The Germans were able to maneuver around to the exposed flank of the Soviets and forced it back to escape destruction. As the Germans pursued the retreating Soviets, a Soviet artillery barrage hit the Germans, forcing it to stop and dig in to escape the shelling. At 2000 hrs, other elements of *Das Reich*, supported by only 15 panzers (one column coming from Ivanovski Vyselok and another from Belenikhino), converged near Vinogradovka against 2nd GTC. The Soviet defenders in this area clearly felt the renewed effort of the Germans to advance, caused by Hoth's ordered to shift direction to the east to destroy 48th RC deployed between the two Donets Rivers. vzz481.

At 1000 hrs, the *LAH* panzer group moved out toward the hills northwest of Oktiabrski while a recon force set out to the west to link up with *SSTK* at Mikhailovka. The panzers made good time to the high ground but when they got there, Soviet tankers on the reverse slopes started firing on the panzers. The barrage was so thick the panzers had to quickly retreat. The recon battalion reached Mikhailovka but Soviet artillery from north of the river began and chased the Germans back to just north of Hill 241.6. agk127. zrl240.

The 10th GMB was moved up to bolster the line with 33rd GRC and 24th GTB to stop the *SSTK*'s advance from getting behind 5th GTA and helping *LAH* in reaching Prokhorovka. Vatutin had ordered Zhadov to continue his attack on *SSTK* that day to prevent the Germans from reaching the Kartashevka-Beregovoe road or crossing to the eastern bank of the Psel River to join up with *LAH*. The 74 assorted panzers of *SSTK* were not strong enough to break the line and, after several more hours of fighting, Priess had to fall back to Hill 226.6. The 13th GRD and 66th GRD of 32nd GRC of 5th GA with the support of 31st TC were to launch an attack toward Hill 235.9 and drive the 11th PzD out of Kochetovka. At the same time, Popov's 33rd GRC would attack Polezhaev, and if possible Hill 226.6 to the southwest. Vatutin had hopes of better success that day, since it was discovered that *SSTK* had sent some of its panzers to the southern bank of the river during the predawn hours. mhz349. vzz460+. vzz1m. lck374. gnk312m. vzz11m

To the south of *SSTK* and *LAH*, *Das Reich* was to resume its attack toward Prokhorovka, hoping that 3rd PzC would catch up and join the attack. At that moment, Rotmistrov considered *SSTK* the greater danger and sent 10th GMB of 5th GMC across the Psel River to join 33rd GRD in stopping *SSTK*. After the fierce fighting the day before, *SSTK* had only 54 working panzers with the division. Priess had left 20 StuGs at the bridgehead to protect the critical bridges if it was necessary to fall back quickly. *SSTK* had advanced to the line: Andreevka-northwest edge of Eleshaev-500 yards north of Polezhaev-northwest of Kluchi-southwest of Ilinski. The *LAH* resumed its march along the railroad to Oktiabrski State Farm but the 29th TC attacked and were able to stop the *LAH* from reaching the farm. mhz349. dgr226. fkk172. fkk178m. lck372.

As part of the 33rd GRC, the 95th GRD along with the 24th GTB, the 10th GMB and fire support from the 18th TC would lead the assault to capture Hill 226.6 while the 132nd GRR of 42nd GRD capture nearby Polezhaev and Kliuchi. The attack launched at 1100 hrs after an hour-long suppressive preparation from artillery of Rodimstev's 32nd GRC while the 13th GRD and 66th GRD launched toward Hill 235.9 and the village of Kochetovka which was defended by 11th PzD. These two divisions were quickly repulsed while the 31st TC positioned nearby stood idle. The 97th GRD had better a little better results with their attack. They reached the outskirts of Veselyi but were prevented from entering. The 95th GRD reached Hill 226.6 and was struggling to take it away from the Germans. vzz460++. gnk312m.

Das Reich fought throughout the night and predawn hours in an attempt to reach Pravorot. To regain Storozhevoe, which was lost the previous day, and to prevent *Das Reich* from advancing on Pravorot, the 2nd TC's 99th TB attacked toward the hamlet. The 58th

MRB was supposed to support the tankers but they did not show up until 1400 hrs. The Germans had planted many mines and erected strong defenses and the Soviet attack failed east of Ivanovski Vyselok. Without artillery support a second attempt also failed. vzz469+.

Das Reich had concentrated its forces in the Iasnaia Poliana, Kalinin and Ozerovski region while the *LAH* had a heavy presence in the Pokrovka-Iakovlevo area. They were preparing to launch an attack on 6th GA the next morning. dgr106.

Though attacked but not threatened, General Priess ordered, with Hausser's approval, his Tigers to continue fighting for the heights along the Kartashevka-Beregovoe road. With these hills secured from Soviet artillery, the division was to force a crossing to the eastern banks of the Psel and clear the resistance in the Petrovka area. This was the route the *LAH* was planning on taking after Prokhorovka fell. At the same time *Das Reich* was to remain on the defensive and stabilize their line in order to send forces over to the 167th ID which was attempting to come even with *Das Reich*. Hitler would squash this order later in the day. Instead of driving north, the *LAH* and *Das Reich* of SS 2nd PzC would shift east in order to encircle the 48th RC of 69th Army which were currently fighting 3rd PzC driving north. Knowing that Citadel was ending, von Manstein was trying now to destroy as many Soviets as possible before the Soviets countered. If the 5th GTA had been more successful the previous day, the 48th RC would not have been in the trouble they were in that day. It was estimated that the Soviets had lost 1,800 tanks in Operation Citadel to this point. vzz456+. sgf351. vzz11m zrl238.

While the 18th TC was battling elements of 2nd SS PzC, the 24th GTB with support of the 42nd GRD launched an offensive to drive the *SSTK* back to Polezhaev and capture Hill 226.6. After regrouping, the 24th GTBs resumed its attack toward Krasnyi Oktiabr. The German resistance strengthen and prevented the 24th GTB from reaching its objective. The 42nd GRD after securing Polezhaev, headed for Hill 226.6 and attacked its southern border. *SSTK* countered, breaking through the 42nd GRD line and were able to reach the Kartashevka-Prokhorovka road, but were forced to retreat from the heavy shelling. dgr226. vzz1m. vzz465. gnk312m.

The 13th GRD and 66th GRD of 32nd GRC (5th GA) supported by the 31st TC launched an attack toward Hill 235.9 and the village of Kochetovka. Both the hill and the village were being defended by 11th PzD. The rest of 32nd GRC launched toward Polezhaev and Hill 226.6 which were defended by *SSTK* and *LAH*. Vatutin, using an active defense, was making certain that Hausser would not capture Prokhorovka. With his tank brigades greatly weakened, Vatutin had to rely on his infantry to stop the Germans. vzz460+. gnk312m.

At 1115 hrs, Hoth transmitted to Hausser that Citadel had been canceled. The main objective was to shift to the east and encircle the 48th RC that was positioned between the two Donets Rivers. The 3rd PzGR of *Das Reich* (*Deutschland*) was ordered to launch an attack from the woods south of Ivanovski Vyselok toward Belenikhino Station while the 4th PzGR (Das Fuhrer) was to attack toward the hills west of Vingradovka to link up with the 3rd PzGR. After linking, *Das Reich* would pass through Vinogradovka and head for Pravorot. The *Luftwaffe* would add its support. Though the Stukas were not flying, the fighters were active. The 167th ID would also advance to provide flank support. It started raining, slowing the advance a little. The 183rd RD was defending Kalinin and Sobachevski sector but had to fall back when *Das Reich* came through around 2000 hrs. The 4th GMRB, 4th GTB and 26th GTB were in the area; they moved to intercept *Das Reich* while the gains were small. It was only a modest gain for *Das Reich* before they were stopped. While *Das Reich* was heading east and eventually south, Kempf continued to advance northward with the objective of linking up with *Das Reich*. vzz480++. vzz488. kuz195. zow167.

At 1130 hrs, Hoth ordered Hausser to have *Das Reich* and all available nearby forces attack toward Pravorot. Kruger was not happy with the order. With the hard fighting of the previous day, his division needed time to regroup. It had been raining hard the past few days and it was raining at that time so the ground was difficult to maneuver and with the cloudy skies, the *Luftwaffe* would not support the drive. Kruger also had difficulties with 167th ID to support their right flank. The assault did not begin until 1630 hrs with infantry in the lead and panzers in the rear and even with light resistance, the division was able to travel less than a mile toward its objective before dark. Kruger refused to travel at night but did choose a good jumping off point for the following morning. After taking Pravorot, *Das Reich* was to shift to the north and drive toward southern Prokhorovka. It was hoped that 3rd PzC would continue its advance and assist *Das Reich* with the taking of Prokhorovka. Pravorot was three miles south of Prokhorovka and seven miles north of Ryndinka where 6th PzD entered the day before. gnk374. zow166.

By 1130 hrs on this Tuesday morning, *SSTK* had followed the Psel River northward and reached the Prokhorovka to Kartashevka road but could go no farther due to a counterattack. Later, Hausser ordered *LAH* to attack the Oktiabrski State Farm, while at the same time the infantry in the division was to advance along the southern bank of the Psel from Andreevka toward Mikhailovka with the object of fortifying *SSTK* at Andreevka. The initial attack on the OSF was good until the panzers met up with a line of dug-in anti-tank guns which stopped their advance. The attack failed and the panzers had to fall back to Hill 241.6 while under heavy fire from Soviet guns on the northern bank of the Psel. The Soviets followed, wanting to annihilate the retreating Germans. *SSTK* was supposed to have gone a little farther then turned to roll over the Soviet defenses on the east side of the river that were blocking *LAH*'s advance, but this was the farthest they achieved and now they would be pushed back to the north banks of the Psel. dgk214. dgk213m. mhz349 fkk172.

Hill 226.6 was now under constant attack by tank and infantry or artillery and aerial assault. The *Eicke* Regiment called Priess for backup but the *Luftwaffe* refused to take to the air. Priess was also unable to send panzers or men from within the bridgehead for the entire bridgehead was under attack and *SSTK* was dangerously threatened. A lucky break for Hill 226.6 defenders occurred in late morning when the panzers that were on the Kartashevka road made it back to Hill 226.6. By 1900 hrs Hill 226.6 was stabilized. It also stopped raining about this time and the skies turned only partly cloudy. A few German planes were then seen flying over the rear areas of the Soviet sectors; no bombers but recon planes surveying ground conditions. By this time fuel and ammo was exhausted at Hill 226.6 and elsewhere, but with the ground so muddy supplies were slow to reach the front. gnk380+.

The 97th GRD struck repeatedly against *SSTK*'s western flank, inflicting heavy casualties to both sides but the Germans desperately held on. With a gap between 11th PzD on the west and *SSTK* on the east side, it made it easier for 97th GRD to attack *SSTK* all day long. A little further east the Soviets continued to attack Kochetovka into the night. gnk381+.

From east of Hill 252.2, Soviet infantry and tanks attacked the hill. The Germans responded with heavy artillery and mortar fire that forced the Soviets back. After falling back a ways, the Soviets started enhancing their trench system, adding more mines and guns expecting that the Germans would attack by next morning after regrouping. In the afternoon, Soviet guns began firing on Hill 252.2 and along the front line to disrupt as much as to kill the enemy. The *LAH* defending Mikhailovka had to fall back to the southwest to Hill 241.6 the shelling became so heavy. *LAH* had suffered 326 casualties. gnk372+. gnk365m. vzz1m.

As part of Vatutin's counter-offensive, the 95th GRD launched toward Kliuchi and Hill 226.6. The 287th GRR headed for Kliuchi and the woods east of the village while 290th GRR followed in second echelon. Fifty tanks from 24th GTB also followed. The 284th GRR headed for Hill 226.6 and by 1115 hrs had thrown the Germans off the hill. From the southeast of the hill, a formation of 50 panzers attacked and separated the 24th GTB from the 284th GRR. By 1200 hrs when the Germans could not retake the hill a second formation of 30 panzers and a battalion of infantry were added to the battle. A third formation of infantry and panzers were needed to push the Soviets off the hill and to fall back. While screening the hill, elements of this German combat group headed toward Kliuchi in order to maneuver around the 284th GRR. For the next three hours bitter fighting occurred but eventually the 284th GRR had to fall back to the line defended by the 290th GRR, south and southeast of Veselyi. The 287th GRR and the 24th GTB fell back a mile to the northwest of Hill 226.6 to the southeast corner of Hill 242.3 which was being defended by the 104th Destroyer Anti-tank Artillery Battalion. vzz463++. gnk312m.

At noon, the bulk of *LAH* launched an attack northeast of Oktiabrski State Farm while the remainder attacked along the south bank of the Psel from Andreevka toward Mikhailovka in order to smooth the line between *LAH* and *SSTK*. The recon forces of *LAH* did penetrate into Mikhailovka but were forced to withdraw to Hill 241.6, being the victim of heavy artillery shelling. The main group was quickly stopped by a long line of dug-in tanks and the 9th GAD and 53rd MRB while the secondary attack penetrated the line of 42nd GRD and made it into Mikhailovka but were forced to withdraw to Hill 241.6 south of Andreevka under a heavy barrage. The remains of the 29th TC then counter-attacked the main *LAH*, pushing them back to just north of the Komsomolets State Farm. *SSTK* had reached the Prokhorovka-Kartashevka road but with the increased Soviet resistance, the *SSTK* decided to fall back to a safer position. dgk214+. vzz8m. vzz1m.

Before the day was out, the 69th Army clearly saw the intentions of the Germans in attempting to encircle the 48th RC. The 3rd PzC consisting of the 168th ID, 6th PzD and 19th PzD would head north and converge on Shakhovo while the northern group of *Das Reich*, *LAH*, 167th ID driving from Teterevino, Iasnaia Poliana and Hill 258.2 would drive south toward Shakhovo, clearing Soviet resistance as it marched. The 27th GAB and 32nd DAB were sent to support the 48th RC with its guns to prevent the encirclement. Nearby the 35th GRC was augmented with several mortar regiments to strengthen the line as well. vzz482+.

Elements of the 18th TC launched an attack toward Andreevka but before reaching the objective, it ran into a column of panzers heading for Mikhailovka. After a short fight the Germans, having an exposed flank, had to withdraw. The 18th TC continued on, capturing Vasilevka. The failure of the *LAH* to crack the Soviet defenses north of the Oktiabrski State Farm condemned the *SSTK* advance north of the Psel River to failure. The 5th GMC along with the 18th TC made further attacks against German positions, recapturing Polezhaev, Hill 226.6 and made further gains in the direction of Krasyni Oktiabr. dgk215+. dgr226.6. vzz1m. gnk312m.

Hoth ordered 2nd SS PzC to clear the area south of Petrovka where the Soviets penetrated the line the previous day and to regain the ground up to the Beregovoe-Kartschevka road. These actions would be necessary if 2nd SS PzC were ever to link up with 3rd PzC, encircling many Soviets. Few of these objectives were achieved. The German army was spent but the *SSTK* was able to eke out a thin salient that extended deep into Soviet forces, north of the Psel reaching the Beregovoe-Kartschevka road but were stopped when the 10th GMB and 24th GTB joined the fight. By the end of the day, the *SSTK* was completely spent and could not cross over to the east bank of the Psel to help *LAH*. Hausser was hoping if the *LAH* and *Das Reich* could reach Prokhorovka that this salient would add pressure and force the Soviets out of the town. The 10th GMB was moved to Ostrenkov, six miles north of Prokhorovka in case they were needed. dgk209+. dgk212. fkk170. dgk211m. vzz11m

In the morning, Bakharov's 170th TB and 181st TB with support from the 110th Brigade attacked toward Andreevka and Vasilevka. Kirichenko pulled back his shattered 31st TB and 32nd TB to Oktiabrski, replacing them with the 53rd MRB and 9th GAD. With losing so many tanks, Rotmistrov was now worried about his flanks, with *SSTK* north of the Psel River and 3rd PzC to the east starting to make progress toward Prokhorovka there was a real possibility of encirclement for some of his brigades. He ordered the 6th GAD to force march during the night to block the way in the morning. dgk195. lck374.

On the 5th GTA's left flank in the Vypolzovka area, the 53rd GTR attacked German positions north of Aleksandrovka but failed to break through. dgr227. vzz3m.

Over the past couple days, Soviet armor had been assembling near Petrovka and still had 120 tanks left after the fighting of the previous day. This group attacked midday and had entered eastern Veselyi. Sturm Abt 3 was called up to plug the gap but while German reinforcements were coming up, Soviet artillery increased on the German positions. That artillery was situated at Ilinski. While Stukas could not fly in this weather, the HS 129s with their new 30mm cannon did fly against the oncoming tanks heading for Veselyi. Rudel, a German ace, put 12 tanks out of action on this day alone. More Soviet tanks and mechanized infantry continued to drive west from Prokhorovka toward Petrovka and Beregovoe. Hill 226.6, west of Prokhorovka, was high priority for both sides and it had changed sides several times in the past few days but it looked like the Soviets were determined to keep it for good. fkk171. fkk319m. gnk312m. vzz11m.

While 2nd SS PzC was struggling for Hill 226.6, a Soviet counter-attack broke through the German line and Pz Abt 3 was called up to help plug the gap. The fighting was fierce and several StuGs were damaged. While the battle raged, two crews got out and repaired their StuGs in the middle of field and then reentered the battle. The gap was plugged and the leading tanks withdrew over the crest of the hill. 38 Soviet tanks were claimed destroyed. fkk171. gnk312m.

The 33rd GRC had a little more success in its attack in the bend of the river than 32nd GRC. The 97th GRD launched heading to the southeast from the line: Hill 209.3 to the left bank of the Olshanka River and then to the southern outskirts of Kartashevka. The assault was halted at Veselyi and the Soviets had to dig in and fight a static battle. The 95th GRD with 30 tanks from the 24th GTB launched about the same time. The 287th GRR headed for Kliuchi while the 284th GRR drove toward Hill 226.6 and the 290th GRR was behind the 287th GRR. The 284th and 287th GRR did reach and capture the first line of trenches in front of Hill 226.6. vzz462++. gnk312m.

At 1300 hrs, the 29th TC had 51 tanks, the 18th TC had 33 tanks while the 2nd TC had 42 tanks and the 2nd GTC had 80 working tanks. Rotmistrov had less than half the armor of the previous morning. vzz458.

The *Das Reich* attacked north of Belenikhino, inflicting heavy casualties while driving the 2nd GTC back. It then attacked and captured Storozhevoe I before moving on toward Vinogradovka. The objective of this action was to link up with 3rd PzC to the east. Late at night, Vatutin ordered the 42nd GRD to travel from Psel Valley southward and move into position and attack *Das Reich* in the morning. dgk216. dgr172m. dgk184m. dgk222m. lck375.

Zhukov arrived at Vatutin's HQ to appraise the situation. Zhukov with Vatutin and Khrushchev immediately inspected the battlefield to confirm Vatutin's appraisal. Stalin had doubts about Vatutin and he was wondering if he should be relieved. After seeing the battlefield, Zhukov backed Vatutin and Stalin relented. Zhukov stayed with Vatutin until 9/24. Stalin was also unhappy with Vasilevsky, who was stationed at Kursk and did not seem to ride Vatutin enough. Stalin sent him to the deep south to oversee the Donbas Offensive. gjz188+. dgk208. gnk355. kcz169. zro210. zrl238.

The regrouping of 18th TC and 29th TC did not take long. In the afternoon while 2nd TC was attacking Storozhevoe and 2nd GTC toward Teterevino, these corps were tasked to advance toward Gresnoe and Malye Maiachki (18th TC) and Hill 252.2, southeast of the Oktiabrski State Farm (29th TC). All attacks failed. The attack area was defended by *Das Reich* and *LAH* which had 133 panzers and 44 anti-tank guns while the Soviets had 154 tanks. Once the Soviet attack was neutralized, *Das Reich* resumed its offensive and was able to gain ground along the Ivanovka-Vinogradovka axis. The *LAH* repulsed all attacks along the Prokhorovka-Teterevino road but at the same time the Soviets were erecting stiffer defenses and establishing minefields in the Oktiabrski State Farm area and eastward. However, the *SSTK* was forced to fall back from the Polezhaev area after being attacked by the 52nd GRD, 95th GRD and the 11th MRB. vzz471++. gnk372. ztc270.

In the afternoon after taking Polezhaev from *SSTK*, the 136th GRR of 42nd GRD moved toward the southern slopes of Hill 226.6 to assist 95th GRD. At the same time other elements of 42nd GRD attacked toward Veselyi. By 1500 hrs, the first line was penetrated but by 1900 hrs, the line was repaired and the 95th GRD had to fall back. vzz465. gnk312m. kuz193. zow167.

With the roads in bad condition, *Das Reich* stayed defensive against repeated attacks by 183rd RD as it drove toward Kalinin and Sobachevski but by 1430 hrs, it launched, with support of the *Luftwaffe* and artillery, its own attack. By 2100 hrs, it had pushed back the 183rd RD, gaining ground in the valley between Ivanovka and Vinogradovka. *Das Reich* shifted to the northeast toward Pravorot but was stopped not far from Ivanovka when the 2nd GTC came in to support the infantry. The Germans made only modest gains that day in this sector. For the whole day, *Das Reich* was trying to improve its position, preparing to make a last run on Prokhorovka. By 1500 hours it had captured Storozhevoe and reached the western outskirts of Vinogradovka. Vatutin sent the 42nd GRD from the Psel River southward to meet *Das Reich*. vzz481. zow167.

Along the southern banks of the Psel, the lead elements of *LAH*, panzers and motorized vehicles, attacked the 42nd GRD but were repulsed. The 181st TB ambushed the on-coming panzers which were heading for Mikhailovka, but the panzers had to fall back. The 181st followed and captured Vasilevka before the Germans could build a defense.

dgk215*+. dgr172m. dgk184m.

Elements of *Das Reich*, with 30 panzers, and the 167th ID crossed the Donets near Shcholokovo and attacked 26th GTB capturing the village. Working its way along a gully toward Shakhovo, it repeatedly tried to reach the village but failed each time against the stiff resistance of the 11th GMB. Near Rzhavets, another group of Germans were heading west toward Hill 216.0 trying to link up with *Das Reich* and encircling 48th RC. At about 2100 hrs, these Germans captured Ryndinka. vzz475. dgr221m.

The 95th GRD and 42nd GRD, along with some tanks of 5th GTA, launched an attack southward from Prokhorovka. Meanwhile, *SSTK* had dug in during the night and was defending the line north of Psel against the 18th TC which had moved in to assist the 11th MRB which was in trouble. Rotmistrov's 5th GTA had lost a lot of tanks the past two days. Throughout the night, Soviet units tried to regroup and fortify for the next day. dgk195.

At the end of the day after the *SSTK* and *LAH* exhausted themselves, the 18th TC and 29th TC, after being on the defensive all day and stopping the *LAH*, went on the offensive. The two tank corps were able to push the Germans back to just north of the Komsomolets State Farm where the Germans regrouped and stopped the Soviet advance. dgk215. vzz8m. zrl240.

Though commanding only a Mk IV panzer, Hans Mennel had destroyed or disabled 24 tanks or assault guns since the start of the campaign. wwf149.

The 2nd VA and 17th VA flew 777 sorties that day; most were against the 3rd PzC. With this strong air support, Trufanov was able to stop 3rd PzC from reaching *Das Reich*. The 3rd PzC was abandoned from the air. The 8th *Flieger* Corps flew 656 sorties in support of 4th PzA, with special attention to *SSTK*. Despite this air support, *SSTK* was unable to gain ground and in fact, in some places, the grenadiers fell back about mile. cbk97++. nzk77.

Vatutin believed that in addition to a properly prepared defense that was heavily echeloned, a timely infusion of reinforcements was another reason for preventing the Germans from reaching Kursk as was the emphasis of having heavy flank protection/incursions, which disrupted the Germans from devoting their full attention to the northern front. The heavy deployment on the sides prevented the enemy in widening their attack zone and disallowed them freedom of movement. Being confined to a relatively narrow front worked to the Soviets' advantage. The same could be said for Rokossovsky's defenses in the north. dgr123+.

Realizing that his present forces would not be able to encircle the Germans, Vatutin asked Stalin for the 4th GTC and one mechanized corps to complete the task. vzz457.

The 95th GRD, 42nd GRD, 52nd GRD of 5th GA along with the 24th GTB and 10th GTB of 5th GMC were to continue their drive to eliminate *SSTK*'s bridgehead north of the Psel River. Taking Polezhaev and Hill 226.6 were of special importance. Polezhaev was taken that afternoon but Hill 226.6 was not occupied until 7/17, when the Germans started to retreat from the area. The 69th Army was to continue to destroy Kempf's bridgehead at Rzhavets-Ryndinka while at the same time avoid any large encirclements. The 6th GA and 1st TA were continue to prevent the 48th PzC from reaching the Psel River. vzz458*. vzz462. dgr221m. gnk312m. vzz578.

With the tank corps getting hit hard yesterday and with 5th GA now in sector, Vatutin places the tank corps in second echelon and the infantry was now on the front line. The

127th GRR and 136th GRR of 42nd GRD defended Vasilevka, Andreevka, Mikhailovka and Oktiabrski State Farm. The 23rd GAR and 28th GAR of 9th GAD were deployed between Mikhailovka and Iamki. The 285th RR of 183rd RD defended from Iamki to Storozhevoe. The 26th GAR of 9th GAD was in second echelon. vzz468+.

By nightfall, most German units were spent; there was nothing left to give. dgk216.

Hoth sent the following orders to Hausser for tomorrow's objectives. *Das Reich* was to continue its advance eastward in the Ivanovka-Vinogradovka area. After capturing those two important villages the division was to turn north and attack Pravorot, south of Prokhorovka. *LAH* was to hold their line until *Das Reich* attacks Pravorot and then join in and attack Iamki which was a little north of Pravorot. *SSTK* was to stay defensive and repulse all attacks, giving up as little ground as possible. zrl241. gnk381.

At dawn, the panzer group of *GD* assembled just outside of Tolstoe Woods that ran along the Berezovka-Kruglik road. Nearby, there was also a road running east to Verkhopenie and just south of this road junction was the troublesome Hill 258.5. The one mile square woods were defended by the 100 tanks of the 10th TC and 30 Pak guns. The Soviets had the advantage, for they had built formidable defenses within the woods while the Germans were completely exposed on open ground for the upcoming battle. Without shelling the woods thoroughly, Knobelsdorff ordered *GD* to attack from the north and 3rd PzD to attack from the south. To make the objective even more difficult to capture, the nearby Hill 258.5 was heavily laden with Soviet artillery. The only way the Germans had a chance to take the woods would be with heavy air support, but the skies were cloudy and the *Luftwaffe* refused to fly until the skies started clearing. gnk384+. gnk365m. hsz132.

At 0600 hrs as planned, the 3rd PzD attacked the southern edge of Tolstoe Woods but *GD*, having already been attacked, had not reached its jumping off point and the 3rd PzD was fighting a desperate battle by itself. By 0700 hrs, the *GD*, commanded by Decker, was still defending itself less than a mile northeast of Hill 258.5. It was subsequently thought that Decker, without the aid of air support, thought the mission was suicidal and refused to join battle. To the south of the woods, General Westhoven was observing the battle when a group of Soviet tanks broke free and starting firing on Westhoven and his staff. As more Soviet tanks left the woods, a group of Marders came by and attacked the T34s of 10th TC. The counter-attack succeeded and the Soviet tanks retreated into the woods. Just before 0900 hrs, elements of the 394th PzGR reached the southern edge of the woods and joined forces with the lead elements of 332nd ID near Hill 237.6. A small Soviet tank force broke out of the woods past this German group and was trying to maneuver to the rear of 3rd PzD which was near Berezovka. General Franz Westhoven, seeing the danger, called Knobelsdorff and demanded Decker of *GD* begin his assault. Instead of calling Decker, Knobelsdorff ordered Westhoven to break off the attack and fall back to Hill 237.6, northwest of Berezovka and regroup before attacking an exposed flank of the Soviets attacking Berezovka. It was just 1000 hrs. While 3rd PzD was redeploying, Decker sent another recon patrol to scout the northern edge of the woods. General Walter Hoernlein reported to Knobelsdorff that his panzers could not take the woods without additional resources. While leaving a scouting party near Hill 258.5, Decker again sandbags and slowly regrouped before moving the rest of his column to Berezovka to help 3rd PzD. gnk385+.

After the previous day's hard fight, the 3rd PzD, *GD*, and 11th PzD were attempting to ready themselves to resume their attack but the Soviets continued to harass the western flank to the point where these German divisions had to postpone their advance and fight to secure their flanks. Von Manstein also had the 24th PzC in reserve, which consisted of the Viking, 17th PzD and 23rd PzD but Hitler would not release these divisions to von Manstein for fear of weakening the Donbas line. The 24th PzC was reporting 181 panzers and assault guns plus 123 field guns. vzz452+. ztc271.

The 3rd PzD was no longer able to advance northwards but had to thrust to the west to keep from being encircled. The Soviets had entered Berezovka the previous night and by that morning had captured it along with Gertsovka. The lead units were now closing in on Rakovo but had to wait for reinforcements to take the village. In *GD* sector, the defenders on Hill 247.0 near Kalinovka were coming under serious attack by the 240th RD and 86th TB coming from west of Kruglik. It soon forced *GD* off the hill. The 48th PzC's left flank was crumbling. In addition to all of Vatutin's other orders for the new offensive, the 6th GA's 23rd GRC, the 3rd MC and 31st TC were tasked to commence an offensive once the Germans showed signs of pulling back. The 5th GA's fresh 13th GRD, 66th GRD and 97th GRD (32nd GRC) were moved up to the line during the previous night and would be an integral part of this new offensive taking place today. dgk206+.

In the attempt to assist 3rd PzD and reduce overall resistance on the west flank, the *GD* attempts to gain ground in the Tolstoe area. hjj122. hjj123m.

On the 48th PzC front, the 1st TA and 6th GA continued to attack using about 70 tanks against the 11th PzD. *GD* was fighting to keep the high ground three miles west of Verkhopenie against attacks by the 5th GTC and elements of 10th TC. At the same time, elements of *GD* attacked the 3rd TC at Novoselovka. The 3rd PzD at Berezovka had to go defensive against attacks from the 184th RD and 219th RD supported by 6th TC. The Soviets penetrated the line but were not able to go far. wdk165+. hjj121m. hjj117m. dgr209m.

To bolster the left flank of 5th GA, the 5th MC of 5th GTA and 33rd GRC advanced past Ostrenkov village, six miles north of Prokhorovka to block the 11th PzD and *Das Reich* from reaching Prokhorovka from the east or west and for the rest of the day fierce fighting occurred; both sides suffering heavy casualties. dgk212. dgk213m.

The 48th PzC went defensive as its flank was being heavily attacked. The 48th finally had to withdraw, losing control of Berezovka and Hill 247. bt89.

The left flank of 4th PzA, the 52nd IC, had no armor and was in serious trouble against persistent Soviet pressure.

North of the Oboyan road, 11 PzD with 50 panzers left was striving for further gains, but were stopped by Soviet resistance. By late afternoon the Soviets counter-attacked but were unable to penetrate the 11th PzD's line. Vatutin knew by now he had broken the Germans' advance; his flank attacks had worked against 48th PzC and that they would not be able to advance to Kursk. Vatutin wanted to continue to put pressure on the Germans to see if they made a mistake and could be encircled. Vatutin resumed his attack against 3rd PzD as well. The 3rd PzD was pushed out of Berezovka then lost control of the Rakova-Kruglik road and finally compelled to give up Hill 247.0 by a Soviet force that was getting stronger by the hour. At the same time, *GD*, after losing Hill 247 but was still defending west of Kalinovka came under strong attack by the 204th RD and the 86th TB coming from the direction of Kruglik. Kalinovka and Hill 254 was soon lost as well. dgk207.

Even without the help of Decker's panzer group (*GD*), Westhoven's 3rd PzD attacked Hill 237.6 and by 1800 hrs, after more of his division arrived, had captured the hill. He quickly brought up artillery pointed at Verkhopenie to help slow down the expected tank attack on the town from the 10th TC, which was currently regrouping in Tolstoe Woods. Westhoven was ordered by Knoelsdorff to attack the Tolstoe woods the next morning and was preparing his attack forces after dark for that attack. gnk387.

The Soviets continued to attack 11th PzD in the Kochetovka area and the division continued to be unable to link up with *SSTK*. The Soviets also attacked 11th PzD further west and small gaps were beginning to appear in the line. Major General Mickl responded to the threat by sending assault guns up to the line but even with this support the Soviets kept coming. With darkness not too far away, the Soviets began to shell the Germans harder and launched the largest attack of the day when sensing the Germans were about to crack. Of special interest to the Soviets was capturing Hill 246.3 but German assault guns were there and were able to repulse the attack in this area. By the end of the day, the German line had buckled in several places but counter-attacks stabilized the weakness and the 11th PzD had lost a little ground but averted a disaster. In fact, all three panzer divisions of 48th PzC had been treated harshly that day but avoided a disaster. With new Soviet reserves moving south, Knobelsdorff knew that his corps would not make Oboyan; he was more concerned about surviving. Knobelsdorff wanted the few panzers of *GD* remaining to bypass Tolstoe Woods and travel further south to support 332nd ID out of their predicament. gnk387+.

At night, Lt General Knobelsdorff visited Walter Hoernlein of *GD* to personally give his orders for the next day. Instead of moving north as expected, *GD* was to attack to the southwest in a repeat performance to assist 3rd PzD in clearing the Berezovka-Kruglik road, especially in the Tolstoe Woods-Dolgi sector, but before linking up with 3rd PzD, *GD* had to retake Hill 243.0. Hoernlein had been part of *GD* since 1941; he was promoted to Lt General in January 1943. fmz226+. fmz227m. zsm254.

Decker's Panther Brigade had to pull out of the line as it had lost most of its Panthers, either through breakdown or damage. There had been bitter tank battles in the Novenkoe area on the western flank on this day and the day before. snk85. gnk312m.

Of the nearly 200 new Panthers that began the campaign, only 38 were still fighting. However only 31 Panthers were total losses and 131 had been recovered from the field and were being repaired. Many of these damaged Panthers would take longer than the usual couple of days to repair, due to type of mechanical problem and the fact that spare parts were not readily available. wdk120.

At 0230 hrs, a Soviet sabotage group with support of six tanks tried to force their way to and destroy the Rzhavets bridge. The attempt failed. gnk384.

At first light, the *Luftwaffe* was out looking for targets and accidently bombed 19th PzD, just west of the Donets. The planes bombed a group of pioneers building a new bridge over the Donets. This was the second friendly fire incident in 24 hours, in the same general area. Shortly after the incident, the 11th GMB attacked the nearby 73rd PzGR which had already lost much of its fighting power to casualties. The 73rd was forced back, taking additional casualties and being threatened with extinction. The 74th PzGR, seeing what happening next door, shifted direction and attacked the Soviets coming through the gap. They were able to stop the bleeding and plug the gap, stabilizing the line. gnk384.

While the 18th TC was attacking, the 29th TC to the east was defending itself against the *LAH* along the railroad line near Oktiabrski State Farm. Further to the east, the 53rd GTB and the 689th AAR attacked 6th PzD near Aleksandrovka but had to go defensive when Tigers came up to support the defense. By the end of the day, the Germans made no appreciable gains and the Soviets were able to stabilize their lines, especially on the flanks.

dgr227.

South of Prokhorovka at night and into the predawn hours of 7/13, the 26th TB and others began an offensive at Shcholokovo, Ryndinka and Vypolsovka against von Manstein's forces which forced the Germans back four miles southward. Ryndinka, near the Donets was captured on this day. Without pausing, the Soviets advanced toward Gostischtschevo, nine miles southwest of Kurakovka. Taking Gostischtschevo bolstered the Soviet line west of the Donets and prevented the 3rd PzC from reaching *Das Reich* for another day. This was a penetration of nine miles into German held ground. fkk296+. dgr221m.

As ordered, the 2nd VA started bombing 3rd PC's sector in early morning and would make many runs throughout the day. Of special interest was the sector that included Kurasovka, Novo Oskochnoe and Kazache. Vatutin was determined to keep Kempf from joining up with Hausser. He was convinced that if the Germans could close the gap and stabilize the line that Prokhorovka would fall. dgk208.

To prevent Kempf from linking up with *Das Reich*, the 48th RC along with the 27th GAB and a few tanks attacked toward the Ryndinka, Rzhavets area. The 48th Destroyer Regiment moved to Plota to block the panzers' path. Artillery moved to shelling distance of the Shakhovo-Vypolzovka line to support the attack. The 32nd Destroyer Brigade moved to the Lvov-Lutovo line to block the path in case the first line was penetrated. The 35th GTC was preparing to advance toward Vypolzovka area but it would take hours before reaching it. The 2nd Air Army was also preparing to increase the sorties in the area as well. vzz482+. dgr221m.

Despite the heavy losses in the morning, Group Bake from 6th PzD, with support from artillery, broke through the Soviet defenses between the Donets and Korocha Rivers, stormed the dominating high ground of Aleksandrovka and opened the way to the north for an advance of 3rd PzC. The 7th PzD and 19th PzD of the 3rd PzC moved from the bridgehead at Rzhavets toward Ryndinka before shifting toward Prokhorovka, but were stopped two miles from town. The lead elements of 19th PzD had been working in predawn hours to stabilize the line between Ryndinka and Shakhovo. The 3rd PzC was exhausted and was no longer capable of mounting an attack; each of its panzer divisions had less than a dozen working panzers. rc209. dlu63m. gnk382+. vzz3m. vzz12m. fzk56. dlu120.

In addition to all the reinforcements that were heading to block Kempf's advance, the 2nd GTC's 26th GTB and the 11th MB would launch from Malye Iablonovo and attack toward Shcholokovo and recapture the village. The attempt failed. During the night, Rotmistrov ordered these forces and the others along the line to stop their offensives and go defensive, if necessary, until the Germans fatigued, then the offensive would begin again. The final objective would be to destroy the bridgehead and take control of the Donets River at Ryndinka and Shcholokovo. The 89th GRD, 81st GRD along with the 26th TB would attack Shcholokovo first. The attack failed and Kempf kept Shcholokovo. Rogozny's 48th RC consists of 81st GRD, 81st GRD, 93rd GRD and the 375th RD. The 35th GRC would join the attack at daybreak next morning and attack toward Rzhavets to prevent the Germans from sending help to Shcholokovo. vzz484+. dgr221m.

The German 3rd PzC was engaged in battle with 69th Army near Aleksandrovka-Bolshie Podiarugi area. Elements of the 5th GMC arrived at Ryndinka while the 11th Mechanized Brigade arrived at Prokhorovka and advanced toward Ryndinka. The 26th GB was shelling Shcholokovo, destroying much of the 19th PzD before it withdrew from the area. The Soviets also penetrated the line near Melikhovo but were eventually repulsed.

shn162. aaa125m. dgr155m. dgr173m. dgr221m. vzz12m.

To prevent Rogozny's 48th RC from being encircled, Vatutin made several redeployments. The 305th RD moved on the line Vypolvzovka-Podsumki-Alekseevka-Ploskoe, replacing 92nd GRD. The 92nd GRD was moving to the line Rzhavets-Avdeevka-Verin,-Polovka-Ryndinka to support the 11th GMB and 12th GMB. Throughout the previous day, the 6th PzD, 7th PzD and 19th PzD attempted to expand its bridgehead but had made few gains. While the other two panzer divisions were preparing to advance, the 19th PzD did so and made it to the woods east of Shakhovo where they stopped. Kempf kept a link with his forces west of the river through Shcholokovo. Kempf was also securing Rzhavets again after a Soviet counter-attack, but the attacks toward Avdeevka and Vypolzovka failed. In late afternoon, a large *Luftwaffe* formation bombed Vypolzovka and Aleksandrovka to the east. By the end of the day Shipy, Avdeevka and Krasnyi Oktiabr were still held by 12th GMB; 6th PzD had to fall back for the night. vzz476++. lck375. dgr221m.

Along the banks of the Northern Donets River, 3rd PzC's 19th PzD and 7th PzD was trying to expand his bridgehead against the 53rd GTR, 96th TB and the 92nd GRD near Aleksandrovka. At the same time the 12th GMB drove into the 6th PzD between Vypolzovka and Aleksandrovka. The 26th GTB and the 11th GMB later joined the battle by attacking German positions at Ryndinka. The 19th PzD was unable to expand the bridgehead but did inflict heavy casualties on the Soviets. The 7th PzD was able to complete assembling into the bridgehead with the 19th PzD. These two divisions were in a good position to launch an attack toward Prokhorovka tomorrow but it was too late. Hitler called off Operation Citadel. dgk216+. dgk222m. dlu63m. vzz3m. dgr221m. wwf173+.

The 3rd PzC's bridgehead on the west side of the Donets, not far from Rzhavets, was too narrow and the Soviet AF found it easy to strike the Germans in such a confined area. lck375.

Another pocket was being closed when a combat group from 7th PzD moved toward Vinogradovka from the south while *Das Reich* moved toward the town from the north. To the southeast, Corps Raus successfully defended against repeated counter-attacks from 25th GRC. It then attacked the Soviets in order to stabilize the line and disrupt their offensive. Over the last day or so, the 7th PzD had divided into three combat groups. One was still defending the eastern flank near Corps Raus. A second group was further north near the Aleksandrovka screening 6th PzD's eastern flank not far from the Rzhavets-Vypolzovka area. The third group had migrated to the Donets River between Strelnikov and Schcholokovo to support 19th PzD. General Raus would command a panzer army in 1944 and 1945. wdk165. zsm258+. vzz12m.

The 7th PzD tried to overrun the line Aleksandrovka-Sviridovo-Hill 235.4 which was heavily defended by the 35th GRC. Despite suffering heavy casualties, the Soviets were able to repulse all attacks from 7th PzD but did lose ground in a couple areas. A little further west, the defenders were also able to hold the Shipy, Avdeevka, Krasnyi Oktiabr line against 6th PzD. The 12th GMB with the support of the 92nd GRD pushed the 6th PzD southward and recaptured Vypolzovka. vzz480.

The weather was very bad with heavy rain showers, making the roads troublesome. The Germans had difficulties resupplying the line. The 2nd SS PzC had troubles regrouping. The 3rd PzC was able to continue to advance toward Prokhorovka. The 19th PzD was able to drive the 81st GRD back toward Schakova. The 6th PzD and 7th PzD were struck by heavy counter-attacks with all the new reserves of the 5th GMC and 2nd GTC coming into the sector from the north. The 6th PzD holding their bridgehead over the Donets at Rzhavets was hardest hit. The Soviet AF made many runs against this bridgehead. Despite all these attacks by evening the Germans had widened their bridgehead in a northwest direction with 19th PzD on the west and 7th PzD in the east. A combat group of the 7th PzD had also moved to the Donets to support the 19th PzD. East of the Donets, the 6th PzD provided flank protection against the advancing 35th GRC. wdk164+.

In the Donets River valley at night, PzR Rothenburg launched an attack that allowed him to reach south of Schachovo before being stopped by strong resistance. Both sides suffered heavy casualties but the Soviets fell back a short ways after losing 19 tanks. fkk297.

Instead of continuing his advance through the night, Kempf paused to regroup his forces for the next day's assault. The 6th PzD was tasked with taking Vypolzovka and Aleksandrovka while the 7th PzD shifted to the northwest to join 19th PzD at Shcholokovo in order to advance on Prokhorovka. dgk204. vzz3m.

The 69th Army continued to experience a desertion problem and deployed blocking patrols to stop and even shoot deserters. vzz486.

Lt General Hermann Breith spent the day trying to consolidate and expand his bridgehead on the Northern Donets River, just seven miles from Prokhorovka. The 92nd GRD, supported by tanks, were trying to stop General Breith. With the bulk of 19th PzD and 7th PzD at the river, 96th TB attacked defenses at Aleksandrovka. The 12th GMB attacked 6th PzD between Vypolzovka and Aleksandrovka. In the north since the start, 9th Army was able to gain only 12 miles at best while Hoth, in the south, gained as much as 30 miles. dgk216+. dgk222m. dlu63m. vzz3m.

On the Prokhorovka axis, the fierce fighting had turned into a stalemate. To the south along the Northern Donets, the 3rd PzC's dramatic advance the day before had turned into a slugging match with 5th GTA and they were now moving nowhere. Von Manstein, Hausser and Kempf all had hopes that the two corps could meet, destroy the trapped forces, reduce their line and resume their assault toward Kursk with a better, cohesive offensive posture. With the ferocious tank battle the previous day, the 2nd SS PzC was down to fewer than 250 panzers including four Tigers and 11 T34s. The Soviets had suffered worse than the Germans but they had more tanks to start with. dgk210++. dgk211m. fkk256.

Shortly after dark, thunderstorms struck causing Vatutin to pause his successful assault for the day, which was led by 5th GA, 6th GA and 10th TC. Vasilevsky and Vatutin discussed plans and decided to continue the assault in the morning to make sure von Manstein could not counter-attack effectively, especially in the Prokhorovka area. Clearing all resistance north of the Psel and then the Pena Rivers would continue, as would clearing 3rd PzC from the Rzhavets area. They both knew the German offensive was dead and that FM von Manstein had lost. dgk208. zow166.

At night, Hoth was discussing battlefield conditions with his staff, lamenting the fact the 2nd Army on 4th PzA's west flank was too weak to participate in the operation, unable to relieve some of the pressure off 48th PzC and 52nd IC that was exerted by 40th Army. zrl240+.

It was a chaotic day for 3rd PzC; the Soviets, with new reinforcements, were attacking the corps from all directions. The advances the 3rd PzC made in the last few days had brought the corps to its physical limits and it was desperate to pause, regroup and resupply, but the Soviets were not obliging. By the end of the day Kempf was more worried about saving his corps than reaching Prokhorovka. Practically every regiment had been broken down into combat groups spread out throughout the sector to put out the many fires the enemy had set. The German cohesion was being torn apart and if the enemy had been a little stronger and better organized it could have shattered the corps. Kempf, realizing his predicament, was doing everything possible to tighten his defenses during the night.

21

July 13th on the Northern Salient

At daybreak and an hour before 4th PzD was scheduled to launch another attack on the hills near Teploe, General Joachim Lemelsen visited Lt General Dieter von Saucken notifying him that his attack was canceled. With 20th PzD being sent to Orel, the 4th PzD was to go defensive and cover both their sector and 20th PzD's old sector. Within a week, the 4th PzD, 5th PzD, 8th PzD and *GD* would be transferred to Orel to rival an offensive that was as large and as important as the Kursk salient. snz255+.

Anticipating a heavy attack near Novosil, Model had the 1st *Flieger* division concentrate on the east sector. It paid off for the 15th VA sent a squadron of IL-2s in to soften up the line shortly after first line. The German fighters who were circling the area quickly attacked and inflicted heavy casualties on the Soviet planes before they had a chance to evade. Not deterred, the 15th VA sent a larger squadron around 1000 hrs, with similar results. Around 1200 hrs, a third wave came in and the Germans had the advantage again. While the air war heated up, Stukas were sent out beyond the salient, attacking Soviet concentrations which forced the Soviet charge to abort. The escorts, Fw 190s, downed additional aircraft while protecting the Stukas. cbk86+. dgk231m. snk433m.

North of the Kursk salient, Operation Kutuzov was expanded. The Western, Bryansk, and later Central Front, attacked Model's 9th Army and 2nd PzA in the Orel sector. In the southern salient, Vatutin ordered his 5th GA and 5th GTA to clear all Germans in the Rzhavets area, southeast of Prokhorovka, which were currently defended by the 3rd PzC. Diversionary attacks were also launched in the Donbas and along the Mius River to prevent reserves from heading to Belgorod. dgk208. dgk227+. dlu63m. zzz101m. dgk231m. snk433m.

Operation Kutuzov expanded by the addition of 50th Army attacking to the west of 11th GA toward Zhizdra into the boundary of 2nd PzA and 4th Army. dgk231m. snk433m.

The 9th PzD, which was still deployed near Ponyri, was ordered to the Orel salient. They arrived later in the day. mkz121. dgk116m. dgk231m. snk433m++.

Planes of *Luftflotte* 6 were already moving to airfields closer to attack area. The field at Karachev and Suponevo, south of Bryansk were chosen. It was a calculated gamble moving closer but Model was willing to take the chance. The 12th Flak Division was moved to the Karachev-Khotynets sector to screen the airfields and to assist the troops against the assault. They practically worked around the clock; their 88s were used as much on tanks as they were on planes. snk171.

In the Orel sector to the north, Boldin's 50th Army on Bagramyan's right flank joined the battle near Ulianovo. Later General Butkov's 1st TC and Maj General Kropotin's 1st GRD also went through the gap. With these new forces, the Soviets were able to break through the second defense belt. Despite 5th PzD's efforts, by the end of the second day, the Soviets had penetrated 10 miles along a 14 mile front. Model would send elements of the 9th Army to assist. dgk234. snk108+. zzz101m. dgk231m. snk433m.

Due to the heavy casualties, the 9th PzD was pulled out of the line in front of

Olkhovatka and sent to north of Orel to help against the Soviet offensive in the Bolkhov area. It arrived in the afternoon and for the next day and half actually slowed the Soviet advance, but then it had to fall back against the unrelenting pressure. mkz121. lck116m.

While the land battle was raging in the Novosil sector, a large air battle was taking place as well. In late morning, for about an hour, the two sides slugged it out, both sides suffering casualties. After it was over, the 1st *Flieger* Division claimed knocking 70 IL-2s out of the sky. Perhaps the *Luftwaffe* did not lose as many planes in the engagement but they lost three of their top aces which was a heavy expense for their victory. cbk88. dgk231m. snk433m.

In the Orel salient, the Red Army resumed its attack. In one 40-tank attack, the Soviets made it to Kotschely, the HQ of 192nd GR of 262nd ID forcing the staff to scatter. It also placed the Soviets behind the artillery line. In other nearby villages of Jevtechov, Voskresensk and Veselaya the grenadiers fought to the last bullet. Through POW interrogations it was discovered that five divisions with 160 tanks were attacking the two divisions of 35th IC sector. Another ten divisions were attacking the rest of 35th IC. So far the worst penetration was in 171th GR sector, but the Soviets were intensifying their assault on the 192nd GR next door. Forty Soviet tanks were destroyed in this sector. fkk351. fkk356. zzz101m. dgk231m. snk433m.

Bagramyan continued to exploit the gap in the line, sending more forces into it. He also drove the 1st TC and 5th TC to deeper penetrations of the second defense belt. The 5th PzD tried to plug the gap but was unable to do so until Model sent elements of 9th Army to support. East of Orel, Rendulic's defenses had better success in fending off the Soviet assault. The 3rd and 63rd Army built a bridge over the Susha River and fought along a nine mile front, but the 35th IC's 56th ID and 262nd ID inflicted heavy casualties once across. Soviet tanks stumbled into a minefield and by the end of the day, had lost 60 tanks but the weight of the attack had forced the Germans back to their second defense belt. At night, Rendulic brought his newly arrived reserves of 36th ID and 8th PzD and 2nd PzDs up to the second line. dgk233++. zzz101m. dgk231m. snk433m. snz260. snz226m. asz366+.

In the Ilyinskoye area not far from Kursk, the pilots of the French volunteers bombed the German positions that were advancing on the Soviet 4th TA and 11th TA.

Around 1200 hrs, after urgently requesting support from the 55th IC, the 1st *Flieger* Division shifted part of it focus to the northwest quadrant to support the ground troops who were getting hit from the ground and the air. A small squadron of 30 planes flew north to attack and maul 50th Army on Western Front's right flank. The 50th had to halt its advance and go defensive. Despite the air raids, the 11th GA continued its attack. Part of the 11th GA were lucky enough to be inside a copse of trees which provided good concealment. cbk87. dgk231m. snk433m.

Flying 2,400 feet over Melekhovo not far from Ulianovo, north of Orel, eight Yak-7Bs were escorting ten IL-2s when four Fw 190s were spotted flying below. The Yaks left the formation and attacked the German fighters just as they were rising to meet the Soviet bombers. Two German planes were shot down as the formation continued to fly south. A single Bf 110 was shot down a few minutes later. With the 1st *Flieger* Divison returning to base leaving the skies unprotected, Bryansk Front resumed its assault with 15th VA providing close support. cbk88. dgk231m. snk433m.

Model completed an emergency defensive belt east of Arkhangelskoye, Kichety, Baranovo and Medyn. The Soviet force heading southwest toward Bolkhov was stopped northwest of the city. The Soviet force heading south, and bypassing Ulianovo in order to enlarge the gap, struck the 293rd ID and 5th PzD along the Vytebet and Resseta Rivers. By 7/15 the Soviets had crossed both rivers though the 5th PzD retained a strategic bridgehead east of Ktsyn. Group Esebeck, consisting of 18th PzD and 20th PzD, managed to temporarily to seal off this penetration. snk109. dgk231m. snk433m.

South of Ulianovo, Soviet pilots discovered a long convoy of trucks and panzers from 9th Army heading for the front line to reinforce the 55th IC. The discovery was called in and the 1st TC was called up to add extra weight against the German line. cbk88. dgk231m. snk433m.

Though knowing him by reputation only, General Model flew up to Mtensk to meet General Rendulic and discuss strategy. If his first impression of Rendulic was favorable, he was going to institute his plan of giving most of the new forces coming into sector to Harpe and giving Rendulic the least amount of help to allow him to keep the Soviets out. Between 7/13 to 7/17, the 36th ID, 2nd PzD and 12th PzD arrived in sector and General Harpe received most of those forces. snz260+.

In the Orel sector to the east, Soviet engineers, while under heavy fire, were able to complete a bridge over the Susha River allowing the 3rd and 63rd Armies to cross against 35th IC's 56th ID and 262nd ID. By the end of the day, the Soviets were repulsed without gaining much ground and suffering heavy casualties. General Lothar Rendulic brought up the 36th ID to the line where it was about to crumble. Soon afterwards the 8th PzD and 2nd PzD arrived to help out. The 2nd PzD came from Model while 8th PzD came from AGC's reserve. Rendulic was promoted to CO of the 2nd PzA because of his fine performance. In the last two days, Model ordered four divisions from 9th Army fighting near Kursk to be brought up to help in the Orel salient. Model was sure further escalation of Soviet forces would occur. dgk234+. zzz101m. dgk231m. snk433m.

Driving out of Orel in the evening, the 56th ID and 262nd ID (35th IC), with support from armor, counter-attacked, surprising the Soviets, but did not gain much ground. fkk335. zzz101m. dgk231m. snk433m.

The 11th GA of the Western Front, with the support of the 1st TC and 5th TC, advanced against the 55th IC toward Bolkhov and Khotynets, a penetration of 10 miles behind German lines along a front of 13 miles. The 61st Army was also moving in the Bolkhov's direction and penetrating five miles behind the lines. After two days, the 2nd PzA had been breached in two major sections and was in trouble. Model began pulling the 9th Army from the Ponyri area to help defend the Orel salient in the hopes of plugging these penetrations. However the skillful defense of the 35th IC and 53rd IC to the southeast had extracted a heavy toll on the attacking 3rd and 63rd Armies. The 15th VA and 16th VA supported the attack after 1300 hrs and by the end of the day, the 53rd IC had to start falling back in an organized manner. The line in their sector had not cracked, but it was close to it. Though the Soviets were beginning to budge the Germans from their front lines, the cost paid for that success was largely derived from the support of the 1st *Flieger* Division. All told, 183 Soviet planes were reported shot down. In addition to the planes, 32 tanks, and 50 vehicles were destroyed, with another 25 tanks damaged. The Germans claimed to have lost 20 aircraft, with nine of them being Fw 190s. The attrition for the Germans had reached a point where they could no longer cover the entire salient at a time. The Red Air Force was in similar straights but it was decided that 1st VA's priority would be in the northwest quadrant, where the biggest gains had been achieved so far. bt89. zzz101m.

dgr199m. cbk88++. kcz169. dgk231m. snk433m.

Col General M.M. Popov, the CO of Bryansk Front, asked *Stavka* for Rybalko's 3rd GTA and late at night it was agreed that Popov could use it. It would take two days to arrive on scene. The 3rd GTA, which had 730 tanks and 37,000 men but no artillery support, was to wheel around the perimeter and attack the Orel salient from the southeast toward Stanovoi Kolodez. and Kromy in 3rd Army's sector between the towns of Mtsenk and Novosil. Naumenko's 15th VA was tasked to support 3rd GTA during the assault. dgk235+. zzz101m. cbk112. kcz171. dgk231m. snk433m++.

In the north the 1st *Flieger* Division flew 1,113 sorties and reported losing 18 planes. nzk77.

22

July 14th on the Southern Salient

Hitler ordered the 24th PzC to move close behind 1st PzA, along the Northern Donets River near Izyum. At the same time *Das Reich* and *SSTK* were notified that they would be heading to the Mius in a few days. To the north, the 8th PzD and 36th ID were moving toward Orel. The 2nd PzD would follow tomorrow. dgk245. snk109. zzz101m.

In the predawn hours, the Soviet AF attacked *LAH* and *Das Reich*'s rear positions. The Soviet pilots attacked Gresnoe, Malye Maichki and Luchki North. A total of 418 missions hit these three targets. cbk99. dgk231m. snk433m.

The *Luftwaffe* was busy attacking rail targets, as well as tank formations moving up to the line. They claimed shooting down 103 Soviet aircraft. jp187.

The Soviets had more planes in the Kursk salient than the Germans, but at least 70% of the pilots would be seeing combat for the first time. Clearly the experienced *Luftwaffe* pilots had the advantage. cbk82.

In *LAH* sector, recon patrols were sent out to get a clear picture of Soviet deployments. It was determined that there were still large concentrations of Soviet tanks south of Prokhorovka near Iamki as well as in the corridor to the west of the important rail junction. The patrols also discovered greatly improved trench systems from Oktiabrski State Farm and Hill 252.2 all the way to Prokhorovka. It was defended by the relatively fresh 110th TB and the 36th GTR. Vatutin was making sure the SS would never make it north of the Kartashevka road. With the discovery of enemy tanks assembling near Mikhailovka, Maj General Wisch wanted to strengthen the boundary with *SSTK* and sent a company west to defend the flank. gnk395+. gnk397m. zrl244.

At 0400 hrs, the 167th ID attacked into the boundary line between the 183rd RD and 375th in the general direction of Ivanovka. After capturing Ivanovka part of the division would pivot south and head for Leski and Shakakhovoto link up with 19th PzD while the rest of division headed north. As the panzers were heading east, a heavy rocket barrage fell on the column. The 375th RD shifted forces and was able to plug the gap on its right flank. The 375th RD was defending the line from half mile north of Teterevino South through Hill 209.7 to Teterevino South (along the railroad line). After taking Ivanovka at 1715 hrs, the 167th ID attacked toward Leski, south of Ivanovka, but was halted at the outskirts of the village. The 183rd RD, directly north of 375th RD, was having trouble keeping the 167th ID out of Leski. The 167th ID's main axis was driving to the northeast toward Hill 234.7 and Maloe Iablonovo and ultimately Pravorot. Fighting past sunset, the 167th ID fought its way to within two miles of Zhimolostnoe, south of Pravorot. By 2000 hrs, the village of Ivanovka and Hill 234.9 had been captured but the division had continued, wanting to reach Pravorot. Hill 234.9 was 2.5 miles from the main road that led into Pravorot. Even with 167th ID paralleling *Das Reich* on its trek toward Pravorot, there was no way the *Das Reich* grenadiers would reach Pravorot that day; the *LAH* panzers, regrouping behind the front lines, waiting for that objective to be taken, would have to wait another day. Wisch only had 53 working panzers and objected strongly to sending them to Iamki to fight for another division while his sector was constantly being attacked. vzz491++. vzz496. vzz3m. gnk396. gnk397m. zrl244. # zow170.

The *Das Reich*'s *Der Führer* Regiment had been stopped the day before but the regiment at 0400 hrs continued its attack along with the 167th ID from Iasnaia Poliana toward Belenikhino and Vinogradovka and the river southwest of Pravorot that morning. The renewed battle saw the Germans penetrate the line. By noon, after a fierce battle for Belenikhino which included house to house fighting, the village fell to the Germans. The regiment moved on and by 1730 hrs had also entered Ivanovka with the support of 167th ID and an hour later captured Hill 234.9. *Der Führer* moved on again but was attacked by armor just two miles west of Zhimolostnoe, where the advance was halted. The 183rd RD was defending nearby Kalinin and Sobachevski sector and the 4th GMRB, 4th GTB, 25th GTB and 26th GTB were defending Belenikhino and Vinogradovka. After losing nine tanks, they eventually had to fall back toward Maloe Iablonovo. A few tankers were encircled in the woods southwest of Vinogradovka but fought their way out. The 375th RD was defending Leski, Teterevino South and Hill 210.7. The whole of the Belenikhino-Ivanovka area was in turmoil until 1800 hrs when the Soviets moved back, leaving the left flank of 4th GTB in Vinogradovka exposed. The *Luftwaffe* had been bombing the Vinogradovka area all afternoon. See Map 23. vzz488++. vz498. dgr106. gnk396. gnk397m. wwf174. zrl241. zow168.

After a short rocket preparation at 0400 hrs, as part of a division wide assault elements of *Das Reich*, with *Der Führer* in the lead, once again attacked Soviet positions at Belenikhino, reaching the outskirts and fighting house to house. Engineers were called up with charges to destroy bunkers and strongpoints. Stukas were called in to assist, destroying 12 T34s and forcing the infantry to withdraw. By 0700 hrs, the Soviet defenses in town began to slowly crumble and by 1200 hrs Belenikhino was captured. At the same time, and with the help of 167th ID, other elements of *Der Führer* were able to capture Hill 220.3, south of Belenikhino. By taking the town and Hill 220.3, there was a sufficient gap in the line to release the panzers that were stationed just outside of Ozerovski, just north of Kalinin. By 1300 hrs, the panzers reached Belenikhino and started supporting the infantry in clearing the surrounding area before quickly moving toward Ivanovka a half mile to the south. rc225. gnk398+.

At 0400 hrs, *Das Reich* also attacked the Iasnaia Poliana area with the objective of reaching Belenikhino and beyond. The defenders, the 89th GRD, initially put up fierce resistance but were eventually forced off the high ground southwest of Pravorot. The *Das Reich* continued to advance and by 1200 hrs was threatening the new rear defenses of 375th RD, which had fallen back a day or so ago and was still fighting to keep 3rd PzC from joining *Das Reich*. See Map 8. wdk166. gnk397m.

In the predawn hours, heavy rains soaked the *SSTK / LAH* area, turning the roads and countryside into deep mud. The supply trucks had a difficult time reaching the line with food, ammo and fuel. mhz360.

Vatutin wanted to destroy *SSTK*'s bridgehead north of Psel River and to capture the two bridges the Germans built. He assembled a large array of forces that launched soon after first light. To prevent the 48th PzC from helping *SSTK*, Vatutin would also attack the western flank as hard as possible. The *SSTK* had discovered a buildup of forces just north of their bridgehead that included 125 tanks and had stayed defensive the whole day; luckily for the division, for if it had launched an attack to the north, it would have been costly. The 5th GA and 5th GTA stayed defensive in the *LAH* and *Das Reich* sectors for the entire day, though Vatutin shelled most of 4th PzA for the entire day. gnk395. kuz193. ztc271. zrl244.

Despite the reverses the German army had suffered in Operation Citadel, both von Manstein and Hoth still believed that a partial victory could be achieved. Kursk was not attainable but both German commanders wanted to destroy as many of the Soviet forces as possible before falling back. gnk395. zow167+.

The *LAH* panzers were ordered to prepare to shift to the east and support *Das Reich* if they penetrated the line and reached Pravorot. From there, the two divisions would turn south away from Prokhorovka. Iamki was supposed to be attacked by *LAH* panzers, but when *Das Reich* failed to take Pravorot today, Iamki was considered non-essential and *LAH* would turn south toward Ryndinka with *SSDR* after taking Pravorot. gnk396. gnk397m.

During the night of 7/13, the 24th GTB was pulled from the front and sent into reserve which left 95th GRD without armor support. With ammo running low, the division launched another assault toward Hill 226.6 but again failed to take it. vzz466.+ gnk312m.

The Tiger company of *LAH* had five running Tigers, while the Panzer Group of *LAH* had 42 panzers, mostly Mk IVs. Panzers were deployed behind the line near Hill 247.6, northeast of Komsomolets State Farm. Their original orders were to drive on Iamki as soon as *Das Reich* captured Pravorot, a little further south. agk129.

Vatutin suspected Hoth's plan to encircle the 48th RC and, to prevent that from happening, he ordered the 2nd TC and 29th TC closer to Storozhevoe and Pravorot to block *Das Reich* from closing the ring. Hausser recognized the increased concentration in this area and ordered *Das Reich*, which was at Maloe Iablonovo, to turn south immediately after capturing Pravorot. To guard *Das Reich* when turning, *LAH*, also turning east, would capture Iamki, northeast of Storozhevoe, and go defensive. Two regiments of 167th ID would continue south to Ivanovka and Hill 234.9, a mile east of Ivanovka, and erect defenses until identification of Soviet intentions. vzz496+. vzz9m.

Elements of *SSTK* at Veselyi, northwest of Prokhorovka and half way between the bend in the Psel River and the Kartashevka road, came under heavy shelling and small attacks but it was quiet otherwise in the rest of its sector. German engineers completed another 60 ton bridge over the Psel by 0840 hrs. Priess wanted another bridge ready in case his division had to quickly retreat to the south side of the Psel. The 33rd GRC moved in southeast of the Veselyi River at Prelestnoe and forced the *SSTK* to give up part of its bridgehead. The 2nd SS PzC claimed only three tanks and one plane destroyed, and only several hundred POWs captured. At the same time north of the Psel, the Thule Regiment of *SSTK* was caught alone and nearly surrounded, but it fought its way clear and inflicted heavy casualties on the Soviets. The bulk of the *SSTK* was attacked by tanks and infantry coming from Veselyi and Mikhailovka but with the help of 111 planes was able to repulse the attack. wdk166. fkk172. fkk319m. gnk397m. vzz1m. ztc271.

In the morning at the *SSTK* bridgehead, the Thule Regiment repulsed a battalion-size attack, supported by some tanks with artillery, mortars and MGs. The *Luftwaffe* was active that morning; they had missed this first attack but were in the air when the second attack occurred. The target was the Veselyi area and the 100-plane formation, made up of Stukas and fighters, quickly turned back the assault, inflicting heavy casualties. The Soviets moved back but did not go very far. They would be back in the morning. kuz218.

The 2nd SS PzC resumed its attack toward Prokhorovka gaining some ground, and was approaching the outskirts. In the afternoon, the 48th PzC made gains near Novenkoe, not far from the Psel River, inflicting heavy casualties and causing the Soviets in the area to retreat northward. The 48th PzC followed, moving north of Novenkoe. This advance gained important high ground which allowed artillery to see Oboyan. With both Prokhorovka and Oboyan within sight, von Manstein was forced to call off the offensive but ordered Hoth to hold his position in the Psel and Pena River areas and to secure it. This securing operation was called Operation Roland but it was called off almost as soon as it started, for the Soviets began a major offensive all along the line that forced von Manstein to detach units from 4th PzA to put out the many penetrations. snk85. dlu121. zrl246.

For most of the day, the 5th GTA regrouped. The 2nd GTC abandoned Belenikhino in order to shorten its front but maintained a front that consisted of Ivanovka, Leski and Shakhovo. dgr227.

As part of the new order to encircle 48th RC, the 167th ID, to the right of *Das Reich*, was now driving east toward the Donets River in the Rozhdestvenka area. Its 339th PzGR's left flank had reached the railroad line one mile west of Belenikhino by evening. The rest of the division was deployed between Ivanovka and Maloe Iablonovo. The 167th ID would attack Leski next morning. On its right flank, the 168th ID had reached the northern outskirts of Gostishchevo. To the north of 167th ID, *Das Reich* had a line that included the northern outskirts of Ivanovka to Hill 234.9. The Soviets had built strong defenses on the west bank of the Donets at Rozhdestvenka and the hills west of the Belgorod-Kursk railroad line. The Soviets had evacuated Leski, Maloe Iablonovo and Shakhovo, moving north and northeast, but they seemed to have stopped their retreat in this area. vzz497+. vzz3m. vzz5m.

As part of their general offensive that was started the previous day, German forces moving from Iasnaia Poliana and Shcholokovo, drove toward Shakhovo, attacking the right wing of 69th Army in the attempt to encircle it. dgk220.

Das Reich opened an assault with artillery preparation with cannon and rockets, then launched their assault. They quickly ran into a minefield, suffering heavy casualties. Once past the minefields, they marched along the ridge southwest of Pravorot and captured the village of Belenikhino by noon after fierce street by street fighting. 12 Soviet tanks that were defending the village were destroyed by infantry. Pravorot, four miles south of Prokhorovka, was their next objective. The Germans continued to push the Soviets back all the next day (15th) until a heavy rainstorm turned the ground into a sea of mud. The 3rd PzC's 7th PzD and 19th PzD were to breakout of their Ryndinka bridgehead, drive west and link up with *Das Reich*, loosely encircling the Soviets between the Lipovyi and Donets Rivers, but no catastrophic damage would be inflicted on 69th Army for the Germans were too weak at this point. dgk220+. hjj121m. mhz358+. lck379. dgr221m. agk129. agk130m. wwf132.

Soviet artillery continued to pound the boundary between *SSTK* and *LAH* for hours. When the artillery stopped at noon, an infantry attack drove toward that weak section. *LAH* had no reserves and was forced to send engineers to help stop the penetration at the boundary. In the afternoon, aerial recon discovered an even larger Soviet force assembling neat Mikhailovka, about a mile northeast of Vasilevka. *LAH* artillery began firing on this concentration with their big guns. Wisch was ordered to keep his remaining panzers on hold in order to support *Das Reich* when they captured Pravorot. Instead of shifting north after Pravorot, the two divisions would now shift south toward Ryndinka, in order to trap as much of 69th Army as possible. Prokhorovka was no longer an objective. gnk396. gnk397m.

While 3rd PzC was advancing to the north, *Das Reich*, with the help of 167th ID, after breaking through Belenikhino Station, was making slow progress toward Pravorot and Leski. Vatutin did not want Pravorot to fall and ordered available elements of the 2nd TC and 29th TC to defend the Storozhevoe-Pravorot line. vzz496. gnk396. gnk397m.

At 1230 hrs, a small Soviet force attacked *SSTK* positions at the barracks that were recently captured south of Veselyi. The attack was preceded by artillery and mortar fire. German artillery returned fire and was able to repulse this initial attack. Reinforcements arrived and a second attempt was made. He111s were called in to attack the tanks that were still north of Veselyi. Stukas also attacked Soviet infantry east of Vasilevka. The *Luftwaffe* stayed for hours but left as it got dark. During the day's fighting it was noticed that grenadiers were not digging in as was SOP; instead, being too exhausted, they would lay on the ground and shoot their rifles. This was causing too many casualties and Hausser had to remind Priess to enforce this entrenching practice. gnk408.

Six miles south of Prokhorovka, the Kempf Army was able to link up with 4th PzA and by night moved a little closer to the town. Nearby, *SSTK* was forced to give up the bridgehead on the north bank of the Psel. The Germans tried to regain the bridgehead but were repulsed with heavy losses. At midnight the rains came and forced the Germans to regroup and go on the defensive. The Soviets were beginning to increase their planned counter-attacks on the exhausted 48th PzC and 2nd SS PzC who had just tried retaking Hill 247.0 and Hill 243.0, west of Prokhorovka. Hill 243.0 was captured but now the Soviets were counter-attacking. bt90. fmz221m. rc225.

While *Das Reich* and 167th ID fought for control of Belenikhino and the surrounding area, Soviet batteries stationed at Leski, one mile south of Ivanovka, shelled the Germans. When the Germans discovered where the shelling came from, their big guns returned fire on Leski, quickly forcing the gun crews to fall back to the northeast. With the Leski guns silenced, Reitzenstein's panzers were able to advance more quickly to capture Ivanovka by 1730 hrs, about the same time that *Der Führer* Regiment reached Hill 234.9. To prevent the enemy from building new defenses, the panzers continued their eastward move, chasing the Soviets. To the northeast from Hill 234.9, large numbers of Soviet forces could be seen heading north, leaving the pocket that *Das Reich*, 167th ID and 3rd PzC were trying to form. A fierce rearguard action was slowing 3rd PzC, while the rest of the forces were settling in along the Storozhevoe-Zhilomostnoe-Novoselovak-Shipy line. This new line also included the Pravorot road. The *SSDR* panzer group reached Hill 234.9 at 1900 hrs but did not stay because their objective was Pravorot and Lt General Kruger thought a quick assault at night might take the village. However, it started raining harder; travel was slower and visibility was poor and the German column never reached the village. gnk399. gnk404+. gnk397m.

During the battle for Belenikhino and Vinogradovka *Das Reich* forced the 4th GMRB and 4th GTB back toward Ivanovka around 1630 hrs, leaving the left flank of 25th GTB exposed at Vinogradovka. After the Soviet retreat to Ivanovka, the *Luftwaffe*'s bombing runs forced the tankers further, back toward Hill 234.9. By 2000 hrs, the elements of 2nd GTC had fallen even further back, close to Zhimolostnoe and Maloe Iablonovo. Elements of *Das Reich* pursued, but stopped at this new line. The lead units of *Das Reich* crossed the Sukhaia Plota ravine but could go no further. vzz491++. vzz3m. gnk397m.

At 1700 hrs, elements of *Das Reich*, including some panzers, were shelled in the Ivanovka-Belenikhino area before a brief engagement that took the Germans into the towns, fighting house to house and forcing the 375th RD to withdraw to the northeast. *Das Reich* continued to advance and tried to take Pravorot but failed to do so. *Das Reich* had to take the town if they were going to outflank the 69th Army to the south and 5th GTA to the north. The 167th ID was on the railroad line southwest of Ivanovka trying to close a pocket at Shakhovo from the west while the 7th PzD was attacking from the east. The *LAH* had a quiet day except for some minor shelling from 5th GTA; Rotmistrov's Army was still recovering from the losses of 7/12. wdk166. hjj121m. dgk222m. gnk397m. vzz12m. vzz3m.

At 1900 hrs, when *Das Reich* was reaching Maloe Iablonovo, Hausser received his latest order. He was to stop all advances toward Prokhorovka and to concentrate on shifting to the east to reach the Zhimolostnoe-Pravorot road, before turning south to link up with Kempf and encircle the 48th RC. vzz496+.

The 2nd GTC abandoned Belenikhino and fell back, forming a line from Ivanovka to Leski to Shakhovo. *Das Reich* was only successful in pushing 2nd GTC back with the heavy support of Stukas. The *Luftwaffe* lost one of their aces in this action. Gunther Schmidt, a Knight's Cross recipient and a pilot with 700 missions, was killed when his plane exploded in mid-air not far from Vinogradovka. dgr227. cbk99+.

At 2000 hrs, the *Luftwaffe* launched a massive raid against the 2nd GTC in the Belenikhino-Shakhovo area. This was followed up by the *Das Reich* attacking the Soviet line which inflicted heavy losses on the tank corps and forcing it to fall back. With 2nd GTC falling back, the 10th GMB was called up to defend the Zhilomostnoe-Novoselovka (east) line. Vatutin was still determined to keep the German two corps from linking up. The 2nd TC repulsed the *Das Reich* along the Storozhevoe-Pravorot line as well. dgr227.

At 2100 hrs, Hoth confirmed Hausser's orders. *Das Reich* was still responsible for capturing Pravorot. Once *Das Reich* reached the Pravorot road, it was to turn north for Pravorot. When the attack was underway, *LAH*'s panzers were to set off eastward and head for Pravorot. This action would also protect *Das Reich*'s northern flank. However Maj General Wisch refused to send his entire panzer group, for he just recently discovered a larger concentration of Soviet tanks massing to his northeast. This would clearly jeopardize *Das Reich* and the successful capture of Pravorot. gnk404+. gnk397m. zow167+.

The 38th Army transferred 167 repaired tanks to 5th GTA. vzz449.

At 0400 hrs, *GD* attacked a hill three miles northwest of Berezovka but was quickly counter-attacked by 20 tanks. German artillery was called in to stop the counter. The 3rd PzD cleared the woods north of Berezovka at about the same time. The 11th PzD fought off an attack on a broad front. The 332nd ID, a little south about a mile northwest of Berezovka made a small advance and improved its defensive position. The 255th ID and 57th ID of 52nd IC held off a couple of small attacks. The 48th PzC claimed destroying 65 tanks which was a rise from the day before and an indication the Soviets were increasing the pressure once again. wdk167.

Knobelsdorff was still threatened by the concentration of Soviet forces in the Tolstoe woods and wanted to make one last attempt in destroying the strongpoint. At 0400 hrs, the *GD* Panzer Brigade, along with support from the 677th GR of 332nd ID, moved into position on the southern border of the woods. *GD* assault guns and its Fusiliers maneuvered to the northern edge. The two groups waited until the *Luftwaffe* appeared and emptied their planes of their deadly cargo. The attack was launched and made good initial progress until the Soviet artillery found the range of the Germans and started pounding the advance. At 0700 hrs, the *Luftwaffe* was called in for a second attack and , having the coordinates of the Soviet artillery, made a solid run against the Soviets. At 0730 hrs, Decker's panzers captured Hill 233.3 southwest of Tolstoe Woods. After a while, the advantage started leaning toward the Germans; the Soviet defenders began to withdraw from the woods heading to the northwest. A rearguard action consisting of a number of T34s prevented the Germans from following. At 0740 hrs, the 3rd PzD began advancing toward the eastern perimeter of the woods but was being held up by stiff resistance at the village of Dolgi and huge minefields. To avoid the minefield the panzers shifted direction, trying to circle the field and drove outside the battle zone leaving the infantry to fend for themselves. With the panzers away, the Soviets counter-attacked, stopping the German advance. Despite the difficulties, 3rd PzD captured Dolgi around 1800 hrs. gnk412.

During the predawn hours and into daylight it rained very hard, making travel slow and difficult throughout the whole day. gnk413.

At 0400 hrs, General Kruger's assault force (*Das Reich*) resumed its march by way of Iasnaia Poliana and skirting just north of Belenikhino toward the high ground southwest of Pravorot. Even with the support of artillery passing Belenikhino took five hours. Without pausing, the shock force made up from *Deutschland* Regiment headed northeast toward the hill southwest of Pravorot. Placing artillery on top of that hill would make their job easier in the taking the heavily fortified village which was located a short distance south of Prokhorovka. zow168.

At 0412 hrs in the *GD* sector on this Wednesday morning, air strikes began. Afterwards, the *GD* resumed its advance but was stopped by heavy artillery fire along the line: Hill 233.3-Hill 240.2. At the same time, after a rocket preparation and a *Luftwaffe* attack that shattered the Soviet anti-tank brigade, the 332nd ID advanced into the Dolgi forest at 1300 hrs and by 1630 hrs, Hill 240.2 and the woods were captured. *GD* destroyed 28 T34s and other heavy field weapons in the engagement. hjj124. hjj123m.

At 0600 hrs on the western flank in 3rd PzD sector, Stukas came in and bombed Soviet positions before 3rd PzD launched a drive to stabilize their line. The Soviets counterattacked, but these attacks were half hearted and were repulsed. In the afternoon, the 3rd PzD moved west and enveloped the Tolstoe Forest, in which the 184th RD and 219th RD had assembled. Panzers from *GD* supported 3rd PzD in clearing the forest. While the Soviet divisions suffered heavy casualties, many soldiers were able to escape to the west. With this action the *GD* was able to close the gap that was between the two divisions. It started raining hard and lasted throughout the night which closed down operations on both sides. The 3rd PzD did search for Soviet survivors in the forest; it did not find many but it did find 70 T34s that got stuck in the swamp ground and abandoned. This successful operation was the last one of 48th PzC and the 4th PzA of Operation Citadel. In the past two weeks, the panzer divisions had lost more than half of their fighting strength. fkk256+.

At 0600 hrs, *GD* moved out as ordered toward the west. The division was configured into three combat groups. The first group, taking the most northern route would head for Hill 247.0 to secure the division's northern flank. The central group headed straight for Hill 243.0 to recapture it and to destroy the defenders. The southern group headed for Tolstoe Woods that ran along the Berezovka-Kruglik road just north of Dolgi. This group attacking from the north, along with elements of 3rd PzD driving from the south, were to encircle and then destroy the tankers that were hiding in the woods. The northern group did not expect heavy resistance until reaching the road to Kruglik but ran into counter-attacks from infiltrating reserves, slowing their progress. They never reached Hill 247.0. The center group did recapture Hill 243.0. The attack on the woods went well. The Soviet tankers came out to face the panzers but many were hit and the survivors returned to the woods where German artillery opened up on them causing greater casualties. In late afternoon, the combat group from *GD* and 3rd PzD moved toward Berezovka where Soviets were causing much trouble. fmz228. fmz227m.

A local attack by elements of 3rd PzD and 52nd IC north of Berezovka, Rakovo line was launched to disrupt Soviet forces on the western flank when Hoth made a final attempt to cross the Psel River in 48th PzC sector. The attack gained about a mile but failed to disrupt Soviet forces. dgr105+. dgr93m.

In the Berezovka sector south of Oboyan the Pz *GD* contacted 3rd PzD and they both repulsed a fierce Soviet counter-attack as they drove toward the Rakovo-Kruglik road which 3rd PzD had lost the day before. The Soviets were now stepping up their counter-attacks; they had evicted the Germans from Hill 247 and recaptured Berezovka five miles away. Now Tolstoe Woods and Hill 258.5 were being attacked. *GD* counter-attacked that started to push the Soviets back to Hill 240 but the advance was stopped when it got within artillery range of the hill. dgk222m. fkk274. lck368.

South of Kruglik, the *GD* division was preparing for an advance when Soviet batteries opened up on it. A Soviet attack from the north and west were repulsed and afterwards, the *GD* advanced toward Hill 247 but made slow progress. Other units of the 48th PzC joined in and routed the Soviets from the area. See Map 8.

The *GD* was ordered from its current position astride the Oboyan road to join up with 3rd PzD in an counter-attack against the 5th GA and 10th TC. The two-day attack launched from the Rakovo-Berezovka region decimated the Soviet defenders, as well as the 6th TC that got in the way. The entire force in front of this onslaught had to retreat almost 2 miles. dgk219. dgr172m. dgk222m.

While the 3rd PzD and *GD* were on the offensive along Tolstoe woods and along the western flank, the 11th PzD fought defensive battles throughout the whole day. The Soviets continued to attack the boundary line between *GD* and 11th PzD's west flank. Not having enough men or panzers to defend his sector, Mickl was forced to use artillery to stop the Soviet attacks. He was successful but by late afternoon, the division was almost out of ammo. If the Soviets had continued to attack, Mickl would have been in trouble for his resupply arrived late. To bridge the gap for the delay of the resupply, Knobelsdroff sent a heavy mortar regiment to Mickl which was gratefully accepted. gnk413.

While the infantry of 3rd PzD completed taking Dolgi, its panzer group had fought its way to Hill 240.2 near the northwest corner of the Tolstoe woods by 1750 hrs. The 332nd ID was then ordered to Hill 240.2 as quick as possible, to join up and relieve the panzers of 3rd PzD and *GD*, which were also fighting in the area. The panzers were ordered to move to Hill 258.2 to close the circle around Tolstoe woods. When the assault guns of 3rd PzD arrived at Hill 240.2 to link up with Decker's Panzer Brigade, Decker was nowhere to be found. On his own initiative, Decker drove back to Berezovka with his 18 Panthers to resupply and refuel. His actions once again completely disrupted the plans of Knobelsdorff to encircle the strongpoint. gnk412+.

The 8th *Flieger* Corps flew 1,452 sorties that day; most of these missions were against

69th Army, which was being squeezed by *Das Reich* on the west and 3rd PzC to the southeast. Von Manstein was trying to enclose the remaining Soviets within this salient. The remainder of the flights assisted *GD* and 3rd PzD in coping with the persistent attacks on their western flanks. About 1,000 sorties were bombers and the rest were fighter attacks. The He 111s were using AB 70 bomb containers and SD 50 fragmentation bombs on Soviet concentrations near Novenkoe. The crews would call these fragmentation bombs "Devil Eggs" which could have a devastating effect on infantry and tanks. The sector was being defended by the 183rd TB and was giving the 3rd PzD a hard time. While the Red Air Force was absent, the German planes received tremendous ground fire. Only one plane was downed in this immediate area but many received damage of varying degrees. Another seven German planes were downed supporting 48th PzC that day. The 1st TA did prevent *GD* and 3rd PzD from gaining much ground, but it cost dearly in men and tanks. The 8th *Flieger* Corps reported downing 31 Soviet planes, which included seven from ground fire. They lost 10 planes. Responding to this increased German air activity, the VVS also increased their missions and flew 1,033 sorties. cbk99+. nzk77. wwf90.

Later in the day *GD* division tried to recapture Hill 243.0 and Hill 247.0 as well as to join up with 3rd PzD at Berezovka. The capture of the hills was in question although the division did join up with 3rd PzD at Berezovka. The forest to the north of Berezovka was cleared at the expense of many Soviet dead from 5th GA and 10th TC but Hill 247 remained in Soviet hands. Von Manstein was trying to smooth out the line and stabilize it before the expected Soviet offensive was launched. This German offensive was called Operation Roland. *Das Reich* was to attack on the Ivanovka-Vinogradovka line and to capture Pravorot. The *LAH* was to regroup and prepare to move through Iamki on Prokhorovka when the other forces were in their starting positions. The *SSTK* was to hold its present position against all counter-attacks. At the same time, the 7th PzD and 19th PzD were to advance from their Ryndinka bridgehead and to trap and destroy all Soviets between the Lipovyi Donets and Donets Rivers. The 6th PzD would attack Aleksandrovka and north of Vypolzovka as a flanking action. rc226. dgk219. dgk222m. vzz3m. dgr221m. wwf174. fmz221m.

At 0100 hrs, fewer than 50 tanks from 26th GTB moved out of Shakhovo toward Leski to prevent the village from falling into 167th ID's control. The 375th RD was still garrisoned at Shakhovo, fighting off 3rd PzC. In just a matter of a few hours it would start a fighting rearguard action to the north. The 2nd GTC was still putting up stiff resistance despite the many casualties. It was defending the line between Ivanovka, Vinogradovka, Maloe Iablonovo, Zhimolostnoe. vzz509.

Breith had 7th PzD and 19th PzD join in order to attack from the Shcholokovo-Ryndinka bridgehead the Soviets were trying to destroy. Then they were to join *Das Reich* between the Lipovyi Donets and the Northern Donets to clear the area, then attack Prokhorovka. The 168th and 167th IDs would follow behind to clear the stragglers. At the same time 6th PzD would attack Aleksandrovka, which had fallen to the Soviets earlier in the week, Hill 222.1 and then move north and capture Vypolzovka, just north of Rzhavets and east of the Northern Donets. This action would protect the rest of 3rd PzC's right flank. Vatutin had anticipated his assault and had sent the 5th GMC to stop the attack. dgk219+. dgk222m. dlu63m. vzz494. vzz3m. dgr221m.

At 0200 hrs, the 2nd GTC moved into their ordered position: Vinogradovka-Belenikhino-Shakhovo-Pokrovka and started enhancing their defenses. They were to keep the 3rd PzC from joining the 2nd PzC. They had gathered 80 working tanks to get the job done. vzz488.

At 0330 hrs, *Das Reich* resumed its attack to the southeast from Iasnaia Poliana, pushing the 89th GRD back and taking the high ground southwest of Pravorot. It pushed the 89th GRD back until it bumped into 375th RD which was trying to halt the advance of 7th PzD. The weather finally improved, clearing by afternoon. At the same time the 3rd PzC drove north toward Shakhovo and beyond in an attempt to link up with *Das Reich* to pocket as much of 69th Army as possible. The pocket did not work as the five divisions of 69th Army were already falling back toward the line that included Storozhevoe, Zhilomostnoe, Novoselovka (east) and Shipy. The divisions would complete their fallback by 7/15. wdk166. hjj121m. dgr106. dgr93m.

At 0500 hrs, the 6th PzD launched an attack toward Aleksandrovka but quickly met stiff resistance and had to fall back. Hunersdorff ordered the sPzAbt 503 to join the new attack. With Tigers in the lead, the Germans penetrated the Soviet line and fought their way into town. Assault guns followed into town and began a systematic process of destroying Soviet resistance house by house. The panzers and assault guns followed the retreating Soviets, strafing them with MG fire as well as running them down. 300 yards north of Aleksandrovka, the remnants of the Soviet garrison assembled on Hill 241.3 and tried to stop the German advance. With the Tigers in the lead, the Soviets could not stop the Germans and quickly moved off the hill. Bake's panzer group continued to advance past the hill and by dark had reached Novo Khmelevo. Bake had destroyed or captured over 50 tanks and assault guns. gnk410. vzz12m. dlu126.

At 0700 hrs, 3rd PzC's panzers broke out of their Donets bridgehead, but Trufanov was able to rally his forces and stopped the Germans after making modest gains. When Trufanov saw *Das Reich* making gains in linking up with 3rd PzC, he ordered his forces back and away from encirclement. This easing of resistance allowed 7th PzD to link with *Das Reich* the next day but it was too late. Operation Roland would fail its primary objective of destroying 48th GRC or moving on Oboyan. lck380+. dgr105.

Near Sachovo at 0700 hrs, the 19th PzD repulse several attacks by Soviet tankers. At 1950 hrs, the 19th PzD met up with 7th PzD and together attacked the fortified town of Schachovo from the south. A strong anti-tank defense was overcome and the Germans moved into the town as well as the nearby woods. fkk290.

South of Prokhorovka at 0700 hrs, a Soviet attack from Shakhovo against 7th PzD was repelled near Rzhavets, southeast of Prokhorovka. An hour later, nearby, the CO of 6th PzD, Hunersdorff, was shot by sniper fire while driving to the front and died three days later in the hospital at Kharkov. He was 45 years old and had just received the Knight's Cross with Oak Leaves. The general took part in the relief attempt of 6th Army the previous December. His wife, a Red Cross nurse, attended the funeral and delivered the eulogy along with General Hoth. Colonel Unrein took over 6th PzD until a permanent replacement was chosen. The Soviets had many snipers in the war and they killed many Germans. pck87. dlu63m. fkk284+. fzk56. dgk201. zfk481.

After fighting throughout the predawn hours, at 0730 hrs, with support of around 30 panzers, the 6th PzD broke through the front line and attacked toward Avdeevka and Aleksandrovka, northeast of Rzhavets. Before reaching Avdeevka, nine panzers broke through the line and crested Hill 222.1. While the 11th GMB and 12th GMB of 5th GMC, which was defending this Shipy-Avdeevka-Hill 222.1 line, tried to stop 6th PzD from breaching this line, the 19th PzD was able to fight its way in and capture Shipy after dark on the 14th. The 6th PzD made several attempts to reach Avdeevka but failed against the units of 35th GRC and of 5th GMC of Group Trufanov. By the afternoon the Soviets were beginning to stabilize the line Avdeevka, Hill 222.1, Hill 241.5, but by evening, the panzers were on the outskirts of Avdeevka and had tenuously captured Hill 222.1. The 53rd GTR moved up to just behind the 92nd GRD and Group Trufanov in the Avdeevka, Aleksandrovka area. See Map 23. vzz494++. vzz498. dgr221m. dlu126. dlu131.

The 7th PzD finally caught up with 6th PzD, deployed in the Ryndinka bridgehead, by assembling to their left. The Soviets were assembling a strike force near Alexsandrovka and 6th PzD would have to defend against the attack. All the Tigers of 3rd PzC (sPzAbt 503) were being assembled with 6th PzD with plans to pre-empt the Soviet attack and take Aleksandrovka while reigning havoc on the Soviets. The 19th PzD, the weakest panzer division in the corps, was ordered to move up into the bridgehead but stay defensive. The 168th ID was ordered to advance from the Belgorod-Prokhorovka rail line to the east and join 19th PzD before traveling north and squeezing 48th RC against *Das Reich*. At 0700 hrs, the 6th PzD attacked toward Alexsandrovka. After being delayed at the tank ditch, the panzers were able to race toward the Soviet tankers and out-maneuver and outgun them. After a brief struggle, the T34s reversed course and headed east. The 11th PzR wounded up prisoners and a cache of weapons as the town was secured. gnk408+. gnk397m. vzz12m. zzt91.

The 7th PzD was trying to improve its position in the Ryndinka bridgehead when they were attacked by 100 tanks. The 21 panzers of 7th PzD were able to repulse the attack and advance to Hill 222.1 which was captured by 1000. At the same time the 19th PzD advanced and then captured the village of Shipy, about half mile northeast of Ryndinka. The Soviets regrouped and launched a counter-attack to retake Shipy. At the same time, the Soviets launched a massive artillery barrage against Shcholokovo, south of Ryndinka, from a nearby woods. The German Werfer Regiment 52 responded with a heavy rocket attack against the woods. The German Flak battalion attached to 19th PzD used its 88s to accurately hit the small group of tanks advancing from the woods toward the village. They were quickly repulsed. A couple of Soviet fighters who were flying by and joined the assault were shot down as well. Even with these minor successes, neither of the panzer divisions of 3rd PzC were able to link up with *Das Reich*. Kempt still had hopes of reaching Pravorot and ordered his panzers to continue their attack next morning. *Das Reich* was still inching its way toward Pravorot but was suffering heavy casualties and would not be able to take the village if it reached it without help. gnk410+. vzz3m.

Throughout the predawn hours and into the afternoon, the 35th GRC, defending in front of Krasnoe Znamia, Avdeevka, Aleksandrovka and Novo Khmelevo, repulsed repeated attacks by 3rd PzC with 6th PzD in the lead. At 0900 hrs, the largest attack yet was launched. The Germans gained a little ground but were unable to make major progress. By 1900 hrs, Hill 222.1 (next to Avdeevka) and the nearby villages were still in Soviet hands and the German attack was faltering. Both sides suffered heavy casualties. The 48th RC had been squeezed but not encircled as Hoth wanted. vzz495+.

On the west side of the Donets, panzers from 7th PzD and 19th PzD met at Shakhovo. The 3rd PzC was now so close to 2nd SS PzC that their guns could be heard firing on the enemy. wdk167. vzz12m.

Elements of 7th PzD attacked and captured the village of Krasnoe Znamia, southeast of Rzhavets, as part of the plan to clear resistance from the Rzhavets sector. fzk56.

The 6th PzD and 7th PzD defeated a Soviet counter-attack as it drove north. It was decided to continue the drive to the northwest and forget about capturing Korocha. The 6th PzD stayed in the Kazache-Aleksandrovka area to protect the northern front, while most of 7th PzD moved to the northwest toward *Das Reich*. The 19th PzD would join the 7th PzD in the Shcholenkovo-Saverskaya sector and advance toward Plota. Plota and Zhilomostnoe were occupied by nightfall. The Germans then encircled and tried reducing a Soviet force but failed to do so for lack of troops, many of them escaping. The 69th Army escaped to the east. shn162+. dgk222m. dlu63m.

West of the Donets River, PzR Gothenburg captured Plota by a surprise attack. The Soviets counter-attacked, encircling the Germans inside Plota. Other elements of the 7th PzD were in the area and drove the Soviets away. fkk297.

Later in the day, after repulsing a Soviet counter-attack, the 19th PzD and 7th PzD encircled and recaptured the woods and town of Shakhovo. After sunset the two groups captured the nearby towns of Plota and Maloe Iablonovo, capturing POWs. See Map 8. dgk222m. dlu63m.

To the east, the 6th PzD and 7th PzD captured Aleksandrovka, east of Rzhavets, inflicting heavy losses and driving the defenders further north. Counter-attacks were made but were repulsed. wdk167. vzz12m.

At night, the 3rd PzC was ordered again by von Manstein to link up with *Das Reich* in the morning and trap the 69th Army. The 6th PzD, which would lead the attack, had 69 panzers including six Tigers and 12 assault guns. fkk285.

At 2000 hrs after an air raid, the 3rd PzC, driving from the direction of Kleimenovo and Shchololkovo with 30 panzers, attacked the 2nd GTC along the Vinogradovka and Shakhovo axes. Shakhovo fell by 2400 hrs. Another combat group with 40 panzers, coming from Ivanovka, captured Hill 234.9. After suffering heavy casualties the 2nd GTC fell back along its entire front. Lt General P.A. Rotmistrov transferred the 10th GMB to the Zhilomostnoe and Novoselovka (east) areas in order to stop *Das Reich* as it advanced. During the day, the *Das Reich* launched an attack against 2nd TC along the Storozhevoe and Pravorot axis but made little progress. dgr227. vzz502. vzz482. vzz12m.

With the top command of 48th RC in chaos and separated from its divisions, Maj General Shchelakovsky was sent to Plota at 2000 hrs to take control of the corps and get it running smoothly again. He was ordered to secure Hill 225.0 and the road to Leski. The 375th RD was to be sent to the west and southwest of Iamki to block *LAH* from reaching there. The 93rd GRD was to be deployed southwest of Shcholokovo to block the Germans' advance. The 89th GRD was to be sent to Kleimenovo. All these deployments were meant to stop the Germans from reaching Leski from Shcholokovo *en masse*. vzz501.

By the end of the day, and after repulsing many attacks from 3rd PzC, the 5th GMC still retained the line: Shcholokovo-Vypolzovka-Avdeevka-Hill 222.1. vzz498. dlu138.

The withdrawal of 48th RC began at 2100 hrs. It went down in stages with the 89th GRD retreating first, followed by 81st GRD, 93rd GRD and 375th RD. By daybreak all divisions were on the road. By 0700 hrs on 7/15, the 89th GRD were setting up their new position along the Iamki-Gridino-Pokrovka-Kuzminka line. This timely retreat saved them partially from the assault the Germans had planned in the morning. The 375th RD, which was screening the retreat, did get hit by 3rd PzC which was advancing from Shakhovo toward Maloe Iablonovo. By 0900 hrs, a small scouting party linked up with the leading troops from *Das Reich* near Belenikhino. Most of the 375th RD made it to Pravorot. vzz505+.

During the night, the 74th PzGR of 19th PzD attacked and captured Shipy, situated on a hill, north of Ryndinka. It made a good OP for the Germans. It was fortified with artillery and panzers. To the east, the 6th PzD repeated its attack on Hill 222.1 not far from Avdeevka. vzz494. vzz12m.

By the end of the day, the 3rd PzC had accumulated about 50 panzers and several battalions of men in the area east of Shcholokovo and northeast of Shakhovo. They were preparing to advance in the morning and hopefully link up with *Das Reich* in a meaningful way. vzz505. dlu133+.

Besides trying to pocket the 48th RC's four divisions between the Donets Rivers, the 2nd GTC and the 5th GMC's 11th GMB and 12th GMB were deployed in the Shipy, Avdeevka and Vypolzovka area and might have been trapped also if they were not careful. The situation for the corps HQ was made worse by poor communications with its front line units and 69th Army, as well as the fact that 48th RC was running out of ammo. Elements of the 89th GRD and 375th RD were sent to this area to help bolster the line and reestablish communications. Elements of the 93rd GRD were being sent to the Shcholokovo-Plota line to relieve the weary troops in the trenches. They would use Plota as their base of operations. These forces were now being squeezed between the 6th PzD, 7th PzD and 19th PzD of 3rd PzC in the south and *Das Reich* and 167th ID to the north and west. vzz498++. dgr221.

23

July 14th on the Northern Salient

During the predawn hours, the Soviet air force flew 259 sorties. The missions were a combination of hitting German infantry on the northern front line, as well as hitting critical rail junctions to the rear. These air attacks in the 11th GA sector were given credit for helping in weakening the line and pushing the 18th PzD back when the 11th GA launched at daybreak. The German 53rd IC had to fall back but part of the corps became isolated when the Soviet tanks drove past them. The 1st *Flieger* Division was urgently called to help free the trapped men, northeast of Orel. Stukas were quickly sent to neutralize the enemy in the sector to allow the men to fall back to their line. Without any Soviet interference from the air, the Stukas were successful in opening a corridor to allow the men to fall back. While this episode was successful for the Germans, another one near Dudorovsky, southwest of Bolkhov, was not. The 1st *Flieger* Division lost six planes to a smaller Soviet squadron. In another situation, a group of IL-2s and Pe-2s of 1st VA attacked a convoy of around 150 vehicles at Zikeyevo, not far from Zhizdra, claiming an unspecified number of trucks destroyed. cbk90+. dgk231m. snk433m.

The 4th PzD was ordered to relieve 20th PzD. The panzers had been ordered north to assist 2nd PzA in stopping the new Soviet offensive in the Orel sector. Model ordered all units to dig in and go defensive against Sokolovsky's Western Front and Popov's Bryansk Front as they drive toward Orel. Model also suspected Rokossovsky's Central Front would join the offensive. The Germans had held this Orel salient for a long time and were able to erect strong defenses to a depth of three to five miles. The towns of Orel, Bolkhov, Mtsensk and Karachev were organized for defense from all directions. The Germans had 16 infantry and four armor divisions in this salient. But after 48 hours of constant fighting, the Red Army had penetrated the line and encircled Bolkhov in the northern section of the salient. fkk70+. zzz101m. dgk87m. lck116m.

The 11th GA advanced alongside the 1st TC and 5th TC with the 83rd GRC and 26th GRD right behind them against the 18th PzD west of Yagodnaya. At the same time the 5th PzD was forced out of the forest west of Dudorovo. The Reserta was then crossed, expanding the gap in the German line to 15 miles from Moilovo and the Vytebet River. fkk339. dgk231m. snk433m.

In the Orel salient, the Red Army continued its attack. This time, eight RDs and up to 250 tanks attacked Rendulic's 35th IC. The 262nd ID continued to get hammered, with a gap opening which allowed the Soviet tankers to head for Shelyabug South and Shelyabug North where the HQ of 56th ID was located, reaching there by noon. At the last minute, before the Soviets could destroy the German defenses, eight Ferdinands of sPzAbt 654 under Major Noak arrived and started shooting from 2,000 yards. 15 of the 40 T34s and KV1s were destroyed before the tankers fell back. Three of the Ferdinands received damage to their tracks and had to be towed away. But as the German staff was celebrating their relief, 18 Stukas came diving in, mistakenly bombing their own forces. Many officers and troops were killed. The command post was moved to Sytschi behind the Aleshnya River after the incident. fkk357+. zzz101m. dgk231m. snk433m.

Near Orel, the 11th GA and 11th Army were bringing up reserves trying to crush the enemy as Model continued his withdrawal. The Soviet air force flew ahead of the advancing ground force. bt90. je113. zzz101m. dgk87m. See Maps 22 and 28.

The 2nd PzA was giving support to 9th Army but with the current deep penetrations by the Soviets, the 9th Army had to come to their aid to avoid annihilation. jp210. dgk87m. lck116m.

In the Orel sector, the 48th, 13th, 70th and 2nd TA, supported by massive artillery, attacked northwesterly toward General Model's Armies which now counted 492,300 combat troops. At the same time the 3rd, 63rd and the newly arrived 3rd TA attacked east of Orel. This pincer action intended on encircling the 9th Army and the 2nd PzA. At this point almost all German action was defensive in the Kursk-Orel area. zzz101m. kcz171. dgk231m. snk433m.

In the Orel sector, the Western Front brought 4th TA and 11th Army to the line to support 11th GA. The Bryansk Front had brought up 3rd GTA to support 3rd and 63rd Armies to crush the apex of the German salient. The Germans continued their slow withdrawal. je113. zzz101m. dgk231m. snk433m.

Model continued to ask OKH for reinforcements from outside the sector. Today a group of fifteen Ju-52s arrived loaded with troops and landed at the Orel airfield. cbk93+. dgk231m. snk433m.

Friessner's 23rd IC, Harpe's 41st PzC and Group Esebeck had all received orders to redeploy as fast as possible to the Orel salient. The 20th IC, 46th PzC and 47th PzC remained and had to expand their sectors to cover the entire 9th Army's responsibility. While Lemelson of 47th PzC disappointed Model as an offensive commander, he was extraordinary as a defensive commander in the northern section of the Orel salient, stationed between Ulianovo and Bolkhov where elements of 11th GA, 11th Army and 4th TA would try penetrate and destroy his forces. General Harpe, who Model trusted, also was given large responsibilities in stopping the Soviet assault. East of both Lemelsen and Harpe, Model, who knew of General Rendulic by reputation only, an Austrian who showed his talented capabilities throughout the entire war, held together the Eastern Front with his 35th IC against 48th Army, 63rd Army and later 3rd TA. Rendulic had to cover 80 miles of front with on average of only 2.5 guns and one assault gun per mile. He too was greatly outmatched for he was facing, during the offensive, up to 1,400 tanks. The extensive trench system was the only thing that saved the front line forces in those first days of the offensive. That and the three experienced generals that frustrated the Soviet commanders for the whole offensive. snz258++.

East of Orel, the 1st TC resumed its advance and ran into the 18th PzD and 20th PzD and were halted. To the north of Orel, just east of Bolkhov and north of Ulianovo, Belov's 9th GRC attacked the 53rd IC's 208th and 34th IDs and despite advancing three or four miles, did not penetrate the German line. Belov ordered the 20th TC into action in the hopes of breaking the line. The German infantry with the help of the 12th PzD was able to stop the tanks, inflicting heavy casualties. *Stavka* ordered the powerful 3rd GTA to Bolkhov but it would take two days to get there and the Germans would stabilize their line by then. dgk235. snk109. zzz101m. dgk231m. snk433m.

East of Orel, Maj General Pankov's 1st GTC (Bryansk Front), driving through the first defense belt, hit head on with the 12th PzD and 18th PzD which stopped 1st GTC's progress. To the north, east of Bolkhov, Lt General Belov's attacked the boundary between 208th ID and 34th ID with his 9th GRC's 12th RD, 76th RD and 77th RD and despite heavy resistance, the Soviets were able to drive about three miles inward. dgk235. zzz101m. dgk231m. snk433m.

In the Orel salient, the 8th PzD moved in to block the 3rd and 63rd Armies. Elements of the 2nd PzD were also committed that were coming from Ponyri in piecemeal fashion. fkk339. zzz101m. dgr199m. dgk231m. snk433m.

East of Orel, eight RDs and 250 tanks again attacked the 431st IR. 30 Sturm IIIs and eight guns had just arrived to the line and together were able to stop the attack. Some 120 Soviet tanks were claimed destroyed in the sector. The destruction was caused by field guns, flak guns and aerial attacks, as well as panzers. Infantry, sneaking up on tanks and using charges, also destroyed a few Soviet tanks. snk222. zzz101m. dgk231m. snk433m.

Around 1400 hrs, a flight of IL-2 escorted by seven Yak-7Bs were attacked over Bolkhov by four Bf 110s. Two of the German planes were shot down and the other two moved off. The pilots of the Yaks were French, fighting against the Germans. While this air battle was playing out, the 11th GA, now with the support of the 5th TC and 1st TC, were pushing the 2nd PzA southward, causing a break in the line that was 25 miles wide and 30 miles deep. The 1st VA's repeated attacks on the reinforcements Model was trying to bring up slowed their progress reaching the gap. A group of He 111's from Olsufyevo airfield to the northwest of Orel were scrambled with orders to slow the 11th GA's advance so the gap could be plugged. cbk91+. dgk231m. snk433m.

In 2nd Army sector repeated small attacks were repulsed by the 82nd ID and 88th ID, especially at Rylsk. In the Orel sector, the 36th ID, 299th ID and 262nd ID were repeatedly attacked and requested air support to reduce the pressure. These divisions were part of Rendulic's 35th IC deployed on the east line of the salient. wdk167. dgk231m. snk433m.

Southeast of Kochely, the 234th PzGR was fighting all day against repeated Soviet attacks. The 35th IC destroyed 100 of the 250 tanks that attacked that day. Rendulic believed if the Soviets attacked again the following day on the same scale as the last two days his corps would crumble. fkk358. dgk231m. snk433m.

To the north of the Kursk salient, both Soviet pincers made good progress toward Orel but, by the end of the day, the action in the Orel area had climaxed as Kluge was forced to go off the offensive and was now fighting defensively. The German shelling continued unabated and was a big factor for slowing the Soviet offensive. zzz101m. dgk231m. snk433m++.

Approximately 120 miles east of Orel, the 3rd TA under Rybalko was ordered to Novosil and be prepared to enter battle at a moment's notice. Forty-eight hours later, the tanks started arriving in the woods just east of Novosil. The 12th TC, 15th TC and 2nd MC each took separate roads to this destination. The 91st TB and the 50th Motorcycle Regiment were trailing but would soon reach Novosil shortly. The 3rd TA had 475 T34s, 224 T70s, 492 guns and 37,200 men. Novosil was 38 miles east of Orel and just outside of the German line. The 2nd MC was a new addition to the 3rd TA. zra180+.

While the previous day saw many downed planes of the Red Air Force, this day saw a complete turnaround of fortunes, with more German planes being destroyed than Soviet planes. Russia claimed destroying 100 German aircraft but that figure is exaggerated. The Germans claimed losing 38 planes and the actual total is probably closer to that number. The VVS reported losing 20 planes. With this day's successes, the VVS began taking control of the skies. cbk92. dgk231m. snk433m.

In the north the 1st *Flieger* Division flew 979 sorties which included targeting positions in the Orel salient. nzk77. The 3rd TA is redesignated 3rd GTA.

24

July 15th on the Southern Salient

According to Hans-Joachim Jung, 4th PzA destroyed 2,000 tanks and 2,000 guns during Operation Citadel. hjj130.

Hitler ordered AGC to quit offensives along its entire front. OKH withdrew 4th PzA and Kempf Corps to new defensive positions to the west. German forces in the Belgorod area were transferred to Orel. zzz101m.

It is claimed by some that the only major strategic mistake the Soviets made at Kursk was the deploying of more assets in the north than the south. This most likely had to do with Stalin's obsession that Hitler would try again to capture Moscow. While this simplistic assessment is true it does not explain the whole truth, the reasons for which will be expanded in the last chapter. gjz198.

The Soviets began a new assault to penetrate the Orel salient and head for Bryansk along the Tereben-Bryansk railroad. The 707th ID and other units were defending the area. snk113. zzz101m.

The Germans launched another campaign against the partisans, in the area between Vilna and Polorsk, named Operation Hermann.

During the predawn hours from east of Hill 252.2, the *LAH* panzer group assembled and prepared to launch an attack at daybreak toward Iamki in order to support *SSDR*'s attack toward Pravorot. The division had 46 working panzers including eight Tigers but four would stay near the hill to safeguard the column's rear as it headed east. As the panzers began their trek toward Ivanovka, a heavy rain started and the panzers were drastically slowed by the muddy roads. By 0900 hrs Hoth had to cancel the attack eastward to prepare for Operation Roland. The panzers turned west again, but by this time the Red Air Force discovered the convoy and harass it up to dark. It was a complete wasted trip for the *LAH* panzers. The grenadiers who stayed behind had a busy day fighting off numerous aerial attacks, artillery shelling and infantry attacks. The German flak guns were busy against the numerous sorties. The Red Air Force owned the skies by now, with the *Luftwaffe* losing so many planes since the start of the campaign that they lost their edge. The *LAH* division suffered 130 casualties. The good news was that the panzer mechanics were able to repair a dozen panzers and by the end of the day, the panzer count had increased to 62 including nine Tigers. gnk418.

During the predawn hours, by order of General Hausser, all available corps artillery was being sent to the *Das Reich* sector to assist the division in taking Pravorot. The movement of the heavy equipment was being slowed by the muddy roads caused by another heavy rain storm. gnk396. gnk397m. kuz193.

Von Manstein ordered Hoth to implement Operation Roland, requiring a major redeployment that morning in order to launch the attack later in the day. Von Manstein continued to underestimate Vatutin's forces and Roland, which made modest gains, ultimately failed. The 48th PzC would resume its advance northward toward Oboyan. The *LAH* would withdraw from the corridor and move behind the 48th PzC and become their reserve. *Das Reich* would give up its east flank position and move west to the 11th PzD's position. *SSTK* would defend the entire east flank position while 11th PzD would move to the old *LAH* position at the mouth of the corridor. The 7th PzD would leave 3rd PzC, move west and deploy in 11th PzD's old position. The rest of 3rd PzC would move west of the Donets and protect the river line. The objective once again would be to travel on both sides of the Oboyan road and capture Oboyan. 48th PzC would be on the left and *Das Reich* and 11th PzD on the right. On the way to Oboyan, 1st TA would be isolated from 5th GTA and destroyed. Operation Roland was a crazy, desperate plan of redisposition that never materialized. The plan would probably have backfired terribly if it had been throughly put into action. gnk417. sgf351.

The weather was cloudy with sporadic heavy rains. Both sides had trouble moving troops and little air activity was allowed. The 3rd PzC and *Das Reich* resumed their joint run up the Donets from last night. Despite heavy rain, *Das Reich* advanced east of Vinogradovka and Ivanovka at 0500 hrs, pushing the 375th RD. By noon, the Soviets were aware of *Das Reich* and reinforcements arrived to stop further movement. *Das Reich* claimed destroying 12 tanks. The 7th PzD pushed ahead on the left flank of 3rd PzC and met up with *Das Reich* at Maloe Iablonovo by 1420 hrs. The gap was closed between the two corps, shortening the front and freeing up the 167th ID and other elements of *Das Reich*. Except for taking the hill north of Gostischtschev with the support of the 168th ID, the 167th ID had little activity and claimed destroying only three tanks. The *LAH* was stalled at Pravorot, south of Prokhorovka by the 69th Army's heavy shelling. wdk167+. hjj121m.

At 0530 hrs, the 3rd PzD launched another attack on Tolstoe Woods. The 394th PzGR attacked the eastern edge of the woods, while the panzer group attacked from the south. With the recent heavy rains, the ground in and around the woods was difficult to travel. *GD* panzers were on the north side. Initially, Soviet resistance was stiff but eventually the Germans entered the woods. Elements of 332nd ID arrived and pushed into the southwest quadrant, forcing the defenders back further. The Germans finally had control of the woods. Much of the Soviet force had left the woods during the night, heading north where Decker had vacated his position against orders to travel back to Berezovka. gnk421.

To relieve some of the pressure off *Das Reich* in its attempt to reach Pravorot, the 1st PzGR of *LAH* launched at 0230 hrs eastward, trying to reach Hill 234.9, east of Ivanovka. Assault guns supported the men and were instructed to assist 2nd PzR in its advance northward toward Pravorot. When Maj General Wisch learned that over 100 tanks had assembled near Mikhailovka; it seemed pretty clear that this formation and the concentration of tanks at Iamki meant that Vatutin was planning a two-prong attack, with the objective of isolating *LAH* from *SSTK* and *Das Reich*. The general immediately canceled the advance by 1st PzGR toward Hill 234.9 with orders to return back to the Storozhevoe area and stay defensive. A little later at 0600 hrs, General Kruger was instructed to cancel *Das Reich*'s advance toward Ivanovka-Vinogradovka. The division, which was on the ridge west of the intended line and when it received the new orders, stopped immediately and went defensive. zrl244+.

Despite heavy rains at 0600 hrs, *Das Reich* had already launched Operation Roland with the objective of driving closer to Prokhorovka and linking up with 3rd PzC which was driving west. Their first objective was the high ground southwest of Pravorot, but the sector east of Belenikhino had to be cleared first. After securing Belenikhino, *Das Reich* had moved on and captured Ivanovka and by nightfall, *Das Reich* was approaching Pravorot.

Not wanting to attack so late, *Das Reich* dug in for the night and would attack in the morning. During the day, 7th PzD was able to link up with the southern flank of *Das Reich* but 6th PzD, after fighting all day, failed to capture Aleksandrovka. By 0600 hrs, 7th PzD had captured the village of Malo Iablonovo, just west of Plota, before linking up with *Das Reich*. Later that morning, the 167th ID also linked up with *Das Reich*, strengthening the line a little. The linking up of *Das Reich* with 3rd PzC trapped some elements of 69th Army and two tank corps between the rivers: between Rzhavets, Belenikhino and Gostishchevo. The *Luftwaffe* still covered air support for *Das Reich*. mhz359+. vzz3m. vzz5m. vzz12m. zow170+.

Hoth ordered all front line units to dig in and stay defensive unless specifically ordered to attack. He also ordered all damaged panzers and tanks that were not immediately recoverable to be destroyed. These were two clear signs that the offensive was over and that Hoth expected a counter-attack soon. *Das Reich* had been ordered to capture the fortified village of Pravorot, which Hoth saw as the key to taking Prokhorovka. Without Pravorot, south of the important rail village, Prokhorovka would never fall. As part of improving the line, Hoth ordered Kempf to take Hill 249.2. wdk168+. mhz361. zow171.

The *SSTK* bridgehead was attacked again. The Veselyi area as well as the terrain east of Mikhailovka were both attacked that day by small forces. kuz218. ztc271.

The Tiger Company of *LAH* now had eight working Tigers, which were guarding the rail line not far from Teterevino North, but it was a fairly quiet day. agk129.

After discovering a large buildup of Soviet forces south of Kharkov, the 8th *Flieger* Corps delivered a bombing run on those positions south of Izyum. While the Red Air Force was getting stronger the past few days, it could be said they took control of the skies only on this day and did not relinquish it. The situation in the Orel salient was getting worse and 8th *Flieger* Corps had to shift planes north to keep the salient from crumbling. It would not be able to make special runs south while Model and von Manstein were involved with Citadel. cbk100.

In *SSTK* sector, it rained all morning and the grenadiers had no relief from Soviet artillery or the rain. The rocket regiment at Gresnoe returned fire but it was no match for the Soviet shelling. Their two biggest targets were Mikhailovka and Andreevka, both northeast of Vasilevka. The 5th GA made repeated attacks on Mikhailovka which was defended by the 6th PzGR, the *Eicke* Regiment, but failed each time to penetrate the line. During the predawn hours, the Soviets had doubled their defenses with wire obstacles, more trenches and probably more mines. Vatutin was making sure that if the Germans tried another attack that it would fail. In the past two weeks he had not pleased Stalin with his performance and Vatutin was making sure that no further criticism could be levied on him. Generally, the sector was free of Soviet infantry or tank attacks that day. The one exception was in late morning, around 1100 hrs, when a small commando raid, supported by several tanks south of Hill 226.6, penetrated the line. Once German artillery was alerted, quick and accurate shelling stopped the attack and the Soviets retreated. gnk420. vzz1m. kuz193. kuz218.

At 0500 hrs, *Das Reich* launched an attack eastward in the Vinogradovka-Ivanovka area and was able to push the 375th RD back a little. Hoth was still trying to encircle as much of 69th Army between 2nd SS PzC and 3rd PzC but the advance was still too slow and would not succeed. wdk168. vzz12m.

For most of the morning, *Das Reich*'s Reitzensten struggled to get his panzers through the thick mud. He was trying to advance on and attack Pravorot but it looked like he would not reach his objective that day. Behind the column of panzers, the convoy of personnel trucks and ammo trucks were having an even more difficult time and were falling further behind. By mid morning, *Das Reich*'s *Der Führer* Regiment entered the village of Leski where the men of the 167th ID had already arrived. By midday, a few panzers of the 7th PzD, after breaking out of the Ryndinka bridgehead, would also arrive. The Soviets had already fallen back toward the north. From Leski, a recon patrol of *Das Reich* traveled north on the road to Pravorot and discovered by 1100 hrs, minefields and further ahead tank ditches and strong fortifications in front of the village on Hill 247.2. The *Luftwaffe*, informed of Hill 247.2, was making preparations to support the attack that afternoon. The air attacks came around 1400 hrs, but with interference from the Red Air Force, the German attack was ineffective. The *Deutschland* Regiment advancing south of *Der Führer* had harsher terrain east of Vinogradovka and was making worse progress. Kruger decided to delay the attack until early next morning. gnk419. zrl244.

It started raining again, making all the roads muddy and harder to travel than the day before. Hausser sent orders to his divisions to stop, dig in and go defensive. fkk172. kuz218.

Elements of the 69th Army that were potentially trapped in the salient between the two Donets Rivers made it to the Storozhevoe-Zhilomostnoe-Novoselovka (east)-Shipy line and out of the grasp of *Das Reich* and 3rd PzC. Novoselovka was about four miles east of Zhilomostone. dgr106.

General Hausser ordered his men in the field to wear their steel helmets. In the past few days in the scorching heat, the men in quiet sectors were not wearing their helmets and a surprising number were being killed by Soviet snipers. To stop this senseless killing, Hausser felt compelled to issue the order. zow170.

The bulk of *Das Reich* resumed its attack against 2nd GTC, 10th GMB and 11th GMB but gained only a little ground. A *Das Reich* Regiment was able to link up with Kempf's 3rd PzC and 7th PzD. This joining effected a loose encirclement and potential destruction of some Soviet forces in the Gostishchevo-Leski area, but this tactical success could not salvage the strategic failure of Citadel. The increased pressure in the Orel area forced Model to forget Citadel and concentrate on saving his Army Group from encirclement, and von Manstein could not attain victory by himself; he would continue the operation for days to keep the Soviets busy in the south and to wring out as much destruction on the Soviets as possible. Citadel was finished. dgr227. rc226. zzz101m. vzz3m. vzz5m.

After dark elements of the 287th GRR of 95th GRD made a commando raid in the hope of at least capturing POWs with the main objective of capturing Hill 226.6. The 287th GRR almost made it to the Kliuchi-Polezhaev road before being stopped by heavy MG fire. The 290th GRR was tasked to capture Kliuchi, southwest of Hill 226.6, but that attempt failed also. It made it to the outskirts of the village but then had to pull back due to the heavy mortar and MG fire. vzz467. gnk312m.

Priess received an order to evacuate the bridgehead during the predawn hours of 7/18 and to move south of the Psel River. kuz193. ztc271.

By 1200 hrs, *Das Reich* had reached the marshes near Vinogradovka and were immediately assaulted by artillery on nearby Hill 242.7. The hill gave the Soviets a huge advantage plus the added difficulty of the marsh, and *Das Reich* decided to pull back out of range and wait for dark. It would try to take the hill that night. zow171.

In a surprise attack at night, the 32nd MRB of 18th TC captured the eastern outskirts of Vasilevka and the slopes of the heights running up to the road southeast of Oktiabrski State Farm, which improved its position. This was accomplished at 0200 hrs on 7/16. dgr228.

The 2nd SS PzC claimed another 44 tanks and five planes destroyed, along with capturing only 344 POWs. In the 48th PzC's sector, the Soviets shelled German positions but the 3rd PzD still engaged the 10th TC, claiming to have destroyed 60 tanks. The sector in front of 52nd IC was quiet but the Soviets continued to harass Col General Walter Weiss' 2nd Army to the west. This time 82nd ID defended against repeated small attacks, losing two tanks. wdk168.

The 5th GTA, among other supporting units, attacked and stopped the advance of 4th PzA in its attempt to reach Prokhorovka from the west, forcing it on the defensive. The German columns coming from the south of the city were also stopped. This ended the German assault on Prokhorovka as well as the Battle for Kursk. The Germans had used its last reserves and though the Soviets had not won, they clearly had the advantage.

At 2130 hrs, Group Woest moved their assault guns to the western slope of Hill 252.2 to give support to 1st PzR of *LAH* and the flak guns that were deployed there to safeguard the panzers against air attack. zrl245.

At the end of the day *LAH* reported 21 dead, 114 wounded and 16 missing. It was also reported to General Hauser that *LAH* still had 47 panzers (no Tigers) and 41 assault guns. The *LAH*'s repair shop had moved to Luchki North on 7/12 and had done an impressive job of returning damaged panzers back to the field. A report was given to Maj General Wisch stating the division had destroyed 500 enemy tanks since the start of the operation. zrl245.

With all the Soviet deployments of the last two days, the lines in the Prokhorovka sector were stabilizing. This would be the last day the Germans made any gains in this sector. vzz512.

In the south the 8th *Flieger* Corps reported flying 706 sorties and losing five planes. nzk77.

In the morning north of the Tolstoe Woods, the Soviets attacked *GD* along the Berezovka-Kruglik road. The remaining panzers of *GD* counter-attacked, surprising the attackers. They headed for Novenkoe and engaged. In a short battle, the Soviets lost a dozen tanks before falling back. gnk422.

It was a fairly quiet day for *GD*. In one engagement, 16 T34s were disabled. In the swampy area between Verkhopenie and Tolstoe woods, a large number of abandoned T34s and KV1s were discovered mired in the thick mud. Not having the facility to recover these tanks, *GD* destroyed them. The Panther Regiment of Lauchert of *GD* reported having destroyed over 400 tanks in the ten days ending 7/14. In addition to the tanks, many cars, trucks, rocket launchers and mortars were also destroyed. hjj126+. dgr209m.

Later that night, 3rd PzD was ordered to relieve *GD* north and west of Tolstoe Woods and 11th PzD was order to stay in place. gnk422.

The 11th PzD had once again been in defensive mode, beating back repeated attacks throughout the day and night. The first Soviet attack began at 0500 hrs on their east flank near the Solotinka River and Hill 227.0. This hill was not far from Kochetovka. German artillery fire was able to stop the assault. The Soviets fell back to regroup and then in early afternoon attacked the line again. Again, German artillery stopped the attack. Accurate artillery fire for the past three days saved the 11th from destruction. gnk422.

The 1st TA in the Rakovo-Berezovka area had to go on the defensive and wait for reinforcements from the 6th GA and 5th GA. The following night it was sent to the rear to regroup. Von Mellenthin remarked that the dangerous situation on 48th PzC's left flank had been rectified temporarily. Of the 180+ Panthers that actually made it to the battlefield, only a few remained. The German forces were spent while the Soviets still had reserves. In reality the Germans had little chance to make it to Kursk and when 2nd SS PzC was recalled, all hope faded. Katukov asked Vatutin for replacement tanks but was told there were not any readily available and that the repair shops would have to recover and repair tanks from the battle field. dgk219. dgr172m. dgk222m. zra63.

The cost of Citadel had been steep for both sides. The Germans claim rose to 32,000 POWs, 85,000 casualties inflicted and 2,000 tanks and 2,000 guns destroyed. The Soviets only had 1,500 tanks left in the Kursk area. The Germans had been hit hard as well. For instance 3rd PzD had 30 panzers left while 7th PzD had 60 and 19th PzD had only 17. Some vehicles were in the repair shop. The *GD* had lost 220 of its 300 panzers, while 2nd SS PzC lost 242 of its 425 panzers and assault guns. The 3rd PzC had destroyed three RDs, one RB and three TBs. It badly mauled four other RDs and one TR. It captured 10,000 POWs and destroyed or captured 334 tanks, 101 guns. It was estimated that 3rd PzC lost 142 of its 243 panzers. bt91*. shn165+. shn173.

At 0100 hrs, a German column supported by panzers moved from Shakhovo toward Leski. By 0900 hrs another column from 3rd PzC continued to gain ground, capturing Maloe Iablonovo and Plota. The Germans quickly started moving men and panzers up from Shakhovo which had just been captured. The lead units of the 167th ID had helped in taking the villages and now the rest of the division was moving up as well. Unable to capture Prokhorovka, they wanted to complete the circle around 48th RC but by this time the 48th RC had moved further north and incapable of being pocketed. On the other hand, Vatutin wanted to keep a bridgehead on the rivers as a jumping off point for his major offensive when *Stavka* gave him the green light. The 168th ID was still making progress along the railroad line. Hoth was finally realizing that the 48th RC had escaped the pocket and ordered *Das Reich* to turn north the next day and capture Pravorot, four miles south of Prokhorovka. *LAH* panzers would join in if *SSDR* neared the town. Operation Roland, the brainchild of von Manstein, would change all this; a complete redeployment would take place. vzz502. gnk417. zow171.

At 0200 hrs, elements of the 107th RD and 94th GRD launched a disruptive attack toward Raevka, Verkhni Olshanets and Shliakhovo, in order to dilute German strength against 48th RC. The Soviet force was stopped before reaching any objective and were forced to fall back to Novoselovka (east), where they were able to repel two attacks. The 94th GRD did reach the outskirts of Shiliakhovo but then withdrew to their starting positions. vzz506. dgk231m. snk433m.

During the predawn hours, a regiment of motorized infantry and a number of panzers regrouped just outside of Shakhovo. While it was still dark, this group left Shakhovo and headed for Leski, in the attempt of linking up with *Das Reich*. Just before dawn another German force attacked toward Plota and Maloe Labonovo which was being reinforced. After a three hour fight, both towns fell to the Germans. vzz502.

In the predawn hours, the 7th PzD was redeployed to the Tschurssino area, three miles from their old position of Schachovo where they performed a screening action against increasing Soviet resistance, along the Lipovyi Donets River in the Soshenkov-Tarnovka sector. A few units moved to Gostischtschevo, further to the west. fkk297.

At 0600 hrs, lead elements of *Das Reich* met up with 19th PzD at Shakhovo. Without resting they joined forces and attacked the 26th GTB southwest of Plota. Soviet positions near Maloe Iablonovo were also attacked. Both defenses had to pull back in the general direction of Novoselovka (east). The only remaining combat-ready corps, the 5th GMC, was defending the line Hill 222.1-Shipy-Plota-Zhimolostnoe. On the eastern side of the line, the 11th GMB and 12th GMB was defending against the 6th PzD and 7th PzD who were driving from Rzhavets-Avdeevka. A little to the west near Zhimolostnoe and Maloe Iablonovo, which the Germans desperately wanted, the 10th GMB was holding on but by 0850 hrs, the Soviet tankers would have to fall back from both villages. The Germans, probably elements of 7th PzD, had out-maneuvered the 11th GMB and were also moving toward Pokrovka (east). vzz510++. dgr221m.

Vatutin believed the best way to stop Kempf's advance and to prevent 48th RC from being encircled was to recapture Shakhovo, which was centrally located to the German advance. To the west or northwest of Shakhovo, Leski, Pravorot and Iamki was also ordered to be taken and held at any cost. He ordered a combined all-out effort from 5th GTA, 69th Army and 2nd Air Army to retake and hold the villages, driving from the line that generally followed Vinogradovka, Maloe Iablonovo, Gridno, Hill 235.0 and Ryndinka. By this point, all three armies were drastically weakened and would be unable to achieve their orders. By the end of the day, the Germans had captured Vinogradovka and Leski and secured Shakhovo. The 48th RC moved back and erected new defenses along, but not including, the Zhimolostnoe-Maloe Iablonovo-Leski-Shakhovo line. The 2nd GTC was ordered into that area. Elements of 29th TC was ordered to hold the line that included Pravorot, Iamki and east of Vinogradovka vzz503++*.

The 168th ID was transferred to the Kazache area in order to relieve the panzers which could be redirected to the northwest. The 167th ID arrived west of the Donets to support the 19th PzD. Together, the Germans were able to repulse Soviet tank attacks. shn164. dlu63m.

With the 375th RD acting as rearguard for the retreating 48th RC, it was attacked not far from Shakhovo by a German column coming from Maloe Iablonovo and by 0900 hrs, a second German column coming from Belenikhino joined the battle. The 375th RD continued to fall back while fighting along the Sukhaia Plota ravine toward Pravorot. The divisional guns which were further north stopped their retreat and gave support to the infantry. When all four divisions reached their destination, the line was formed about 1,000 meters east of the front line. The 375th RD was between Storozhevoe-Zhimolostnoe. The 81st GRD was east of Dalnil while the 89th GRD defended from Novoselovka to Gnezdilovka. The remaining units fell back to second echelon. vzz506+.

That morning, the divisions of 48th RC started arriving at their new positions along the Pravorot-Zhimolostnoe-Novoselovka line. It included the 375th RD, 93rd GRD, 81st GRD and the 183rd RD. vzz507.

The 96th TB and elements of the 5th GTA attacked 3rd PzC in which the battle lasted into the night. The Germans repulsed the Soviet attack, inflicting heavy losses on the Soviets. The Tiger crews claimed disabling 100 tanks.

At 1440 hrs after fighting all day, the 7th PzD reached Malye Iablonovo and linked up with *Das Reich*. The gap between the two German corps had loosely closed which shortened the line, freeing up the 167th ID and part of *Der Führer* (*SSDR*). Elements of the 167th

ID worked with 168th ID and captured the high ground north of Gostishchevo. These small victories were happening too late in the campaign and would have little strategic meaning. Vatutin had moved his 69th Army further north to block the way to Pravarot and Prokhorovka, preventing *LAH* and *Das Reich* from advancing on those objectives. wdk168. vzz12m. vzz3m.

The 3rd PzC continued to chip away at the 35th GRC as they pushed toward Vypolzovka and Novo Khmelevoe, but the Germans continued to fail to gain control of the villages. Nearby, the Germans had, by 0900 hrs, gained control of Plota but the 10th GMB and the 51st GTR just arrived on scene and began to attack the Germans before suitable defenses were erected. The 3rd PzC began the day with less than 75 working panzers including six Tigers. vzz512. vzz502. fzk56.

After two days of bitter fighting with 7th PzD and 19th PzD, the five divisions of 69th Army were nearly encircled and Vatutin finally gave permission to withdraw to the east. The assault began in the Iasnaia Poliana and Schchelakovo regions and moved into Shakhovo, where the Soviets disengaged and retreated to the Storozhevoe-Zhilomeste-Novoselovka (east)-Shipy line. dgk220. dgk184m.

Operation Roland began this morning, with 7th PzD and 19th PzD moving west from the Ryndinka bridgehead to link up with *Das Reich*, which was still fighting near Pravorot. The 167th ID and 168th ID would support the panzers. At the same time the 6th PzD would drive to the northeast toward Aleksandrovka, acting as a flank blocker. The 7th PzD did link up with *Das Reich* that day, but it was three or four days too late. If the line had been joined before 7/12, *Das Reich*, with 3rd PzC screening its right flank, would have had a better chance of taking Pavrovot and assisting *LAH* in taking Prokhorovka. The 168th ID could also have been of greater help for *Das Reich*. *SSTK* had been defending itself throughout the night and morning along the Psel and had not the time to redeploy which disrupted von Manstein's new plans. mhz358. lck378. gnk417+. dgr221m. kuz193. vzz12m.

Though Operation Citadel had been canceled, von Manstein still wanted to pursue the enemy and destroy as much of it for as long as his forces were able. However, that time was just about over and von Manstein would be required to watch over AGS's retreat, just as he did during the withdrawal from Stalingrad.

For the past few days, *Das Reich* had been driving east trying to reach and control the important Ivanovka-Belenikhino-Vinogradovka ridge line and that objective was accomplished on this day by 1200 hrs. From the ridge, a patrol was sent out to the east toward Mal Iablonovo to recon the area. At 1420 hrs, this patrol met up with 7th PzD, driving north from the Donets River. The pocket that von Manstein wanted so badly was beginning to close but the problem was it was closing much too late and there were not many enemy troops in the pocket. zow170.

Just as in the south against 198th ID in the Batratskaia Dacha area, Vatutin also thought that further north in the Kazache sector, the 168th ID was the easiest way to penetrate the eastern line. The last few days and days to come, 7th GA would make repeated attacks against German infantry. If General Vatutin felt this way, why did he reject proposals for a major assault in this sector on or about 7/12? dlu123.

That night elements of the 2nd SS PzC joined up with 7th PzD of 3rd PzC in the Gostischevo-Leski area and destroyed the Soviet complement that were encircled, but the bigger salient between Hoth's and Kempf's forces was still in tact. The fact is, von Manstein did not have the forces or time to liquidate the entire salient and still fight off the Soviets assaults from outside the salient. Though the 7th PzD had succeeded to gain ground, most of 69th Army along with 5th GMC was able to withdraw from the area as well as keep the Germans out of Pravorot. By the end of the day, the *LAH* was down to 57 panzers and the other two divisions of 2nd SS PzC were not much better. The *LAH* estimated that they had destroyed 501 tanks in the campaign while the whole SS corps destroyed 1149. Late at night Priess was ordered to prepare to evacuate the salient north of the Psel River and to move across the river to defend the southern banks. Operation Citadel was finally over with this move. dgk221++. hjj121m. mhz360.

By the end of the day, 92nd GRD had less than 2,200 men. On 7/9 it had 8,430 men while on 7/7 just before entering battle, the division was at full strength of 10,506 men. Much of this division's battle action had been defending the west bank of the Donets. The west bank of the river was much higher than the eastern bank, giving the Soviets an advantage over the Germans. The Soviet CO claimed that was the only way his men were able to limit the German advance in their sector. vzz421.

25

July 15th on the Northern Salient

During the predawn hours, the Red Air Force flew many missions; many of them were against the Orel train station which Model desperately needed to stay open. cbk95. dgk231m. snk433m.

As part of Operation Kutuzov, Rokossovsky's Central Front, after regrouping, launched a heavy assault against Model's 9th Army, which had several days to prepare for it. The main attack struck 41st PzC and the interior wings of 47th PzC and 23rd IC but the Soviets had been repulsed after a full day of attacks, losing 250 tanks. After today's fighting, Model moved his 9th Army back to their starting line. In 2nd PzA's 35th IC sector on the eastern perimeter of the salient the Soviets did not attack in strength, preparing for a massive attack in the morning. snk110. snk222dgk87m. dgk231m. lck116m.

In the Orel salient, the Bryansk and Western Fronts resumed their attack in the north, northeast and east parts of the salient. Rokossovsky's Central Front joined the campaign. Driving from Olkhovatka, elements of the 13th and 2nd TA assaulted Gremiache. The 13th Army's prime objective was to capture Kromy, south of Orel. The Central Front also supported attacks with forces of its 48th and 70th Armies. One attack was from Nikoslkoye area against Gnilets and Sacharovka. Another attack launched from the area northeast of Ponyri against Busuluk and Kamenka and the third attack from the area south of Arkhangelskoye against Glasunovka. Model could see there was no way of stopping the attacks and wanted to pull his forces back to the neck of the salient in a controlled manner; defenses were better there. fkk339. zzz101m. dgr199m. dgk231m. snk110. snk433m. je113.

Rokossovsky's Central Front, supported by 16th VA, launched its offensive on the southern border of the Orel salient against 9th Army, although its forces were tired and ineffective against the well dug-in positions. Nevertheless, this assault did complicate Model's defense for in the north near Bolkhov, the 11th GA, the 1st TC and 5th TC continued to create havoc, which required his undivided attention. The situation was was made worse when Maj General Anikushkin's 25th TC drove through the gap in second echelon. As the 70th, 13th, 48th and 2nd Tank Armies attacked Rudenko's 16th VA, which had had a five-day rest, resumed its attack against 9th Army ahead of the ground forces. The Red Air Force completely controlled the skies today. The 16th VA made three major bombing runs with at least 300 planes in each raid. The situation was getting desperate for the *Luftwaffe*; they ordered additional planes from 8th *Flieger* Corps to Orel but this transfer had to be cut short when it was discovered a major Soviet buildup was occurring south of Kharkov. dgk237. zzz101m. cbk95. kcz170. snk170+. dgk231m. snk110. snk433m.

In the Orel salient, the Soviets, except for local attacks, did not resume their offensive in a major way that morning, which surprised the Germans. This gave the Germans a little time to bring reinforcements up to the line, especially in 35th IC sector. During the day the 36th ID moved up and squeezed in between the 56th ID and 262nd ID. fkk360. zzz101m. dgk231m. snk433m++. dgk237.

With Central Front launching its assault today, the Orel salient was now being attacked on three sides, forcing the 9th Army and 2nd PzA to retire to secondary positions. Rybalko was ordered to shift his axis of attack to the southeast quadrant next to 63rd Army. The sector was being defended by 35th IC. By this time eight additional divisions (most from 9th Army) had deployed to support the three original corps stationed here. dgk230. dgk236. zzz101m. je113. dgk231m. snk433m.

The German resistance east of Orel remained high and the Soviet progress was slow. A flight of Soviet bombers attacked a panzer concentration near Podmaslovo. Using the new PTAB bombs, seven of the 25 panzers were hit and put out of action. cbk95. dgk231m. snk433m.

East of Orel, the 2nd SS PzC had arrived in sector and was divided into two groups. Group Buck went into action near Bogdanovo, south of Mstensk while Group Schmidthuber attacked near Zheliabugskie, east of Orel. By 7/21, both Groups had to fall back, occupying positions on the western bank of the Oka River, northeast of Orel. By the 29th, the 2nd SS PzC had to fall back again toward Orel and by 8/3 occupied positions north of town. kn99. zzz101m. dgk231m. snk433m++.

In the Orel salient, the 20th TC was committed, but ran into heavy resistance from the 112th ID and the 12th PzD. The 20th TC suffered heavy casualties and had to withdraw from the line. dgk235. zzz101m. dgk231m. snk433m.

Model realized that his 9th Army and 2nd PzA defending the Orel salient was in critical trouble now that three Soviet fronts were attacking. Model had been asking for further reinforcements from the OKL and finally the planes started arriving that day, with a few more were due the next day. With the added planes, a major counter-offensive was planned to strike the important railheads at Kaluga, Sukhinichi and Kozelsk in order to disrupt Soviet communications. During the late evening and predawn hours, 155 German planes headed for targets. Half of the group attacked Sukhinichi, a third of the planes hit Kaluga and the remainder attacked Kozelsk and other targets of opportunity. The ADD of VVS flew their own night missions. The 222 bombers targeted Mokhovaya rail station, 19 miles east of Orel, and the area around Bolkhov. cbk102. dgk231m. snk433m.

South of Kharkov, Soviet spearheads of the South Front had advanced 15 to 30 miles against the German line. The new 6th Army was defending the Mius River and losing ground as it desperately needed more armor. The SS PzC and other units were rushed in to support the 6th Army. This reinforcement helped stop the Soviet advance, but it weakened the German defense in the Belgorod-Orel area which was the target of the current Soviet counter offensive. zzz101m. dgk231m. snk433m++.

The battle east and north of Orel had ignited once again with both sides sending in reserves, trying to gain an advantage. The Soviets, using a pincer action, were trying to encircle the Germans but Model's cunning was hampering the Soviet success. zzz101m. dgk231m. snk433m.

After four days of bitter fighting in the Orel salient, the 11th GA and 61st Army had penetrated the German line in three major places and had gone around Bolkhov on both sides. A smaller gap had opened by the 63rd Army west of Novosil but the 35th IC had repaired the breach. That day, the panzers sent from the Kursk conflict arrived, but could only slow not stop the Soviet advance because the 4th TA, 11th CC and 2nd GCC also arrived in sector. See Map 28. fkk338. zzz101m. dgk231m. snk433m.

Due to attrition, the 1st *Flieger* Division flew only 703 sorties, compared with 1,113 missions on 7/13. The *Luftwaffe* reported losing ten planes in this sector. cbk95. nzk77.

dgk231m. snk433m.

26

July 16th-July 31st

July 16th – Southern Salient

At 0200 hrs, a Soviet battalion moving from out of a ravine east of Veselyi, was trying to get close to the line before attacking, but was quickly discovered and repulsed by elements of *SSTK*. The raiding party suffered heavy losses and did not attempt to attack the rest of the day in this area. Vatutin did continue to assemble forces near Veselyi and Mikhailovka for what Priess considered was a large assault in the offing. At this point *SSTK* had 27 Mk IVs, 30 Mk IIIs, 23 StuGs, 7 command panzers and nine Tigers still working, though a few panzers were in the repair shop and would be returning to the division in the near future. fkk173. fkk319m. kuz218. zow171+.

The 32nd MRB of 18th TC launched a night attack and by 0200 hrs had captured the eastern outskirts of Vasilevka and the slopes of the heights leading to Oktiabrski State Farm. dgr228.

The 2nd VA and 17th VA flew 926 sorties while the 8th *Flieger* Corps flew just 500 missions. To avoid Soviet fighters as much as possible, most of these sorties were flown early in the morning or at dusk. There were a few defensive patrols made up of Bf 109 fighters but they were unable to completely block Soviet formations from bombing German positions. In just the *SSTK* sector alone the Red Air Force flew almost 300 sorties. cbk100. kuz218. zrl246.

Vatutin set up a stiff defense from Vasilevka to Storozhevoe, using the 5th GA and 69th Army in front with 5th GTA's corps in second echelon. Until the major counter-offensive began, Vatutin wanted to make sure the Germans would not capture Prokhorovka and with the tanks in the rear, he was forced to rely on his artillery to squelch German activity. The 2nd GTC and 5th GTC's 6th GMRB were the exceptions, having to take the front line in the Belenikhino-Leski area. The 183rd RD was in second echelon. vzz468*+. zrl246.

Das Reich was ordered to stay defensive, protecting their current position which included the ridge line: east of Ivanovka-Vinogradovka, east of Storozhevoe. kuz193.

Hausser was told to be prepare to redeploy his corps back to the Iakovlevo-Belgorod road in preparations for Operation Roland and wait for further orders on a moment's notice. The operation died before ever getting started because Hitler started dismantling 4th PzA for deployment elsewhere. The German retreat was beginning. But in the meantime Hausser ordered his corps to redeploy on von Manstein's orders to launch Operation Roland, in case Hitler changed his mind. *SSTK*, after dark and into the predawn hours of the 17th, would sneak back to the south side of the Psel River. The other two divisions of the corps had more complicated realignments. During the retreat, another major thunderstorm hit the men, making it a truly miserable experience. Von Manstein still had faint hopes of destroying 1st TA before reaching Oboyan, and perhaps more with this new offensive, before Hitler closed it down and splintered 4th PzA apart. gnk418. zrl246+. zow172+.

The 2nd SS PzC began falling back, heading for their start positions near Belgorod. They claimed destroying 18 tanks and 29 anti-tank guns as well as capturing 1,136 POWs.

That day, 3rd PzC came under 4th PzA's control. Earlier, the 2nd SS PzC had attacked the 29th TC and 2nd TC in the direction of Novo Khmelevoe but failed and then retreated. wdk169. mh361. dgr228. vzz512.

Marshal Zhukov arrived in the Prokhorovka sector and questioned Zhadov of his handling of 5th GA on 7/12. Zhukov was displeased with Zhadov' and reprimanded him for his poor performance. vzz468.

Orders arrived to evacuate the bridgehead sooner than originally ordered, and the *SSTK* grenadiers began retreating non-combat personnel to the south bank of the Psel. The retreat was covered by rocket fire from Gresnoe. Despite the rockets, at 2100 hrs, the Soviets launched a small attack into the bridgehead, hoping to catch Germans unaware. The attackers made it to the first trench line where hand-to-hand combat erupted. Priess, seeing the success the Soviets had made and fearing Soviet reserves would enter the fray, canceled the withdrawal and ordered Tokenkopf Regiment to the front line. Realizing the Germans were crossing back to the south side, the Soviet AF increased their sorties to destroy the bridges and keep the Germans on the north side, where they could be destroyed easier. Their attempts failed to destroy either bridge and it was almost midnight when the panzers started crossing the bridges. *LAH* and *DR* were also ordered to prepare for a withdrawal to a new defense line. In the predawn hours of 7/17, the last vehicle crossed and the engineers destroyed both bridges to slow the pursuit of the Soviets. On the south side, *SSTK* remained for several more days preventing the Soviets from crossing over. The changes in redeployments in recent days were in preparation for Operation Roland. gnk420+. kuz193. ztc271. zow172.

LAH reported to headquarters that casualties were 16 killed and 86 wounded with 3 missing. The division also reported 60 working panzers including 9 Tigers and 49 assault guns. zrl247.

General Hoth discontinued his advance and in some areas began a slow retreat to better defensive areas. This gradual retirement took until 7/23 to reach its starting points for Operation Citadel. Col General N.F. Vatutin's forces followed the Germans but did not engage in a major counter offensive. The Soviets were regrouping, receiving supplies and waiting for the order to counter-attack as planned. dgr106.

The 2nd SS PzC launched a night attack in the direction of Novo Khmelevoe against 29th TC and 2nd TC but was repulsed. dgr228.

General Walter Kruger of *Das Reich* informed Hausser that since the campaign started, it had destroyed 448 Soviet tanks and assault guns while losing only 46 unrecoverable panzers. wwf149. zow171.

With von Manstein's forces falling back in all sectors and with Operation Rumyantsev starting soon, this day could be considered the unofficial end of Operation Citadel. vzz175. wwf174+. dgn232.

At 1700 hrs on the west side of the Donets, the 114th PzGR advanced from Hill 240.0 toward Hill 222.1, which had been contested for couple days and now had a platoon of Germans surrounded. The 114th GR reached the hill and rescued the survivors which were almost all wounded. After the rescue, the regiment moved on Hill 241.5 which was also captured. zzt91+.

After having taken a few days off, the Red Air Force came back with a vengeance that day. It particularly hit hard the *LAH* and *Das Reich* sectors. *Das Reich* suffered heavy casualties and great loss of equipment from these raids. zow171.

In the Kursk sector, the dawn broke with heavy clouds and more heavy rains. The German offensive had fallen off drastically that day and Zhukov knew the German offensive had ended. In fact, the German line was ordered to retreat to their start lines. The closest the two German pincers got to each other was 78 miles. Even though Soviet casualties were much higher, the German offensive was a failure, not entirely achieving any of their major objectives. mhz361. cbk100. zfk177.

Col Crisolli was chosen to replace General Hunersdorff. When the colonel arrived he was appalled at the fighting condition of the division and the fact that there was only a handful of panzers still working. Just four days later the division, under the supervision of Major Bake, had repaired over 25 panzers and now had 34 working panzers. Crisolli was promoted to Major General in February 1944 and transferred to Italy where he was killed shortly after by partisans. fzk57. zsm76+.

July 16th – Northern Salient

East of Orel, the Soviets opened a mighty barrage that stretched across the 15 miles of 35th IC sector. 300 tanks, supported by rushing infantry, launched their attack while the waiting Germans watched as the Soviets closed in. Their machine gunners and mortar men were ready and would hit the Soviets as hard as possible as soon as they were within range. fkk361. zzz101m.

In 262nd ID sector, the newly arrived 36th ID under Golnick moved up to bolster the front line. The support was desperately needed. The Soviets resumed their attack in this sector after a day off. Of the 300 tanks that participated, half of them were destroyed. In the afternoon the Soviets expanded their attack to include 52nd ID, under Newiger, which was deployed just north of 262nd ID. Fichtner's shattered 8th PzD was also moved north to help. snk222. dgk231m. snk433m.

The 53rd IC of 2nd PzA was reinforced. The 8th PzD, 2nd PzD and sPzAbt 653, all from 9th Army arrived in sector that day. The 36th ID from AGC Reserve also arrived. The key to saving 2nd PzA and 9th Army was in the stopping of Western Front from linking up with Central and pocketing the forces within the salient. Model thought the best way to stop 11th GA and the supporting tanks was through air power. cbk104. dgk231m. snk433m.

Knowing the Orel salient, a distance of 250 miles, could not be held indefinitely, and in fact was in imminent danger of collapse, Model ordered the Hagan line to be implemented. This was a defense belt along the Desna River, about 12 miles west of Bryansk, which ran along the base of the Orel salient. The northern tip of the defense belt was Kirov. The Soviets resumed their attack on 9th Army east of the important rail line that they were trying to capture. In the next two days of fighting another 280 Soviet tanks were destroyed. dgk238. dgk239m. snk110. zzz101m. kcz171. dgk231m. snk433m.

The 16th VA performed three large air raids against German positions around Kunach and Kudeyarovo, both south of Orel. The first raid occurred about 1230 hrs and included over 400 planes. The second raid struck around 1600 hrs and the last raid around 1900 hrs. The last two raids were only slightly smaller. The first two raids saw no German planes but the last attack the Germans were ready, but still couldnt stop the raid. In total the 16th VA flew 1713 sorties and was a major contributor in helping the ground forces to gain ground. The 15th VA supported the Bryansk Front in the northeast quadrant of the salient. The biggest single raid for 15th VA that day occurred in 63rd Army sector against

German positions near Zhelyabug, when 153 bombers and fighters attacked. Four panzers were destroyed and 28 damaged. Despite the aerial success, the 63rd Army made few gains against the highly developed defenses. The Germans had 18 months to build the defenses. cbk103+. dgk231m. snk433m.

Bagramyan's 11th GA continued to make progress. The general was hoping his forces would reach the Bryansk-Orel highway as well as the rail line at Khotynets. Reaching this far south, along with the progress that Rokossovsky's Central Front was making, would almost encircle all of 2nd PzA and much of 9th Army. Model was well aware of the situation, which was the reason for the extra planes being redeployed closer to Orel without actually being in the salient. At daybreak, the fortified 1st *Flieger* Division took to the skies, flying north, looking for the supporting tanks of the 11th GA that had broken through. The area in question was heavily wooded, making it difficult for German pilots to find their prey. Despite flying 1595 sorties, the *Luftwaffe* was able to destroy only 19 tanks and 70 trucks. Another 25 tanks were damaged. Most of the planes in the raids were either Stukas or Hs 129s. For scoring so few hits, the Hs 129s suffered heavy casualties from heavy ground fire. The extensive raids only slowed the 11th GA's advance. cbk102. dgk231m. snk433m.

By the end of the day in the Orel sector, 2nd PzA's line had been penetrated in three places. On both sides of Bolkhov the 11th GA and 61st Army had broken through and surrounded the city. To the southwest of Bolkhov, the deepest penetration had been made. The 4th TA had been inserted through a gap and now racing toward Karachev. If they could reach the Oka River and its tributary, the Optucha, the salient would be untenable, forcing a urgent retreat. To the west of Novosil, the 63rd Army achieved a small penetration against 35th IC, forcing Rendulic to shift forces to plug the gap. Both rivers run between Mtensk and Bolkhov. fkk364. zzz101m. dgk231m. snk433++.

German fighters flew 369 sorties, the largest number flown in days. 1st *Flieger* Division reported destroying 40 planes while losing 16. cbk103. dgk231m. snk433m.

July 17th – Southern Salient

By 0245 hrs, *LAH* reported completing redeployment orders of shifting forces further to the west in preparation for Operation Roland, should it be launched that day. The 1st PzGR of *LAH* moved up close to the right flank of *SSTK* and was actually attached to that division for the next few days. The regiment had not been in their new position long, when at first light they were attacked by a combination of infantry and a few tanks, but the attack was successfully repulsed. The 2nd PzGR of *LAH* had destroyed the bridge over the tank ditch near Hill 252.2 and planted mines to slow the enemy in anticipation of their new deployment orders. Those new orders came shortly but they were not for Operation Roland but for general retreat orders. It was a slow phased retreat in small groups to the southwest. The *LAH* HQ moved to the woods of Bol Dolzhik while the 2nd PzGR would move back to Luchki North by next day with the finally destination being Kharkov. The panzers would be loaded on trains at Belgorod for the trip to Kharkov. zrl248.

In an attempt to disguise the upcoming offensive south of Belgorod called Operation Rumyantsev, the Southwestern/Southern Fronts attacked AGS further south along the Mius River sector. This would be southwest of Kharkov; the Soviets were hoping the Germans would divert forces from Belgorod southward, weakening their defenses at the exact spot the Soviet were going to attack on 8/3. dgk244+*. dgk223.

Malinovsky's Southwestern and Tolbukhin's Southern Fronts launched initially a 16-

day offensive against the eastern most bulge of AGS's defenses in the Donbas, along the Northern Donets near Izyum River and Mius River. It would cause Hitler to breakup 4th PzA quickly to send forces to this area and in so doing making it easier on Konev's offensive to take Belgorod and advance on Kharkov. dgk245. kcz170+.

At daybreak the 167th ID began relieving *Das Reich* of their present positions in order for the panzer division to fall back to the Iakovlevo-Belgorod road line as ordered. During the whole process Soviet artillery was active and causing havoc among the troops. German flak guns were busy trying to keep Soviet ground attack fighters from harassing the convoys. *Der Führer* Regiment was the first to pull out and made it without incident. *Deutschland* Regiment was used as rearguard and had a tough time of it, for the Soviet infantry followed closely using mortar fire as much as possible. They made it also but suffered casualties in the process as they pulled into the new line by 1600 hrs. gnk419.

The *LAH* had suffered 474 killed, 2,202 wounded and 77 missing. Wittmann, who was now commander of the Tiger Company, had nine working Tigers. The 13th Panzer Company destroyed 151 tanks, 87 assault guns and four batteries of artillery. Personally, Wittmann reported destroying 28 tanks, 28 assault guns and many anti-tank guns. These numbers do not include damaged vehicles or destroyed trucks. Wittmann died south of Caen on August 8th, 1944 and by his death had compiled 138 tank victories. Despite Soviet propaganda that stated over 100 Tigers were deployed in the southern salient on this morning it is estimated the greatest number of Tigers deployed at any one time on the battlefield was 146 across the two salients, and that was earlier in the campaign. agk129. wwf123. wdk170.

The Soviets attacked the German defenses along the Mius River line as well as toward Izyum. Hitler began to break up 4th PzA to different sectors to help put out fires. By the end of the month, *LAH* would be transferred out of Russia, leaving Stalino for Italy. All of *LAH*'s panzers would be left in Russia and distributed between *SSTK* and *SSDR*. gnk418+. erz209.

The Soviets watched as 500 panzers and 1,000 trucks, traveling in five columns, left Komsomolets State Farm area for Pokrovka and Bolshie Maiachki. By the end of the day, Storozhevoe and Komsomolets State Farm was once again in Soviet hands. Operation Citadel was clearly over. vzz515. dgk183m.

The 8th *Flieger* Corps flew 138 sorties against 2nd VA's 484 missions. The *Luftwaffe* claimed to have shot down six planes while losing two. cbk100.

The *OKH* ordered the 2nd SS PzC to shut down Operation Roland, assemble at Belgorod and prepare to head for Italy. This order would be quickly changed so that only *LAH* would leave Russia. Since his meeting with Hitler on the 13th, Manstein had done everything possible to encircle the Soviets between Hoth's and Kempf's forces and nearly succeeded in closing a net around the Soviets. The *GD* was transferred north to AGC while 3rd PzD went south. Estimated losses for the Soviet Voronezh and Steppe Fronts include 85,000 casualties and 32,000 POWs in the southern salient against Manstein for the first 19 days of the campaign. The Central Front suffered approximately the same number against 9th Army. The Germans took heavy casualties as well and would never again be capable of having a strategic reserve or a strategic offensive. For the same time period casualties in the south were roughly 44,000 and in the north during the offensive against only Central Front 35,000. The battle for Kursk is claimed to be a visible turning point in the war and culminated a series of costly battles for the Wehrmacht that also included Stalingrad and

North Africa. The US and British Lend Lease aid was also a major factor in Russia's victory; the 200,000 trucks Stalin possessed in July 1943 improved logistics and infantry mobility significantly. dgk218. dgk223. snk54. snk85. mhz358. pck93+. lck378. sgf352.

For the period from 7/5 to this day, the 2nd SS PzC claimed destroying 1,149 tanks, capturing 18 tanks, destroying 459 anti-tank guns, killing 4,262 soldiers, capturing 6,441 POWs and 561 deserters as well as destroying 85 planes. The 48th PzC claimed 500 tanks destroyed for a total of over 1,650 destroyed but this number is a little high as the Soviets were able to recover some units. By August, Rotmistrov and the other tank commanders would already be receiving new replacements. This large loss of tanks would go unnoticed in the near future. wdk169.

Since the start of 7/12 one estimate claimed AGS had lost about 150 panzers, while the 5th GTA lost 334 tanks. Others claim the Soviet loss was closer to 600-650 tanks with some of them recoverable. gjz187*.

In the morning, *GD* was hit hard by several waves of fighters, west of Verkhopenie. At 1200 hrs, the division received orders to stop the advance and prepare to fall back the next morning. Group Lauchert of *GD* had lost 43 Panthers that were unrecoverable during Operation Citadel. Most of the damaged vehicles had to be shipped back to Germany for repairs. hjj128.

July 17th – Northern Salient

During the predawn hours, the 3rd TA moved to their assembly area six miles from the Oleshen River and would be advancing in the morning. The orders to attack were postponed; the next morning Rybalko was ordered to the alternate start point. Driving north through 3rd Army sector, Rybalko was now ordered to drive east of the Oleshen River in the Strelnikov area and attack toward the Spasskoe-Otrada area and cut the Orel-Mtsensk highway in order to starve the German garrison at Mtsensk which was defended by 34th ID of 35th IC. The 12th TC, assembled north of 15th TC, had specific orders to drive toward Sychi and capture the German airfield near Grachevka and then cross the Rybnitsa River near Lyubanovo and Stupino. The 15th TC was to attack toward Bortnoye and Khotetovo and cross the Rybnitsa River at Golokhvastovo and Yeropkino Station. The 2nd MC was launched at the same time defending 15th TC southern flank and to capture Novopetrovka and Znobishino. The villages mentioned are located in Mtensk sector. zra181. snk433++.

In the Orel salient at daybreak, the Soviets opened a two-hour barrage along the entire 65 mile sector of 35th IC. The 36th ID and the late arriving 8th PzD got hit the hardest. Afterwards, ten divisions supported by 400 tanks charged the German positions repeatedly. Many of the tanks were damaged or destroyed; the overpowering force of the Soviets could not be denied. The 36th ID was pushed back five miles and a gap of six miles opened in the line. The 192nd GR of 56th ID was also struggling to defend the villages of Shelyabug and Suvorovo. Eventually the 192nd GR would have to fall back to Aleksandrovka behind the Aleshnya River. The 171st GR was also being pressured at Melyn and Plyanka and was forced to bend its line back to Borodinski to save itself. fkk365++. zzz101m. dgk231m. snk433m.

The 16th VA organized three major raids similar to the previous day. At least 350 planes took part in each raid, with the first one launching at 0600 hrs. The second launched five hours later and the third attack launched five hours after the second. The attacks were aimed at the Ozerki, Vesyoly, Berezhok, Ochki and Sokolniki line which 2nd TA's 3rd TC was trying to achieve. With 11th GA having made a deeper penetration, the *Luftwaffe* spent more time in the north. cbk106. dgk231m. snk433m.

The 234th GR was hit hard for the first time since the offensive began. It was defending the line between Soimonovo to Borodinski. It initially held back the Soviets but then it had to give ground and fall back as well. By noon in the 53rd IC sector, its right flank was in trouble and it was falling back even quicker. This action exposed the left flank of 34th ID, which also had to fall back to the west bank of the Oka River. An hour later, the 2nd PzD started arriving in sector and would be ordered to support the 56th ID which had allowed 50 Soviet tanks into the German rear area that day. The 12th PzD, with its 20 panzers, were being redeployed and would be arriving next morning as well to support the 35th IC. The next day, Rendulic decided to pull the entire 56th ID back behind the Oka River. fkk367++. dgk231m. snk433m++.

For three days, Central Front slammed into the defenses of 9th Army with special interest in the sector east of the Kursk-Orel railroad, but 9th Army held against the terrific pressure. Model claimed his army had destroyed 530 tanks in those three days. snk110.

Bagramyan launched the 25th TC, which had been sitting in reserve the whole month. It was heading for Bolkhov in the northeast corner of the salient. The city had been encircled but it had to be reduced for the offensive to continue in this quadrant without complications. cbk108. dgk231m. snk433m.

The Soviets attacked the 35th IC sector again with ten RDs and 400 tanks. The 36th ID was driven back a mile but the front line was maintained. Again about half of the Soviet tanks were destroyed but 50 tanks penetrated the 56th ID line and drove about ten miles in before being stopped and destroyed. Nearby, the 34th ID had to fall back when 53rd IC lost Bolkhov. Luebbe's 2nd PzD and Bodenhausen's 12th PzD arrived in the area but between them had only 20 working panzers. snk222. dgk231m. snk433m.

To prevent Central Front from linking up with Western Front east of Orel, the entire focus of 1st *Flieger* Division was the northern and southern fronts with little attention to the eastern line. Many dogfights erupted, especially in the south half. With the absence of *Luftwaffe* in the eastern sector of the salient, the 15th VA hit hard the 53rd IC that had been holding back 63rd Army. Areas of special attention to the Soviet pilots included Hill 269.5, Arkhangelskoe, Podmaslovo and Tsarevka. cbk104. dgk231m. snk433m.

The 25th TC, fresh into combat went through the 61st Army gap and turned to break into the rear areas of Bolkhov. The 9th PzD, 10th PzGD and the 253rd ID were defending. The Germans were greatly overmatched. dgk237. zzz101m. dgk231m. snk433m.

Because of the many casualties over the last two weeks, the 9th PzD was unable to function as an independent division and was attached to Group Esebeck, a part of 2nd PzA. The next day elements of 4th PzD was transferred to enhance the Kahler Group. That same day, the Kahler Group was moved to Bolkhov alongside of 9th PzD to strengthen the line. mkz121. lck116m.

The Soviets made their first penetrations on the Mius River line. Hollidt's 6th Army was beginning to fall back and needed panzer support if they were to hold back the Soviet attack. The Southwest Front also attacked toward Izyum. These two major attacks convinced Hitler to completely cancel all operations in the southern Kursk region. The 24th PzC was immediately recalled from Belgorod and sent south to the Mius River and Izyum regions. gnk420++. dgk231m. snk433m. (July 17)

The 11th GA's advance in the northern half of the Orel salient was slowing down due to stiff resistance and an active *Luftwaffe* that had destroyed many tanks and Bagramyan was still 13 miles from Khotynets. The 4th TA had been ordered to the sector to assist 11th GA but it had not arrived yet. It would not arrive until 7/26. kcz170. dgk231m. snk433m.

In the late afternoon twelve miles northwest of Orel, a small squadron of bombers and their seven escorts were attacked by 16 Fw 190s. The Soviet bombers released their bombs and escaped while the dogfight between the fighters played out. The *Luftwaffe* escaped injuries but several of the Yaks were downed. One of the French pilots parachuted to safety but the other two did not make it. cbk108. dgk231m. snk433m.

The 1st *Flieger* Division with its new planes flew 1,693 sorties. Besides just a few planes shot down, 24 tanks and 31 trucks were destroyed. The German air division lost 12 planes. Even with the increased sorties, the *Luftwaffe* was unable to stop the Red Air Force from attacking their ground forces. cbk108. dgk231m. snk433m.

July 18th on the Southern Salient

During last night and into the predawn hours, Priess stepped up his evacuation of the bridgehead north of the Psel, crossed the river and erected defenses on the southern banks. Katukov's 1st TA had already left the line to regroup so it was a relatively easy evacuation against a major armor assault, but the 5th GA did attack the rearguard *Eicke* Regiment, still deployed in the bridgehead. The attack was repulsed. The Red Air Force did harass the column moving south and there were probing attacks but nothing major beyond that one attempt. For days Vatutin had been testing the *SSTK* bridgehead with small scale assaults but nothing that came close to the counter-attacks prior to 7/12. Vatutin was resting his men and repairing his tanks for the big offensive that would start in early August. To the right of *SSTK*, *LAH* and *Das Reich* were also pulling back. The *LAH* reported to Hausser having 28 StuGs and 57 panzers including eight Tigers, five of which were just repaired and returned to the field. Thirty-two of the panzers were the long barrel Mk IVs. *SSTK* reported having 81 panzers and StuGs. It included seven repaired Tigers and 28 long barreled Mk IIIs. Over a dozen more Mark IIIs and StuGs were expected back from the repair shop any day now. snk55++. mhz360. fkk173.

At 1800 hrs the 2nd SS PzC was officially released from Hoth's 4th PzC. The corps would be broken up with *LAH* moving to Italy and the other two divisions moving south to the Mius River sector where the Southwest Front were beginning their own major offensive. zow176.

SSTK abandoned its bridgehead on the north side of the Psel, crossed the river and quickly erected new defenses on the southern bank. It would retreat again the next day for defenses along the line that included Luchki North. Priess lost more than half his panzers and had casualties of almost 2,700 men, including 512 killed. In return, he destroyed 241 tanks and captured over 1,700 POWs. fkk173. ztc271.

In the previous four days, the VVS claimed to have flown a total of 2,209 sorties in and around the Kursk salient during the daylight hours. The sorties flown at night were an impressive 1,298. The respective numbers for the 8th *Flieger* Corps were 1,422 and 241. The Soviet planes did go farther afield than the *Luftwaffe*, striking the Barvenkovo and Ilovayskaya rail stations as well as the airfield at Stalino further south. cbk100+.

At night *LAH* grenadiers began leaving the Belgorod area. The men had to march about 38 miles toward Kharkov. The next two days the regiments started arriving in assembly areas north and west of Kharkov but that was only the first step in the journey. *LAH* received new orders to head for Slavyansk, further south. where the Soviets were assembling the 8th GA, the 1st GMC and the 13th GTC. These forces had already made probing attacks across the Southern Donets and the 40th IC and Viking division had been rushed south to block any further penetrations. The next day, the Tigers were loaded on a train at Belgorod, heading for Stalino. The Tigers would arrive at Slavyansk on 7/21. agk131. zrl248+.

At the end of the day Hausser reported his Corps since the start of Operation Citadel had destroyed 1,150 tanks, counted approximately 4,200 enemy dead and captured 6,400 POWs. It was not the haul General Hoth or Hausser were expecting. kuz218+.

Konev's Steppe Front began its planned offensive to destroy 4th PzA. Konev had already given up his two largest armies to Vatutin; he had left only the 53rd and 47th Armies. Two days later the Voronezh Front would join in and by 7/23 the Soviets were back to their starting points before Citadel began. vzz515. cbk101. kcz170.

The 19th PzD was recalled from Kempf, forcing him to move back. The 11th IC's 106th ID, 320th ID plus 168th ID lost 8754 troops including officers in the operation. erz210. shn173.

July 18th on the Northern Salient

General von Greim of *Luftflotte* 6, before getting official permission, began the evacuation of non-combat personnel, wounded and critical equipment and supplies from the Orel salient back behind the Hagen Line, the Desna River. The *Luftwaffe* was successful in saving all supplies except the large bombs, but they were used in destroying all essential buildings, bridges and railways. Model wanted to slow the assault and did not want to leave anything useful for the Soviets. The Ju-52s were used for much of this evacuation. snk172. snk433m. dgk231m.

Within the last week *Stavka* released the 11th Army and 4th TA to the Western Front to bolster its attack on the northern perimeter of the Orel salient. On this day, Maj General Kriukov's 2nd GCC was also released and was ordered to support the 4th TA with its offensive. dgk420+.

The 234th GR, defending in front of Susha, was attacked by infantry running behind tanks. The Soviets wanted to go through Susha to get to the Oka River. The ground in front of the German position was heavily mined and on the first assault damaged seven tanks. Nearby, the 171st GR and the 156th AR were also struggling. The intensity of the Soviet soldier was extreme, something that some Germans had not seen before. This was especially hectic day for the 35th IC. A total of 24 Soviet tanks were destroyed in this small engagement and 304 tanks by all of the 35th IC. On the way to Kamenka the Soviet tank column struck the village of Protasovo. A number of T34s were destroyed but the Soviets kept on going. The Germans for the most part were able to continue to fall back to the Oka in an orderly manner. fkk374++. dgk231m. snk433m.

Model ordered the Pz Abt 4 to cross the Orel as quick as possible to join up with 9th PzD at Snamenskoye, 15 miles southwest of Bolkhov. Two hours later the 4th PzD was ordered to Trosna to wait for further orders. It was discovered a large concentration of Soviet tanks were forming north of Karachev (west of Orel) that intended to drive south and help split the Orel salient. The 4th PzD with the support of sPzAbt 505 and StuGAbt 909 would be tasked in blocking this assault force. fkk388. zzz101m. dgk231m. snk433m.

On the southern boundary of the 9th Army sector, the Soviets, unable to crack the line, shifted direction to the west in the Trosna-Fatezh and Chern River bend. The forces in the new area were spotted and reinforcements were quickly sent to stop the incursion. When the Soviets attacked that same afternoon with approximately three divisions and 60 tanks, the quickly prepared defenses were able to stop them. snk112. dgk87m.

The Soviets attacked again along the entire 35th IC's front but, despite pushing some forces back, could not penetrate the line in strength. Model had launched a counter that surprised the Soviets, but did little to push them back. snk223. fkk71. dgk87m.

The 1st *Flieger* Division flew 1,104 combat sorties that day. Most of these raids targeted three specific areas: Ulianovo, Bolkhov and Novosil. The Germans claimed shooting down 25 planes as well as destroying 15 tanks, 18 trucks and five guns, with another seven tanks damaged. An unknown number of Soviet infantry were killed as well. Despite the heavy bombing, five tanks from the 70th TB penetrated the line and started driving toward the rear, trying to reach and cut the Orel rail line. A group of Hs 129 spotted the tanks and attacked. Four of the tanks were destroyed from the air. While the last tank was under attack, the German pilot misjudged his point of turning up and slammed into the tank. One of the Hs 129 planes received flak damage and had to perform an emergency landing next to a marsh. Getting out of his plane, the pilot noticed a concentration of 80 T34s camouflaged, which had been undetected up to this point. Meyers called in this intel and a flight of Fw 190s heading for another target was ordered to the down pilot's location to attack the Soviet tanks. That night and for the next two days those tanks were hunted down and destroyed. They were destroyed by either 250 pound bombs or from 37mm cannon being fired from Ju-87s. cbk108+. dgk231m. snk433m.

July 19th on the Southern Salient

The 8th *Flieger* Corps flew a total of 92 missions which included recon patrols. cbk101.

General Kruger of *Das Reich* computed the casualties for his division since the start of the campaign. There were 456 killed, 1,844 wounded and 23 missing. General Hausser added up the casualties for his corps and the numbers were high: 1,447 killed, 6,198 wounded and 138 missing. The total was 7,774 and breaks down where each division had about the same number of casualties. *SSTK* was highest with 2,668. FM von Manstein informed his corps commanders that it was estimated that 2,000 tanks were destroyed, along with 1,500 guns and 1,000 planes, besides 32,000 POWs and 18,000 (counted) dead which extrapolates to an estimated 100,000 dead. zow174+.

Panzer remains of *GD* were loaded on trains for Bryansk. For the next few days, the rest of the division would follow. It is estimated that 56 of the nearly 200 Panthers were destroyed in Operation Citadel. The number up until this point had been 43 Panthers but when *GD* was ordered to fall back and be prepared to embark the number jumped to 56 panzers. Those panzers were heavily damaged but recoverable, if time permitted, but when it was determined recovery was not possible due to the retreat, they were destroyed by the division. The Panther Brigade was no longer an independent unit; it became an integral part of the division. Berlin was already shipping a new batch of Panthers to the division destined to arrive at Bryansk in a couple weeks. hjj128. mhz292.

The 69th Army was relieved from Voronezh Front and was transferred to Steppe Front. gjz190.

After being recalled from the front, the 19th PzD started arriving at Belgorod and three days later the rest of 3rd PzC returned to its start positions. During the campaign, it was estimated the corps shattered nine infantry divisions and four tank brigades. In addition 10,000 POWs and hundreds of guns and some tanks were captured. shn164+.

July 19th on the Northern Salient

Beginning on this day and for the next two days, the *Luftwaffe* retook control of the skies. The Soviet offensive had been so close to closing the gap between the northern and southern salient but with the supreme effort, the German pilots fought off the Soviet air cover and hit the ground assault hard which forced a temporary retreat. It gave Model enough breathing room to call for a retreat to the Hagen Line on 7/21. During these three days, the 1st *Flieger* Division claimed destroying or damaging 200 tanks and killing countless number of troops, much of the damage occurring in 11th GA sector, northwest of Orel. cbk109. dgk231m. snk433m.

At 0745 hrs, the Soviets attacked the 258th ID and penetrated its line with 40 tanks that were now heading for south of Trosna. By evening it had captured Trosna north and had entered Trosna south and fighting for the rest of the village. The 4th PzD had now entered the Orel salient and was heading for the Rakitnaya River at Chernodie West and Chernodie East. The 258th ID was on the left and the 102nd ID on the right. Other elements of the 4th PzD went to Hill 247.2 and Hill 236.7. The bulk of the 4th PzD attacked in the Rakitnaya River Valley and pushed the the Soviets back a little. They were facing the 19th TC which was tasked to reach Kromy. The 53rd Werfer Regiment was also sent to Trosna. fkk389. zzz101m. dgk231m. snk433m.

After 250 planes of the 15th VA raided the eastern perimeter of the Orel salient, the 3rd GTA's 12th TC and 15th TC launched almost 700 tanks toward the area south of Mtsensk (southeast quadrant). A group of tanks penetrated the front line, crossed the Oleshen River and advanced a total of seven miles. The air cap was able to keep 1st *Flieger* Division at bey without losing many bombers. The Soviets claimed destroying or damaging 35 panzers in the raid. With the increased pressure caused by the entry of 3rd TA, the Soviets now had overwhelming strength on three sides of the salient and Model was enacting a organized retreat to the west to the Hagen line. It is quite an accomplishment that the Germans were able to fall back in such an orderly manner under such stiff pressure from three sides. The German garrison at Mtsensk was at the greatest risk from encirclement and there was concern that the order to pull back was given too late. Flying at night and into the predawn hours of 7/20, the 1st *Flieger* Division attacked the 3rd GTA to allow the ground troops to pull back but even with air support, the ground troops sustained heavy casualties. The *Luftwaffe* reported shooting down 54 planes after dark from the air and ground fighting. The VVS claimed destroying 30 panzers and 100 trucks that were withdrawing west on the Mtsensk-Orel road. With most of the night-qualified planes and pilots back in Germany, fighting the Allied bombing, there were not many planes available to fly at night at Orel. cbk112+. dgk231m. snk433m.

The 36th ID had arrived just a few days ago to the Orel salient but it was already in trouble. The 78th AD of 9th Army arrived today and General Rendulic quickly inserted it with the 36th ID. fkk381. zzz101m. dgk231m. snk433m.

At 1030 hrs, after a thirty-minute preparation, the 3rd TA launched and quickly crossed the Oleshen River attacking the German defenses. The *Luftwaffe* was quickly called in and attacked the tanks trying to break through the front trenches. While the German planes attacked and slowed the Soviet assault, Model sent two panzer divisions to the area to help the 35th IC stop the massive attack. Despite the aerial, artillery and panzer resistance, by nightfall the 3rd TA advanced six miles, pursuing the retreating Germans. During the night, Zinkovich's 12th TC traveled another six miles while Rudkin's 15th TC gained little against stiffening resistance. zra182.

With aerial support, the tankers of 3rd TA crossed the Oleshen River and advanced six miles by nightfall. The 8th PzD counter-attacked, forcing the 15th TC column to stop for the night. Rybalko, next morning under orders, would split his forces (promoted to 3rd GTA) and shift direction to capture Otrada, northeast of Orel but he would be unable to cross the Oka River. One group with 100 tanks attacked the boundary line between 36th ID and 262nd ID, broke through and headed for the critical rail junction at Archangelskoye. The 2nd PzD with its few panzers and Pak guns intercepted to prevent the Soviets from reaching the junction. While the panzers were keeping the Soviet tanks busy, German engineers would sneak up and, using demo charges, attacked the tanks. The Germans had stopped the column less than a mile from Archangelskoye by destroying 47 tanks. dgk236. fkk372+. zzz101m. dgk231m. snk433m.

To bolster the strength of 9th PzD, Group Kahler was attached to the division. The 9th PzD was then joined to 9th Armored Reconnaissance Battalion and together were called Group Schmall. mkz121. snk433m++.

While the new offensive on the eastern perimeter was escalating, the 16th VA flew 1,222 sorties in support of Central Front's advance to the north. With the help of air support, a small gap in the line was opened south of Kromy cbk112. dgk231m. snk433m.

In 2nd PzA's sector, a Soviet assault penetrated the Karachev-Bryansk road and confirming the wide offensive the Soviets were developing. The 2nd PzA had to fall back again to contain the penetration which necessitated 9th Army to fall back as well. At the same time, the Soviets were attacking the boundary line between 2nd PzA and 9th Army and advancing toward Smiyevka. The last of Model's reserves were sent there and by 7/24 would slow down the advance, but by that date the 2nd PzA had fallen back to the next trench line. At the same time General K.K Rokossovsky sent two or three divisions of 13th Army along with a few tanks up the Trosna-Fatezh road to attack Model's southern perimeter. Receiving aerial intel that the force was coming, Model was ready for it when it struck. Model was a master in shifting his forces quickly to meet the new threats that were constantly forming. snk112. dgk231m. snk433m.

In the Orel salient, the 3rd TA drove into the line of 35th IC under Rendulic. Its divisions, 34th ID, 56th ID, 262nd and 299th ID, had finally been penetrated in several places. The 2nd PzD, under Luebbe, 8th PzD and 36th ID were sent to plug the gap. The 9th PzD was also sent to the sector from the southeast. The 183rd ID, 253rd ID and 707th ID were also sent but they would be a day behind. While the reinforcements were moving, the Soviets cut the Orel-Karachev rail near Ilinskoye but the Soviet contingent was destroyed by a *Luftwaffe* raid. The 253rd ID shifted direction, moved in to secure the area. It recaptured Ilinskoye on 7/21. By 7/23, the 35th IC had fallen back to the second trench system but the line in the area had been stabilized by all the transfers from 9th Army but southeast of there the Germans were still in trouble. snk110+. zzz101m. dgk231m. snk433m.

The 1st *Flieger* Division made another successful attack on Soviet assets near Karachev, northwest of Orel. It then had to fly missions against the concentrations of Soviets near Khotynets, also northwest of Orel, to prevent the 11th GA from breaking through. Then the 1st *Flieger* Division had to fly east to attack the latest threat, Rybalko's 3rd TA (3rd

GTA). There were not enough planes left to cover all threats at the same time. The pilots had to fly multiple missions, putting out one fire then another. By now there was not much left to the Orel salient but Model was still very concerned in evacuating his men. cbk112+. dgk231m. snk433m++.

July 20th on the Southern Salient
The day before *Das Reich* had been detached from 4th PzA and was currently *en route* to Barvenkovo to prepare for a counter-attack toward Izyum, which the Soviets had just attacked. Hitler changed his mind on *Das Reich's* deployment and had them transported on 7/23 to the Mius River line where the Soviets were also active. gnk420. dgk231m. snk433m.

While the 6th PzD and 19th PzD were falling back with Soviet tanks closely following Major Bake with six Tigers from the sPzAbt 503 ambushed the enemy. The Tigers coming from the nearby woods attacked the passing column of T34s and within a short period of time 23 T34s were destroyed. Slow to react, the Soviet tanks finally countered, trying to maneuver to the sides and rears of the panzers. The attempt was unsuccessful and the Soviets lost another ten tanks before breaking away. Though receiving hits, none of the Tigers were damaged enough to require a tow. fzk57.

The 48th PzC reported to General Hoth that of the nearly 200 Panthers received at the start of the operation, 56 were completely destroyed and were left on the battlefield. The many other Panthers that were disabled and towed off the battlefield would be able to be repaired or used for parts or for further testing. zzt101.

July 20th on the Northern Salient
Bryansk Front commander, Popov, ordered 3rd TA to shift direction to the northwest, cut across the Orel-Mtensk road and capture Otrada by nightfall. Mtensk was to be captured within 24 hours. These were very ambitious plans but Rybalko was confident that they could be accomplished. He had the assets of 3rd Army in the sector and between the two armies it should be easy. By noon, the leading forces of both armies had crossed the highway and were fighting toward the Oka River, east of Orel. The initial quick advance was slowing down against the stiff resistance of new resources coming into the sector. In order to capture Stanovoi Kolodez by the end of day on 7/22, Rybalko brought up the 2nd MC from second echelon to help with the attack. zra182+.

In the Orel salient, Model launched another counter-attack but it was repulsed. The Red Air Force sent many sorties against the weakening German positions today. fkk71. fkk389. zzz101m. dgk231m. snk433m++.

Hitler ordered Model to halt all further withdrawals by 9th Army and 2nd PzA but two days later Model convinced Hitler to rescind the order. The 9th Army immediately began evacuating an estimated 20,000 casualties in Operation Citadel. Some sources claim the number was twice as much. dgk238. dgk217. dgk231m. snk433m.

The 2nd PzD and 8th PzD were expected in the Orel salient east of the Oka River but they had not arrived yet. The intended line of Protasovo-Dobrovody-Bogoroditskoe-Spasskoe could not be held without the panzers and more troops were retreating for the far banks of the Oka-Optucha line. fkk380. zzz101m. dgk231m. snk433m.

A Soviet air raid against the German airfield at Kramatorskaya, not far from Stalino, destroyed ten Stukas. cbk101. dgk231m. snk433m.

Despite the heavy pressure on the eastern line the past two days. the Germans were able to prevent 3rd Army, fighting on 3rd GTA's right flank, from penetrating the line. Though the line was bending, it had not ruptured and the 3rd Army had been prevented from crossing the Oka River to the west of Mtsensk. By now, the Soviet three Front attack had evolved into four axes of attack around the entire salient. The *Luftwaffe* was no longer able to support the entire ground forces at the same time. Situations with the greatest urgency received priority support. It also had to abandon all attempts to hit Soviet airfields and railroads outside the sector. cbk113. snk170+. dgk231m. snk433m.

The 20th PzD had reported losing another twelve unrecoverable panzers in the past eight days. mhz262. fkk285. dgk87m.

In the Orel salient, the 1st TC reported having only 33 working tanks. cbk109. dgk231m. snk433m.

July 21st on the Southern Salient
Further dismantling of Hoth's forces continued. While 7th PzD marched toward the Borisovka-Graivoron area, the 6th PzD, which now had 34 working panzers, and 167th ID, were transferred from 3rd PzC to 4th PzA, forcing Kempf, once he received OKH permission, to speed up his retreat to behind the Donets River. With those two divisions leaving 3rd PzC, the 11th IC, which had lost half its strength in the campaign, had to expand its sector. snk55. erz210. fkk297.

July 21st on the Northern Salient
At 0300 hrs, Rybalko once again received new orders. His 3rd TA was to turn south, cross the Rybnitsa River and capture Stanovoi Kolodez. Rybalko had always been good in reacting to changing orders and this time was no different. Leaving a security force at the Oka bridgehead, the 3rd TA shifted direction at first light and moved toward the new objective. Fighting along the river with elements of 63rd Army, the 3rd TA's pace slowed to a crawl, falling behind schedule and failing to reach Stanovoi Kolodez. The 91st TB was called up and the pace quickened a little, allowing the 91st TB to enter and capture Sobakino on Rybalko's flank. It was an expensive day for 3rd TA, suffering many casualties. General Rybalko, while driving to the front to see for himself why his army was stalling, was nearly killed when a German plane strafed his entourage. His car was totaled, but he was uninjured and continued to the front. His usual practice was to visit the front in a single Jeep, believing that a German plane would not bother with a single jeep. However that day he had a convoy of two other jeeps and a guard truck, and the Germans attacked. zra184+. zra186.

General Scheller of 9th PzD was ordered to launch a suicide attack north of Orel toward Krasnilkovo. He refused the original order and proposed a sensible order. The proposed order was accepted but then General Harpe of 41st PzC rejected the proposal and would convince Model to fire him. It is ironic because at daybreak the Soviets attacked, preempting the German attack and the 9th PzD, and then later the 10th PzGD, were forced on the defensive with no chance of ever launching the objectionable attack. The 10th PzGR was also involved with the attack toward Hill 222.4, south of Krasnilkovo. By 1430 hrs, Harpe ordered the two divisions to make a stand along the Karentievo-Koptevo line. mkz122. dgk231m. snk433m++.

Realizing the Western and Central Fronts were not closing the salient off quickly enough and seeing that some of the German troops were falling back, *Stavka* ordered the

3rd GTA to immediately shift direction and head for Stanovoi Kolodez with the objective of pocketing the 35th IC east of Orel. The 1st *Flieger* Division flew 1,500 sorties in support of the eastern perimeter and especially the 35th IC. The 3rd GTA was constantly being hit and lost 38 tanks and 85 trucks. cbk113. dgk231m. snk433m++.

In the Orel salient, the fortified town of Mzensk finally fell to the Soviets. The fighting for Orel continued. fkk71. zzz101m. dgk231m. snk433m++.

Model relieved Lt General Scheller of 9th PzD for refusing to launch a suicidal attack against Bagramyan's tanks west of Krasnikov. Model called in the *Luftwaffe* to help support the desperate ground defense but the *Luftwaffe* was so short of fuel that its participation was negligible. The flak gunner batteries were called in to defend against onrushing tanks. dgk237. dgk231m. snk433m++.

The 56th ID had been pushed back behind the Oka River and now it defended a five mile section of it that included the destroyed village of Voin. As the Soviet tanks approached Voin, the 234th GR waited until the tanks got to 300 yards and started firing on them with everything they had. The 7.5cm PaKs hit five tanks before the T34s and KV1s returned fire. German kill teams left the line to search out and destroy the incoming tanks. Soviet infantry behind the tanks came out to stop the Germans and a hand-to-hand combat ensued. After two hours of fighting, the Soviet tanks gave up and bypassed the strongpoint. Stukas finally arrived to search for the tanks. They found them and attacked, stopping a few of them. Another friendly fire incident occurred that cost the lives of some of the German soldiers. Pz Abt 156 which had warned out their guns, received four new anti-tank guns that day. fkk381+. dgk231m. snk433m++.

Model ordered the 46th PzC to fall back behind the Rakitnaya. The move would start after dark the following night. The 4th PzD would move back as well as soon as 46th PzC was in place. General von Saucken of 4th PzD complained to Lt General Hans Zorn of 46th PzC of the way his division had been deployed in a piecemeal fashion. An inventory of the 4th PzD that night revealed that it had 12,000 men, 1,800 horses, 48 panzers, 20 Pak guns and 24 Mk IVs in the repair shop. fkk390. lck116m.

Popov ordered Maj General Rudkin's 15th TC and Maj General Korchagin's 2nd MC (3rd GTA) which were committed around Otrada, to the northeast of Orel; the rest of 3rd GTA was to shift and expand to the south and punch through the southern shoulder of the penetration. The advance was slow due to stiff resistance. The northern flank saw Maj General Zinkovich's 12th TC stay on it original axis. dgk236*. zzz101m. dgk231m. snk433m++.

The 1st *Flieger* Division reported losing 13 planes while downing 16 Soviet planes. Six of those 13 planes were destroyed by ground fire. cbk113. dgk231m. snk433m++.

July 22nd on the Southern Salient
Over the previous few days, the 6th PzD had retreated back to Gonki, north of Belgorod. That morning, the 69th Army attacked along the line that included Gonki but the attack was initially repulsed. knz189.

July 22nd on the Northern Salient
At first light, the Soviets opened with an hour-long barrage before the assault was launched. Red fighters strafed the German positions as well. During the night the Soviets had moved up through the ravines to be very close to the German line; it was a big surprise for the

Germans, with the Soviets so close at the time of the attack. In one section, Pz Abt 49 defended itself, knocking out 17 tanks. The main axis hit the 7th ID, which was on the right of 4th PzD, head on causing a gap in the line. The Soviet tankers headed for Hill 254 and Hill 250. Those hills were defended by the 35th PzR. The commander of the 35th, Major Cossel, was in the lead and quickly destroyed three tanks when his panzer took a direct hit that caused his own rounds to explode, killing everyone in the panzer. At Lomovea, the Soviets were stopped by 4th PzD. General von Saucken expected another counter-attack at Lomovea the next morning and sent StuGAbt 244 up there to support the line. fkk384. fkk390+. dgk231m. snk433m++.

At 0630 hrs, the 1st *Flieger* Division flew its first mission of the day against a concentration of tanks in a village northeast of Orel. There was little resistance in the air but a number of German planes received damage from ground flak. Several runs were made against the targets and an unknown number of tanks were hit. During the raids, the advance on the German line was slowed. By this point in the campaign the pilots of both sides were exhausted and could barely stay awake even during combat. It could not be helped for by now both sides were low on pilots and planes. cbk114. dgk231m. snk433m++.

Stavka shifted 3rd TA a little south to the 2nd PzA-9th Army boundary. They also brought up 4th TA to drive on Bolkhov. The fighting would continue to be the focal point in the northern salient until the end of the month. Model brought up 95th ID to just south of Bolkhov, alongside Jaschke's 55th IC to hold back the renewed attack that was expected there. The *GD*, 293rd ID and 129th ID were brought up and initiated a disruptive counter-attack to prevent them from capturing the important Khotynets-Karachev railway and highway. The 25th PzGD, the 10th PzGD, the 18th PzD and the 20th PzD under the direction of Harpe, formerly of 41st PzC, would also take part in the defense. An estimated 200 Soviet tanks per day were destroyed by this group. The 3rd TA was redeployed to 9th Army's Nikolskoe-Filosopov sector. snk113*+. kcz171. dgk231m. snk433m++.

Model ordered the southeast quadrant of the Orel salient to withdraw westward. The 48th Army tried to follow, but the 1st *Flieger* Division constantly raided the Soviets, slowing their progress. In the northern sector, northeast of Karachev, the Soviet pressure had subsided, allowing the *Luftwaffe* to concentrate on the east and southeast sides of the salient. cbk115. dgk231m. snk433m++.

The 51st Werfer Regiment with their four rocket launchers were brought close to the Oka River and started firing on the enemy. It was their first day in battle. For that day and the following two days the Soviets repeatedly attacked this sector of the Oka and the 51st WR was in constant battle; this made a big difference in the German defense which kept the Soviets from crossing at this point for another couple days. fkk385. dgk231m. snk433m++.

In the early afternoon, the Soviets attempted a second attack along the line: Lomovea-Kasmino Juryevski. The line flexed but held by the end of the day. A total of 62 Soviet tanks were destroyed in the engagement in 4th PzD sector. Next morning the 4th PzD and Maj General Hitzfeld's 102nd ID would counter, trying to regain ground lost today. fkk392. dgk231m. snk433m++.

The Soviets entered Bolkhov and began a house to house clearing; the city would not be secured until 7/25. fkk399. dgk231m. snk433m++.

With Soviet tanks now arriving at the Oka, Soviet artillery was moved westward as well and was now pounding the German positions west of the river. Model was bringing all reserves up to the Oka, in an all out effort to stop the Soviets. Both the 2nd PzD which was deployed to the right of 56th ID and 8th PzD had arrived and were on the river. The 34th ID was on the left side of 56th ID. The Soviets had still been able to establish two small bridgeheads on the western banks of the Oka by the end of the day. fkk383+. dgk231m. snk433m++.

Hitler had forbidden Model to enhance the trenches at the base of the salient and ordered him to stand fast on the outside perimeter's defenses. However Model brought more troops to the base defenses and started enhancing the trenches. Model knew they would be needed and he did not want to lose his armies. sgf354. dgk231m. snk433m++.

The 1st *Flieger* Division reported losing 11 planes while shooting down 14 Soviet planes. cbk114. dgk231m. snk433m++.

July 23rd on the Southern Salient

The 4th PzA and 3rd PzC in the last week had retreated to their pre Citadel start line, south of Tomorovka. Konev's Steppe Front held a line from just north of Tomarovka to Volchansk to the east. At this line Konev paused for almost two weeks to regroup and resupply his forces before resuming his advance. Vatutin's Voronezh Front was deployed to the west of Tomarovka. The 4th PzA estimated that it captured 32,000 POWs, destroyed up to 2,000 tanks and 2,000 guns but it appeared that these casualties had little impact on the Red Army for it seemed to the Germans the Red Army had an unlimited pool of men and production capacity. kcz171+. wwf174. fmz229.

As the Red Army continued to push 4th PzA away from Prokhorovka, the German repair shops continued to repair panzers, returning them to active duty. Hausser reported to von Manstein that his corps had 221 assorted panzers and 78 assault guns. The breakdown included 72 Pz IIIs, 98 Pz IVs, 30 Tigers, 17 T34s. The cost in men was even worse. During the campaign the corps had lost 196 officers and 6,232 men and was short of its authorized strength by 1,041 officers and 5,609 men. wdk170. vzz175. dgk241.

July 23rd on the Northern Salient

In the Orel sector the 253rd ID counter-attacked and regained Hill 223.6, establishing a link with the left flank of 9th PzD. The 253rd ID now held the line Strykovo-Hill 223.6-Ilinskoye. For days, the Soviets had attacked the boundary line between the 9th PzD and 253rd ID without much success. mkz123. dgk231m. snk433m++.

The *GD*, arriving by train, reached the Orel salient and was sent to the swampy woods northeast of Karachev where they were most needed. Soviet tanks from the 6th Anti Tank Division supported by the 31st GRR were only four miles from the Orel-Karachev road. Despite the heavy rainfall that day the Soviets were now approaching the woods. The *GD* division was still deploying when they had to engage the 31st GRR who were determined to sever the critical Orel-Karachev road. While the woods were being defended, other elements of *GD* went on the attack and were able to clear the nearby villages of Krutoye, Umrichino and Shishkino where the Soviets were bringing up supplies to use to advance their attack. hsz134+. hsz140m.

From Bolkhov, the 12th PzD was rushed to east of Orel to help plug a new gap in the line. The 78th AD from 9th Army was also traveling there to help out. With these penetrations, Model ordered Rendulic to withdraw his forces to Bolkhov to shorten the line and to prevent the Soviets into his rear area. The 10th PzGD moved over from Krasnikovo and was used as rearguard to slow the Soviet advance while Rendulic prepared defenses.

snk111+. zzz101m. dgk231m. snk433m++.

Late at night, the 3rd TA stopped its advance at Novo Petrovtsa to rest and prepare for the planned assault on Stanovoi Kolodez next morning. Rybalko was also ordered to reach the Stish River by midnight the next day. zra186.

The 1st *Flieger* Division recorded losing 19 planes while downing 18 Soviet planes. cbk114. dgk231m. snk433m++.

July 24th on the Southern Salient
SSTK was being loaded onto trains at Belgorod. It was rumored they would be traveling south to the Mius River sector, where the Soviets were assembling on the east side of the river. kuz219.

July 24th on the Northern Salient
During the predawn hours, the Soviets tried to surprise the German line and force a crossing of the Oka. The Germans quickly responded and only a few Soviets made it across and into captivity. They suffered heavy casualties and the crossing was aborted. fk386. dgk231m. snk433m++.

The *GD* division arrived that day in the Karachev-Khotynets area and immediately set up defenses against the tanks attached to 11th GA. cbk115. dgk231m. snk433m++.

Aerial photos showed 176 Soviet tanks were assembling in the Trosna area. This was the area that 4th PzD was going to attack that day. The attack was canceled and a new defensive belt erected. fkk392. dgk231m. snk433m++.

The 3rd TA got a late start and launched its attack toward Stanovoi Kolodez around midday. On this extremely hot day, the 12th TC and 2nd MC led the advance but failed to reach their objective. zra186.

July 25th on the Southern Salient
Hitler ordered the 2nd SS PzC to Italy but rescinded the order to have just the *LAH* transferred to Italy; the other two divisions were needed in the Kharkov sector. *LAH* left their 42 panzers, including a few Tigers, in sector. The division would be picking up new panzers in Italy. cbk101. kuz219.

SSTK was ordered to the Mius River area to help stop the Southern Front from destroying 6th Army. *Das Reich* and 3rd PzD were being deployed there as well. gnk421.

The 11th PzR of 6th PzD went into reserve to rest and refit. Major Bake did such a good job during the campaign, especially in keeping the Ryndinka bridgehead on 7/12, that Hoth promoted him to regimental CO and on 8/1 he received the Oak Leaves to his Knight's Cross. Just six days later, Bake's commander and friend, Colonel Oppeln-Bronikovski received the Cross in Gold. fzk57. fzk315. zfk479.

July 25th on the Northern Salient
In early morning, heavy rains came, turning the dirt roads to mud. At 0800 hrs, the 4th PzD's line in the Trosna sector was heavily bombed. At 0900, the attack was launched with the support of 100 tanks. The Pz Abt 6 allowed the Soviet tanks to break the line and head inland but the panzers turned and demolished the Red tanks from the rear. Nearby, 35th PzR was attacked as it defended Hill 250. It repulsed the attack, destroying seven tanks. 4th PzD destroyed a total of 20 tanks that day. fkk393. dgk231m. snk433m++.

Mussolini was arrested and removed from power. Hitler considered sending more divisions to Italy. dgk238. cbk101.

Now several days behind schedule, the 3rd TA resumed their advance at dawn. The Germans were putting up stiff resistance and the advance continued slowly, but toward evening Yeropkino fell and 3rd TA was on the verge of accomplishing one of its original objectives which was cutting the Orel-Kursk rail line and capturing Stanovoi Kolodez. zra186.

Shortly after daybreak, Soviet guns opened up on the German line with the primary recipient being the 34th ID and part of the 56th ID to its right. The shelling turned into a rolling barrage as the Red Army started crossing the Oka. The 78th SD, which had just arrived a couple days before, swung the tide of victory to the German side when it assisted the 34th ID as it was about to crumble. After the end of the day, the Soviets paused for a few days to regroup. General Rendulic's 35th IC accounted for taking down 819 tanks since 7/11. All of the 22 Soviet divisions that battled the 35th IC had suffered heavy casualties. Rendulic was promoted and was awarded the Oak Leaves to his Knight's Cross. The 35th IC stayed on the Oka until 7/31. fkk386.

General Rybalko's two corps continued to slowly gain ground and were finally able to cut the rail line from Orel to Kursk. The constant pressure from the Soviet forces would eventually wear down the German defenses and force a more determined retreat. The bulk of 3rd GTA was shifted southwards to support the 48th Army in quickening its pace northward. This move probably should have been done days earlier when it was discovered that some of the German forces were pulling back and escaping. dgk236*+. zzz101m.

The 3rd Army crossed the Oka River and established a bridgehead on the western banks before moving on. The 1st *Flieger* Division immediately attacked the Soviets on the west bank of the river and prevented them from advancing further that day. The Oka River ran north-south just west of Orel. fkk399. zzz101m. cbk115.

July 26th on the Southern Salient

Wittmann's Tigers along with the rest of panzers of *LAH* were handed over to *SSTK* and *SSDR* as they were about to be ordered to Italy on 7/29, where they would receive their new panzers. Wittmann, during the campaign to this point, had destroyed 30 tanks, 28 assault guns and many field guns. agk131. fzk317. zow175.

For the next eight days, the 38th Army, from the southwestern end of the Kursk bulge, would demonstrate an attack to mislead Hausser. The real attack would come from the east. Soviet engineers built 22 under the surface bridges along the Northern Donets River and its tributaries in preparation for the massive attack that was coming: Operation Rumyantsev. It would include the 6th GA, 5th GA and 53rd Army in the lead with the 7th GA following. The replenished 1st TA and the 5th GTA would support. The Soviets had a 5 to 1 advantage in men and 10 to 1 advantage in tanks when the operation launched. dgk245+.

July 26th on the Northern Salient

The grenadiers of *GD* launched an attack toward the Vitebyet River, which the enemy was using as an assembly area. The assault, which lasted all day, for the most part failed; the enemy was too strong. One battalion of *GD* did reach the river at Ismorosny. Knowing that the captured site was important to the Soviets and that they would try to get it back, additional forces were quickly brought up to resist the attack. In the afternoon, the Soviets attacked at Ismorosny and nearby Alisovo, as well as the woods northeast of Karachev. Once it was realized that *GD* had moved into the area plus the fact it was an important area, 11th GA brought up its reserves to put greater pressure on the line. hsz137+.

The three tank corps of General Badanov's 4th TA (496 tanks) struck west of Bolkhov, in the northern sector of the salient, threatening a breakthrough which would take the Soviets to the important rail town of Karachev. Initially the 23rd PzC and 41st PzC resisted, but the Soviets eventually broke through, forcing the Germans to abandon Bolkhov to a new defense belt northwest of Orel and less than six miles from the vital Bryansk-Orel rail line. The arrival of *GD* finally stopped the advance of 11th GA and 2nd GCC. Karachev remained in German hands despite Bagramyan throwing new reserves into battle. It started raining after dark. dgk238+. fkk393. zzz101m. dgk231m. snk433m++.

The OKH unofficially notified Model that Operation Herstreise (Autumn Journey) would begin in a few days. During the previous three weeks, Model's two armies lost 62,300 soldiers, but yet they prevented three fronts from surrounding them. The Soviet casualties were even higher. A major reason for Model's success in holding back the Soviets so long was his disobedience of the order from OKH not to dig defenses in the Orel salient. Model quietly built four trenches before and during Operation Citadel because he realized the Soviets would eventually counter-attack. The order not to build defenses by the OKH made no sense at all except to a fanatic like its leader. dgk238. snk112+. mkz123+. zzz101m.

The 4th PzD finally crossed the Rakitnaya to newly-built defenses in order to rest and regroup. There were no major fighting in 46th PzC sector that day. Model believed the Soviets were preparing to shift their attack to the Solotnoye Dno area. The general sent the 103rd PzAR to the area to bolster the line that was defended by the 102nd ID, 7th ID and 258th ID. Soviet tanks broke through the line southeast of Martinovski and it was sealed off, but not before Hill 260 was captured. A counter-attack led by 4th PzD chased the Soviets off the hill to stabilize the 102nd ID line. Another break in the line occurred in 258th ID sector but that gap was sealed as well. That night 4th PzD counted 37 panzers and 10 StuGs. fkk393+. dgk87m. lck116m.

Stavka, recognizing Rybalko and his army's significant contributions, renamed 3rd TA to 3rd GTA and renamed its corps as well. The 12th TC became 6th GTC and the 15th TC became 7th GTC, while 2nd MC became 7th GMC. zra187.

The 23rd IC and 41st PzC, defending Bolkhov area were slowly pushed back, abandoning the town and falling back to newly constructed defenses, northwest of Orel and only six miles from the critical Bryansk-Orel rail line. Only the timely arrival of *GD* contained the southward drive of Bagramyan's 11th GA and 2nd GCC. dgk238+. zzz101m. dgk231m. snk433m++.

Badanov's 4th TA finally arrived in sector and pulled up behind the 11th GA. The army consisted of the 11th TC, 30th TC and 6th GMC. The 4th TA had 500 new tanks that had never been in battle. In the week that it took the tanks to reach this sector, Model transferred four panzer divisions to this area and was able to put up stiff resistance. Badanov lost many tanks and was unable to help push the Germans back very far, but he was succeeding in enclosing some Germans near Bolkhov. kcz171. dgk231m. snk433m++.

July 27th on the Southern Salient

Preliminaries of Operation Rumyantsev began. The Voronezh and Steppe Fronts launched a massive counter-attack along the Belgorod-Kharkov line. The Germans had anticipated this offensive and the Orel offensive as well but what really surprised them was the speed and resilience of the fighting units in the Kursk defense as they participated in these new offensives. dgk229. zzz101m.

July 27th on the Northern Salient
Model, to avoid senseless deaths, ordered his garrison at Orel to fall back to the Hagen line while there was an escape route. Hitler approved all forces to the Hagen line. The rear area services began the next day. The rearguard was formed by 12th PzD and 78th AD. The 3rd and 63rd Armies arrived in front of Orel on 8/4. fkk387. fkk399. zzz101m.

The PzAbt 653 had lost a total of 13 Ferdinands since 7/5. They had more damaged machines but they were repaired. mhz262*.

At night, a panzer battalion of *GD* moved into the Varky area on a search and destroy mission. It was discovered that elements of 11th GA had shifted direction to the west and were trying to outmaneuver German forces. For the most part Soviet forces evaded the shock group and the search party was eventually recalled. hsz139.

July 28th on the Southern Salient
General Hausser was decorated with Oak Leaves to his Knight's Cross for his determination and leadership in the campaign. He was the 261st recipient so honored. fzk184.

July 28th on the Northern Salient
Model was ordered to launch Operation Herbstreise. It was the complete evacuation of the Orel salient by German forces. While the front line was moving back toward the Hagen Line, 17 divisions were moving into sector to stiffen the line for the expected assault that the three fronts could generate. Model's leadership during this evacuation was excellent and was probably the main reason why few Germans were lost during the operation. In addition to the 9th Army and the 2nd PzA, 20,000 injured and 53,000 tons of supplies were saved during the retreat along the Orel-Bryansk highway. The 1st *Flieger* Division played an important role in safeguarding the evacuation. cbk115. kcz171. dgk231m. snk433m++. zzk385.

It had been raining off and on all day in the Karachev sector where *GD* was defending, and the swamping ground was getting worse. At 0630 hrs, when it had temporarily stopped raining, the *Luftwaffe* made a bombing run north of Shudre where the enemy was assembling forces; results were inconclusive. At 0900 hrs, a heavy artillery barrage targeted the *GD* division which hunkered down and endured the shelling. During the shelling, a combined force of tanks and infantry advanced and recaptured Alisovo from the Germans. Though the nearby village of Kusmenkovo was also hit hard, it was still being held by *GD*. By noon, the Soviet shelling had stopped and lead units had reached Ismorosny and were fighting with the small garrison holding the village. By 1500 hrs, Ismorosny had fallen and the Soviets were fighting with *GD* for the woods near the village. At about this same time a small squadron of German fighters were strafing Alisovo, trying to cause as much death and destruction as possible. Increased Soviet activity was felt at Semenovka, Tvanosvskoye Dvoriki, Krasaskye and Novogorodskye as the Karachev sector attack was renewed. These villages had fallen by dark. The newly arrived 293rd ID was sent to the area to try to plug the forming gap in the line. hsz140+.

The 3rd TA (3rd GTA) was pulled from the line, given a few days to rest and was then transferred to the command of General Rokossovsky of Central Front in an attempt to speed Central Front's pace. zra187.

In the Orel salient, the 102nd ID and 7th ID was repeatedly attack by Soviet squads, but the attacks were initially repulsed. At 1400 hrs gaps opened on either side of Iablonovez which allowed the tankers to head for Golenischtschevo, Brussovez and establish a bridgehead at Golenischtschevo. fkk394. dgk231m. snk433m++.

July 29th on the Northern Salient

In the Orel salient, elements of the 4th PzD attacked toward Topkovo to stop Soviet attempts to capture Hill 260 which help 7th ID's defensive posture. On the way 4th PzD fought a hard battle to capture Martinovski. The capture was made even harder by the shelling being delivered by nearby Yalta Woods. An attempt was made to clear the woods but after entering the woods, it was decided that after an air attack that failed to shake the Soviets loose, the odds were against them so they pulled back. fkk395. dgk87m. lck116m.

The 129th ID had just arrived in the Karachev sector and was immediately sent on the attack. It was joined by the 293rd ID and together they launched an attack on the newly lost villages of Semenovka, Krasaskye and Novogorodskye. Two of the three villages were recaptured but Krasaskye remained in Soviet hands. hsz141.

The Fusiliers of *GD* received bad news that day. Their Col Kassnitz had died in a Breslau hospital from wounds received when he was leading his group on July 5th. The regiment had just passed Butovo and was heading for Cherkasskoe when it ran into a minefield covered by small arms and mortars. He was awarded the Knight's Cross while in hospital on 7/21. hsz142. dgk94. lck228.

July 30th on the Northern Salient

The PzR of *GD* had arrived in the Karachev region, west of Orel four days before and been immediately placed in the line. That morning, while maintaining a defensive posture it was attacked by 30 T34s supported by infantry, near Hill 211.7. The Soviet attackers fought in a suicidal fashion, not giving up when they realized they were facing mostly Panthers. The Germans destroyed almost all the tanks and repulsed the infantry as well, forcing them to fall back. Lt Risch and his crew of a Mk IV destroyed 18 tanks this day but three days later defending against another tank attack, Lt Risch was killed. hjj143. hsz142.

July 31st on the Northern Salient

It is estimated that since 7/11 in the Orel salient, Model's 9th Army and 2nd PzA suffered casualties of 62,300 men and as many as 400 panzers. These numbers far exceed the casualties 9th Army experienced in the first week of Operation Citadel. It is estimated that for the whole month of July, 9th Army lost 304 panzers. sna262. snz226m.

The Fusiliers of *GD* had a restless night. They were defending the line on either side of Alechino and were hearing tanks moving closer. At first light, those tanks attacked. The Fusiliers were ready and were supported by a few panzers that were brought up during the predawn hours. Quickly the *GD* destroyed a dozen or more tanks before the rest fell back. hsz142.

In the Alisovo sector, it was discovered that there was a strong enemy presence on the road north of Shudre that crossed the Vitebyet River. Besides sending a strike force from *GD*, the *Luftwaffe* sent a squadron to hit the concentration. hsz143.

At night in the Orel salient, Model began to fall back to the Desna River, the Hagen line (Operation Herbstreise). It was the first of a four part phased retreat to a new line 60 miles to the rear. This fall back would free up up to 20 divisions for deployment where needed. It required a tremendous amount of time and planning by the officers, in addition to running the battlefield to achieve this successful endeavor. By this time, most of the fighting was occurring in the Bolkhov salient. This four-phased withdrawal would take until 8/17 to complete. The task of stopping a major Soviet offensive, moving huge ammunition stores, withdrawing two armies and building new defenses all at the same time was a monumental effort. Once the Soviets realized the withdrawal was on, they increased their efforts to penetrate the line. For the month of July, the elite 4th PzD which contributed so much lost 2,521 men. dgk240. snk112++*. fkk396. zzz101m. dgk231m. snk172. snk433m++. zzk385+.

27

August 1st-August 27th

August 1st on the Northern Salient
Quickly discovering Model's evacuation (Operation Hagen), the Soviets renewed their attack on 9th Army in the Shepelovo-Gomel sector. Four rifle divisions and 120 tanks attacked the 7th ID, 31st ID and the 258th ID. Though the Germans were outnumbered in both men and panzers, they did a good job in stopping the attack. It's claimed the Soviets lost 77 tanks. On August 4th, the divisions reached Kromy, south of Orel but the pressure was maintained from the Chern River area and Model had to temporarily redirect Luftwaffe support away from 2nd PzA to 9th Army. Though no penetration was made, the line did bend with the Soviets capturing Hill 269.5 and with the advanced recon battalion heading for Hill 263. They were now only seven miles from their main objective of Kromy. snk115. fkk398. dgr209m. aaa124m. lck116m.

The 33rd PzGR, under Mauss, was ordered to the Krasnikovo West-Gunyavka West-Krasnyi Kommunar to east of Hill 269 with explicit orders that Hill 269.5 must stay in German hands. fkk398.

The 9th PzD, west of Orel, had suffered casualties of 3,642 men since Citadel was launched. It had 22 Mk IIIs and 32 Mk IVs and 241 other armored vehicles. mkz122. dgk231m. snk433m++.

August 2nd on the Southern Salient
At Belgorod, the 4th PzA had several defense belts, but only the first one was manned and with infantry only. Von Manstein was forced to give up panzer units to other areas and was now in a much weakened condition. The 11th PzD, 19th PzD and 6th PzD were still available near Belgorod. He sent the *Das Reich* and *SSTK* to assist the 3rd PzD northwest of Kharkov to stop the new massive Soviet assault. Viking was sent to help Group Kempf. dgk246+.

August 2nd on the Northern Salient
West of Orel, the 35th PzR and Pz Abt 49 were attacked by Soviet tanks. Though the Germans destroyed 16 tanks, the Soviets were able to fight their way past. The CO of 46th PzC, General Zorn, was killed on this day by a shellburst, as he drove to the line. Lt General Hossbach, the CO of 31st ID, eventually replaced him. The temporary commander until Lt General Hossbach was chosen was Lt General Esebeck. Hossbach would lead the 56th PzC in June 1944. fkk398. zsm266.. zmb239+.

At night, Soviet partisans exploded 5,000 charges, destroying 30 miles of track, interrupting rail traffic for 48 hours and preventing the Germans from emptying their huge Orel warehouse. Another 1,700 charges were set off on the 3rd and another 4,100 charges exploded on the 4th. dgk240. zzz101m. dgk231m. snk433m++.

August 3rd on the Southern Salient

Operation Rumyantsev began that day. The combined efforts of Vatutin's Vorenzh Front and Konev's Steppe Front launched with the sole purpose of destroying 4th PzA and, if possible, the rest of AGS deployed down to the Black Sea. The 1st TA, 5th GTA, 5th GA, 6th GA, 7th GA, 69th and 53rd Armies would be involved in the main spearhead. The 38th and 40th Armies as well as the 47th Army and 3rd GMC would attack on the western flank. The Soviets advanced over 15 miles that day and were in the vicinity of the Tomarovka-Belgorod line. The first phase objective was to secure Kharkov. dgk241+. dgk243m. zra65+. dgn242m. gmn260. gmn260m.

When Operation Rumyantsev began, the Soviet forces numbered 980,000 men and 2,439 tanks. The Germans had only 210,000 men and 250 panzers. At 0500 hrs, the Soviets opened with a massive barrage and by 0800 hrs, the assault force jumped off into narrow attack zones where men and tanks would far outweigh the enemy. Von Manstein knew a counter offensive would eventually come but it was a surprise that it came so soon. 4th PzA and Kempf Group suffered heavy casualties by not being ready for the assault. *Das Reich* and *SSTK* divisions went south but were quickly called back. The 5th SS PzGD moved up to assist Kempf. While a few facts of this operation are presented, the operation was much too large to cover in depth here. dgk247*. dgk241*. gjz192. gmn260. gmn260m. zro211.

At 0500 hrs, Operation Rumyantsev began with a heavy barrage that lasted three hours. Elements of 1st TA and 6th GA quickly penetrated the front line but the 53rd Army was stalled against the stiff German defense of the Erik River. Vatutin had to shift resources to assist 53rd Army. dgk247.

Konev's Steppe Front was having trouble crossing the Northern Donets River against stiff resistance. To help Konev, the 5th GMC pivoted to the east, toward the village of Krasnoe while Rotmistrov's 18th TC and 29th TC continued toward the south, parallel to 1st TA. This diversion hastened the Germans evacuation of Belgorod. The stiff resistance in the towns of Borisovka and Graivoron forced RDs from both 27th Army and 6th GA to stay behind to clear while the tankers moved ahead unprotected. The two field armies had encircled five German divisions and were trying to reduce the pocket. The 11th PzD and *GD* attacked the Soviets from the rear and were able to open a corridor for the trapped comrades. Maj General Poluboiarov's 4th GTC was able to force a flank of 11th PzD back from the main attack and had to fight for survival themselves. dgk248.

The 4th PzA was fighting for survival. The 19th PzD and 6th PzD joined to establish a defense northeast of Tomarovka that stopped the 31st TC of 1st TA. On the following day, the 6th TC and 3rd MC continued to exploit the gap southwest of Borisovka. The 6th GA were riding with the tankers. To the east of 1st TA, Konev's Steppe Front was having trouble crossing the Northern Donets River. Vatutin sent his 5th GTA over to Konev to assist his 7th GA in breaking the German defense at the river. The 5th GMC pivoted and advanced on Krasnoe while Rotmistrov's 18th and 29th TC continued to drive south, parallel to 1st TA. These forces were nearing Belgorod, threatening encirclement. The Germans started to evacuate the city that day. dgk248.

The Bake Group was exiting the Gonki woods when they were attacked. After a brief struggle, nine T34s were destroyed before the tanks pulled off. By this time the Bake Group had destroyed 150 tanks and a number of guns during this campaign. fzk58.

August 3rd on the Northern Salient
During the predawn hours, the PzR of *GD*, under Major Possel, moved to Ismorosny. At first light the panzers moved out toward the northwest through the woods near Alechino. While in the woods, the column was ambushed but the attack was repulsed. The column continued, fighting its way north of Alisovo toward the important hill south of Shudre. The *GD* reached the hill but it was costly. hsz145.

To the west of the Orel salient, 100,000 partisans began a series of bombings to destroy the rail line leading into the salient in order to block all supplies from reaching AGC. Despite a critical situation in the salient, Model was forced to send troops to the rear to stop the partisans. The destruction was so extensive that all supplies were blocked from reaching Model for the next three days. sgf354.

Rokossovsky's Central Front reached the Kroma River and tried to cross but the initial attempt fails. The last of the Germans were crossing the Oka River and would have been vulnerable if the Central Front was not stopped at the Kroma. The bridges over the Oka were blown. fkk399.

The Red Air Force flew 1,000 sorties against Orel that day. The town was nearly surrounded and it was meant to soften the front trenches for when the ground forces made their last assault on the city in the morning. The following day, the 3rd and 63rd Armies would drive into the hard fought city and by 8/5 the city would be secured. As a small contingent of soldiers came into the city, the citizens came out and started cheering their liberators. fkk399. awk692.

August 4th on the Southern Salient
For the leadership displayed during the campaign, Capt Kageneck of the sPzAbt 503 was awarded the Knight's Cross. zfk177.

August 4th on the Northern Salient
The 4th PzD reached the new defenses behind the Neschivka River. All German units were able to make it out of the Orel salient. In the previous three weeks the 4th PzD and its attachments had destroyed 240 tanks. fkk399.

During the withdrawal from the Orel salient, the 9th Army reached Kromy. With the Soviets having shifted their main assault from 2nd PzA to 9th Army, Model had the *Luftwaffe* turn south and help support 9th Army. The 3rd and 63rd Armies entered the evacuated Orel. Next day, Stalin gave a 120 gun salute for liberating Orel. Belgorod also fell that day to the Voronezh and Steppe Fronts. Losing Operation Citadel and being pushed out of the Orel salient was the first time the Germans were defeated in a summer campaign. snk115. fkk388. fkk400. zzz101m.

August 5th on the Northern Salient
Now part of Central Front, during the predawn hours, 3rd TA assembled in the Koroskovo area. Rybalko's orders were to advance alongside 13th Army toward Kromy and capture it before crossing over the Oka River. Kromy was in the deep southern sector of the salient and was south of Orel. Capturing Kromy would deprive the Germans east of the city a valuable exit route to the west. Rybalko received 200 new tanks the previous day in preparation for this new assault. The 3rd TA now had 417 tanks and assault guns in their arsenal but one problem with the new tanks was that they were accompanied by poorly trained new recruits.

He launched at midday, with his 12th TC, 15th TC and 2nd MC in the lead while his 91st TR and 50th Motorcycle Regiment were in reserve. The 3rd TA and its corps had been renamed at this point, but I' have kept their old designations to avoid confusion. zra187+.

The recently arrived 8th PzD moved up to the line at daybreak to relieve GD in the Ismorosny area. The 10th PzR and the 28th PzGR relieved the exhausted Fusiliers and few panzers while their third regiment stayed behind in reserve. hsz146.

The Red Army shifted direction southwest of Kromy against 9th Army and especially against the 258th ID of 46th PzC, but again the Soviet attack was repulsed, however the constant pressure on 9th Army and 2nd PzA would eventually weaken the German line. It was only a matter of time. Model also transferred 12th PzD from 2nd PzA to 9th Army to bolster the line. Model also made a science of quickly redeploying his mobile forces to areas of urgency; using these forces as "fire brigades". *Stavka* had created a two pincer offensive with the objective of penetrating the German line and swinging in behind 9th Army to destroy it. The two main focal points of attack were Khotynets and Kromy. Model recognized the plan and was able to rebuff it. snk115.

The Soviets renewed their assault on 9th Army southwest of Kromy. The Red Army made 15 assaults on this day, primarily against 258th ID of 46th PzC. Partisan action against the rails increased, causing shortages of fuel and ammo from reaching 9th Army. Model had to transfer 12th PzD to the area east of Smablykin to help 292nd ID and 383rd ID which were in trouble. snk115.

Popov's forces in the north and General Rokossovsky in the southern part of the Orel salient, resumed their attack to liberate the Orel sector. That same day, the 2nd PzA completed evacuating 53,000 tons of supplies and 20,000 wounded from Orel and blew the remaining bridges heading west. As they headed for the Hagen line, they executed a scorch earth policy. The Soviets quickly moved into Orel with the German evacuation of the key city. With the capture of Orel, Moscow broadcasted the good news and delivered a 120 gun salute to the victors. Regaining Orel and eliminating the Orel salient within the month was a huge relief to Stalin. Ever since October 1941 when the city was captured, Stalin always considered the possibility that the Germans would move from there toward Moscow. In 1941, the population of Orel was 140,000 but in August 1943, when the city was liberated, the population had dwindled to 30,000. Nearly 40,000 people were either executed or deported back to the camps, a few thousand escaped and the rest died of starvation. As a sign of how important Orel was to the Germans, very few German soldiers were taken prisoners. Most, that could not fall back at the last minute, fought to the last bullet. The Germans also left thousands of mines in the city that took the Soviet engineers weeks to clear out. dgk240*. snk115. fkk400. zzz101m. kcz170+. dgk231m. snk433m++. awk685. zro211.

August 6th on the Southern Salient

The 6th GA had finally broken through in the west and its battered 5th GTC passed under control of the 1st TA. dgk248+.

Now south of Belgorod, the grenadiers of 6th PzD were falling back in disorder; several panzers from 11th PzR moved up and slowed the enemy advance, giving the soldiers a chance to compose themselves. The same thing happened the next day on a bigger scale and the panzers came up to block the Soviet attack again. fzk59. zro211.

August 6th on the Northern Salient
The initial advance by 3rd TA was good but as it approached the Kromy River, the *Luftwaffe* continued to strike it and German artillery zoomed in on it, causing heavy casualties and dramatically slows its pace. To cross the river and attack the city of Kromy, Rybalko formed a new shock group using elements of all his units. It had 100 tanks and its only mission was to capture Kromy. The rest of 3rd TA would keep the enemy busy while this new combat group sneaked off in the night, getting a head start on the main group. zra188. awk685.

August 7th on the Southern Salient
Bogodukhov, on the Mearla River, fell to the 1st TA. The 1st TA also fought the *GD* Division east of Akhtyrka, as well as the 2nd SS PzD east of Bogodukhov. Heavy fighting at Zolochev continued between the 3rd PzC and 5th GTA. Other units of 1st Tank Army ran into the 2nd SS *Das Reich* Div of the 3rd PzC east of Bogodukhov, sparking a furious tank battle. The 5th GTC had slipped by the panzers and were southwest of Bogodukhov. The gap between 4th PzA and Group Kempf had widened to 30 miles. bt99. dgk249.

The 11th PzD and the *GD* began an advance toward Graivoron and Borisovka to free the remains of five divisions entrapped there. The 4th GTC of 27th Army was able to push back elements of 11th PzD as it tried to protect the western flank of 1st TA. dgk248+.

The gap between the two German armies had grown to 30 miles near Bogodukhov. The 5th GTC, attached to 1st TA was driving south, trying to extend the gap, southwest of the town. Over the next three days, reinforcements arrived on both sides, intensifying an already bitter see-saw battle that started near Bogodukhov and moved toward Akhtyrka. dgk249.

General Gustav Schmidt of 19th PzD was killed in action near Borisovka. fkk87. dlu29.

Official Soviet records show casualties for the last month in both the Kursk and Orel salient reached 430,000 men and 2,600 tanks. German losses for the same period are estimated at 86,000 casualties and 343 panzers. sgf355.

August 7th on the Northern Salient
To the north of Kursk, the Western Front and Kalinin Front launched Operation Suvorov. From Dukhovshchina in the north and Roslavl to the south, the two fronts drove west in order to encircle Smolensk. Though the Kursk sector saw the heaviest fighting, the rest of the line saw action as well. dgk254.

Group Harpe completed its retreat to the Moshcherka River despite the repeated attacks. The Soviets were heading toward Khotynets but failed to reach it by 8/10. With 9th Army falling back, 2nd PzA's southern flank near Smitrovsk was exposed. The next day, a large Soviet assault began from Bryantsovo toward Dmitrovsk, which was defended by Lt General Muller-Gebhard's 72nd ID. Aided by a thunderstorm, the Soviets penetrated the line. With a gap opening, the next day saw three more RDs and tanks enter the battle to exploit their advantage. The 72nd ID with the help of the 31st ID regrouped and stopped the advance. The 20th PzGD then moved up to the line and acting as a rearguard allowed the infantry to continue to fall back while still holding on to Dmitrovsk. A breakthrough of the line at Dmitrovsk would present tremendous problems to Model's evacuation to the Hagen Line. He ordered the town to be held for as long as possible, but the Soviet pressure became too much and by the evening of 8/11, 20th PzGD had to fall back, giving the town to the Soviets. In the days that followed, the Red Army expanded their offensive.

To the north of 9th Army, 4th Army was attacked and in the south, 4th PzA was attacked. snk116+. dgk231m. snk433m++.

The 6th PzD was heading south toward Kharkov. The Bake Group was in the lead when the column was ambushed on its eastern flank by 40 T34s. With the help of a nearby battery of 88s, the 6th PzD was able to repulse the attack. The division was heading for Kharkov as part of the force to defend the city. fzk59.

August 10th on the Southern Salient
Ever since Operation Rumyantsev began in early August, the 6th PzD had been falling back from Belgorod. On this day, it settled into the outer defense line, north of Kharkov. For the next three days, the 6th PzD had been up against fierce resistance north and east of Kharkov against the Soviet major offensive. On 8/22, the division would be withdrawn from the line and sent back to near Merefa, southwest of Kharkov, to refit. knz189.

August 10th on the Northern Salient
Elements of the 4th TA resumed the assault on Dmitrovsk which was an important blocking point, allowing Model to continue its fall back to the Hagen Line. The next night, the Germans evacuated Dmitrovsk and the Soviets quickly moved in. snk116.

Three days earlier, the Soviet offensive launched toward Spas-Demensk and were making gains. That day, the remains of the 9th PzD moved to the area west of Kirov (southwest of the original penetration) and for the next eight days, slowed the Soviet progress. By the end of 8/17, the 9th PzD had only five panzers and 12 assault guns working. It was then incorporated into 56th PzC. mkz124.

August 11th on the Southern Salient
It was determined that of the 212 Panthers *GD* received since 7/5, 156 were write-offs. This clearly shows how vicious the fighting was in this five week period. mhz292+.

August 11th on the Northern Salient
Due to its heavy losses, the 3rd TA (3rd GTA) was ordered to disengage and was transferred to *Stavka* Reserve. It was sent to near Kursk to regroup. It was not with the Kutuzov operation very long but being part of the leading spearhead against Model's forces, it suffered heavy casualties. Besides the stiff resistance of the enemy, the 3rd TA had to overcome harsh terrain and heavy rainstorms that turned the ground and dirt roads into muddy swamps. Even with all these things going against Rybalko, *Stavka* was still disturbed with the general's performance. *Stavka* also believed Vatutin's premature tank attacks cost his front valuable tanks and crews. zra188+.

August 12th on the Southern Salient
The *SSTK* launched a counter-attack against the over stretched 1st TA, near the rail line that went from Belgorod to Kharkov. The Germans quickly surrounded part of the column and destroyed 100 tanks. During the battle, Soviet reinforcements arrived, launching an attack of their own. *SSTK* withdrew, allowing the Soviets to capture Vysokopole, another small village on the rail line. At the same time, the *Das Reich* and *Wiking* divisions attacked the 1st TA south of Bogodukhov. Further elements of the 3rd PzC arrived and a few days later, were able to push the 6th GA and 1st TA back to the Merchik River and stopping the

Soviet advance in this area. dgk249.

Von Manstein prepared 4th PzA to a two-prong counter-attack from Akhtryka to isolate 27th Army and 6th GA that were in the Akhtryka-Bogodukhov area. The 3rd PzC would be the other half of the attack. The attack was scheduled to start by 8/17. dgk251.

With Soviets approaching Kharkov, Kempf prepared to evacuate the city, fearing encirclement. Konev's Steppe Front had cut the rail line into Kharkov. Konev was in no hurry to attack the city; he wanted to lay seige to it at first to wear down the Germans. dgk251.

After von Manstein informed his dictator that AGS was unable to hold Donbas without further reinforcements, Hitler ordered the East Wall to be built. Hitler up to this point refused to allow the East Wall because to him it was a sign of defeatism, but reality finally seeped into his conscience. The wall would run for the most part along the Dnepr River and run from Chernigov, Kiev, Zaporozhe and Melitopol. wwf177.

August 13th on the Northern Salient
Model's 9th HQ took control of 2nd PzA as well as they began the final phase of the withdrawal to the Hagen Line. Bitter fighting was now occurring in the Karachev area, west of Orel, as both sides tried to build up forces. The Soviets, under the umbrella of artillery shelling, launched another offensive toward Krarachev, crashing into 8th PzD and 18th PzD. For two days the panzers prevented the Soviets from gaining much ground, allowing Model to reach the Hagen Line on 8/14. The rearguard arrived on 8/18. Karachev was on the Bryansk-Orel Highway, about halfway between the two cities. By this time the Orel salient was gone and the front line was just east of Karachev or near the shoulder of the old salient. While the German front was holding back the enemy, the defenses of the Hagen Line were being enhanced. snk117. dgk231m.

August 14th on the Southern Salient
Hitler was outraged by the evacuation of Kharkov and fired Kempf. Von Manstein chose Lt General Woehler as Kempf's replacement. Kempf's forces would now be designated 8th Army. In 1941, Kempf had been the CO of 48th PzC before becoming the commander of Army Detachment Kempf. dgk251+. zsm266.

August 14th on the Northern Salient
The Soviets paused their attack against Model to regroup and redeploy to new attack points. The southern pincer moved southwest of Karachev while the northern pincer moved to Kirov. snk117. dgk231m. snk431m.

August 16th on the Southern Salient
The 47th Army launched an attack to clear Germans near Boromlia and north of Akhtyrka and by the 18th, the German 57th ID was shattered. By the 19th, the 47th Army was threatening the rear of the German Akhtryka forces. The *GD* had to fall back from the town to escape destruction. Maj General Obukhov's 3rd GMC was attached to 47th Army and was a major influence in pushing the Germans back. dgk251*.

August 16th on the Northern Salient
In the 9th Army sector, along the Hagen Line, the OKH transferred the following units

to other areas: 1st ID, 102nd ID, 183rd ID, 258th ID, 293rd ID, 4th PzD, 9th PzD and 12th PzD. It also took from the line covered by 56th PzC and 12th IC of 4th Army. snk118.

The 9th Army and 2nd PzA completed arriving at the Hagen line, east of Bryansk. The Soviets, not realizing this defense belt was prepared, crashed into it and were quickly stopped, suffering heavy casualties. The Soviets fell back, regrouped and made separate concentrated attacks near Shablykino, Karachev and Kirov. This small delay allowed Model to resupply and strengthen the Hagen Line. With the front line shortened, AGC was able to free up 19 divisions for other deployments. dgk240. snk117. mkz124. sgf354. kcz171.

August 17th on the Southern Salient
In a concerted effort, 7th PzD, 19th PzD and *GD* attacked from southeast of Akhtryka toward Bodgodukhov, to meet up with *SSTK* and 223rd ID in order to trap Red forces there. The encirclement worked, but the Germans were too weak to liquidate the pocket. Lt General Kulik's 4th GA with its 3rd GTC moved in to free the pocket. General Gustav Schmidt of 19th PzD was killed in action that day. dgk251. fkk87.

August 18th on the Southern Salient
Woehler of the new 8th Army, formerly Kempf Group, asked Hitler to evacuate Kharkov and to fall back to the Dnepr. The savage battles west of Kharkov did have one advantage for the Germans; it kept their escape route to the Dnepr open. On the 22nd, the 5th GA and 5th GTA tried desperately to close the escape route but failed to do so. Though 4th PzA succeeded to evacuate both Belgorod and Kharkov to the Dnepr River, it came at a high price. The Soviets had inflicted heavy casualties but by the end of operations they would have casualties of 250,000 men. dgk251+.

August 18th on the Northern Salient
By this time, Operation Kutuzov had expanded to a front that was 250 miles long. It had begun on 7/12 with just 11th GA, 3rd and 63rd Armies but then the 13th, 48th, 60th, 65th Armies and the 2nd TA joined in to dissolve the Orel salient. The German line was defended by 2nd PzA and a few days later with also 9th Army. The *GD* left 48th PzC in the south to add its weight with 2nd PzA. On 7/20, the 3rd GA, 11th and 4th TA were also brought up to the line. gjz192. zzz101m. fmz229.

Now that the Germans were behind the Hagen line and the front line had shrunk by over 100 miles, *Stavka* pulled the battered 61st Army from the line and sent it to southern Ukraine. Coincidentally, the 47th PzC was sent to southern Ukraine at about this same time. kcz171. dgk231m. snk433m++.

The city of Bryansk fell to the Soviets. zro211.

August 19th on the Southern Salient
Maj General Kozlov's 47th Army was threatening the German rear area at Akhtryka, forcing the *GD* to evacuate. dgk251.

August 19th on the Northern Salient
The Red Army launched an offensive on the Hagen Line against 23rd IC, expanding the attack on 8/26 to include 46th PzC and attacking Group Harpe on 8/28. snk118.

August 21st on the Southern Salient
Maj General von Waldenfels became the CO of 6th PzD, replacing its former chief, Major General Hunersdorff, who died in battle in July. General Hunersdorff had been a veteran of WWI and had been born in Cairo in 1898. fkk285. dlu42.

August 22nd on the Northern Salient
West of Orel, the 9th PzD loaded onto a train, heading south toward the Mius River. It would now be attached to 24th IC. mkz124.

August 23rd on the Southern Salient
Operation Rumyantsev was officially terminated and with it concluded Soviet activities related to Operation Citadel. However, that did not end the Soviet offensives. On 8/7 Operation Suvorov launched against AGC. On 8/13 the Southwest Front and South Front launched the Donbas Strategic Offensive. These offensives lasted until around the start of October and gained about 175 miles of territory. gjz193.

The 11th PzD had only 820 men and 19 panzers, while 19th PzD had 760 men and 7 panzers. The 19th PzD also lost its CO, General Schmidt, who was killed at Borisovka. *Das Reich* had 55 panzers and *SSTK* had 61. The 1st TA had lost 646 tanks in Citadel and, after reinforcement, another 1,042 tanks in the Belgorod-Kharkov Offensive; it was now down to 120 tanks. Rotmistrov's 5th GTA had only 50 of its 503 tanks remaining. dgk252*.

The Soviets had made repeated assaults on Kharkov and the Germans were losing their grip on the city. Using the remains of 6th PzD, the Germans evacuated the city for the last time. The 183rd RD pushed the rearguard out of Kharkov and the city once again was free. By 8/27 the 6th PzD arrived at Tamovka, where it went into reserve. A few days later, Maj General von Waldenfels took over command of the division. fzk59. dgn359. zro211.

August 26th on the Northern Salient
In the 20th IC sector, the Soviets began a major offensive with Maj General Felzmann's 251st ID and Lt General Weidling's 86th ID taking the brunt of the attack, while Maj General Falkenstein's 45th ID and Lt General Kamecke's 137th ID received only minor pressure. After several days of fighting, penetrations in the 251st and 86th ID area appeared, especially near Sevsk and on a line that headed toward Seredina Buda, about twelve miles to the west. South of Sevsk, in the deep forest that was the boundary line between 20th IC and 13th IC, fighting remained heavy and obscured. Lt General Rappard's 7th ID moved into this contested area but it did not slow the Soviets down. snk230+.

Operation Hagen officially ended. *Luftflotte* 6 covered the retreat for nearly all of the last month. It lost many planes protecting the convoys and trains heading toward the Desna River, but it was still intact and functioning fairly well. snk172+. dgk231m. snk433m++.

The 1st *Flieger* Division, covering both the Kursk and Orel salients, made the following claims for the period starting July 4th: The division flew 37,421 sorties and shot down 1,733 Soviet airplanes, destroyed or damaged over 1,100 tanks and destroyed 1,300 armored vehicles and trucks. The 12th Flak Division shot down 383 planes and destroyed or damaged 225 tanks. This flak division and others used huge amount of ammo; they were lucky the ammunition was available. It's safe to say that the *Luftwaffe* had a major impact in preventing the 2nd PzA and 9th Army from destruction. snk173. dgk116m. dgk231m. snk433m++.

August 27th on the Southern Salient

After regrouping for five days near Merefa, the 6th PzD was sent to Taranovka, southeast of Merefa, to defend the line. knz189.

Northwest of the Sevsk River, the Soviets made many separate attacks of up to a division against the left flank of 251st ID and the right flank of 86th ID. The attacks were repulsed and the Soviets suffered heavy casualties. snk231.

The month of August saw the Soviet offensive expand to include fighting from around Smolensk in the north to the Sea of Azov in the south and beyond. Seven complete Soviet Fronts would be fully involved, steming from Operation Citadel. The Soviets continued to maintain a superiority of men and tanks and in some sectors of the line that superiority was greater than it was between Orel and Belgorod in early July. Stalin believed the best way to defeat Germany was with a war of attrition along the entire front line. It was lucky for Stalin that his armies had a superiority for they continued to lose two to three times or more in men and armor than the Germans in these summer and fall months. I believe Vatutin's many ill-prepared armored counter-attacks in the first week of the campaign, plus the Soviet strategy of starting Operation Rumyanstev in early August, was a mistake and that if Konev's Steppe Front had been in position to attack the German flanks while 4th PzA had been deployed along the Psel River, the Soviets would have seen far greater gains. We will return to this in subsequent pages. With the success of Stalingrad so recent it's likely the *Stavka* would have wanted to repeat that success at Kursk.

28

Final Thoughts

See Map 29

Using hindsight, it is obvious that Operation Citadel should never have been launched, but even in mid-1943 after several delays many of the generals were against the operation. Von Manstein, Guderian, von Mellenthin, Kempf, Jodl and Heinrici are just a few. The aerial photos showed the massive defensive measures that were taking place in the salient. Hitler, Zeitzler and his staff should have known the Soviets were alerted and preparing and would be ready for the assault, but the dictator would not listen to his generals, believing his new panzers would overcome every obstacle. In addition to political considerations, he was obsessed with his heavy armor, despite the fact that the Panther had never been in battle and was already showing major mechanical problems or that the Ferdinand did not have a machine gun to protect itself from infantry and would be tremendously handicapped as the front runner in the assault.

Knowing his armies would be up against superior forces, Col General Kurt Zeitzler scraped together every possible man, gun and panzer from the rest of the Eastern Line, but it still was not nearly enough. It was not enough to take Prokhorovka in the south or Olkhovatka in the north, let alone have the two armies link up at Kursk and destroy the pocketed Soviets trapped in the salient as ordered. An over-reliance on the new panzers and an extreme underestimation of the Soviet defensive preparations and subsequent response were the two major reasons for German failure in this campaign. It can also be argued that the German strategic plan was flawed as well. They were abandoning the virtues of Blitzkrieg and using their armor as battering rams and General Hoth made the situation worse by deploying the Panther Brigade in the worst terrain sector possible for armor, placing his new panzers at a larger disadvantage. This difficult situation was made even worse when 2nd SS PzC was directed toward Prokhorovka, further weakening their primary axis of advance when 48th PzC was allowed to continue its trek toward Oboyan. While there was good reason to move toward Prokhorovka, Hoth should have abandoned his attack toward Oboyan, contracting 48th PzC sector to the east and allowed this corps to support 2nd SS PzC in its drive across the Psel River and through the corridor. Clearly 4th PzA did not have the resources to continue an assault on both Oboyan and Prokhorovka. To make matters worse, the 3rd PzC on the other flank had to launch from a start line further south than the other two panzers corps, cross the Donets River, head further east toward Korocha, enlarging their attack sector needlessly to catch up to the SS and do it with a deficiency of infantry and air support.

It is difficult for me to view the German perspective without the benefit of hindsight but it is clear that Hitler, and especially Hoth, had already forgotten the defensive stance the Soviets were capable of, as at Stalingrad, or the costs incurred by a bad strategic move. An objective became too difficult, too costly, too time consuming yet efforts continued to capture it, allowing the Soviets to wear down the German forces and affording them time to concentrate forces for a counter-attack such as that which resulted in the loss of 6th Army or the subsequent drubbing AGS received as they were pushed back to the Donets River. Even without hindsight, knowing large concentrations of Soviet forces were assembling in the Orel and south of Kharkov areas, as well as the fact that for this operation to be successful the two German armies would each have had to travel close to 70 miles to link up while maintaining flank protection on both sides of their assault spearhead, it seems over ambitious and an unreasonable risk at that stage of the war. Field Marshals von Manstein and Kluge knew their opponents, had gone up against Rokossovsky and Vatutin before and knew them as smart and aggressive commanders that would put up a difficult and costly defense. Ironically, it seems the *Stavka* has a short memory as well. Operation Uranus was so successful, why did not the Soviets attempt an encirclement of 4th PzA in a similar manner? With both Voronezh and Steppe Fronts properly deployed and attacking at the proper time, it seems highly likely that 4th PzA would have been destroyed or at least fatally wounded and with no German reserves available the Soviets had little to fear of a counter-attack on the scale that had occurred at Kharkov the previous two springs.

If you extend your thinking beyond actual events, it is probably a good thing 4th PzA did not get beyond Prokhorovka or 9th Army past Olkhovatka, for that would have extended their lines of communications and flanks thus weakening their defenses on both eastern and western flanks of the corridor that they were developing. When Operation Kutuzov launched, Lt General Walter Model would not have had as many panzer divisions to deploy to Orel and when Operation Rumyantsev launched in early August, Hoth probably would have been unable to fight his way south to Kharkov, let alone send forces south to 6th Army to defend against the major assault by Southwestern Front.

I would argue Col General Heinz Guderian was right when he strongly defended his position that the German Army should have stayed defensive during the summer of 1943 and waited for Stalin to make the first move. The *Wehrmacht* would not have gone up against such formidable defenses at Kursk which levied such a heavy toll, the bugs of the Panther and Ferdinand could have been worked out and new supplies of panzers could have helped restore the panzer divisions as well as give the infantry a little more time to refit and train.

Let us replace the pessimism and say Hoth and Model had a chance to succeed and the operation should have launched as planned, but when it got off to an unsatisfactory start for the two flanks, I submit, von Manstein and Hoth did not do enough to resolve the existing battlefield conditions. Going against von Manstein's wishes, Hoth, favoring 48th PzC, allowed 3rd PzC to languish in the east. The original plan for Kempf to fight his way to Korocha to provide flank protection also seems unreasonable after seeing how the campaign started for General Kempf. For Hoth to continue to ignore this corps as the days passed and as the corps continued to fall behind, leaving a critical gap in the German line and the subsequent problems it caused for the 2nd SS PzC, was truly an error of judgement.

On the western flank, Col General Hoth could see 48th PzC struggling to reach the Psel River in the Oboyan sector, which was predominately caused by an over-extended front line when the 2nd SS PzC shifted to the northeast away from 48th PzC. The situation worsened when Hoth wanted 48th PzC to drive further west to control the Berezovka-Kruglik road. It was potentially an important road and one that should be kept from the Soviets (but less so with the shift toward Prokhorovka) but when you do not have enough forces to get the job done without interfering with your primary objective then you should back away. With the combined stiff resistance in the north as well as on the western flank General Hoth should have pulled his forces back to east of the Pena River line, but did not and this was another error of judgement.

Starting on the afternoon of 7/8, *GD* had to shift assets to the west to assist 3rd PzD in protecting and expanding the flank. By the next day, most of the division had been diverted from the northern assault and for the rest of the campaign *GD* had little to do with the northern advance. At this point, the chance for the 48th PzC to cross the Psel in force was unattainable and there were no clear alternative solutions to 4th PzA's problems, but it could clearly be seen that 48th PzC had failed their mission as planned and remedial action needed to be taken immediately. With the far eastern flank also failing their mission, it is reasonable to consider a restriction of the flanks, to between the Pena River line in the west and the Lipovyi Donets River or Northern Donets River line in the east, as a plausible alternative. If these restrictions had been in place earlier, or better still from the beginning of the campaign, it would appear *SSTK* could have fought alongside *LAH* through much of the campaign, while allowing 3rd PzC to safeguard the flank with the help of the natural barrier of the Lipovyi Donets River. Here again, there are no guarantees and despite the increase in traffic congestion, my supposition is that it would have fostered greater results than the original way. I believe this narrower attack axis should have been part of the original plan, not an after thought. Having the entire SS Corps driving north and having the Panther Brigade as their backup, while the two other corps covered the flanks of a smaller area, the chances would have been good that the SS could have reached the Psel River and the Prokhorovka corridor before 5th GA and 5th GTA arrived. To avoid road congestion within the smaller attack zone, the 3rd PzC could have been phased into the battle along the Lipovyi Donets as the SS advanced northward. If battlefield conditions warranted it, once the SS reached Teterevino South or more likely the Kalinin line, the 3rd PzC could have shifted eastward beyond the Lipovyi and expanded their attack zone to the Invanovka-Zhilomostnoe axis or even to the western bank of the Northern Donets in preparation for the attack on Pravorot, Iamki and Prokhorovka. This expansion would reduce congestion and place an extra tactical burden on the Soviets while reducing the pressure on the SS as the 3rd PzC headed north, but under this scenario the German line between the two corps would be unified and the entire 2nd SS Corps would be advancing in step toward Prokhorovka, its corridor and the Psel River. If conditions were not conducive to expansion the 3rd PzC could stay behind the Lipovyi River line and protect the SS's flank, as its been doing since the start of the campaign. Extending this scenario, if the 3rd PzC had advanced with the SS, it would have been even harder for the 5th GTA to launch an attack from where they did, causing 5th GTA to be more disadvantaged than they actually were. With all three divisions of the 2nd SS PzC advancing northward and allowing the 3rd PzC to handle the eastern flank from west of the river, advancement should have achieved a more dramatic pace, which would have given General Vatutin a whole new set of problems to contend with. With his plate already full, it would have been interesting to see how Vatutin handled this scenario; this extra burden with 4th PzA already across the Psel and into the corridor past Prokhorovka, probably as far as Kartashevka, without the aid of his two reserve armies could be traumatizing even for a man like Vatutin. Plus, how would 5th GA and 5th GTA have attacked the Germans from their new positions and how would *Stavka* have reacted to this situation? The possibilities are intriguing.

As an alternative to the Pena River to Lipovyi River attack zone, the Vorskla River to Ramzumnaia River or the Vorskla to Koren River attack zone could have been used. They had the disadvantage of having two rivers between the 2nd SS PzC and 3rd PzC but would have given the German forces more room to work while avoiding the worse parts of the original western attack zone. They would also have allowed the Panther Brigade, or at least half of it, to fight on favourable terrain east of the Donets. With the Panthers divided between the three panzer divisions, it would have allowed the Tiger Battalion, the sPzAbt 503, to stay intact. A spearhead of 45 Tigers could have been successful in clearing a path to Rzhavets. Both the Ramzumnaia River and Koren River run parallel to the Donets River. The Ramzumnaia is about seven miles east while the Koren is about 14 miles east of the Donets. dgr172m. lck164m. zzy123m.

While there are pros and cons to a narrower attack zone, several advantages of a reduced attack zone come to mind. The reduced land area would mean fewer strongpoints would have to be fought over and that includes fewer mines to avoid and clear as well as fewer tank traps and dug-in Pak fronts to overcome. The men and weapons in those strongpoints would have to leave the relative safety of their defenses and advance on the Germans, giving the Germans greater parity. Also, with too few planes to support the ground assault, a smaller attack area would allow the available planes a better chance to cover the battlefield and when those Soviet forces left their prepared defenses to attack the German line, those planes could exploit the situation to the fullest. On the western front, strongpoints at Cherkasskoe, Korovino, Rakovo, Berezovka, Kruglik and a number of fortified hills could have been avoided. On the far eastern flank, strongpoints including Staryi Gorod, Iastrebovo, Blizhniaia Igumenka, Miasoedovo, Melikhovo, Shliakhovo, Kazache, Aleksandrovka and Rzhavets, to name a few, could have been avoided. The above battle sites cost the German forces dearly in time and many casualties of men and armor. When the garrisons of these sites were forced to leave their defenses and attack the enemy, it would have naturally cost the Germans time and casualties to defend themselves but most likely not as much as actual results and correspondingly would be more expensive to the Soviet side. By June the Germans had photographed the entire battlefield and should have known the areas of difficult terrain, useable road networks and of course the many difficult strongpoints to overcome and yet they made no appreciable changes to their existing attack plan, forging ahead to have Oboyan their primary axis of attack. The only practical way for 48th PzC to reach Oboyan en masse, especially with all the rain and subsequent muddy conditions, was by way of the Belgorod-Oboyan Road and General Vatutin had amassed so many reserves on this route that it would have been impossible for 48th PzC in its present condition to breakthrough, cross the Psel and enter the town. I find it hard to accept that with all the aerial reconnaissance Hoth received in addition to the stiff resistance of the enemy that he did not take major remedial actions concerning the Oboyan axis and 48th PzC's deployment. The photos the German Command received clearly showed the 48th PzC sector had the worse terrain for armor and even with the extra punch of the Panther Brigade to compensate this was not the best axis to take. Add the fact that the corps would also have flank duties and one can clearly see this section should not have been the main axis of attack. In conjunction with the corps placement, the German strategy was not well thought out. Although I do not believe it was the case, let's assume the attack axes of the three corps were well chosen for the beginning of the offensive. However, it does not appear the battle plans once past Oboyan and Prokhorovka were ever seriously considered. By the time the Germans crossed the Psel River line the salient that had been carved out had expanded greatly in both width and certainly in length; it makes you wonder what the Germans were thinking of when they chose this operation. When one adds in the difficulties of crossing the Psel and having two corps separated by the two Donets rivers besides giving the enemy months to prepare, the odds of success drastically plummeted. With the expanded line to defend plus the already considerable attrition and with no reserves what was Hoth planning to do? How could Hoth allow the two divisions of the SS attempt to fight their way into the corridor, even as far as only the Kartashevka road, with his two flanks completely stymied and fending off flank attacks, preventing any appreciable flank protection for the SS while in the corridor? Again, a battle plan based on a narrower front from the start had its advantages and probably would have given the 4th PzA a deeper penetration toward Kursk.

FM von Manstein wanted to continue the campaign on 7/13 when Adolf Hitler canceled it. In this circumstance, I would argue that Hitler was correct and von Manstein wrong. The chance to encircle the bulk of 48th RC, which had already fallen back, was practically gone and to attempt to chase it down afterwards with the remains of General Konev's Steppe Front close enough to intercede if necessary, was too dangerous considering the condition and disposition of 2nd SS PzC and 3rd PzC at the time. It could also be argued that Hitler waited too long to cancel the operation. With the attrition, both German Armies suffered by 7/10 and the fact that Soviet resistance was still strong, it could clearly be seen that the original plan to meet at Kursk and destroy the trapped enemy was never going to happen. And though 69th Army had fallen back from their original defense line, the new defense line south of Prokhorovka was still strong enough to prevent *Das Reich* from providing strong support to *LAH* in its attempt to take the rail village on 7/12. As it turned out, the tank battles of 7/12 favored the Germans, but 4th PzA was at an offensive end by the end of 7/12 and cancelation of the operation was the right action. The worse results of 9th Army only fortifies the position that Operation Citadel should have been canceled earlier.

Col General Vatutin made some mistakes as well; he made enough mistakes that Stalin felt compelled to send Marshal Zhukov to Kursk to oversee the battle zone. He had built an impressive defense system that included Pak fronts, dug-in tanks, an effective maze of mutually defending trenches, many anti-tank trenches and huge minefields and yet he made numerous redeployments and numerous counter-attacks, forcing his tank brigades to launch offensives prematurely, before they were ready or coordinated with each other. The results on several occasions were costly. Vatutin forced General Rotmistrov's 5th GTA to attack practically as soon as it arrived in sector from an area that was not well suited for an offensive against the strongest part of the German line. Considering where the German line was at the end of day of 7/11, I submit that if 5th GA and 5th GTA had had a defensive posture for the next few days, say to 7/14, to wear down the SS Corps even further after the Germans resumed their advance on 7/12, then the Germans could have been eventually pushed back enough to allow 5th GTA to gain a better launch point. This would have probably resulted in losing fewer tanks and valuable tank crews when Rotmistrov's offensive was finally launched. I know that a passive defense was looked down on by Vatutin, Zhukov and Stalin but in this case, waiting a day or two before counter-attacking would have been beneficial. Vatutin felt compelled to attack as soon as possible to avoid allowing 3rd PzC to reach *Das Reich* and solidify the eastern line, but that threat was not as large as he thought. The entire Kempf detachment had less than 100 working panzers on 7/12 and these panzer groups were spread out over much of the sector. Elements of 69th Army and all of 7th GA were constantly resisting and in fact, in a few areas of the line, were nearing penetration. Though the 7th PzD, with about 35 working panzers, was Kempf's strongest division by this time, it still could not concentrate enough strength to be able to reach and then assist the 2nd SS PzC in time to take Prokhorovka.

It could also be said that Vatutin's use of his tank corps was ill-advised. From July 7th onwards these tank corps made repeated attacks to slow or stop the Germans from driving through the second defensive belt or reaching the third belt. By July 7th it was too late to stop the enemy from breaking through the second belt and to attack the leading Tigers companies on the flats leading to the third belt was foolhardy. By the 12th, these Soviet corps were, for the most part, at half strength. With the third defensive belt's many advantages – the high northern banks of the Psel, numerous hills critically located plus the prepared defenses – these tank corps at or near full strength could have had a more destructive impact from behind these defenses when the Germans attacked on the morning of the 12th than going head to head in open ground. This is especially true in preventing *SSTK* in crossing the Psel and establishing a bridgehead on the northern banks of the river.

Several other alternative attack plans that Vatutin could have tried, that probably would have worked better, resulting in fewer casualties for him and greater destruction of 4th PzA, seem feasible. Here is one crazy idea that might have worked: While the terrain in parts of the Belenikhino sector was rugged and not conducive for major tank offensives on the scale of 5th GTA, the terrain east of the Donets in the 7th GA sector was better. What if the 18th TC and 29th TC, along with adequate air cover, had struck 3rd PzC or even 11th IC on its eastern flank? The 5th GTA could probably have rolled Kempf's forces fairly easily for they were spread out, exhausted and not prepared for a major flank/rear armor attack. By the end of 7/12, Kempf had his less than 100 working panzers and assault guns already engaged and having a difficult time in securing their objectives. It does not seem possible that General Breith could have created a new shock group while maintaining his current defenses to either reach *Das Reich* or combat this new attack spearhead. After reducing 3rd PzC, the tankers could have continued west, penetrated the 167th ID line and got behind the 2nd SS PzC, cutting off communications and crushing Hausser's corps between itself, 7th GA, 69th Army and 5th GA. It may be a novel idea, but it was certainly feasible. I do not suggest that this flank assault would be easy. Though there were clear avenues of attack, there were not any major paved highways and there were several rivers to cross, but with the proper bridge equipment the assault could still have been effective. The 5th GMC would have been detached from 5th GTA and sent to the Kartashevka-Prokhorovka road area to stop *SSTK* from accomplishing their objectives. In fact, with the support of elements of the 32nd GRC and 33rd GRC of 5th GA, the three recently arrived corps had a good chance to prevent the *SSTK's* bridgehead from reaching Kartashevka road in any meaningful way. In this scenario, when it was discovered that the 5th GTA had attacked and penetrated the 3rd PzC eastern and or northern line, the entire 4th PzA would have to go on the defensive, eliminating the chance for further gains to the north.

Another alternative attack plan also deals with the *SSTK* bridgehead but as the primary assault, not secondary. Instead of attacking *LAH* as they did on 7/12, the 5th GTA (18th TC, 29th TC) should have attacked *SSTK* in their northern bridgehead. The defenses of *SSTK* were not nearly as elaborate or as well defended as *LAH*'s, plus the Soviet tanks, though still having to cope with a ravine or two, had greater freedom of movement within the bend of the Psel River. When *SSTK* advanced northward from Hill 226.6 toward Hill 236.7 which straddled the Kartashevka road, the division was spread out and became vulnerable to a massive counter-attack. If General Rotmistrov, supported by a coordinated air attack and the many guns deployed along the river, had waited until *SSTK* was approaching Hill 236.7 before attacking, he had an excellent chance to isolate and destroy much of Priess's division north of the river, which by this time was vulnerable. Much of 5th GA was already deployed in the area and the combined strength of the two armies against *SSTK* in its own mini-salient should have been overwhelming. With *SSTK* losing many men and panzers as well as their bridgehead in this offensive, it seems reasonable that the entire northern German line from Novoselovka to Prokhorovka would soon become untenable, as 5th GTA / 5th GA crossed the swollen Psel River, forcing 4th PzA to fall back within days to save itself. As a precautionary measure, the 5th GMC would have deployed near Hill 252.4 to make sure *LAH* did not advance too much or in case 69th Army needed help against *Das Reich* or 3rd PzC. Generals Vatutin and Rotmistrov had wanted to destroy the entire 2nd SS PzC in this single attack, but that battle plan had been too ambitious, especially from the improvised launch point. Vatutin had anticipated what *SSTK* was going to do on 7/12; Priess had to drive north to screen *LAH*'s left flank as it drove on Prokhorovka. General Vatutin should have seen the vulnerability of *SSTK* in the salient that they would develop and taken advantage of it, but he was over confident and impatient, wanting to destroy the entire 2nd SS PzC in one morning. He should have allowed the panzers of *SSTK* become extended north of the Psel and separated from their grenadiers before launching a major assault.

Generals Vatutin and Rotmistrov defended their actions by saying that perhaps the main objective of destroying the 2nd SS PzC had failed but at least the Germans were stopped from advancing further north. While there is some truth behind their defense, it is also true to say that a golden opportunity to destroy a good deal of 4th PzA was wasted by poor planning. It is no wonder Stalin was considering sacking both of his generals.

I saved my favorite scenario until last. It is similar to one of the above-mentioned alternatives, but it is on a larger scale which was probably necessary, as while the German force had taken many casualties by 7/12, it was still a force to be respected. Here is the last alternative:

It can also be argued that *Stavka* made a strategic mistake by waiting too long to launch Operation Rumyantsev. Ideally, if this counter offensive had started between 7/12 and 7/15, while 4th PzA was still deployed along the Novoselovka-Prokhorovka line, then there was a very good chance of pocketing much of the 4th PzA. As it was, *Stavka* waited another several weeks and by that time the 4th PzA was backing away from their vulnerability.

Let me suggest that the ideal offensive would have been a two-prong pincer attack, on the order of Operation Uranus, that would drive behind the German front line from the east and west, but that assault would have taken months to plan and deploy. It was not done, but an operation of lesser dimensions and complexity could have been put together in less time that could have resulted with a major upheaval against the Germans.

Briefly this multi-army attack could have come from the east not north, attacking the vulnerable east flank of 3rd PzC where 198th and 106th IDs were defending. If Steppe Front's 47th and 53rd Armies, which also had attached the 4th GTC and 1st MC (400 tanks), had deployed and been ready to attack not far from the Koren River by 7/12 and if Vatutin had used the 18th TC and 29th TC of 5th GTA along with these other two armies, there would have been an excellent chance of penetrating the eastern line defended by the German infantry (11th IC and 198th ID) and overwhelming the 3rd PzC which by 7/12 had been widely deployed for the most part along the Donets River from Krivtsovo to Ryndinka and along the Rzhavets-Aleksandrovka-Kazache line. With the resources of the three new armies, plus the remains of 69th and 7th GA along with a massive artillery preparation and competent aerial support, the Soviets could have finished off 3rd PzC and then driven west into the Shishino-Petropavlovka-Khokhlovo area to take on the 168th ID and then the 167th ID. The southern flank of the advancing 5th GTA could have driven west between Staryi Gorod and Shishino. With 3rd PzC gone and 167th ID threatened, 4th PzA would have had to immediately react and probably fall back. With the 1st TA, 6th GA, 5th GA and the new 27th Army, which should have deployed just north of Prokhorovka-Kartashevtka road and northwest of Veselyi as well, driving south at the same time the 48th PzC and 2nd SS PzC would have been pressured to breaking point and in their desperation to fall back many men and heavy equipment would have been lost against the onrushing hordes of new armies that had just arrived in sector. One can extend this scenario to include the trouble the German line would have faced if the 4th PzA/3rd PzC suffered devastating losses and a gap of 30 to 50 miles had opened in the line but I'll stop here for now. Admittedly, for this scenario to work, *Stavka* would have had to plan, prepare and deploy weeks in advance. I submit that this counter-offensive could have been more beneficial and with fewer casualties for Vatutin than the actual offensive, due to the extended position 4th PzA had carved out by 7/12. This counter-offensive could also have been fitting retribution, under similar circumstances, for Timoshenko's loss at Kharkov (May 1942), where his initial gains were cut off and his forces isolated and destroyed by a dual pincer counter-attack by Col General Paulus's 6th Army and FM Kleist's 1st PzA. See Map 29.

Criticism can be levied in the north as well. Even though Model opened his campaign using nearly 300 panzers and assault guns, he should have used more. Rokossovsky was only truly vulnerable on the first day. He held back heavy reserves in second echelon to see where the main attacks would take place. He intended to see how the German assault unfolded and then quickly send reserves to the assault areas. The two biggest formations being held in reserve for Rokossovsky were the 17th GRC and 2nd TA, which both eventually played pivotal roles in stopping 9th Army. If Model had used the 2nd PzD, 9th PzD and 18th PzD with the opening assault in the 41st PzC and 46th PzC sectors and attacked toward Ponyri and Samodurovka respectively, there was an opportunity to reach and penetrate the second defensive belt before the 17th GRC and 2nd TA were called up. There was no guarantee this alternative action would have gotten 9th Army to Kursk, but it seems plausible that if Model could have controlled the high ground around Olkhovatka by the end of the first day, his chances for reaching Kursk would have greatly improved. At the very least it would have cost Rokossovsky many more men, tanks, ammunition and time to push 9th Army off the high ground and if the casualties had been great enough, it could have made a difference during Operation Kutuzov.

During the campaign, General Model made a practice of leaving his HQ for the whole day, visiting the front line. There were many instances where he would be out of touch with his staff and several events occurred that desperately needed his attention and he missed them. The biggest incident occurred when 4th PzD was attached to General Lemelsen's 47th PzC. Lemelsen, on his own responsibility, decided to separate the panzer regiment from the rest of the division in order to fight the division in two separate sectors. Without proper armored support that first day, 4th PzD went into battle disadvantaged: the two infantry regiments suffered heavy casualties, including its division commander. If Model had been at his headquarters, he could have prevented this costly error and others that occurred during the campaign.

General Rokossovsky probably made fewer mistakes than the other three commanders but he was also up against an enemy with slightly fewer combat soldiers, panzers and aircraft as compared to the southern salient as well as a commander, though a master at defense, who was partially restricted with his order of battle by von Kluge, besides being a little too cautious. To his credit, Model's handling of the Orel defense was superb and saved AGC from practical destruction. Continuing with Rokossovsky for a moment, I believe that there are several distinct reasons why Central Front did so much better in stopping 9th Army than Voronezh Front did in stopping 4th PzA. The first reason is battlefield defenses were more evolved, providing better coverage for man and machine. Rokossovsky had more guns than Vatutin and he made sure his gun crews used them, consuming many more tons of ammunition than the southern batteries. German survivors of 9th Army all complained of the horrendous wall of fire that they faced.

Mistakes were made at German Group level as well, and fall directly on von Manstein's shoulders. During the campaign he questioned certain of Hoth's decisions, mostly pertaining to the flanks. Hoth neglected air support and refused to send elements of the 167th ID to General Kempf as well ordering the 48th PzC to expand its western border beyond the Rakovo-Kruglik road at a time when the northern advance had stalled and 11th PzD and especially 3rd PzD were in trouble. Manstein discussed the issues with his subordinate but did not take any action to correct these issues when Hoth failed to respond. This reluctance to take corrective action seems unfathomable from such a noted strategist and commander and had a clear impact on the final outcome.

More importantly, errors were being made prior to the launch that would have a profound impact on the campaign, and consequently revisiting the German High Command one last time seems appropriate. While Hoth and von Manstein did not have complete freedom of command, they did have a lot of control over their destiny. They also had plenty of time before attacking to study the battlefield in order to make major changes or receive permission to make those changes. It should be emphatically stated that the German attack plan was flawed and Hoth and von Manstein should have seen it, especially when one takes into account the fact that Soviets had months to prepare, that the new panzers and assault guns were unreliable or flawed and that von Manstein had only three panzer corps to advance along mostly rugged terrain that sported five major rivers, few highways and only a few narrow off-road avenues for his armor. To make the situation worse the distance needed to travel to reach Kursk was relatively large, and the further north the army traveled the front would expand.

And if that was not bad enough, Hoth was asking the 48th PzC to advance along the primary axis and also deploy along the western flank which means the advance would be twice as hard. To confirm this theory is true, the 48th with the inclusion of the Panther Brigade and the *GD* division could not keep up or go as far as the 2nd SS PzC. Just from this aspect alone, its seems more logical to have the primary axis from the very start of the campaign to have been in the center, allowing the two outer corps provide the necessary flank protection.

FINAL THOUGHTS

As 48th PzC veered slightly to the northwest, the 2nd SS PzC was heading to the northeast and the 3rd PzC, which was starting the campaign as much as 20 miles further south of the other two corps, had to immediately cross the Donets, head east before pivoting to the north with at least two major rivers between itself and the SS. Having the weakest corps traveling the greatest distance while being separated from 4th PzA and having it advance northward and defend itself along both expanding flanks with inadequate air support was a recipe for failure. To provide that timely protection 3rd PzC needed at least half of the available Panthers to assist the Tigers attached to the 3rd PzC in penetrating the difficult defense located near the Belgorod sector.

In the later planning stage, by the time the three German corps (assuming the 3rd could have caught up) reached the Psel River line, the front would have expanded approximately another ten miles or more from their start positions. Once past Prokhorovka the front might have been reduced a little but by the idea that by then the exhausted vanguard of five weakened corps would continue to carve out and maintain a corridor at least thirty miles wide all the way to Kursk seems a gross misjudgement, and this does not even take into account the need to reduce the pocketed Soviet 38th and 40th Armies in the south and the 60th and 65th Armies in the north that were deployed to the west of the corridor after Hoth reached Kursk. If AGS had three full strength panzer divisions, three infantry divisions in reserve plus greater air support (at a minimum) the plan might have worked initially but reserves were not realistically available and it was doomed to fail. Hitler demanded and Hoth complied with supplying daily casualty figures for armor and men. By the 10th or even earlier, it should have been patently obvious to Hoth and von Manstein, as it was to Model, that Citadel would fail to reach Kursk and that drastic remedial action was required.

If the 48th PzC had the good fortune to cross the Psel en masse while the 2nd SS PzC entered the Prokhorovka corridor while the 3rd PzC continued to struggle, lagging far behind the other two, then serious gaps would have formed which Vatutin would have exploited by bringing up reserves. With two corps north of the Psel River and the 3rd PzC east of the Lipovyi River, Kemp's forces would have been dangerously isolated and in dire trouble. But realistically by the 10th, bearing in mind the troubles the 48th and 52nd Corps were actually having, it made no sense for Hoth to expand westward and continue to concentrate efforts on the Oboyan route. The open flanks on the 2nd SS PzC and 3rd PzC sectors were causing a greater long term disruption to success yet Hoth continued to obsess about the 48th PzC expanding its sector.

I have already suggested an ideal German disposition but the following scenario had a better chance for acceptance for it was closer to the original yet diverted the main focus away from 48th PzC. After studying the aerial photos plus situation reports from patrols, along with the experiences gained in 1941 and 1942 when the area was originally cleared and occupied, it could clearly be seen that the central and eastern sectors were best suited for armor and therefore should be used for the primary attack axis. The western sector, which had the shortest route to Kursk but the worse terrain, and was the most obvious sector to be protected by the Soviets, should have been reduced in scale and importance and used as flank protection for the 2nd SS PzC. The Panther brigade should have redeployed to the eastern sector to support 3rd PzC and Prokhorovka should have been the primary axis from the beginning. With all three divisions of 2nd PzC along with the 167th ID devoted to the northern front along with the reinforced 3rd PzC (includes the Panthers), it seems very plausible that the two corps could have cleared the ground between the Donets River and the Prokhorovka railroad forming a unified front within days of the launch.

It also seems plausible that these two corps would have captured Prokhorovka and the southern portion of the corridor before the arrival of 5th GA and 5th GTA and have done so suffering fewer casualties. The 3rd PzC along with the Panthers could have erected a defense that would have stopped the 5th GTA if it attacked from the east. If Rotmistrov had mannuvered his tanks to the north so that it defended the Seim River line, the full force of the SS Corps would have been in position to engage. That is not to say von Manstein would have successfully reached Kursk and liquidated the 38th and 40th Armies but I believe the 4th PzA could have had much better results that would have inflicted far more Soviet casualties and caused a definite disruption to the enemy's plans.

It is hard to know for sure whether the Germans would have been better off staying on the defensive and preparing for the eventual Soviet offensive on the Orel salient - Operation Kutuzov. However, after studying the Belgorod-Kursk-Orel sector it seems plausible that the Germans would have been better off by never launching Operation Citadel. It seems obvious that when the Germans did not attack in July Stalin, who was anxious to attack in June, would have prepared to attack Orel in August or September to eliminate the last major bulge situated less than 350 miles south of Moscow. The Germans could have used this time to good use. In the interval, the Germans could have improved defenses, repaired the Panthers, trained their crews as well as installed machine guns on the Elefants. Having a month or two to work on the Panthers could have made an appreciable difference to their dependability. Deploying the new panzers in the Orel salient where the terrain was more suited to armor as compared to the muddy Pena River valley, the German defense could have been greatly enhanced, inflicting even greater casualties on the Soviets while suffering fewer casualties and delaying the inevitable. Routine maintenance on the other vehicles and rest for their exhausted men as well as restore logistics were also in order. With dilligent intelligence, the Germans should have been fairly prepared to take on the assaults when launched along the line.

After months of being on the defensive, the tactical victory at Kharkov earlier in the year was just a brief respite, not an indication or omen to Hitler that the German onward march had resumed. It would have taken a blunder by the Soviets of unimaginable scale for the Germans to scratch their way up to parity, but that would not happen in 1943. The Soviets had just about completed tranforming their war doctrine and organization and by July 1943 the massive aid delivered by the Western Allies would help to see that those improvements put in place would be efficiently carried out. Considering what the *Stavka* had planned for the last half of the year, especially in the south, the war of attrition would have continued unabated, keeping the Germans constantly off balance.

By carefully expanding one's view to the entire front in the middle of 1943, after the huge losses at Stalingrad and North Africa and the loss of hundreds of miles of territory, a leader who less of a gambler than Hitler could see that Germany no longer had the capability to launch a major offensive that would have strategic significance. Without launching Operation Citadel, the German forces had just enough strength to defend the entire shortened line (after pulling back from Orel) and if their intelligence was dilligent they could slow their retreat. However, they did not have enough strength to gain ground in any meaningful way through an offensive and Operation Citadel's poor results clearly proves that point. Despite having a winning ledger on destroying many more enemy tanks and inflicting many more casualties on the enemy, this campaign had knocked the Germans down another peg in this war of attrition that would force the Wehrmacht on the strategic defensive for the rest of the war.

Appendix I
German Order of Battle July 4th 1943

Army Group Center (Field Marshal Günther von Kluge)
2nd PzA (Lt Gen Rudolf Schmidt)
    55th IC (General Erich Jaschke)
        321st ID
        339th ID
        110th ID
        296th ID
        134th ID
        5th PzD (reserve)
    53rd IC (General Friedrich Gollwitzer)
        211th ID
        293rd ID
        25th PzGD
        208th ID
        112th ID
    35th IC (General Lothar Rendulic)
        34th ID
        56th ID
        262nd ID
        299th ID
        36th ID
OKH Reserve
    8th PzD
    305th SD
    707th SD

9th A (Col General Walter Model)
    20th IC (General Freiherr von Roman)
        45th ID
        72nd ID
        137th ID
        251st ID
    46th PzC (General Hans Zorn)
        7th ID
        31st ID
        102nd ID
        258th ID
    47th PzC (General Joachim Lemelsen)
        2nd PzD
        9th PzD
        20th PzD
        6th ID
    41st PzC (General Josef Harpe)
        18th PzD
        86th ID
        292nd ID
    23rd IC (General Johannes Friessner)
        216th ID
        383rd ID
        78th AD
    21st Panzer Brigade
    sPzAbt 505
    sPzAbt 653
    sPzAbt 654
    sPzAbt 656
    StuGAbt 177
    StuGAbt 244
    StPzAbt 216
    StuGAbt 909

Reserve
    10th PzGD
    12th PzD
    4th PzD

Army Group South (Field Marshal Erich von Manstein)
4th PzA (Col General Hermann Hoth)
    52nd IC (General Eugen Ott)
        57th ID
        255th ID
        332nd ID
    48th PzC (General Otto von Knobelsdorff)
        3rd PzD
        11th PzD
        PzGD *Grossdeutschland*

167th ID
2nd SS PzC (General Paul Hausser)
   1st SS PzGD *Leibstandarte Adolf Hitler*
   2nd SS PzGD *Das Reich*
   3rd SS PzGD *Totenkopf*
Army Detachment Kempf (General Werner Kempf)
   3rd PzC (General Hermann Breith)
     6th PzD
     7th PzD
     19th PzD
     168th ID
     198th ID (attached)
   11th IC (General Erhard Raus)
     106th ID
     320th ID
   42nd IC (General Mattenklott)
     39th ID
     161st ID
     282nd ID
1st Werfer Regiment
52nd Werfer Regiment
54th Werfer Regiment
4th Anti-aircraft Regiment
StuGAbt 905
StuGAbt 393
sPzAbt 503

Abbreviations

AD	Assault Division
IC	Infantry Corps
ID	Infantry Division
PzA	Panzer Army
PzC	Panzer Corps
PzD	Panzer Division
PzGD	Panzer Grenadier Division
SD	Security Division
sPzAbt	Heavy Tank Detachment
StPzAbt	Assault Panzer Detachment
StuGAbt	Assault Gun Detachment

Luftwaffe
Luftflotte 4 (General Otto Dessloch)
   8th *Flieger* Corps (Maj General Hans Seidemann) - South
Luftflotte 6 (Col General Ritter von Greim)
   1st *Flieger* Division (Lt General Deichmann) - North

Appendix II
Soviet Order of Battle July 4th 1943

Bryansk Front (Lt General M.M. Popov)
3rd Army (Lt General A. V. Gorbatov)
    41st RC (Maj General V. K. Urbanovich)
        235th RD
        308th RD
        380th RD
    269th RD
    283rd RD
    342nd RD
    82nd Separate TR
    114th Separate TR

15th Air Army (Lt General N. F. Naumenko)

61st Army (Lt General P. A. Belov)
    9th GRC (Maj General A. A. Boreiko)
        12th GRD
        76th GRD
        77th GRD
    110th RD
    336th RD
    356th RD
    415th RD
    68th TB
    36th TR

63rd Army (Lt General V. I. Kolpakchi)
    5th RD
    41st RD
    129th RD
    250th RD
    287th RD
    348th RD
    397th RD
    231st TR

Central Front (General K. K. Rokossovsky)
2nd Tank Army (Lt General Rodin)
    3rd TC (Maj General M. D. Sinenko)
    16th TC (Maj General V. E. Grigorev)
    9th TC (attached) (Maj General S. I. Bogdanov)
    19th TC (attached) (Maj General I. D. Vasilev)

13th Army (Lt General N. P. Pukhov)
    17th GRC (Lt General A. L. Bondarev)
        6th GRD
        70th GRD
        75th GRD
    18th GRC (Maj General I. M. Afonin)
        2nd GAD
        3rd GAD
        4th GAD
    15th RC (Maj General I. I. Liudnikov)
        8th RD
        74th RD
        148th RD
    29th RC (Maj General A. N. Slyshkin)
        15th RD
        81st RD
        307th RD

16th Air Army (Lt General Sergey Rudenko)
    3rd Bombing Air Corps
    6th Air Corps
    6th Fighter Air Corps

48th Army (Lt General P. L. Romanenko)
    42nd RC (Maj General K. S. Kolganov)

16th RD
202nd RD
399th RD
73rd RD
137th RD
143rd RD
170th RD
45th Separate TR
193rd Separate TR
299th Separate TR

60th Army (Lt General I. D. Chernyakhovsky)
    24th RC (Maj General N. I. Kiriukhin)
        42nd RD
        112th RD
        129th RB
    30th RC (Maj General G. S. Lazko)
        121st RD
        141st RD
        322nd RD
    55th RD
    150th TB

65th Army (Lt General P. I. Batov)
    18th RC (Maj General I. I. Ivanov)
        69th RD
        149th RD
        246th RD
    27th RC (Maj General F. M. Cherokmanov)
        60th RD
        115th RB
        193rd RD
    37th GRD
    181st RD
    194th RD
    354th RD

70th Army (General Galanin)
    28th RC (Maj General A. N. Nechaev)
        132nd RD
        211th RD
        280th RD
        102nd RD
        106th RD
        140th RD
        162nd RD
    240th Separate TR
    251st Separate TR
    259th Separate TR

Voronezh Front (General N. F. Vatutin)
1st Tank Army (Lt Gen Katukov)
    3rd MC (Maj General S. M. Krivoshein)
        1st MB
        3rd MB
        10th MB
        1st GTB
        17th TR
        49th TB
    6th TC (Maj General A. L. Getman)
        22nd TB
        112th TB
        200th TB
        6th MRB
    31st TC (Maj General D. K. Chernienko)
        100th TB
        237th TB
        242nd TB
    5th GTC (Maj General A. G. Kravchenko)
        20th GTB
        21st GTB
        22nd GTB
        6th GMRB
        48th TR

2nd Air Army (Lt General S. A. Krasovsky)
    1st Bombing Air Corps (Col I. S. Polbin)
    1st Assault Air Corps (Lt General V. G. Gribakin)
    4th Fighter Air Corps (Maj General I. D. Podgorny)
    5th Fighter Air Corps (Maj General D.

P. Galunov)

6th Guards Army (Lt General I. M. Chistiakov)
    22nd GRC (Maj General N. B. Ibiansky)
        67th GRD
        71st GRD
        90th GRD
    23rd GRC (Maj General P. P. Vakhrameev)
        51st GRD
        52nd GRD
        375th RD
    89th GRD
    96th TB
    230th TR
    245th TR
    184th RD
    219th RD
    31st AAB

7th Guards Army (Lt General M. S, Shumilov)
    24th GRC (Maj General N. A. Vasilev)
        15th GRD
        36th GRD
        72nd GRD
    25th GRC (Maj General G. B. Safiullin)
        73rd GRD
        78th GRD
        81st GRD
    213th RD
    27th GTB
    201st TB
    148th TR
    167th TR
    262nd TR

38th Army (Lt General Chibisov)
    50th RC (Maj General S. S. Martirosian)
        167th RD
        232nd RD
        340th RD
    51st RC (Maj General P. P. Andreenko)
        180th RD
        240th RD
        204th RD
    180th TB
    192nd TB

40th Army (Lt General K. S. Moskalenko)
    47th RC (Maj General A. S. Griaznov)
        161st RD
        206th RD
        237th RD
    52nd RC (Lt General F. I. Perkhorovich)
        100th RD
        219th RD
        309th RD
    184th RD
    86th TB
    59th TR
    60th HTR

69th Army (Lt Gen V. D. Kriuchenkin)
    48th RC (Maj General Z. Z. Rogozny)
        107th RD
        183rd RD
        305th RD
    49th RC (Maj General G. P. Terentev)
        111th RD
        270th RD
    35th GRC (Maj Gen S. G. Goriachev)
        92nd GRD
        94th GRD
        93rd GRD
    81st GRD
    89th GRD

Southwestern Front (General R. I. Malinovsky)
17th Air Army (Lt General V. A. Sudets)

Steppe Front (Col General Konev)
4th Guard Army (Lt General G. I. Kulik)
    20th RC (Maj General N. I. Biriukov)

5th GAD
7th GAD
8th GAD
21st RC (Maj General P. I. Fomenko)
  68th GRD
  69th GRD
  80th GRD
3rd GTC
  3rd GTB
  18th GTB
  19th GTB
  2nd GMRB

5th Air Army (Lt General Goriunov)
  7th Air Corps
  8th Air Corps
  3rd Fighter Corps
  7th Fighter Air Corps

5th Guards Army (Lt General A. S. Zhadov) (originally Steppe Front)
  32nd GRC (Maj General A. I. Rodinstev)
    13th GRD
    66th GRD
    6th GAD
  33rd GRC (Maj General I. I. Popov)
    95th GRD
    97th GRD
    9th GAD
    42nd GRD (attached)
  10th TC (Maj General G. V. Burkov)
    178th TB
    183rd TB
    186th TB
    11th MRB

5th Guards Tank Army (Lt General P. A. Rotmistrov) (originally Steppe Front)
  5th GMC (Maj General B. M. Skvortsov)
    10th GMB
    11th GMB
    12th GMB
    24th GTB
    55th GTR

29th TC (Maj General I. F. Kirichenko)
  25th TB
  31st TB
  32nd TB
  53rd MRB
18th TC (Maj General B. S. Bakharov)
  110th TB
  170th TB
  181st TB
  32nd MRB
  36th GTR
2nd TC (attached) (Maj General A. F. Popov)
  26th TB
  99th TB
  169th TB
  58th MRB
2nd GTC (attached) (Maj General A. S. Burdeiny)
  4th GTB
  25th GTB
  26th GTB
  4th GMRB
  47th GTR

Southwestern Front (General R. I. Malinovsky)
17th Air Army (Lt General V. A. Sudets)

Western Front (Col General V. D. Sokolovsky)
1st Air Army (Lt General M. M. Gromov)

50th Army (Lt General I. V. Bolden)
  38th RC (Maj General A. D. Tereshkov)
    17th RD
    326th RD
    413th RD
  49th RD
  64th RD
  212th RD
  324th RD
  196th TB

11th Guards Army (Lt Gen I. K. Bagramyan)
    8th GRC (Maj General P.F. Malyshev)
        11th GRD
        26th GRD
        83rd GRD
    16th GRC (Maj General A. V. Lapshov (initially))
        1st GRD
        16th GRD
        31st GRD
        169th RD
    36th GRC (Maj General A. S. Ksenefontov)
        5th GRD
        18th GRD
        84th GRD
    108th RD
    217th RD
    10th GTB
    29th GTB
    43rd GTB

Abbreviations

AAB	Anti-Aircraft Brigade
GAD	Guards Airborne Division
GMRB	Guards Mechanized Rifle Brigade
GRC	Guards Rifle Corps
GRD	Guards Rifle Division
GTB	Guards Tank Brigade
GTR	Guards Tank Regiment
HTR	Heavy Tank Regiment
MB	Mechanized Brigade
MRB	Mechanized Rifle Brigade
RB	Rifle Brigade
RC	Rifle Corps
RD	Rifle Division
TB	Tank Brigade
TC	Tank Corps
TD	Tank Division
TR	Tank Regiment

Appendix III

German Armored Strengths

Tigers			Approx number combat-ready
9th Army	sPzAbt 505		45
	21st Pz Brigade		31
4th PzA	13th Company, 1st SS PzR		13
	8th Company, 2nd SS PzR		14
	9th Company, 3rd SS PzR		15
	13th Company, *GD* PzR		14
3rd PzC	sPzAbt 503		45
Total Tigers			177
Mark IIIs & IVs		III	IV
9th Army	2nd PzD	40	66
	4th PzD	15	86
	5th PzD (reserve)	26	76
	8th PzD (reserve)	59	28
	9th PzD	38	44
	12th PzD	36	41
	18th PzD	31	38
	20th PzD	95	56
	21st PzB	8	7
4th PzA			
	3rd PzD	59	24
	11 PzD	79	26
	GD	42	68
	LAH	13	76
	DR	72	33
	TK	63	52
3rd PzC			
	6th PzD	65	28
	7th PzD	62	38

	19th PzD	38	38
Total Mk IIIs & IVs	(includes working only but excludes obsoletes)	841	825
StuGs	(Includes StuGs and all other Assault Gun types)		
9th Army	21st PzB 41st PzC		36
	StuGAbt 177 41st PzC		36
	StuGAbt 185 23rd IC		36
	StuGAbt 189 23rd IC		36
	StPzAbt 216 41st PzC		45
	StuGAbt 244 41st PzC		31
	StuGAbt 245 47th PzC		36
	312th Pz Co 47th PzC		22
	sPzAbt 653 41st PzC		55
	sPzAbt 654 41st PzC		55
	StuGAbt 904 47th PzC		36
	StuGAbt 909 46th PzC		31
4th PzA	StuGAbt 911 48th PzC		31
	GD 48th PzC		35
	LAH 2nd SS PzC		35
	DR 2nd SS PzC		34
	TK 2nd SS PzC		35
3rd PzC	StuGAbt 228 3rd PzC		31
	StuGAbt 905 Corps Raus		32
	StuGAbt 393 Corps Raus		12
Total StuGs			700

Panthers			
4th PzA	*GD* (working panzers)		192
	Total Panthers		192
T34s	(captured)		
4th PzA	*DR*		26
	Total T34s		26
Grand Total for both salients			2,761
It is estimated that 250 panzers were destroyed and unrepairable on a best case scenario.			

Appendix IV

Soviet Armored Strengths

Primary Fronts		Tanks	Assault Guns
Central Front			
2nd GA		455	21
13th Army		258	12
48th Army		124	50
60th Army		65	0
65th Army		120	0
70th Army		120	0
9th TC		165	0
19th TC		168	0
Front Reserves		187	20
Total		1,662	103
Voronezh Front			
1st TA	Includes 3rd MC, 6th TC, 31st TC	625	21
6th GA		134	20
7th GA		216	30
38th Army		106	0
40th Army		113	0
2nd TC		168	0
2nd GTC		200	0
5th GTC		200	0
10th TC		165	21
5th GTA	(available on 7/12)	625	37
Total		2,552	129
It is estimated that 1600 tanks from the primary fronts were destroyed and unrepairable by the end of 7/12.			
Peripheral Fronts			
Western Front			
4th TA		624	28
11th GA		268	12
50th Army		75	12
1st TC		168	16
5th TC		168	16

Front Reserves		350	0
Total		1,653	84
Bryansk Front			
3rd Army		88	12
3rd GTA		695	32
61st Army		98	12
63rd Army		48	12
1st GTC		205	0
20th TC		168	16
Front Reserves		150	36
Total		1,452	120
Steppe Front			
27th Army		92	0
53rd Army		78	0
4th GTC		168	21
1st MC		204	0
Total		542	21
Peripheral sub-totals		3,647	225
Grand Totals of Primary and Supporting Fronts		6,199	354

Appendix V
AFV Technical Data

German Vehicle	Weight (tons)	L W H (feet)	Main Gun (typical)	Ammo Load	Machine Gun	Max Armor (mm)	Max Speed (MPH)	Range (Miles)
Pz III	25	18' 1" x 9' 8" x 8'2"	50mm L60	78	7.92mm	50	25	90
Pz IV	26	19' 4" x 10' 9" x 8' 9"	75mm L48	87	7.92mm	50	24	123
Panther	50	22'7" x 11'3" x 10'2"	75mm L70	79	7.92mm	80	28	123
Tiger	63	20'.4" x 12'.3" x 9' 3"	88mm L56	92	7.92mm	102	22	72
StuG III	26	17'5" x 9'5" x 6'4"	75mm L48		None	50	25	95
StuG III	26	17'5" x 9'5" x 6'4"	105mm L28		None	50	25	95
StuG IV	30		150mm L12		None	100	25	123
Marder (III)	12		75mm L46	41	None	35	28	150
Hornisse	26		88mm L71	40	None	30	25	132
Ferdinand	72		88mm L71	44	None	200	12	92

488

German

Vehicle	Weight (tons)	L W H (feet)	Main Gun (typical)	Ammo Load	Machine Gun	Max Armor (mm)	Max Speed (MPH)	Range (Miles)
Wespe	12		105mm leFH	32	None	20	25	85
Hummel	25		150mm 18L30	20	None	20	25	132

Soviet

Vehicle	Weight (tons)	L W H (feet)	Main Gun (typical)	Ammo Load	Machine Gun	Max Armor (mm)	Max Speed (MPH)	Range (Miles)
T34	34	19'5" x 9'10" x 8'	76.2mm	100	7.62mm (2)	70	33	185
KV1	52	21'11" x 10'10" x 8'10"	76.2mm L42	114	7.62mm (2)	120	17	155
T70	10	14'1" x 7'7" x 6'8"	45mm	94	7.62mm	60	28	155
SU76	10		76mm	60	None	35	28	180
SU122	34	21'10" x 10'6" x 8'8"	122mm M30		None	45	33	92
SU152	46		152mm		None	60	27	75

Appendix VI

Ground forces strengths as of July 4th 1943

German		Approximate Totals
Army Group South		
4th PzA		223,900
Army Kemp		126,000
Total		349,900
Army Group Center		
9th Army		335,000
2nd Army		96,000
Totals		431,000
Grand total		780,900
Soviets		
Voronezh Front		**Estimated Totals**
38th Army		60,000
40th Army		77,000
6th GA		79,000
7th GA		76,000
69th Army		52,000
1st TA		40,000
35th GRC		35,000
Front Reserve		204,000
Total		623,000
Central Front		
48th Army		84,000
13th Army		114,000
70th Army		96,000
65th Army		100,000
60th Army		96,000
2nd TA		37,000
Front Reserves		184,000
Total		711,000

Steppe Front		573,000
Western Front	(estimate)	277,000
Bryansk Front	(estimate)	400,000
Southwestern Front		700,000
Totals		1,950,000
This total represents forces deployed near Kharkov, Belgorod, Kursk, Orel and Bryansk for July and August period. The number shrinks to 1.9 million for just the Voronezh and Central Fronts and direct reinforcements from other Fronts for the first ten days.		
Grand total		3,284,000

Appendix VII
Aviation Strengths

(Includes operational aircraft only as of July 4th 1943)

German		*Luftflotte* 6	*Fliegerkorps* 8	Distant Airfields
Ju 88		134	72	92
Ju 52		167	13	
He 111		0	221	152
Ju 87		0	242	166
Fw 190		0	105	186
Hs 129		0	79	
Bf 109		0	184	31
Misc*		0	63	99
Sub Totals		301	979	726
Grand Total			1,280	2,006

Soviet				
	2nd VA	16th VA	17th VA	
Fighters	389	455	163	
Sturmoviks	276	241	239	
Bombers	206	334	136	
Reconnaissance	10	4	0	
Sub Totals	881	1034	538	
Grand Total			2,453	

* includes non combat aircraft

Appendix VIII
Casualties

German	4th PzA			Corps Kempf			9th Army		
	Killed	Wounded	Missing	Killed	Wounded	Missing	Killed	Wounded	Missing
From 7/5 to 7/12	2,011	10,123	253	1,912	9,517	578	3,977	18,005	851
From 7/13 to 7/31	1,689	7,460	637	1,496	7,528	511	2,294	9,321	1,115
Totals	3,700	17,583	890	3,408	17,045	1,089	6,271	27,326	1,966
Grand total	79,278								
Soviet									
Soviets casualties are estimated at 178,000									
Estimated 5th GTA tank losses on 7/12									

	Participated	Lost
29th TC	153	77
18th TC	84	35
2nd GTC	54	29
2nd TC	22	11
1446 Self Propelled Art Reg	19	14
5th GMC	105	73
Totals	437	239

Damaged but repairable tanks are estimated at an additional 160

The 2nd SS PzC have estimates that range up to 153 panzers destroyed or damaged.

Bibliography

Agte, P., *Michael Wittmann and the Waffen-SS Tiger Commanders of the Leibstandarte in WWII* Volume 1 (Mechanicsburg PA, 2006)
Armstrong, Col R.N., *Red Army Tank Commanders: The Armored Guards* (Atglen PA, 1994)
Barnet, C., *Hitler's Generals* (London, 1989)
Bellamy, C., *Absolute War: Soviet Russia in the Second World War* (London, 2007)
Bergstrom, C., *Kursk: The Air Battle, July 1943* (Hersham, 2008)
Boatner, M.M., III, *The Biographical Dictionary of World War II* (Novato CA, 1996)
Butler, R., *Hitler's Death's Head Division* (Barnsley, 2004)
Carius, O., *Tigers in the Mud* (Winnipeg, 1992)
Citino, R.M., *The Wehrmacht Retreats: Fighting a Lost War, 1943* (Lawrence KS, 2012)
Clark, L., *Kursk: The Greatest Battle* (London, 2011)
Cross, R., *Citadel: The Battle of Kursk* (London, 1993)
Cumins, K., *Cataclysm: The War on the Eastern Front 1941-45* (Solihull, 2011)
Dunn, W.S., Jr, *Kursk: Hitler's Gamble, 1943* (Westport CT, 1997)
Erickson, J., *The Road to Berlin: Stalin's War with Germany* Volume 2 (London, 1983)
Fey, W., *Armor Battles of the Waffen-SS* (Winnipeg, 1990)
Fowler, W., *Kursk: The Vital 24 Hours* (Staplehurst, 2005)
Fritz, S.G., *Ostkrieg: Hitler's War of Extermination in the East* (Lexington KY, 2011)
Glantz, D.M. & J. House, *The Battle of Kursk* (Lawrence KS, 1999)
Glantz, D.M., *From the Don to the Dnepr: Soviet Offensive Operations, December 1942 - August 1943* (London, 1991)
Glantz, D.M., *The Battle for Kursk, 1943: The Soviet General Staff Study* (London, 1999)
Glantz, D.M., *After Stalingrad: The Red Army's Winter Offensive 1942-1943* (Solihull, 2009)
Goodenough, S., *War Maps* (New York, 1982)
Healy, M., *Zitadelle: The German Offensive Against the Kursk Salient 4-17 July 1943* (Stroud, 2008)
Jentz, T.L., *Panzertruppen 2: The Complete Guide to the Creation & Combat Employment of Germany's Tank Force 1943-1945* (Atglen PA, 1996)
Jones, M., *Total War: From Stalingrad to Berlin* (London, 2011)
Jukes, G., *Stalingrad to Kursk: Triumph of the Red Army* (London, 1969)
Jung, H.-J., *The History of Panzerregiment "Grossdeutschland"* (Winnipeg, 2000)
Keegan, J., *Atlas of the Second World War* (London, 2003)
Kurowski, F., *Operation Zitadelle, July 1943* (Winnipeg, 2003)
Kurowski, F., *Panzer Aces* (Mechanicsburg PA, 2004)
Kurowski, F., *Panzer Aces II* (Mechanicsburg PA, 2004)
Kurowski, F., *Panzerkrieg: An Overview of German Armored Operations in World War 2* (Winnipeg, 2005)
Kurowski, F., *Infantry Aces* (Winnipeg, 2006)
Lehmann, R., *The Leibstandarte III* (Winnipeg, 1990)

Lochmann, F.-W. et al, *The Combat History of German Tiger Tank Battalion 503 in World War II* (Mechanicsburg PA, 2008)
Lodieu, D., *III. Pz.Korps at Kursk* (Paris, 2007)
Mann, C., *SS-Totenkopf: The History of the 'Death's Head' Division 1940-45* (Staplehurst, 2001)
Manstein, E. von, *Lost Victories: The War Memoirs of Hitler's Most Brilliant General* (London, 1958)
McCarthy, P. & M. Syron , *Panzerkrieg: The Rise and Fall of Hitler's Tank Divisions* (London, 2002)
Mellenthin, F.W. von, *Panzer Battles: A Study of the Employment of Armor in the Second World War* (London, 1955)
Mitcham, S.W., Jr, *Panzer Legions: A Guide to the German Army Tank Divisions of World War II and Their Commanders* (Westport CT, 2000)
Mitcham, S.W., Jr, *The Men of Barbarossa: Commanders of the German Invasion of Russia, 1941* (Philadelphia PA, 2010)
Nevenkin, K., *Fire Brigades: The Panzer Divisions 1943-1945* (Winnipeg, 2008)
Newton, S.H., *Hitler's Commander: Field Marshal Walther Model-Hitler's Favorite General* (New York, 2005)
Newton, S.H., *Kursk: The German View* (New York, 2002)
Nipe, G.M., Jr, *Decision in the Ukraine: German Panzer Operations on the Eastern Front, Summer 1943* (Winnipeg, 1996)
Nipe, G.M., Jr, *Last Victory in Russia: The SS-Panzerkorps and Manstein's Kharkov Counteroffensive, February-March 1943* (Atglen PA, 2000)
Nipe, G.M., Jr, *Blood, Steel, and Myth: The II.SS-Panzer-Korps and the Road to Prochorowka* (Southbury CT, 2011)
Overy, R., *Russia's War: A History of the Soviet Effort: 1941-1945* (London, 1998)
Piekalkiewicz, J., *Operation Citadel: Kursk and Orel, the Greatest Tank Battle of the Second World War* (Novato CA, 1987)
Porter, D., *Fifth Guards Tank Army at Kursk 12 July, 1943* (London, 2011)
Porter, D., *Das Reich Division at Kursk: 12 July 1943* (London, 2011)
Raus, E. & S.H. Newton, *Panzer Operations: The Eastern Front Memoir of General Raus, 1941-1945* (New York, 2003)
Seaton, A., *The Russo-German War 1941-45* (New York, 1972)
Showalter, D., *Hitler's Panzers* (New York, 2009)
Shukman, H., *Stalin's Generals* (London, 1993)
Spaeter, H., *History of the Panzerkorps Grossdeutschland* (Winnipeg, 1992, 3 volumes)
Trang, C., *Totenkopf* (Bayeux, 2008)
Ullrich, K., *Like a Cliff in the Ocean: A History of the 3rd SS-Panzer-Division Totenkopf* (Winnipeg, 2002)
Weidinger, O., *Das Reich IV* (Winnipeg, 2008)
Werth, A., *Russia at War 1941-1945* (New York, 1964)
Zamulin, V., *Demolishing the Myth: The Tank Battle at Prokhorovka, Kursk, July 1943: An Operational Narrative* (Solihull, 2011)
Ziemke, E., *Stalingrad to Berlin : The German Defeat in the East* (Washington DC, 1968)

Index

Index of People – German

Bake, Franz, Major, 200, 304, 360-361, 363, 366, 369, 394, 411, 433, 443, 448, 455, 459
Balck, General, 226
Baum, Otto, Lt Colonel, 212, 243, 251
Becker, Hellmuth, Lt Colonel, 214, 243, 246, 251-252, 278
Becker, Hans, Captain, 199
Bieberstein, Rogalla von, Major, 235, 361
Biermeier, Fritz, Captain, 212
Blissinger, Hans, Major, 336
Bochmann, Georg, Major, 177, 381
Breith, Hermann, Lt General, 29, 79, 235, 264-266, 304, 308, 366-367, 396, 410, 469, 477
Buffa, Ernst, Lt General, 139

Clossner, Erich, General, 269, 376
Cossel, Major, 446
Crisolli, Colonel, 433

Decker, Karl, Colonel, 38, 61, 66, 71, 121, 123, 391-393, 408-409, 420
Deichmann, Paul, Lt General, 41, 238, 477
Dessloch, Otto, General, 31, 477
Dieterich, Josef "Sepp",, General, ,30

Elverfeldt, Maj General, 93
Esebeck, General, 204, 400, 416, 437

Falkenstein, Maj General, 462
Felzmann, Max, Maj General, 462
Fermello, Corporal, 41
Fichtner, Sebastian, Maj General, 433
Forst, Werner, Lt General, 234
Franz, Major, 196-197, 391
Fretter-Pico, Max, Maj General, 62, 158
Frey, Lt, 106, 144, 177
Frey, Lt Colonel, 245, 276
Friessner, Johannes, Lt General, 83, 86, 89, 476
Funck, Freiherr von, Lt General, 76-77, 80, 163, 302, 364

Gehlen, Reinhard, General, 33
Gollnick, Hans, Maj General, 270, 433
Greim, Ritter von,, Col General, ,21, 31, 439, 477
Grossmann, Horst, Lt General, 84, 88, 93, 130, 134
Guderian, Heinz, Col General, 19-21, 33, 86, 260-261, 353, 464-465

Harpe, Joseph, Lt General, 84-85, 88, 92-93, 132-133, 238-239, 400, 416, 444, 446, 458, 461, 476
Hausherr, Lt, 191
Hausser, Paul, General, 14, 25, 43, 45-47, 50, 54-57, 60, 65, 98, 102, 105-106, 109-110, 112-113, 143, 147, 149-150, 161, 163, 173-175, 178, 180-181, 183-186, 188-189, 193, 197, 201, 209-211, 215, 218, 220, 241, 244-245, 247-249, 251-253, 255, 272-273, 276, 279, 283-286, 288, 290, 292-295, 313, 315, 317, 319-322, 325, 330, 336-339, 341-344, 348-352, 358-359, 364, 369, 383, 385-386, 388, 391, 396, 404, 406-407, 419, 422, 431-432, 438-440, 447, 451, 469, 477
Hitler, Adolf, 17, 19-21, 23-25, 28, 31, 33, 37, 43, 86, 141, 158, 173, 206, 228, 232, 240-241, 249, 254-255, 262, 266, 271, 293, 303-304, 308, 352, 364, 377, 382-383, 385, 392, 395, 402, 419, 431, 435, 437, 443, 447-449, 451, 460-461, 464, 468, 473, 474, 477
Hitzfeld, Otto, Maj General, 446
Hocker, Hans, Lt General, 95
Hoepner, Erich, General, 31
Hoernlein, Walter, Lt General, 23, 64, 66, 71, 231, 354, 391, 393
Hoffmeister, Edmund, Lt General, 84
Hollidt, Karl, General, 437
Horn, Maj General, 263, 364, 371
Horst, Johannes, Major, 303-304, 306, 364
Hossbach, Friedrich, Lt General, 87, 454
Hoth, Hermann, Col General, 14, 17-18, 21-23, 27-29, 31-36, 38, 41-42, 45-46, 57-62, 64, 69-70, 72, 74, 78, 83, 95, 100, 109-115, 119, 123, 127, 134, 136, 143-145, 147-149, 151-153, 158, 160-161, 173-175, 177-178, 180-184, 187-190, 197-198, 200, 209, 212, 214-220, 225, 227-229, 231-233, 235, 241, 245, 249, 255-257, 262-263, 265-266, 270, 272, 275, 279, 285, 292-297, 300-301, 304, 306, 313, 315, 319-320, 332, 338, 348, 350, 352-353, 355, 359, 369, 382, 384-386, 388, 391, 396, 404-405, 407, 409, 412, 419, 421, 424, 426, 432, 435, 438-439, 443-444, 448, 464-468, 472-473, 476
Hunersdorff, Walter von, Maj General, 39, 76-77, 126, 164, 199, 202, 235, 264, 307, 316, 360-362, 371, 411, 433, 462
Hutner, Maj General, 264

Jaschke, Erich, General, 446, 476
Jeschonnek, Hans, Col General, 21
Jodl, Alfred, Col General, 19, 464
Jung, Hans-Joachim, 419
Jungenfeldt, von, Lt, 83

Kageneck, Clemens, Captain, 41, 307, 456
Kamecke, Hans, Lt General, 462
Karck, Georg, Colonel, 31, 47
Kassnitz, Erich, Colonel, 452
Keitel, Wilhelm, Field Marshal, 19
Kempf, Werner, General, 14, 28, 29, 38, 39, 42, 47, 75-80, 89, 99, 101, 111, 117, 124-125, 127, 150-153, 158, 162-163, 185, 189, 199-202, 215, 217-219, 227, 232, 234-235, 246, 254, 262-267, 279, 289-290, 293-295, 299, 301-304, 306-308, 314, 316, 318, 333, 340, 349, 351, 353, 360-362, 364, 366-368, 370-372, 382, 386, 390, 394-397, 406-407, 419, 421-422, 425-426, 435, 439, 444, 455, 458, 460-461, 464-465, 468-469, 472, 477, 493
Kessel, Mortimer von, Maj General, 83-84, 87, 94, 130, 134-135, 137-138
Kleber, Captain, 103
Kleist, Ewald, Field Marshal, 471
Klinfeld, D, Colonel, 380
Kling, Heinz, Captain, 59, 113, 179, 190, 246-247, 275-276, 279, 327
Klostermeyer, Heinz, Corporal, 115
Kluge, Guenther von, Field Marshal, 19-20, 93, 133-134, 140, 206, 238-239, 270, 309-310, 352-353, 376-377, 382, 417, 465, 472, 476
Knobelsdorff, Otto von, General, 14, 19, 38, 67, 71-72, 115-121, 123, 143, 181, 198, 221-222, 224-226, 230-233, 256-257, 260-261, 293, 296-297, 299, 353-355, 358-360, 391, 393, 407, 409, 476
Kohler, Rudolf, Maj General, 163
Krass, Hugo, Lt Colonel, 277, 330
Kruger, Walter, Lt General, 49, 102, 104-105, 143, 151, 177, 210, 283, 288, 343, 349, 386, 406, 408, 420, 422, 432, 440

Lauchert, Meinrad von, Colonel, 66-67, 156, 423, 436
Lemelsen, Joachim, Lt General, 29, 84-85, 93-94, 138, 166, 205-206, 239, 398, 416, 471, 476
Lubbe, Vollrath von, Lt General, 130, 134-136, 205, 437, 442

Manstein, Erich von, Field Marshal, 17-21, 23, 25, 28, 33, 37-38, 43, 58-59, 70, 72-74, 83, 111, 117, 121, 127, 151, 153, 158, 163, 189-190, 199, 201, 215, 217-218, 223, 228-229, 232, 241, 253-255, 257, 262-266, 285, 292, 295, 303-308, 312, 318, 337-338, 343, 348, 352-353, 358-359, 372, 376, 382-383, 385, 392, 394, 396, 404-405, 410, 413, 419, 421-422, 424, 426, 431-432, 440, 447, 454-455, 460, 464-465, 468, 472-474, 476
Mattenklott, Franz, General, 79, 477
Mauss 454
Meierdress, Erwin, Captain, 273, 321
Mennel, Hans, Captain, 352, 390

Mellenthin, Frriedrich von, Maj General, 19, 33, 255, 296, 348, 359, 424, 464
Mickl, Johann, Maj General, 65, 121, 155, 192, 221, 232, 256, 261, 296, 355, 359, 393, 409
Model, Walter, Col General, 17, 19, 21, 24, 29, 31, 33, 35, 40-42, 44, 59, 82-85, 88-96, 128-141, 147, 151, 165-171, 186, 203-207, 237-240, 268-271, 306, 309-311, 338, 353, 373-379, 382-383, 398-400, 415-417, 421-422, 428-429, 433-434, 437, 439-447, 450-454, 456-461, 465, 471-473, 476
Muller-Gebhard, Lt General, 458

Newiger, Albert, Maj General, 433
Noak, Major, 82, 88, 415

Oppeln-Bronikovski, von, Colonel, 162-163, 199-200, 361, 369, 448
Ott, Eugen, Lt General, 28, 37, 62, 476

Paulus, Friedrich, Col General, 471
Peiper, Joachim, Lt Colonel, 50, 142, 146, 179, 278-282, 286, 321, 323, 328, 334, 380
Poppe, Walter, Lt General, 356
Possel, Major, 456
Postel, Georg, Maj General, 39
Priess, Hermann, Maj General, 25, 98, 143, 146, 150, 157, 177, 210, 213, 218, 220, 243, 249, 252-253, 273, 279, 283, 285-286, 294, 312-313, 316, 319-321, 335, 349, 381-386, 404, 406, 422, 427, 431-432, 438, 470

Rappard, Lt General, 95, 462
Raus, Erhard, General, 30, 39, 73-74, 78, 81, 123, 125-126, 163, 201, 234, 254, 265, 267, 302, 362, 364, 366, 395, 477, 484
Remer, Otto, Major, 118, 122, 191
Rendulic, Lothar, General, 269-270, 310, 376, 377, 399-400, 415-417, 434, 437, 441, 447, 449, 476
Ribbentrop, Rudolf von, Lt, 146, 216, 286, 323, 326-328, 331, 334, 349
Richthofen, Wolfram von, Field Marshal, 31
Risch, Lt, 452
Rudel, Hans, Captain, 59, 326, 388

Sametreiter, Kurt, Sergeant Major, 328
Sandig, Rudolf, Major, 247
Saucken, Dieter von, Lt General, 139, 170, 203, 206, 269, 398, 445-446
Schack, Friedrich, Maj General, 88
Schaefer, Hans, Lt General, 354, 356
Scheller, Walter, Lt General, 138, 444-445
Schimmelmann, Graf von, Colonel, 119, 159, 221
Schlieben, Maj General, 88
Schmidt, Rudolf, Col General, 39, 77-78, 164, 235, 263, 269, 303, 306-307, 309, 311, 369, 373, 407, 458, 461-462, 476

INDEX 499

Schmidt, Gustav, Lt General, 39, 77, 78, 164, 235, 263, 269, 303, 306-307, 309, 311, 369, 373, 407, 458, 461-462, 476
Schmidt-Ott, Lt General, 224, 261
Schreiber, Captain, 47
Schultz, Waldemar, Lt ,276
Schultze, Major, 276
Seidemann, Hans , Maj General, 97, 222, 477
Speer, Albert, 19-20
Staudegger, Sergeant, 189, 249
Steinwachs, Major, 82
Strachwitz, Graf von, Colonel, 38, 61, 71, 121, 123, 156-157, 192, 195-196, 221, 223, 226, 228-229, 257-258, 261

Traut, Hans, Lt General, 88
Trierenberg, Wolf, Lt General, 143-144, 188, 252, 346

Ullrich, Karl, Major, 215
Unrein, Martin , Colonel, 368, 411

Waldenfels, Maj General, 462
Warmbrunn, Karl, Corporal, 103
Weidinger, Otto, Major, 47
Weidling, Helmuth, Lt General, 90, 462
Weiss, Walter, Col General, 41, 423
Westhoven, Franz, Lt General, 64, 117, 120, 158, 197-198, 222, 231, 355, 391-393
Wietersheim, Walter von, Captain, 229, 261
Wisch, Theodore, Maj General, 30, 106, 114, 175-177, 186, 217-218, 245, 277, 285, 288, 351, 402, 405, 407, 420, 423
Wisliceny, Gunther , Major, 47
Wittmann, Michael Lt 53, 60, 103, 106-107, 150, 190, 276, 327, 334, 345, 435, 449
Woehler, Otto, Lt General, 460-461

Zeitzler, Kurt, Col General, 17, 19, 464
Zorn, Hans, Lt General, 84, 91-92, 95, 445, 454, 476

Index of People – Soviet
Akopov, M.K., Lt Colonel, 244
Alekseev, V.M., Maj General, 354
Andriushchenko, G.I., Colonel, 355
Anikushkin, F.G, Maj General, 428

Badanov, V.M., Lt General, 376, 450
Bagramyan, I.K., Lt General, 374-375, 398, 399, 434, 437-438, 445, 450, 482
Baidak, K.M., Colonel, 214, 221
Bakharov, B.S., Maj General, 186, 324, 340, 345-346, 381, 388, 481
Baksov, A.I., Colonel, 64, 119
Barinov, A.B., Maj General, 84-85
Batov, P.I., Lt General, 131, 479

Belov, P.A., Lt General, 376, 416-417, 478
Bobrov, A.F., Maj General, 254, 316
Bogdanovo, S.I., Lt Colonel, 429
Boldin, I.V., Lt General, 376, 398
Bondarev, A.L., Lt General, 87, 478
Borisenko, G.I., Colonel, 361, 371
Borodkin, P.G., Colonel, 246
Brazhnikov, A.K., Colonel, 325
Bulygin, S.M., Lt Colonel, 325, 334, 346
Burdeiny, A.S., Maj General, 48, 67, 99-100, 104, 108, 148, 153, 174, 176-177, 179, 182, 184-186, 217, 244, 287, 291, 315-316, 320-321, 323, 333, 341, 344, 347, 362-363, 368-369, 481
Burkov, V.G., Maj General, 110, 153, 177, 182, 186, 214, 221, 230, 256, 354, 481
Butkov, V.V., General, 398

Cherniakhovsky, I.D., Lt General, 131
Chernienko, D.K., Maj General, 67, 106, 177, 180, 193, 197, 213, 260, 479
Chernov, V.G., Colonel, 56, 69, 119
Chibisov, N.E., Lt General, 69, 480
Chistiakov, I.M., Lt General, 14, 30, 35, 45, 52, 56, 63-67, 100, 106, 108, 115, 149, 151, 154, 217, 226, 295, 298, 480

Dremin, D.F., Colonel, 221, 256
Dzhandzhgava, V.N., Colonel, 84-85

Elin, Colonel, 296
Enshin, M.A., Maj General, 132, 170

Fediuninsky, I.I., Lt General, 376

Galanin, I.V., Lt General, 168, 479
Getman, A.L., Maj General, 37, 156, 255, 257-259, 479
Gorbatov, A.V., Lt General, 376, 478
Gorelov, V.M., Colonel, 107
Goriachev, S.G., Maj General, 123, 235, 480
Govorunenko, P.D., Colonel, 34, 99
Grigoyev, V.E., Maj General, 129
Grishchenko, N.V., Colonel, 361, 371

Ibiansky, N.B., General, 64, 480
Ivanov, I.I., Maj General, 479
Ivanov, N.M., Colonel, 108
Ivanov, S.P., Lt General, 280,

Jenshin, 137

Kashpersky, G.M., Lt Colonel, 284, 295
Katukov, M.E., General, 14, 25, 31, 45, 51, 58, 67, 69-71, 100, 105-108, 110, 112, 122, 144, 149, 154-155, 160, 176, 185, 197, 214, 227, 258, 295, 297, 355, 424, 438, 479

Kazakov, K.V., Lt Colonel, 349
Khrushchev, N.S., Lt General, 25, 185, 350, 389
Kirichenko, I.F., Maj General, 324, 327, 381, 388, 481
KrIovsheev, G.F., Col General, 352
Kiselev, A.I., Maj General, 168
Kolpakchi, V.I., Lt General, 377, 478
Konev, I.S., General, 27, 29, 42, 110-111, 292, 301, 350-351, 435, 439, 447, 455, 460, 463, 468, 480
Korchagin, I.M., Maj General, 445
Kozak, S.A., Colonel, 125-126
Kozlov, P.M., Maj General, 461
Kravchenko, A.G., Maj General, 48, 59, 67, 99-100, 102-103, 106, 109, 112, 148, 153, 174, 179, 182, 184, 355, 479
Kriuchenkin, V.D., Lt General, 151, 214, 233, 255, 302, 362, 365, 371, 480
Kriukov, V.V., Maj General, 439
Krivoshein, S.M., Maj General, 61, 99, 107, 119, 121, 144, 154-155, 161, 479
Kropotin, N.A., Maj General, 398
Kulik, G.I., Lt General, 461, 480
Kurnosov, N.A., Major, 370

Lazarov, I.G., Maj General, 376
Lebedev, V.G., Maj General, 49, 98, 233
Leonov, M.T., Colonel, 160
Liakhov, A.N., Colonel, 272, 283
Linev, A.A., Lt Colonel, 323, 327, 334
Lipichev, N.P., Lt Colonel, 278, 327, 340
Lunev, M.S., Captain, 290

Malinovsky, Rodion I., Col General, 143
Malov, L.I., Lt Colonel, 212, 246, 287, 344
Mitroshenko, I.S. Lt 325
Moiseev, S.F., Colonel, 327, 334
Morgunov, N.V., Colonel, 105
Morozov, I.K., Maj General, 255, 266, 360
Moskalenko, K.S., Lt General, 69, 191, 298, 480

Nekrasov, I.M., Colonel, 34, 37, 51, 54, 59, 119
Nesterov, S.K., Colonel, 334, 362, 371
Novikov, Lt Colonel, 267

Obukhov, V.T., Maj General, 460
Okhrimenko, P.F., Lt Colonel, 68, 108-109
Ovcharenko, K.I., Colonel, 323

Pankov, N.F., Maj General, 416
Pantiukhov, G.G., Lt Colonel, 251
Piskarev, V., Colonel, 371
Plissov, Major, 325
Poloskov, Colonel, 364
Poluboiarov, G.G., Maj General, 455
Popiel 45

Popov, M.M., Col General, 23, 376, 384, 401, 415, 443, 445, 457, 478, 481
Popov, I.I., Maj General, 219, 272, 289, 313, 384, 481
Popov, A.F., Maj General, 111, 148, 153, 176, 179, 182, 197, 214, 243-244, 246-247, 254, 277, 315-316, 331, 345, 347, 360, 481
Pukhov, N.P., Lt General, 40, 137, 478
Puzyrev, V.A., Lt Colonel, 324

Rodimstev, A.I., Maj General, 384
Rodin, A.G., Lt General, 129, 131, 136, 478
Rogozny, Z.Z., Maj General, 245, 266, 289, 394-395, 480
Rokossovsky, K.K., General, 15, 21, 26, 28-29, 34, 40-42, 75, 82-83, 86-88, 90-92, 94-96, 128-133, 135-136, 139-141, 151, 165, 167-168, 170, 186, 203-204, 206-207, 215, 237-240, 268, 270, 309, 348, 350-351, 376, 378-379, 390, 415, 428, 434, 442, 452, 456-457, 465, 471-472, 478
Romanenko, P.L., Lt General, 83, 478
Rudenko, Sergey, Lt General, 41, 85, 128, 132, 140, 150, 165, 237, 270-271, 428, 478
Rudkin, F.N., Maj General, 442, 445
Russkikh, I.G., Colonel, 34, 79, 123, 306
Rybalko, P.S., Lt General, 376, 401, 417, 429, 436, 442-444, 448-450, 456, 458-459

Safiullin, G.B., Maj General, 480
Sakhno, M.S., Maj General, 374
Savchenko, Colonel, 325, 341
Sazonov, A.M., Colonel, 253-254, 316
Seriugin, M.P., Colonel, 181
Shchelakovsky, A.V., Maj General, 413
Shumilov, M.S., Lt General, 14, 30, 57, 75-76, 79, 124, 164, 202, 265, 289, 295, 480
Sibakov, I.S., Colonel, 64, 70, 119
Simonov, M.E., Major, 267
Sinenko, M.D., Maj General, 87, 129, 138, 478
Skvortsov, A.V., Maj General, 75-76, 314, 316, 481
Sokolovsky, V.D., Col General, 23, 376, 415, 481
Stalin, Joseph 18-19, 24-25, 27, 29, 42, 57-58, 108, 110-111, 114, 122, 132, 150-151, 153, 185-187, 207, 239, 271, 288, 295, 315, 350, 365, 389-390, 419, 421, 436, 456-457, 463, 465, 468, 470, 474
Stepanov, I.I., Lt Colonel, 382

Tarasov, V.D., Lt Colonel, 323, 349
Tavartkiladze, N.T., Maj General, 52, 55, 100
Teliakov, N.M., Lt Colonel, 130, 137
Terentev, G.P., Maj General, 365, 480
Tikhomirov, V.V., Maj General, 123, 338, 341
Timoshenko, S.K., Marshal, 471
Tolbukhin, F.I., Lt General, 143, 434
Trufanov, K.G., Maj General, 315, 347, 360-361, 363, 365, 367, 370-371, 390, 411, 412
Trunin, V.F., Colonel, 79, 123

Vasilev, N.A., Maj General, 123, 129, 478, 480
Vasilevsky, A.M., Marshal, 18, 42, 58, 110, 183, 274, 280, 288-289, 294, 350, 389, 396
Vatutin, N.F., Col General, 14-15, 25-26, 28-30, 32, 34-35, 37-38, 42, 48, 50-51, 53-54, 56-58, 61-62, 67-72, 78-81, 97, 100, 102-106, 108-111, 114-115, 119-124, 126, 131, 136, 142, 145, 147-148, 150-155, 157-158, 160-162, 164, 173-176, 178-181, 183-193, 196-197, 199-201, 207, 209, 213-216, 218-222, 224, 227, 229-230, 232-235, 240-242, 244-247, 249, 253-257, 259-260, 263, 265-266, 272, 278, 280-282, 284-285, 287-290, 292-295, 298-301, 303, 305, 307, 312, 314, 316-317, 322, 325, 329, 332, 336, 338, 340, 346, 349-352, 354-358, 360-361, 363, 367-369, 371, 379, 383-385, 387, 389-390, 392, 394-396, 398, 402-404, 406-407, 410, 419-421, 424-426, 431, 432, 438-439, 447, 455, 459, 463, 465-473, 479
Volodin, N.K., Colonel, 290, 327, 329
Voronov, N.N., General, 23

Zhadov, A.S., Lt General, 14, 186, 188-189, 197, 220, 272, 279, 289-290, 295, 316, 320, 335, 338-339, 381, 384, 432, 481
Zhilin, F.A., Colonel, 145
Zhukov, G.K., Marshal, 18-19, 23, 29, 42-43, 207, 216, 219, 232, 239, 301, 350, 389, 432-433, 468
Zinkovich, M.I., Maj General, 442, 445
Zotov, Major, 325

Index of Places

Akhtyrka, 458, 460
Alechino, 452
Aleksandrovka, 56, 86, 90-91, 307-308, 360, 363, 366-367, 370-371, 388, 393-396, 410-413, 426, 436, 467
Aleksandrovski, 112, 369-370
Aleksandrovski Vyselok, 369-370
Alekseevka, 36, 51, 62-63, 66, 70, 97, 104, 115, 118-120, 144, 194, 222, 225, 229, 259, 297, 363
Alekseevski Vyselok , 301, 361-362
Aleshnya River, 415
Alisovo, 450-452, 456
Andreevka, 174, 248, 273, 275, 277-278, 286, 291, 325, 327, 329, 332, 334, 336, 340, 342-343, 349, 351-352, 380-381, 386-388, 391, 421
Andreevski, 202, 235
Antipenko, 379
Arkhangelskoe, 87, 437
Arkhangesk, 20
Arsenevski, 134
Avdeevka, 361-362, 365, 367-368, 370-371, 395, 411-414, 425

Balka Razumnaia , 302
Barchevka, 282

Barvenkovo, 18, 44, 438, 443
Batratskaia Dacha, 123-124, 126-127, 162-164, 199, 201, 265, 302, 371, 426
Bazhenova, 170, 237
Beaulieu, 39
Belaia, 37
Belenikhino, 105-106, 108-109, 112, 114, 147, 151, 153-154, 174, 179, 182, 188, 230, 242, 245, 250, 252-253, 255, 262, 266, 279-280, 287-290, 294, 305, 315, 322, 324-325, 329-331, 333-334, 339-340, 344-346, 350, 352, 362, 381, 384-385, 389, 403, 405-410, 420-421, 425-426, 431, 469
Belenikhino Station, 106, 108-109, 147, 188, 331, 385, 406
Belev, 375
Belgorod, 17-18, 23, 28, 30, 34-35, 38-39, 42, 44, 47, 58-59, 64, 70-71, 73-80, 98, 111, 123-125, 127, 143, 199-201, 234, 246, 249, 262, 266, 279, 303, 307, 322, 351, 359, 365, 382, 419, 434-435, 437-440, 454-457, 459, 461, 463, 473, 491
Belinska, 127, 163
Belomestnazha, 302
Belomestniai, 54
Belovskaia, 125, 127, 162, 266
Beregovoe, 209, 222, 243, 283, 337
Beregovoi , 213
Beresovyi, 61, 66
Berezhok, 437
Berezov, 25, 34, 36, 43-46, 48-52, 54-55, 62-63, 65, 67, 99, 115, 137
Berezov Log, 137
Berezovka, 147, 194, 197, 221, 223, 226-229, 232-233, 256, 258-261, 294, 296-298, 314, 354-357, 391-392, 407, 409, 410, 467
Berezovyi, 65, 166, 169-170, 269
Berezovyi Log, 170, 269
Berlin, 18, 21, 31, 33, 86, 173, 234, 261, 373, 440
Besliyodovo, 78
Bezliudovka, 48
Bezlydovka, 125
Bitiug, 133, 169, 170
Blizhniaia Igumenka, 77, 80, 127, 162, 164, 199-202, 235, 263, 467
Bobrik, 83-85, 87, 90-91, 93, 95, 128, 130, 132, 134-135, 137, 168, 238
Bobryshevo, 112, 218
Bodenhausen, 270, 437
Bogodukhov, 458
Bogoroditskoe, 158, 251, 286, 321, 333
Bol Dolzhik, 434
Bolkhov, 167, 374-376, 399-400, 415-417, 428-429, 434, 437, 440, 446-447, 450, 453
Boloto, 90-91
Bolshie Maiachki, 53, 99, 101, 104, 107, 114, 142, 148, 150-151, 157-158, 175-176, 183-184, 192, 217, 277, 317, 322

Bolshie Podiarugi , 361, 394
Bolshie Seti, 112
Bolskhoi Makinovez , 373
Borisovka, 97, 455, 458
Borodinski, 436
Boromlia, 460
Breslau, 33, 452
Brezhnev, 185
Brochorovka, 322
Brody , 315
Brussovez, 452
Bryansk, 28-29, 41, 269, 309-311, 373-377, 398-399, 401,
    415-416, 419, 428, 433, 440, 443, 461, 478, 487, 491
Bryantsovo, 458
Bubny, 62, 117, 194, 259, 261, 297, 356-357
Bulanovka, 199
Burmeister, 205, 207, 268
Busuluk , 428
Butovo, 32, 36-38, 51, 60-62, 65, 71, 115-116, 452
Butyrki, 82, 84-85, 89-91, 93, 130, 137-138
Buzova, 237
Bykonov, 37

Chapaev, 115, 297-298, 314, 355-357
Cherkasskoe, 22-23, 36-37, 42, 51, 56, 61, 63-72, 115-118,
    120-121, 233, 452, 467
Chern Creek , 87
Chern River, 440, 454
Chernaia Poliana, 74, 76, 79
Chernigov, 460
Chernodie East , 441
Chernodie West, 441
Chiornaya Poliana , 164
Cholchlovka, 234
Chuguyev, 126
Churaevo, 124, 127, 164
Chursino, 181

Dal Igumnovo , 163
Dalni Dolzhik , 233, 242
Dalniaia Igumenka, 199, 201, 202, 234-235, 301, 304, 308
Dalnie Peski, 75, 77
Delnazhaya Igumenka, 77
Demensk , 459
Demyansk, 17
Desna River, 433, 453, 462
Dmitrievka, 47, 115, 119-121, 155, 228, 358
Dmitrovsk, 458-459
Dnepr River, 460-461
Dobrovody, 443
Dolbino, 303
Dolgi, 198, 225, 393, 408-409
Donets River, 25, 27-31, 35, 38-39, 48, 50-51, 56-57, 68,
    71, 73-80, 103, 105-106, 108-109, 111-112, 114, 123,
    127, 143, 149, 164, 183, 185, 186, 202, 212-213, 223,
    233-235, 248, 255, 262, 265, 267, 292, 302, 307-308,
    332, 360-361, 365, 367, 394-396, 402, 405, 413, 424,
    449, 455, 464, 466, 471, 474
Dorogobuzhino, 30, 74-76, 79-80
Dragunskoe, 32, 38, 62, 69, 71-72
Druzhnyi, 68, 103
Dubino, 304
Dubki, 44
Dubno , 315
Dubrova, 55, 66, 70, 99, 103, 115-122, 145, 154, 156, 158-
    161, 222, 224, 225-227, 233, 299, 358
Dudino , 373, 379
Dudorovsky, 415
Dukhovshchina, 458

Eleshaev , 384
Elets, 350
Erik, 43, 49-51, 60, 98-99, 110, 455
Erik River, 43, 60

Fatezh, 167, 169
Filosopov , 446

Generalovka, 124-127, 162
Gertsovka, 32, 35-38, 43, 60-65, 68, 119, 353
Gertsovka Station, 36
Glafirovka , 220
Glasunovka, 92
Glinev, 44
Glinnaya, 373, 375
Glinnaya River , 375
Glubki , 374
Gnezdilovka , 425
Gnilets, 85-87, 90-91, 129-130, 134-135, 137-138, 166,
    168-169, 238, 428
Goianino, 194
Golenischtschevo, 452
Golokhvastovo, 436
Gomel , 454
Gonki, 49, 98, 146, 177, 445, 455
Goreloie, 133
Gorki, 20
Gostishchevo, 58, 62, 67, 70-71, 100, 104, 151, 177, 179,
    185, 294, 302, 306, 308, 313, 361, 365, 371
Gostishchevo II , 294
Gotnya , 36-37
Grachevka, 375, 436
Graivoron, 455, 458
Gremiache, 302, 361, 365, 428
Gremuchi, 45, 48, 50-52, 54, 62-63, 123-125, 127, 145,
    156, 159, 160, 181, 191-192, 196
Gresnoe, 107, 142, 145, 147-148, 151-152, 154, 161, 174-
    175, 178, 180-181, 184, 189-190, 192, 210, 212-213,
    215-217, 230, 232, 247, 251, 253, 279, 299, 314,

316, 319, 324, 327, 332, 336, 342, 345, 347, 349, 389, 402, 421
Gridino , 413
Grinevka , 40
Grushki, 345
Gunyavka , 454

Hill 122.5, 263
Hill 135.0, 363
Hill 147.0 , 234, 255, 266
Hill 174.0 , 357
Hill 185.7, 234
Hill 187.7 , 242
Hill 190.5, 302
Hill 198.3, 98
Hill 202.8 , 262
Hill 207, 163
Hill 207.8, 242
Hill 208.0, 299
Hill 209.5, 177, 181, 183, 210, 213
Hill 209.6, 365
Hill 209.7, 402
Hill 209.9, 126
Hill 210.3, 63
Hill 210.7, 101, 121
Hill 211.5, 235, 265, 267, 301, 304
Hill 211.6, 302
Hill 211.9, 242
Hill 212.1, 162
Hill 213.4 , 234
Hill 214.5, 55
Hill 215.4, 51-53, 282-283
Hill 215.5 , 162
Hill 216.0, 370, 390
Hill 216.5, 25, 45, 49, 52
Hill 217.1, 43, 45, 48, 51-53
Hill 217.4, 265, 301
Hill 217.9, 347
Hill 218.0, 55
Hill 218.3, 55
Hill 218.5, 156, 222
Hill 219.8, 218
Hill 220.3, 403
Hill 220.4, 183
Hill 220.5, 43, 45, 48, 51-52, 66
Hill 221.0 , 235
Hill 222.1, 368, 370, 410, 412, 414, 432
Hill 223.4 , 317
Hill 223.6, 447
Hill 224.2, 54
Hill 224.4, 263
Hill 224.5, 182, 212, 214
Hill 225.0, 413
Hill 225.9, 49, 98, 210
Hill 226.0, 101

Hill 226.6, 144, 197, 212, 217, 219, 242-243, 248-252, 272-274, 276, 282, 283, 285, 289-290, 294-295, 312-313, 316, 319-321, 328, 332, 335, 337-338, 340-342, 344-345, 350, 381-390, 404, 421-422, 470
Hill 227.0 , 252, 423
Hill 227.4, 25, 43, 177-179
Hill 227.6 , 357
Hill 228.4, 363-364
Hill 228.6, 31, 33, 35, 43-45, 55
Hill 229.4, 101, 155
Hill 230.1, 156
Hill 230.3, 265, 304, 306
Hill 230.5, 107-108, 157-160, 191-192, 195
Hill 231.3, 286
Hill 231.7, 137
Hill 232.0, 68, 100, 102-103, 106, 108
Hill 232.4 , 367
Hill 232.8, 231, 252, 256, 261-262
Hill 233.3, 46-47, 51, 55, 304, 408
Hill 233.6, 55
Hill 234.1, 169-170
Hill 234.8, 54-55
Hill 234.9, 340, 402, 404, 406, 420
Hill 235.0, 425
Hill 235.3, 319
Hill 235.4 , 395
Hill 235.9, 230, 359, 384-385
Hill 236.7, 137, 284, 312, 319, 335, 339, 344, 470
Hill 237.6, 178, 297, 299, 314, 357, 391-392
Hill 237.8, 71, 118
Hill 238.4, 55
Hill 239.6, 176-179, 296
Hill 239.8, 83, 139, 238
Hill 240.0, 230, 432
Hill 240.4, 194, 209, 221-222, 224, 228-229
Hill 240.8, 195
Hill 241.1, 116, 119, 121, 191
Hill 241.5, 363, 366-367, 370, 412, 432
Hill 241.6, 152, 197, 212, 217-218, 220, 243, 245-251, 253-255, 278, 280, 283, 285-287, 318-319, 324, 330-331, 336, 340, 342, 346, 351, 384-387
Hill 242.3, 387
Hill 242.5, 286, 330
Hill 242.7, 360
Hill 243.0, 193, 222, 226, 229-230, 256-258, 313, 353, 357, 406, 408, 410
Hill 243.2, 60, 100-103, 107, 109, 223
Hill 243.5, 244, 313
Hill 243.8, 297-298, 360
Hill 244.8, 224, 229, 231, 256-259, 262, 296, 299
Hill 245.8, 273, 275-276
Hill 246.0, 115-116, 118
Hill 246.3, 57, 100-102, 109, 143, 393
Hill 246.4 , 357

Hill 247.0, 229, 256-258, 260, 298, 355, 358, 392, 406, 408, 410
Hill 247.2, 66, 116, 118, 120, 122, 196, 223-224, 229, 422, 441
Hill 248.3, 252
Hill 249.3, 192
Hill 249.7, 89
Hill 251.2, 155, 183, 192, 213, 317
Hill 251.4, 194, 229-230, 299
Hill 251.5, 256
Hill 252.2, 31, 185, 197, 248, 250, 254, 272, 274-289, 291, 294-295, 312-315, 318-319, 321-324, 326-335, 338-340, 343, 346, 348-349, 352, 380-381, 386-387, 389, 402, 419, 423, 434
Hill 252.4, 218, 244, 272, 275, 278, 282-287, 295, 312-313, 317-318, 320, 322, 470
Hill 252.5, 183
Hill 253.5, 82, 132-134, 139, 170, 203, 206-207, 238-239, 270, 309
Hill 254.2, 53, 159-160
Hill 254.4, 55
Hill 254.5, 156, 342
Hill 255.9, 174, 317
Hill 257.0, 166, 170, 204, 207, 237
Hill 258, 170
Hill 258.2, 102, 110, 112, 149, 180, 182, 209, 217, 226, 243, 248, 387, 409
Hill 258.5, 257-262, 291, 297-298, 358-359, 382, 391, 409
Hill 258.8, 317
Hill 258.9, 317
Hill 260.8, 159, 193, 195-196, 209, 221-226, 228-229, 232, 256, 296, 299-300, 355, 359
Hill 261.0, 194
Hill 263, 454
Hill 269.5, 437, 454
Hill 272, 82, 130, 134, 239
Hill 274, 82, 130-131, 134-135, 139, 170, 203-204, 206, 238-239

Iablochki, 148, 161, 183
Iablonovez, 452
Iadova, 58
Iakhontov, 32-33, 35, 38, 43-44, 50-51, 60, 110
Iakovlevo, 31, 34-35, 43, 46-47, 50-62, 64-65, 68, 70, 97-105, 107-109, 112-113, 115, 117, 122, 144-145, 147, 151-152, 154-155, 157-158, 177, 180, 186, 192-193, 209, 221, 255, 287, 289, 291, 294, 298-299, 301, 314-316, 320, 322, 325, 333, 342, 356, 358, 385, 431, 435
Iamki, 243-244, 249, 272, 275, 278, 280-281, 283, 286, 288, 290, 292-293, 312, 314-315, 317-318, 322, 324, 327-328, 331-332, 382, 391, 402-404, 410, 413, 419-420, 425, 466
Iaoki, 120
Iar Orlov, 34
Iar Zaslonnyi, 182

Iarki, 67
Iasnaia Poliana (Northern Salient), 40, 85-87, 90
Iasnaia Poliana (Southern Salient), 102, 105, 109, 114, 144-147, 149, 151-152, 174, 182, 184, 210-211, 214, 217, 230, 244, 294, 313, 325, 333-334, 337, 352, 380, 385, 387, 403, 405, 408, 411, 426
Iastrebovo, 77, 124-127, 162-164, 467
Ielisaveto, 88
Ilinski, 192, 195, 198, 210, 221, 225
Ilinskoye, 442
Ilovayskaya, 438
Ismorosny, 450-451, 457
Italy, 19, 31, 241, 382, 433, 438, 448-449
Ivanovka, 245, 280, 292, 296, 320, 325, 329, 331, 333, 340, 347, 381, 383, 389, 402-407, 410, 413, 419-420
Ivanovski Vyselok, 114, 147, 149, 211-212, 242-245, 248, 250-251, 279, 290, 291, 294, 316, 319, 324, 329, 332, 334, 336, 338, 340, 342, 381, 384-385
Ivany, 379
Ivnia, 37, 157
Izmailovo, 83, 90
Izyum, 18, 359, 435, 437, 443
Izyum River, 435

Jagodnaya, 378
Jelez, 373
Juryevski, 446

Kalashnoye, 116
Kalesnoie, 121
Kalinin, 102, 104, 106, 108-109, 114, 146, 148-149, 179-180, 184, 187, 211, 213, 242, 248, 252, 280, 292, 306, 313, 325, 331, 336-339, 341, 343-344, 346, 352, 381, 383, 385, 389, 403, 458, 466
Kalinina, 199-200
Kalinovka, 223, 230-231, 255-259, 262, 291, 296, 298, 300, 353-356, 359, 392
Kaluga, 310, 429
Kamarichi, 167
Kamenka, 110, 199, 428, 439
Kamennyi Log, 44, 51, 56
Kamyshevka, 178
Karachev, 310, 398, 415, 439, 442, 446-447, 450-452, 460-461
Karashevka, 284
Karentievo, 444
Kartashevka, 217, 245, 249, 285, 295, 313, 319, 321, 328, 341, 348-349, 380-382, 386, 402, 404, 466, 468-470
Kasazkaia, 49
Kashara, 84, 129-131, 133, 136, 169-170, 204-205
Kasikino, 234
Kasmino Juryevski, 446
Kazache, 76, 152, 234, 263, 303-308, 361, 363, 367-368, 370-371, 425-426, 467, 471

Kazatskoe, 72
Kelekovo, 234
Kharkov, 17-18, 21, 28, 39, 41, 176, 307, 324, 329, 352, 359, 369, 421, 429, 434, 439, 448, 454, 459-462, 465, 471, 474, 491
Khmelevoe, 199, 426, 432
Khokhlovo, 202, 233, 263, 265, 301, 307-308, 362, 365
Khotynets, 310, 376, 400, 442, 457-458
Kiev, 28, 460, 516
Kirov, 459
Kirovograd, 28
Kiselevo, 233-235, 263-265, 267, 301-308, 361-362, 365
Kleimenovo, 413
Kliuchi, 212, 219, 243, 248-253, 273-274, 282, 285, 316, 319, 321, 387-388, 422
Knasavka, 136
Knochlein, 49, 273
Kobylevka, 117-118
Kochely, 417
Kochetovka, 107, 176, 178, 180-181, 183-184, 189, 193-194, 196, 209-210, 212-214, 216-218, 220-221, 223, 226, 229, 242, 246, 250, 255, 259-260, 273, 294, 296, 316, 327-328, 337, 355, 384, 386, 393
Kolch, 163
Kolomytsevo, 303
Kolonozh-Dubovzh, 126
Komintern, 235, 303
Komsomolets State Farm, 102, 107, 147, 149, 151-152, 182, 190, 212, 214, 218, 221, 242-243, 245-248, 251, 254-255, 279, 281, 284-285, 291, 294, 314-315, 317, 319-320, 324-325, 330, 332-334, 336, 340, 342-345, 390, 435
Koptevo, 444
Koren River, 77, 79, 123-124, 127, 164, 200, 267, 302, 308, 362, 371, 467, 470
Korocha, 25, 39, 57-58, 71, 73, 76, 78, 80, 97, 123, 127, 199, 201, 215, 235, 254, 280, 394, 464-465
Korocha River, 25, 39, 127, 394
Koronio, 201
Koroskovo, 456
Korovino, 37, 60-61, 63-64, 66, 68, 71, 117, 119, 158, 194, 259, 356-359, 467
Korytnoe, 244-245
Kosachev, 54-55
Koshelevo, 134
Kostornoe, 20
Kotelnikov, 357
Kotenko, 50-51
Kozelsk, 310, 377, 429
Kozinka woods, 106
Kozlovka, 184, 210, 213-216, 220, 243, 245-247, 249, 251-252, 254, 260, 273-274, 321, 343, 347
Kozmo-Demianovka, 51, 55, 72, 98, 101, 109, 118
Kramatorskaya, 443
Kramotorskaya, 45

Kransnoe Znamia, 363
Krasaskye, 451-452
Krasavka, 40, 168
Krasnaia Dubrova, 224-225, 227, 299
Krasnaia Poliana, 104, 195, 222
Krasnaia Saria, 135
Krasnaia Slobodka, 83
Krasnikov, 445, 447, 454
Krasnilkovo, 444
Krasniye Ugolok, 134
Krasnoe Znamia, 368, 412
Krasnopolye, 159, 355
Krasnyi Kommunar, 454
Krasnyi Oktiabr, 142, 147, 176, 178, 181, 183, 210, 212-216, 220, 246, 253, 255, 260, 273-274, 287, 294, 335, 337, 383, 395
Krasnyi Pochinok, 36-37, 56, 62, 64, 66, 68-69, 72, 115, 117-119, 158, 356-357, 359
Krasnyi Uzliv, 297
Krassny, 137
Kreida, 125, 126, 161-162
Kreida Station, 125
Kriukovo, 181
Krivonosovka, 199
Krivtsovo, 76, 302, 305, 471
Kroma River, 456
Kromy, 134, 378, 401, 428, 442, 454, 456-458
Kron, 328
Kruglik, 198, 230-232, 255-260, 262, 290, 294, 298, 355, 358, 409, 467
Krutoi Log, 75-77, 79-80, 123-125, 127, 365
Krutoye, 447
Ktsyn, 400
Kuban, 24
Kubaossovski, 258, 260, 291, 298, 353
Kudeyarovo, 433
Kunach, 433
Kurakovka, 306, 316, 360
Kurasovka, 37, 394
Kursk, 17-28, 31, 33, 35, 38-39, 41-44, 58-59, 78, 89, 93, 95-96, 111, 127, 129, 133, 139, 141-143, 149, 151, 153, 163, 166, 168, 173, 185, 188-190, 206, 209, 216, 218, 239, 241, 246, 252-253, 257, 271, 274-275, 282, 295, 311-312, 315, 349-351, 359-360, 373, 376-378, 389-390, 396, 398-400, 402, 404, 417, 419, 424, 429, 433, 435, 437-438, 449, 451, 458-459, 462, 464-465, 468, 471-474, 491
Kusmenkovo, 451
Kutyriki, 87
Kutyrka, 204
Kuzmenkov, 110
Kuzminka, 366
Kuznetsovo forest, 299

Ladyrevo, 134

Leningrad, 18
Leninski, 204-205, 237
Leski, 242, 253, 283, 329, 346, 402-403, 405-407, 410, 413, 422, 424-425
Lipovyi Donets River, 25, 31, 50-54, 56, 59, 67-68, 70, 79, 97-106, 108, 110-111, 143, 146, 148-151, 157, 174, 180, 183, 187-188, 201-202, 210, 213-214, 217, 223, 233, 242, 246-249, 255, 264, 302-303, 332, 339, 366, 383, 410, 424, 466
Lischansk, 110
Livny, 94
Loknia, 116
Lomovea, 446
Lomovo, 307
Luchki North, 102-103, 107-108, 112, 144-147, 149-150, 175-176, 179-180, 184, 210, 213, 215, 217, 277, 287-288, 315, 423, 434
Luchki South, 52, 58, 70, 98-99, 101-108, 111, 143, 145, 149, 151, 154, 180, 186, 209
Lukhanino, 32, 35-36, 62, 64, 66, 97, 99-100, 104, 115-122, 144-145, 149, 157-159, 161, 193, 197-198, 222, 225, 233, 297-299, 353-354
Lukhanino River, 66, 118, 144
Luninka, 169
Lutovo, 277, 281, 283, 313
Lyubanovo, 436

Malaia Psinka, 339
Malakhova Sloboda, 40
Malenkie Maiachki, 158
Malinovka, 51, 101
Malinovoe, 223, 227, 231
Maloarkhangelsk, 82-83, 85-86, 88, 90, 93-94, 129, 131, 135, 140-141, 171, 206
Maloe Iablonovo, 244, 291, 402, 404-405, 407, 410, 413, 420, 424-425
Malye Maiachki, 114, 142, 147-148, 151-152, 175-176, 180, 193, 197, 210-211, 214, 247, 255, 266, 316-317, 324, 332, 342, 389
Martinovski, 450
Maslovo, 30, 264
Maslovo Pristan, 30, 264
May 1st State Farm, 165
Mearla River, 458
Melikhovo, 77, 123, 125, 152, 162-163, 199-202, 231, 233-235, 263-266, 301-302, 304-305, 358, 367, 394, 467
Melitopol, 460
Melovoe, 50-51, 68, 70, 100, 223, 227, 256, 262, 296-297, 354
Melovoe Woods, 223
Melyn, 436
Merchik River, 459
Merefa, 459, 463
Miasoedovo, 34, 111, 123, 125, 163-164, 199, 201-202, 263, 265-266, 301-302, 305-306, 308, 467

Mikayanovka, 44
Mikhailovka, 44, 47, 74-75, 78, 80, 107, 117-118, 127, 144, 145, 148, 162, 214, 251, 273-274, 277-278, 281, 289, 291, 294, 319, 325, 340, 343, 355-357, 380-381, 384, 386-387, 389, 391, 402, 404-405, 420-421, 431
Mius River, 241, 359, 398, 429, 434-435, 437-438, 443, 448
Mokhovaya, 429
Molotyschi, 129
Molozhavaia gully, 212, 243
Moschchenoye, 24, 37, 48, 61
Moscow, 18-19, 143, 293, 457
Moshcherka River, 458
Mtsensk, 375, 415, 436, 441

Nasiana Polian, 103
Naumenko, 401, 478
Nekliudovo, 127, 164
Nepkhaevo, 55-56, 68, 99, 106, 146, 174, 179, 182, 211, 333
Nezhegol River, 39
Nikolskaia, 86-87
Nikolskoe, 129, 138, 446
Nizhnee Tagino, 135
Nizhni Olshanets, 127
Novaia, 61, 69, 116
Novaia Gorianka, 61, 69, 116
Novaya Sloboda, 379
Novenkoe, 230, 255, 258, 262, 297-299, 353-355, 357, 393, 405, 423
Novi Chutor, 83
Novo Alekseevski, 362
Novo Cherkasskoe, 72
Novo Khmelevo, 412
Novo Oskochnoe, 234-235, 394
Novo Slobodka, 303
Novo Troevka, 164
Novogorodskye, 451
Novopetrovka, 436
Novoselovka (east), 187, 266, 302, 362, 407, 411, 413, 422, 424-426
Novoselovka (west), 159-160, 175, 193-196, 209, 221-233, 256-259, 296, 299-300, 302, 353, 356, 392, 411, 413, 470
Novosil, 311, 374-375, 377, 398-399, 417, 429, 434
Novotroitzki, 128
Novye Lozy, 108, 262
Novyi Lug, 378
Novyi Oskol, 44, 253

Oboyan, 17, 19, 22-23, 28, 34-35, 37-39, 49, 69-72, 98-99, 103, 105, 108, 115, 119, 121-123, 145, 147-151, 154-155, 157-160, 173, 175-176, 183, 185-188, 190-198, 209, 213-215, 219-221, 223-232, 235, 241, 244, 246, 253-259, 262, 274, 280, 296-297, 299-301, 305, 312,

347-348, 353-358, 360, 380, 392-393, 405, 409, 420, 431, 464-465, 467, 473
Oboyan Road, 70-71, 115, 145, 150, 154, 159-160, 176, 190, 192-193, 195-197, 221, 223-232, 241, 246, 256, 258-259, 296, 300, 347, 354-358, 392, 409, 420
Obydenki Ismailovo, 87
Ochki, 437
Oikova, 121
Oka River, 83-84, 89-90, 128, 376, 429, 434, 443-446, 449, 456
Oktiabrski State Farm, 188, 218, 243, 251, 255, 272, 276-278, 280-289, 291, 293-295, 313-315, 317, 319, 322-333, 335-336, 338-340, 342-343, 346-348, 351-352, 384, 386-387, 389, 391, 393, 402, 423
Oleshen River, 436, 441-442
Olianovo, 379
Olkhovatka (Northern Salient), 29, 34, 40-41, 82, 86-88, 91, 93-96, 128-139, 141, 165-168-170, 199, 203-207, 234, 237-239, 268-270, 309, 353, 378, 399, 428, 464-465, 471
Olkhovatka (Southern Salient in 3rd PzC sector), 302, 304
Olkhovatka (Southern Salient in 48th PzC sector), 255, 297, 299
Olkhovka, 47, 60, 70, 98-99, 104, 115, 118, 120-121, 155
Olshanaya, 304
Olsufyevo, 417
Optucha, 434
Orel, 18-19, 21, 23, 26, 28-29, 41-42, 59, 92, 132, 140, 187, 204, 206, 237, 239-241, 268-270, 309-311, 338, 351, 373-379, 398-401, 415-419, 421-422, 428-429, 433-434, 436-447, 449-454, 456-458, 460-463, 465, 472, 474, 491
Orel sector, 18, 21, 23, 29, 41, 140, 206, 237, 309-310, 338, 373-379, 398-401, 415-419, 421-422, 428-429, 433-434, 436, 438-439, 441-447, 450-453, 456-458, 460-462, 474,
Orlovka, 37, 70, 213, 231, 256, 296
Orlovski, 87, 167
Orsha, 28
Oshigovo, 375
Oskochnoye, 304
Oskol River, 22-23, 28, 58, 112, 151, 186, 218
Ossinovi, 204-205
Ostnova, 44
Ostrenki, 323, 339, 344
Ostrenkov, 347, 388, 392
Ostrogozhsk, 27, 110
Otrada, 442-443, 445
Otschki, 90
Ozerki, 86-87, 90, 92-93, 437
Ozerovski, 99, 104, 106, 108, 145, 148, 150, 158, 180, 184, 187, 211, 214, 230, 241, 280, 332-333, 385, 403

Paltschikovo, 374

Panskaia, 84, 134
Pena River, 22-23, 25, 31, 35, 42, 56, 63-64, 66-67, 69, 97, 100, 115-122, 143-144, 154-155, 157-161, 190-198, 210, 215, 219-220, 222-223, 225, 227-228, 230-231, 233, 246, 258-259, 263, 286, 295-300, 354-357, 359, 396, 405, 466, 474
Penkovsky, 226
Perestriash, 373
Peresyp, 221
Petropavlovka, 34, 302
Petrovka, 48, 177, 228, 249-250, 274-276, 281-282, 286-287, 289, 291, 295, 318, 322, 326, 330, 336-337, 341, 343-344, 348, 381-383, 385, 388
Petrovski, 114, 149, 181, 249, 292, 366
Ploski, 363
Ploskoe, 202, 362, 395
Plota, 321, 334, 362-364, 367-368, 394, 406, 413-414, 421, 424-426
Plyanka, 436
Podimovka, 118
Podmaslovo, 437
Podolian, 85-87, 89-91, 134-135, 137-138, 167
Podsoborovka, 94, 166, 204
Podsumki, 395
Pogorelovka, 144, 148, 342
Pogorelovtsy, 204
Pokrovka, 50, 53-54, 68, 99-102, 105-107, 110, 114, 117, 118, 142, 144-145, 147-151, 154-155, 157, 159, 175-177, 192, 247, 279, 299, 314, 317, 370, 425, 435
Pokrovskoye, 44
Poland, 20
Polevaia, 168
Polezhaev, 144, 150, 212, 214, 219, 242, 272, 274, 295, 319, 321-322, 327-328, 332, 337-341, 343, 345, 347, 349-350, 381, 383-385, 387, 389-390, 422
Poliana State Farm, 123-124
Polorsk, 419
Polsela Goriannova, 91, 95
Pomerki, 44-45
Ponyri, 87-88, 91-92, 94-95, 129-135, 137-141, 165-171, 203-207, 237-239, 268-269, 271, 309, 311, 376-377, 398, 400, 417, 428, 471
Ponyri II, 87, 94-95, 134, 165-166, 171, 205-206
Ponyri PC, 171, 268, 309
Ponyri Station, 130, 132, 203
Poselka, 87
Postnikov, 234-235
Pravorot, 47, 49, 210, 244, 283, 292, 294, 296, 313, 331, 338, 340, 346, 349, 366, 372, 381-382, 384, 386, 389, 391, 402-407, 412, 413, 420-422, 424-427, 466
Prelestnoe, 112, 219, 272, 274-276, 278, 281, 286-287, 291, 295, 325, 336, 343, 381, 404
Priiutovka, 75
Prilepy, 132, 133, 239
Pristennoe, 20

Priytovka, 78
Priznachnoe, 186, 291
Probuzhdenie, 90, 134
Prokhorovka, 19, 22-23, 27-28, 34, 38-40, 49, 54, 57-58, 65, 70, 75, 79, 97, 99, 102, 105-106, 108, 110, 112, 114, 123, 143-149, 151, 158, 173-177, 179-184, 186-189, 193, 197, 199, 201, 209,-210, 212-221, 223, 227, 230-233, 241-249, 251-256, 262-263, 266, 272-296, 300-301, 303-307, 312-318, 320, 323, 327-330, 333, 335-337, 339, 347-353, 355, 358-366, 368-371, 380-386, 388, 392, 394-396, 398, 402, 404-407, 410-411, 420-421, 423-424, 426, 431-432, 447, 464-468, 470, 473-474
Protasovo, 86, 88, 91, 140, 171, 237
Protochino, 151
Psel River, 22-25, 27, 29, 31, 34, 37-39, 45, 50, 54-55, 65, 69, 72, 80, 99-100, 105, 112, 115, 121-123, 142-148, 150, 158-159, 161, 173-178, 180-186, 188-189, 191-194, 196-198, 209-210, 212-221, 223, 229-232, 242-261, 263, 266, 272-274, 277-280, 283-290, 292-301, 312-316, 318-322, 324-325, 327-329, 332, 335-337, 341-343, 345, 347-350, 355, 357-360, 382-390, 396, 403-406, 409, 422, 426-427, 431-432, 438, 463-467, 470, 473
Psyolknee, 150
Puliaevka, 75
Pushkarnogo, 97
Pushkarnoye, 73-74, 77

Raevka, 424
Rakitnaya River, 441
Rakitnoe, 230
Rakovo, 48, 51, 70, 115, 117-118, 194, 223, 227-228, 232, 260, 286, 296-298, 300, 355-357, 359-360, 392, 409, 467, 472
Rastenburg, 382
Razdol, 117-118
Razumnaia River, 34, 77, 123-124, 126, 161-162, 234, 266, 303, 368
Razumnoe, 74-75, 77, 79, 125, 127, 265, 289, 304, 307, 361-362, 364-365, 367
Redilovka, 49
Reitzenstein, 102, 145, 179, 406
Retschiza, 378
Rogan, 44-45, 160
Roslavl, 458
Rozhdestvenka, 68, 103, 143, 233, 366, 405
Ruhr Pocket, 71
Rybnitsa River, 436, 444
Rylsk, 417
Rylski, 179, 210-211
Ryndinka, 28, 255, 287, 302-303, 307, 318, 321, 333-334, 344, 355, 360-371, 386, 390, 394-395, 404-405, 410, 412, 414, 422, 425-426, 448, 471

Rzhavets, 27, 31, 164, 263, 265, 302-303, 305-308, 314, 316, 325, 360-371, 390, 393-396, 398, 410-411, 413, 421, 425, 467, 471
Rzhev Salient, 21

Sabachevski, 180, 183
Saborovka, 85, 128, 169
Sabynino, 76, 199, 202, 234-235, 264, 301, 303-308, 361-362, 364-366
Sadelnoe, 44, 48
Sakovnino, 375
Salegosch, 374
Samodurovka, 94, 129-130, 134, 165-166, 168-171, 203-207, 237-238, 268, 471
Saratov, 20
Saria, 135
Sartytoie, 118
Sashenkovo, 99
Saverskaya, 413
Saverskoye, 305, 367
Sazhnoe, 51
Sbatshevski, 266
Schischino, 234
Seim River, 350-351, 474
Semenovka, 69, 194, 451-452
Seredina Buda, 462
Sergeevskoe, 134
Serukovo, 162
Sevana, 85
Severny Donets River, 200
Sevriukovo, 162, 200
Sevsk, 167, 462-463
Shablykino, 461
Shakhovo, 51, 201, 233, 242, 287, 289, 291, 294, 302-303, 308, 361, 363-364, 368, 370-371, 387, 390, 394-395, 405, 407, 410-414, 424-426
Shamshin, 134
Shcholokovo, 125, 234-235, 266, 303, 360, 363-364, 367-371, 390, 394- 396, 405, 410, 412-414
Shebekino, 127, 164
Shelyabug, 415, 436
Shepelevka, 51, 70, 115, 299
Shepelevo, 40
Shevekino, 81
Shilkov, 373
Shipy, 187, 285, 361, 363, 365, 369, 395, 406, 411- 412, 414, 422, 425-426
Shirokoe, 90-91
Shishino, 235, 308
Shishkino, 447
Shliakhovo, 233, 235, 263, 265, 304-308, 358, 424, 467
Shopino, 25, 35, 52, 98-99, 101, 104, 110, 112-113, 146, 150, 158, 177, 180-181, 233, 249, 264, 280
Shudre, 451-452
Shukhtsovo, 235

INDEX 509

Sinkovo, 374
Skordnoye, 307
Slavyansk, 439
Smitrovsk, 458
Smogodino, 210
Smolensk, 28-29, 463
Smorodino, 98, 112, 338-339
Snamenskoye, 439
Snovo, 94, 135, 138, 140, 165, 169, 204-205, 269
Sobachevski, 106, 109, 325, 383, 385, 389, 403
Sobakino, 444
Sobyshno, 307, 369
Sohilno, 367
Soimonovo, 437
Sokolniki, 437
Sokomki, 45
Sololniki, 44
Solomino, 30, 48, 73, 75, 124, 126
Solonets, 53-55, 60, 101, 122
Soloschonki, 166
Solotinka River, 152, 173, 175-179, 181-182, 184-185, 187, 190, 193, 196-198, 210-214, 216-217, 245, 280, 328, 423
Solotnoye Dno, 450
Solovev State Farm, 364
Solovzhev, 126
Soshenkov, 112, 338
Sovkhoz Okatybrsi, 339
Soyshno, 305
Spasskoe, 436, 443
Sredniaia Olshanka, 290
St Gorodishche, 74
Stalingrad, 17-18, 24, 30, 33, 199, 216, 293, 300, 435, 463-464, 474
Stalino, 28, 352, 435, 438, 443
Stalinskoe State Farm, 37, 51, 182, 250, 275, 281, 291-292, 296, 312-313, 318, 327, 338, 342, 351
Stanovoe, 134, 148, 155
Stanovoe Woods, 155
Stanovoi Kolodez, 443, 445, 448
Stariza, 378
Staryi Gorod, 39, 74, 77, 79-80, 125, 127, 164, 200, 202, 234, 266-467, 471
Staryi Oskol, 143, 186, 197, 253, 317
Step, 85, 87, 95, 209, 265, 276, 439, 466
Stish, 448
Storozhevoe, 31, 106, 174, 211-212, 214, 219, 242-243, 245, 247-251, 253, 255, 266, 273-281, 283-296, 303, 313, 315-319, 321-325, 327, 329-333, 335-338, 340, 342-346, 348, 350, 352, 366, 381, 384, 389, 391, 404, 406-407, 411, 413, 420, 422, 425-426, 431, 435
Storozhevoe Woods, 250, 275-276, 280, 283, 286, 288, 291, 321, 325, 342, 352
Streletskoe, 31, 37, 43-44, 48, 56, 106
Strelnikov, 305, 395, 436

Strykovo, 447
Studenok, 37, 51, 70
Stupino, 436
Sukhinichi, 309, 429
Sukho Solotino, 107, 194, 210-211, 222, 248
Sukhodol forest, 299
Susha, 373, 399-400, 439
Susha River, 373, 399-400
Suvorovo, 436
Svapa River, 139, 166, 169, 204
Sviridovo, 395
Sychi, 436
Syrtsev, 32, 69, 122, 156, 158-159
Syrtsevo, 51, 56, 62, 67-68, 99, 115-116, 119, 121, 154-161, 191-192, 194-198, 225, 233, 259, 296, 298, 358
Sytschi, 415

Taganrog, 352
Tagino, 41, 85, 87-88, 128, 135
Tamovka, 462
Taranovka, 463
Tarnovka, 424
Teploe, 82, 88, 129-130, 132-134, 136, 138, 140, 167, 168, 170-171, 203-207, 237-239, 268, 270-271, 377, 398
Tereben, 419
Ternovka, 54, 62, 98, 101, 104, 180, 183, 187
Teterevino North, 106-108, 110, 113, 142-149, 151-153, 175-178, 180, 182, 185-187, 210-211, 214, 216-217, 221, 242, 245, 247, 249, 251, 253, 274-276, 278, 284, 288, 314, 342, 381, 421
Teterevino South, 31, 51, 101-102, 105, 107-108, 114, 145, 149, 179, 181, 183, 187, 209, 242, 317, 333, 338, 402-403, 466
Tolstoe, 225, 233, 256-257, 259-261, 296-297, 299-300, 354, 356, 358, 391-393, 407-409, 420, 423
Tomarovka, 24-25, 34, 36, 48-49, 57, 71, 97, 181, 279, 447, 455
Topkovo, 452
Toplinka, 30
Trefilovka, 37, 261
Trirechnoe, 72, 121
Trosna, 83, 88-89, 130, 133, 170, 207, 237, 268, 309, 439, 441, 448
Trubitsyn, 134
Tsarevka, 437
Tula, 90, 324
Tureika, 87
Tvanosvskoye Dvoriki, 451
Tysnokoye, 87

Ulianov, 107, 145, 147, 299
Ulianovka, 145
Ulianovo, 374-375, 378, 399-400, 416, 440
Umrichino, 447
Urochishche, 148

Uroshazah, 73
Urozhai Collective Farm, 127
Ushakovo, 307

Vakhrameev, 34, 480
Vararovka, 160, 245
Varky, 451
Vasilevka, 151, 174, 210, 212, 214, 216, 220-221, 233, 242-247, 252, 272-274, 278, 281-283, 286, 294, 313-314, 318, 321, 327-329, 332-334, 336, 341-343, 345-347, 349, 358, 380, 389, 391, 423, 431
Velikie Luki, 377
Velikomikhailovka, 352
Velize, 206
Vengerovka, 123
Verkhne Gnilusha, 40
Verkhne Smorodnoe, 134
Verkhne Tagino, 86-87
Verkhni Olshanets, 152, 235, 305-306, 368, 424
Verkhopenie, 68, 152, 154-155, 157, 159, 175, 190-198, 221-232, 256-261, 297, 299, 353-354, 356, 358, 382, 391-392, 423
Veselyi, 175-180, 184, 210, 213-214, 219, 243, 245, 252-253, 273, 285, 290, 295, 312, 319, 350, 381, 384, 388, 404, 421, 431, 471
Vesyoly, 437
Vetrenka, 40
Vilna, 419
Vinogradovka, 202, 217, 247, 250, 253, 266, 279-283, 287, 290-292, 296, 315, 317-319, 325, 329, 333-334, 343-344, 346, 348, 350, 384-385, 395, 403, 406, 410, 413, 420, 422, 425
Visloe, 98-99, 113, 177, 180-181, 183, 185, 210
Vladimirovka, 37, 51, 70, 221, 230, 257
Voin, 445
Volchansk, 125, 127, 447
Voronezh, 22
Voroshilov State Farm, 323, 328, 335, 338-339, 341, 344
Vorskla, 23, 25, 27, 31, 35, 44, 46, 48-50, 52-56, 59-60, 63-65, 68, 72, 100, 103-104, 106-107, 114, 117-120, 219, 233, 466, 467
Vorskla River, 23, 44, 46, 48, 52-53, 55, 59-60, 63, 72, 103, 106-107, 114, 117-118, 219, 233, 466
Vorsklitsa River, 56, 62, 119
Vorskolets River, 120
Voskhod, 224
Vosnesenskiall, 45
Vosnessenovka, 353
Vosschod, 261
Voznesenski, 53
Vyashi, 378
Vyazma, 17
Vypolzovka, 303-304, 360, 362-363, 365, 367-370, 388, 394-396, 410, 414, 426
Vyshniaia Olshanka, 290

Vytebet River, 378

Yalta Woods, 452
Yarkity, 116
Yaroslavl, 20
Yeropkino, 436, 449

Zadelnoe, 56, 63
Zagotskot, 38
Zaporozhe, 28, 33, 460
Zapselets River, 219
Zavidovka, 36, 62, 64, 69, 100, 115-119, 228, 296-297, 356-357
Zheliabugskie, 429
Zhilomeste, 380
Zhimolostnoe, 361, 402, 406, 425
Zhizdra, 375, 398, 415
Zhuravlinyi Woods, 46, 48, 50, 55
Ziborovka, 30
Zikeyevo, 415
Zmievka, 134
Znobishino, 436
Zolochev, 458
Zorinskie Dvory, 70, 157, 256
Zybino, 36-37, 48, 60, 116,

Index of German Military Units
For abbreviations see pages vii-viii.

Armies
2nd PzA, 29, 41-42, 133, 240, 268-270, 309-311, 373-374, 377-379, 382, 398, 400, 415-417, 429, 433-434, 437, 442-443, 446, 451-452, 454, 456-458, 460-462, 476
4th, 20, 398, 459, 461
4th PzA, 22-23, 26, 28, 31-32, 35-36, 39, 42, 52-53, 58, 60, 62, 67, 71-72, 97-98, 109, 113-114, 117, 122-123, 131, 147-148, 154, 159-160, 173-174, 183-184, 186-190, 193, 197-198, 209, 216, 218, 220-221, 228-229, 231, 241, 246, 255-256, 262, 266, 270, 289, 293-295, 299-300, 305, 307, 312, 314, 317, 349, 351, 353, 359, 364, 372, 382-383, 390, 392, 396, 404-406, 408, 419, 423, 431-432, 435, 443-444, 447, 454-455, 458-461, 463-466, 468-471, 473-474, 476, 483-485, 490, 493
6th (1st formation lost at Stalingrad), 219, 300, 411, 465, 471
6th (2nd formation, deployed on Mius River), 429, 437, 448, 465
8th, 461
9th, 19, 29, 40-42, 82, 83, 85-86, 93-96, 131, 135-136, 140-141, 151, 158, 165, 171, 186-187, 206-207, 239, 268-271, 300, 306, 309-311, 373-374, 376-382, 396, 398-400, 416, 428-429, 433-434, 437, 439, 441-447, 451-452, 454, 456-462, 465, 468, 471-472, 476, 483-484, 490, 493

INDEX   511

Luftwaffe Luftflotten
Luftflotte 4, 31, 44, 101, 477
Luftflotte 6, 31, 95, 310-311, 398, 439, 462, 477, 492

Corps
Corps Raus, 30, 39, 201, 265, 267, 364, 395, 484
2nd SS PzC, 14, 17, 22, 25, 28, 34, 37-38, 42-43, 45-47, 50, 54, 56-57, 60, 62, 64-65, 67, 72-73, 76-79, 97-101, 103-115, 117-118, 120-122, 127, 142, 144-154, 157-158, 160-161, 163, 174-175, 179-190, 192-193, 196-197, 201, 209, 215-220, 223, 226, 229, 231-232, 235-236, 242, 244-246, 253-255, 258, 261, 263-264, 266, 272, 274-275, 277-280, 282-285, 289-291, 294, 298, 300-301, 303, 306-307, 312-317, 319-320, 322-324, 326-329, 332-333, 335, 337, 343, 348-352, 355, 359, 364-365, 367-371, 383, 385, 388, 395-396, 404, 406, 412, 421, 423-424, 426-427, 429, 431-432, 435-436, 438, 448, 458, 464-473, 477, 483-484
3rd PzC, 17, 22-23, 26-28, 30-31, 38-39, 47, 49, 57-60, 73, 75-80, 111, 113, 123, 125-127, 147, 150-153, 162-164, 181, 185, 187, 192, 200-202, 214, 219-220, 227, 231, 233-236, 241, 246, 250, 262-266, 274, 280, 287-288, 292-293, 301, 303-308, 312, 316, 318, 324, 337, 346, 348, 361-372, 384-390, 394-396, 403, 405-406, 410-414, 420-422, 424-426, 432, 440, 444, 447, 458-460, 464-471, 473-474, 477, 483-484
8th *Flieger*, 33, 101, 145, 150, 153, 158, 190, 220, 222, 255, 278, 294, 326, 348, 352, 390, 409-410, 421, 423, 428, 431, 435, 438, 440, 477
11th IC, 17, 39, 73-74, 78, 80-81, 124-126, 163, 200, 233, 302, 308, 364, 439, 444, 469, 471, 477
12th IC, 461
20th IC, 41, 87, 138, 167, 416, 462, 476
23rd IC, 41, 82-89, 91-92, 95-96, 130, 132-133, 135-136, 140-141, 169, 171, 205, 239, 268, 309, 364, 416, 428, 450, 461, 476, 484
24th PzC, 21, 110, 228, 232, 246, 254-255, 262-264, 266, 293, 303, 305, 308, 343, 352, 359, 382-383, 392, 402, 437
35th IC, 269-270, 309-310, 373-376, 379, 399-400, 416-417, 428-429, 433-434, 437, 440, 442, 445, 449, 476
41st PzC, 41, 84-88, 90-94, 96, 134-135, 139-141, 165, 168-169, 171, 204-205, 238-239, 268, 309, 311, 416, 428, 444, 446, 450, 471, 476, 484
42nd IC, 79-80, 123, 477
46th PzC, 41, 84-87, 89, 91-92, 95-96, 130, 134, 138-139, 166, 169, 204, 238-239, 268, 309, 377, 416, 445, 450, 454, 457, 461, 471, 476, 484
47th PzC, 29, 41, 84-88, 90-96, 129-130, 132-133, 135-138, 140, 165-171, 204-205, 207, 237-239, 268, 309-311, 416, 428, 461, 476, 484
48th PzC, 14, 17, 19, 22-23, 25-28, 30, 32-33, 35-38, 42-43, 46-47, 50-51, 57, 60-65, 68-73, 79, 99-100, 102-103, 111-123, 144-145, 147-155, 157-161, 173, 175-176, 179-181, 184, 187-188, 190-198, 209-211, 213, 215, 217, 219-221, 223-233, 244, 246, 250, 253, 255-264, 274, 286, 289, 290, 293-296, 298-301, 303, 316, 328, 340, 353-360, 364, 382, 390, 392-393, 396, 403, 405-410, 419-420, 423-424, 436, 443, 460, 461, 464-467, 471-473, 476, 484
52nd IC, 22, 28, 35, 37, 62, 72, 115, 117, 158, 187, 193-194, 197-198, 210, 215, 223-224, 227-228, 231, 256, 259, 261, 285, 296-297, 356, 358-359, 392, 396, 407, 409, 423, 476
53rd IC, 41, 269, 309, 373, 376, 379-400, 415-416, 433, 437, 476
55th IC, 41, 309, 373, 375-376, 399-400, 446, 476
56th PzC, 454, 461

Divisions
PzGD *Grossdeutschland*, 17, 22-25, 31-32, 35-38, 46-47, 60-71, 99, 105, 113, 115-123, 152-160, 174, 181-182, 190-198, 215, 221-233, 256-262, 286, 291, 296-301, 313, 353-359, 382, 391-393, 398, 407-410, 420, 423-424, 435-436, 440, 446-452, 455-461, 466, 472, 483-485
1st *Flieger*, 33, 41, 96, 166, 171, 204-205, 207, 237, 271, 377-379, 398-401, 415, 418, 429, 434, 437-438, 440-442, 445-449, 451, 462, 477
1st ID, 461
1st SS PzGD *Leibstandarte Adolf Hitler*, 14, 27, 30-31, 33, 35, 37, 43-45, 47-62, 65, 70, 97-114, 117-119, 121-123, 142-155, 157-158, 161, 173-190, 192-193, 195, 197-198, 201, 209-211, 213-220, 222-224, 226, 228-231, 233, 241-255, 264, 272-296, 300-301, 304, 312-340, 342-346, 348-352, 380, 382-391, 393, 402-405, 407, 410, 413, 419-421, 423-424, 426-427, 432, 434-435, 438-439, 448-449, 466, 468-470, 483-484
2nd PzD, 29, 85, 86, 90, 93-94, 128-140, 165-171, 203-205, 208, 237-238, 268-269, 400, 402, 417, 433, 437, 442-443, 446, 471, 476, 483
2nd SS PzGD *Das Reich*, 14, 25, 31, 33, 36, 38, 43-44, 46-47, 49-58, 61, 98-114, 117, 121, 123, 142, 144-149, 151-154, 174-190, 195, 198, 201, 209-211, 213-214, 217-219, 223, 231, 235, 241-245, 247-253, 255, 264, 266, 274-275, 277-279, 280-286, 288, 290, 292-296, 301, 304, 306, 312-313, 315-318, 320-322, 324-325, 327, 329-335, 336-350, 352, 360, 362-364, 366, 368-370, 372, 381-392, 394-395, 402-408, 410-414, 419-426, 431-432, 435, 438, 440, 443, 448-449, 454-455, 458-459, 462, 468-470, 477
3rd PzD, 22-23, 31-32, 35-38, 41, 60-66, 68-70, 72, 115-122, 154-155, 157-161, 190-191, 193-198, 215, 222-233, 256, 258-261, 286, 294-300, 314, 353-359, 382, 391-393, 407-410, 420, 423-424, 435, 448, 454, 466, 472, 476, 483
3rd SS PzGD *Totenkopf*, 25, 27, 31-32, 38, 44-46, 49-55, 57-58, 62, 79-80, 97-101, 104-105, 109-113, 117, 143,

145-146, 148-151, 153, 157-158, 174-175, 177-178, 180-181, 183-189, 192, 198, 202, 209-220, 231, 233, 242-255, 260, 263, 272-274, 278-292, 294, 295, 300-301, 312-316, 318-324, 326-329, 332-343, 345-350, 355, 357, 359, 380-391, 402-406, 410, 420-421, 426, 431-432, 434-435, 438, 440, 448-449, 454-455, 459, 461-462, 466, 469-470
4th PzD, 41, 90, 128, 132-134, 138-140, 166-171, 203-208, 237-238, 268-269, 309, 398, 415, 437, 439, 441, 445-446, 448, 450, 452-453, 456, 461, 471-472, 476, 483
5th PzD, 41, 133, 269-270, 310, 373-374, 378-379, 398-400, 415, 476, 483
6th ID, 29, 41, 83-86, 88-93, 129-130, 134-135, 137-138, 165, 167, 169-170, 203-204, 237-239, 476
6th PzD, 18, 28, 30-31, 39, 41, 47, 49, 73-74, 76-80, 123-127, 161-164, 199-201, 233-235, 249, 263-266, 301-308, 316, 321, 325, 334, 344, 360-369, 371-372, 386-387, 393-396, 410-414, 421, 425-426, 443-445, 448, 454-455, 457, 459, 462,-463, 477, 483
7th ID, 87, 91-92, 95, 138, 166, 204, 268, 446, 450, 452, 454, 462, 476
7th PzD, 18, 28, 30-31, 39, 41, 73-81, 123-127, 162-164, 199-201, 233-236, 263-266, 301-306, 308, 360-361, 364-368, 371, 394-396, 405, 407, 410-414, 420-422, 424-427, 444, 461, 469, 477, 483
8th PzD, 41, 133, 206, 254, 269-270, 310, 377, 398-400, 402, 417, 433, 436, 442-443, 447, 457, 460, 476, 483
9th PzD, 29, 85-86, 90, 93-94, 128-131, 133-135, 137-140, 165, 167-171, 203-206, 208, 237-239, 269-270, 398, 437, 439, 442, 444-445, 447, 454, 459, 461-462, 471, 476, 483
10th PzGD, 41, 133, 134, 140, 168, 203, 205-206, 238, 268, 270, 311, 437, 444, 446-447, 476
11th PzD, 23, 31-32, 35-38, 47-48, 50-51, 54, 58, 60-63, 65-71, 97, 99, 105, 115-123, 153-156, 158-161, 173, 175, 178-179, 181-182, 184, 187, 192, 195-196, 198, 210-213, 215-217, 221-227, 229-233, 242, 244, 250-252, 256, 258-262, 291, 294, 296-300, 313, 316, 327-328, 355-359, 380, 384, 386, 391-393, 407, 409, 420, 423, 454-455, 458, 462, 472, 476
12th PzD, 41, 131, 133-134, 138, 140, 166-167, 206, 238, 254, 270, 309, 310, 374, 377, 400, 416, 437, 447, 451, 457, 476, 483
17th PzD, 110, 305, 343, 359, 392
18th PzD, 85, 88, 90, 92-94, 130, 132, 134, 138-140, 165, 167-171, 204, 206, 238-239, 374, 377, 400, 415-416, 446, 471, 476, 483
19th PzD, 18, 28, 30-31, 39, 44, 73-80, 123-127, 161-164, 199-201, 233-235, 249, 263-266, 301-308, 316, 334, 360-364, 366-371, 387, 393-396, 402, 405, 410-414, 424-426, 439, 440, 443, 454-455, 458, 461-462, 477, 484
20th PzD, 29, 83-85, 87-88, 91-95, 128-132, 134-135, 137-141, 165-170, 203-207, 237-238, 268, 374, 377, 398, 400, 416, 444, 446, 476, 483
23rd PzD, 110, 228, 305, 359, 372, 382, 392
25th PzGD, 41, 446, 476
31st ID, 87, 91-92, 130, 135, 137-138, 166-168, 204, 238, 268, 311, 454, 458, 476
34th ID, 310, 377, 417, 436-437, 442, 447, 449, 476
36th ID, 83, 166, 171, 238, 270, 309, 374, 377, 399-400, 402, 417, 428, 433, 436-437, 441-442, 476
45th ID, 87, 462, 476
52nd ID, 433
56th ID, 377, 379, 399-400, 415, 428, 436-437, 442, 445, 447, 449, 476
57th ID, 37, 62, 117, 356-357, 407, 460, 476
72nd ID, 87, 458, 476
78th AD, 83-84, 86, 88-89, 92, 129, 131-133, 140-141, 169-171, 207, 239, 268, 441, 447, 476
86th ID, 88, 90, 92-93, 130-134, 138-141, 165, 167-168, 170-171, 205, 268, 462, 476
102nd ID, 92, 441, 446, 450, 452, 461, 476
106th ID, 31, 39, 78, 80, 123, 125-126, 162-164, 201, 234, 265, 302, 439, 477
137th ID, 87, 462, 476
167th ID, 31, 37, 43-44, 48, 50, 54-56, 58-63, 65, 68, 70, 80, 98-99, 105-106, 115, 117-118, 120, 122, 143-144, 146, 150, 153, 158, 161, 174-175, 177, 181, 184-185, 188, 192, 198, 209-214, 223, 241, 247-250, 252-253, 264, 280, 285, 292, 303, 307-308, 324, 331-333, 338-339, 341, 344, 346, 348, 352, 365-366, 371, 383, 385-387, 390, 402-407, 410, 414, 420-422, 424-426, 435, 444, 469, 471-473, 477
168th ID, 28, 30-31, 39, 73-76, 78-80, 125-127, 149-150, 162-164, 200, 234-235, 263-266, 292, 301-303, 306-307, 332, 348, 365-366, 371, 383, 387, 405, 412, 420, 424-426, 439, 471, 477
183rd ID, 442, 461
198th ID, 28, 125-126, 200-202, 235, 263, 265-267, 302, 364, 371, 426, 471, 477
211th ID, 374-375, 379, 476
216th ID, 83, 86, 88-89, 92-93, 138, 239, 268, 476
251st ID, 87, 462-463, 476
253rd ID, 437, 442, 447
255th ID, 37, 62, 64, 66, 69, 117, 158, 194, 224, 228, 232, 259-261, 297, 299-300, 355-358, 407, 476
258th ID, 87, 95, 268, 441, 450, 457, 461, 476
262nd ID, 270, 311, 377-379, 399-400, 415, 417, 433, 442, 476
292nd ID, 84-86, 88, 90, 92-93, 130-134, 139-141, 165, 167, 170, 203, 206, 238-239, 270, 457, 476
293rd ID, 374-375, 379, 400, 446, 451-452, 461, 476
320th ID, 31, 39, 78-80, 123, 125, 163-164, 265, 302, 439, 477
332nd ID, 31, 36, 60-62, 64-66, 69, 117, 119, 157, 161, 194, 198, 223-226, 228-229, 259-261, 297-298, 300, 314, 354-359, 391, 393, 407-409, 420, 476
383rd ID, 84, 86, 138, 170, 207, 457, 476

INDEX 513

Brigades
10th PzB, 25, 28, 37, 66, 120, 256
21st PzB, 138, 167, 483-484

Combat Groups/*Kampfgruppen*
Kahler, 167, 268, 437, 442
Schmall, 442
Schmidthuber, 429
Schulz, 162
Westphalian, 234
Woest, 423

Regiments
PzR *Rothenburg*, 74, 396
1st SS PzGR, 43, 54-55, 98, 100-101, 103, 107-108, 118, 144, 147, 174, 186, 210-211, 243, 245, 247-248, 250, 253-254, 276-277, 283-285, 287, 291, 312, 322-323, 340, 345, 352, 381, 420, 434
1st SS PzR, 54, 106-109, 113, 147, 174, 176, 276-277, 287, 291, 312, 318, 322, 326, 331, 352, 423
1st *Werfer*, 49, 50, 477
2nd SS PzGR, 33, 35, 44-45, 47-49, 52-53, 55, 98, 100, 102-103, 106, 143, 147, 174, 177, 186, 209, 218, 243, 245, 247-249, 251, 253-254, 275-278, 280-281, 283-284, 286-287, 289, 291, 312, 322, 326, 330, 352, 381, 434
2nd SS PzR, 55, 147, 174, 176, 215, 243, 251, 277, 282, 323, 344, 352, 420
3rd SS PzGR *Deutschland*, 46-47, 51, 55, 57, 116, 146, 179-181, 210-211, 241, 244-245, 250, 252, 281, 284, 290, 292, 317, 324, 329, 334, 336-337, 340, 343-344, 385, 408, 422, 435
3rd SS PzR, 44, 60, 109, 143, 146, 183, 210, 215, 239, 313, 321, 339
4th SS PzGR *Der Führer*, 52, 57, 100, 102, 105, 142, 144, 146, 176, 179, 183, 211, 241, 244-245, 247, 292, 324, 333-334, 337, 339, 343, 352, 380, 385, 403, 406, 422, 425, 435
5th SS PzGR *Thule*, 52, 216, 243, 404
6th PzGR, 75, 77
6th PzR, 18, 61, 66, 68, 119, 157-158, 191, 195, 298
6th SS PzGR *Eicke*, 46, 49, 52-53, 98, 210, 216, 252, 260, 272-274, 348, 381, 386, 421, 438
6th SS PzR, 216
7th PzGR, 75, 77
12th PzR, 269
25th PzR, 77, 79
27th PzR, 77-78, 162, 361
33rd PzGR, 203, 454
33rd PzR, 167, 207, 268-269, 309
35th PzR, 205-207, 238-239, 309, 448, 454
51st PzGR, 92
53rd Werfer, 441
55th Werfer, 48-50, 101, 276-277, 285

73rd PzGR, 78, 125, 162-163, 302, 328, 366, 368, 370, 393
74th PzGR, 125, 162, 301, 366, 368, 370, 393, 414
101st PzGR, 92
110th PzGR, 221-222, 256
171st GR, 436, 439
234th GR, 437, 439, 445
315th GR, 241, 292
326th GR, 263, 302
331st GR, 241, 292
339th GR, 241, 292
394th PzGR, 36, 61, 68, 71, 119, 155, 222, 298, 354, 391, 420
429th GR, 162, 302
431st IR, 375
432nd GR, 270, 379
442nd PzGR, 125
508th GR, 85, 92, 238-239
677th GR, 407
Pioneer Regiment 680, 251

Battalions/*Abteilungen*
Pz Abt 2, 50, 183
9th Armored Reconnaissance, 442
Pz Abt 19, 162, 263
Pz Abt 49, 207, 269, 446, 454
StPzAbt 216, 83, 476, 484
Pz Abt 238, 292
Pz Abt 327, 354
sPzAbt 503, 28, 31, 38-39, 41, 74-78, 126, 164, 199, 201-202, 234-235, 302, 304, 307-308, 362-363, 368, 411-412, 443, 456, 467, 477, 483
sPzAbt 505, 40, 43, 84, 86, 88, 90-91, 93-95, 128, 130-132, 134, 136-138, 167, 170, 206-207, 239, 269, 309, 439, 476, 483
Pz Abt 560, 89
627th Pioneer, 338, 341
sPzAbt 653, 40, 84, 92, 133, 309, 377, 433, 451, 476, 484
sPzAbt 654, 40, 82, 88, 92, 133, 270, 309, 377, 415, 476, 484
sPzAbt 656, 82-84, 93, 131, 476
StuGAbt 911, 38, 484
StuGAbt 909, 138, 439, 476, 484

Miscellaneous
Fremde Heere Ost, 33

Index of Soviet Military Units
For abbreviations see pages vii-viii.

Command Functions
Stavka, 18, 27, 29, 32, 40, 42, 58, 72, 110, 143, 186, 197, 199, 209, 216, 269, 316, 361, 401, 416, 424, 439, 444, 446, 450, 457, 459, 461, 463, 465-466, 470-471, 474

Fronts

Bryansk Front, 29, 269, 309, 311, 373-377, 399, 401, 415-416, 433, 443, 478, 487, 491

Central Front, 26, 29, 40-42, 129, 140, 165, 171, 269-271, 352, 373, 376, 398, 415, 428, 434-435, 437, 442, 452, 456, 472, 478, 486, 490

Kalinin Front, 458

Southern Front, 143, 448

Southwestern Front, 111, 143, 148, 480-481, 491

Steppe Front, 22, 26-27, 29, 42, 58, 110, 199, 216, 292, 301, 350-352, 439, 447, 455, 460, 463, 468, 470, 480-481, 487, 491

Voronezh Front, 22, 26-27, 34, 42, 69, 97, 105, 110, 160, 186, 199, 246, 270-271, 308, 352, 435, 439-440, 447, 472, 479, 486, 490

Western Front, 29, 269, 309, 316, 373-378, 399-400, 415-416, 433, 437, 439, 458, 467, 481, 486, 491

Armies

1st TA, 30-31, 37, 50, 56, 58, 67-72, 97, 100, 102-105, 108-109, 112-113, 115, 118, 120, 122, 142, 144-145, 149, 152, 154-160, 173, 181, 183, 185-186, 189-190, 197-198, 214-216, 218-219, 221, 225, 229, 232, 246, 256, 258, 260-262, 279, 290-291, 295, 297-299, 301, 316, 320, 322, 328, 337, 340, 351, 353, 355-356, 358, 390, 392, 410, 420, 424, 431, 438, 449, 455, 458-459, 462, 471, 486, 490

2nd TA, 40, 87, 91, 95, 129, 131, 133-138, 169, 206, 269, 376, 416, 428, 437, 461, 471, 490

2nd VA, 20, 33, 73, 97, 114, 294, 317, 339, 352, 390, 394, 431, 435, 492

3rd , 376-377, 401, 436, 443-444, 449

3rd GTA (*see also* 3rd TA), 401, 416, 441-442, 444-445, 449-451, 459, 487

3rd TA (became 3rd GTA during the campaign – *see also* 3rd GTA), 137, 309, 416-418, 436, 441-444, 446, 448-451, 456-459

4th GA, 461

4th TA, 376, 399, 416, 429, 434, 438-439, 446, 450, 459, 461, 486

5th GA, 27, 58, 110-111, 176, 186, 188-189, 197, 199, 214, 216, 218-221, 230, 249, 253-254, 257, 263, 272-273, 279-280, 284-285, 287, 289-290, 292-293, 297, 307, 313-314, 316, 319-320, 327-328, 337-339, 341, 343, 347, 349, 353, 356-357, 366, 383-385, 390, 392, 396, 398, 404, 409-410, 421, 431-432, 438, 449, 455, 461, 466, 468-471, 474

5th GTA, 27, 58, 108, 110-112, 142, 151, 178, 186, 188-189, 199, 209, 214-216, 218-221, 227, 232, 235, 241, 246, 253-255, 257, 262, 274-275, 279-280, 282, 284-285, 287, 289-295, 298, 301, 303, 305, 307-308, 312, 314-319, 322-325, 328, 338-342, 344-345, 347-348, 350-351, 353, 356, 360, 363, 367-368, 380, 382, 384-385, 388, 390, 392, 396, 398, 404-405,
407, 420, 423, 425, 431, 436, 449, 455, 461-462, 466, 468-471, 474, 486, 493

6th GA, 26-27, 30-32, 34-35, 38, 42, 44-45, 51-52, 56-57, 60-61, 64-65, 67-69, 72, 98-101, 103, 105-110, 115, 123, 144, 149, 151, 154-155, 157, 161, 164, 173, 191, 198, 215-217, 219-220, 224-225, 229, 232-233, 242, 255, 261-262, 295, 297-299, 316, 320, 322, 328, 337, 340, 347, 351, 353-354, 356, 358, 385, 390, 392, 396, 424, 449, 455, 457, 459-460, 471, 486, 490

7th GA, 26-27, 30-32, 34, 39, 44, 49, 57, 71, 73 77, 79 81, 97, 113, 123-124, 162-164, 185, 187, 197, 200, 202, 216, 220, 227, 233, 254, 262, 267, 289, 295, 299, 301, 322, 360, 362, 364-366, 426, 449, 455, 469, 471, 486, 490

11th GA, 309-310, 373-379, 398-400, 415-417, 428-429, 433-434, 437-438, 441-442, 450-451, 461, 486

13th, 29, 40, 82-85, 88, 90, 93, 95-96, 129-133, 136-137, 165-168, 203-204, 416, 428, 442, 456, 461, 478, 486, 490

15th VA, 132, 171, 207, 237, 268, 375, 398-401, 433, 437, 441

16th VA, 20, 33, 171, 207, 237, 257, 271, 378, 400, 428, 433, 436, 442, 492

17th VA, 20, 33, 34, 59, 75, 111, 114, 160, 266, 294, 317, 352, 364, 390, 431, 492

27th, 58, 131, 350, 455, 458, 460, 471, 481, 487

38th, 69, 108, 148, 154, 164, 191, 194, 214, 221, 228, 232-233, 241, 256, 300, 407, 449, 455, 473-474, 480-481, 486, 490

40th, 22, 69, 108, 117-118, 123, 144, 148, 154, 159, 164, 173, 191, 193-195, 198-199, 216, 223, 227-228, 230, 232-233, 256, 259, 261, 298, 300, 356, 359, 396, 439, 455, 473-474, 480, 486, 490

47th, 199, 351, 455, 460-461, 470, 480-481, 484

48th, 83-84, 129, 134, 138, 207, 416, 446, 449, 461, 478-479, 486, 490

50th, 309, 376, 398-399, 417, 457, 480-481, 486

53rd, 350, 449, 455, 487

61st, 374-376, 400, 429, 434, 437, 461, 478, 487

63rd, 373-377, 379, 399-400, 416-417, 429, 433-434, 437, 444, 451, 456, 461, 478, 487

69th, 30-31, 34, 45, 53, 78-79, 97, 100-101, 103, 123, 150-152, 158, 185, 187, 200-201, 214, 216, 220, 227-228, 232-235, 242, 244, 246, 249, 254-255, 262, 281, 289, 292-293, 298-299, 301, 303, 305-306, 308, 312, 316, 318, 331, 338, 340, 346, 360-368, 371, 385, 387, 390, 394, 396, 405-407, 410-411, 413-414, 420-422, 425-427, 431, 440, 445, 455, 468-471, 479-481, 490

70th, 86-87, 89-90, 92-93, 95-96, 130-131, 133-137, 166-168, 203, 205, 237, 268-269, 376, 416, 428, 479, 486, 490

Corps

1st GTC, 416, 487

1st MC, 351, 470, 487

1st TC, 374-375, 398-400, 415-417, 428, 444, 486
2nd GTC, 30-31, 48, 51, 58, 67-68, 70-71, 97-105, 108, 110-112, 115, 144, 148, 151, 153, 174, 176-179, 181-182, 184-185, 187, 189, 193, 198, 201, 210-211, 213-214, 217, 228, 234, 241-242, 244, 250, 255, 266, 280, 287, 289, 290, 305, 308, 314-315, 317-318, 320-321, 323-325, 329-331, 333-334, 336, 338-344, 346-349, 351-352, 360-361, 363, 367-369, 381, 389, 394, 396, 405-407, 410, 413-414, 422, 425, 431, 481, 486
2nd MC, 417, 436, 443, 445, 448, 450, 457
2nd TC, 23, 58, 67, 98, 111, 146, 148, 151, 153, 174, 176-178, 180, 182, 186-187, 189, 193, 196-197, 201, 211-214, 217, 219, 221, 233, 242-244, 246-248, 251, 254, 273-274, 276, 280-281, 283-284, 286-290, 294, 302, 305-306, 314-315, 317, 323, 329-331, 335-336, 339-340, 344-345, 347, 351, 360, 381, 384, 389, 404, 406-407, 413, 432, 481, 486
3rd GMC, 351, 455, 460
3rd GTC, 461, 481
3rd MC, 31, 35, 37, 50-51, 58-59, 61, 67, 69-71, 97, 99, 101, 104-105, 107, 110, 112, 117, 119-120, 122, 144, 148, 150-151, 154-155, 157, 159, 161, 175, 177-178, 189-198, 213-214, 221-227, 229-230, 255-258, 262, 298-301, 353-354, 356, 358, 368, 392, 455, 479, 486
3rd TC, 27, 40, 87, 91, 95, 129, 131, 137-138, 169, 203, 231, 392, 437, 478
4th GTC, 350, 390, 455, 458, 470, 487
5th GMC, 27, 110, 112, 143, 186, 213, 219, 249, 291, 305, 314, 316, 323, 328, 335, 338-341, 344, 347, 349, 351, 355, 360-361, 363, 367, 370, 383-384, 387, 390, 394, 396, 410-414, 425, 427, 455, 469-470, 481
5th GTC, 30, 37, 48, 51, 58-59, 67-68, 70-71, 97, 99-100, 102-106, 108-113, 115, 144-146, 148, 151, 153-154, 174, 177, 179-180, 182, 184, 186-187, 189, 193, 196, 198-199, 211, 213-214, 219, 228, 230, 241-242, 255-256, 260, 296, 298-300, 303, 316, 353-354, 356-359, 392, 431, 457-458, 479, 486
5th TC, 374-375, 378, 399-400, 415, 417, 428, 486
6th GMC, 450
6th GTC, 450
6th TC, 31, 37, 50-51, 67, 69-71, 97, 105-106, 115, 117-118, 120, 122, 144, 148, 151-152, 154-155, 157, 159, 161, 174-175, 189-191, 193, 196-198, 223-225, 227, 229-231, 250, 255-261, 296-297, 300-301, 357-358, 409, 455, 479, 486
7th GMC, 450
7th GTC, 450
9th TC, 40, 91, 129, 132, 134, 204, 206, 345, 478, 486
10th TC, 22, 58, 110, 119, 143, 151, 153, 159, 174, 176-178, 181-183, 186-187, 193, 196-199, 211-212, 214-215, 219, 221, 224, 227, 229-232, 241-242, 244, 247, 255-257, 259-260, 273, 290, 295, 297-300, 316, 336, 342, 353-358, 391, 393, 410, 423, 481, 486
11th TC, 450
12th TC, 417, 436, 441-442, 445, 448, 450, 457

15th TC, 417, 436, 441-442, 445, 450, 457
16th TC, 40, 87, 91, 95, 128-132, 134, 136-137, 167, 169, 204, 206, 478
17th GRC, 87, 91, 94-95, 128-134, 137, 140, 165-166, 168-171, 204-205, 207, 471, 478
18th GRC, 40, 91-92, 129, 137, 169, 478
18th TC, 112, 142, 186, 219-220, 276, 279, 281, 284, 287-291, 314-317, 320-324, 326-328, 333-338, 340-349, 351, 355, 366, 381, 383-385, 387, 389-390, 393, 422, 431, 455, 469-470, 481
19th TC, 87, 91, 95, 129-131, 134, 136-140, 169, 204, 206, 269, 316, 441, 478, 486
20th TC, 375-376, 416, 429, 487
22nd GRC, 56, 64, 69, 259, 298, 355, 359, 480
23rd GRC, 34, 56, 64, 144, 356, 392, 480
24th GRC, 30, 74, 76, 123, 480
25th GRC, 30, 76, 78, 124, 162, 164, 266, 480
25th TC, 428, 437
29th RC, 85, 88, 94, 132, 478
29th TC, 27, 110, 112, 142, 279, 281-282, 284, 287-288, 290-291, 299, 301, 313-315, 317, 319-324, 326-336, 338-340, 342-343, 346-349, 351, 355, 381, 383-384, 387, 389-390, 393, 404, 406, 425, 432, 455, 469-470, 481
30th TC, 450
31st TC, 31, 37, 50-51, 67, 69-70, 97, 104-108, 110, 112, 122, 142, 144, 147-151, 154, 159-161, 175-178, 180-185, 192-194, 196-198, 210, 213-214, 216-217, 223, 227, 229-231, 255, 259-260, 272-273, 282, 297, 299, 320, 349, 353-354, 356-357, 384-385, 392, 455, 479, 486
32nd GRC, 219, 297, 327, 337, 357, 384-385, 392, 469, 481
33rd GRC, 219, 254, 272-273, 279, 289, 297, 313-314, 316, 327, 339, 342, 357, 384, 388, 392, 404, 469, 481
35th GRC, 30, 71-72, 79, 97, 123, 163-164, 197, 200, 202, 266, 304-305, 308, 364, 387, 394, 412, 426, 480, 490
48th RC, 243-244, 255, 262, 266, 289, 306, 338, 340, 348, 361, 366, 368, 384-385, 387, 394-395, 404-405, 412-414, 424-425, 468, 480
49th RC, 187, 262, 289, 295, 364-365, 480

Divisions
3rd GRD, 40
4th GAD, 40, 203, 478
5th Artillery Division, 90, 268
6th GRD, 40, 87, 94, 165-166, 169-170, 204-205, 238, 478
8th RD, 40, 83-84, 88, 478
9th Anti-aircraft Division, 144
9th GAD, 214, 219, 253-254, 272, 275, 277, 279, 282, 284, 286, 288-289, 291, 295, 312, 316, 324, 329, 331, 333-334, 336, 340, 342, 345, 351, 381, 387, 391, 481
13th GRD, 316, 355, 357, 384-385, 392, 481
15th GRD, 30, 78, 95, 123, 127, 164, 200, 202, 265, 267, 302, 305-306, 362, 480

15th RD, 40, 83-91, 95, 135, 478
16th GRD, 379, 482
40th GRD, 269
42nd GRD, 254, 279, 303, 313, 316, 319, 323-325, 328, 330, 336, 338, 340, 351, 381, 384-385, 387, 389-391, 481
51st GRD, 43, 52-60, 67-68, 97-104, 106-108, 113-114, 145, 148, 194, 213-214, 221, 227, 231, 242, 254, 260, 272-273, 279-280, 297, 299, 313, 480
52nd GRD, 30, 32, 34-35, 37, 43-44, 46-56, 58, 61-65, 68-69, 72, 97, 99, 101, 104, 107-109, 114, 116-117, 119-122, 144, 150, 157, 161, 174, 212-214, 216, 219, 242, 244, 248, 250-251, 254, 273-274, 277, 279-280, 290, 313, 316, 319-321, 327-328, 335, 337, 342-344, 380, 389-390, 480
66th GRD, 219, 316, 357, 384-385, 392, 481
67th GRD, 30, 32, 36, 47-48, 50, 61-66, 68-70, 72, 97, 99, 107, 112, 115-116, 118-122, 155, 157, 194, 225, 227, 230-231, 257, 260, 298, 327, 480
70th GRD, 40, 87, 131, 134, 136-137, 171, 203, 237, 269, 478
71st GRD, 30, 36-37, 58, 60-64, 68-70, 72, 115-120, 141, 158, 193, 259, 297-299, 356, 359, 480
72nd GRD, 30, 75, 78, 127, 163-164, 265, 302, 480
73rd GRD, 30, 76, 78, 123, 125-127, 234, 289, 364-365, 480
74th RD, 40, 86, 90-91, 95, 130-131, 169, 205, 268, 478
75th GRD, 40, 131-132, 136-137, 166, 169, 171, 269, 478
77th GRD, 374, 478
78th GRD, 30, 75-76, 78-79, 125-127, 267, 480
81st GRD, 30, 34, 47, 49, 74-76, 78, 80, 125, 127, 161, 163-164, 185, 200, 202, 228, 234-235, 249-250, 255, 266, 280, 302, 305-307, 360, 362-363, 365, 367-369, 371, 394-395, 413, 425, 480
81st GRD, 40, 74, 84-86, 88, 90-91, 93, 95, 131, 137, 168, 265, 360-362, 478
89th GRD, 98, 110, 151, 181, 214, 228, 234, 242, 265, 302-303, 306, 360-362, 365-366, 371, 394, 403, 411, 413-414, 425, 480
90th GRD, 35, 56, 63, 67-69, 98, 112, 116-117, 119-122, 157, 161, 191, 195, 197, 228, 255, 258, 296-298, 358-359, 480
92nd GRD, 34, 57, 79, 97, 123-124, 162-164, 199-202, 228, 234-235, 263, 266-267, 301, 303, 306-308, 360-368, 370-371, 395-396, 412, 427, 480
93rd GRD, 57, 68, 97, 110, 123, 214, 228, 233-234, 241-242, 244, 247, 307, 338, 341, 361-362, 365, 394, 413-414, 425, 480
94th GRD, 34, 57, 79, 97, 123, 162, 164, 199-202, 228, 234, 263, 302, 305-306, 361-362, 364-365, 367, 424, 480
95th GRD, 201, 219, 254, 272, 282-291, 312-313, 316, 319-321, 328, 335, 337-339, 341, 343, 345, 380, 384, 387-390, 404, 422, 481
96th GRD, 201, 308

97th GRD, 219, 254, 272, 313, 316, 357, 384, 386, 388, 392, 481
107th RD, 202, 234, 235, 302-303, 361-362, 365, 424, 480
111th RD, 79, 123, 127, 162, 164, 202, 289, 306, 364-365, 480
129th RD, 375, 478
132nd RD, 86-87, 89-91, 93, 135, 138, 168, 204, 479
140th RD, 168, 171, 203, 479
148th RD, 40, 83-84, 88, 90-91, 95, 130-131, 268, 478
161st RD, 69, 158, 193, 480
175th RD, 87, 138, 167, 204, 268
183rd RD, 79, 102, 105, 114, 123, 158, 174, 187, 212, 214, 217, 234, 242-245, 247, 250, 254-255, 266, 274, 277-278, 282, 291, 331, 333, 338, 340-341, 348, 383, 385, 389, 391, 402-403, 431, 462, 480
184th RD, 227, 258-259, 261, 296-298, 354, 356-357, 359, 392, 408, 480
204th RD, 214, 221, 227, 230, 255-256, 296, 298-299, 353-354, 356, 392, 480
213th RD, 30, 37, 75, 78, 123, 127, 163-164, 200, 480
254th RD, 136
270th RD, 79, 123, 127, 162, 164, 200, 202, 267, 289, 306, 364-365, 480
275th RD, 98
276th GRD, 304
280th RD, 86-87, 90-91, 93, 166-167, 268, 479
287th RD, 375, 478
294th RD, 136
305th RD, 201-202, 234-235, 263, 302-303, 307-308, 361-363, 365, 395, 480
307th RD, 40, 131-132, 137-138, 165-166, 168-170, 203-205, 207, 268, 478
309th RD, 69, 117-118, 144, 148, 157, 159, 194, 221, 223-224, 226-227, 230-231, 255-256, 260, 299, 353, 356, 480
336th RD, 374, 478
348th RD, 375, 478
375th RD, 30, 34, 49, 53-55, 57-58, 68, 80, 98-99, 101, 104, 110, 113, 150-151, 217, 234-235, 249, 264-265, 280, 301-303, 307, 361, 365, 367, 402-403, 407, 410-411, 413-414, 421, 425, 480

Brigades

1st GTB, 70, 97, 99-100, 104, 106-107, 110, 112, 144-145, 147-148, 256, 479
1st MB, 52, 70, 104, 119-120, 159, 191, 196, 479
3rd TDB, 169, 171, 204
4th GMRB, 181, 325, 333, 341, 343-344, 385, 403, 406, 481
4th GTB, 287, 289, 324-325, 333-334, 337, 341, 343-344, 385, 403, 406, 481
6th MRB, 157, 194, 257, 296, 479
10th GMB, 314, 323, 339, 341, 344, 349, 360, 366, 381, 383-384, 388, 407, 413, 422, 425-426, 481

10th GTB, 317, 390, 482
10th MB, 104, 195, 197, 347, 479
10th TB, 70, 255, 317
11th GMB, 314, 361, 363, 365, 367-371, 393, 395, 411, 414, 422, 425, 481
11th GTB, 87, 129
11th Mechanized, 394
11th MRB, 174, 212-214, 216, 219, 242, 246-248, 254, 276, 290, 313, 316, 321, 338, 341-344, 390, 481
12th GMB, 314, 361, 363, 365, 367-368, 370-371, 395-396, 411, 414, 425, 481
20th GTB, 68, 108-109, 479
22nd GTB, 109, 145, 299, 357, 479
22nd TB, 35, 69-70, 106, 108, 194, 479
24th GTB, 210, 220, 317, 328, 335, 338-339, 341, 344, 346-347, 349, 361, 366, 381, 383-385, 387-388, 390, 404, 481
25th GTB, 287, 289, 291, 321, 324-325, 333-334, 336, 340, 346-347, 403, 406, 481
25th TB, 290, 313-315, 323-324, 327, 329-330, 332, 334-335, 338, 340, 342-343, 345, 481
26th GTB, 109, 146, 181, 183, 287, 289, 315, 318, 321, 325, 333-334, 344, 347, 361-364, 367-371, 385, 390, 394-395, 403, 410, 425, 481
26th TB, 182, 219, 243, 248, 273, 277, 330-331, 336, 340, 345, 394, 481
27th ATB, 69, 121, 228, 234
27th GTB, 76, 78, 364-365, 480
27th TDB, 36, 61
28th ATB, 52, 54
29 ATB, 105, 118, 149, 227
29th TDB, 69, 147, 175
30th TDB, 228, 234
31st ATB, 126, 202, 365
31st TB, 163, 281-282, 314, 324, 326-327, 330-332, 334, 336, 339-342, 346, 388, 481
32nd DATB, 394
32nd MRB, 314, 323, 336, 340, 345-347, 422, 431, 481
32nd TB, 314, 321, 323-327, 330-334, 336, 339, 341, 343, 346, 388, 481
49th TB, 53, 97, 104-107, 110, 112, 144-145, 147, 150, 154-155, 157, 192, 194, 223, 256, 479
53rd GTB, 393
53rd MRB, 278, 314, 317, 323-325, 327, 330, 332, 340-341, 343, 345-346, 387-388, 481
58th MRB, 273, 275, 278, 291, 331, 338, 340, 342, 481
86th TB, 69, 144, 154, 157, 183, 194, 223-224, 230, 354, 392, 480
91st TB, 417, 444
96th TB, 30, 37, 49, 54, 55, 98, 101, 104, 105, 199, 201-202, 228, 233-235, 301, 306, 308, 360-363, 365-368, 371, 395-396, 425, 480
99th TB, 174, 182, 212, 219, 244, 246-248, 251, 273, 276, 280-284, 286-288, 290, 313, 344-345, 349, 384, 481

100th TB, 104, 106-108, 110, 142, 144, 150, 157, 282, 285, 479
103rd TB, 137
107th TB, 130-131, 137
110th TB, 314, 333, 336, 343, 346, 402, 481
112th TB, 69, 70, 122, 154-157, 159-160, 190-192, 194-197, 257-258, 260-261, 479
129th TB, 88, 93, 205-207
164th TB, 129-130, 137
169th TB, 174, 182, 219, 250-251, 273, 276-277, 279, 283, 291, 327, 329, 332, 338, 340, 342, 347, 481
170th TB, 281, 314, 321, 323-328, 335-337, 340, 343, 345-346, 349, 388, 481
180th TB, 69, 148, 155, 194, 198, 223, 480
181st TB, 314, 323-324, 326-328, 332, 334-337, 340, 343, 346, 349, 388-389, 481
183rd TB, 299, 353-355, 410, 481
192nd TB, 175, 183, 191-192, 213, 480
200th TB, 69-70, 105, 155, 157, 160, 190-197, 225, 227-228, 257-259, 261, 479
237th TB, 70, 97, 106, 110, 150, 161, 179, 183, 212, 217, 479
242nd TB, 70, 97, 106, 110, 150, 176-177, 217, 479
456th MRB, 343

Regiments
4th AR, 199
4th GTR, 379
6th TR, 375
7th GAAR, 253
11th TR, 375
12th TDR, 69, 198
12th TR, 375
16th Guards Mortar, 325
23rd GAR, 272, 282, 288, 291, 295, 334, 391
26th GAR, 272, 276-277, 281-284, 288, 293, 295, 391
28th GAR, 277, 288, 291, 295, 331, 335, 339, 342, 391
32nd Guards Fighter, 375
36th GTR, 314, 325, 336, 340, 342, 345-347, 481
38th RLR, 199
43rd TR, 141, 169, 171
47th RR, 84
48th GTR, 104, 106, 109, 112, 146, 149
51st GTR, 339, 380-381, 426
53rd GTR, 316, 323, 360-361, 363, 365, 370-371, 388, 395, 412
59th TR, 69, 183, 199, 480
60th TR, 69, 199, 256-257
66th GMR, 256
66th RLR, 198
76th GMR, 323
82nd TR, 375
104th GTDR, 367
111th Guards Artillery, 198
114th Guards Artillery, 125

114th TR, 375
136th GRR, 330, 336, 389, 391
148th TR, 30, 228, 234, 480
151st GRR, 45-48, 54-56, 99, 219, 251, 273, 319, 321
153rd GRR, 55-56, 219, 319, 341
155th GRR , 46-47, 49, 54-55, 58, 68, 99, 101, 104, 219, 251, 319, 341
167th TR, 30, 124, 162, 480
196th GRR, 63, 67, 116
203rd RR, 131
203rd TR, 69, 107, 223
205th RR, 131
210th GRR, 63, 68-69, 119
222nd TDR, 198
230th TR, 30, 37, 45, 52, 54, 56, 104, 480
235th GRR, 162
245th TR, 37, 67, 244, 251, 273, 480
262nd TR, 30, 76, 78, 480
276th GRR, 267, 304
280th GRR, 267, 306
282nd GRR, 234, 304
283rd GRR, 306
284th GRR, 285, 343, 387-388
285th RR, 102, 114, 149, 174, 212, 242, 244, 248, 250-251, 278-279, 340, 391
286th GRR, 306
287th RR, 278, 282
288th GRR, 306
290th GRR, 282, 285, 387-388, 422
301st DATR, 272
332nd RR, 88
438th TDR, 199
496th TDR, 101, 104
538th TDR, 50, 63
611th ATR, 67, 116
676th RR, 84, 90
689th AAR, 393
712th RR, 86, 90
869th TDR, 69
1008th DATR, 50-51, 53, 63
1032nd RR, 207, 239
1446th AR, 290
1461st SU, 69
1500th DAR, 325
1669th TDR, 124
1689th TDR , 69
1694th Anti-aircraft Artillery, 290
1695th Anti-aircraft Artillery, 325
1837th ATR , 67

Battalions

2nd Guard Motorcycle Battalion, 367
4th Guard Mechanized Battalion, 367
51st Motorized Sapper, 318
104th Destroyer Anti-tank Artillery Battalion, 387

737th Anti-tank , 367
755th DAB, 291, 293
755th Destroyer Anti-tank Artillery Battalion, 325

Miscellaneous

B-IV, 89, 91
Donbas Strategic Offensive, 389, 462
Gestapo, 269, 373
Goliaths, 84, 88-89
Hagen line, 439, 441, 451, 453, 457, 460-461
Luftwaffe, 20-21, 24-25, 27-28, 31-33, 41-45, 47-48, 50-51, 55-56, 59-64, 73, 75, 82-83, 85-87, 89-91, 93-95, 97-98, 102, 104, 106-107, 111, 113-114, 122-124, 128-130, 132, 135-136, 139-140, 142, 145-147, 149, 151-153, 155, 158, 164-166, 168, 173-177, 179-183, 185-186, 189-192, 195, 197-199, 204-205, 211-213, 221-223, 225-226, 228, 230-231, 238, 243-244, 249-250, 252, 256-257, 260-261, 264, 269-271, 275, 277-283, 285-286, 293, 297, 301, 304, 306-307, 310, 313, 317, 320, 325, 327-328, 330-331, 333, 335-336, 339, 341-344, 350, 352, 357, 360, 362, 365-366, 378-379, 381, 385-386, 389, 391, 393, 395, 399, 402-404, 406-408, 419, 421-422, 428-429, 434-435, 437-439, 441-442, 444-446, 451-452, 454, 456, 458, 462, 477
Operation Barbarossa, 17
Operation Citadel, 15, 17-24, 31, 33-34, 38, 139, 241, 259, 272, 311, 352-353, 355, 382-383, 385, 404, 426-427, 435, 439, 450, 456, 464, 468, 474
Operation Herstreise, 450
Operation Kutuzov, 15, 18, 239, 268-269, 309, 311, 373, 398, 428, 461, 465
Operation Roland, 405, 411, 419-420, 424, 426, 431, 434-435
Operation Rumyantsev, 15, 432, 434, 450, 455, 459, 462, 465
Operation Suvorov, 462
Operation Uranus, 216, 465, 470
Panther tank, 20, 23, 25, 36-38, 57, 60, 64-66, 71,-72, 116, 120-121, 123, 156, 160-161, 215, 293, 393, 423, 440, 464-467, 472-473, 488
PTAB bombs, 96, 157, 339, 429
SD-1, 47, 82
SD-2, 82
Smersh, 365
Tiger tank, 20, 27-28, 38, 52, 60, 94, 100, 103, 106-107, 131, 159, 179, 183, 189-190, 204, 211, 239, 241, 265, 275, 318, 328, 330, 334, 345, 383, 404, 421, 425, 435, 467, 488

Related titles published by Helion & Company

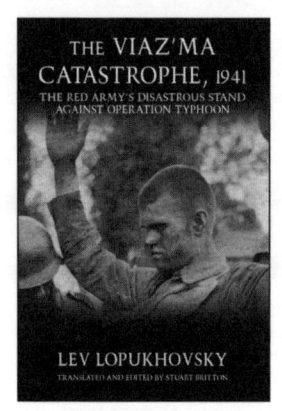

The Viaz'ma Catastrophe. The Red Army's Disastrous Stand Against Operation Typhoon
Lev Lopukhovsky (edited and translated by Stuart Britton)
ISBN 978-1-908916-50-1

The Rzhev Slaughterhouse. The Red Army's Forgotten 15-Month Campaign against Army Group Center, 1942-1943
Svetlana Gerasimova (edited and translated by Stuart Britton)
ISBN 978-1-908916-51-8

Demolishing the Myth. The Tank Battle at Prokhorovka, Kursk, July 1943: An Operational Narrative
Valeriy Zamulin (edited and translated by Stuart Britton)
ISBN 978-1-906033-89-7

Zhitomir-Berdichev. German Operations West of Kiev 24 December 1943-31 January 1944 Volume 1
Stephen Barratt
ISBN 978-1-907677-66-3

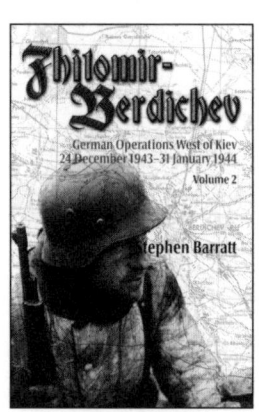

Zhitomir-Berdichev. German Operations West of Kiev 24 December 1943-31 January 1944 Volume 2
Stephen Barratt
ISBN 978-1-909384-10-1

HELION & COMPANY
26 Willow Road, Solihull, West Midlands B91 1UE, England
Telephone 0121 705 3393   Fax 0121 711 4075
Website: http://www.helion.co.uk